THE BRIEF

AMERICAN PAGEANT

A HISTORY OF THE REPUBLIC

Seventh Edition

David M. Kennedy
Stanford University

Lizabeth Cohen
Harvard University

Mel Piehl
Valparaiso University

Houghton Mifflin Company   Boston   New York

Publisher: Suzanne Jeans
Senior Marketing Manager: Katherine Bates
Marketing Assistant: Lauren Bussard
Senior Development Editor: Jeffrey Greene
Senior Project Editor: Bob Greiner
Editorial Assistant: Emily Meyer
Senior Art and Design Coordinator: Jill Haber
Cover Design Director: Anthony F. Saizon
Senior Photo Editor: Jennifer Meyer Dare
Composition Buyer: Chuck Dutton
New Title Project Manager: James Lonergan

Cover Image: *Flag Gate,* artist unidentified, Jefferson County, New York, circa 1876. Paint on wood with iron and brass. Collection American Folk Art Museum, New York. Gift of Herbert Waide Hemphill, Jr. Photo by John Parnell, New York.

Printed in the U.S.A.

Library of Congress Control Number: 2006924976

Instructor's Exam Copy
ISBN-10: 0-618-83407-9
ISBN-13: 978-0-618-83407-5

For orders, use student text ISBNs:
ISBN-10: 0-618-77612-5
ISBN-13: 978-0-618-77612-2

2 3 4 5 6 7 8 9-CRK-10 09 08 07

THE BRIEF

AMERICAN PAGEANT

CONTENTS

PART ONE

Founding the New Nation
c. 33,000 B.C.–A.D. 1783

2

PART TWO

Building the New Nation
1776–1860

112

PART THREE

Testing the New Nation

1820–1877

234

PART FOUR

Forging an Industrial Society

1865–1909

336

PART FIVE

Struggling for Justice at Home and Abroad

1899–1945

440

PART SIX

★

Making Modern America

1945 to the Present

⸻ ⁕ ⸻

570

39 The Stalemated Seventies 1968–1980   629

Economic stagnation • Nixon and the Vietnam War • New policies toward China and the Soviet Union • Nixon and the Supreme Court • Nixon's domestic program • Nixon trounces McGovern, 1972 • The Watergate scandal • Israelis, Arabs, and oil • Nixon resigns • Feminism • Desegregation and affirmative action • The election of Jimmy Carter, 1976 • The energy crisis and inflation • The Iranian hostage humiliation

★ EXAMINING THE EVIDENCE   The "Smoking Gun" Tape, June 23, 1972, 10:04–11:39 A.M. **639**

★ MAKERS OF AMERICA   The Vietnamese **640**

★ MAKERS OF AMERICA   The Feminists **642**

40 The Resurgence of Conservatism 1980–1992   647

The "New Right" and Reagan's election, 1980 • Budget battles and tax cuts • Reagan and the Soviets • The Iran-Contra scandal • Reagan's economic legacy • Reagan and the "social issues" • The election of George Bush, 1988 • The end of the Cold War • The Persian Gulf War, 1991 • Bush's battles at home

★ VARYING VIEWPOINTS   Where Did Modern Conservatism Come From? **663**

41 America Confronts the Post–Cold War Era 1992–2006   664

The election of Bill Clinton, 1992 • Republicans win control of Congress, 1994 • The reelection of Clinton, 1996 • Clinton's foreign policy • The Clinton impeachment trial • The 2000 election • September 11, 2001, and its consequences • The Iraq War • The reelection of Bush, 2004

42 The American People Face a New Century   679

Economic revolutions • Widening inequality • The feminist revolution • The transformation of the family • The new immigration • Cities and suburbs • Minorities and multiculturalism • American culture in the new century • The American prospect

★ MAKERS OF AMERICA   The Latinos **688**

MAPS

CHARTS AND TABLES

PREFACE

This new edition of *The Brief American Pageant,* a concise version of *The American Pageant,* Thirteenth Edition, includes significant innovations. As always, this Brief Edition presents the core content of *The American Pageant* in an efficient and attractive fashion. For the first time in the Brief Edition, we have included numerous additional features designed to enhance core academic skills and foundational knowledge essential to serious academic work in history, as well as closely related areas of the social sciences and humanities. This Brief Edition aims not only to teach students American history, but also to teach them how to learn history and other subjects more effectively.

The text incorporates these features while preserving the liveliness and readability that have long been *The American Pageant's* hallmark. We are often told that the *Pageant* is the sole American history text that has a distinctive personality—defined by clarity, concreteness, a consistent chronological narrative, strong emphasis on major themes, avoidance of clutter, access to a variety of interpretive perspectives, and a colorful writing style leavened, as appropriate, with wit. That personality, we strongly believe, is what has made the Pageant both appealing and useful to countless students for more than four decades. In *The Brief American Pageant,* Seventh Edition, David M. Kennedy, Lizabeth Cohen, and Mel Piehl have preserved the parent text's essential character, while making this edition far more useful to students and instructors alike.

Changes in this Edition

Like *The American Pageant,* the Brief Edition provides overview essays designed to encourage students to think coherently about six eras in American history. Those essays, revised for this edition, demonstrate that the study of history is not just a matter of piling up mountains of facts, but is principally concerned with discovering complex patterns of change over time and organizing seemingly disparate events, actions, and ideas into meaningful chains of cause and consequence.

The Brief Edition includes for the first time the feature "Examining the Evidence." This feature is intended to deepen students' understanding of the historical craft in another way, by conveying how historians develop interpretations of the past through research in many kinds of primary sources. Students will learn about the insights historians derive from a wide range of historical artifacts: what a letter from a black freedman to his former master in 1865 reveals about his family's enslavement as well as their hopes for a new life; how a song popular during World War I contains clues to soldiers' experiences in the military; why the *Gettysburg Address* sheds light not only on President Lincoln's brilliant oratory but also on his vision of the American nation; what the manuscript census teaches us about immigrant households on the Lower East Side of New York in 1900; and how a new kind of architectural structure—the shopping mall—changed both consumers' behavior and politicians' campaign tactics after World War II. Other featured sources include maps, furniture, clothing, private correspondence, travelogues, paintings and photographs, court decisions, political broadsides and cartoons, novels, motion pictures, newspapers, public opinion polling, and transcripts of important diplomatic conferences and political meetings.

The popular "Makers of America" feature shows how Americans have forged their group identities through shared experiences, intellectual interests, and technical skills as well as through ethnicity and neighborhoods. The twenty-nine essays constitute a comprehensive mosaic of the diverse peoples and groups that have composed our strikingly pluralistic society.

Readers will also find in this edition of *The Brief American Pageant* enriched discussion of the experiences and contributions of women, the Seven Years' War, the election of 1800, law and the national economy in the antebellum period, the Compromise of 1850, the rise of colleges and universities, American involvement in Asia, the Spanish-American War, and the Cold War.

Our greatest attention in this revision has gone to expanding two areas of inquiry that are often overlooked in U.S. history textbooks: the cultural innovations and ideas that have engaged Americans and the international context in which U.S. history has unfolded. We hope to give readers a greater appreciation for the contributions of American writers, artists, and thinkers, while also conveying how extensively the American experience has been shaped by interaction with other peoples on the world stage.

In addition, this Brief Edition introduces for the first time boxed quotations that provide more varied perspectives to the events chronicled in the *Pageant's* historical narrative. We have also compressed and reorganized the material concerning United States foreign involvements from 1890–1909 into a single Chapter 27. Treatment of the post-World War II period has expanded to include an additional chapter, as that era lengthens in time. The final chapter has been thoroughly revised, to portray the present state of the nation in historical perspective. Updated "Varying Viewpoints" essays reflect new interpretations of significant trends and events. Selecting visual material that illuminates complex and important historical ideas continues to be a high priority, and readers will find many new and revised maps and charts, as well as fresh documentary images. Completely updated bibliographies are located at the end of the book. "An American Profile: The United States and Its People," containing abundant statistical data on many aspects of the American historical experience is located on the companion web site.

New Pedagogical Features

In this edition of *The Brief American Pageant,* we are introducing a new four-color design, many new pedagogical features, and a larger format to display these features most effectively. This is all part of our effort to help students become more effective and efficient learners. The special pedagogical features of the Brief Edition are many and varied, and may be used in different ways by students and instructors.

- **"What if . . . ?"** questions at the end of each overview essay prompt students to consider how history might have changed if certain events had turned out differently. These questions illustrate the contingent nature of history.

- **Chapter Outlines** begin each chapter to provide a roadmap for the student.

- **Focus Questions** come at the beginning of each chapter, pointing to the key issues and ideas in the account that follows, and guiding the student's reading and understanding.

- The **Chronology** has been moved to the beginning of the chapter, so that students will have an idea of the succession of important events as they start to read the chapter.

- The **Marginal Glossary** highlights and defines key words to expand students' general historical and social science vocabulary.

- **Icons** in the margins direct students to primary sources and interactive maps on the companion web site.

- **Examining the Evidence,** the feature that acquaints students with historical evidence, offers questions to develop historical and critical thinking skills.

- **Map-Reading Skill Builders** are questions designed to improve students' map-reading ability.

- **Chapter Summaries** provide a handy review that highlights the chapter's main points.

Goals of *The Brief American Pageant*

Like its predecessors, this seventh edition of *The Brief American Pageant* cultivates its readers' capacity for balanced judgment and informed understanding about American society by holding up to the present the mirror and measuring rod that is the past. The book's goal is not to teach the art of prophecy but the much subtler and more difficult arts of seeing things in context, of understanding the roots and direction and pace of change, and of distinguishing what is truly new under the sun from what is not. The study of history, it has been rightly said, does not make one smart for the next time, but wise forever.

We hope that *The Brief American Pageant* will develop those intellectual assets in its readers, and that those who use the book will take from it both a fresh appreciation of what has gone before and a seasoned perspective on what is to come. And we hope, too, that readers will take as much pleasure in reading *The Brief American Pageant* as we have had in writing it.

Teaching and Learning Aids

These supplements have been created with the diverse needs of today's students and instructors in mind.

For the Instructor

- The **Online Teaching Center** (http://college.hmco.com/pic/kennedybrief7e) includes PowerPoint slides of hundreds of maps, images, and other media that are related to each chapter in the book as well as web links and questions for use with Personal Response Systems. Instructors have access to 100 interactive maps and over 500 primary sources to use for assignments. In addition, there is an Instructor's Resource Guide that can aid in encouraging classroom discussions or constructively enhance a class presentation.

• **HM Testing** is a new program with improved functionality that provides instructors all the tools they will need to create, write, customize, and deliver multiple types of tests. Instructors can import questions directly from the test bank, create their own questions, or edit existing questions, all within Diploma's powerful electronic platform.

• **Blackboard/WebCT** provides instructors who want to offer all or part of their entire course online with much of the fundamental material for their course. From this base, instructors can customize the course to meet their needs including program-level, graded homework questions organized by topic.

• **Eduspace** provides the ability for instructors to create part or all of their courses online, using the widely recognized tools of Blackboard Learning System and content from Houghton Mifflin. Instructors can quickly and easily assign homework exercises, quizzes and tests, tutorials, and supplementary study materials, and can modify or add content of their own. A powerful grade book in Eduspace allows instructors to monitor student progress and easily tabulate grades.

• **The Houghton Mifflin U.S. History Transparency Set, Volumes I and II,** is a set of standard U.S. history transparencies, taken from illustrations and maps in the Houghton Mifflin survey texts. It includes 150 full-color maps.

• **BiblioBase for U.S. History** is a database of hundreds of primary source documents—including speeches, essays, travel accounts, government documents, and memoirs—covering U.S. history from the fifteenth century to the present. This comprehensive database enables you to create a customized course pack of primary sources to complement any U.S. history text. You can search for documents by period, region, approach, theme, and type and then view the documents in their entirety before choosing your course pack selections.

• The **Rand McNally Atlas of American History** is offered for packaging with the textbook. Please contact your sales representative for additional information.

For the Student

• The **Online Study Center** (http://college.hmco.com/pic/kennedybrief7e) is a student web site that includes a wide array of interactive study content such as preclass quizzes, ACE Practice Tests, vocabulary-building exercises, identification exercises, and interactive map activities, among many others. This web site also contains the same primary sources and interactive maps that are on the Online Teaching Center.

• **Icons** in the text direct students to interactive maps, primary sources, and ACE practice test questions.

Acknowledgments

Many people contributed to the seventh edition of *The Brief American Pageant*. Foremost among them are the countless students and teachers who have written unsolicited letters of comment or inquiry. We also offer thanks to the following colleagues for their particular contributions to improving the text:

Carol Bender, *Saddleback College*
Wesley B. Borucki, *Palm Beach Atlantic University*
Janet Newlan Bower, *San Diego Mesa College*
Linzy Brekke-Aloise, *Harvard University*
Jon L. Brudvig, *University of Mary*
Scott Buchanan, *South Plains College*
Andrea J. DeKoter, *SUNY Cortland*
Yonatan Eyal, *Harvard University*
Ronald H. Fritze, *Athens State University*
Frederick B. Gates, *Southwestern Oklahoma State University*
Robert Gudmestad, *University of Memphis*
David Holland, *Stanford University*
David Hollinger, *University of California, Berkeley*
David Hunter, *San Bernardino City Unified Schools*
Timothy K. Kinsella, *Ursuline College*
Robert MacDougall, *Harvard University*
Frank Ninkovich, *St. John's University*
Selina Pearson, *Northwest-Shoals Community College*
Kimberly Sims, *Harvard University*
Ann Engram Smith, *Darton College*
Richard A. Straw, *Radford University*
Ruth Suyama, *Los Angeles Mission College*
F. Walter VanderHeijden, *Hempfield High School*
Gerald R. Virgilio, *New Mexico State University at Alamogordo*
Larry Wade, *Darton College*
Daniel Wewers, *Harvard University*

D.M.K.
L.C.
M.P.

Sail, sail thy best, ship of Democracy,
Of value is thy freight, 'tis not the Present only,
The Past is also stored in thee,
Thou holdest not the venture of thyself alone, not
   of the Western continent alone,
Earth's résumé entire floats on thy keel, O ship, is
   steadied by thy spars,
With thee Time voyages in trust, the antecedent
   nations sink or swim with thee,
With all their ancient struggles, martyrs, heroes,
   epics, wars, thou bear'st the other continents,
Theirs, theirs as much as thine, the destination-port
   triumphant. . . .

———✦———

Walt Whitman
Thou Mother with Thy Equal Brood, 1872

FOR STUDENTS

A Guide to Your Textbook

Welcome to U.S. History! What follows is a guide to how to use the features of your textbook, _The Brief American Pageant_. Spending a few minutes on these next few pages will help you get the most out of your book, and do well in your class.

PART ONE

Founding the New Nation

c. 33,000 B.C.–A.D. 1783

The European explorers who followed Christopher Columbus to North America in the sixteenth century had no notion of founding a new nation. Neither did the first European settlers who peopled the thirteen English colonies on the eastern shores of the continent in the seven-

individual liberty, self-government, religious tolerance, and economic opportunity. They also commonly displayed a willingness to subjugate outsiders—first Indians, who were nearly annihilated through war and disease, and then Africans, who were

■ The chapters in this book are grouped into six parts, representing six distinct eras in American history. Each part opens with an essay that identifies the major themes and events of the era. Reading the essay will help you understand the larger patterns and trends discussed in the chapters to follow.

■ Following the part essay is a list of **"What if..."** questions. These questions ask what our country would look like if certain events had turned out differently. They prompt you to consider that history is not a story of inevitable events; there are always other possibilities.

What if . . . ?

■ What if some sort of compromise between the North and South had prevented the Civil War?

What might such a compromise have looked like?

What might have been its consequences for the future of slavery, and for American nationhood?

Was _any_ such compromise politically possible—or morally defensible?

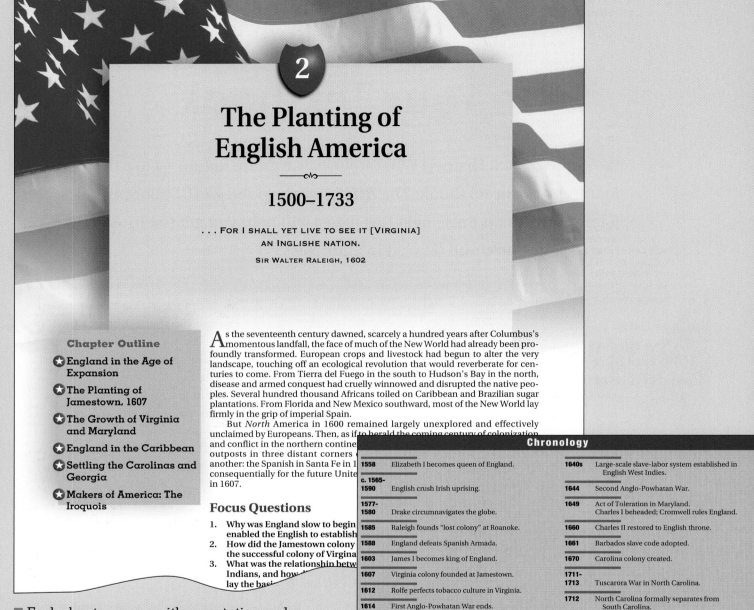

2

The Planting of English America

—⚬◇⚬—

1500–1733

. . . FOR I SHALL YET LIVE TO SEE IT [VIRGINIA]
AN INGLISHE NATION.

SIR WALTER RALEIGH, 1602

Chapter Outline

- ★ England in the Age of Expansion
- ★ The Planting of Jamestown, 1607
- ★ The Growth of Virginia and Maryland
- ★ England in the Caribbean
- ★ Settling the Carolinas and Georgia
- ★ Makers of America: The Iroquois

As the seventeenth century dawned, scarcely a hundred years after Columbus's momentous landfall, the face of much of the New World had already been profoundly transformed. European crops and livestock had begun to alter the very landscape, touching off an ecological revolution that would reverberate for centuries to come. From Tierra del Fuego in the south to Hudson's Bay in the north, disease and armed conquest had cruelly winnowed and disrupted the native peoples. Several hundred thousand Africans toiled on Caribbean and Brazilian sugar plantations. From Florida and New Mexico southward, most of the New World lay firmly in the grip of imperial Spain.

But *North* America in 1600 remained largely unexplored and effectively unclaimed by Europeans. Then, as if to herald the coming century of colonization and conflict in the northern continent [...] outposts in three distant corners [...] another: the Spanish in Santa Fe in 1[...] consequentially for the future Unite[...] in 1607.

Focus Questions

1. Why was England slow to begin [...] enabled the English to establish [...]
2. How did the Jamestown colony [...] the successful colony of Virgini[...]
3. What was the relationship betw[...] Indians, and how [...] lay the basi[...]

Chronology

1558	Elizabeth I becomes queen of England.	**1640s**	Large-scale slave-labor system established in English West Indies.
c. 1565–1590	English crush Irish uprising.	**1644**	Second Anglo-Powhatan War.
1577–1580	Drake circumnavigates the globe.	**1649**	Act of Toleration in Maryland. Charles I beheaded; Cromwell rules England.
1585	Raleigh founds "lost colony" at Roanoke.	**1660**	Charles II restored to English throne.
1588	England defeats Spanish Armada.	**1661**	Barbados slave code adopted.
1603	James I becomes king of England.	**1670**	Carolina colony created.
1607	Virginia colony founded at Jamestown.	**1711–1713**	Tuscarora War in North Carolina.
1612	Rolfe perfects tobacco culture in Virginia.	**1712**	North Carolina formally separates from South Carolina.
1614	First Anglo-Powhatan War ends.		
1619	First Africans arrive in Jamestown. Virginia House of Burgesses established.	**1715–1716**	Yamasee War in South Carolina.
1624	Virginia becomes royal colony.	**1733**	Georgia colony founded.
1634	Mary[...]		

■ Each chapter opens with a quotation and a brief introduction that sets the stage for what is to come in the chapter. The opening page also includes a **Chapter Outline** and **Focus Questions**. The outline shows the major topics that will be discussed and the focus questions introduce you to the issues you should be thinking about as you read the chapter.

■ The **Chronology** lists the important events that are discussed in the chapter. It is a convenient reminder of what happened when. When you are done reading the chapter, you can use it to review the major events.

oyed farmers took to the
like Bristol and London.
at only eldest sons were el-
us younger sons, among
eir fortunes elsewhere. By
f such courtiers were re-
nsiderable number of in-

nity for English coloniza-
oyment, as well as a thirst
ovided the motives. Joint-
tage was set for a historic
ncharted North American

Seedling

destiny beckoned toward
ny of London, received a
orld. The main attractions
ge through America to the
Virginia Company was in-
ckholders hoped to liqui-
e on the luckless colonists,

---

primogeniture *The legal principle that the oldest son inherits all family property or land.*

joint-stock company *An economic arrangement by which a number of investors pool their capital for investment.*

charter *A legal document granted by a government to some group or agency to implement a stated purpose, and spelling out the attending rights and obligations.*

■ The **On-Page Glossary** provides definitions of important terms and concepts in the margin of the page on which the term appears. This makes it easy to review these important terms. Also they appear in boldface type so you can find them quickly.

■ The **Boxed Quotation**s give you a feeling for the era being discussed by presenting the perspectives of the people who participated in and were affected by the historical events under discussion.

In the years immediately following the defeat of the Spanish Armada, the English writer Richard Hakluyt (1552?–1616) extravagantly exhorted his countrymen to cast off their "sluggish security" and undertake the colonization of the New World:

"There is under our noses the great and ample country of Virginia; the inland whereof is found of late to be so sweet and wholesome a climate, so rich and abundant in silver mines, a better and richer country than Mexico itself. If it shall please the Almighty to stir up Her Majesty's heart to continue with transporting one or two thousand of her people, she shall by God's assistance, in short space, increase her dominions, enrich her coffers, and reduce many pagans to the faith of Christ."

The charter of the Virginia Company is a significant document in American history. It guaranteed to the overseas settlers the same rights of Englishmen that they would have enjoyed if they had stayed at home. This precious boon was gradually extended to the other English colonies, helping to reinforce the colonists' sense that even on the far shore of the Atlantic they remained comfortably within the embrace of traditional English institutions. But ironically, a century and a half later, the colonists' insistence on the "rights of Englishmen" fed their hot resentment against an increasingly meddlesome mother country and nourished their appetite for independence.

Setting sail in late 1606, the Virginia Company's tiny band of colonists eventually arrived at a site on the wooded and malarial banks of a swampy river. There, on May 24, 1607, about a hundred English settlers, all men, disembarked. They called the place Jamestown and the river the James in honor of King James I.

The early years of Jamestown proved to be a nightmare for all concerned—except the buzzards. Once ashore, the settlers died by the dozens from disease, malnutrition, and starvation. The woods rustled with game, and the rivers flopped with fish, but the greenhorn settlers, many of them self-styled "gentlemen" unaccustomed to fending for themselves, wasted valuable time grubbing for nonexistent gold when they should have been gathering provisions.

■ At the end of every chapter is a **Chapter Summary**. It's a convenient place to review quickly the major themes of the chapter.

✪ Chapter Summary ✪

The defeat of the Spanish Armada and the exuberant spirit of Elizabethan nationalism finally drew England into the colonial race. After some early failures, the first permanent English colony was established at Jamestown, Virginia. Harsh conditions, gentlemanly aversion to work, and Indian hostility nearly caused it to fail, but stern leadership and tobacco cultivation finally brought prosperity and population growth.

The early encounters of English settlers with the Powhatan Indians in Virginia established many of the patterns that characterized later Indian-white relations in North America, including disease, warfare, and removal. Indian societies underwent their own substantial changes as a result of warfare, disease, and trade. For a time after the Atlantic coastal tribes were nearly wiped out, the larger Indian peoples of the Appalachian area formed a formidable barrier to white expansion.

Maryland and South Carolina were founded by aristocratic proprietors. Maryland was originally a Catholic refuge. South Carolina flourished by establishing close ties with the British sugar colonies in the West Indies, and brought the West Indian pattern of harsh slave codes and large plantation agriculture to North America. North Carolina was a less hierarchical settlement of largely poor white colonists who owned small farms and disdained authority. Latecomer Georgia served initially as a buffer against the Spanish and a haven for debtors.

Despite some differences, all the southern colonies depended on staple plantation agriculture for their survival and on the institutions of indentured servitude and African slavery for their labor. With widely scattered rural settlements, they had relatively weak religious and social institutions and tended to develop hierarchical economic and social orders.

EXAMINING THE EVIDENCE

A Seventeenth-Century Valuables Cabinet In 1999 a boatyard worker on Cape Cod and his sister, a New Hampshire teacher, inherited a small (20-pound, 16–1/2 inch-high) chest that had always stood on their grandmother's hall table, known in the family as the "Franklin chest." Eager to learn more about it, they set out to discover the original owner, tracing their family genealogy and consulting with furniture experts. In January 2000 this rare seventeenth-century cabinet, its full provenance now known, appeared on the auction block and sold for a record $2.4 million to the Peabody Essex Museum in Salem, Massachusetts. No less extraordinary than the price was the history of its creator and its owners embodied in the piece. Salem cabinetmaker James Symonds (1636–1726) had made the chest for his relatives Joseph Pope (1650–1712) and Bathsheba Folger (1652–1726) to commemorate their 1679 marriage. Symonds carved the Popes' initials and the date on the door of the cabinet. He also put elaborate S curves on the sides remarkably similar to the Mannerist carved oak paneling produced in Norfolk, England, from where his own cabinetmaker father had emigrated. Behind the chest's door are ten drawers where the Popes would have kept jewelry, money, deeds, and writing materials. Surely they prized the chest

as a sign of refinement to be shown off in their best room, a sentiment passed down through the next thirteen generations even as the Popes' identities were lost. The chest may have become known as the "Franklin chest" because Bathsheba was Benjamin Franklin's aunt, but also because that identification appealed more to descendants ashamed that the Quaker Popes, whose own parents had been persecuted for their faith, were virulent accusers during the Salem witch trials of 1692.

1. What significant features of this seventeenth-century chest could be determined simply by careful examination of the material object itself, and which could be learned only by historical research?

2. After studying the chest itself, which elements of the construction and carving might provide significant clues about what historical inquiries to pursue?

3. What does the nature of the chest and its original function as a storage place for valuables tell you about the economic status of the original owners, Joseph and Bathsheba Pope? Why might this chest have been handed down through their descendants for over 300 years, when most other material arti-

■ **Examining the Evidence** shows how historians might interpret primary sources, the original material of history. Official documents, letters, song lyrics, polls, and photographs are some of the sources examined. See if you can answer the questions that follow the description of each source.

MAKERS OF AMERICA

MAKERS OF AMERICA

■ **Makers of America** introduces you to the wide diversity of people who compose our pluralistic society. The achievements of scientists, philosophers, soldiers, and ordinary people are highlighted to show how Americans have forged their group identities through shared experiences.

The Iroquo[is]

Well before the crowned heads of Europe turned their eyes and their dreams of empire toward North America, a great military power had emerged in...

■ **Varying Viewpoints** raises questions about events, people, and movements that might cause you to rethink common conceptions about these trends and events. This feature demonstrates that the interpretation of historical events is never fixed, that new ideas are always possible.

VARYING VIEWPOINTS

Europeanizing America or Americanizing Europe?

The history of discovery and the earliest colonization raises perhaps the single most fundamental question about all American history. Should it be understood as the extension of European civilization into the New World or as the gradual development of a uniquely "American" culture? One school of thought tended to emphasize the Europeanization of America. Historians of that persuasion paid close attention to the situation in Europe, particularly in England and Spain, in the fifteenth and sixteenth centuries. They also focused on the various means by which the values and institutions of the mother continent were exported to the new lands in the western sea. Some European writers varied this general question by asking what transforming effect the discovery of America had on Europe itself. Both of these approaches are Eurocentric. More recently, historians have concentrated on the distinctiveness of America. The concern with European origins has evolved into a comparative treatment of English, Spanish, Dutch, and French settlements in the New World. The newest trend to emerge is a transatlantic history that views European empires and their American

ropean, African, and Native American ways of life. Scholars including Richard White, Alfred W. Crosby, William Cronon, Karen Kupperman, and Timothy Silver have enhanced understanding of the cultural as well as the physical transformations that resulted from contact.

The variety of American societies that emerged out of the interaction of Europeans, Africans, and Native Americans has also become better appreciated. Studies such as Richard S. Dunn's *Sugar and Slaves* (1972) emphasize the importance of the Caribbean in early English colonization efforts. Similarly, Edmund S. Morgan's *American Slavery, American Freedom* (1975) stresses the role of economic ambition in explaining the English peopling of the Chesapeake and the eventual importation of African slaves to that region. Studies by Bernard Bailyn and David Hackett Fischer demonstrate that there was scarcely a "typical" English migrant to the New World. English colonists migrated both singly and in families, and for economic, social, political, and religious reasons.

The picture of colonial America that is emerging

■ **The *Brief American Pageant* Website** offers students, through the Online Study Center, and instructors, through the Online Teaching Center, a wide array of teaching and learning resources.

■ **For Students:**

ACE practice test questions

Chapter themes and a summary

Flashcards for testing your vocabulary

Chronology exercises

Examining the Evidence activities

Primary sources with pedagogy and questions

Interactive maps with questions

■ **For Instructors:**

Historical images in PowerPoint

Maps in PowerPoint

Primary sources with pedagogy and questions

Interactive maps with questions

Test Items and HM Testing (available on a CD-ROM)

Instructors Resource Manual

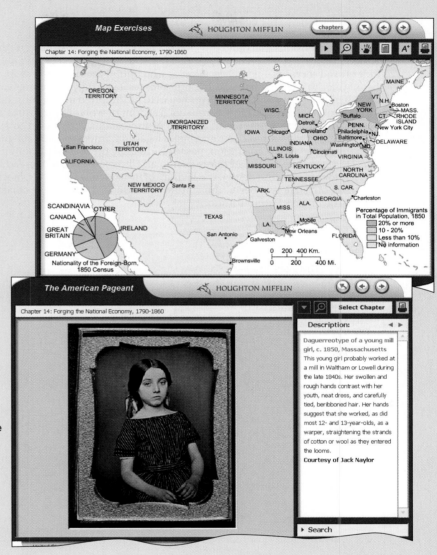

organized and conomic func- ods to offer in s' desire for a

◌╫◌ *Online Study Center*

**Primary source
European Settlements and Indian Tribes in North America**
college.hmco.com/pic/kennedybrief7e

nous peoples went forward.

■ Throughout the book, you will see icons for the **Online Study Center** in the margin that direct you to **primary sources** and **interactive maps** on the website. The interactive maps provide a dynamic way to improve your knowledge of geography and the primary sources offer another opportunity to engage the raw material of history.

cracy, were intended to arise amidst the fertile forests. As in Virginia, ists proved willing to come only if offered the opportunity to acquire land ir own. Soon they were dispersed around the Chesapeake region on mod- rms, and the haughty land barons, mostly Catholic, were surrounded by tful backcountry planters, mostly Protestant. Resentment flared into open ion near the end of the century, and the Baltimore family for a time lost its ietary rights.

Despite these tensions Maryland prospered. Like Virginia, it blossomed forth in of tobacco. Also like Virginia, it depended for labor in its early years mainly on **indentured servants**—penniless persons who bound themselves to work for ber of years to pay their passage. In both colonies it was only in the later years seventeenth century that black slaves began to be imported in large numbers. ord Baltimore at first permitted unusual freedom of worship for Protestant rs in Maryland. But when the heavy tide of Protestants threatened to sub- e the Catholics, the Catholic settlers sought legal guarantees for their religious ce in the famed Act of Toleration, passed in 1649 by the local representative bly. This statute guaranteed **toleration** to all Christians, but it decreed the penalty for anyone who denied the divinity of Jesus. While falling far short of standards of religious liberty, the statute did extend a temporary cloak of ction to the uneasy Catholic minority.

feudal *Concerning the decentralized medieval social system of personal obligations between rulers and ruled.*

indentured servants *Poor persons obligated to a fixed term of unpaid labor, often in exchange for a benefit such as transportation, protection, or training.*

toleration *Originally, religious freedom granted by an established church to a religious minority.*

■ Early Maryland and Virginia

✪ Map Skill-Builder:
Understanding Political Maps

1. Where did the original land grant to Lord Baltimore follow natural geographical features, and where did it follow certain "artificial" straight lines of latitude or longitude on the map?

2. Did the eventual *political* boundary of Maryland mostly follow the natural features, or did it add more artificially drawn boundaries?

■ The **Map-Reading Skill Builders** are questions that appear adjacent to selected maps and are designed to help you better understand the information conveyed by the map.

THE BRIEF AMERICAN PAGEANT

Founding the New Nation

—⚬—

c. 33,000 B.C.–A.D. 1783

The European explorers who followed Christopher Columbus to North America in the sixteenth century had no notion of founding a new nation. Neither did the first European settlers who peopled the thirteen English colonies on the eastern shores of the continent in the seventeenth and eighteenth centuries. These original colonists may have fled poverty or religious persecution in the Old World, but they continued to view themselves as Europeans, and as subjects of the English king. They regarded America as but the western rim of a transatlantic European world.

Yet life in the New World made the colonists different from their European cousins, and eventually, during the American Revolution, the Americans came to embrace a vision of their country as an independent nation. How did this epochal transformation come about? How did the colonists overcome the conflicts that divided them, unite against Britain, and declare themselves at great cost to be an "American" people?

They had much in common to begin with. Most were English-speaking. Most came determined to create an agricultural society modeled on English customs. Conditions in the New World deepened their common bonds. Most colonists strove to live lives unfettered by the tyrannies of royal authority, official religion, and social hierarchies that they had left behind. They grew to cherish ideals that became synonymous with American life—

individual liberty, self-government, religious tolerance, and economic opportunity. They also commonly displayed a willingness to subjugate outsiders—first Indians, who were nearly annihilated through war and disease, and then Africans, who were brought in chains to serve as slave labor, especially on the tobacco, rice, and indigo plantations of the southern colonies.

But if the settlement experience gave people a common stock of values, both good and bad, it also divided them. The thirteen colonies were quite different from one another. Puritans carved tight, pious, and relatively democratic communities of small family farms out of rocky-soiled New England. Theirs was a homogeneous world in comparison with most of the southern colonies, where large landholders, mostly Anglicans, built plantations along the coast from which they lorded over a labor force of black slaves and looked down upon the poor white farmers who settled the backcountry. Different still were the middle colonies stretching from New York to Delaware. There diversity reigned. Well-to-do merchants put their stamp on New York City, as Quakers did on Philadelphia, while out in the countryside sprawling estates were interspersed with modest homesteads. Within individual colonies, conflicts festered over economic interests, ethnic rivalries, and religious practices. All those clashes made it difficult for colonists to imagine that they were a single people with a common destiny, much less that they ought to break free from Britain.

The American colonists in fact had little reason to complain about Britain. Each of the thirteen colonies enjoyed a good deal of self-rule. Many colonists profited from trade within the British Empire. But by the 1760s this stable arrangement began to crumble, a victim of the imperial rivalry between France and Britain. Their struggle for supremacy in North America began in the late seventeenth century and finally dragged in the colonists during the French and Indian War from 1756 to 1763. That war in one sense strengthened ties with Britain, since colonial militias fought triumphantly alongside the British army against their mutual French and Indian enemies. But once the French were driven from the North American continent, the colonists no longer needed Britain for protection. More important still, after 1763 a financially overstretched British government made the fateful choice of imposing taxes on colonies that had been accustomed to answering mainly to their own colonial assemblies. By the 1770s issues of taxation, self-rule, and trade restrictions brought the crisis of imperial authority to a head. Although as late as 1775 most people in the colonies clung to the hope of some kind of accommodation short of outright independence, royal intransigence soon thrust the colonists into a war of independence that neither antagonist could have anticipated just a few years before.

Eight years of revolutionary war did more than anything in the colonial past to bring Americans together as a nation. Comradeship in arms and the struggle to shape a national government forced Americans to subdue their differences as best they could. But the spirit of national unity was hardly universal. One in five colonists sided with the British as "Loyalists," and a generation would pass before the wounds of this first American "civil war" fully healed. Yet in the end, Americans won the Revolution, with no small measure of help from the French, because in every colony people shared a firm belief that they were fighting for the "unalienable rights" of "life, liberty, and the pursuit of happiness," in the words of Thomas Jefferson's magnificent Declaration of Independence. Almost two hundred years of living a new life had prepared Americans to found a new nation.

What if...?

■ **What if France had won the French and Indian War and maintained its colonial power in Canada and west of the Appalachians?**

Would Britain's American colonies still have protested taxes and declared their independence?

New World Beginnings

33,000 B.C.–A.D. 1769

I HAVE COME TO BELIEVE THAT THIS IS A MIGHTY CONTINENT
WHICH WAS HITHERTO UNKNOWN. . . .
YOUR HIGHNESSES HAVE AN OTHER WORLD HERE.

CHRISTOPHER COLUMBUS, 1498

About six thousand years ago—only a minute in geological time—recorded history began among certain peoples of the ancient Middle East who developed a written culture. Just five hundred years ago—only a few seconds figuratively speaking—European explorers stumbled on the Americas. This dramatic accident forever altered the future of both the Old World and the New, and of Africa and Asia as well.

Focus Questions

1. What geological, geographical, and climatic conditions set the stage for human history in America?
2. What were the primary features of the diverse Indian cultures of the Americas, and how did they change over time?
3. What developments in European and global history paved the way for Columbus's voyage and the subsequent collision of two worlds?
4. How did the mutual relations of Indians, Europeans, and Africans shape a genuinely new biological, cultural, and economic world in the Americas?
5. How did Spain's conquest of the Indian civilizations of Mexico and South America shape the essential features of its vast New World empire?

The Shaping of North America

Planet earth took on its present form slowly. Some 225 million years ago, a single supercontinent contained all the world's dry land. Then enormous chunks of terrain began to drift away from this colossal continent, opening the Atlantic and Indian Oceans, narrowing the Pacific Ocean, and forming the great landmasses of Eurasia, Africa, Australia, Antarctica, and the Americas.

Continued shifting and folding of the earth's crust thrust up mountain ranges. The Appalachians were probably formed even before continental separation, perhaps 350 million years ago. The majestic ranges of western North America—the Rockies, the Sierra Nevada, the Cascades, and the Coast Ranges—arose much more recently, geologically speaking, some 135 million to 25 million years ago.

Chronology

c. 33,000–8000 B.C.	First humans cross over to the Americas from Asia.
c. 5000 B.C.	Corn is developed as a staple crop in highland Mexico.
c. 4000 B.C.	First civilized societies develop in the Middle East.
c. 1200 b.c.	Corn planting reaches present-day American Southwest.
c. A.D. 1000	Norse voyagers discover and briefly settle in North America. Corn cultivation reaches Midwest and southeastern Atlantic seaboard.
c. A.D. 1100	Height of Mississippian settlement at Cahokia.
c. A.D. 1100–1300	Christian crusades arouse European interest in Asia.
1295	Marco Polo returns to Europe.
late 1400s	Spain becomes united.
1488	Díaz rounds southern tip of Africa.
1492	Columbus lands in the Bahamas.
1494	Treaty of Tordesillas between Spain and Portugal.
1498	Da Gama reaches India. Cabot explores northeastern coast of North America for England.
1513, 1521	Ponce de León explores Florida.
1519–1521	Cortés conquers Mexico for Spain.
1532	Pizarro crushes Incas.
1540–1542	Coronado explores present-day Southwest.
1542	Cabrillo explores California coast for Spain.
1565	Spanish build fortress at St. Augustine.
late 1500s	Iroquois Confederacy founded, according to Iroquois legend.
1609	Spanish found New Mexico.
1680	Popé's Rebellion in New Mexico.
1680s	French expedition down Mississippi River under La Salle.
1769	Serra founds first California mission, at San Diego.

By about 10 million years ago, nature had sculpted the basic geological shape of North America. The continent was anchored in its northeastern corner by the massive Canadian Shield—a zone undergirded by ancient rock, probably the first part of what became the North American landmass to have emerged above sea level. A narrow eastern coastal plain, or "tidewater" region, creased by many valleys, sloped gently upward to the timeworn ridges of the Appalachians. Those ancient mountains slanted away on their western side into the huge midcontinental basin that rolled downward to the Mississippi Valley bottom and then rose relentlessly to the towering peaks of the Rockies. From the Rocky Mountain crest—the "roof of America"—the land fell off jaggedly into the intermountain Great Basin, bounded by the Rockies on the east and the Sierra and Cascade ranges on the west. The valleys of the Sacramento and San Joaquin rivers and the Willamette–Puget Sound trough seamed the interiors of present-day California, Oregon, and Washington. The land at last met the foaming Pacific, where the Coast Ranges rose steeply from the sea.

Beginning about 2 million years ago, two-mile-thick ice sheets crept across much of northern Europe, Asia, and the Americas. In North America, the glaciers spread as far southward as a line stretching from Pennsylvania through the Ohio country and the Dakotas to the Pacific Northwest.

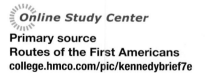

Online Study Center

Primary source
Routes of the First Americans
college.hmco.com/pic/kennedybrief7e

When the glaciers finally retreated about 10,000 years ago, they left the North American landscape transformed, and much as we know it today. The grinding and flushing action of the moving and melting ice pitted the rocky surface of the Canadian Shield with thousands of shallow depressions, into which the melting glaciers flowed to form lakes. The same glacial action scooped out and filled the Great Lakes. When the Great Lakes eventually found an outlet to the Atlantic Ocean through the St. Lawrence River, they left the Missouri-Mississippi-Ohio river system to drain the enormous midcontinental basin between the Appalachians and the Rockies.

Similarly, in the West, water from the melting glaciers filled sprawling Lake Bonneville, covering much of present-day Utah, Nevada, and Idaho. Eventually deprived of both inflow and drainage as the glaciers retreated, the giant lake became a shrinking inland sea. It grew increasingly saline, slowly evaporated, and left an arid, mineral-rich desert, with only the Great Salt Lake as a relic of its former vastness. Today Lake Bonneville's ancient beaches are visible on mountainsides up to 1,000 feet above the dry floor of the Great Basin.

✪ Map Skill-Builder:
Using Map Distance Scales
When the first migrants crossed the Bering Land Bridge from Siberia to North America, approximately how many miles did they have to walk before they were south of the large ice caps to either side of the only open route?
a) 200 miles b) 500 miles
c) 2,000 miles d) 3,000 miles

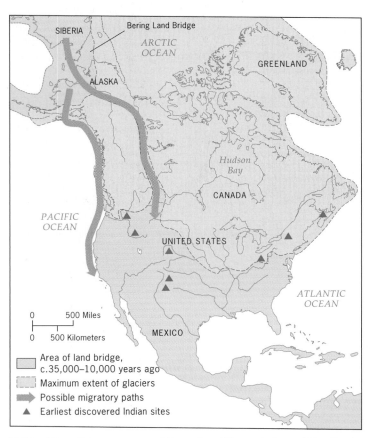

■ **The First Discoverers of America** The origins of the first Americans remain something of a mystery. According to the most plausible theory of how the Americas were populated, for some 25,000 years, people crossed the Bering Strait land bridge from Eurasia to North America. Gradually, they dispersed southward down ice-free valleys, populating both of the American continents.

Online Study Center

Interactive map
First Americans Enter the New World
college.hmco.com/pic/kennedybrief7e

Peopling the Americas

The Great Ice Age shaped more than the geological history of North America. It also contributed to the origins of the continent's human history. Some 35,000 years ago, the Ice Age congealed much of the world's oceans into massive ice-pack glaciers, lowering the level of the sea. As the sea level dropped, it exposed a land bridge connecting Eurasia with North America. Across that bridge spanning the present-day Bering Sea between Siberia and Alaska ventured small bands of nomadic Asian hunters—the "immigrant" ancestors of the Native Americans. They continued to trek across the Bering isthmus for some 250 centuries, slowly peopling the American continents.

As the Ice Age ended and the glaciers melted, the sea level rose again, inundating the land bridge about 10,000 years ago. Nature thus barred the door to further immigration for many thousands of years, leaving this part of the human family to develop its separate existence on the American continents.

Time did not stand still for these original Americans. Roaming slowly through this awesome wilderness, they eventually reached the far tip of South America, some 15,000 miles from Siberia. By the time the Europeans arrived in America in 1492, perhaps 54 million people inhabited the two American continents. Over the centuries they split into countless tribes, evolved more than 2,000 separate languages, and developed many diverse religions, cultures, and ways of life.

Incas in Peru, Mayans in Central America, and Aztecs in Mexico shaped stunningly sophisticated civilizations. Their advanced agricultural practices, based primarily on the cultivation of maize (Indian corn), fed large populations, perhaps as many as 20 million in Mexico alone. Though lacking technologies such as the wheel, these peoples built elaborate cities and carried on far-flung commerce. Talented mathematicians, they made strikingly accurate astronomical observations. The Aztecs also sought the favor of their gods by offering human sacrifices, cutting the hearts out of the chests of living victims, who were often captives conquered in battle.

EXAMINING THE EVIDENCE

Making Sense of the New World This map from 1546 by Sebastian Münster represents one of the earliest efforts to make geographic sense out of the New World (*Nouus Orbis* and *Die Nůw Welt* on the map). The very phrase *New World* suggests just how staggering a blow to the European imagination was the discovery of the Americas. Europeans reached instinctively for the most expansive of all possible terms—*world*, not simply *places*, or even *continents*—to comprehend Columbus's startling report that lands and peoples previously unimagined lay beyond the horizon of Europe's western sea.

Gradually the immense implications of the New World's existence began to impress themselves on Europe, with consequences for literature, art, politics, the economy, and, of course, cartography. Maps can only be *representations* of reality and are therefore necessarily distortions. This map bears a recognizable resemblance to modern mapmakers' renderings of the American continents, but it also contains gross geographic inaccuracies (note the location of Japan—*Zipangri*—relative to the North American west coast) as well as telling com-

mentaries on what sixteenth-century Europeans found remarkable (note the Land of Giants—*Regio Gigantum*—and the indication of cannibals—*Canibali*—in present-day Argentina and Brazil, respectively).

1. What further clues to the European mentality of the time does the map offer? In what ways might misconceptions about the geography of the Americas have influenced further exploration and settlement patterns?

2. Which portions of "New World" geography were more accurately mapped by European cartographers in 1546? Which were most distorted? Why?

3. Notice the closeness of *Zipangri* (Japan) and India to the West Coast of North America on the map. What does this tell you about Europeans' continuing belief in a "western route to the Indies" a half century after Columbus stumbled upon the Americas?

4. Look closely at the very small illustration of *Canibali* (cannibals) located on the map in today's South America. What does it reveal about Europeans' views of Native Americans?

■ **A Rocky Mountain Lake near Aspen, Colorado** The geologically young Rockies form the rugged backbone of the North American Continent.

The Earliest Americans

Agriculture, especially corn growing, accounted for the size and sophistication of the Native American civilizations in Mexico and South America. About 5000 B.C. hunter-gatherers in highland Mexico developed a wild grass into the staple of corn, which became the foundation of the complex, large-scale, centralized Aztec and Incan **nation-states**. As cultivation of corn spread across the Americas from the Mexican heartland, it transformed some nomadic hunting bands into settled agricultural villagers.

Corn planting reached the present-day American Southwest by about 1200 B.C. and powerfully molded Pueblo culture. The Pueblo peoples in the Rio Grande Valley constructed intricate irrigation systems to water their cornfields, and they built villages of terraced, multistory buildings. Corn cultivation reached other parts of North America considerably later, and the timing of its arrival explains much about the relative rates of development of different Native American peoples. North and east of the Pueblos, elaborately developed "societies" in the modern sense of the word scarcely existed. The lack of dense concentrations of population or complex nation-states was one reason for the relative ease with which the European colonizers subdued the native North Americans.

The Mound Builders of the Ohio River valley, the Mississippian culture of the lower Midwest, and the desert-dwelling Anasazi peoples of the Southwest did sustain some large settlements after the incorporation of corn-planting into their way of life during the first millennium A.D. The Mississippian settlement at Cahokia, near present-day East St. Louis, was at one time home to as many as 25,000 people. The Anasazis built an elaborate pueblo of more than six hundred inter-connected rooms in Chaco Canyon in modern-day New Mexico. But mysteriously, perhaps due to prolonged drought, all those ancient cultures fell into decline by about 1300.

Maize cultivation, as well as high-yielding strains of beans and squash, reached the southeastern Atlantic seaboard region of North America about A.D. 1000. The rich diet provided by these three crops produced some of the highest population densities on the continent, among them the Creek, Choctaw, and Cherokee peoples. In the northeastern woodlands, the Iroquois, inspired by their

nation-states *The form of political society that traditionally combines centralized government with a high degree of ethnic and cultural unity.*

✪ Map Skill-Builder:
**Understanding Demographic-Topographic Maps
(See map, p. 9)**

List five Indian tribes that lived in each of the following regions of North America: (a) Southwest (b) Great Plains (c) Northeast (d) Southeast

■ **North American Indian Peoples at the Time of First Contact with Europeans** Because this map depicts the location of various Indian peoples *at the time of their first contact with Europeans,* and because initial contacts ranged from the sixteenth to the nineteenth centuries, it is necessarily subject to considerable chronological skewing and is only a crude approximation of the "original" territory of any given group. The map also cannot capture the fluidity and dynamism of Native American life even before Columbus's "discovery." For example, the Navajo and Apache peoples had migrated from present-day northern Canada only shortly before the Spanish first encountered them in the present-day American Southwest in the 1500s. The map also places the Sioux on the Great Plains, where Europeans met up with them in the early nineteenth century—but the Sioux had spilled onto the Plains not long before then from the forests surrounding the Great Lakes. The indigenous populations of the southeastern and mid-Atlantic regions are especially difficult to represent accurately in a map like this because pre-Columbian intertribal conflicts had so scrambled the native inhabitants that it is virtually impossible to determine which groups were originally where.

■ **Cahokia** This artist's rendering of Cahokia, based on archaeological excavations, shows the huge central square and the imposing Monk's Mound, which rivaled in size the pyramids of Egypt.

Online Study Center

Interactive map
Indian Economies in North America
college.hmco.com/pic/kennedybrief7e

Online Study Center

Primary source
Cahokia
college.hmco.com/pic/kennedybrief7e

---

confederacy *An alliance or league of nations or peoples looser than a federation.*

matrilinear *The form of society in which family line, power, and wealth are passed primarily through the female side.*

primeval *Concerning the earliest origin of things; of ancient age.*

saga *A lengthy story or poem recounting the great deeds and adventures of a people and their heroes.*

legendary leader Hiawatha, created in the sixteenth century perhaps the closest North American approximation to the great nation-states of Mexico and Peru. The Iroquois **Confederacy** developed the political and organizational skills to sustain a robust military alliance that menaced its neighbors, Native American and European alike, for well over a century (see "Makers of America: The Iroquois," pp. 28–29).

But for the most part, the native peoples of North America were living in scattered and impermanent settlements on the eve of the Europeans' arrival. In more settled agricultural groups, women tended the crops while men hunted, fished, gathered fuel, and cleared fields for planting. This pattern of life frequently conferred substantial authority on women, and many North American native peoples, including the Iroquois, developed **matrilinear** cultures, in which power and possessions passed down the female side of the family line.

Unlike the Europeans, who would soon arrive with the presumption that humans had dominion over the earth and with the technologies to alter the very face of the land, Native Americans had neither the desire nor the means to manipulate nature aggressively. They revered the physical world and endowed nature with spiritual properties. Yet they did sometimes ignite massive forest fires, deliberately torching trees to create better hunting habitats, especially for deer. This practice accounted for the open, park-like appearance of the eastern woodlands that so amazed early European explorers.

But in a broad sense, the land did not feel the hand of the Native Americans heavy upon it, partly because they were so few in number. In the fateful year 1492, probably no more than 4 million Native Americans padded through the whispering, **primeval** forests and paddled across the sparkling, virgin waters of North America. They were blissfully unaware that the historic isolation of the Americas was about to end forever, as both the land and the native peoples alike felt the full shock of the European "discovery."

Indirect Discoverers of the New World

Europeans were equally unaware of the existence of the Americas. Blond-bearded Norse seafarers from Scandinavia chanced upon northeastern North America about 1000 A.D., and briefly settled in a place they called Vinland, near L'Anse aux Meadows in present-day Newfoundland. But no strong nation-state, yearning to expand, supported these venturesome voyagers. Their flimsy settlements consequently were soon abandoned, and their discovery was forgotten, except in Scandinavian **saga** and song.

For several centuries thereafter, other restless Europeans, with the growing power of ambitious governments behind them, sought contact with a wider world, whether for conquest or trade. They thus set in motion the chain of events that led to a drive toward Asia, the exploitation of Africa, and the completely accidental discovery of the New World.

Christian crusaders of the eleventh to the fourteenth centuries rank high among America's indirect discoverers. Though ultimately foiled in their attempts to wrest the Holy Land from Muslim control, the crusaders nevertheless acquired a taste for the exotic delights of Asia—silk for clothing, drugs for aching flesh, perfumes for unbathed bodies, colorful draperies for gloomy castles, and sugar and spices for preserving and flavoring food. The Italian adventurer Marco Polo further whetted European appetites for Asian luxury goods when he returned from China in 1295 telling tales of its golden pagodas and rose-tinted pearls.

But the distance and difficulties of transportation, for which Muslim and Italian **middlemen** charged dearly, made European consumers and distributors eager to find a less expensive route to the riches of Asia. Their hopes for an ocean route to Asia were long frustrated. Before the mid-fifteenth century, European sailors refused to sail southward along the coast of West Africa because they could not beat their way home again against the prevailing northerly winds and south-flowing currents.

Europeans Enter Africa

About 1450, Portuguese mariners overcame these obstacles by developing the **caravel**, a ship that could sail more closely into the wind. They also learned that they could return to Europe by sailing northwesterly from the African coast toward the Azores islands, where the prevailing westward breezes would carry them home.

The new world of sub-Saharan Africa, previously remote and mysterious to Europeans, now came within their questing grasp. African gold, perhaps two-thirds of Europe's supply, crossed the Sahara on camelback, and tales may have reached Europe about the flourishing West African kingdom of Mali in the Niger River valley, with its impressive Islamic university at Timbuktu. But Europeans had no direct access to sub-Saharan Africa until the Portuguese mariners began to creep down the West African coast in the mid-fifteenth century.

The Portuguese promptly set up trading posts along the African shore for the purchase of gold—and slaves. Arab and African merchants had traded slaves for centuries before the Europeans arrived. They routinely charged higher prices for slaves from distant sources, who could not flee to their native villages. Slave brokers also deliberately separated persons from the same tribes to frustrate organized resistance.

The Portuguese adopted these Arab and African practices in the sugar **plantations** that they, and later the Spanish, established on the African coastal islands of Madeira, the Canaries, São Tomé, and Principe. The Portuguese appetite for slaves was enormous, and slave trading became big business. Some forty thousand Africans were carried away to the Atlantic sugar islands in the last half of the fifteenth century. Millions more would be wrenched from their home continent after the discovery of the Americas. These fifteenth-century Portuguese adventures in Africa contained the origins of the modern plantation system, based on large-scale commercial agriculture and the wholesale exploitation of slave labor. This kind of plantation economy would shape the destiny of much of the New World.

After years of cautious exploration down the African coast, the Portuguese mariner Bartholomeu Días rounded the southernmost tip of Africa in 1488. Ten years later Vasco da Gama reached India and returned home with a small but tantalizing cargo of jewels and spices.

Meanwhile, the kingdom of Spain was united as a result of the marriage of two sovereigns, Ferdinand of Aragon and Isabella of Castile. After the brutal expulsion of the Muslim Moors from Spain, the new Spanish nation was eager to outstrip its Portuguese rivals in the race to tap the wealth of the Indies. Because Portugal controlled the round-Africa water route to India, Spain of necessity looked westward.

Online Study Center

Primary source
European Explorations in America
college.hmco.com/pic/kennedybrief7e

middlemen *In trading systems, those dealers who operate between the original producers of goods and the retail merchants who sell to consumers.*

caravel *A small vessel with a high deck and three triangular sails.*

plantation(s) *A large-scale agricultural enterprise growing commercial crops and usually employing coerced or slave labor.*

Columbus Comes upon a New World

The stage was now set for a cataclysmic shift in the course of history—the history not only of Europe but of all the world. Europeans clamored for more and cheaper products from the lands beyond the Mediterranean. Africa had been established as a source of cheap slave labor for plantation agriculture. The Portuguese voyages had demonstrated the feasibility of long-range ocean navigation. In Spain a modern national state was taking shape, with the unity, wealth, and power to shoulder the formidable tasks of discovery, conquest, and colonization. The dawn of the Renaissance in the fourteenth century nurtured an ambitious spirit of optimism and adventure. Printing presses, introduced about 1450, facilitated the spread of scientific knowledge. The mariner's compass, possibly borrowed from the Arabs, eliminated some of the uncertainties of sea travel.

Onto this stage stepped Christopher Columbus. This skilled Italian seafarer persuaded the Spanish monarchs to outfit him with three tiny but seaworthy ships. Columbus sailed westward into the oceanic unknown, and after six weeks at sea his fearful sailors grew increasingly mutinous. But on October 12, 1492, the crew sighted an island in the Bahamas. A new world thus swam within the vision of Europeans.

Only gradually did Europeans realize that Columbus had in fact bumped into enormous new continents. For decades explorers tried to get through or around the "islands" that, they assumed, blocked the ocean pathway to Asia. Columbus himself was at first so certain that he had skirted the rim of the "Indies" that he called the native peoples Indians, a gross geographical misnomer that somehow stuck.

Columbus's discovery would eventually convulse four continents—Europe, Africa, and the two Americas. Thanks to his epochal voyage, an interdependent global economic system emerged on a scale undreamed-of before he set sail. Its workings touched every shore washed by the Atlantic Ocean. Europe provided the markets, the capital, and the technology; Africa furnished the labor; and the New World offered its raw materials—especially its precious metals and its soil for the cultivation of sugar cane. For Europeans, as well as for Africans and Native Americans, the world after 1492 would never be the same, for better or worse.

When Worlds Collide

ecosystems A naturally evolved network of relations among organisms in a stable environment.

Two **ecosystems**—the fragile, naturally evolved networks of relations among organisms in a stable environment—commingled and clashed when Columbus waded ashore. The flora and fauna of the Old and New Worlds had been separated for thousands of years. European explorers marveled at the strange sights that greeted them, including exotic beasts such as iguanas and "snakes with castanets" (rattlesnakes). Native New World plants such as tobacco, maize, beans, tomatoes, and especially the lowly potato eventually revolutionized the international economy and fed the rapid population growth of the Old World. These foodstuffs were among the most important Indian gifts to the Europeans and the rest of the world. Ironically, the introduction into Africa of New World foodstuffs like maize, manioc, and sweet potatoes may have fed an African population boom that numerically, though not morally, more than offset the losses inflicted by the slave trade.

In exchange the Europeans introduced Old World crops and animals, such as cattle and horses, to the Americas. Horses reached the North American mainland through Mexico. North American tribes like the Apaches, Sioux, and Blackfoot swiftly adopted the horse, transforming their cultures into highly mobile, wide-ranging hunter societies that pursued the shaggy buffalo across the Great Plains. Columbus also brought sugar cane to the Americas. Thriving in the warm Caribbean climate, it prompted a "sugar revolution" in the European diet that fueled the forced migration of millions of Africans to work the canefields and sugar mills of the New World.

Online Study Center
**Primary source
Plant Exchange: The New World
and Old World Crops**
college.hmco.com/pic/kennedybrief7e

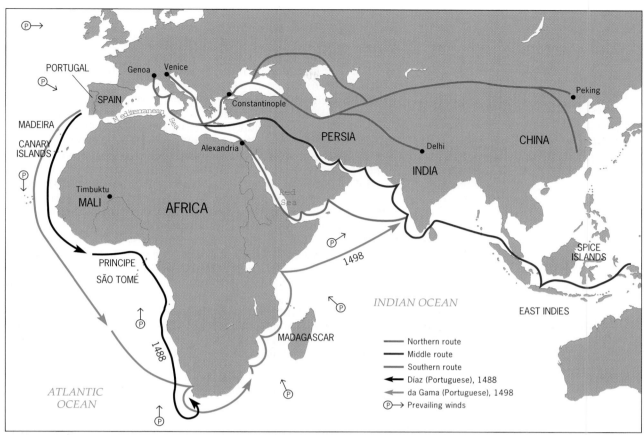

■ **Trade Routes with the East** Goods on the early routes passed through so many hands along the way that their ultimate source remained mysterious to Europeans.

Unwittingly, the Europeans also brought in their bodies the germs that caused smallpox, yellow fever, and malaria—diseases that quickly devastated the Native Americans. During the Indians' millennia of separate existence in the Americas, most of the Old World's killer maladies had disappeared from among them. But generations of freedom from those illnesses had also wiped out protective antibodies. Devoid of natural resistance to Old World sicknesses, Indians died in droves. Within fifty years of the Spanish arrival, the population of the Taino natives in Hispaniola dwindled from some 1 million people to about 200. The lethal germs spread among New World peoples with the speed and force of a hurricane, swiftly sweeping far ahead of the human invaders; most of those afflicted never laid eyes on a European. In the centuries after Columbus's landfall, as many as 90 percent of Native Americans perished, a **demographic** catastrophe without parallel in human history. Depopulation was so severe that entire cultures and ancient ways of life were extinguished forever. The Indians, by contrast, unintentionally infected the early explorers with syphilis, injecting that lethal sexually transmitted disease for the first time into Europe.

✪

The Spanish *Conquistadores*

Gradually, Europeans realized that the American continents held rich prizes, especially the gold and silver of the advanced civilizations in Mexico and Peru. Spain secured its claim to Columbus's discoveries in the Treaty of Tordesillas (1494), dividing with Portugal the "heathen lands" of the New World.

Spain became the dominant exploring and colonizing power of the 1500s. Seeking both the glitter of gold and the glory of God, Spanish *conquistadores* (conquerors) fanned out across the Caribbean and eventually onto the mainland of the

✪ Map Skill-Builder:
Understanding Economic Maps

In the early European trading routes with Asia and the East Indies, what one *common* destination could be reached by the Middle route, the Southern route, and da Gama's ocean route?
a) Constantinople b) Persia
c) China d) India

Online Study Center

Interactive map
Africa and Its Peoples, c. 1400
college.hmco.com/pic/kennedybrief7e

―――――

demographic *Concerning the general characteristics of a given population, including such factors as numbers, age, gender, birth and death rates, and so on.*

Bartolomé de Las Casas (1474–1566), a reform-minded Dominican friar, wrote The Destruction of the Indies *in 1542 to chronicle the awful fate of the Native Americans and to protest Spanish policies in the New World. He was especially horrified at the catastrophic effects of disease on the native peoples:*

"Who of those in future centuries will believe this? I myself who am writing this and saw it and know the most about it can hardly believe that such was possible."

Online Study Center

Primary source
Spanish Monk Pleads for Better Treatment of the Indians
college.hmco.com/pic/kennedybrief7e

conquistadores *Spanish conquerors or adventurers in the Americas.*

capitalism *An economic system characterized by private property, generally free trade, and open and accessible markets.*

encomienda *The Spanish labor system in which persons were held to unpaid service under the permanent control of their masters, though not legally owned by them.*

■ Conquistadores, c. 1534
This illustration for a book called the Köhler Codex of Nuremberg may be the earliest depiction of the *conquistadores* in the Americas. It portrays men and horses alike as steadfast and self-assured in their work of conquest.

American continents (see "Makers of America: The Spanish *Conquistadores*," pp. 16–17). Some early explorers, among them Ponce de León, Coronado, and de Soto, ventured into territory that eventually became part of the United States. But the permanent Spanish conquests of Peru and Mexico were by far the most consequential achievements of the *conquistadores*.

In South America, the ironfisted conqueror Francisco Pizarro crushed the Incas of Peru in 1532 and added a huge horde of booty, especially silver, to Spanish coffers. This flood of precious metal touched off a price revolution in Europe that increased consumer costs by as much as 500 percent in the hundred years after the mid-sixteenth century. Some scholars see in this ballooning European money supply the fuel that fed the growth of the economic system known as **capitalism**.

The islands of the Caribbean Sea—the West Indies—served as offshore bases where supplies could be stored and men and horses rested for the Spanish invasion of the mainland Americas. The vulnerable native communities of the West Indies also provided laboratories for testing the techniques that would eventually subdue Mexico and Peru. Most important was the institution of the *encomienda*, which allowed the government to give Indians to certain colonists in return for the promise to try to Christianize them. It was slavery in all but name, and the Spanish missionary Bartolome de Las Casas called it "a moral pestilence invented by Satan."

The Conquest of Mexico

The conquest of Mexico was engineered by Hernán Cortés, who set sail from Cuba in 1519 with sixteen horses and several hundred men. From an island near the coast of Mexico, he picked up a female Indian slave named Malinche, who knew both Mayan and Nahuatl, the language of the powerful Aztecs. Aided by Malinche and another interpreter, Cortés learned of the unrest among subordinate peoples within the Aztec empire, and of the gold and other wealth in its capital of Tenochtitlán. "We Spanish suffer from a strange disease of the heart,"

Cortés allegedly informed emissaries of the Aztec ruler Moctezuma, "for which the only known remedy is gold." The ambassadors reported this comment to Moctezuma, along with the astonishing fact that the newcomers rode on the backs of "deer" (horses). Believing that Cortés was the god Quetzalcoatl, whose return from the eastern sea was predicted in Aztec legends, Moctezuma allowed the *conquistadores* to approach his capital unopposed.

The Spaniards were amazed by the beauty and wealth of Tenochtitlán, with its 300,000 inhabitants and marvelous temples, aqueducts, and floating gardens. Moctezuma treated Cortés hospitably at first, but soon the Spanish were unable to contain their lust for gold. After warfare broke out on the *noche triste* (sad night) of June 30, 1520, Cortés laid siege to the city. It capitulated on August 13, 1521.

The Aztec empire thus gave way to three centuries of Spanish rule. Its people suffered not only from the armed conquest but from smallpox and other epidemics that burned through the Valley of Mexico. The native population of Mexico shrank from more than 20 million to fewer than 2 million people in less than a century. The temples of Tenochtitlán were destroyed to make way for the Christian cathedrals of Mexico City, built on the site of the ruined Aztec capital.

Yet the invader brought more than conquest and death. He brought his language, laws, customs, and religion, all of which proved adaptable to the peoples of Mexico. He intermarried with the surviving Indians, creating a distinctive culture of **mestizos**, people of mixed Indian and European heritage. To this day Mexican civilization remains a unique blend of the Old World and the New, producing both ambivalence and pride among people of Mexican heritage. Cortés's translator Malinche, for example, has given her name to the Mexican language in the word *malinchista*, or "traitor." But Mexicans also celebrate Columbus Day as the *Dia de la Raza*—the birthday of a wholly new race of people.

mestizo(s) *A person of mixed Native American and European ancestry.*

province *A medium-sized subunit of territory and governmental administration within a larger nation or empire.*

The Spread of Spanish America

Spain's colonial empire grew swiftly and impressively. Within about half a century of Columbus's landfall, hundreds of Spanish cities and towns flourished in the Americas. Majestic cathedrals dotted the land, printing presses turned out books, and scholars studied at distinguished universities, including those at Mexico City and Lima, Peru, both founded in 1551, eighty-five years before Harvard, the first college established in the English colonies.

But how secure were these imperial possessions? Other powers were already sniffing around the edges of the Spanish domain, eager to bite off their share of the promised wealth of the new lands. The upstart English sent Giovanni Caboto (known in English as John Cabot) to explore the northeastern coast of North America in 1497 and 1498. The French king dispatched Giovanni da Verrazano to probe the eastern seaboard in 1524 and Jacques Cartier to explore the St. Lawrence River in 1534. To protect sea lanes and secure their northern borderlands against such encroachments, the Spanish erected a fortress at St. Augustine, Florida, in 1565, thus founding the oldest continually inhabited European settlement in the future United States.

In Mexico, the tales of Francisco Coronado's expedition of the 1540s beckoned *conquistadores* northward from Mexico into the Rio Grande and Colorado River regions. A Spanish expedition led by Don Juan de Oñate entered the Rio Grande Valley in 1598 and cruelly abused the Pueblo peoples they encountered. In the battle of Acoma in 1599, the Spanish severed one foot of each survivor. They proclaimed the area to be the **province** of New Mexico in 1609 and founded its capital at Santa Fe the following year. The Spanish settlers found precious little gold, but missionaries did discover a wealth of souls to be harvested for the Christian religion. Their efforts to suppress Pueblo religious customs provoked an uprising called Popé's Rebellion in 1680. The Pueblo rebels destroyed every Catholic church in the province and killed a score of priests and hundreds of Spanish settlers. It took nearly half a century for the Spanish to reclaim New Mexico from the insurrectionary Indians.

Meanwhile, as a further hedge against the ever-threatening French, who had sent an expedition under Robert La Salle down the Mississippi River in the 1680s,

The Spanish *Conquistadores*

In 1492, the same year that Columbus sighted America, the great Moorish city of Grenada fell after a ten-year siege. For five centuries, the Christian kingdoms of Spain had tried to drive the North African Muslim Moors off the Iberian peninsula, and with the fall of Grenada this "Reconquista" succeeded. Centuries of religious war nurtured an obsession with status and honor, bred religious zealotry and intolerance, and created a large class of men who regarded manual labor and commerce contemptuously. With the Reconquista ended, some of these men turned their restless gaze to Spain's New World frontier.

Between 1519 and 1540, Spanish *conquistadores* swept across the Americas in two wide arcs of conquest—one driving from Cuba through Mexico into what is now the southwestern United States, the other starting from Panama, previously conquered by Vasco Balboa, and pushing south into Peru. The military conquest of this vast region was achieved by just ten thousand men, organized in a series of private expeditions. Hernán Cortés, Francisco Pizarro, and other aspiring conquerors signed contracts with the Spanish monarch, raised money from investors, and then proceeded to recruit private armies. Only a minority of the *conquistadores* were nobles. About half were professional soldiers or sailors; the rest comprised peasants, artisans, and members of the middling classes. Most were in their twenties and early thirties.

Some of these motley adventurers hoped to win royal titles or favors. Others sought to ensure God's favor by spreading Christianity to the pagans. Some men aspired to escape dubious pasts, while others sought the kind of historical adventure experienced by heroes of classical antiquity. Nearly all shared a lust for gold.

■ **An Aztec View of the Conquest, 1531** Produced just a dozen years after Cortés's arrival in 1519, this drawing by an Aztec artist pictures the Indians rendering tribute to their conquerors. The inclusion of the banner showing Madonna and child also illustrates the early incorporation of Christian beliefs by the Indians.

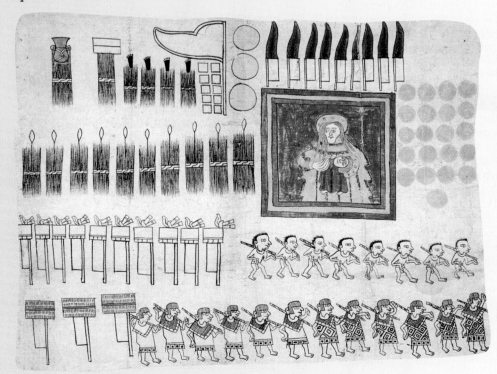

But most never achieved their dreams of glory or riches. Even when an expedition captured exceptionally rich booty, the spoils were unevenly divided: men from the commander's home region often received more, and men on horseback generally got two shares to the infantryman's one. The *conquistadores* lost still more power as the crown tightened its control in the New World. By the 1550s, the day of the *conquistador* had ended.

Nevertheless, the *conquistadores* achieved a kind of immortality. Because of a scarcity of Spanish women in the early days of the conquest, many *conquistadores* married Indian women. Their offspring, the "new race" of *mestizos*, formed a cultural and biological bridge between Latin America's European and Indian races.

the Spanish began around 1716 to establish a few settlements and missions in Texas, including the one at San Antonio later known as the Alamo. To the west, in California, no serious foreign threat loomed, and Spain directed its attention there only belatedly. Juan Rodriguez Cabrillo had explored the California coast in 1542, but for some two centuries thereafter California slumbered undisturbed by European intruders.

Then in 1769, Spanish missionaries led by Father Junipero Serra founded at San Diego the first of a chain of twenty-one missions that wound up the coast as far as Sonoma, north of San Francisco Bay. Father Serra's brown-robed Franciscan friars toiled with zealous devotion to Christianize three hundred thousand native Californians and teach them horticulture and crafts. These "mission Indians" did adopt Christianity, but they lost their native cultures and often lost their lives as well, as the white man's diseases doomed these biologically vulnerable peoples.

The misdeeds of the Spanish in the New World obscured their substantial achievements and helped give birth to the "Black Legend." This false concept held that the conquerors merely tortured and butchered the Indians, stole their gold, infected them with smallpox, and left little but misery behind. The Spanish invaders did indeed kill, enslave, and infect countless natives, but they also grafted their culture, laws, religion, and language onto a vast array of native societies, laying the foundations for a score of Spanish-speaking nations.

■ **The Devastation of Disease**
This engraving of a burial service records the horrendous impact of Old World diseases on the vulnerable Native Americans.

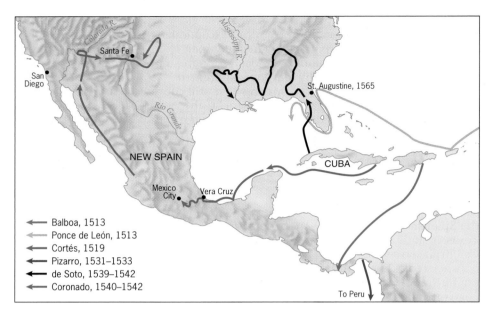

■ **Principal Early Spanish Explorations and Conquests** Notice that Coronado traversed northern Texas and Oklahoma. In present-day eastern Kansas, he found, instead of the great golden city he sought, a drab encampment, probably of Wichita Indians.

Clearly, the Spanish, who had more than a century's head start over the English, were genuine empire builders and cultural innovators in the New World. Compared with their Anglo-Saxon rivals, their colonial establishment was larger and richer, and it was destined to endure more than a quarter of a century longer. And in the last analysis, the Spanish paid the Native Americans the high compliment of fusing with them through marriage and incorporating indigenous culture into their own, rather than shunning and eventually isolating the Indians as their English adversaries would do.

★ Chapter Summary ★

Millions of years ago, the two American continents became geologically separated from the Eastern Hemisphere landmasses where humanity originated. The first people to enter these continents came across a temporary land bridge from Siberia about 35,000 years ago. Spreading across the two continents, they developed a great variety of societies based largely on corn agriculture and hunting. In North America, some ancient Indian peoples like the Pueblos, the Anasazi, and the Mississippian culture developed elaborate settlements. But on the whole, North American Indian societies were less numerous and urbanized than those in Central and South America, though equally diverse in culture and social organization.

The impetus for European exploration came from the desire for new trade routes to Asia, the spirit and technological discoveries of the Renaissance, and the power of the new European national monarchies. The European encounters with America and Africa, beginning with the Portuguese and Spanish explorers, convulsed the entire world. Biological change, disease, population loss, conquest, African slavery, cultural change, and economic expansion were just some of the consequences of the commingling of two ecosystems.

After they conquered and then intermarried with Indians of the great civilizations of South America and Mexico, the Spanish *conquistadores* expanded northward into the northern border territories of Florida, New Mexico, Texas, and California. There they established small but permanent settlements in competition with the French and English explorers who also were venturing into North America.

2

The Planting of English America

1500–1733

As the seventeenth century dawned, scarcely a hundred years after Columbus's momentous landfall, the face of much of the New World had already been profoundly transformed. European crops and livestock had begun to alter the very landscape, touching off an ecological revolution that would reverberate for centuries to come. From Tierra del Fuego in the south to Hudson's Bay in the north, disease and armed conquest had cruelly winnowed and disrupted the native peoples. Several hundred thousand Africans toiled on Caribbean and Brazilian sugar plantations. From Florida and New Mexico southward, most of the New World lay firmly in the grip of imperial Spain.

But *North* America in 1600 remained largely unexplored and effectively unclaimed by Europeans. Then, as if to herald the coming century of colonization and conflict in the northern continent, three European powers planted primitive outposts in three distant corners of the continent within three years of one another: the Spanish in Santa Fe in 1610, the French at Quebec in 1608, and, most consequentially for the future United States, the English at Jamestown, Virginia, in 1607.

Focus Questions

1. Why was England slow to begin colonization, and what factors finally enabled the English to establish successful colonies?
2. How did the Jamestown colony evolve from its disastrous beginnings into the successful colony of Virgina?
3. What was the relationship between early Virginia settlers and the Powhatan Indians, and how did Indian policies in the southern colonies eventually lay the basis for forced removal and reservations?
4. What was the basis for the economic and labor systems of Virginia and the other southern colonies?
5. What were the fundamental similarities and lesser differences among the five southern colonies of Virginia, Maryland, North Carolina, South Carolina, and Georgia?

★

England's Imperial Stirrings

Feeble indeed were England's efforts in the 1500s to compete with the sprawling Spanish Empire. As Spain's ally in the first half of the century, England took little interest in establishing its own overseas colonies. But in 1558 the Protestant Elizabeth ascended to the English throne and solidified her father King Henry VIII's break with the Roman Catholic Church. Protestantism became dominant in England, and rivalry with Catholic Spain intensified.

An early scene of that rivalry was Ireland, where the Catholic Irish sought help from Catholic Spain to throw off the yoke of the new Protestant English queen. In crushing the Irish uprising of the 1570s and 1580s with terrible ferocity, many English soldiers developed a sneering contempt for the "savage" natives, an attitude they brought with them to the New World.

Encouraged by the ambitious Queen Elizabeth, hardy English buccaneers now swarmed out upon the shipping lanes to plunder Spanish treasure ships and raid Spanish settlements. The most famous of these semipiratical "sea dogs" was the courtly Francis Drake, who plundered his way around the planet and returned in 1580 laden with Spanish gold.

The first English attempt at colonization, in bleak Newfoundland, collapsed when its promoter, Sir Humphrey Gilbert, lost his life at sea in 1583. Inspired by Gilbert's ill-starred dream, his gallant half-brother, Sir Walter Raleigh, organized another group of settlers, who went ashore in 1585 on North Carolina's Roanoke Island. But the hapless Roanoke colony mysteriously vanished, swallowed up by the wilderness.

These pathetic English failures at colonization contrasted embarrassingly with the glories of the Spanish Empire, whose profits were fabulously enriching Spain. Philip II of Spain, self-anointed foe of the Protestant Reformation, used part of his imperial gains to amass an "Invincible Armada" of ships for an invasion of England in 1588. But the skillful English sea dogs inflicted heavy damage on the armada, and a devastating storm (the "Protestant wind") scattered the crippled Spanish ships.

The rout of the Spanish Armada marked the beginning of the end of Spanish imperial dreams, though Spain's New World empire would not fully collapse for three more centuries. England's victory also started that country on its way to becoming master of the world oceans—a fact of enormous importance to the American people. Indeed England now possessed many of the strengths that Spain displayed on the eve of its colonizing adventure a century earlier: a strong, unified national state under a popular monarch; a measure of religious unity after a protracted struggle between Protestants and Catholics; and a vibrant sense of **nationalism** and national destiny.

This new sense of national pride and patriotism blossomed in the Elizabethan golden age of culture and politics. William Shakespeare, who made occasional poetic references to England's American colonies, was only one of many contemporary poets and writers who expressed boundless faith in the future of the English nation.

But England's scepter'd isle, as Shakespeare called it, also throbbed with social and economic tensions as the seventeenth century opened. Its population was mushrooming, from some 3 million people in 1550 to about 4 million in 1600. In the evergreen English countryside, landlords were "enclosing" croplands for sheep grazing, forcing many small farmers into precarious tenancy or off the land altogether. It was no accident that the woolen districts of eastern and western England—where Puritanism had taken strong root—supplied many of the earliest immigrants to America. When economic depression hit the

■ Elizabeth I (1533–1603), by Marcus Gheeraets the Younger, c. 1592 Although accused of being vain, fickle, prejudiced, and miserly, she proved to be an unusually successful ruler. She never married (hence, the "Virgin Queen"), although various royal matches were projected.

nationalism *Fervent belief and loyalty devoted to the political unit of the nation-state.*

Chronology

1558	Elizabeth I becomes queen of England.
c. 1565–1590	English crush Irish uprising.
1577–1580	Drake circumnavigates the globe.
1585	Raleigh founds "lost colony" at Roanoke.
1588	England defeats Spanish Armada.
1603	James I becomes king of England.
1607	Virginia colony founded at Jamestown.
1612	Rolfe perfects tobacco culture in Virginia.
1614	First Anglo-Powhatan War ends.
1619	First Africans arrive in Jamestown. Virginia House of Burgesses established.
1624	Virginia becomes royal colony.
1634	Maryland colony founded.
1640s	Large-scale slave-labor system established in English West Indies.
1644	Second Anglo-Powhatan War.
1649	Act of Toleration in Maryland. Charles I beheaded; Cromwell rules England.
1660	Charles II restored to English throne.
1661	Barbados slave code adopted.
1670	Carolina colony created.
1711–1713	Tuscarora War in North Carolina.
1712	North Carolina formally separates from South Carolina.
1715–1716	Yamasee War in South Carolina.
1733	Georgia colony founded.

woolen trade in the late 1500s, thousands of unemployed farmers took to the roads, often ending up as beggars and paupers in cities like Bristol and London.

At the same time, laws of **primogeniture** decreed that only eldest sons were eligible to inherit landed estates. Landholders' ambitious younger sons, among them Gilbert, Raleigh, and Drake, were forced to seek their fortunes elsewhere. By the early 1600s the unsuccessful lone-wolf ventures of such courtiers were replaced by the **joint-stock company,** which enabled a considerable number of investors to pool their capital.

Peace with a chastened Spain provided the opportunity for English colonization. Population growth provided the workers. Unemployment, as well as a thirst for adventure, for markets, and for religious freedom, provided the motives. Joint-stock companies provided the financial means. The stage was set for a historic effort to establish an English beachhead in the still uncharted North American wilderness.

primogeniture *The legal principle that the oldest son inherits all family property or land.*

joint-stock company *An economic arrangement by which a number of investors pool their capital for investment.*

charter *A legal document granted by a government to some group or agency to implement a stated purpose, and spelling out the attending rights and obligations.*

England Plants the Jamestown Seedling

In 1606, two years after peace with Spain, the hand of destiny beckoned toward Virginia. A joint-stock company, the Virginia Company of London, received a **charter** from King James I for a settlement in the New World. The main attractions were the promise of gold and the desire to find a passage through America to the Indies. Like most joint-stock companies of the day, the Virginia Company was intended to endure for only a few years, after which its stockholders hoped to liquidate it for a profit. This arrangement put severe pressure on the luckless colonists, who were threatened with abandonment in the wilderness if they did not quickly strike it rich on the company's behalf. Few of the investors thought in terms of long-term colonization. Apparently no one even faintly suspected that the seeds of a mighty nation were being planted.

> *In the years immediately following the defeat of the Spanish Armada, the English writer Richard Hakluyt (1552?–1616) extravagantly exhorted his countrymen to cast off their "sluggish security" and undertake the colonization of the New World:*
>
> "There is under our noses the great and ample country of Virginia; the inland whereof is found of late to be so sweet and wholesome a climate, so rich and abundant in silver mines, a better and richer country than Mexico itself. If it shall please the Almighty to stir up Her Majesty's heart to continue with transporting one or two thousand of her people, she shall by God's assistance, in short space, increase her dominions, enrich her coffers, and reduce many pagans to the faith of Christ."

> *The authorities meted out harsh discipline in the young Virginia colony. One Jamestown settler who publicly criticized the governor was sentenced to*
>
> "be disarmed [and] have his arms broken and his tongue bored through with an awl [and] shall pass through a guard of 40 men and shall be butted [with muskets] by every one of them and at the head of the troop kicked down and footed out of the fort."

The charter of the Virginia Company is a significant document in American history. It guaranteed to the overseas settlers the same rights of Englishmen that they would have enjoyed if they had stayed at home. This precious boon was gradually extended to the other English colonies, helping to reinforce the colonists' sense that even on the far shore of the Atlantic they remained comfortably within the embrace of traditional English institutions. But ironically, a century and a half later, the colonists' insistence on the "rights of Englishmen" fed their hot resentment against an increasingly meddlesome mother country and nourished their appetite for independence.

Setting sail in late 1606, the Virginia Company's tiny band of colonists eventually arrived at a site on the wooded and malarial banks of a swampy river. There, on May 24, 1607, about a hundred English settlers, all men, disembarked. They called the place Jamestown and the river the James in honor of King James I.

The early years of Jamestown proved to be a nightmare for all concerned—except the buzzards. Once ashore, the settlers died by the dozens from disease, malnutrition, and starvation. The woods rustled with game, and the rivers flopped with fish, but the greenhorn settlers, many of them self-styled "gentlemen" unaccustomed to fending for themselves, wasted valuable time grubbing for nonexistent gold when they should have been gathering provisions.

Virginia was saved from utter collapse at the start largely by the leadership and resourcefulness of an intrepid young adventurer, Captain John Smith. Taking over in 1608, he whipped the gold-hungry colonists into line with the rule "He who shall not work shall not eat." He had been kidnapped in December 1607 and subjected to a mock execution by the Indian chieftain Powhatan, whose daughter Pocahontas "saved" Smith by dramatically interposing her head between his and the war clubs of his captors. Pocahontas became an intermediary between the Indians and the settlers, helping to preserve a shaky peace and provide needed food.

Still, the colonists died in droves, and living skeletons were driven to desperate acts. They were reduced to eating "dogges, Catts, Ratts, and Myce" and even to digging up corpses for food. One hungry man killed, salted, and ate his wife, for which misbehavior he was executed. Of the four hundred settlers who managed to make it to Virginia by 1609, only sixty survived the "starving time" winter of 1609–1610. Diseased and despairing, the remaining colonists were ready to return to England in the spring of 1610 when a relief party suddenly arrived, headed by a new governor, Lord De La Warr.

De La Warr ordered the settlers to stay in Jamestown, imposed a harsh military regime on the colony, and soon undertook aggressive military action against the Indians. But disease continued to reap a gruesome harvest. By 1625 Virginia contained only some twelve hundred hard-bitten survivors of the nearly eight thousand adventurers who had tried to start life anew in the ill-fated colony.

Cultural Clash in the Chesapeake

When the English landed in 1607, the chieftain Powhatan dominated the few dozen small tribes in the James River area. Powhatan at first may have considered the English potential allies in his struggle to extend his power over his Indian rivals, and he tried to be conciliatory. But relations between the Indians and the English remained tense, especially as the starving colonists took to raiding Indian food supplies.

The atmosphere grew even more strained after Lord De La Warr arrived in 1610. He carried orders from the Virginia Company that amounted to a declaration of war against the Indians in the Jamestown region. A veteran of the vicious campaigns against the Irish, De La Warr introduced "Irish tactics" against the Indians. His troops raided Indian villages, burned houses, confiscated provisions, and torched cornfields. A peace settlement ended this First Anglo-Powhatan War in 1614, sealed by the marriage of Pocahontas to the colonist John Rolfe—the first known interracial union in Virginia.

A fragile peace prevailed for eight years. But the Indians, pressed by the land-hungry whites and ravaged by European diseases, struck back in 1622. A series of Indian attacks left 347 settlers dead, including John Rolfe. Pushed westward by retaliatory settler raids, the Indians made one last effort to dislodge the Virginians in the Second Anglo-Powhatan War in 1644. They were again defeated. The peace treaty of 1646 repudiated any hope of assimilating the native peoples into Virginian society or of peacefully coexisting with them. Instead it effectively banished the Chesapeake Indians from their ancestral lands and formally separated Indian from white areas of settlement—the origins of the later reservation system. By 1669 an official **census** revealed that only about two thousand Indians remained in Virginia, perhaps 10 percent of the population the original English settlers had encountered in 1607. By 1685 the English considered the Powhatan peoples extinct.

It had been the Powhatans' calamitous misfortune to fall victim to three Ds: disease, disorganization, and disposability. Like native peoples throughout the New World, they were struck down by European epidemics of smallpox and measles. They also lacked the unity to oppose the relatively well-organized and militarily disciplined whites. Finally, the Powhatans served no economic function for the Virginia colonists, having no gold, labor, or valuable goods to offer in commerce. Indeed the Indian presence frustrated the colonists' desire for a local commodity the Europeans desperately wanted: land.

■ Pocahontas (c. 1595–1617) Taken to England by her husband, she was received as a princess. She died when preparing to return to Virginia. Her infant son ultimately reached Virginia, where hundreds of his descendants have lived, including the second Mrs. Woodrow Wilson.

census *An official count of population, often also including other information about the population.*

✺ **Online Study Center**

Primary source
European Settlements and Indian Tribes in North America
college.hmco.com/pic/kennedybrief7e

The Indians' New World

The fate of the Powhatans foreshadowed the destinies of indigenous peoples throughout the continent as the process of European settlement went forward. Native Americans, of course, were no strangers to change, adaptation, and even catastrophe throughout their history, well before Columbus's arrival. But the shock of large-scale European colonization disrupted Native American life on a vast scale, inducing unprecedented demographic and cultural transformations.

Some changes were fairly benign. Horses acquired from the Spanish catalyzed a substantial migration of previously sedentary forest-dwelling peoples such as the Lakotas (Sioux) onto the Great Plains in the eighteenth century. There they thrived impressively, adopting an entirely new way of life as mounted nomadic hunters. But the effects of contact with Europeans proved less salutary for most other native peoples.

Disease was by far the biggest disrupter, as Old World pathogens licked lethally through biologically defenseless Indian populations. Disease took more than human life; it extinguished entire cultures and occasionally helped to shape new ones. Epidemics often robbed native peoples of the elders who preserved their oral traditions, and the survivors then faced the daunting task of literally re-inventing themselves without benefit of accumulated wisdom or kin networks. The decimation and forced migration of native peoples sometimes scrambled them together in wholly new ways. The Catawba nation of the southern Piedmont region, for example, was formed from the remnants of several different groups uprooted by the Europeans.

Trade also transformed Indian life, as traditional barter-and-exchange networks gave way to the temptations of European commerce. The drive to acquire European firearms in exchange for fur pelts fueled competition among the tribes for prime hunting grounds and led to an escalating cycle of Indian-on-Indian violence.

Indians along the Atlantic seaboard felt the most ferocious effects of European contact. Further inland, native peoples had the advantages of time, space, and numbers as they sought to adapt to the European incursion. The Algonquians in the Great Lakes area, for instance, became a substantial regional power, able to deal from a position of strength with the few Europeans who managed to penetrate the interior. As a result, a British or French trader wanting to do business with the inland tribes had little choice but to conform to Indian ways, often taking an Indian wife. Thus was created a middle ground, a zone where both Europeans and Native Americans were compelled to accommodate one another—at least until the Europeans arrived in large numbers.

Online Study Center

Primary source
Origins of Ottawa Society, as
Related by N. Perrot
college.hmco.com/pic/kennedybrief7e

Virginia: Child of Tobacco

John Rolfe, the husband of Pocahontas, became the father of the tobacco industry and an economic savior of the Virginia colony. By 1612 he had perfected methods of raising and curing the pungent weed. A tobacco rush swept over Virginia, as crops were planted in the streets of Jamestown and even between the numerous graves. Colonists who had once hungered for food now hungered for ever more land on which to plant ever more tobacco. Relentlessly, they pressed the frontier of settlement up the river valleys to the west, abrasively edging against the Indians.

Virginia's prosperity was finally built on tobacco smoke. This "bewitching weed" played a vital role in putting the colony on firm economic foundations. But tobacco—King Nicotine—was something of a tyrant. It was ruinous to the soil when greedily planted in successive years, and it chained Virginia's fortunes to the fluctuating price of a single crop. Tobacco also promoted the broad-acred plantation system and with it a brisk demand for slave labor.

In 1619, the year before the Plymouth Pilgrims landed in New England, what was described as a Dutch warship appeared off Jamestown and sold some twenty Africans. The scanty record does not reveal whether they were purchased as lifelong slaves or as servants committed to limited years of servitude. This commercial transaction planted the seeds of the North American slave system. Yet blacks were too costly for most of the hard-pinched white colonists to acquire, and for decades few were brought to Virginia. In 1650 Virginia counted but three hundred blacks, although by the end of the century blacks, most of them enslaved, made up approximately 14 percent of the colony's population.

Representative self-government was also born in primitive Virginia, in the same cradle with slavery and in the same year—1619. The London Company authorized the settlers to summon an assembly, known as the House of Burgesses. A momentous precedent was thus feebly established, for this assemblage was the first of many miniature parliaments to flourish in the soil of America.

As time passed, James I grew increasingly hostile to Virginia. He detested tobacco, and he distrusted the representative House of Burgesses, which he branded a "seminary of sedition." In 1624 he revoked the charter of the bankrupt Virginia Company, thus making Virginia a royal colony directly under his control.

Maryland: Catholic Haven

Maryland—the second plantation colony but the fourth English colony to be planted—was founded in 1634 by Lord Baltimore, of a prominent English Catholic family. He embarked on the venture partly to reap financial profits and partly to create a refuge for his fellow Catholics, who were harshly persecuted in Protestant England.

Absentee proprietor Lord Baltimore hoped that the two hundred settlers who founded Maryland at St. Marys, on Chesapeake Bay, would be the vanguard of a vast new **feudal** domain. Huge estates were to be awarded to his largely Catholic relatives, and gracious manor houses, modeled on those of England's aristocracy, were intended to arise amidst the fertile forests. As in Virginia, colonists proved willing to come only if offered the opportunity to acquire land of their own. Soon they were dispersed around the Chesapeake region on modest farms, and the haughty land barons, mostly Catholic, were surrounded by resentful backcountry planters, mostly Protestant. Resentment flared into open rebellion near the end of the century, and the Baltimore family for a time lost its proprietary rights.

Despite these tensions Maryland prospered. Like Virginia, it blossomed forth in acres of tobacco. Also like Virginia, it depended for labor in its early years mainly on white **indentured servants**—penniless persons who bound themselves to work for a number of years to pay their passage. In both colonies it was only in the later years of the seventeenth century that black slaves began to be imported in large numbers.

Lord Baltimore at first permitted unusual freedom of worship for Protestant settlers in Maryland. But when the heavy tide of Protestants threatened to submerge the Catholics, the Catholic settlers sought legal guarantees for their religious practice in the famed Act of Toleration, passed in 1649 by the local representative assembly. This statute guaranteed **toleration** to all Christians, but it decreed the death penalty for anyone who denied the divinity of Jesus. While falling far short of later standards of religious liberty, the statute did extend a temporary cloak of protection to the uneasy Catholic minority.

Online Study Center

**Primary source
Divorce in Maryland**
college.hmco.com/pic/kennedybrief7e

Online Study Center

**Interactive map
European Settlements and
Indian Tribes in Eastern North
America, 1650**
college.hmco.com/pic/kennedybrief7e

───────

feudal *Concerning the decentralized medieval social system of personal obligations between rulers and ruled.*

indentured servants *Poor persons obligated to a fixed term of unpaid labor, often in exchange for a benefit such as transportation, protection, or training.*

toleration *Originally, religious freedom granted by an established church to a religious minority.*

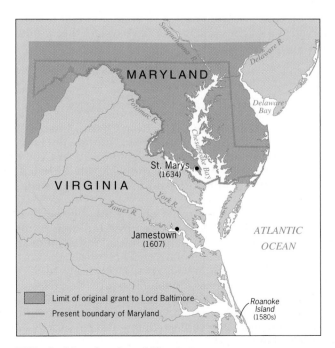

■ **Early Maryland and Virginia**

⭐ Map Skill-Builder:
Understanding Political Maps

1. Where did the original land grant to Lord Baltimore follow natural geographical features, and where did it follow certain "artificial" straight lines of latitude or longitude on the map?

2. Did the eventual *political* boundary of Maryland mostly follow the natural features, or did it add more artificially drawn boundaries?

African slaves destined for the West Indian sugar plantations were bound and branded on West African beaches and ferried out in canoes to the waiting slave ships. An English sailor described the scene:

"The Negroes are so wilful and loth to leave their own country, that they have often leap'd out of the canoes, boat and ship, into the sea, and kept under water till they were drowned, to avoid being taken up and saved by our boats, which pursued them; they having a more dreadful apprehension of Barbadoes than we can have of hell."

Online Study Center

Primary source
Estimated Slave Imports to the
New World
college.hmco.com/pic/kennedybrief7e

The West Indies: Way Station to Mainland America

While the English were nursing the first frail colonial shoots in the Chesapeake, they were also busily colonizing the West Indies. By the mid-seventeenth century, England had secured its claim to several West Indian islands, including the large prize of Jamaica in 1655.

Sugar formed the foundation of the West Indian economy. What tobacco was to the Chesapeake, sugar cane was to the Caribbean—with one crucial difference. Tobacco was a poor man's crop that could be planted and processed easily. Sugar cane was a rich man's crop, requiring extensive planting and an elaborate refining process in a mill. Because of the need for land, and for the labor to clear it and to run the mills, sugar cultivation was a capital-intense business. Only wealthy growers with abundant resources to invest could succeed in sugar.

The sugar lords extended their dominion over the West Indies in the seventeenth century. To work their sprawling plantations, they imported enormous numbers of African slaves—more than a quarter of a million in the five decades after 1640. By about 1700, black slaves outnumbered white settlers in the English West Indies by nearly four to one, and the region's population has remained predominantly black ever since. West Indians thus take their place among the numerous children of the African diaspora—the vast scattering of African peoples throughout the New World in the three and a half centuries following Columbus's discovery.

To control this large and potentially restive population of slaves, English authorities devised formal "codes" that defined the slaves' legal status and the masters' prerogatives. The notorious Barbados slave code of 1661 denied even the most fundamental rights to slaves and gave masters virtually complete control over their laborers.

A group of English settlers from Barbados arrived in Carolina in 1670, bringing with them a few African slaves, as well as the model of the Barbados code. In 1696 Carolina officially adopted a version of the code, which eventually inspired statutes governing slavery throughout the mainland colonies. The Caribbean islands thus served as a staging area for the slave system that would take root elsewhere in British North America.

Colonizing the Carolinas

Civil war convulsed England in the 1640s. King Charles I had dismissed Parliament in 1629, and when he recalled it in 1640, the members were mutinous. Finding their great champion in the Puritan soldier Oliver Cromwell, they ultimately beheaded Charles in 1649, and Cromwell ruled England for nearly a decade. Finally, Charles II, son of the decapitated king, was restored to the throne in 1660.

Colonization had been interrupted during this period of bloody unrest. Now, in the so-called Restoration period, empire building resumed with even greater intensity—and royal involvement. Carolina was formally created in 1670, after King Charles II granted to eight of his court favorites, the Lords Proprietors, an expanse of wilderness ribboning across the continent to the Pacific. These aristocratic founders hoped to grow foodstuffs to provision the sugar plantations in Barbados and to export non-English products like wine, silk, and olive oil.

Carolina prospered by developing close economic ties with the flourishing sugar islands of the English West Indies. Among the colonists' ventures was the capture and sale of inland Indians, which they turned into a thriving export business. As many as ten thousand Indians were dispatched to lifelong labor in the

West Indies, and others were sold to New England. A war with the Savannah Indians that began in 1707 ended this deplorable commerce. By 1710 the Indian tribes of coastal Carolina were all but annihilated.

After much experimentation, rice emerged as the principal export crop in Carolina. Since rice was grown in Africa, the Carolinians were soon paying premium prices for West African slaves experienced in rice cultivation. The Africans' agricultural skill and their relative immunity to malaria made them ideal laborers on the hot and swampy rice plantations. By 1710 they constituted a majority of Carolinians.

Moss-festooned Charles Town—named for King Charles II—rapidly became the busiest seaport in the South. Many high-spirited sons of English landed families, deprived of an inheritance, came to the Charleston area and gave it a rich aristocratic flavor. The village became a colorfully diverse community, to which French Protestant refugees and others were attracted by religious toleration.

Nearby, in Florida, the Catholic Spaniards abhorred the intrusion of these Protestant heretics. Carolina's frontier was often aflame. Armor-clad Spanish soldiers, often aided by their Indian allies, attacked English settlements during the successive Anglo-Spanish wars. But by 1700 Carolina was too strong to be wiped out.

The wild northern expanse of the huge Carolina grant bordered on Virginia. From the older colony drifted down a ragtag group of poverty-stricken outcasts and religious dissenters, many of them repelled by the wealthy plantation gentry of Virginia, who belonged to the established Church of England. These small farmers, who frequently were "**squatters**" without legal right to the soil, raised their tobacco and other crops with little need for slaves. Regarded as riffraff by their snobbish neighbors, the North Carolinians earned a reputation for being resistant to authority, hostile to religion, and hospitable to pirates. Their location between aristocratic Virginia and aristocratic South Carolina caused the area to be dubbed "a vale of humility between two mountains of conceit." North Carolina was officially separated from South Carolina in 1712, and subsequently each segment became a royal colony.

North Carolina, unlike its sister colony, did not at first import large numbers of African slaves. But both Carolinas shared in the ongoing tragedy of bloody relations between Indians and Europeans. After Tuscarora Indians fell upon the fledgling settlement of Newbern in 1711, North and South Carolinians retaliated by crushing the Tuscaroras in battle and selling hundreds of them into slavery. In another ferocious encounter four years later, the South Carolinians defeated and scattered the Yamasees, thereby devastating the last of the coastal Indian tribes in the southern colonies. In the interior Appalachian Mountains, however, the powerful Cherokees, Creeks, and Iroquois remained (see "Makers of America: The Iroquois," pp. 28–29). Stronger and more numerous than their coastal cousins, they managed for half a century more to contain British settlement on the coastal plain east of the mountains.

squatter *A frontier farmer who illegally occupied land owned by others or not yet officially opened for settlement.*

buffer *In politics, a small territory or state between two larger, antagonistic powers and intended to minimize the possibility of conflict between them.*

Late-Coming Georgia: The Buffer Colony

Pine-forested Georgia, with the harbor of Savannah nourishing its chief settlement, was formally founded in 1733. It proved to be the last of the thirteen colonies to be planted—126 years after the first, Virginia, and 52 years after the twelfth, Pennsylvania.

The British crown intended Georgia to serve chiefly as a **buffer**. It would protect the more valuable Carolinas against vengeful Spaniards from Florida and hostile French from Louisiana. Georgia indeed suffered much buffeting, especially when wars broke out between Spain and Britain in the European arena.

Named in honor of King George II of Britain, Georgia was launched by a high-minded group of philanthropists. Besides protecting their neighboring northern colonies and producing silk and wine, they were also determined to carve out a haven for wretched souls imprisoned for debt. The ablest of the founders was the dynamic soldier-statesman James Oglethorpe, who became keenly interested in prison reform after one of his friends died in a debtors' jail. As an able military

The Iroquois

Well before the crowned heads of Europe turned their eyes and their dreams of empire toward North America, a great military power had emerged in the Mohawk Valley of what is now New York State. The Iroquois Confederacy, dubbed by whites the "League of the Iroquois," bound together five Indian nations—the Mohawks, the Oneidas, the Onondagas, the Cayugas, and the Senecas. According to Iroquois legend, the alliance was founded in the late 1500s by two leaders, Deganawidah and Hiawatha. This proud and potent league vied with neighboring Indians for territorial supremacy, then with invading Europeans for control of the fur trade. Ultimately, decimated by the white man's diseases, whiskey, and muskets, the Iroquois struggled for their very survival as a people.

Online Study Center

Primary source
Dekanawida Myth and the
Achievement of Iroquois Unity
college.hmco.com/pic/kennedybrief7e

■ **The Longhouse (reconstruction)** The photo shows a modern-day reconstruction of a Delaware Indian longhouse (almost identical in design and building materials to the Iroquois longhouses), at Historic Waterloo Village on Winakung Island in New Jersey. (The Iroquois conquered the Delawares in the late 1600s.) Bent saplings and sheets of elm bark made for sturdy, weathertight shelters. Longhouses were typically furnished with deerskin-covered bunks and shelves for storing baskets, pots, fur pelts, and corn.

The building block of Iroquois society was the long-house. Twenty-five feet wide and up to two hundred feet long, these wooden structures sheltered several closely related nuclear families, their connections of blood running exclusively through the maternal line. The oldest woman in a clan was the honored matriarch. Men dominated the society, but they owed their positions of prominence to their mothers' families.

As if sharing one great longhouse, the five nations joined in the Iroquois Confederacy but kept their own separate fires. Although they celebrated together and shared a common policy toward outsiders, they remained essentially independent of one another. On the eastern flank, the Mohawks, known as the Keepers of the Eastern Fire, specialized as middlemen with European traders, whereas the outlying Senecas, the Keepers of the Western Fire, became fur suppliers. In the early 1700s, the Tuscaroras from the Carolina region gained affiliation with the Iroquois Confederacy.

Throughout the seventeenth and eighteenth centuries the Iroquois allied alternately with the British against the French and vice versa, for a time successfully working this perpetual rivalry to their advantage. But the confederacy divided during the American Revolution, with most tribes siding with the British. Their ultimate defeat left the Iroquois Confederacy in tatters. Most Iroquois moved to British Canada or were relegated to reservations in western New York.

Reservation life proved unbearable to the proud Iroquois, who fell into feuding and alcoholism. But in 1799 an Iroquois prophet named Handsome Lake arose, warning his people to mend their ways, affirm family values, and revive their old Iroquois customs. Handsome Lake died in 1813, but his teachings, in the form of the Longhouse religion, survive to this day.

leader, Oglethorpe repelled Spanish attacks. As an imperialist and a philanthropist, he saved "the Charity Colony" by his energetic leadership and by heavily mortgaging his own personal fortunes.

The hamlet of Savannah, like Charleston, was a **melting-pot** community that included German Lutherans and kilted Scottish Highlanders, among others. All Christian worshipers except Catholics enjoyed religious toleration. Many Bible-carrying missionaries arrived to work among debtors and Indians, including young John Wesley, who later returned to Britain and founded the Methodist church.

Georgia grew with painful slowness and at the end of the colonial era was perhaps the least populous of the colonies. The development of a plantation economy was thwarted by an unhealthful climate, by early restrictions on black slavery, and by demoralizing Spanish attacks.

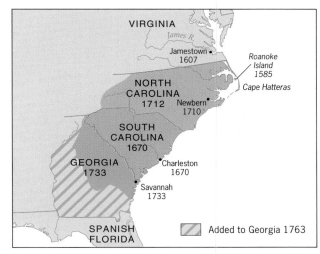

■ **Early Carolina and Georgia Settlements**

The Plantation Colonies

Certain distinctive features were shared by all of Britain's southern mainland colonies: Maryland, Virginia, North Carolina, South Carolina, and Georgia. Broad-acred, these outposts of empire were all to some degree devoted to exporting commercial agricultural crops like tobacco, rice, and indigo. Slavery was found in all the plantation colonies, though only after 1750 in reform-minded Georgia. Immense acreage in the hands of a favored few fostered a strong aristocratic atmosphere, except in North Carolina and to some extent in debtor-tinged Georgia. The wide scattering of plantations and farms, often along stately rivers, retarded the growth of cities and made the establishment of churches and schools both difficult and expensive.

Although the tax-supported Church of England became the dominant faith, all the plantation colonies permitted some religious toleration. The plantation colonies were to some degree expansionary. "Soil butchery" by excessive tobacco growing drove settlers westward, and the long, lazy rivers invited penetration of the continent—and continuing confrontation with Native Americans.

melting pot *Popular American term for an ethnically diverse population that is presumed to be "melting" toward some eventual commonality.*

Online Study Center

Interactive map
The Settlements of the Lower South
college.hmco.com/pic/kennedybrief7e

✪ Chapter Summary ✪

The defeat of the Spanish Armada and the exuberant spirit of Elizabethan nationalism finally drew England into the colonial race. After some early failures, the first permanent English colony was established at Jamestown, Virginia. Harsh conditions, gentlemanly aversion to work, and Indian hostility nearly caused it to fail, but stern leadership and tobacco cultivation finally brought prosperity and population growth.

The early encounters of English settlers with the Powhatan Indians in Virginia established many of the patterns that characterized later Indian-white relations in North America, including disease, warfare, and removal. Indian societies underwent their own substantial changes as a result of warfare, disease, and trade. For a time after the Atlantic coastal tribes were nearly wiped out, the larger Indian peoples of the Appalachian area formed a formidable barrier to white expansion.

Maryland and South Carolina were founded by aristocratic proprietors. Maryland was originally a Catholic refuge. South Carolina flourished by establishing close ties with the British sugar colonies in the West Indies, and brought the West Indian pattern of harsh slave codes and large plantation agriculture to North America. North Carolina was a less hierarchical settlement of largely poor white colonists who owned small farms and disdained authority. Latecomer Georgia served initially as a buffer against the Spanish and a haven for debtors.

Despite some differences, all the southern colonies depended on staple plantation agriculture for their survival and on the institutions of indentured servitude and African slavery for their labor. With widely scattered rural settlements, they had relatively weak religious and social institutions and tended to develop hierarchical economic and social orders.

3

Settling the Northern Colonies

1619–1700

GOD HATH SIFTED A NATION THAT HE MIGHT SEND CHOICE
GRAIN INTO THIS WILDERNESS.

WILLIAM STOUGHTON [OF MASSACHUSETTS BAY], 1669

Although colonists both north and south were bound together by a common language and a common allegiance to Mother England, they established different patterns of settlements, different economies, different political systems, and even different sets of values—defining distinctive regional characteristics that would persist for generations. The promise of riches—especially from golden-leafed tobacco—drew the first settlers to the southern colonies. But to the north, in the fertile valleys of the middle Atlantic region and especially along the rocky shores of New England, it was not worldly wealth but religious devotion that principally shaped the earliest settlements.

Focus Questions

1. What motivated English Pilgrims and Puritans to emigrate to the New World, and how did their religious beliefs affect the character and organization of the Plymouth and Massachusetts Bay Colonies?
2. How did religious dissent, economic circumstances, and Indian relations shape the founding and development of the other New England colonies?
3. What were the early efforts to promote intercolonial unity in New England, and why did they generally fail?
4. What were the original motives for the founding of New York and Pennsylvania? In what ways were the two colonies different, and in what ways were they similar?
5. What were the central features of the four middle colonies, and how did they differ from the New England colonies?

The Protestant Reformation Produces Puritanism

Little did the German monk Martin Luther suspect, when he nailed his protests against Catholic doctrines to the door of Wittenberg's castle church in 1517, that he was shaping the destiny of a yet unknown nation. Denouncing the authority of priests and popes, Luther declared that the Bible alone was the source of God's word. He ignited a fire of religious reform (the "Protestant Reformation") that licked its way across Europe for more than a century, dividing people, toppling sovereigns, and kindling the spiritual fervor of millions of men and women—some of whom helped to found America.

The reforming flame burned especially brightly in the bosom of John Calvin of Geneva. This somber and severe religious leader elaborated Martin Luther's ideas in ways that profoundly affected the thought and character of generations of Americans yet unborn. Calvinism became the dominant theological credo not only of the New England Puritans but of other American settlers as well, including Scottish Presbyterians, French Huguenots, and Dutch Reformed.

Calvin argued in the *Institutes of the Christian Religion* (1536) that God was all-powerful and all-good. Humans, because of the corrupting effect of original sin, were weak and wicked. God was also all-knowing, and since the first moment of creation had destined some souls—the elect—for eternal bliss and others for eternal torment. Good works could not save those whom **predestination** had marked for the infernal fires.

But neither could the **elect** count on their determined salvation and lead lives of wild, immoral abandon. For one thing, no one could be certain of his or her status in the heavenly ledger. Gnawing doubts about their eternal fate caused Calvinists constantly to seek signs of "**conversion**," or the receipt of God's free gift of saving grace, in themselves and others. Those who had the intense personal experience of conversion were expected to lead "sanctified" lives, demonstrating by their holy behavior that they were among the "**visible saints.**"

These doctrines swept into England just as King Henry VIII was breaking his ties with the Roman Catholic Church in the 1530s, making himself the head of the Church of England. Henry would have been content to retain Roman rituals and creeds, but some English religious reformers sought a total purification of English Christianity. As they grew increasingly unhappy with the snail-like progress of the Protestant Reformation in England, these "Puritans" burned with pious zeal to see the Church of England wholly de-Catholicized.

The most devout Puritans, including those who eventually settled New England, believed that only "visible saints" (that is, persons who felt the stirrings of grace in their souls and could demonstrate its presence to their fellow Puritans) should be admitted to church membership. But the Church of England enrolled all the king's subjects, which meant that the "saints" had to share pews and communion rails with the "damned." Appalled by this unholy fraternizing, a tiny group of dedicated Puritans, known as Separatists, vowed to break away entirely from the Church of England. King James I, who was head of both the church and the state in England from 1603 to 1625, threatened to harass the more bothersome Separatists out of the land.

predestination *The Calvinist doctrine that God has foreordained some people to be saved and some to be damned.*

elect *In Calvinist doctrine, those people who have been chosen by God for salvation.*

conversion *A religious turn to God, thought by Calvinists to involve an intense, identifiable personal experience of grace.*

visible saints *In Calvinism, those who publicly proclaimed their experience of conversion and were expected to lead godly lives.*

The Pilgrims End Their Pilgrimage at Plymouth

The most famous congregation of Separatists, fleeing royal wrath, departed for Holland in 1608. During the ensuing twelve years of toil and poverty, they were increasingly distressed by the "Dutchification" of their children. They longed to find a haven where they could live and die as English men and women—and as purified Protestants. America was the logical refuge.

A group of the Separatists in Holland, after negotiating with the Virginia Company, at length secured rights to settle under its jurisdiction. But their crowded *Mayflower*, sixty-five days at sea, missed its destination and arrived off the rocky coast of New England in 1620, with a total of 102 persons. Because their settlement at inhospitable Plymouth Bay was outside the domain of the Virginia Company,

Chronology

1517	Martin Luther begins Protestant Reformation.		**1639**	Connecticut's Fundamental Orders drafted.
1536	John Calvin of Geneva publishes *Institutes of the Christian Religion.*		**1642-1648**	English Civil War.
1620	Pilgrims sail on the *Mayflower* to Plymouth Bay.		**1643**	New England Confederation formed.
1624	Dutch found New Netherland.		**1655**	New Netherland conquers New Sweden.
1629	Charles I dismisses Parliament and persecutes Puritans.		**1664**	England seizes New Netherland from Dutch. East and West Jersey colonies founded.
1630	Puritans found Massachusetts Bay Colony.		**1675-1676**	King Philip's War.
1635-1636	Roger Williams convicted of heresy and founds Rhode Island colony.		**1681**	William Penn founds Pennsylvania colony.
1635-1638	Connecticut and New Haven colonies founded.		**1686**	Royal authority creates Dominion of New England.
1637	Pequot War.		**1688-1689**	Glorious Revolution overthrows Stuarts and Dominion of New England.
1638	Anne Hutchinson banished from Massachusetts colony.			

the Pilgrims became squatters without legal right to the land or specific authority to establish a government.

Before disembarking, the Pilgrim leaders drew up and signed the brief Mayflower Compact. Although setting an invaluable precedent for later written constitutions, this document was not a constitution at all. It was a simple agreement to form a crude government and to submit to the will of the majority under the regulations agreed upon. The compact was signed by forty-one adult males, eleven of them with the exalted rank of "mister," though not by the servants and two seamen. The pact was a promising step toward genuine self-government, for

■ Plymouth Plantation Carefully restored, the modest village at Plymouth looks today much as it did nearly four hundred years ago.

Online Study Center

Primary source
Mortality at Plymouth Plantation
college.hmco.com/pic/kennedybrief7e

Online Study Center

Primary source
The Great Puritan Migration
college.hmco.com/pic/kennedybrief7e

Online Study Center

Interactive map
English Migration, 1610–1660
college.hmco.com/pic/kennedybrief7e

calling *In Protestantism, the belief that saved individuals have a religious obligation to engage in worldly work.*

soon the adult male settlers were assembling to make their own laws in open-discussion town meetings—a great laboratory of liberty.

The Pilgrims' first winter of 1620–1621 took a grisly toll. Only 44 out of the 102 survived. Yet when the *Mayflower* sailed back to England in the spring, not a single one of the courageous band of Separatists left. As one of them wrote, "It is not with us as with other men, whom small things can discourage."

God made his children to prosper, so the Pilgrims believed. The next autumn, that of 1621, brought bountiful harvests and with them the first Thanksgiving Day in New England. In time the frail colony found sound economic legs in fur, fish, and lumber. The beaver and the Bible were the early mainstays: the one for the sustenance of the body, the other for the sustenance of the soul. The Pilgrims were also extremely fortunate in their leaders, especially William Bradford, a self-taught scholar who read Hebrew, Greek, Latin, French, and Dutch and was elected governor thirty times.

Quiet and quaint, the little colony of Plymouth was never important economically or numerically. Its population numbered only seven thousand by 1691, when, still charterless, it merged with its giant neighbor, the Massachusetts Bay Colony. But the tiny settlement of Pilgrims was big both morally and spiritually.

The Bay Colony Bible Commonwealth

The Separatist Pilgrims were dedicated extremists—the purest Puritans. More moderate Puritans sought to reform the Church of England from within. But their efforts faced catastrophe when Charles I dismissed Parliament in 1629 and sanctioned the anti-Puritan persecutions of the reactionary Archbishop William Laud.

In 1629 an energetic group of non-Separatist Puritans, fearing for their faith and for England's future, secured a royal charter to form the Massachusetts Bay Company. Stealing a march on both king and church, the newcomers brought their charter with them when they emigrated to Massachusetts. For many years they used it as a kind of constitution, out of easy reach of royal authority.

The Massachusetts Bay enterprise was singularly blessed. The well-equipped expedition of 1630, with eleven vessels carrying nearly a thousand immigrants, started the colony off on a larger scale than any of the other English settlements. Continuing turmoil in England tossed up additional enriching waves of Puritans on the shores of Massachusetts in the following decade (see "Makers of America: The English," p. 36). During the "Great Migration" of the 1630s, about seventy thousand refugees left England. But not all of them were Puritans, and only about twenty thousand came to Massachusetts. Many were more attracted to the warm and fertile West Indies, especially Barbados.

Many fairly prosperous, educated persons emigrated to the Bay Colony, including John Winthrop, a well-to-do pillar of English society. A successful attorney and manor lord in England, Winthrop eagerly accepted the offer to become the first governor of the Massachusetts Bay Colony, believing that he had a "**calling**" from God to lead the new religious experiment. He served as governor or deputy governor for nineteen years. The resources and skills of talented settlers like Winthrop helped Massachusetts prosper, and the Bay Colony rapidly shot to the fore as the biggest and the most influential of the New England outposts.

Massachusetts also benefited from a shared sense of purpose among most of the first settlers. "We shall be as a city upon a hill," a beacon to humanity, declared Governor Winthrop. The Puritan bay colonists believed that they had a covenant with God, an agreement to build a holy society that would be a model for humankind.

Building the Bay Colony

These common convictions deeply shaped the infant colony's life. Soon after arrival the settlers extended the franchise to all "freemen"—adult males who belonged to the Puritan congregations, which in time came to be called collectively the Congregational Church. On this basis about two-fifths of adult males enjoyed the franchise in provincial affairs, a far larger proportion than in contemporary England. Town governments, which conducted much important business, were even more inclusive. There all male property holders, and in some cases other residents as well, discussed and voted on public issues.

Yet the provincial government, liberal by the standards of the time, was not a democracy. "If the people be governors," asked one Puritan clergyman, "who shall be the governed?" True, the freemen annually elected the governor and his assistants, as well as a representative assembly called the General Court. But only Puritans—the "visible saints" who were alone eligible for church membership—could be freemen. And according to the doctrine of the covenant, the whole purpose of government was to enforce God's laws—which applied to believers and nonbelievers alike. Moreover, nonbelievers as well as believers paid taxes for the government-supported church.

Religious leaders thus wielded enormous influence in the Massachusetts "Bible commonwealth." They powerfully influenced admission to church membership, by conducting public interrogations of persons claiming to have experienced conversions. But the power of preachers, such as the eminent and learned John Cotton, was not absolute. Because Puritans had suffered so much at the hands of a "political" Anglican clergy, they barred clergymen from holding formal political office. In a limited way, the bay colonists thus endorsed the idea of the separation of church and state.

The Puritans were a worldly lot, despite—or even because of—their spiritual intensity. Like John Winthrop, they believed in the doctrine of a "calling" to do God's work on this earth. They shared in what was later called the "Protestant ethic," which involved serious commitment to work and to engagement in worldly pursuits. Legend to the contrary, they also enjoyed simple pleasures; they ate plentifully, drank heartily, sang songs occasionally, and made love monogamously.

Yet to the Puritans life was serious business, and hellfire was real—a hell where sinners shriveled and shrieked in vain and forever for divine mercy. Puritan clergyman Michael Wigglesworth's poem "Day of Doom" (1662) described the horrifying fate of the damned:

> They cry, they roar for anguish sore,
> and gnaw their tongues for horrour,
> But get away without delay,
> Christ pitties not your cry:
> Depart to hell, there may you yell,
> and roar Eternally.

★

Trouble in the Bible Commonwealth

The Bay Colony enjoyed a high degree of social harmony, stemming from common beliefs, in its early years. But even in this tightly knit community, dissension soon appeared. Quakers, who flouted the authority of the Puritan clergy, were persecuted with fines, floggings, and banishment. In one extreme case, four Quakers were hanged on Boston Common for their beliefs.

A sharp challenge to Puritan orthodoxy came from Anne Hutchinson. An exceptionally intelligent, strong-willed, and talkative woman, she claimed that the truly saved need not bother to obey the law of either God or man. This assertion, known as *antinomianism* (from the Greek, "against the law"), was high **heresy.** Brought to trial in 1638, the quick-witted Hutchinson bamboozled her clerical inquisitors for days, until she eventually boasted that she had come by her beliefs through a direct revelation from God. This was even higher heresy. After the Puritan magistrates banished her, she traveled on foot to Rhode Island, and finally moved to New York, where she and all but one of her household were killed by Indians.

More threatening to the Puritan leaders was a personable and popular Salem minister, Roger Williams. An extreme Separatist with an unrestrained tongue, Williams demanded a clean break with the corrupt Church of England and challenged the legality of the Bay Colony's charter, which he condemned for its unfairness to the Indians. As if all this were not enough, he went on to deny the

---

William Bradford (1590–1657) wrote in Of Plymouth Plantation,

"Thus out of small beginnings greater things have been produced by His hand that made all things of nothing, and gives being to all things that are; and, as one small candle may light a thousand, so the light here kindled hath shone unto many, yea in some sort to our whole nation."

Online Study Center

Primary source
Land Division for a Typical Puritan Town
college.hmco.com/pic/kennedybrief7e

heresy *Departure from correct or officially defined belief.*

The English

During the late Middle Ages, the Black Death and other epidemics that ravaged England kept the island's population in check. But by 1500 increased resistance to such diseases allowed the population to soar; and a century later the island nation was bursting at the seams. This population explosion, combined with economic depression and religious repression, sparked the first major European migration to England's New World colonies.

Some of those who voyaged to Virginia and Maryland in the seventeenth century were independent artisans or younger members of English gentry families. But roughly three-quarters of the English migrants to the Chesapeake during this period came as servants, signed to "indentures" ranging from four to seven years. One English observer described such indentured servants as "idle, lazie, simple people," and another complained that many of those taking ship for the colonies "have been pursued by hue-and-cry for robberies, burglaries, or breaking prison."

Whereas English immigration to the Chesapeake was spread over nearly a century, most English voyagers to New England arrived within a single decade. In the twelve years between 1629 and 1642, some twenty thousand Puritans swarmed to the Massachusetts Bay Colony. Fleeing a sustained economic depression and the cruel religious repression of Charles I, the Puritans came to plant a godly commonwealth in New England's rocky soil.

In contrast to the single indentured servants of the Chesapeake, the New England Puritans migrated in family groups, and in many cases whole communities were transplanted from England to America. Although they remained united by the common language and common Puritan faith they carried to New England, their English baggage was by no means uniform. Most New Englanders were farmers, but some towns recreated the specialized economies of particular localities in England. Marblehead, Massachusetts, for example, became a fishing village because most of its settlers had been fishermen in Old England. The townsfolk of Rowley, Massachusetts, brought from Yorkshire their distinctive way of life revolving around textile manufacturing.

Political practices, too, reflected the towns' variegated English roots. In Ipswich, Massachusetts, settled by East Anglian Puritans, the ruling selectmen served long terms and ruled with an iron hand. By contrast, local politics in the town of Newbury was often contentious and turnovers among officeholders high; the town's founders were from western England, a region with little tradition of local government. Although the Puritans' imperial masters in London eventually circumscribed such precious local autonomy, this diverse heritage of fiercely independent New England towns endured, reasserting itself during the American Revolution.

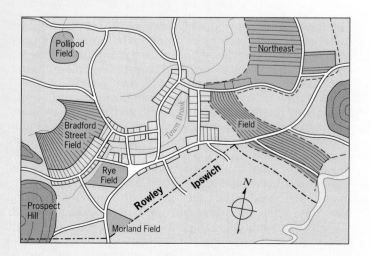

■ **Land Use in Rowley, Massachusetts, c. 1650** The settlers of Rowley brought from their native Yorkshire the practice of granting families very small farming plots and reserving large common fields for use by the entire community. On the map, the yellow areas show private land; the green areas show land held in common.

authority of civil government to regulate religious behavior—a **seditious** blow at the Puritan idea of government's very purpose. Their patience exhausted by 1635, the Bay Colony authorities found Williams guilty of disseminating "newe & dangerous opinions" and ordered him banished.

seditious *Concerning resistance to or rebellion against the government.*

New England Spreads Out

Aided by friendly Indians, Roger Williams fled to the Rhode Island area in 1636, where he built a Baptist church. He established complete freedom of religion, even for Jews and Catholics, a degree of toleration far ahead of the other English settlements in the New World. He demanded no oaths regarding religious beliefs, no compulsory attendance at worship, and no taxes to support a state church. He even sheltered the abused Quakers, although disagreeing sharply with their views.

Those outcasts who clustered about Roger Williams also enjoyed additional blessings. They exercised simple manhood suffrage from the start, though this broadminded practice was later narrowed by a property qualification. Opposed to special privilege of any sort, the malcontents and exiles who largely populated "Rogues' Island" had little in common with Roger Williams—except being unwelcome anywhere else. The Puritan clergy back in Boston sneered at Rhode Island as "that sewer" in which the "Lord's debris" had collected and rotted. Stubbornly individualistic, the squatters in "Little Rhody" finally established rights to the soil when they secured a charter from Parliament in 1644. A huge bronze statue of the "Independent Man" appropriately stands today on the dome of the state house in Providence.

The fertile valley of the Connecticut River had meanwhile attracted a different type of Dutch and English settlers. Hartford was founded in 1635, and the next year an energetic group of Boston Puritans, led by the Reverend Thomas Hooker, swarmed into the area. In 1639 the settlers of the new Connecticut River colony drafted a trailblazing document known as the Fundamental Orders, which established a regime controlled by the "substantial" citizens.

Another flourishing Connecticut settlement began to spring up at New Haven in 1638. It was a prosperous community, founded by Puritans who contrived to set up an even closer church-government alliance than in Massachusetts. The colonists dreamed of making New Haven a bustling seaport, but they fell into disfavor with Charles II because they sheltered two of the judges who had condemned his father, Charles I, to death. In 1662 the crown granted a charter that merged New Haven with the more democratic settlements in the Connecticut Valley.

Two smaller settlements grew up north of Massachusetts Bay. The fishermen and fur traders who had been active along the coast of Maine even before the founding of Plymouth were absorbed by Massachusetts Bay in 1677. The Maine territory remained part of Massachusetts for nearly a century and a half before becoming a separate state. In 1641 the Bay Colony also annexed its immediate northern neighbor, New Hampshire, under a strained interpretation of the Massachusetts charter. The king, annoyed by this display of greed, separated New Hampshire from Massachusetts in 1679 and made it a royal colony.

■ **Anne Hutchinson, Dissenter** Mistress Hutchinson (1591–1643) held unorthodox views that challenged the authority of the clergy and the very integrity of the Puritan experiment in the Massachusetts Bay Colony.

Online Study Center

Interactive map
Pattern of Settlement in Surry County, Virginia, 1620–1660
college.hmco.com/pic/kennedybrief7e

Puritans Versus Indians

The spread of English settlements inevitably led to clashes with the Indians, who were particularly weak in New England. Shortly before the Pilgrims arrived at Plymouth in 1620, an epidemic, probably triggered by contact with English fishermen, had swept through the coastal tribes and killed more than three-fourths of the native people. The deserted fields that greeted the Plymouth settlers provided grim evidence of the impact of the disease.

In no position to resist the English incursion, the local Wampanoag Indians at first befriended the settlers. Cultural accommodation was facilitated by Squanto, a Wampanoag who had learned English from a ship's captain who had kidnapped him some years earlier. The Wampanoag chieftain Massasoit signed a treaty with

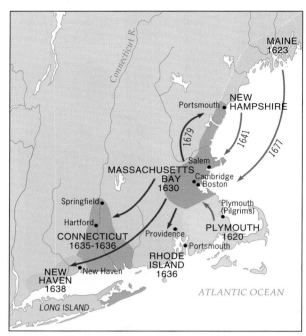

■ **Seventeenth-Century New England Settlements**
The Massachusetts Bay Colony was the hub of New England. All earlier colonies grew into it; all later colonies grew out of it.

the Plymouth Pilgrims in 1621 and helped them celebrate the first Thanksgiving after the autumn harvests that same year.

As more English settlers arrived and pushed inland into the Connecticut River valley, confrontations between Indians and whites ruptured these peaceful relations. Hostilities exploded in 1637 between the settlers and the powerful Pequot tribe. In a brutal war the English militiamen and their Naragansett Indian allies virtually annihilated the Pequots.

During the ensuing four decades of tense peace, the Puritans made some feeble efforts to convert the remaining Indians to Christianity. But their missionary zeal never equaled that of the Spanish and French Catholics, and a mere handful of Indians were gathered into Puritan "praying towns."

The Indians' only hope for resisting English encroachment lay in intertribal unity—a pan-Indian alliance against the swiftly spreading settlements. In 1675 Massasoit's son Metacom, called King Philip by the English, forged such an alliance and mounted a series of coordinated assaults on English villages throughout New England. When the war ended in 1676, fifty-two Puritan towns had been attacked, and twelve destroyed entirely. Hundreds of colonists and many more Indians lay dead. Metacom was captured, beheaded, and drawn and quartered. His head was carried on a pike back to Plymouth, where it was displayed for years.

King Philip's War slowed the westward march of English settlement in New England for several decades. But the war inflicted a lasting defeat on New England's Indians. Drastically reduced in numbers, dispirited, and disbanded, they thereafter posed only sporadic threats to the New England colonists.

Seeds of Colonial Unity and Revolt

A path-breaking experiment in union was launched in 1643, when four colonies banded together to form the New England Confederation. The confederation was intended to provide defense against foes like the Indians, French, and Dutch, as well as to solve intercolonial problems like runaway servants and criminals. Each member colony, regardless of size, wielded two votes.

Weak though it was, the confederation was the first notable milestone on the long and rocky road toward colonial unity. The delegates took tottering but long-overdue steps toward acting together on matters of intercolonial importance.

English monarchs had paid little attention to the American colonies during the early years of settlement. This era of benign neglect allowed the colonies, in effect, to become semiautonomous **commonwealths.** But when Charles II was restored to the throne in 1660, the royalists and their Church of England allies determined to take an aggressive hand in the management of the colonies. The king's agents took particular aim at proud and stubborn Massachusetts by extending rival Connecticut's charter in 1662 and granting a charter to the outcasts in Rhode Island in 1663. A final and crushing blow fell on the stiff-necked Bay Colony in 1684, when its precious charter was revoked by royal authorities. Massachusetts suffered further humiliation in 1686, when the royal government created the Dominion of New England, which was soon expanded to include New York and East and West Jersey. Unlike the homegrown New England Confederation, the Dominion was imposed from London and designed primarily to stitch England's overseas possessions more tightly to the motherland by throttling American trade with countries not ruled by the British crown.

The new Dominion's governor was **autocratic** Sir Edmund Andros, an able but tactless English military man who established his headquarters in Puritan Boston and promptly outraged the colonials with his profane soldiers and iron-handed tactics. Andros ruthlessly curbed the cherished town meetings, restricted the courts, and taxed the people without the consent of their duly elected representatives in the assemblies.

Online Study Center

**Primary source
Timucuan Shows Frenchmen How His People Respect a . . .**
college.hmco.com/pic/kennedybrief7e

commonwealth(s) *An organized civil government or social order united for a shared purpose.*

autocratic *Absolute or dictatorial rule.*

Online Study Center

**Primary source
Narragansett Leader Complains of English Encroachment**
college.hmco.com/pic/kennedybrief7e

Online Study Center

**Primary source
How the Savages Roast Their Enemies**
college.hmco.com/pic/kennedybrief7e

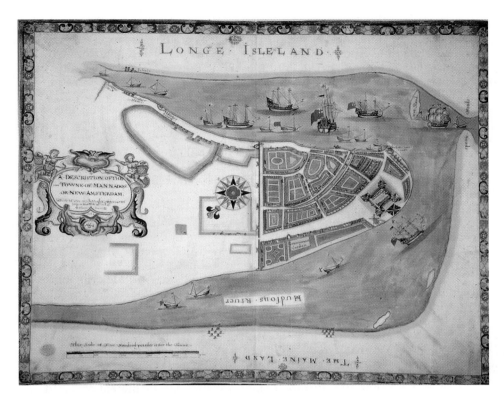

 **New York (then New Amsterdam), 1664** This drawing clearly shows the tip of Manhattan Island protected by the wall after which Wall Street was named.

On the verge of revolt, the New Englanders were beaten to the punch by the people of old England. In the Glorious Revolution of 1688–1689 they overthrew the despotic Catholic King James II and then invited the Dutch Protestant rulers William III and Mary to assume the English throne. When news of the Glorious Revolution reached America, a Boston mob rose against the existing regime, and the ramshackle Dominion of New England collapsed like a house of cards. Sir Edmund Andros attempted to flee in women's clothing but was betrayed by boots protruding beneath his dress. He was hastily shipped off to England. Though rid of the despotic Andros, Massachusetts did not gain as much from the upheaval as it had hoped. In 1691 it was arbitrarily made a royal colony, and the proud Puritans were forced to yield the privilege of voting—once a monopoly of church members—to all qualified male property holders.

The new English monarchs relaxed the royal grip on colonial trade and inaugurated a period of "salutary neglect" in which the much-resented Navigation Laws were only weakly enforced. Yet residues remained of Charles II's effort to assert tighter administrative control over his empire. More English officials—judges, clerks, customs officials—staffed the courts and strolled the wharves of English America. Many were incompetent, corrupt hacks who knew little and cared less about American affairs. Aggrieved Americans viewed them with mounting contempt and resentment as the eighteenth century wore on.

★ New Netherland Becomes New York

Late in the sixteenth century, the oppressed people of the Netherlands unfurled the standard of rebellion against Catholic Spain. After bloody and protracted fighting, they finally succeeded, with the aid of Protestant England, in winning their independence. This vigorous little lowland nation quickly emerged as a major commercial and naval power that ungratefully challenged the supremacy of its former benefactor, England.

The Dutch Republic also became a leading colonial power through the activities of the enterprising Dutch East India Company. The company's vast riches came mostly from the East Indies, where it maintained an enormous and

Online Study Center

Primary source
English Trade with Indians, as
Seen by Theodore de Bry
college.hmco.com/pic/kennedybrief7e

profitable empire for over three hundred years. In 1609 it employed an English explorer, Henry Hudson, who ventured into Delaware Bay and New York Bay and then ascended the Hudson River, hoping that he had at last chanced upon the coveted shortcut through the continent. But there was no transcontinental waterway, so Hudson merely filed a Dutch claim to the magnificently watered and wooded area.

New Netherland was permanently planted in 1623–1624 by the Dutch West India Company, the less wealthy counterpart of the East India Company. Never more than a secondary interest of the founders, the colony was exploited for its quick-profit fur trade. The company's most brilliant stroke was to buy Manhattan Island from the Indians (who did not actually "own" it) for trinkets— twenty-two thousand acres of what is now perhaps the most valuable real estate in the world for pennies per acre.

New Amsterdam—later New York City—was a company town. It was run by and for the Dutch company, in the interests of the stockholders. The investors had no enthusiasm for religious toleration, free speech, or democratic practices; and the governors appointed by the company were usually harsh and despotic. Religious dissenters like the Quakers were savagely abused.

The picturesque Dutch colony of New Netherland soon took on a strongly aristocratic tinge and retained it for generations. Vast feudal estates fronting the Hudson River, known as patroonships, were granted to promoters who agreed to settle fifty people on them. One patroonship in the Albany area was slightly larger than the later state of Rhode Island.

A threat to New Netherland soon came from the Swedes, who trespassed on Dutch preserves by planting the colony of New Sweden on the Delaware River in 1638. Resenting the Swedish intrusion, the Dutch dispatched a small military expedition in 1655, led by the able but despotic director-general Peter Stuyvesant. The main fort fell after a bloodless siege, and Swedish rule came to an abrupt end, leaving behind in later Delaware only a sprinkling of Swedish place-names and Swedish log cabins (the first in America), as well as an admixture of Swedish blood.

Just as New Netherland absorbed New Sweden, it was soon the turn of the Dutch to be swallowed up by the English. In 1664, after the imperially ambitious King Charles II granted the area to his brother, the Duke of York, a strong English squadron appeared off the decrepit defenses of New Amsterdam. A fuming Peter Stuyvesant, short of all munitions except courage, was forced to surrender without firing a shot. New Amsterdam was thereupon renamed New York, in honor of the Duke of York. England won a splendid harbor, strategically located in the middle of the mainland colonies, with the stately Hudson River penetrating the interior. With the removal of this foreign wedge, the English banner waved triumphantly over a solid stretch of territory from Maine to the Carolinas.

The conquered Dutch province tenaciously retained many of the illiberal features of earlier days. An autocratic spirit survived, and the aristocratic element gained strength when certain corrupt English governors granted immense acreage to their favorites. Influential landowning families—such as the Livingstons and the De Lanceys—wielded disproportionate power in the affairs of colonial New York. These monopolistic land policies, combined with the lordly atmosphere, discouraged many European immigrants from coming. The physical growth of New York was correspondingly retarded.

Penn's Holy Experiment in Pennsylvania

A remarkable group of dissenters, commonly known as Quakers, arose in England during the mid-1600s. Their name derived from the report that they "quaked" when touched by deep religious emotion. Officially they were known as the Religious Society of Friends.

Quakers were especially offensive to the authorities, both religious and civil. They refused to support the established Church of England with taxes. They built simple meetinghouses, without a paid clergy, and "spoke up" themselves in meetings when moved. Believing that all were equal as children in the sight of God, Quakers kept their broad-brimmed hats on in the presence of their "betters" and addressed others with simple "thee's" and "thou's," rather than with conventional titles. They would take no oaths because Jesus had commanded, "Swear not at all." This peculiarity often embroiled them with government officials, for "test oaths" were still required to establish the fact that a person was not a Roman Catholic.

The Quakers, beyond a doubt, were a people of deep conviction. They abhorred strife and warfare and refused military service. As advocates of **passive resistance,** they would turn the other cheek and rebuild their meetinghouse on the sites where their enemies had torn it down. Their courage and devotion to principle finally triumphed. Although at times they seemed stubborn and unreasonable, they were a simple, devoted, democratic people, contending in their own way for religious and civic freedom.

William Penn, a well-born and athletic young Englishman, was attracted to the Quaker faith in 1660, when only sixteen years old. His father, disapproving, administered a sound flogging. After various adventures in the army (the best portrait of the peaceful Quaker has him in armor), the youth firmly embraced the despised faith and suffered much persecution.

Penn felt keenly the plight of his fellow Quakers, thousands of whom were executed, flogged, or cast into dank prisons. Penn's thoughts naturally turned to the New World, where a sprinkling of Quakers had already fled, notably to Rhode Island, North Carolina, and New Jersey. Eager to establish an **asylum** for his people, he also hoped to experiment with liberal ideas in government and at the same time make a profit. Finally, in 1681, he managed to secure from the king an immense grant of fertile land, in consideration of a monetary debt that the crown owed to his deceased father. The king called the area Pennsylvania ("Penn's Woodland") in honor of the father.

Pennsylvania was by far the best advertised of all the colonies. Its founder sent out paid agents and distributed countless pamphlets printed in English, Dutch, French, and German. Unlike the lures of many an American real estate promoter, then and later, Penn's inducements were generally truthful. He especially welcomed substantial citizens, including industrious carpenters, masons, and shoemakers. His liberal land policy, which encouraged substantial holdings, was instrumental in attracting a heavy inflow of immigrants.

Penn formally launched his colony in 1681. He farsightedly bought land along the Delaware River from the Indians for his town of Philadelphia ("brotherly love" in Greek). His treatment of the native people was so fair that the Quaker "broad brims" went among them unarmed and even employed them as babysitters. For a brief period, Pennsylvania seemed the promised land of amicable Indian-white relations. Some southern tribes even migrated there, seeking the Quaker haven. But ironically, Quaker tolerance proved the undoing of Quaker Indian policy. As

passive resistance *Nonviolent action in opposition to authority or laws, often in accord with religious or moral beliefs.*

asylum *A place of refuge and security, especially for the persecuted or unfortunate.*

■ **Penn's Treaty, by Edward Hicks** The peace-loving Quaker founder of Pennsylvania made a serious effort to live in harmony with the Indians, as this treaty-signing scene illustrates. But the westward thrust of white settlement eventually caused friction between the two groups, as in other colonies.

In a Boston lecture in 1869, Ralph Waldo Emerson (1803–1882) declared,

"The sect of the Quakers in their best representatives appear to me to have come nearer to the sublime history and genius of Christ than any other of the sects."

naturalization *The granting of citizenship to foreigners or immigrants.*

ethnic *Concerning diverse peoples or cultures, specifically—in America—those of non-Anglo-Saxon background.*

blue laws *Laws designed to restrict personal behavior in accord with a strict code of morality.*

non-Quaker European immigrants flooded into the welcoming province, they undermined the Quakers' own benevolent policy toward the Indians. The feisty Scots-Irish were particularly unpersuaded by Quaker idealism.

Among other noteworthy features, no provision was made by the Quakers of Pennsylvania for a military defense. No restrictions were placed on immigration, and **naturalization** was made easy. The humane Quakers early developed a strong dislike of black slavery, and in the genial glow of Pennsylvania some progress was made toward social reform.

With its many liberal features, Pennsylvania attracted a rich mix of **ethnic** groups. They included numerous religious misfits who were repelled by the harsh practices of neighboring colonies. This Quaker refuge boasted a surprisingly modern atmosphere in an unmodern age, and to an unusual degree it afforded economic opportunity, civil liberty, and religious freedom. Even so, "**blue laws**" prohibited "ungodly revelers," stage plays, playing cards, dice, games, and excessive hilarity.

Under such generally happy auspices, Penn's brainchild grew lustily. The Quakers were shrewd businesspeople, and in a short time the settlers were exporting grain and other foodstuffs. Within two years Philadelphia claimed three hundred houses and twenty-five hundred people. Within nineteen years—by 1700—the colony was surpassed in population and wealth only by long-established Virginia and Massachusetts.

William Penn spent only about four years in the colony and eventually died full of sorrows back in England. But Pennsylvania, his enduring monument, was not only a noble experiment in government but also a new commonwealth. Based on civil and religious liberty, and dedicated to freedom of conscience and worship, it held aloft a hopeful torch in a world of semidarkness.

Small Quaker settlements flourished next door to Pennsylvania. New Jersey was started in 1664, when two noble proprietors received the area from the Duke of York. One of the proprietors sold West New Jersey in 1674 to a group of Quakers, and Quakers also acquired East New Jersey a few years later. In 1702, the crown clipped the Quakers' wings and combined the two Jerseys in a royal colony.

Swedish-tinged Delaware consisted of only three counties—two at high tide, the witticism goes—and was named after Lord De La Warr, the harsh military governor who had arrived in Virginia in 1610. Harboring some Quakers, and closely associated with Penn's flourishing colony, Delaware was granted its own assembly in 1703. But until the American Revolution it remained under the governor of Pennsylvania.

The Middle Way in the Middle Colonies

The middle colonies—New York, New Jersey, Delaware, and Pennsylvania—enjoyed certain features in common. In general, the soil was fertile and the expanse of land was broad, unlike rock-strewn New England. Pennsylvania, New York, and New Jersey came to be known as the "bread colonies" because of their heavy exports of grain.

Rivers also played a vital role. Broad, languid streams—notably the Susquehanna, the Delaware, and the Hudson—tapped the fur trade of the interior and beckoned adventuresome spirits into the backcountry. The rivers, unlike New England's, had few cascading waterfalls and hence presented little inducement to manufacturing with water-wheel power.

A surprising amount of industry nonetheless hummed in the middle colonies. Virginal forests abounded for lumbering and shipbuilding. The presence of deep river estuaries and landlocked harbors stimulated both commerce and the growth of seaports, such as New York and Philadelphia. Even Albany, more than a hundred miles up the Hudson, was a port of some consequence in colonial days.

The middle colonies stood midway between New England and the southern plantation group in many respects besides geography. Except in aristocratic New

EXAMINING THE EVIDENCE

A Seventeenth-Century Valuables Cabinet In 1999 a boatyard worker on Cape Cod and his sister, a New Hampshire teacher, inherited a small (20-pound, 16–1/2 inch-high) chest that had always stood on their grandmother's hall table, known in the family as the "Franklin chest." Eager to learn more about it, they set out to discover the original owner, tracing their family genealogy and consulting with furniture experts. In January 2000 this rare seventeenth-century cabinet, its full provenance now known, appeared on the auction block and sold for a record $2.4 million to the Peabody Essex Museum in Salem, Massachusetts. No less extraordinary than the price was the history of its creator and its owners embodied in the piece. Salem cabinetmaker James Symonds (1636–1726) had made the chest for his relatives Joseph Pope (1650–1712) and Bathsheba Folger (1652–1726) to commemorate their 1679 marriage. Symonds carved the Popes' initials and the date on the door of the cabinet. He also put elaborate S curves on the sides remarkably similar to the Mannerist carved oak paneling produced in Norfolk, England, from where his own cabinetmaker father had emigrated. Behind the chest's door are ten drawers where the Popes would have kept jewelry, money, deeds, and writing materials. Surely they prized the chest as a sign of refinement to be shown off in their best room, a sentiment passed down through the next thirteen generations even as the Popes' identities were lost. The chest may have become known as the "Franklin chest" because Bathsheba was Benjamin Franklin's aunt, but also because that identification appealed more to descendants ashamed that the Quaker Popes, whose own parents had been persecuted for their faith, were virulent accusers during the Salem witch trials of 1692.

1. What significant features of this seventeenth-century chest could be determined simply by careful examination of the material object itself, and which could be learned only by historical research?

2. After studying the chest itself, which elements of the construction and carving might provide significant clues about what historical inquiries to pursue?

3. What does the nature of the chest and its original function as a storage place for valuables tell you about the economic status of the original owners, Joseph and Bathsheba Pope? Why might this chest have been handed down through their descendants for over 300 years, when most other material artifacts disappeared?

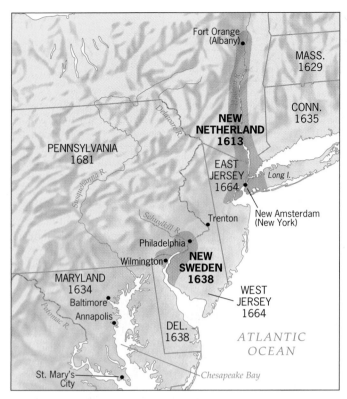

■ Early Settlements in the Middle Colonies, with Founding Dates

York, the landholdings were generally intermediate in size—smaller than in the big-acreage South but larger than in small-farm New England. Local government lay somewhere between the personalized town meeting of New England and the diffused county government of the South. There were fewer industries in the middle colonies than in New England, more than in the South.

Yet the middle colonies could claim certain distinctions in their own right. Generally speaking, the population was more ethnically mixed than that of other settlements. The people were blessed with an unusual degree of religious toleration and democratic control. Earnest and devout Quakers, in particular, made a contribution to human freedom out of all proportion to their numbers. Desirable land was more easily acquired in the middle colonies than in New England or in the tidewater South. One result was that a considerable amount of economic and social democracy prevailed, though less so in aristocratic New York.

Modern-minded Benjamin Franklin, often regarded as the most representative American personality of this era, was a child of the middle colonies. Although it is true that Franklin was born a Yankee in puritanical Boston, he entered Philadelphia as a seventeen-year-old in 1720 with a loaf of bread under each arm and immediately found a congenial home in the urbane, open atmosphere of what was then North America's biggest city. One Pennsylvanian later boasted that Franklin "came to life, at seventeen, in Philadelphia."

By the time Franklin arrived in the City of Brotherly Love, the American colonies themselves were "coming to life." Population was growing robustly. Transportation and communication were improving. The British, for the most part, left the colonists to fashion their own local governments, run their own churches, and develop networks of intercolonial trade. As people and products crisscrossed the colonies with increasing frequency and increasing volume, Americans began to realize that—far removed from Mother England—they were not merely surviving, but truly thriving.

✪ Chapter Summary ✪

The New England colonies were founded primarily by English Calvinist religious dissenters called Puritans. While most Puritans sought to "purify" the Church of England from within, and not to break away from it, a small group of Separatists—the Pilgrims—founded the first small, pious Plymouth Colony in New England. More important was the larger group of nonseparating Puritans, led by John Winthrop, who founded the Massachusetts Bay Colony as part of a "great migration" of Puritans fleeing persecution in England in the 1630s.

A strong sense of common religious and moral purpose shaped the Massachusetts Bay Colony. Because of the close alignment of religion and politics in the colony, those who challenged religious orthodoxy, among them Anne Hutchinson and Roger Williams, were considered guilty of sedition as well, and driven out of Massachusetts. The banished Williams founded Rhode Island, by far the most religiously and politically tolerant of the colonies. Other New England settlements, all originating in Massachusetts Bay, were established in Connecticut, Maine, and New Hampshire. Although they shared a common way of life, and occasionally engaged in common action (for instance, against the Indians), each of the New England colonies developed with a substantial degree of independence.

The middle colonies took shape quite differently. New York, founded as New Netherland by the Dutch and later conquered by England, was economically and ethnically diverse, socially hierarchical, and politically quarrelsome. Pennsylvania, founded as a Quaker haven by William Penn, attracted an economically ambitious and religiously tolerant but politically troublesome population of diverse ethnic groups.

With their economic variety, ethnic and religious diversity, and political factionalism, the middle colonies were the most typically "American" of England's thirteen Atlantic seaboard colonies.

VARYING VIEWPOINTS

Europeanizing America or Americanizing Europe?

The history of discovery and the earliest colonization raises perhaps the single most fundamental question about all American history. Should it be understood as the extension of European civilization into the New World or as the gradual development of a uniquely "American" culture? One school of thought tended to emphasize the Europeanization of America. Historians of that persuasion paid close attention to the situation in Europe, particularly in England and Spain, in the fifteenth and sixteenth centuries. They also focused on the various means by which the values and institutions of the mother continent were exported to the new lands in the western sea. Some European writers varied this general question by asking what transforming effect the discovery of America had on Europe itself. Both of these approaches are Eurocentric. More recently, historians have concentrated on the distinctiveness of America. The concern with European origins has evolved into a comparative treatment of English, Spanish, Dutch, and French settlements in the New World. The newest trend to emerge is a transatlantic history that views European empires and their American colonies as players in a process of cultural cross-fertilization affecting not only the colonies but Europe and Africa as well.

This less Eurocentric approach has changed the way historians explain the colonial development of America. Historians increasingly view the colonial period as one of "contact" and "adaptation" between European, African, and Native American ways of life. Scholars including Richard White, Alfred W. Crosby, William Cronon, Karen Kupperman, and Timothy Silver have enhanced understanding of the cultural as well as physical transformations that resulted from contact.

The variety of American societies that emerged out of the interaction of Europeans, Africans, and Native Americans has also become better appreciated. Studies such as Richard S. Dunn's *Sugar and Slaves* (1972) emphasize the importance of the Caribbean in early English colonization efforts. Similarly, Edmund S. Morgan's *American Slavery, American Freedom* (1975) stresses the role of economic ambition in explaining the English peopling of the Chesapeake and the eventual importation of African slaves to that region. Studies by Bernard Bailyn and David Hackett Fischer demonstrate that there was scarcely a "typical" English migrant to the New World. English colonists migrated both singly and in families, and for economic, social, political, and religious reasons.

The picture of colonial America that is emerging from all this new scholarship is of a society unique—and diverse—from its inception. No longer simply Europe transplanted, American colonial society by 1700 is now viewed as an outgrowth of many intertwining roots—of different European and African heritages, of varied encounters with native peoples, and of complicated mixtures of settler populations, each with its own distinctive set of ambitions.

American Life in the Seventeenth Century

1607–1692

BEING THUS PASSED THE VAST OCEAN, AND A SEA OF
TROUBLES BEFORE IN THEIR PREPARATION . . ., THEY HAD NOW
NO FRIENDS TO WELLCOME THEM, NOR INNS TO ENTERTAINE OR
REFRESH THEIR WEATHERBEATEN BODIES, NO HOUSES OR MUCH
LESS TOWNS TO REPAIRE TOO, TO SEEKE FOR SUCCORE.

WILLIAM BRADFORD, *OF PLYMOUTH PLANTATION*, C. 1630

As the seventeenth century wore on, the crude encampments of the first colonists slowly gave way to permanent settlements. Durable and distinctive ways of life emerged, as Europeans and Africans adapted to the New World and as Native Americans adapted to the newcomers. Even the rigid doctrines of Puritanism softened somewhat in response to the circumstances of life in America. And though all the colonies remained tied to England and stitched tightly into the fabric of an Atlantic economy, regional differences continued to crystallize, notably the increasing importance of slavery to the southern way of life.

Focus Questions

1. What were the major features of the economy, population, and social structure of England's North American colonies in the seventeenth century?
2. How did the social order and ways of life differ between the southern and northern colonies?
3. How did the labor system of white indentured servitude work, and why did plantation owners eventually replace it with African slavery?
4. How did the African slave trade develop, and how did African slaves develop their own culture and practices in America?
5. What were the major features of the "New England way of life," and how did religion, family life, and women's roles change in the later seventeenth century?

The Unhealthy Chesapeake

Life in the American wilderness was nasty, brutish, and short for the earliest Chesapeake settlers. Malaria, dysentery, and typhoid took a cruel toll, cutting ten years off the life expectancy of newcomers from England. Half the people born in early Virginia and Maryland did not survive to celebrate their twentieth birthdays. Few of the remaining half lived to see their fiftieth—or even their fortieth, if they were women.

Chronology

1619	First Africans arrive in Virginia.	**1689–1691**	Leisler's Rebellion in New York.
1625	Population of English colonies in America about 2,000.	**1692**	Salem witch trials in Massachusetts.
		1693	College of William and Mary founded.
1636	Harvard College founded.	**1698**	Royal African Company slave trade monopoly ended.
1662	Half-Way Covenant for Congregational Church membership established.	**1700**	Population of English colonies in America about 250,000.
1670	Virginia assembly disfranchises landless freemen.		
1676	Bacon's Rebellion in Virginia.	**1712**	New York City slave revolt.
1680s	Mass expansion of slavery in colonies.	**1739**	South Carolina slave revolt.

The disease-ravaged settlements of the Chesapeake grew only slowly in the seventeenth century, mostly through fresh immigration from England. The great majority of immigrants were single men in their late teens and early twenties, and most perished soon after arrival. Surviving males competed for the affections of the extremely scarce women, whom they outnumbered nearly six to one in 1650 and still outnumbered by three to two at the end of the century. Eligible women did not remain single for long.

Families were few and fragile in this ferocious environment. Most men could not find mates. Most marriages were destroyed by the death of a partner within seven years. Scarcely any children reached adulthood under the care of two parents, and almost no one knew a grandparent. Weak family ties were reflected in the many pregnancies among unmarried young girls. In one Maryland county, more than a third of all brides were already pregnant when they wed.

Yet despite these hardships, the Chesapeake colonies struggled on. The native-born inhabitants eventually acquired immunity to the killer diseases that had ravaged the original immigrants. The presence of more women allowed more families to form, and by the end of the seventeenth century the white population of the Chesapeake was growing on the basis of its own birthrate. As the eighteenth century opened, Virginia, with some fifty-nine thousand people, was the most populous colony. Maryland, with about thirty thousand, was the third largest (after Massachusetts).

The Tobacco Economy

Although unhealthy for human life, the Chesapeake was immensely hospitable to tobacco cultivation. Profit-hungry settlers often planted tobacco to sell before they planted corn to eat. But intense tobacco cultivation quickly exhausted the soil, creating a nearly insatiable demand for new land. Relentlessly seeking fresh fields to plant in tobacco, commercial growers plunged ever farther up the river valleys, provoking ever more Indian attacks.

This continual expansion created tobacco yields that reached almost 40 million pounds a year by the end of the seventeenth century. This enormous production depressed prices, but colonial Chesapeake tobacco growers responded to falling prices by planting still more acres in tobacco and bringing still more product to market.

More tobacco meant more labor, but where was it to come from? Families procreated too slowly to provide it by natural population increase. Indians died too quickly on contact with whites, and African slaves cost too much money. But England still had a "surplus" of displaced farmers desperate for employment. Many of them, as indentured servants, voluntarily mortgaged the sweat of their bodies for

Online Study Center

Primary source
Excerpts of Virginia Law on Indentured Servitude
college.hmco.com/pic/kennedybrief7e

> An agent for the Virginia Company in London submitted the following description of the Virginia colony in 1622:
>
> "I found the plantations generally seated upon mere salt marshes full of infectious bogs and muddy creeks and lakes, and thereby subjected to all those inconveniences and diseases which are so commonly found in the most unsound and most unhealthy parts of England."

Online Study Center

Primary source
Indentured Servant's Confession
college.hmco.com/pic/kennedybrief7e

---

headright *The right to acquire a certain amount of land that was granted to the person who financed the passage of an indentured servant or laborer.*

disenfranchise *To take away the right to vote.*

civil war *Any significant conflict between rival forces of the same country, both claiming to be the sovereign government of the territory in whole or in part.*

tidewater *The territory adjoining water affected by tides—that is, near the seacoast or coastal estuaries and rivers.*

Online Study Center

Interactive map
African Origins of North American Slaves 1690–1807
college.hmco.com/pic/kennedybrief7e

several years to Chesapeake masters. In exchange they received transatlantic passage and eventual "freedom dues," including a few barrels of corn, a suit of clothes, and perhaps a small parcel of land.

Both Virginia and Maryland employed the "**headright**" system to encourage the importation of servant workers. Under its terms, whoever paid the passage of a laborer received the right to acquire fifty acres of land. Taking advantage of this system, some masters soon parlayed their investments in servants into vast holdings in real estate. They became the great merchant-planters who came to dominate the agriculture and commerce of the southern colonies. Chesapeake planters had brought some 100,000 indentured servants to the region by 1700. These "white slaves" represented more than three-quarters of all European immigrants to Virginia and Maryland in the seventeenth century.

Indentured servants led a hard but hopeful life in the early days of the Chesapeake settlements. They looked forward to becoming free and acquiring land of their own after completing their term of servitude. But as prime land became scarcer toward the end of the seventeenth century, masters became increasingly resistant to including land grants in "freedom dues." Even after formal freedom was granted, penniless freed workers often had little choice but to hire themselves out for pitifully low wages to their former masters.

Frustrated Freemen and Bacon's Rebellion

An accumulating mass of footloose, impoverished freemen was drifting discontentedly about the Chesapeake region by the late seventeenth century. Mostly single young men, they were frustrated by their broken hopes of acquiring land as well as by their gnawing failure to find single women to marry.

The swelling number of these wretched bachelors rattled the established planters. Encouraged by Governor William Berkeley, the Virginia assembly in 1670 **disenfranchised** most of the landless knockabouts. About a thousand poverty-stricken Virginians then broke out of control in 1676, led by a twenty-nine-year-old planter, Nathaniel Bacon. Angered by Berkeley's mild Indian policies as well as economic grievances, Bacon and his followers first mercilessly attacked Indians on the frontier. They then chased Berkeley from Jamestown and put the torch to the capital. Chaos swept the raw colony as frustrated freemen and resentful servants—described as "a rabble of the basest sort of people"—went on a rampage of plundering and pilfering.

As this **civil war** in Virginia ground on, Bacon suddenly died of disease. Berkeley thereupon crushed the uprising with brutal cruelty, hanging more than twenty rebels. Back in England King Charles II complained, "That old fool has put to death more people in that naked country than I did here for the murder of my father."

The distant English king could scarcely imagine the depths of passion and fear that Bacon's Rebellion excited in Virginia. Bacon had ignited the smoldering unhappiness of landless former servants, and he had pitted the hardscrabble backcountry frontiersmen against the haughty gentry of the **tidewater** plantations. The rebellion was suppressed, but these tensions remained. Lordly planters, surrounded by a still-seething sea of malcontents, anxiously looked about for less troublesome laborers to toil in their restless tobacco kingdom. Their eyes soon lit on Africa.

Colonial Slavery

Perhaps 10 million Africans were carried in chains to the New World in the three centuries or so following Columbus's landing. Only about 400,000 of them ended up in North America. Most were hauled to Spanish and Portuguese South America or the sugar-rich West Indies. Africans had been brought to Jamestown as early as 1619, but

EXAMINING THE EVIDENCE

An Indentured Servant's Contract, 1746 Legal documents, such as this contract signed in Virginia in 1746, not only provide evidence about the ever-changing rules by which societies have regulated their affairs, but also furnish rich information about the conditions of life and the terms of human relationships in the past. This agreement between Thomas Clayton and James Griffin provides a reminder that not all indentured servants in early America came from abroad. Indentured servitude could be equivalent to an apprenticeship, in which a young person traded several years of service to a master in exchange for instruction in the master's craft. Here Clayton pledges himself to five years in Griffin's employ in return for a promise to initiate the young man into the "Mystery" of the master's craft.

1. Why might the master's trade be described as a "mystery"?

2. From the evidence of this contract, what are the principal objectives of each of the parties to it?

3. What problems do the master and the servant/apprentice each anticipate? What obligations does each assume?

4. What does the consent of Clayton's mother to the contract suggest about the young man's situation?

5. The first sentence of the contract says that Clayton "doth voluntarily and of his own free will and accord, and with the consent and approbation of his mother, put himself apprentice to James Griffin. . . ." Why was it legally important that Clayton affirm that he had *voluntarily* made himself an unpaid servant/laborer for a term of five years?

6. The contract also declares that Griffin may not, among other things, "commit fornication," marry, or play cards or dice during his term of servitude. What does this provision reveal about the relationship of master to servant? Should this document be considered an "employment contract" or something else?

Online Study Center

Primary source
Early Evidence of Sexual Tensions Within Slavery
college.hmco.com/pic/kennedybrief7e

middle passage *That portion of a slave ship's journey in which slaves were carried from Africa to slave markets in the Americas. (The slave-carrying shipments from Africa to American slave markets were the "middle" leg of a round-trip voyage from Europe or New England and back.)*

as late as 1670 they numbered only about 7 percent of the 50,000 people in the southern plantation colonies as a whole. For hard-pinched colonists, white servants were far less costly than high-priced slaves who might die soon after arrival.

Drastic change came in the 1680s. Rising wages in England shrank the pool of potential indentured servants, while large planters grew increasingly fearful of the potentially mutinous former servants in their midst. By the mid-1680s, for the first time, black slaves outnumbered white servants among the plantation colonies' new arrivals. In 1698 the Royal African Company, first chartered in 1672, lost its crown-granted monopoly on carrying slaves to the colonies. Enterprising Americans, especially Rhode Islanders, rushed to cash in on the lucrative slave trade, and the supply of slaves rose steeply. By 1750 blacks accounted for nearly half the population of Virginia, and in South Carolina they outnumbered whites two to one.

Most of the slaves who reached North America came from the west coast of Africa, especially the area stretching from present-day Senegal to Angola. They were originally captured by African coastal tribes, who traded them in crude markets to itinerant European—and American—flesh merchants. Usually branded and bound, the captives were herded aboard sweltering ships for the gruesome "**middle passage,**" on which death rates ran as high as 20 percent. Terrified survivors were eventually shoved onto auction blocks in New World ports like Newport, Rhode Island, or Charleston, South Carolina, where a giant slave market traded in human misery for more than a century.

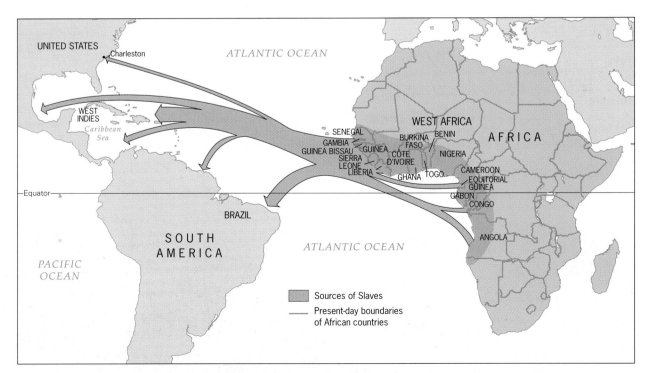

■ **Main Sources of African Slaves, c. 1500 to c. 1800** The three centuries of the African diaspora scattered blacks all over the New World, with about 400,000 coming to North America. Boundaries shown are those of modern African states.

A few of the earliest African immigrants gained their freedom, and some even became slaveowners themselves. But as the number of Africans in their midst increased dramatically toward the end of the seventeenth century, white colonists reacted remorselessly to this supposed racial threat. Beginning in Virginia in 1662, the iron conditions of bondage were spelled out in slave codes that made blacks *and their children* the property (or "chattels") for life of their white masters. Not even conversion to Christianity could qualify a slave for freedom. Slavery might have begun in America for economic reasons, but by the end of the seventeenth century, it was clear that racial discrimination also powerfully molded the American slave system.

Africans in America

In the deepest South, slave life was especially severe. The climate was hostile to health, and the labor was life draining. The widely scattered South Carolina rice and indigo plantations were lonely hells on earth where gangs of mostly male Africans toiled and perished. Only fresh imports could sustain the slave population under these loathsome conditions.

Blacks in the tobacco-growing Chesapeake region had a somewhat easier lot. Tobacco was less physically demanding than the crops of the deeper South. Tobacco plantations were smaller and closer to one another than rice plantations. By about 1720 the proportion of females in the Chesapeake slave population had begun to rise, making family life possible. The captive black population of the Chesapeake area soon began to grow not only through new imports but also through its own **fertility**—making it one of the few slave societies in history to perpetuate itself by its own natural reproduction.

Native-born African Americans contributed to the growth of a stable and distinctive slave culture, a mixture of African and American elements of speech, religion, and folkways (see "Makers of America: From African to African American," pp. 52–53). On the sea islands off South Carolina's coast, blacks evolved a unique language, Gullah, that blended English with several African languages, including Yoruba, Ibo, and Hausa. The ringshout, a West African religious dance performed by shuffling in a circle while answering a preacher's shouts, was brought to colonial America by slaves and eventually contributed to the development of jazz.

Slaves also helped mightily to build the country with their labor. A few became skilled artisans—carpenters, bricklayers, and tanners. But chiefly they performed the sweaty toil of clearing swamps, grubbing out trees, and other **menial** tasks. Condemned to life under the lash, slaves naturally pined for freedom. Slave revolts erupted in New York City in 1712, and again in South Carolina in 1739. But in the end the slaves in the South proved to be a more manageable labor force than the white indentured servants they gradually replaced. No slave uprising in American history matched the scale of Bacon's Rebellion.

> *The Mennonites of Germantown, Pennsylvania, recorded the earliest known protest against slavery in America in 1688:*
>
> "There is a saying, that we should do to all men like as we will be done ourselves. . . . But to bring men hither, or to rob and sell them against their will, we stand against. . . . Pray, what thing in the world can be done worse towards us, than if men should rob or steal us away, and sell us for slaves to strange countries, separating husbands from their wives and children?"

Online Study Center

Interactive map
West Africa and the Atlantic Slave Trade
college.hmco.com/pic/kennedybrief7e

---

fertility *The ability to mate and produce abundant young.*

menial *Fit for servants; humble or low.*

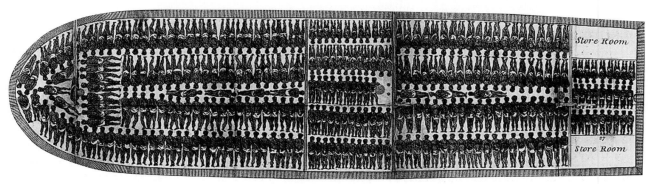

■ The "Middle Passage" Human cargo in the hold of a slave ship.

From African to African American

Dragged in chains from West African shores, the first African Americans struggled to preserve their diverse heritages from the ravages of slavery. Their children, the first generation of American-born slaves, melded these various traditions—Guinean, Ibo, Yoruba, Angolan—into a distinctive African American culture. Their achievement sustained them during the cruelties of enslavement and has endured to this day to enrich American life.

With the arrival of the first Africans in the seventeenth century, a cornucopia of African traditions poured into the New World: handicrafts and skills in numerous trades; a plethora of languages, musics, and cuisines; even rice-planting techniques that conquered the inhospitable soil

■ **Yarrow Mamout, by Charles Willson Peale, 1819** When Peale painted this portrait, Mamout was over 100 years old. A devout Muslim brought to Maryland as a slave, he eventually bought his freedom and settled in Georgetown.

O carry me back, O carry me back, to old Virginia —
Shore, home Spun, and humani block, & Corn.
this very valuable grain in Virginia and much is raised.

Lynchburg — negro dance, August 18 1853.

■ **The Emergence of an African American Culture** In this scene from the mid-nineteenth century, African Americans play musical instruments of European derivation, like the fiddle, as well as instruments of African origin, like the bones and banjo—a vivid illustration of the blending of the two cultures in the crucible of the New World.

of South Carolina. It was North America's rice paddies, tilled by experienced West Africans, that introduced the staple rice into the English diet.

These first American slaves were mostly males who lived and worked on small, isolated farms. But by the beginning of the eighteenth century, a settled slave society was emerging in the southern colonies. Laws tightened; slave traders stepped up their deliveries of human cargo; large plantations formed. Most significantly, a new generation of American-born slaves joined their forebears at labor in the fields. By 1740 large groups of slaves lived together on sprawling plantations, the American-born outnumbered the African-born, and the importation of African slaves slowed.

Plantation life was an endless cycle of miserable toil for the slaves. After a day's backbreaking work, women were expected to sit up for hours spinning, weaving, or sewing clothes for themselves and their families. Enslaved women also lived in constant fear of sexual exploitation by conscienceless masters.

Slave religion illustrates how new ideas were combined with a traditional heritage. Most slaves became Christians but fused elements of African and Western traditions and drew their own conclusions from Scripture. White Christians might encourage slaves to "stay in their place," but black Christians emphasized God's role in freeing the Hebrews from slavery and saw Jesus as the Messiah who would deliver them from bondage.

At their Sunday and evening prayer meetings, slaves also patched African remnants onto conventional Christian ritual. Black Methodists, for example, evaded the traditional Methodist ban on dancing by practicing the "ringshout." Some worshipers clapped their hands and beat time in a circle while others walked around the ring, singing in unison. Christian slaves also often used outwardly religious songs as encoded messages about escape or rebellion. The hymn "Wade in the Water," for instance, taught fleeing slaves one way of covering their trails. The "Negro spirituals" that took shape as a distinctive form of American music thus had their origins in both Christianity and slavery. Indeed, much American music was born in the slave quarters from African importations. But this rich cultural harvest came at the cost of generations of human agony.

hierarchy *A social group arranged in ranks or classes.*

Southern Society

As slavery spread, the gaps in the South's social structure widened. The rough equality of poverty and disease of the early days was giving way to a defined **hierarchy** of wealth and status in the early eighteenth century. At the top of this southern social ladder perched a small but powerful covey of great planters. Owning gangs of slaves and vast domains of land, the planters ruled the region's economy and virtually monopolized political power. Yet, legend to the contrary, these great seventeenth-century merchant-planters were not silk-swathed cavaliers gallantly imitating the ways of English country gentlemen. For the most part they were a hard-working, businesslike lot, laboring long hours over the problems of plantation management.

Far beneath the planters in wealth, prestige, and political power were the small farmers, the largest social group. They might or might not own one or two slaves, but they lived a ragged, hand-to-mouth existence on their modest plots. Still lower on the social scale were landless whites and, below them, indentured servants still serving out their terms. The oppressed black slaves, of course, remained enchained in society's basement.

Few cities sprouted in the colonial South, and consequently an urban professional class, including lawyers and financiers, was slow to emerge. Southern life revolved around the great plantations, distantly isolated from one another. Waterways, rather than the wretched roads, provided the principal means of transportation from one plantation to another.

The New England Family

Nature smiled more benignly on pioneer New Englanders than on their disease-plagued fellow colonists to the south. Clean water and cool temperatures, which retarded the spread of microbes, created healthier living conditions that enabled settlers in seventeenth-century New England to *add* ten years to their life spans by migrating from the Old World, in stark contrast to the fate of Chesapeake immigrants. The first generations of Puritan colonists enjoyed, on the average, about seventy years on this earth—not very different from the life expectancy of present-day Americans.

In further contrast with the Chesapeake, New Englanders tended to migrate not as single individuals but as families, and the family remained at the center of New England life. Early marriage and prolific childbearing enabled New England's population to grow from natural reproductive increase almost from the outset. Women typically wed by their early twenties and produced babies about every two years thereafter until menopause. A married woman could expect to experience up to ten pregnancies and rear as many as eight surviving children. A New England woman might well have dependent children living in her household from the earliest days of her marriage until the day of her death, and child raising became virtually her full-time occupation.

The longevity of the New Englanders contributed to family stability. Children received nurturing love and guidance not only from their parents but from their grandparents as well. Family stability was reflected in low premarital pregnancy rates (again in contrast with the Chesapeake) and in the generally strong, tranquil social structure characteristic of colonial New England.

Oddly enough, the strength of New England families actually weakened the economic independence of women in that region compared with women in the South. Because southern men frequently died young, leaving widows with small children to support, the southern colonies allowed married women to retain separate titles to their property and gave widows the right to inherit their husband's estates. But in New England, Puritan lawmakers worried that recognizing women's separate property rights would undercut the unity of husband and wife. New England women, therefore, usually gave up their property rights when they married.

"A true wife accounts subjection her honor," one Massachusetts Puritan leader declared, expressing a sentiment then common in Europe as well as America. But in the New World, a rudimentary conception of women's rights as indi-

Online Study Center
Primary source
Puritan Prescription for Marital Concord
college.hmco.com/pic/kennedybrief7e

Online Study Center
Primary source
Family Ties: A Puritan Woman's Advice on Dealing . . .
college.hmco.com/pic/kennedybrief7e

Online Study Center
Primary source
Early Prenuptial Agreement
college.hmco.com/pic/kennedybrief7e

viduals was beginning to appear in the seventeenth century. Women still could not vote, and the popular attitude persisted that they were morally weaker than men. But a husband's power over his wife was not absolute. The New England authorities could and did intervene to restrain abusive spouses, and women had some spheres of autonomy. Midwifery—assisting with childbirths—was a virtual female monopoly, and midwives often fostered networks of women bonded by the common travails of motherhood.

Above all, the laws of Puritan New England sought to defend the integrity of marriages. Divorce was exceedingly rare: outright abandonment and adultery were among the few permissible grounds for divorce. Convicted adulterers—especially if they were women—were whipped in public and forced forever after to wear the capital letter "A" cut out in cloth and sewn on their outer garments—the basis for Nathaniel Hawthorne's famous 1850 tale, *The Scarlet Letter.*

Life in the New England Towns

Sturdy New Englanders evolved a tightly knit society, the basis of which was small villages and farms. Puritanism especially made for unity of purpose—and for concern about the moral health of the whole community.

Even territorial expansion occurred in orderly, communal fashion, in contrast to the Chesapeake's normal mode of expansion by lone-wolf planters on their own initiative. New towns were legally chartered by the colonial authorities, and the distribution of land was entrusted to the steady hands of sober-minded town fathers, or

■ **Mrs. Elizabeth Freake and Baby Mary** This portrait of a Boston mother and child in about 1674 suggests the strong family ties that characterized early New England society.

militia *An armed force of citizens called out only in emergencies.*

jeremiad *A sermon or prophecy recounting wrongdoing, warning of doom, and calling for repentance.*

hinterland *An inland region set back from a port, river, or seacoast.*

Online Study Center

Primary source
Mr. John Freake
college.hmco.com/pic/kennedybrief7e

Online Study Center

Primary source
Ann Putnam's Deposition
college.hmco.com/pic/kennedybrief7e

The Massachusetts School Law of 1647 (later called "The Old Deluder Law"), stated,

"It being one chief project of the old deluder, Satan, to keep men from the knowledge of the Scriptures, as in former times by keeping them in an unknown tongue, it is therefore ordered that every township in this jurisdiction, after the Lord has increased them [in] number to fifty householders, shall then forthwith appoint one within their town to teach all such children as shall resort to him to write and read, whose wages shall be paid either by the parents or masters of such children, or by the inhabitants in general."

"proprietors." After receiving a grant of land from the colonial legislature, the proprietors usually laid out their town around a meetinghouse, which served as both the place of worship and the town hall. Also marked out was a village green, where the **militia** could drill. Each family received several parcels of land.

Towns of more than fifty families were required to provide elementary education, and roughly half of the adults knew how to read and write. As early as 1636, just six years after the colony's founding, the Massachusetts Puritans established Harvard College to train local boys for the ministry. Only in 1693, eighty-six years after the founding of Jamestown, did the Virginians establish their first college, William and Mary.

Puritans ran their own churches, and democracy in Congregational Church government led logically to democracy in political government. The town meeting, in which the adult males met together and each man voted, was a showcase and a classroom for democracy. The New England town meeting, observed Thomas Jefferson, was "the best school of political liberty the world ever saw."

The Changing New England Way of Life

Yet worries plagued the God-fearing pioneers of these tidy New England settlements. The pressure of a growing population was gradually dispersing the Puritans onto outlying farms, far from the control of church and neighbors. And although the core of Puritan belief still burned brightly, the passage of time was dampening the first generation's religious zeal. About the middle of the seventeenth century, earnest preachers began scolding parishioners for their waning piety in a new form of sermon—the "**jeremiad**." In response to the apparent decline in conversions, troubled ministers in 1662 announced a new formula for church membership, the "Half-Way Covenant." This new arrangement admitted to baptism, but not to "full communion," the unconverted children of existing members. By conferring partial membership rights in the once-exclusive Puritan congregations, the Half-Way Covenant weakened the distinction between the "elect" and other members of society. In effect, strict religious purity was sacrificed somewhat to the cause of wider religious participation. Interestingly, from about this time onward, women were in the majority in the Puritan congregations.

Women also played a prominent role in one of New England's most frightening religious episodes. A group of adolescent girls in Salem, Massachusetts, claimed to have been bewitched by certain older women. A hysterical "witch hunt" ensued, leading to the execution in 1692 of twenty individuals.

The reign of horror in Salem grew not only from the superstitions and prejudices of the age but also from the unsettled social and religious conditions of the rapidly evolving Massachusetts village. Most of the accused witches came from families associated with Salem's burgeoning market economy; their accusers came largely from the ranks of subsistence farming families in Salem's **hinterland.** The episode thus reflected the widening social stratification of New England, as well as the fear of many religious traditionalists that the Puritan heritage was being eclipsed by Yankee commercialism. The Salem witchcraft delusion marked an all-time high in the American experience of popular passions run wild.

New England soil, like New England religion, was hard and unyielding. Scratching a living from the rock-strewn land put a premium on industry and penny-pinching frugality, for which New Englanders became famous. The grudging land also left colonial New England less ethnically mixed than its southern neighbors. European immigrants were not attracted in great numbers to a site where the soil was so stony—and the sermons so sulfurous.

Yet the harsh climate and unproductive soil of New England eventually encouraged a diversified agriculture and industry. Staple products like tobacco did not flourish, as in the South. Black slavery, although attempted, could not exist profitably on small farms. Turning away from the land, New Englanders more and more looked to the sea for a living. Hacking timber from their dense forests, they became experts in shipbuilding and commerce. They also ceaselessly exploited the self-perpetuating codfish lode off the coast of Newfoundland—the fishy "gold mines of New England." As a reminder of the importance of fishing, a handsome replica of the "sacred cod" is proudly displayed to this day in the Massachusetts State House in Boston.

Just as the land shaped New Englanders, so they shaped the land. Native Americans of the region had left an early imprint on the earth, beating trails through the woods and periodically burning woodlands to restore leafy first-growth forests. But in contrast with Native Americans, who *used* the land but recognized no right to *own* it, the English settlers felt a virtual duty to "improve" the land by clearing woodlands for pasturage and tillage, building roads and fences, and laying out permanent settlements. The introduction of livestock also led colonists to clear ever more forests for pastureland, while the animals' voracious appetites and heavy hooves compacted the soil, speeding erosion and flooding.

The combination of Calvinism, soil, and climate in New England made for energy, purposefulness, sternness, stubbornness, self-reliance, and resourcefulness. Righteous New Englanders prided themselves on being God's chosen people. They long boasted that Boston was "the hub of the universe"—at least in spirit. A famous jingle of later days ran:

> *I come from the city of Boston*
> *The home of the bean and the cod*
> *Where the Cabots speak only to Lowells*
> *And the Lowells speak only to God.*

New England has had an incalculable impact on the rest of the nation. Ousted by their sterile soil, thousands of New Englanders scattered from Ohio to Oregon and even Hawaii. The democratic town meeting, the tidy schoolhouse, and "Yankee ingenuity," all originally fostered by the flinty fields and comfortless climate of New England, came to be claimed by all Americans as a proud national heritage. And the fabled "New England conscience," born of the steadfast Puritan faith, left a legacy of high idealism in the national character and inspired many later reformers.

The Early Settlers' Days and Ways

The cycles of the seasons and the sun set the schedules of all the earliest American colonists—men as well as women, blacks as well as whites. The overwhelming majority of colonists were farmers. They planted in the spring, tended their crops in the summer, harvested in the fall, and prepared in the winter to begin the cycle anew. They usually rose at dawn and went to bed at dusk. Chores might be performed after nightfall only if they were "worth the candle," a phrase that has persisted in American speech.

Women, slave or free, on southern plantations or northern farms, cooked, cleaned, and cared for children. Men worked the land, cut firewood, and butchered livestock as needed. Children helped with all these tasks, while picking up such schooling as they could.

Life was humble but comfortable by the standards of the time. Compared to most seventeenth-century Europeans, Americans lived in affluent abundance. Land was relatively cheap, though somewhat less available in the planter-dominated South than elsewhere. Wages for workmen were roughly three times those of their English counterparts.

"Dukes don't emigrate," the saying goes, for if people enjoy wealth and security, they are not likely to risk exposing their lives in the wilderness. Similarly, the very poorest members of a society may not possess even the modest means needed to pull up stakes and seek a fresh start in life. Accordingly, most white migrants to early colonial America came neither from the aristocracy nor from the dregs of European society—with the partial exception of the impoverished indentured servants.

Seventeenth-century society in all the colonies had a certain simple sameness to it, especially in the more egalitarian New England and middle colonies. Yet many settlers who considered themselves to be of the "better sort" tried to re-create on a

social structure *The basic pattern of the distribution of status and wealth in a society.*

blue bloods *Of noble or upper-class descent.*

modified scale the **social structure** they had known in the Old World. Resentment against such upper-class pretensions helped to spark outbursts like Bacon's Rebellion in Virginia in 1676, the uprising of Maryland's Protestants toward the end of the seventeenth century, and Leisler's Rebellion, an ill-starred and bloody insurgence that rocked New York City from 1689 to 1691.

For their part, would-be American **blue bloods** resented the pretensions of the "meaner sort" and passed laws to try to keep them in their place. Massachusetts in 1651 prohibited poorer folk from "wearing gold or silver lace," and in eighteenth-century Virginia a tailor was fined and jailed for arranging to race his horse—"a sport only for gentlemen." But these efforts to reproduce the finely stratified societies of Europe proved feeble in the early American wilderness, where equality and democracy found fertile soil—at least for white people.

★ Chapter Summary ★

Life was hard in the seventeenth-century southern colonies. Disease drastically shortened life spans in the Chesapeake region, even for the young single men who made up the majority of settlers. Families were few and fragile, with men greatly outnumbering women, who were much in demand and seldom remained single for long.

The tobacco economy first thrived using the labor of white indentured servants, who hoped to work their way up to become landowners and perhaps even become wealthy. But by the late seventeenth century, this hope was increasingly frustrated, and the discontents of the poor whites exploded in Bacon's Rebellion in Virginia.

With white labor increasingly troublesome, slaves (earlier a small fraction of the workforce) began to be imported from West Africa by the tens of thousands in the 1680s, and soon became essential to the colonial economy. Slaves in the Deep South died rapidly of disease and overwork, but those in the Chesapeake tobacco region survived longer. Their numbers eventually increased by natural reproduction, and they developed a distinctive African American way of life that combined African elements with features developed in the New World.

By contrast with the South, New England's clean water and cool air contributed to a healthy way of life, which actually *added* ten years to the average English life span. The New England way of life centered on strong families and tightly knit towns and churches, which were relatively democratic and equal by seventeenth-century standards. By the late seventeenth century, however, social and religious tensions developed in these narrow communities, as the Salem witch hysteria dramatically illustrates.

Rocky soil forced many New Englanders to turn to fishing and merchant shipping for their livelihoods. Their difficult lives and stern religion made New Englanders tough, idealistic, purposeful, and resourceful. In later years they spread these same values across much of American society.

All of seventeenth-century American society was relatively simple and almost entirely agrarian. Would-be aristocrats who tried to recreate the social hierarchies of Europe were generally frustrated.

5

Colonial Society on the Eve of Revolution

—◆—

1700–1775

DRIVEN FROM EVERY OTHER CORNER OF THE EARTH, FREEDOM
OF THOUGHT AND THE RIGHT OF PRIVATE JUDGMENT IN
MATTERS OF CONSCIENCE DIRECT THEIR COURSE TO THIS
HAPPY COUNTRY AS THEIR LAST ASYLUM.

SAMUEL ADAMS, 1776

Chapter Outline

⭐ Population Growth and Ethnic Diversity

⭐ Colonial Society and Economy

⭐ The Atlantic Economy

⭐ The Great Awakening

⭐ Education and Culture

⭐ Political Patterns

⭐ Makers of America: The Scots-Irish

⭐ Varying Viewpoints: Colonial America: Communities of Conflict or Consensus?

The common term *thirteen original colonies* is misleading. Britain ruled thirty-two colonies in North America by 1775, including Canada, the Floridas, and various Caribbean islands. But only thirteen of them unfurled the standard of rebellion. A few of the nonrebels, such as Canada and Jamaica, were larger, wealthier, or more populous than some of the revolting thirteen. Why, then, did some British colonies eventually strike for their independence, while others did not? Part of the answer is to be found in the distinctive social, economic, and political structures of the thirteen Atlantic seaboard colonies—and in the halting, gradual appearance of a recognizably *American* way of life.

Focus Questions

1. What were the major demographic and social structures that characterized Britain's eighteenth-century colonies, and how had these changed since the early seventeenth-century settlements?
2. How did the expanding economy of the colonies alter the patterns of social prestige and wealth, and introduce greater class divisions?
3. What were the causes of the first religious "Great Awakening" in American history, and how did it affect colonial identity, education, and politics?
4. What were the major features of education, culture, and daily life in the eighteenth century?
5. What issues and conflicts dominated colonial politics, and how did both formal institutions (legislatures and governors) and informal practices of public opinion affect those issues?

Conquest by the Cradle

Among the distinguishing characteristics that the eventually rebellious settlements shared was lusty population growth. In 1700 they contained fewer than 300,000 souls, about 20,000 of whom were black. By 1775, 2.5 million people inhabited the thirteen colonies, of whom about half a million were black. White immigrants made up nearly 400,000 of the increased number, and black "forced immigrants" accounted for almost as many again. But most of the spurt stemmed from the remarkable natural fertility of all Americans, white and black. The youthful Americans, whose average age in 1775 was about sixteen, were doubling their numbers every twenty-five years. Unfriendly Dr. Samuel Johnson, back in Britain, growled that the Americans were multiplying like their own rattlesnakes.

This population boom had political consequences. In 1700 there were twenty Britons for each American colonist. By 1775 the British advantage in numbers had fallen to three to one—setting the stage for a momentous shift in the balance of power between the colonies and Britain.

The bulk of the population was cooped up east of the Alleghenies. The most populous colonies in 1775 were Virginia, Massachusetts, Pennsylvania, North Carolina, and Maryland—in that order. Only four communities could properly be called cities: Philadelphia, including suburbs, was first with about 34,000 residents, trailed by New York, Boston, and Charleston. About 90 percent of the people lived in rural areas.

Huguenots *French Calvinist dissenters from that country's dominant Catholicism. Eventually outlawed by King Louis XIV in 1685, many fled elsewhere, including to British North America.*

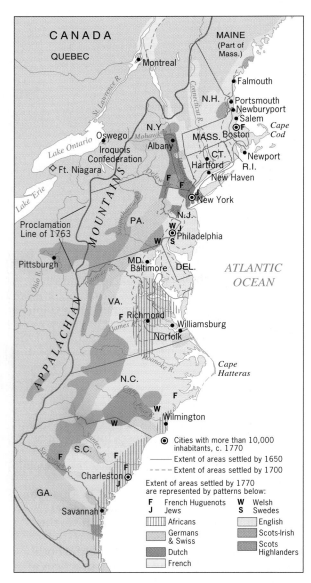

A Potpourri of Peoples

Colonial America was a melting pot and had been from the outset. The population, although basically English in stock and language, was picturesquely mottled with numerous foreign groups.

Germans constituted about 6 percent of the total population, or 150,000, by 1775. Fleeing religious persecution, economic oppression, and the ravages of war, they had flocked to America in the early 1700s and had settled chiefly in Pennsylvania. They belonged to several different Protestant groups—primarily Lutheran—and thus further enhanced the religious diversity of the colony. Known popularly but erroneously as the Pennsylvania Dutch (a corruption of the German word *Deutsch,* for "German"), they totaled about one-third of the colony's population. In parts of Philadelphia, street signs were painted in both German and English. In the Pennsylvania backcountry, where many of them moved, German immigrants clung tenaciously to their language and customs.

The Scots-Irish, who in 1775 numbered about 175,000, or 7 percent of the population, were an important non-English group, although they spoke English (see "Makers of America: The Scots-Irish," p. 62). They were not Irish at all but turbulent Scots Lowlanders who had been transplanted over many decades to Northern Ireland, where they had not prospered. The Irish Catholics already there, hating Scottish Presbyterianism, resented the intruders (and still do). Early in the 1700s tens of thousands of these embittered Scots-Irish finally abandoned Ireland and came to America, chiefly to tolerant and deep-soiled Pennsylvania.

Finding the best acres already taken by Germans and Quakers, the Scots-Irish pushed out onto the Appalachian frontier, often drifting southward into the backcountry of Virginia, Maryland, and the Carolinas. There many of them illegally but defiantly squatted on the unoccupied lands and quarreled with both Indian and white owners. Pugnacious, lawless, and individualistic, the Scots-Irish brought with them the Scottish secrets of whiskey distilling and dotted the Appalachian hills and hollows with their stills. They cherished no love for the British government that had uprooted them, and many of them—including the young Andrew Jackson—eventually joined the embattled American revolutionists.

Approximately 5 percent of the colonial population consisted of other European groups, including French **Huguenots,** Welsh, Dutch, Swedes, Jews, Irish, Swiss, and Scots Highlanders. Except for the Scots Highlanders, these ethnic groups felt little loyalty to

■ **Immigrant Groups in 1775** America was already a nation of diverse ethnic groups in the colonial period. This map shows the great variety of immigrant groups, especially in Pennsylvania and New York. It also illustrates the tendency of later arrivals, particularly the Scots-Irish, to push into the backcountry. The basic ethnic makeup of many of these colonial settlements persists even today, each with distinct cultural patterns and attitudes.

Chronology

1693	College of William and Mary founded.
1701	Yale College founded.
1721	Smallpox inoculation introduced.
1732	First edition of Franklin's *Poor Richard's Almanack*.
1734	Jonathan Edwards begins Great Awakening.
1734–1735	Zenger free-press trial in New York.
1738	George Whitefield spreads Great Awakening.
1746	Princeton College founded.
1760	Britain vetoes South Carolina anti–slave trade measures.
1764	Brown College founded.
1766	Rutgers College founded.
1769	Dartmouth College founded.

the British crown. By far the largest single non-English group was African, accounting for nearly 20 percent of the colonial population in 1775 and heavily concentrated in the South.

The population of the thirteen colonies, though mainly Anglo-Saxon, was among the most mixed to be found anywhere in the world. The South, holding about 90 percent of the slaves, already displayed its historic black-and-white racial composition. New England, mostly staked out by the original Puritan migrants, showed the least ethnic diversity. The middle colonies, especially Pennsylvania, received the bulk of later white immigrants and boasted an astonishing variety of people. Outside of New England, about half of the population was non-English in 1775.

As these various immigrant groups mingled and intermarried, they laid the foundations for a new multicultural American national identity unlike anything known in Europe. Nor were white colonists alone in creating new societies out of diverse ethnic groups. The African slave trade long had mixed peoples from many different tribal backgrounds, giving birth to an African-*American* community far more variegated in its cultural origins than anything to be found in Africa itself. Similarly, in the New England "praying towns" where Indians were gathered to be Christianized, and in Great Lakes villages such as Detroit, home to dozens of different displaced indigenous peoples, polyglot Native American communities emerged, blurring the boundaries of individual tribal identities.

> *The young Frenchman Michel-Guillaume Jean de Crèvecoeur (1735–1813) wrote of the diverse population in about 1770:*
>
> "They are a mixture of English, Scotch, Irish, French, Dutch, Germans, and Swedes. From this promiscuous breed, that race now called Americans have arisen. . . . I could point out to you a family whose grandfather was an Englishman, whose wife was Dutch, whose son married a French woman, and whose present four sons have now four wives of different nations."

Online Study Center

Interactive map
Immigration and Frontier
Expansion, to 1755
college.hmco.com/pic/kennedybrief7e

The Structure of Colonial Society

In comparison to contemporary Europe, eighteenth-century America seemed like a shining land of equality and opportunity—with the notorious exception of slavery. No titled nobility dominated society from on high, and no pauperized underclass threatened it from below. Most white Americans, and even a handful of free blacks, were small farmers. The cities contained a small class of skilled artisans, as well as a few shopkeepers, tradespeople, and unskilled day laborers. The most remarkable feature of the social ladder was its openness. An ambitious colonist, even a former indentured servant, could rise from a lower rung to a higher one, a rare step in Britain.

Yet in contrast with seventeenth-century America, colonial society on the eve of the Revolution was beginning to show signs of **stratification** and barriers to **mobility** that raised worries about the "Europeanization" of America. A new class of merchant princes in New England and the middle colonies, many of whom had

stratification *The visible arrangement of society into a hierarchical pattern, with distinct social groups layered one on top of the other.*

mobility *The capacity to pass readily from one social or economic condition to another; "upward mobility" means a rise in social or economic status, while "downward mobility" is a decline in status.*

The Scots-Irish

As the British Empire spread its dominion across the seas in the seventeenth and eighteenth centuries, great masses of people poured into its ever-widening realms. Their migration unfolded in stages. They journeyed from farms to towns, from towns to great cities such as London and Bristol, and eventually from the seaports to Ireland, the Caribbean, and North America. Among these intrepid wanderers, few were more restless than the Scots-Irish, the settlers of the first American West. Never feeling at home in the British Empire, these perennial outsiders always headed for its most distant outposts. They migrated first from their native Scottish Lowlands to Northern Ireland and from there to the New

World. But even in North America, the Scots-Irish remained on the periphery, ever distancing themselves from the reach of the English crown and the Church of England.

The Scottish migration from Scotland itself was driven by severe poverty. Always forced to struggle with a harsh and unyielding land, poorer Scots were oppressed further in the 1600s by merciless rent increases at the hands of the landowning lairds. Adding insult to injury, the British authorities repeatedly persecuted the Presbyterian Scots, squeezing taxes from their barren purses to support the hated Church of England.

Not surprisingly, then, some 200,000 Scots immigrated to neighboring Ireland in the 1600s. So great was the exodus that Protestant Scots eventually outnumbered Catholic natives in the several northern Irish counties that compose the province of Ulster. But soon the Scots discovered that their migration had not freed them from their ancient woes. Their Irish landlords raised rents just as ruthlessly as their Scottish lairds had done. Under such punishing pressures, waves of these already once-transplanted Scots, now known as Scots-Irish, fled again, this time to America.

Most debarked in Pennsylvania, seeking the religious tolerance and abundant land of William Penn's commonwealth. But these unquiet people did not stay put for long. They fanned out from Philadelphia into the farmlands of western Pennsylvania. Blocked temporarily by the Allegheny Mountains, they migrated south along the backbone of the Appalachian range, slowly filling the backcountry of Virginia, the Carolinas, and Georgia.

Almost every Scots-Irish community, however isolated or impermanent, maintained a Presbyterian church. Religion was the bond that yoked these otherwise fiercely independent folk. In backcountry towns, churches were erected before law courts, and clerics were pounding their pulpits before civil authorities had the chance to raise their gavels. But despite their intense faith, the Scots-Irish were not theocrats or advocates of religious rule. Their bitter struggles with the Church of England made them stubborn opponents of established religions in the United States, just as their seething resentment against the king of England ensured that they would be well represented among the Patriots in the American Revolution.

■ Georgia governor James Oglethorpe, in Scottish attire, visits Scottish settlers at New Inverness, Georgia.

made their fortunes as military suppliers in the colonial wars, roosted regally atop the social ladder. They sported imported clothing and dined at tables laid with English china and gleaming silverware. Prominent individuals came to be seated in churches and schools according to their social rank.

The plague of war also created a class of widows and orphans, who became dependent for their survival on charity. Both Philadelphia and New York built **almshouses** in the 1730s to care for the destitute. Yet the numbers of poor people remained tiny compared with the numbers in England, where about a third of the population lived in squalor.

In the New England countryside the descendants of the original settlers faced more limited prospects than had their pioneering forebears. As families grew and existing landholdings were repeatedly divided, the average size of farms shrank drastically. Younger sons as well as daughters were forced to hire out as wage laborers. By 1750 Boston contained a large number of homeless poor, who were supported by public charity and forced to wear a large red "P" on their clothing.

In the South the power of the great planters continued to be bolstered by their disproportionate ownership of slaves. Wealth was concentrated in the hands of the largest slaveowners, widening the gap between the prosperous **gentry** and the "poor whites," who were more and more likely to become **tenant farmers.** In all the colonies the ranks of the lower classes were further swelled by the continuing stream of indentured servants.

Far less fortunate than the voluntary indentured servants were the paupers and convicts involuntarily shipped to America. Altogether, about fifty thousand "jayle birds"—including robbers, rapists, and murderers—were dumped on the colonies by the London authorities. But many of the convicts were the unfortunate victims of a viciously unfair British **penal code,** and some eventually became highly respectable citizens.

Least fortunate of all, of course, were the black slaves. Oppressed and downtrodden, the slaves were America's closest approximation to Europe's volatile lower classes, and fears of black rebellion plagued the white colonists. Some colonial legislatures, notably South Carolina's in 1760, attempted to restrict or halt the importation of slaves, but British authorities vetoed all such efforts. Thomas Jefferson, himself a slaveholder, assailed the British **vetoes** in an early draft of the Declaration of Independence, but was forced to withdraw the proposed clause by a torrent of protest from southern slaveholders.

almshouses *A home for the poor, supported by charity or public funds.*

gentry *Landowners of substantial property, social standing, and leisure, but not titled nobility.*

tenant farmer(s) *One who rents rather than owns land.*

penal code *The body of criminal laws specifying offenses and prescribing punishments.*

vetoes *The executive power to prevent acts passed by the legislature from becoming law.*

apprentice(s) *A person who works under a master to acquire instruction in a trade or profession.*

Online Study Center

Primary source
Virginia Case Involving Runaway Indentured Servants
college.hmco.com/pic/kennedybrief7e

Clergy, Physicians, and Jurists

Most honored of the professions was the Christian ministry. In 1775 the clergy wielded less influence than in the early days of Massachusetts, when piety had burned more warmly. But they still occupied a position of high prestige.

Most physicians, on the other hand, were poorly trained and not highly esteemed. Not until 1765 was the first medical school established, although European centers attracted some students. Aspiring young doctors served for a while as **apprentices** to older practitioners and were then turned loose on their "victims." Bleeding was a favorite and frequently fatal remedy; when the physician was not available, a barber was often summoned.

Epidemics were a constant nightmare. Especially dreaded was smallpox, which afflicted one out of five persons, including the heavily pock-marked George Washington. A crude form of inoculation was introduced in 1721 despite the objections of many physicians and some of the clergy, who opposed tampering with the will of God. Powdered dried toad was a favorite prescription for smallpox. Diphtheria was also a deadly killer, especially of young people. One epidemic in the 1730s took the lives of thousands.

At first the law profession was not favorably regarded. In this pioneering society of farmers and manual laborers, the parties to a dispute often presented their own cases in court. Lawyers were commonly regarded as noisy windbags or troublemaking rogues; an early Connecticut law classed them with drunkards and brothel keepers.

Online Study Center

Primary source
Cotton Mather on the Education of His Children
college.hmco.com/pic/kennedybrief7e

Workaday America

Agriculture was the leading industry, involving about 90 percent of the people. Tobacco continued to be the staple crop in Maryland and Virginia, though wheat cultivation also spread in the Chesapeake, often on lands depleted by the excessive cultivation of tobacco. The fertile middle ("bread") colonies produced large quantities of grain, and by 1759 New York alone was exporting eighty thousand barrels of flour a year. Seemingly the farmer had only to tickle the soil with a hoe and it would laugh with a harvest. Overall, Americans probably enjoyed a higher average standard of living than the masses of any country in history up to that time.

Fishing (including whaling), though ranking in scale far below agriculture, was rewarding. Pursued in all the colonies, this harvesting of the sea was a major industry in New England, which exported smelly shiploads of dried cod to the Catholic countries of Europe. The fishing fleet also stimulated shipbuilding and served as a nursery for the seamen who manned the navy and merchant marine.

Yankee seamen were famous in many climes not only as skilled mariners but as tightfisted traders. They provisioned the Caribbean sugar islands with food and forest products. They hauled Spanish and Portuguese gold, wine, and oranges to London, to be exchanged for industrial goods, which were then sold for a juicy profit in America.

The so-called triangular trade was infamously profitable, though small in relation to total colonial commerce. A skipper would leave a New England port with a cargo of rum and sail to the Gold Coast of Africa. Bartering the fiery liquor with African chiefs for captured African slaves, he would proceed to the West Indies with his suffocating cargo sardined below deck. There he would exchange the slaves for molasses, which he would then carry to New England, where it would be distilled into rum. He would then repeat the trip, making a handsome profit on each leg of the triangle.

Manufacturing in the colonies was of only secondary importance, although there was a surprising variety of small enterprises. Huge quantities of "kill devil" rum were distilled in Rhode Island and Massachusetts, and even some of the "elect of the Lord" developed an overfondness for it. Beaver hats, iron, and clothing, spun and woven by women in the household, constituted other colonial manufactures. As in all pioneering countries, strong-backed laborers and skilled craftspeople were scarce and highly prized.

Lumbering was perhaps the most important single manufacturing activity. Countless cartloads of virgin timber were consumed by shipbuilders, who by 1770 were sending four hundred new vessels splashing into the sea each year. Colonial naval stores—such as tar, pitch, resin, and turpentine—were highly valued. Towering trees, ideal as masts for His Majesty's Navy, were marked with the king's broad arrow for future use. The luckless colonist who was caught cutting down this reserved timber was subject to a fine.

Americans held an important flank of a thriving, many-sided Atlantic economy by the dawn of the eighteenth century. Yet strains appeared in this complex network as early as the 1730s. Fast-breeding Americans demanded more and more British products—yet the slow-growing British population early reached the saturation point for absorbing imports from America. How, then, could the colonists sell the goods to make the money to buy what they wanted in Britain? The answer was obvious: by seeking foreign (non-British) markets.

By the eve of the Revolution the bulk of Chesapeake tobacco was filling pipes in France and other European countries, though it passed through the hands of British re-exporters, who took a slice of the profits for themselves. More important was the trade with the West Indies, especially the French islands. West Indian purchases of North American timber and foodstuffs provided the crucial cash for the colonists to continue to make their own purchases in Britain. But in 1733, bowing to pressure from influential British West Indian planters, Parliament passed the Molasses Act, aimed at squelching North American trade with the French West Indies. If successful, this scheme would have struck a crippling blow to American

Online Study Center

Interactive map
Atlantic Trade Routes
college.hmco.com/pic/kennedybrief7e

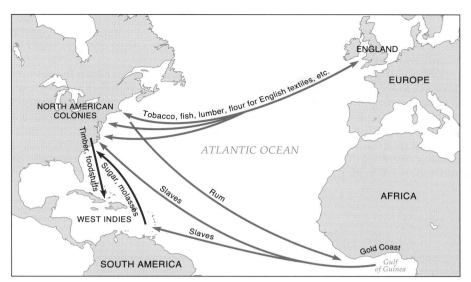

Future president John Adams noted about this time that "the commerce of the West Indies is a part of the American system of commerce. They can neither do without us, nor we without them. The Creator has placed us upon the globe in such a situation that we have occasion for each other."

international trade and to the colonists' standard of living. American merchants responded by bribing and smuggling their way around the law. Thus was foreshadowed the impending imperial crisis, when headstrong Americans would revolt rather than submit to the dictates of a far-off Parliament apparently bent on destroying their very livelihood.

Horsepower and Sailpower

As a sprawling and sparsely populated pioneer community, America was cursed with oppressive problems of transportation. Not until the 1700s did roads connect even the major cities. The few dirt thoroughfares that did exist were treacherously deficient, throwing up clouds of dust in summer and turning into quagmires of mud in winter. Stagecoach travelers braved additional dangers such as fallen trees, rickety bridges, carriage overturns, and runaway horses. Travel was so slow that it actually took twenty-nine days after the Fourth of July in 1776 for the news of the Declaration of Independence to reach Charleston from Philadelphia.

Estimated Religious Census, 1775

Name	Number	Chief Locale
Congregationalists	575,000	New England
Anglicans	500,000	N.Y., South
Presbyterians	410,000	Frontier
German churches (incl. Lutheran)	200,000	Pa.
Dutch Reformed	75,000	N.Y., N.J.
Quakers	40,000	Pa., N.J., Del.
Baptists	25,000	R.I., Pa., N.J., Del.
Roman Catholics	25,000	Md., Pa.
Methodists	5,000	Scattered
Jews	2,000	N.Y., R.I.
EST. TOTAL MEMBERSHIP	1,857,000	
EST. TOTAL POPULATION	2,493,000	
PERCENTAGE CHURCH MEMBERS	74%	

Where man-made roads were wretched, heavy reliance was placed on God-grooved waterways. Population tended to cluster along the banks of navigable rivers. There was also much coastwise traffic, which was cheap and pleasant but slow and undependable.

Taverns sprang up along the main routes of travel as well as in the cities. Along with such attractions as bowling alleys, pool tables, and gambling equipment, taverns were clearinghouses of information, misinformation, and rumor—frequently stimulated by alcoholic refreshment and impassioned political talk. Before a cheerful, roaring log fire all social classes would mingle, including the village loafers and drunks. Taverns were important in crystallizing public opinion, and alehouses like Boston's Green Dragon proved to be hotbeds of agitation as the revolutionary movement gathered momentum.

Dominant Denominations

Two "established," or tax-supported, churches were conspicuous in 1775: the Church of England and the Congregational Church. The Church of England, the Anglican Church, was the official faith in Georgia, North and South Carolina, Virginia, Maryland, and part of New York. British officials made vigorous attempts to impose it on additional colonies but ran into a stone wall of opposition. On the eve of the American Revolution, there was serious talk of creating a resident Anglican bishop in North America, but this scheme was also violently opposed by non-Anglicans, who feared a tightening of the royal reins. This controversy poured holy oil on the smoldering fires of rebellion.

Secure, self-satisfied, and often worldly, the Anglican Church itself fell distressingly short of its promise. So dismal was the reputation of the Anglican clergy in seventeenth-century Virginia that the College of William and Mary was founded in 1693 to train a better class of clerics.

The influential Congregational Church, the successor of the Puritans, was formally established in all the New England colonies except independent-minded Rhode Island. Presbyterianism, though closely associated with Congregationalism, was never the official church of any colony. Sometimes turning from the Bible to worldly politics, many Congregationalist and Presbyterian ministers of the gospel joined in stirring up opposition to the British crown in the 1760s and 1770s. Presbyterianism, Congregationalism, and rebellion became a neo-trinity. But most Anglican clergymen, aware of which side their tax-provided bread was buttered on, naturally supported their king.

Despite the presence of established churches, religious toleration had made enormous strides in America. Roman Catholics were still generally discriminated against, as in Britain, though the anti-papist laws were less severe and less strictly enforced. In general, people could worship—or not worship—as they pleased.

The Great Awakening

In all the colonial churches, religion was less fervid in the early eighteenth century than it had been a century earlier, when the colonies were first planted. The Puritan churches in particular sagged under the weight of two burdens: their elaborate theological doctrines and their compromising efforts to liberalize membership requirements. Churchgoers increasingly complained about the "dead dogs" who droned out tedious sermons from the pulpit. Some ministers, on the other hand, worried that their parishioners had gone soft and no longer embraced orthodox Calvinism. These twin trends toward clerical rigidity and lay indifference were sapping the spiritual vitality of many denominations.

The stage was thus set for a rousing religious **revival.** Known as the Great Awakening, it exploded in the 1730s and 1740s and swept through the colonies like a fire through prairie grass. The Awakening was first ignited in Northampton, Massachusetts, by a tall, delicate, and intellectual pastor, Jonathan Edwards. Perhaps the deepest theological mind ever nurtured in America, Edwards

revival *In religion, a movement of renewed enthusiasm and commitment, often accompanied by special meetings or vigorous evangelical and mission activity.*

proclaimed with burning righteousness the need for complete dependence on God's grace. His preaching style was learned and closely reasoned, but his stark doctrines sparked a warmly sympathetic reaction among his parishioners in 1734.

Four years later, the itinerant English parson George Whitefield loosed a different style of evangelical preaching on America and touched off a conflagration of religious ardor that revolutionized the spiritual life of the colonies. A former alehouse attendant, Whitefield was a magnificent orator whose voice boomed sonorously over thousands of enthralled listeners in the open fields where he preached. Triumphantly touring the colonies, Whitefield displayed an eloquence that reduced Jonathan Edwards to tears and even caused the skeptical and thrifty Benjamin Franklin to empty his pockets into the collection plate. During Whitefield's roaring revival meetings, countless sinners professed conversion, and hundreds of the "saved" groaned, shrieked, or rolled in the snow from religious excitement. Soon, American imitators took up Whitefield's electrifying new style of preaching and shook enormous audiences with emotional appeals.

Orthodox clergymen, known as "old lights," were deeply skeptical of the emotionalism and the theatrical antics of the revivalists. But "new light" ministers defended the Awakening for its role in revitalizing American religion. The Awakening left many lasting effects. Its emphasis on direct, emotive spirituality seriously undermined the older clergy, whose authority had derived from their education and erudition. The schisms that the Awakening set off in many denominations increased the numbers and competitiveness of American churches. The Awakening also encouraged a fresh wave of missionary work among the Indians and black slaves, many of whom attended open-air revivals. It also led to the founding of "new light" centers of higher learning such as Dartmouth, Brown, Rutgers, and Princeton. Perhaps most significant, the Great Awakening was the first spontaneous mass movement of the American people. By breaking down sectional boundaries and denominational lines, it contributed to the growing sense Americans had of themselves as a single people united by a common history and shared experience.

■ **George Whitefield Preaching** Americans of both genders and all races and regions were spellbound by Whitefield's fervent oratory.

Schools and Colleges

Only slowly and painfully did American colonists break away from the English idea that education should be reserved for the aristocratic few. In Puritan New England, education was dominated by the Congregational Church, which stressed the need for Bible reading to make good Christians. Education, principally for boys, thus flourished almost from the outset in New England, which boasted an impressive number of graduates from the British universities, especially Cambridge. New Englanders, at a relatively early date, established primary and secondary schools, which varied widely in the quality of instruction and in the length of time their doors remained open each year.

Fairly adequate elementary schools were also hammering knowledge into the heads of reluctant "scholars" in the middle colonies and in the South. Some of these institutions were tax supported; others were privately operated. The South, with its white and black populations diffused over wide areas, was severely handicapped in attempting to establish an effective school system. Wealthy families leaned heavily on private tutors.

John Adams (c. 1736–1826) the future second president, wrote to his wife:

"The education of our children is never out of my mind. . . . I must study politics and war that my sons may have the liberty to study mathematics and philosophy. My sons ought to study mathematics and philosophy, geography, natural history, naval architecture, navigation, commerce, and agriculture, in order to give their children a right to study painting, poetry, music, architecture, statuary, tapestry, and porcelain."

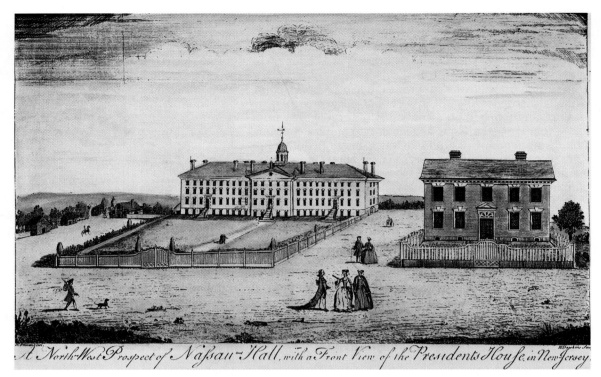

A North-West Prospect of Nassau-Hall, with a Front View of the Presidents House, in New-Jersey.

■ **The College of New Jersey at Princeton, 1764** Later known as Princeton University, it was chartered in 1746 by the Presbyterian Synod, though open to students of all religious persuasions. The fourth college to be founded in British North America, it met in Elizabeth and Newark, New Jersey, until a gift of ten acres of land precipitated a move to Princeton in 1756. All classes were held in the large building, Nassau Hall. Here the Continental Congress met for three months during the summer of 1783, making Princeton for a short time the capital of the nation. This copper engraving, based on a drawing by one of Princeton's earliest students, was part of a series of college views that reflected colonial Americans' growing pride in institutions of higher learning.

The general atmosphere in the colonial schools and colleges continued grim and gloomy. Most of the emphasis was on religion and the classical languages, Latin and Greek. Instruction was poor, independent thinking was discouraged, and severe discipline was often administered with a switch cut from a birch tree. But by 1750 a distinct trend had emerged toward "live" languages and other modern subjects in the nine small colonial colleges. A significant contribution was made by Benjamin Franklin, who played a major role in launching what became the University of Pennsylvania, the first American college free from denominational control.

A Provincial Culture

When it came to art and culture, colonial Americans were still in thrall to European tastes, especially British. The simplicity of pioneering life had not yet bred many homespun patrons of the arts, nor artists either. One aspiring painter, John Trumbull of Connecticut (1756–1843), was discouraged in his youth by his father's chilling remark, "Connecticut is not Athens." Trumbull, as well as his talented artistic contemporaries Charles Willson Peale (1741–1827), Benjamin West (1738–1820), and John Copley (1738–1815), all eventually succeeded in their ambition to become famous painters. But they had to go to Britain to complete their training and find patrons to support them.

Colonial architecture, too, was largely imported from the Old World. The red-brick Georgian style, so common in the pre-Revolutionary decades, was introduced about 1720 and is best exemplified by the beauty of now-restored Williamsburg, Virginia.

Colonial literature, like art, was generally undistinguished, but a few out-standing individuals produced original and enduring work. Precocious black poet Phillis Wheatley (c. 1753–1784) was an uneducated slave girl who was brought to Boston at age eight and then taken to London when she was twenty. She overcame her disadvantages and produced polished poems that revealed the influence of Alexander Pope.

Versatile Benjamin Franklin, often called "the first civilized American," also shone as a literary light. His autobiography was his greatest literary achieve-ment, but he was best known to his contemporaries for *Poor Richard's Almanack,* which he edited from 1732 to 1758. Emphasizing the homespun virtues of thrift, industry, and common sense, "Poor Richard" was most famous for his pithy sayings: "Plough deep while sluggards sleep"; "Fish and visitors stink in three days." *Poor Richard's* was well known in Europe and was more widely read in America than anything except the Bible. Dispensing witty advice to old and young alike, Franklin had an incalculable influence in shaping the American character.

Franklin's scientific efforts, including his spectacular kite-flying experiments with electricity, made him the colonies' only first-rate scientist and won him nu-merous honors in Europe. Among the inventions produced by his practical mind were bifocal spectacles, the Franklin stove, and the lightning rod.

Online Study Center

Primary source
Poor Richard's Almanack
college.hmco.com/pic/kennedybrief7e

Pioneer Presses

Stump-grubbing Americans were generally too poor to buy quantities of books and too busy to read them. A few fine private libraries, however, like that of the Byrd family in Virginia, could be found. Bustling Benjamin Franklin established in Philadelphia the first privately supported circulating library, and by 1776 there were about fifty public libraries and collections supported by subscription.

On the eve of the Revolution there were about forty newspapers, chiefly week-lies that consisted of a single large sheet folded once. The "news," especially from overseas, often lagged many weeks behind the event, and the papers devoted much column space to somber essays. Nevertheless, newspapers proved to be a powerful agency for airing colonial grievances and rallying opposition to British control.

A celebrated legal case in 1734–1735 involved John Peter Zenger, a newspa-per printer. Significantly, the case arose in New York, reflecting the tumultuous give-and-take of politics in the middle colonies, where so many different ethnic groups jostled against one another. Zenger's newspaper had assailed the corrupt royal governor. Charged with seditious libel, the accused was hauled into court, where he was defended by a former indentured servant, now a distinguished Philadelphia lawyer, Andrew Hamilton. Zenger argued that he had printed the truth, but the royal chief justice ruled that the mere fact of printing, regardless of the truth, was enough to convict. But the jury, swayed by Hamilton's eloquence, defied the bewigged judge and daringly returned a verdict of not guilty. Cheers burst from the spectators.

The Zenger decision was a banner achievement for freedom of the press. It pointed the way to the kind of open public discussion required by the diverse society that colonial New York already was and that all America was to become. Although contrary to existing law and not immediately accepted by other judges and juries, in time the ruling helped establish the doctrine that true statements about public officials could not be prose-cuted as libel. Newspapers were thus eventually free to print responsible criticisms of powerful officials, though full freedom of the press was unknown during the pre-Revolutionary era.

Andrew Hamilton (c. 1676–1741) concluded his eloquent plea in the Zenger case with these words:

"The question before the court and you, gentlemen of the jury, is not of small nor private concern. It is not the cause of a poor printer, nor of New York alone, which you are now trying. No! It may, in its consequence, affect every freeman that lives under a British government on the main [land] of America. It is the best cause. It is the cause of liberty."

The Great Game of Politics

American colonists may have been backward in natural or physical science, but they were making noteworthy contributions to political science.

The thirteen colonial governments took a variety of forms. By 1775 eight of the colonies had royal governors appointed by the king. Three—Maryland, Pennsylvania, and Delaware—were under proprietors who themselves chose the governors. And two—Connecticut and Rhode Island—elected their own governors under self-governing charters.

Practically every colony utilized a two-house legislative body. The upper house, or council, was normally appointed by the crown in the royal colonies and by the proprietor in the proprietary colonies. It was chosen by the voters in the self-governing colonies. The lower house, as the popular branch, was elected by the people—or rather by those who owned enough property to qualify as voters. In several of the colonies, the backcountry settlers were seriously underrepresented, and they hated the ruling colonial clique perhaps more than they did kingly authority. Legislatures, in which the people enjoyed direct representation, voted such taxes as they deemed necessary for the expenses of colonial government. Self-taxation through representation was a precious privilege that Americans had come to cherish above most others.

Governors appointed by the king were generally able men. Some, unfortunately, were incompetent or corrupt—broken-down politicians badly in need of jobs. The worst of the group was probably impoverished Lord Cornbury, first cousin of Queen Anne, who was made governor of New York and New Jersey in 1702. He proved to be a drunkard, a spendthrift, a grafter, an embezzler, a religious bigot, and a vain fool. He was also accused (probably inaccurately) of dressing as a woman. Even the best appointees had trouble with the colonial legislatures, basically because every royal governor embodied a bothersome transatlantic authority some three thousand miles away.

The colonial assemblies found various ways to assert their authority and independence. Some of them employed the trick of withholding the governor's salary unless he yielded to their wishes. Because he was normally in need of money, the power of the purse usually forced him to terms.

Administration at the local level was also varied. County government remained the rule in the plantation South; town-meeting government predominated in New England; and a modification of the two developed in the middle colonies. In the town meeting, with its open discussion and open voting, direct democracy functioned at its best. In this unrivaled cradle of self-government, Americans learned to cherish their privileges and exercise their duties as citizens of the New World commonwealths.

Yet the ballot was by no means a birthright. Religious or property qualifications for voting, with even stiffer qualifications for officeholding, existed in all the colonies in 1775. The privileged upper classes, fearful of democratic excesses, were unwilling to grant the ballot to every "biped of the forest." Perhaps half of the adult white males were thus disfranchised. But because of the ease of acquiring land and thus satisfying property requirements, the right to vote was not beyond the reach of most industrious and enterprising colonists.

By 1775 America was not yet a true democracy—socially, economically, or politically. But it was far more democratic than Britain and the European continent. Colonial institutions were giving freer rein to the democratic ideals of tolerance, education, equality of economic opportunity, freedom of speech, freedom of the press, freedom of assembly, and representative government. And these democratic seeds, planted in rich soil, were to bring forth a lush harvest in later years.

Colonial Folkways

Everyday life in the colonies may now seem glamorous, especially as reflected in antique shops. But judged by modern standards, it was drab and tedious. For most people, the labor was heavy and constant—from "can see" to "can't see."

Basic comforts now taken for granted were lacking. Food was plentiful, though the diet could be coarse and monotonous. Churches were unheated except for charcoal foot-warmers that the women carried. During the frigid New England winters, the preaching of hellfire may not have seemed altogether unattractive. There was no running water in the houses, no plumbing, and probably not a single bathtub in all colonial America. Candles and whale-oil lamps provided faint and flickering illumination. Garbage disposal was primitive. Long-snouted hogs customarily ranged the streets to consume refuse, while buzzards, protected by law, flapped greedily over tidbits of waste.

Amusement was eagerly pursued where time and custom permitted. Militia "musters," house-raisings, quilting bees, funerals, and weddings everywhere afforded opportunities for social gatherings, which customarily involved the swilling of much strong liquor. Winter sports were common in the North, whereas the South favored hunting, horse racing, dancing, theater, card playing, and cockfighting. The agile George Washington, not surprisingly, was equally skilled at riding and dancing.

Lotteries were universally approved, even by the clergy, and were used to raise money for churches and colleges, including Harvard. Holidays were celebrated everywhere, but Christmas was frowned upon in New England as an offensive reminder of "Popery." Thanksgiving Day came to be a truly American festival, for it combined giving thanks to God with an opportunity for jollification, gorging, and guzzling.

By the mid-eighteenth century Britain's North American colonies, despite their differences, revealed some striking similarities. All were basically English in language and customs and Protestant in religion, while the widespread presence of other peoples and faiths compelled every colony to cede at least some degree of ethnic and religious toleration. Compared with contemporary Europe, the colonies all afforded unusual opportunities for economic advancement and a measure of self-government, though by no means complete democracy. British North America by 1775 looked like a patchwork quilt—each section slightly different but stitched together by common origins, common ways of life, and common beliefs in toleration, economic development, and, above all, self-rule. Fatefully, all the colonies were also separated from the seat of imperial authority by a vast ocean moat some three thousand miles wide. These simple facts of shared history, culture, and geography set the stage for the colonists' struggle to unite as an independent people.

✪ Chapter Summary ✪

By 1775 there were thirty-two British colonies in the Americas, but only thirteen eventually revolted to form the United States of America. These latter territories were inhabited by a rapidly expanding, youthful population of about two million whites and half a million blacks. The white population was a melting pot of diverse ethnic groups, with Germans and Scots-Irish the largest non-English contingent.

Compared with Europe, America was a land of equality and opportunity (for whites); but relative to the seventeenth-century colonies, there was a rising economic hierarchy and increasing social complexity. Ninety percent of Americans worked in agriculture. But a growing class of wealthy planters and merchants appeared at the top of the social pyramid, in contrast with slaves and "jayle birds" forcibly shipped from Britain, who formed a visible lower class. The large "middle class" of whites consisted mostly of small farmers, along with artisans and tradespeople in the few small cities.

By the early eighteenth century, the established New England Congregational church was losing religious fervor. The Great Awakening, sparked by fiery preachers like Jonathan Edwards and George Whitefield, spread a new style of emotional worship that revived religious zeal. While the Awakening led to greater religious diversity, it also created a greater sense of a shared "American" identity across the colonies. Colonial education and culture were generally undistinguished, although science and journalism displayed some vigor. Politics was everywhere an important activity, as representative colonial assemblies battled with politically appointed governors from Britain. Despite their differences, the thirteen colonies already shared something of a common "American way of life."

Colonial America: Communities of Conflict or Consensus?

The earliest historians of colonial society portrayed close-knit, homogeneous, and hierarchical communities. Richard Bushman in *From Puritan to Yankee* (1967) challenged that traditional view. He described colonial New England as an expanding, open society in which the colonists gradually lost the religious discipline and social structure of the founding generations. Rhys Isaac viewed the Great Awakening in the South as similar evidence of erosion in the social constraints and deference that once held colonial society together.

Some scholars dispute that a loss of common faith and morals undermined colonial communities. Christine Heyrmann in particular argued in *Commerce and Culture* (1984) that the decline of traditional mores was overstated and that religious beliefs and commercial activities coexisted throughout the late seventeenth and early eighteenth centuries. Similarly, colonial historian Jack Greene has suggested that the obsession with the decline of deference obscures the fact that colonies outside New England, like Virginia and Maryland, actually experienced a consolidation of religious and social authority throughout the seventeenth and eighteenth centuries, becoming more hierarchical and paternalistic, not less.

Since the 1970s, some historians have also attacked the traditional idea that New England was the home of American freedom and that the South spawned hierarchical, aristocratic communities. They argue that not only did the South produce many of the founders—Washington, Jefferson, and Madison—but that republican principles were actually strongest in Virginia. Some scholars, notably Edmund S. Morgan in *American Slavery, American Freedom* (1975), consider the willingness of wealthy planters to concede the equality and freedom of all white males a device to ensure racial solidarity and to mute class conflict.

Few historians still argue that the colonies offered boundless opportunities for inhabitants, white or black. Whether one accepts Morgan's arguments that "Americans bought their independence with slave labor" or those interpretations that point to the rising social conflict between whites as the salient characteristic of colonial society on the eve of the Revolution, the once-common assumption that America was a world of equality and consensus no longer reigns undisputed. Yet because one's life chances were still unquestionably better in America than in Europe, immigrants who viewed America as a land of opportunity continued to pour in.

6

The Duel for North America

———— ⌐∿⌐ ————

1608–1763

A TORCH LIGHTED IN THE FORESTS OF AMERICA SET ALL
EUROPE IN CONFLAGRATION.

VOLTAIRE, C. 1756

As the seventeenth century neared its sunset, a titanic struggle was shaping up for mastery of the North American continent. The contest involved three Old World nations—Britain (England),* France, and Spain—and it unavoidably swept up Native American peoples as well. From 1688 to 1763, four bitter wars convulsed Europe. All four of those conflicts were world wars. Fought on the waters and on the soil of two hemispheres, they amounted to a death struggle for domination in Europe as well as in the New World. Counting these first four clashes, nine world wars have been waged since 1688. The American people, whether as British subjects or as American citizens, proved unable to stay out of a single one of them. And one of those wars—known as the Seven Years' War in Europe and the French and Indian War in America—set the stage for America's independence.

Focus Questions

1. What were the fundamental causes of the imperial conflict between France and Britain for control of North America?
2. What was the social and political character of New France, and how did it compare with Britain's North American colonies?
3. How were eighteenth-century political and military events in North America shaped by rivalries on the larger European stage?
4. Why did Britain finally win the French and Indian War, and what role did the American colonists play in the victory?
5. How did the British victory in the Seven Years' War ironically become one of the precipitating causes of the American Revolution?

———————

*After the political union of England and Scotland in 1707, the nation's official name became "Great Britain."

France Finds a Foothold in Canada

domestic *Concerning the internal affairs of a country.*

edict *A publicly announced order or law, especially one issued unilaterally by an authoritarian government, requiring immediate obedience.*

peasants *A farmer or agricultural laborer, often owing payment or services to a landlord and sometimes legally tied to the land.*

coureurs des bois *French-Canadian fur trappers; literally, "runners of the woods."*

voyageurs *French-Canadian explorers, adventurers, and traders.*

ecological (ecology) *The mutual sustaining relationships between biological organisms and their environment.*

Like England and Holland, France was a latecomer in the scramble for New World real estate, and for basically the same reasons. It was convulsed during the 1500s by foreign wars and **domestic** strife, including frightful clashes and sometimes massacres between Roman Catholics and Protestant Huguenots.

A new era dawned in 1598 when the **Edict** of Nantes, issued by the crown, granted limited toleration to French Protestants (Huguenots). Religious wars ceased, and in the new century France blossomed into the mightiest and most feared nation in Europe.

After rocky beginnings, success finally rewarded the exertions of France in the New World. In 1608, the year after the founding of Jamestown, the permanent beginnings of a vast empire were established at Quebec, a granite sentinel commanding the St. Lawrence River. The leading figure was Samuel de Champlain, an intrepid soldier and explorer whose energy and leadership fairly earned him the title "Father of New France."

Champlain entered into friendly relations—a fateful friendship—with the nearby Huron Indian tribes. At their request, he joined them in battle against their foes, the federated Iroquois tribes of the upper New York area. Two volleys from the "lightning sticks" of the whites routed the Iroquois, who left behind three dead and one wounded. France, to its sorrow, thus earned the lasting enmity of the Iroquois tribes, who thereafter hampered French penetration of the Ohio Valley, sometimes ravaging French settlements, and frequently serving as allies of the British in the prolonged struggle for supremacy on the continent.

The government of New France (Canada) finally fell under the direct control of the king after various commercial companies had faltered or failed. This royal regime was almost completely autocratic. The people elected no representative assemblies, as the English colonies did; nor did they enjoy the right of trial by jury.

The population of Catholic New France grew at a listless pace. As late as 1750 only sixty thousand or so whites inhabited New France. Landowning French **peasants,** unlike the dispossessed English tenant farmers who embarked for the British colonies, had little economic motive to move. Protestant Huguenots, who might have had a religious motive to migrate, were denied a refuge in this raw colony. The French government, in any case, favored its Caribbean island colonies, rich in sugar and rum, over the snow-cloaked wilderness of Canada.

New France Fans Out

New France did contain one valuable resource: the beaver. To adorn the heads of fashionable Europeans, French fur trappers ranged over the woods and waterways of North America in pursuit of the thick-furred beavers. These colorful *coureurs des bois* (runners of the woods) were also runners of risks—two-fisted drinkers, free spenders, free livers and lovers. They littered the land with scores of place names, including Baton Rouge (red stick), Terre Haute (high land), Des Moines (some monks), and Grand Teton (big breast).

Singing, paddle-swinging French **voyageurs** also recruited Indians into the fur business. But the Indians were decimated by the white man's diseases and debauched by his alcohol. Slaughtering beaver by the boatload also violated many Indian religious beliefs and sadly demonstrated the shattering effect that contact with Europeans wreaked on traditional Indian ways of life.

Pursuing the sharp-toothed beaver ever deeper into the heart of the continent, French trappers and their Indian partners covered amazing distances. They trekked in a huge arc across the Great Lakes, into present-day Saskatchewan and Manitoba, along the valleys of the Platte, the Arkansas, and the Missouri, west to the Rockies, and south to the border of Spanish Texas. In the process, they all but extinguished the beaver population in many areas, inflicting incalculable **ecological** damage.

Chronology

1598	Edict of Nantes.
1608	Champlain colonizes Quebec for France.
1682	La Salle explores Mississippi River to the Gulf of Mexico.
1689–1697	King William's War (War of the League of Augsburg).
1702–1713	Queen Anne's War (War of Spanish Succession).
1718	French found New Orleans.
1739	War of Jenkins's Ear.
1740–1748	King George's War (War of Austrian Succession).
1754	Washington battles French on frontier. Albany Congress.
1754–1763	Seven Years' War (French and Indian War).
1755	Braddock's defeat.
1757	Pitt emerges as leader of British government.
1759	Battle of Quebec.
1763	Peace of Paris. Pontiac's uprising. Proclamation of 1763.

French Catholic missionaries, notably the Jesuits, labored zealously to save the Indians for Christ and from the fur trappers. Some of the Jesuit missionaries, their efforts scorned, suffered unspeakable tortures at the hands of the Indians. But though they made few permanent converts, the Jesuits played a vital role as explorers and geographers.

Other explorers sought neither souls nor fur, but empire. To check Spanish penetration into the region around the Gulf of Mexico, ambitious Robert La Salle floated down the Mississippi in 1682 to the point where it mingles with the Gulf. Three years later he tried to return to the territory he had named "Louisiana," but he failed to find the Mississippi delta. He landed instead in Spanish Texas and in 1687 was murdered by his **mutinous** men.

Persistent French officials planted several fortified posts in what is now Mississippi and Louisiana, the most important of which was New Orleans (1718). Commanding the mouth of the Mississippi River, this **strategic** semitropical outpost controlled the trade of the huge interior valley, especially the fertile Illinois country. There the French also established forts and trading posts at Vincennes, Cahokia, and Kaskaskia.

The Clash of Empires

The earliest contests among the European powers for control of North America, the War of the League of Augsburg and the War of Spanish Succession, known to the British colonists respectively as King William's War (1689–1697) and Queen Anne's War (1702–1713), mostly pitted British colonists against the French *coureurs des bois,* with both sides recruiting whatever Indian allies they could. Neither France nor Britain considered America worth the commitment of large detachments of regular troops, so the combatants in these conflicts waged a kind of guerrilla warfare. France's Indian allies ravaged with torch and tomahawk the British colonial frontiers from New York to Massachusetts. Spain, eventually allied with France, probed from its Florida base at outlying South Carolina settlements. For their part, the British colonists failed miserably in **sallies** against Quebec and Montreal but did temporarily seize the stronghold of Port Royal in Acadia (present-day Nova Scotia).

mutinous (mutiny) *Revolt by subordinate soldiers or seamen against their commanding officers.*

strategic *Concerning the placement and planned movement of large-scale military forces so as to gain advantage, usually prior to actual engagement with the enemy.*

sallies (sally) *In warfare, very rapid military movements, usually by small units, against an enemy force or position.*

Online Study Center

Primary source
Land Division in New Orleans Clearly Shows. . .
college.hmco.com/pic/kennedybrief7e

■ **Chief of the Taensa Indians Receiving La Salle, March 20, 1682, by George Catlin, 1847–1848 (detail)** Driven by the dream of a vast North American empire for France, La Salle spent years exploring the Great Lakes region and the valleys of the Illinois and Mississippi Rivers. This scene of his encounter with an Indian chieftain was imaginatively re-created by the nineteenth-century artist George Catlin.

In the Peace of Utrecht (1713), victorious Britain acquired French-populated Acadia and the wintry wastes of Newfoundland and Hudson Bay. These immense tracts pinched the St. Lawrence settlements of France. The British also won limited trading rights in Spanish America, but these later created much friction over smuggling. Ill feeling between Britain and Spain led to war in 1739, when the British Captain Robert Jenkins, whose ear had been sliced off by a Spanish sword, returned to London with a tale of woe on his tongue and a shriveled ear in his hand. The War of Jenkins's Ear was confined to the Caribbean Sea and to the much-buffeted buffer colony of Georgia.

This small-scale scuffle with Spain in America soon merged with the large-scale War of the Austrian Succession in Europe (called King George's War in America). Once again, France allied itself with Spain. And again operating on their own, a rustic force of New Englanders, with the help of the British fleet, captured the reputedly impregnable French fortress of Louisbourg on Cape Breton Island, which commanded the approaches to the St. Lawrence River. When the peace treaty of 1748 handed Louisbourg back to their French foe, the victorious New Englanders were outraged. The glory of their arms seemed tarnished by the wiles of Old World diplomats. Worse still, Louisbourg remained a cocked pistol pointed at the heart of the American continent. France, powerful and unappeased, still clung to its vast holdings in North America.

George Washington Inaugurates War with France

As the dogfight intensified in the New World, the Ohio Valley became the chief bone of contention between the French and British. The Ohio Country was the critical area into which the westward-pushing British would inevitably penetrate. It was the key to the continent that the French had to retain, particularly if they were going to link their Canadian holdings with those of the lower Mississippi Valley. By the mid-1700s the British colonists, painfully aware of these basic truths, were no longer so reluctant to bear the burdens of empire. Alarmed by French

Restless Colonists

Britain's colonists, baptized in fire, emerged with increased confidence in their military strength. They had borne the brunt of battle at first; they had fought bravely alongside the crack British regulars; and officers and men alike had gained valuable experience. In the closing days of the conflict some twenty thousand American recruits were under arms.

The French and Indian War, while bolstering colonial self-esteem, simultaneously shattered the myth of British invincibility. On Braddock's bloody field the "buckskin" militia had seen the demoralized regulars huddling helplessly together or fleeing their unseen enemy.

Ominously, friction had developed during the war between arrogant British officers and the raw colonial "boors." Displaying the professional soldier's contempt for amateurs, the British refused to recognize any American militia **commission** above the rank of captain—a demotion humiliating to "Colonel" George Washington. They also showed the usual condescension of snobs from the civilized Old Country toward the "scum" who had confessed failure by fleeing to the "outhouses of civilization." Energetic and hard-working American settlers, by contrast, believed themselves to be on the cutting edge of British civilization. They felt that they deserved credit rather than contempt for risking their lives to erect a New World empire.

British officials were further distressed by the reluctance of the colonists to support the common cause wholeheartedly. American shippers developed a treasonable but lucrative trade with the Spanish and French West Indies at the very time the British navy was trying to subdue them. Other self-centered colonists refused to provide troops and money for the conflict until Pitt reimbursed the colonies for their mounting expenditures.

The curse of intercolonial disunity, present from early days, had continued throughout the recent hostilities. It had been caused mainly by enormous distances and geographical barriers; by religious differences spanning everyone from Catholic to Quaker; by various nationalities, from German to Irish; by differing types of colonial governments; by many boundary disputes; and by the resentment that the crude backcountry settlers felt against the aristocratic bigwigs.

commission *An official certification granting a commanding rank in the armed forces.*

The Reverend Andrew Burnaby, an observant Church of England clergyman who visited the colonies in the closing months of the Seven Years' War, scoffed at any possibility of unification (1760):

". . . for fire and water are not more heterogeneous than the different colonies in North America. Nothing can exceed the jealousy and emulation which they possess in regard to each other. . . . In short . . . were they left to themselves there would soon be a civil war from one end of the continent to the other, while the Indians and Negros would . . . impatiently watch the opportunity of exterminating them all together."

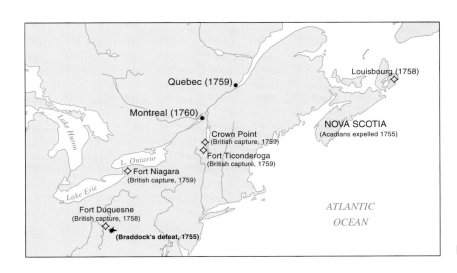

■ Events of 1755–1760

The French

King Louis XIV's dream of a bountiful empire in New France flickered out like a candle after the British conquered his French colonies in the eighteenth century. His former subjects in Quebec and the maritime provinces of Acadia had to suffer foreign governance in the aftermath of the French defeats in 1713 and 1763. Over the course of the next two centuries many eventually found their way to the United States.

■ **Modern-Day Quebec** A bit of the Old World in the New.

The first French to leave Canada were the Acadians, the settlers of the seaboard region that now comprises Nova Scotia, New Brunswick, Prince Edward Island, and part of Maine. In 1713 the French crown ceded this territory to the British, who demanded that the Acadians either swear allegiance to Britain or withdraw to French territory. At first doing neither, they managed to escape reprisals until Le Grand Dérangement ("The Great Displacement") in 1755, when the British expelled them from the region at bayonet point. The Acadians fled far south to the French colony of Louisiana, where they settled among the sleepy bayous, planted sugar cane and sweet potatoes, practiced Roman Catholicism, and spoke the French dialect that came to be called Cajun (a corruption of the English word *Acadian*). The Cajun settlements were tiny and secluded, many of them accessible only by small boat.

For generations these insular people were scarcely influenced by developments outside their tight-knit communities. Not until the twentieth century did Cajun parents surrender their children to public schools and submit to a state law restricting French speech. Only in the 1930s, with a bridge-building spree engineered by Governor Huey Long, was the isolation of the bayou communities broken.

In 1763, as the French settlers of Quebec fell under British rule, a second group began to leave Canada. By 1840 what had been an irregular southward trickle of Quebecois swelled to a steady stream of people who were driven away mostly by lean harvests.

Most of them emigrated to work in New England's lumberyards and textile mills, gradually establishing permanent settlements in the northern woods. Like the Acadians, these later migrants from Quebec stubbornly preserved their Roman Catholicism. Both groups shared a passionate love of their French language, believing it to be the cement that bound them, their religion, and their culture together. As one French-Canadian explained: "Let us worship in peace and in our own tongue. All else may disappear but this must remain our badge."

Today, almost all Cajuns and New England French Canadians speak English. But their ethnic communities and traditions eloquently testify to the continued vitality of French culture in North American history.

Yet unity received some encouragement during the French and Indian War. When soldiers and statesmen from widely separated colonies met around common campfires and council tables, they were often agreeably surprised to discover that they were all fellow Americans who generally spoke the same language and shared common ideals. Barriers of disunity began to melt, although a long and rugged road lay ahead before a coherent nation would emerge.

Americans: A People of Destiny

The removal of the French menace in Canada profoundly affected American attitudes. While the French hawk had been hovering in the North and West, the colonial chicks had been forced to cling close to the wings of their British mother hen. Now that the hawk was killed, they could range far afield with a new spirit of independence.

The French, humiliated by the British and saddened by the fate of Canada, consoled themselves with one wishful thought. Perhaps the loss of their American empire would one day result in Britain's loss of its American empire. In a sense the history of the United States began with the fall of Quebec and Montreal; the infant Republic was conceived on the Plains of Abraham.

The Spanish and Indian menaces were also substantially reduced. Spain was eliminated from Florida, although entrenched in Louisiana and New Orleans. As for the Indians, the Treaty of Paris dealt a harsh blow to the Creeks, Iroquois, and other interior tribes. Sensing the newly precarious position of the Indian peoples, the Ottawa chief Pontiac in 1763 led several tribes in a violent campaign to drive the British out of the Ohio Country. Pontiac's warriors seized Detroit in the spring of 1763 and eventually overran all but three British outposts west of the Appalachians.

■ **North America Before 1754**

■ **North America After 1763 (after French losses)**

Online Study Center

Interactive map
European Claims in North America
college.hmco.com/pic/kennedybrief7e

The British retaliated swiftly and cruelly. Waging a primitive version of biological warfare, one British commander ordered blankets infected with smallpox to be distributed among the Indians. Such tactics crushed the uprising, and Pontiac's death in 1769 brought an uneasy truce to the frontier. The bloody episode convinced the British of the need to stabilize relations with the western Indians and to station regular troops along the restless frontier, a measure for which they soon asked the colonists to foot the bill.

Land-hungry American colonists were now free to burst over the dam of the Appalachian Mountains and flood out over the verdant western lands. A tiny rivulet of pioneers like Daniel Boone had already trickled into Tennessee and Kentucky. Other courageous pioneers made their preparations for the long, dangerous trek over the mountains.

Then, out of a clear sky, the London government issued its Proclamation of 1763, which flatly prohibited settlement in the area beyond the Appalachians, pending further adjustments. The truth is that this hastily drawn document was not designed to oppress the colonists at all, but to work out the Indian problem fairly and prevent another bloody eruption like Pontiac's uprising.

But countless Americans, especially land speculators, were dismayed and angered. Was not the land beyond the mountains their birthright? Had they not, in addition, bought it with their blood in the recent war? In complete defiance of the proclamation, they clogged the westward trails. In 1765 an estimated one thousand wagons rolled through the town of Salisbury, North Carolina, on their way "up west." This wholesale flouting of royal authority boded ill for the longevity of British rule in America.

The Seven Years' War caused the colonists to develop a new vision of their destiny. With the path cleared for the conquest of a continent, with their birthrate high and their energy boundless, they sensed that they were a potent people on the march. Lordly Britons, whose suddenly swollen empire had tended to produce swollen heads, were in no mood for back talk. Puffed up over their recent victories, they were already annoyed with their unruly colonial subjects. The stage was thus set for a violent family quarrel.

✪ Chapter Summary ✪

Like Britain, France entered late into the American colonial scramble, eventually developing an extensive though thinly settled empire based primarily on the fur trade. During much of the eighteenth century, Britain and France engaged in a bitter power struggle that frequently erupted into worldwide wars. In North America these wars constituted an extended military duel for imperial control of the continent.

The culminating phase of this struggle was inaugurated by young George Washington's venture into the sharply contested Ohio country. After early reversals in this French and Indian War (the Seven Years' War in Europe), the British under William Pitt revived their fortunes and won a decisive victory at Quebec, finally forcing the French from North America.

The American colonists had played a subordinate role in Britain's earlier imperial wars with France. But during the French and Indian War they emerged with increased confidence in their own abilities, and increased resentment of the British treatment of them as provincial inferiors. The removal of the French threat to British control of North America also decreased the colonists' reliance on Britain for their defense. The Ottawa chief Pontiac's unsuccessful uprising in 1763 convinced the British of the need to continue stationing troops in America. But the colonists saw no need for new taxes to pay for British protection, and increasingly resented Britain's authority over them.

7

The Road to Revolution

—⟳—

1763–1775

THE REVOLUTION WAS EFFECTED BEFORE THE WAR
COMMENCED. THE REVOLUTION WAS IN THE MINDS AND
HEARTS OF THE PEOPLE.

JOHN ADAMS, 1818

Victory in the Seven Years' War made Britain the master of a vastly enlarged imperial domain in North America. But victory—including the subsequent need to garrison ten thousand troops along the sprawling American frontier—was painfully costly. The London government therefore struggled after 1763 to compel the American colonists to shoulder some of the financial costs of empire. This change in British colonial policy reinforced an emerging sense of American political identity and helped to precipitate the American Revolution.

The eventual conflict was by no means inevitable. Indeed, given the tightening commercial, military, and cultural bonds between the colonies and mother country since the first crude settlements a century and a half earlier, it might be considered remarkable that the Revolution happened at all. The truth is that Americans were reluctant revolutionaries. Until late in the day, they sought only to claim the "rights of Englishmen," not to separate from the mother country. But what began as a squabble about economic policies soon exposed irreconcilable differences between Americans and Britons over cherished political principles. The ensuing clash gave birth to a new nation.

Focus Questions

1. What deeply rooted historical factors moved America toward independence from Britain?
2. Why did Britain seek tighter control and heavier taxation of its North American colonies after 1763, and why did these policies produce such a strong reaction from the colonists?
3. What were the major methods and specific events that shaped colonial resistance to taxation, and how did Britain respond to the protests?
4. Why did the Boston Tea Party provoke the fierce British response of the "Intolerable Acts," when earlier conflicts had been compromised or dampened down?
5. What advantages and disadvantages did the American "patriots" and Britain each possess as the two sides entered upon armed conflict?

The Deep Roots of Revolution

In a broad sense, America was a revolutionary force from the day of its discovery. The New World nurtured new ideas about the nature of society, citizen, and government. In the Old World many humble folk had long lived in the shadow of graveyards that contained the bones of their ancestors for a thousand years past. Few people born into such changeless surroundings dared to question their social status. But in the American wilderness ordinary people encountered a world that was theirs to make afresh.

Two ideas in particular had taken root in the minds of the American colonists by the mid-eighteenth century: One was what historians call *republicanism*. Looking to the models of the ancient Greek and Roman republics, exponents of republicanism defined a just society as one in which all citizens willingly subordinated their private, selfish interests to the common good. The stability of society and the authority of government thus depended on the virtue of the citizenry, especially its appetite for civic involvement.

A second idea that fundamentally shaped American political thought derived from a group of British political commentators known as the "radical Whigs." Widely read by the colonists, the Whigs feared the threat to liberty posed by the arbitrary power of the monarch and his ministers, especially the "corruption" revealed by **patronage** and bribes. Whigs warned citizens to be eternally vigilant against corruption and possible conspiracies to denude them of their hard-won liberties. Together, republican and Whig ideas predisposed the American colonists to be on hair-trigger alert against any threat to their rights.

The circumstances of colonial life had done much to bolster those attitudes. Dukes and princes, barons and bishops were unknown in the colonies, while property ownership and political participation were relatively widespread. The Americans had also grown accustomed to running their own affairs, largely unmolested by remote officials in London. Distance weakens authority; great distance weakens authority greatly. So it came as an especially jolting shock when Britain after 1763 tried to enclose its American colonists more snugly in its grip.

Mercantilism and Colonial Grievances

Britain's empire was acquired in a "fit of absentmindedness," an old saying goes, and there is much truth in the jest. Not one of the original thirteen colonies except Georgia was formally planted by the British government. All the others were haphazardly founded by trading companies, religious groups, or land speculators.

The British authorities nevertheless embraced a theory, called "**mercantilism**," that justified their control of the colonies. Mercantilists believed that wealth was power and that a country's economic wealth could be measured by the amount of gold or silver in its treasury. To amass gold or silver, a country needed to export more than it imported. Possessing colonies thus conferred distinct advantages, since the colonies could both supply raw materials to the mother country (thereby reducing the need for foreign imports) and provide a guaranteed market for exports.

The London government therefore looked on the American colonists more or less as tenants. They were expected to furnish raw products needed in the mother country; refrain from making finished products like cloth or beaver hats for export; buy imported manufactured goods exclusively from Britain; and not indulge in dangerous dreams of economic independence or, worse, self-government.

From time to time Parliament passed laws to regulate the mercantile system. The first of these, the Navigation Law of 1650, required that all commerce flowing to and from the colonies must be transported only in British (including colonial) vessels. Subsequent laws stipulated that European goods destined for America first had to be landed in Britain, where tariff duties could be collected and British middlemen would take a slice of the profits. American merchants also had to ship

patronage *A system in which benefits, including jobs, money, or protection are granted in exchange for political support.*

mercantilism *The economic theory that all parts of an economy should be coordinated for the good of the whole state; hence, that colonial economies should be subordinated to the benefit of an imperial power.*

Online Study Center

Primary source
William Shepherd Attempts to Collect Customs Duties
college.hmco.com/pic/kennedybrief7e

Chronology

1650	First Navigation Laws to control colonial commerce.	**1770**	Boston Massacre. All Townshend Acts except tea tax repealed.
1763	Seven Years' War (French and Indian War) ends.	**1772**	Committees of correspondence formed.
1764	Sugar Act.	**1773**	British East India Company granted tea monopoly. Governor Hutchinson's actions provoke Boston Tea Party.
1765	Quartering Act. Stamp Act. Stamp Act Congress.		
1766	Declaratory Act.	**1774**	"Intolerable Acts." Quebec Act. First Continental Congress. The Association boycotts British goods.
1767	Townshend Acts. New York legislature suspended by Parliament.		
1768	British troops occupy Boston.	**1775**	Battles of Lexington and Concord.

certain "enumerated" products, notably tobacco, exclusively to Britain, even though prices might be better elsewhere.

British policy also inflicted a currency shortage on the colonies. Since the colonists bought more from Britain than they sold there, the difference had to be made up in hard cash. Every year gold and silver coins, mostly earned in illicit trade with the Spanish and French West Indies, drained out of the colonies, creating an acute money shortage. To facilitate everyday purchases, the colonists resorted to using butter, nails, pitch, and feathers for purposes of exchange.

Currency issues came to a boil when dire financial need finally forced many of the colonies to issue paper money, which swiftly **depreciated.** British merchants and creditors squawked so loudly that Parliament prohibited the colonial legislatures from printing paper currency and from passing indulgent bankruptcy laws—practices that might harm British merchants.

The British crown also reserved the right to nullify any colonial legislation that might work mischief with the mercantile system. This royal **veto** was used rather sparingly—just 469 times in connection with 8,563 laws. But the colonists nevertheless fiercely resented its very existence—another example of how principle could weigh more heavily than practice in fueling colonial grievances.

depreciated *To decrease in value, as in the decline of the purchasing power of money.*

veto *The constitutional right of a ruler or executive to block legislation passed by another unit of government.*

monopoly *The complete control of a product or sphere of economic activity by a single producer or business.*

The Merits and Menace of Mercantilism

In theory, the British mercantile system seemed thoroughly selfish and deliberately oppressive. But the truth is that until 1763 the various Navigation Laws imposed no intolerable burden, mainly because they were loosely enforced. Enterprising colonial merchants learned early to disregard or evade troublesome restrictions. Some of the first American fortunes, like that of John Hancock, were amassed by wholesale smuggling.

Americans also reaped direct benefits from the mercantile system. If the colonies existed for the benefit of the mother country, it was hardly less true that Britain existed for the benefit of the colonies. London paid liberal bounties to colonial producers of ships' parts, over the protests of British competitors. Virginia tobacco planters enjoyed a **monopoly** in the British market. The colonists also benefited from the protection of the world's mightiest navy and a strong, seasoned army of redcoats—all without a penny of cost.

But even when painted in its rosiest colors, the mercantile system burdened the colonists with annoying liabilities. Mercantilism stifled economic initiative and imposed a rankling dependency on British agents and creditors. Most grievously, many Americans simply found the mercantilist system debasing. They

■ **Paul Revere, by John Singleton Copley, c. 1768**
This painting of the famed silversmith-horseman challenged convention—and reflected the new democratic spirit of the age—by portraying an artisan in working clothes. Notice how Copley has depicted the serene confidence of the master craftsman and Revere's quiet pride in his work. Photograph © 2006 Museum of Fine Arts, Boston.

duty (duties) *A customs tax on the export or import of goods.*

admiralty courts *In British law, special administrative courts designed to handle maritime cases without a jury.*

felt used, kept in a state of perpetual economic adolescence, and never allowed to come of age. As Benjamin Franklin wrote in 1775:

We have an old mother that peevish is grown;
She snubs us like children that scarce walk alone;
She forgets we're grown up and have sense of our own.

Revolution broke out, as Theodore Roosevelt later remarked, because Britain failed to recognize an emerging nation when it saw one.

The Stamp Tax Uproar

Victory-flushed Britain emerged from the Seven Years' War holding one of the biggest empires in the world—and also, less happily, the biggest debt, some £140 million, about half of which had been incurred defending the American colonies. To justify and service that debt, British officials now moved to redefine their relationship with their North American colonies.

Prime Minister George Grenville first aroused the resentment of the colonists in 1763 by ordering the British navy to enforce the Navigation Laws. He also secured from Parliament the so-called Sugar Act of 1764, the first law ever passed by that body for raising tax revenue in the colonies for the crown. Among various provisions, it increased the **duty** on foreign sugar imported from the West Indies. After bitter protests from the colonists, the duties were lowered substantially, and the agitation died down. But resentment was kept burning by the Quartering Act of 1765, which required certain colonies to provide food and quarters for British troops.

Then in the same year, 1765, Grenville proposed the most odious measure of all: a stamp tax, to raise revenues to support the new military force. The Stamp Act mandated the use of stamped paper or the affixing of stamps certifying payment of tax. Stamps were required on bills of sale for about fifty trade items as well as on certain types of commercial and legal documents, including playing cards, pamphlets, newspapers, diplomas, bills of lading, and marriage licenses.

Grenville regarded all these measures as reasonable and just. He was simply asking the Americans to pay their fair share of the costs for their own defense, through taxes that were already familiar in Britain. In fact, Englishmen for two generations had endured a stamp tax far heavier than that passed for the colonies.

Yet the Americans were angrily aroused at what they regarded as Grenville's fiscal aggression. The new laws did not merely pinch their pocketbooks. Far more ominously, Grenville seemed also to be striking at the local liberties they had come to assume as a matter of right. Thus some colonial assemblies defiantly refused to comply with the Quartering Act, or voted for only a fraction of the supplies that it called for.

Worst of all, Grenville's noxious legislation seemed to jeopardize the basic rights of the colonists as Englishmen. Both the Sugar Act and the Stamp Act provided for trying offenders in the hated **admiralty courts,** where juries were not allowed. The burden of proof was on the defendants, who were assumed to be guilty unless they could prove themselves innocent. Trial by jury and the precept of "innocent until proved guilty" were ancient privileges that British people everywhere, including the American colonists, held most dear.

And why was a British army needed at all in the colonies, now that the French were expelled from the continent and Pontiac's warriors crushed? Could its real purpose be to whip rebellious colonists themselves into line? Many Americans, weaned on the radical Whigs' suspicion of all authority, began to sniff the strong scent of a conspiracy to strip them of their historic liberties. They lashed back violently, and the Stamp Act became the target that drew their most ferocious fire.

Angry throats raised the cry, "No taxation without representation." There was some irony in the slogan, because the seaports and tidewater towns that were most wrathful against the Stamp Act had long denied full representation to their own backcountry pioneers. But now the aggravated colonists took the high ground of principle.

The Americans made a distinction between "legislation" and "taxation." They conceded the right of Parliament to legislate about matters that affected the entire empire, including the regulation of trade. But they steadfastly denied the right of Parliament, in which no Americans were seated, to impose taxes on Americans. Only their own elected colonial legislatures, the Americans insisted, could legally tax them.

Grenville dismissed these American protests as hairsplitting absurdities. The power of Parliament was supreme and undivided, he asserted, and in any case the Americans were represented in Parliament. Elaborating the theory of "**virtual representation,**" Grenville claimed that every member of Parliament represented all British subjects, even those Americans in Boston or Charleston who had never voted for a member of the London Parliament. The Americans scoffed at this notion of virtual representation.

Thus the principle of no taxation without representation was supremely important, and the colonists clung to it with tenacious consistency. When the British replied that the sovereign power of government could not be divided between "legislative" authority in London and "taxing" authority in the colonies, they forced the Americans to deny the authority of Parliament altogether and to begin to consider their own political independence. This chain of logic eventually led to revolutionary consequences.

virtual representation *The political theory that a class of persons is represented in a lawmaking body without direct vote.*

nonimportation agreements *Pledges to boycott, or decline to purchase, certain goods from abroad.*

boycotts *An organized refusal to deal with some person or organization, or to buy a product or service.*

Parliament Forced to Repeal the Stamp Act

Among colonial outcries against the hated stamp tax, the most conspicuous was the Stamp Act Congress, held in New York City in 1765. Twenty-seven distinguished delegates from nine colonies petitioned the king and Parliament to repeal the repugnant legislation. The Stamp Act Congress made little splash in America at the time, but it was one more significant step toward intercolonial unity.

More effective than the congress was the widespread adoption of **nonimportation agreements** against British goods. Homespun woolen garments became fashionable, and the eating of lamb chops was discouraged so that the wool-bearing sheep would be allowed to mature. Nonimportation agreements were in fact a promising stride toward union; they spontaneously united the American people for the first time in common action.

Mobilizing in support of nonimportation gave ordinary men and women new opportunities to participate in colonial protests by signing petitions or refusing to purchase British goods. Joining consumer **boycotts,** groups of women assembled in public to hold spinning bees and make homespun cloth as a replacement for shunned British textiles. Such public defiance helped spread angry resistance throughout American colonial society.

Sometimes violence accompanied colonial protests. Crying, "Liberty, Property, and No Stamps," ardent Sons and Daughters of Liberty enforced the nonimportation agreements against violators, often with a generous coat of tar and feathers. Patriot mobs ransacked the houses of unpopular officials and hanged effigies of stamp agents on liberty poles.

Shaken by colonial commotion, the machinery for collecting the tax broke down. On that dismal day in 1765 when the new act was to go into effect, the stamp agents had all been forced to resign, and there was no one to sell the stamps. While flags flapped at half-mast, the law was openly and flagrantly defied—or rather, nullified.

Britain was hard hit. Merchants, manufacturers, and shippers suffered from the colonial nonimportation agreements, and hundreds of laborers were thrown out of work. Loud demands converged on Parliament for repeal of the Stamp Act.

Online Study Center

Primary source
John Holt's Account of the Stamp Act Riots in New York
college.hmco.com/pic/kennedybrief7e

Online Study Center

Primary source
Grace Galloway Defies the Radicals in Philadelphia
college.hmco.com/pic/kennedybrief7e

Online Study Center

Primary source
Stamp Act Protest
college.hmco.com/pic/kennedybrief7e

But many of the members could not understand why 7.5 million Britons had to pay heavy taxes to protect the colonies, whereas some 2 million colonists refused to pay for only one-third of the cost of their own defense.

After a stormy debate, Parliament in 1766 grudgingly repealed the Stamp Act. But virtually in the same breath, it provocatively passed the Declaratory Act, reaffirming Parliament's right "to bind" the colonies "in all cases whatsoever." The British government thereby drew its line in the sand. It defined the constitutional principle it would not yield: absolute and unqualified sovereignty over its North American colonies. The colonists had already drawn their own battle line by making it clear that they wanted a measure of sovereignty of their own, and would undertake drastic action to secure it. The stage was set for a continuing confrontation.

The Townshend Tea Tax and the Boston "Massacre"

Control of the British ministry was now seized by the gifted but erratic "Champagne Charley" Townshend, a man who could deliver brilliant speeches in Parliament even while drunk. Rashly promising to pluck feathers from the colonial goose with a minimum of squawking, he persuaded Parliament in 1767 to pass the Townshend Acts. The most important of these new regulations was a light import duty on glass, white lead, paper, paint, and tea. Townshend made this tax, unlike the Stamp Act, an indirect customs duty payable at American ports.

Flushed with their recent victory over the stamp tax, the colonists were in a rebellious mood. The impost on tea was especially irksome, for an estimated 1 million people drank the refreshing brew twice a day.

The new Townshend revenues, worse yet, would be used to pay the salaries of the royal governors and judges in America. The ultrasuspicious Americans, who had beaten the royal governors into line by controlling the purse, regarded Townshend's tax as another attempt to enchain them. Their worst fears took on a greater reality when the London government, after passing the Townshend taxes, suspended the New York legislature in 1767 for failure to comply with the Quartering Act.

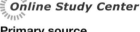

Online Study Center

Primary source
Boston Gazette Describes the Boston Massacre

Online Study Center

Primary source
Map of the Boston Massacre
Primary source
Blood Massacre Perpetrated in King Street, Boston

Nonimportation agreements, previously potent, were quickly revived against the Townshend Acts. But they proved less effective than those devised against the Stamp Act. The colonists, again enjoying prosperity, took the new tax less seriously than might have been expected, largely because it was light and indirect. They found, moreover, that they could secure smuggled tea at a cheap price, and consequently smugglers increased their activities, especially in Massachusetts.

British officials, faced with a breakdown of law and order, landed two regiments of troops in Boston in 1768. With liberty-loving colonists mercilessly taunting the often profane and drunken redcoats, a clash between citizens and soldiers was inevitable. On the evening of March 5, 1770, a crowd of some sixty townspeople, angry over the earlier death of an eleven-year old boy, began taunting and throwing snowballs at a squad of ten redcoats. Acting apparently without orders but nervous and provoked by the jeering crowd, the troops opened fire and killed or wounded eleven citizens. One of the first to die was Crispus Attucks, described by contemporaries as a "**mulatto**" and a leader of the mob. Both sides were in some degree to blame, and in the subsequent trial (in which future president John Adams served as defense attorney for the soldiers) only two redcoats were found guilty of manslaughter.

mulatto *A person of mixed African and European ancestry.*

> *Giving new meaning to the proverbial tempest in a teapot, a group of 126 Boston women signed an agreement, or "subscription list," which announced,*
>
> "We the Daughters of those Patriots who have and now do appear for the public interest . . . do with Pleasure engage with them in denying ourselves the drinking of Foreign Tea, in hopes to frustrate a Plan that tends to deprive the whole Community of . . . all that is valuable in Life."

The Seditious Committees of Correspondence

By 1770 King George III was strenuously attempting to assert the power of the British monarchy. Earnest, industrious, stubborn, and lustful for power, he surrounded himself with cooperative yes men, notably his corpulent Tory prime minister, Lord North.

■ **Two Views of the Boston Massacre, 1770 and 1856** Both of these prints of the Boston Massacre were art as well as propaganda. Paul Revere's engraving (left) began circulating within three weeks of the event in March 1770, depicting not a clash of brawlers but armed soldiers taking aim at peaceful citizens. Absent also was any evidence of the mulatto ringleader, Crispus Attucks. Revere wanted his print to convince viewers of the indisputable justice of the colonists' cause. By the mid-1850s, when the chromolithograph (right) circulated, it served a new political purpose. In the era of the abolitionist movement, freedman Crispus Attucks held center place in the scene, which portrayed his death as an American martyr in the revolutionary struggle for freedom.

The ill-timed Townshend Acts had failed to produce revenue, though they did produce near-rebellion. Net proceeds from the tax in one year were a paltry £295, and during that time the annual military costs to Britain in the colonies had mounted to £170,000. Nonimportation agreements, though feebly enforced, were pinching British manufacturers. The government of Lord North, bowing to various pressures, finally persuaded Parliament to repeal the Townshend revenue duties. But the three-pence tax on tea was retained to keep alive the principle of parliamentary taxation.

Flames of discontent in America, fanned by periodic incidents involving British officials, were further kindled by a master **propagandist** and engineer of rebellion, Samuel Adams. This cousin of John Adams was so unimpressive in appearance that his friends had to buy him a presentable suit of clothes when he left Massachusetts on intercolonial business. Zealous, tenacious, and courageous, Samuel Adams cherished a deep faith in the common people.

Samuel Adams's signal contribution was to organize in Massachusetts the local committees of correspondence. After he had formed the first one in Boston during 1772, some eighty towns in the colony speedily set up similar organizations. Their chief function was to spread the spirit of resistance by exchanging letters and thus keep alive opposition to British policy.

Intercolonial committees of correspondence were the next logical step. Virginia led the way in 1773 by creating such a body as a standing committee of the House of Burgesses. Within a short time every colony had established a central committee through which it could exchange ideas and information with other colonies. These intercolonial groups were supremely significant in stimulating and disseminating sentiment in favor of united action. They evolved directly into the first American congresses.

propaganda (propagandist) *A systematic program or particular materials designed to promote certain ideas; sometimes, but not always, the term is used negatively, implying the use of manipulative or deceptive means. (A propagandist is one who engages in such practices.)*

Tea Parties at Boston and Elsewhere

Thus far—that is, by 1773—nothing had happened to make rebellion inevitable. Nonimportation was weakening. Increasing numbers of colonists were

> *Ann Hulton (d. 1779?), a Loyalist, described colonial political divisions and her hopes and fears for her own future in a letter she sent to a friend in England in 1774:*
>
> "Those who are well disposed towards Government are termed Tories. They daily increase & have made some efforts to take the power out of the hands of the Patriots, but they are intimidated & overpowered by Numbers. . . . However I don't despair of seeing Peace & tranquility in America, tho' they talk very high & furious at present. They are all preparing their Arms & Ammunition & say if any of the Leaders are seized, they will make reprisals on the friends of Government."

reluctantly paying the tea tax because the legal tea was cheaper than the smuggled tea.

A new ogre entered the picture in 1773. The powerful British East India Company, overburdened with 17 million pounds of unsold tea, was facing bankruptcy. If it collapsed, the London government would lose heavily in tax revenue. The ministry therefore decided to assist the company by awarding it a complete monopoly of the American tea business. The giant corporation would now be able to sell the coveted leaves more cheaply than ever before, even with the three-pence tax tacked on. But to the determined Americans, principle remained far more important than price.

Fatefully, the British officials decided to enforce the letter of the law. Once more, the colonists rose up in wrath to defy it. Not a single one of the thousands of chests of tea shipped by the East India Company ever reached the hands of the consignees. In Philadelphia and New York, mass demonstrations forced the tea-bearing ships to return to Britain. At Annapolis, Marylanders burned both cargo and vessel, while proclaiming "Liberty and Independence or death in pursuit of it."

Only in Boston did a British official stubbornly refuse to be cowed. Massachusetts governor Thomas Hutchinson agreed that the tea tax was unjust, but believed even more strongly that the colonists had no right to flout the law. Hutchinson further inflamed the situation when he declared that "an abridgement of what are called English liberties" was necessary for the preservation of law and order in the colonies—apparently confirming the darkest conspiracy theories of the American radicals. On December 16, 1773, roughly a hundred Bostonians, disguised as Indians, boarded the docked ships, smashed open 342 chests of tea, and dumped their contents into the Atlantic. A crowd watched approvingly from the shore as Boston harbor became a vast teapot.

Reactions varied. All up and down the eastern seaboard, sympathetic colonists applauded destruction of the tea as "the hated badge of slavery." But conservatives complained that the destruction of private property violated the law and threatened anarchy. Hutchinson, disgusted with the colonies, retreated to Britain. The British authorities saw little alternative to whipping the upstart colonists into shape. Granting the Americans some measure of home rule at this stage might still have prevented rebellion, but few British politicians were willing to take that high road. The perilous path they chose instead led only to reprisals, bitterness, and escalating conflict.

■ **The Boston Tea Party, December 16, 1773** Crying "Boston harbor a tea-pot this night," Sons of Liberty disguised as Indians hurled chests of tea into the sea to protest the tax on tea and to make sure that the tea's cheap price did not prove an "invincible temptation" to the people.

Parliament Passes the "Intolerable Acts"

An irate Parliament responded speedily to the Boston Tea Party with measures that brewed a revolution. By huge majorities in 1774 it passed a series of acts designed to chastise Boston in particular and Massachusetts in general.

Most drastic of all was the Boston Port Act. It closed the tea-stained harbor until damages were paid and order could be ensured. In the other "Intolerable Acts"—as they were called in America—many of the chartered rights of colonial Massachusetts were swept away. Restrictions were likewise placed on the precious town meetings. Contrary to previous practice, enforcing officials who killed colonists in the line of duty could now be sent to Britain for trial. Particularly intolerable to Bostonians was a new Quartering Act that gave local authorities the power to lodge British soldiers in private homes.

By a fateful coincidence, the "Intolerable Acts" were accompanied in 1774 by the Quebec Act. Passed at the same time, it was erroneously regarded in English-speaking America as part of the British reaction to the turbulence in Boston. Actually, the Quebec Act was a good law in bad company. For many years the British government had debated how it should administer the sixty thousand or so conquered French subjects in Canada, and it had finally framed this farsighted and statesmanlike measure. The French Canadians were guaranteed their Catholic religion. They were also permitted to retain many of their old customs and institutions, which did not include a representative assembly or trial by jury in civil cases. In addition, the old boundaries of the Province of Quebec were extended southward all the way to the Ohio River.

The Quebec Act, from the viewpoint of the French Canadians, was a shrewd and conciliatory measure. If Britain had only shown as much foresight in dealing with its English-speaking colonies, it might not have lost them.

But from the viewpoint of the American colonists as a whole, the Quebec Act was especially noxious. All the other "Intolerable Acts" slapped directly at Massachusetts, but this one had a much wider range. By sustaining unrepresentative assemblies and denials of jury trials, it seemed to set a dangerous precedent in America. It alarmed land speculators, who were distressed to see the huge trans-Allegheny area snatched from their grasp. It aroused anti-Catholics, who were shocked by the extension of Roman Catholic jurisdiction southward into a huge region once earmarked for Protestantism.

The Continental Congress and Bloodshed

Chafing over the Quebec Act and the other "Intolerable Acts," American dissenters responded to the plight of Massachusetts with acts of sympathy and solidarity. Their most memorable step was the summoning of a Continental Congress. Delegates from all of the thirteen colonies except Georgia—including Samuel Adams, George Washington, and Patrick Henry—met in Philadelphia from September 5 to October 26, 1774. A stellar role at this First Continental Congress was played by John Adams. Eloquently swaying his colleagues to a revolutionary course, he helped defeat by the narrowest of margins a proposal by moderates for a species of American home rule under British direction.

The most significant action of the Congress was the creation of The Association. Unlike previous nonimportation agreements, The Association called for a complete boycott of all British goods: nonimportation, nonexportation, and nonconsumption. Yet it is important to note that the delegates were not yet calling for independence. They sought merely to repeal the offensive legislation and return to the happy days before parliamentary taxation. Resistance had not yet ripened into open rebellion.

But the fatal drift toward war continued. Parliament rejected the First Continental Congress's petitions. In America, chickens squawked and tar kettles bubbled as violators of The Association were tarred and feathered. Muskets were gathered, men began to drill openly, and a clash seemed imminent.

In April 1775, the British commander in Boston sent a detachment of troops to nearby Lexington and Concord. They intended to seize stores of colonial gunpowder and also to bag the "rebel" ringleaders, Samuel Adams and John Hancock. At Lexington the colonial "Minute Men" refused to disperse rapidly enough, and shots were fired that killed eight Americans and wounded several more. The redcoats then pushed on to Concord, from which they were soon forced to retreat by the rough-and-ready Americans, whom Emerson immortalized:

> By the rude bridge that arched the flood,
> Their flag to April's breeze unfurled,
> Here once the embattled farmers stood,
> And fired the shot heard round the world.*

The bewildered British, fighting off murderous fire from militiamen crouched behind thick stone walls, finally regained the sanctuary of Boston. Licking their wounds, they could count about three hundred casualties, including some seventy killed. Britain now had a war on its hands.

Imperial and Colonial Strengths and Weaknesses

Aroused Americans had brashly rebelled against a mighty empire. The population odds were about three to one against the rebels—some 7.5 million Britons to 2.5 million colonists. The odds in monetary wealth and naval power overwhelmingly favored the mother country.

Britain then boasted a professional army of some fifty thousand men, as compared with the numerous but wretchedly trained American militia. King George III, in addition, hired some thirty thousand German soldiers—so-called Hessians—to bolster his army. The British also enlisted the services of about fifty thousand American Loyalists and many Indians in their cause.

Yet Britain was weaker than it seemed at first glance. British troops had to be detached to watch the smoking volcano of oppressed Ireland. Recently defeated France was bitterly awaiting an opportunity to stab Britain in the back. The London government, under stubborn George III and his pliant Tory prime minister, Lord North, was confused and inept.

Many earnest and God-fearing Britons had no desire to kill their American cousins. Many British Whigs actually believed that the battle for their own liberties was being fought in America. If George III triumphed there, they believed, his rule at home might become more tyrannical. This outspoken sympathy in Britain, though plainly a minority voice, greatly encouraged the Americans. If they continued their resistance long enough, the Whigs might come to power and deal generously with them.

Britain's army in America had to operate under endless difficulties. The generals were second-rate; the soldiers, though on the whole capable, were brutally treated. Provisions were often scarce, rancid, and wormy.

Other handicaps loomed. The redcoats had to conquer the Americans; restoring the pre-1763 status quo would be a victory for the colonists. Britain was operating some 3,000 miles from its home base, and distance often delayed military orders from London for months, so that they no longer fit the changing situation.

America's geographical expanse was enormous: roughly 1,000 by 600 miles. The united colonies had no urban nerve center like France's Paris. During the war British armies captured every city of any size, yet like a

The great conservative political theorist and champion of the American cause, Edmund Burke, made a stirring speech in Britain's House of Commons in 1775, pleading in vain for reconciliation with the colonies:

"As long as you have the wisdom to keep the sovereign authority of this country as the sanctuary of liberty . . . they will turn their faces towards you. . . . Slavery they can have anywhere; freedom they can have from none but you. This is the commodity of price, of which you have the monopoly. This is the true Act of Navigation, which binds to you the commerce of the colonies, and through them secures to you the wealth of the world. Deny them this participation of freedom, and you break that sole bond which originally made, and must still preserve, the unity of the empire."

---

* Ralph Waldo Emerson, Concord Hymn.

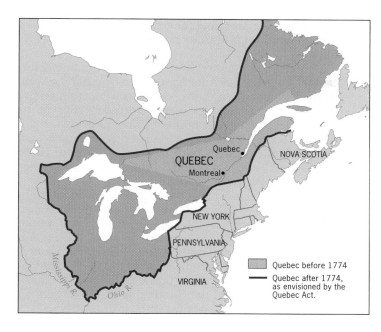

■ **Quebec Before and After 1774** Young Alexander Hamilton voiced the fears of many colonists when he warned that the Quebec Act of 1774 would introduce "priestly tyranny" into Canada, making that country another Spain or Portugal. "Does not your blood run cold," he asked, "to think that an English Parliament should pass an act for the establishment of arbitrary power and Popery in such a country?"

boxer punching a feather pillow, they made little more than a dent in the entire country. The Americans wisely traded space for time.

The revolutionaries were also blessed with outstanding leadership. George Washington was a giant among men. Master diplomat Benjamin Franklin eventually secured open foreign aid from France. In a class by himself was Marquis de Lafayette, a wealthy young French nobleman who loved both glory and liberty. Lafayette became a major general in the colonial army at age nineteen, and the services of the teenage "French gamecock" helped secure further aid from France.

Other conditions aided the Americans. They were fighting defensively on their own terrain. In agriculture, the colonies were mainly self-sustaining, like a kind of Robinson Crusoe's island. The Americans also enjoyed the moral advantage that came from belief in a just cause.

Yet the American rebels were badly organized for war. Almost fatally lacking in unity, the new nation lurched forward uncertainly like an uncoordinated centipede. Even the Continental Congress, which directed the conflict, was hardly more than a debating society, and it grew feebler as the struggle dragged on. The disorganized colonists fought almost the entire war before adopting a written constitution—the Articles of Confederation—in 1781.

Economic difficulties were nearly insuperable. With metallic money drained away and taxation an explosive issue, the Continental Congress was forced to print "Continental" paper money in great amounts. As this currency poured from the presses, it depreciated until the expression "not worth a Continental" became current. **Inflation** of the currency inevitably skyrocketed prices, hitting the families of soldiers at the front especially hard. Debtors easily acquired handfuls of the quasi-worthless money and gleefully paid their debts "without mercy."

inflation *An increase in the supply of currency relative to the goods available, leading to a decline in the purchasing power of money and a corresponding rise in prices.*

A Thin Line of Heroes

Basic military supplies in the colonies were dangerously scanty, especially firearms. While many families and towns did own firearms, the colonists had long relied heavily on Britain for troops, armaments, and military subsidies. When the supply of British funds and war materiel evaporated, sufficient stores of gunpowder, cannons, and ships could not be found.

Other shortages bedeviled the rebels. Manufactured goods were generally in short supply in agricultural America, and clothing and shoes were appallingly scarce. The path of the Patriot fighting men was often marked by bloody snow. At

Enslaved blacks hoped that the Revolutionary crisis would make it possible for them to secure their own liberty. On the eve of the war in South Carolina, merchant Josiah Smith, Jr., noted such a rumor among the slaves:

"[Freedom] is their common Talk throughout the Province, and has occasioned impertinent behavior in many of them, insomuch that our Provincial Congress now sitting hath voted the immediate raising of Two Thousand Men Horse and food, to keep those mistaken creatures in awe."

Despite such repressive measures, slave uprisings continued to plague the southern colonies through 1775 and 1776.

frigid Valley Forge during the cruel winter of 1777–1778, twenty-eight hundred soldiers went barefoot and nearly naked.

American militiamen were numerous but highly unreliable. Able-bodied American males—perhaps several hundred thousand of them—had received rudimentary training, and many of these recruits served for short terms in the rebel armies. But poorly trained plowboys could not stand up in the open field against professional British troops advancing with bare bayonets. Many of these undisciplined warriors would, in the words of Washington, "fly from their own shadows."

A few thousand regulars—perhaps seven or eight thousand at the war's end—were finally whipped into shape by stern drillmasters. Notable among them was an organizational genius, the salty German Baron von Steuben. He spoke no English when he arrived in America, but he soon taught his men that bayonets were not for broiling beefsteaks over open fires. As they gained experience, these soldiers of the Continental Army more than held their own in battle against crack British troops.

Blacks also fought and died for the American cause. Although many states initially barred them from militia service, by war's end more than five thousand blacks, most from the northern states, had enlisted in the American armed forces. Blacks fought at Trenton, Brandywine, Saratoga, and other important battles.

African Americans also served on the British side. In November 1775 Lord Dunmore, royal governor of Virginia, issued a proclamation offering freedom to any enslaved black in Virginia who joined the British army. In time, thousands of blacks fled plantations in response to British promises of emancipation. At war's end the British kept their word, to some at least, evacuating as many as fourteen thousand "Black Loyalists" to Nova Scotia, Jamaica, and Britain itself.

Morale in the Revolutionary army was badly undermined by American profiteers. Putting profits before patriotism, these speculators sold supplies to the British and made profits of 50 to 200 percent on army garb while the American army was freezing at Valley Forge. The failures of revolutionary zeal meant that Washington never had as many as twenty thousand effective troops in one place at one time.

The brutal truth is that only a select minority of colonists attached themselves to the cause of independence with a spirit of selfless devotion. These were the dedicated souls who bore the burden of battle and the risks of defeat. Seldom have so few done so much for so many.

✪ Chapter Summary ✪

The American War of Independence was a military conflict fought from 1775 to 1783, but the American Revolution was a deeper transformation of thought and loyalty that began when the first settlers arrived in America and finally led to the colonies' political separation from Britain.

One source of long-term conflict was the tension between the considerable freedom and self-government the colonists enjoyed in the American wilderness and their participation in the British Empire's mercantile system. While British mercantilism actually provided economic benefits to the colonies along with certain liabilities, its limits on freedom and its patronizing goal of keeping America in a state of perpetual economic adolescence stirred growing resentment.

The short-term movement toward the War of Independence began with British attempts to impose higher taxes and tighter imperial controls after the French and Indian War. To the British these were reasonable measures, requiring the colonists simply to bear their fair share of the costs of the empire. To the colonists, however, the measures constituted attacks on fundamental rights.

Through well-orchestrated agitation and boycotts, the colonists forced repeal of the Stamp Act of 1765 as well as the Townshend Acts that replaced it, except for a symbolic tax on tea. A temporary lull in conflict between 1770 and 1773 ended with the Boston Tea Party in December 1773. This radical action was instigated by a network of Boston agitators who refused to bow to the stubborn Massachusetts governor's attempt to enforce a law that benefited primarily the British East India Company monopoly.

In response to the Tea Party, the British imposed the harsh Intolerable Acts, and coincidentally passed the Quebec Act, which roused deep fears of religious as well as political tyranny. These twin actions stirred fe-rocious American resistance throughout the colonies, and led directly to the calling of the First Continental Congress in September 1774 and the clash of arms at Lexington and Concord in April 1775.

As the two sides headed into war, the British enjoyed the advantages of a larger population, a professionally trained army, and much greater economic strength. American rebels had advantages of territory and leadership, but their greatest asset was the fervent commitment of that minority of Patriots who were ready to sacrifice everything for their rights.

America Secedes from the Empire

1775–1783

THESE ARE THE TIMES THAT TRY MEN'S SOULS. THE SUMMER SOLDIER AND THE SUNSHINE PATRIOT WILL, IN THIS CRISIS, SHRINK FROM THE SERVICE OF THEIR COUNTRY; BUT HE THAT STANDS IT NOW, DESERVES THE LOVE AND THANKS OF MAN AND WOMAN.

THOMAS PAINE, DECEMBER 1776

Bloodshed at Lexington and Concord in April 1775 was a clarion call to arms. About twenty thousand musket-bearing "Minute Men" swarmed around Boston, there to coop up the outnumbered British.

The Second Continental Congress met in Philadelphia the next month, on May 10, 1775; and this time the full slate of thirteen colonies was represented. The conservative element in the Congress was still strong, despite the shooting in Massachusetts. There was still no well-defined sentiment for independence—merely a desire to continue fighting in the hope that king and Parliament would consent to a redress of grievances. Congress hopefully drafted new appeals to the British people and king—appeals that were spurned. Anticipating a possible rebuff, the delegates also adopted measures to raise money and to create an army and a navy. The British and the Americans now teetered on the brink of all-out warfare.

Focus Questions

1. How and why did Americans move in 1775–1776 from fighting only for "the rights of Englishmen" within the British Empire to declaring their independence?
2. What specific arguments and general political principles did Thomas Paine's *Common Sense* and Thomas Jefferson's Declaration of Independence use to promote and justify American independence?
3. In what ways was the Revolution a political and military "civil war" between American Patriots and American Loyalists, as well as a war for independence against Britain?
4. How and why did the British strategy to swiftly crush the rebellion fail, and how were Washington and his generals able to sustain the war after 1778 and take advantage of French assistance?
5. Why were Americans able to win not only the war but a stunning diplomatic victory in the peace settlement of 1783?

Chronology

1775	Battles of Lexington and Concord.
	Second Continental Congress.
	Battle of Bunker Hill.
	King George III formally proclaims colonies in rebellion.
	Failed invasion of Canada.
1776	Paine's *Common Sense*.
	Declaration of Independence.
	Battle of Trenton.
1777	Battle of Brandywine.
	Battle of Germantown.
	Battle of Saratoga.

1778	Formation of French-American alliance.
	Battle of Monmouth.
1778-1779	Clark's victories in the West.
1781	Battle of King's Mountain.
	Battle of Cowpens.
	Greene leads Carolina campaign.
	French and Americans force Cornwallis to surrender at Yorktown.
1782	North's ministry collapses in Britain.
1783	Treaty of Paris.

Congress Drafts George Washington

Perhaps the most important single action of the Congress was to select George Washington, one of its members already in officer's uniform, to head the hastily improvised army besieging Boston. This choice was made with considerable misgivings. The tall, powerfully built, dignified Virginia planter, then forty-three, had never risen above the rank of colonel in the militia. His largest command had numbered only twelve hundred men, and that had been some twenty years earlier. Falling short of true military genius, Washington would actually lose more pitched battles than he won.

But the distinguished Virginian was gifted with outstanding powers of leadership and immense strength of character. He radiated patience, courage, self-discipline, and a sense of justice. He was a great moral force rather than a great military mind—a symbol and a rallying point. People instinctively trusted him; they sensed that when he put himself at the head of a cause, he was prepared, if necessary, to go down with the ship. He insisted on serving without pay, though he would keep a careful wartime expense account amounting to more than $100,000.

The Continental Congress initially selected Washington more for political reasons than for his leadership qualities. Americans from other sections distrusted the large New England army gathering around Boston, and prudence suggested a commander from Virginia.

Bunker Hill and Hessian Hirelings

The clash of arms continued on a strangely contradictory basis. On the one hand, the Americans were emphatically affirming their loyalty to the king and earnestly voicing their desire to patch up difficulties. On the other hand, they were raising armies and shooting down His Majesty's soldiers. This curious war of inconsistency was fought for fourteen long months—from April 1775 to July 1776—before the fateful plunge into independence was taken.

Gradually the tempo of warfare increased. In May 1775 a tiny American force under Ethan Allen and Benedict Arnold surprised and captured the British garrisons at Ticonderoga and Crown Point, on the scenic lakes of upper New York. A priceless store of gunpowder and artillery for the siege of Boston was thus secured.

Online Study Center

Interactive map
The First Battles in the War for Independence, 1775
college.hmco.com/pic/kennedybrief7e

Online Study Center

Interactive map
The War in the North, 1776–1779
college.hmco.com/pic/kennedybrief7e

In June 1775 the colonists seized a hill, now known as Bunker Hill (actually Breed's Hill), from which they menaced the enemy in Boston. The British blundered bloodily when they launched a frontal attack with three thousand men. Sharpshooting Americans, numbering fifteen hundred and strongly entrenched, mowed down the advancing redcoats with frightful slaughter. But the colonists' scanty store of gunpowder finally gave out, and they were forced to abandon the hill in disorder. With two more such victories, remarked the French foreign minister, the British would have no army left in America.

Following Bunker Hill, King George III slammed the door on all hope of reconciliation. In August 1775 he formally proclaimed the colonies in rebellion. The next month he widened the chasm by hiring thousands of troops from the German principality of Hesse, shocking colonists who feared the Hessians' exaggerated reputation for butchery. Actually, the Hessian hirelings turned out to be more interested in booty than in duty. Hundreds of them eventually deserted and remained in America as respected citizens.

Online Study Center

Interactive map
The War in the North
college.hmco.com/pic/kennedybrief7e

The Abortive Conquest of Canada

The unsheathed sword continued to take its toll. In October 1775 the British burned the town of Falmouth (Portland), Maine. That same autumn the rebels daringly undertook a two-pronged invasion of Canada. American leaders believed, erroneously, that the conquered French were explosively restive under the British yoke. A successful assault on Canada would add a fourteenth colony, while depriving Britain of a valuable base for striking at the colonies in revolt. But this large-scale attack, involving some two thousand American troops, contradicted the claim of the colonists that they were merely fighting defensively for a redress of grievances. Invasion northward was undisguised offensive warfare.

This bold stroke for Canada narrowly missed success. One invading column under the Irish-born General Richard Montgomery pushed up the Lake Champlain route and captured Montreal. He was joined at Quebec by the bedraggled army of General Benedict Arnold, whose men had been reduced to eating dogs and shoe leather during their grueling march through the Maine woods. An assault on Quebec, launched on the last day of 1775, was beaten off. The able Montgomery was killed; the dashing Arnold was wounded in one leg. Scattered remnants under Arnold's command retreated up the St. Lawrence River. But French Canadian leaders, who had been generously treated by the British in the Quebec Act of 1774, showed no real desire to welcome the plundering anti-Catholic invaders.

Bitter fighting persisted in the colonies, though the Americans still continued to disclaim a desire for independence. In January 1776 the British set fire to the Virginia town of Norfolk. In March they were finally forced to evacuate Boston, taking with them the leading friends of the king. In the South the rebellious colonists won two victories in 1776: one in February against some fifteen hundred Loyalists at Moore's Creek Bridge in North Carolina, and the other in June against an invading British fleet in Charleston harbor.

■ **Washington at Verplanck's Point, New York, 1782, Reviewing the French Troops After the Victory at Yorktown, by John Trumbull, 1790** This noted American artist accentuated Washington's height (6 feet, 2 inches) by showing him towering over his horse. Washington so appreciated this portrait of himself that he hung it in his dining room at his home at Mount Vernon, Virginia.

Thomas Paine Preaches Common Sense

Why did Americans continue to deny any intention of independence? Loyalty to the empire was deeply ingrained; many

Americans continued to consider themselves part of a transatlantic community in which the mother country of Britain played a leading role; colonial unity was poor; and open rebellion was dangerous, especially against a formidable Britain. Irish rebels of that day were customarily hanged, drawn, and quartered. American rebels might have fared no better. As late as January 1776—five months before independence was declared—the king's health was being toasted by the officers of Washington's mess near Boston. "God save the king" had not yet been replaced by "God save the Congress."

Gradually the Americans were shocked into recognizing the necessity of separating from the crown. Their eyes were jolted open by harsh British acts like the burning of Falmouth and Norfolk, and especially by the hiring of the Hessians. Then in 1776 came the publication of *Common Sense*, one of the most influential pamphlets ever written. Its author was the radical Thomas Paine, once an impoverished corset-maker's apprentice, who had come over from Britain a year earlier. His tract became a whirlwind bestseller and within a few months reached the astonishing total of 120,000 copies.

Paine flatly branded the shilly-shallying of the colonists as contrary to "common sense." Nowhere in the physical universe did the smaller heavenly body control the larger one. Then why should the tiny island of Britain control the vast continent of America? As for the king, whom the Americans professed to revere, he was nothing but "the Royal Brute of Great Britain."

Paine's passionate protest was as compelling as it was eloquent and radical—even doubly radical. It called not simply for independence but for the creation of a new kind of political society, a *republic,* where power flowed from the people themselves, not from a corrupt and despotic monarch. In language laced with biblical imagery familiar to common folk, Paine argued that all government officials—governors, senators, and judges, not just representatives in a house of commons—should derive their authority from popular consent.

The colonists' experience with governance had prepared them well for Paine's summons to create a republic. Many settlers, particularly New Englanders, had practiced a kind of republicanism in their democratic town meetings and annual elections, while the popularly elected committees of correspondence during 1774 and 1775 had demonstrated the feasibility of republican government. The absence of a hereditary aristocracy and the relative equality of condition enjoyed by landowning farmers meshed well with the republican repudiation of a fixed hierarchy of power.

Most Americans considered citizen "virtue" fundamental to any successful republican government. Because political power no longer rested with the king, individuals in a republic needed to sacrifice their personal self-interest to the public good. The collective good of "the people" mattered more than the private rights and interests of individuals. Paine inspired his contemporaries to view America as fertile ground for the cultivation of such civic virtue.

In Common Sense *Thomas Paine (1737–1809) argued for the superiority of a republic over a monarchy:*

"The nearer any government approaches to a republic the less business there is for a king. It is somewhat difficult to find a proper name for the government of England. Sir William Meredith calls it a republic; but in its present state it is unworthy of the name, because the corrupt influence of the crown, by having all the places in its disposal, hath so effectively swallowed up the power, and eaten out the virtue of the house of commons (the republican part of the constitution) that the government of England is nearly as monarchical as that of France or Spain."

■ Portrait of Thomas Paine, by Auguste Millière.

Online Study Center

Primary source
Gouverneur Morris Warns Against
Democratic Revolution
college.hmco.com/pic/kennedybrief7e

Yet not all Patriots agreed with Paine's ultrademocratic approach to republicanism. Some favored a republic ruled by a "natural aristocracy" of talent. Republicanism for them meant an end to hereditary aristocracy but not an end to all social hierarchy. These more conservative republicans feared that the fervor for liberty would overwhelm the stability of the social order. They watched with trepidation as the "lower orders" of society—poorer farmers, tenants, and laboring classes in towns and cities—seemed to embrace a kind of runaway republicanism that amounted to radical "leveling." The contest to define the nature of American republicanism would noisily continue for the next hundred years.

Jefferson's "Explanation" of Independence

Members of the Philadelphia Congress, instructed by their respective colonies, gradually edged toward a clean break. On June 7, 1776, fiery Richard Henry Lee of Virginia moved that "These United Colonies are, and of right ought to be, free and independent states. . . ." After considerable debate, the motion was adopted nearly a month later, on July 2, 1776.

The passing of Lee's resolution was the formal "declaration" of independence by the American colonies, and technically this was all that was needed to cut the British tie. John Adams wrote confidently that ever thereafter July 2 would be celebrated annually with fireworks. But something more was required. An epochal rupture of this kind called for some formal explanation to "a candid world." An inspirational appeal was also needed to enlist other British colonies in the Americas, to invite assistance from foreign nations, and to rally resistance at home.

Shortly after Lee made his memorable motion on June 7, Congress appointed a committee to prepare a more formal statement of separation. The task of drafting it fell to Thomas Jefferson, a tall, freckled, sandy-haired Virginia lawyer of thirty-three. Despite his youth, he was already recognized as a brilliant writer, and he measured up splendidly to the awesome assignment. After some debate and amendment, the Declaration of Independence was formally approved by the Congress on July 4, 1776.

Jefferson's pronouncement, couched in a lofty style, was magnificent. He gave his appeal universality by invoking the "natural rights" of humankind—not just British rights. He argued persuasively that because the king had flouted these rights, the colonists were justified in cutting their connection. He then set forth a long list of the presumably tyrannous misdeeds of George III. The overdrawn bill of **indictment** included imposing taxes without consent, dispensing with trial by jury, abolishing valued laws, establishing a military **dictatorship,** maintaining standing armies in peacetime, cutting off trade, burning towns, hiring **mercenaries,** and inciting hostility among the Indians.*

The formal declaration of independence cleared the air as a thundershower does on a muggy day. Foreign aid could be solicited with greater hope of success. Those Patriots who defied the king were now rebels, not loving subjects shooting their way into reconciliation. They must all hang together, Franklin is said to have grimly remarked, or they would all hang separately. Or, in the eloquent language of the great declaration, "We mutually pledge to each other our lives, our fortunes and our sacred honor."

indictment *A formal written accusation charging someone with a crime.*

dictatorship *A form of government characterized by absolute state power and the unlimited authority of the ruler.*

mercenaries *A professional soldier who serves in a foreign army for pay.*

Patriots and Loyalists

The War of Independence, strictly speaking, was a civil war between two factions of Americans as well as a war between Americans and the British. Besides battling the British redcoats, the American rebels, called Patriots or "Whigs," fought Americans loyal to the king, called Loyalists or "Tories" (see "Makers of America: The Loyalists," p. 102).

---

*For an annotated text of the Declaration of Independence, see the Appendix.

Like many revolutions, the American Revolution was a minority movement. Many colonists were apathetic or **neutral,** including the Byrds of Virginia, who sat on the fence. The opposing forces contended not only against each other but also for the allegiance and support of the **civilian** population. In this struggle for the hearts and minds of the people, the Patriot militia proved far more successful than the inept British. The British military proved able to control only those areas where it could maintain a massive military presence. Elsewhere, as soon as the redcoats had marched on, the rebel militiamen appeared and took up the task of "political education"—sometimes by coercive means. Often lacking bayonets but always loaded with political zeal, the ragtag militia units convinced many colonists, even those indifferent to independence, that the British army was an unreliable friend and that they had better throw in their lot with the Patriot cause.

Loyalists, numbering perhaps 15 percent of the American people, remained true to their king. Some fifty thousand Loyalist volunteers at one time or another bore arms for the British. They also helped the king's cause by serving as spies, by inciting the Indians, and by keeping Patriot soldiers at home to protect their families.

Many people of education and wealth, of culture and caution, remained loyal. Loyalists were more numerous among the older generation, for young people make revolutions. They also included the king's officers and other beneficiaries of the crown—people who knew which side their daily bread came from. Loyalists were most numerous where the Anglican Church was strongest, except in Virginia, where debt-burdened Anglican aristocrats flocked into the rebel camp. The king's followers were well entrenched in aristocratic New York City and Charleston, and also in Quaker Pennsylvania and New Jersey, where General Washington felt that he was fighting in "the enemy's country." Loyalists were least numerous in New England, where Presbyterianism and Congregationalism flourished, producing strong support for rebellion.

Before the Declaration of Independence in 1776, persecution of the Loyalists was relatively mild. But once independence was declared, Loyalists were more roughly handled. Hundreds of Loyalists were imprisoned and a few were hanged. About eighty thousand loyal supporters of George III were driven out or fled the country, and their estates were **confiscated** to finance the war. But no reign of terror comparable to that of the later French and Russian revolutions occurred. Confiscation often worked great economic hardship, but most Loyalists did not regret their stand. Ardent Loyalists had their hearts in their cause, and a major blunder of the haughty British was not to make full use of them in the fighting.

> *The American signers of the Declaration of Independence had reason to fear for their necks. In 1802, twenty-six years later, George III (1738–1820) approved this death sentence for seven Irish rebels:*
>
> "... [You] are to be hanged by the neck, but not until you are dead; for while you are still living your bodies are to be taken down, your bowels torn out and burned before your faces, your heads then cut off, and your bodies divided each into four quarters, and your heads and quarters to be then at the King's disposal; and may the Almighty God have mercy on your souls."

Online Study Center

**Primary source
Maryland Preacher Resists the Patriots**
college.hmco.com/pic/kennedybrief7e

neutral *A nation or person not taking sides in a war.*

civilian *A citizen not in military service.*

confiscated *To seize private property for public use, often as a penalty.*

Online Study Center

**Primary source
New Jersey Artisan Is Tarred and Feathered**
college.hmco.com/pic/kennedybrief7e

General Washington at Bay

After evacuating Boston in March 1776, the British made New York City their central base of operations. Here was a splendid seaport, centrally located, where the king could count on cooperation from the numerous Loyalists. An awe-inspiring British fleet appeared off New York in July 1776. It consisted of some five hundred ships and thirty-five thousand men—the largest armed force to be seen in America until the Civil War. General Washington, dangerously outnumbered, could muster only eighteen thousand ill-trained troops with which to meet the crack army of the invader.

Disaster befell the Americans in the summer and fall of 1776. Outgeneraled and outmaneuvered, they were routed at the Battle of Long Island, where panic seized the raw recruits. By the narrowest of margins, and thanks to a favoring wind and fog, Washington escaped to Manhattan Island. Retreating northward, he crossed the Hudson River to New Jersey and finally reached the Delaware River

The Loyalists

In late 1776 Catherine Van Cortlandt wrote to her husband, a New Jersey merchant fighting in a Loyalist brigade, about the Patriot troops who had quartered themselves in her house. "They were the most disorderly of species," she complained, "and their officers were from the dregs of the people."

Like the Van Cortlandts, many Loyalists thought of themselves as "the better sort of people." Conservative, wealthy, and well-educated, Loyalists of this breed thought a break with Britain would invite anarchy. But Loyalism was hardly confined to the well-to-do. It also appealed to many people of modest means who identified strongly with Britain or who had reason to fear a Patriot victory. They included British veterans of the Seven Years' War who had received land grants from the crown, and recent immigrants from Scotland and Ireland who had settled the backcountry of Georgia or the Carolinas. Resenting the plantation elites who ran these colonies, they filled the ranks of Tory brigades organized by the British army.

Online Study Center

**Primary source
Legislative Attacks on the
Loyalists**
college.hmco.com/pic/kennedybrief7e

Online Study Center

**Primary source
Loyalist Widow Decries the Fate
of Tory Exiles in Canada**
college.hmco.com/pic/kennedybrief7e

Other ethnic minorities found their own reasons to support the British. Some Dutch, German, and French religious sects believed that religious tolerance would be greater under the British than under the Americans. Encouraged by British officials, thousands of African Americans joined the Loyalist ranks in hopes that their service might bring an escape from bondage. Many of them joined black regiments that specialized in making small sorties against Patriot militia.

As the war drew to an end in 1783, the fate of black Loyalists varied enormously. Many thousands who came to Loyalism as fugitive slaves managed to find a way to freedom, especially in Nova Scotia. Other African American Loyalists suffered betrayal. British general Lord Cornwallis abandoned over four thousand former slaves in Virginia, and others found themselves sold back into slavery in the West Indies.

White Loyalists faced no threat of enslavement, but they did often suffer arrest, exile, confiscation of property, and loss of legal rights. Faced with such retribution, some eighty thousand Loyalists fled abroad, mostly to Britain or Canada. Some settled contentedly as exiles, but many, especially in Britain, had difficulty becoming accepted and lived lonely and diminished lives.

Most Loyalists, though, remained in America, despite the daunting burden of reestablishing themselves in a society that viewed them as traitors. Some succeeded remarkably, such as Hugh Gaine, a New York City printer who reopened his business and even won printing contracts from the new government. Gaine reintegrated himself into public life by siding with the Federalist call for a strong central government and a powerful executive. When New York ratified the Constitution in 1788, Gaine rode the float at the head of the city's celebration parade. He had, like many other former Loyalists, become an American.

with the British close at his heels. Tauntingly, enemy buglers sounded the fox-hunting call so familiar to Virginians of Washington's day. The Patriot cause was at low ebb when the rebel remnants fled across the river after collecting all available boats to forestall pursuit.

The wonder is that Washington's adversary, General William Howe, did not speedily crush the demoralized American forces. But Howe was no military genius, and he well remembered the horrible slaughter at Bunker Hill, where he had commanded. The country was rough, supplies were slow in coming, and Howe did not relish the rigors of winter campaigning. Washington, who was now almost counted out, stealthily recrossed the ice-clogged Delaware River. At Trenton, on December 26, 1776, he surprised and captured a thousand Hessians who were sleeping off the effects of their Christmas celebration. A week later, leaving his campfires burning as a ruse, he slipped away and inflicted another sharp defeat on a smaller British detachment at Princeton. This brilliant New Jersey campaign, crowned by these two lifesaving victories, revealed "Old Fox" Washington at his military best.

Burgoyne's Blundering Invasion

London officials adopted an intricate scheme for capturing the vital Hudson River Valley in 1777. If successful, the British would sever New England from the rest of the states and paralyze the American cause. The main invading force, under the soldier-actor-playwright General John ("Gentleman Johnny") Burgoyne, would push down the Lake Champlain route from Canada. General Howe's troops in New York would advance up the Hudson River to meet Burgoyne near Albany. A third and much smaller British force, commanded by Colonel Barry St. Leger, would come in from the west by way of Lake Ontario and the Mohawk Valley.

British planners did not reckon with General Benedict Arnold. Retreating slowly from Quebec after being repulsed there in 1775, Arnold had by heroic efforts kept his army in the field and assembled a small fleet on Lake Champlain. The British finally constructed a fleet that defeated Arnold's tiny flotilla. But by then winter was descending, and the British were forced to retire back to Canada. This delay was critical to the American cause.

Compelled to start over in the spring of 1777, General Burgoyne began his fateful invasion with seven thousand regular troops who were encumbered by a heavy baggage train and many accompanying officers' wives. Progress was painfully slow, for sweaty axmen had to chop a path through the forest, while American militiamen began to swarm like hornets on Burgoyne's flanks.

Meanwhile, astonished eyebrows rose as General Howe marched the main British army toward the rebel capital of Philadelphia at a time when it seemed obvious he should be starting up the Hudson River from New York to meet the advancing Burgoyne. As scholars now know, Howe wanted to engage and destroy Washington's army, apparently assuming he had ample time to assist Burgoyne directly should he be needed.

General Washington, keeping a wary eye on the British in New York, hastily transferred his army to the vicinity of Philadelphia. There, late in 1777, he was defeated in two pitched battles at Brandywine Creek and Germantown. Pleasure-loving General Howe then settled down comfortably in the lively capital, leaving Burgoyne to flounder through the wilds of upstate New York. Benjamin Franklin, recently sent to Paris as an **envoy**, truthfully jested that Howe had not captured Philadelphia but that Philadelphia had captured Howe. Washington finally retired to winter quarters at Valley Forge, a strong hilly position some twenty miles northwest of Philadelphia. There his frostbitten and hungry men were short of about everything except misery. This **rabble** was nevertheless whipped into a professional army by the recently arrived Prussian drillmaster, the profane but patient Baron von Steuben.

Burgoyne, meanwhile, had begun to bog down north of Albany, while a host of American militiamen, scenting the kill, hounded him on all sides. In a series of sharp engagements, the British army was trapped. Meanwhile, the Americans had driven back St. Leger's force at Oriskany, New York. Unable to advance or retreat, Burgoyne was forced to surrender his entire command at Saratoga, on October 17, 1777, to the American general Horatio Gates.

envoy *A messenger or agent sent by a government on official business.*

rabble *A mass of disorderly and crude common people.*

Online Study Center

Primary source
Abigail Smith Adams (Mrs. John Adams)
college.hmco.com/pic/kennedybrief7e

EXAMINING THE EVIDENCE

A Revolution for Women? Abigail Adams Chides Her Husband, 1776   In the midst of the revolutionary fervor of 1776, at least one woman—Abigail Adams, wife of noted Massachusetts Patriot (and future president) John Adams—raised her voice on behalf of women. Yet she apparently raised it only in private—in this personal letter to her husband. Private documents like the correspondence and diaries of individuals both prominent and ordinary offer invaluable sources for the historian seeking to discover sentiments, opinions, and perspectives that are often difficult to discern in the official public record.

1. What does it suggest about the historical circumstances of the 1770s that Abigail Adams confined her claim for women's equality to this confidential exchange with her spouse?

2. What ideas and events inspired the arguments Adams employed?

3. Despite her privileged position and persuasive power, and despite her threat to "foment a rebellion," Abigail Adams's plea went largely unheeded in the Revolutionary era—as did comparable pleadings to extend the revolutionary principle of equality to blacks. What accounts for this limited application of the ideas of liberty and equality in the midst of a supposedly democratic revolution?

 **Washington Crossing the Delaware, by Emanuel Gottlieb Leutze, 1851** On Christmas Day, 1776, George Washington set out from Pennsylvania with twenty-four hundred men to surprise the British forces, chiefly Hessians, in their quarters across the river in New Jersey. The subsequent British defeat proved to be a turning point in the Revolution, as it checked the British advance toward Philadelphia and restored American morale. Seventy-five years later, Leutze, a German-born American painter, mythologized the heroic campaign in this painting.

Saratoga ranks high among the decisive battles of both American and world history. The victory immensely revived the faltering colonial cause. Even more important, it made possible the urgently needed foreign aid from France, which in turn helped ensure American independence.

Revolutionary America and the World

France, thirsting for revenge against Britain, was eager to inflame the quarrel that had broken out in America and cripple British imperial power. The American revolutionaries badly needed help to throw off the British yoke. The stage seemed set for the embattled new nation to make its diplomatic debut by sealing an alliance with France against the common foe.

Yet just as they stood for revolutionary political ideals at home, the rebellious Americans also harbored revolutionary ideas about international affairs. They wanted to end colonialism, promote free trade and freedom of the seas, and substitute the rule of law for the ancient reliance on raw power to arbitrate the affairs of nations. The Continental Congress accordingly instructed its emissaries to France to seek no political or military alliance, but only a commercial connection. These remarkable restrictions reflected a belief among enlightened American and European thinkers of the time that history had reached a momentous turning point when military conflict would be abandoned in favor of peaceful commerce between nations. While some critics considered this dream hopelessly naïve and utopian, it infused an element of idealism into American attitudes toward international affairs that has proved stubbornly persistent.

When wily old Benjamin Franklin arrived in Paris to negotiate the treaty with France, he was determined that his very appearance should herald the diplomatic revolution the Americans hoped to achieve. Forsaking the ermined robes and

⭐ Map Skill-Builder:
Understanding Military Maps

1. Examine the map carefully in relation to the text's discussion of Britain's grand strategy for crushing the rebellion quickly (pp. 101–105). Approximately where were the three British armies under Burgoyne, St. Leger, and Howe supposed to converge and trap the Americans?

2. Which one of the three British generals moved in the opposite direction he was supposed to go, and therefore failed to arrive at the appointed rendezvous?

3. Which of the three was defeated far short of the intended goal?

4. Which one got closest to the intended rendezvous point, but found himself alone and trapped by the Americans, instead of trapping them as the British plan intended?

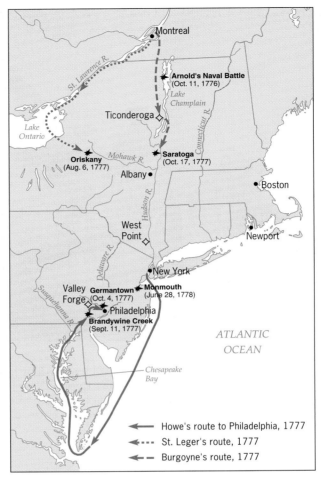

■ **New York–Pennsylvania Theater, 1777–1778** Distinguished members of the Continental Congress fled from Philadelphia in near-panic as the British army approached. Thomas Paine reported that at three o'clock in the morning the streets were "as full of Men, Women, and Children as on a Market Day." John Adams had anticipated that "I shall run away, I suppose, with the rest," since "we are too brittle ware, you know, to stand the dashing of balls and bombs." Adams got his chance to decamp with the others into the interior of Pennsylvania and tried to put the best face on things. "This tour," he commented, "has given me an opportunity of seeing many parts of this country which I never saw before."

fancy wigs expected in the royal court, he sported homespun garments and a simple cap of marten fur. Pompous French diplomats were shocked, but ordinary Parisians adored him as a specimen of a new democratic social order, devoid of pretense and ornament. Franklin's personal popularity was a valuable card in the diplomatic game.

Franklin also played skillfully on French fears of reconciliation between Britain and America. After the humiliation of Saratoga in 1777, the British had belatedly offered the Americans a species of home rule within the empire. To counter this, the French offered Franklin a treaty that bound both parties to wage war until the United States had fully secured its freedom and until both agreed to terms with the common enemy. In an example of practical self-interest trumping abstract idealism in the conduct of foreign affairs, the young Republic agreed to join its first entangling military alliance. The treaty with France, signed in February 1778, constituted an official recognition of America's independence and lent powerful military heft to the Patriot cause.

With France now supporting the Americans' cause, the shot fired at Lexington rapidly widened into a global conflagration. Spain entered the fray against Britain in 1779, as did Holland. Combined Spanish and French fleets outnumbered those of Britain, and on two occasions the British Isles seemed to be at the mercy of hostile warships. Catherine the Great of Russia lined up the remaining European neutrals into the "Armed Neutrality" that assumed an attitude of passive hostility toward Britain.

To Britain, now struggling for its very life, the scuffle in the New World soon became secondary. The Americans deserve credit for having kept the war going until 1778. But they did not achieve their independence until the conflict erupted into a multipower world war that was too big for Britain to handle. From 1778 to 1783, France provided the rebels with guns, money, immense amounts of equipment, about one-half of America's regular armed forces, and practically all of the new nation's naval strength.

France's entrance into the conflict forced the British to change their basic strategy in America. With powerful French fleets in American waters, Britain could no longer **blockade** the colonial coast and command the seas. To shorten their lines of supply, the British evacuated Philadelphia and escaped to New York City after the indecisive Battle of Monmouth in June 1778. Washington followed them to the New York area and hemmed them in.

blockade *The isolation of a place by hostile ships or troops.*

Blow and Counterblow

In the summer of 1780 a powerful French army of six thousand regular troops, commanded by the Comte de Rochambeau, arrived in Newport, Rhode Island. Preparations began for a Franco-American attack on New York.

Improving American morale was staggered later in 1780 when General Benedict Arnold turned traitor. A leader of undoubted dash and brilliance, he was ambitious, greedy, and unscrupulous, and he suffered from a well-grounded but petulant feeling that his valuable services were not fully appreciated. He plotted with the British to sell out the key stronghold of West Point, which commanded the Hudson River, for £6,300 and an officer's commission. By the sheerest accident the plot was detected in the nick of time, and Arnold fled to the British. "Whom can we trust now?" cried General Washington in anguish.

The British meanwhile had devised a new plan to roll up the colonies, beginning with the South, where the Loyalists were numerous. Georgia was ruthlessly overrun in 1778–1779. Charleston, South Carolina, fell in 1780. The surrender of that city to the British involved the capture of five thousand men and four hundred cannon, and was a heavier loss to the Americans, in relation to existing strength, than Burgoyne's was to the British.

Warfare now intensified in the Carolinas, where Patriots bitterly fought their Loyalist neighbors. It was not uncommon for prisoners on both sides to be butchered in cold blood after they had thrown down their arms. The tide turned later in 1780 and early in 1781, when American riflemen wiped out a British detachment at King's Mountain and then defeated a smaller force at Cowpens. In the Carolina campaign of 1781, General Nathanael Greene, a Quaker-reared tactician, distinguished himself by his strategy of delay. Standing and then retreating, he exhausted his foe, General Cornwallis, in vain pursuit. By losing battles but winning campaigns, the "Fighting Quaker" finally succeeded in clearing most of Georgia and South Carolina of British troops.

The Land Frontier and the Sea Frontier

The West was ablaze during much of the war. Indian allies of George III, hoping to protect their land, were busy attacking and burning frontier settlements. They were egged on by British agents, branded as "hair buyers" because they allegedly paid bounties for American scalps. Although two nations of the Iroquois Confederacy, the Oneidas and the Tuscaroras, sided with the Americans, the Senecas, Mohawks, Cayugas, and Onondagas joined the British. They were led by Mohawk

Online Study Center

**Primary source
Charleston, South Carolina, Sons of Liberty**
college.hmco.com/pic/kennedybrief7e

Online Study Center

**Interactive map
The War in the South, 1778–1781**
college.hmco.com/pic/kennedybrief7e

Online Study Center

**Interactive map
The War in the South**
college.hmco.com/pic/kennedybrief7e

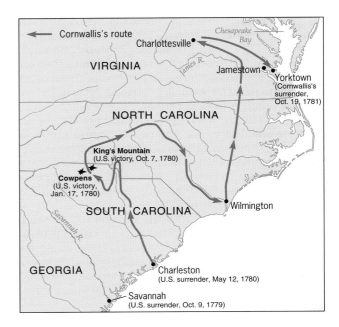

■ War in the South,
1780–1781

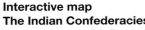
privateers *A private vessel temporarily authorized to capture or plunder enemy ships in wartime.*

graft *Taking advantage of one's official position to gain money or property by illegal means.*

chief Joseph Brant, a convert to Anglicanism who believed that a victorious Britain would restrain American expansion into the West. Brant and the British ravaged large areas of back-country Pennsylvania and New York until checked by an American force in 1779.

In the wild Illinois country the British were especially vulnerable to attack, for they held only scattered posts that they had captured from the French. An audacious frontiersman, George Rogers Clark, conceived the idea of seizing these forts by surprise. In 1778–1779 he floated down the Ohio River with about 175 men and captured in quick succession Forts Kaskaskia, Cahokia, and Vincennes.

America's infant navy, commanded by daring officers like the hard-fighting young Scotsman John Paul Jones, was more successful in destroying British merchant shipping than in engaging Britain's powerful fleets. More numerous and damaging than ships of the regular American navy were swift **privateers.** Authorized by Congress, over a thousand of these privately owned armed ships preyed on enemy shipping and captured some six hundred British prizes. Although they diverted manpower from the main war effort and involved Americans in speculation and **graft,** privateers brought in urgently needed gold, harassed the enemy, and raised American morale. Unhappy British shippers and manufacturers brought increasing pressure on Parliament to end the war on honorable terms.

Yorktown and the Final Curtain

One of the darkest periods of the war was 1780–1781, just before the last decisive victory. Inflation of the currency continued at full gallop, and the government was virtually bankrupt. Despair prevailed; the sense of unity withered; and mutinous sentiments infected the army.

Meanwhile, the British General Cornwallis was blundering into a trap. After futile operations in Virginia, he had fallen back to Chesapeake Bay at Yorktown to await seaborne supplies and reinforcements. He assumed Britain would continue to control the sea. But these few fateful weeks just happened to be one of the brief periods during the war when British naval superiority slipped away.

The French were now prepared to cooperate energetically in a brilliant stroke. Admiral de Grasse, operating with a powerful fleet in the West Indies, sent word to the Americans that he was free to join with them in an assault on Cornwallis at Yorktown. Quick to seize this opportunity, General Washington made a swift march of more than three hundred miles to the Chesapeake from the New York area. Accompanied by Rochambeau's French army, Washington beset the British by land, while de Grasse blockaded them by sea after beating off the British fleet. Completely cornered, Cornwallis surrendered his entire force of seven thousand men on October 19, 1781, as his band appropriately played "The World Turn'd Upside Down." The triumph was no less French than American: France provided essentially all the seapower and about half of the regular troops in the besieging army of some sixteen thousand men.

Stunned by news of the disaster, Prime Minister Lord North cried, "Oh God! It's all over! It's all over!" But it was not. George III stubbornly planned to continue the struggle, for Britain was far from being crushed. It still had fifty-four thousand troops in North America, including thirty-two thousand in the United States. Washington returned with his army to New York, there to continue keeping a vigilant eye on a British force of ten thousand men.

Fighting actually continued for more than a year after Yorktown, with Patriot-Loyalist warfare in the South especially savage. "No quarter for Tories" was the common battle cry. One of Washington's most valuable contributions was to keep the cause alive, the army in the field, and the states together during these critical months. Otherwise, a satisfactory peace treaty might never have been signed.

Peace at Paris

After Yorktown, many Britons were weary of war and increasingly ready to come to terms. They had suffered heavy reverses in India and in the West Indies. Lord North's Tory ministry collapsed in March 1782, and was replaced by a Whig ministry rather favorable to the Americans.

Three American peace negotiators had meanwhile gathered at Paris: the aging but astute Benjamin Franklin; the flinty John Adams, vigilant for New England interests; and the impulsive John Jay of New York, deeply suspicious of Old World intrigue. The three envoys had explicit instructions from Congress to make no separate peace and to consult with their French allies at all stages of the negotiations. But the American representatives chafed under this directive. They well knew that it had been written by a subservient Congress, with the French Foreign Office indirectly guiding the pen.

France was in a painful position. It had induced Spain to enter the war on its side, and the Spanish coveted the immense trans-Appalachian area for itself. Wanting an America that would be independent but feeble, the French therefore joined the scheme to keep the new republic cooped up east of the Appalachian Mountains.

But John Jay was unwilling to play France's game. Suspiciously alert, he perceived that the French could not satisfy the conflicting ambitions of both Americans and Spaniards. He saw signs—or thought he did—indicating that the Paris Foreign Office was about to betray America's trans-Appalachian interests to satisfy those of Spain. He therefore secretly made separate overtures to London, contrary to his instructions from Congress. The hard-pressed British, eager to entice one of their enemies from the alliance, speedily came to terms with the Americans. The final Treaty of Paris concluding the war was signed in 1783.

By terms of the treaty, the British formally recognized the independence of the United States. In addition, they granted

Baron von Steuben (1730–1794), a Prussian general who helped train the Continental Army, found the Americans to be very different from other soldiers he had known. As von Steuben explained to a fellow European,

"The genius of this nation is not in the least to be compared with that of the Prussians, Austrians, or French. You say to your soldier, 'Do this' and he doeth it; but I am obliged to say, 'This is the reason why you ought to do that,' and then he does it."

■ Benjamin Franklin (1706–1790), by Charles Willson Peale, 1789　He left school at age ten, and became a wealthy businessman, a journalist, an inventor, a scientist, a legislator, and preeminently a statesman-diplomat. He was sent to France in 1776 as the American envoy at age seventy, and he remained there until 1785, negotiating the alliance with the French and helping to negotiate the treaty of peace. His fame had preceded him, and when he discarded his wig for the fur cap of a simple "American agriculturist," he took French society by storm. French aristocratic women, with whom he was a great favorite, honored him by adopting the high coiffure à la Franklin in imitation of his cap.

generous boundaries, stretching majestically to the Mississippi on the west, to the Great Lakes on the north, and to Spanish Florida on the south. (Spain had recently captured Florida from Britain.)

The Americans, on their part, had to yield important concessions. Loyalists were not to be further persecuted, and Congress was to *recommend* to the state legislatures that confiscated Loyalist property be restored. As for the debts long owed to British creditors, the states vowed to put no lawful obstacles in the way of their collection. Unhappily for future harmony, the assurances regarding both Loyalists and debts were not carried out in the manner hoped for by London.

A New Nation Legitimized

Britain's terms were liberal almost beyond belief. The enormous trans-Appalachian area was thrown in as a virtual gift, for George Rogers Clark had captured only a small segment of it. Why the generosity? Had the United States beaten Britain to its knees?

The key to the riddle may be found in the Old World. At the time the peace terms were drafted, Britain was trying to seduce America from its French alliance, so it made the terms as alluring as possible. The shaky Whig ministry, hanging on by its fingernails for only a few months, was more friendly to the Americans than were the Tories. It was determined, by a policy of liberality, to salve recent wounds, reopen old trade channels, and prevent future wars over the coveted trans-Appalachian region. This far-visioned policy was regrettably not followed by the successors of the Whigs.

In spirit, the Americans made a separate peace—contrary to the French alliance. In fact, they did not. The Paris Foreign Office formally approved the terms of peace, though disturbed by the lone-wolf course of its American ally. France was immensely relieved by the prospect of bringing the costly conflict to an end, and of freeing itself from its embarrassing promises to the Spanish crown.

America alone gained from the world-girdling war. The British, though soon to stage a comeback, were battered and beaten. The French savored sweet revenge but plunged headlong down the slippery slope to bankruptcy and revolution. The Americans fared much better. Snatching their independence from the furnace of world conflict, they began their national career with a splendid territorial birthright and a priceless heritage of freedom. Seldom, if ever, have any people been so favored.

✪ Chapter Summary ✪

Even after the shooting began at Lexington and Concord in April 1775, the Second Continental Congress did not at first pursue independence. Instead, it continued to appeal to the king to respect "the rights of Englishmen." The Congress's most important action was selecting George Washington as military commander.

After further armed clashes, George III formally proclaimed the colonists in rebellion. In early 1776, Thomas Paine's *Common Sense* finally persuaded Americans to fight for independence as well as liberty. Paine and other leaders promoted the Revolution as an opportunity for self-government by the people, though more conservative republicans disliked revolutionary egalitarianism and hoped to retain a strong political hierarchy without monarchy. Jefferson's Declaration of Independence deepened the meaning of the American Revolution by proclaiming it a fight for self-evident and universal human rights applicable to all peoples everywhere.

The committed revolutionary Patriots, only a minority of the American population, had to fight a civil war with Loyalist Americans as well as the professionally trained and better-armed British army and navy. Loyalists were strongest among conservatives, city-dwellers, and Anglicans (except in Virginia). Patriots were strongest in New England and among Presbyterians and Congregationalists.

In the first phase of the war, Washington was barely able to hold off the British, who botched their grand plan to isolate New England and quash the rebellion quickly. Victory in the Battle of Saratoga brought Americans new respect and the prospect of international assistance. Partially compromising their idealistic revolutionary beliefs that traditional military alliances were wrong, Franklin and other U.S. emissaries joined an alliance with France. With active French involvement, the Revolutionary War became a world war.

VARYING VIEW

Whose Revolution?

Historians once assumed that the American Revolution was just another chapter in the unfolding story of human liberty—an important way station on a divinely ordained pathway toward moral perfection in human affairs. This approach, often labeled the "Whig view of history," was best expressed in George Bancroft's ten-volume *History of the United States,* published between the 1830s and the 1870s.

In the nineteenth century, an "imperial school" of historians like Charles Andrews and Lawrence Gipson argued that the revolution was primarily a constitutional conflict within the British Empire. By the early twentieth century, both the Whig and imperial-school interpretations were sharply challenged by so-called progressive historians, who argued that neither divine destiny nor constitutional squabbles had much to do with the Revolution. Rather, progressives like Carl Becker and J. Franklin Jameson claimed the Revolution stemmed from deep-seated class tensions within American society that, once released by revolt, produced a truly transformed social order. The Revolution, therefore, was not only about "home rule" within the British Empire but about "who should rule at home" in America.

In the 1950s, the progressive historians fell out of favor as the political climate became more conservative. Historians such as Robert Brown and Edmund Morgan downplayed the role of class conflict in the Revolutionary era, but emphasized that colonists of all ranks shared a commitment to certain fundamental political principles of self-government. The unifying power of ideas was now back in fashion almost a hundred years after Bancroft.

Since the 1950s two broad interpretations have contended with each other and perpetuated the controversy over whether political ideals or economic and social realities were most responsible for the Revolution. The first, articulated most prominently by Bernard Bailyn, has emphasized inherent ideological and psychological factors. Bailyn argued that the colonists, incited by their reading of earlier English theorists, grew extraordinarily suspicious of any attempts to tighten the imperial reins. When confronted with new taxes and imperial regulations, the colonists screamed "conspiracy against liberty" and took up armed insurrection in defense of their intellectual commitment to liberty.

A second school of historians, inspired by the social movements of the turbulent 1960s and 1970s, revived the progressive interpretation of the Revolution. Gary Nash in *An Urban Crucible* (1979) and Edward Countryman in *A People in Revolution* (1981) pointed to attacks by laborers on political elites and expressions of resentment toward wealth as evidence of a society breeding revolution from within, quite aside from British provocations. The neoprogressives argue that the varying material circumstances of American participants gave the Revolution a less unified and more complex ideological underpinning than the idealistic historians had previously suggested.

More recently, scholars have taken a more transatlantic view of the Revolution's origins, asking when and how colonists shifted from identifying as "British" to viewing themselves as "American." Fred Anderson argued that the Seven Years' War helped create a sense of American identity apart from Britain, and T. H. Breen said that American nationalism emerged because the British failed to see Americans as equal imperial citizens, entitled to the same rights as Englishmen.

PART TWO

Building The New Nation

—⚬—

1776–1860

By 1783 Americans had won their freedom. Now they had to build their country. To be sure, they were blessed with a vast and fertile land, and they inherited from their colonial experience a proud legacy of self-rule. But history provided scant precedent for erecting a democracy on a national scale. No law of nature guaranteed that the thirteen rebellious colonies would stay glued together as a single nation, or that they would preserve, not to mention expand, their democratic way of life. New institutions had to be created, new habits of thought cultivated. Who could predict whether the American experiment in government by the people would succeed?

The ramshackle national government cobbled together under the Articles of Confederation during the Revolutionary War soon proved woefully inadequate to the task of nation building. Less than ten years after the war's conclusion, the Articles were replaced by a new constitution, but even its adoption did not end the debate over what form American democracy should take. Would the president, or the congress, or the courts be the dominant branch of government? What should be the proper division of authority between the federal government and the states? How could the rights of individuals be protected against a potentially powerful government? What economic policies would best serve the infant Republic? How should the nation defend itself against foreign foes? What principles should guide

foreign policy? Was America a nation at all, or was it merely a geographic expression, destined to splinter into several bitterly quarreling sections, as had happened to so many other would-be countries?

After a shaky start under George Washington and John Adams in the 1790s, buffeted by foreign troubles and domestic crises, the new Republic passed a major test when power was peacefully transferred from the conservative Federalists to the more liberal Jeffersonians in the election of 1800. A confident President Jefferson proceeded boldly to expand the national territory with the landmark Louisiana Purchase in 1803. But before long Jefferson, and then his successor, James Madison, were embroiled in what eventually proved to be a fruitless effort to spare the United States from the ravages of the war then raging in Europe.

America was dangerously divided during the War of 1812 and suffered a humiliating defeat. But a new sense of national unity and purpose was unleashed in the land thereafter. President Monroe, presiding over this "Era of Good Feelings," proclaimed in the Monroe Doctrine of 1823 that both of the American continents were off-limits to further European intervention. The foundations of a continental-scale economy were laid, as a "transportation revolution" stitched the country together with canals and railroads and turnpikes. Settlers flooded over those new arteries into the burgeoning

West, often brusquely shouldering aside the native peoples. Immigrants, especially from Ireland and Germany, flocked to American shores. The combination of new lands and new labor fed the growth of a market economy, including the commercialization of agriculture and the beginnings of the factory system of production. Old ways of life withered as the market economy drew women as well as men, children as well as adults, blacks as well as whites, into its embrace. Ominously, the slave system grew robustly as cotton production, mostly for sale on European markets, exploded into the booming Southwest.

Meanwhile, the United States in the era of Andrew Jackson gave the world an impressive lesson in political science. Between roughly 1820 and 1840 Americans virtually invented mass democracy, creating huge political parties and enormously expanding political participation by enfranchising nearly all adult white males. Nor was the spirit of innovation confined to the political realm. A wave of reform and cultural vitality swept through many sectors of American society. Utopian experiments proliferated. Religious revivals and even new religions, like Mormonism, flourished. A national litera-ture blossomed. Crusades were launched for temperance, prison reform, women's rights, and the abolition of slavery.

By the second quarter of the nineteenth century, the outlines of a distinctive American national character had begun to emerge. Americans were a diverse, restless people, tramping steadily westward, eagerly forging their own nascent industrial revolution, proudly exercising their democratic political rights, impatient with the old, in love with the new, testily asserting their superiority over all other peoples—and increasingly divided, in heart, in conscience, and in politics, over the single greatest blight on their record of nation making and democracy building: slavery.

What if . . . ?

- What if the American people had failed to ratify the Constitution in 1788, and the United States had persisted as a loosely tied group of states under the Articles of Confederation? What would have been the implications for the development of political democracy, the character of the economy, the nature of foreign policy—and the fate of slavery?

The Confederation and the Constitution

1776–1790

THIS EXAMPLE OF CHANGING THE CONSTITUTION BY
ASSEMBLING THE WISE MEN OF THE STATE, INSTEAD OF
ASSEMBLING ARMIES, WILL BE WORTH AS MUCH TO THE WORLD
AS THE FORMER EXAMPLES WE HAVE GIVEN IT.

THOMAS JEFFERSON

The American Revolution did not usher in a radical or total change. It did not suddenly and violently overturn an entire political and social framework, as later occurred in the French and Russian revolutions. What happened was accelerated evolution rather than outright revolution.

Yet some striking changes were ushered in, affecting social customs, political institutions, and ideas about society and government and even gender roles. The exodus of some eighty thousand substantial Loyalists after the war robbed the new ship of state of conservative ballast. This weakening of the aristocratic upper crust, with all its culture and elegance, paved the way for new, Patriot elites to emerge. It also cleared the field for more egalitarian ideas to sweep across the land.

Focus Questions

1. What were the political and social consequences of the American Revolution?
2. What were the primary achievements and failures of the United States under the Articles of Confederation?
3. What essentially motivated the drive to create a new foundation for government, and how did the Constitution written in Philadelphia reflect the Founders' central intentions?
4. What were the fundamental disagreements between the federalists and antifederalists, and why were the federalists successful in achieving ratification of the Constitution?
5. If the Constitution represented in part a "conservative" reaction to the American Revolution, how did it at the same preserve and protect the essential "radical" principles of the Revolution?

Chronology

1774 First Continental Congress calls for abolition of slave trade.	**1783** Military officers form Society of the Cincinnati.
1775 Philadelphia Quakers found world's first antislavery society.	**1785** Land Ordinance of 1785.
1776 New Jersey constitution temporarily gives women the vote.	**1786** Virginia Statute for Religious Freedom. Shays's Rebellion. Meeting of five states to discuss revision of the Articles of Confederation.
1777 Articles of Confederation adopted by Second Continental Congress.	**1787** Northwest Ordinance. Constitutional Convention in Philadelphia.
1780 Massachusetts adopts first constitution drafted in convention and ratified by popular vote.	**1788** Ratification by nine states guarantees a new government under the Constitution.
1781 Articles of Confederation put into effect.	

The Pursuit of Equality

"All men are created equal," the Declaration of Independence proclaimed, and equality was everywhere the watchword. Most states reduced (but usually did not eliminate altogether) property-holding requirements for voting. Ordinary men and women demanded to be addressed as "Mr." and "Mrs."—titles once reserved for the wealthy and highborn. Most Americans ridiculed the lordly pretensions of Continental Army officers who formed an exclusive hereditary order, the Society of the Cincinnati. Social democracy was further stimulated by the growth of trade organizations for artisans and laborers.

A protracted fight for separation of church and state resulted in notable gains. The well-entrenched Congregational Church continued to be legally established in some New England states, but the Anglican Church, tainted by association with the British crown, was humbled. De-anglicized, it re-formed as the Protestant Episcopal Church and was everywhere **disestablished**. The struggle for divorce between religion and government proved fiercest in Virginia. It was prolonged to 1786, when free-thinking Thomas Jefferson and his co-reformers, including the Baptists, won a complete victory with the passage of the Virginia Statute for Religious Freedom.

The egalitarian sentiments unleashed by the war likewise challenged the institution of slavery. Philadelphia Quakers in 1775 founded the world's first antislavery society. The Continental Congress in 1774 called for the complete abolition of the slave trade, a summons to which most of the states responded positively. Several northern states went further and either abolished slavery outright or provided for the gradual **emancipation** of blacks. Even on the plantations of Virginia, a few idealistic masters freed their human **chattels**—the first frail sprouts of the later **abolitionist** movement.

But this revolution of sentiments was sadly incomplete. No states south of Pennsylvania abolished slavery, and in both North and South the law discriminated harshly against freed blacks and slaves alike. Emancipated African Americans could be barred from purchasing property, holding certain jobs, or educating their children. Laws against interracial marriage also sprang up at this time.

Why in this dawning democratic age did abolition not go further and clearly blot the evil of slavery from the fresh face of the new nation? The sorry truth is that the fledgling idealism of the Founders was sacrificed to political expediency. A fight over slavery would have fractured the fragile national unity that was so desperately needed. "Great as the evil [of slavery] is," the young Virginian James

disestablish *To separate an official state church from its connection with the government.*

emancipation *Setting free from servitude or slavery.*

chattels *An article of personal or movable property; hence a term applied to slaves, since they were considered the personal property of their owners.*

abolitionist *An advocate of the end of slavery.*

Madison wrote in 1787, "a dismemberment of the union would be worse."

Likewise incomplete was the extension of the doctrine of equality to women. Some women did serve (disguised as men) in the military, and New Jersey's new constitution in 1776 even for a time enabled women to vote. But though Abigail Adams teased her husband John in 1776 that "the ladies" were determined "to foment a rebellion" of their own if they were not given political rights, most of the women in the Revolutionary era were still doing traditional women's work.

Yet women did not go untouched by revolutionary ideals. Republican ideology advanced the concept of "civic virtue"—the notion that democracy depended on the unselfish commitment of each citizen to the public good. Mothers, to whom society entrusted the education of the young, were often cited as the very models of proper republican behavior. The idea of "republican motherhood" thus took root, elevating women to a newly prestigious role as special keepers of the nation's conscience. Educational opportunities for women expanded, in the expectation that educated wives and mothers could better cultivate the virtues demanded by the Republic in their husbands, daughters, and sons. Republican women now bore crucial responsibility for the survival of the nation.

Constitution Making in the States

The Continental Congress in 1776 called on the colonies to draft new constitutions. In effect, Congress was actually asking the colonies to summon themselves into being as new states, whose sovereignty, according to the theory of republicanism, would rest on the authority of the people. In most of the states, writers of new constitutions worked tirelessly to capture on black-inked parchment the republican spirit of the age.

Massachusetts contributed one especially noteworthy innovation when it called a special convention to draft its constitution and then submitted the final draft directly to the people for **ratification.** Once adopted in 1780, the Massachusetts constitution could be changed only by another special convention. This procedure was later imitated in the drafting and ratification of the federal Constitution.

The newly penned state constitutions enjoyed many features in common. As *written* documents, they were intended to represent a *fundamental* law, superior to the transient whims of ordinary legislation. Most of these documents included bills of rights, specifically guaranteeing long-prized liberties against later legislative encroachment. All of them deliberately created weak executive and judicial branches. A generation of quarreling with His Majesty's officials had implanted a deep distrust of despotic governors and arbitrary judges. But the legislatures, presumably the most democratic branch of government, were given sweeping powers.

The democratic character of the new state legislatures was vividly reflected in the presence of many members from the recently enfranchised poorer western districts. Their influence was powerfully felt in their several successful movements to relocate state capitals from the haughty eastern seaports into the less pretentious interior. These geographical shifts portended political shifts that deeply discomfited many more conservative Americans.

■ Elizabeth "Mumbet" Freeman (c. 1744–1829), by Susan Anne Livingston Ridley Sedgwick, 1811 In 1781, having overheard Revolutionary-era talk about the "rights of man," Mumbet sued her Massachusetts master for her freedom from slavery. She won her suit and lived the rest of her life as a paid domestic servant in the home of the lawyer who had pleaded her case.

ratification *The confirmation or validation of an act (such as a constitution) by authoritative approval.*

The Revolution enhanced the expectations and power of women as wives and mothers. As one "matrimonial republican" wrote in 1792,

"I object to the word 'obey' in the marriage-service because it is a general word, without limitations or definition. . . . The obedience between man and wife, I conceive, is, or ought to be mutual. . . . Marriage ought never to be considered a contract between a superior and an inferior, but a reciprocal union of interest, an implied partnership of interests, where all differences are accommodated by conference; and where the decision admits of no retrospect."

EXAMINING THE EVIDENCE

Copley Family Portrait, c. 1776–1777   A portrait painting like this one by John Singleton Copley (1738–1815) documents physical likenesses, clothing styles, and other material possessions typical of an era. But it can do more than that. In the execution of the painting itself, the preeminent portrait painter of colonial America revealed important values of his time. Copley's composition and use of light emphasized the importance of the mother in the family. Mrs. Copley is the visual center of the painting; the light falls predominantly on her, and she provides the focus of activity for the family group. Although Copley had moved to England in 1774 to avoid the disruptions of war, he had made radical friends in his hometown of Boston and surely had imbibed the sentiment of the age about "republican motherhood"—a sentiment that revered women as homemakers and mothers, the cultivators of good republican values in young citizens.

1. What prevalent eighteenth-century attitudes about gender and age might this painting reveal?

2. How does the scene visible through the opening in the rear suggest that this family is intended to be representative of an American future?

3. What attitudes toward children are revealed in the painting? What does it suggest about proper relationships among mothers, fathers, and children?

Economic Crosscurrents

Economic changes begotten by the war were likewise noteworthy, but not overwhelming. States seized control of former crown lands, and although rich **speculators** had their day, many of the large Loyalist holdings were confiscated and eventually cut up into small farms. Roger Morris's huge estate in New York, for example, was sliced into 250 parcels—thus accelerating the spread of economic democracy. The frightful excesses of the French Revolution were avoided, partly because cheap land was easily available. People do not chop off heads so readily when they can chop down trees. It is highly significant that in the United States economic democracy, broadly speaking, preceded political democracy.

speculators (speculation) *Those who buy property, goods, or financial instruments not primarily for use but in anticipation of profitable resale after a general rise in value.*

A sharp stimulus was given to manufacturing by the prewar nonimportation agreements and later by the war itself. Goods that formerly had been imported from Britain were mostly cut off, and the ingenious Yankees were forced to make their own. Ten years after the Revolution the tumbling Brandywine Creek, south of Philadelphia, was turning the waterwheels of numerous mills along an eight-mile stretch. Yet America remained overwhelmingly a nation of soil-tillers.

Economically speaking, independence had drawbacks. Much of the coveted commerce of Britain was still reserved for the loyal parts of the empire. American ships were now barred from British and British West Indian harbors. But new commercial outlets, fortunately, partially compensated for the loss of old ones. Americans could now trade freely with foreign nations, subject to local restrictions—a boon they had not enjoyed in the days of mercantilism. Enterprising Yankee shippers ventured boldly—and profitably—into the Baltic and China Seas.

Yet the general economic picture was far from rosy. War had spawned demoralizing extravagance, speculation, and profiteering, with profits for some as indecently high as 300 percent. Runaway inflation had been ruinous to many citizens, and Congress had failed in its feeble attempts to curb economic laws. While a newly rich class of profiteers was noisily conspicuous, the average citizen was probably worse off financially at the end of the shooting than before.

A Shaky Start Toward Union

What would the Americans do with the independence they had so dearly won? Prospects for erecting a lasting regime were far from bright. It is always difficult to set up a new government, doubly difficult to set up a new type of government. The picture was further clouded in America by leaders preaching "natural rights" and looking suspiciously at all persons clothed with authority. America was more a name than a nation, and unity ran little deeper than the color on the map.

Disruptive forces stalked the land. The departure of the conservative Loyalists left the political system inclined toward experimentation and innovation. Patriots had fought the war with a high degree of disunity, but they at least had concurred on allegiance to a common cause. Now even that was gone. It would have been almost a miracle if any government fashioned in all this confusion had long endured.

Hard times, the bane of all regimes, set in shortly after the war and hit bottom in 1786. As if other troubles were not enough, British manufacturers, with dammed-up surpluses, began flooding the American market with cut-rate goods. War-baby American industries, in particular, suffered industrial colic from such ruthless competition.

Yet hopeful signs could be discerned. The thirteen sovereign states were basically alike in governmental structure and functioned under similar constitutions. Americans enjoyed a rich political inheritance, derived partly from Britain and partly from their own homegrown devices for self-government. Finally, they were blessed with political leaders of a high order in men like George Washington, James Madison, John Adams, Thomas Jefferson, and Alexander Hamilton.

Online Study Center

Primary source
Socioeconomic Profile of Loyalist Claimants
college.hmco.com/pic/kennedybrief7e

Creating a Confederation

The Second Continental Congress of Revolutionary days was little more than a conference of ambassadors from the thirteen states. In nearly all respects the thirteen states were sovereign, for they coined money, raised armies and navies, and erected tariff barriers.

Shortly before declaring independence in 1776, Congress appointed a committee to draft a written constitution for the new nation. The finished product was the Articles of Confederation. Adopted by Congress in 1777, it was translated into French after the Battle of Saratoga so as to convince France that America had a genuine government in the making. The articles were not ratified by all thirteen states until 1781, less than eight months before the victory at Yorktown.

The chief apple of discord was western lands. Six of the jealous states, including Pennsylvania and Maryland, had no holdings beyond the Appalachian Mountains. Seven, notably New York and Virginia, were favored with enormous acreage on the basis of earlier sea-to-sea charter grants. The six land-hungry states argued that the more fortunate states would not have retained possession of this splendid prize if all the other states had not fought for it also. Why not turn the whole western area over to the central government?

Unanimous approval of the Articles of Confederation by the thirteen states was required, and land-starved Maryland stubbornly held out until March 1, 1781. Maryland at length gave in when New York surrendered its western claims and Virginia seemed about to do so. To sweeten the pill, Congress pledged itself to dispose of these vast areas for the "common benefit." It further agreed to carve from the new public domain not colonies but a number of "republican" states, which in time would be admitted to the Union on terms of complete equality with all the others. This extraordinary commitment faithfully reflected the anticolonial spirit

Online Study Center

Interactive map
Western Land Claims After
American Independence
college.hmco.com/pic/kennedybrief7e

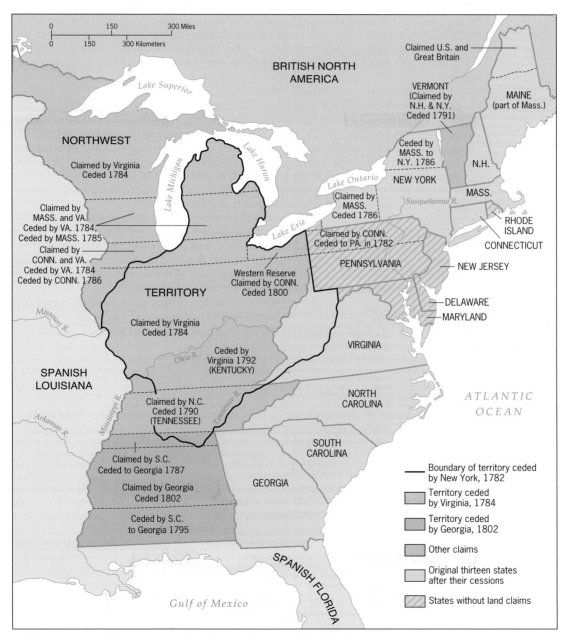

■ **Western Land Cessions to the United States, 1782–1802**

of the Revolution, and the pledge was later fully redeemed in the famed Northwest Ordinance of 1787.

Fertile public lands thus transferred to the central government proved to be an invaluable bond of union. The states that had thrown their heritage into the common pot had to remain in the Union if they were to reap their share of the advantages from the land sales. An army of westward-moving pioneers purchased their farms from the federal government, directly or indirectly, and they learned to look to the national capital, rather than to the state capitals—with a consequent weakening of local influence. Finally, a uniform national land policy was made possible.

The Articles of Confederation: America's First Constitution

The Articles of Confederation provided for a loose confederation or "firm league of friendship." Thirteen independent states were thus linked together for joint action in dealing with common problems, such as foreign affairs. A clumsy Congress was to be the chief agency of government. There was no executive branch—George III had left a bad taste—and the vital judicial arm was left almost exclusively to the states.

Congress, though dominant, was severely hobbled. Each state had a single vote. All bills dealing with subjects of importance required the support of nine states; any amendment of the Articles themselves required unanimous ratification. Purposely designed to be weak, Congress was crippled by its lack of power to regulate commerce, which left the states free to establish conflicting laws regarding tariffs and navigation. Lacking any power to enforce its tax-collection program, Congress set a tax quota for the individual states and then asked them please to contribute their shares on a voluntary basis. This "government by supplication" was lucky if in any year it received one-fourth of its requests.

In spite of their defects, the anemic Articles of Confederation were a significant steppingstone toward the present Constitution. They clearly outlined the general powers that were to be exercised by the central government, such as making treaties and establishing a postal service. As the first written constitution of the Republic, the Articles kept alive the flickering ideal of union and held the states together—until such time as they were ripe for the establishment of a strong constitution by peaceful, evolutionary methods. Without this intermediary jump, the states probably would never have consented to the breathtaking leap from the old boycott Association of 1774 to the Constitution of the United States.

Landmarks in Land Laws

Handcuffed though the Congress of the Confederation was, it succeeded in passing supremely farsighted pieces of legislation. These related to an immense part of the public domain recently acquired from the states commonly known as the Old Northwest. This area of land lay north of the Ohio River, east of the Mississippi River, and south of the Great Lakes.

The first of these red-letter laws was the Land Ordinance of 1785. It provided that the acreage of the Old Northwest should be sold and that the proceeds should be used to help pay off the national debt. The vast area was to be surveyed before sale and settlement, thus forestalling endless confusion and lawsuits. It was to be divided into **townships** six miles square, each of which in turn was to be split into thirty-six sections of one square mile each. The sixteenth section of each township was set aside to be sold for the benefit of the public schools—a priceless gift to education in the Old Northwest.

Even more noteworthy was the Northwest Ordinance of 1787, which related to the governing of the Old Northwest. This law came to grips with the problem of how a nation should deal with its colonies—the same problem that had bedeviled the king and Parliament in London. The solution provided by the Northwest

townships *In America, a surveyed territory six miles square; the term also refers to a unit of local government, smaller than a county, that is often based on these survey units.*

Online Study Center

Primary source
Township and Range Map of the Old Northwest
college.hmco.com/pic/kennedybrief7e

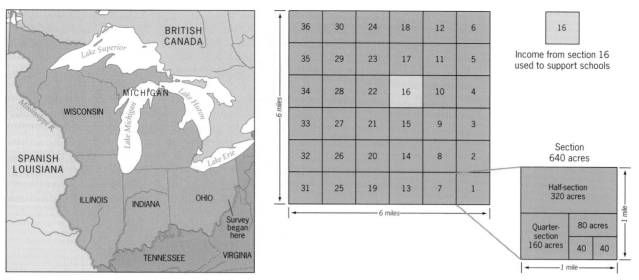

■ **Surveying the Old Northwest** Sections of a township under the Land Ordinance of 1785.

Ordinance was a judicious compromise: temporary tutelage, then permanent equality. First, there would be two evolutionary territorial stages, during which the area would be subordinate to the federal government. Then, when a **territory** could boast sixty thousand inhabitants, it might be admitted by Congress as a state, with all the privileges of the thirteen charter members. The ordinance also forbade slavery in the Old Northwest—a path-breaking step, though it exempted slaves already present.

The wisdom of Congress in handling this explosive problem deserves warm praise. If it had attempted to chain the new territories in permanent subordination, a second American Revolution almost certainly would have erupted in later years, fought this time by the West against the East. Congress thus neatly solved the seemingly insoluble problem of empire. The scheme worked so well that its basic principles were ultimately carried over from the Old Northwest to other frontier areas.

territory *In American government, an organized political entity not yet enjoying the full and equal status of a state.*

annex *To make a smaller territory or political unit part of a larger one.*

★ The World's Ugly Duckling

Foreign relations, especially with London, continued troubled during these anxious years of the Confederation. Britain flatly declined to send a minister to America, to make a commercial treaty, or to repeal its ancient Navigation Laws. The British Lord Sheffield argued that Britain would win back America's trade anyhow, because commerce would naturally return to old channels. The British also officially closed their profitable West Indian trade from the United States, though the Yankees still engaged in smuggling.

Along the far-flung northern frontier, scheming British agents intrigued with the disgruntled Allen brothers of Vermont and sought to **annex** that rebellious area to Britain. Redcoats continued to hold a chain of trading posts on U.S. soil, maintaining their fur trade and bolstering the Indians as a barrier against future American attacks on Canada.

Maddened by these grievances, some patriotic Americans demanded that the United States force the British into line by imposing restrictions on their imports to America. But Congress could not control commerce, and the states refused to adopt a uniform tariff policy.

Spain, though recently an enemy of Britain, was openly unfriendly to the new Republic. It controlled the mouth of the all-important Mississippi, down which the pioneers of Tennessee and Kentucky were forced to float their produce. In 1784 Spain closed the river to American commerce, threatening the

Online Study Center

Interactive map
Indian Land Cessions, 1768–1799
college.hmco.com/pic/kennedybrief7e

West with strangulation. Spain likewise claimed a large area north of the Gulf of Mexico, including Florida. From its important fort at Natchez, Spain schemed with neighboring Indians to hem in the Americans east of the Appalachians. Spain and Britain together, radiating their influence out among the powerful Indian tribes, prevented America from exercising effective control over about half of its total territory.

Even France, America's comrade-in-arms, demanded the repayment of money loaned during the war and restricted trade with its bustling West Indies ports. North African pirates, including the arrogant Dey of Algiers, were ravaging America's Mediterranean commerce and enslaving Yankee sailors. The British purchased protection for their subjects, but as an independent nation the United States was too weak to fight and too poor to bribe. John Jay, secretary for foreign affairs, hoped that these insults would at least humiliate the American people into framing a new government at home that would be strong enough to command respect abroad.

The Horrid Specter of Anarchy

Economic storm clouds continued to loom in the mid-1780s. Interest on the public debt was piling up at home, and the nation's credit was evaporating abroad. Quarreling states were levying duties on goods from their neighbors: New York, for example, taxed firewood from Connecticut and cabbages from New Jersey.

An alarming uprising, known as Shays's Rebellion, flared up in western Massachusetts in 1786 and set off widespread fear of further insurrection. Impoverished backcountry farmers, many of them Revolutionary War veterans, were losing their farms through mortgage **foreclosures** and tax delinquencies. Led by Captain Daniel Shays, a veteran of the Revolution, these desperate debtors demanded cheap paper money, lighter taxes, and a suspension of mortgage foreclosures. Hundreds of angry agitators, again seizing their muskets, attempted to enforce their demands.

foreclosures *Depriving someone of the right to redeem mortgaged property because the legal payments on the loan have not been kept up.*

Massachusetts authorities responded with drastic action. Supported partly by contributions from wealthy citizens, they raised a small army. After a few skirmishes the revolt collapsed. Daniel Shays, who believed that he was fighting anew against tyranny, was condemned to death but later pardoned.

Shays's followers were crushed—but the nightmarish memory lingered on. The outbursts of Shays and other distressed debtors struck fear in the hearts of the propertied class, who began to suspect that the Revolution had raised up a Frankenstein's monster "mobocracy." Unbridled republicanism, it seemed to many of the elite, had fed an insatiable appetite for liberty that was fast becoming license. Civic virtue was no longer sufficient to rein in self-interest and greed. It had become "undeniably evident," one skeptic sorrowfully lamented, "that some malignant disorder has seized upon our body politic." If republicanism was too shaky a ground on which to construct a new nation, a stronger central government would provide the needed foundation. How critical were conditions under the Confederation? Conservatives, anxious to safeguard their wealth and position, naturally exaggerated the seriousness of the nation's plight. They were eager to persuade their fellow citizens to amend the Articles of Confederation in favor of a muscular central government. But the poorer states' rights people pooh-poohed the talk of anarchy. Many of them were debtors who feared that a powerful federal government would force them to pay their creditors.

Yet friends and critics of the Confederation agreed that it needed strengthening. Popular toasts were "Cement to the Union" and "A hoop to the barrel." The chief differences arose over how this goal should be attained and how a maximum amount of states' rights could be reconciled with a strong central government.

Social tensions reached a fever pitch during Shays's Rebellion in 1787. In an interview with a local Massachusetts paper, instigator Daniel Shays (1747–1825) explained how the debt-ridden farmers hoped to free themselves from the demands of a merchant-dominated government. The rebels would seize arms and

"march directly to Boston, plunder it, and then . . . destroy the nest of devils, who by their influence, make the Court enact what they please, burn it and lay the town of Boston in ashes."

A Convention of "DemiGods"

Control of commerce, more than any other problem, touched off the chain reaction that led to a constitutional convention. Interstate squabbling over this issue had become so alarming by 1786 that Virginia issued a call for a convention at Annapolis, Maryland. When delegates from only five states showed up, nothing could be done about the ticklish question of commerce. A charismatic New Yorker, thirty-one-year-old Alexander Hamilton, brilliantly saved the convention from failure by engineering a call for another convention to meet the next year in Philadelphia to bolster the entire fabric of the Articles of Confederation.

Congress was reluctant to take a step that might lead to signing its own death warrant. But after six states appointed delegates anyhow, Congress belatedly issued the call for a convention "for the sole and express purpose of revising" the Articles of Confederation.

Every state chose representatives, except independent-minded Rhode Island, a stronghold of paper-moneyites. These leaders were all appointed by the state legislatures, whose members had been elected by voters who could qualify as property holders. This double distillation inevitably brought together a select group of propertied men.

A **quorum** of the fifty-five emissaries from twelve states finally convened at Philadelphia on May 25, 1787, in the imposing red-brick statehouse. The smallness of the assemblage facilitated intimate acquaintance and hence compromise. Sessions were held in complete secrecy, with armed sentinels posted at the doors. Delegates knew that they would generate heated differences, and they did not want to advertise their own dissensions or put the ammunition of harmful arguments into the mouths of the opposition.

The caliber of the participants was extraordinarily high—"demigods," Jefferson called them. The crisis was such as to induce the ablest men to drop their personal pursuits and come to the aid of their country. Most of the members were lawyers, and most of them fortunately were old hands at constitution making in their own states.

George Washington, towering austere and aloof among the "demigods," was unanimously elected chairman. His enormous prestige as "the Sword of the Revolution" served to quiet overheated tempers. Benjamin Franklin, then eighty-one, added the urbanity of an elder statesman, though he was inclined to be indiscreetly talkative in his declining years. Concerned for the secrecy of their deliberations, the convention assigned chaperones to accompany Franklin to dinner parties and make sure he held his tongue. James Madison, then thirty-six and a profound student of government, made contributions so notable that he has been dubbed "the Father of the Constitution." Alexander Hamilton was present as an advocate of a super-powerful central government. His five-hour speech in behalf of his plan, though the most eloquent of the convention, left only one delegate convinced—himself.

Most of the fiery Revolutionary leaders of 1776 were absent. Thomas Jefferson, John Adams, and Thomas Paine were in Europe; Samuel Adams and John Hancock were not elected by Massachusetts. Patrick Henry, ardent champion of states' rights, was chosen as a delegate from Virginia but declined to serve, declaring that he "smelled a rat." It was perhaps well that these architects of revolution were absent. The time had come to yield the stage to leaders interested in fashioning solid political systems.

quorum *The minimum number of persons who must be present in a group before it can conduct valid business.*

■ **Statehouse in 1778, from a drawing by Charles Willson Peale, by William L. Breton, c. 1830** Originally built in the 1730s as a meeting place for the Pennsylvania colonial assembly, this building witnessed much history: here Washington was given command of the Continental Army, the Declaration of Independence was signed, and the Constitution was hammered out. The building began to be called "Independence Hall" in the 1820s.

anarchy *The theory that formal government is unnecessary and wrong in principle; the term is also used generally for lawlessness or antigovernmental disorder.*

bicameral, unicameral *Referring to a legislative body with two houses (bicameral) or one (unicameral).*

Patriots in Philadelphia

The fifty-five delegates were a conservative, well-to-do body: lawyers, merchants, shippers, land speculators, and moneylenders. Not a single spokesperson was present from the poorer debtor groups. Nineteen of the fifty-five owned slaves. They were young (the average age was about forty-two) but experienced statesmen. Above all, they were nationalists, more interested in preserving and strengthening the young Republic than in further stirring the roiling cauldron of popular democracy.

The delegates hoped to crystallize the evaporating pools of revolutionary idealism into a stable political structure that would endure. They strongly desired a firm, dignified, and respected government. They believed in republicanism but sought to protect the American experiment from its weaknesses abroad and excesses at home. They aimed to clothe the central authority with genuine power, especially in controlling tariffs, so that the United States could wrest satisfactory commercial treaties from foreign nations.

Other motives hovered in the Philadelphia hall. Delegates were determined to preserve the Union, forestall **anarchy,** and ensure security of life and property against dangerous uprisings by the "mobocracy." Above all, they sought to curb the unrestrained democracy rampant in the various states. The specter of the recent outburst in Massachusetts was especially alarming, and in this sense, Daniel Shays was another Founding Father. Grinding necessity extorted the Constitution from a reluctant nation. Fear occupied the fifty-sixth chair.

Hammering Out a Bundle of Compromises

Some of the travel-stained delegates, when they first reached Philadelphia, decided on a daring step. They would completely scrap the old Articles of Confederation, despite explicit instructions from Congress to *revise.* Technically, these bolder spirits were determined to overthrow the existing government of the United States by peaceful means.

A scheme proposed by populous Virginia, and known as "the large-state plan," was first pushed forward as the framework of the Constitution. Its essence was that representation in both houses of a **bicameral** Congress should be based on population—an arrangement that would naturally give the larger states an advantage. Tiny New Jersey, suspicious of brawny Virginia, countered with "the small-state plan." This provided for equal representation in a **unicameral** Congress by states, regardless of size and population.

After bitter and prolonged debate, and with the danger of complete failure looming, the "Great Compromise" of the convention was hammered out and agreed upon. The larger states were conceded representation by population in the House of Representatives (Art. I, Sec. II, para. 3; see the Appendix at the end of this book), and the smaller states were appeased by equal representation in the Senate (see Art. I, Sec. III, para. 1). Each state, no matter how poor or small, would have two senators. The big states obviously yielded more. As a sop to them, the delegates agreed that every tax bill or revenue measure must originate in the House, where population counted more heavily (see Art. I, Sec. VII, para. 1). This critical compromise broke the logjam, and from then on success seemed within reach.

In a significant reversal of the arrangement most state constitutions had embodied, the new Constitution provided for a robust—though still legally restrained—executive in the presidency. The president was to have broad authority to appoint officials and judges, veto legislation, and wage war as commander in chief of the military. But Congress retained

the crucial right to *declare* war—a division of responsibilities that has been an invitation to conflict between president and Congress ever since.

The Constitution as drafted was a bundle of compromises; they stand out in every section. A key compromise was the method of electing the president indirectly by the Electoral College, rather than by direct means (see Art. II, Sec. I, para. 2). While the large states would have the advantage in the first round of popular voting, the small states would gain a larger voice if no candidate got a majority of electoral votes and the election was thrown to the House of Representatives, where each state had only one vote (see Art. II, Sec. I, para. 2). Although the framers of the Constitution expected election by the House to occur frequently, it has happened just twice, in 1800 and 1824.

Sectional jealousy also intruded. Should the voteless slave of the southern states count as a person in apportioning direct taxes and representation in the House of Representatives? The South, not wishing to be deprived of influence, answered "yes." The North replied "no," arguing that slaves were not citizens. As a compromise between total representation and none at all, it was decided that a slave might count as three-fifths of a person. Hence the memorable, if arbitrary, "three-fifths compromise" (see Art. I, Sec. II, para. 3).

Most of the states wanted to shut off the African slave trade. But slaveholding South Carolina and Georgia raised vehement protests. In another compromise the convention stipulated that the slave trade might continue until the end of 1807, at which time Congress could stop the trade (see Art. I, Sec. IX, para. 1). It did so as soon as the prescribed interval had elapsed.

Safeguards for Conservatism

Heated clashes among the delegates have been overplayed. The area of agreement was actually large; otherwise the convention would have speedily disbanded. Economically, the members of the Constitutional Convention generally saw eye to

■ **Signing of the Constitution of the United States, 1787** George Washington presided from the dais as the Constitutional Convention's president. At a table in the front row sat James Madison, later called the Father of the Constitution, who recorded the proceedings in shorthand. Daily from 10 A.M. to 3 P.M., from late May through mid-September 1787, the fifty-five delegates wrangled over ideas for a new federal government.

Strengthening the Central Government

Under Articles of Confederation	Under Federal Constitution
A loose confederation of states	A firm union of people
1 vote in Congress for each state	2 votes in Senate for each state; representation by population in House (see Art. I, Secs. II, III)
Vote of 9 states in Congress for all important measures	Simple majority vote in Congress, subject to presidential veto (see Art. I, Sec. VII, para. 2)
Laws administered loosely by committees of Congress	Laws executed by powerful president (see Art. II, Secs. II, III)
No congressional power over commerce	Congress to regulate both foreign and interstate commerce (see Art. I, Sec. VIII, para. 3)
No congressional power to levy taxes	Extensive power in Congress to levy taxes (see Art. I, Sec. VIII, para. 1)
Limited federal courts	Federal courts, capped by Supreme Court (see Art. III)
Unanimity of states for amendment	Amendment less difficult (see Art. V)
No authority to act directly upon individuals and no power to coerce states	Ample power to enforce laws by coercion of individuals and to some extent of states

eye; they demanded sound money and the protection of private property. Politically, they were in basic agreement; they favored a stronger government, with three branches and with checks and balances among them—what critics branded a "triple-headed monster." Finally, the convention was virtually unanimous in believing that manhood-suffrage democracy—government by "democratick babblers"—was something to be feared and fought.

Daniel Shays, the prime bogeyman, still frightened the conservative-minded delegates. They deliberately erected safeguards against the excesses of the "mob," and they made these barriers as strong as they dared. The awesome federal judges were to be appointed for life. The powerful president was to be elected *indirectly* by the Electoral College; the lordly senators were to be chosen *indirectly* by state legislatures (see Art. I, Sec. III, para. 1). Only in the case of one-half of one of the three great branches—the House of Representatives—were qualified (propertied) citizens permitted to choose their officials by *direct* vote (see Art. I, Sec. II, para. 1).

Yet the new charter also contained democratic elements. Above all, it stood foursquare on the two great principles of republicanism: that the only legitimate government was one based on the consent of the governed, and that the powers of the government should be limited by a written constitution. The virtue of the people, not the authority of the state, was to be the ultimate guarantor of liberty, justice, and order. "We the people," the preamble began, in a ringing affirmation of these republican doctrines.

At the end of seventeen muggy weeks—May 25 to September 17, 1787—only forty-two of the original fifty-five members remained to sign the Constitution. Three of the forty-two, refusing to do so, returned to their states to resist ratification. The remainder, adjourning to the City Tavern, celebrated the toastworthy occasion.

The Clash of Federalists and Antifederalists

The Framing Fathers early foresaw that nationwide acceptance of the Constitution would not be easy to obtain. A formidable barrier was unanimous ratification by all thirteen states, as required for amendment by the still-standing Articles of Confederation. But since absent Rhode Island was certain to veto the Constitution, the delegates boldly adopted a different scheme. They stipulated that when nine states had registered their approval through specially elected conventions, the Constitution would become the supreme law of the land in those states ratifying (see Art. VII).

This was extraordinary, even revolutionary. It was in effect an appeal over the heads of the Congress that had called the convention, and over the heads of the legislatures that had chosen its members, to the people—or those of the people who could vote. In this way the framers could claim greater popular sanction for their handiwork. A divided Congress submitted the document to the states on this basis, without recommendation of any kind.

The American people were somewhat astonished, so well had the secrets of the convention been kept. The public had expected the old Articles of Confederation to be patched up; now it was handed a startling new document in which, many thought, the precious jewel of state sovereignty was swallowed up. One of the hottest debates of American history forthwith erupted. The antifederalists, who opposed the stronger federal government, were arrayed against the federalists, who obviously favored it.

A motley crowd gathered in the antifederalist camp. Its leaders included prominent revolutionaries like Samuel Adams, Patrick Henry, and Richard Henry Lee. Their followers consisted primarily, though not exclusively, of states' rights devotees, backcountry dwellers, and one-horse farmers—in general, the poorest classes. They were joined by paper-moneyites and debtors. Many antifederalists saw in the Constitution a plot by the upper crust to steal power back from the common folk.

Silver-buckled federalists had power and influence on their side. They enjoyed the support of such commanding figures as George Washington and Benjamin Franklin. Most of them lived along the seaboard. Overall, they were wealthier than the antifederalists, better educated, and more organized. They also controlled the press. Of about a hundred newspapers published in America in the 1780s, only a dozen supported the antifederalist cause.

Antifederalists voiced vehement objections to the "gilded trap" known as the Constitution. They cried with much truth that it had been drawn up by the aristocratic elements and hence was antidemocratic. They likewise charged that the sovereignty of the states was being submerged and that the freedoms of the individual were jeopardized by the absence of a **bill of rights.** They decried the dropping of annual elections for congressional representatives, the erecting of a federal stronghold ten miles square (later the District of Columbia), the creation of a standing army, the omission of any reference to God, and the highly questionable procedure of ratifying with only two-thirds of the states.

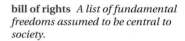

bill of rights *A list of fundamental freedoms assumed to be central to society.*

The Great Debate in the States

Special elections, some apathetic but others hotly contested, were held in the various states for members of the ratifying conventions. The candidates—federalist or antifederalist—were elected on the basis of their pledges for or against the Constitution.

With the ink barely dry on the parchment, four small states quickly accepted the Constitution, for they had come off much better than they expected. Pennsylvania, number two on the list of ratifiers, was the first large state to act, but not until high-handed irregularities had been employed by the federalist legislature in calling a convention. These included the forcible seating of two antifederalist members, their clothes torn and their faces red with rage, in order to complete a quorum.

Massachusetts, the second most populous state, provided an acid test. If the Constitution had failed in Massachusetts, the entire movement might easily have bogged down. The Boston ratifying convention at first contained an antifederalist majority, including grudging Shaysites and the aging Samuel Adams, as suspicious of government power in 1787 as he had been in 1776. The absence of a bill of rights especially alarmed the antifederalists. But the federalists gave solemn assurances that the new Congress would add such a safeguard by amendment, and Massachusetts then ratified by the narrow margin of 187 to 168.

■ **The Struggle over Ratification**
This mottled map shows that federalist support tended to cluster around the coastal areas, which had enjoyed profitable commerce with the outside world, including the export of grain and tobacco. Impoverished frontiersmen, suspicious of a powerful new central government under the Constitution, were generally antifederalists.

Online Study Center

Interactive map
Federalists and Antifederalists Strongholds, 1787–1790
college.hmco.com/pic/kennedybrief7e

Three more states—Maryland, South Carolina, and New Hampshire—fell into line, though the struggle in New Hampshire was fierce. Nine states—all but Virginia, New York, North Carolina, and Rhode Island—had now taken shelter under the "new federal roof," and the document was officially adopted on June 21, 1788. But federalist rejoicing was premature so long as the four dissenters, conspicuously New York and Virginia, dug in their heels.

The Four Laggard States

Proud Virginia, the biggest and most populous state, provided fierce antifederalist opposition. There the college-bred federalist orators, for once, encountered worthy antagonists, including the fiery Patrick Henry. He professed to see in the fearsome document the death warrant of liberty. George Washington, James Madison, and John Marshall, on the federalist side, lent influential support. The new Union was going to be formed anyhow, and Virginia could not very well continue comfortably as an independent state. After exciting debate in the state convention, ratification carried, 89 to 79.

New York also experienced an uphill struggle, burdened as it was with its own heavily antifederalist state convention. Alexander Hamilton at heart favored a much stronger central government than that under debate, but he contributed his sparkling personality and persuasive eloquence to whipping up support for federalism as framed. He also joined John Jay and James Madison in penning a masterly series of articles for the New York newspapers. Though designed as propaganda, these essays remain the most penetrating commentary ever written on the Constitution and are still widely sold in book form as *The Federalist.* Probably the most famous of these is Madison's *Federalist* No. 10, which brilliantly refuted the conventional wisdom that a republic could not extend over a large territory.

New York finally yielded. Realizing that the state could not prosper apart from the Union, the convention ratified the document by the close count of 30 to 27.

Last-ditch dissent developed in only two states. A hostile convention met in North Carolina, then adjourned without taking a vote. Rhode Island did not even summon a ratifying convention, rejecting the Constitution by popular referendum. The two most ruggedly individualist centers of the colonial era—homes of the "otherwise minded"—thus ran true to form. They were to change their course, albeit unwillingly, only after the new government had been in operation for some months.

The race for ratification was close and quite bitter in some localities. No lives were lost, but riotous disturbances broke out in New York and Pennsylvania, involving bruises and bloodshed. There was much behind-the-scenes pressure on delegates who had promised their constituents to vote against the Constitution. The last four states ratified not because they wanted to but because they had to. They could not survive as lone wolves.

A Conservative Triumph

Online Study Center
**Primary source
University President Denounces
Conservative Coercion**
college.hmco.com/pic/kennedybrief7e

A minority had triumphed—twice. A militant minority of American radicals had engineered the military Revolution that cast off the unwritten British constitution. A militant minority of conservatives—now embracing many of the earlier radicals—had engineered the peaceful revolution that overthrew the inadequate Articles of Confederation. Eleven states, in effect, had seceded from the Confederation, leaving the two still in actually out in the cold.

A majority had not spoken. Only about one-fourth of the adult white males in the country, chiefly the propertied people, had voted for delegates to the ratifying conventions. Careful estimates indicate that if the new Constitution had been submitted to a manhood-suffrage vote, as in New York, it would have encountered much more opposition, probably defeat.

Conservatism was victorious. Safeguards had been erected against mob-rule excesses, while the republican gains of the Revolution were conserved. Radicals like Patrick Henry, who had ousted British rule, saw themselves upended in turn by American conservatives. The federalists were convinced that by setting the drifting ship of state on a steady course they could restore economic and political stability.

Yet if the architects of the Constitution were conservative, it is worth emphasizing that they conserved the principle of republican government through a redefinition of popular sovereignty. Unlike the antifederalists, who believed that the sovereignty of the people resided in a single branch of government—the legislature—the federalists contended that every branch—executive, judiciary, and legislature—effectively represented the people. By ingeniously embedding the doctrine of self-rule in a self-limiting system of checks and balances, the Constitution reconciled the potentially conflicting principles of liberty and order. It elevated the ideals of the Revolution even while setting boundaries to them. One of the distinctive—and enduring—paradoxes of American history was thus revealed: in the United States, conservatives and radicals alike have championed the heritage of republican revolution.

✪ Chapter Summary ✪

The American Revolution did not overturn the social order, but it did produce substantial changes in social customs, political institutions, and ideas about society and government. Among the changes were the separation of church and state in some places, the abolition of slavery in the North, written political constitutions, and a shift in political power from the eastern seaboard toward the frontier. The ideas of liberty and equality also affected many areas of society, but stopped short of promoting true equality for women or ending slavery (except where it was weakest, in the North).

The first weak national government, the Articles of Confederation, was unable to exercise real authority, although it did successfully deal with the western lands issue. The Confederation's weaknesses in handling foreign policy, commerce, and the Shays rebellion spurred the movement to alter the Articles.

Instead of revising the Articles, the young, nationalistic, and well-off delegates to the Constitutional Convention created a permanent charter for a whole new government. In a series of compromises, the convention produced a plan that provided for a vigorous central government, a strong executive, and protection for property, while still upholding republican principles and states' rights. The pro-Constitution federalists, generally representing wealthier and more commercial forces, were opposed by less sophisticated and well educated portions of the population who feared that a strong federal government would undermine their rights and their interests.

The federalists met their strongest opposition from antifederalists in Virginia and New York, but they triumphed through the use of more effective organization and argument, as well as through promises to incorporate a bill of rights into the document. By establishing the new national government, the federalists checked the Revolutionary momentum toward equality and decentralization of authority. But their "conservative" regime actually embraced the central Revolutionary values of popular republican government and liberty, making the Constitution the permanent bedrock of American political values.

VARYING VIEWPOINTS

The Constitution: Revolutionary or Counterrevolutionary?

Although the Constitution has endured over two centuries as the basis of American government, historians have differed sharply over how to interpret its origins and meaning. Early historians of the Nationalist School like John Fiske viewed the Constitution as the logical culmination of the Revolution and a crucial step in the God-given progress of Anglo-Saxon peoples.

By the early twentieth century, however, the progressive historians had turned a more critical eye to the Constitution. For historians like Carl Becker and Charles Beard, the Constitution was part of a revolutionary struggle between the lower classes (small farmers, debtors, and laborers) and the upper classes (merchants, financiers, and manufacturers). Beard's *An Economic Interpretation of the Constitution of the United States* (1913) argued that the Articles of Confederation had protected debtors and displeased wealthy elites heavily invested in trade, the public debt, and manufacturing. Reviewing the economic holdings of the Framers, Beard argued that the Constitution represented a successful attempt by conservative elites to buttress their own economic supremacy at the expense of less fortunate Americans.

Beard's economic interpretation of the Constitution held sway through the 1940s. In the 1950s, however, this analysis fell victim to "consensus" historians such as Robert Brown and Forrest McDonald, who convincingly disputed Beard's evidence and argued that the Constitution derived from an emerging consensus that the country needed a stronger central government.

Scholars since the 1950s have searched for new ways to understand the origins of the Constitution. The most influential work has been Gordon Wood's *The Creation of the American Republic* (1969). Wood reinterpreted the ratification controversy as a struggle to define the true essence of republicanism. While antifederalists feared human corruption and, consequently, a strong central government, federalists believed that a strong, balanced government would rein in selfish human instincts and channel them toward pursuit of the common good. James Madison in particular (especially in *Federalist* No. 10) developed the novel idea of an "extensive republic," a polity that would achieve stability by virtue of its great size and diversity. In this sense, Wood argued, the Constitution represented a bold experiment—fulfillment, rather than the repudiation, of the most advanced ideas of the Revolutionary era—even though it emanated from traditional elites determined to curtail dangerous disruptions to the social order.

10

Launching the New Ship of State

—◆—

1789–1800

I SHALL ONLY SAY THAT I HOLD WITH MONTESQUIEU, THAT A
GOVERNMENT MUST BE FITTED TO A NATION, AS MUCH AS A
COAT TO THE INDIVIDUAL; AND, CONSEQUENTLY, THAT WHAT
MAY BE GOOD AT PHILADELPHIA MAY BE BAD AT PARIS, AND
RIDICULOUS AT PETERSBURG [RUSSIA].

ALEXANDER HAMILTON, 1799

America's new ship of state did not spread its sails to the most favorable breezes. Within twelve troubled years the American people had risen up and thrown overboard both the British yoke and the Articles of Confederation. A decade of lawbreaking and constitution smashing was not the best training for government making. Americans had come to regard central authority, replacing that of George III, as a necessary evil—something to be distrusted, watched, and curbed.

The finances of the infant government were likewise precarious. The revenue had declined to a trickle, whereas the **public debt,** with interest heavily in arrears, was mountainous. Worthless paper money, both state and national, was as plentiful as metallic money was scarce. Nonetheless, the Americans were brashly trying to erect a republic on an immense scale, something that no other people had attempted and that traditional political theory deemed impossible. The eyes of a skeptical world were on the upstart United States.

Focus Questions

1. How did George Washington's personal prestige and Alexander Hamilton's financial policies get the new federal government off to a strong beginning?
2. What were the policy differences between Hamilton and Thomas Jefferson within Washington's cabinet, and how did their disagreements lead to the formation of the first American political parties, the Federalists and Republicans?
3. How did the French Revolution and related events create conflict and polarization between Federalists and Republicans over American foreign policy, and how did President Washington maintain American neutrality?
4. How did the Alien and Sedition Acts reflect popular anti-French hysteria as well as Federalist political interests?
5. What were the underlying philosophical and political differences between Hamiltonian Federalists and Jeffersonian Republicans?

public debt *The debt of a government or nation to individual creditors, also called the national debt.*

census *An official count of population; in the United States, the federal census occurs every ten years.*

cabinet *The body of official advisers to the head of a government; in the United States, it consists of the heads of the major executive departments.*

Online Study Center

**Interactive map
African American Population, 1790**

college.hmco.com/pic/kennedy7e

Growing Pains

When the Constitution was launched in 1789, the Republic was continuing to grow at an amazing rate. Population was doubling about every twenty-five years, and the first official **census** of 1790, recorded almost 4 million people. Cities had blossomed proportionately: Philadelphia numbered 42,000; New York, 33,000; Boston, 18,000; Charleston, 16,000; and Baltimore, 13,000.

America's population was still about 90 percent rural, despite the flourishing cities. All but 5 percent of the people lived east of the Appalachian Mountains. The trans-Appalachian overflow was concentrated chiefly in Kentucky, Tennessee, and Ohio, all of which were welcomed as states within fourteen years. (Vermont had preceded them, becoming the fourteenth state in 1791.) Foreign visitors to the new Republic looked down their noses at the roughness and crudity resulting from ax-and-rifle pioneering life.

Washington for President

General Washington, the esteemed war hero, was unanimously drafted as president by the Electoral College in 1789—the only presidential nominee ever to be honored by unanimity.

His presence was imposing: 6 feet, 2 inches, 175 pounds, broad and sloping shoulders, strongly pointed chin, and pockmarks (from smallpox) on nose and cheeks. Much preferring the quiet of Mount Vernon to the turmoil of politics, he was perhaps the only president who did not in some way angle for this exalted office. Balanced rather than brilliant, he commanded his followers by strength of character rather than by the arts of the politician.

Washington's long journey from Mount Vernon to New York City, the temporary capital, was a triumphal procession. He was greeted by roaring cannon, pealing bells, flower-carpeted roads, and singing and shouting citizens. With appropriate ceremony, he solemnly and somewhat nervously took the oath of office on April 30, 1789, on a crowded balcony overlooking Wall Street.

Washington soon put his stamp on the new government by establishing the **cabinet.** The Constitution does not mention a cabinet; it merely provides that the president "may require" written opinions of the heads of the executive branch departments (see Art. II, Sec. II, para. 1). But this system proved so cumbersome that cabinet meetings gradually evolved during the Washington administration. At first only three department heads served under the president: Secretary of State Thomas Jefferson, Secretary of the Treasury Alexander Hamilton, and Secretary of War Henry Knox.

The Bill of Rights

The new nation faced some unfinished business. Many antifederalists had sharply criticized the Constitution drafted at Philadelphia for its failure to provide guarantees of individual rights such as freedom of religion and trial by jury. Many states had ratified the federal Constitution with the understanding that it would soon be amended to include such guarantees. Drawing up a bill of rights headed the list of imperatives facing the new government.

The proposed amendments were drafted and submitted to Congress by James Madison, whose intellectual and political skills were quickly making him the leading figure in the new body. Adopted by the necessary number of states in 1791, the first ten amendments to the Constitution, popularly known as the Bill of Rights, safeguard some of the most precious American principles. Among these are protections for freedom of religion, speech, and the press; the right to bear arms and to be tried by a jury; and the right to assemble and petition the government for redress of grievances. The Bill of Rights also prohibits cruel and unusual punishments and arbitrary government seizure of private property.

Chronology

1789	Constitution formally put into effect. Judiciary Act of 1789. Washington elected president. French Revolution begins.	**1794**	Whiskey Rebellion. Battle of Fallen Timbers. Jay's Treaty with Britain.
1790	First official census.	**1795**	Treaty of Greenville: Indians cede Ohio. Pinckney's Treaty with Spain.
1791	Bill of Rights adopted. Vermont becomes fourteenth state. Bank of the United States created. Excise tax passed.	**1796**	Washington's Farewell Address.
		1797	Adams becomes president. XYZ Affair.
1792	Washington reelected president.	**1798**	Alien and Sedition Acts.
1792- **1793**	Federalist and Democratic-Republican parties formed.	**1798-** **1799**	Kentucky and Virginia resolutions.
1793	Louis XVI beheaded; radical phase of French Revolution. Washington's Neutrality Proclamation. Citizen Genêt affair.	**1798-** **1800**	Undeclared war with France.
		1800	Convention of 1800: peace with France

To guard against the danger that enumerating such rights might lead to the conclusion that they were the only ones protected, Madison inserted the crucial Ninth Amendment. It declares that specifying certain rights "shall not be construed to deny or disparage others retained by the people." To reassure states' righters, he included the equally significant Tenth Amendment, which reserves all rights not explicitly delegated or prohibited by the federal Constitution "to the States respectively, or to the people." By preserving a strong central government while specifying certain protections for minority and individual liberties, Madison's amendments partially swung the federalist pendulum back in an antifederalist direction. (See Amendments I–X, in the Appendix.)

The first Congress also nailed other newly sawed governmental planks into place. It created effective federal courts under the Judiciary Act of 1789. The act organized the Supreme Court, with a chief justice and five associates, as well as federal district and **circuit courts,** and established the office of attorney general. New Yorker John Jay, Madison's collaborator on *The Federalist* papers, became the first chief justice of the United States.

circuit courts *A court that hears cases in several designated locations rather than a single place.*

fiscal *Concerning public finances—expenditures and revenues.*

Hamilton Revives the Corpse of Public Credit

The key figure in the new government was still smooth-faced Treasury Secretary Alexander Hamilton, a native of the British West Indies. Hamilton's genius was unquestioned, but critics claimed he loved his adopted country more than he loved his countrymen. Doubt about his character and his loyalty to the republican experiment always swirled about his head. Hamilton regarded himself as a kind of prime minister in Washington's cabinet, and on occasion he thrust his hands into the affairs of other departments, including that of his archrival, Secretary of State Thomas Jefferson.

A financial wizard, Hamilton set out immediately to correct the economic vexations that had crippled the Articles of Confederation. His plan was to shape the **fiscal** policies of the administration in such a way as to favor the wealthier groups. They, in turn, would gratefully lend the government monetary and political support. The new federal regime would flourish, the propertied classes would fatten, and prosperity would trickle down to the masses.

Evolution of the Cabinet

Position	Date Established	Comments
Secretary of state	1789	
Secretary of treasury	1789	
Secretary of war	1789	Loses cabinet status, 1947
Attorney general	1789	Not head of Justice Dept. until 1870
Secretary of navy	1798	Loses cabinet status, 1947
Postmaster general	1829	Loses cabinet status, 1970
Secretary of interior	1849	
Secretary of agriculture	1889	
Secretary of commerce and labor	1903	Office divided in 1913
Secretary of commerce	1913	
Secretary of labor	1913	
Secretary of defense	1947	Subordinate to this secretary, without cabinet rank, are secretaries of army, navy, and air force
Secretary of health, education, and welfare	1953	Office divided in 1979
Secretary of housing and urban development	1965	
Secretary of transportation	1966	
Secretary of energy	1977	
Secretary of health and human services	1979	
Secretary of education	1979	
Secretary of veterans affairs	1989	
Secretary of homeland security	2002	

The youthful financier's first objective was to bolster the national credit. Without public confidence in the government, Hamilton could not secure the funds with which to float his risky schemes. He therefore boldly urged Congress to "fund" the entire national debt "at par" and to assume completely the debts incurred by the states during the recent war.

"Funding at par" meant that the federal government would pay off its debts at face value, plus accumulated interest—a then-enormous total of more than $54 million. So many people believed the infant Treasury incapable of meeting those obligations that government bonds had depreciated to ten or fifteen cents on the dollar. Yet speculators held fistfuls of them, and when Congress passed Hamilton's measure in 1790, they grabbed for more. Some of them galloped into rural areas ahead of the news, buying for a song the depreciated paper holdings of farmers, war veterans, and widows.

Hamilton was willing, even eager, to have the new government shoulder additional obligations. While pushing the funding scheme, he urged Congress to assume the debts of the states, totaling some $21.5 million. The secretary made a convincing case for "**assumption**." The state debts could be regarded as a proper national obligation, for they had been incurred in the war for independence. But foremost in Hamilton's thinking was the belief that assumption would chain the states more tightly to the "federal chariot." Thus the secretary's maneuver would shift the attachment of wealthy creditors from the states to the federal government. The support of the rich for the national administration was a crucial link in Hamilton's political strategy of strengthening the central government.

States burdened with heavy debts, like Massachusetts, were delighted by Hamilton's proposal. States with small debts, like Virginia, were less charmed. The stage was set for some old-fashioned horse trading. Virginia did not want the state

assumption *The appropriation or taking on of obligations not originally one's own.*

debts assumed, but it did want the forthcoming federal district*—now the District of Columbia—to be located on the Potomac River. Hamilton persuaded a reluctant Jefferson to line up enough votes in Congress for assumption. In return, Virginia would have the federal district in its backyard. The bargain was carried through in 1790.

Customs Duties and Excise Taxes

> *One of the most eloquent tributes to Hamilton's apparent miracle working came from Daniel Webster (1782–1852) in the Senate (1831):*
>
> "He smote the rock of the national resources, and abundant streams of revenue gushed forth. He touched the dead corpse of public credit, and it sprung upon its feet."

The new ship of state thus set sail dangerously overloaded. The national debt had swelled to $75 million owing to Hamilton's insistence on honoring the outstanding federal and state obligations alike. But Hamilton, the "Father of the National Debt," was not greatly worried. His objectives were as much political as economic. He believed that, within limits, a national debt was a "national blessing"—a kind of union adhesive. The more creditors to whom the government owed money, the more people there would be with a personal stake in the success of his ambitious enterprise.

Where was the money to come from to pay interest on this huge debt and to run the government? Hamilton's first answer was customs duties, derived from a tariff. Tariff revenues, in turn, depended on a vigorous foreign trade, another crucial link in Hamilton's overall economic strategy for the new Republic.

The first tariff law, which imposed a low tariff of about 8 percent on dutiable imports, was speedily passed by Congress in 1789. Revenue was by far the main goal, but the measure was also designed to erect a low protective wall around infant industries, which bawled noisily for more shelter than they received. Hamilton had the vision to see that the industrial revolution would soon reach America, and he argued strongly in favor of more protection for the well-to-do manufacturing groups—another vital element in his economic program. But Congress was still dominated by agricultural and commercial interests, and it voted only two slight increases in the tariff during Washington's presidency.

Hamilton, with characteristic vigor, sought additional internal revenue and in 1791 secured from Congress an **excise** tax on a few domestic items, notably whiskey. The new levy of seven cents a gallon was borne chiefly by the distillers who lived in the mountains and backcountry. Whiskey flowed so freely on the frontier that it was used for money.

excise *A tax on the manufacture, sale, or consumption of certain products.*

Hamilton Battles Jefferson for a Bank

As the capstone for his financial system, Hamilton proposed a Bank of the United States. With the Bank of England as his model, he envisioned a private institution with the government as its major stockholder. The bank would provide a convenient strongbox for surplus federal funds, stimulate business by keeping money in circulation, and print an urgently needed sound paper currency.

Jefferson, whose written opinion on this question Washington requested, argued vigorously against the bank. The Constitution, he insisted, provided no specific authorization for such a financial octopus. He was convinced that all powers not specifically granted to the central government were reserved to the states, as provided in the about-to-be-ratified Bill of Rights (see Amendment X). He therefore concluded that the states, not Congress, had the power to charter banks. Believing that the Constitution should be interpreted "literally" or "strictly," Jefferson and his states' rights disciples zealously embraced the theory of "strict construction."

Hamilton, also at Washington's request, prepared a brilliantly reasoned reply to Jefferson's arguments. He boldly invoked the clause of the Constitution that

---

* Authorized by the Constitution, Art. I. Sec. VIII, para. 17.

■ Alexander Hamilton (1755–1804), by John Trumbull, 1792 He was one of the youngest and most brilliant of the Founding Fathers, who might have been president but for his ultraconservatism, a scandalous adultery, and a duelist's bullet. Hamilton favored a strong central government with a weak legislature to unify the infant nation and encourage industry. His chief rival, Thomas Jefferson, who extolled states' rights as a bulwark of liberty and thought the United States should remain an agricultural society, regarded Hamilton as a monarchist plotter and never forgave him for insisting that "the British Govt. was the best in the world: and that he doubted much whether any thing short of it would do in America."

medium of exchange *Any item, paper or otherwise, used as money.*

stipulates that Congress may pass any laws "necessary and proper" to carry out the powers vested in the various governmental agencies (see Art. I, Sec. VIII, para. 18). The government was explicitly empowered to collect taxes and regulate trade. In carrying out these basic functions, Hamilton argued, a national bank would be not only "proper" but "necessary." By inference or by implication—that is, by virtue of "implied powers"—Congress would be fully justified in establishing the Bank of the United States. In short, Hamilton contended for a "loose" or "broad" interpretation of the Constitution. He and his federalist followers thus evolved the theory of "loose construction" by invoking the "elastic clause" of the Constitution—a precedent for enormous federal powers.

Hamilton's financial views prevailed. Washington accepted his eloquent and realistic arguments and signed the bank measure into law. This explosive issue had been debated with much heat in Congress, where the old North-South cleavage still lurked ominously. The most enthusiastic support for the bank naturally came from the commercial and financial centers of the North; the strongest opposition arose from the agricultural South.

The Bank of the United States, as created by Congress in 1791, was chartered for twenty years. Located in Philadelphia, it was to have capital of $10 million, one-fifth of it owned by the federal government, the rest by private investors.

Mutinous Moonshiners in Pennsylvania

The Whiskey Rebellion, which flared up in southwestern Pennsylvania in 1794, sharply challenged the new national government. Hamilton's excise bore harshly on these homespun pioneer folk. They regarded it not as a tax on a luxury but as a burden on an economic necessity and a **medium of exchange.** Even preachers of the gospel were paid in "Old Monongahela rye." Defiant distillers finally erected whiskey poles, similar to the liberty poles of anti–stamp tax days in 1765, and raised the cry "Liberty and No Excise." Boldly tarring and feathering revenue officers, they brought collections to a halt.

President Washington, once a revolutionary, was alarmed by what he called these "self-created societies." With the hearty encouragement of Hamilton, he summoned the militia of several states. An army of about thirteen thousand men rallied to the colors, and two widely separated columns marched briskly forth in a gorgeous, leaf-tinted Indian summer. But when the troops reached the hills of western Pennsylvania, they found no insurrection. The "Whiskey Boys" were overawed, dispersed, or captured. Only three rebels were killed.

The Whiskey Rebellion was minuscule, but its consequences were mighty. George Washington's government, now substantially strengthened, commanded a new respect. Yet the foes of the administration condemned its brutal display of force—for using a sledgehammer to crush a gnat.

The Emergence of Political Parties

Almost overnight, Hamilton's fiscal feats had established the government's sound credit rating. The Treasury could now borrow needed funds in the Netherlands on favorable terms.

But Hamilton's financial successes—funding, assumption, the excise, the bank, suppression of the Whiskey Rebellion—created some political liabilities. All these schemes encroached sharply on states' rights. Many Americans, dubious about the Constitution in the first place, might never have approved it if they had foreseen how the states were going to be overshadowed by the federal colossus. Now, out of resentment against Hamilton's revenue-raising and centralizing policies, an organized opposition began to build. What once was a personal feud between Hamilton and Jefferson developed into a full-blown and frequently bitter political rivalry.

National political parties, in the modern sense, were unknown to America when George Washington took the inaugural oath. There had been Whigs and Tories, federalists and antifederalists, but these groups were factions rather than parties. They had sprung into existence over hotly contested special issues; they had faded away when their cause had triumphed or fizzled.

The Founders at Philadelphia had not envisioned the existence of permanent political parties. Organized opposition to the government seemed tainted with disloyalty, an affront to the spirit of national unity that the glorious cause of the Revolution had inspired.

The notion of a formal party apparatus was thus a novelty in the 1790s, and when Jefferson and Madison first organized their opposition to the Hamiltonian program, they did not anticipate creating a long-lived and popular party. But as their antagonism toward Hamilton stiffened, and as the amazingly boisterous and widely read newspapers of the day spread their political message, and Hamilton's, among the people, primitive semblances of political parties emerged.

The two-party system has existed in the United States since that time. Ironically, in light of the early suspicions about the very legitimacy of parties, their competition for power has actually proved to be among the indispensable ingredients of a sound democracy. The party out of power— "the loyal opposition"—traditionally plays the invaluable role of the balance wheel on the machinery of government, ensuring that politics never drifts too far out of kilter with the wishes of the people.

■ **Republicanism Triumphant** Artists often used classical motifs to celebrate the triumph in America of republicanism—a form of government they traced back to ancient Greece and Rome.

The Impact of the French Revolution

When Washington's first administration ended, early in 1793, domestic controversies had already formed two political camps—Hamiltonian Federalists and Jeffersonian Democratic-Republicans. As Washington's second term began, foreign-policy issues brought the differences between them to a fever pitch.

Only a few weeks after Washington's inauguration in 1789, the curtain had risen on the first act of the French Revolution. Twenty-six years were to pass before the seething continent of Europe collapsed into a peace of exhaustion. Few non-American events have left a deeper scar on American political and social life. In a sense the French Revolution was misnamed: it was a revolution that sent tremors through much of the civilized world.

Most Americans, loving liberty and deploring despotism, cheered the early, peaceful stages of the French Revolution, involving as it did a successful attempt to impose constitutional shackles on King Louis XVI. The Revolution entered a more ominous phase in 1792, when France declared war on hostile Austria. Late that year the electrifying news reached America that French citizen armies had hurled back the invading foreigners, and that France had proclaimed itself a republic. Americans enthusiastically sang the rousing revolutionary anthem "The Marseillaise" and renamed roads "Liberty Street" and "Equality Lane."

But centuries of pent-up poison could not be purged without baleful results. The guillotine was set up, the king was beheaded in 1793, the Roman Catholic Church was attacked, and the head-rolling Reign of Terror was begun. Back in America, God-fearing Federalist aristocrats nervously fingered their tender white necks and eyed the Jeffersonian masses apprehensively. Lukewarm Federalist approval of the early Revolution turned, almost overnight, to heated talk of "blood-drinking cannibals."

Sober-minded Jeffersonians regretted the bloodshed. But they felt, with Jefferson, that one could not expect to be carried from "**despotism** to liberty in a feather bed," and that a few thousand aristocratic heads were a cheap price to pay for human freedom.

Such approbation was shortsighted, for dire peril loomed ahead. The earlier battles of the French Revolution had not hurt America directly, but now Britain was sucked into the contagious conflict. The conflagration speedily spread to the New World, where it vividly affected the expanding young American republic.

despotism *Arbitrary or tyrannical rule.*

Washington's Neutrality Proclamation

Ominously, the Franco-American alliance of 1778 was still on the books, and many Jeffersonian Democratic-Republicans favored honoring the pact. Aflame with the liberal ideals of the French Revolution, red-blooded Jeffersonians were eager to enter the conflict against Britain, the recent foe, at the side of France, the recent friend.

But levelheaded President Washington was not swayed by the clamor of the crowd. Backed by Hamilton, he believed that war had to be avoided at all costs. Accordingly, Washington boldly issued his Neutrality Proclamation in 1793, shortly after the outbreak of war between Britain and France. This epochal document not only proclaimed the government's official neutrality in the widening conflict but sternly warned American citizens to be impartial toward both armed camps. As America's first formal declaration of aloofness from Old World quarrels, Washington's Neutrality Proclamation proved to be a major prop of the spreading isolationist tradition.

The pro-French Jeffersonians were enraged by the Neutrality Proclamation; the pro-British Federalists were heartened. Debate intensified when an impetuous, thirty-year-old representative of the French republic, Citizen Edmond Genêt, landed at Charleston, South Carolina. With unrestrained zeal, he undertook to outfit privateers and otherwise take advantage of the existing Franco-American alliance. Swept away by his enthusiastic reception by the Jeffersonian Democratic-Republicans, Genêt foolishly came to believe that the Neutrality Proclamation did not reflect the true wishes of the American people. He consequently embarked on an outrageously unneutral campaign to appeal over the head of "Old Washington" to the sovereign voters, and to recruit armies to invade Spanish Florida and British Canada. The president quickly demanded Genêt's withdrawal, and the Frenchman was replaced by a less impulsive emissary.

Embroilments with Britain

President Washington's far-visioned policy of neutrality was sorely tried by the British. For ten years they had been retaining the chain of northern frontier posts on U.S. soil, all in defiance of the peace treaty of 1783. British agents openly sold firearms and firewater to the Miami Confederacy, an alliance of eight Indian nations who attacked Americans invading their lands northwest of the Ohio River. In 1790 and 1791 Little Turtle's braves defeated armies led by Generals Josiah Harmer and Arthur St. Clair, handing the United States what remains one of its worst military defeats in the history of the frontier.

But in 1794 General "Mad Anthony" Wayne's army routed the Miamis at the Battle of Fallen Timbers. In the Treaty of Greenville, signed in August 1795, the confederacy gave up most of the present-day states of Ohio and Indiana. In exchange the Indians received monetary compensation, the right to hunt on the lands they had ceded, and what they hoped was recognition of their sovereign status.

On the sea frontier, the British were eager to starve out the French West Indies and naturally expected the United States to defend them under the Franco-American alliance. Hard-boiled commanders of the Royal Navy, acting under instructions from London in 1793, struck savagely. They seized about three hundred American merchant ships in the West Indies, **impressed** scores of seamen into service on British vessels, and threw hundreds of others into foul dungeons. A mighty outcry arose, chiefly from Jeffersonians, that America should once again fight George III in defense of its liberties.

President Washington, in a last desperate gamble to avert war, sent Chief Justice John Jay to London in 1794. The Jeffersonians were acutely unhappy over the choice, partly because they feared that so notorious a Federalist and Anglophile would sell out his country.

Unhappily, Jay entered the negotiations with weak cards and could win only a few concessions. The British did promise to evacuate the chain of posts on U.S. soil—a pledge that inspired little confidence, since it had been made before in Paris (to the same John Jay!) in 1783. In addition, Britain consented to pay damages for the recent seizures of American ships. But the British stopped short of pledging anything about future maritime seizures and impressments or about supplying arms to Indians.

When the Jeffersonians learned of Jay's concessions, their rage was fearful to behold. The treaty seemed like an abject surrender to Britain, as well as a betrayal of the Jeffersonian South. Jeffersonian mobs hanged, burned, and guillotined in effigy that "damn'd archtraitor, Sir John Jay." His unpopular pact, more than any other issue, vitalized the newborn Democratic-Republican party of Thomas Jefferson.

Jay's Treaty had other unforeseen consequences. Fearing that the treaty foreshadowed an Anglo-American alliance, Spain moved hastily to strike a deal with the United States. Pinckney's Treaty of 1795 with Spain granted the Americans virtually everything they demanded, including free navigation of the Mississippi and the large disputed territory north of Florida.

Exhausted after the diplomatic and partisan battles of his second term, President Washington decided to retire. His choice contributed powerfully to establishing a two-term tradition for American presidents.* In his Farewell Address to the nation in 1796, Washington strongly advised the avoidance of "permanent alliances" like the still-vexatious Franco-American treaty of 1778. Contrary to general misunderstanding, Washington did not oppose all alliances, but rather favored only "temporary alliances" for "extraordinary emergencies."

Washington's contributions as president were enormous, even though the sparkling Hamilton at times seemed to outshine him. The central government, its fiscal feet now under it, was solidly established. The West was expanding. The merchant marine was plowing the seas. Above all, Washington had kept the nation out of both overseas entanglements and foreign wars. The experimental stage had passed, and the presidential chair could now be turned over to a less impressive figure. But republics are notoriously ungrateful. When Washington left office in 1797, he was showered with the brickbats of partisan abuse, quite in contrast with the bouquets that had greeted his arrival.

■ **American Posts Held by the British After 1783**

---

impress *To force people or property into public service without choice; conscript.*

---

* This tradition, not broken until 1940 by Franklin D. Roosevelt, was made part of the Constitution in 1951 by the Twenty-second Amendment.

Although Thomas Jefferson (1743–1826) and John Adams hardly saw eye to eye, Jefferson displayed grudging respect for Adams in a piece of private correspondence in 1787:

"He is vain, irritable, and a bad calculator of the force and probable effect of the motives which govern men. This is all the ill which can possibly be said of him. He is as disinterested as the Being who made him."

John Adams Becomes President

Who should succeed the exalted "Father of His Country"? Alexander Hamilton was the best-known Federalist leader now that Washington had bowed out. But his financial policies, some of which had fattened speculators, had made him so unpopular that he could not hope to be elected president. The Federalists were forced to turn to Washington's experienced but ungracious vice president John Adams, a rugged chip off old Plymouth Rock. The Democratic-Republicans naturally rallied behind their master organizer and leader, Thomas Jefferson.

Political passions ran feverishly high in the presidential campaign of 1796. The lofty presence of Washington had hitherto imposed some restraints on partisan attacks; now the lid was off. Cultured Federalists referred to the Jeffersonians as "fire-eating salamanders, poison-sucking toads." Federalists and Democratic-Republicans even drank their ale in separate taverns. The Jeffersonians again assailed the too-forceful crushing of the Whiskey Rebellion and, above all, the negotiation of Jay's hated treaty.

John Adams, with most of his support in New England, squeezed through by the narrow margin of 71 votes to 68 in the Electoral College. Jefferson, as runner-up, became vice president.* One of the ablest statesmen of his day, Adams at sixty-two was bald, short, and thickset ("His Rotundity"). He impressed observers as a man of stern principles who did his duty with stubborn devotion. Although learned and upright, he was a tactless and prickly intellectual aristocrat with no appeal to the masses and no desire to cultivate any. Many citizens regarded him with "respectful irritation."

The crusty New Englander suffered from other handicaps. He had stepped into Washington's shoes, which no successor could hope to fill. In addition, Adams was hated by Hamilton, who now headed the pro-war faction of the Federalist party. The famed financier even secretly plotted with certain members of the cabinet against the new president, who soon had a conspiracy rather than a cabinet on his hands. Most ominous of all, Adams inherited a violent quarrel with France—a quarrel whose gunpowder lacked only a spark.

Unofficial Fighting with France

The French were infuriated by Jay's Treaty. They condemned it as the initial step toward an American alliance with Britain, their perpetual foe. French warships, in retaliation, seized about three hundred defenseless American merchant vessels by mid-1797.

President Adams kept his head, temporarily, even though the nation was mightily aroused. Trying to reach an agreement with the French, he appointed a diplomatic commission of three men, including John Marshall, the future chief justice. When Adams's envoys reached Paris in 1797, they were secretly approached by three French go-betweens, later referred to as X, Y, and Z in the published dispatches. The French spokesmen demanded an unneutral loan of 32 million florins, plus what amounted to a bribe of $250,000, for the privilege of merely talking with Talleyrand, the French foreign minister.

These terms were intolerable. The American trio knew that bribes were standard diplomatic devices in Europe, but they gagged at paying a quarter of a million dollars for mere talk, without any assurances of a settlement. Negotiations quickly broke down.

---

* The possibility of such an inharmonious two-party combination in the future was removed by the Twelfth Amendment to the Constitution in 1804. (See text in the Appendix.)

War hysteria swept through the United States, catching up even President Adams. The slogan of the hour became "Millions for defense, but not one cent for tribute." Despite considerable Jeffersonian opposition in Congress, war preparations were pushed along at a feverish pace. The Navy Department was created, the three-ship navy expanded, and the United States Marine Corps re-established (it had been created in 1775 but disbanded after the Revolutionary War).

Bloodshed was confined to the sea, principally in the West Indies. In two and a half years of undeclared hostilities (1798–1800), American privateers and men of-war of the new navy captured over eighty armed vessels flying the French colors, though several hundred Yankee merchant ships were lost to the enemy. Only a slight push, it seemed, might plunge both nations into a full-dress war.

Adams Puts Patriotism Above Party

Embattled France, its hands full in Europe, wanted no war. An outwitted Talleyrand realized that to fight the United States would add one more foe to his enemy roster. He therefore let it be known, through roundabout channels, that if the Americans would send a new minister, he would be received with proper respect.

Despite the popular acclaim that he might have enjoyed by leading the nation into a full-fledged war, Adams exploded a bombshell in early 1799 by sending to the Senate the name of a new minister to France. Hamilton and his war-hawk faction were enraged. But public opinion—Jeffersonian and reasonable Federalist alike—was favorable to one last try for peace.

America's envoys (now three) found the political skies brightening when they reached Paris early in 1800. The ambitious "Little Corporal," the Corsican Napoleon Bonaparte, had recently seized dictatorial power. He was eager to free his hands of the American squabble so that he might continue to redraw the map of Europe and perhaps create a New World empire in Louisiana. The afflictions and ambitions of the Old World were again working to America's advantage.

After a great deal of haggling, a memorable treaty known as the Convention of 1800 was signed in Paris. France agreed to annul the twenty-two-year-old

■ **Preparation for War to Defend Commerce: The Building of the Frigate *Philadelphia*** In 1803 this frigate ran onto the rocks near Tripoli harbor, and about three hundred officers and men were imprisoned by the Tripolitans. The ship was refloated for service against the Americans, but Stephen Decatur led a party of men that set it afire.

marriage of (in)convenience, but as a kind of alimony the United States agreed to pay the damage claims of American shippers. So ended the nation's only peacetime military alliance for a century and a half. Its troubled history does much to explain the traditional antipathy of the American people to foreign entanglements.

John Adams, flinty to the end, deserves immense credit for his belated push for peace, even though he was moved in part by jealousy of Hamilton. Adams not only avoided the hazards of war but unwittingly smoothed the path for the peaceful purchase of Louisiana three years later. If America had drifted into a full-blown war with France in 1800, Napoleon would not have sold Louisiana to Jefferson on any terms in 1803.

President Adams, the bubble of his popularity pricked by peace, was aware of his signal contribution to the nation. He later suggested as the epitaph for his tombstone (not used), "Here lies John Adams, who took upon himself the responsibility of peace with France in the year 1800."

The Federalist Witch Hunt

Exulting Federalists had meanwhile capitalized on the anti-French frenzy to drive through Congress in 1798 a sheaf of laws designed to muffle or minimize their Jeffersonian foes.

The first of these oppressive laws was aimed at supposedly pro-Jeffersonian "aliens." The Federalist Congress, hoping to discourage the "dregs" of Europe, erected a disheartening barrier. They raised the residence requirements for aliens who desired to become citizens from a tolerable five years to an intolerable fourteen. This drastic new law violated the traditional American policy of open-door hospitality and speedy **assimilation.**

Two additional Alien Laws struck heavily at undesirable immigrants. The president was empowered to deport dangerous foreigners in time of peace and to deport or imprison them in time of hostilities. This was an arbitrary grant of executive power contrary to American tradition and to the spirit of the Constitution, even though the stringent Alien Laws were never enforced.

The "lockjaw" Sedition Act, the last measure of the harsh Federalist clampdown, was a direct slap at two priceless freedoms guaranteed in the Constitution by the Bill of Rights in the First Amendment—freedom of speech and freedom of the press. This law provided that anyone who impeded the policies of the government or falsely defamed its officials, including the president, would be liable to a heavy fine and imprisonment.

Many outspoken Jeffersonian editors were indicted under the Sedition Act. Ten were brought to trial and convicted by packed juries swayed by prejudiced Federalist judges. Among them was Vermont congressman Matthew Lyon (the "Spitting Lion"), who had earlier gained fame by spitting in the face of a Federalist and fighting on the floor of Congress.

The Sedition Act seemed to be in direct conflict with the Constitution. But the Supreme Court, dominated by Federalists, was of no mind to declare this Federalist law unconstitutional. (The law expired in March 1801.) This attempt by the Federalists to crush free speech and silence the opposition party undoubtedly made many converts for the Jeffersonians.

Yet the Alien and Sedition Acts, despite pained outcries from the Jeffersonians they muzzled, commanded widespread popular support. Anti-French hysteria played directly into the hands of **witch-hunting** conservatives. In the congressional elections of 1798–1799, the Federalists, riding a wave of popularity, scored the most sweeping victory of their entire history.

assimilation *The merging of diverse cultures or peoples into one.*

witch-hunting *An investigation carried on with much publicity, supposedly to uncover dangerous activity but actually intended to weaken the political opposition.*

In 1800 James Callender (1758–1803) published a pamphlet that assailed the president in strong language. For blasts like the following tirade, Callender was prosecuted under the Sedition Act, fined $250, and sentenced to prison for nine months:

"The reign of Mr. Adams has, hitherto, been one continued tempest of *malignant* passions. As president, he has never opened his lips, or lifted his pen, without threatening and scolding. The grand object of his administration has been to exasperate the rage of contending parties, to calumniate and destroy every man who differs from his opinions. . . . Every person holding an office must either quit it, or think and vote exactly with Mr. Adams."

The Virginia (Madison) and Kentucky (Jefferson) Resolutions

Resentful Jeffersonians naturally refused to take the Alien and Sedition Acts lying down. Jefferson himself feared that if the Federalists managed to choke free speech and free press, they would then wipe out other precious constitutional guarantees. His own fledgling political party might even be stamped out of existence.

Fearing prosecution for sedition, Jefferson secretly penned a series of resolutions, which the Kentucky legislature approved in 1798 and 1799. His friend and fellow Virginian James Madison drafted a similar but less extreme statement, which was adopted by the Virginia legislature in 1798.

Both Jefferson and Madison stressed the compact theory—a theory popular among English political philosophers in the seventeenth and eighteenth centuries. As applied to America by the Jeffersonians, this concept meant that the thirteen sovereign states, in creating the federal government, had entered into a "**compact**," or contract, regarding its jurisdiction. The national government was consequently the agent or creation of the states. Since water can rise no higher than its source, the individual states were the final judges of whether their agent had broken the "compact" by overstepping the authority originally granted. Invoking this logic, Jefferson's Kentucky resolutions concluded that the federal regime *had* exceeded its constitutional powers and that, with regard to the Alien and Sedition Acts, "**nullification**" was the "rightful remedy."

The Virginia and Kentucky resolutions were a brilliant formulation of the extreme states' rights view regarding the Union—indeed more sweeping in their implications than their authors had intended. They were later used by southerners to support nullification—and ultimately secession. Yet neither Jefferson nor Madison, as Founding Fathers of the Union, had any intention of breaking it up: they were groping for ways to preserve it. Their resolutions were basically campaign documents designed to crystallize opposition to the Federalist party and to unseat it in the upcoming presidential election of 1800. The only real nullification that Jefferson had in view was the nullification of Federalist abuses.

compact *An agreement or covenant between states to perform some legal act.*

nullification *In American politics, the assertion that a state may legally invalidate a federal act deemed inconsistent with its rights or sovereignty.*

Federalists Versus Democratic-Republicans

As the presidential contest of 1800 approached, the differences between Federalists and Democratic-Republicans were sharply etched. As might be expected, most federalists of the pre-Constitutional period (1787–1789) became Federalists in the 1790s. Largely welded by Hamilton into an effective group by 1793, they openly advocated rule by the "best people." "Those who own the country," remarked Federalist John Jay, "ought to govern it." With their intellectual arrogance and Tory tastes, Hamiltonians distrusted full-blown democracy as the fountain of all mischiefs and feared the "swayability" of the untutored common folk.

Hamiltonian Federalists also advocated a strong central government with the power to crush democratic excesses like Shays's Rebellion, protect the lives and estates of the wealthy, and subordinate the sovereignty-loving states. They believed the national government should support private enterprise but not interfere with it. This attitude came naturally to the seaboard merchants, manufacturers, and shippers who made up the majority of Federalist support. Farther inland, few Hamiltonians dwelled.

Leading the anti-Federalists, who eventually came to be known as Democratic-Republicans or sometimes simply Republicans, was Thomas Jefferson. Lanky and relaxed in appearance, lacking personal aggressiveness, and unable to deliver a rabble-rousing speech, he became a master political organizer through his ability to lead people rather than drive them. His strongest appeal was to the middle class and to the underprivileged—the "dirt" farmers, the laborers, the artisans, and the small shopkeepers.

Liberal-thinking Jefferson, with his aristocratic head set on a farmer's frame, was a bundle of inconsistencies. By one set of tests he should have been a

■ Monticello, Jefferson's Self-Designed Architectural Marvel

Federalist, for he was a Virginia aristocrat and slave-owner who lived in an imposing hilltop mansion at Monticello. A so-called traitor to his own upper class, Jefferson cherished uncommon sympathy for the common people, especially the downtrodden, the oppressed, and the persecuted. As he wrote in 1800, "I have sworn upon the altar of God eternal hostility against every form of tyranny over the mind of man."

Jeffersonian Democratic-Republicans demanded a weak central regime. They believed that the best government was one that governed least, and that the bulk of power should be retained by the states. There the people could keep a more vigilant eye on their public servants. The national debt should be paid off, and government should provide no special privileges for special classes, especially manufacturers. Agriculture, to Jefferson, was the favored branch of the economy and formed the foundation of his political thought. "Those who labor in the earth are the chosen people of God," he said. Most of his followers naturally came from the agricultural South and Southwest.

Above all, Jefferson advocated the rule of the people. But he did not propose thrusting the ballot into the hands of every adult white male. He favored government *for* the people but not by *all* the people. Since the ignorant were incapable of self-government, only people literate enough to inform themselves about citizenship should have the ballot. Universal education would have to precede universal suffrage. Jefferson had a profound faith in the reasonableness and teachableness of the masses and in their collective wisdom when taught.

Landlessness among American citizens threatened popular democracy as much as illiteracy, in Jefferson's eyes. He feared that propertyless dependents would be political pawns in the hands of their landowning superiors. How could the emergence of a landless class of voters be avoided? The answer, in part, was by slavery. A system of black slave labor ensured that southern white yeoman farmers would remain independent landowners and not be forced to labor for low wages in others' tobacco and rice fields. Jefferson thus tortuously reconciled slaveholding—his own included—with his more democratic impulses.

Yet for his time, Jefferson's confidence that white, free men could become responsible and knowledgeable citizens was open-minded. He championed freedom of speech, for without free speech and a free press, the misdeeds of tyranny could not be exposed. Although Jefferson suffered much foul abuse from editorial pens, he said that he would choose "newspapers without a government" rather than "a government without newspapers."

Differences over foreign policy defined another sharp distinction between Hamilton and Jefferson. Hamilton looked outward and eastward. He sought to build a strong national state that would assert America's commercial interests and expand foreign trade, especially with Britain. Jeffersonian Republicans, unlike "British bootlickers," were basically pro-French. They earnestly believed that it was to America's advantage to support the liberal ideals of the French Revolution rather than reactionary British Tories. Jefferson, in effect, faced inward and westward. His priorities were to strengthen democracy at home, especially in the frontier regions beyond the Appalachians, rather than to flex America's muscles abroad.

So as the young Republic's first full decade of nationhood came to a close, the Founders' hopes seemed already imperiled. Conflicts over domestic politics and foreign policy undermined the unity of the Revolutionary era and called into question the very viability of the American experiment in democracy. As the presidential election of 1800 approached, the danger loomed that the fragile and battered American ship of state would founder on the rocks of controversy. The shores of history are littered with the wreckage of nascent nations torn asunder before they could grow to stable maturity. Why should the United States expect to enjoy a happier fate?

Thomas Jefferson's vision of a republican America was peopled with virtuous farmers, not factory hands. As early as 1784, he wrote:

"While we have land to labor then, let us never wish to see our citizens occupied at a work-bench, or twirling a distaff. . . . For the general operations of manufacture, let our workshops remain in Europe. . . . The mobs of great cities add just so much to the support of pure government, as sores do to the strength of the human body."

⭐ Chapter Summary ⭐

The fledgling federal government under the new Constitution faced severe difficulties and deep skepticism about its durability, especially because traditional political theory held that large-scale republics were bound to fail. But President Washington brought credibility to the new government, while his cabinet, led by Alexander Hamilton, strengthened its political and economic foundations.

The government's first achievements were the Bill of Rights and Hamilton's financial system. Through effective leadership, Hamilton carried out his program of funding the national debt, assuming state debts, imposing customs and excise taxes, and establishing a Bank of the United States.

The bank was the most controversial part of Hamilton's program because it raised basic constitutional issues. Opposition to the bank from Jefferson and his followers reflected more fundamental political disagreements about republicanism, economics, federal power, and foreign policy. As the French Revolution evolved from moderation to radicalism, it intensified the ideological divisions between the pro-French Jeffersonians and the pro-British Hamiltonians. Their disagreements solidified into the first American political parties, the Republicans and the Federalists—a development not anticipated in the Constitution.

Washington's Neutrality Proclamation angered Republicans, who wanted America to aid Revolutionary France. Washington's policy was sorely tested by the British, who routinely violated American neutrality. In order to avoid war, Washington endorsed the conciliatory Jay's Treaty, further outraging the Jeffersonian Republicans in the United States as well as revolutionary France.

After the humiliating XYZ affair, the United States began to fight a "quasi-war" with France, but President John Adams sacrificed his political popularity and divided his party by choosing to negotiate peace.

These foreign-policy disagreements deeply embittered domestic politics: Federalists passed the repressive Alien and Sedition Acts, to which Jefferson and Madison responded with the Virginia and Kentucky resolutions, which challenged federal authority.

11

The Triumphs and Travails of the Jeffersonian Republic

⎯⎯ ❦ ⎯⎯

1800–1812

TIMID MEN . . . PREFER THE CALM OF DESPOTISM
TO THE BOISTEROUS SEA OF LIBERTY.

THOMAS JEFFERSON, 1796

In the critical presidential election of 1800, the first in which Federalists and Democratic-Republicans functioned as two national political parties, John Adams and Thomas Jefferson again squared off against each other. The choice seemed clear and dramatic. Adams's Federalists waged a defensive struggle for a strong central government and public order. Their Jeffersonian opponents presented themselves as the guardians of agrarian purity, liberty, and states' rights.

The next dozen years, however, would turn what seemed like a clear-cut choice in 1800 into a messier reality, as the Jeffersonians in power were confronted with a series of opportunities and crises requiring the assertion of federal authority. As the first challengers successfully to rout a reigning party, the Republicans were also the first to learn that it is far easier to condemn from the stump than to govern consistently.

Focus Questions

1. How did Jefferson adapt his principles and ideals to practical realities as he carried out the "Revolution of 1800"?
2. Why did Republicans and Federalists clash so sharply over the judiciary, and how did John Marshall perpetuate Federalist principles on the Supreme Court?
3. What were Jefferson's basic foreign-policy goals, and how successful was he in achieving them?
4. What were the causes and effects of the Louisiana Purchase?
5. How did America become embroiled in the turbulent crisis of the Napoleonic Wars, and why did President Madison see a new war with Britain as essential to maintaining America's republican experiment?

Chronology

1800	Jefferson defeats Adams for presidency.	**1805– 1807**	Pike's explorations.
1801	Judiciary Act of 1801.	**1806**	Burr treason trial.
1801– 1805	Naval war with Tripoli.	**1807**	*Chesapeake* affair. Embargo Act.
1802	Revised naturalization law. Judiciary Act of 1801 repealed.	**1809**	Non-Intercourse Act replaces Embargo Act.
1803	*Marbury* v. *Madison*. Louisiana Purchase.	**1810**	Macon's Bill No. 2. Napoleon announces (falsely) repeal of blockade decrees. Madison reestablishes nonimportation against Britain.
1804	Jefferson reelected president.		
1804– 1806	Lewis and Clark expedition.	**1811**	Battle of Tippecanoe.
1805	Peace treaty with Tripoli.	**1812**	United States declares war on Britain.

Federalist and Republican Mudslingers

In fighting for survival, the Federalists labored under heavy handicaps. Their Alien and Sedition Acts had aroused a host of enemies, although most of these critics were dyed-in-the-wool Jeffersonians anyhow. The Hamiltonian wing of the Federalist party, robbed of its glorious war with France, split openly with President Adams, and Hamilton himself attacked the president.

The most damaging blow to the Federalists, however, was the refusal of Adams to give them a rousing fight with France. Their feverish war preparations had swelled the public debt and required disagreeable new taxes, including a stamp tax. After all these unpopular measures, the war scare had petered out, and the country was left with an all-dressed-up-but-no-place-to-go feeling.

Thrown on the defensive, the Federalists concentrated their fire on Jefferson himself, who became the victim of one of America's earliest "whispering campaigns." He was accused of having robbed a widow and her children of a trust fund and of having fathered numerous mulatto children by his own slave women. (Jefferson's long-rumored intimacy with his slave Sally Hemings has recently been confirmed by DNA testing; see "Examining the Evidence," p. 149.) As a liberal in religion, Jefferson had earlier incurred the wrath of the orthodox clergy, largely through his successful struggle to separate church and state in Virginia. From the New England stronghold of Federalism and Congregationalism, preachers thundered against his alleged atheism. Old ladies of Federalist families, fearing Jefferson's election, even buried their Bibles or hung them in wells.

Online Study Center

Primary source
Jefferson Campaign Poster
college.hmco.com/pic/kennedybrief7e

The Jeffersonian "Revolution of 1800"

Jefferson won by a majority of 73 electoral votes to 65. In defeat, the colorless and presumably unpopular Adams polled more electoral strength than he had gained four years earlier—except for New York. The Empire State fell into the Jeffersonian basket, and with it the election, largely because Aaron Burr, a master wire-puller, turned New York to Jefferson by the narrowest of margins. The Virginian polled the bulk of his strength in the South and West, particularly in those states where universal white manhood suffrage had been adopted.

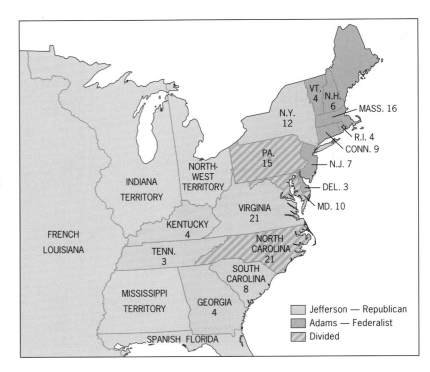

■ **Presidential Election of 1800 (with electoral vote by state)** New York was the key state in this election, and Aaron Burr helped to swing it away from the Federalists with tactics that anticipated the political machines of a later day. Federalists complained that Burr "travels every night from one meeting of Republicans to another, haranguing . . . them to the most zealous exertions. [He] can stoop so low as to visit every low tavern that may happen to be crowded with his dear fellow citizens." But Burr proved that the price was worth it. "We have beat you," Burr told kid-gloved Federalists after the election, "by superior Management."

lame duck *A political official during the time he or she remains in office after an electoral defeat or legal inability to seek another term, and whose power is therefore diminished.*

Decisive in Jefferson's victory was the three-fifths clause of the Constitution. By counting three-fifths of the slave population for the purposes of congressional and Electoral College representations, the Constitution gave white southern voters a bonus that helped Jefferson win the White House. Northern critics fumed that Jefferson was an illegitimate embodiment of the "slave power" that southern states wielded in the Union.

Jeffersonian joy was dampened by an unexpected deadlock. Through a technicality Jefferson, the presidential candidate, and Burr, his vice-presidential running mate, received the same number of electoral votes for the presidency. Under the Constitution the tie could be broken only by the House of Representatives (see Art. II, Sec. I, para. 2). This body would be controlled for several more months by the **lame duck** Federalists, who preferred Burr to the hated Jefferson.*

Voting in the House moved slowly to a climax as exhausted representatives snored in their seats. The agonizing deadlock was broken at last when a few Federalists, despairing of electing Burr and hoping for moderation from Jefferson, refrained from voting. The election then went to the rightful candidate. John Adams proved to be the last Federalist president of the United States, and his party sank slowly into political oblivion and ultimately disappeared.

Jefferson later claimed that the election of 1800 was a "revolution" comparable to that of 1776. But it was no revolution in the sense of a massive popular upheaval or an upending of the political system, for Jefferson had only narrowly squeaked through to victory. Jefferson meant that his election represented a return to what he considered the original spirit of the Revolution. In his eyes, Hamilton and Adams had betrayed the ideals of 1776 and 1787. Jefferson's mission, as he saw it, was to restore the republican experiment, to check the growth of government, and to halt the decay of virtue that had set in under Federalist rule.

No less "revolutionary" was the peaceful and orderly transfer of power on the basis of an election whose results all parties accepted. This was a remarkable achievement for a raw young nation, especially after all the partisan bitterness that had agitated the country during Adams's presidency. After a decade of division and doubt, Americans could take justifiable pride in the vigor of their experiment in democracy.

---

*A "lame duck" has been humorously defined as a politician whose goose has been cooked at the recent elections. The possibility of another such tie was removed by the Twelfth Amendment in 1804 (for text, see the Appendix). Before then, each elector had two votes, and the second-place finisher became the vice president.

EXAMINING THE EVIDENCE

The Thomas Jefferson–Sally Hemings Controversy
Debate over whether Thomas Jefferson had sexual relations with Sally Hemings, a slave at Monticello, began as early as 1802, when James Callender published the first accusations and Federalist newspapers gleefully broadcast them throughout the country. Two years later this print, "The Philosophic Cock," attacked Jefferson by depicting him as a rooster and Hemings as a hen. The rooster, or cock, was also a symbol of revolutionary France. Jefferson's enemies sought to discredit him for personal indiscretions as well as radical sympathies. Although he resolutely denied any affair with Hemings, a charge that at first seemed only to be a politically motivated defamation refused to go away. In the 1870s two new oral sources of evidence came to light. Madison Hemings, Sally's next-to-last child, claimed that his mother had identified Jefferson as the father of all five of her children. Soon thereafter James Parton's biography of Jefferson revealed that among Jefferson's white descendants it was said that his nephew had fathered all or most of Sally's children. In the 1950s several large publishing projects on Jefferson's life and writings uncovered new evidence and inspired renewed debate. Most convincing was Dumas Malone's calculation that Jefferson had been present at Monticello nine months prior to the birth of each of Sally's children. Speculation continued throughout the rest of the century, with little new evidence, until scientific advances made possible DNA testing of the remains of Jefferson's white and possible black descendents to establish paternity. Two centuries after James Callender first cast aspersions on Jefferson's morality, cutting-edge science helped establish the high probability that Jefferson had fathered Sally's youngest son and the likelihood that he was the father of all of her children.

1. Are there ways that historians can use unproven rumors and charges made during political campaigns—such as those leveled against Thomas Jefferson regarding Sally Hemings—to better understand a person or event, even if the accusations themselves are false or unproven? Or should such material be totally disregarded?

2. Which piece of "unscientific" historical information that existed in the nineteenth and early twentieth centuries regarding Jefferson's affair with Sally Hemings was most persuasive: the oral traditions of a liaison within both the Hemings and Jefferson families, or the recorded evidence that Jefferson had been at Monticello nine months before the birth of each of Hemings's five children? How should historians treat such material?

3. How might the scientific evidence strongly suggest that Jefferson did father Hemings's children alter historians' perceptions of Jefferson, his political opponents, and the larger issues of race relations?

> The toleration of Thomas Jefferson (1743–1826) was reflected in his inaugural address:
>
> "If there be any among us who would wish to dissolve this Union or to change its republican form, let them stand undisturbed as monuments of the safety with which error of opinion may be tolerated where reason is left free to combat it."

■ **Jefferson in Casual Attire** As befitted a champion of the new democracy, Jefferson typically dressed casually, shunning the sartorial pretensions affected by many Federalists.

precedent *In law and government, a decision or action that establishes a sanctioned rule for determining similar cases in the future.*

Responsibility Breeds Moderation

"Long Tom" Jefferson was inaugurated president on March 4, 1801, in the swampy village of Washington, the crude new national capital. Tall (six feet two and a half inches), with large hands and feet, red hair ("the Red Fox"), and prominent cheekbones and chin, he was an arresting figure. Believing that the customary pomp did not befit his democratic ideals, he spurned a horse-drawn coach and strode to the Capitol from his boardinghouse.

Jefferson's inaugural address, beautifully phrased, was a classic statement of democratic principles. Seeking to allay Federalist fears of a bull-in-the-china-shop overturn, Jefferson ingratiatingly intoned, "We are all Republicans, we are all Federalists." As for foreign affairs, he pledged "honest friendship with all nations, entangling alliances with none."

With its rustic setting, Washington lent itself admirably to the simplicity and frugality of the Jeffersonian Republicans. In this respect, it contrasted sharply with the elegant atmosphere of Federalist Philadelphia, the former temporary capital.

As president, Jefferson was shockingly unconventional. He would receive callers in sloppy attire—once in a dressing gown and slippers. He started the **precedent,** unbroken until Woodrow Wilson's presidency 112 years later, of sending messages to Congress to be read by a clerk. Personal appearances, in the Federalist manner, suggested too strongly a monarchical speech from the throne.

As if compelled by an evil twin, Jefferson was forced to reverse many of the political principles he had so vigorously championed. There were in fact two Thomas Jeffersons. One was the scholarly private citizen who philosophized in his study. The other was the harassed public official, who made the disturbing discovery that bookish theories worked out differently in the noisy arena of practical politics. The open-minded Virginian was therefore consistently inconsistent; it is easy to quote one Jefferson to refute the other.

Jefferson quickly proved an able politician. He was especially effective in the informal atmosphere of a dinner party, where he would woo congressional representatives while personally pouring imported wines and serving French food. In part, Jefferson had to rely on his charm because his party was so weak-jointed. Jefferson's refusal to practice widespread patronage made it difficult for Democratic-Republicans to build a political following. Opposition to the Federalists was the chief glue holding them together, and as the Federalists faded, so did Republican unity. The era of well-developed, well-disciplined political parties still lay in the future.

At the outset, Jefferson was determined to undo the Federalist abuses begotten by the anti-French hysteria. The hated Alien and Sedition Acts had already expired. The incoming president speedily pardoned the "martyrs" serving sentences under the Sedition Act. Shortly after Congress met, the Jeffersonians enacted the new naturalization law of 1802, which reduced the requirement of fourteen years of residence to a more reasonable five years.

Jefferson actually kicked away only one substantial prop of the Hamiltonian economic system. He hated the excise tax, which bred bureaucrats and bore heavily on his farmer following, and he early persuaded Congress to repeal it. But except for excising the excise tax, Jefferson and his talented treasury secretary, Albert Gallatin, left the Hamiltonian framework essentially intact. They launched no attack on the Bank of the United States, nor did they repeal the mildly protective Federalist tariff.

Paradoxically, Jefferson's moderation thus further cemented the gains of the "Revolution of 1800." By shrewdly absorbing many major Federalist programs, Jefferson showed that a change of regime need not be disastrous for the defeated group. His restraint pointed the way toward the two-party system that was later to become a characteristic feature of American politics.

The "Dead Clutch" of the Judiciary

The "deathbed" Judiciary Act of 1801 was one of the last important laws passed by the expiring Federalist Congress. It created sixteen new federal judgeships and other judicial offices. President Adams remained at his desk until nine o'clock in the evening on his last day in office, supposedly signing the **commissions** of the Federalist "midnight judges."

This Federalist-sponsored Judiciary Act, though a long-overdue reform, aroused bitter resentment. "Packing" of these lifetime posts with anti-Jeffersonian partisans was, in Republican eyes, a brazen attempt by the ousted party to entrench itself in one of the three powerful branches of government. Jeffersonians condemned the last-minute appointees in violent language.

The newly elected Republican Congress bestirred itself to repeal the Judiciary Act of 1801 in the year after its passage. Jeffersonians thus swept sixteen benches from under their recently appointed midnight judges.

Jeffersonians likewise had their knives sharpened for the scalp of Chief Justice John Marshall, whom Adams had appointed to the Supreme Court in the dying days of his term. The strong-willed Marshall, with his rasping voice and steel-trap mind, was Thomas Jefferson's cousin. As a lifelong Federalist and fervent advocate of a powerful central government, Marshall was cordially disliked by the states' rights Jeffersonians. The Federalist party died out, but Marshall lived on, handing down Federalist decisions serenely for thirty-four years under Democratic-Republican administrations. For over three decades, the ghost of Alexander Hamilton spoke through the lanky, black-robed judge.

One of the "midnight judges" of 1801 presented John Marshall with a historic opportunity. When obscure William Marbury, whom President Adams had named a justice of the peace for the District of Columbia, learned that his commission was being shelved by the new Secretary of State James Madison, he sued for its delivery. Chief Justice John Marshall knew that his Jeffersonian rivals, entrenched in the executive branch, would hardly spring forward to enforce a **writ** to deliver the commission to his fellow Federalist Marbury. He therefore dismissed Marbury's suit, avoiding a direct showdown. But the wily Marshall snatched victory from the jaws of this judicial defeat. In explaining his ruling, Marshall said that the part of the Judiciary Act of 1789 on which Marbury tried to base his appeal was unconstitutional. The act had attempted to assign to the Supreme Court powers that the Constitution had not foreseen.

In this self-denying opinion, Marshall greatly magnified the authority of the Court—and slapped at the Jeffersonians. Until the case of *Marbury* v. *Madison* (1803), controversy had clouded the question of who had the final authority to determine the meaning of the Constitution.

commission *The official legal authorization appointing a person to an office or military position, indicating the nature of the duty, term of office, chain of command, and so on.*

writ *A formal legal document ordering or prohibiting some act.*

In his decision in Marbury *v.* Madison, *Chief Justice John Marshall (1755–1835) vigorously asserted his view that the Constitution embodied a "higher" law than ordinary legislation, and that the Court must interpret the Constitution:*

"The Constitution is either a superior paramount law, unchangeable by ordinary means, or it is on a level with ordinary legislative acts, and like other acts, is alterable when the legislature shall please to alter it.

"If the former part of the alternative be true, then a legislative act contrary to the constitution is not law; if the latter part be true, then written constitutions are absurd attempts, on the part of the people, to limit a power in its own nature illimitable. . . .

"It is emphatically the province and duty of the judicial department to say what the law is. . . .

"If, then, the courts are to regard the Constitution, and the Constitution is superior to any ordinary act of the legislature, the Constitution, and not such ordinary act, must govern the case to which they are both applicable."

Jefferson in the Kentucky resolutions (1798) had tried to assign that right to the individual states. But now his cousin on the Court had cleverly promoted the contrary principle of "judicial review"—the idea that the Supreme Court alone had the last word on the question of constitutionality. In this landmark case, Marshall inserted the keystone into the arch that supports the tremendous power of the Supreme Court in American life.*

Jefferson: A Reluctant Warrior

One of Jefferson's first actions as president was to reduce the military establishment to a mere twenty-five hundred officers and men. Jefferson's reluctance to invest in soldiers and ships was less about money than about republican ideals. He fondly hoped that America would transcend Europe's bloody wars and set an example for the world by winning friends through "peaceful coercion" rather than military force. The Republicans also distrusted standing armies as standing invitations to dictatorships. A large navy, the farm-loving Jeffersonians feared, might embroil the Republic in costly and corrupting wars far from America's shores.

But harsh realities forced Jefferson's principles to bend. Pirates of the North African Barbary States had long made a national industry of blackmailing and plundering merchant ships that ventured into the Mediterranean. Preceding Federalist administrations had been forced to buy protection. At the time of the French crisis of 1798, when Americans were shouting, "Millions for defense, but not one cent for tribute," twenty-six barrels of blackmail dollars were being shipped to Algiers.

War across the Atlantic was not part of the Jeffersonian vision—but neither was paying tribute to a pack of pirate states. The showdown came in 1801. The pasha of Tripoli, dissatisfied with his share of protection money, informally declared war on the United States by cutting down the flagstaff of the American **consulate.** A gauntlet was thus thrown squarely into the face of Jefferson—the noninterventionist, the critic of a big-ship navy, and the political foe of Federalist shippers. He reluctantly rose to the challenge by dispatching the infant navy to "the shores of Tripoli," as related in the song of the U.S. Marine Corps. After four years of intermittent fighting, Jefferson succeeded in obtaining a peace treaty with Tripoli in 1805.

The Louisiana Godsend

A secret pact, fraught with peril for America, was signed in 1800. Napoleon Bonaparte induced the king of Spain to **cede** to France, for attractive considerations, the immense trans-Mississippi region of Louisiana, which included the New Orleans area. Then, in 1802, the right of deposit at New Orleans, guaranteed America by the treaty of 1795, was withdrawn. Deposit (warehouse) privileges were vital to frontier farmers who floated their produce down the Mississippi to its mouth, there to await oceangoing vessels. A roar of anger rolled up the mighty river and into its tributary valleys. American pioneers talked wildly of descending on New Orleans, rifles in hand.

Thomas Jefferson was again on the griddle. Louisiana in the grip of senile Spain posed no real threat, but Louisiana in the iron fist of Napoleon, the preeminent military genius of his age, foreshadowed a dark and blood-drenched future. Hoping to quiet the clamor of the West, Jefferson moved decisively. Early in 1803 he sent James Monroe to Paris to join forces with the regular minister there, Robert R. Livingston. The two envoys were instructed to buy New Orleans and as much land to the east as they could get for a maximum of $10 million.

At this critical juncture, Napoleon suddenly abandoned his dream of a New World empire and decided to sell all Louisiana. Two developments prompted his

consulate (consul) *A place where a government representative is stationed in a foreign country, but not the main headquarters of diplomatic representation headed by an ambassador (the embassy).*

cede *To yield or grant something, often upon request or under pressure. (Anything ceded is a cession.)*

---

* The next invalidation of a federal law by the Supreme Court came fifty-four years late with the explosive *Dred Scott* decision (see p. 280).

change of mind. First, he had failed to reconquer the sugar-rich island of Santo Domingo, for which Louisiana was to serve as a source of foodstuffs. Infuriated ex-slaves, ably led by the gifted Toussaint L'Ouverture, had put up a stubborn resistance. Santo Domingo could not be reconquered, except perhaps at a staggering cost. Second, Bonaparte was about to end the twenty-month lull in his deadly conflict with Britain. Because the British controlled the seas, he feared that he might be forced to make them a gift of Louisiana. Rather than drive America into the arms of Britain by attempting to hold the area, he decided to sell the huge wilderness to the Americans and pocket the money for his schemes nearer home.

Events now unrolled dizzily. Suddenly, out of a clear sky, the French foreign minister asked the American minister Robert Livingston how much he would give for all Louisiana. Scarcely able to believe his ears (he was partially deaf anyhow), Livingston nervously entered upon the negotiations. After about a week of haggling, the treaties were signed on April 30, 1803, ceding Louisiana to the United States for about $15 million.

When news of the bargain reached America, Jefferson was startled. He had authorized his envoys to offer not more than $10 million for New Orleans, and as much to the east in the Floridas as they could get. Instead, they had signed three treaties that pledged $15 million for New Orleans and a vast wilderness entirely to the west—an area that would more than double the size of the United States. They had bought a wilderness to get a city.

Once again two Jeffersons wrestled with each other: the theoretical strict constructionist versus the democratic visionary. Where in his beloved Constitution was the president authorized to negotiate treaties incorporating a huge new expanse into the Union—an expanse containing tens of thousands of Indian, white, and black inhabitants? There was no such clause. Yet Jefferson also perceived that the vast domain now within his reach could form a sprawling "empire of liberty" that would ensure the health and life of America's experiment in democracy. So Jefferson shamefacedly submitted the treaties to the Senate while privately admitting that the purchase was unconstitutional.

The senators were less finicky than Jefferson. Reflecting enthusiastic public support, they registered their prompt approval of the transaction. Land-hungry Americans were not disposed to split constitutional hairs when confronted with perhaps the most magnificent real estate bargain in history—828,000 square miles at about three cents an acre.

Online Study Center

Interactive map
Louisiana Purchase and the Lewis and Clark Expedition
college.hmco.com/pic/kennedybrief7e

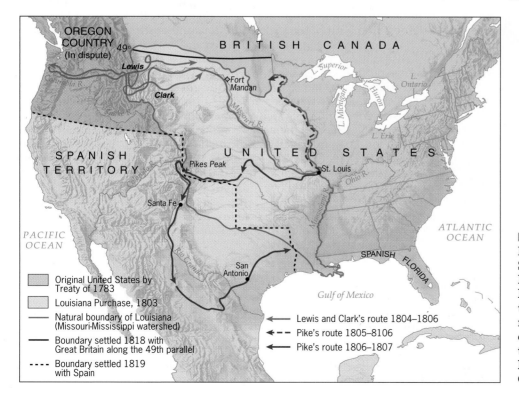

▓	Original United States by Treaty of 1783
░	Louisiana Purchase, 1803
—	Natural boundary of Louisiana (Missouri-Mississippi watershed)
▬	Boundary settled 1818 with Great Britain along the 49th parallel
- - -	Boundary settled 1819 with Spain

←	Lewis and Clark's route 1804–1806
←- -	Pike's route 1805–8106
←	Pike's route 1806–1807

■ **Exploring the Louisiana Purchase and the West**
Seeking to avert friction with France by purchasing all of Louisiana, Jefferson bought trouble because of the vagueness of the boundaries. The disputants included Spain in the Floridas, Spain and later Mexico in the Southwest, and Great Britain in Canada.

secession *The withdrawal, by legal or
illegal means, of one portion of a political entity from the government to which
it has been bound.*

■ **Meriwether Lewis** This painting portrays him as he looked on his return from
the great expedition through the Louisiana
Purchase and the West. Collection of The
New York Historical Society, neg. 51322.

Jefferson's bargain with France was epochal. By scooping up Louisiana, America secured at one bloodless stroke the western half of the richest river valley in the
world and further laid the foundations of a future major power. The ideal of a great
agrarian republic, as envisioned by Jefferson, could now be realized in the vast
"Valley of Democracy." At the same time, the transfer established a valuable
precedent for acquiring foreign territories and peoples by purchase and incorporating them into the Union as full equals.

The purchase also contributed to making operational the isolationist principles
of Washington's Farewell Address. With virtually the last potentially hostile European power removed from the North American continent, the United States could
happily disengage from the ancient system of European power politics and rivalries.

The extent of the huge new area was more fully unveiled by a series of explorations under Jefferson's direction. In the spring of 1804, Jefferson sent Meriwether Lewis and William Clark on a voyage of discovery that took them up the
Missouri River (the "Great Muddy"), across the Rockies, and down the Columbia
River to the Pacific coast. Aided by the Shoshoni woman guide Sacajawea, Lewis
and Clark's two-and-one-half-year expedition yielded rich scientific observations,
demonstrated the viability of an overland trail to the Pacific, and bolstered American claims to Oregon. Other explorers also pushed into the uncharted West. Ze-
bulon M. Pike explored the headwaters of the Mississippi River in 1805–1806 and
the southern portion of the Louisiana territory in 1807.

The Aaron Burr Conspiracies

In the long run, the Louisiana Purchase greatly expanded the fortunes of the
United States and the power of the federal government. In the short term, the vast
expanse of territory, and the feeble reach of the government obliged to
control it, raised fears of **secession** and foreign intrigue.

Aaron Burr, Jefferson's first-term vice president, played no small part
in provoking—and justifying—such fears. Dropped from the ticket for Jefferson's second term, Burr joined a group of Federalist extremists to plot
the secession of New England and New York. Alexander Hamilton,
though no friend of Jefferson, exposed and foiled this conspiracy. Incensed, Burr challenged his foe to a duel, and Hamilton reluctantly accepted. Burr killed Hamilton with a single shot. Burr's pistol blew the
brightest brain out of the Federalist party and destroyed its one remaining hope of effective leadership.

His political career as dead as Hamilton's, Burr now turned his disunionist plottings to the trans-Mississippi West, where he struck up an alliance with General James Wilkinson, the unscrupulous military governor
of Louisiana. Burr's schemes are still shrouded in mystery, but he and
Wilkinson apparently planned to break the West away from the United
States and then expand their new confederacy by invading Spanish Mexico and Florida. In the fall of 1806 Burr and his followers floated down the
Mississippi to meet Wilkinson's army at Natchez, but Wilkinson betrayed
Burr and fled to New Orleans. The former vice president was arrested and
tried for treason, but finally acquitted. Chief Justice Marshall ruled that
there was insufficient proof that Burr had committed overt acts of treason
according to the Constitution (see Art. III, Sec. III). Burr then fled to Europe. His insurrectionary brashness demonstrated that purchasing a
large expanse of western territory was far easier than controlling it.

America: A Nutcrackered Neutral

Jefferson was triumphantly reelected in 1804, with 162 electoral votes to
only 14 votes for his Federalist opponent. But the laurels of Jefferson's
first administration soon withered under the blasts of the new storm that
broke in Europe. After unloading Louisiana in 1803, Napoleon deliberately provoked a new war with Britain, an awesome conflict that raged for

eleven long years. After the Battle of Trafalgar in 1805, Britain's navy controlled the seas, while Napoleon's victory in the Battle of Austerlitz made him master of the whole European continent. Like the tiger and the shark, France and Britain each reigned supreme in their chosen elements.

Unable to hurt each other directly, the two antagonists were forced to strike indirect blows. Britain ruled the waves and waived the rules. The London government, beginning in 1806, issued a series of Orders in Council that closed all ports under French control to foreign shipping, including American, unless the vessels first stopped at a British port. Napoleon struck back, ordering the seizure of all merchant ships, including American, that entered British ports. There was thus no way to trade with either nation without facing the other's guns. American vessels were, quite literally, caught between the devil and the deep blue sea.

Even more galling to American pride than the seizure of wooden ships was the seizure of flesh-and-blood American seamen. Impressment—the forcible enlistment of sailors—was a crude form of **conscription** that the British, among others, had employed for over four centuries. Clubs and stretchers (for men knocked unconscious) were standard equipment of press gangs from His Majesty's crew-hungry ships. Some six thousand bona fide U.S. citizens were impressed by the "piratical man stealers" of Britain from 1808 to 1811 alone.

Britain's determination was spectacularly highlighted in 1807 when a British warship, seeking deserters, fired on a U.S. frigate, the *Chesapeake,* killing three Americans and wounding eighteen. Britain was clearly in the wrong, as the London foreign office admitted. But London's contrition availed little; a roar of national wrath went up from infuriated Americans. Jefferson, the peace lover, could easily have had war if he had wanted it.

conscription *Compulsory enrollment of men and women into the armed forces.*

embargo *A government order prohibiting commerce in or out of a port.*

The Hated Embargo

National honor would not permit a slavish submission to British and French mistreatment. Yet a large-scale foreign war was contrary to the settled policy of the new Republic—and in addition it would be futile. The navy was weak, and the army was even weaker. A disastrous defeat would not improve America's plight.

The warring nations in Europe depended heavily on the United States for raw materials and foodstuffs. In his eager search for an alternative to war, Jefferson seized on this essential fact. He reasoned that if America voluntarily cut off its exports, the offending powers would be forced to bow, hat in hand, and agree to respect U.S. rights. Responding to the presidential lash, Congress hastily passed the Embargo Act late in 1807. This rigorous law forbade the export of all goods from the United States, whether in American or in foreign ships. More than just a compromise between submission and shooting, the **embargo** embodied Jefferson's idea of "peaceful coercion." If it worked, the embargo would vindicate the rights of neutral nations and point to a new way of conducting foreign affairs.

The American economy staggered under the effect of the embargo long before Britain or France began to bend. Forests of dead masts gradually filled once-flourishing harbors; docks that had once rumbled were deserted (except for illegal trade); and soup kitchens cared for some of the hungry unemployed. Jeffersonian Republicans probably hurt the commerce of New England, which they avowedly were trying to protect, far more than Britain and France together were doing.

Farmers of the South and West, the strongholds of Jefferson, suffered no less disastrously than New England. They were alarmed by the mounting piles of exportable cotton, grain, and tobacco. Jefferson in truth seemed to be waging war on his fellow citizens rather than on the offending foreign powers.

An enormous illicit trade mushroomed in 1808, especially along the Canadian border, where bands of armed Americans on loaded rafts overawed or overpowered federal agents. Irate citizens cynically transposed the letters of "Embargo" to read "O Grab Me," "Go Bar 'Em," and "Mobrage," while heartily cursing the "Dambargo."

Jefferson nonetheless induced Congress to pass iron-toothed enforcing legislation. It was so inquisitorial and tyrannical as to cause some Americans to think more kindly of George III, whom Jefferson had berated in the Declaration of Independence. One indignant New Hampshirite denounced the president with this ditty:

> *Our ships all in motion,*
> *Once whiten'd the ocean;*
>   *They sail'd and return'd with a cargo;*
> *Now doom'd to decay*
> *They are fallen a prey,*
>   *To Jefferson, worms, and EMBARGO*

The embargo even had the effect of reviving the moribund Federalist party. Gaining new converts, its leaders hurled their nullification of the embargo into the teeth of the "Virginia lordlings" in Washington. In 1804 the discredited Federalists had polled only 14 electoral votes out of 176; in 1808, the embargo year, the figure rose to 47 out of 175. New England seethed with talk of secession, and Jefferson later admitted that he felt the foundations of government tremble under his feet.

An alarmed Congress, yielding to the storm of public anger, finally repealed the embargo on March 1, 1809, three days before Jefferson's retirement. A half-loaf substitute was provided by the Non-Intercourse Act. This measure formally re-opened trade with all the nations of the world, except the two most important, Britain and France. Though thus watered down, economic coercion continued to be the policy of the Jeffersonians from 1809 to 1812, when the nation finally plunged into war.

Why did the embargo, Jefferson's most daring act of statesmanship, collapse after fifteen dismal months? First, the president overestimated the dependence of both belligerents on America's trade. Bumper grain crops blessed the British Isles during these years, and the revolutionary Latin American republics unexpectedly threw open their ports for compensating commerce. With most of Europe under his control, Napoleon simply tightened his belt and went without American trade even as he mocked the United States by seizing American ships and cargo with the claim that he was simply helping them enforce the embargo.

More critically, perhaps, Jefferson miscalculated the unpopularity of such a self-crucifying weapon and the difficulty of enforcing it. The hated embargo was not continued long enough or tightly enough to achieve the desired results—and a leaky embargo was perhaps more costly than none at all.

Curiously enough, New England plucked a new prosperity from the ugly jaws of the embargo. With shipping tied up and imported goods scarce, the resourceful Yankees reopened old factories and erected new ones. The real foundations of modern America's industrial might were laid behind the protective wall of the embargo, followed by nonintercourse and the War of 1812. Jefferson, the avowed critic of factories, may have unwittingly done more for American manufacturing than Alexander Hamilton, industry's outspoken friend.

Madison's Gamble

Following Washington's precedent, Jefferson left the presidency after two terms, happy to escape what he called the "splendid misery" of the highest office in the land. As his successor, he strongly favored the nomination and election of his friend and fellow Virginian, the quiet, intellectual, and unassuming James Madison.

Madison took the presidential oath on March 4, 1809, as the awesome conflict in Europe was roaring to its climax. The scholarly Madison was short, thin, bald, and weak of voice. Despite a distinguished career as a legislator, he was crippled as president by factions within his party and his cabinet. Unable to dominate Congress as Jefferson had done, Madison often found himself holding the bag for risky foreign policies not of his own making.

The Non-Intercourse Act of 1809—a diluted embargo aimed solely at Britain and France—was due to expire in 1810. To Madison's dismay, Congress dismantled the embargo completely with a bargaining measure known as Macon's Bill No. 2. While reopening American trade with all the world, it dangled what

Congress hoped was an attractive lure. If either Britain or France repealed its commercial restrictions, America would restore its embargo against the nonrepealing nation. A dismayed Madison recognized that this measure emphasized America's economic weakness and left the determination of who would be America's trading partner to the potentates of London and Paris.

The crafty Napoleon saw his chance. Without actually promising to do so, he signaled in August 1810 that France might repeal its trade restrictions if Britain in turn lifted its Orders in Council. Madison knew better than to trust Napoleon, but he chose to accept the French offer as evidence of repeal, gambling that the threat of seeing the United States trade exclusively with France would lead the British to repeal their restrictions. But in fact they did not. In firm control of the seas, London saw little need to bargain. Madison's gamble had failed. He saw no choice but to reestablish the embargo against Britain alone—a decision that meant the end of American neutrality and a dangerous step toward war.

Tecumseh and the Prophet

Not all of Madison's party was reluctant to fight. The complexion of the Twelfth Congress, which met late in 1811, differed markedly from that of its predecessor. Recent elections had swept away many of the older "submission men" and replaced them with young hotheads, many from the South and West. Dubbed "war hawks" by their Federalist opponents, the newcomers were indeed on fire for a new war with the old enemy—actually two old enemies. The war hawks detested the British for their manhandling of American sailors and their Orders in Council that dammed the flow of American farm products headed for Europe. They also yearned to wipe out a renewed Indian threat to the flood of pioneer settlers then washing into the trans-Appalachian wilderness.

Two remarkable Shawnee brothers, Tecumseh and Tenskwatawa, known to non-Indians as "the Prophet," concluded that the time had come to stop this onrushing tide. They began to weld together a far-flung confederacy of all the tribes east of the Mississippi, inspiring a vibrant movement of Indian unity and cultural renewal. Their followers gave up textile clothing for traditional buckskin garments and foreswore alcohol, the better to fight a last-ditch battle with the white invaders. Rejecting whites' concept of "ownership," Tecumseh urged his supporters never to cede land to whites unless all Indians agreed.

Meanwhile, frontiersmen and their war-hawk spokesmen in Congress became convinced that British "scalp buyers" in Canada were nourishing the Indians' growing strength. In the fall of 1811 General William Henry Harrison, governor of the Indiana Territory, gathered an army and advanced on Tecumseh's headquarters at the junction of the Wabash and Tippecanoe Rivers in present-day Indiana. Tecumseh was absent, recruiting supporters in the South, but the Prophet attacked Harrison's army—foolishly, in Tecumseh's

Rivals for the presidency, and for the soul of the young Republic, Thomas Jefferson and John Adams died on the same day— the Fourth of July, 1826—fifty years to the day after both men had signed the Declaration of Independence. Adams's last words were,

"Thomas Jefferson still survives."
But he was wrong, for three hours earlier, Jefferson had drawn his last breath.

In a speech at Vincennes, Indiana Territory, Tecumseh (1768?–1813) said,

"Sell a country! Why not sell the air, the clouds, and the great sea, as well as the earth? Did not the Great Spirit make them all for the use of his children?"

■ **Tecumseh (1768?–1813)** A Shawnee Indian born in the Ohio country, he was probably the most gifted organizer and leader of his people in U.S. history. A respected warrior, he fought the tribal custom of torturing prisoners and opposed the practice of permitting any one tribe to sell land that, he believed, belonged to all Indians.

William Henry Harrison (1773–1841), Indian fighter and later president, called Tecumseh

"one of those uncommon geniuses who spring up occasionally to produce revolutions and overturn the established order of things. If it were not for the vicinity of the United States, he would perhaps be founder of an Empire that would rival in glory that of Mexico or Peru."

eyes—with a small force of Shawnees. The Shawnees were routed and their settlement burned.

The Battle of Tippecanoe made Harrison a national hero. It also discredited the Prophet and drove Tecumseh into an alliance with the British. When America's war with Britain came, Tecumseh fought fiercely for the redcoats until his death in 1813 at the Battle of the Thames. With him perished the dream of an Indian confederacy.

Mr. Madison's War

By the spring of 1812, Madison believed war with Britain to be inevitable. The British arming of hostile Indians pushed him toward this decision, as did the whoops of the war hawks in his own party who believed the only way to remove the menace of the Indians was to wipe out their Canadian base. "On to Canada, on to Canada" was the war hawks' chant. Southern expansionists, less vocal, cast a covetous eye on Florida, then held by Britain's ally Spain.

Above all, Madison turned to war to restore confidence in the republican experiment. For five years the Republicans had tried to steer a noble course between submission and battle with the warring European powers. But the only result was international derision and internal strife. Madison and the Republicans came to believe that only a vigorous assertion of American rights could demonstrate the viability of American nationhood—and of democracy as a form of government. If America could not fight to protect itself, its experiment in republicanism would be discredited in the eyes of a scoffing world.

Madison asked Congress to declare war on June 1, 1812. Congress obliged him two weeks later. The vote in the House was 79 to 49 for war, in the Senate 19 to 13. The close tally revealed deep divisions over the wisdom of fighting. The split was both sectional and partisan. Support for war came from the South and West, but also from Republicans in the populous middle states such as Pennsylvania and Virginia. Federalists in both North and South damned the conflict, but their stronghold was New England, which greeted the declaration of war with muffled bells, flags at half-mast, and public fasting.

Why should seafaring New England oppose the war for a free sea? The answer is that Federalists in the Northeast sympathized with Britain and resented the Republicans' sympathy with Napoleon, whom they regarded as the "Corsican butcher" and the "anti-Christ of the age." The Federalists also opposed the acquisition of Canada, which would only add more agrarian states and increase Jeffersonian Republican voting strength. The bitterness of New England Federalists against "Mr. Madison's War" led them to treason or near-treason. They were determined, charged one Republican versifier,

To rule the nation if they could,
But see it damned if others should.

New England gold holders probably lent more dollars to the British Exchequer than to the federal Treasury. Federalist farmers sent huge quantities of supplies and foodstuffs to Canada, enabling British armies to invade New York. New England governors stubbornly refused to permit their militias to serve outside their own states. In a sense America had to fight two enemies simultaneously, old England and New England.

Thus perilously divided, the barely United States plunged into armed conflict against Britain, then the world's most powerful empire. No sober American could have had much reasonable hope of victory, but by 1812 the Jeffersonian Republicans saw no other choice.

✪ Chapter Summary ✪

The ideological conflicts of the early Republic culminated in the bitter election of 1800 between Adams and Jefferson. Despite the fierce rhetoric of the campaign, Jefferson's defeat of an incumbent president in the "Revolution of 1800" demonstrated that the infant Republic could peacefully transfer power from one party to another. The election of 1800 also signaled the decline of the conservative Federalist Party, which proved unable to adjust to the democratic future of American politics.

Jefferson, as a renowned political philosopher and idealist, came to Washington determined to restore what he saw as the original American revolutionary doctrines and to implement his Republican principles of limited and frugal government, strict construction, and an antimilitarist foreign policy. But Jefferson the practical politician had to compromise many of these goals, thereby moderating the Republican-Federalist ideological conflict.

The sharpest political conflicts occurred over the judiciary, where John Marshall worked effectively to enshrine the principles of judicial review and a strong federal government. Against his original intentions, Jefferson himself also enhanced federal power by waging war against the Barbary pirates and especially by his dramatic purchase of Louisiana from Napoleon. The Louisiana Purchase was Jefferson's greatest success, increasing national unity and pointing to America's long-term future in the West. But in the short term the vast geographical expansion fostered problems like Aaron Burr's secessionist scheme to break the West away from the United States.

Nevertheless, Jefferson became increasingly entangled in the horrific European wars between Napoleonic France and Britain, as both great powers obstructed American trade and violated freedom of the seas. Jefferson attempted to avoid war through his embargo policy, which damaged the American economy and stirred bitter opposition in New England.

Jefferson's successor, James Madison, faced more British assaults on American neutrality, as well as cries from western "War Hawks" in his own party who wanted to defeat the Indians and seize Canada. Fearing for the very future of American republicanism, Madison reluctantly called for war in order to regain American national confidence. The nation went to war totally unprepared, bitterly divided, and devoid of any coherent strategy.

12

The Second War for Independence and the Upsurge of Nationalism

1812–1824

THE AMERICAN CONTINENTS . . . ARE HENCEFORTH NOT TO BE
CONSIDERED AS SUBJECTS FOR FUTURE COLONIZATION
BY ANY EUROPEAN POWERS.

JAMES MONROE, DECEMBER 2, 1823

The War of 1812 was an especially divisive and ill-fought war. There was no burning national anger, as there had been in 1807 following the *Chesapeake* outrage. The supreme lesson of the conflict was the folly of leading a divided and apathetic people into war. And yet, despite the unimpressive military outcome and the even less decisive negotiated peace, Americans came out of the war with a renewed sense of nationhood. For the next dozen years an awakened spirit of nationalism would inspire activities ranging from protecting manufacturing to building roads to defending the authority of the federal government over the states.

Focus Questions

1. Why was the War of 1812 so politically divisive and poorly fought by the United States, and how did the course of the war reflect these problems?
2. Why did the War of 1812, despite its stalemated outcome, lead to an outburst of proud postwar nationalism and an "era of good feelings" in the United States?
3. Why did a serious conflict over slavery suddenly burst on the American scene in 1819, and how did the Missouri Compromise resolve it (at least temporarily)?
4. How did John Marshall's Supreme Court promote the spirit of nationalism and counter growing sectionalism through its rulings in favor of federal power?
5. What were the origins and essential principles of the Monroe Doctrine, and what were its short- and long-term effects in Latin America and elsewhere?

On to Canada over Land and Lakes

On the eve of the War of 1812, the regular army was ill-trained, ill-disciplined, and widely scattered. It had to be supplemented by the even more poorly trained militia, who were sometimes distinguished by their speed of foot in leaving the battlefield. Some of the ranking generals were semisenile heirlooms from the Revolutionary War, rusting on their laurels and lacking in vigor and vision.

Chronology

1812	United States declares war on Britain. Madison reelected president.
1812–1813	American invasions of Canada fail.
1813	Battle of the Thames. Battle of Lake Erie.
1814	Battle of Plattsburgh. British burn Washington. Battle of Horseshoe Bend. Treaty of Ghent signed ending War of 1812.
1814–1815	Hartford Convention.
1815	Battle of New Orleans.
1816	Second Bank of the United States founded. Protectionist Tariff of 1816. Monroe elected president.
1817	Rush-Bagot agreement limits naval armament on Great Lakes.
1818	Treaty of 1818 with Britain. Jackson invades Florida.
1819	Panic of 1819. Spain cedes Florida to United States. *McCulloch* v. *Maryland*. *Dartmouth College* v. *Woodward*.
1820	Missouri Compromise. Missouri and Maine admitted to Union. Monroe reelected.
1823	Secretary of State Adams proposes Monroe Doctrine.
1825	Erie Canal completed.

The opening offensive strategy against the British in Canada was especially poorly conceived. Had the Americans captured Montreal, the center of population and transportation, everything to the west might have died, just as the leaves of a tree wither when the trunk is girdled. But instead of laying ax to the trunk, the Americans frittered away their strength in the three-pronged invasion of 1812. The trio of invading forces that set out from Detroit, Niagara, and Lake Champlain were all beaten back shortly after they crossed the Canadian border.

By contrast, the British and Canadians displayed energy from the outset. Early in the war they captured the American fort of Michilimackinac, which commanded the upper Great Lakes and the Indian-inhabited area to the south and west. Their brilliant defensive operations were led by the inspired British General Isaac Brock, assisted (in the American camp) by "General Mud" and "General Confusion."

When several American land invasions of Canada were again hurled back in 1813, Americans looked for success on the water. Man for man and ship for ship, the American navy did better than the army. Compared to the larger British navy, American craft on the whole were more skillfully handled, had better gunners, and were manned by non–press-gang crews who were burning to avenge numerous indignities. Similarly, the American frigates, notably the *Constitution* ("Old Ironsides"), had thicker sides, heavier firepower, and larger crews, of which one sailor in six was a free black.

Control of the Great Lakes was vital, and an energetic American naval officer, Oliver Hazard Perry, managed to build a fleet of green-timbered ships on the shores of Lake Erie, manned by even greener seamen. When Perry captured a British fleet in a furious engagement on Lake Erie, he reported to his superior, "We have met the enemy and they are ours." Perry's victory and his slogan infused new life into the drooping American cause. Forced to withdraw from Detroit and Fort

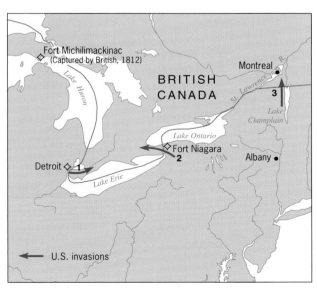

■ **The Three U.S. Invasions of 1812**

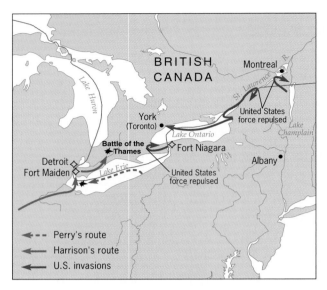

■ Campaigns of 1813

Malden, the retreating redcoats were overtaken by General Harrison's army and beaten at the Battle of the Thames in October 1813.

Despite these successes, the Americans by late 1814, far from invading Canada, were grimly defending their own soil against the invading British. In Europe the diversionary power of Napoleon was destroyed in mid-1814, and the dangerous despot was exiled to the Mediterranean isle of Elba. The United States, which had so brashly provoked war behind the protective skirts of Napoleon, was now left to face the music alone. Thousands of victorious veteran redcoats began to pour into Canada from Europe.

Assembling some ten thousand crack troops, the British prepared in 1814 for a crushing blow into New York, along the familiar lake-river route. In the absence of roads, the invader was forced to bring supplies over the Lake Champlain waterway. A weaker American fleet, commanded by the thirty-year-old Thomas Macdonough, challenged the British. The ensuing battle was desperately fought near Plattsburgh on September 11, 1814, on floating slaughterhouses. The American flagship at one point was in grave trouble. But Macdonough, unexpectedly turning his ship about with cables, confronted the enemy with a fresh broadside and snatched victory from the fangs of defeat.

The results of this heroic naval battle were momentous. The invading British army was forced to retreat. Macdonough thus saved at least upstate New York from conquest, New England from further disaffection, and the Union from possible dissolution. He also profoundly affected the concurrent negotiations of the Anglo-American peace treaty in Europe.

■ *Constitution and Guerrière,* 1812 The *Guerrière* was heavily outweighed and outgunned, yet its British captain eagerly—and foolishly—sought combat. His ship was totally destroyed. Historian Henry Adams later concluded that this duel "raised the United States in one half hour to the rank of a first-class Power in the world." Today, the *U.S.S. Constitution,* berthed in Boston harbor, remains the oldest actively commissioned ship in the U.S. Navy.

Despite its success on the Great Lakes, the American navy could not match the powerful British fleet in the Atlantic. Its wrath aroused, the Royal Navy finally retaliated by throwing a ruinous naval blockade along America's coast and by landing raiding parties almost at will. American economic life, including fishing, was crippled. Customs revenues were choked off, and as the war continued the bankrupt Treasury was unable to meet its obligations.

Washington Burned and New Orleans Defended

A second formidable British force, numbering about four thousand, landed in the Chesapeake Bay area in August 1814. Advancing rapidly on Washington, it easily dispersed some six thousand panicky militia at Bladensburg ("the Bladensburg races"). The invaders then entered the capital and set fire to most of the public buildings, including the Capitol and the White House. But while Washington burned, the Americans at Baltimore held firm. The British fleet hammered Fort McHenry with their cannons but could not capture the city. Francis Scott Key, a detained American anxiously watching the bombardment from a British ship, was inspired to write the words of "The Star-Spangled Banner." Set to the tune of a saucy English tavern refrain, the song quickly attained popularity.

A third British blow of 1814, aimed at New Orleans, menaced the entire Mississippi Valley. Gaunt and hawk-faced Andrew Jackson, fresh from crushing the southwest Indians at the Battle of Horseshoe Bend, was placed in command. His hodgepodge force consisted of seven thousand sailors, regulars, pirates, and Frenchmen, as well as militiamen from Louisiana, Kentucky, and Tennessee. Among the defenders were two Louisiana **regiments** of free black volunteers, numbering about four hundred men. The Americans threw up their entrenchment, and in the words of a popular song:

> Behind it stood our little force—
> None wished it to be greater;
> For ev'ry man was half a horse,
> And half an alligator.

The overconfident British, numbering some eight thousand battle-seasoned veterans, blundered badly. They made the mistake of launching a frontal assault, on January 8, 1815, on the entrenched American riflemen and cannoneers. The attackers suffered the most devastating defeat of the entire war, losing over two thousand killed and wounded in half an hour, compared with seventy for the Americans. It was an astonishing victory for Jackson and his men.

News of the victory struck the country "like a clap of thunder," according to one contemporary. Andrew Jackson became a national hero, as poets and politicians lined up to sing the praises of the defenders of New Orleans. It hardly mattered when word arrived that a peace treaty had been signed at Ghent, Belgium, ending the war two weeks before the battle. The United States had fought for honor as much as material gain. The Battle of New Orleans restored that honor, at least in American eyes, and unleashed a wave of nationalism and self-confidence.

The Treaty of Ghent

Tsar Alexander I of Russia, hard-pressed by Napoleon's army and not wanting his British ally to fritter away its strength in America, proposed **mediation** between the clashing Anglo-Saxon cousins in 1812. The tsar's feeler eventually set in motion the machinery that brought five American peacemakers to the quaint Belgian city of Ghent in 1814. The bickering group was headed by early rising, puritanical John Quincy Adams, son of John Adams, who deplored the late-hour card playing of his high-living colleague Henry Clay.

regiment *A medium-sized military unit, larger than a company or battalion and smaller than a division.*

mediation *An intervention, usually with consent of the parties, to aid in voluntarily settling differences between groups or nations. (**Arbitration** involves a mandatory settlement determined by a third party.)*

> *In a letter to her friend Mercy Otis Warren, Abigail Adams (1744–1818) fretted that the British were taking advantage of Americans' disagreement over the War of 1812:*
>
> "We have our firesides, our comfortable habitations, our cities, our churches and our country to defend, our rights, privileges and independence to preserve. And for these are we not justly contending? Thus it appears to me. Yet I hear from our pulpits, and read from our presses, that it is an unjust, a wicked, a ruinous, and unnecessary war. . . . A house divided upon itself—and upon that foundation do our enemies build their hopes of subduing us."

armistice *A temporary stopping of warfare by mutual agreement, sometimes in preparation for an actual peace negotiation between the parties.*

Confident after their military successes, Britain's envoys made sweeping demands for a neutralized Indian buffer state in the Great Lakes region, control of the Great Lakes, and a substantial part of conquered Maine. The Americans flatly rejected these terms, and the talks appeared stalemated. But news of British reverses in upstate New York and at Baltimore, and increasing war-weariness in Britain, made London more willing to compromise. Preoccupied with the Congress of Vienna that concluded the Napoleonic wars, and eyeing still-dangerous France, the British lion resigned itself to licking its wounds.

The Treaty of Ghent, signed on Christmas Eve in 1814, was essentially an **armistice**. Both sides simply agreed to stop fighting and to restore conquered territory. No mention was made of those grievances for which America had ostensibly fought: the Indian menace, search and seizure, Orders in Council, impressment, and confiscations. With neither side able to impose its will, the treaty negotiations—like the war itself—ended as a virtual draw. Relieved Americans boasted, "Not One Inch of Territory Ceded or Lost"—a watchword that contrasted strangely with the "On to Canada" rallying cry of the war's outset.

Federalist Grievances and the Hartford Convention

Defiant New England remained a problem. It prospered during the conflict, owing largely to illicit trade with the enemy in Canada and to the absence of a British blockade until 1814. But the embittered opposition of the Federalists to the war continued unabated.

As the war dragged on, New England extremists became more vocal. The most spectacular manifestation of Federalist discontent was the ill-omened Hartford Convention. Late in 1814, when the British capture of New Orleans seemed imminent, Massachusetts issued a call for a convention at Hartford, Connecticut. Twenty-six prominent delegates from all of the New England states except Vermont met in complete secrecy for about three weeks—December 15, 1814, to January 5, 1815—to discuss their grievances and to seek redress for their wrongs. The convention's final report was actually quite moderate. It demanded financial compensation to New England for lost trade, abolition of the "three-fifths" clause of the Constitution that gave the South added representation, and a single-term limit for the presidency—a stab at the much-resented "Virginia dynasty" of presidents. These and other measures reflected Federalist fears that a once-proud New England was falling subservient to an agrarian South and West.

Three special envoys from Massachusetts brought these demands to the burned-out capital of Washington in early January 1815. The trio arrived just in time to be overwhelmed by the glorious news from New Orleans, followed by that from Ghent. As the rest of the nation congratulated itself on a glorious victory, New England's wartime complaints seemed petty at best, and treasonous at worst. Pursued by the sneers and jeers of the press, the envoys sank away into obscurity.

The Hartford resolutions, as it turned out, were the death dirge of the Federalist party. The Federalists were never again to mount a successful presidential campaign, and the party disappeared altogether in the 1820s.

Federalist doctrines of disunity, which long survived the party, blazed a fateful trail. Until 1815 there was far more talk of nullification and secession in New England than in any other section, including the South. The outright flouting of the Jeffersonian embargo and the later crippling of the war effort were the two most damaging acts of nullification in America prior to the events leading to the Civil War.

The Second War for American Independence

The War of 1812 was a small war, involving about 6,000 Americans killed or wounded. It was but a footnote to the mighty European conflagration. In 1812, when Napoleon invaded Russia with about 500,000 men, Madison tried to invade Canada with about 5,000 men. But if the American conflict was globally unimportant, its results were highly important to the United States.

The Republic had shown that it would resist, sword in hand, what it regarded as grievous wrongs. Other nations developed a new respect for America's fighting prowess. America's emissaries abroad were henceforth treated with less scorn. In a diplomatic sense, if not in a military sense, the conflict could be called the Second War for American Independence.

A new nation, moreover, was welded in the fiery furnace of armed conflict. Sectionalism, now identified with discredited New England Federalists, was given a black eye. The painful events of the war glaringly revealed, as perhaps nothing else could have done, the folly of sectional disunity. In a sense, the most conspicuous casualty of the war was the Federalist party.

War heroes emerged, especially the two Indian-fighters, Andrew Jackson and William Henry Harrison. Both of them were to become president. Left in the lurch by their British friends at Ghent, the Indians were forced to make such terms as they could. They reluctantly consented, in a series of treaties, to relinquish vast areas of forested land north of the Ohio River.

Manufacturing prospered behind the fiery wooden wall of the British blockade. In both an economic and a diplomatic sense, the War of 1812 bred greater American independence. The industries stimulated by the fighting rendered America less dependent on Europe's workshops.

Canadian patriotism and nationalism also received a powerful stimulus from the clash. Many Canadians felt betrayed by the Treaty of Ghent. They were especially aggrieved by the failure to secure an Indian buffer state or even mastery of the Great Lakes. Canadians fully expected the frustrated Yankees to return, and for a time the Americans and British engaged in a naval arms race on the Great Lakes. But in 1817 the Rush-Bagot agreement between Britain and the United States severely limited naval armament on the lakes. Better relations brought the last border fortifications down in the 1870s, with the happy result that the United States and Canada came to share the world's longest unfortified boundary—stretching 5,527 miles long.

After Napoleon's final defeat at Waterloo in 1815, Europe slumped into a peace of exhaustion. Deposed monarchs returned to battered thrones, as the Old World took the rutted road back to conservatism, illiberalism, and **reaction.** But the American people, largely unaffected by these European developments, turned their backs on the Old World and faced resolutely toward the untamed West—and toward the task of building their democracy.

Nascent Nationalism

The most impressive by-product of the War of 1812 was heightened nationalism—the spirit of nation-consciousness or national oneness. America may not have fought the war as one nation, but it emerged as one nation. The changed mood even manifested itself in the birth of a distinctively national literature. Washington Irving and James Fenimore Cooper attained international recognition in the 1820s, significantly as the nation's first writers of importance to use American scenes and themes. School textbooks, often British in an earlier era, were now being written by Americans for Americans. In the world of magazines, the highly intellectual *North American Review* began publication in 1815—the year of the triumph at New Orleans. Even American painters increasingly celebrated their native landscapes on their canvases.

A fresh nationalistic spirit could be recognized in many other areas as well. The revived Bank of the United States established by Congress in 1816 reflected

Online Study Center

Primary source
Urania White Headstone
college.hmco.com/pic/kennedybrief7e

Online Study Center

Primary source
Rachel Weeping
college.hmco.com/pic/kennedybrief7e

─────

reaction (reactionary) *In politics, extreme conservatism, looking to restore the political or social conditions of some earlier time.*

■ **View of the Capitol, by Charles Burton, 1824** This painting of the Capitol building, much smaller than it is today, reveals the rustic conditions of the early days in the nation's capital. A series of architects worked on the Capitol, following William Thornton's original design along neoclassical, or "Greek Revival," lines. After the British burned the building in 1814, Boston's Charles Bulfinch oversaw the reconstruction of the Capitol, finally completed in 1830.

nationalism in finance. A more handsome capital began to rise from the ashes of Washington. The army was expanded to ten thousand men. The navy covered itself with glory in 1815 when it administered a thorough beating to the piratical plunderers of North Africa. Stephen Decatur, naval hero of the War of 1812 and of the Barbary Coast expeditions, pungently captured the country's nationalist mood in a famous toast made on his return from the Mediterranean campaigns: "Our country, right or wrong!"

The American System

Nationalism likewise manifested itself in manufacturing. Patriotic Americans took pride in the factories that had recently mushroomed, largely as a result of the self-imposed embargoes and the war. When hostilities ended in 1815, British competitors tried to strangle the American war-baby factories in the cradle by cutting prices below cost and dumping goods on U.S. markets. In response, the infant industries bawled lustily for **protection.**

A nationalist Congress, out-Federalizing the old Federalists, responded by passing the path-breaking Tariff of 1816—the first tariff in American history instituted primarily for protection, not revenue. Its rates—roughly 20 to 25 percent on the value of dutiable imports—were not high enough to provide completely adequate safeguards, but the law was a bold beginning. A strongly protective trend was started that stimulated the appetites of the protected for more protection.

Nationalism was further highlighted by Henry Clay's grandiose plan for developing a profitable home market. Still radiating the nationalism of war-hawk days, Clay threw himself behind an elaborate scheme known by 1824 as the American System. This system had three main parts. The first was a strong banking system to provide easy and abundant credit. Then a high protective tariff would enable eastern manufacturing to flourish. Finally, revenues gushing from the tariff would provide funds for a network of roads and canals, especially in the burgeoning Ohio Valley. Through these new arteries of transportation would flow foodstuffs and

protection (protective) *In economics, the policy of stimulating or preserving domestic producers by placing barriers against imported goods, often through high tariffs.*

raw materials from the South and West to the North and East. In exchange, a stream of manufactured goods would flow in the return direction, knitting the country together economically and politically.

Persistent and eloquent demands by Henry Clay and others for **internal improvements** struck a responsive chord with the public, especially in the road-poor West. The recent attempts to invade Canada had all failed partly because of oath-provoking roads—or no roads at all.

But attempts to secure federal funding for roads and canals stumbled on Republican constitutional scruples. Congress voted in 1817 to distribute $1.5 million to the states for internal improvements. But President Madison sternly vetoed the measure as unconstitutional, forcing the individual states to undertake building programs on their own, including the Erie Canal, triumphantly completed by New York in 1825. Jeffersonian Republicans, who had gulped down Hamiltonian loose construction on other important problems, choked on the idea of direct federal support for **intrastate** internal improvements. New England also opposed federally constructed roads and canals because such outlets would further drain away population and create competing states beyond the mountains.

Boston's Columbian Centinel *was not the only newspaper to regard President Monroe's early months as the Era of Good Feelings.* Washington's National Intelligencer *observed in July 1817,*

"Never before, perhaps, since the institution of civil government, did the same harmony, the same absence of party spirit, the same national feeling, pervade a community. The result is too consoling to dispute too nicely about the cause."

raw materials *Products in their natural, unmanufactured state.*

internal improvements *The basic public works, such as roads, canals, and bridges that create the infrastructure for economic development.*

intrastate *Something existing wholly within a single state of the United States.* (**Interstate** *refers to movement between two or more states.*)

dynasty *A succession of rulers in the same family line; by extension, any system of predetermined succession in power.*

The So-Called Era of Good Feelings

James Monroe—six feet tall, somewhat stooped, courtly, and mild mannered—was nominated for the presidency in 1816 by the Republicans. They thus undertook to continue the so-called Virginia **dynasty** of Washington, Jefferson, and Madison. The fading Federalists ran a candidate for the last time in their checkered history, and he was crushed by 183 electoral votes to 34. The vanquished Federalist party was gasping its dying breaths, leaving the field to the triumphant Republicans and one-party rule.

In James Monroe, the man and the times auspiciously met. As the last president to wear an old-style cocked hat, he straddled two generations: the bygone age of the Founding Fathers and the emergent age of nationalism. The serene Virginian with gray-blue eyes was in intellect and personal force among the least distinguished of

■ Fairview Inn or Three Mile House on Old Frederick Road, by Thomas Coke Ruckle, c. 1829 This busy scene on the Frederick Road, leading westward from Baltimore, was typical as pioneers flooded into the newly secured West in the early 1800s.

the first eight presidents. But Monroe was an experienced, level-headed executive, in tune with the public in a time that required sober administration, not heroics.

President Monroe further cemented America's emerging nationalism with a goodwill tour in 1817 that took him deep into Federalist New England. The heartwarming welcome he received even in "the enemy's country" ushered in what one Boston newspaper hailed as the "Era of Good Feelings," as the Monroe administrations have commonly been called ever since.

The Era of Good Feelings, unfortunately, was something of a misnomer. Considerable tranquility and prosperity did in fact smile on the early years of Monroe, but the period was a troubled one. The acute issues of the tariff, the bank, internal improvements, and the sale of public lands were being hotly contested. Sectionalism was crystallizing, and the conflict over slavery was beginning to raise its hideous head.

The Panic of 1819 and the Curse of Hard Times

depression *In economics, a severe and very prolonged period of declining economic activity, high unemployment, and low wages and prices.*

boom *In economics, a period of sudden, spectacular expansion of business activity.*

Much of the goodness went out of the good feelings in 1819, when a paralyzing economic panic descended. It brought deflation, **depression,** bankruptcies, bank failures, unemployment, and the overcrowded pesthouses known as debtors' prisons.

This was the first national financial panic since President Washington took office. Many factors contributed to the catastrophe of 1819, but looming large was overspeculation in frontier lands. The Bank of the United States, through its western branches, had become deeply involved in this popular type of outdoor gambling.

Financial paralysis from the panic, which lasted in some degree for several years, dealt a rude setback to the nationalistic ardor. The West was especially hard hit. When the pinch came, the Bank of the United States forced the speculative ("wildcat") western banks to the wall and foreclosed mortgages on countless farms. All this was technically legal but politically unwise. In the eyes of western debtors, the nationalist Bank of the United States soon became a kind of financial devil.

The panic of 1819 also created backwashes in the political and social world. The poorer classes—the one-suspender men and their families—were severely strapped, and in their troubles was sown the seedbed of Jacksonian democracy. Hard times also directed attention to the inhumanity of imprisoning debtors. Mounting agitation against that often cruel practice bore fruit in remedial legislation in an increasing number of states.

Growing Pains of the West

The onward march to the West continued: nine frontier states had joined the original thirteen between 1791 and 1819. With an eye to preserving the North-South sectional balance, most of these commonwealths had been admitted alternately, free or slave. (See Admission of States in the Appendix.)

Why this explosive expansion? In part, it was simply a continuation of the generations-old westward movement, which had been going on since early colonial days. In addition, the siren call of cheap land—"the Ohio fever"—had a special appeal to European immigrants. With the return of peace in Europe and America, eager newcomers from abroad were beginning to stream down the gangplanks in impressive numbers. Land exhaustion in the older southern tobacco states, where the soil was "mined" rather than cultivated, likewise drove people westward. Glib speculators accepted small down payments, making it easier to buy new holdings.

The western **boom** was stimulated by additional developments. Acute economic distress during the embargo years turned many pinched faces toward the setting sun. The crushing of the Indians in the Northwest by General Harrison and in the Southwest by General Jackson pacified the frontier and opened up vast virgin tracts of land. The building of highways improved the land routes to the Ohio Valley. Noteworthy was the Cumberland Road, begun in 1811, which ran ultimately from western Maryland to Illinois. The use of the first steamboat on western waters, also in 1811, heralded a new era of upstream navigation.

But the West, despite the inflow of settlers, was still weak in population and influence. It could only make its voice heard when it formed alliances with other sections. Western pioneers' principal demands were for cheap federal land, cheap transportation, and cheap money issued by its own **"wildcat" banks** rather than the restrictive Bank of the United States. With the passage of the Land Act of 1820, which offered 80 acres at the minimum price of $1.25 an acre, the West began to make headway in achieving these goals (see "Makers of America: Settlers of the Old Northwest," p. 170).

wildcat bank *An unregulated, speculative bank that issues notes without sufficient capital to back them.*

peculiar institution *Widely used term for the institution of American black slavery.*

Slavery and Sectional Balance

Sectional tensions were stunningly revealed in 1819, when the territory of Missouri knocked on the doors of Congress seeking admission as a slave state. This fertile area contained sufficient population to warrant statehood. But the House of Representatives stymied the plans of the Missourians by passing the incendiary Tallmadge amendment. It stipulated that no more slaves should be brought into Missouri and also provided for the gradual emancipation of children born to slave parents already there. A roar of anger burst from slaveholding southerners.

Southerners saw in the Tallmadge amendment, which they eventually managed to defeat in the Senate, an ominous threat to the sectional balance. When the Constitution was adopted in 1788, the North and South were running neck and neck in wealth and population. But with every passing decade, the North was becoming wealthier and also more thickly settled—an advantage reflected in an increasing northern majority in the House of Representatives. Yet in the Senate, with eleven free states and eleven slave states, the southerners had maintained equality. They were therefore in a good position to thwart any northern effort to interfere with the expansion of slavery, and they did not want to lose this equal balance in the Senate.

The future of the slave system caused southerners profound concern. Missouri was the first state entirely west of the Mississippi River to be carved out of the Louisiana Purchase, and the Missouri emancipation amendment might set a damaging precedent for all the rest of the area. Even more disquieting was another possibility. If Congress could abolish the "**peculiar institution**" in Missouri, might it not attempt to do likewise in the older states of the South? The wounds of the Constitutional Convention of 1787 were once more ripped open.

Burning moral questions also protruded, even though the main issue was political and economic balance. A small but growing group of antislavery agitators in the North seized the occasion to raise an outcry against the evils of slavery. They were determined that the plague of human bondage should not spread farther into the untainted territories.

The Uneasy Missouri Compromise

Deadlock in Washington was at length broken in 1820 by the time-honored American solution of compromise—actually a bundle of three compromises. Courtly and gifted Henry Clay of Kentucky played a leading role as a conciliator. Congress did agree to admit Missouri as a slave state. But at the same time, free-soil Maine, which until then had been part of Massachusetts, was admitted as a separate state. The balance between North and South was thus kept at twelve states each and remained there for the next fifteen years. Although Missouri was permitted to retain slaves, all future bondage was prohibited in the remainder of the Louisiana Purchase north of the line of 36° 30′—the southern boundary of Missouri.

Neither North nor South was completely happy with this horse-trading adjustment, though they had each gained something as well as yielded something. Fortunately, the Missouri Compromise lasted thirty-four years—a vital formative period in the life of the young Republic—and during that time it preserved the

Online Study Center

Primary source
Missouri Compromise, The
college.hmco.com/pic/kennedybrief7e

Settlers of the Old Northwest

The Old Northwest beckoned to settlers after the War of 1812. The withdrawal of the British protector weakened the Indians' grip on the territory. Then the canal and highway boom of the 1820s opened broad arteries along which the westward movement flowed.

The first wave of newcomers came mainly from Kentucky, Tennessee, and the upland regions of Virginia and the Carolinas. Most migrants were roughhewn white farmers who had been pushed from good land to bad by an expanding plantation economy. Some settlers acquired land for the first time. John Palmer, whose family left Kentucky for Illinois in 1831, recalled his father telling him "of land so cheap that we could all be landholders, where men were *equal*." Migrants from the South settled mainly in the southern portions of Ohio, Indiana, and Illinois.

Having escaped from a lowly social position in a slaveholding society, many of these new immigrants sought to prevent the spread of slavery by enacting Black Codes in their new territories that prevented blacks from following them. They wanted their own democratic communities, free of rich planters and African Americans alike.

If southern "Butternuts," as these settlers were called, dominated settlement in the 1820s, the next decade brought equally land-starved Yankees from the Northeast. Yankee settlers came especially to the northern parts of Ohio, Indiana, and Illinois. Unlike the Butternuts who wanted to quit forever the imposing framework of southern society, northerners hoped to re-create the world they had left behind.

Conflict soon emerged between Yankees and southerners. As self-sufficient farmers who did not produce for the market, southerners viewed the northern newcomers as inhospitable, greedy, and excessively ambitious. Northerners, in turn, viewed the southerners as uncivilized, a "coon dog and butcher knife tribe" with no interest in education, self-improvement, or agricultural innovation. While Yankees advocated taxes to establish public schools and fund roads and canals, southerners opposed such efforts, especially public schooling. Religion also divided settlers. Northerners typically embraced denominations like Congregationalism and Presbyterianism that supported a learned ministry. Southerners preferred the more revivalist Methodists and Baptists, and preferred humble, uneducated preacher-farmers who would, in their eyes, stay closer to the Lord and his people.

As the population swelled and the region acquired its own character, the stark contrasts between northerners and southerners started to fade. Some residents like Abraham Lincoln, with roots in Kentucky, came to adopt views more akin to those of the Yankees than the southerners. Railroads and Great Lakes shipping tied the region economically ever more tightly to the Northeast. Yankees and southerners sometimes allied as new kinds of economic, ethnic, and religious cleavages emerged.

Still, echoes of the clash between Yankees and Butternuts persisted. During the Civil War, the southern counties of Ohio, Indiana, and Illinois, where southerners had first settled, harbored sympathizers with the South and served as a key area for Confederate military infiltration into the North. Decades later these same counties became a stronghold of the Ku Klux Klan. The Old Northwest may have become firmly anchored to the economy of the Northeast, but vestiges of its early dual personality persisted.

shaky compact of the states. Yet the embittered dispute over slavery heralded the future breakup of the Union. Ever after, the morality of the South's peculiar institution was an issue that could not be swept under the rug. The Missouri Compromise only ducked the question—it did not resolve it. Sooner or later, Thomas Jefferson predicted, it will "burst on us as a tornado."

The Missouri Compromise and the concurrent panic of 1819 should have dimmed the political star of President Monroe. Certainly both unhappy events had a dampening effect on the Era of Good Feelings. But smooth-spoken James Monroe was so popular, and the Federalist opposition so weak, that he received every electoral vote in the election of 1820 except one. Unanimity remained an honor reserved for George Washington.

John Marshall and Judicial Nationalism

The upsurging nationalism of the post-Ghent years, despite the ominous setbacks concerning slavery, was further reflected and reinforced by the Supreme Court. The high tribunal continued to be dominated by the tall, thin, and aggressive Chief Justice John Marshall. And many of Marshall's most famous decisions bolstered the power of the federal government at the expense of the states.

A notable case in this category was *McCulloch* v. *Maryland* (1819). The suit involved an attempt by the state of Maryland to destroy a branch of the Bank of the United States by imposing a tax on its notes. John Marshall, speaking for the Court, declared the bank constitutional by invoking the Hamiltonian doctrine of implied powers (see p. 136). At the same time, he strengthened federal authority and slapped at state infringements when he denied the right of Maryland to tax the bank, with the ringing declaration that "the power to tax is the power to destroy."

Marshall's ruling in this case gave the doctrine of "loose construction" its most famous formulation. The Constitution, he said, was "intended to endure for ages to come and, consequently, to be adapted to the various crises of human affairs." Finally, he declared, "Let the end be legitimate, let it be within the scope of the Constitution, and all means which are appropriate, which are plainly adapted to

> *While the debate over Missouri was raging, Thomas Jefferson (1743–1826) wrote to a correspondent,*
>
> "The Missouri question . . . is the most portentous one which ever yet threatened our Union. In the gloomiest moment of the revolutionary war I never had any apprehensions equal to what I feel from this source. . . . [The] question, like a fire-bell in the night, awakened and filled me with terror. . . . [With slavery] we have a wolf by the ears, and we can neither hold him nor safely let him go."
>
> *John Quincy Adams confided to his diary,*
>
> "I take it for granted that the present question is a mere preamble—a title-page to a great, tragic volume."

Online Study Center

Interactive map
Missouri Compromise 1820–1821
college.hmco.com/pic/kennedybrief7e

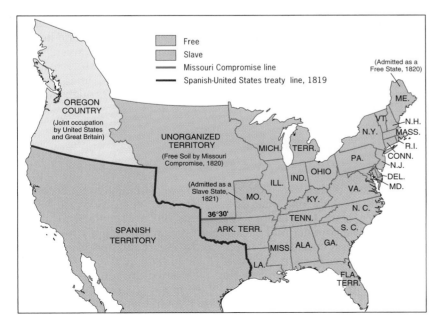

■ **The Missouri Compromise and Slavery, 1820–1821** Note the 36° 30' line. In the 1780s Thomas Jefferson had written of slavery in America: "Indeed I tremble for my country when I reflect that God is just; that his justice cannot sleep forever; that . . . the Almighty has no attribute which can take side with us in such a contest." Later, at the time of the Missouri Compromise, Jefferson feared that his worst forebodings were coming to pass. "I considered it at once," he said of the Missouri question, "as the knell of the Union."

■ **John Marshall (1755–1835)** Born in a log cabin on the Virginia frontier, he attended law lectures for just a few weeks at the College of William and Mary—his only formal education. Yet Marshall would go on to prove himself a brilliant chief justice. One admiring lawyer wrote of him, "His black eyes . . . possess an irradiating spirit, which proclaims the imperial powers of the mind that sits enthroned therein."

demagogic (demagogue) *Concerning a leader who stirs up the common people by appeals to emotion and prejudice, often for selfish or irrational ends.*

contract *In law, an agreement in which each of two or more parties binds itself to perform some act in exchange for what the other party similarly pledges to do.*

that end, which are not prohibited, but consist with the letter and spirit of the Constitution, are constitutional." Five years later, in the "steamboat case" of *Gibbons* v. *Ogden* (1824), Marshall again upheld federal supremacy by striking down New York's awarding of a monopoly on waterborne commerce between New Jersey and New York to a private company.

Another set of Marshall's decisions bolstered judicial barriers against democratic or **demagogic** attacks on property rights. The notorious case of *Fletcher* v. *Peck* (1810) arose when a Georgia legislature, swayed by bribery, granted 35 million acres in the Yazoo River country (present-day Mississippi) to private speculators. The next legislature, yielding to an angry public outcry, canceled the crooked transaction. But the Supreme Court, with Marshall presiding, decreed that the legislative grant was a **contract** (even though fraudulently secured) and that the Constitution forbids state laws "impairing" contracts (see Art. I, Sec. X, para. 1). The decision is perhaps most noteworthy for further protecting property rights against popular pressures. It is also one of the earliest clear assertions of the right of the Court to invalidate state laws conflicting with the federal Constitution.

A similar principle was upheld in the case of *Dartmouth College* v. *Woodward* (1819), perhaps the best-remembered of Marshall's decisions. The college had been granted a charter by King George III in 1769, but the democratic New Hampshire state legislature had seen fit to change it. Dartmouth appealed the case, employing as counsel its most distinguished alumnus, Daniel Webster, himself an ardent nationalist. The "Godlike Daniel" pulled out all the stops in his tear-inducing summary when he declaimed, "It is, sir, as I have said, a small college. And yet there are those who love it." Marshall put the states firmly in their place when he ruled that the original charter must stand. It was a contract, and the Constitution protected contracts against state encroachments. The *Dartmouth* decision had the fortunate effect of safeguarding business enterprise from domination by the states. But it had the unfortunate effect of creating a precedent that enabled chartered corporations, in later years, to escape the handcuffs of needed public control.

Marshall's decisions are felt even today. In this sense his nationalism was the most tenaciously enduring of the era. He buttressed the federal Union and helped to create a stable, nationally uniform environment for business. In an age when America was veering toward popular democratic control, Marshall almost single-handedly shaped the Constitution along conservative, centralizing lines that ran somewhat counter to the dominant spirit of the new country. Through him the conservative Hamiltonians partly triumphed from the tomb.

Sharing Oregon and Acquiring Florida

The robust nationalism of the years after the War of 1812 was likewise reflected in foreign policy. To this end, the nationalistic President Monroe teamed with his nationalistic secretary of state, John Quincy Adams, the cold and scholarly son of the frosty ex-president. The younger Adams, a superb statesman, happily rose above the ingrown Federalist sectionalism of his native New England and proved to be one of the great secretaries of state.

To its credit, the Monroe administration negotiated the much-underrated Treaty of 1818 with Britain. This agreement fixed the vague northern limits of Louisiana along the forty-ninth parallel from the Lake of the Woods (in present-day Minnesota) to the Rocky Mountains. The treaty also provided for a ten-year

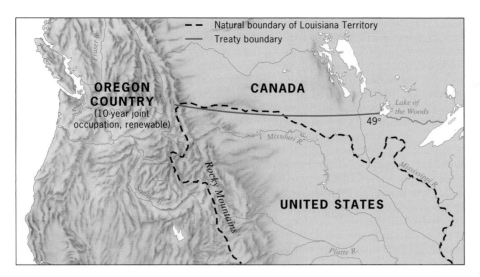

Natural boundary of Louisiana Territory
Treaty boundary

OREGON COUNTRY (10-year joint occupation, renewable)

CANADA

49°

Lake of the Woods

UNITED STATES

Rocky Mountains

Fraser R.

Missouri R.

Mississippi R.

Snake R.

Platte R.

■ **U.S.-British Boundary Settlement, 1818** Notice that the United States gained considerable territory by securing a treaty boundary rather than the natural boundary of the Missouri River watershed. The line of 49° was extended westward to the Pacific Ocean under the Treaty of 1846 with Britain.

joint occupation of the untamed Oregon country, without a surrender of the rights or claims of either America or Britain.

To the south lay semitropical Spanish Florida, which many Americans believed geography and providence had destined to become part of the United States. Americans already claimed West Florida, where uninvited American settlers had torn down the hated Spanish flag in 1810. Congress ratified this grab in 1812, and during the War of 1812 a small American army seized the Mobile region. But the bulk of Florida remained under Spanish rule.

When an epidemic of revolutions in South America, beginning in 1816, led to the birth of several new republics there, Spain was forced to denude Florida of troops to fight the rebels. General Andrew Jackson, idol of the West and scourge of the Indians, saw opportunity in the undefended swamplands. On the pretext that hostile Seminole Indians and fugitive slaves were using Florida as a refuge, Jackson secured a commission to enter Spanish territory, punish the Indians, and recapture the runaways. But he was to respect all posts under the Spanish flag.

Early in 1818 Jackson swept across the Florida border with all the fury of an avenging angel. He hanged two Indian chiefs and executed two British subjects for assisting the Indians. He also seized the two most important Spanish forts in the area, St. Marks and Pensacola, where he deposed the Spanish governor.

Jackson had clearly exceeded his instructions from Washington. Alarmed, President Monroe consulted his cabinet. Its members were for disavowing or disciplining the overzealous Jackson—all except the lone wolf John Quincy Adams, who refused to howl with the pack. An ardent patriot and nationalist, the flinty New Englander took the offensive and demanded huge concessions from Spain.

In the mislabeled Florida Purchase Treaty of 1819, Spain ceded Florida as well as shadowy Spanish claims to Oregon, in exchange for America's abandonment of equally murky claims to Texas, soon to become part of independent Mexico. The hitherto vague western boundary of Louisiana was made to run zigzag along the Rockies to the forty-second parallel and then to turn due west to the Pacific, dividing Oregon from Spanish holdings.

The Menace of Monarchy in America

After the Napoleonic nightmare, the rethroned autocrats of Europe banded together in a kind of monarchical protective association. Determined to restore the good old days, they undertook to stamp out the democratic tendencies that had sprouted from soil they considered richly manured by the ideals of the French Revolution. The world must be made safe *from* democracy.

The crowned despots acted promptly. With complete ruthlessness, they smothered the embers of rebellion in Italy (1821) and in Spain (1823). According to the European rumor factory, they were also gazing across the Atlantic. Russia,

Austria, Prussia, and France, acting in partnership, would presumably send powerful fleets and armies to the revolted colonies of Spanish America and there restore the autocratic Spanish king to his ancestral domains.

Many Americans were alarmed. Sympathetic to democratic revolutions everywhere, they cheered when the Latin American republics rose from the ruins of monarchy. Americans feared that if the European powers intervened in the New World, the cause of republicanism would suffer irreparable harm. The physical security of the United States—the mother lode of democracy—would be endangered by the proximity of powerful and unfriendly forces.

The southward push of the Russian bear from the chilly region now known as Alaska had already publicized the menace of monarchy to North America. In 1821 the tsar of Russia issued a decree extending Russian jurisdiction over one hundred miles of the open sea down to the line of 51°, an area that embraced most of the coast of present-day British Columbia.

Britain, still Ruler of the Seas, recoiled from joining the continental European powers in crushing the newly won liberties of the Spanish-Americans. These revolutionaries had thrown open their monopoly-bound ports to outside trade, and British shippers, as well as Americans, had found the profits sweet. Accordingly, in August 1823, George Canning, the haughty British foreign secretary, approached the American minister in London to ask if the United States would join Britain in warning the European despots to keep their harsh hands off the Latin American republics? The American minister, lacking instructions, referred this fateful scheme to his superiors in Washington.

Monroe and His Doctrine

The tenacious nationalist, Secretary Adams, was hardheaded enough to be wary of Britons bearing gifts. Why should the lordly British, with the mightiest navy afloat, need America as an ally—an America that had neither naval nor military strength? Such a union, argued Adams, was undignified—like a tiny American "cockboat" sailing "in the wake of the British man-of-war."

Adams, ever alert, thought that he detected a joker in the Canning proposal. If Canning could seduce the United States into guaranteeing existing territorial arrangements in the New World, America's hands would be morally tied against its own expansion. Adams suspected—correctly—that European powers had no definite plans for invading the Americas. In any event the British navy would prevent hostile fleets from interfering with South American markets, so Adams decided it was safe for Uncle Sam to blow a defiant nationalistic blast at all Europe.

The Monroe Doctrine was born late in 1823, when the nationalistic Adams won the nationalistic Monroe over to his way of thinking. The president, in his regular annual message to Congress on December 2, 1823, incorporated a stern warning to the European powers. Its two basic features were (1) noncolonization and (2) nonintervention.

Monroe first directed his verbal volley primarily at Russia in the Northwest. He proclaimed, in effect, that the era of colonization in the Americas had ended and that henceforth the hunting season was permanently closed. What the great powers had they might keep, but neither they nor any other Old World governments could seize or otherwise acquire more.

At the same time Monroe trumpeted a warning blast against foreign intervention. He was clearly concerned with regions to the south, where the fledgling Latin American republics were extremely vulnerable. Monroe bluntly directed the crowned heads of Europe to keep their hated monarchical systems out of the Western Hemisphere. For its part the United States would not intervene in the war that the Greeks were then fighting against the Turks for their independence.

Online Study Center

Primary source
Monroe Doctrine
college.hmco.com/pic/kennedybrief7e

Monroe's Doctrine Appraised

The ermined monarchs of Europe were angered at Monroe's doctrine. Having resented the incendiary American experiment from the beginning, they were deeply offended by Monroe's high-flown declaration—all the more so because of the gulf between America's pretentious pronouncements and its puny military strength. But though offended by the upstart Yankees, the European powers found their hands tied, and their frustration increased their annoyance. Even if they had worked out plans for invading the Americas, they would have been helpless before the booming broadsides of the British navy.

Monroe's solemn warning made little splash in the newly hatched republics to the south. Anyone could see that Uncle Sam was only secondarily concerned about his neighbors, because he was primarily concerned about defending himself against future invasion. Only a relatively few educated Latin Americans knew of the message, and they generally recognized that it was the British navy—not the paper pronouncement of James Monroe—that stood between them and a hostile Europe.

In truth, Monroe's message actually did not have very much contemporary significance. Americans applauded it and then forgot it as they turned back to such activities as felling trees and fighting Indians. Not until 1845 did President James Polk revive it, and not until midcentury did it become an important national dogma.

The Monroe Doctrine might more accurately have been called the Self-Defense Doctrine. President Monroe was concerned mainly with the security of his own country—not of Latin America. The United States has never willingly permitted a powerful foreign nation to secure a foothold near its strategic Caribbean vitals. Yet in the absence of the British navy or other allies, the strength of the Monroe Doctrine has never been greater than America's power to eject the trespasser.

The Monroe Doctrine has had a long career of ups and downs. It was never law—domestic or international. It was not, technically speaking, a pledge or an agreement. It was merely a simple statement of the policy of President Monroe. What one president says, another may unsay. And Monroe's presidential successors have ignored, revived, distorted, or expanded the original version, chiefly by adding interpretations. In 1823 the Monroe Doctrine was largely an expression of post-1812 American nationalism directed at a specific menace, and hence is a kind of period piece. But the doctrine proved to be the most famous and long-lived offspring of that nationalism. While giving vent to a spirit of patriotism, it simultaneously deepened the American illusion of isolationism. Many Americans falsely concluded, then and later, that the Republic was in fact insulated from European dangers simply because it wanted to be.

✪ Chapter Summary ✪

Americans began the War of 1812 with high hopes of conquering Canada and delivering a severe blow to their British tormentors. But their strategy and efforts were badly flawed, and before long British and Canadian forces had thrown the United States on the defensive. The Americans fared somewhat better in naval warfare on the Great Lakes, but by 1814 the British had burned Washington and were threatening elsewhere. The Treaty of Ghent in 1814 ended the war in a stalemate that solved none of the original issues. But largely because of Andrew Jackson's "postwar" victory in the Battle of New Orleans in 1815, Americans counted the war a success and increasingly turned away from European affairs and toward isolationism.

Despite some secessionist talk by New Englanders at the Hartford Convention, the ironic outcome of the divisive and near-disastrous war was a strong surge of American nationalism and unity. Partisan political conflict disappeared during the "Era of Good Feelings" under President Madison. A fervent new nationalism appeared in diverse areas of culture, economics, and foreign policy.

But the Era of Good Feelings was soon threatened by the economic panic of 1819, caused largely by excessive land speculation and unstable banks. An even more serious threat to national unity came from the first major sectional dispute over slavery, which was postponed but not really resolved by the Missouri Compromise of 1820.

Under Chief Justice John Marshall, the Supreme Court further enhanced its role as the major force upholding a powerful national government and conservative defense of property rights. Marshall's rulings partially checked the general movement toward states' rights and popular democracy.

Nationalism also led to a more assertive American foreign policy. Andrew Jackson's military adventures in Spanish Florida resulted in the forced purchase of that territory by the United States. American fears of European intervention in Latin America encouraged Monroe and J. Q. Adams to declare the Monroe Doctrine. The announcement had little immediate practical effect, but it carried large consequences for the future of United States foreign policy in the Americas.

13

The Rise of a Mass Democracy

1824–1840

IN THE FULL ENJOYMENT OF THE GIFTS OF HEAVEN AND THE FRUITS OF SUPERIOR INDUSTRY, ECONOMY, AND VIRTUE, EVERY MAN IS EQUALLY ENTITLED TO PROTECTION BY LAW; BUT WHEN THE LAWS UNDERTAKE TO ADD TO THOSE NATURAL AND JUST ADVANTAGES ARTIFICIAL DISTINCTIONS . . . AND EXCLUSIVE PRIVILEGES . . . THE HUMBLE MEMBERS OF SOCIETY—THE FARMERS, MECHANICS, AND LABORERS . . . HAVE A RIGHT TO COMPLAIN OF THE INJUSTICE OF THEIR GOVERNMENT.

ANDREW JACKSON, 1832

The so-called Era of Good Feelings was never entirely tranquil, but even the illusion of national consensus was shattered by the panic of 1819 and the Missouri Compromise of 1820. Economic distress and the slavery issue raised the political stakes in the 1820s and 1830s. Vigorous political conflict, once feared, came to be celebrated as necessary for the health of democracy. New political parties emerged. New styles of campaigning took hold. A new chapter opened in the history of American politics. The political landscape of 1824 was similar, in its broad outlines, to that of 1796. By 1840 it would be almost unrecognizable.

The **deference,** apathy, and virtually nonexistent party organizations of the Era of Good Feelings yielded to the boisterous democracy, frenzied vitality, and strong political parties of the Jacksonian era. The old suspicion of political parties as illegitimate disrupters of society's natural harmony gave way to an acceptance of the sometimes wild contentiousness of political life.

In 1828 an energetic new party, the Democrats, captured the White House. By the 1830s the Democrats faced an equally vigorous opposition party in the form of the Whigs. This two-party system institutionalized divisions that had vexed the Revolutionary generation and came to constitute an important part of the nation's checks and balances on political power.

New forms of politicking emerged in this era, as candidates used banners, badges, parades, barbecues, free drinks, and baby kissing to get out the vote. Voter turnout rose dramatically; only about one-quarter of eligible voters cast a ballot in the presidential election of 1824, but that proportion doubled in 1828, and in the election of 1840 it reached 78 percent. Everywhere people flexed their political muscles.

Focus Questions

1. How did John Quincy Adams's victory through an alleged "corrupt bargain" in the election of 1824 set the stage for Andrew Jackson's election as the popular hero of the Democratic party in 1828 and the emergence of a new democratic politics?
2. How did Jackson's policies of westward expansion and Indian removal lead to the "Trail of Tears" to Oklahoma and the Seminole Wars in Florida?

Chronology

1822	Vesey slave rebellion conspiracy in Charleston, South Carolina.	**1833**	Compromise Tariff of 1833. Jackson removes federal deposits from Bank of the United States.
1823	Mexico opens Texas to American settlers.	**1836**	Bank of the United States expires. Specie Circular issued. Bureau of Indian Affairs established. Battle of the Alamo. Battle of San Jacinto. Texas wins independence from Mexico. Van Buren elected president.
1824	Lack of electoral majority for presidency throws election into the House of Representatives.		
1825	House elects John Quincy Adams president.		
1828	Tariff of 1828 ("Tariff of Abominations"). Jackson elected president.	**1837**	Seminole Indians defeated and most eventually removed from Florida. Panic of 1837. United States recognizes republic of Texas but refuses annexation.
1829	Indian Removal Act.		
1832	"Bank War"—Jackson vetoes bill to recharter Bank of the United States. Tariff of 1832. Jackson defeats Clay for presidency. Black Hawk War.	**1838-1839**	Cherokee Indians removed on "Trail of Tears."
1832-1833	South Carolina nullification crisis.	**1840**	Independent Treasury established. Harrison defeats Van Buren for presidency.

3. How did Andrew Jackson's "war" against the Second Bank of the United States fuel popular democracy as well as the anti-Jackson Whig party?
4. What were the causes of the Texas revolution and independence, and why did efforts to bring Texas into the Union stir such sharp controversy?
5. What were the central features of America's new mass democracy and two-party system, and how were these developments reflected in the flamboyant "log cabin and hard cider" campaign of 1840?

⭐ **William Henry Harrison's "Log Cabin" Campaign, 1840**

⭐ **The Establishment of the Two-Party System**

⭐ **Examining the Evidence: Satiric Bank Note, 1837**

⭐ **Makers of America: Mexican or Texican?**

⭐ **Varying Viewpoints: What Was Jacksonian Democracy?**

The "Corrupt Bargain" of 1824

The last of the old-style elections was marked by the controversial "corrupt bargain" of 1824. The woods were full of presidential timber as James Monroe, last of the Virginia dynasty, completed his second term. Four candidates towered above the others: John Quincy Adams of Massachusetts, highly intelligent, experienced, and aloof; Henry Clay of Kentucky, the gamy and gallant "Harry of the West"; William H. Crawford of Georgia, an able though ailing giant of a man; and Andrew Jackson of Tennessee, the gaunt and gutsy hero of New Orleans.

All four rivals professed to be "Republicans." Well-organized parties had not yet emerged; their identities were so fuzzy, in fact, that John C. Calhoun appeared as the vice-presidential candidate on both the Adams and the Jackson tickets.

The results of the noisy campaign were interesting but confusing. Jackson, the war hero, clearly had the strongest personal appeal, especially in the West, where his campaign against the forces of corruption and privilege in government resonated deeply. He polled almost as many popular votes as his next two rivals combined, but he failed to win a majority of the electoral vote (see table on p. 178). In such a deadlock the House of Representatives, as directed by the Twelfth Amendment (see the Appendix), must choose among the top three candidates. Clay was thus eliminated, yet as Speaker of the House he presided over the very chamber that had to pick the winner.

deference *The yielding of opinion to the judgment of someone else; in politics, the inclination of lower social or economic classes to conform to the political views and choices of social elites.*

■ **Canvassing for a Vote, by George Caleb Bingham, 1852** This painting shows the "new politics" of the Jacksonian era. Politicians now had to take their message to the common man.

puritanical *Extremely or excessively strict in matters of morals or religion.*

Online Study Center

Primary source
Election Day at the State House
college.hmco.com/pic/kennedybrief7e

The influential Clay was in a position to throw the election to the candidate of his choice. He reached the decision by the process of elimination. Crawford, recently felled by a paralytic stroke, was out of the picture. Clay hated the "military chieftain" Jackson, who in turn bitterly resented Clay's public denunciation of his Florida foray in 1818. The only candidate left was the **puritanical** Adams, with whom Clay—a free-living gambler and duelist—had never established cordial personal relations. But the two men had much in common politically: both were fervid nationalists and advocates of the American System. Shortly before the final ballot in the House, Clay met privately with Adams and assured him of his support.

Decision day came early in 1825. The House of Representatives met amid tense excitement, with sick members being carried in on stretchers. On the first ballot, thanks largely to Clay's behind-the-scenes influence, Adams was elected president. A few days later, the victor announced that Henry Clay would be the new secretary of state.

Masses of angered Jacksonians, most of them common folk, roared in protest against this "corrupt bargain." Jackson condemned Clay as the "Judas of the West," and John Randolph of Virginia declared that Clay "shines and stinks like . . . a rotten mackerel by moonlight." No positive evidence has ever been unearthed to prove that Adams and Clay entered into a formal bargain. Clay was a natural choice for secretary of state, and Adams was scrupulously honest and not given to patronage. Even if a bargain had been struck, it was not necessarily corrupt. Deals of this nature have long been the stock-in-trade of politicians. But the outcry over Adams's election showed that change was in the wind. What had once been common practice was

Election of 1824

Candidates	Electoral Vote	Popular Vote	Popular Percentage
Jackson	99	153,544	42.16%
Adams	84	108,740	31.89%
Crawford	41	46,618	12.95%
Clay	37	47,136	12.99%

now condemned as furtive, elitist, and subversive of democracy. The next president would not be chosen behind closed doors.

A Yankee Misfit in the White House

John Quincy Adams was a chip off the old family glacier. Short, thickset, and billiard-bald, he was even more frigidly austere than his presidential father, John Adams. Shunning people, he often went for early morning swims, sometimes stark naked, in the then-pure Potomac River. Essentially a closeted thinker rather than a politician, he was irritable, sarcastic, and tactless. Yet few individuals have ever come to the presidency with a more brilliant record in statecraft, especially in foreign affairs. He ranks as one of the most successful secretaries of state, yet one of the least successful presidents.

A man of scrupulous honor, Adams entered upon his four-year "sentence" in the White House smarting under charges of "bargain," "corruption," and "**usurpation.**" Fewer than one-third of the voters had voted for him. As the first "minority president," he would have found it difficult to win popular support even under the most favorable conditions. He possessed almost none of the arts of the politician and scorned those who did. He refused to engage in the growing practice of patronage, appointing almost none of his political supporters to office. In the dawning age of back-slapping and baby-kissing democracy, the cold fish John Quincy Adams could hardly hope for success at the polls.

Adams's nationalistic views contributed to his woes in the White House. Much of the nation was turning away from post-Ghent nationalism toward states' rights and sectionalism. But Adams swam against the tide. Confirmed nationalist that he was, the new president urged Congress in his first annual message to construct a national network of roads and canals. He also renewed George Washington's proposal for a national university and went so far as to advocate federal support for an astronomical observatory.

The public reaction to these proposals was prompt and unfavorable. To many workaday Americans grubbing out stumps, astronomical observatories seemed like a scandalous waste of public funds. The South in particular bristled. If the federal government could meddle in local concerns like education and roads, it might some day try to lay its hand on the "peculiar institution" of black slavery.

usurpation *The act of seizing, occupying, or enjoying the place, power, or functions of someone without legal right.*

mudslinging *Malicious, unscrupulous attacks against an opponent.*

Going "Whole Hog" for Jackson in 1828

The presidential campaign for Andrew Jackson had started early—on February 9, 1825, the day of John Quincy Adams's controversial election by the House—and it continued noisily for nearly four years.

Even before the election of 1828, the temporarily united Republicans of the Era of Good Feelings had split into two camps. One was the National Republicans, with Adams as their standard-bearer. The other was the Democratic-Republicans, with the fiery Jackson heading their ticket. Chanting "All hail, Old Hickory" and planting hickory poles for their hickory-tough hero, Jackson's zealots argued that the will of the people had been thwarted in 1825 by the backstairs "corrupt bargain" between Adams and Clay. The only way to right the wrong was to seat Jackson, who would then bring about "reform" by sweeping out the "dishonest" Adams gang.

Mudslinging reached new lows in 1828, and the electorate developed a taste for bare-knuckle politics. Adams would not stoop to gutter tactics, but many of his backers were less squeamish. They described Jackson's mother as a prostitute and his wife as an adulteress, and they recounted "Old Hickory's" numerous duels and brawls and his hanging of six militiamen.

Jackson men also hit below the belt. A billiard table that President Adams had purchased with his own money became, in the mouths of rabid Jacksonites, "gambling tables" in the "presidential palace." Jackson campaigners mocked Adams's large federal salaries and even accused him of having served as a pimp for the Russian tsar during his time as minister to St. Petersburg.

On voting day the electorate split on largely sectional lines. Jackson's strongest support came from the West and South. The middle Atlantic states and the Old Northwest were divided, while Adams won the backing of his own New England as well as the propertied "better elements" of the Northeast. But when the popular vote was converted to electoral votes, General Jackson's triumph could not be denied. Old Hickory had trounced Adams by an electoral count of 178 to 83. Although a considerable part of Jackson's support was lined up by **machine** politicians in eastern cities, particularly in New York and Pennsylvania, the political center of gravity clearly had shifted away from the conservative eastern seaboard toward the emerging states across the mountains.

machine *A hierarchical political organization, often controlled through patronage or spoils, where professional workers deliver large blocs of voters to preferred candidates.*

The Advent of Old Hickory Jackson

The new president cut a striking figure—tall, lean, with bushy iron-gray hair brushed high above a prominent forehead, craggy eyebrows, and blue eyes. His irritability and emaciated condition resulted in part from long-term bouts with dysentery, malaria, tuberculosis, and lead poisoning from two bullets that he carried in his body from near-fatal duels. His autobiography was written in his lined face.

Jackson's upbringing had its shortcomings. Born in the Carolinas and early orphaned, "Mischievous Andy" grew up without parental restraints. As a youth, he displayed much more interest in brawling and cockfighting than in his scanty opportunities for reading and spelling. Although he eventually learned to express himself in writing with vigor and clarity, his grammar was always rough-hewn and his spelling original. He sometimes misspelled a word two different ways in the same letter.

The youthful Carolinian shrewdly moved "up West" to Tennessee, where fighting was prized above writing. There—through native intelligence, force of personality, and powers of leadership—he became a judge and a member of Congress. Afflicted with a violent temper, he early became involved in numerous duels, stabbings, and bloody frays. His passions were so profound that on occasion he would choke into silence when he tried to speak.

The first president from the West, the first nominated in a formal party convention (in 1832), and only the second without a college education (Washington was the first), Jackson was unique. His university was adversity. He had risen from the masses but was not one of them, except insofar as he shared many of their prejudices. Essentially a frontier aristocrat, he owned many slaves, cultivated broad acres, and lived in one of the finest mansions in America—the Hermitage, near Nashville, Tennessee.

Jackson's inauguration symbolized the ascendancy of the masses. "Hickoryites" poured into Washington from far away, sleeping on hotel floors and in hallways. They were eager to see their hero take office, and perhaps to pick up a well-paying office for themselves. Nobodies mingled with notables as the White House, for the first time, was thrown open to the multitude. A milling crowd of rubbernecking clerks and shopkeepers, hobnailed artisans, and grimy laborers surged in, allegedly wrecking the china and furniture and threatening the "people's champion" with cracked ribs. Jackson was hastily spirited through a side door, and the White House miraculously emptied itself when the word was passed that huge bowls of well-spiked punch had been placed on the lawns. Such was the "inaugural brawl."

■ **Presidential Election of 1828 (with electoral vote by state)** Jackson swept the South and West, while Adams retained the old Federalist stronghold of the Northeast. Yet Jackson's inroads in the Northeast were decisive. He won twenty of New York's electoral votes and all twenty-eight of Pennsylvania's. If those votes had gone the other way, Adams would have been victorious—by a margin of one vote.

In 1824 Thomas Jefferson (1743–1826) said of Jackson,

"When I was President of the Senate he was a Senator; and he could never speak on account of the rashness of his feelings. I have seen him attempt it repeatedly, and as often choke with rage. His passions are no doubt cooler now . . . but he is a dangerous man."

To conservatives, this orgy seemed like the end of the world. "King Mob" reigned triumphant as Jacksonian vulgarity replaced Jeffersonian simplicity. Faint-hearted traditionalists shuddered, drew their blinds, and recalled with trepidation the opening scenes of the French Revolution.

Jackson Nationalizes the Spoils System

Once in power, the Democrats, famously suspicious of the federal government, demonstrated they were not above striking some bargains of their own. Under Jackson the **spoils** system—that is, rewarding political supporters with public office—was introduced into the federal government on a large scale. Its name came from Senator William Marcy's classic remark in 1832, "To the victors belong the spoils of the enemy." The system had already secured a firm hold in New York and Pennsylvania, where well-greased machines ladled out the "gravy" of office.

Jackson defended the spoils system on democratic grounds. "Every man is as good as his neighbor," he declared—perhaps "equally better." As this was believed to be so, and as the routine of office was thought to be simple enough for any upstanding American to learn quickly, why encourage the development of an aristocratic, bureaucratic, officeholding class? Better to bring in new blood, Jackson argued. But the spoils system was less about qualifications than about rewarding old cronies. The questions Democrats asked each appointee were not "What can he do for the country?" but "What has he done for the party?" and "Is he loyal to Jackson?"

Scandal inevitably accompanied the new system. Men who had openly bought their posts by campaign contributions were appointed to high office. Illiterates, incompetents, and plain crooks were given positions of public trust; men on the make lusted for the spoils—rather than the toils—of office. Samuel Swartwout, despite ample warnings of his untrustworthiness, was awarded the lucrative post of collector of customs for the port of New York. Nearly nine years later he "Swartwouted out" for Britain, leaving his accounts more than a million dollars short—the first person to steal a million from the Washington government.

But despite its undeniable abuses, the spoils system was an important element of the emerging two-party order, cementing as it did loyalty to party over competing claims from economic class or geographic region. The promise of patronage provided a compelling reason for Americans to pick a party and stick with it through thick and thin.

■ **Andrew Jackson (1767–1845), by Thomas Sully, 1845** A self-taught and popularly elected major general of the Tennessee militia, Andrew Jackson became a major general of the U.S. Army in 1814. He was noted for his stern discipline, iron will ("Old Hickory"), and good luck.

spoils *Public offices given as a reward for political support.*

The Tricky "Tariff of Abominations"

The touchy tariff issue had been one of John Quincy Adams's biggest headaches. Now Andrew Jackson felt his predecessor's pain. In 1824 Congress had increased the general tariff significantly, but wool manufacturers bleated for still-higher barriers. Ardent Jacksonites now played a cynical political game. They promoted a high-tariff bill, expecting it to be defeated, which would give a black eye to then President Adams. To their surprise the tariff passed in 1828, and Andrew Jackson inherited the political hot potato.

Southerners, as heavy consumers of manufactured goods with little manufacturing of their own, were hostile to tariffs, particularly to this high Tariff of 1828. Hotheads branded it the "Black Tariff" and the "Tariff of Abominations." Several southern states adopted formal protests, and in South Carolina flags were lowered to half-mast.

Why did the South react so angrily to the tariff? Southerners believed, not illogically, that the "Yankee tariff" discriminated against them. Southerners who sold their cotton in an unprotected world market were forced to buy expensive manufactured goods from Yankee and middle state producers heavily protected by tariffs, and the tariff provided a convenient and plausible scapegoat for the hard times befalling the Old South.

But much deeper issues underlay the southern outcry—in particular, a growing anxiety about possible federal interference with the institution of slavery. The congressional debate on the Missouri Compromise had kindled those anxieties, and they were further fanned by an abortive slave rebellion in Charleston in 1822, led by a free black named Denmark Vesey. South Carolinians, still closely tied to the British West Indies, knew full well that slaveholding West Indians were feeling the mounting pressures of British abolitionism on the London government. American abolitionists might similarly use the power of the Washington government to suppress slavery. If so, now was the time, and the tariff was the issue, for making a strong stand against all federal encroachments on states' rights.

South Carolinians took the lead in protesting the "Tariff of Abominations." Vice President John C. Calhoun, a topflight political theorist, secretly authored a pamphlet known as the "South Carolina Exposition" that the state legislature published in 1828. (As vice president he was forced to conceal his authorship.) Going a stride beyond the Kentucky and Virginia resolutions of 1798, it bluntly and explicitly proposed that the states should nullify the tariff—that is, they should declare it null and void within their borders.

"Nullies" in South Carolina

The stage was set for a showdown. Through Jackson's first term the South Carolina nullifiers—"nullies" they were called—tried strenuously to muster the necessary two-thirds vote in the legislature, but they were blocked by a determined minority of Unionists. Congress pared away the worst "abominations" by passing the new, somewhat lower Tariff of 1832, but it was still frankly protectionist and fell far short of satisfying southern demands.

South Carolina was now nerved for drastic action. After the "nullies" won a commanding majority in the state election of 1832, the legislature called a special convention. Meeting in Columbia, the delegates solemnly declared the existing tariff null and void in South Carolina, and threatened to take their state out of the Union if Washington attempted to collect the customs duties by force.

Such tactics might have intimidated John Quincy Adams, but Andrew Jackson was the wrong president to stare down. The cantankerous general would never permit defiance or disunion. Privately threatening to invade the state and hang the nullifiers, he publicly dispatched naval and military forces to the Palmetto State and issued a ringing proclamation against nullification. Governor Robert Hayne responded with a counterproclamation, and the lines were drawn. If civil war was to be avoided, one side would have to surrender, or both would have to compromise.

Conciliatory Senator Henry Clay of Kentucky stepped forward. Although himself a supporter of tariffs, he had no desire to see his old enemy Andrew Jackson win laurels by crushing the Carolinians and returning with the scalp of John C. Calhoun. The gallant Kentuckian therefore pushed through Congress a compromise bill that would gradually reduce the Tariff of 1832 by about 10 percent over eight years, to the mildly protective level of 1816.

South Carolinians welcomed this opportunity to extricate themselves from a dangerously tight corner without loss of face. To the consternation of the Calhounites, no other southern states had sprung to their support, and an appreciable Unionist minority within South Carolina was gathering guns and nailing the Stars and Stripes to flagpoles. Faced with civil war within and invasion from without, the Columbia convention met again and repealed the ordinance of nullification.

Neither Jackson nor the "nullies" won a clear-cut victory in 1833. Clay was the true hero of the hour, hailed in Charleston and Boston alike for saving the country. Armed conflict had been avoided, but the fundamental issues had not been resolved. When next the "nullies" and the Union clashed, compromise would prove more elusive.

The Trail of Tears

Jackson's Democrats were committed to western expansion, but such expansion necessarily meant confrontation with the current inhabitants of the land. More than 125,000 Native Americans lived in the forests and prairies east of the Mississippi in the 1820s. Federal policy toward them varied. Beginning in the 1790s, the Washington government ostensibly recognized the tribes as separate nations and agreed to acquire land from them only through formal treaties. The Indians were shrewd and determined negotiators, but this availed them little when Americans routinely violated their own covenants as white settlement pushed west.

Many white Americans felt respect and admiration for the Indians and believed that the Native Americans could be assimilated into white society. Much energy was therefore devoted to Christianizing and "civilizing" the Indians. Many **denominations** sent missionaries into Indian villages, and in 1793 Congress appropriated $20,000 for Indian literacy programs and agricultural instruction.

Although many tribes violently resisted white encroachment, others followed the path of accommodation. The Cherokees of Georgia made especially remarkable efforts to learn white ways. They composed a written legal code and constitution, adopted a system of settled agriculture, and vigorously promoted education, using a Cherokee alphabet devised by the Indian Sequoyah. Some Cherokees became prosperous cotton planters and even turned to slaveholding. Nearly thirteen hundred black slaves toiled for their Native American masters in the Cherokee nation in the 1820s. For these efforts, the Cherokees—along with the Creeks, Choctaws, Chickasaws, and Seminoles—were numbered by the whites among the "Five Civilized Tribes."

All this embrace of "civilization" apparently was not good enough for whites. In 1828 the Georgia legislature declared the Cherokee tribal council illegal and asserted its own jurisdiction over Indian affairs and Indian lands. The Cherokees appealed this move to the Supreme Court, which thrice upheld the rights of the Indians. But President Jackson, who clearly wanted to open Indian lands to white settlement, refused to recognize the Court's decisions. In a callous jibe at the Indians' defender, Jackson reportedly snapped, "John Marshall has made his decision; now let him enforce it."[*]

Feeling some obligation to "this much injured race," Jackson proposed a bodily removal of the "Five Civilized Tribes" of the Southeast beyond the Mississippi. Emigration was supposed to be voluntary because it would be "cruel and unjust to compel the aborigines to abandon the graves of their fathers," Jackson declared.

Jackson's policy, passed by Congress as the Indian Removal Act of 1830, led to the forced uprooting of more than 100,000 Indians. In the ensuing decade, countless Indians died on the "Trail of Tears" to the newly established Indian Territory (present-day Oklahoma) where they were to be "permanently" free of white encroachments. The Bureau of Indian Affairs was established in 1836 to administer relations with America's original inhabitants. But as the land-hungry "palefaces" pushed rapidly west, the government's guarantees of a "permanent" Indian homeland went up in smoke.

Suspicious of white intentions from the start, the Sauk and Fox tribes of Illinois and Wisconsin, ably led by Black Hawk, resisted eviction. They were bloodily crushed in 1832 by regular troops, including Lieutenant Jefferson Davis of Mississippi, and by militia volunteers, including Captain Abraham Lincoln of Illinois. In Florida the Seminoles, under the leadership of Osceola, retreated into the swampy Everglades, and for seven years (1835–1842) waged a bitter guerrilla war that took the lives of some fifteen hundred soldiers. The American commander's treacherous seizure of Osceola under a flag of truce finally led to the Seminoles' defeat. Some Seminoles fled deeper into the Everglades, where their descendants now

denominations *In American religion, the branches of Christianity, organized into distinct church structures and traditions, such as Presbyterians, Baptists, Disciples of Christ, and so forth.*

Online Study Center

Primary source
Jesuit's Interpretation of Gender Roles Among . . .
college.hmco.com/pic/kennedybrief7e

Online Study Center

Primary source
Ball Play of the Choctaw—Ball Up
college.hmco.com/pic/kennedybrief7e

Online Study Center

Primary source
Indian Land Cessions
college.hmco.com/pic/kennedybrief7e

---

[*] One hundred sixty years later, in 1992, the state of Georgia formally pardoned the two white missionaries, Samuel Austin Worcester and Elihu Butler, who had figured prominently in the decision Jackson condemned. They had been convicted of living on Cherokee lands without a license from the state of Georgia. They served sixteen months at hard labor on a chain gang and later accompanied the Cherokees on the "Trail of Tears" to Oklahoma.

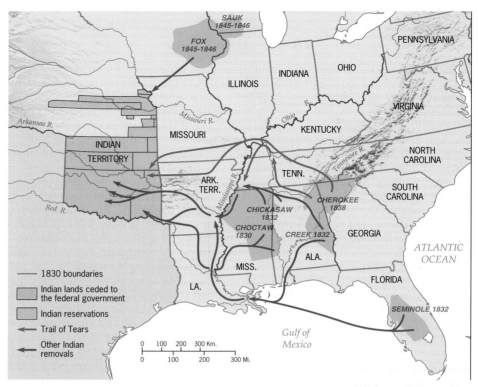

■ Indian Removals, 1830–1846

live, but about four-fifths of them were moved to Oklahoma, where several thousand of the tribe survived.

The Bank War

President Jackson did not hate all banks and all businesses, but he distrusted monopolistic banking and overbig business, as did his followers. A man of virulent dislikes, he came to share the prejudices of his own West against the "moneyed monster" known as the Bank of the United States.

What made the bank a monster in Jackson's eyes? The national government minted gold and silver coins in the mid-nineteenth century but did not issue paper money. Paper notes issued by private banks in effect functioned as money, giving private bankers considerable power over the nation's economy.

No bank in America had more power than the Bank of the United States. In many ways the bank acted like a branch of government. It was the principal depository for the funds of the Washington government and controlled much of the nation's gold and silver. A source of credit and stability, the bank was an important and useful part of the nation's expanding economy.

But the Bank of the United States was a private institution, accountable not to the people but only to its elite circle of moneyed investors. Its president, the brilliant but arrogant Nicholas Biddle—dubbed "Czar Nicholas I" by his enemies—held immense power over the nation's financial affairs.

To some the bank's very existence seemed to sin against the egalitarian credo of American democracy.

One survivor of the Indians' forced march in 1838–1839 on the "Trail of Tears" to Indian Territory, farther west, remembered,

"One each day, and all are gone. Looks like maybe all dead before we get to new Indian country, but always we keep marching on. Women cry and make sad wails. Children cry, and many men cry, and all look sad when friends die, but they say nothing and just put heads down and keep on toward west. . . . She [his mother] speak no more; we bury her and go on."

as an identifiable group in the Senate, where Clay, Webster, and Calhoun joined forces in 1834 in opposition to Jackson's bank policies. Thereafter, the Whigs rapidly evolved into a potent national political force by attracting other groups alienated by Jackson: supporters of Clay's American System, southern states' righters offended by Jackson's stand on nullification, the larger northern industrialists and merchants, and eventually many of the evangelical Protestants associated with the Anti-Masonic party.

Whigs thought of themselves as conservatives, yet they were progressive in their support of active government programs and reforms. Instead of boundless territorial acquisition, they called for internal improvements like canals, railroads, and telegraph lines, and they supported institutions like prisons, asylums, and public schools. The Whigs welcomed the market economy, drawing support from manufacturers in the North, planters in the South, and merchants and bankers in all sections. But they were not simply a party of wealthy fat cats, however dearly the Democrats wanted to paint them as such. By absorbing the egalitarian Anti-Masonic party, the Whigs blunted much of the Democratic appeal to the common man. Turning Jacksonian rhetoric on its head, the Whigs portrayed Jackson and his successor, Martin Van Buren, as imperious aristocrats, and the Democrats as the party of cronyism and corruption.

The Election of 1836

The smooth-tongued and keen-witted <u>vice</u> president, <u>Martin Van Buren of</u> New York, was Jackson's choice for "appointment" as his successor in 1836. Jackson was too old and ailing to consider a third term, but he was not loath to try to serve a third term through Van Buren, something of a "yes man." Leaving nothing to chance, Jackson carefully rigged the nominating convention and rammed his favorite down the throats of the delegates. Van Buren was supported by the Jacksonites without wild enthusiasm, even though he had promised "to tread generally" in the military-booted footsteps of his predecessor.

As the election neared, the still-ramshackle organization of the Whigs showed in their inability to nominate a single presidential candidate. Their long-shot strategy was instead to run several prominent "**favorite sons**" from different regions, hoping thereby to scatter the vote and throw the election into the House of Representatives. With Henry Clay elbowed aside, the leading Whig "favorite son" was heavy-jawed General William Henry Harrison, hero of the Battle of Tippecanoe (see p. 158). The fine-spun schemes of the Whigs availed nothing, however. Van Buren, the dapper "Little Magician," squirmed into office by the close popular vote of 765,483 to 735,795, but by the comfortable margin of 170 to 124 votes (for all the Whigs combined) in the Electoral College.

favorite sons *In American politics, presidential candidates nominated by their own state, primarily out of local loyalty, but not usually expected to win.*

Big Woes for the "Little Magician"

Martin Van Buren was the <u>first</u> president to be <u>born under the American flag</u>. Short and slender, bland and bald, the adroit little New Yorker has been described as "a first-class second-rate man." An accomplished strategist and spoilsman—"the wizard of Albany"—he was also a statesman of wide experience in both legislative and administrative life. Unfortunately, he fell victim to a series of misfortunes over which he had little control.

From the outset the new president labored under severe handicaps. As a machine-made candidate, he incurred the resentment of many Democrats. Jackson, the master showman, had been the dynamic type of chief executive whose administration had resounded with furious quarrels and cracked heads. Mild-mannered Martin Van Buren seemed to rattle about in the military boots of his bull-in-the-china-shop predecessor. The people felt let down. Inheriting Jackson's mantle without his popularity, Van Buren also inherited the ex-president's numerous and vengeful enemies.

Van Buren's four years overflowed with toil and trouble. A rebellion in Canada in 1837 caused ugly incidents along the border that threatened to trigger war with

Britain. Antislavery agitators in the North were in full cry, condemning among other things the prospective annexation of Texas.

Worst of all, Jackson bequeathed to Van Buren the makings of a searing depression. Much of Van Buren's energy had to be devoted to the purely negative task of battling the panic, and there were not enough rabbits in the "Little Magician's" tall silk hat. Hard times ordinarily blight the reputation of a president, and Van Buren was no exception.

Depression Doldrums and the Independent Treasury

The panic of 1837 was a symptom of the financial sickness of the times. Its basic cause was rampant speculation prompted by a mania of get-rich-quick-ism. Gamblers in western lands were doing a "land-office business" on borrowed capital, much of it in the shaky currency of "wildcat" banks. The speculative craze spread to canals, roads, railroads, and slaves.

But speculation alone did not cause the crash. Jacksonian finance, including the Bank War and the Specie Circular, gave an additional jolt to an already teetering structure. The collapse of two British banks late in 1836 caused investors to call in loans in the United States. Failures of wheat crops deepened the distress. Grain prices were forced so high that three weeks before Van Buren took the oath of office mobs in New York City stormed warehouses and broke open flour barrels.

Soon the depression's full fury burst about Van Buren's bewildered head. Hardship was acute and widespread. American banks collapsed by the hundreds, including some of the "pet banks," which carried down with them several millions in government funds. Commodity prices drooped, sales of public lands fell off, and customs revenues dried to a rivulet. Factories closed their doors, and unemployed workers milled about in the streets.

The Whigs came forward with proposals for active government remedies for the economy's ills. They called for the expansion of bank credit, higher tariffs, and subsidies for internal improvements. But Van Buren, shackled by the Jacksonian philosophy of keeping the government's paws off the economy, spurned all such ideas.

The beleaguered Van Buren tried to apply vintage Jacksonian medicine to the ailing economy through his controversial "Divorce Bill." Convinced that some of the financial fever was fed by the injection of federal funds into private banks, he championed the principle of "divorcing" the government from banking altogether. By establishing a so-called independent treasury, the government could lock its surplus money in vaults. Government funds would thus be safe, but they would also be denied to the banking system as reserves, thereby shriveling available credit resources.

Van Buren's "divorce" scheme was never highly popular. His fellow Democrats, many of whom longed for the risky but lush days of the "pet banks," supported it only lukewarmly. The Whigs condemned it because it shriveled their hopes for a revived Bank of the United States. After a prolonged struggle, the Independent Treasury Bill passed Congress in 1840. Repealed the next year by the victorious Whigs, the scheme was reenacted by the triumphant Democrats in 1846 and then continued until merged with the Federal Reserve System in the next century.

Gone to Texas

Americans, greedy for land, continued to covet the vast expanse of Texas, which the United States had abandoned to Spain when acquiring Florida in 1819. The Spanish authorities wanted to populate this virtually unpeopled area, but before they could carry through their

Philip Hone (1780–1851), a New York businessman, described in his diary (May 10, 1837) a phase of the financial crisis:

"The savings-bank also sustained a most grievous run yesterday. They paid 375 depositors $81,000. The press was awful; the hour for closing the bank is six o'clock, but they did not get through the paying of those who were in at that time till nine o'clock. I was there with the other trustees and witnessed the madness of the people—women nearly pressed to death, and the stoutest men could scarcely sustain themselves; but they held on as with a death's grip upon the evidences of their claims, and, exhausted as they were with the pressure, they had strength to cry 'Pay! Pay!' "

EXAMINING THE EVIDENCE

Satiric Bank Note, 1837 Political humor can take more forms than the commonly seen caustic cartoon. Occasionally historians stumble upon other examples, such as this fake bank note. A jibe at Andrew Jackson's money policies, it appeared in New York in 1837 after Jackson's insistence on shutting down the Bank of the United States resulted in the suspension of specie payments. The clever creator of this satiric bank note for six cents left little doubt about the worthlessness of the note or Jackson's responsibility for it. The six cents payable by the "Humbug Glory Bank"—whose symbols were a donkey and a "Hickory Leaf" (for Old Hickory)— were redeemable "in mint drops or Glory at cost." The bank's cashier was "Cunning Reuben," possibly an anti-Semitic allusion to usurious Jewish bankers. Can you identify other ways in which this document takes aim at Jackson's banking policies? What symbols did the note's creator assume the public would comprehend?

1. Identify at least three *visual* images or symbols that serve to link this satirical currency with Andrew Jackson's "pet banks."

2. Point to at least three *verbal* terms or phrases that highlight the supposed fraudulency of Jacksonian banking practices.

3. What historical conclusions about the "Bank War" might you draw from the printing of this kind of "money" by Jackson's opponents? Exactly what political purpose does this form of satire serve that more straightforward argument would not?

Collection of the New York Historical Society, neg. 44812.

contemplated plans, the Mexicans won their independence. A new regime in Mexico City thereupon concluded arrangements in 1823 for granting a huge tract of land to Stephen Austin, with the understanding that he would bring into Texas three hundred American families. Immigrants were to be of the established Roman Catholic faith and upon settlement were to become properly Mexicanized.

Those two stipulations were largely ignored. Hardy Texan pioneers remained Americans at heart, resenting the trammels imposed by a "foreign" government. They were especially annoyed by the presence of Mexican soldiers, many of whom were ragged ex-convicts.

Energetic and prolific, Texan Americans numbered about thirty thousand by 1835 (see "Makers of America: Mexican or Texican?" p. 190). Most of them were law-abiding, God-fearing people, but some of them had left the "states" only one or two jumps ahead of the sheriff. "G.T.T." (Gone To Texas) became current descriptive slang. Among the adventurers were Davy Crockett, the famous rifleman and former Congressman, and James Bowie, the presumed inventor of the murderous knife that bears his name. A distinguished latecomer and leader was an ex-governor of Tennessee, Sam Houston. His life had been temporarily shattered in 1829 when his bride of a few weeks left him and he took up transient residence with the Arkansas Indians, who dubbed him "Big Drunk."

The pioneer individualists who came to Texas were not easy to push around. Friction rapidly increased between Mexicans and Texans over such issues as slavery, immigration, and local rights. Slavery was a particularly touchy topic.

Mexican or Texican?

Moses Austin, born a Connecticut Yankee in 1761, was determined to be Spanish—if that's what it took to acquire cheap land and freedom from pesky laws. In 1798 he tramped into untracked Missouri, still part of Spanish Louisiana, and pledged his allegiance to the king of Spain. In 1820, with his old Spanish passport in his saddlebag, he rode into Spanish Texas and asked for permission to establish a colony of three hundred families.

The Spanish authorities had repeatedly stamped out previous attempts at American settlement in Texas. But the governor somewhat reluctantly allowed Austin's colonists to enter the territory, hoping that they might "civilize" the land and wrest it from the Indians. Upon Moses Austin's death in 1821, the task of realizing his dream fell to his twenty-seven-year-old son, Stephen. "I bid an everlasting farewell to my native country," Stephen Austin said, and he crossed into Texas on July 15, 1821, "determined to fulfill rigidly all the duties and obligations of a Mexican citizen." (Mexico declared its independence from Spain in early 1821.) Soon he learned fluent Spanish and was signing his name as "Don Estévan F. Austin."

Austin fell just three families short of recruiting the three hundred households that his father had contracted to bring to Texas. The original settlers in the colony between the Brazos and Colorado Rivers were nevertheless dubbed "the Old Three Hundred," the Texas equivalent of New England's Mayflower Pilgrims or the "First Families of Virginia." Mostly Scots-Irish southerners from the trans-Appalachian frontier, the Old Three Hundred were cultured folk by frontier standards; all but four of them were literate. Other settlers followed, from Europe as well as America. Within ten years the "Anglos" (many of them French and German) outnumbered the Mexican residents, or *tejanos,* ten to one and soon evolved a distinctive "Texican" culture. The wide-ranging horse patrols organized to attack Indians became the Texas Rangers. Samuel

Maverick, whose unbranded cattle roamed the limited prairies, left his surname as a label for rebellious loners. Jared Groce, who came from Alabama with fifty covered wagons and a hundred slaves, etched the original image of the larger-than-life big-time Texas operator.

The original Anglo-Texans brought with them the old Scots-Irish frontiersman's hostility to officialdom and authority. When the Mexican government tried to impose its will on the Anglo-Texans in the 1830s, they took up their guns. Like the American revolutionaries of the 1770s, who at first demanded only the rights of Englishmen, the Texans began by asking simply for Mexican recognition of their rights as guaranteed by the Mexican constitution of 1824. But bloodshed at the Alamo in 1836, like that at Lexington in 1775, transformed protest into rebellion.

Texas lay—and still lies—along the frontier where Hispanic and Anglo-American cultures met, mingled, and clashed. In part the Texas Revolution was a contest between those two cultures. But it was also a contest about philosophies of government, pitting liberal frontier ideals of freedom against the conservative concept of centralized control. Stephen Austin sincerely tried to "Mexicanize" himself and his followers—until the Mexican government grew too arbitrary and authoritarian. Some of those who adhered to this philosophy were not "Anglos" but *tejanos.* Seven *tejanos* died at the Alamo, and several others signed the Texas declaration of independence. Lorenzo de Zavala, an ardent Mexican liberal who had long resisted the centralizing tendencies of Mexico's dominant political party, became vice president of the Texas republic's interim government in 1836. Like the Austins, these *tejanos* and Mexicans sought in Texas an escape from overbearing governmental authority. Their role in the Texas revolution underscores the fact that it was a struggle between defenders of local rights and agents of central authority as much as it was a fight between Anglo and Mexican cultures.

Mexico emancipated its slaves in 1830 and prohibited their further importation into Texas, as well as further colonization by troublesome Americans. The Texans refused to honor this decree. They kept their slaves in bondage, and new American settlers kept bringing more slaves into Texas. The explosion finally came in 1835, when Mexican dictator Santa Anna wiped out all local rights and started to raise an army to suppress the upstart Texans.

The Lone Star Rebellion

Early in 1836 the Texans unfurled their Lone Star flag and declared their independence, naming Sam Houston as commander in chief. Santa Anna, at the head of about six thousand men, stormed ferociously into Texas. Trapping a band of nearly two hundred pugnacious Texans at the Alamo in San Antonio, he wiped them out to a man after a thirteen-day siege. A short time later a band of about four hundred surrounded and defeated American volunteers, having thrown down their arms at Goliad, were butchered as "pirates."

Slain heroes like Jim Bowie and Davy Crockett, well known in life, became legendary in death. Texan war cries—"Remember the Alamo!" "Remember Goliad!" and "Death to Santa Anna!"—swept up into the United States. Scores of vengeful Americans seized their rifles and rushed to the aid of relatives, friends, and compatriots.

General Sam Houston's small army retreated to the east, luring Santa Anna to San Jacinto, near the site of the city that now bears Houston's name. The Mexicans numbered about thirteen hundred men, the Texans about nine hundred. Suddenly, on April 21, 1836, Houston turned, wiping out the pursuing force. The captured Santa Anna was forced to sign two treaties in which he agreed to withdraw Mexican troops and to recognize the Rio Grande as the extreme southwestern boundary of Texas. When released, he repudiated the whole agreement as illegal because it was extorted under duress.

These events put the U.S. government in a sticky situation. As the Mexicans bitterly complained, the Washington government's weak enforcement of neutrality laws had permitted American men and supplies to leak across the border and

■ **Mexican Forces Assault the Alamo** The defenders fought bravely but were overwhelmed by Santa Anna's army. Among those who died defending the historic mission were Colonel William Travis, Captain James Bowie, and former congressman David Crockett.

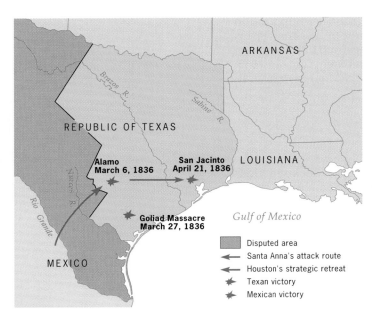

■ The Texas Revolution, 1835–1836 General Houston's strategy was to retreat and use defense in depth. His line of supply from the United States was shortened as Santa Anna's lengthened. The Mexicans were forced to bring up supplies by land because the Texas navy controlled the sea. This force consisted of only four small ships, but it was big enough to do the job.

aid the Texans. But American public opinion, overwhelmingly favorable to the Texans, left the federal authorities powerless to act. On the day before he left office in 1837, President Jackson extended the right hand of recognition to the Lone Star Republic, led by his old comrade-in-arms against the Indians, Sam Houston.

Many Texans wanted not just recognition of their independence, but outright union with the United States. The radiant Texan bride, officially petitioning for annexation in 1837, presented herself for marriage. But the expectant groom, Uncle Sam, was jerked back by the strong arm of the slavery issue. Antislavery crusaders in the North were opposing annexation with increasing vehemence; they contended that the whole scheme was merely a conspiracy cooked up by the southern "slavocracy" to bring new slave pens into the Union.

At first glance, the "slavery plot" charge seemed plausible. Most of the early settlers in Texas, as well as American volunteers during the revolution, had come from slaveholding states of the South and Southwest. But scholars have concluded that the settlement of Texas was merely the normal and inexorable march of the westward movement. The explanation was proximity rather than conspiracy. Yet the fact remained that many Texans were slaveholders, and admitting Texas to the Union inescapably meant enlarging American slavery.

Log Cabins and Hard Cider of 1840

Martin Van Buren was renominated by the Democrats in 1840, albeit without terrific enthusiasm. The party had no acceptable alternative to the man the Whigs called "Martin Van Ruin."

The Whigs, hungering for the spoils of office, scented victory in the breeze. Pangs of the panic were still being felt, and voters blamed their woes on the party in power. Learning from their mistake in 1836, the Whigs united behind one candidate, Ohio's William Henry Harrison. He was not their ablest statesman—that would have been Webster or Clay—but he was believed to be their ablest vote-getter.

The aging hero, nearly sixty-eight when the campaign ended, was known for his successes against Indians and the British at the Battles of Tippecanoe (1811) and the Thames (1813). Harrison's views on current issues were only vaguely known. "Old Tippecanoe" was nominated primarily because he was issueless and enemyless—a tested recipe for electoral success that still appeals today. John Tyler of Virginia, an afterthought, was selected as his vice-presidential running mate.

The Whigs, eager to avoid offense, published no official platform, hoping to sweep their hero into office with a frothy huzza-for-Harrison campaign reminiscent of Jackson's triumph in 1828. A dull-witted Democratic editor played directly into Whig hands. Stupidly insulting the West, he lampooned Harrison as an impoverished old farmer who should be content with a pension, a log cabin, and a barrel of hard cider—the poor westerner's champagne. Whigs gleefully adopted honest hard cider and the sturdy log cabin as symbols of their campaign. Harrisonites portrayed their hero as the poor "Farmer of North Bend" who had been called from his cabin and his plow to drive corrupt Jackson spoilsmen from the "presidential palace." They denounced Van Buren as a supercilious aristocrat, a simpering dandy who wore corsets and ate French food from golden plates. As a jeering Whig campaign song proclaimed,

> *Old Tip, he wears a homespun shirt,*
> *He has no ruffled shirt, wirt, wirt.*
> *But Matt, he has the golden plate,*
> *And he's a little squirt, wirt, wirt.*

■ **William Henry Harrison Campaign in Philadelphia, 1840**
The parties of Democratic incumbent Martin Van Buren and his Whig challenger, "The Hero of Tippecanoe," took their electoral rivalry into the streets of cities like Philadelphia, launching modern-style popular politics. Harrison won, but a mere month after delivering the longest inaugural address ever (two hours), he succumbed to pneumonia and died. He served the shortest term of any president (thirty-one days). One of his forty-eight grandchildren, Benjamin Harrison, became the twenty-third president of the United States.

The Whig campaign was a masterpiece of hoopla. Log cabins were dished up in every conceivable form. Bawling Whigs, stimulated by fortified cider, rolled huge balls from village to village and state to state, representing the snowballing majority for "Tippecanoe and Tyler too." In truth, Harrison was not lowborn but from one of the FFV's ("First Families of Virginia"). He was not a poverty-stricken dweller in a one-room log cabin, but rather lived in a sixteen-room mansion on a three-thousand acre estate. He did not swill down gallons of hard cider (he evidently preferred whiskey). And he did not plow his fields with his own "huge paws." But such details had not mattered when General Jackson rode to victory, and they did not matter now.

The Democrats who hurrahed Jackson into the White House in 1828 now discovered to their chagrin that whooping it up for a backwoods Westerner was a game two could play. Harrison won by the surprisingly close margin of 1,275,016 popular votes to 1,129,102, but by an overwhelming electoral margin of 234 to 60. With hardly a real issue debated, though with hard times blighting the incumbent's fortunes, Van Buren was washed out of Washington in a wave of apple juice.

Interactive map
Settled Areas of the United
States, 1820, and 1840
college.hmco.com/pic/kennedybrief7e

populist *A political program or style*
focused on the common people, and
attacking perspectives and policies
associated with the well-off, well-born,
or well-educated. (The Populist party
was a specific third-party organization
of the 1890s.)

divine right *The belief that government*
or rulers are directly established by God.

Although campaigners in 1840 did their best to bury substantive issues beneath the ballyhoo, voters actually faced a stark choice between economic visions of how to cope with the nation's first major depression. Whigs sought to expand and stimulate the economy, while Democrats favored retrenchment and an end to high-flying banks and aggressive corporations.

Politics for the People

The election of 1840 conclusively demonstrated two major changes in American politics since the Era of Good Feelings. The first was the triumph of a **populist** democratic style. Democracy had been something of a taint in the days of the lordly Federalists. But by the 1840s, aristocracy was the taint, and democracy was respectable. Politicians were forced to unbend and curry favor with the voting masses. Lucky indeed was the aspiring office seeker who could boast of birth in a log cabin. The semiliterate frontiersman Davy Crockett of Tennessee had been elected to Congress mainly on the basis of his bear-hunting prowess. Hopelessly handicapped was the candidate who appeared too well dressed, too grammatical, too high-browishly intellectual. In truth, most high political offices continued to be filled by "leading citizens," but now these wealthy and prominent men had to forsake all social pretensions and cultivate the common touch if they hoped to win elections.

Snobbish bigwigs sneered at the "coonskin Congressmen" elected by newly enfranchised "bipeds of the forest." But these critics protested in vain. The common man was moving to the center of the national political stage: the sturdy American who donned plain trousers rather than breeches, who sported a plain haircut and a coonskin cap rather than a silk top hat. Instead of the old **divine right** of kings, America was now bowing to the divine right of the people.

The Two-Party System

The second dramatic change resulting from the 1840 election was the formation of a vigorous and durable two-party system. The Jeffersonians of an earlier day had been so successful in absorbing the programs of their Federalist opponents that a full-blown two-party system had never truly emerged in the subsequent Era of Good Feelings. The idea had prevailed that parties of any sort smacked of conspiracy and "faction" and were injurious to the health of the body politic in a virtuous republic. By 1840 political parties had fully come of age, a lasting legacy of Andrew Jackson's tenaciousness.

Both national parties, the Democrats and the Whigs, grew out of the rich soil of Jeffersonian republicanism, and each laid claim to different aspects of the republican inheritance. Jacksonian Democrats glorified the liberty of the individual and were fiercely on guard against the inroads of "privilege" into government. Whigs trumpeted the natural harmony of society and the value of community, and were willing to use government to realize their objectives. Whigs also berated those leaders—and they considered Jackson to be one—whose appeals to self-interest fostered conflict among individuals, classes, or sections.

Democrats clung to states' rights and federal restraint in social and economic affairs as their basic doctrines. Whigs tended to favor a renewed national bank; protective tariffs; internal improvements; public schools;

President Andrew Jackson advised a supporter in 1835 on how to tell the difference between Democrats and "Whigs, nullies, and blue-light federalists." In doing so, he neatly summarized the Jacksonian philosophy:

"The people ought to inquire [of political candidates]—are you opposed to a national bank; are you in favor of a strict construction of the Federal and State Constitutions; are you in favor of rotation in office; do you subscribe to the republican rule that the people are the sovereign power, the officers their agents, and that upon all national or general subjects, as well as local, they have a right to instruct their agents and representatives, and they are bound to obey or resign; in short, are they true Republicans agreeable to the true Jeffersonian creed?"

and, increasingly, moral reforms such as the prohibition of liquor and eventually the abolition of slavery.

The two parties were thus separated by real differences of philosophy and policy. But they also had much in common. Both were mass-based "catchall" parties that tried deliberately to mobilize as many voters as possible for their cause. Although it is true that Democrats tended to be more humble folk and Whigs more prosperous, both parties nevertheless commanded the loyalties of all kinds of Americans, from all social classes and in all sections. The social diversity of the two parties fostered horse-trading compromises *within* each party that prevented either from assuming extreme or radical positions. By the same token, the geographical diversity of the two parties retarded the emergence of purely sectional political parties—temporarily suppressing, through compromise, the ultimately uncompromisable issue of slavery. When the two-party system began to creak in the 1850s, the Union was mortally imperiled.

✪ Chapter Summary ✪

Beginning in the 1820s, a powerful movement celebrating the common person and promoting the "New Democracy" transformed the earlier elitist character of American politics. The controversial election of the Yankee sophisticate John Quincy Adams in 1824 angered the followers of Andrew Jackson, who had received more popular votes.

Jackson's sweeping presidential victory in 1828 represented the political triumph of the New Democracy, including the spoils-rich political machines that thrived in the new environment. Jackson's simple, popular ideas and rough-hewn style reinforced the patronage system's growing belief that any ordinary person could hold public office. The "Tariff of Abominations" and the nullification crisis with South Carolina revealed a growing sectionalism and anxiety about slavery that challenged Jackson's fierce nationalism.

Jackson vigorously wielded the powers of the presidency against his opponents, particularly Calhoun and Clay. He made the Bank of the United States a symbol of evil financial power and killed it after a bitter political fight. Destroying the bank reinforced Jacksonians' hostility to all forms of concentrated political or financial power in the hands of elites, but also left the United States without any effective financial system. In opposition to Jackson's aggressive assertion of power and his numerous controversial policies, a new Whig party emerged to compete with the Jacksonian Democrats.

Jackson's presidency also focused on issues of westward expansion. Pressured to adopt paths of "civilization," Native Americans of the Southeast engaged in extensive agricultural and educational development. But white settlers and state governments still encroached upon the Cherokees and other tribes, and Jackson ordered the forced removal of all southeastern Indians to Oklahoma along the "Trail of Tears."

Jackson's ill-considered economic policies came home to roost under the unlucky Martin Van Buren, his handpicked successor. As the country plunged into a serious depression following the panic of 1837, Van Buren continued futile Jacksonian policies by forcing the removal of all federal funds from private banks.

In Texas, American settlers successfully rebelled against Mexico and declared their independence. Jackson recognized the Texas Republic, but because of the slavery controversy, he refused its application for annexation to the United States.

The Whigs saw these economic and political troubles as a path to the White House. But rather than campaign on issues, they used the political hoopla of the new mass democratic process to turn a western aristocrat and military hero, William Henry Harrison, into a democratic symbol of the "log cabin and hard cider." The Whig victory signaled the emergence of a new two-party system, in which the two parties' genuine philosophical differences and somewhat different constituencies proved less important than their widespread popularity and shared roots in the new American democratic spirit.

VARYING VIEWPOINTS

What Was Jacksonian Democracy?

Aristocratic, eastern-born historians of the nineteenth century damned Jackson as a backwoods barbarian and Jacksonianism as democracy run riot. In the late nineteenth and early twentieth centuries, however, another generation of historians, many of them midwesterners, rejected the elitist views of their predecessors. Frederick Jackson Turner and his disciples saw the western frontier as the fount of democratic virtue, and they hailed Jackson as a true popular hero sprung from the forests of the West to protect the people against the moneyed interests.

When Arthur M. Schlesinger, Jr., published *The Age of Jackson* in 1945, however, the debate on Jacksonianism shifted dramatically. Schlesinger cast the Jacksonian era not as a sectional conflict but as a class conflict between poor farmers, laborers, and noncapitalists on the one hand and the business community on the other.

Soon after Schlesinger's book appeared, the discussion again shifted ground and entirely new interpretations of Jacksonianism emerged. Richard Hofstadter argued in *The American Political Tradition and the Men Who Made It* (1948) that Jacksonian democracy was not a rejection of capitalism, as Schlesinger insisted, but rather the effort of aspiring entrepreneurs to serve their own interests against their entrenched, monopolistic, eastern competitors. Lee Benson contended in *The Concept of Jacksonian Democracy* (1961) that the political conflicts of the Jacksonian era were rooted not in class or region but in religious and ethnic splits within American society that led to local conflicts over cultural issues.

In the 1980s Sean Wilentz and other scholars began to resurrect some of Schlesinger's arguments about the importance of class to Jacksonianism. In *Chants Democratic* (1984), Wilentz maintained that Jacksonian politics could not be understood without reference to the changing national economy. Artisans and small producers, Wilentz argued, believed that impersonal institutions and large-scale employers threatened the very existence of a republic founded on virtuous self-sufficiency. Jackson's attack on the Bank of the United States symbolized the antagonism these individuals felt toward the emerging capitalist economy.

The scholarly cycle came full circle in Charles Sellers's *The Market Revolution: Jacksonian America, 1815–1846* (1991). In many ways this ambitious synthesis offered an updated version of Schlesinger's argument about class conflict. American democracy and free-market capitalism, Sellers suggested, were not natural twins but rather adversaries, with Jacksonians inventing mass democracy in order to hold capitalist expansion in check. Like Schlesinger's thesis, Sellers's interpretation provoked a storm of controversy. Critics like William E. Gienapp charged that Sellers suffered from a hopelessly romantic view of preindustrial society, and that no political party could prevail by appealing exclusively to rich or poor. The complex connections between capitalism and American democracy reflected in the Jacksonian era remain a lively subject for historical research and analysis.

14

Forging the National Economy

—⚭—

1790–1860

THE PROGRESS OF INVENTION IS REALLY A THREAT [TO MONARCHY]. WHENEVER I SEE A RAILROAD I LOOK FOR A REPUBLIC.

RALPH WALDO EMERSON, 1866

The new nation went bounding into the nineteenth century in a burst of movement. New England Yankees, Pennsylvania farmers, and southern yeomen all pushed west in search of cheap land and prodigious opportunity, soon to be joined by vast numbers of immigrants from Europe. But not only people were in motion. Newly invented machinery quickened the cultivating of crops and the manufacturing of goods, while workers found themselves laboring under new, more demanding expectations for their pace of work. Better roads, faster steamboats, farther-reaching canals, and tentacle-stretching railroads all helped move people, raw materials, and manufactured goods from coast to hinterland and Gulf to Great Lakes by the mid-nineteenth century. The momentum gave rise to a more dynamic, market-oriented economy.

Focus Questions

1. How did the westward migration and German and Irish immigration alter the geographical distribution and composition of the American population in the early nineteenth century?
2. Why was America relatively slow to embrace urbanization, industrialization, and the factory system of production?
3. How did Eli Whitney's system of interchangeable parts and other inventions and innovations, especially in transportation and communications, lay the foundations for the first wave of American industrialization?
4. How did early industrialization affect workers and alter the role of women both inside and outside the home?
5. What were the large-scale effects of the emerging national American market economy, including its impact on regional and social class relationships?

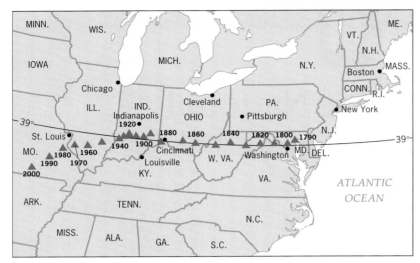

■ **Westward Movement of the Center of Population, 1790–2000** The triangles indicate the points at which a map of the United States weighted for the population of the country in a given year would balance. Note the remarkable equilibrium of the north-south pull from 1790 to about 1940, and the strong spurt west and south thereafter. The 1980 census revealed that the nation's center of population had at last moved west of the Mississippi River. The map also shows the slowing of the westward movement between 1890 and 1940—the period of heaviest immigration from Europe, which ended up mainly in East Coast cities.

The Westward Movement

The rise of Andrew Jackson, the first president from beyond the Appalachian Mountains, exemplified the inexorable westward march of the American people. The West, with its raw frontier, was the most typically American part of the nation. As Ralph Waldo Emerson wrote in 1844, "Europe stretches to the Alleghenies; America lies beyond."

The Republic was young, and so were the people—as late as 1850, half of Americans were under the age of thirty. They were also restless and energetic, seemingly always on the move, and always westward. By 1840 the "demographic center" of the American population had crossed the Alleghenies. By the eve of the Civil War, it had marched beyond the Ohio River.

Legend portrays an army of muscular axmen triumphantly carving civilization out of the western woods. But in reality life was downright grim for most pioneer families. Poorly fed, ill-clad, housed in hastily erected shanties, they were perpetual victims of disease, depression, and premature death. Above all, unbearable loneliness haunted them, especially the women, who were often cut off from human contact, even their neighbors, for days or even weeks, while confined to the cramped orbit of a dark cabin erected in a secluded clearing. Breakdowns and even madness were all too frequently the "opportunities" that the frontier offered to pioneer women.

■ **A Pioneer Homestead in Wisconsin, c. 1847** This frontier family felled trees both to build a crude cabin and to provide fuel for cooking. After the remaining stumps were burned, the cleared fields were ready for planting. Cooking outdoors (weather permitting) spared the rough shelter from smoke and odors.

Chronology

c. 1750	Industrial Revolution begins in Britain.
1791	Samuel Slater builds first U.S. textile factory.
1793	Eli Whitney invents the cotton gin.
1798	Whitney develops interchangeable parts for muskets.
1807	Robert Fulton's first steamboat. Embargo spurs American manufacturing.
1811	Cumberland Road construction begins.
1817	Erie Canal construction begins.
1825	Erie Canal completed.
1828	First railroad in United States.
1830s	Cyrus McCormick invents mechanical mower-reaper.
1834	Anti-Catholic riot in Boston.
1837	John Deere develops steel plow.
1840	President Van Buren establishes ten-hour day for federal employees.
1842	Massachusetts declares labor unions legal in *Commonwealth* v. *Hunt*.
1844	Samuel Morse invents telegraph. Anti-Catholic riot in Philadelphia.
1845–1849	Potato famine in Ireland.
1846	Elias Howe invents sewing machine.
1848	First general incorporation laws in New York. Democratic revolutions collapse in Germany.
1849	American (or Know-Nothing party) formed.
1852	Cumberland Road completed.
1858	Cyrus Field lays first transatlantic cable.
1860	Pony Express established.
1861	First transcontinental telegraph.
1866	Permanent transatlantic cable established.

Frontier life could be tough and crude for men as well. No-holds-barred wrestling, which permitted such niceties as the biting off of noses and the gouging out of eyes, was a popular entertainment. Pioneering Americans, marooned by geography, were often ill-informed, superstitious, provincial, and fiercely individualistic. Emerson's popular lecture-essay "Self-Reliance" struck a deeply responsive chord. Popular literature of the period abounded with portraits of heroically unique, isolated figures such as James Fenimore Cooper's courageous Natty Bumppo and Herman Melville's restless Captain Ahab—just as Jacksonian politics aimed to emancipate the lone-wolf, enterprising businessperson. Yet even in this heyday of "rugged individualism," there were important exceptions. Pioneers, in tasks clearly beyond their own individual resources, would call upon neighbors for logrolling and barn raising and upon their governments for help in building internal improvements.

Shaping the Western Landscape

The westward movement also molded the physical environment. Pioneers in a hurry often exhausted the land and then pushed on, leaving behind barren and rain-gutted fields. In the Kentucky bottomlands, settlers discovered that they could burn off the native cane and plant "Kentucky bluegrass," which made ideal pasture for livestock.

The American West felt the pressure of civilization in additional ways. By the 1820s American fur trappers were setting their trap lines all over the vast Rocky Mountain region. Each summer, trappers came down from the mountains and swapped their beaver pelts for manufactured goods from the East. This trade thrived for some two decades, until the hapless beavers had all but disappeared from the region. Trade in buffalo robes also flourished. On the California coast, other traders pursued sea-otter pelts, driving the once-bountiful otters nearly to extinction. Some historians have called this aggressive and often heedless exploitation of the West's natural bounty "ecological imperialism."

Yet Americans in this period also revered nature and admired its beauty. Indeed the spirit of nationalism fed a growing belief in the uniqueness of the American wilderness. Searching for the United States' distinctive characteristics in this nation-conscious age, many observers found the wild, unspoiled land of the West to be among the young nation's defining attributes. Devotion to the pristine natural beauty of the American wilderness became in time a national mystique, inspiring literature and painting and eventually kindling a powerful conservation movement.

George Catlin, a painter and student of Native American life, was among the first Americans to advocate the preservation of nature as a deliberate national policy. Appalled at the reckless slaughter of Indians and buffalo alike, Catlin proposed the creation of a national park to preserve nature and wildlife. His idea later bore fruit with the creation of a national park system, beginning with Yellowstone Park in 1872.

The March of the Millions

Online Study Center

Primary source
Continental Expansion
college.hmco.com/pic/kennedybrief7e

As the American people moved west, they also multiplied at an amazing rate. By midcentury the population was still doubling approximately every twenty-five years, as in fertile colonial days. By 1860 the original thirteen states had more than doubled in number: thirty-three stars graced the American flag. The United States was the fourth most populous nation in the western world, exceeded only by three European countries—Russia, France, and Austria.

Urban growth continued explosively. In 1790 only two American cities could boast populations of twenty thousand or more: Philadelphia and New York. By 1860 there were forty-three, and about three hundred other places claimed over five thousand inhabitants apiece. New York was the metropolis; New Orleans, the "Queen of the South"; and Chicago, the swaggering lord of the Midwest, destined to be "hog butcher for the world."

Such overrapid urbanization unfortunately brought undesirable by-products. It intensified the problems of smelly slums, feeble street lighting, impure water, foul sewage, ravenous rats, and improper garbage disposal. Hogs poked their scavenging snouts about many city streets as late as the 1840s. Boston in 1823 pioneered with a sewage system, and New York in 1842 abandoned wells and cisterns for a piped-in water supply. The city thus unknowingly eliminated many of the breeding places of disease-carrying mosquitoes.

A continuing high birthrate accounted for most of the increase in population, but by the 1840s the tides of immigration were adding hundreds of thousands more. Before this decade, immigrants had been flowing in at the rate of about sixty thousand a year, but suddenly the influx tripled in the 1840s and then quadrupled in the 1850s. During these two feverish decades, over a million and a half Irish, and nearly as many Germans, swarmed down the gangplanks. Why did they come?

Irish and German Immigration by Decade, 1830–1900

Years	Irish	Germans
1831–1840	207,381	152,454
1841–1850	780,719	434,626
1851–1860	914,119	951,667
1861–1870	435,778	787,468
1871–1880	436,871	718,182
1881–1890	655,482	1,452,970
1891–1900	388,416	505,152
TOTAL	3,818,766	5,000,519

The immigrants came partly because Europe seemed to be running out of room. The population of the Old World more than doubled in the nineteenth century, and Europe began to generate a seething pool of apparently "surplus" people. They were displaced and footloose in their homelands before they felt the tug of the American magnet. Indeed, at least as many people moved about *within* Europe as crossed the Atlantic.

Yet America still beckoned most strongly to the struggling masses of Europe. About 35 million of the nearly 60 million emigrants who abandoned Europe in the century after 1840 headed for "the land of freedom and opportunity," where no aristocratic **caste** or state church oppressed the individual. Much-read letters sent home by immigrants—"America letters"—often described in glowing terms the richer life: low taxes, no compulsory military service, and "three meat meals a day." The introduction of transoceanic steamships also meant that the immigrants could come speedily, in a matter of ten or twelve days instead of ten or twelve weeks. On board, they were still jammed into unsanitary quarters, thus suffering an appalling death rate from infectious diseases, but the nightmare was more endurable because it was shorter.

caste *An exclusive or rigid social distinction based on birth, wealth, occupation, and so forth.*

The Emerald Isle Moves West

Ireland, already groaning under the heavy hand of British overlords, was prostrated in the mid-1840s. A terrible rot attacked the potato crop, on which the people had become dangerously dependent, and about one-fourth of them were swept away by disease and hunger. Dead bodies were found by the roadsides with grass in their mouths. All told, about 2 million perished.

Tens of thousands of destitute souls, fleeing the Land of Famine for the Land of Plenty, flocked to America in the "Black Forties." Ireland's great export has been population, and the Irish take their place beside the Africans and the Jews as a dispersed people (see "Makers of America: The Irish," pp. 202–203). These uprooted newcomers swarmed into the larger seaboard cities, such as Boston and New York, which rapidly became the largest Irish city in the world. Before many decades, more people of Irish descent lived in America than on the "ould sod" of Erin's isle.

The luckless Irish immigrants received no red-carpet treatment. They were scorned by the older American stock, especially "proper" Protestant Bostonians, who regarded the scruffy Catholic arrivals as a social menace. Barely literate "Biddies" (Bridgets) took jobs as kitchen maids. Broad-shouldered "Paddies" (Patricks) were pushed into pick-and-shovel drudgery on canals and railroads, where thousands left their bones as victims of disease and accidental explosions. It was said that an Irishman lay buried under every railroad tie. As wage-depressing competitors for jobs, the Irish were hated by native workers. "No Irish Need Apply" was a sign commonly posted at factory gates. The Irish, for similar reasons, fiercely resented the blacks, with whom they shared society's basement. Race riots between black and Irish dockworkers flared up in several port cities, and the Irish were generally cool to the abolitionist cause.

The friendless "famine Irish" were forced to fend for themselves. The Ancient Order of Hibernians, a semisecret society founded in Ireland to fight rapacious landlords, served in America as a benevolent society, aiding the downtrodden. It also helped to spawn the "Molly Maguires," a shadowy Irish miners' union that rocked the Pennsylvania coal districts in the 1860s and 1870s.

The Irish tended to remain in low-skill occupations but gradually improved their lot, usually by acquiring modest amounts of property. The education of children was cut short as families struggled to save money to

Margaret McCarthy, a recent arrival in America, captured much of the complexity of the immigrant experience in a letter she wrote from New York to her family in Ireland in 1850:

"This is a good place and a good country, but there is one thing that's ruining this place. The emigrants have not money enough to take them to the interior of the country, which obliges them to remain here in New York and the like places, which causes the less demand for labor and also the great reduction in wages. For this reason I would advise no one to come to America that would not have some money after landing here that would enable them to go west in case they would get no work to do here."

The Irish

During the wars that ravaged Europe from 1793 to 1815, Irish tenant farmers temporarily prospered by planting every available acre with wheat and potatoes to feed ravenous armies. But when peace came, wheat prices plummeted, and hard-pressed landlords, aided by British police, forced their tenants off the unprofitable land. Many displaced Irish farmers sought work in England; some went to America. Then in 1845 a blight that ravaged the potato crop sounded the final knell for the Irish peasantry. The resultant famine spread desolation throughout the island. In five years, more than a million people died. Another million sailed for America.

Most of the emigrants were under thirty-five years old. Families typically pooled money to send strong young sons to the New World, where they would earn wages to pay the fares for those who waited at home. These "famine Irish" mostly remained in the port cities of the Northeast, abandoning the farmer's life for the dingy congestion of the urban metropolis.

The disembarking Irish were poorly prepared for urban life. They found progress up the economic ladder painfully slow. Their work as domestic servants or construction laborers was dull and arduous, and mortality rates were astoundingly high. Escape from the potato famine hardly guaranteed a long life to an Irish-American; a gray-bearded Irishman was a rare sight in nineteenth-century America. For Irish-born women, opportunities were even scarcer; they worked mainly as domestic servants.

But it was their Roman Catholicism, even more than their penury or their perceived fondness for alcohol, that earned the Irish the distrust and resentment of their native-born Protestant American neighbors. The cornerstone of social and religious life for Irish immigrants was the Catholic parish. Worries about safeguarding their children's faith inspired the construction of parish schools, financed by the pennies of struggling working-class Irish parents.

If Ireland's green fields scarcely equipped her sons and daughters for the scrap and scramble of economic life in America's cities, life in the Old Country had instilled in them an aptitude for politics. Irish Catholic resistance against centuries of English-Anglican domination had instructed many Old Country Irish in the ways

■ Outward Bound, The Quay at Dublin, 1854
Thousands fled famine in Ireland by coming to America in the 1840s and 1850s.
Collection of the New York Historical Society, neg. 41082.

of mass politics. That political experience readied them for the boss system of the political "machines" in America's northeastern cities. Irish voters soon became a bulwark of the Democratic party, reliably supporting the party of Jefferson and Jackson in cities like New York and Boston. As Irish-Americans like New York's "Honest John" Kelly themselves became bosses, white-collar jobs in government service opened up to the Irish. They became building inspectors, aldermen, and even policemen—an astonishing irony for a people driven from their homeland by the nightsticks and bayonets of the British police.

purchase a home. But for humble Irish peasants, cruelly cast out of their homeland, property ownership counted as a grand "success."

Politics quickly attracted these gregarious Gaelic newcomers. They soon began to gain control of powerful city machines, notably New York's Tammany Hall, and reaped the patronage rewards. Before long, brogued Irishmen dominated police departments in many big cities, where they drove the "Paddy wagons" that had once carted their forebears to jail.

The German Forty-Eighters

The influx of refugees from Germany between 1830 and 1860 was hardly less spectacular than that from Ireland. During these troubled years, over a million and a half Germans stepped onto American soil (see "Makers of America: The Germans," p. 206). Most were uprooted farmers, displaced by crop failures and by other hardships, but a strong sprinkling were liberal political refugees. Saddened by the collapse of the democratic revolutions of 1848, they had decided to leave the autocratic fatherland and flee to America—the brightest hope of democracy. Germany's loss was America's gain. Zealous German liberals like the public-spirited and antislavery Carl Schurz contributed richly to the elevation of American political life.

Unlike the Irish, many of the German newcomers possessed a modest amount of material goods. Most of them pushed out to the lush lands of the Midwest, notably Wisconsin, where they settled and established model farms.

The hand of Germans in shaping American life was widely felt in other ways. Like the Irish, they formed an influential body of voters. Having fled German militarism and European wars, they came to be a bulwark of isolationist sentiment in the upper Mississippi Valley. Better educated on the whole than the stump-grubbing Americans, they warmly supported public schools, including their *Kindergarten* ("children's garden"). They likewise did much to stimulate art and music. As outspoken champions of freedom, they became relentless enemies of slavery during the fevered years before the Civil War.

Yet the Germans—often dubbed "damned Dutchmen"—were occasionally regarded with suspicion by their old-stock American neighbors. Seeking to preserve their language and culture, they sometimes settled in compact "colonies" and kept aloof from the surrounding community. Accustomed to the "Continental Sunday" and uncurbed by Puritan tradition, they made merry on the Sabbath and drank huge quantities of their favorite amber beverage, *Bier* (beer). Their Old World drinking habits, like those of the Irish newcomers, spurred advocates of temperance in the use of alcohol to redouble their reform efforts.

Flare-ups of Antiforeignism

The invasion by this so-called immigrant "rabble" in the 1840s and 1850s inflamed the prejudices of American "**nativists**." Not only did the newcomers take jobs from "native" Americans, but most of the displaced Irishmen were Roman Catholics, as were a substantial minority of the Germans. The Church of Rome was still widely regarded by many old-line Americans as a "foreign" and "popish" church.

nativist(s) *One who advocates favoring native-(born) citizens over aliens or immigrants.*

Strong antiforeignism was reflected in the platform of the American (Know-Nothing) party in 1856:

"Americans must rule America; and to this end, native-born citizens should be selected for all state, federal, or municipal offices of government employment, in preference to naturalized citizens."

Roman Catholics were now on the move. Seeking to protect their children from Protestant indoctrination in the public schools, they began in the 1840s to construct an entirely separate Catholic educational system—an enormously expensive undertaking for a poor immigrant community, but one that revealed the strength of its religious commitment. A negligible minority during colonial days, Catholics became a powerful religious group with the enormous influx of the Irish and Germans in the 1840s and 1850s. In 1840 they had ranked fifth, behind the Baptists, Methodists, Presbyterians, and Congregationalists. By 1850, with some 1.8 million communicants, they had bounded into first place—a position they have never lost.

Older-stock Americans were alarmed by these mounting figures. They professed to believe that in due time the "alien riffraff" would "establish" the Catholic Church at the expense of Protestantism and introduce "popish idols." The noisier American "nativists" rallied for political action. In 1849 they formed the Order of the Star-Spangled Banner, which soon developed into the formidable American, or "Know-Nothing" party—a name derived from its secretiveness. "Nativists" agitated for rigid restrictions on immigration and naturalization, and for laws authorizing the deportation of alien paupers. They also promoted a lurid literature of exposure, most of it pure fiction. The authors, sometimes posing as "escaped nuns," described shocking sins they imagined the cloisters concealed, including the secret burial of babies. One of these sensational books—Maria Monk's *Awful Disclosures* (1836)—sold over 300,000 copies.

Even uglier was occasional mass violence. As early as 1834 a Catholic convent near Boston was burned by a howling mob, and in ensuing years a few scattered attacks fell upon Catholic schools and churches. The most frightful flare-up occurred during 1844 in Philadelphia, where the Irish Catholics fought back against the threats of the "nativists." The City of Brotherly Love did not quiet down until two Catholic churches had been burned and some thirteen citizens had been killed and fifty wounded in several days of fighting. These outbursts of intolerance, though infrequent and generally localized, remain an unfortunate blot on the record of America's treatment of minority groups.

■ **Crooked Voting** A bitter "nativist" cartoon charging Irish and German immigrants with "stealing" elections.

Immigrants were undeniably making America a more pluralistic society—one of the most ethnically and racially varied in the history of the world. Why, in fact, were such episodes of intolerance not even more frequent and more violent? Part of the answer lies in the robust American economy. The vigorous growth of the economy in these years ensured that immigrants could claim their share of American wealth without jeopardizing the wealth of others. Their hands and brains, in fact, helped fuel economic expansion. Immigrants and the American economy, in short, needed one another. Without the newcomers, a preponderantly agricultural United States might have been condemned to watch in envy as the Industrial Revolution swept through nineteenth-century Europe.

The March of Mechanization

A group of gifted British inventors, beginning about 1750, perfected a series of machines for the mass production of textiles. This enslavement of steam multiplied the power of human muscles some ten-thousandfold and ushered in the modern **factory** system—and with it the so-called Industrial Revolution.

The factory system gradually spread from Britain to other lands. It took a generation or so to reach Western Europe, and then the United States. Why was the youthful American Republic, eventually to become an industrial giant, so slow to embrace the machine?

For one thing, land was cheap in America. Land-starved descendants of land-starved peasants were not going to coop themselves up in smelly factories when they might till their own acres in God's fresh air and sunlight. Labor was therefore generally scarce, and enough nimble hands to operate the machines were hard to find—until immigrants began to pour ashore in the 1840s. Money for capital investment, moreover, was not plentiful in pioneering America. Raw materials lay undeveloped, undiscovered, or unsuspected.

If labor was scarce, consumers were not. But the young country had difficulty producing goods of high enough quality and cheap enough to compete with European products. Long-established British factories, in particular, provided cutthroat competition. Their superiority was attested by the fact that a few unscrupulous Yankee manufacturers, out to make a dishonest dollar, stamped their own products with faked English **trademarks.**

The British also enjoyed a monopoly of the textile machinery, whose secrets they were anxious to hide from foreign competitors. Parliament enacted laws forbidding the export of the machines or the emigration of mechanics able to reproduce them.

Although a number of small manufacturing enterprises existed in the early Republic, the future industrial colossus was still snoring. Not until well past the middle of the nineteenth century did the value of the output of factories exceed that of farms.

Whitney Ends the Fiber Famine

Samuel Slater has been acclaimed the "Father of the Factory System" in America, and seldom can the paternity of a movement more properly be ascribed to one person. A skilled British mechanic of twenty-one, he was attracted by bounties being offered to British workers familiar with the textile machines. After memorizing the plans for the machinery, he escaped in disguise to America, where he won the backing of Moses Brown, a Quaker **capitalist** in Rhode Island. Laboriously reconstructing the essential apparatus with the aid of a blacksmith and a carpenter, he put into operation in 1791 the first efficient American machinery for spinning cotton thread.

The ravenous mechanism was now ready, but where was the cotton fiber? Handpicking one pound of lint from three pounds of seed was a full day's work for one slave, and this process was so expensive that American-made cotton cloth was relatively rare.

Another mechanical genius, Massachusetts-born Eli Whitney, now made his mark. After graduating from Yale, he journeyed to Georgia to serve as a private

Online Study Center

Interactive map
Origin and Settlement of
Immigrants, 1820–1850
college.hmco.com/pic/kennedybrief7e

factory *An establishment for the mass manufacturing of goods, including buildings and substantial machinery.*

trademark *A distinguishing symbol or word used by a manufacturer on its goods, usually registered by law to protect against imitators.*

capitalist *An individual or group who uses accumulated funds or private property to produce goods for profit in a market.*

The Germans

Between 1820 and 1920, a sea of Germans lapped at America's shores and seeped into its very heartland. Their numbers surpassed those of any other immigrant group, even the prolific and often detested Irish. Yet this Germanic flood, unlike its Gaelic equivalent, stirred little panic in the hearts of native-born Americans because the Germans largely stayed to themselves, far from the madding crowds and nativist fears of northeastern cities.

These "Germans" actually hailed from many different lands, because there was no unified nation of Germany until 1871, when the ruthless and crafty Prussian Otto von Bismarck assembled the German state out of a mosaic of independent principalities, kingdoms, and duchies. Until that time, "Germans" came to America as Prussians, Bavarians, Hessians, Rhinelanders, Pomeranians, and Westphalians. They arrived at different times and for many different reasons. Some, particularly the so-called Forty-Eighters—refugees from the abortive democratic revolution of 1848—hungered for the democracy they had failed to win in Germany. Others, particularly Jews, Pietists, and Anabaptist groups like the Amish and the Mennonites, coveted religious freedom.

Typical German immigrants arrived with fatter purses than their Irish counterparts. Small landowners or independent artisans in their native countries, they did not have to settle for bottom-rung industrial employment in the grimy factories of the Northeast and instead could afford to push on to the open spaces of the West.

In Wisconsin these immigrants found a home away from home, a place with a climate, soil, and geography much like central Europe's. Milwaukee, a crude frontier town before their arrival, became the "German Athens." It boasted a German theater, German beer gardens, a German volunteer fire company, and a German-English academy. In distant Texas, German settlements like New Braunfels and Friedrichsburg flourished. These German colonies in the frontier Southwest mixed high European elegance with Texas ruggedness. When landscape architect and writer Frederick Law Olmsted toured these frontier outposts, he came across a German household where the settlers sat on "barrels for seats, to hear a Beethoven symphony on the grand piano."

These German colonizers of America's heartland also formed religious communities, none more distinctive or durable than the Amish settlements of Pennsylvania, Indiana, and Ohio. The Amish took their name from their founder and leader, the Swiss Anabaptist Jacob Amman. Like other Anabaptist groups, they shunned extravagance and reserved baptism for adults, repudiating the tradition of infant baptism. For this they were persecuted, even imprisoned, in Europe. Seeking escape from their oppression, some five hundred Amish ventured to Pennsylvania in the 1700s, followed by three thousand in the years from 1815 to 1865.

In America they formed enduring religious communities—isolated enclaves where they could shield themselves from the corruption and the conveniences of the modern world. To this day the German-speaking Amish travel in horse-drawn carriages and farm without heavy machinery. No ringing telephones punctuate the reverent tranquility of their mealtime prayer; no ornaments relieve the simplicity of their black garments. The Amish remain a stalwart, traditional religious community in a rootless, turbulent society.

■ "Little Germany" Cincinnati's "Over-the-Rhine" district in 1887.

tutor while preparing for the law. There he was told that the poverty of the South would be relieved if someone could only invent a workable device for separating the seed from the short-staple cotton fiber. Within ten days, in 1793, he built a crude machine called the cotton gin (short for engine), which was fifty times more effective than the handpicking process.

Few machines have ever wrought so wondrous a change. Almost overnight the raising of cotton became highly profitable, and the South was tied hand and foot to the throne of King Cotton. Human bondage had been dying out, but the insatiable demand for cotton reriveted the chains on the limbs of the downtrodden southern blacks.

South and North both prospered. Slave-driving planters cleared more acres for cotton, pushing the Cotton Kingdom westward off the depleted tidewater plains, over the Piedmont, and onto the black loam bottomlands of Alabama and Mississippi. Humming gins poured out avalanches of snowy fiber for the spindles of the Yankee machines. The American phase of the Industrial Revolution, which first blossomed in cotton textiles, was well on its way.

Factories at first flourished most actively in New England. Its stony soil made farming difficult and manufacturing attractive, and the rapid rivers provided abundant water power to turn the cogs of the machines. By 1860 more than 400 million pounds of southern cotton poured annually into the gaping maws of over a thousand mills. Factories eventually branched out into the populous areas of New York, New Jersey, and Pennsylvania. But the South, increasingly wedded to the production of cotton, developed little manufacturing because most of its capital was bound up in slaves.

Marvels in Manufacturing

America's factories spread slowly until about 1807, when there began the fateful sequence of the embargo, non-intercourse, and the War of 1812. The stoppage of European commerce drove both capital and labor from the waves onto the factory floor. Generous bounties were offered by local authorities for homegrown goods. "Buy American" and "Wear American" became popular slogans, and patriotism prompted the wearing of baggy homespun garments. President Madison donned some at his inauguration, where he was said to have been a walking argument for the better processing of native wool.

But the manufacturing boomlet broke abruptly with the peace of Ghent in 1815, as British competitors unloaded their dammed-up surpluses at ruinously low prices. Responding to pained outcries, Congress provided some relief when it passed the mildly protective Tariff of 1816—among the earliest political contests to control the shape of the economy.

As the factory system flourished, it embraced numerous other industries in addition to textiles. Prominent among them was the manufacturing of firearms, and here the wizardly Eli Whitney again appeared with an extraordinary contribution. Frustrated in his earlier efforts to monopolize the cotton gin, he turned to the mass production of muskets for the U.S. Army. Up to this time each part of a firearm had been hand-tooled, and if the trigger of one broke, the trigger of another might or might not fit. About 1798 Whitney seized upon the idea of having machines make each part, so that all the triggers, for example, would be as much alike as the successive imprints of a copperplate engraving. Journeying to Washington, he reportedly dismantled ten of his new muskets in the presence of skeptical officials, scrambled the parts together, and then quickly reassembled ten different muskets.

The principle of interchangeable parts was widely adopted by 1850, and it ultimately became the basis of modern mass-production, assembly-line methods. Ironically, the Yankee Eli Whitney, by perfecting the cotton gin, gave slavery a renewed lease on life, and thus perhaps made inevitable the Civil War. At the same time, by popularizing the principle of interchangeable parts, Whitney helped factories to flourish in the North, giving the Union a decided advantage when that showdown came.

The sewing machine, invented by Elias Howe in 1846 and perfected by Isaac Singer, gave another strong boost to industrialization. The sewing machine

---

patents *The legal certification of an original invention, product, or process, guaranteeing its holder sole rights to profits from its use or reproduction for a specified period of time.*

liability *Legal responsibility for loss or damage.*

incorporation *The formation of individuals into an organized entity with legally defined privileges and responsibilities.*

labor union *An organization of workers—usually wage-earning workers—to promote the interests and welfare of its members, often by collective bargaining with employers.*

strike *An organized work stoppage by employees in order to obtain better wages, working conditions, and so on.*

became the foundation of the ready-made clothing industry, which took root about the time of the Civil War. It drove many a seamstress from the shelter of the private home to the factory where, like a human robot, she tended the clattering mechanisms.

Each momentous new invention seemed to stimulate still more imaginative inventions. For the decade ending in 1800 only 306 **patents** were registered in Washington; but the decade ending in 1860 saw the amazing total of 28,000. Yet in 1838 the clerk of the Patent Office resigned in despair, complaining that all worthwhile inventions had been discovered.

Technical advances spurred equally important changes in the form and legal status of business organizations. The principle of limited **liability** aided the concentration of capital by permitting the individual investor, in cases of legal claims or bankruptcy, to risk no more than his or her own share of the corporation's stock. Laws of "free **incorporation**," first passed in New York in 1848, meant that businessmen could create corporations without applying for individual charters from the legislature.

Samuel F. B. Morse's telegraph was among the inventions that tightened the sinews of an increasingly complex business world. A distinguished but poverty-stricken portrait painter, Morse finally secured from Congress, to the accompaniment of the usual jeers, an appropriation of $30,000 to support his experiment with "talking wires." In 1844 Morse strung a wire forty miles from Washington to Baltimore and tapped out the historic message, "What hath God wrought?" The invention brought fame and fortune to Morse, as he put distant people into almost instant communication with one another. By the eve of the Civil War, a web of singing wires spanned the continent, revolutionizing news gathering, diplomacy, and finance.

Workers and "Wage Slaves"

One ugly outgrowth of the factory system was an increasingly acute labor problem. Hitherto manufacturing had been done in the home, or in the small shop, where the master craftsman and his apprentice, rubbing elbows at the same bench, could maintain an intimate and friendly relationship. The Industrial Revolution submerged this personal association in the impersonal ownership of stuffy factories in "spindle cities." Around these, like tumors, the slumlike hovels of the "wage slaves" tended to cluster.

Clearly the early factory system did not shower its benefits evenly on all. While many owners grew plump, working people often wasted away at their workbenches. Hours were long, wages were low, and meals were skimpy and hastily gulped. Workers were forced to toil in unsanitary buildings that were poorly ventilated, lighted, and heated. They were forbidden by law to form **labor unions** to raise wages, for such cooperative activity was regarded as a criminal conspiracy. Not surprisingly, only twenty-four recorded **strikes** occurred before 1835.

Especially vulnerable to exploitation were child workers. In 1820 half the nation's industrial toilers were children under ten years of age. Victims of factory labor, many children were mentally blighted, emotionally starved, physically stunted, and even brutally whipped in special "whipping rooms." In Samuel Slater's mill of 1791, the first machine tenders were seven boys and two girls, all under twelve years of age.

By contrast, the lot of most adult wage workers improved markedly in the 1820s and 1830s. In the full flush of Jacksonian democracy, many of the states granted the laboring man the vote. Brandishing the ballot and strongly backing Andrew Jackson, workers pushed for the ten-hour workday, better wages and working conditions, public education for their children, and an end to the inhuman practice of imprisonment for debt.

Employers, abhorring the rise of the "rabble" in politics, fought the ten-hour day to the last ditch. But labor registered a red-letter gain in 1840 when President Van Buren established the ten-hour day for federal employees on public works. In ensuing years a number of states gradually fell into line by reducing the hours of working people.

Day laborers at last learned that their strongest weapon was to lay down their tools, even at the risk of prosecution under the law. Dozens of strikes erupted in the 1830s and 1840s, most of them for higher wages, some for the ten-hour day. The workers usually lost more strikes than they won, for the employer could resort to such tactics as importing strikebreakers—often derisively called "scabs" or "rats," and often fresh off the boat from the Old World. Labor long raised its voice against the unrestricted inpouring of wage-depressing and union-busting immigrant workers.

Labor's early and painful efforts at organization had netted some 300,000 trade unionists by 1830. But such encouraging gains were dashed on the rock of hard times following the severe depression of 1837. Yet toilers won a promising legal victory in 1842 when the Massachusetts Supreme Court ruled in *Commonwealth* v. *Hunt* that labor unions were not illegal conspiracies, provided that their methods were "honorable and peaceful." This enlightened decision did not legalize the strike overnight throughout the country, but it was a significant signpost of the times. Trade unions still had nearly a century to go before they could meet management on relatively even terms.

> *A woman worker in the Lowell mills wrote a friend in 1844:*
>
> "You wish to know minutely of our hours of labor. We go in [to the mill] at five o'clock; at seven we come out to breakfast; at half-past seven we return to our work, and stay until half-past twelve. At one, or quarter-past one four months in the year, we return to our work, and stay until seven at night. Then the evening is all our own, which is more than some laboring girls can say, who think nothing is more tedious than a factory life."

★ Women and the Economy

Women were also sucked into the clanging mechanism of factory production. Farm women and daughters had an important place in the pre-industrial economy, spinning yarn, weaving cloth, and making candles, soap, butter, and cheese. New factories undermined these activities, cranking out manufactured goods faster than they could be made by hand at home. Yet these same factories offered employment to the very young women whose work they were displacing. Factory jobs promised greater economic independence for women, as well as the means to buy the manufactured products of the new market economy.

"Factory girls" typically toiled six days a week, earning a pittance for dreary, ear-splitting stints of twelve or thirteen hours—"from dark to dark." The Boston Associates' textile mills at Lowell, Massachusetts, employed New England farm girls, carefully supervised on and off the job by watchful matrons who escorted them to church from their company boardinghouses.

But factory jobs of any kind were still unusual for women. Opportunities for women to be economically self-supporting were scarce and consisted mainly of nursing, domestic service, and especially teaching. The dedicated Catharine Beecher, daughter of a famous preacher and sister of Harriet Beecher Stowe, tirelessly urged women to enter the teaching profession. She eventually succeeded beyond her dreams, as men left teaching for other lines of work and school teaching became a thoroughly "feminized" occupation. By 1850 about 10 percent of white women were working for pay outside their own homes, and about 20 percent of all women had been employed at some time prior to marriage.

The vast majority of working women were single. Upon marriage, they left their paying jobs and took up their new work (without wages) as wives and mothers. In the home they were enshrined in a "cult of domesticity," a widespread cultural creed that glorified the traditional functions of the homemaker. From their pedestals, married women commanded immense moral power, and they increasingly made decisions that altered the character of the family itself.

Women's changing roles and the spreading Industrial Revolution brought some important changes in the life of the nineteenth-century home—the traditional "women's sphere." Love, not parental "arrangement," more and more frequently determined the choice of a spouse—yet parents often retained the power

Online Study Center

Primary source
Weighing and Printing
college.hmco.com/pic/kennedybrief7e

of veto. Families thus became more closely knit and affectionate, providing the emotional refuge that made the threatening impersonality of big-city industrialism tolerable to many people.

Most striking, families grew smaller. The average household had nearly six members at the end of the eighteenth century but fewer than five members a century later. The "fertility rate," or number of births among women age fourteen to forty-five, dropped sharply among white women in the years after the Revolution and, in the course of the nineteenth century as a whole, fell by half. Birth control was still a taboo topic for polite conversation, and contraceptive technology was primitive, but clearly some form of family limitation was being practiced quietly and effectively in countless families, rural and urban alike. Women undoubtedly played a large part—perhaps the leading part—in decisions to have fewer children. This newly assertive role for women has been called "domestic feminism" because it signified the growing power and independence of women, even while they remained trapped in the "cult of domesticity."

Smaller families, in turn, meant child-centered families, since where children are fewer, parents can lavish more care on them individually. European visitors to the United States in the nineteenth century often complained about the unruly behavior of American "brats." But though American parents may have increasingly spared the rod, they did not spoil their children. What Europeans saw as permissiveness was in reality the consequence of an emerging new idea of child-rearing, in which the child's will was not to be simply broken, but shaped.

In the little republic of the family, as in the Republic at large, good citizens were raised not to be meekly obedient to authority, but to be independent individuals who could make their own decisions on the basis of internalized moral standards. Thus the outlines of the "modern" family were clear by midcentury: it was small, affectionate, and child-centered, and it provided a special arena for the talents of women. Feminists of a later day might decry the stifling atmosphere of the nineteenth-century home, but to many women of the time it seemed a big step upward from the conditions of grinding toil—often alongside men in the fields—in which their mothers had lived.

■ **The Sewing Floor of Thompson's Skirt Factory, 1859** The burgeoning textile industry provided employment for thousands of women in antebellum America—and also produced the clothes that women wore. This view of a New York City shop in 1859 illustrates the transition from hand-sewing (on the right) to machine-stitching (on the left). It also vividly illustrates the contrast between the kinds of "sewing circles" in which women had traditionally sought companionship to the impersonal mass-production line of the modern manufacturing plant. Note especially the stark exhortation on the wall: "Strive to Excel."

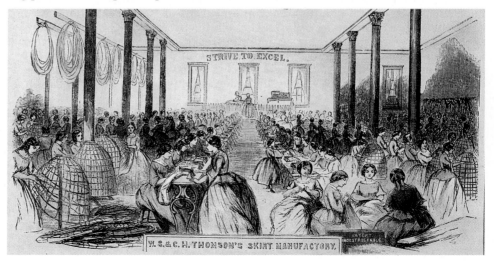

EXAMINING THE EVIDENCE

The Invention of the Sewing Machine Historians of technology examine not only the documentary evidence of plans and patents left behind by inventors, but surviving machines themselves. In 1845 Elias Howe, a twenty-six-year-old apprentice to a Boston watchmaker, invented a sewing machine that could make 250 stitches a minute, five times what the swiftest handsewer could do. A year later Howe received a patent for his invention, but because the hand-cranked machine could only stitch straight seams for a short distance before requiring resetting, it had limited commercial appeal. Howe took his sewing machine abroad, where he worked with British manufacturers to improve it, and then returned to America and combined his patent with those of other inventors, including Isaac M. Singer. Hundreds of thousands of sewing machines were produced beginning in the 1850s for commercial manufacturing of clothing, books, shoes, and many other products and also for home use. The sewing machine became the first widely advertised consumer product. Due to its high cost, the Singer company introduced an installment buying plan, which helped place sewing machines in most middle-class households. Why was the sewing machine able to find eager customers in commercial workshops and home sewing rooms alike? How might the sewing machine have changed other aspects of American life, such as work patterns, clothing styles, and retail selling? What other advances in technology might have been necessary for the invention of the sewing machine?

1. Examine the photo of this sewing machine, built only one year after Elias Howe invented the first such machine in 1845. What are the key components that Howe had to combine in order to improve on hand sewing? In what ways was this machine more limited than hand sewing?

2. What functional and economic differences were there between Howe-Singer machines aimed at sewing within the home and those that came to be built for factory production of the ready-made clothing industry?

3. What made the sewing machine the rare invention that was *both* a capital-intensive industrial product *and* the "first widely advertised consumer product" sold "on the installment plan"?

Western Farmers Reap a Revolution in the Fields

As smoke-belching factories altered the eastern skyline, flourishing farms were changing the face of the West. The trans-Allegheny region—especially the Ohio-Indiana-Illinois tier—was fast becoming the nation's breadbasket. Before long, it would become a granary to the world.

Pioneer farmers first hacked a clearing out of the forest and then planted their painfully furrowed fields to corn. The yellow grain was amazingly versatile. It could be fed to hogs ("corn on the hoof") or distilled into liquor ("corn in the bottle"). Both these products could be transported more easily than the bulky grain itself, and they became the early western farmer's staple market items. So many corn-fed hogs were butchered, traded, or shipped at Cincinnati that the city was known as the "Porkopolis" of the West.

Most western produce was at first floated down the Ohio-Mississippi river system to feed the booming Cotton Kingdom. Spurred on by the easy availability of the seemingly boundless acres, farmers continuously sought ways to bring more and more acres into cultivation. They were often frustrated by the thickly matted soil of the West that snagged and snapped fragile wooden plows. John Deere of Illinois in 1837 finally produced a light, steel plow that broke the stubborn soil.

In the 1830s Virginia-born Cyrus McCormick contributed the most wondrous contraption of all: a mechanical mower-reaper. The clattering cogs of McCormick's horse-drawn machine were to the western farmers what the cotton gin was to the southern planters. Seated on his red-chariot reaper, a single harvester could do the work of five men with sickles and scythes.

No other American invention cut so wide a swath. It made ambitious capitalists out of humble plowmen, who now scrambled for more acres on which to plant more fields of billowing wheat. Specialized cash-crop agriculture came to dominate the West, producing mounting indebtedness as farmers bought more land and more machinery to work it. With hustling farmers producing more than the South could devour, they began to dream of markets in the mushrooming eastern factory towns, or across the faraway Atlantic. But they were still largely landlocked. Commerce moved north and south on the river systems. Before it could begin to move east-west in bulk, a transportation revolution would have to occur.

Online Study Center

**Primary source
McCormick's Harvesting
Machines
college.hmco.com/pic/kennedybrief7e**

Highways and Steamboats

In 1789, when the Constitution was launched, primitive methods of travel were still in use. Waterborne commerce, whether along the coast or on the rivers, was slow, uncertain, and often dangerous. Stagecoaches and wagons lurched over bone-shaking roads. Passengers would be rousted out to lay nearby fence rails across muddy stretches, and occasionally horses would drown in muddy pits while wagons sank slowly out of sight.

Cheap and efficient carriers were imperative if raw materials were to be transported to the factories, and if the finished product was to be delivered to consumers. A promising improvement came in the 1790s, when a private company completed the Lancaster **turnpike,** a broad, hard-surfaced highway that ran sixty-two miles from Philadelphia to Lancaster, Pennsylvania. The highly successful Lancaster turnpike returned dividends as high as 15 percent annually to its stockholders, attracted a rich trade to Philadelphia, and touched off the westward migration of the canvas-covered Conestoga wagons.

Westerners scored a notable triumph in 1811 when the federal government began to construct the elongated National Road, or Cumberland Road. When finally completed in 1852, after interruptions caused by the War of 1812 and states' rights shackles on internal improvements, the highway stretched 591 miles from Cumberland, Maryland, to Vandalia, Illinois.

The steamboat craze, which overlapped the turnpike craze, was touched off by an ambitious painter-engineer named Robert Fulton. In 1807 he installed a powerful steam engine in the *Clermont,* dubbed "Fulton's Folly" by a dubious public. Belching

turnpike *A toll road.*

sparks from its single smokestack, the quaint little ship steadily churned up the Hudson River from New York City to Albany, making the run of 150 miles in 32 hours.

The success of the steamboat was sensational. People could now in large degree defy wind, wave, tide, and downstream current. Within a few years Fulton had changed all of America's navigable streams into two-way arteries, thereby doubling their carrying capacity. Hitherto keelboats had been pushed up the Mississippi, with quivering poles and raucous profanity, at less than one mile an hour—a process that was prohibitively expensive. Now the steamboats could churn rapidly against the current, ultimately attaining speeds in excess of ten miles an hour. The mighty Mississippi had finally met its master. By 1820 there were some sixty steamboats on the Mississippi and its tributaries; by 1860 about a thousand steamboats, including some luxurious river palaces, were plying the inland waters.

Canals and the Iron Horse

A canal-cutting craze paralleled the boom in turnpikes and steamboats. Blessed with the driving leadership of Governor De-Witt Clinton, New York State started the trend when it dug the Erie Canal linking the Hudson River to the Great Lakes.

Begun in 1817, the canal eventually ribboned 363 miles. On its completion in 1825, a garland-bedecked canal boat glided from Buffalo, on Lake Erie, to the Hudson River and on to New York harbor. There, with colorful ceremony, Governor Clinton emptied a cask of water from the lake to symbolize "the marriage of the waters."

The water from Clinton's keg baptized the Empire State. Mule-drawn passengers and bulky freight could now be handled with thrift and dispatch, at the dizzy speed of five miles an hour. The cost of shipping a ton of grain from Buffalo to New York City fell from $100 to $5, and the time of transit from about twenty days to six.

Ever-widening economic ripples followed the completion of the Erie Canal. The value of land along the route skyrocketed, and new cities—such as Rochester and Syracuse—blossomed. Industry in the state boomed. The new profitability of farming in

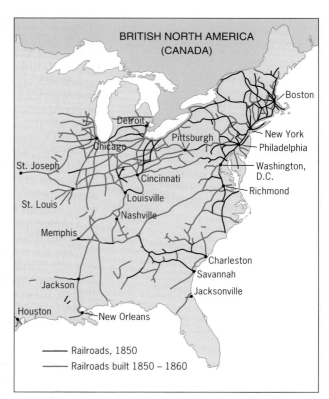

■ **The Railroad Revolution** Note the explosion of new railroad construction in the 1850s and its heavy concentration in the North.

Online Study Center

Interactive map
Population Distribution, 1790
and 1850
college.hmco.com/pic/kennedybrief7e

Online Study Center

Primary source
Railroad Growth
college.hmco.com/pic/kennedybrief7e

the Old Northwest—notably in Ohio, Michigan, Indiana, and Illinois—attracted thousands of European immigrants to the unaxed and untaxed lands now available. Flotillas of steamships soon traversed the Great Lakes, connecting with waiting canal barges at Buffalo. Interior waterside villages like Cleveland, Detroit, and Chicago exploded into mighty cities.

The greatest single contribution to the developing continental economy initiated by the canals proved to be the railroad. It was fast, reliable, cheaper than canals to construct, and not frozen over in winter. Able to go almost anywhere, even through the Appalachian barrier, it defied terrain and weather. The first railroad appeared in the United States in 1828. By 1860, only thirty-two years later, the United States boasted thirty thousand miles of railroad track, three-fourths of it in the rapidly industrializing North.

At first the railroad faced strong opposition from vested interests, especially canal backers. Anxious to protect its investment in the Erie Canal, the New York legislature in 1833 prohibited the railroads from carrying freight—at least temporarily. Early railroads were also considered a dangerous public menace, for flying sparks could set fire to haystacks and houses, and appalling railway accidents could turn the wooden "miniature hells" into flaming funeral pyres for their riders.

Railroad pioneers had to overcome other obstacles as well. Arrivals and departures were conjectural, and numerous differences in gauge (the distance between the rails) meant frequent changes of trains for passengers. In 1840 there were seven transfers between Philadelphia and Charleston. But gauges gradually became standardized, safety devices were adopted, and the Pullman "sleeping palace" was introduced in 1859. America at long last was being bound together with ribs of iron, later to be made of steel.

Cables, Clippers, and Pony Riders

Other forms of transportation and communication were binding together the United States and the world. A crucial step came in 1858 when Cyrus Field, called "the greatest wire puller in history," stretched a telegraph cable under the deep North Atlantic waters from Newfoundland to Ireland. Although this initial cable went dead after three weeks of public rejoicing, a heavier cable laid in 1866 permanently linked the American and European continents.

American commercial shipping fell behind in the early nineteenth century, and American naval designers made few contributions to maritime progress. A pioneer American steamer, the *Savannah,* crept across the Atlantic in 1819, but it used sail most of the time and was pursued for a day by a British captain who thought it afire.

In the 1840s and 1850s, a golden age dawned for American shipping. Yankee naval yards, notably Donald McKay's at Boston, began to send down the ways sleek new crafts called clipper ships. Long, narrow, and majestic, they glided across the sea under towering masts and clouds of canvas. In a fair breeze they could outrun any steamer. The stately clippers sacrificed cargo space for speed, and their captains made killings by hauling high-value cargoes across the oceans in record times.

But the hour of glory for the clipper was relatively brief. On the eve of the Civil War, the British had clearly won the world race for maritime ascendancy with their iron tramp steamers ("teakettles"). Although slower and less romantic than the clipper, these vessels were steadier, roomier, more reliable, and hence more profitable.

No story of rapid American communication would be complete without including the Far West. By 1858 horse-drawn overland stage coaches, immortalized in Mark Twain's *Roughing It,* were a familiar sight. Their dusty tracks stretched from the banks of the muddy Missouri River clear to California.

Even more dramatic was the Pony Express, established in 1860 to carry mail speedily the two thousand lonely miles from St. Joseph, Missouri, to Sacramento, California. Daring, lightweight riders, leaping onto wiry ponies saddled at stations approximately ten miles apart, could make the trip in an amazing ten days. These unarmed horsemen galloped on, summer or winter, day or night, through dust or snow, past Indians and bandits. The speeding postmen missed only one trip, though the whole enterprise lost money and folded after only eighteen legend-leaving months.

Just as the clippers had succumbed to steam, the Pony Express riders were un-horsed by Morse's clacking keys, which began tapping messages to California in 1861. The swift ships and fleet ponies ushered out a dying technology of wind and muscle. In the future, machines would be in the saddle.

The Transport Web Binds the Union

More than anything else, the desire of the East to tap the West stimulated the "transportation revolution." Until about 1830, the produce of the western region drained southward to the cotton belt or to the heaped-up wharves of New Orleans. The steamboat vastly aided the reverse flow of finished goods up the watery western arteries and helped bind the West and South together. But the truly revolutionary changes in commerce and communication came in the three decades before the Civil War, as canals and railroad tracks radiated out from the East, across the Appalachians, and into the blossoming heartland. The ditch-diggers and tie-layers were attempting nothing less than a conquest of nature itself. They would offset the "natural" flow of trade on the interior rivers by laying down an impressive grid of "internal improvements."

The builders succeeded beyond their wildest dreams. The Mississippi was increasingly robbed of its traffic, as goods moved eastward on chugging trains, puffing lake boats, and mule-tugged canal barges. By the 1840s Buffalo was handling more western produce than New Orleans. Between 1836 and 1860, grain shipments through Buffalo increased a staggering sixtyfold. New York City became the seaboard queen of the nation, a gigantic port through which a vast hinterland poured its wealth and to which it daily paid economic tribute.

By the eve of the Civil War, a truly continental economy had emerged. The principle of division of labor, which spelled **productivity** and profits in the factory, applied on a national scale as well. Each region now specialized in a particular type of economic activity. The South raised cotton for export to New England and Britain; the West grew grain and livestock to feed factory workers in the East and in Europe; the East made machines and textiles for the South and West.

The economic pattern thus woven had fateful political and military implications. Many southerners regarded the Mississippi as a silver chain that naturally linked together the upper valley states and the Cotton Kingdom. They would become convinced, as secession approached, that some or all of these states would have to secede with them or be strangled. But they overlooked the man-made links that now bound the upper Mississippi Valley to the East in intimate commercial union. Southern rebels would have to fight not only Northern armies but the tight bonds of an interdependent continental economy. Economically, the two northerly sections were Siamese twins.

productivity *In economics, the relative capacity to produce goods and services, measured in terms of the number of workers and machines needed to create goods in a certain length of time.*

barter *The direct exchange of goods and services for one another, without the use of cash or any medium of exchange.*

The Market Revolution

No less revolutionary than the political upheavals of the antebellum era was the "market revolution" that transformed a subsistence economy of scattered farms and tiny workshops into a national network of industry and commerce. As more and more Americans linked their economic fates to the burgeoning market economy, the self-sufficient households of colonial days were transformed. Most families had once raised all their own food, spun their own wool, and **bartered** with their neighbors for the few necessities they could not make themselves. In growing numbers, they now scattered to work for wages in the mills, or they planted just a few crops for sale at market and used the money to buy goods made by strangers in far-off factories.

As store-bought fabrics, candles, and soap replaced homemade products, a quiet revolution occurred in the household division of labor and status. Traditional women's work was rendered superfluous and devalued. The home itself, once a center of economic production in which all family members cooperated, grew into a place of refuge from the world of work, a refuge that became increasingly the special and separate sphere of women.

Revolutionary advances in manufacturing and transportation brought increased prosperity to all Americans, but they also widened the gulf between the rich and the poor. Millionaires had been rare in the early days of the Republic, but by the eve of the Civil War, several specimens of colossal financial success were strutting across the national stage. Spectacular was the case of fur-trader and real estate speculator John Jacob Astor, who left an estate of $30 million on his death in 1848.

Cities bred the greatest extremes of economic inequality. Unskilled workers, then as always, fared worst. Many of them came to make up a floating mass of "drifters," buffeted from town to town by the shifting prospects for menial jobs. These wandering workers accounted at various times for up to half the population of the brawling industrial centers. Although their numbers were large, they left little behind them but the homely fruits of their transient labor. Largely unstoried and unsung, they are among the forgotten men and women of American history.

Many myths about "social mobility" grew up over the buried memories of these unfortunate day laborers. Mobility did exist in industrializing America—but not in the proportions that legend often portrays. Rags-to-riches success stories were relatively few.

Yet America, with its dynamic society and its wide open spaces, undoubtedly provided more "opportunity" than did the contemporary countries of the Old World—which is why millions of immigrants packed their bags and headed for New World shores. Moreover, a rising tide lifts all boats, and the improvement in overall standards of living was real. Wages for unskilled workers in labor-hungry America rose about 1 percent a year from 1820 to 1860. This general prosperity helped to defuse the potential class conflict that otherwise might have exploded—and that did explode in many European countries.

✪ Chapter Summary ✪

The youthful American republic expanded dramatically on the frontier in the early nineteenth century. Frontier life was often crude and hard on the pioneers, especially women.

Westward-moving pioneers often ruthlessly exploited the environment, exhausting the soil and exterminating wildlife. Yet the wild beauty of the West was also valued as a symbol of American national identity, and eventually environmentalists would create a national park system to preserve pieces of the wilderness.

Other changes altered the character of American society and its workforce. Old cities expanded, and new cities sprang up in the wilderness. Irish and German immigrants poured into the country in the 1830s and 1840s, and the Irish in particular aroused nativist hostility because of their Roman Catholic faith.

Inventions and business innovations like free incorporation laws spurred economic growth. Women and children were the most exploited early factory laborers. Male wage workers made some genuine gains in wages and hours but generally failed in unionization attempts.

The economic changes brought new roles not only for those women who worked in factories (usually only in their early years) but within the traditional sphere of the home. Families became smaller as well as more close-knit and affectionate, and women gained a larger authority within the home, exerting a kind of "domestic feminism." Families also became more child-centered, as child-rearing practices changed from authority to nurture.

The most far-reaching economic advances before the Civil War occurred in agriculture and transportation. The early railroads, despite many obstacles, gradually spread their tentacles across the country. Foreign trade remained only a small part of the American economy, but changing technology gradually created growing economic links to Europe. By the early 1860s the telegraph, railroad, and steamship had gone far toward replacing older means of travel and communication like the canals, clipper ships, stagecoach, and pony express.

The new means of transportation and distribution laid the foundations for a continental market economy. The new national economy created a pattern of sectional specialization and altered the traditional economic functions of the family. There was growing concern over the class differences spawned by industrialization, especially in the cities. But the general growth of opportunities and the increased standard of living made America a magnetic "land of opportunity" to many people at home and abroad.

15

The Ferment of Reform and Culture

⤬

1790–1860

WE [AMERICANS] WILL WALK ON OUR OWN FEET; WE WILL
WORK WITH OUR OWN HANDS; WE WILL SPEAK OUR OWN MINDS.

RALPH WALDO EMERSON, "THE AMERICAN SCHOLAR," 1837

A third revolution accompanied the reformation of American politics and the transformation of the American economy in the mid-nineteenth century. This was a diffuse yet deeply felt commitment to improve the character of ordinary Americans, to make them more upstanding, God-fearing, and literate. Some high-minded souls were disillusioned by the rough-and-tumble realities of democratic politics. Others, notably women, were excluded from the political game altogether. As the young Republic grew, increasing numbers of Americans poured their considerable energies into religious revivals and reform movements.

Reform campaigns of all types flourished in sometimes bewildering abundance. There was not "a reading man" who was without some scheme for a new utopia in his "waistcoat pocket," claimed Ralph Waldo Emerson. Reformers promoted better public schools and rights for women, as well as **polygamy,** celibacy, rule by prophets, and guidance by spirits. Societies were formed against alcohol, tobacco, profanity, and the transit of mail on the Sabbath. Eventually overshadowing all other reforms was the great crusade against slavery (see pp. 242–244). Many reformers drew their crusading zeal from religion. Beginning in the late 1790s and boiling over into the early nineteenth century, the Second Great Awakening swept through America's Protestant churches, transforming the place of religion in American life and sending a generation of believers out on their mission to perfect the world.

Focus Questions

1. What were the most important changes in American religion in the early nineteenth century, and how did they lead to movements for social reform?
2. What were the most important social and educational reform movements of the period, and how successful were they?
3. How did the early women's movement react against the widespread "separate spheres" gender ideology, and what successes and failures did female reformers experience?
4. How were the early utopian experiments and ideologies related to the general religious, social, and intellectual ferment of early American democracy?
5. How did American intellectual and literary life generally reflect the spirit of American democracy, and why did some notable writers dissent from the idealistic spirit of transcendentalism and other optimistic ideologies?

polygamy *The practice of having two or more spouses at one time. (**Polygyny** refers specifically to two or more wives; **polyandry** to two or more husbands.)*

Reviving Religion

Church attendance was still a regular ritual for about three-fourths of the 23 million Americans in 1850. Alexis de Tocqueville declared that there was "no country in the world where the Christian religion retains a greater influence over the souls of men than in America." Yet the austere Calvinist rigor had long been seeping out of the nation's churches.

The rationalist ideas of the French Revolutionary era had done much to soften the older orthodoxy. Thomas Paine's widely circulated book *The Age of Reason* (1794) shockingly declared that all churches were set up "to terrorize and enslave mankind." American anticlericalism was seldom that vehement, but many of the Founders, including Jefferson and Franklin, embraced the liberal doctrines of Deism. Deists relied on reason rather than revelation, rejected the concept of original sin, and denied Christ's divinity. Yet they believed in a Supreme Being who had endowed human beings with a capacity for moral behavior

Deism helped to inspire an important spinoff from Puritanism—the Unitarian faith, which began to gather momentum in New England at the end of the eighteenth century. Unitarians held that God existed in only *one* person (hence *unitarian*) and not in the orthodox Trinity (God the Father, God the Son, and God the Holy Spirit). Although denying the deity of Jesus, Unitarians stressed the essential goodness of human nature, the possibility of salvation through good works, and God as a loving Father rather than a stern Creator. Embraced by many leading thinkers (including Ralph Waldo Emerson), the Unitarian movement appealed mostly to intellectuals whose rationalism and optimism contrasted sharply with the Calvinist doctrines of predestination and human depravity.

A boiling reaction against the growing liberalism in religion set in about 1800. A fresh wave of roaring revivals, beginning on the southern frontier but soon rolling even into the cities of the Northeast, sent the Second Great Awakening surging across the land. Sweeping up more people than the First Great Awakening almost a century earlier (see p. 66), the Second Awakening was one of the most momentous episodes in the history of American religion. This tidal wave of spiritual fervor left in its wake countless converted souls, shattered and reorganized churches, and numerous new sects.

The Second Great Awakening was spread to the masses on the frontier by huge "camp meetings" where as many as twenty-five thousand people would gather for an encampment of several days. Thousands of spiritually starved souls "got

■ **A Camp Meeting at Sing Sing, New York** The preacher stands with hands uplifted under the canopy at the left. A British visitor wrote in 1839 of a revival meeting, "In front of the pulpit there was a space railed off and strewn with straw, which I was told was the anxious seat, and on which sat those who were touched by their consciences."

Chronology

1770s	First Shaker communities formed.		**1835**	Lyceum movement flourishes.
1795	University of North Carolina founded.		**1837**	Emerson delivers "The American Scholar" address.
1800	Second Great Awakening begins.			Mary Lyon establishes Mount Holyoke Seminary.
1819	Jefferson founds University of Virginia.			Oberlin College admits female students.
1821	Cooper publishes *The Spy*, his first successful novel.		**1841**	Brook Farm commune established.
	Emma Willard establishes Troy (New York) Female Seminary.		**1843**	Dorothea Dix petitions Massachusetts legislature on behalf of the insane.
1825	New Harmony commune established.		**1846– 1847**	Mormon migration to Utah.
1826	American Temperance Society founded.		**1848**	Seneca Falls Woman's Rights Convention held.
1828	American Peace Society founded.			Oneida community established.
	Noah Webster publishes dictionary.		**1850**	Hawthorne publishes *The Scarlet Letter*.
1830	Joseph Smith founds Mormon church.		**1851**	Melville publishes *Moby Dick*.
	Godey's Lady's Book first published.			Maine passes first law prohibiting liquor.
1830– 1831	Finney conducts revivals in eastern cities.		**1855**	Whitman publishes *Leaves of Grass*.

religion" at these gatherings, which boosted church membership and stimulated a variety of humanitarian reforms. Responsive easterners were moved to engage in missionary work among the Indians, in Hawaii, and in Asia. Everywhere the Second Awakening encouraged an effervescent evangelicalism that bubbled up into innumerable areas of American life—including prison reform, the temperance cause, the women's movement, and the crusade to abolish slavery.

Methodists and Baptists reaped the most abundant harvest of souls from the fields fertilized by revivalism. Both sects stressed personal conversion (contrary to predestination), a relatively democratic control of church affairs, and a rousing emotionalism. As a frontier jingle ran,

*The devil hates the Methodists
Because they sing and shout the best.*

Powerful Peter Cartwright (1785–1872), was the best known of the Methodist "circuit riders," or traveling frontier preachers. This sinewy servant of the Lord ranged for a half-century from Tennessee to Illinois, calling upon sinners to repent. Bell-voiced Charles Grandison Finney, the greatest of the revival preachers, abandoned his career as a lawyer to become an evangelist after a deeply moving conversion experience as a young man. Tall and athletically built, Finney held huge crowds spellbound with the power of his oratory and the pungency of his message. He led massive revivals in Rochester and New York City in 1830 and 1831. Holding out the promise of a perfect Christian kingdom on earth, Finney denounced both alcohol and slavery. He eventually served as president of Oberlin College in Ohio, which he helped to make a hotbed of revivalist activity and abolitionism.

In his lecture "Hindrances to Revivals," delivered in the 1830s, Charles Grandison Finney (1792–1875) proposed the excommunication of drinkers and slaveholders:

"Let the churches of all denominations speak out on the subject of temperance, let them close their doors against all who have anything to do with the death-dealing abomination, and the cause of temperance is triumphant. A few years would annihilate the traffic. Just so with slavery. . . . It is a great national sin. It is a sin of the church. The churches by their silence, and by permitting slaveholders to belong to their communion, have been consenting to it. . . . The church cannot turn away from this question. It is a question for the church and for the nation to decide, and God will push it to a decision."

A key feature of the Second Great Awakening was the feminization of religion, in terms of both church membership and theology. Middle-class women were the first and most fervent enthusiasts of religious revivalism, and they were the most likely to stay within the fold when the tents were packed up and the traveling evangelist left town. Perhaps women's greater ambivalence than men about the changes wrought by the expanding market economy made them such eager converts to piety. It helped as well that evangelicals preached a gospel of female spiritual worth and offered women an active role in bringing their husbands and families back to God. That accomplished, many women turned to saving the rest of society. They formed a host of benevolent and charitable organizations and spearheaded crusades for most, if not all, of the era's ambitious reforms.

Denominational Diversity

Revivals also furthered the fragmentation of religious faiths. Western New York, where many descendants of New England Puritans had settled, was so blistered by sermonizers preaching "hellfire and damnation" that it came to be known as the "Burned-Over District." Millerites, or Adventists, who mustered several hundred thousand adherents, rose from the superheated soil of the Burned-Over District in the 1830s. The failed prophecy of their eloquent leader, William Miller, that Christ would return to earth on October 22, 1844, dampened but did not destroy the movement.

Like the First Great Awakening, the Second Great Awakening tended to widen the gaps between classes and regions. The more prosperous and conservative denominations in the East were little touched by revivalism, and Episcopalians, Presbyterians, Congregationalists, and Unitarians continued to rise mostly from the wealthier, better-educated levels of society. Methodists, Baptists, and members of the new denominations spawned by the swelling evangelistic fervor tended to come from less prosperous, less "learned" communities in the rural South and West.

Religious diversity further reflected social cleavages when the churches faced up to the slavery issue. By 1844–1845 both the southern Baptists and the southern Methodists had split with their northern brethren over human bondage. In 1857 the Presbyterians, North and South, parted company. The secession of the southern churches foreshadowed the secession of the southern states. First the churches split, then the political parties split, and then the Union split.

A Desert Zion in Utah

The smoldering spiritual embers of the Burned-Over District kindled one especially ardent flame in 1830. In that year Joseph Smith—a rugged visionary, proud of his prowess at wrestling—reported that he had received some golden plates from an angel. When deciphered, they constituted the Book of Mormon, and the Church of Jesus Christ of Latter-Day Saints (Mormons) was launched. It was a native American product, a new religion, destined to spread its influence worldwide.

After establishing a religious oligarchy, Smith ran into serious opposition from his non-Mormon neighbors, first in Ohio and then in Missouri and Illinois. His cooperative sect antagonized rank-and-file Americans, who were individualistic and dedicated to free enterprise. The Mormons aroused further antagonism by voting as a unit and by openly but understandably drilling their militia for defensive purposes. Accusations of polygamy likewise arose and increased in intensity, for Joseph Smith was reputed to have several wives.

Continuing hostility finally drove the Mormons to desperate measures. In 1844 Joseph Smith and his brother were murdered and mangled by a mob in Carthage, Illinois, and the movement seemed near collapse. The falling torch was seized by a remarkable Mormon Moses named Brigham Young. Stern and austere, in contrast to Smith's charm and affability, the barrel-chested Young quickly proved to be an aggressive leader, eloquent preacher, and gifted administrator. Determined to

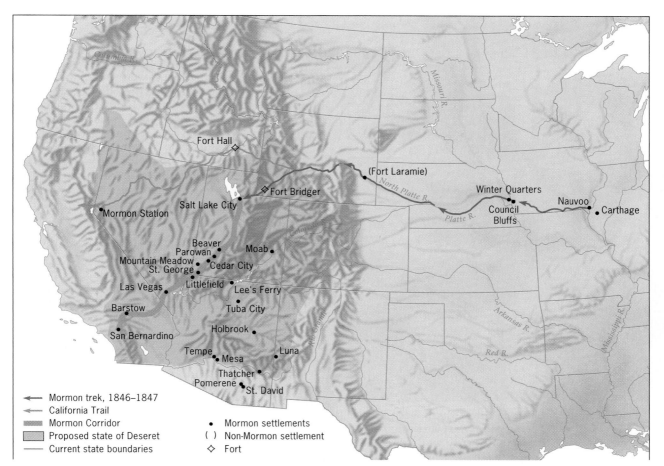

Mormon trek, 1846–1847
California Trail
Mormon Corridor
Proposed state of Deseret
Current state boundaries
• **Mormon settlements**
( ) **Non-Mormon settlement**
◇ **Fort**

■ **The Mormon World** After the murder of Joseph Smith in 1844, the Mormons abandoned their thriving settlement at Nauvoo, Illinois (which had about twenty thousand inhabitants in 1845), and set out for the valley of the Great Salt Lake, then still part of Mexico. When the Treaty of Guadalupe Hidalgo in 1848 brought the vast Utah Territory into the United States, the Mormons rapidly expanded their desert colony, which they called Deseret, especially along the "Mormon Corridor" that stretched from Salt Lake to southern California.

escape further persecution, Young in 1846–1847 led his oppressed Latter-Day Saints over vast rolling plains to Utah as they sang "Come, Come, Ye Saints."

Overcoming pioneer hardships, the Mormons soon made the desert bloom like a new Eden by means of ingenious and cooperative methods of irrigation. The crops of 1848, threatened by hordes of crickets, were saved when flocks of gulls appeared, as if by a miracle, to gulp down the invaders.

Semiarid Utah grew remarkably. By the end of 1848 some five thousand settlers had arrived, and other large bands were to follow them. Many dedicated Mormons in the 1850s actually made the 1,300-mile trek across the plains pulling two-wheeled carts.

Under the rigidly disciplined management of Brigham Young, the community became a prosperous frontier **theocracy** and cooperative commonwealth. Young married as many as twenty-seven women and begot fifty-six children.

A crisis developed when the Washington government seemed unable to control the hierarchy of Brigham Young, who had been made territorial governor in 1850. A federal army marched in 1857 against the Mormons, who harassed its lines of supply and rallied to die in their last dusty ditch. Fortunately, the quarrel was finally adjusted without serious bloodshed. The Mormons later ran afoul of the antipolygamy laws passed by Congress in 1862 and 1882, and their unique marital customs delayed statehood for Utah until 1896.

theocracy *Literally, rule by God; the term is often applied to a state where religious leaders exercise direct or indirect political authority.*

Online Study Center

Interactive map
Major American Cities in 1830 and 1860
college.hmco.com/pic/kennedybrief7e

■ School Days Schoolteaching in the early nineteenth century was a poorly paid occupation that was often pursued by single men who were not very well educated themselves. This drawing depicts John Pounds (1766–1839), who taught school and supplemented his income by mending shoes.

Free Schools for a Free People

Tax-supported primary schools were scarce in the early years of the Republic. They had the odor of pauperism about them, since they existed chiefly to educate the children of the poor—the so-called ragged schools. Advocates of "free" public education met stiff opposition.

Between 1825 and 1850, the spread of democratic ideals and manhood suffrage for whites gradually won acceptance for the public schools, except in the slavery-cursed South. A free vote cried aloud for free education. A civilized nation that was both ignorant and free, declared Thomas Jefferson, "never was and never will be."

But most of the one-room, one-teacher "little red schoolhouses" of the time were imperfect shrines of democracy. Early free schools stayed open only a few months of the year. Schoolteachers, most of them men in this era, were often ill-trained, ill-tempered, and ill-paid. These knights of the blackboard often "boarded around" in the community, and some knew scarcely more than their older pupils. They usually taught only the "three Rs—readin', 'ritin', and 'rithmetic."

Reform was urgently needed. Into the breach stepped Horace Mann (1796–1859), a brilliant and idealistic graduate of Brown University. As secretary of the Massachusetts Board of Education, he campaigned effectively for more and better schoolhouses, longer school terms, higher pay for teachers, and an expanded curriculum. His influence radiated out to other states, and impressive improvements were chalked up. Yet education remained an expensive luxury for many communities. As late as 1860 the nation counted only about a hundred public secondary schools—and nearly a million white adult illiterates. Black slaves in the South were legally forbidden to receive instruction in reading or writing, and even free blacks, in the North as well as the South, were usually excluded from the schools.

Educational advances were aided by improved textbooks, notably those of Noah Webster (1758–1843), a Yale-educated Connecticut Yankee who was known as the "Schoolmaster of the Republic." His "reading lessons," used by millions of children in the nineteenth century, were partly designed to promote patriotism. Webster devoted twenty years to his famous dictionary, published in 1828, which helped to standardize the American language.

Equally influential was Ohioan William H. McGuffey (1800–1873), a teacher-preacher of rare power. His grade-school readers, first published in the 1830s, sold 122 million copies in the following decades. *McGuffey's Readers* hammered home lasting lessons in morality, patriotism, and idealism.

Higher Goals for Higher Learning

Higher education was likewise stirring. The religious zeal of the Second Great Awakening led to the planting of many small, denominational, liberal arts colleges, chiefly in the South and West. The first state-supported universities sprang up in the South, beginning with North Carolina in 1795. Conspicuous among the early group was the University of Virginia, founded in 1819 by Thomas Jefferson, who also designed its beautiful architecture. He dedicated the university to freedom from religious or political shackles, and modern languages and the sciences received unusual emphasis.

Women's higher education was frowned upon in the early decades of the nineteenth century. A woman's place was believed to be in the home, and training in needlecraft seemed more important than training in algebra. Prejudices prevailed that too much learning injured the feminine brain, undermined health, and rendered a young lady unfit for marriage. The teachers of Susan B. Anthony, the future feminist, refused to instruct her in long division.

Women's schools at the secondary level began to attain some respectability in the 1820s, thanks in part to the dedicated work of Emma Willard (1787–1870). In 1821 she established the Troy (New York) Female Seminary. Oberlin College in Ohio shocked traditionalists in 1837 when it opened its doors to women as well as men. (Oberlin had already created shock waves by admitting black students.) In the same year, Mary Lyon established an outstanding women's school, Mount Holyoke Seminary (later College), in South Hadley, Massachusetts.

Adults who craved more learning satisfied their thirst for knowledge at private subscription libraries or, increasingly, at tax-supported libraries. House-to-house peddlers also did a lush business in feeding the public appetite for culture. Traveling lecturers helped to carry learning to the masses through the lyceum lecture associations, which numbered about three thousand by 1835. The lyceums provided platforms for speakers in such areas as science, literature, and moral philosophy. Talented talkers like Ralph Waldo Emerson journeyed thousands of miles on the lyceum circuits, casting their pearls of civilization before appreciative audiences.

Magazines flourished in the pre–Civil War years. The *North American Review,* founded in 1815, was the long-lived leader of the intellectuals. *Godey's Lady's Book,* founded in 1830, survived until 1898 and attained the enormous circulation (for those days) of 150,000. It was devoured devotedly by millions of women, many of whom read the dog-eared copies of their relatives and friends.

An Age of Reform

As the young Republic grew, reform campaigns of all types flourished in sometimes bewildering abundance. Some of the reformers, usually touched by the fire of evangelical religion, were simply cranks, but most were intelligent, inspired idealists. The optimistic fervor of the Second Great Awakening inspired countless souls to do battle against earthly evils. These modern idealists dreamed anew the old Puritan vision of a perfected society free from cruelty, war, intoxicating drink, discrimination, and—ultimately—slavery. Women were particularly prominent in these reform crusades, especially in their own struggle for suffrage. For many middle-class women, the campaigns provided a unique opportunity to escape the confines of the home and enter the arena of public affairs.

In part the practical, activist Christianity of these reformers resulted from their desire to reaffirm traditional values as they plunged ever further into a world disrupted and transformed by the turbulent forces of a market economy. Often blissfully unaware that they were witnessing the dawn of the industrial era, they either ignored the factory workers or blamed their problems on bad habits. Reformers sometimes applied conventional virtue to refurbishing an older order—while events hurtled them headlong into the new.

Imprisonment for debt continued to be a nightmare. As late as 1830 hundreds of penniless people were languishing in filthy holes. The poorer working classes were especially hard hit by this merciless practice. But as the embattled laborer won the ballot and asserted himself, state legislators gradually abolished the debtors' prisons and softened the criminal codes. The number of capital offenses was reduced, and brutal punishments, such as whipping and branding, were slowly eliminated. A refreshing idea began taking hold that prisons should reform as well as punish—hence "reformatories," "houses of correction," and "penitentiaries" (for penance).

Sufferers from so-called insanity were still being treated with incredible cruelty. The mentally deranged were considered willfully perverse and depraved—to be treated only as beasts. A formidable New England teacher-author, Dorothea

■ **Dorothea Dix (1802–1887)** A tireless reformer, she worked mightily to improve the treatment of the mentally ill. At the outbreak of the Civil War, she was appointed superintendent of women nurses for the Union forces.

---

zealot *One who is carried away by a cause to an extreme or excessive degree.*

In presenting her case to the Massachusetts legislature for more humane treatment for the mentally ill, Dorothea Dix (1802–1887) quoted from the notebook she carried with her as she traveled around the state:

"Lincoln. A woman in a cage. *Medford.* One idiotic subject chained, and one in a close stall for seventeen years. *Pepperell.* One often doubly chained, hand and foot; another violent; several peaceable now. . . . *Dedham.* The insane disadvantageously placed in the jail. In the almshouse, two females in stalls . . . ; lie in wooden bunks filled with straw; always shut up. One of these subjects is supposed curable. The overseers of the poor have declined giving her a trial at the hospital, as I was informed, on account of expense."

Dix (1802–1887) spent eight years observing these conditions at first hand and then presented her classic petition to the Massachusetts legislature in 1843. Her description of cells so foul that visitors were driven back by the stench turned legislative stomachs and hearts. Her persistent prodding resulted in improved conditions and in a gain for the concept that the demented were not willfully perverse but mentally ill.

Agitation for peace also gained momentum in the pre–Civil War years. In 1828 the American Peace Society was formed, with a ringing declaration of war on war. The American peace crusade, linked with a European counterpart, was making promising progress by midcentury, but it was set back by the bloodshed of the Crimean War in Europe and the Civil War in America.

Demon Rum: The "Old Deluder"

The ever-present drink problem also attracted dedicated reformers. Excessive drinking of hard liquor was common even among women, clergymen, and members of Congress. Weddings and funerals all too often became disgraceful brawls, and occasionally a drunken mourner would fall into the open grave with the corpse. Drunkenness also fouled the sanctity of the family, threatening the spiritual welfare—and physical safety—of women and children.

After earlier and feebler efforts, the American Temperance Society was formed at Boston in 1826. Within a few years about a thousand local groups sprang into existence. They implored drinkers to sign the temperance pledge and organized children's clubs, known as the "Cold Water Army."

The most popular anti-alcohol tract of the era was T. S. Arthur's melodramatic novel, *Ten Nights in a Barroom and What I Saw There* (1854). It described in shocking detail how a once-happy village was ruined by Sam Slade's tavern. The book was second only to Harriet Beecher Stowe's *Uncle Tom's Cabin* as a bestseller in the 1850s, and it enjoyed a highly successful run on the stage.

Early foes of Demon Drink adopted two major lines of attack. One was to stiffen the individual's will to resist the wiles of the little brown jug. The moderate reformers thus stressed temperance rather than the total elimination of intoxicants. But less patient **zealots** came to believe that temptation should be removed by legislation. Prominent among this group was Neal S. Dow of Maine, a blue-nosed reformer who, as mayor of Portland and an employer of labor, had often witnessed the debauching effect of alcohol.

Dow—the "Father of Prohibition"—sponsored the so-called Maine Law of 1851. This drastic new statute, hailed as "the law of Heaven Americanized," prohibited the manufacture and sale of intoxicating liquor. Other states in the North followed Maine's example, and by 1857 about a dozen had passed various prohibitory laws.

On the eve of the Civil War the prohibitionists had registered inspiriting gains. There was much less drinking among women than earlier in the century and probably much less per capita consumption of hard liquor.

Women in Revolt

When the nineteenth century opened, it was still a man's world, both in America and in Europe. A wife was supposed to immerse herself in her home and subordinate herself to her husband. Like black slaves, she could not vote; like black slaves, she could be legally beaten by her overlord "with a reasonable instrument." When she married, she could not retain title to her property; it passed to her husband. Women in America were still the "submerged sex" in the early part of the century, though their position was somewhat better than that of their European cousins. French visitor Alexis de Tocqueville noted that in his native France rape was punished only lightly, whereas in America it was one of the few crimes punishable by death.

But as the decades unfolded, American women increasingly surfaced to breathe the air of freedom and self-determination. In contrast to women in colonial times, many women now avoided marriage altogether—about 10 percent of adult women remained "spinsters" at the time of the Civil War.

Gender differences were strongly emphasized in nineteenth-century America—largely because the burgeoning market economy was increasingly separating women and men into sharply distinct economic roles. Women were thought to be physically and emotionally weak, but also artistic and refined. Endowed with finely tuned moral sensibilities, they were the keepers of society's conscience, with special responsibility to teach the young how to be good citizens of the Republic. Men were considered strong but crude, always in danger of slipping into some savage or beastly way of life if not guided by the gentle hands of their loving ladies.

The home was a woman's special sphere, the centerpiece of the "cult of domesticity." Even reformers like Catharine Beecher, who urged her sisters to seek employment as teachers, endlessly celebrated the role of the good homemaker. But some women increasingly felt that the glorified sanctuary of the home was in fact a gilded cage. They yearned to tear down the bars that separated the private world of women from the public world of men.

Clamorous female reformers—most of them white and well-to-do—began to gather strength as the century neared its halfway point. Most were broad-gauge battlers; while demanding rights for women, they joined in the general reform movement of the age, fighting for temperance and the abolition of slavery. Like men, they had been touched by the evangelical spirit that offered the promise of earthly reward for human endeavor. Neither foul eggs nor foul words, when hurled by disapproving men, could halt women heartened by these doctrines.

The women's rights movement was mothered by some arresting characters. Prominent among them was Lucretia Mott, a sprightly Quaker whose ire had been aroused when she and her fellow female delegates to the London antislavery convention of 1840 were not recognized. Elizabeth Cady Stanton, a mother of seven who had insisted on leaving "obey" out of her marriage ceremony, shocked fellow feminists by going so far as to advocate suffrage for women. Quaker-reared Susan B. Anthony, a militant lecturer for women's rights, fearlessly exposed herself to rotten garbage and vulgar epithets.

Other feminists challenged the man's world. Dr. Elizabeth Blackwell, a pioneer in a previously forbidden profession for women, was the first female graduate of a medical college. Precocious Margaret Fuller edited a transcendentalist journal, *The Dial,* and took part in the struggle to bring unity and republican government to Italy. The talented Grimké sisters, Sarah and Angelina, championed antislavery. Lucy Stone retained her maiden name after marriage—hence the latter-day "Lucy Stoners," who follow her example. Amelia Bloomer revolted against the current "street-sweeping" female attire by donning a short skirt with Turkish trousers—"bloomers," they were called—amid much bawdy ridicule about "Bloomerism" and "loose habits." A jeering male rhyme of the times jabbed

> *Gibbey, gibbey gab*
> *The women had a confab*
> *And demanded the rights*
> *To wear the tights*
> *Gibbey, gibbey gab.*

Unflinching feminists met at Seneca Falls, New York, in a memorable Woman's Rights Convention (1848). The defiant Stanton read a "Declaration of Sentiments," which in the spirit of the Declaration of Independence declared that "all men and women are created equal." One resolution formally demanded the

> When early feminist Lucy Stone (1818–1893) married fellow abolitionist Henry B. Blackwell (1825–1909) in West Brookfield, Massachusetts, in 1855, they added the following vow to their nuptial ceremony:
>
> "While acknowledging our mutual affection by publicly assuming the relation of husband and wife, yet in justice to ourselves and a great principle, we deem it a duty to declare that this act on our part implies no . . . promise of voluntary obedience to such of the present laws of marriage, as refuse to recognize the wife as an independent, rational being, while they confer upon the husband an injurious and unnatural superiority."

utopian *Referring to any place or plan that aims at an ideal social order.*

communistic *Referring to the theory or practice in which the means of production are owned by the community as a whole.*

communitarian *Referring to the belief in or practice of the superiority of community life or values over individual life, but not necessarily the common ownership of material goods.*

coitus reservatus *A form of sexual intercourse in which male ejaculation is suppressed.*

eugenic *Concerning the improvement of the human species through selective breeding or genetic control.*

 *Online Study Center*

Primary source
Orestes Brownson Views Brook Farm as an Expression
college.hmco.com/pic/kennedybrief7e

 *Online Study Center*

Primary source
Noyes Acknowledges the Associationist Debt to the Shakers
college.hmco.com/pic/kennedybrief7e

 *Online Study Center*

Primary sources
John H. Noyes Discusses Free Love, as Practiced at Oneida
college.hmco.com/pic/kennedybrief7e

ballot for females. Amid scorn and denunciation from press and pulpit, the Seneca Falls meeting launched the modern women's rights movement.

The crusade for women's rights was eclipsed by the campaign against slavery in the decade before the Civil War. Still, any white male over twenty-one could vote, while no woman could. Yet women were being gradually admitted to colleges, and some states, beginning with Mississippi in 1839, were even permitting wives to own property after marriage.

Wilderness Utopias

Bolstered by the **utopian** spirit of the age, various reformers, ranging from the high-minded to the "lunatic fringe," set up more than forty communities of a cooperative, **communistic,** or "**communitarian**" nature. Seeking human betterment, a wealthy and idealistic Scottish textile manufacturer, Robert Owen, founded in 1825 a communal society of about a thousand people at New Harmony, Indiana. Little harmony prevailed in the colony, which, in addition to hard-working visionaries, attracted a sprinkling of radicals, work-shy theorists, and outright scoundrels. The colony sank in a morass of contradiction and confusion.

Brook Farm in Massachusetts, comprising two hundred acres of grudging soil, was started in 1841 by about twenty intellectuals committed to the philosophy of transcendentalism. They prospered reasonably well until 1846, when they lost by fire a large new communal building shortly before its completion. The whole venture in "plain living and high thinking" then collapsed in debt. The Brook Farm experiment inspired Nathaniel Hawthorne's classic novel *The Blithedale Romance* (1852), whose main character was modeled on the feminist writer Margaret Fuller.

A more radical experiment was the Oneida Colony, founded in New York in 1848. It practiced free love ("complex marriage"), birth control (through "male continence," or *coitus reservatus*), and the **eugenic** selection of parents to produce superior offspring. This curious enterprise flourished for more than thirty years, largely because its artisans made superior steel traps and Oneida Community (silver) Plate. In 1879–1880 the group embraced monogamy and abandoned communism (see "Makers of America: The Oneida Community," p. 228).

Among the longest-lived communitarian sects were the Shakers. Led by Mother Ann Lee, they began in the 1770s to set up a score or so of religious communities. The Shakers attained a membership of about six thousand in 1840, but since their monastic customs prohibited both marriage and sexual relations, they were virtually extinct by 1940.

Artistic Achievements

The arts in practical, pioneering early America were slow to gain momentum, and even slower to achieve real distinction. Architecturally, America contributed little of note in the first half of the century. The rustic Republic, still under pressure to erect shelters in haste, was continuing to imitate European models. Public buildings and other important structures followed Greek and Roman lines, which seemed curiously out of place in a wilderness setting. A remarkable Greek revival came between 1820 and 1850. About midcentury strong interest developed in a revival of Gothic forms, with their emphasis on pointed arches and large windows.

EXAMINING THE EVIDENCE

Dress as Reform Among the many social movements that swept nineteenth-century America, dress reform emerged in the 1840s as a critique of materialism and the constraints that fashion imposed on women. Medical professionals, social reformers, and transcendentalist intellectuals all argued that corsets constricting vital organs and voluminous skirts dragging along garbage-strewn streets unfairly restricted women's mobility, prevented women from bearing healthy children, and even induced serious sickness and death. The "Bloomer costume" depicted in this illustration from *Harper's New Monthly Magazine* in 1851 included Turkish-style trousers, a jacket, and a short overskirt that came to the knees. Named after reformer Amelia Bloomer (1818–1894), who publicized the new style in her magazine, *The Lily,* the bloomer dress was first adopted by utopian communities such as the Owenites in New Harmony, Indiana, and the Oneidans in New York. Radical social critic Henry David Thoreau also advocated rational dress as a way of rejecting the artificial desires created by industrialization. But while applauded by reformers, new-style dress was viciously ridiculed by mainstream society, as this print demonstrates. Critics claimed that women blurred gender distinctions by adopting "male" attire, endangering the family and even American civilization. After only a decade, practitioners gave up wearing bloomers in public, adopting plain and simplified clothing instead. But Owenites, some Mormons, women's rights advocates, farmers, and travelers on the overland trail continued to wear bloomers in private. How did dress reform intersect with other religious and social movements of the era? Why did bloomers upset so many antebellum Americans? Have there been other historical eras when new styles of dress came to symbolize broader social change?

1. In this illustration of the "Bloomer costume" from *Harper's* (1851), what evidence is there of the hostility of the illustrator to the new and socially significant fashion? Besides the trousers, how is the supposed loss of "femininity" conveyed?

2. How does the bloomer outfit itself contrast with the more conventional mid-nineteenth-century female attire worn by the woman on the right?

3. What are the responses of the witnesses, including the children, to this innovation? How do the bloomer wearers themselves apparently respond to these attitudes?

The Oneida Community

John Humphrey Noyes (1811–1886), the founder of the Oneida Community, repudiated the old Puritan doctrines that God was vengeful and that sinful mankind was doomed to dwell in a vale of tears. Noyes believed in a benign deity, in the sweetness of human nature, and in the possibility of a perfect Christian community on earth. "The more we get acquainted with God," he declared, "the more we shall find it our special duty to be happy."

That sunny thought was shared by many early-nineteenth-century American utopians (a word derived from Greek that slyly combines the meanings of "a good place" and "no such place"). But Noyes added some wrinkles of his own. The key to happiness, he taught, was the suppression of selfishness. True Christians should possess no private property—nor should they indulge in exclusive emotional relationships, which bred jealousy, quarreling, and covetousness. Material things and sexual partners alike, Noyes preached, should be shared. Marriage should not be monogamous. Instead all members of the community should be free to love one another in "complex marriage." Noyes called his system "Bible Communism."

Tall and slender, with piercing blue eyes and reddish hair, the charismatic Noyes began voicing these ideas in his hometown of Putney, Vermont, in the 1830s. He soon attracted a group of followers who called themselves the Putney Association, a kind of extended family whose members farmed five hundred acres by day and sang and prayed together in the evenings.

The Putney Association also indulged in sexual practices that outraged the surrounding community's sense of moral propriety. Indicted for adultery in 1847, Noyes led his followers to Oneida, in the supposedly more tolerant region of New York's Burned-Over District, the following year.

The Oneidans struggled in New York until the manufacture of steel animal traps and other goods put the Community on a sound financial footing. By the 1860s Oneida was a flourishing commonwealth of some three hundred people. Men and women shared equally in all the community's tasks, from field to factory to kitchen. Children at the age of three were removed from direct parental care and raised communally until the age of thirteen or fourteen, when they took up jobs in the community's industries. They imbibed their religious doctrines with their school lessons:

> I-spirit
> With me never shall stay,
> We-spirit
> Makes us happy and gay.

Oneida's apparent success fed the utopian dreams of others, and for a time it became a great tourist attraction. Visitors from as far away as Europe came to picnic on the shady lawns, speculating on the sexual secrets that the Community guarded, while their hosts fed them strawberries and cream and entertained them with music.

But eventually the same problems that had driven Noyes and his band from Vermont began to shadow their lives at Oneida. Their New York neighbors grew increasingly horrified at the Oneidans' licentious sexual practices, including the selective breeding program by which the community matched mates and gave permission—or orders—to procreate, without regard to the niceties of matrimony.

Yielding to their neighbors' criticisms, the Oneidans gave up complex marriage in 1879. Soon other "communistic" practices withered away as well. In 1880 the Oneidans abandoned communism altogether and became a joint-stock company specializing in the manufacture of silver tableware. Led by Noyes's son Pierrepont, Oneida Community, Ltd., grew into the world's leading manufacturer of stainless steel knives, forks, and spoons, with annual sales by the 1990s of some half a billion dollars. Ironically, what grew from Noyes's religious vision was not utopia but a mighty capitalist corporation.

Talented Thomas Jefferson, architect of revolution, was probably the ablest American architect of his generation. He brought a **classical** design to his Virginia hilltop home, Monticello—perhaps the most stately mansion in the nation. The quadrangle of the University of Virginia at Charlottesville, another of Jefferson's creations, remains one of the finest examples of classical architecture in America.

Painting, like the theater, suffered from the Puritan prejudice that art was a sinful waste of time—and often obscene. When Edward Everett, the eminent Boston scholar and orator, placed a statue of Apollo in his home, he had its naked limbs draped.

Competent painters nevertheless emerged. Gilbert Stuart (1775–1828), a Rhode Islander and one of the most gifted of the early group, wielded his brush in Britain in competition with the best artists. He produced several portraits of Washington, all of them somewhat idealized and dehumanized. Charles Willson Peale (1741–1827), a Marylander, painted some sixty portraits of Washington, who patiently sat for about fourteen of them. John Trumbull (1756–1843), who had fought in the Revolutionary War, recaptured its scenes and spirit on scores of striking canvases.

During the nationalistic upsurge after the War of 1812, American painters turned increasingly from human subjects to romantic landscapes. The Hudson River School excelled in this type of art. At the same time, portrait painters gradually encountered some unwelcome competition from the invention of a crude photograph known as the daguerreotype, perfected about 1839 by a Frenchman, Louis Daguerre.

Music was slowly shaking off the restraints of colonial days, when the prim Puritans had frowned upon nonreligious singing. Rhythmic and nostalgic "darky" tunes were becoming immense hits by midcentury. Special favorites were the uniquely American minstrel shows, featuring white actors with darkened faces. The most famous black songs, ironically, came from a white Pennsylvanian, Stephen C. Foster (1826–1864). Foster made a valuable contribution to American folk music by capturing the plaintive spirit of the slaves in songs like "Old Folks at Home." An odd and pathetic figure, he finally lost both his art and his popularity and died in a charity ward after drowning his sorrows in drink.

The Blossoming of a National Literature

"Who reads an American book?" sneered a British critic in 1820. The painful truth was that the nation's rough-hewn, pioneering civilization gave little encouragement to "polite" literature. America produced praiseworthy political essays like *The Federalist,* political orations like the masterpieces of Daniel Webster, and classics like Benjamin Franklin's *Autobiography* (1818). But most reading matter before 1820 was imported or plagiarized from Britain.

A genuinely American literature received a strong boost from the wave of nationalism that followed the Revolutionary War and especially the War of 1812. By 1820 the older seaboard areas were sufficiently removed from the survival mentality of tree chopping so that literature could be supported as a profession. The Knickerbocker Group in New York blazed brilliantly across the literary heavens, enabling America for the first time to boast of a literature to match its magnificent landscapes.

Washington Irving (1783–1859), born in New York City, was the first American to win international recognition as a literary figure. Steeped in the traditions of New Netherland, he published in 1809 his *Knickerbocker's History of New York,* with its amusing caricatures of the Dutch. Irving won fame at home and abroad with his *Sketch Book* (1819–1820), which included such immortal Dutch-American tales as "Rip Van Winkle" and "The Legend of Sleepy Hollow." Europe was amazed to find at last an American with a feather in his hand, not in his hair.

The novelist James Fenimore Cooper (1789–1851) was the first American novelist, as Washington Irving was the first general writer, to gain world fame and make New World themes respectable. After an initial failure, Cooper launched his illustrious career in 1821 with his second novel *The Spy*—an absorbing tale of the American Revolution. His fame rests most enduringly on the *Leatherstocking Tales.* A deadeye rifleman named Natty Bumppo, one of nature's noblemen, meets with Indians in stirring adventures like *The Last of the Mohicans.* Some Europeans who read Cooper's novels came to think of all Americans as born with a tomahawk

Online Study Center

**Primary sources
Oneida Sisters Comment on Love and Labor**
college.hmco.com/pic/kennedybrief7e

Online Study Center

**Primary source
Shaker Village at Alfred, Maine**
college.hmco.com/pic/kennedybrief7e

Online Study Center

**Primary source
Dwight's Reflections on the Promise and . . .**
college.hmco.com/pic/kennedybrief7e

Online Study Center

**Primary source
Ohio Associationist Sees Women's Activism as . . .**
college.hmco.com/pic/kennedybrief7e

Online Study Center

**Primary source
Lowell Offering Correspondent Describes a Shaker**
college.hmco.com/pic/kennedybrief7e

Online Study Center

**Interactive map
Religious and Utopian Communities, 1800–1845**
college.hmco.com/pic/kennedybrief7e

classical *Concerning the culture of ancient Greece and Rome, or any artistic or cultural values presumed to be based on those enduring principles.*

in hand. Actually Cooper was exploring the viability and destiny of America's republican experiment by contrasting the values of "natural men" of the wilderness with the artificiality of modern civilization.

A third member of the Knickerbocker Group in New York was the belatedly Puritan William Cullen Bryant (1794–1878). At age sixteen he wrote the meditative and melancholy "Thanatopsis," (published in 1817), one of the first high-quality poems produced in the United States. Critics could hardly believe that it had been written on "this side of the water."

Trumpeters of Transcendentalism

A golden age in American literature dawned in the second quarter of the nineteenth century, when an amazing outburst shook New England. One of the mainsprings of this literary flowering was transcendentalism, especially around Boston, which preened itself as "the Athens of America."

The transcendentalist movement of the 1830s resulted in part from a liberalizing of the straitjacket Puritan theology. It also owed much to foreign influences, including the German romantic philosophers and the religions of Asia. The transcendentalists rejected the prevailing theory, derived from John Locke that all knowledge comes to the mind through the senses. Truth, rather, "transcends" the senses: it cannot be found by observation alone. Every person possesses an inner light that can illuminate the highest truth and put him or her in direct touch with God, or the "Oversoul."

These **mystical** doctrines of transcendentalism defied precise definition, but they underlay concrete beliefs. Foremost was a stiff-backed individualism in matters religious as well as social. Closely associated was a commitment to self-reliance, self-culture, and self-discipline. These traits naturally bred hostility to authority and to formal institutions of any kind, as well as to all conventional wisdom. Finally came exaltation of the dignity of the individual, whether black or white—the mainspring of a whole array of humanitarian reforms.

Best known of the transcendentalists was Boston-born Ralph Waldo Emerson (1803–1882). Tall, slender, and intensely blue-eyed, he mirrored serenity in his noble features. Trained as a Unitarian minister, he early forsook his pulpit and ultimately reached a wider audience by pen and platform. He was a never-failing favorite as a lyceum lecturer and for twenty years took a western tour every winter. Perhaps his most thrilling public effort was a Phi Beta Kappa address, "The American Scholar," delivered at Harvard College in 1837. This brilliant appeal was an intellectual Declaration of Independence, for it urged American writers to throw off European traditions and delve into the riches of their own backyards.

Hailed as both a poet and a philosopher, Emerson was not of the highest rank as either. He was more influential as a practical philosopher and through his fresh and vibrant essays enriched thousands of humdrum lives. Catching the individualistic mood of the Republic, he stressed self-reliance, self-improvement, optimism, and freedom. The secret of Emerson's popularity lay largely in the fact that his ideals reflected those of an expanding America. By the 1850s he was an outspoken critic of slavery, and he ardently supported the Union cause in the Civil War.

Henry David Thoreau (1817–1862) was Emerson's close associate—a poet, a mystic, a transcendentalist, and a **nonconformist.** Condemning a government that supported slavery, he refused to pay his Massachusetts poll tax and was jailed for a night.* A gifted prose writer, he is

mystical *Referring to the belief in the direct apprehension of God or divine mystery, without reliance on reason or human comprehension.*

nonconformist *One who refuses to follow established or conventional ideas or habits.*

In 1849 Henry David Thoreau (1817–1862) published "Resistance to Civil Government," (later renamed "Civil Disobedience"), asserting:

"All men recognize the right of revolution; the right to refuse allegiance to and to resist the government, when its tyranny or its inefficiency are great and endurable. But almost all say that such is not the case now. . . . I say, when a sixth of the population of a nation which has undertaken to be the refuge of liberty are slaves, and a whole country is unjustly overrun and conquered by a foreign army, and subjected to military law, I think that it is not too soon for honest men to rebel and revolutionize. What makes this duty more urgent is the fact, that the country so overrun is not our own, but ours is the invading army."

---

* The story (probably apocryphal) is that Emerson visited Thoreau at the jail and asked, "Why are you here?" The reply came, "Why are you not here?"

well known for *Walden: Or Life in the Woods* (1854). The book is a record of Thoreau's two years of simple existence in a hut that he built on the edge of Walden Pond, near Concord, Massachusetts. A stiff-necked individualist, he believed that he should reduce his bodily wants so as to gain time for a pursuit of truth through study and meditation. Thoreau's *Walden* and his essay *On the Duty of Civil Disobedience* exercised a strong influence in furthering idealistic thought, both in America and abroad. His writings later encouraged Mohandas Gandhi to resist British rule in India and, still later, inspired the development of American civil rights leader Martin Luther King, Jr.'s thinking about **nonviolence.**

Bold, brassy, and swaggering was the open-collared figure of Brooklyn's Walt Whitman (1819–1892). In his famous collection of poems, *Leaves of Grass* (1855), he gave free rein to his gushing genius with what he called a "barbaric yawp." Highly romantic, emotional, and unconventional, he dispensed with titles, stanzas, rhymes, and at times even regular meter. He handled sex with shocking frankness, and his book was banned in Boston.

Whitman's *Leaves of Grass* was at first a financial failure. The only three enthusiastic reviews that it received were written by the author himself—anonymously. But in time the once-withered *Leaves of Grass,* revived and honored, won for Whitman an enormous following in both America and Europe.

Leaves of Grass gained for Whitman the informal title "Poet Laureate of Democracy." Singing with transcendental abandon of his love for the masses, he caught the exuberant enthusiasm of an expanding America that had turned its back on the Old World:

All the Past we leave behind;
We debouch upon a newer, mightier world, varied world;
Fresh and strong the world we seize—world of labor and the
march—
Pioneers! O Pioneers!

Here at last was the native art for which critics had been crying.

Two women writers whose work remains enormously popular today were also tied to the New England literary world. Louisa May Alcott (1832–1888) grew up in Concord, Massachusetts, in the bosom of transcendentalism, alongside neighbors Emerson, Thoreau, and Fuller. Her philosopher father Bronson Alcott occupied himself more devotedly to ideas than to earning a living, leaving his daughter to write *Little Women* (1868) and other books to support her mother and sisters. Not far away, in Amherst, Massachusetts, poet Emily Dickinson (1830–1886) lived as a recluse but created her own original world through precious gems of poetry. In deceptively spare language and simple rhyme schemes, she explored universal themes of nature, love, death, and immortality. Although she refused during her lifetime to publish any of her poems, when she died, nearly two thousand of them were found among her papers and eventually made their way into print.

■ **Walt Whitman** This portrait of the young poet appeared in the first edition of *Leaves of Grass* (1855).

nonviolence *The principle of resolving or engaging in conflict without resort to physical force.*

Literary Individualists and Dissenters

Not all writers in these years believed so keenly in human goodness and social progress as Whitman and the New England transcendentalists. Edgar Allan Poe (1809–1849), who spent much of his youth in Virginia, was an eccentric genius. Orphaned at an early age, cursed with ill health, and married to a child-wife of thirteen who fell fatally ill of tuberculosis, he suffered hunger, cold, poverty, and debt. Poe was a gifted lyric poet, as "The Raven" attests. If he did not invent the modern detective novel, he at least set new high standards for it in tales like "The Gold Bug." A master stylist, he also excelled in the short story, especially of the horror genre, in which he shared his nightmares with fascinated readers.

Poe was fascinated by the ghostly and ghastly, as in "The Fall of the House of Usher" and other stories; Poe reflected a dark sensibility distinctly at odds with the usually optimistic tone of American culture. Partly for this reason, Poe has perhaps been even more prized by Europeans than by Americans. His brilliant career was cut short when he was found drunk in a Baltimore gutter and shortly thereafter died.

Two other writers reflected the continuing Calvinist obsession with original sin and with the never-ending struggle between good and evil. In somber Salem, Massachusetts, Nathaniel Hawthorne (1804–1864) grew up in an atmosphere heavy with the memories of his Puritan forebears and the tragedy of his father's premature death on an ocean voyage. His masterpiece was *The Scarlet Letter* (1850), which described the Puritan practice of forcing an adulteress to wear a scarlet "A" on her clothing. In *The Marble Faun* (1860), Hawthorne dealt with a group of young American artists who witness a mysterious murder in Rome. The book explores the concepts of the omnipresence of evil and the dead hand of the past weighing upon the present.

Herman Melville (1819–1891), an orphaned and ill-educated New Yorker, went to sea as a youth and served eighteen adventuresome months on a whaler. "A whale ship was my Yale College and my Harvard," he wrote. Jumping ship in the South Seas, he lived among cannibals, from whom he **providentially** escaped uneaten. His fresh and charming tales of the South Seas were immediately popular, but his masterpiece, *Moby Dick* (1851), was not. The epic novel is a complex allegory of good and evil, told in terms of the conflict between a whaling captain, Ahab, and a giant white whale, Moby Dick. Captain Ahab, having lost a leg to the marine monster, lives only for revenge. His pursuit finally ends when Moby Dick rams and sinks his ship, leaving only one survivor. The whale's exact identity and Ahab's motives remain obscure. In the end the sea, like the terrifyingly impersonal and unknowable universe of Melville's imagination, simply rolls on.

Moby Dick was widely ignored at the time of its publication; people were accustomed to more straightforward and upbeat prose. A disheartened Melville continued to write unprofitably for some years, part of the time eking out a living as a customs inspector, and then died in relative obscurity and poverty. Ironically, his brooding masterpiece about the mysterious white whale had to wait until the more jaded twentieth century for readers and for proper recognition.

providential *Under the care and direction of God or other benevolent natural or supernatural forces.*

Portrayers of the Past

A distinguished group of American historians was emerging at the same time that other writers were winning distinction. Energetic George Bancroft (1800–1891), who as secretary of the navy helped found the Naval Academy at Annapolis in 1845, has deservedly received the title "Father of American History." He published a spirited, superpatriotic history of the United States to 1789 in six volumes (1834–1876), a work that grew out of his vast researches in dusty archives in Europe and America.

Two other historians are read with greater pleasure and profit today. William H. Prescott (1796–1859) published classic accounts of the conquest of Mexico (1843) and Peru (1847). Francis Parkman (1823–1893) penned a brilliant series of volumes beginning in 1851. In epic style he chronicled the struggle between France and Britain in colonial times for the mastery of North America.

Early American historians of prominence were almost without exception New Englanders, largely because the Boston area provided well-stocked libraries and a stimulating literary tradition. These writers numbered abolitionists among their relatives and friends and hence were disposed to view the South unsympathetically. The writing of American history suffered for generations from an antisouthern bias perpetuated by this early "made in New England" interpretation.

✪ Chapter Summary ✪

In early-nineteenth-century America, movements of moral and religious reform accompanied the democratization of politics and the creation of a national market economy. After a period of growing rationalism in religion, a new wave of revivals beginning about 1800 swept out of the West and effected great change not only in religious life but also in other areas of society. Existing religious groups were further fragmented, and new groups like the Mormons emerged. Women were especially prominent in these developments, becoming a major presence in the churches and discovering in reform movements an outlet for energies that were often stifled in masculinized political and economic life.

Among the first areas to benefit from the reform impulse was education. The public elementary school movement gained strength, while a few women made their way into still tradition-bound colleges. Women were also prominent in movements for improved treatment of the mentally ill, peace, temperance, and other causes. By the 1840s some women also began to agitate for their own rights, including suffrage. The movement for women's rights, closely linked to the antislavery crusade, gained adherents even while it met strong obstacles and vehement opposition.

While many reformers worked to improve society as a whole, others created utopian experiments to model their religious and social ideals. Some of these groups promoted radical sexual and economic doctrines, while others appealed to high-minded intellectuals and artists.

American culture was still quite weak in theoretical sciences and the fine arts, but a vigorous national literature blossomed after the War of 1812. In New England the literary renaissance was closely linked to the philosophy of transcendentalism promoted by Emerson and others. Many of the great American writers like Walt Whitman reflected the national spirit of utopian optimism, but a few dissenters like Hawthorne and Melville explored the darker side of life and of their own society.

✪ VARYING VIEWPOINTS ✪

Reform: Who? What? How? and Why?

Early chronicles of the antebellum period universally lauded the era's reformers, portraying them as idealistic, altruistic crusaders intent on improving American society. After World War II, however, some historians began to detect selfish and even conservative motives underlying the apparent benevolence of the reformers. They described reforms like temperance, asylums, prisons, and mandatory public education as efforts by anxious upper-class men and women to assert social control over the ferment of antebellum life.

The wave of reform activity in the 1960s prompted a reevaluation of the reputations of the antebellum reformers. These more recent interpretations found much to admire in the authentic religious commitments of reformers and especially in the participation of women, who sought various social improvements as an extension of their function as protectors of the home and family.

Abolitionism, for example, which had once been blamed by some historians for the Civil War, received new favorable treatment as the racial climate began to change during the 1960s. By the end of the twentieth century abolitionist men and women were revered as ideologically committed individuals dedicated not just to freeing the enslaved but to saving the soul of America.

Scholars animated by the modern feminist movement have also inspired a reconsideration of women's reform activity. Historians like Nancy Cott, Kathryn Sklar, and Mary Ryan began to look more closely at what Cott called "the bonds of womanhood" and uncover the links between women's domestic lives and their public benevolent behavior. When men behaved in immoral or illegal ways, women reformers claimed that they had the right and duty to leave the confines of their homes and actively purify society.

More recently, historians Nancy Hewitt and Lori Ginzburg have challenged the idea of a single female reform identity, pointing to class-based tensions within female ranks and detecting a shift from an early focus on moral uplift to a more class-based appeal for social control. Historians of the suffrage movement have emphasized another kind of exclusivity among women reformers—the boundaries of race. Ellen DuBois has shown that after a brief alliance with the abolitionist movement, many female suffrage reformers abandoned the cause of black liberation in order to achieve their own goal. Whatever historians may conclude about the liberating or leashing character of the early reform, it is clear that they now have to contend with the ways in which class, gender, and race divided reforms, making the plural—*reform movements*—the more accurate depiction of the impulse to "improve" that pervaded American society in the early nineteenth century.

PART THREE

Testing the New Nation

—◈—

1820–1877

The Civil War of 1861 to 1865 was the awesome trial by fire of American nationhood and of the American soul. All Americans knew, said Abraham Lincoln, that slavery "was somehow the cause of this war." The war tested, in Lincoln's ringing phrase at Gettysburg, whether any nation "dedicated to the proposition that all men are created equal . . . can long endure." How did this great and bloody conflict come about? And what were its results?

American slavery was by any measure a "peculiar institution." It was rooted in both racism and economic exploitation and depended for its survival on brutal repression. Yet the American slave population was the only enslaved population in history that grew by means of its own biological reproduction—a fact that suggests to many historians that conditions under slavery in the United States were somehow less punitive than in other slave societies. Indeed, a distinctive and durable African American culture managed to flourish under slavery, further suggesting that the slave regime provided some "space" for African American cultural development. But however benignly it might be painted, slavery remained a cancer in the heart of American democracy, a moral outrage that mocked the nation's claim to be a model of social and political enlightenment. As time went on, more and more voices called more and more stridently for its abolition.

The nation lived uneasily with slavery from the outset. Thomas Jefferson was only one among many in the founding generation who felt acutely the conflict between the high principle of equality and the ugly reality of slavery. The federal government in the early Republic took several steps to check the growth of slavery. It banned slavery in the Old Northwest in 1787, prohibited the further importation of slaves after 1808, and declared in the Missouri Compromise of 1820 that the vast western territories secured in the Louisiana Purchase were forever closed to slavery north of the state of Missouri. Antislavery sentiment even abounded in the South in the immediate post-Revolutionary years. But as time progressed, and especially after Eli Whitney's invention of the cotton gin in the 1790s, the southern planter class became increasingly dependent on slave labor to wring profits from the sprawling plantations that carpeted the South. As cotton cultivation spread westward, the South's stake in slavery grew deeper, and the abolitionist outcry grew louder.

The controversy over slavery significantly intensified following the war with Mexico in the 1840s. "Mexico will poison us," predicted the philosopher Ralph Waldo Emerson, and he proved distressingly prophetic. The lands acquired from Mexico—most of the present-day American Southwest, from Texas to California—

reopened the question of extending slavery into the western territories. The decade and a half following the Mexican War—from 1846 to 1861—witnessed a series of ultimately ineffective efforts to come to grips with that question, including the ill-starred Compromise of 1850, the conflict-breeding Kansas-Nebraska Act of 1854, and the Supreme Court's inflammatory decision in the *Dred Scott* case of 1857. Ultimately, the slavery question was settled by force of arms, in the Civil War itself.

The Civil War, as Lincoln observed, was assuredly about slavery. But as Lincoln also repeatedly insisted, the war was about the viability of the Union as well and about the strength of democracy itself. Could a democratic government, built on the principle of popular consent, rightfully deny some of its citizens the same right to independence that the American revolutionaries had exercised in seceding from the British Empire in 1776? Southern rebels, calling the conflict "The War for Southern Independence," asked that question forcefully, but ultimately it, too, was answered not in the law courts or in the legislative halls but on the battlefield.

The war unarguably established the supremacy of the Union, and it ended slavery as well. But as the victorious Union set about the task of "reconstruction" after the war's end in 1865, a combination of weak northern will and residual southern power frustrated the goal of making the emancipated blacks full-fledged American citizens. The Civil War in the end brought nothing but freedom—but over time, freedom proved a powerful tool indeed.

What if . . . ?

■ **What if some sort of compromise between the North and South had prevented the Civil War?**

What might such a compromise have looked like?

What might have been its consequences for the future of slavery, and for American nationhood?

Was *any* such compromise politically possible—or morally defensible?

The South and the Slavery Controversy

—◦⌣◦—

1793–1860

> IF YOU PUT A CHAIN AROUND THE NECK OF A SLAVE, THE
> OTHER END FASTENS ITSELF AROUND YOUR OWN.
>
> RALPH WALDO EMERSON, 1841

At the dawn of the Republic, slavery faced an uncertain future. Touched by Revolutionary idealism, some southern leaders, including Thomas Jefferson, were talking openly of freeing the slaves. Others predicted that the iron logic of economics would eventually expose slavery's unprofitability, speeding its demise.

But the introduction of Eli Whitney's cotton gin in 1793 scrambled all those predictions. Whitney's invention made possible the wide-scale cultivation of short-staple cotton. The white fiber rapidly became the dominant southern crop, eclipsing tobacco, rice, and sugar. The explosion of cotton cultivation created an insatiable demand for labor, chaining the slave to the gin and the planter to the slave. As the nineteenth century opened, the reinvigoration of southern slavery carried fateful implications for blacks and whites alike—and threatened the survival of the nation itself.

Focus Questions

1. How did a small, elite planter aristocracy come to dominate the "Cotton Kingdom" of the South, and what were the strengths and weaknesses of the region's plantation-controlled economic and social system?
2. Why did the majority of nonslaveholding whites in the South support slavery, and what was their relationship with both the slaveholding planters and the black slaves?
3. What were the central features of slavery, and what was life like for African Americans under slavery (as well as for the small number of free blacks)?
4. What were the effects of the "peculiar institution" on blacks, whites, and the nation as a whole?
5. How and why did abolitionism gradually gain strength, despite the strong initial hostility of most northerners, and why did southerners respond so fiercely to the movement's very existence?

Chronology

1793	Whitney's cotton gin transforms southern economy.
1800	Gabriel slave rebellion in Virginia.
1808	Congress outlaws slave trade.
1817	American Colonization Society formed.
1820	Missouri Compromise.
1822	Republic of Liberia established in Africa. Vesey slave rebellion in Charleston, South Carolina.
1831	Garrison begins publishing the *Liberator*. Nat Turner slave rebellion in Virginia.
1833	British abolish slavery in West Indies. American Anti-Slavery Society founded.
1834	Abolitionist students expelled from Lane Theological Seminary.
1835	U.S. Post Office orders destruction of abolitionist mail. "Broadcloth Mob" attacks Garrison.
1836	House of Representatives passes "Gag Resolution."
1837	Mob kills abolitionist Lovejoy in Alton, Illinois.
1839	Weld publishes *American Slavery As It Is*.
1845	Douglass publishes *Narrative of the Life of Frederick Douglass*.
1848	Free Soil party organized.

"Cotton Is King!"

As time passed, the Cotton Kingdom developed into a huge agricultural factory, pouring out avalanches of the fluffy fiber. Quick profits drew planters to the virgin bottomlands of the Gulf states. As long as the soil was still vigorous, the yield was bountiful, and the rewards were high. Caught up in an economic spiral, the planters bought more slaves and land to grow more cotton, so as to buy still more slaves and land.

To a large degree, the prosperity of both North and South rested on the bent backs of southern slaves. Cotton accounted for half the value of all American exports after 1840, and northern shippers reaped a large part of the profits from the cotton trade.

Cotton even held foreign nations in partial bondage. Britain's most important single manufacture in the 1850s was cotton cloth, from which about one-fifth of its population, directly or indirectly, drew their livelihood. About 75 percent of this precious supply of fiber came from the white-carpeted acres of the South.

Southern leaders were fully aware that Britain was tied to them by cotton threads, and this dependence gave them a heady sense of power. In their eyes "Cotton Was King," the gin was his throne, and the black slaves were his henchmen. If war should ever break out between North and South, northern warships would presumably cut off the outflow of cotton. Fiber-famished British factories would then close their gates, starving mobs would force the London government to break the blockade, and the South would triumph. Cotton was a powerful monarch indeed.

Online Study Center
Primary source
Southern Cotton Production
college.hmco.com/pic/kennedybrief7e

Slaves of the Slave System

Before the Civil War the South was in some respects not so much a democracy as an **oligarchy**—or a government by the few, in this case a planter aristocracy. In 1850 only 1,733 families owned more than 100 slaves each, and this select

oligarchy *Rule by a small elite.*

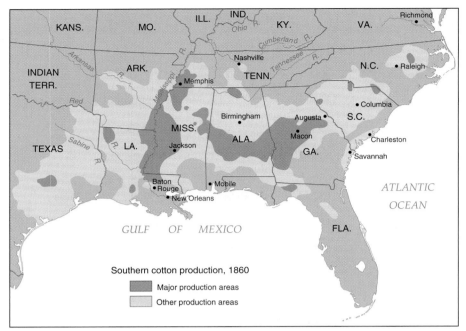

■ **Southern Cotton Production, 1860** The concentration of cotton-growing was in the "black belt" stretching from South Carolina to Louisiana.

Southern cotton production, 1860
- Major production areas
- Other production areas

Online Study Center

Interactive map
The Legal Status of Slavery, from the Revolution to the Civil War
college.hmco.com/pic/kennedybrief7e

commissions *Fee paid to an agent in a transaction, usually as a percentage of the sale.*

middlemen *In commerce, those who stand between the original producer of goods and the retailer or consumer.*

Basil Hall (1788–1844), an Englishman, visited part of the cotton belt on a river steamer (1827–1828). Noting the preoccupation with cotton, he wrote,

"All day and almost all night long, the captain, pilot, crew, and passengers were talking of nothing else; and sometimes our ears were so wearied with the sound of cotton! cotton! cotton! that we gladly hailed a fresh inundation of company in hopes of some change— but alas! . . . 'What's cotton at?' was the first eager inquiry. 'Ten cents [a pound],' 'Oh, that will never do!'"

group provided the cream of the political and social leadership of the section and nation. Here was the mint-julep South of the tall-columned and white-painted plantation mansion—the "big house," where dwelt the "cottonocracy."

The planter aristocrats, with their blooded horses and Chippendale chairs, enjoyed the lion's share of southern wealth. They could educate their children in the finest schools, often in the North or abroad. Their money provided the leisure for study, reflection, and statecraft, as was notably true of men like John C. Calhoun (a Yale graduate) and Jefferson Davis (a West Point graduate).

The plantation system also shaped the lives of southern women. The mistress of a great plantation commanded a sizable household staff of mostly female slaves. She gave daily orders to cooks, maids, seamstresses, laundresses, and personal servants. Some mistresses showed tender regard for their bondswomen, while others treated their slaves atrociously. But virtually no slaveholding women believed in abolition, and relatively few protested when the husbands and children of their slaves were sold.

Despite the occasional benevolent relations between owners and slaves, the moonlight-and-magnolia tradition concealed much that was worrisome, distasteful, and sordid. The domination of southern society by a favored aristocracy was fundamentally undemocratic, widening the gap between rich and poor and hampering public education. Plantation agriculture was wasteful, largely because King Cotton and his money-hungry subjects despoiled the good earth. Quick profits led to excessive cultivation or "land butchery," which in turn caused a heavy leakage of population to the West and Northwest.

The economic structure of the South became increasingly monopolistic. As the land wore thin, many small farmers sold their holdings to more prosperous neighbors. The big got bigger and the small got smaller. When the Civil War finally erupted, a large percentage of southern farms had passed from the hands of the families that had originally cleared them.

Another cancer in the bosom of the South was the financial instability of the plantation system. The temptation to overspeculate in land and slaves caused many planters, including Andrew Jackson in his later years, to plunge in beyond their depth. The slaves represented a heavy investment of capital, perhaps $1,200 each in the case of "prime field hands," and they might deliberately injure themselves or run away.

Dominance by King Cotton likewise led to a dangerous dependence on a one-crop economy, whose price level was at the mercy of world conditions. The whole system discouraged the healthy diversification of agriculture and particularly of manufacturing.

Southern planters resented watching the North grow fat at their expense. They were pained by the heavy outward flow of **commissions** and interest to northern **middlemen,** bankers, agents, and shippers. True souls of the South, especially by the 1850s, deplored the fact that when they were born they were wrapped in Yankee-made

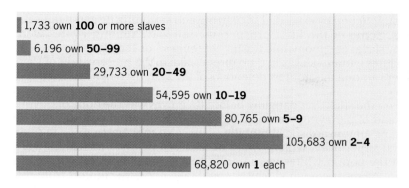

1,733 own **100** or more slaves	
6,196 own **50–99**	
29,733 own **20–49**	
54,595 own **10–19**	
80,765 own **5–9**	
105,683 own **2–4**	
68,820 own **1** each	

■ **Slaveowning Families, 1850** More than half of all slaveholding families owned fewer than four slaves. In contrast, 2 percent of slaveowners owned more than fifty slaves each. A tiny slaveholding elite held a majority of slave property in the South. The great majority of white southerners owned no slaves at all.

swaddling clothes, spent their lives in servitude to Yankee manufacturing, and when they died they were laid in coffins made with Yankee nails and buried in graves dug with Yankee shovels. The South furnished the corpse and the hole in the ground.

The Cotton Kingdom also repelled large-scale European immigration, which added so richly to the manpower and wealth of the North. In 1860 only 4.4 percent of the southern population was foreign-born, compared with 18.7 percent for the North. The diverting of non-British immigration to the North caused the white South to become the most Anglo-Saxon section of the nation.

The White Majority

Only a handful of southern whites lived in pillared mansions. Below those 1,733 families in 1850 who owned one hundred or more slaves were some 345,000 less wealthy slaveowning families, representing about 1,725,000 white persons. Over two-thirds of these families—255,268 in all—owned fewer than ten slaves each. All told, only about one-fourth of white southerners owned any slaves or belonged to a slaveowning family.

The smaller slaveowners did not own a majority of the slaves, but they made up a majority of the masters. With the striking exception that their households contained a slave or two, or perhaps an entire slave family, the small slaveowners' lifestyles resembled that of small farmers in the North more than it did that of the southern planter aristocracy. They lived in modest farmhouses and sweated beside their bondsmen in the cotton fields, laboring callous for callous just as hard as their slaves.

Beneath the slaveowners in the social pyramid was the great body of whites who owned no slaves at all. By 1860 their numbers had swelled to 6,120,825—three-quarters of all southern whites. Shouldered off the richest bottomlands by the mighty planters, they scratched a simple living from the thinner soils of the backcountry and the mountain valleys. These red-necked farmers participated in the market economy scarcely at all. As subsistence farmers, they raised corn and hogs, not cotton, and often lived

Online Study Center

**Primary source
Hermitage, Main House**
college.hmco.com/pic/kennedybrief7e

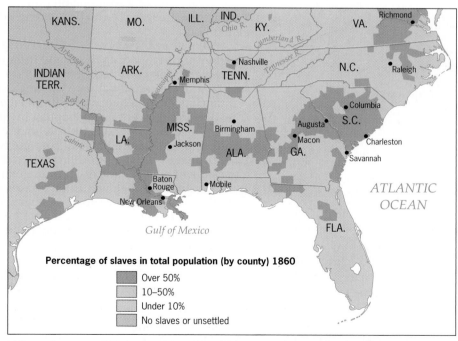

Percentage of slaves in total population (by county) 1860

- Over 50%
- 10–50%
- Under 10%
- No slaves or unsettled

■ **Distribution of Slaves, 1860** The philosopher Ralph Waldo Emerson, a New Englander, declared in 1856, "I do not see how a barbarous community and a civilized community can constitute a state. I think we must get rid of slavery or we must get rid of freedom."

isolated lives, punctuated by extended socializing and sermonizing at religious revival meetings. Some of the least prosperous non-slaveholding whites were scorned even by slaves as "poor white trash," "hillbillies," or "crackers."

All these whites without slaves had no direct stake in the preservation of slavery, yet they were among the stoutest defenders of the system. Why? The answer is not far to seek.

The carrot on the stick ever dangling before their eyes was the hope of buying a slave or two and of parlaying their holdings into riches—all in accord with the "American dream" of upward social mobility. They also took fierce pride in their presumed racial superiority, which would be watered down if the slaves were freed. Many of the poorer whites were hardly better off economically than the slaves, but even the most wretched whites could take perverse comfort from the knowledge that they outranked someone in status: the still more wretched African American slave. Thus did the logic of economics join with the illogic of **racism** in buttressing the slave system.

In a special category among white southerners were the mountain whites, more or less marooned in the valleys of the Appalachian range that stretched from western Virginia to northern Georgia and Alabama. As independent small farmers, hundreds of miles distant from the heart of the Cotton Kingdom and rarely if ever in sight of a slave, these mountain whites had little in common with the whites of the flatlands. Many of them, including future president Andrew Johnson of Tennessee, hated both the haughty planters and their gangs of blacks. When the Civil War came, the tough-fibered mountain men constituted a vitally important peninsula of Unionism jutting down into the secessionist southern sea. They ultimately played a significant role in crippling the Confederacy.

racism *Belief in the superiority of one race over another; or behavior reflecting such a belief.*

Free Blacks: Slaves Without Masters

Precarious in the extreme was the standing of the South's free blacks, who numbered about 250,000 by 1860. In the upper South, the free black population traced its origins to a wavelet of emancipation inspired by the idealism of Revolutionary days. In the deep South, many free blacks were mulattoes, usually the emancipated children of a white planter and his black mistress. Throughout the South were some free blacks who had purchased their freedom with earnings from labor after hours.

These free blacks in the South were a kind of "third race." They were prohibited from certain occupations and from testifying in court, and were always vulnerable to being hijacked back into slavery by unscrupulous slave traders. As free men and women, they were walking examples of what might be achieved by emancipation, and hence were detested by defenders of the slave system.

Free blacks were also unpopular in the North, where about another 250,000 of them lived. Several states forbade their entrance, most denied them the right to vote, and some barred blacks from public schools. Much of the agitation in the North against the spread of slavery into the new territories in the 1840s and 1850s grew out of race prejudice, not humanitarianism.

Antiblack feeling was in fact frequently stronger in the North than in the South. It was sometimes observed that white southerners, who were often suckled and reared by black nurses, liked black people as individuals but despised the race. The white northerner, on the other hand, often professed to like the race but disliked individual blacks.

Plantation Slavery

In society's basement in the South of 1860 were nearly 4 million black human chattels. Their numbers had quadrupled since the dawn of the century, as the booming cotton economy created a seemingly unquenchable demand for slave labor. Congress ended the legal slave trade in 1808, but the price of "black ivory" was so high in the years before the Civil War that thousands of slaves were smuggled illegally into the South. Yet the huge bulk of the increase in the slave population came not from imports but instead from natural reproduction—a fact that distinguished slavery in America from slavery in other New World societies and implied much about the tenor of the regime and the conditions of family life under slavery.

Above all, the planters regarded the slaves as investments, into which they had sunk nearly $2 billion by 1860. Slaves were the primary form of wealth in the South, and as such they were cared for as any asset is cared for by a prudent capitalist. Masters sometimes hired cheap Irish wage laborers to perform dangerous work like tunnel blasting or swamp draining, rather than risk the life of a valuable slave, worth $1,800 by 1860 (a price that had quintupled since 1800).

Slavery was profitable for the great planters, though it hobbled the economic development of the region as a whole. The profits from the cotton boom sucked ever more slaves from the upper to the lower South. Thousands of blacks from the soil-exhausted states of the Old South, especially Virginia, were "sold down the river" to the cotton frontier of the lower Mississippi Valley. By 1860 the Deep South states of South Carolina, Georgia, Florida, Mississippi, Alabama, and Louisiana each had a majority or near-majority of blacks and accounted for about half of all slaves in the South.

The forced "breeding" of slaves was not openly encouraged. But white masters all too frequently forced their attention on female slaves, fathering a sizable mulatto population, most of which remained enchained.

Slave auctions were brutal sights. The open selling of human flesh under the hammer was among the most revolting aspects of slavery. On the auction block, families were separated with distressing frequency, usually for economic reasons such as **bankruptcy** or the division of "property" among heirs. The sundering of families in this fashion was perhaps slavery's greatest psychological horror. Abolitionists decried the practice, and Harriet Beecher Stowe seized on the emotional power of this theme by putting it at the heart of the plot of *Uncle Tom's Cabin.*

■ **A Market in People** Held captive in a net, a slave sits on the Congo shore, waiting to be sold and shipped.

bankruptcy *Legally, the condition of being declared unable to meet legitimate financial obligations or debts, requiring special supervision by the courts.*

overseer *Someone who governs or directs the work of another.*

Life Under the Lash

White southerners often romanticized about the happy life of their singing, dancing, banjo-strumming "darkies." But how did the slaves actually live? There is no simple answer to this question. Conditions varied greatly from region to region, from large plantation to small farm, and from master to master. Everywhere, of course, slavery meant hard work, ignorance, and oppression. The slaves—both men and women—usually toiled from dawn to dusk in the fields, under the watchful eyes and ready whip-hand of a white **overseer** or black "driver." They had no civil or political rights, and even minimal protection from murder or unusually cruel punishment was difficult to enforce. Slaves were forbidden to testify in court, and their marriages were not legally recognized.

Floggings were common, for the whip was the substitute for the wage-incentive system and the most visible symbol of the planter's mastery. Strong-willed slaves were sometimes sent to "breakers," whose technique consisted mostly in lavish laying on of the lash. As an abolitionist song of the 1850s lamented,

> To-night the bond man, Lord
> Is bleeding in his chains;
> And loud the falling lash is heard
> On Carolina's plains!

But savage beatings made sullen laborers, and lash marks hurt resale values. There are, to be sure, sadistic monsters in any population, and the planter class

Online Study Center

Primary source
Slave Perspective on Family Ties,
college.hmco.com/pic/kennedybrief7e

In 1852 Maria Perkins, a woman enslaved in Virginia, wrote plaintively to her husband about the disruption that the commercial traffic in slaves was visiting upon their family:

"I write you a letter to let you know of my distress my master has sold albert to a trader on Monday court day and myself and other child is for sale also and I want you to let hear from you very soon before next cort if you can I dont know when I dont want you to wait till Christmas I want you to tell Dr Hamelton and your master if either will buy me they can attend to it know and then I can go after-wards I dont want a trader to get me they asked me if I had got any person to buy me and I told them no they took me to the court houste too they never put me up a man buy the name of brady bought albert and is gone I dont know whare they say he lives in Scottesville my things is in several places some is in staunton and if I should be sold I dont know what will become of them I dont expect to meet with the luck to get that way till I am quite heart sick nothing more I am and ever will be your kind wife Maria Perkins."

Online Study Center

Primary source
Slaves Dancing the Juba
college.hmco.com/pic/kennedybrief7e

contained its share. But the typical planter had too much of his own prosperity riding on the backs of his slaves to beat them bloody on a regular basis.

By 1860 most slaves were concentrated in the "black belt" of the deep South that stretched from South Carolina and Georgia into the new southwest states of Alabama, Mississippi, and Louisiana. A majority of blacks lived on larger plantations that harbored communities of twenty or more slaves. In some counties of the deep South, especially along the lower Mississippi River, blacks accounted for more than 75 percent of the population. There the family life of slaves tended to be relatively stable, and a distinctive African American culture developed. Forced separations of spouses, parents, and children were evidently more common on smaller plantations and in the upper South. Slave marriage vows sometimes proclaimed, "Until death or *distance* do you part."

With impressive resilience, blacks managed to sustain family life in slavery, and most slaves were raised in stable two-parent households. Continuity of family identity across generations was evidenced in the widespread practice of naming children for grandparents or adopting the surname not of a current master but of a forebear's master. African Americans also displayed their African cultural roots when they avoided marriage between first cousins, in contrast to the frequent intermarriage of close relatives among the ingrown planter aristocracy.

African roots were also visible in the slaves' religious practices. Though heavily Christianized by itinerant evangelists of the Second Great Awakening, blacks in slavery molded their own distinctive religious forms from a mixture of Christian and African elements. They emphasized those aspects of the Christian heritage that seemed most pertinent to their own situation—especially the captivity of the Israelites in Egypt. One of the most haunting spirituals implored,

Tell old Pharaoh,
"Let my people go."

And another lamented,

Nobody knows de trouble I've seen
Nobody knows but Jesus.

African practices also persisted in the "responsorial" style of preaching, in which the congregation frequently punctuates the minister's remarks with assents and amens—an adaptation of the give-and-take between caller and dancers in the African ringshout dance.

The Burdens of Bondage

Slavery was intolerably degrading to the victims. They were deprived of the dignity and sense of responsibility that come from independence and the right to make choices. Slaves were denied an education, because reading brought ideas, and ideas brought discontent. Many states passed laws forbidding their instruction, and perhaps nine-tenths of adult slaves at the beginning of the Civil War were illiterate. For all slaves—indeed for virtually all blacks, slave or free—the "American dream" of bettering one's lot through study and hard work was a cruel and empty mockery.

Not surprisingly, victims of the "peculiar institution" devised countless ways to throw sand in its gears. Slaves often slowed the pace of their labor to the barest minimum that would spare them the lash, thus fostering the myth of black "laziness" in the minds of whites. They filched food from the "big house" and pilfered other goods that had been produced by their labor. They sometimes **sabotaged** expensive equipment and occasionally even poisoned their masters' food.

The slaves also universally pined for freedom. Many took to their heels as runaways, frequently in search of a separated family member. Others rebelled, though never successfully. In 1800 an armed insurrection led by a slave named Gabriel in Richmond, Virginia, was foiled by informers, and in 1822 Denmark Vesey, a free black, led another ill-fated rebellion in Charleston. In both cases the rebels were betrayed by informers and hanged. In 1831 Nat Turner, a visionary black preacher, led an uprising that slaughtered about sixty Virginians, mostly women and children. Reprisals were swift and bloody.

The dark taint of slavery also left its mark on the whites. It fostered the brutality of the whip, the bloodhound, and the branding iron. White southerners increasingly lived in a state of imagined siege, surrounded by potentially rebellious blacks inflamed by abolitionist propaganda from the North. Their fears bolstered an intoxicating theory of biological racial superiority and turned the South into a reactionary backwater in an era of progress—one of the last bastions of slavery in the Western world. The defenders of slavery were forced to degrade themselves, along with their victims. As Booker T. Washington, a distinguished black leader and former slave, later observed, whites could not hold blacks in a ditch without getting down there with them.

■ **Slave Nurse and Young White Master** Southern whites would not allow slaves to own property or exercise civil rights, but, paradoxically, they often entrusted them with the raising of their own precious children. Many a slave "mammy" served as a surrogate mother for the offspring of the planter class.

Early Abolitionism

The inhumanity of the "peculiar institution" gradually caused antislavery societies to sprout forth. Abolitionist sentiment first stirred at the time of the Revolution, especially among Quakers. Because of the widespread loathing of blacks, some of the earliest abolitionist efforts focused on transporting blacks back to Africa. The American Colonization Society was founded for this purpose in 1817, and in 1822 the Republic of Liberia was established for former slaves on the West African coast. Most native-born African Americans had no wish to be transplanted into a strange civilization, and only some fifteen thousand were actually transported there over the next four decades. Yet the colonization idea appealed to some antislaveryites, including Abraham Lincoln, until the time of the Civil War.

In the 1830s the abolitionist movement took on new energy and momentum, mounting to the proportions of a crusade. American abolitionists took heart in 1833 when their British counterparts unchained the slaves in the West Indies. Most important, the religious spirit of the Second Great Awakening inflamed the hearts of many abolitionists against the sin of slavery.

Prominent among them was lanky, tousle-haired Theodore Dwight Weld, who had been evangelized by Charles Grandison Finney in the 1820s. In 1832 Weld enrolled at Lane Theological Seminary in Cincinnati, whose president was the formidable Lyman Beecher, father of novelist Harriet Beecher Stowe, reformer Catharine Beecher, and preacher-abolitionist Henry Ward Beecher. Expelled along with several other students in 1834 for organizing an eighteen-day debate on

sabotage *Intentional destruction or damage of goods, machines, or productive processes.*

slavery, Weld and his fellow "Lane Rebels"—full of the energy and idealism of youth—fanned out across the Old Northwest preaching the antislavery gospel. Weld also assembled a potent propaganda tract, *American Slavery As It Is* (1839), which greatly influenced Harriet Beecher Stowe's *Uncle Tom's Cabin*.

Radical Abolitionism

fratricidal *Literally, concerning the killing of brothers; the term is often applied to the killing of relatives or countrymen in feuds or civil wars. (The killing of sisters is **sororicide**; of fathers **patricide**; and of mothers **matricide**.)*

■ Sojourner Truth Also known simply as "Isabella," she held audiences spellbound with her deep, resonant voice and the religious passion with which she condemned the sin of slavery. This photo was taken about 1870.

On New Year's Day, 1831, a shattering abolitionist blast came from the bugle of William Lloyd Garrison, a mild-looking reformer of twenty-six. A spiritual child of the Second Great Awakening, Garrison published in Boston the first issue of his militantly antislavery newspaper the *Liberator*. With this mighty paper broadside, Garrison triggered a thirty-year war of words and in a sense fired one of the opening barrages of the Civil War.

Stern and uncompromising, Garrison proclaimed in strident tones that under no circumstances would he tolerate the poisonous weed of slavery:

> I will be as harsh as truth and as uncompromising
> as justice. . . . I am in earnest—I
> will not equivocate—I will not excuse—I
> will not retreat a single inch—and I WILL
> BE HEARD!

Other dedicated abolitionists rallied to Garrison's standard, and in 1833 they founded the American Anti-Slavery Society. Prominent among them was eloquent Wendell Phillips, a Boston patrician known as "abolition's golden trumpet."

Black abolitionists distinguished themselves as living monuments to the cause of African American freedom. Their ranks included David Walker, whose incendiary *Appeal to the Colored Citizens of the World* advocated a bloody end to white supremacy. Also noteworthy were Sojourner Truth, a freed black woman who fought tirelessly for black emancipation and women's rights, and Martin Delany, one of the few black leaders to take seriously the notion of black recolonization in Africa.

The greatest of the black abolitionists was Frederick Douglass. Escaping from bondage in 1838 at the age of twenty-one, Douglass was "discovered" by the abolitionists in 1841 when he gave a stunning impromptu speech at an antislavery meeting in Massachusetts. Thereafter he lectured widely for the cause, despite frequent beatings and threats against his life. In 1845 he published his classic autobiography, *Narrative of the Life of Frederick Douglass*. It depicted his remarkable origins as the son of a black slave woman and a white father, his struggle to learn to read and write, and his eventual escape to the North.

Douglass was as flexibly practical as Garrison was stubbornly principled. Garrison often appeared to be more interested in his own righteousness than in the substance of the slavery evil itself. He repeatedly demanded that the "virtuous" North secede from the "wicked" South. Renouncing politics, on the Fourth of July, 1854, he publicly burned a copy of the Constitution as "a covenant with death and an agreement with hell." Douglass, on the other hand, along with other abolitionists, increasingly looked to politics to end the blight of slavery. These political abolitionists backed the antislavery Liberty party in 1840, the Free Soil party in 1848, and eventually the Republican party in the 1850s. In the end, most abolitionists, including even the pacifist Garrison himself, followed out the logic of their beliefs and supported a frightfully costly **fratricidal** war as the price of emancipation.

High-minded and courageous, the abolitionists were men and women of goodwill and various colors who faced the cruel choice that people in many ages have had thrust upon them:

EXAMINING THE EVIDENCE

Bellegrove Plantation, Donaldsville, Louisiana, Built 1857 The sugar-growing Bellegrove Plantation—on the banks of the Mississippi River ninety-five miles north of New Orleans—was laid out on a grander scale than many southern plantations. In this rendering from an advertisement for Bellegrove's sale in 1867, the planter John Orr's home was identified as a "mansion," and quarters for his field hands proved extensive: twenty double cabins built for slaves (now for "Negroes") and a dormitory, described in the ad but not pictured here, housing 150 laborers. Because of the unhealthy work involved in cultivating sugar cane, such as constant digging of drainage canals to keep the cane from rotting in standing water, many planters hired immigrant (usually Irish) labor to keep their valuable slaves out of physical danger. The presence of a hospital between the slave cabins and the mansion indicates the very real threat to health. The layout of Bellegrove reflects the organization of production as well as the social relations on a sugar plantation. The storehouse where preserved sugar awaited shipping stood closest to the Mississippi River, the principal transportation route, whereas the sugar house, the most important building on the plantation, with its mill, boilers, and cooking vats for converting syrup into sugar, dominated the canefields. Although the "big house" and slave quarters stood in close proximity, hedges surrounding the planter's home shut out views of both sugar production and labor. Within the slave quarters, the overseer's larger house signified his superior status, while the arrangement of cabins ensured his supervision of domestic as well as work life.

1. What else does the physical layout of the plantation reveal about settlement patterns, sugar cultivation, and social relationships along the Mississippi?

2. Besides living quarters and facilities for the production and shipping of sugar, what other major supporting activities had to be carried out on a large plantation such as Bellegrove—such that separate buildings were dedicated to those functions?

3. In rough terms, what proportion of the total land of Bellegrove Plantation was given over to growing sugar cane, and what proportion to dwellings, sugar production facilities, and woodlands?

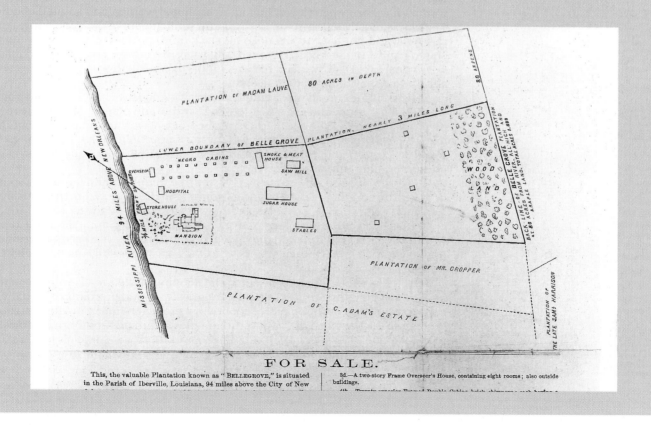

After hearing Frederick Douglass speak in Bristol, England, in 1846, Mary A. Estlin wrote to an American abolitionist,

"[T]here is but one opinion of him. Wherever he goes he arouses sympathy in your cause and love for himself. . . . Our expectations were highly roused by his narrative, his printed speeches, and the eulogisms of the friends with whom he has been staying: but he far exceeds the picture we had formed both in outward graces, intellectual power and culture, and eloquence."*

barbarism (barbarian) *The condition of being crude, uneducated, or uncivilized.*

when is evil so enormous that it must be denounced, even at the risk of precipitating bloodshed and butchery?

The South Lashes Back

Antislavery sentiment was not unknown in the South up to the 1820s, but after 1830 the voice of white southern abolitionism was silenced. The Virginia legislature actually debated and eventually defeated various emancipation proposals in 1831–1832. Nat Turner's rebellion in 1831 sent a wave of hysteria sweeping over the snowy cotton fields, and planters in growing numbers slept with pistols by their pillows.

The nullification crisis of 1832 further implanted haunting fears in white southern minds, conjuring up nightmares of black incendiaries and abolitionist devils. Jailings, whippings, and lynchings now greeted rational efforts to discuss the slavery problem in the South.

Proslavery whites responded to the abolitionist groundswell by launching a massive defense of slavery as a positive good. In doing so they forgot their own section's previous doubts about the morality of the "peculiar institution." Slavery, they claimed, was supported by the authority of the Bible and the wisdom of Aristotle. It was good for the Africans, who were lifted from the "**barbarism** of the jungle" and clothed with the blessings of Christian civilization.

Slavemasters strongly encouraged religion in the slave quarters, emphasizing those teachings that encouraged obedience. White apologists also contended that master-slave relationships really resembled those of a family. Southern whites were quick to contrast the "happy" lot of their "servants" with that of the overworked northern wage slaves, including exploited women and stunted children. The blacks mostly toiled in the fresh air and sunlight, not in dark and stuffy factories. They did not have to worry about slack times or unemployment, as did the "hired hands" of the North. Provided with a jail-like form of Social Security, slaves were cared for in sickness and old age, unlike the northern workers, who were set adrift when they outlived their usefulness.

These curious proslavery arguments only widened the chasm between a backward-looking South and a forward-looking North—and indeed much of the rest of the Western world. The southerners reacted defensively to the pressure of their own fears and the merciless nagging of the northern abolitionists. Increasingly the white South turned in upon itself and grew hotly intolerant of any embarrassing questions about the status of slavery.

Regrettably, also, the controversy over free people endangered free speech in the entire country. Piles of petitions poured into Congress from the antislavery reformers, and in 1836 sensitive southerners drove through the House the so-called Gag Resolution. It required all such antislavery appeals to be tabled without debate. This attack on the right of petition aroused the aged ex-president, Representative John Quincy Adams, who waged a successful eight-year fight for its repeal.

Southern whites likewise resented the flooding of their mails with incendiary abolitionist literature. In 1835 a mob in Charleston, South Carolina, looted the local post office and burned a pile of abolitionist propaganda. Capitulating to southern pressures, the Washington government in 1835 ordered southern postmasters to destroy abolitionist material and called on southern state officials to arrest federal postmasters who did not comply. Such was "freedom of the press" as guaranteed by the Constitution.

---

*From Clare Taylor, ed., British and American Abolitionists, An Episode in Transatlantic Understanding (Edinburgh University Press, 1974), p. 282.

The Abolitionist Impact in the North

Abolitionists—especially the extreme Garrisonians—were for a long time unpopular in many parts of the North. Northerners had been brought up to revere the Constitution and to regard the clauses on slavery as a lasting bargain. The ideal of Union, hammered home by the thundering eloquence of Daniel Webster and others, had taken deep root; and Garrison's wild talk of secession grated harshly on northern ears.

The North also had a heavy economic stake in Dixieland. By the late 1850s, southern planters owed northern bankers and other creditors about $300 million, and much of this immense sum would be lost—as, in fact, it later was—should the Union dissolve. New England textile mills were fed with cotton raised by the slaves, and a disrupted labor system might cut off this vital supply and bring unemployment. The Union during these critical years was partly bound together with cotton threads, tied by lords of the loom in collaboration with the so-called lords of the lash. It was not surprising that strong hostility developed in the North against the boat-rocking tactics of the radical antislaveryites.

Repeated tongue-lashings by the extreme abolitionists provoked many mob outbursts in the North, some led by respectable gentlemen. A gang of young toughs broke into abolitionist Lewis Tappan's New York house in 1834 and demolished its interior, while a crowd in the street cheered. In 1835 Garrison, with a rope tied around him, was dragged through the streets of Boston by the so-called Broadcloth Mob but escaped almost miraculously. Reverend Elijah P. Lovejoy, of Alton, Illinois, had his printing press destroyed four times. In 1837 he was killed by a mob and became "the martyr abolitionist." So unpopular were the antislavery zealots that ambitious politicians, like Abraham Lincoln, usually avoided the taint of Garrisonian abolition like the plague.

Yet by the 1850s the abolitionist outcry had made a deep dent in the northern mind. Many citizens had come to see the South as the land of the unfree and the home of a hateful institution. Few northerners were prepared to abolish slavery outright, but a growing number, including Lincoln, opposed extending it to the western territories. People of this stamp, commonly called "free-soilers," swelled their ranks as the Civil War approached.

Online Study Center

Interactive map
Escaping from Slavery
college.hmco.com/pic/kennedybrief7e

Online Study Center

Primary source
Border Ruffians Invading Kansas
college.hmco.com/pic/kennedybrief7e

✪ Chapter Summary ✪

Whitney's cotton gin made cotton production enormously profitable, and created an ever-increasing demand for slave labor. The South's dependence on cotton production tied it economically to the plantation system and racially to white supremacy. The cultural gentility and political domination of the relatively small plantation aristocracy concealed slavery's great social and economic costs for whites as well as blacks.

Most slaves were held by a few large planters. But most slaveowners had few slaves, and most southern whites had no slaves at all. Nevertheless, except for a few mountain whites, the majority of southern whites strongly supported slavery and racial supremacy because they cherished the hope of becoming slaveowners themselves, and because white racial identity gave them a sense of superiority to the blacks.

The treatment of the economically valuable slaves varied considerably. Within the bounds of the cruel system, slaves yearned for freedom and struggled to maintain their humanity, including family life.

The older black colonization movement was largely replaced in the 1830s by a radical Garrisonian abolitionism demanding an immediate end to slavery. Abolitionism and the Nat Turner rebellion caused a strong backlash in the South. Earlier southern criticism of slavery disappeared, and proslavery whites increasingly defended slavery as a positive good that actually benefited the slaves. In defending slavery, the South turned its back not only on many of the liberal political and social ideas gaining strength in the North, but on most of progressive Western civilization.

Most northerners were hostile to radical abolitionism as a threat to the cherished Union, and respected the Constitution's evident protection of slavery where it existed. But many also gradually came to see the South as a land of oppression, and any attempt to extend slavery as a threat to free society.

VARYING VIEWPOINTS

What Was the True Nature of Slavery?

By the early twentieth century, the predictable accounts of slavery written by partisans of the North or South had receded in favor of a romantic vision of the Old South. A scholarly version of this vision was Ulrich Bonnell Phillips's landmark study, *American Negro Slavery* (1918), which portrayed slavery as a dying, unprofitable economic institution where benevolent masters treated their slaves with kindly paternalism and racially inferior blacks submissively accepted the system that enslaved them.

Later in the twentieth century historians challenged many of these views. Economic historians have decisively refuted Phillips's claim that slavery was unprofitable by showing that it was a viable, profitable, expanding system. Beginning in the late 1950s, historians came increasingly to emphasize the harshness of the slave system. One study, Stanley Elkins's *Slavery* (1959), went so far as to compare the "peculiar institution" to the Nazi concentration camps of World War II.

More recently, scholars such as Eugene Genovese have contended that slavery did indeed embrace a strange form of paternalism, one reflecting not slaveholders' benevolence but their need to control and coax work out of their reluctant and often recalcitrant "investments." Furthermore, within this paternalist system, black slaves were able to make reciprocal demands of their white owners and to protect a "cultural space" of their own in which family and religion particularly could flourish.

The revised conceptions of the master-slave relationship also spilled over into the debate about slave personality. Kenneth Stampp rejected Stanley Elkins's view that slaves were "infantilized" like concentration camp inmates, and stressed the frequency and variety of slave resistance. In another perspective, Lawrence Levine imaginatively argued in *Black Culture and Black Consciousness* (1977) that the Sambo character was an act, an image that slaves used to confound their masters without incurring punishment. More recently, historians have attempted to avoid the polarity of repression versus autonomy. The challenge before historians today is to capture the vibrancy of slave culture and its legacy for African American society after emancipation, without diminishing the brutality of life under the southern slave regime.

A new sensitivity to gender, spurred by the growing field of women's history, has also expanded the horizons of slavery studies. Historians such as Elizabeth Fox-Genovese, Jacqueline Jones, and Catherine Clinton have focused on the ways in which slavery differed for men and women, both slaves and slaveholders. Enslaved black women, for example, had the unique task of negotiating an identity out of their dual responsibilities as plantation laborer, even sometimes caretaker of white women and children, and anchor of the black family. By tracing the interconnectedness of race and gender in the American South, these historians have also shown how slavery shaped conceptions of masculinity and femininity within southern society, further distinguishing its culture from that of the North.

Scholarship on slavery continues to grow. The newest work by Philip D. Morgan and Ira Berlin has drawn attention to how both the institution of slavery and the experience of the enslaved changed over time. Slavery adapted to particular geographic and environmental factors, and also changed from one generation to the next. As southern slaveholders responded to new social and economic conditions, they gradually altered the legal status of slaves, outlawing manumission in many places and rendering freedom for the enslaved increasingly difficult to attain.

17

Manifest Destiny and Its Legacy

1841–1848

OUR MANIFEST DESTINY [IS] TO OVERSPREAD THE CONTINENT
ALLOTTED BY PROVIDENCE FOR THE FREE DEVELOPMENT OF
OUR YEARLY MULTIPLYING MILLIONS.

JOHN L. O'SULLIVAN, 1845*

Territorial expansion dominated American diplomacy and politics in the 1840s. Settlers swarming into the still-disputed Oregon country aggravated relations with Britain, which had staked its own claims in the Pacific Northwest. The clamor to annex Texas to the Union provoked bitter tension with Mexico, which continued to regard Texas as a Mexican province in revolt. And when Americans began casting covetous eyes on Mexico's northernmost province, the great prize of California, open warfare erupted between the United States and its southern neighbor. Victory over Mexico added vast new domains to the United States, but it also raised thorny questions about the status of slavery in the newly acquired territories—questions that would be answered in blood in the Civil War of the 1860s.

Focus Questions

1. What was "Manifest Destiny," and why did it inspire a burst of American expansionism in the 1840s?
2. Why did American expansionist efforts provoke increasing tensions with Britain over Oregon and other issues, as well as increasing domestic conflict over the possible annexation of Texas?
3. How did the issues of Oregon and Texas become central to the election of 1844, and why was Polk's victory taken to be a mandate for Manifest Destiny?
4. How did the issues of California and the Texas boundary lead to war with Mexico, and how did the American victory lead to the territorial acquisition of the entire Southwest?
5. What were the consequences of the Mexican War? In particular, why did it reignite the slavery question?

---

* This is the earliest known use of the term *Manifest Destiny*.

The Accession of "Tyler Too"

A horde of office-hungry hard-ciderites descended on Washington in 1841, bewildering newly elected President William Henry Harrison. The real leaders of the Whig party regarded "Old Tippecano" as little more than an impressive figurehead. Daniel Webster, as secretary of state, and Henry Clay, the uncrowned king of the Whigs and their ablest spokesman in the Senate, would grasp the helm.

Unluckily for Clay and Webster, their schemes soon hit a fatal snag. Before the new term had fairly started, Harrison contracted pneumonia and died after only four weeks in the White House—by far the shortest administration in American history.

The "Tyler too" part of the Whig ticket, hitherto only a rhyme, now claimed the spotlight. With blue eyes, classical features, and a high forehead, John Tyler was a Virginia gentleman of the old school—gracious and kindly, yet stubbornly attached to principle. He had earlier resigned from the Senate, quite unnecessarily, rather than accept distasteful instructions from the Virginia legislature. Still a lone wolf, he had forsaken the Jacksonian Democratic fold for that of the Whigs, largely because he could not stomach the dictatorial tactics of Jackson.

Tyler's enemies accused him of being a Democrat in Whig clothing. But the Whig party, like the Democratic party, was something of a catchall, and the accidental president simply belonged to the minority wing, which embraced a number of Jeffersonian states' righters. Tyler had in fact been put on the ticket partly to attract the vote of this fringe group, many of whom were influential southern gentry.

It was true, however, that on virtually every major issue the obstinate Virginian was at odds with the majority of his Whig party, which was pro-bank, pro–protective tariff, and pro–internal improvements. "Tyler too" rhymed with "Tippecanoe," but there the harmony ended. As events turned out, President Harrison, the Whig, served for only 4 weeks, whereas Tyler, the ex-Democrat who was still largely a Democrat at heart, served for 204 weeks.

John Tyler: A President Without a Party

platform *The campaign document stating a party's or candidate's position on the issues, and upon which they "stand" for election.*

caucus *An unofficial organization or consultation of like-minded people to plan a political course or advance their cause, often within some larger body.*

After their hard-won, hard-cider victory, the Whigs brought their not-so-secret **platform** out of Clay's waistcoat pocket. To the surprise of no one, it outlined a strongly nationalistic program.

Financial reform came first. The Whig Congress hastened to pass a law ending the independent treasury system, and President Tyler, disarmingly agreeable, signed it. Clay next drove through Congress a bill to establish a new Bank of the United States.

Tyler's hostility to a centralized bank was notorious, and Clay—the "Great Compromiser"—would have done well to conciliate him. But the Kentuckian, robbed repeatedly of the presidency by lesser men, was in an imperious mood and riding for a fall. When the bank bill reached the presidential desk, Tyler flatly vetoed it on both practical and constitutional grounds. A drunken mob gathered late at night near the White House and shouted insultingly, "Huzza for Clay!" "A Bank! A Bank!" "Down with the Veto!"

Whig extremists, seething with indignation, condemned Tyler as "His Accidency" and as an "Executive Ass." To the delight of Democrats, the stiff-necked Virginian was formally expelled from his party by a **caucus** of Whig congressmen, and a serious attempt to impeach him was broached in the House of Representatives. His entire cabinet resigned in a body, except Secretary of State Webster, who was in the midst of delicate negotiations with Britain.

The proposed Whig tariff also felt the prick of the president's well-inked pen. Tyler vetoed a tariff bill that included a scheme for distributing to the states revenues from the sale of public land. But he reluctantly signed the revised Clay-sponsored Tariff of 1842, which pushed rates back down to the moderately protective level of 1832, about 32 percent.

Chronology

1841	Harrison dies after four weeks in office. Tyler assumes presidency.
1842	Aroostook War over Maine boundary. Webster-Ashburton Treaty.
1844	Polk defeats Clay in "Manifest Destiny" election.
1845	United States annexes Texas.
1846	United States settles Oregon dispute with Britain.
1846	United States and Mexico clash over Texas boundary.

1846	Kearny takes Santa Fe. Frémont conquers California. Wilmot Proviso passes House of Representatives.
1846– 1848	Mexican War.
1847	Battle of Buena Vista. Scott takes Mexico City.
1848	Treaty of Guadalupe Hidalgo.

Tensions With Britain

Hatred of Britain during the nineteenth century periodically came to a head and had to be lanced by treaty settlement or by war. The poison festered ominously in the late 1830s, especially because of private American involvement in an unsuccessful Canadian rebellion in 1837. When an American steamer, the *Caroline*, attempted to deliver supplies to Canadian insurgents, British troops sank the ship in the Niagara River, killing one American.

Anglo-American controversy then exploded in the early 1840s over the disputed Maine boundary. Hoping to bypass the icebound St. Lawrence River, the British planned to build a road westward from the seaport of Halifax to Quebec. But the proposed route ran through territory claimed by Maine under the treaty of 1783. Tough-knuckled lumberjacks from both Maine and Canada commenced fighting in the disputed **no-man's-land** of the tall-timbered Aroostook River valley. When both sides summoned the local militias, the small-scale lumberjack clash, dubbed the "Aroostook War," threatened to widen into a full-dress shooting war.

no-man's-land *A territory to which neither of two disputing parties has clear claim and where they may meet as combatants.*

As the crisis deepened in 1842, the London Foreign Office sent to Washington a conciliatory diplomat, Lord Ashburton, who had married a wealthy American woman. He speedily established cordial relations with Secretary of State Webster. After protracted and nerve-wracking negotiations in the heat of a Washington summer, the two statesmen finally agreed to compromise on the Maine boundary. On the basis of a rough, split-the-difference arrangement, the Americans retained some 7,000 square miles of the 12,000 square miles of wilderness in dispute. The British got less land but won the desired Halifax-Quebec route.

An overlooked bonus sneaked by in small print of the same treaty: the British, in adjusting the U.S.-Canadian boundary farther west, surrendered 6,500 square miles. The area was later found to contain the priceless Mesabi iron range of Minnesota.

Old Glory Adds the Lone Star of Texas

During the uncertain eight years since 1836, Texas had led a precarious existence. Mexico, refusing to recognize Texas's independence, regarded the Lone Star Republic as a province in revolt, to be reconquered in the future. Mexican

protectorate *The relation of a strong nation to a weak one under its control and protection.*

colossus *Anything of extraordinary size and power; therefore, in international affairs, a major or hegemonic great power.*

mandate *In politics, the belief that an official has been issued a clear charge by the electorate to pursue some particular policy goal.*

resolution *In government, a formal statement of policy or judgment by a legislature, but requiring no legal statute.*

intrigue *A plot or scheme formed by secret, underhanded means.*

Online Study Center

Interactive map
Texas Revolution
college.hmco.com/pic/kennedybrief7e

officials loudly threatened war if the American eagle should ever gather the fledgling republic under its protective wings.

Confronted with such perils, Texas was driven to open negotiations with Britain and France in the hope of securing the defensive shield of a **protectorate**. In 1839 and 1840 the Texans concluded treaties with France, Holland, and Belgium.

Britain was intensely interested in an independent Texas. Such a republic would check the southward surge of the American **colossus**, whose bulging biceps posed a constant threat to nearby British possessions in the New World. Clashes between a puppet Texas and the Yankees would create a smoke-screen diversion behind which foreign powers could move into the Americas and challenge the insolent Monroe Doctrine. French schemers likewise hoped that an independent Texas would result in the fragmentation and militarization of America.

British abolitionists were also busily intriguing in Texas, hoping that gaining freedom for blacks there would inflame the nearby slaves of the South. In addition, British merchants regarded Texas as a potentially important free-trade area—an offset to the tariff-walled United States. British textile manufacturers believed that an independent Texas, with its vast cotton-producing plains, would relieve British looms of their dependence on American fiber—a supply that might be cut off by embargo or war.

Partly because of the fears aroused by these British and French schemers, Texas became a leading issue in the presidential campaign of 1844. The proexpansion Democrats under James K. Polk finally triumphed over the Whigs under Henry Clay, the hardy perennial candidate. Lame duck President Tyler thereupon promptly interpreted the narrow Democratic victory as a "**mandate**" to acquire Texas.

Eager to crown his troubled administration with this splendid prize, Tyler quickly shepherded Texas into the fold. Many "conscience Whigs" feared that Texas in the Union would be red meat to nourish the lusty "slave power." Aware of their opposition, Tyler despaired of securing the needed two-thirds vote for a treaty in the Senate. He therefore arranged for annexation by a joint **resolution**. This solution required only a simple majority in both houses of Congress. After a spirited debate, the resolution passed early in 1845, and Texas was formally invited to become the twenty-eighth star on the American flag.

Mexico angrily charged that the Americans had despoiled it of Texas. Yet realistic observers could see that the Mexicans would not be able to reconquer their lost province. By 1845 the Lone Star Republic had become a danger spot, inviting foreign **intrigue** that menaced the American people. The continued existence of Texas as an independent nation threatened to involve the United States in a series of ruinous wars, both in America and in Europe.

What other power would have spurned the imperial domain of Texas? The bride was so near, so rich, so fair, so willing. Whatever the peculiar circumstances of the Texas Revolution, the United States can hardly be accused of unseemly haste in achieving annexation. Nine long years were surely a decent wait between the beginning of the courtship and the consummation of the marriage.

Oregon Fever Populates Oregon

The Oregon Country was an enormous wilderness. It sprawled magnificently west of the Rockies to the Pacific Ocean, and north of California to the line of 54°40′— the present southern tip of the Alaska panhandle. All or substantial parts of this immense area were claimed at one time or another by four nations: Spain, Russia, Britain, and the United States.

Two claimants dropped out of the scramble. Spain, though the first to raise its banner in Oregon, bartered away its claims to the United States in the Florida Treaty of 1819. Russia retreated to the line of 54°40′ by the treaties of 1824 and 1825 with America and Britain. These two remaining rivals now had the field to themselves.

British claims to Oregon were strong—at least to that portion north of the Columbia River. They were based squarely on prior discovery and exploration, on treaty rights, and on actual occupation. The most important colonizing agency was the far-flung Hudson's Bay Company, which was trading profitably with the Indians of the Pacific Northwest for furs.

Americans, for their part, could also point to exploration and occupation. Captain Robert Gray in 1792 had stumbled upon the majestic Columbia River, which he named after his ship; and the famed Lewis and Clark expedition of 1804–1806 had ranged overland through the Oregon Country to the Pacific. This shaky American toehold was ultimately strengthened by the presence of missionaries and other settlers, a sprinkling of whom reached the grassy Willamette River valley, south of the Columbia, in the 1830s. These men and women of God, in saving the souls of the Indians, were also instrumental in saving the soil of Oregon for the United States. They stimulated interest in a faraway domain that Americans had earlier assumed would not be settled for centuries.

Scattered American and British pioneers in Oregon continued to live peacefully side by side. At the time of negotiating the Treaty of 1818 (see pp. 172–173), the United States had sought to divide the vast domain at the forty-ninth **parallel**. But the British, who regarded the Columbia River as the St. Lawrence of the West, were unwilling to yield this vital artery. A scheme for peaceful "joint occupation" was thereupon adopted, pending future settlement.

The handful of Americans in the Willamette Valley was suddenly multiplied in the early 1840s, when "Oregon fever" seized hundreds of restless pioneers. In increasing numbers, their creaking covered wagons jolted over the two-thousand-mile Oregon Trail as the human rivulet widened into a stream. By 1846 about five thousand Americans, some of them tough ruffians, had settled south of the Columbia River.

The British, in the face of this rising torrent of humanity, could muster only seven hundred or so subjects north of the Columbia. Losing out lopsidedly in the population race, they were beginning to see the wisdom of arriving at a peaceful settlement before being engulfed by their neighbors.

A curious fact is that only a relatively small segment of the Oregon Country was in actual controversy by 1845. The area in dispute consisted of the rough quadrangle between the Columbia River on the south and east, the forty-ninth parallel on the north, and the Pacific Ocean on the west—most of the present state of Washington (see the map on p. 253). Britain had repeatedly offered the line of the Columbia; America had repeatedly offered the forty-ninth parallel. The whole fateful issue was now tossed into the presidential election of 1844, where it was largely overshadowed by the question of annexing Texas.

A Mandate (?) for Manifest Destiny

The two major parties nominated their presidential standard-bearers in May 1844. Ambitious but often-frustrated Henry Clay, easily the most popular man in the country, was enthusiastically chosen by the Whigs at Baltimore. The Democrats, meeting there later, nominated James K. Polk of Tennessee, America's first "**dark horse**," or "surprise," presidential candidate.

Polk may have been a dark horse, but he was hardly an unknown or decrepit nag. Speaker of the House of Representatives for four years and governor of Tennessee for two terms, Polk was a determined, industrious, ruthless, and intelligent public servant. Whigs attempted to jeer him into oblivion with the taunt, "Who is James K. Polk?" They soon found out.

The campaign of 1844 was in part an expression of the mighty emotional upsurge known as "Manifest Destiny."

> *In winning Oregon, the Americans had great faith in their procreative powers. Boasted one congressman in 1846,*
>
> "Our people are spreading out with the aid of the American multiplication table. Go to the West and see a young man with his mate of eighteen; after the lapse of thirty years, visit him again, and instead of two, you will find twenty-two. That is what I call the American multiplication table."

parallel *In geography, the imaginary lines parallel to the earth's equator, marking latitude. (There are 360 degrees of latitude on the globe.)*

dark horse *In politics, a candidate with little apparent support who unexpectedly wins a nomination or election.*

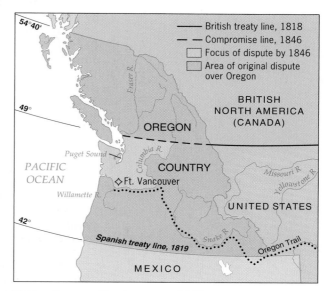

■ The Oregon Controversy, 1846

■ **Westward the Course of Empire Takes Its Way** This romantic tribute to the spirit of Manifest Destiny was commissioned by Congress in 1860 and may still be seen in the Capitol.

Countless citizens in the 1840s and 1850s, feeling a sense of mission, believed that Almighty God had "manifestly" destined the American people for a hemispheric career. They would irresistibly spread their uplifting and ennobling democratic institutions over at least the entire North American continent, and possibly over South America as well. Land greed and ideals—"empire" and "liberty"—were thus conveniently conjoined.

Expansionist Democrats were strongly swayed by the intoxicating spell of Manifest Destiny. They came out flat-footedly in their platform for the "Re-annexation of Texas"* and the "Reoccupation of Oregon," all the way to 54°40′. The Whigs countered with such slogans as "Polk, Slavery, and Texas, or Clay, Union, and Liberty."

On the crucial issue of Texas, the acrobatic Clay tried to ride two horses at once. The "Great Compromiser" compromised away the presidency when he wrote letters saying that while he personally favored annexing slave-holding Texas (an appeal to the South), he also favored postponement (an appeal to the North). By straddling the issue this way, Clay alienated ardent antislaveryites.

In the stretch drive, "Dark Horse" Polk nipped Henry Clay at the wire, 170 to 105 votes in the Electoral College and 1,338,464 to 1,300,097 in the popular column. Clay would have won if he had not lost New York by a scant 5,000 votes. There the tiny antislavery Liberty party absorbed nearly 16,000 votes, many of which would otherwise have gone to the unlucky Kentuckian. Ironically, the anti-Texas Liberty party, by helping to elect the pro-Texas Polk, hastened the annexation of Texas. The victorious Democrats proclaimed that they had received a mandate from the voters to take Texas, and three days before leaving office President Tyler signed the joint resolution of annexation.

Polk the Purposeful

"Young Hickory" Polk, unlike "Old Hickory" Jackson, was not an impressive figure. Lean, white-haired, gray-eyed, and stern-faced, he took life seriously and drove

---

* The United States had given up its claims to Texas in the Florida Purchase Treaty with Spain in 1819 (see p. 173). The slogan "fifty-four forty or fight" was evidently not coined until two years later, in 1846.

himself mercilessly into a premature grave. His burdens were increased by an unwillingness to delegate authority. Methodical and hard-working but not brilliant, he was shrewd, narrow-minded, and persistent. "What he went for he fetched," wrote a contemporary. Purposeful in the highest degree, he developed a positive four-point program and with remarkable success achieved it completely in less than four years.

Polk's first goal was a lower tariff. Robert J. Walker, his secretary of the Treasury, lobbied through Congress a tariff bill that reduced the average rates of the Tariff of 1842 from about 32 percent to 25 percent. The Walker Tariff of 1846 proved to be an excellent revenue producer.

A second objective of Polk was restoration of the independent treasury, unceremoniously dropped by the Whigs in 1841. Pro-bank Whigs in Congress raised a storm of opposition, but victory at last rewarded the president's efforts in 1846.

The third and fourth points on Polk's "must list" were the settlement of the Oregon dispute and the acquisition of California.

"Reoccupation" of the "whole" of Oregon had been promised northern Democrats in the campaign of 1844. But southern Democrats, once they had annexed Texas, rapidly cooled off. Polk, himself a southerner, had no intention of insisting on the 54°40′ pledge of his own platform. He again proposed the compromise line of 49°, but the British minister in Washington brusquely spurned this olive branch.

Fortunately for peace, British anti-expansionists ("Little Englanders") were now persuaded that the Columbia River after all was not the St. Lawrence of the West. Early in 1846 the British came around and themselves proposed the line of 49°. The senators speedily accepted the offer and approved the subsequent treaty, despite a few diehard shouts of "Fifty-four forty forever!"

Satisfaction with the Oregon settlement among Americans was not unanimous. The northwestern states, hotbeds of Manifest Destiny and "fifty-four fortyism," joined the antislavery forces in condemning what they regarded as a base betrayal by the South. Why *all* of Texas and not *all* of Oregon? Because, retorted the expansionist Senator Thomas Hart Benton of Missouri, "Great Britain is powerful and Mexico is weak."

So Polk, despite all the campaign bluster, got neither "fifty-four forty" nor a fight. But he did get something that in the long run was better: a reasonable compromise without a rifle being raised.

Misunderstandings with Mexico

Faraway California was Polk's final objective. He and other disciples of Manifest Destiny had long coveted its verdant valleys and especially the spacious bay of San Francisco. This splendid harbor was widely regarded as America's future gateway to the Pacific Ocean.

The population of California in 1845 was curiously mixed. It consisted of perhaps thirteen thousand sun-blessed Spanish Mexicans and as many as seventy-five thousand dispirited Indians. There were fewer than a thousand "foreigners," mostly Americans, some of whom had "left their consciences" behind them as they rounded Cape Horn. Given time, these transplanted Yankees might bring California into the Union by "playing the Texas game."

Polk was eager to buy California from Mexico, but relations with Mexico City were dangerously embittered. One point of friction was some $3 million in claims against Mexico for damages to American citizens and their property. The most serious bone of contention was Texas. After threatening war if the United States acquired the Lone Star Republic, the Mexican government completely severed diplomatic relations following annexation.

Deadlock with Mexico over Texas was further tightened by a question of boundaries. During the long era of Spanish occupation of Mexico, the southwestern boundary of Texas had been the Nueces River. But the expansive Texans, on rather far-fetched grounds, were claiming the more southerly Rio Grande instead. Polk, for his part, felt a strong obligation to defend Texas in its claim, once it was annexed.

deadlock *To completely block or stop action as a consequence of the mutual pressure of equal and opposed forces.*

The Mexicans were far less concerned about this boundary quibble than the United States. In their eyes all of Texas was still theirs, although temporarily in revolt, and a dispute over the two rivers seemed pointless. Yet Polk was careful to keep American troops out of virtually all of the explosive no-man's-land between the Nueces and the Rio Grande, as long as there was any real prospect of peaceful adjustment.

The golden prize of California continued to cause Polk much anxiety. Disquieting rumors (now known to have been ill-founded) were circulating that Britain was about to buy or seize California—a grab that Americans could not tolerate under the Monroe Doctrine. In a last desperate throw of the dice, Polk dispatched John Slidell to Mexico City as minister late in 1845. The new envoy, among other alternatives, was instructed to offer a maximum of $25 million for California and territory to the east. But the proud Mexican people would not even permit Slidell to present his "insulting" proposition.

American Blood on American (?) Soil

A frustrated Polk was now prepared to force a showdown. On January 13, 1846, he ordered four thousand men, under General Zachary Taylor, to march from the Nueces River to the Rio Grande, provocatively near Mexican forces. Polk's presidential diary reveals that he expected at any moment to hear of a clash. When none occurred after an anxious wait, he informed his cabinet on May 9, 1846, that he proposed to ask Congress to declare war on the basis of (1) unpaid claims and (2) Slidell's rejection. These, at best, were rather flimsy pretexts. Two cabinet members spoke up and said that they would feel better satisfied if Mexican troops should fire first.

That very evening news of bloodshed arrived. On April 25, 1846, Mexican troops had crossed the Rio Grande and attacked General Taylor's command, with a loss of sixteen Americans killed or wounded.

Polk, further aroused, sent a vigorous war message to Congress. He declared that despite "all our efforts" to avoid a clash, hostilities had been forced upon the country by the shedding of "American blood upon the American soil." A patriotic Congress overwhelmingly voted for war, and enthusiastic volunteers cried, "Ho for the Halls of the Montezumas!" and "Mexico or Death!" Inflamed by the war fever, even antislavery Whig bastions joined with the rest of the nation, though they later condemned "Jimmy Polk's war." As James Russell Lowell of Massachusetts lamented,

> *Massachusetts, God forgive her,*
> *She's akneelin' with the rest.*

In his message to Congress, Polk was making history—not writing it. If he had been a historian, he would have explained that American blood had been shed on soil that the Mexicans had good reason to regard as their own. A gangling, rough-featured Whig congressman from Illinois, one Abraham Lincoln, introduced certain resolutions that requested information as to the precise "spot" on American soil where American blood had been shed. He pushed his "spot" resolutions with such persistence that he came to be known as the "spotty Lincoln" who could die of "spotted fever." More extreme antislavery agitators branded the president a liar—"Polk the Mendacious."

Did Polk provoke war? California was an imperative point in his program, and Mexico would not sell it at any price. The only way to get it was to use force or wait for an internal American revolt. But in 1846, patience had ceased to be a virtue as far as Polk was concerned. Bent on grasping California by fair means or foul, he pushed the quarrel to a bloody showdown.

Both sides, in fact, were spoiling for a fight. Feisty Americans, especially southwestern expansionists, were

> On June 1, 1860, less than a year before he became president, Abraham Lincoln (1809–1865) wrote,
>
> "The act of sending an armed force among the Mexicans was unnecessary, inasmuch as Mexico was in no way molesting or menacing the United States or the people thereof; and . . . it was unconstitutional, because the power of levying war is vested in Congress, and not in the President."

eager to teach the Mexicans a lesson. The Mexicans, in turn, were burning to humiliate the "Bullies of the North." Possessing a considerable standing army, they boasted of invading the United States, freeing the black slaves, and lassoing whole regiments of Americans. They were hoping that the quarrel with Britain over Oregon would blossom into a full-dress war, as it came near doing, and further pin down the hated *yanquis*. Fired by indignation, Mexicans and Americans each believed the other was the aggressor.

The Mastering of Mexico

Polk wanted California—not war. But when war came, he hoped to fight it on a limited scale and then pull out when he had captured the prize. The conflict would not be so simple. The dethroned and devious Mexican dictator Santa Anna, then exiled in Cuba, returned to Mexico and proceeded to rally his countrymen to a desperate defense of their soil.

American operations in the Southwest and in California were completely successful. In 1846 General Stephen W. Kearny led a detachment of seventeen hundred troops over the famous Santa Fe Trail from Fort Leavenworth to Santa Fe. This sun-baked outpost, with its drowsy plazas, was easily captured. But before Kearny could reach California, the fertile province was won. When war broke out, Captain John C. Frémont, the dashing explorer, just "happened" to be there with several dozen well-armed men. In helping to overthrow Mexican rule in 1846, he collaborated with American naval officers and with the local Americans, who had hoisted the banner of the short-lived California Bear Flag Republic.

General Zachary Taylor meanwhile had been spearheading the main thrust. Known as "Old Rough and Ready" because of his iron constitution and unsoldierly appearance—he sometimes wore a Mexican straw hat—he fought his way across the Rio Grande into Mexico. After several gratifying victories, he reached Buena Vista. There, on February 22–23, 1847, his weakened force of five thousand men was attacked by some twenty thousand march-weary troops under Santa Anna. The Mexicans were finally repulsed with extreme difficulty, and overnight Zachary Taylor became the "Hero of Buena Vista."

Sound American strategy now called for a crushing blow at the enemy's vitals—Mexico City. Though a good leader, General Taylor could not decisively win the war in the semideserts of northern Mexico. The command of the main expedition, which pushed inland from the coastal city of Vera Cruz early in 1847, was entrusted to General Winfield Scott. A handsome giant of a man, Scott had emerged as a hero from the War of 1812 and later earned the nickname "Old Fuss and Feathers" because of his resplendent uniforms and strict discipline. Scott succeeded in battling a more numerous enemy through mountainous terrain up to Mexico City by September 1847 in one of the most brilliant campaigns in American military annals. He proved to be the most distinguished general produced by his country between 1783 and 1861.

Fighting Mexico for Peace

Polk was anxious to end the shooting as soon as he could secure his territorial goals. Accordingly, he sent along with Scott's invading army a State Department official, Nicholas P. Trist. Grasping a fleeting opportunity to negotiate, Trist signed the Treaty of Guadalupe Hidalgo on February 2, 1848, and forwarded it to Washington.

The terms of the treaty were breathtaking. They confirmed the American title to Texas and yielded the enormous area stretching northward to Oregon and west to the ocean, embracing coveted California. This total expanse, including Texas, was about one-half of Mexico. The United States agreed to pay $15 million for the land and to assume the claims of its citizens against Mexico in the amount of $3,250,000 (see "Makers of America: The Californios," pp. 260–261).

Polk quickly submitted the treaty to the Senate. Speed was imperative. The antislavery Whigs in Congress—dubbed "Mexican Whigs" or "conscience Whigs"—

Online Study Center

Primary source
Texas Revolution, The
college.hmco.com/pic/kennedybrief7e

Online Study Center

Primary source
General Scott's Triumph
college.hmco.com/pic/kennedybrief7e

Online Study Center

Interactive map
The Mexican War
college.hmco.com/pic/kennedybrief7e

Online Study Center

Primary source
Southwest and the Mexican War
college.hmco.com/pic/kennedybrief7e

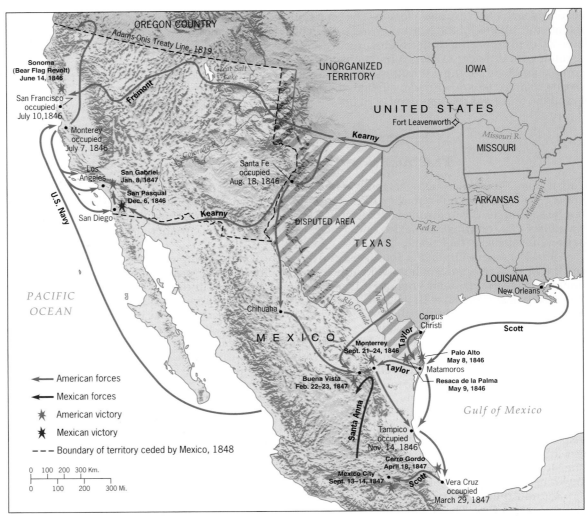

■ **Major Campaigns of the Mexican War**

were denouncing this "damnable war" with increasing heat. Having secured control of the House in 1847, they were even threatening to vote down supplies for the armies in the field. If they had done so, Scott probably would have been forced to retreat, and the fruits of victory might have been tossed away.

Another peril impended. A swelling group of expansionists, intoxicated by Manifest Destiny, was clamoring for the United States to take all of Mexico. If America had seized it, the nation would have been saddled with a vexatious problem. Farseeing southerners like Calhoun, alarmed by the mounting anger of antislavery agitators, realized that the South would do well not to be too greedy. The treaty was finally approved by the Senate, 38 to 14. Oddly enough, it was condemned both by those opponents who wanted all of Mexico and by opponents who wanted none of it.

Profit and Loss in Mexico

As wars go, the Mexican War was a small one. It cost some thirteen thousand American lives, most of them taken by disease. But the fruits of the fighting were enormous.

America's total expanse, already vast, was increased by about one-third (counting Texas)—an addition even greater than that of the Louisiana Purchase. A sharp stimulus was given to the spirit of Manifest Destiny for, as the proverb has it, the appetite comes with eating.

The Mexican War proved to be the blood-spattered schoolroom of the Civil War. The campaigns provided priceless field experience for most of the officers destined to become leading generals in the forthcoming conflict, including Captain Robert E. Lee and Lieutenant Ulysses S. Grant. The Military Academy at West Point, founded in 1802, fully justified its existence through the well-trained officers. Useful also was the navy, which did valuable work in throwing a crippling blockade around Mexican ports. The Marine Corps, in existence since 1798, won new laurels and to this day sings, in its stirring hymn, about the Halls of Montezuma.

The army waged war without defeat and without a major blunder, despite formidable obstacles and a half-dozen or so achingly long marches. Chagrined British critics, as well as other foreign skeptics, reluctantly revised upward their estimate of Yankee military prowess. Opposing armies, moreover, emerged with increased respect for each other. The Mexicans, though poorly led, fought heroically. At Chapultepec, near Mexico City, the teenage lads of the military academy there (*los niños*) perished to a man.

> *Early in 1848 the* New York Evening Post *demanded,*
>
> "Now we ask, whether any man can coolly contemplate the idea of recalling our troops from the [Mexican] territory we at present occupy . . . and . . . resign this beautiful country to the custody of the ignorant cowards and profligate ruffians who have ruled it for the last twenty-five years? Why, humanity cries out against it. Civilization and Christianity protest against this reflux of the tide of barbarism and anarchy."
> *Such was one phase of Manifest Destiny.*

■ **War News from Mexico, by Richard Caton Woodville** The newfangled telegraph kept the nation closely informed of events in far-off Mexico.

The Californios

When the United States acquired the Mexican Cession in 1848, it took in a vast land that stretched from the arid desert Southwest to the fruited valleys and port cities of California. There, at the conclusion of the Mexican War, dwelled some thirteen thousand Californios—descendants of the Spanish and Mexican conquerors who had once ruled California.

The Spanish had first arrived in California in 1769, extending their New World empire and outracing Russian

Online Study Center

Primary source
Richard Henry Dana Looks at California
college.hmco.com/pic/kennedybrief7e

traders to bountiful San Francisco Bay. Father Junipero Serra, an enterprising Franciscan friar, soon established twenty-one missions along the coast. Indians in the iron grip of the missions were encouraged to adopt Christianity and often forced to toil endlessly as farmers and herders, in the process suffering disease and degradation. These frequently maltreated mission Indians occupied the lowest rungs on the ladder of Spanish colonial society.

Upon the loftiest rungs perched the Californios. Pioneers from the Mexican heartland of New Spain, they had trailed Serra to California, claiming land and civil offices in their new home. Yet even the proud Californios had deferred to the all-powerful Franciscan missionaries until Mexico threw off the Spanish colonial yoke in 1826 and transferred power from the missions to secular (that is, governmental) authorities.

■ California Indians Dancing at the Mission in San José, by Sykes, 1806

This "secularization" program attacked and eroded the immense power of the Franciscans, who had confidently commanded their rich fiefdoms and resisted even minor efforts to reform their harsh treatment of the Indians. But during the 1830s much of their land and many of their assets were confiscated by the Californios. Vast *ranchos* (ranches) formed, and from those citadels the Californios ruled until the Mexican War.

The Californios' glory faded in the wake of the American victory. Overwhelmed by the inrush of Anglo gold-diggers after the discovery at Sutter's Fort in 1848, the Californios saw their recently acquired lands and political power slip through their fingers. When the Civil War broke out in 1861, so harshly did the word *Yankee* ring in their ears that many Californios supported the South.

By 1870 the Californios' brief ascendancy had utterly vanished—a short and sad tale of riches to rags in the face of the Anglo onslaught. Half a century later, beginning in 1910, hundreds of thousands of young Mexicans would flock into California and the Southwest. They would enter a region liberally endowed with Spanish architecture and artifacts, bearing the names of Spanish missions and Californio ranchos. But they would find it a land dominated by Anglos, a place far different from that which their Californio ancestors had settled so hopefully in earlier days.

Long-memoried Mexicans have never forgotten that their northern enemy tore away about half of their country. The argument that they were lucky not to lose all of it, and that they had been paid something for their land, has scarcely lessened their bitterness. The war also marked an ugly turning point in the relations between the United States and Latin America as a whole. Hitherto, Uncle Sam had been regarded with some friendliness. Henceforth, he was increasingly feared as the "Colossus of the North." Suspicious neighbors to the south condemned him as a greedy and untrustworthy bully, who might next despoil them of their soil.

Most ominous of all, the war rearoused the snarling dog of the slavery issue, and the beast did not stop yelping until drowned in the blood of the Civil War. Abolitionists assailed the Mexican conflict as one provoked by the southern "slavocracy" for its own evil purposes.

Quarreling over slavery extension also erupted on the floors of Congress. In 1846, shortly after the shooting started, Polk requested an appropriation of $2 million with which to buy a peace. Representative David Wilmot of Pennsylvania, fearful of the southern "slavocracy," introduced a fateful amendment. It stipulated that slavery should never exist in any of the territory wrested from Mexico.

The disruptive Wilmot amendment twice passed the House but not the Senate. Southern members, unwilling to be robbed of prospective slave states, fought the restriction tooth and nail. Antislavery men, in Congress and out, battled no less bitterly for the exclusion of slaves. The "Wilmot Proviso" never became law, but it soon came to symbolize the burning issue of slavery in the territories.

In a broad sense, the opening shots of the Mexican War were the opening shots of the Civil War. President Polk left the nation the splendid physical heritage of California and the Southwest but also the ugly moral heritage of an embittered slavery dispute. "Mexico will poison us," said the philosopher Ralph Waldo Emerson. Mexicans could later take some satisfaction in knowing that the territory wrenched from them had proved to be a venomous apple of discord that could well be called Santa Anna's revenge.

⭐ Chapter Summary ⭐

As Tyler assumed the presidency after Harrison's early death, the United States became engaged in a series of sharp disputes with Britain. A conflict over the Maine boundary was resolved, but British involvement in Texas revived the movement to annex the Lone Star Republic to the United States.

The Texas and Oregon questions became embroiled in the hotly contested 1844 campaign, as the Democrats nominated and elected the militantly expansionist Polk. After Texas was added to the Union, Polk pursued an aggressive policy of expansion. He successfully acquired part of the disputed Oregon country from Britain. Unable to obtain Mexican California peaceably, Polk led the nation into war with an equally belligerent Mexico in 1846.

American forces quickly conquered California and New Mexico. Winfield Scott's and Zachary Taylor's invasion of Mexico was also successful, and the United States obtained large new territories in the peace treaty.

Besides adding California, New Mexico, and Utah to American territory, the Mexican War trained a new generation of military leaders and aroused long-term Latin American resentment of the United States. But its most important consequence was to force the slavery controversy to the center of national politics, as first indicated by the Wilmot Proviso proposing to ban slavery from the newly acquired territories.

18

Renewing the Sectional Struggle

∾

1848–1854

SECESSION! PEACEABLE SECESSION! SIR, YOUR EYES AND
MINE ARE NEVER DESTINED TO SEE THAT MIRACLE.

DANIEL WEBSTER, 1850

Chapter Outline

⭐ "Popular Sovereignty"

⭐ The Compromise of 1850

⭐ The Inflammatory Fugitive
Slave Law

⭐ President Pierce and
Expansion, 1853–1857

⭐ Senator Douglas and the
Kansas-Nebraska Act,
1854

The year 1848, highlighted by a rash of revolutions in Europe, was filled with unrest in America. The Treaty of Guadalupe Hidalgo had officially ended the war with Mexico but initiated a new and perilous round of political warfare in the United States. The vanquished Mexicans had been forced to relinquish an enormous tract of real estate, including Texas, California, and all the area between. The acquisition of this huge domain raised anew the burning issue of extending slavery into the territories. Northern antislaveryites had rallied behind the Wilmot Proviso, which flatly prohibited slavery in any territory acquired in the Mexican War. Southern senators had blocked the passage of the proviso, but the issue did not die. Ominously, debate over slavery in the area of the Mexican Cession threatened to disrupt the ranks of both Whigs and Democrats and to split national politics along North-South sectional lines.

Focus Questions

1. What were the major terms of the Compromise of 1850, and how did they try to defuse the furious controversies over the territories acquired from Mexico in 1848?
2. How successful was the Compromise of 1850?
3. Why did the Whig party disintegrate and then disappear?
4. How and why did the Democratic Pierce administration, as well as private American adventurers, pursue overseas schemes designed to expand slavery?
5. What was the content and purpose of Douglas's Kansas-Nebraska Act, and why did it stir the sectional controversy to new heights?

The Popular Sovereignty Panacea

Each of the two great political parties was a vital bond of national unity, for each enjoyed powerful support in both North and South. If they should be replaced by two purely sectional groupings, the Union would be in peril. To politicians, the wisest strategy seemed to be to sit on the lid of the slavery issue and ignore the boiling beneath. Even so, the cover bobbed up and down ominously in response

⚙ *Online Study Center*

**Primary source
Mexican News**
college.hmco.com/pic/kennedybrief7e

---

self-determination *In politics, the right of a people to assert its own national identity or form of government without outside influence.*

to the agitation of zealous northern abolitionists and impassioned southern "fire-eaters."

President Polk, broken in health, did not seek a second term. The Democratic National Convention in Baltimore turned to aging General Lewis Cass, an experienced but pompous senator whose enemies dubbed him "General Gass." The Democratic platform, in line with the lid-sitting strategy, was silent on the burning issue of slavery in the territories. But Cass himself was well-known as the reputed father of "popular sovereignty," the doctrine that the people of a territory, under the principles of the Constitution, should themselves determine the status of slavery.

Popular sovereignty had a persuasive appeal. The public liked it because it accorded with the democratic tradition of **self-determination**. Politicians liked it because it seemed a comfortable compromise between the abolitionist bid for a ban on slavery in the territories and southern demands that Congress protect slavery in the territories. Popular sovereignty tossed the slavery problem into the laps of the people in the various territories. Advocates of the principle thus hoped to dissolve the most stubborn national issue of the day into a series of local issues. Yet popular sovereignty had one fatal defect: it might serve to spread the blight of slavery.

Meeting in Philadelphia, the Whigs turned away from the controversial Henry Clay and nominated the frank General Zachary Taylor, the Hero of Buena Vista, who had never held civil office or even voted for president. As usual, the Whigs pussyfooted in their platform. Eager to win at any cost, they dodged all troublesome issues and extolled the homespun virtues of their candidate. Taylor had not committed himself on the issue of slavery extension, but as a wealthy Louisiana sugar planter he owned scores of slaves.

Aroused by the conspiracy of silence in the Democratic and Whig platforms, ardent antislavery northerners organized the Free Soil party. They came out foursquare for the Wilmot Proviso and against slavery in the territories. The new party nominated former President Martin Van Buren as its candidate, and went into the campaign shouting "Free soil, free speech, free labor, and free men."

These freedoms provided the bedrock of its principles, but the new party assembled a strange assortment of new fellows in the same political bed. It contained a large element of "conscience Whigs," heavily influenced by the abolitionist crusade, who condemned slavery on moral grounds. But it also harbored many northerners who condemned slavery not so much for enslaving blacks as for destroying the chances of free white workers to rise up from wage-earning dependence to the esteemed status of self-employment. Free-Soilers argued that only with free soil in the West could a traditional American commitment to upward mobility continue to flourish. To avoid ruinous competition with unpaid labor, they believed that slavery—and African Americans—should be kept out of the West. As the first widely inclusive party organized around the issue of slavery and confined to a single section, the Free Soil party foreshadowed the emergence of the Republican party six years later.

With the slavery issue officially shoved under the rug by the two major parties, politicians on both sides opened fire on personalities. The amateurish Taylor had to be carefully watched, lest his indiscreet pen puncture the reputation won by his sword. Taylor's wartime popularity pulled him through. He harvested 1,360,967 popular and 163 electoral votes, compared with Cass's 1,222,342 popular and 127 electoral votes. Free-Soiler Van Buren, although winning no state, polled 291,263 votes and apparently diverted enough Democratic strength from Cass in the crucial state of New York to throw the election to Taylor.

Sectional Balance and the Underground Railroad

The South of 1850 was relatively well off. It had seated in the White House the war hero Zachary Taylor, a Virginia-born, slaveowning planter from Louisiana. It boasted a majority in the cabinet and on the Supreme Court. If outnumbered in the House, the South had equality in the Senate, where it could at least neutralize

Chronology

1848	Treaty of Guadalupe Hidalgo ends Mexican War. Taylor defeats Cass and Van Buren for presidency.	**1853**	Gadsden Purchase from Mexico.
1849	California gold rush. Fillmore assumes presidency after Taylor's death. Compromise of 1850, including Fugitive Slave Law. Clayton-Bulwer Treaty with Britain.	**1854**	Commodore Perry "opens" Japan. "Ostend Manifesto" proposes seizure of Cuba. Kansas-Nebraska Act. Republican party organized.
1852	Pierce defeats Scott for presidency.	**1856**	William Walker becomes president of Nicaragua and legalizes slavery.

northern maneuvers. Its cotton fields were expanding, and cotton prices were profitably high. Few sane people, North or South, believed that slavery was seriously threatened where it already existed below the Mason-Dixon line. The fifteen slave states could easily veto any proposed constitutional amendment.

Yet the South was deeply worried, as it had been for several decades, by the ever-tipping political balance. There were then fifteen slave states and fifteen free states. But the discovery of gold in California immediately after the Mexican War drew tens of thousands of forty-niners to the area. Soon the newcomers were clamoring for the direct admission of California to the Union. California's admission as a free state would destroy the delicate equilibrium in the Senate, perhaps forever. With agitation already developing in the territories of New Mexico and Utah for admission to the Union as nonslave states, the fate of California might well establish a precedent for the rest of the Mexican Cession territory.

Texas nursed an additional grievance of its own. It claimed a huge area east of the upper Rio Grande and north to the forty-second parallel, about half the territory of present-day New Mexico. The federal government was proposing to detach this prize, while hot-blooded Texans were threatening to descend on Santa Fe and seize what they regarded as rightfully theirs. The explosive quarrel foreshadowed shooting.

Many southerners were also angered by the nagging agitation in the North for the abolition of slavery in the District of Columbia. They looked with alarm on the prospect of a ten-mile-square oasis of free soil thrust between slaveholding Maryland and slaveholding Virginia.

Even more disagreeable to the South was the loss of runaway slaves, many of whom were assisted north by the Underground Railroad. This virtual freedom train consisted of an informal chain of "stations" (antislavery homes), through which scores of "passengers" (runaway slaves) were spirited by "conductors" (usually white and black abolitionists) from the slave states to the free-soil **sanctuary** of Canada.

The most amazing of these "conductors" was a runaway slave from Maryland, fearless Harriet Tubman. During nineteen forays into the South, she rescued more than three hundred slaves, including her aged parents, and deservedly earned the title "Moses." Lively imaginations later exaggerated the role of the Underground Railroad, but its importance was undisputed.

By 1850 southerners were demanding a new and more stringent **fugitive**-slave law. The old one, passed by Congress in 1793, had proved inadequate to cope with runaways, especially since unfriendly state authorities failed to cooperate.

Estimates indicate that the South in 1850 was losing perhaps 1,000 runaways a year out of its total of some 4 million slaves. In fact, more blacks probably gained their freedom by self-purchase or voluntary emancipation than ever escaped. But the principle weighed heavily with the slavemasters. "Although the loss of property is felt," said a southern senator, "the loss of honor is felt more."

Online Study Center

Primary source
Levi Coffin Remembers the Underground Railroad
college.hmco.com/pic/kennedybrief7e

Online Study Center

Primary source
Runaway Slave Advertisements
college.hmco.com/pic/kennedybrief7e

sanctuary *A place of refuge or protection, where people are safe from punishment by the law.*

fugitive *A person who flees from danger or prosecution.*

■ **Harriet Tubman, Premier Assistant of Runaway Slaves** John Brown called her "General Tubman" for her effective work in helping slaves escape to Canada on the Underground Railroad. During the Civil War, she served as a Union spy behind Confederate lines. Herself illiterate, she worked after the war to bring education to the freed slaves in North Carolina.

────────

topography *The precise surface features and details of a place—for example, rivers, canyons, hills—in relation to one another.*

Twilight of the Senatorial Giants

Southern fears were such that Congress was confronted with catastrophe in 1850. Free-soil California was banging on the door for admission. "Fire-eaters" in the South were voicing ominous threats of secession. The failure of Congress to act could easily mean the failure of the United States as a country. The crisis brought into the congressional forum the most distinguished assemblage of statesmen since the Constitutional Convention of 1787—the Old Guard of the dying generation and the young gladiators of the new. That "immortal trio"—Clay, Calhoun, and Webster—appeared together for the last time on the public stage.

Henry Clay, now seventy-three years of age, played a crucial role by proposing a series of compromises. He was ably seconded by thirty-seven-year-old Senator Stephen A. Douglas of Illinois, the "Little Giant" (five feet four inches), whose role was less spectacular but even more important. Clay persuasively urged both North and South to make concessions.

Senator John C. Calhoun, then sixty-eight and dying of tuberculosis, championed the South in his last formal speech. Too weak to deliver it himself, he sat bundled up in the Senate chamber, his eyes glowing within a stern face, while a younger colleague read his fateful words. Rejecting Clay's proposed concessions, Calhoun's impassioned plea was to leave slavery alone, return runaway slaves, give the South its rights as a minority, and restore the political balance. Calhoun died in 1850, before the debate was over, murmuring the sad words, "The South! The South! God knows what will become of her!"

Daniel Webster, sixty-eight years old and also ailing, next took the Senate spotlight to uphold Clay's compromise measures in his own last great speech. Webster urged all reasonable concessions to the South, including a new fugitive-slave law with teeth. Because climate and **topography** would prevent the spread of cotton production to the Mexican Cession territory, Webster argued, it was unnecessary to legislate on slavery there.* Webster's famed speech of the Seventh of March, 1850, was his finest effort. It visibly strengthened Union sentiment and especially pleased northern banking and commercial centers, which stood to lose millions of dollars by secession. But the Free-Soilers and abolitionists, who had

Compromise of 1850

Concessions to the North	Concessions to the South
California admitted as a free state	The remainder of the Mexican Cession area to be formed into the territories of New Mexico and Utah, without restriction on slavery, hence open to popular sovereignty
Territory disputed by Texas and New Mexico to be surrendered to New Mexico	Texas to receive $10 million from the federal government as compensation
Abolition of the domestic slave trade (but not slavery) in the District of Columbia	A more stringent fugitive-slave law, going beyond that of 1793

────────

* Webster was wrong here; within one hundred years California had become one of the great cotton-producing states of the Union.

assumed Webster was one of them, upbraided him as a traitor.

The stormy congressional debate of 1850 was not finished, for the Young Guard from the North were yet to have their say. Led by wiry freshman Senator William Seward of New York, this new generation of antislavery leaders was more interested in purifying the Union than in patching and preserving it. Seward unequivocally opposed further concessions to the South. Seward argued earnestly that Christian legislators must obey God's moral law as well as man's mundane law, and therefore appealed to a "higher law" than the Constitution to exclude slavery from the territories.

As the great debate in Congress ran its heated course, deadlock seemed certain. Blunt old President Taylor seemed bent on vetoing any compromise passed by Congress. In response to threats of Texas to seize Santa Fe, the crusty soldier-president seemed ready to lead an army into Texas in person and hang all the "damned traitors." If troops had marched, the South probably would have rallied to the defense of Texas, and the Civil War might have erupted in 1850.

> *Ralph Waldo Emerson, the philosopher and moderate abolitionist, was outraged by Webster's support of concessions to the South in the Fugitive Slave Act. In February 1851 he wrote in his Journal,*
>
> "I opened a paper to-day in which he [Webster] pounds on the old strings [of liberty] in a letter to the Washington Birthday feasters at New York. 'Liberty! liberty!' Pho! Let Mr. Webster, for decency's sake, shut his lips once and forever on this word. The word *liberty* in the mouth of Mr. Webster sounds like the word *love* in the mouth of a courtesan."

Breaking the Congressional Logjam

At the height of the controversy in 1850, President Taylor unknowingly helped the cause of concession by dying suddenly. The portly and colorless Vice President Millard Fillmore took the reins. As presiding officer of the Senate, he had been impressed with the arguments for conciliation, and he gladly signed the series of compromise measures that passed Congress after seven long months of stormy debate.

The struggle to get these measures accepted by the country was hardly less heated than in Congress. In the northern states, "Union savers" like Senators Clay, Webster, and Douglas orated on behalf of the compromise. The ailing Clay himself delivered more than seventy speeches, as a powerful sentiment for acceptance gradually crystallized in the North. It was strengthened by a growing feeling of goodwill and an upsurge of prosperity enriched by California gold.

But the southern "fire-eaters" were still violently opposed to concessions. In June 1850 the assemblage of southern extremists met in Nashville, Tennessee, to condemn the compromise. Meeting again in November, the convention proved to be a dud. By that time southern opinion had reluctantly accepted the verdict of Congress.

Like the calm after a storm, a second Era of Good Feelings dawned. Peace-loving people, both North and South, were determined that the compromises should finally bury the explosive issue of slavery. But this placid period proved all too brief.

Balancing the Compromise Scales

Who got the better deal in the Compromise of 1850? The answer is clearly the North. California, as a free state, tipped the Senate balance permanently against the South. The territories of New Mexico and Utah were open to slavery on the basis of popular sovereignty. But the iron law of nature—the "highest law" of all—had loaded the dice in favor of free soil. Southerners urgently needed more slave territory to restore the "sacred balance." If they could not carve new states out of the recent conquests from Mexico, where else could they get them? The Caribbean was one answer.

Even the apparent gains of the South rang hollow. Disgruntled Texas was to be paid $10 million toward discharging its indebtedness, but in the long run this was a

 **A Ride for Liberty, by Eastman Johnson** In this famous painting, Johnson, a New England artist, brilliantly evokes the anxiety of fleeing slaves.

modest sum. The immense area in dispute had been torn from the side of slave-holding Texas and was almost certain to be free. The South had halted the drive toward abolition in the District of Columbia, at least temporarily, by permitting the outlawing of the slave *trade* in the federal district. But even this move was an entering wedge toward complete emancipation in the nation's capital.

Most alarming of all, the drastic new Fugitive Slave Law of 1850—"the Bloodhound Bill"—stirred up a storm of opposition in the North. The fleeing slaves could not testify on their own behalf, and they were denied a jury trial. These harsh practices threatened to create dangerous precedents for white Americans. Freedom-loving northerners who aided the slave to escape were liable to heavy fines and jail sentences. They might even be ordered to join the slave-catchers, and this possibility rubbed salt into old sores.

So abhorrent was this "Man-Stealing Law" that it touched off an explosive chain reaction in the North. Many shocked moderates, hitherto passive, were driven into the swelling ranks of the antislaveryites.

The Underground Railroad stepped up its timetable, and infuriated northern mobs rescued slaves from their pursuers. Massachusetts, in a move toward nullification suggestive of South Carolina in 1832, made it a penal offense for any state official to enforce the new federal statute. Other states passed "personal liberty laws," which denied local jails to federal officials and otherwise hampered enforcement. The abolitionists rent the heavens with their protests against the man-stealing statute. A meeting presided over by William Lloyd Garrison in 1851 declared, "We execrate it, we spit upon it, we trample it under our feet."

Beyond question, the Fugitive Slave Law was an appalling blunder on the part of the South. No single irritant of the 1850s was more persistently galling to both sides, and none did more to awaken in the North a spirit of antagonism against the South. The southerners in turn were embittered because the northerners would not in good faith execute the law—the one real and immediate southern "gain" from the Great Compromise. Slave-catchers, with some success, redoubled their efforts.

Should the shooting showdown have come in 1850? From the standpoint of the secessionists, yes; from the standpoint of the Unionists, no. Time was fighting for the North. With every passing decade, this huge section was forging further ahead in population and wealth—in crops, factories, foundries, ships, and railroads.

Online Study Center

**Primary source
Compromise of 1850, The**
college.hmco.com/pic/kennedybrief7e

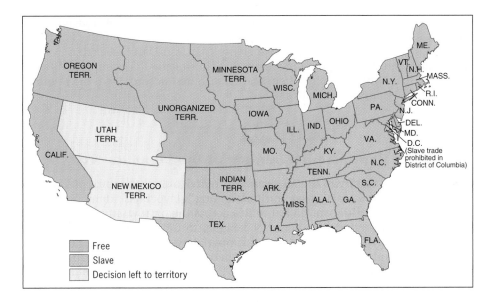

Free
Slave
Decision left to territory

■ **Slavery After the Compromise of 1850** Regarding the Fugitive Slave Act provisions of the Compromise of 1850, Ralph Waldo Emerson declared (May 1851) at Concord, Massachusetts, "The act of Congress . . . is a law which every one of you will break on the earliest occasion—a law which no man can obey, or abet the obeying, without loss of self-respect and forfeiture of the name of gentleman." Privately he wrote in his *Journal,* "This filthy enactment was made in the nineteenth century, by people who could read and write. I will not obey it, by God."

Delay also added immensely to the moral strength of the North—to its will to fight for the Union. In 1850 thousands of northern moderates were unwilling to pin the South to the rest of the nation with bayonets. But the inflammatory events of the 1850s did much to bolster the Yankee will to resist secession, whatever the cost. This one feverish decade gave the North time to accumulate the material and moral strength that provided the margin of victory. Thus the Compromise of 1850, from one point of view, won the Civil War for the Union.

Defeat and Doom for the Whigs

Meeting in Baltimore, the deadlocked Democratic convention of 1852 finally stampeded to the second "dark horse" candidate in American history, Franklin Pierce, an unrenowned New Hampshire lawyer-politician. Weak and indecisive, Pierce was called the "Fainting General" by his opponents because a painful groin injury had caused him to fall off a horse during the Mexican War. As a prosouthern northerner, Pierce was acceptable to the slavery wing of the Democratic party. His platform emphatically endorsed the Compromise of 1850, Fugitive Slave Law and all.

The Whigs, also convening in Baltimore, might logically have nominated figures associated with the Compromise of 1850, such as President Fillmore or Senator Webster. But having won in the past only with military heroes, they turned to another, "Old Fuss and Feathers," Winfield Scott. Although Scott was the ablest American general of his generation as well as an impressive statesman, his haughty personality repelled the masses. Democrats ridiculed Scott's pomposity and cried exultantly, "We Polked 'em in '44; we'll Pierce 'em in '52."

Luckily for the Democrats, the Whig party was hopelessly split. Antislavery Whigs of the North swallowed Scott as their nominee but deplored his platform, which endorsed the hated Fugitive Slave Law. Southern Whigs, who doubted Scott's loyalty to the Compromise of 1850 and especially to the Fugitive Slave Law, accepted the platform but spat on the candidate. In the end the politically inexperienced Scott was stabbed in the back by his fellow Whigs, notably in the South. The Free Soil candidate, New Hampshire Senator John P. Hale, also siphoned off northern Whig votes that might have gone to Scott. The pliant Pierce won in a landslide, 254 electoral votes to 42, although the popular vote was closer, 1,601,117 to 1,385,453.

The election of 1852 was fraught with frightening significance, though it seemed tame at the time. It marked the effective end of the disorganized Whig party and, within a few years, its complete death. The Whigs' demise augured the eclipse of *national* parties and the worrisome rise of purely *sectional* political alignments. The Whigs were governed at times by the crassest opportunism, and they won only two presidential elections in their colorful career (1840, 1848), both with war heroes. They finally choked to death trying to swallow the distasteful

Fugitive Slave Law. But their great contribution—and a noteworthy one indeed—was to uphold the ideal of Union through their electoral strength in the South and through the eloquence of leaders like Henry Clay and Daniel Webster. Both of these statesmen, by unhappy coincidence, died during the 1852 campaign. But the good they had done lived after them and contributed powerfully to the eventual preservation of a *united* United States.

The Expansionist Legacy of the Mexican War

The intoxicating victory in the Mexican War reinvigorated the spirit of Manifest Destiny and a lust for new slave territory among "slavocrats." Many Americans were also looking for transportation routes across the narrow isthmus of Central America, through either Panama or Nicaragua, to California's new gold fields. Whoever controlled that route would hold imperial sway over all maritime nations, including the United States. A sharp conflict between the United States and Britain, which had been encroaching on Nicaragua's "Mosquito Coast," was avoided by the Clayton-Bulwer Treaty of 1850. It stipulated that neither America nor Britain would fortify or seek exclusive control over any future **isthmian** waterway (later rescinded by the Hay-Pauncefote Treaty of 1901; see p. 270).

Southerner "slavocrats" cast especially covetous eyes southward in the 1850s. They lusted for new slave territory after the Compromise of 1850 seemingly closed most of the Mexican Cession to the "peculiar institution." In 1856 a Texan proposed a toast "to the Southern republic bounded on the north by the Mason and Dixon line and on the South by the Isthmus of Tehuantepec [southern Mexico], including Cuba and all the lands on our Southern shore."

Nicaragua beckoned beguilingly. A brazen American adventurer, William Walker, tried repeatedly to grab control of this Central American country in the 1850s. Backed by an armed force recruited largely in the South, he installed himself as president in July 1856 and promptly legalized slavery. One southern newspaper proclaimed to the planter aristocracy that Walker—the "gray-eyed man of destiny"—"now offers Nicaragua to you and your slaves." But a coalition of Central American nations formed an alliance to overthrow him. President Pierce withdrew diplomatic recognition, and the gray-eyed man's destiny was to crumple before a Honduran firing squad in 1860.

Sugar-rich Cuba, lying just off the nation's southern doorstep, was also an enticing prospect for annexation. This remnant of Spain's once-mighty New World empire, with its large population of enslaved blacks, might be carved into several states, restoring the political balance in the Senate. President Polk had considered offering Spain $100 million for Cuba, but the proud Spaniards replied that they would sooner see the island sunk into the sea than in the hands of the hated Yankees.

Some southern adventurers now undertook to shake the tree of Manifest Destiny. During 1850–1851, two "**filibustering**" expeditions, each numbering several hundred armed men, descended on Cuba. Both feeble efforts were repelled, and fifty of the invaders were summarily shot or strangled.

When Spanish officials in Cuba rashly seized an American steamer in 1854, southern-dominated President Pierce decided that now was the time to provoke a war with Spain and seize Cuba. An incredible **cloak-and-dagger** episode followed. Pierce's secretary of state instructed the American ministers to Spain, Britain, and France to meet in Ostend, Belgium, and draw up a plan to acquire Cuba. Their top-secret dispatch, known as the "Ostend **Manifesto**," urged the administration to offer $120 million for Cuba. If Spain refused to sell, the United States would "be justified in wresting" the island from the Spanish.

When the secret Ostend Manifesto leaked out, Northern free-soilers rose up in wrath against the "manifesto of brigands." The red-faced Pierce administration hurriedly dropped its reckless schemes for Cuba. The slavery issue thus checked territorial expansion in the 1850s.

Besides Latin America, another arena of American international assertiveness in the 1850s was in the Pacific and East Asia. The acquisition of California and Oregon had made the United States a Pacific power—or would-be power. In 1842 Britain gained free access to so-called treaty ports in China as well as outright control of the

isthmus (isthmian) *A narrow strip of land connecting two larger bodies of land.*

filibustering (filibuster) *Adventurers who conduct a private war against a foreign country. (In a different meaning, the term also refers to deliberately prolonged speechmaking in order to block legislation.)*

cloak-and-dagger *Concerning the activities of spies or undercover agents, especially involving elaborate deceptions.*

manifesto *A proclamation or document aggressively asserting a controversial position or advocating a daring course of action.*

island of Hong Kong. To secure comparable concessions for the United States, President Tyler in 1844 dispatched dashing Massachusetts diplomat Caleb Cushing, along with four warships, to the southern Chinese port of Macao. In July 1844 Cushing signed the Treaty of Wanghia with China. It secured the United States equal trading rights with other nations and the principle of "extraterritoriality" that provided for trying accused Americans in American, not Chinese, courts. American trade with China flourished, and thousands of American missionaries soon arrived through the treaty ports to convert the "heathen Chinese."

Success in China inspired a still more consequential mission to pry open the bamboo gates of Japan, which had been closed to outsiders for centuries. In 1852 President Millard Fillmore dispatched to Japan a fleet of four awesome, smoke-belching warships, commanded by Commodore Matthew C. Perry, to Edo (later Tokyo) Bay. Perry returned in February 1854 with an even larger force of seven men-of-war, and with a combination of bluster and grace, persuaded the Japanese to sign the landmark Treaty of Kanagawa on March 31, 1854. It provided for proper treatment of shipwrecked sailors, American coaling rights in Japan, and the establishment of consular relations. This commercial toe in the door cracked Japan's two-century shell of isolation open, and began to propel the Land of the Rising Sun headlong into the modern world.

The first platform of the newly born (antislavery) Republican party in 1856 lashed out at the Ostend Manifesto, with its transparent suggestion that Cuba be seized. The plank read,

"Resolved, That the highwayman's plea, that 'might makes right,' embodied in the Ostend Circular, was in every respect unworthy of American diplomacy, and would bring shame and dishonor upon any Government or people that gave it their sanction."

Pacific Railroad Promoters and the Gadsden Purchase

Acute transportation problems were another legacy of the Mexican War. The newly acquired prizes of California and Oregon might just as well have been islands some eight thousand miles west of the nation's capital. The sea routes to and from the Isthmus of Panama, to say nothing of those around South America, were too long. Covered-wagon travel past bleaching animal bones was possible, but slow and dangerous. A popular song recalled the formidable trek.

> *They swam the wide rivers and crossed the tall peaks,*
> *And camped on the prairie for weeks upon weeks.*
> *Starvation and cholera and hard work and slaughter,*
> *They reached California spite of hell and high water.*

Feasible land transportation was imperative—or the newly won possessions on the Pacific Coast might break away. Camels were even imported from the Near East as an attempted answer, but mule-driving Americans did not adjust to the temperamental beasts. A transcontinental railroad was clearly the only real solution to the problem.

Should its terminus be in the North or in the South? The favored section would reap rich rewards in wealth, population, and influence. The South, losing the economic race with the North, was eager to extend a railroad through adjacent southwestern territory all the way to California.

Another chunk of Mexico now seemed desirable, because the best railway route across the Southwest ran slightly south of the Mexican border. Secretary of War Jefferson Davis therefore appointed a South Carolina railroad man, James Gadsden, as minister to Mexico. He negotiated a treaty in 1853 that ceded to the United States the Gadsden Purchase area for $10 million. The transaction aroused northern criticism, but the Senate approved the pact.

Southerners now argued that because their proposed rail line ran through the state of Texas and the organized New Mexico Territory, the southern route should be built first. Northern railroad **boosters** quickly replied that if organized territory was the test, then Nebraska, site of the proposed northern route, should also be organized. But southerners in Congress greeted all schemes for organizing Nebraska with apathy or hostility. Why should the South help create new free-soil states and thus cut its own throat by facilitating a northern railroad?

booster *One who promotes a person or enterprise, especially in a highly enthusiastic way.*

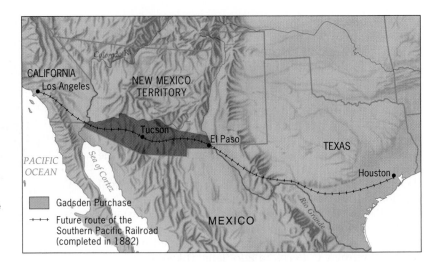

■ **Gadsden Purchase, 1853** The purchase made possible a southern rail route to the West Coast. But the Southern Pacific railroad (whose route is shown here) was not built until 1882, after the Civil War.

Douglas's Kansas-Nebraska Scheme

At this point in 1854, Senator Stephen A. Douglas of Illinois delivered a counterstroke to offset the Gadsden thrust for southern expansion westward. A squat, bull-necked, and heavy-chested figure, the "Little Giant" radiated the energy and breezy optimism of the self-made man. An ardent booster for the West, he longed to break the North-South deadlock over westward expansion and stretch a line of settlements across the continent. He also had invested heavily in Chicago real estate and in railway stock and was eager to have the Windy City become the eastern terminus of the proposed Pacific railroad. He would thus endear himself to the voters of Illinois, benefit his section, and enrich his own purse.

A veritable "steam engine in breeches," Douglas threw himself behind a legislative scheme that would enlist the support of a reluctant South. The proposed Territory of Nebraska would be carved into two territories, Kansas and Nebraska. Their status regarding slavery would be settled by popular sovereignty—a democratic concept to which Douglas and his western constituents were deeply attached. Kansas, which lay due west of slaveholding Missouri, would presumably choose to

Online Study Center

Interactive map
The Kansas-Nebraska Act, 1854
college.hmco.com/pic/kennedybrief7e

■ **Kansas and Nebraska, 1854** The route of the future Union Pacific Railroad (completed in 1869) is shown. Notice the Missouri Compromise line of 36°30′ (1820).

become a slave state. But Nebraska, lying west of free-soil Iowa, would presumably become a free state.

Douglas's Kansas-Nebraska scheme flatly contradicted the Missouri Compromise of 1820, which had forbidden slavery in the proposed Nebraska Territory north of the sacred 36°30ʹ line. The only way to open the region to popular sovereignty was to repeal the ancient compact outright. This bold step Douglas was prepared to take, even at the risk of shattering the uneasy **truce** patched together by the Compromise of 1850.

Many southerners, who had not conceived of Kansas as slave soil, rose to the bait. Here was a chance to gain one more slave state. The pliable President Pierce, under the thumb of southern advisers, threw his full weight behind the Kansas-Nebraska Bill.

But the Missouri Compromise, now thirty-four years old, could not be brushed aside lightly. Whatever Congress passes it can repeal, but by this time the North had come to regard the sectional pact as almost as sacred as the Constitution itself. Free-soil members of Congress struck back with a vengeance. They met their match in the violently gesticulating Douglas, who was the ablest rough-and-tumble debater of his generation. Employing twisted logic and oratorical fireworks, he rammed the bill through Congress with strong support from many southerners. So heated were political passions that bloodshed was barely averted. Some members carried a concealed revolver or a bowie knife—or both.

Douglas's motives in prodding anew the snarling dog of slavery have long puzzled historians. His personal interests have already been mentioned. In addition, his foes accused him of angling for the presidency in 1856. Yet his admirers have argued in his defense that if he had not championed the ill-omened bill, someone else would have.

The truth seems to be that Douglas acted somewhat impulsively and recklessly. His heart did not bleed over the issue of slavery, and he declared repeatedly that he did not care whether it was voted up or down in the territories. What he failed to perceive was that hundreds of thousands of his fellow citizens in the North *did* feel deeply on this moral issue. They regarded the repeal of the Missouri Compromise as an intolerable breach of faith, and they would henceforth resist to the last trench all future southern demands for slave territory.

Genuine leaders, like skillful chess players, must foresee the possible effects of their moves. Douglas predicted a "hell of a storm," but he grossly underestimated its proportions. His critics in the North, branding him a "Judas" and a "traitor," greeted his name with frenzied boos, hisses, and "three groans for Doug." But he still enjoyed a high degree of popularity among his following in the Democratic party, especially in Illinois, a stronghold of popular sovereignty.

■ **Stephen A. Douglas (1813–1861)** Despite having stirred up sectional bitterness, Douglas was so devoted to the Union that he warmly supported his rival, Lincoln, when war broke out. He attended the inauguration and reportedly held Lincoln's stovepipe hat while the president spoke.

truce *A temporary suspension of warfare by agreement of the hostile parties.*

Congress Legislates a Civil War

The Kansas-Nebraska Act—curtain raiser to a terrible drama—was one of the most momentous measures ever to pass Congress. By one way of reckoning, it greased the slippery slope to civil war.

Antislavery northerners were angered by what they condemned as an act of bad faith by the "Nebrascals" and their "Nebrascality." All future compromise with the South would be immeasurably more difficult, and without compromise there was bound to be conflict.

Henceforth the Fugitive Slave Law of 1850, previously enforced in the North only halfheartedly, was a dead letter. The Kansas-Nebraska Act wrecked two compromises: that of 1820, which it repealed specifically, and that of

Massachusetts senator Charles Sumner (1811–1874) described the Kansas-Nebraska Bill as "at once the worst and the best Bill on which Congress ever acted." It was the worst because it represented a victory for the slave power in the short run. But it was the best, he said prophetically, because it

"annuls all past compromises with slavery, and makes all future compromises impossible. Thus it puts freedom and slavery face to face, and bids them grapple. Who can doubt the result?"

Online Study Center

**Primary source
Kansas-Nebraska Act, The**
college.hmco.com/pic/kennedybrief7e

1850, which northern opinion repealed indirectly. Emerson wrote, "The Fugitive [Slave] Law did much to unglue the eyes of men, and now the Nebraska Bill leaves us staring."

Northern abolitionists and southern "fire-eaters" alike saw less and less they could live with. The growing legion of antislaveryites gained numerous recruits, who resented the grasping move by the "slavocracy" for Kansas. The southerners, in turn, became inflamed when the free-soilers attempted to control Kansas, contrary to the presumed "deal."

The proud Democrats—a party now over half a century old—were shattered by the Kansas-Nebraska Act. They did elect a president in 1856, but he was the last one they were to boost into the White House for twenty-eight long years.

Undoubtedly the most durable offspring of the Kansas-Nebraska blunder was the new Republican party. It sprang up spontaneously in the Midwest, notably in Wisconsin and Michigan, as a mighty moral protest against the gains of slavery. Gathering together dissatisfied elements, it soon included disgruntled Whigs (among them Abraham Lincoln), Democrats, Free-Soilers, Know-Nothings, and other foes of the Kansas-Nebraska Act. The hodgepodge party spread eastward with the swiftness of a prairie fire and with the zeal of a religious crusade. Unheard of and unheralded at the beginning of 1854, it elected a Republican Speaker of the House of Representatives within two years. Never really a third-party movement, it erupted with such force as to become almost overnight the second major political party—and a purely sectional one at that.

At long last the dreaded sectional rift had appeared. The new Republican party would not be allowed south of the Mason-Dixon line. Countless southerners subscribed wholeheartedly to the sentiment that it was "a nigger stealing, stinking, putrid, abolition party." The Union was in dire peril.

⭐ Chapter Summary ⭐

The acquisition of territory from Mexico created acute new dilemmas concerning the expansion of slavery, especially for the two major political parties, which had long tried to avoid the issue. The antislavery Free Soil party pushed the issue into the election of 1848. The application of gold-rich California for admission to the Union forced the controversy into the Senate, which engaged in stormy debates over slavery and the Union.

After the timely death of President Taylor, who had blocked a settlement, Congress resolved the crisis by passing the delicate Compromise of 1850. The compromise eased sectional tension for the moment, although the Fugitive Slave Law aroused opposition in the North.

As the sectionally divided Whig party died, the Democratic Pierce administration became the tool of proslavery expansionists. Attempts at further expansion into Nicaragua, Cuba, and the Gadsden Purchase showed the increasing assertiveness of proslavery expansionists, who stirred strong resistance in the North.

For complex and somewhat mysterious reasons that included the desire for a northern railroad route, Senator Stephen Douglas rammed the Kansas Nebraska Act through Congress in 1854. By repealing the Missouri Compromise and making new territory subject to "popular sovereignty" on slavery, this act aroused the fury of the North, sparked the rise of the Republican party, and set the stage for the Civil War.

19

Drifting Toward Disunion

1854–1861

A HOUSE DIVIDED AGAINST ITSELF CANNOT STAND.

I BELIEVE THIS GOVERNMENT CANNOT ENDURE PERMANENTLY
HALF SLAVE AND HALF FREE.

ABRAHAM LINCOLN, 1858

The slavery question continued to churn the cauldron of controversy throughout the 1850s. As moral temperatures rose, prospects for a peaceful political solution to the slavery issue simply evaporated. Kansas Territory erupted in violence between proslavery and antislavery factions in 1855. Two years later the Supreme Court's *Dred Scott* decision invalidated the Missouri Compromise of 1820, which had imposed a shaky lid on the slavery problem for more than a generation. Attitudes on both sides progressively hardened. When in 1860 the newly formed Republican party nominated for president Abraham Lincoln, an outspoken opponent of the further expansion of slavery, the stage was set for all-out civil war.

Focus Questions

1. What were the major crises in the 1850s that led from the Kansas-Nebraska Act to secession, and how did each work to tear apart the Union and create the climate for the Civil War?
2. How and why did "bleeding Kansas" become a small-scale dress rehearsal for the Civil War?
3. How did the new Republican party emerge as a powerful new voice against the expansion of slavery, and what enabled Abraham Lincoln to emerge from obscurity to become its most effective leader and presidential nominee?
4. What were the central issues in the campaign of 1860, and how did the Democratic party's divisions as well as Republican unity lead to Lincoln's victory?
5. Why did the lower South secede immediately after Lincoln's victory, and why did last-ditch efforts like the Crittenden Compromise fail to prevent Civil War?

Stowe and Helper: Literary Incendiaries

Online Study Center

Primary source
Southern Critique of *Uncle Tom's Cabin,* A
college.hmco.com/pic/kennedybrief7e

Sectional tensions were further strained in 1852, and later, by an inky phenomenon. Harriet Beecher Stowe, a wisp of a woman and the mother of a half-dozen children, published her heart-rending novel *Uncle Tom's Cabin.* Dismayed by the passage of the Fugitive Slave Law, she was determined to awaken the North to the wickedness of slavery by laying bare its terrible inhumanity, especially the cruel splitting of families. Her wildly popular book relied on powerful imagery and touching pathos. "God wrote it," she explained in later years—a reminder that the deeper sources of her antislavery sentiments lay in the evangelical religious crusades of the Second Great Awakening.

The success of the novel at home and abroad was sensational. Several hundred thousand copies were published in the first year, and the totals soon ran into the millions as the tale was translated into more than a score of languages. It was also put on the stage in "Tom shows" for lengthy runs. No other novel in American history—perhaps in all history—can be compared with it as a political force. To millions of people it made slavery appear almost as evil as it really was.

When Mrs. Stowe was introduced to President Lincoln in 1862, he reportedly remarked, "So you're the little woman who wrote the book that made this great war." The truth is that *Uncle Tom's Cabin* did help start the Civil War—and win it.

Uncle Tom, endearing and enduring, left a profound impression on the North. Thousands of readers swore that henceforth they would have nothing to do with the enforcement of the Fugitive Slave Law. The tale was devoured by millions of impressionable youths in the 1850s—some of whom later became the Boys in Blue who volunteered to fight the Civil War through to its grim finale. The memory of a beaten and dying Uncle Tom helped sustain them in their determination to wipe out the plague of slavery.

Another trouble-brewing book appeared in 1857, five years after the debut of *Uncle Tom.* Titled *The Impending Crisis of the South,* it was written by Hinton R. Helper, a nonaristocratic white from North Carolina. Hating both slavery and blacks, he attempted to prove by an array of statistics that indirectly the non-slaveholding whites were the ones who suffered most from the millstone of slavery. Helper's book, with its "dirty allusions," was banned in the South and fed to the flames at book-burning parties. But in the North thousands of copies, many in condensed form, were distributed as campaign literature by the Republicans.

Online Study Center

Primary source
Uncle Tom's Cabin at the Theater
college.hmco.com/pic/kennedybrief7e

■ Harriet Beecher Stowe (1811–1896), Daguerreotype by Southworth and Hawes Stowe was a remarkable woman whose pen helped to change the course of history.

The North-South Contest for Kansas

The rolling plains of Kansas had meanwhile been providing an example of the worst possible workings of popular sovereignty. Newcomers who ventured into Kansas were a motley lot. Most of the northerners were just ordinary westward-moving pioneers. But a small part of the inflow was financed by groups of northern abolitionists or free-soilers, especially the New England Emigrant Aid Company, which sent about two thousand people to the troubled area to forestall the South. Shouting "Ho for Kansas!" many of them carried the deadly new breech-loading Sharps rifles, nicknamed "Beecher's Bibles" after the Reverend Henry Ward Beecher (Harriet Beecher Stowe's brother), who had helped raise

Chronology

1852	Harriet Beecher Stowe publishes *Uncle Tom's Cabin*.
1854	Kansas-Nebraska Act. Republican party forms.
1856	Buchanan defeats Frémont and Fillmore for presidency. Sumner beaten by Brooks in Senate chamber. Brown's Pottawatomie massacre.
1856-1860	Civil war in "bleeding Kansas."
1857	*Dred Scott* decision. Lecompton Constitution rejected.
1857	Panic of 1857. Hinton R. Helper publishes *The Impending Crisis of the South*.
1858	Lincoln-Douglas debates.
1859	Brown raids Harpers Ferry.
1860	Lincoln wins four-way race for presidency. South Carolina secedes from the Union. Crittenden Compromise fails.
1861	Seven seceding states form Confederate States of America.

money for their purchase. Many of the Kansas-bound pioneers sang Whittier's marching song (1854):

> *We cross the prairie as of old*
> *The pilgrims crossed the sea,*
> *To make the West, as they the East,*
> *The homestead of the free!*

Southern spokesmen, now more than ordinarily touchy, raised furious cries of betrayal. They had supported the Kansas-Nebraska scheme of Douglas with the unspoken understanding that Kansas would become slave and Nebraska free. The northern "Nebrascals" were now apparently out to "abolitionize" *both* Kansas and Nebraska.

A few southern hotheads, quick to respond in kind, attempted to "assist" small groups of well-armed slaveowners to Kansas. But despite such efforts slavery never took hold in Kansas. The census of 1860 found only 2 slaves among 107,000 souls in all Kansas Territory, and only 15 in Nebraska. Nevertheless, crisis conditions in Kansas rapidly worsened. When the day came in 1855 to elect members of the first territorial legislature, proslavery "border ruffians" poured in from Missouri to vote early and often. The slavery supporters triumphed and then set up their own **puppet government** at Shawnee Mission. The free-soilers, unable to stomach this fraudulent conspiracy, established an extralegal regime of their own in Topeka. The confused Kansans thus had their choice between two governments—one based on fraud, the other on illegality. Tensions reached the breaking point in 1856 when a gang of proslavery raiders shot up and burned a part of the free-soil town of Lawrence. This outrage was but the prelude to a bloodier tragedy.

puppet government *A government set up and controlled by outside forces.*

> *In the closing scenes of Harriet Beecher Stowe's novel, Uncle Tom's brutal master, Simon Legree, orders the $1,200 slave savagely beaten (to death) by two fellow slaves. Through tears and blood, Tom exclaims,*
>
> *"No! no! no! my soul an't yours, Mas'r! You haven't bought it,—ye can't buy it! It's been bought and paid for, by one that is able to keep it,—no matter, no matter, you can't harm me!" "I can't," said Legree, with a sneer; "we'll see,— we'll see! Here, Sambo, Quimbo, give this dog such a breakin' in as he won't get over, this month!"*

Kansas in Convulsion

The fanatical figure of John Brown now stalked upon the Kansas battlefield. Spare, gray-bearded, and iron-willed,

■ **Bleeding Kansas, 1854–1860**
"Enter every election district in Kansas . . . and vote at the point of a bowie knife or revolver," one proslavery agitator exhorted a Missouri crowd. Proslavery Missouri senator David Atchison declared that "there are 1,100 men coming over from Platte County to vote, and if that ain't enough we can send 5,000—enough to kill every Goddamned abolitionist in the Territory."

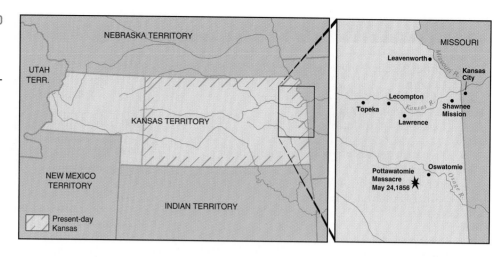

he was obsessively dedicated to the abolitionist cause. The power of his glittering gray eyes was such, so he claimed, that his stare could force a dog or cat to slink out of a room. Brooding over the recent attack on Lawrence, "Old Brown" of Osawatomie led a band of his followers to Pottawatomie Creek, in May 1856. There they literally hacked to pieces five surprised men, presumed to be proslaveryites. This fiendish butchery brought vicious retaliation from proslavery forces. Civil war in Kansas thus flared forth in 1856 and continued intermittently until it merged with the large-scale Civil War of 1861–1865.

The proslavery forces intensified the conflict in 1857 when they attempted to bring Kansas into the Union under a tricky document known as the Lecompton Constitution. Although the majority of Kansans were free-soilers, the vote on the proposed constitution was arranged so that it was impossible to prohibit all black bondage and still obtain statehood. With infuriated free-soilers boycotting the election, the proslaveryites approved the constitution with slavery late in 1857.

■ **Preston Brooks Caning Charles Sumner, 1856** Cartoonist John Magee of Philadelphia depicted Brooks's beating of Sumner in the Senate as a display of southern ruthlessness in defending slavery, ironically captioned "southern chivalry."

EXAMINING THE EVIDENCE

As works of fiction, novels pose tricky problems to historians, whose principal objective is to get the factual record straight. Works of the imagination are notoriously unreliable as descriptions of reality, and only rarely is it known with any degree of certainty what a reader might have felt when confronting a particular fictional passage or theme. Yet a novel like Harriet Beecher Stowe's *Uncle Tom's Cabin* had such an unarguably large impact on the American (and worldwide) debate over slavery that historians have inevitably looked to it for evidence of the mid-nineteenth-century ideas and attitudes to which Stowe appealed. The passage quoted here is especially rich in such evidence—and even offers an explanation for the logic of the novel's title. Stowe cleverly aimed to mobilize not simply her readers' sense of injustice, but also their sentiments, on behalf of the antislavery cause.

The February morning looked gray and drizzling through the window of Uncle Tom's cabin. It looked on downcast faces, the images of mournful hearts. The little table stood out before the fire, covered with an ironing-cloth; a coarse but clean shirt or two, fresh from the iron, hung on the back of a chair by the fire, and Aunt Chloe had another spread out before her on the table. Carefully she rubbed and ironed every fold and every hem, with the most scrupulous exactness, every now and then raising her hand to her face to wipe off the tears that were coursing down her cheeks.

Tom sat by, with his Testament open his knee, and his head leaning upon his hand;—but neither spoke. It was yet early, and the children lay all asleep together in their little rude trundle-bed.

Tom, who had, to the full, the gentle, domestic heart, which, woe for them! has been a peculiar characteristic of his unhappy race, got up and walked silently to look at his children.

"It's the last time," he said.

1. What sentimental values does the *cabin* represent, and why is it so central to Stowe's novel?
2. What is the nature of the threat to those values?
3. How does Stowe convey the importance of both religion and family for her slave characters, and why might these elements particularly appeal to the novel's middle-class readers?

The new president, James Buchanan, was just as much under southern influence as President Pierce had been, and he threw the weight of his administration behind the notorious Lecompton Constitution. But Senator Douglas, who had championed true popular sovereignty, would have none of this semipopular fraudulency. Deliberately tossing away his strong support in the South for the presidency, he fought courageously to submit the entire Lecompton Constitution to a fair popular vote. The free-soil voters thereupon snowed it under at the polls. Kansas remained a territory until 1861, when the southern secessionists left Congress.

President Buchanan, by antagonizing the numerous Douglas Democrats in the North, hopelessly divided the once-powerful Democratic party. Until then, it had been the only remaining national party, for the Whigs were dead and the Republicans were sectional. With the disruption of the Democrats came the snapping of one of the last important strands in the rope that was barely binding the Union together.

"Bully" Brooks and His Bludgeon

"Bleeding Kansas" also spattered blood on the floor of the Senate in 1856. The abolitionist Senator Charles Sumner of Massachusetts, a tall and imposing figure, delivered a blistering speech titled "The Crime Against Kansas," in which he viciously condemned proslavery men as "hirelings picked from the drunken spew and vomit of an uneasy civilization." The speech also insulted white-haired Senator Andrew Butler of South Carolina.

Hot-tempered South Carolina Congressman Preston S. Brooks, Butler's distant cousin, took vengeance into his own hands. On May 22, 1856, he approached Sumner, then sitting at his Senate desk, and pounded the orator with an eleven-ounce cane until it broke. The victim fell bleeding and unconscious to the floor, suffering serious injuries to his head and nervous system.

Bleeding Sumner thus joined bleeding Kansas as a hotly divisive political issue. South Carolina triumphantly reelected Brooks to Congress, and Massachusetts defiantly did the same for Sumner, even though the battered abolitionist was unable to take his seat for over three years. Meanwhile, Sumner's abusive speech sold by the thousands in the North, while southern admirers deluged Brooks with canes to replace the one he had broken over Sumner's head.

The Sumner-Brooks clash and the ensuing reactions revealed how dangerously inflamed passions were becoming, North and South. It was ominous that the cultured Sumner should have used the language of a barroom bully and that the gentlemanly Brooks should have employed the tactics and tools of a thug. Emotion was displacing thought. The blows rained on Sumner's head were, broadly speaking, among the first blows of the Civil War.

"Old Buck" Versus "The Pathfinder"

With bullets whining in Kansas, the Democrats met in Cincinnati to nominate their presidential standard-bearer of 1856. Both weak-kneed President Pierce and dynamic Senator Douglas were too indelibly tainted by the Kansas-Nebraska Act, so the delegates finally turned to a well-to-do Pennsylvania lawyer and diplomat, James Buchanan, who had been serving as minister to London during the recent Kansas-Nebraska uproar. Although his "Kansasless" neutrality made him acceptable to the party, "Old Buck" Buchanan was mediocre, irresolute, and confused.

The fast-growing Republican party, in their enthusiastic convention in Philadelphia, passed over "Higher Law" Senator William Seward, their most conspicuous leader, and instead chose John C. Frémont, a dashing but erratic explorer-soldier-surveyor. Republicans hoped that the so-called "Pathfinder of the West" would blaze them a path to the White House. Vigorously condemning the extension of slavery into the territories, Republicans sang,

> *Arise, arise ye brave!*
> *And let our war-cry be*
> *Free speech, free press, free soil, free men,*
> *Fré-mont and victory!*

An ugly dose of antiforeignism was injected into the campaign, even though slavery extension loomed largest. The recent influx of immigrants from Ireland and Germany had alarmed the old-stock Protestant nativists who had organized the American or Know-Nothing party. Antiforeign and anti-Catholic, these super-patriots nominated former President Millard Fillmore as their candidate, and campaigned under the slogan, "Americans Must Rule America." With remnants of the dying Whig party also endorsing Fillmore, the Know-Nothings cut into Republican party strength.

The bland Buchanan, although polling less than a majority of the popular vote, won handily. His tally in the Electoral College was 174 to 114 for Frémont, with Fillmore garnering 8. The popular vote was 1,832,955 for Buchanan to 1,339,932 for Frémont, with 871,731 for Fillmore.

Democrats had carried the hapless "Old Buck" into office, but the Republicans could rightfully claim a "victorious defeat" in 1856. The new party—a mere two-year-old toddler—had made an astonishing showing against the well-oiled Democratic machine. John Greenleaf Whittier exulted:

> *Then sound again the bugles,*
> *Call the muster-roll anew;*
> *If months have well-nigh won the field,*
> *What may not four years do?*

That question cast a long shadow forward, as politicians, North and South, peered anxiously toward 1860.

The Dred Scott Bombshell

The *Dred Scott* decision, handed down by the Supreme Court on March 6, 1857, abruptly ended the two-day presidential honeymoon of the unlucky bachelor, James Buchanan. Basically, the case was simple. Dred Scott, a black slave, had lived with his master for five years in free-state Illinois and Wisconsin Territory. Backed by interested abolitionists, he sued for freedom on the basis of his long residence on free soil.

The Supreme Court proceeded to turn a simple legal case into a complex political issue. It ruled, not surprisingly, that Dred Scott was a black slave and not a citizen, and hence could not sue in federal courts.* The tribunal could then have thrown out the case on these technical grounds alone. But a majority decided to go further, under the leadership of emaciated Chief Justice Roger Taney from the slave state of Maryland.

Taney's sweeping judgment on the larger question of slavery rocked the free-soilers back on their heels. Speaking for a majority of the Court, Taney decreed that because a slave was private property, he or she could be taken into *any* territory and legally held there in slavery. The reasoning was that the Fifth Amendment clearly forbade Congress to deprive people of their property without due process of law. The Court, to be consistent, went further. The Missouri Compromise of 1820, banning slavery north of 36°30′, had been repealed three years earlier by the Kansas-Nebraska Act, but its spirit was still venerated in the North. Now the Court ruled that the Missouri Compromise had been unconstitutional all along: Congress had no power to ban slavery from the territories, regardless even of what the territorial legislatures might want.

Southerners were delighted with this unexpected victory. Champions of popular sovereignty, including Senator Douglas and most northern Democrats, were aghast. Another lethal wedge was thus driven between the northern and southern wings of the once-united Democratic party.

Foes of slavery extension, especially the Republicans, were infuriated by the *Dred Scott* setback. Because a majority of the Supreme Court justices were southerners, Republicans insisted that the ruling was merely an opinion, not a decision, and no more binding than the views of a "southern debating society." Southerners in turn wondered how much longer they could remain joined to a section that refused to honor the Supreme Court, to say nothing of the constitutional compact that had established it.

> *Spiritual overtones developed in the Frémont campaign, especially over slavery. The* Independent, *a prominent religious journal, saw in Frémont's nomination "the good hand of God." As election day neared, it declared,*
>
> "Fellow-Christians! Remember it is for Christ, for the nation, and for the world that you vote at this election! Vote as you pray! Pray as you vote!"

The Financial Crash of 1857

Bitterness caused by the *Dred Scott* decision was deepened by hard times, which dampened a period of feverish prosperity. Late in 1857, a financial panic burst about Buchanan's harassed head. The storm was not so bad economically as the panic of 1837, but psychologically it was probably the worst of the nineteenth century.

The North, including its grain growers, was hardest hit by the sharp economic downturn. The South, enjoying favorable cotton prices abroad, rode out the storm with flying colors. Panic conditions seemed further proof that cotton was king, and that its economic kingdom was stronger than that of the North. This fatal delusion helped drive the overconfident southerners closer to a shooting showdown.

---

* This part of the ruling, denying blacks their citizenship, seriously menaced the precarious position of the south's quarter-million free blacks.

public domain *Land or other property belonging to the whole nation, controlled by the federal government.*

Financial distress in the North, especially in agriculture, gave a new vigor to the demand for free farms of 160 acres from the **public domain**. Overcoming the objections of both eastern industrialists and southern slaveholders, Congress in 1860 finally passed a homestead act that made public lands available at the nominal sum of twenty-five cents an acre. But it was stabbed to death by the veto pen of Buchanan, near whose elbow sat leading southern sympathizers.

The panic of 1857 also created a clamor for higher tariff rates. The Tariff of 1857 had lowered duties to about 20 percent, but hardly had the revised rates been placed on the books when financial misery descended like a black pall. Northern manufacturers noisily blamed their misfortunes on the low tariff and clamored for increased protection. Thus the panic of 1857 gave the Republicans two surefire economic issues for 1860: protection for the unprotected and farms for the farmless.

An Illinois Rail-Splitter Emerges

The Illinois senatorial election of 1858 now claimed the national spotlight. Senator Douglas's term was about to expire, and the Republicans decided to run against him a rustic Springfield lawyer, one Abraham Lincoln. The Republican candidate—6 feet, 4 inches in height and 180 pounds in weight—presented an awkward but arresting figure. Lincoln's legs, arms, and neck were grotesquely long; his head was crowned by coarse, black, and unruly hair; and his face was sad, sunken, and weather-beaten.

Lincoln was no silver-spoon child of the elite. Born in 1809 in a Kentucky log cabin to impoverished parents, he attended a frontier school for not more than a year; being an avid reader, he was mainly self-educated. All his life he said "git," "thar," and "heered." Although narrow-chested and somewhat stoop-shouldered, he shone in his frontier community as a wrestler and weight lifter, and spent some time, among other pioneering pursuits, as a splitter of logs for fence rails. A superb teller of earthy and amusing stories, he would sometimes plunge into protracted periods of melancholy.

Lincoln's private and professional lives had not been especially noteworthy. He married "above himself" socially, into the influential Todd family of Kentucky. After reading a little law, he gradually emerged as one of the dozen or so better-known trial lawyers in Illinois, although still accustomed to carrying important papers in his stovepipe hat. He was widely referred to as "Honest Abe," partly because he would refuse cases that he had to suspend his conscience to defend.

The rise of Lincoln as a political figure was less than rocketlike. After making his mark in the Illinois legislature as a Whig politician of the logrolling variety, he served one undistinguished term in Congress, 1847–1849. Until 1854, when he was forty-five years of age, he had done nothing to establish a claim to statesmanship. But the passage of the Kansas-Nebraska Act in that year lighted within him unexpected fires. After mounting the Republican **bandwagon**, he emerged as one of the foremost politicians and orators of the Northwest. At the Philadelphia convention of 1856, where Frémont was nominated, Lincoln actually received 110 votes for the vice-presidential nomination.

The Great Debate: Lincoln Versus Douglas

Lincoln, as Republican nominee for the Senate seat, boldly challenged Douglas to a series of joint debates. This was a rash act because the stumpy senator was prob-

bandwagon *In politics, a movement or candidacy that gains rapid momentum because of people's purported desire to join a successful cause.*

Lincoln expressed his views on the relation of the black and white races in 1858, in his first debate with Stephen A. Douglas:

"I, as well as Judge Douglas, am in favor of the race to which I belong, having the superior position. I have never said anything to the contrary, but I hold that notwithstanding all this, there is no reason in the world why the negro is not entitled to all the natural rights enumerated in the Declaration of Independence, the right to life, liberty, and the pursuit of happiness. I hold that he is as much entitled to those rights as the white man. I agree with Judge Douglas he is not my equal in many respects—certainly not in color, perhaps not in moral or intellectual endowment. But in the right to eat the bread, without leave of anybody else, which his own hand earns, he is my equal and the equal of Judge Douglas, and the equal of every living man."

ably the nation's most devastating debater. Douglas promptly accepted Lincoln's challenge, and seven meetings were arranged from August to October 1858.

The most famous debate came at Freeport, Illinois, where Lincoln nearly impaled his opponent on the horns of a dilemma. Suppose, he queried, the people of a territory should vote slavery down? The Supreme Court in the *Dred Scott* decision had decreed that they could not. Who would prevail, the Court or the people?

Douglas's reply, which came to be known as the "Freeport Doctrine," was that no matter how the Supreme Court ruled, slavery would stay down if the people voted it down. Laws to protect slavery would have to be passed by the territorial legislatures. These would not be forthcoming in the absence of popular approval, and black bondage would soon disappear.

The upshot was that Douglas defeated Lincoln for the Senate seat. The "Little Giant's" loyalty to popular sovereignty, which still had a powerful appeal in Illinois, probably was decisive. But Douglas, in winning Illinois, hurt his chances of winning the presidency, while further splitting his **splintering** Democratic party. After his opposition to the Lecompton Constitution for Kansas, and his further defiance of the Supreme Court at Freeport, southern Democrats were determined to break up the party (and the Union) rather than accept him. For his part, Lincoln lost the election but shambled into the national limelight as a leading northern spokesman and potential Republican nominee for president. The Lincoln-Douglas debate platform thus proved to be one of the preliminary battlefields of the Civil War.

splintering *Concerning the small political groups left after a larger group has divided or broken apart.*

John Brown: Murderer or Martyr?

The gaunt, grim figure of John Brown of bleeding Kansas infamy now appeared again in an even more terrible way. His fanatical scheme was to invade the South secretly with a handful of followers, call upon the slaves to rise, furnish them with arms, and establish a kind of black free state as a sanctuary. Brown secured several thousand dollars for firearms from northern abolitionists and finally arrived in hilly western Virginia with some twenty men. He seized the federal arsenal at scenic Harpers Ferry in October 1859, incidentally killing seven innocent people, including a free black, and injuring ten or so more. But the slaves failed to rise, and the wounded Brown and the remnants of his tiny band were quickly captured by U.S. Marines under the command of Lieutenant Colonel Robert E. Lee. "Old Brown" was convicted of murder and treason after a hasty but legal trial.

But Brown—"God's angry man"—was given every opportunity to pose and to enjoy martyrdom. He was clever enough to see that he was worth much more to the abolitionist cause dangling from a rope than in any other way. His demeanor during the trial was dignified and courageous, and he marched up the scaffold steps without flinching. So the hangman's trap was sprung, and Brown plunged not into oblivion but into world fame. A memorable marching song of the impending Civil War ran,

John Brown's body lies a-mould'ring in the grave,
His soul is marching on.

■ **Last Moments of John Brown, by Thomas Hovenden** Sentenced to be hanged, John Brown wrote to his brother, "I am quite cheerful in view of my approaching end, being fully persuaded that I am worth inconceivably more to hang than for any other purpose. . . . I count it all joy. 'I have fought the good fight,' and have, as I trust, 'finished my course.' " This painting of Brown going to his execution may have been inspired by the journalist Horace Greeley, who was not present but wrote that "a black woman with a little child stood by the door. He stopped for a moment, and stooping, kissed the child." That scene never took place, as Brown was escorted from the jail only by a detachment of soldiers. But this painting has become famous as a kind of allegorical expression of the pathos of Brown's martyrdom for the abolitionist cause.

> *Upon hearing of John Brown's execution, escaped slave and abolitionist Harriet Tubman (c. 1820–1913) paid him the highest tribute for his self-sacrifice:*
>
> "I've been studying, and studying upon it, and its clar to me, it wasn't John Brown that died on that gallows. When I think how he gave up his life for our people, and how he never flinched, but was so brave to the end; its clar to me it wasn't mortal man, it was God in him."
>
> *Not all opponents of slavery, however, shared Tubman's reverence for Brown. Republican presidential candidate Abraham Lincoln dismissed Brown as deluded:*
>
> "[The Brown] affair, in its philosophy, corresponds with the many attempts, related in history, at the assassination of kings and emperors. An enthusiast broods over the oppression of a people till he fancies himself commissioned by Heaven to liberate them. He ventures the attempt, which ends in little else than his own execution."

Online Study Center

**Primary source
Election of 1860**
college.hmco.com/pic/kennedybrief7e

martyr *One who is tortured or killed for adherence to a belief.*

border state *The northernmost slave states contested by North and South; during the Civil War the four border states (Maryland, Delaware, Kentucky, and Missouri) remained within the Union, though they contained many Confederate sympathizers and volunteers.*

The effects of Harpers Ferry were calamitous. In the eyes of the South, already embittered, "Osawatomie Brown" was a wholesale murderer and an apostle of treason. Many southerners asked how they could possibly remain in the Union while a "murderous gang of abolitionists" were financing armed bands to "Brown" them. Moderate northerners, including Republican leaders, openly deplored this mad exploit. But the South naturally concluded that the violent abolitionist view was shared by the entire North, dominated by "Brown-loving" Republicans.

Abolitionists and other ardent free-soilers were infuriated by Brown's execution. On the day of his hanging, free-soil centers in the North tolled bells, fired guns, lowered flags, and held rallies. Some spoke of "Saint John" Brown, and Ralph Waldo Emerson compared the new **martyr**-hero with Jesus. The gallows became a cross. E. C. Steman wrote,

> And Old Brown,
>   Osawatomie Brown,
> May trouble you more than ever
>   when you've nailed his coffin down!

The ghost of the martyred Brown would not be laid to rest.

Democrats Divide and Republicans Rise

Beyond question the presidential election of 1860 was the most fateful in American history. Deeply divided, the Democrats met in Charleston, South Carolina. Northern Democrats looked to Douglas as the leading candidate of their party, but southern "fire-eaters" regarded him as a traitor. After a bitter platform fight, delegates from most of the cotton states walked out of the convention. When the remainder could not scrape together the necessary two-thirds vote for Douglas, the entire body dissolved. The southerners' departure from the Democratic convention was the first tragic act of secession. Departure became habit forming.

The Democrats tried again in Baltimore. With northern Douglas Democrats firmly in the saddle, the cotton-state delegates again took a walk, and the rest of the convention enthusiastically nominated their hero. Angered southern Democrats promptly organized a rival convention in Baltimore and selected as their nominee the stern-jawed vice president, John C. Breckinridge, from the **border state** of Kentucky. The platform favored the extension of slavery into the territories and the annexation of slave-populated Cuba.

A middle-of-the-road group, fearing for the Union, hastily organized the Constitutional Union party. It consisted mainly of former Whigs and Know-Nothings. This "gathering of graybeards" met in Baltimore and nominated John Bell of Tennessee for the presidency on a platform of "the Union, the Constitution, and the enforcement of the law."

Elated Republicans, scenting victory in the breeze as their opponents split hopelessly, gathered in Chicago in a huge boxlike wooden structure called the Wigwam. William H. Seward was by far the best known of the contenders, but Seward's radical utterances, including his "irrepressible conflict" speech at Rochester in 1858,* had ruined his prospects. Lincoln, the favorite son of Illinois,

---

* Seward had referred to an "irrepressible conflict" between slavery and freedom, though not necessarily a bloody one.

was a stronger candidate because he had made fewer enemies than Seward. Overtaking Seward on the third ballot, he was nominated amid scenes of the wildest excitement.

The Republican platform had a seductive appeal for almost every important nonsouthern group: for the free-soilers, the nonextension of slavery; for northern manufacturers, a protective tariff; for immigrants, no abridgment of rights; and for farmers, free homesteads from the public domain.

Southern secessionists promptly served notice that the election of the "baboon" Lincoln would split the Union. In fact, "Honest Abe," though hating slavery, was no outright abolitionist. He campaigned quietly and issued no new statements in response to these threats. The most active opposition to southern extremism came from the "Little Giant" Douglas, who waged a vigorous speaking campaign, even in the South, and threatened to put the rope with his own hands around the neck of the first secessionist.

The returns, breathlessly awaited, proclaimed a sweeping victory for Lincoln (see the table and map, p. **000**).

The Electoral Upheaval of 1860

Awkward "Abe" Lincoln had run a curious race. To a greater degree than any other holder of the nation's highest office (except John Quincy Adams), he was a minority president. Sixty percent of the voters preferred some other candidate. He was also a sectional president, for in ten southern states, where he was not allowed on the ballot, he polled no popular votes. The election of 1860 was virtually two elections: one between Lincoln and Douglas in the North, the other between Bell and Breckinridge in the South. South Carolinians rejoiced over Lincoln's victory; they now had their excuse to secede. In winning the North the "rail-splitter" had split off the South.

Douglas, though scraping together only twelve electoral votes, made an impressive showing. He drew important strength from all sections and ranked a fairly close second in the popular-vote column. In fact, the Douglas Democrats and the Breckinridge Democrats together amassed 366,484 more popular votes than did Lincoln. But contrary to myth, Lincoln's electoral vote victory did not occur because his opponents were divided. Even if all the Democrats and Constitutional Unionists had united behind Douglas, Lincoln would have carried the populous northern states and therefore would still have won the electoral vote 169 to 134 instead of 180 to 123.

Significantly, the verdict of the ballot box did not indicate a strong sentiment for secession. Breckinridge, while favoring the extension of slavery, was no disunionist. Although the candidate of the "fire-eaters," he polled fewer votes in the slave states than Douglas and Bell combined. Despite its electoral defeat, the South was not badly off. Southerners still controlled the Supreme Court, both houses of Congress, and more than enough states to block any attempt to end slavery by constitutional amendment.

Online Study Center

Primary source
Preserving the Union
college.hmco.com/pic/kennedybrief7e

The Secessionist Exodus

But a tragic chain reaction of secession now began to erupt. South Carolina had threatened to go out if the "Illinois baboon" were elected, and in December 1860 a special convention called by the legislature carried out the threat by voting unanimously to secede. During the next six weeks, six other states of the Lower South followed the leader over the precipice: Alabama, Mississippi, Florida, Georgia, Louisiana, and Texas. Four more were to join them later, bringing the total to eleven.

With the eyes of destiny upon them, the seven seceders, formally meeting in Montgomery, Alabama, in February 1861, created a government known as

Online Study Center

Primary source
Louisiana Newspapers Respond
to Lincoln's Victory
college.hmco.com/pic/kennedybrief7e

Election of 1860

Candidate	Popular Vote	Percentage of Popular Vote	Electoral Vote
Lincoln	1,865,593	39.79%	180 (every vote of the free states except for 3 of New Jersey's 7 votes)
Douglas	1,382,713	29.40	12 (only Missouri and 3 of New Jersey's 7 votes)
Breckinridge	848,356	18.20	72 (all the cotton states)
Bell	592,906	12.61	39 (Virginia, Kentucky, Tennessee)

■ **Presidential Election of 1860 (with electoral vote by state)** A surprising fact is that Lincoln, often rated among the greatest presidents, ranks near the bottom in percentage of popular votes. In all eleven states that seceded, he received only a scattering of one state's votes—about 1.5 percent in Virginia.

■ **Presidential Election of 1860 (showing popular vote by county)** The vote by county for Lincoln was virtually all cast in the North. The northern Democrat, Douglas, was also nearly shut out in the South, which divided its votes between Breckenridge and Bell.

the Confederate States of America. As their president they chose Jefferson Davis, a dignified and austere former secretary of war and recent U.S. senator from Mississippi.

The crisis, already critical enough, was deepened by the "lame duck" interlude. Lincoln, although elected president in November 1860, could not take office until four months later, March 4, 1861. During this period of protracted uncertainty, when Lincoln was still a private citizen in Illinois, seven of the eleven deserting states pull out of the Union.

Meanwhile, the aging incumbent President Buchanan chose to wring his hands rather than secessionist necks. Surrounded by prosouthern advisers, Buchanan found constitutional and practical justifications for inaction. One important reason why he did not resort to force was that the tiny standing army of fifteen thousand men was widely scattered, fighting Indians in the West. Public opinion in the North, at that time, was far from willing to unsheathe the sword. Fighting would shatter all prospects of adjustment, and until the guns began to boom, there was still a flickering hope of reconciliation rather than a contested divorce. The weakness lay not so much in Buchanan as in the Constitution and in the Union itself. Ironically, when Lincoln became president in March, he essentially continued Buchanan's wait-and-see policy.

A Failed Compromise and Secession

Impending bloodshed spurred final and frantic attempts at compromise, most notably by Senator James Henry Crittenden of Kentucky. Crittenden proposed several constitutional amendments designed to appease the South. Slavery in the territories was to be prohibited north of 36°30′, but south of that line it was to be given federal protection in all territories existing or "hereafter to be acquired" (such as Cuba). Future states, north or south of 36°30′, could come into the Union with or without slavery, as they should choose. In short, the slavery supporters were to be guaranteed full rights in the southern territories, as long as they were territories, regardless of the wishes of the majority under popular sovereignty. Federal protection in a territory south of 36°30′ might conceivably, though improbably, turn the entire area permanently to slavery.

Lincoln flatly rejected the Crittenden scheme, which offered some slight prospect of success, and all hope of compromise evaporated. He had been elected on a platform that opposed the extension of slavery, and he felt that as a matter of principle he could not afford to yield, even though gains for slavery in the territories might be only temporary. Larger gains might come later in Cuba and Latin America. Crittenden's proposal, said Lincoln, "would amount to a perpetual covenant of war against every people, tribe, and state owning a foot of land between here and Tierra del Fuego."

Secessionists who parted company with their sister states left for a number of avowed reasons, mostly relating in some way to slavery. They were alarmed by the inexorable tipping of the political balance against them—"the despotic majority of numbers." The "crime" of the North, observed James Russell Lowell, was the census returns. Southerners were also dismayed by the triumph of the new sectional Republican party, which seemed to threaten their rights as a slaveholding minority. They were weary of free-soil criticism, abolitionist nagging, and northern interference, ranging from the Underground Railroad to John Brown's raid. "All we ask is to be let alone," declared President Jefferson Davis in an early message to his congress.

---

* The lame duck period was shortened to ten weeks in 1933 by the Twentieth Amendment (see the Appendix).

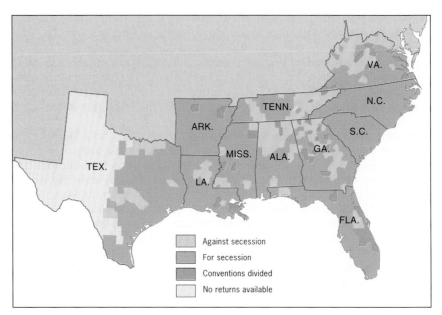

■ **Southern Opposition to Secession, 1860–1861 (showing vote by county)**
This county vote shows the opposition of the antiplanter, antislavery mountain whites in the Appalachian region. There was also considerable resistance to secession in Texas, where Governor Sam Houston, who led the Unionists, was deposed by secessionist hotheads.

vassalage *The service and homage given by a feudal subordinate to an overlord; by extension, any similar arrangement between political figures or entities.*

Many southerners supported secession because they felt sure that their departure would be unopposed, despite "Yankee yawp" to the contrary. They were confident that the clodhopping and cod fishing Yankee would not or could not fight. They also believed that northern manufacturers and bankers, so heavily dependent on southern cotton and markets, would not dare to cut their own economic throats with their own unionist swords.

Southern leaders regarded secession as a golden opportunity to cast aside their generations of "**vassalage**" to the North. An independent Dixieland could develop its own banking and shipping, trade directly with Europe, and forever rid itself of the threat of high tariffs. For decades this fundamental friction had pitted the manufacturing North against the agricultural South.

The principles of self-determination—of the Declaration of Independence—seemed to many southerners to apply perfectly to them. Few, if any, of the seceders felt that they were doing anything wrong or immoral. The thirteen original states had voluntarily entered the Union and now seven—ultimately eleven—southern states were voluntarily withdrawing from it.

Historical parallels ran even deeper. In 1776 thirteen American colonies, led by the rebel George Washington, had seceded from the British Empire by throwing off the yoke of King George III. In 1860–1861 eleven American states, led by the rebel Jefferson Davis, were seceding from the Union by throwing off the yoke of "King" Abraham Lincoln. With that burden gone, the South was confident that it could work out its own peculiar destiny more quietly, happily, and prosperously.

✪ Chapter Summary ✪

The 1850s were punctuated by a series of increasingly violent incidents and confrontations that deepened sectional hostility, until it broke out in the Civil War.

Harriet Beecher Stowe's *Uncle Tom's Cabin* fanned northern antislavery feeling. In Kansas, Douglas's "popular sovereignty" scheme proved a disaster, as proslavery and antislavery forces fought a bloody little preview of the Civil War. Prosouthern President Buchanan's support of the proslavery Lecompton Constitution alienated moderate northern Democrats like Douglas. Congressman Brooks's beating of Senator Sumner aroused passions in both sections.

The 1856 election signaled the rise of the sectionally based Republican party. The *Dred Scott* case delighted the South, while northern Republicans pledged defiance. The Lincoln-Douglas debates of 1858 made Lincoln a national Republican leader and deepened the controversy over slavery. The fanatical abolitionist John Brown's raid on Harpers Ferry made him a heroic martyr in the North but caused outraged southerners to fear a slave uprising.

In the campaign of 1860, the Democratic party split along sectional lines. Lincoln won the resulting four-way election with support only from the North. Seven southern states quickly seceded and organized the Confederate States of America.

As southerners enthusiastically cast off their ties to the hated North, lame-duck President Buchanan proved unable to act. The last-minute Crittenden Compromise effort failed because of Lincoln's conviction that it would allow slavery to expand into Latin America.

VARYING VIEWPOINTS

The Civil War: Repressible or Irrepressible?

Few topics have generated as much controversy among American historians as the causes of the Civil War. Interpretations of the great conflict have naturally differed according to section and have been charged with both emotional and moral fervor. Yet despite long and keen interest in the origins of the conflict, the causes of the Civil War remain as passionately debated today as they were a century ago.

The so-called Nationalist School of the late nineteenth century, typified by James Ford Rhodes, claimed that slavery caused the Civil War and credited the conflict with ending "the peculiar institution" and preserving the Union. But in the early twentieth century, progressive historians like Charles and Mary Beard argued that the war was not fought over slavery per se, but rather was a deeply rooted economic struggle between an industrial North and an agricultural South. Anointing the Civil War "the Second American Revolution," the Beards claimed that the war transferred the dominant class power in America from the southern plantation aristocracy to the rising class of northern industrialists.

Shaken by the disappointing results of World War I, a new wave of historians argued that the Civil War, too, had actually been a big mistake. James G. Randall and Avery Craven asserted that the war had been a "repressible conflict," and they attributed the bloody confrontation to overzealous reformers and blundering political leaders.

Following the Second World War, however, a neonationalist view, echoing the earlier views of Rhodes, began depicting the Civil War as an unavoidable conflict between two societies, one slave and one free. For Allan Nevins and David M. Potter, irreconcilable differences in morality, politics, culture, social values, and economic systems increasingly eroded the ties between the sections and inexorably set the United States on the road to Civil War.

Eric Foner and Eugene Genovese have emphasized each section's nearly paranoid fear that the survival of its way of life was threatened by the expansion of the other section. In *Free Soil, Free Labor, Free Men* (1970), Foner emphasized that most northerners detested slavery not because it enslaved blacks but because its rapid extension threatened the position of free white laborers. Genovese has argued that the South, convinced that its labor system was superior to the northern factory system, saw northern designs to destroy their way of life lurking at every turn.

More recently, historians of the "Ethnocultural School," especially Michael Holt, have offered a different analysis of how the collapse of the two established political parties caused the Civil War. They note that the two great political parties had earlier muted sectional differences over slavery by focusing on issues such as the tariff, banking, and internal improvements. According to this argument, it was the temporary *consensus* on almost all national issues *other than* slavery that enabled the slavery issue to rise to the fore. Slavery fueled the rise of purely regional parties that saw their political opponents as threats to their way of life, even to the life of the Republic itself.

20

Girding for War: The North and the South

1861–1865

I CONSIDER THE CENTRAL IDEA PERVADING THIS STRUGGLE IS THE NECESSITY THAT IS UPON US, OF PROVING THAT POPULAR GOVERNMENT IS NOT AN ABSURDITY. WE MUST SETTLE THIS QUESTION NOW, WHETHER IN A FREE GOVERNMENT THE MINORITY HAVE THE RIGHT TO BREAK UP THE GOVERNMENT WHENEVER THEY CHOOSE. IF WE FAIL IT WILL GO FAR TO PROVE THE INCAPABILITY OF THE PEOPLE TO GOVERN THEMSELVES.

ABRAHAM LINCOLN, MAY 7, 1861

Chapter Outline

⭐ The Attack on Fort Sumter, April 1861

⭐ The Crucial Border States

⭐ The Balance of Forces

⭐ Diplomacy and the Threat of European Intervention

⭐ Lincoln and Civil Liberties

⭐ Men in Uniform

⭐ Wartime Finance and Economy

⭐ Women and the War

⭐ The Fate of the South

Abraham Lincoln solemnly took the presidential oath of office on March 4, 1861, after having slipped into Washington at night, partially disguised to thwart assassins. He thus became president not of the *United* States of America, but of the dis-United States of America. Seven had already departed; eight more teetered on the edge. The girders of the unfinished Capitol dome loomed nakedly in the background, as if to symbolize the imperfect state of the Union. Before the nation was restored—and the slaves freed at last—the American people would endure four years of anguish and bloodshed, and Lincoln would face tortuous trials of leadership such as have been visited upon few presidents.

Focus Questions

1. Why did the South fire the first shots of the Civil War? How did that assault and Lincoln's call for troops galvanize both sides for war and lead to the secession of four more Southern states?
2. What were the strengths and weaknesses of both sides as they went to war, and why were the Border States so critical to the balance of forces?
3. Why was the issue of British or French recognition of the Confederacy so central to the diplomacy of both sides?
4. How did Lincoln and Davis each mobilize their nation's forces and shape the moral and political character of the struggle?
5. What were the economic and social consequences of the war for both sides, including its effects on the roles of women?

Chronology

1861	Confederate government formed.	**1862–**	
	Lincoln takes office (March 4).	**1864**	*Alabama* raids Northern shipping.
	Fort Sumter fired upon (April 12).		
	Four upper South states secede (April–June).	**1863**	Union enacts conscription.
	Morrill Tariff Act passed.		New York City draft riots.
	Trent affair.		National Banking System established.
	Lincoln suspends writ of habeas corpus.		
		1863–	Napoleon III installs Archduke Maximilian as
1862	Confederacy enacts conscription.	**1864**	emperor of Mexico.
	Homestead Act.		
		1864	*Alabama* sunk by Union warship.

The Menace of Secession

Lincoln's inaugural address was firm yet conciliatory: there would be no conflict unless the South provoked it. Secession, the president declared, was wholly impractical because, "physically speaking, we cannot separate."

Here Lincoln put his finger on a profound geographical truth. The North and South were bound inseparably together. If they had been divided by the Pyrenees Mountains or the Danube River, a sectional divorce might have been more feasible. But the Appalachian Mountains and the mighty Mississippi River both ran the wrong way.

Uncontested secession would create new controversies. What share of the national debt should the South be forced to take with it? What portion of the jointly held federal territories, if any, should the Confederate states be allotted—areas so largely won with Southern blood? How would the fugitive-slave issue be resolved? The Underground Railroad would certainly redouble its activity, and it would have to transport its passengers only across the Ohio River, not all the way to Canada. Was it conceivable that all such problems could have been solved without ugly armed clashes?

A *united* United States had hitherto been the paramount republic in the Western Hemisphere. If this powerful democracy broke into two hostile nations, the European nations would be delighted. They could gleefully transplant to America their ancient concept of the **balance of power**. Playing the no-less-ancient game of divide and conquer, they could incite one snarling fragment of the dis–United States against the other. The colonies of the European powers in the New World, notably those of Britain, would thus be made safer against the rapacious Yankees. And European imperialists, with no unified republic to stand across their path, could more easily defy the Monroe Doctrine and seize territory in the Americas.

balance of power *The distribution of political or military strength among several nations so that no one of them becomes too strong or dangerous.*

Secretary of State William H. Seward (1801–1872) entertained the dangerous idea that if the North picked a fight with one or more European nations, the South would once more rally around the flag. On April Fools' Day, 1861, he submitted to Lincoln a memorandum:

"I would demand explanations from Spain and France, categorically, at once. I would seek explanations from Great Britain and Russia. . . . And, if satisfactory explanations are not received from Spain and France . . . would convene Congress and declare war against them." Lincoln quietly but firmly quashed Seward's scheme.

South Carolina Assails Fort Sumter

The issue of the divided Union came to a head over the matter of federal forts in the South. As the seceding states left, they seized the United States' arsenals, mints, and other public property within their borders. When Lincoln took office, only two significant forts in the South still flew the Stars and Stripes. The more important of the pair was square-walled Fort Sumter, in Charleston harbor, with fewer than a hundred men.

Ominously, the choices presented to Lincoln by Fort Sumter were all bad. This stronghold had provisions that would last only a few weeks—until the middle of April 1861. If no supplies were forthcoming, its commander would have to surrender without firing a shot. Lincoln, quite understandably, did not feel that such a weak-kneed course squared with his obligation to protect federal property. But if he sent reinforcements, the South Carolinians would undoubtedly fight back; they could not tolerate a federal fort blocking the mouth of their most important Atlantic seaport.

After agonizing indecision, Lincoln adopted a middle-of-the-road solution. He notified the South Carolinians that an expedition would be sent to *provision* the garrison, though not to *reinforce* it. But to Southern eyes "provision" still spelled "reinforcement."

A Union naval force started on its way to Fort Sumter—a move that the South regarded as an act of aggression. On April 12, 1861, the cannon of the Carolinians opened fire on the fort, while crowds in Charleston applauded and waved handkerchiefs. After a thirty-four-hour bombardment, the dazed garrison surrendered.

The shelling of the fort electrified the North, which at once responded with cries of "Remember Fort Sumter!" and "Save the Union!" Hitherto, countless Northerners had been saying that if the Southern states wanted to go, they should not be pinned to the rest of the nation with bayonets. "Wayward sisters, depart in peace" was a common sentiment. But the assault on Fort Sumter provoked the North to a fighting pitch: the fort was lost, but the Union was saved.

Lincoln had turned a tactical defeat into a strategic victory. Southerners had wantonly fired upon the glorious Stars and Stripes, and honor demanded an armed response. Lincoln promptly (April 15) issued a call to the states for seventy-five thousand militiamen, and volunteers sprang to the colors in such enthusiastic numbers that many were turned away. On April 19 and 27, the president proclaimed a leaky blockade of Southern seaports.

The call for troops, in turn, aroused the South much as the attack on Fort Sumter had aroused the North. Lincoln was now waging war—from the Southern view an aggressive war—on the Confederacy. Virginia, Arkansas, and Tennessee, all of which had earlier voted down secession, reluctantly joined their embattled sister states, as did North Carolina. Thus the seven states became eleven as the "submissionists" and "Union shriekers" were overcome. Richmond, Virginia, replaced Montgomery, Alabama, as the Confederate capital—too near Washington for strategic comfort on either side.

Brothers' Blood and Border Blood

The only slave states left were the crucial Border States. This group consisted of Missouri, Kentucky, Maryland, Delaware, and later West Virginia—the "mountain white" area that somewhat illegally uprooted itself from Virginia in mid-1861. If the North had fired the first shot, some or all of these doubtful states probably would have seceded, and the South might well have succeeded. The border group actually contained a white population more than half that of the entire Confederacy. Lincoln reportedly said that he *hoped* to have God on his side but he *had* to have Kentucky.

In dealing with the Border States, President Lincoln did not rely solely on moral suasion but successfully used methods of dubious legality. In Maryland he declared **martial law** where needed and sent in troops because this state threatened to cut off Washington from the North. Lincoln also deployed Union soldiers in western Virginia and notably in Missouri, where they fought beside Unionists in a local civil war within the larger Civil War.

Any official statement of the North's war aims was profoundly influenced by the teetering Border States. At the very outset, Lincoln was obliged to declare publicly that he was not fighting to free the blacks. An antislavery declaration would no doubt

martial law *The imposition of military rule above or in place of civil authority during times of war and emergency.*

Lincoln wrote to the antislavery editor Horace Greeley in August 1862, even as he was about to announce the Emancipation Proclamation,

"If I could save the Union without freeing any slave, I would do it; and if I could save it by freeing all the slaves, I would do it; and if I could do it by freeing some and leaving others alone, I would also do that."

have driven the Border States into the welcoming arms of the South. An antislavery war was also extremely unpopular in the so-called Butternut region of southern Ohio, Indiana, and Illinois, originally settled largely by racially prejudiced Southerners (see "Makers of America: Settlers of the Old Northwest," p. 170). Lincoln insisted repeatedly—even though undercutting his high moral ground—that his paramount purpose was to save the Union at all costs. Thus the war began not as one between slave soil and free soil, but one for the Union—with slaveholders on both sides and many proslavery sympathizers in the North.

Slavery also colored the character of the war in the West. In Indian Territory (present-day Oklahoma), most of the Five Civilized Tribes—the Cherokees, Creeks, Choctaws, Chickasaws, and Seminoles—sided with the Confederacy. Some of these Indians, notably the Cherokees, owned slaves and thus felt themselves to be making common cause with the slaveowning South. The Confederate government invited the Native Americans to send delegates to the Confederate congress, and they in return supplied troops to the Confederate army. A rival faction of Cherokees and most of the Plains Indians, however, sided with the Union.

Unhappily, the conflict between "Billy Yank" and "Johnny Reb" was a brothers' war. There were many Northern volunteers from the Southern states, and many Southern volunteers from the Northern states. The "mountain whites" of the South sent north some 50,000 men, and the loyal slave states contributed some 300,000 soldiers to the Union. In many a family of the Border States, one brother rode north to fight with the Blue, another south to fight with the Gray. Senator Crittenden of Kentucky, who fathered the abortive Crittenden Compromise, fathered two sons: one became a general in the Union army, the other a general in the Confederate army.

The Balance of Forces

Online Study Center

Primary source
Enlisted Man Describes Life in a
Confederate Prison Camp
college.hmco.com/pic/kennedybrief7e

When war broke out, the South seemed to have great advantages. The Confederacy could fight defensively behind interior lines. The North had to invade the vast territory of the Confederacy, conquer it, and drag it bodily back into the Union. In fact, the South did not have to win the war in order to win its independence. If it merely fought the invaders to a draw and stood firm, Confederate independence would be won. Fighting on their own soil for self-determination and preservation of their way of life, Southerners at first enjoyed an advantage in morale as well.

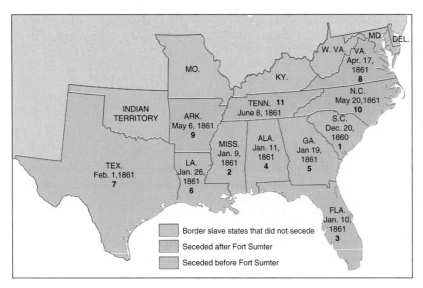

■ Seceding States (with dates and order of secession) Notice the long interval—nearly six months—between the secession of South Carolina, the first state to go, and that of Tennessee, the last state to leave the Union. These six months were a time of terrible trial for moderate Southerners. When a Georgia statesman pleaded for restraint and negotiations with Washington, he was rebuffed with the cry, "Throw the bloody spear into this den of incendiaries!"

Militarily, the South from the opening volleys of the war had the most talented officers. Most conspicuous among a dozen or so first-rate commanders was gray-haired General Robert E. Lee, whose knightly bearing and chivalric sense of honor embodied the Southern ideal. Lincoln had unofficially offered him command of the Northern armies, but when Virginia seceded Lee felt honor-bound to go with his native state. Lee's chief lieutenant for much of the war was black-bearded Thomas J. ("Stonewall") Jackson, a gifted tactical theorist and a master of speed and deception.

Besides their brilliant leaders, ordinary Southerners were also bred to fight. Accustomed to managing horses and bearing arms from boyhood, they made excellent cavalrymen and foot soldiers. Their high-pitched "rebel yell" ("yeeeahhh") was designed to strike terror into the hearts of fuzz-chinned Yankee recruits.

As one immense farm, the South seemed to be handicapped by the scarcity of its factories. Yet by seizing federal weapons, running Union blockades, and developing their own ironworks, Southerners managed to obtain sufficient weaponry. "Yankee ingenuity" was not confined to Yankees.

Nevertheless, as the war dragged on, grave shortages of shoes, uniforms, and blankets afflicted the South. Even with immense stores of food on Southern farms,

■ The Technology of War One of the new machines of destruction that made the Civil War the first mechanized war, this eight-and-a-half ton federal mortar sat on a railroad flatcar in Petersburg, Virginia, ready to hurl two-hundred-pound missiles as far as two and a half miles. This powerful artillery piece rode on the tracks of a captured Southern railroad—itself another artifact of modern technology that figured heavily in the war. Of the 31,256 miles of railroad track in the United States in 1861, less than 30 percent, or 9,283 miles, were in the Confederate states, soon reduced by Union capture and destruction to 6,000 miles. The Confederate government's failure to understand the military importance of railroads contributed substantially to its defeat.

Online Study Center

Primary source
Union Soldier's Opinion of the War, A
college.hmco.com/pic/kennedybrief7e

Immigration to United States, 1860–1866

Year	Total	Britain	Ireland	Germany	All Others
1860	153,640	29,737	48,637	54,491	20,775
1861	91,918	19,675	23,797	31,661	16,785
1862	91,985	24,639	23,351	27,529	16,466
1863	176,282	66,882	55,916	33,162	20,322
1864	193,418	53,428	63,523	57,276	19,191
1865*	248,120	82,465	29,772	83,424	52,459
1866	**318,568**	**94,924**	**36,690**	**115,892**	**71,062**

*Only the first three months of 1865 were war months.

civilians and soldiers often went hungry because of supply problems. "Forward, men! They have cheese in their haversacks," cried one Southern officer as he attacked the Yankees. Much of the hunger was caused by a breakdown of the South's rickety transportation system, especially where the railroad tracks were cut or destroyed by the Yankee invaders.

The economy was the greatest Southern weakness; it was the North's greatest strength. The North was not only a huge farm but a sprawling factory as well. Yankees boasted about three-fourths of the nation's wealth, including three-fourths of the thirty thousand miles of the railroads.

The North also controlled the sea. With its vastly superior navy, it established a blockade that, though a sieve at first, soon choked off Southern supplies and eventually shattered Southern morale. Its sea power also enabled the North to exchange huge quantities of grain for munitions and supplies from Europe, thus adding the output from the factories of Europe to its own.

The Union also enjoyed a much larger reserve of manpower. The loyal states had a population of some 22 million; the seceding states had 9 million people, including about 3.5 million slaves. Adding to the North's overwhelming supply of soldiery were immigrants from Europe, who continued to pour into the North even during the war (see the table on p. 296). Over 800,000 newcomers arrived between 1861 and 1865, most of them British, Irish, and German. Large numbers of them were induced to enlist in the Union armies. Altogether about one-fifth of the Union forces were foreign-born, and in some units military commands were given in four different languages.

Whether immigrant or native, ordinary Northern boys were much less prepared than their Southern counterparts for military life. Yet the Northern "clodhoppers" and "shopkeepers" eventually adjusted themselves to soldiering and became known for their discipline and determination.

The North was much less fortunate in its higher commanders. Lincoln was forced to use a costly trial-and-error method to sort out effective leaders from the many incompetent political officers, until he finally uncovered a general, Ulysses Simpson Grant, who was determined to slog his way to victory at whatever cost to life and limb.

In the long run, as the Northern strengths were brought to bear, they outweighed those of the South. But when the war began, the chances for Southern independence were unusually favorable—certainly better than the prospects for success of the thirteen colonies in 1776. The turn of a few events could easily have produced a different outcome.

The might-have-beens are fascinating. *If* the Border States had seceded, or *if* the uncertain states of the upper Mississippi Valley had turned against the Union, or *if* a wave of Northern defeatism had demanded an armistice, or *if* Britain and/or France had broken the naval blockade, the South might well have won. All of these possibilities almost became realities, but none of them actually occurred, and lacking their impetus, the South could not win.

Dethroning King Cotton

Successful revolutions, including the American Revolution of 1776, have generally succeeded because of foreign intervention. The South counted on it, did not get it, and lost. Of all the Confederacy's potential assets, none counted more weightily than the prospect of assistance from abroad. Europe's ruling classes, which had long abhorred the incendiary example of American democracy, were openly sympathetic to the semifeudal, aristocratic South.

In contrast, the masses of working people in Britain, and to some extent in France, were pulling and praying for the North. Many of them had read *Uncle Tom's Cabin*, and they sensed that the war—though at the outset officially fought only over the question of union—might extinguish slavery if the North emerged victorious. The hostility of British common folk to any official intervention on behalf of the South had a sobering effect on the British government. Yet the fact remained that British textile mills depended on the American South for 75 percent of their cotton supplies. Humanitarian sympathies aside, Southerners counted on hard economic need to bring Britain to their aid. Why did King Cotton fail them?

He failed in part because he had been so lavishly productive in the immediate prewar years of 1857–1860. When the shooting started in 1861, British manufacturers had on hand enormous surpluses of cotton piled up in their warehouses. The real pinch did not come until about a year and a half later, when thousands of hungry operatives were thrown out of work. But by this time Lincoln had announced his slave-emancipation policy, and the "wage slaves" of Britain were not going to demand a war to defend the slaveowners of the South.

The direct effects of the "cotton famine" in Britain were relieved in several ways. As Union armies penetrated the South, they captured or bought considerable supplies of cotton and shipped them to Britain; the Confederates also ran a limited quantity through the blockade. In addition, the cotton growers of Egypt and India, responding to high prices, increased their output. Finally, booming war industries in Britain, which supplied both the North and the South, relieved unemployment.

King Wheat and King Corn—the monarchs of Northern agriculture—proved to be more potent potentates than King Cotton. Blessed with ideal weather and the efficient harvesting of McCormick's mechanical reaper, the North produced bountiful crops during the war years. The grain was purchased by Britain, which suffered a series of bad harvests in the same period. If the British had broken the blockade to gain cotton, they would have provoked the North to war and would have lost this precious granary.

Foreign Flare-ups

America's diplomatic front has seldom been so critical as during the Civil War. The South never wholly abandoned its dream of foreign intervention, and Europe's rulers schemed to take advantage of America's distress.

The first major crisis with Britain came over the *Trent* affair, late in 1861. A Union warship cruising on the high seas north of Cuba stopped a British mail steamer, the *Trent*, and forcibly removed two Confederate diplomats bound for Europe.

Britons were outraged: upstart Yankees could not so boldly offend the Mistress of the Seas. War preparations buzzed, and red-coated troops embarked for Canada with bands blaring "I Wish I Was in Dixie." The London Foreign Office prepared an **ultimatum** demanding surrender of the prisoners and an apology. But luckily, slow communications gave passions on both sides a chance to cool. Lincoln came to see the *Trent* prisoners as "white elephants" and reluctantly released them.

Another major crisis in Anglo-American relations arose over the unneutral building in Britain of Confederate commerce-raiders, notably the *Alabama*. These

ultimatum *A final proposal or demand, as by one nation to another, that if rejected, will likely lead to war.*

loopholed *Characterized by small exceptions or conditions that enable escape from the general rule or principle.*

squadron *A special unit of warships assigned to a particular naval task.*

vessels were not warships within the meaning of **loopholed** British law because they left their shipyards unarmed and picked up their guns elsewhere. The *Alabama* escaped in 1862 to the Portuguese Azores and there took on weapons and a crew from two British ships that followed it.

The *Alabama* lighted the skies from Europe to East Asia with the burning hulks of Yankee merchantmen. All told, this "British pirate" captured over sixty vessels. Competing British shippers were delighted, while an angered North had to divert naval strength from its blockade for wild-goose chases. The *Alabama* was finally sunk by a Union cruiser off the coast of France in 1864.

A final Anglo-American crisis was touched off in 1863 by the Laird rams—two Confederate warships being constructed in Great Britain. Designed to destroy the wooden ships of the Union navy with their iron rams and large-caliber guns, they were far more dangerous than the swift and lightly armed *Alabama*. If delivered to the South, they probably would have sunk the blockading **squadrons** and then brought Northern cities under their fire. In retaliation, the North doubtless would have invaded Canada, and a full-dress war with Britain would have erupted. But America's minister to Britain, Charles Francis Adams, took a hard line, warning that "this is war" if the rams were released. At the last minute the London government relented and bought the two ships for the Royal Navy. Everyone seemed satisfied—except the disappointed Confederates.

Emperor Napoleon III of France, taking advantage of America's preoccupation with its own internal problems, dispatched a French army to occupy Mexico City in 1863. The following year he installed on the ruins of the crushed republic his puppet, the Austrian Archduke Maximilian, as emperor of Mexico. Sending the army and enthroning Maximilian were both flagrant violations of the Monroe Doctrine. Napoleon was gambling that the Union would collapse and thus America would be too weak to enforce its hands-off policy in the Western Hemisphere.

The North, as long as it was convulsed by war, pursued a walk-on-eggs policy toward France. But when the shooting stopped in 1865, Secretary of State Seward, speaking with the authority of nearly a million war-tempered bayonets, prepared to march south. Napoleon realized that his costly gamble was doomed. He reluctantly took French leave of his ill-starred puppet in 1867, and Maximilian soon crumpled ingloriously before a Mexican firing squad.

President Davis Versus President Lincoln

The Confederate government, like King Cotton, harbored fatal weaknesses. Its constitution, borrowing liberally from that of the Union, contained one deadly defect. Created by secession, it could not logically deny future secession to its constituent states. Jefferson Davis, while making his bow to states' rights, had in view a well-knit central government. But determined states' rights supporters fought him bitterly to the end. The Richmond regime encountered difficulty even in persuading certain state troops to serve outside their own borders.

Sharp-featured President Davis—tense, humorless, legalistic, and stubborn—was repeatedly in hot water. Although an eloquent orator and an able administrator, he at no time enjoyed real personal popularity and was often at loggerheads with his congress. At times there was serious talk of impeachment. Unlike Lincoln, Davis was somewhat imperious and inclined to defy rather than lead public opinion. Suffering acutely from neuralgia and other nervous disorders (including a tic), he overworked himself with the details of both civil government and military operations. No one could doubt his courage, sincerity, integrity, and devotion to the South, but the task proved beyond his powers.

Lincoln also had his troubles, but on the whole they were less prostrating. The North enjoyed the prestige of a long-established government, financially stable and fully recognized both at home and abroad. Lincoln, the inexperienced prairie politician, proved superior to the more experienced but less flexible Davis. Able to relax with droll stories at critical times, "Old Abe" grew as the war dragged on.

Online Study Center

Primary source
Allen Pinkerton and Others at Antietam
college.hmco.com/pic/kennedybrief7e

Tactful, quiet, patient, yet firm, he developed a genius for interpreting and leading a fickle public opinion. Holding aloft the banner of Union with inspiring utterances, he revealed charitableness toward the South and forbearance toward backbiting colleagues. "Did [Secretary of War Edwin] Stanton say I was a damned fool?" he reportedly replied to a talebearer. "Then I dare say I must be one, for Stanton is generally right and he always says what he means."

One of "Honest Abe" Lincoln's greatest challenges was to preserve the Union while upholding America's Constitutionally protected freedoms in wartime. He reluctantly concluded that if he did not abridge some civil liberties in order to quell the rebellion, there might not be a Constitution of a *united* United States to mend.

Congress was not in session when war broke out, so Lincoln proclaimed a blockade and increased the size of the federal army—something that only Congress can do under the Constitution (see Art. I, Sec. VIII, para. 12). He also advanced federal funds to private citizens without authorization, and suspended the precious writ of habeas corpus, so that anti-Unionists might be summarily arrested. These questionable acts led critics to call him a "Simple Susan Tyrant." But Lincoln believed that his ironhanded authority would be lifted once the Union was preserved. He pointedly remarked in 1863 that a man suffering from a "temporary illness" would not persist in taking bitter medicines for "the remainder of his healthful life."

Volunteers and Draftees: North and South

Ravenous, the gods of war demanded men—lots of men. Northern armies were at first manned solely by volunteers, with each state assigned a **quota** based on population. But in 1863, after volunteering had slackened off, Congress passed a federal conscription law for the first time on a nationwide scale in the United States. The provisions were grossly unfair to the poor. Rich boys, including young John D. Rockefeller, could hire substitutes to go in their places or purchase exemption outright by paying $300.

The draft was especially damned in the Democratic strongholds of the North, notably in New York City. A frightful riot broke out in 1863, touched off largely by underprivileged and antiblack Irish Americans who shouted "Down with Lincoln!" and "Down with the draft!" For several days the city was at the mercy of a burning, drunken, pillaging mob. Scores of lives were lost, and the victims included many lynched blacks. Elsewhere in the North, conscription met with resentment and an occasional minor riot.

More than 90 percent of the Union troops were volunteers, since social and patriotic pressures to enlist were strong. As able-bodied men became scarcer, generous bounties for enlistment were offered by federal, state, and local authorities. With money flowing so freely, an unsavory crew of "bounty brokers" and "substitute brokers" sprang up at home and abroad. They combed the poorhouses of the British Isles and western Europe, and many an Irishman or German was befuddled with whiskey and induced to enlist.

Like the North, the South at first relied mainly on volunteers. But since the Confederacy was much less populous, it scraped the bottom of its manpower barrel much more quickly. The Richmond regime, robbing both "cradle and grave" (ages seventeen to fifty), was forced to resort to conscription as early as April 1862, nearly a year earlier than the Union.

Confederate draft regulations also worked serious injustices. As in the North, a rich man could hire a substitute or purchase exemption. Slave owners or overseers with twenty slaves might also claim exemption. These special privileges, later modified, made for bad feelings among the less prosperous, many of whom complained that this was "a rich man's war and a poor man's fight." No large-scale draft riots broke out in the South, as in New York City. But Confederate conscription agents often found it prudent to avoid areas inhabited by sharp shooting mountain whites, who were branded "Tories," "traitors," and "Yankee lovers."

quota *The proportion or share of a larger number of things that a smaller group is assigned to contribute.*

The Dollar Goes to War

Blessed with the lion's share of the wealth, the North rode through the financial breakers much more smoothly than the South. Excise taxes on tobacco and alcohol were substantially increased by Congress. An income tax was levied for the first time in the nation's experience.

Customs receipts likewise proved to be important revenue-raisers. Early in 1861, after enough antiprotection Southern members had seceded, Congress passed the Morrill Tariff Act. It increased the existing duties some 5 to 10 percent, but these modest rates were soon pushed sharply upward by the necessities of war. The increases were designed partly to raise additional revenue and partly to provide more protection for the prosperous manufacturers who were being plucked by the new internal taxes. A protective tariff thus became identified with the Republican party, as American industrialists, mostly Republicans, waxed fat on these welcome benefits.

The Washington Treasury also issued **greenback** paper money totaling nearly $450 million at face value. This printing-press currency was inadequately supported by gold, and hence its value was determined by the nation's credit. Greenbacks thus fluctuated with the fortunes of Union arms and at one low point were worth only 39 cents on the gold dollar.

Borrowing far outstripped both greenbacks and taxes as a money raiser. The federal Treasury netted $2,621,916,786 through the sale of **bonds**, which bore interest and were payable at a later date. A financial landmark of the war was the National Banking System, authorized by Congress in 1863. Launched partly as a stimulant to the sale of government bonds, it was also designed to establish a standard bank-note currency. (The country was then flooded with depreciated "rag money" issued by unreliable bankers.) Banks that joined the National Banking System could buy government bonds and issue sound paper money backed by them. The war-born National Banking Act thus turned out to be the first significant step taken toward a unified banking network since 1836, when the "monster" Bank of the United States was killed by Andrew Jackson. Spawned by the war, this new system continued to function for fifty years, until replaced by the Federal Reserve System in 1913.

The impoverished South was beset by different financial woes. Customs duties were choked off as the coils of the Union blockade tightened. Large issues of Confederate bonds were sold at home and abroad, amounting to nearly $400 million. The Richmond regime also increased taxes sharply and imposed a 10 percent levy on farm produce. But in general, the states' rights Southerners were immovably opposed to heavy direct taxation by the central authority: only about 1 percent of the total income was raised this way.

As revenue began to dry up, the Confederate government was forced to print blueback paper money with complete abandon. "Runaway inflation" occurred as Southern presses continued to grind out the poorly backed treasury notes, totaling in all more than $1 billion. The Confederate paper dollar finally sank to the point where it was worth only 1.6 cents when Lee surrendered. Overall, the war inflicted a 9,000 percent inflation rate on the Confederacy, contrasted with 80 percent for the Union.

greenback *United States paper currency, especially that printed before the establishment of the Federal Reserve System.*

bond *In finance, an interest-bearing certificate issued by a government or business that guarantees repayment to the purchaser on a specified date at a predetermined rate of interest.*

A contemporary (October 22, 1863) Richmond diary portrays the ruinous effects of inflation:

"A poor woman yesterday applied to a merchant in Carey Street to purchase a barrel of flour. The price he demanded was $70. 'My God!' exclaimed she, 'how can I pay such prices? I have seven children; what shall I do?' 'I don't know, madam,' said he coolly, 'unless you eat your children.'"

"The North's Economic Boom

Wartime prosperity in the North was little short of miraculous. New factories, sheltered by the friendly umbrella of the new protective tariffs, mushroomed forth. Soaring prices, resulting from inflation, unfortunately pinched the laborers and white-collar workers to some extent, but manufacturers and businesspeople raked in "the fortunes of war." The Civil War bred a millionaire class for the first time in American history.

Yankee "sharpness" appeared at its worst during the war. Dishonest agents, putting profits above patriotism, palmed off aged and blind horses on government purchasers. Unscrupulous Northern manufacturers supplied shoes with cardboard soles and fast-disintegrating uniforms of reprocessed or "shoddy" wool, rather than virgin wool. Hence the reproachful term "shoddy millionaires" was doubly fair.

Newly invented laborsaving machinery enabled the North to expand economically, even though the cream of its manpower was being drained off to the fighting front. The sewing machine wrought wonders in fabricating uniforms and military footwear. Clattering mechanical reapers, which numbered about 250,000 by 1865, proved hardly less potent than thundering guns. They not only released tens of thousands of farm boys for the army but fed them their field rations.

Other industries were humming. The discovery of petroleum gushers in 1859 had led to a rush of "Fifty-Niners" to Pennsylvania. The result was the birth of a new industry, with its "petroleum plutocracy" and "coal oil Johnnies." Pioneers continued to push westward during the war, altogether an estimated 300,000 people. Major magnets were free gold nuggets and free lands under the Homestead Act of 1862.

The Civil War was a woman's war, too. The protracted conflict opened new opportunities for women. When men departed in uniform, women often took their jobs. In Washington, D.C., five hundred women clerks ("government girls") became government workers, with over one hundred in the Treasury Department alone. The booming military demand for shoes and clothing, combined with technological marvels like the sewing machine, likewise drew countless women into industrial employment. Before the war, one industrial worker in four had been female; during the war, the ratio rose to one in three.

Other women on both sides stepped up to the fighting front—or close behind it. More than four hundred women accompanied husbands and sweethearts into battle by posing as male soldiers. Other women took on dangerous spy missions. One woman was executed for smuggling gold to the Confederacy. Dr. Elizabeth Blackwell, America's first female physician, helped organize the U.S. Sanitary Commission to assist Union armies in the field. The commission trained nurses, collected medical supplies, and equipped hospitals. Commission work helped many women to acquire the organizational skills and the self-confidence that would propel the women's movement forward after the war. Heroically energetic Clara Barton and dedicated Dorothea Dix, superintendent of nurses for the Union army, helped transform nursing from a lowly service into a respected profession—and in the process opened up another major sphere of employment for women in the postwar era. Equally renowned in the South was Sally Tompkins, who ran a Richmond infirmary for wounded Confederate soldiers and was awarded the rank of captain by Confederate president Jefferson Davis. Still other women, North as well as South, organized bazaars and fairs that raised millions of dollars for the relief of widows, orphans, and disabled soldiers.

Online Study Center

Primary source
Zouave Soldier
college.hmco.com/pic/kennedybrief7e

Online Study Center

Primary source
Women and the Attack on Slavery
college.hmco.com/pic/kennedybrief7e

A Crushed Cotton Kingdom

The South fought to the point of exhaustion. The suffocation caused by the blockade, together with the destruction wrought by invaders, took a terrible toll. Possessing 30 percent of the national wealth in 1860, the South claimed only 12 percent in 1870. Transportation collapsed. The South was even driven to the economic cannibalism of pulling up rails from the less-used lines to repair the main lines. Window weights were melted down into bullets; gourds replaced dishes; pins became so scarce that they were loaned with reluctance.

To the brutal end, the South mustered remarkable resourcefulness and spirit. Women buoyed up their menfolk, many of whom had seen enough of war at first hand to be heartily sick of it. A number of women proposed that they cut off their

■ **Booth at the Sanitary Fair in Chicago, 1863**   The Chicago Sanitary Fair was the first of many such fairs throughout the nation to raise funds for soldier relief efforts. Mainly organized by women, the fair sold captured Confederate flags, battle relics, handicrafts like these potholders (right), and donated items, including President Lincoln's original draft of the Emancipation Proclamation (which garnered $3,000 in auction). When the fair closed, the Chicago headquarters of the U.S. Sanitary Commission had raised $100,000, and its female managers had gained organizational experience that many would put to work in the postwar movement for women's rights.

Online Study Center

**Primary source
Women's War, The**
college.hmco.com/pic/kennedybrief7e

long hair and sell it abroad to support the cause. Self-sacrificing Southern women took pride in denying themselves the silks and satins of their Northern sisters.

The chorus of a song, "The Southern Girl," touched a cheerful note:

*So hurrah! hurrah! For Southern Rights,
Hurrah!
Hurrah! for the homespun dress the Southern
ladies wear.*

At war's end, the Northern Captains of Industry had conquered the Southern Lords of the Manor. A crippled South left the capitalistic North free to work its own way, with high tariffs and other benefits. The manufacturing moguls of the North, ushering in the full-fledged Industrial Revolution, were headed for increased dominance over American economic and political life. Hitherto the agrarian "slavocracy" of the South had partially checked the rising plutocracy of the North. Now cotton capitalism lost out to industrial capitalism. The South of 1865 was to be rich in little but amputees, war heroes, ruins, and memories.

⭐ Chapter Summary ⭐

South Carolina's firing on Fort Sumter aroused the North for war. Lincoln's call for troops to suppress the rebellion drove four upper South states into the Confederacy. Lincoln used an effective combination of political persuasion and force to keep the deeply divided Border States in the Union.

The Confederacy enjoyed initial advantages of upper-class European support, military leadership, and a defensive position on its own soil. The North enjoyed the advantages of lower-class European support, industrial and population resources, and political leadership.

The British upper classes sympathized with the South and abetted Confederate naval efforts, while France's Emperor Napoleon III took advantage of the war to intervene in Mexico. But effective diplomacy and Union military success prevented foreign recognition and further assistance for the Confederacy.

Lincoln's political leadership proved effective in mobilizing the North for war, despite political opposition and resistance to his infringement on civil liberties. The North eventually mobilized its larger troop resources for war and ultimately turned to an unpopular and unfair draft system.

Northern economic and financial strengths enabled it to gain an advantage over the less-industrialized South. The changes in society opened new opportunities for women, who had contributed significantly to the war effort in both the North and South. Since most of the war was waged on Southern soil, the South was left devastated by the war.

21

The Furnace of Civil War

⌘

1861–1865

MY PARAMOUNT OBJECT IN THIS STRUGGLE IS TO SAVE THE
UNION, AND IS NOT EITHER TO SAVE OR TO DESTROY SLAVERY.

ABRAHAM LINCOLN, 1862

When President Lincoln issued his call to the states for seventy-five thousand militiamen on April 15, 1861, he envisioned them serving for only ninety days. Reaffirming his limited war aims, he declared that he had "no purpose, directly or indirectly, to interfere with slavery in the States where it exists." With a swift flourish of federal force, he hoped to show the folly of secession and rapidly return the rebellious states to the Union. But the war was to be neither brief nor limited. When the guns fell silent four years later, hundreds of thousands of soldiers on both sides lay dead, slavery was ended forever, and the nation faced the challenge of reintegrating the defeated but still recalcitrant South into the Union.

Focus Questions

1. Why did the Northern defeats in the First Battle of Bull Run and the Peninsula Campaign transform the Civil War from a limited struggle for the Union to a total war against slavery?
2. What was the significance of the Battles of Antietam, Vicksburg, and Gettysburg as key turning points of the Civil War?
3. What were the strengths and limits of the Emancipation Proclamation, and what role did African Americans play in the Union army and navy?
4. What were Lincoln's central political problems with the Copperheads and Peace Democrats, and how did he successfully outmaneuver them to win reelection in 1864?
5. How did Sherman's "March to the Sea" and Grant's 1864–1865 campaign in Virginia finally complete the Union's grand military strategy and force Lee's surrender?

Bull Run Ends the "Ninety-Day War"

Northern newspapers, at first sharing Lincoln's expectation of quick victory, raised the cry "On to Richmond!" In this yeasty atmosphere, a Union army of some thirty thousand men drilled near Washington in the summer of 1861. It was ill prepared for battle, but the press and the public clamored for action. Lincoln eventually concluded that an attack on a smaller Confederate force at Bull Run

Chronology

1861	First Battle of Bull Run.	**1863**	Final Emancipation Proclamation.
			Battle of Chancellorsville.
1862	Grant takes Forts Henry and Donelson.		Battle of Gettysburg.
	Battle of Shiloh.		Fall of Vicksburg.
	McClellan's Peninsula Campaign.		Fall of Port Hudson.
	Seven Days' Battles.		
	Second Battle of Bull Run.	**1864**	Sherman's march through Georgia.
	Naval battle of the *Merrimack* (the *Virginia*) and		Grant's Wilderness Campaign.
	the *Monitor.*		Battle of Cold Harbor.
	Battle of Antietam.		Lincoln defeats McClellan for presidency.
	Preliminary Emancipation Proclamation.		
	Battle of Fredericksburg.	**1865**	Lee surrenders to Grant at Appomattox.
	Northern army seizes New Orleans.		Lincoln assassinated.
			Thirteenth Amendment ratified.

(Manassas Junction), some thirty miles southwest of Washington, might be worth a try. If successful, it would demonstrate the superiority of Union arms. It might even lead to the capture of the Confederate capital at Richmond, one hundred miles to the south. If Richmond fell, secession would be thoroughly discredited, and the Union could be restored without damage to the economic and social system of the South.

Raw Yankee recruits swaggered out of Washington toward Bull Run on July 21, 1861, as if they were headed for a sporting event. Congressmen and spectators trailed along with their lunch baskets to witness the fun. At first the battle went well for the Yankees. But "Stonewall" Jackson's gray-clad warriors stood like a stone wall (here he won his nickname), and Confederate reinforcements arrived unexpectedly. Panic seized the green Union troops, many of whom fled in shameful confusion. The Confederates, themselves too exhausted or disorganized to pursue, feasted on captured lunches.

The "military picnic" at Bull Run, though not decisive militarily, had significant psychological and political consequences. Victory was worse than defeat for the South because it inflated an already dangerous overconfidence. Many of the Southern soldiers promptly deserted, feeling that the war was now surely over. Southern enlistments fell off sharply, and preparations for a protracted conflict slackened. Defeat was better than victory for the Union, because it dispelled all illusions of a one-punch war and caused the Northerners to buckle down to the staggering task at hand. It also set the stage for a war that would be waged not merely for the cause of Union but also, eventually, for the abolitionist ideal of emancipation.

"Tardy George" McClellan and the Peninsula Campaign

Northern hopes brightened later in 1861, when General George B. McClellan was given command of the Army of the Potomac, as the major Union force near Washington was now called. Red-haired and red-mustached, strong and stocky, McClellan ("Young Napoleon") was a brilliant, thirty-four-year-old West Pointer who had seen plenty of fighting in the Mexican War.

Cocky George McClellan embodied a curious mixture of virtues and defects. He was a superb organizer and drillmaster, and he injected splendid **morale** into the Army of the Potomac. Hating to sacrifice his troops, he was idolized by his men, who affectionately called him "Little Mac." But he was a perfectionist who seems not to have realized that an army is never ready to the last button and that wars cannot be won without running some risks. He consistently but erroneously believed that the

Online Study Center

Primary source
War in the East, The (early phase)
college.hmco.com/pic/kennedybrief7e

Online Study Center

Primary source
War in the East, The (middle phase)
college.hmco.com/pic/kennedybrief7e

Online Study Center

Interactive map
The War in the East, 1861–1862
college.hmco.com/pic/kennedy/brief7e

morale *The condition of courage, confidence, and willingness to endure hardship.*

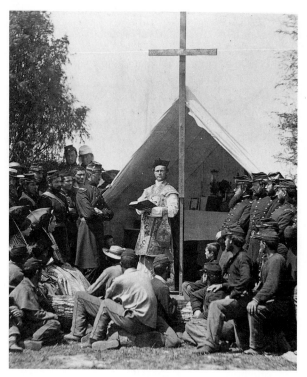

■ **Preparing for Battle** These troops of the 69th New York State Militia, a largely Irish regiment, were photographed attending Sunday morning Mass in May 1861, just weeks before the Battle of Bull Run. Because the regiment was camped near Washington, D.C., women were able to visit.

---

intelligence *In military affairs or diplomacy, specific information about an adversary's forces, deployments, production, and so on.*

proclamation *An official announcement or publicly declared order.*

Abraham Lincoln (1809–1865) treated the demands of George McClellan for reinforcements and his excuses for inaction with infinite patience. One exception came when the general complained that his horses were tired. On October 24, 1862, Lincoln wrote,

"I have just read your dispatch about sore-tongued and fatigued horses. Will you pardon me for asking what the horses of your army have done since the battle of Antietam that fatigues anything?"

---

enemy outnumbered him, partly because his **intelligence** reports from the head of Pinkerton's Detective Agency were unreliable. He was overcautious—Lincoln once accused him of having "the slows"—and he addressed the president in an arrogant tone that a less forgiving person than Lincoln would never have tolerated. Privately the general referred to his chief as a "baboon."

After threatening to "borrow" the army if it was not going to be used, Lincoln finally issued firm orders to move. A reluctant McClellan at last decided on a waterborne approach to Richmond. Moving up the narrow peninsula formed by the James and York Rivers, McClellan warily inched toward the Confederate capital in the spring of 1862 with about 100,000 men in what was called the Peninsula Campaign. After taking a month to capture historic Yorktown, which bristled with imitation wooden cannon, he finally came within sight of the spires of Richmond. Aided by "Jeb" Stuart's Confederate cavalry, General Robert E. Lee suddenly launched a devastating counterattack—the Seven Days' Battles—June 26–July 2, 1862. The Confederates slowly drove McClellan back to the sea. The Union forces abandoned the Peninsula Campaign as a costly failure, and Lincoln temporarily removed McClellan as commander of the Army of the Potomac.

Lee had achieved a brilliant, if bloody, triumph. Yet the ironies of his accomplishment are striking. If McClellan had succeeded in taking Richmond and ending the war in mid-1862, the Union would probably have been restored with minimal disruption, and slavery would have survived, at least for a time. By his successful defense of Richmond and defeat of McClellan, Lee had in effect ensured that the war would endure until slavery was uprooted and the Old South thoroughly destroyed. Lincoln himself now declared that the rebels "cannot experiment for ten years trying to destroy the government and if they fail still come back into the Union unhurt." He began to draft an emancipation **proclamation**.

Union strategy now turned toward total war. As finally developed, the Northern military plan had six components: first, slowly suffocate the South by blockading its coasts; second, liberate the slaves and hence undermine the economic foundations of the Old South; third, cut the Confederacy in half by seizing control of its Mississippi River backbone; fourth, chop the Confederacy to pieces by sending troops from Tennessee through Georgia and then the Carolinas; fifth, decapitate it by capturing its capital at Richmond; and sixth (this was Ulysses Grant's idea, especially), try everywhere to engage the enemy's main strength and grind it into submission.

The War at Sea

The blockade started leakily; it was not clamped down all at once but extended by degrees. Blockading was simplified by concentrating on the principal ports and inlets, where dock facilities were available for loading bulky bales of cotton. The blockade was further strengthened when Britain recognized it as binding and warned its shippers that they ignored it at their peril.

Blockade-running was risky but profitable, as the growing scarcity of Southern goods drove prices skyward. A leading rendezvous for successful runners was the West Indies port of Nassau, in the British Bahamas, where at one time thirty-five of the speedy ships rode at anchor. But the lush days of blockade-running finally passed as Union squadrons gradually pinched off the leading Southern ports from New Orleans to Charleston.

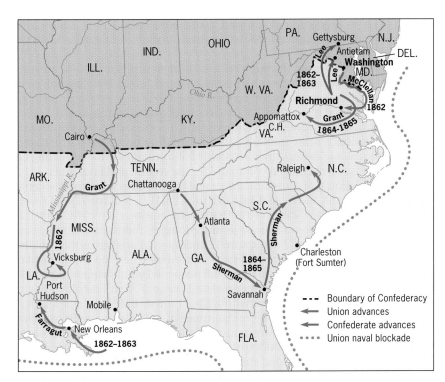

Online Study Center

Interactive map
The Anaconda Plan and the Battle of Antietam
college.hmco.com/pic/kennedy/brief7e

■ **Main Thrusts, 1861–1865** Northern strategists at first believed that the rebellion could be snuffed out quickly by a swift, crushing blow. But the stiffness of Southern resistance to the Union's early probes, and the North's inability to strike with sufficient speed and severity, revealed that the conflict would be a war of attrition, long and bloody.

The most alarming Confederate threat to the blockade came in 1862. Resourceful Southerners raised and reconditioned a former wooden United States warship, the *Merrimack*, and plated its sides with old iron railroad rails. Renamed the *Virginia*, this clumsy but powerful monster easily destroyed two wooden ships of the Union navy in the Virginia waters of Chesapeake Bay; it also threatened the entire Yankee blockading fleet.

A tiny Union ironclad, the *Monitor*, built in about one hundred days, arrived on the scene in the nick of time. For four hours, on March 9, 1862, the little "Yankee cheesebox on a raft" fought the wheezy *Merrimack* to a standstill. Britain and France had already built several powerful ironclads, but the first battle test of these new craft heralded the doom of wooden warships.

The Pivotal Point: Antietam

Robert E. Lee, having broken the back of McClellan's assault on Richmond, next moved northward. Emboldened by a victory at the Second Battle of Bull Run (August 29–30, 1862), Lee daringly thrust into Maryland. He hoped to strike a blow that would not only encourage foreign intervention but also seduce the still wavering Border State and its sisters from the Union. The Confederate troops sang lustily,

Thou wilt not cower in the dust,
Maryland! my Maryland!
Thy gleaming sword shall never rust,
Maryland! my Maryland!

A Confederate soldier assigned to burial detail after the Seven Days' Battles (1862) wrote,

"The sights and smells that assailed us were simply indescribable . . . corpses swollen to twice their original size, some of them actually burst asunder with the pressure of foul gasses. . . . The odors were so nauseating and so deadly that in a short time we all sickened and were lying with our mouths close to the ground, most of us vomiting profusely."

But the Marylanders did not respond to the siren song. The presence among the invaders of so many blanketless, hatless, and shoeless soldiers dampened the state's ardor.

Events finally converged toward a critical battle at Antietam Creek, Maryland. Lincoln, yielding to popular pressure, hastily restored "Little Mac" to active command of the main Northern army. His soldiers tossed their caps skyward and hugged his horse as they hailed his return. McClellan succeeded in halting Lee at Antietam on September 17, 1862, in one of the bitterest and bloodiest days of the war. Antietam was more or less a draw militarily. But Lee, finding his thrust parried, retired across the Potomac. McClellan, unaccountably failing to pursue the retreating Confederate army, was removed from command for the second and final time.

The landmark Battle of Antietam was one of the most decisive engagements of world history—probably the most decisive of the Civil War. Jefferson Davis was perhaps never again so near victory as on that fateful summer day. The British and French governments were on the verge of diplomatic mediation, and a certain Washington rebuff might well have spurred London and Paris into armed collusion with Richmond. But both Britain and France cooled off when the Union displayed unexpected power at Antietam, and their chill deepened with the passing months.

Bloody Antietam was also the long-awaited "victory" that Lincoln needed for launching his Emancipation Proclamation. Abolitionists like Wendell Phillips had long been clamoring for action. By midsummer of 1862, with the Border States safely in the fold, Lincoln was ready to move. But he believed that issuing such an edict on the heels of military failure would seem like an act of desperation.

Antietam served as the needed emancipation springboard. The halting of Lee's offensive was just enough of a victory to justify Lincoln's issuing, on September 23, 1862, the preliminary Emancipation Proclamation. This hope-giving document announced that on January 1, 1863, the president would issue a final proclamation. On the scheduled date he fully redeemed his promise, and the Civil War became a moral crusade and what Lincoln called a "remorseless revolutionary struggle." After January 1, 1863, Lincoln said, "The character of the war will be changed. It will be one of subjugation. . . . The [old] South is to be destroyed and replaced by new propositions and ideas."

Online Study Center

**Primary source
Confederate Offensive in the
West, The
college.hmco.com/pic/kennedybrief7e**

A Proclamation Without Emancipation

Lincoln's Emancipation Proclamation of 1863 declared "forever free" the slaves in those Confederate states still in rebellion. Bondsmen in the loyal Border States were not affected, nor were those in specific conquered areas in the South—all told, about 800,000. The tone of the document was dull and legalistic. But if Lincoln stopped short of a clarion call for a holy war to achieve freedom, he pointedly concluded his historic document by declaring that the Proclamation was an "act of justice" and calling for "the considerate judgment of mankind and the gracious favor of Almighty God."

The presidential pen did not formally strike the shackles from a single slave. Where Lincoln could presumably free the slaves—that is, in the loyal Border States—he refused to do so, lest he spur disunion. Where he could not—that is, in the Confederate states—he tried to. In short, where he *could* he would not, and where he *would* he could not. Thus the Emancipation Proclamation was stronger on proclamation than emancipation.

Yet much unofficial do-it-yourself liberation did take place. Thousands of jubilant slaves, learning of the proclamation, flocked to the invading Union armies, stripping already rundown plantations of their work force. In this sense the Emancipation Proclamation was heralded by the drumbeat of running feet. The slaves' presence in Union army camps helped put emancipation atop Lincoln's agenda and strengthened the moral cause of the Union at home and abroad. At the same time Lincoln's proclamation clearly foreshadowed the ultimate doom of slavery. This was legally achieved by actions of the individual states and by their ratification of the Thirteenth Amendment (see the Appendix) in 1865. The Emancipation Proclamation also fundamentally changed the nature of the war because it effectively removed any chance of a negotiated settlement. Both sides now knew that the war would be a fight to the finish.

Public reactions to the long-awaited proclamation of 1863 were varied. "God bless Abraham Lincoln," exulted the antislavery editor Horace Greeley in his *New York Tribune*. But many ardent abolitionists complained that Lincoln had not gone far enough. On the other hand, formidable numbers of Northerners, especially in the "Butternut" regions of the Old Northwest and the Border States, felt that he had gone too far. A Democratic rhymester quipped,

> *Honest old Abe, when the war first began,*
> *Denied abolition was part of his plan;*
> *Honest old Abe has since made a decree,*
> *The war must go on till the slaves are all free.*
> *As both can't be honest, will someone tell how,*
> *If honest Abe then, is he honest Abe now?*

Opposition mounted in the North against supporting an "abolition war." Many Boys in Blue, especially from the Border States, had volunteered to fight for the Union, not against slavery. Desertions increased sharply. The crucial congressional elections in the autumn of 1862 went heavily against the administration, particularly in New York, Pennsylvania, and Ohio. Democrats even carried Lincoln's Illinois, although they did not secure control of Congress.

The Emancipation Proclamation caused an outcry to rise from the South that "Lincoln the fiend" was trying to stir up the "hellish passions" of a slave insurrection. Many European aristocrats sympathized with the Southern protests. But the Old World working classes, especially in Britain, reacted otherwise. They sensed that the proclamation spelled the ultimate doom of slavery, and many laborers became more determined than ever to oppose intervention. Gradually the diplomatic position of the Union improved.

The North now had much the stronger moral cause. In addition to preserving the Union, it had committed itself to freeing the slaves. The moral position of the South was correspondingly diminished.

■ **The Killing Fields of Antietam** These Confederate corpses testify to the awful slaughter of the battle. The twelve-hour fight at Antietam Creek ranks as the bloodiest single day of the war, with more than ten thousand Confederate casualties and even more on the Union side. "At last the battle ended," one historian wrote, "smoke heavy in the air, the twilight quivering with the anguished cries of thousands of wounded men."

Blacks Battle Bondage

As Lincoln moved to emancipate the slaves, he also took steps to enlist blacks in the armed forces. Although some African Americans had served in the Revolution and the War of 1812, the regular army contained no blacks at the war's outset, and the War Department refused to accept those free Northern blacks who tried to volunteer. (The Union navy, however, enrolled many blacks, mainly as cooks, stewards, and firemen.)

But as manpower ran low and emancipation was proclaimed, black enlistees were accepted, sometimes over ferocious protests from Northern as well as Southern whites. By war's end some 180,000 blacks served in the Union armies, most of them from the slave states, but many from the free-soil North. Blacks accounted for about 10 percent of the total enlistments in the Union forces, on land and sea, and included two black Massachusetts regiments raised largely through the efforts of ex-slave Frederick Douglass.

Black fighting men unquestionably had their hearts in the war against slavery that the Civil War had become after Lincoln proclaimed emancipation. Participating in about five hundred engagements, they received twenty-two Congressional Medals of Honor—the highest military award.

> *Abraham Lincoln defended his policies toward blacks in an open letter to Democrats on August 26, 1863:*
>
> "You say you will not fight to free negroes. Some of them seem willing to fight for you; but, no matter. Fight you, then, exclusively to save the Union. I issued the proclamation on purpose to aid you in saving the Union."

Their casualties were extremely heavy; more than thirty-eight thousand died, whether from battle, sickness, or reprisals from vengeful masters. Many, when captured, were put to death as slaves in revolt. In one notorious case, several black soldiers were massacred after they had formally surrendered at Fort Pillow, Tennessee. Thereafter vengeful black units cried "Remember Fort Pillow!" as they swung into battle and vowed to take no prisoners.

For reasons of pride, prejudice, and principle, the Confederacy could not bring itself to enlist slaves until a month before the war ended. Meanwhile tens of thousands were impressed into building fortifications, supplying armies, and other war-connected activities. Slaves, moreover, were "the stomach of the Confederacy," for they kept the farms going while the white men fought.

In many ways the actions of Southern slaves hamstrung the Confederate war effort and subverted the institution of slavery. Fear of slave insurrection required many eligible young white men to serve as Confederate "home guards" far from the fighting front. Everyday forms of slave resistance and defiance increased, diminishing productivity and undermining discipline. As Union armies approached, escaping slaves served as spies, guides, and scouts. By war's end nearly half a million slaves took the ultimate risk of revolting "with their feet," abandoning their plantations. Although they stopped short of violent uprising, slaves contributed powerfully to the collapse of slavery and the disintegration of the antebellum Southern way of life.

Lee's Last Lunge at Gettysburg

After Antietam, Lincoln replaced McClellan as commander of the Army of the Potomac with General A. E. Burnside, whose ornate side-whiskers came to be known as "burnsides" or "sideburns." Protesting his unfitness for this responsibility, Burnside proved it when he launched a rash frontal attack on Lee's strong position at Fredericksburg, Virginia, on December 13, 1862. A chicken could not have lived in the line of fire, remarked one Confederate officer. More than ten thousand Northern soldiers were killed or wounded in "Burnside's Slaughter Pen."

A new slaughter pen was prepared when General Burnside yielded his command to "Fighting Joe" Hooker, an aggressive but headstrong officer. At Chancel-

■ **A Bit of War History: Contraband, Recruit, Veteran, by Thomas Waterman Wood, 1865–1866** This painting dramatically commemorates the contributions and sacrifices of the 180,000 African Americans who served in the Union army during the Civil War.

EXAMINING THE EVIDENCE

Abraham Lincoln's Gettysburg Address

Political speeches are unfortunately all too often composed of claptrap, platitudes, and just plain bunk—and they are frequently written by someone other than the person delivering them. But Abraham Lincoln's address at the dedication of the cemetery at Gettysburg battlefield on November 19, 1863, has long been recognized as a masterpiece of political oratory and as a foundational document of the American political system, as weighty a statement of the national purpose as the Declaration of Independence (which it deliberately echoes in its statement that all men are created equal) or even the Constitution itself. In just 272 simple but eloquent words that Lincoln himself indisputably wrote, he summarized the case for American nationhood.

1. What did Lincoln believe was at stake in the Civil War? (Conspicuously, he made no direct mention of slavery in this address.) Another speech that Lincoln gave in 1861 offers some clues. He said, "I have often inquired of myself what great principle or idea it was that kept this [nation] together. It was not the mere separation of the colonies from the motherland, but that sentiment in the Declaration of Independence which gave liberty not alone to the people of this country, but hope to the world, for all future time."

2. Using the text of the Gettysburg Address, consider: how does Lincoln use language and images of parent and child, conception, rebirth, and sacrifice to present the American nation as a living entity?

3. In Lincoln's view, how does the dead soldiers' "last full measure of devotion" hallow the cause of liberty and Union, and create new obligations for "we the living"?

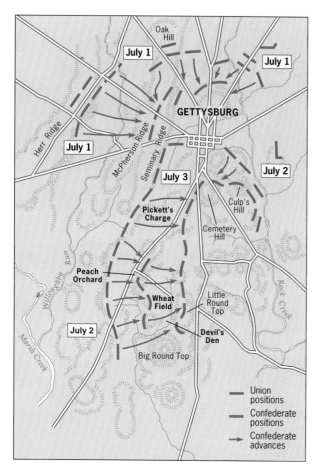

■ **The Battle of Gettysburg, 1863** With the failure of Pickett's charge, the fate of the Confederacy was sealed—though the Civil War dragged on for almost two more bloody years.

flank *The side of an army, where it is vulnerable to attack.*

court-martial *A military court or a trial held in such a court under military law.*

lorsville, Virginia, on May 2–4, 1863, Lee daringly divided his numerically inferior force and sent "Stonewall" Jackson to attack the Union **flank**. The strategy worked. Hooker, temporarily dazed by a near-hit from a cannonball, was badly beaten but not crushed. This victory was probably Lee's most brilliant, but it was dearly bought. Jackson was mistakenly shot by his own men in the gathering dusk and died a few days later. "I have lost my right arm," lamented Lee. Southern folklore relates how Jackson outflanked the angels while galloping into Heaven.

Lee now prepared to follow up his brilliant victory by invading the North again, this time through Pennsylvania. A decisive blow would add strength to the noisy peace prodders in the North and would also encourage foreign intervention—still a Southern hope. Quite by accident, the Northern army, now under the scholarly and unspectacular General George G. Meade, took its stand on the rolling hills near quiet little Gettysburg, Pennsylvania. There his 92,000 men in blue locked horns in furious combat with Lee's 76,000 gray-clad warriors. The battle seesawed across the rolling green slopes for three agonizing days, July 1–3, 1863, and the outcome was in doubt until the very end. The failure of General George Pickett's magnificent but futile charge finally broke the back of the Confederate attack—and broke the heart of the Confederate cause.

Pickett's charge has been called the "high tide of the Confederacy." It defined both the northernmost point reached by any significant Southern force and the last real chance for the Confederates to win the war. After Gettysburg, Lincoln spurned Southern efforts to reach a negotiated peace settlement between the parties. From now on the Southern cause was doomed. Yet the men of Dixie fought for nearly two years longer, through sweat, blood, and weariness of spirit.

Later in that dreary autumn of 1863, with the graves still fresh, Lincoln journeyed to Gettysburg to dedicate the cemetery. He read a two-minute address, following a two-hour speech by the orator of the day. Lincoln's noble remarks were branded by the *London Times* as "ludicrous" and by Democratic editors as "dishwatery" and "silly." The address attracted relatively little attention at the time, but the president was speaking for the ages.

The War in the West

Events in the western theater of the war at last provided Lincoln with an able general who did not have to be shelved after every reverse. Ulysses S. Grant had been a mediocre student at West Point, although he did do well in mathematics and horsemanship. After fighting creditably in the Mexican War, he was stationed at isolated frontier posts, where boredom and loneliness drove him to drink. Resigning from the army to avoid a **court-martial** for drunkenness, he failed at various business ventures, and when war came he was working in his father's leather store in Illinois for $50 a month.

Grant did not cut much of a figure. The shy and silent shopkeeper was short, stooped, awkward, stubble-bearded, and sloppy in dress. He managed with some difficulty to secure a colonelcy in the volunteers. From then on his military experience—combined with his boldness, resourcefulness, and doggedness—catapulted him on a meteoric rise.

Grant's first signal success came in the northern Tennessee theater. After heavy fighting, he captured Fort Henry and Fort Donelson on the Tennessee and Cumberland Rivers in February 1862. When the Confederate commander at Fort Donelson asked for terms, Grant bluntly demanded "an unconditional and immediate surrender."

Grant's triumph in Tennessee was crucial. It not only riveted Kentucky more securely to the Union but also opened the gateway to the strategically important region of Tennessee, and eventually to Georgia and the heart of Dixie. Grant next attempted to exploit his victory by capturing the junction of the main Confederate north-south and east-west railroads in the Mississippi Valley at Corinth, Mississippi. But a Confederate force foiled his plans in the gory Battle of Shiloh, just over the Tennessee border from Corinth, on April 6–7, 1862. The impressive Confederate showing at Shiloh confirmed that there would be no quick end to the war in the West.

Lincoln resisted all demands for the removal of "Unconditional Surrender" Grant, insisting, "I can't spare this man; he fights." When talebearers later told Lincoln that Grant drank too much, the president allegedly replied, "Find me the brand, and I'll send a barrel to each of my other generals."

Other Union thrusts were in the making. In the spring of 1862, a flotilla commanded by David G. Farragut joined with a Northern army to strike the South a staggering blow by seizing New Orleans. With Union gunboats both ascending and descending the Mississippi, the eastern part of the Confederacy was left with a jeopardized back door. Through this narrowing entrance, between Vicksburg and Port Hudson, flowed herds of vitally needed cattle and other provisions from Louisiana and Texas. The fortress of Vicksburg, located on a hairpin turn of the Mississippi, was the South's sentinel protecting the lifeline to the western sources of supply.

In command of the Union forces attacking Vicksburg, General Grant displayed rare skill and daring in the teeth of grave difficulties. The siege of Vicksburg was his best-fought campaign of the war. The beleaguered city at length surrendered, on July 4, 1863, with the **garrison** reduced to eating mules and rats. Five days later came the fall of Port Hudson, the last Southern bastion on the Mississippi. The spinal cord of the Confederacy was now severed, and, in Lincoln's quaint phrase, the Father of Waters at last flowed "unvexed to the sea."

The Union's victory at Vicksburg (July 4, 1863) came the day after the Confederate defeat at Gettysburg. The political significance of these back-to-back military successes was monumental. Reopening the Mississippi helped to quell strong peace agitation in southern Ohio, Indiana, and Illinois. Confederate control of the Mississippi had cut off that region's usual trade routes down the Ohio-Mississippi River system to New Orleans, thus adding economic pain to that border section's already shaky support for the "abolition war." The twin victories also conclusively tipped the diplomatic scales in favor of the North, as Britain stopped delivery of the Laird rams to the Confederates and as France killed a deal for the sale of six naval vessels to the Richmond government. By the end of 1863 all Confederate hopes for foreign help were irretrievably lost.

Sherman Scorches Georgia

General Grant, the victor of Vicksburg, was now transferred to the east Tennessee theater, where Confederates had driven Union forces from the battlefield of Chickamauga into the city of Chattanooga. Grant won a series of desperate engagements in November 1863 in the vicinity of besieged Chattanooga, including Missionary Ridge and Lookout Mountain ("the Battle Above the Clouds"). Chattanooga was liberated, the state was cleared of Confederates, and the way was thus opened for an invasion of Georgia. Grant was rewarded by being made general in chief. Georgia's conquest was entrusted to General William Tecumseh Sherman. Red-haired and red-bearded, grim-faced and ruthless, he captured Atlanta in September 1864 and burned the city in November of that year. He then daringly left his supply base, lived off the country for some 250 miles, and emerged at Savannah on the sea.

Online Study Center

Primary source
War in the West, The
college.hmco.com/pic/kennedybrief7e

---

garrison *A military fortress, or the troops stationed at such a fortress, usually designed for defense or occupation of a territory.*

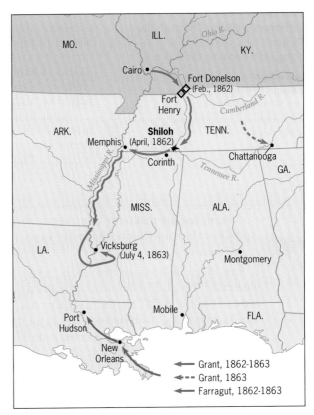

■ The Mississippi River and Tennessee, 1862–1863

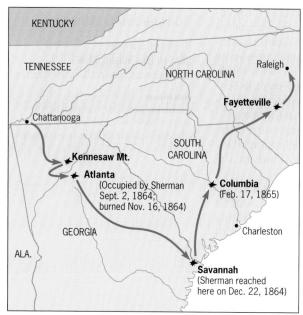

■ Sherman's March, 1864–1865

⚙ *Online Study Center*

Interactive map
Sherman's Campaign in the South
college.hmco.com/pic/kennedy/brief7e

⚙ *Online Study Center*

Primary source
Sherman's March Through the South
college.hmco.com/pic/kennedybrief7e

─────
pillaging *Plundering, looting, destroying property by violence.*

A letter picked up on a dead Confederate in North Carolina and addressed to his "deer sister" concluded that

it was "dam fulishness" trying to "lick shurmin." He had been getting "nuthin but hell & lots uv it" ever since he saw the "dam yanks," and he was "tirde uv it." He would head for home now, but his old horse was "plaid out." If the "dam yankees" had not got there yet, it would be a "dam wunder." They were thicker than "lise on a hen and a dam site ornerier."

Sherman's hated "Blue Bellies," sixty thousand strong, cut a sixty-mile-wide swath of destruction through Georgia. They burned buildings, leaving only the blackened chimneys ("Sherman's Sentinels"). They tore up railroad rails, heated them red-hot, and twisted them into "iron doughnuts" and "Sherman's hairpins." They bayoneted family portraits and ran off with valuable "souvenirs." "War . . . is all hell," admitted Sherman later, and he proved it by his efforts to "make Georgia howl." His major purposes were to destroy supplies destined for the Confederate army and to weaken the morale of the men at the front by waging war on their homes.

Sherman was a pioneer practitioner of total war. His success in "Shermanizing" the South was attested by increasing numbers of Confederate desertions. Although effective, his methods were unquestionably brutal. At times the discipline of his army broke down, as roving riffraff (Sherman's "bummers") engaged in an orgy of **pillaging**. "Sherman the Brute" was universally damned in the South.

After seizing Savannah as a Christmas present for Lincoln, Sherman's army veered north into South Carolina, where the destruction was even more vicious. Many Union soldiers believed that this state, the "hell-hole of secession," had wantonly provoked the war. The capital city, Columbia, was put to the torch. Crunching northward, Sherman's conquering army had rolled deep into North Carolina by the time the war ended.

The Politics of War

Presidential elections come by the calendar and not by the crisis. The election of 1864 fell most inopportunely in the midst of war.

Political infighting in the North added greatly to Lincoln's cup of woe. Factions within his own party, distrusting his ability or doubting his commitment to abolition, sought to tie his hands or even remove him from office. Conspicuous among his critics was a group led by the overambitious secretary of the Treasury, Salmon Chase. Especially burdensome to Lincoln was the creation of the Congressional Committee on the Conduct of the War, formed in late 1861. It was dominated by "radical" Republicans who pressed Lincoln zealously on emancipation.

Most dangerous of all to the Union cause were the Northern Democrats. Deprived of the talent that had departed with the Southern wing of the party, those Democrats remaining in the North were left with the taint of association with the seceders. Tragedy befell the Democrats—and the Union—when their gifted leader, Stephen A. Douglas, died of typhoid fever seven weeks after the war began. Unshakably devoted to the Union, he probably could have kept much of his following on the path of loyalty.

Lacking a leader, the Democrats divided. A large group of "War Democrats" patriotically supported the Lincoln administration, but tens of thousands of "Peace Democrats" did not. At the extreme were the so-called Copperheads, named for the poisonous snake that strikes without a warning rattle. Copperheads openly obstructed the war through attacks against the draft, against Lincoln, and especially, after 1863, against emancipation. They denounced the president as the "Illinois Ape" and condemned the "Nigger War." They commanded considerable political strength in the southern parts of Ohio, Indiana, and Illinois.

Notorious among the Copperheads was a sometime congressman from Ohio, Clement L. Vallandigham. This tempestuous character possessed brilliant oratorical gifts and unusual talents for stirring up trouble. A Southern partisan, he publicly demanded an end to the "wicked and cruel" war. In 1863 he was convicted and sentenced to prison by a **military tribunal** for treasonable utterances. Lincoln decided that if Vallandigham liked the Confederates so much, he ought to be banished to their lines. This was done. But Vallandigham was not so easily silenced. Making his way to Canada, he ran for the governorship of Ohio on foreign soil and polled a substantial but insufficient vote.

The Election of 1864

As the election of 1864 approached, Lincoln's precarious authority depended on his retaining Republican support while spiking the threat from the Peace Democrats and the Copperheads. Fearing defeat, the Republican party executed a clever maneuver. Joining with the War Democrats, it proclaimed itself to be the Union party. Thus the Republican party passed temporarily out of existence.

Lincoln's renomination at first encountered surprisingly strong opposition. Hostile factions whipped up considerable agitation to shelve him in favor of Secretary of the Treasury Chase. Lincoln was accused of lacking force, of not having won the war, and of having shocked many sensitive souls by his ill-timed and earthy jokes. But the "ditch Lincoln" move collapsed, and he was nominated by the Union party without serious dissent.

Lincoln's **running mate** was ex-tailor Andrew Johnson, a loyal War Democrat from Tennessee who had been a small slaveowner when the conflict began. He was placed on the Union party ticket to "sew up" the election by attracting War Democrats and voters in the Border States and, sadly, with no proper regard for the possibility that Lincoln might die in office.

Embattled Democrats—regulars and Copperheads—nominated the deposed and overcautious war hero, General McClellan. The Copperheads managed to force into the Democratic platform a plank denouncing the prosecution of the war as a failure. But McClellan, who could not otherwise have faced his old comrades-in-arms, repudiated this defeatist declaration.

The campaign was noisy and nasty. Lincoln's reelection was at first gravely in doubt. The war was going badly, and Lincoln himself gave way to despondency, fearing that political defeat was imminent. But the atmosphere of gloom was changed electrically, as balloting day neared, by a succession of Northern victories. Admiral Farragut captured Mobile, Alabama, after defiantly shouting the now famous order, "Damn the torpedoes! Go ahead." General Sherman seized Atlanta. General ("Little Phil") Sheridan laid waste the verdant Shenandoah Valley of Virginia so thoroughly that in his words, "a crow could not fly over it without carrying his rations with him."

The president pulled through, but nothing more than necessary was left to chance. At election time many Northern soldiers were furloughed home to support Lincoln at the polls. Other Northern soldiers cast their ballots at the front.

Bolstered by the "bayonet vote," Lincoln vanquished General McClellan by 212 electoral votes to 21, losing only Kentucky, Delaware, and New Jersey. But "Little Mac" ran a much closer race than the electoral count indicates. He netted a healthy 45 percent of the popular vote, 1,803,787 to Lincoln's 2,206,938, piling up much support in the Old Northwest, in New York, and also in his native state of Pennsylvania (see the map).

military tribunal *A special military court or commission charged with trying cases outside ordinary civilian or military courts.*

running mate *In American politics, the candidate for the lesser of two offices when they are decided together—for example, the U.S. vice presidency.*

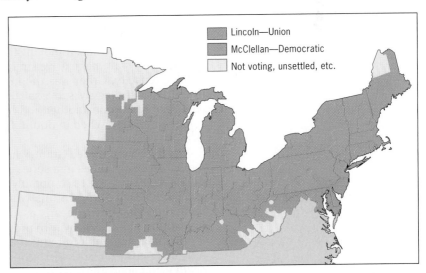

■ **Presidential Election of 1864 (showing popular vote by county)** Lincoln also carried California, Oregon, and Nevada, but there was a considerable McClellan vote in each. Note McClellan's strength in the Border States and in the southern tier of Ohio, Indiana, and Illinois—the so-called "Butternut" region.

■ **General Ulysses S. Grant and General Robert E. Lee** Trained at West Point, Grant (left) proved to be a better general than a president. Oddly, he hated the sight of blood and recoiled from rare beef. Lee (right), a gentlemanly general in an ungentlemanly business, remarked when the Union troops were bloodily repulsed at Fredericksburg, "It is well that war is so terrible, or we should get too fond of it."

One of the most crushing defeats suffered by the South was the defeat of the Northern Democrats in 1864. The removal of Lincoln was the last ghost of a hope for a Confederate victory, and Southern soldiers would wishfully shout, "Hurrah for McClellan!" When Lincoln triumphed, desertions from the sinking Southern ship increased sharply.

Grant Outlasts Lee

After Gettysburg, Grant was brought in from the West over Meade, who was blamed for failing to pursue the defeated but always dangerous Lee. Lincoln needed a general who, employing the superior resources of the North, would have the intestinal stamina to drive straight ahead, regardless of casualties. A soldier of bulldog tenacity, Grant was the man for this meat-grinder type of warfare. His overall basic strategy was to assail the enemy's armies simultaneously, so that they could not assist one another and hence could be destroyed piecemeal. His personal motto was "When in doubt, fight." Lincoln urged him "to chew and choke, as much as possible."

A grimly determined Grant, with more than 100,000 men, struck toward Richmond. He engaged Lee in a series of furious battles in the Wilderness of Virginia during May and June 1864, notably in the leaden hurricane of the "Bloody Angle" and "Hell's Half Acre." In this Wilderness Campaign Grant suffered about fifty thousand casualties, or nearly as many men as Lee had commanded at the start. But Lee lost about as heavily in proportion.

In a ghastly gamble, on June 3, 1864, Grant ordered a frontal assault on the impregnable position of Cold Harbor. Union soldiers advanced to almost certain death with papers pinned on their backs bearing their names and addresses. In a few minutes, about seven thousand men were killed or wounded.

Public opinion in the North was appalled by this "blood and guts" fighting, and critics assailed "Grant the Butcher." But Grant's reputation was undeserved, while Lee's was overrated. Lee's rate of loss (one casualty for every five soldiers) was the highest of any general in the war. By contrast, Grant lost one in ten. It was

Lee, not Grant, who turned the eastern campaign into a war of attrition fought in the trenches. Lee's new defensive posture in turn forced Grant into some brutal arithmetic. Grant could trade two men for one and still beat the enemy to his knees. "I propose to fight it out on this line," he wrote, "if it takes all summer." It did—and it also took all autumn, all winter, and a part of the spring.

In February 1865 the Confederates, tasting the bitter dregs of defeat, tried desperately to negotiate for peace between the "two countries." But Lincoln could accept nothing short of Union and emancipation, and the Southerners could accept nothing short of independence. So the tribulation wore on—amid smoke and agony—to its terrible climax.

The end came with dramatic suddenness. Rapidly advancing Northern troops captured Richmond and then cornered Lee at Appomattox Courthouse in Virginia, in April 1865. Grant—stubble-bearded and informally dressed—met with Lee on the ninth, Palm Sunday, and granted generous terms of surrender. Among other concessions, the hungry Confederates were allowed to keep their own horses for spring plowing.

Tattered Southern veterans—"Lee's Ragamuffins"—wept as they took leave of their beloved commander. The elated Union soldiers cheered, but they were silenced by Grant's stern admonition, "The war is over; the rebels are our countrymen again."

Lincoln traveled to conquered Richmond and sat in Jefferson Davis's evacuated office just forty hours after the Confederate president had left it. As he walked the blasted streets of the city, crowds of freed slaves gathered to see and touch "Father Abraham." One black man fell to his knees before the Emancipator, who said to him, "Don't kneel to me. This is not right. You must kneel to God only, and thank Him for the liberty you will enjoy hereafter." Sadly, as many freed slaves would discover, the hereafter of their full liberty was a long time coming.

The Martyrdom of Lincoln

On the night of April 14, 1865 (Good Friday), only five days after Lee's surrender, Ford's Theater in Washington witnessed its most sensational drama. A half-crazed, fanatically pro-Southern actor, John Wilkes Booth, slipped behind Lincoln as he sat in his box and shot him in the head. After lying unconscious all night, the Great Emancipator died the following morning. "Now he belongs to the ages," remarked the once-critical Secretary of War Edwin Stanton.

Lincoln expired in the arms of victory at the very pinnacle of his fame. From the standpoint of his reputation, his death could not have been better timed if he had hired the assassin. A large number of his countrymen had not suspected his greatness, and many others had even doubted his ability. But his dramatic death helped to erase the memory of his shortcomings and caused his nobler qualities to stand out in clearer relief.

The full impact of Lincoln's death was not at once apparent to the South. Hundreds of bedraggled ex-Confederate soldiers cheered, as did some Southern civilians and Northern Copperheads, when they learned of the assassination. But as time wore on, increasing numbers of Southerners perceived that Lincoln's death was a calamity for them. Belatedly they recognized that his kindliness and moderation would have been the most effective shields between them and vindictive treatment by the victors. The assassination unfortunately increased the bitterness of the North, partly because of the fantastic rumor that Jefferson Davis had plotted it.

A few historians have argued that if the rail-splitter had lived, he would have suffered Andrew Johnson's fate of being impeached by the embittered members of his own party who demanded harshness, not forbearance, toward the South. Lincoln no doubt would have clashed with Congress. But the surefooted and experienced Lincoln could hardly have blundered into the same quicksands that engulfed Johnson. Lincoln was a victorious president, and there is no arguing with victory. In addition to his powers of leadership refined in the war crucible, Lincoln possessed in full measure tact, sweet reasonableness, and an uncommon amount of common sense. Andrew Johnson, hot-tempered and impetuous, lacked all of

Online Study Center

Primary source
Wounded Escaping from the Burning Woods of the Wilderness
college.hmco.com/pic/kennedybrief7e

Online Study Center

Interactive map
Grant's Campaign Against Lee
college.hmco.com/pic/kennedy/brief7e

The Funeral of President Lincoln, New-York, April 25th, 1865.

■ **New York Mourns Lincoln's Death, April 25, 1865** Lincoln's body traveled by train to lie in state in fourteen cities before arriving at his final resting place of Springfield, Illinois. In New York City, 160,000 mourners accompanied the hearse as the funeral procession slowly made its way down Broadway. Scalpers sold choice window seats for four dollars and up. Blacks were barred from participating, until the mayor changed his mind at the last minute—but only if they marched at the rear. This souvenir stereo view, bringing the scene to three-dimensional life when seen through the popular device of a hand-held stereopticon, allowed many more Americans to observe the funeral than could be there in person.

these priceless qualities. Ford's Theater, with its tragic murder of Lincoln, set the stage for the wrenching ordeal of Reconstruction.

The Aftermath of the Nightmare

The Civil War took a grisly toll in gore, about as much as all of America's subsequent wars combined. Over 600,000 men died in action or of disease, and in all over a million were killed or seriously wounded. To its lasting hurt, the nation lost the cream of its young manhood and potential leadership.

Direct monetary costs of the conflict totaled about $15 billion. But this colossal figure does not include continuing expenses, such as pensions and interest on the national debt. The intangible costs—dislocations, wasted energies, lowered ethics, blasted lives, bitter memories, and burning hates—cannot be calculated.

The greatest constitutional decision of the century, in a sense, was written in blood and handed down at Appomattox Courthouse, near which Lee surrendered. The extreme states' righters were crushed. The national government, tested in the fiery furnace of war, emerged unbroken. Nullification and secession, those twin nightmares of previous decades, were laid to rest.

Beyond doubt the Civil War—the nightmare of the Republic—was the supreme test of American democracy. It finally answered the question, in the words of Lincoln at Gettysburg, whether a nation dedicated to such principles "can long endure." The preservation of democratic ideals, though not an officially announced war aim, was subconsciously one of the major objectives of the North.

Victory for Union arms also provided inspiration to the champions of democracy and liberalism the world over. The great English Reform Bill of 1867, under which Britain became a true political democracy, was passed two years after the

Online Study Center

Primary source
Appomattox Court House
college.hmco.com/pic/kennedybrief7e

Civil War ended. American democracy had proved itself, and its success was an additional argument used by the disfranchised British masses in securing similar blessings for themselves.

The "Lost Cause" of the South was lost, but few Americans today would argue that the end result was not for the best. The shameful cancer of slavery was sliced away by the sword, and African Americans were at last in a position to claim their rights to life, liberty, and the pursuit of happiness. The nation was again united politically, though for many generations it was still divided spiritually by the passions of the war. Grave dangers were averted by a Union victory, including the indefinite prolongation of the "peculiar institution," the unleashing of the "slave power" on weak Caribbean neighbors, and the transformation of the area from Panama to Hudson's Bay into an armed camp, with several hostile states constantly snarling and sniping at one another. America still had a long way to go to make the promises of freedom a reality for all its citizens, black and white. But emancipation laid the necessary groundwork, and a united and democratic United States was free to fulfill its destiny as the dominant republic of the hemisphere—and eventually of the world.

★ Chapter Summary ★

The Union defeats at Bull Run and the Peninsula Campaign ended Northern complacency about a quick victory, and also prevented a quick return of the South to the Union with slavery intact. George McClellan and other early Union generals proved unable to defeat the tactically brilliant Confederate armies under Lee. The Union naval blockade put a slow but devastating economic noose around the South.

The political and diplomatic dimensions of the war quickly became critical. In order to retain the border states, Lincoln first de-emphasized any intention to destroy slavery. But the Battle of Antietam in 1862 enabled Lincoln to prevent foreign intervention and turn the struggle into a total war against slavery. Blacks and abolitionists joined enthusiastically in a war for emancipation, but white resentment in part of the North created political problems for Lincoln.

The Union first gained military success in the West, succeeding at Vicksburg in cutting the Confederacy in half. Lee's failed invasion of the North ended at Gettysburg, and completely turned the military tide against the South. Southern resistance remained strong, with the hope that political defeatist ("Copperheads") would force a negotiated peace settlement. But the Union victories at Atlanta and Mobile assured Lincoln's success in the election of 1864 and ended the last Confederate hopes. The war ended the issues of disunion and slavery, but at a tremendous cost to both North and South.

VARYING VIEWPOINTS

What Were the Consequences of the Civil War?

With the end of the Civil War in 1865, the United States was permanently altered despite the reunification of the Union and the Confederacy. Slavery was officially banned, secession was a dead issue, and industrial growth surged forward. With the Union's victory, power rested firmly with the North, and it would orchestrate the future development of the country.

According to historian Eric Foner, the war redrew the economic and political map of the country. For example, the first twelve amendments to the Constitution, ratified before the war, had all served to limit government power. In contrast, the Thirteenth Amendment, which abolished slavery, and the revolutionary Fourteenth Amendment, which conferred citizenship on and guaranteed civil rights to all those born in the United States, marked unprecedented expansions of federal power.

Historian James M. McPherson has noted still other ways in which the Civil War extended the authority of the central government. It expanded federal powers of taxation, conscripted soldiers, developed a National Banking System and printed currency, bolstered federal courts, and established the first federal social welfare agency—the Freedmen's Bureau—to aid former slaves.

Some scholars have disputed whether the Civil War marked an absolute watershed in American history. They correctly note that racial inequality scandalously persisted after the Civil War despite the supposed protections extended by federal civil rights legislation. Others have argued that the industrial growth of the post–Civil War era had its real roots in the Jacksonian era. Regional differences between North and South endured, moreover, even down to the present day.

Yet the argument that the Civil War launched a modern America remains convincing. The lives of Americans, white and black, North and South, were transformed by the war experience. Industry entered a period of unprecedented growth. The emergence of new, national legal and governmental institutions marked the birth of the modern American state. All considered, it is hard to deny that the end of the Civil War brought one chapter of the nation's history to a close while opening another.

22

The Ordeal of Reconstruction

1865–1877

WITH MALICE TOWARD NONE, WITH CHARITY FOR ALL, WITH
FIRMNESS IN THE RIGHT AS GOD GIVES US TO SEE THE RIGHT,
LET US STRIVE ON TO FINISH THE WORK WE ARE IN, TO BIND UP
THE NATION'S WOUNDS, TO CARE FOR HIM WHO SHALL HAVE
BORNE THE BATTLE AND FOR HIS WIDOW AND ORPHAN, TO DO
ALL WHICH MAY ACHIEVE AND CHERISH A JUST AND LASTING
PEACE AMONG OURSELVES AND WITH ALL NATIONS.

ABRAHAM LINCOLN, SECOND INAUGURAL ADDRESS, MARCH 4, 1865

The battle was done, the buglers silent. Bone-weary and bloodied, the American people, North and South, now faced the staggering challenges of peace. Four questions loomed large. How would the South, physically devastated by war and socially revolutionized by emancipation, be rebuilt? How would the liberated blacks fare as free men and women? How would the Southern states be reintegrated into the Union? And who would direct the process of Reconstruction—the Southern states themselves, the president, or Congress?

Focus Questions

1. What were the major problems facing the South and the nation after the Civil War?
2. How did African Americans and whites, Southern and Northern, respond to the end of slavery and conduct race relations under new conditions of freedom?
3. How did Andrew Johnson's blunders enable the Radical Republicans to gain control of Reconstruction policy?
4. What were the actual effects of congressional Reconstruction in the South, and how did militant white opposition and growing northern apathy eventually bring an end to Reconstruction in the Compromise of 1877?
5. What were the primary successes and failures of Reconstruction, and what legacy did it leave for later generations of Americans?

The Problems of Peace

Other questions also clamored for answers. What should be done with the captured Confederate ringleaders? All Confederate officials were subject to charges of treason, and during the war a popular Northern song had been "Hang Jeff Davis to a Sour Apple Tree." Davis was clapped into prison for two years, but no **treason** trials were ever held. President Andrew Johnson pardoned all "rebel" leaders as a sort of Christmas present in 1868. Congress removed their **civil disabilities** thirty years later.

treason *The crime of betrayal of one's country, involving some overt act violating an oath of allegiance or providing illegal aid to a foreign state. In the United States, treason is the only crime specified in the Constitution.*

civil disabilities *Legally imposed restrictions of a person's civil rights or liberties.*

Online Study Center

**Primary source
Ruins in Charleston, South
Carolina**
college.hmco.com/pic/kennedybrief7e

Online Study Center

**Primary source
Ruins of the Arsenal at Richmond**
college.hmco.com/pic/kennedybrief7e

Online Study Center

**Primary source
Ruins of Atlanta**
college.hmco.com/pic/kennedybrief7e

Online Study Center

**Primary source
Ruins of Petersburg Railroad
Bridge**
college.hmco.com/pic/kennedybrief7e

Dismal indeed was the picture presented by the war-wracked South when the rattle of musketry faded. Not only had an age perished, but a civilization had collapsed, in both its economic and its social structure. The moonlight-and-magnolia Old South, largely imaginary in any case, had forever gone with the wind.

Handsome cities of yesteryear, such as Charleston and Richmond, were rubble-strewn and weed-choked. An Atlantan returned to his once-fair hometown and remarked, "Hell has laid her egg, and right here it hatched." Economic life had creaked to a halt. Banks and businesses had locked their doors, ruined by runaway inflation. Factories were smokeless, silent, dismantled. The transportation system had broken down completely. Efforts to untwist the rails corkscrewed by Sherman's soldiers proved bumpily unsatisfactory.

Agriculture—the economic lifeblood of the South—was almost hopelessly crippled. Once-white cotton fields yielded a lush harvest of nothing but green weeds. The slave-labor system had collapsed, seed was scarce, and livestock had been driven off by plundering Yankees. Pathetic instances were reported of men hitching themselves to plows, while women and children gripped the handles.

The princely planter aristocrats were humbled by the war—at least temporarily. Reduced to proud poverty, they faced charred and gutted mansions, lost investments, and almost worthless land. Their investment of more than $2 billion in slaves, their primary form of wealth, had evaporated with emancipation.

Beaten but unbent, many high-spirited white Southerners remained dangerously defiant. They cursed the "damn yankees" and spoke of "your government" in Washington instead of "our government." Conscious of no crime, these former Confederates continued to believe that their view of secession was correct and that the "lost cause" was still a just war. One popular anti-Union song ran,

*I'm glad I fought agin her, I only wish we'd won,
And I ain't axed any pardon for anything I've done.*

Such attitudes boded ill for the prospects of painlessly binding up the Republic's wounds.

Freedmen Define Freedom

Confusion abounded in the still-smoldering South about the precise meaning of "freedom" for blacks. Emancipation took effect haltingly and unevenly in different parts of the conquered Confederacy. As Union armies marched in and out of various localities, many blacks found themselves emancipated and re-enslaved. A North Carolina slave estimated that he had celebrated freedom about twelve times. In some regions planters stubbornly protested that slavery was legal until state legislatures or the Supreme Court might act. For many slaves the shackles of bondage were not struck off in a single mighty blow; long-suffering blacks often had to pry off their chains link by link.

The variety of responses to emancipation, by whites as well as blacks, illustrated the sometimes startling complexity of the master-slave relationship. Loyalty to the plantation master prompted some slaves to resist the liberating Union armies, while other slaves' pent-up bitterness burst violently forth on the day of liberation. In one instance, a group of Virginia slaves laid twenty lashes on the back of their former master—a painful dose of his own favorite medicine.

Prodded by the bayonets of Yankee armies of occupation, all

■ **Richmond Devastated** Charleston, Atlanta, and other Southern cities looked much the same, resembling bombed-out Berlin and Dresden in 1945.

Chronology

1863	Lincoln announces "10 percent" Reconstruction plan.
1864	Lincoln vetoes Wade-Davis Bill.
1865	Lincoln assassinated. Johnson issues Reconstruction proclamation. Congress refuses to seat Southern congressmen. Freedmen's Bureau established. Southern states pass Black Codes.
1866	Congress passes Civil Rights Bill over Johnson's veto. Congress passes Fourteenth Amendment. Johnson-backed candidates lose congressional election. *Ex parte Milligan* case. Ku Klux Klan founded.
1867	Reconstruction Act. Tenure of Office Act. United States purchases Alaska from Russia.
1868	Johnson impeached and acquitted. Johnson pardons Confederate leaders.
1870	Fifteenth Amendment ratified.
1870–1871	Force Acts.
1872	Freedmen's Bureau ended.
1877	Reconstruction ends.

masters were eventually forced to recognize their slaves' permanent freedom. The once-commanding planter would assemble his former human chattels in front of the porch of the "big house" and announce their liberty. Though some blacks initially responded to news of their emancipation with suspicion and uncertainty, they soon celebrated their newfound freedom. Many took new names in place of the ones given by their masters and demanded that whites formally address them as "Mr." or "Mrs."

Tens of thousands of emancipated blacks took to the roads, some to test their freedom, others to search for long-lost spouses, parents, and children. Emancipation thus strengthened the black family, and many newly freed men and women formalized "slave marriages" for personal and pragmatic reasons, including the desire to make their children legal heirs.

Whole communities sometimes moved together in search of opportunity. From 1878 to 1880, some twenty-five thousand blacks from Louisiana, Texas, and Mississippi surged in a mass exodus to Kansas.

The church became the focus of black community life in the years following emancipation. As slaves, blacks had worshiped alongside whites, but now they formed their own churches pastored by their own ministers. Black churches grew robustly. The 150,000-member black Baptist Church of 1850 reached 500,000 by 1870, while the African Methodist Episcopal Church quadrupled in size from 100,000 to 400,000 in the first decade after emancipation. These churches formed the bedrock of black community life, and they soon gave rise to other benevolent, fraternal, and **mutual aid societies.** All these organizations helped blacks protect their newly won freedom.

Emancipation also meant education for many blacks. Learning to read and write had been a privilege generally denied to them under slavery. Freedmen wasted no time establishing societies for self-improvement, which undertook to raise funds to purchase land, build schoolhouses, and hire teachers. With qualified black teachers in short supply, they turned for help to Northern white women sent by the American Missionary Association and to the federal government.

Online Study Center

Primary source
Black Recollections of Freedom's Impact
college.hmco.com/pic/kennedybrief7e

Online Study Center

Primary source
Black Recollections of Freedom's Impact
college.hmco.com/pic/kennedybrief7e

Houston H. Holloway, age twenty at the time of his emancipation, recalled his feelings upon hearing of his freedom:

"I felt like a bird out of a cage. Amen. Amen. Amen. I could hardly ask to feel any better than I did that day.... The week passed off in a blaze of glory."

The reunion of long-lost relatives also inspired joy; one Union officer wrote home,

"Men are taking their wives and children, families which had been for a long time broken up are united and oh! such happiness. I am glad I am here."

mutual aid societies *Nonprofit organizations designed to provide their members with financial and social benefits, often including medical aid, life insurance, funeral costs, and disaster relief.*

The Freedmen's Bureau

confiscation *Legal government seizure of private property without compensation.*

Abolitionists had long preached that slavery was a degrading institution. Now the emancipators were faced with the brutal reality that the former slaves were overwhelmingly unskilled, unlettered, without property or money, and with scant knowledge of how to survive as free people. To cope with this problem throughout the conquered South, Congress created the Freedmen's Bureau on March 3, 1865.

On paper at least, the bureau was intended to be a kind of primitive welfare agency. It was to provide food, clothing, and education both to freedmen and to white refugees. It was also authorized to distribute up to forty acres of abandoned or **confiscated** land to black settlers. Headed by General O. O. Howard, who later founded and served as president of Howard University in Washington, D.C., the bureau achieved its greatest successes in education. It taught an estimated 200,000 blacks how to read. Many former slaves had a passion for learning, partly because they wanted to close the gap between themselves and the whites and partly because they longed to read the Word of God.

But in other areas the bureau's accomplishments were meager—or even mischievous. Little confiscated Confederate land actually passed into black hands. Instead local administrators often collaborated with planters in expelling blacks from towns and cajoling them into signing labor contracts to work for their former masters. Still, the white South resented the bureau as a meddlesome federal interloper that threatened to upset white racial dominance. President Andrew Johnson, who shared the white supremacist views of most white Southerners, repeatedly tried to kill it, and it expired in 1872.

■ **Educating Young Freedmen and Women, 1870s** Freed slaves in the South regarded schooling as the key to improving their children's lives and the fulfillment of a long-sought right that had been denied blacks in slavery. These well-dressed school children are lined up outside their rural, one-room schoolhouse alongside their teachers, both black and white.

EXAMINING THE EVIDENCE

Letter from a Freedman to His Old Master, 1865
What was it like to experience the transition from slavery to freedom? Four million southern blacks faced this exhilarating and formidable prospect with the end of the war. For historians, recovering the African American perspective on emancipation is challenging. Unlike their white masters, freed blacks left few written records. But one former slave captured in a letter to his "Old Master" (whose surname he bore) the heroic determination of many blacks to build new independent and dignified lives for themselves and their families.

During the war Jourdon Anderson escaped slavery in Tennessee with his wife and two daughters. After relocating to the relative safety of Ohio, he received a communication from his former owner asking him to return. In his bold reply, reportedly "dictated by the old servant" himself, Anderson expressed his family's new expectations for life as free people and an uneasiness about his former master's intentions. He made reference to his "comfortable home," his daughters' schooling, the church that he and his wife were free to attend regularly, and the peace of mind that came with knowing that "my girls [would not be] brought to shame by the violence and wickedness of their young masters." To test the white man's sincerity, Anderson and his wife asked for the astronomical figure of $11,680 in back wages from decades as slaves. He closed by reiterating that "the great desire of my life is to give my children an education and have them form virtuous habits." This rare letter demonstrates that many black correspondents may have been illiterate, but they were hardly inarticulate. And they asserted themselves as parents, workers, and citizens not only from the distance of a former free state like Ohio but also deep within the former slave states of the South.

1. Was the tone of Anderson's letter (and postscript) serious, sarcastic, or tongue-in-cheek? What specific phrases support your answer?

2. How did the eventual accomplishments of Reconstruction correspond with the initial expectations of people like Anderson and his former owner?

3. What does this letter reveal about the complicated relationships between freedmen and their former masters? Is the relationship a "personal" one, or was it entirely dominated by Jourdan Anderson's having been held by Colonel P.H. Anderson as "property"?

Letter from a Freedman to his Old Master.

The following is a genuine document. It was *dictated* by the old servant, and contains his ideas and forms of expression. [Cincinnati Commercial.

DAYTON, Ohio, August 7, 1865.
To my Old Master, Col. P. H. ANDERSON, Big Spring, Tennessee.

SIR: I got your letter and was glad to find that you had not forgotten Jordan, and that you wanted me to come back and live with you again, promising to do better for me than anybody else can. I have often felt uneasy about you. I thought the Yankees would have hung you long before this for harboring Rebs, they found at your house. I suppose they never heard about your going to Col. Martin's to kill the Union soldier that was left by his company in their stable. Although you shot at me twice before I left you, I did not want to hear of your being hurt, and am glad you are still living. It would do me good to go back to the dear old home again and see Miss Mary and Miss Martha and Allen, Esther, Green and Lee. Give my love to them all, and tell them I hope we will meet in the better world, if not in this. I would have gone back to see you all when I was working in the Nashville Hospital, but one of the neighbors told me Henry intended to shoot me if he ever got a chance.

I want to know particularly what the good chance is you propose to give me. I am doing tolerably well here; I get $25 a month, with victuals and clothing; have a comfortable home for Mandy (the folks here call her Mrs. Anderson), and the children, Milly Jane and Grundy, go to school and are learning well; the teacher says Grundy has a head for a preacher. They go to Sunday-School, and Mandy and me attend church

As to my freedom, which you say I can have, there is nothing to be gained on that score, as I got my free-papers in 1864 from the Provost-Marshal-General of the Department at Nashville. Mandy says she would be afraid to go back without some proof that you are sincerely disposed to treat us justly and kindly—and we have concluded to test your sincerity by asking you to send us our wages for the time we served you. This will make us forget and forgive old sores, and rely on your justice and friendship in the future. I served you faithfully for thirty-two years, and Mandy twenty years, at $25 a month for me, and $2 a week for Mandy. Our earnings would amount to $11,680. Add to this the interest for the time our wages has been kept back and deduct what you paid for our clothing and three doctor's visits to me, and pulling a tooth for Mandy, and the balance will show what we are in justice entitled to. Please send the money by Adams Express, in care of V. Winters, esq., Dayton, Ohio. If you fail to pay us for faithful labors in the past we can have little faith in your promises in the future.

P. S.—Say howdy to George Carter, and thank him for taking the pistol from you when you were shooting at me.

Women from the North enthusiastically embraced the opportunity to go south and teach in Freedmen's Bureau schools for emancipated blacks. One volunteer explained her motives:

"I thought I must do something, not having money at my command, what could I do but give myself to the work. . . . I would go to them, and give them my life if necessary."

Johnson: The Tailor President

Few presidents have ever been faced with a more perplexing sea of troubles than that confronting Andrew Johnson. What manner of man was this dark-eyed, black-haired Tennessean, now chief executive by virtue of the bullet that killed Lincoln?

No citizen, not even Lincoln, ever reached the White House from humbler beginnings. Born to impoverished parents in North Carolina and orphaned early, Johnson never attended school but was apprenticed to a tailor at age ten. Ambitious to get ahead, he taught himself to read, and later his wife taught him to write and do simple arithmetic. Like many another self-made man, he was inclined to overpraise his maker.

Johnson early became active in politics in Tennessee, where he had moved when seventeen years old. He shone as an impassioned champion of the poor whites against the planter aristocrats, and as a two-fisted stump speaker before angry and heckling crowds. Elected to Congress, he attracted much favorable attention in the North when he refused to secede with his own state. After Tennessee was partially liberated by Union armies, he was appointed war governor of the state.

Political exigency next thrust Johnson into the vice presidency. Lincoln's Union party in 1864 needed to attract support from the War Democrats and other pro-Southern elements, and Johnson, a Democrat, seemed to be the ideal man.

"Old Andy" Johnson was no doubt a man of parts—unpolished parts. He was intelligent, able, forceful, and steadfastly devoted to duty and to the Constitution. Yet the man who had raised himself from the tailor's bench to the president's chair was a misfit. A Southerner who did not understand the North, a Tennessean who had earned the distrust of the South, a Democrat who had never been accepted by the Republicans, a president who had not been elected to the office, he was not at home in a Republican White House. Hotheaded, contentious, and stubborn, he was the wrong man in the wrong place at the wrong time. A Reconstruction policy devised by the angels might well have failed in his tactless hands.

Presidential Reconstruction

Even before the shooting war had ended, the political war over Reconstruction had begun. Abraham Lincoln believed that the Southern states had never legally withdrawn from the Union. Their formal restoration to the Union would therefore be relatively simple. Accordingly, Lincoln in 1863 proclaimed his "10 percent" Reconstruction plan. It decreed that a state could be reintegrated into the Union when 10 percent of its voters in the presidential election of 1860 had taken an oath of allegiance to the United States and pledged to abide by emancipation. The next step would be formal erection of a state government. Lincoln would then recognize the purified regime.

Lincoln's proclamation provoked a sharp reaction in Congress, where Republicans feared the restoration of the planter aristocracy to power and the possible re-enslavement of blacks. Republicans therefore rammed through Congress in 1864 the Wade-Davis Bill. The bill required that 50 percent of a state's voters take the oath of allegiance and demanded stronger safeguards for emancipation than Lincoln's as the price of readmission. Republicans were outraged when Lincoln "**pocket-vetoed**" this bill by refusing to sign it after Congress had adjourned.

The controversy surrounding the Wade-Davis Bill had revealed deep differences between the president and Congress. Unlike Lincoln, many in Congress insisted that the seceders had indeed left the Union—had "committed suicide" as republican states—and had therefore forfeited all their rights. They could be readmitted only as "conquered provinces" on such conditions as Congress should decree.

pocket veto *The presidential act of blocking a Congressionally passed law not by direct veto but by simply refusing to sign it at the end of a session. (A president can pocket-veto a bill within ten days of a session's end or after.)*

The episode further revealed differences among two emerging Republican factions, moderates and radicals. The majority moderate group tended to agree with Lincoln that the seceded states should be restored to the Union as simply and swiftly as reasonable—though on Congress's terms, not the president's. The minority radical group believed that before the South could be restored, its social structure should be uprooted, the haughty planters punished, and the newly emancipated blacks protected by federal power.

After President Lincoln's assassination in April 1865, some radicals hoped that spiteful Andy Johnson, who shared their hatred for the planter aristocracy, would also share their desire to reconstruct the South with a rod of iron. But Johnson soon disillusioned them. He quickly recognized several of Lincoln's 10 percent governments, and on May 29, 1865, he issued his own Reconstruction proclamation. It disfranchised certain leading Confederates and called for special state conventions, which were required to repeal secession, repudiate all Confederate debts, and ratify the slave-freeing Thirteenth Amendment.

Johnson, savoring his dominance over the high-toned aristocrats who now begged his favor, granted pardons in abundance. Bolstered by the political resurrection of the planter elite, the recently rebellious states moved rapidly in the second half of 1865 to organize governments. But as the pattern of the new governments became clear, Republicans of all stripes grew furious.

The Baleful Black Codes

Among the first acts of the new Southern regimes sanctioned by Johnson was the passage of the iron-toothed Black Codes. These laws were designed to regulate the affairs of the emancipated blacks, much as the slave statutes had done in pre–Civil War days. The Black Codes aimed, first of all, to ensure a stable and subservient labor force. Dire penalties were therefore imposed by the codes on blacks who "jumped" their labor contracts, which usually committed them to work for the same employer for one year, and generally at pittance wages.

The codes also sought to restore as nearly as possible the pre-emancipation system of race relations. Freedom was legally recognized, as were some other privileges, such as the right to marry. But all the codes forbade a black to serve on a jury or vote, and some even barred blacks from renting or leasing land.

These oppressive laws mocked the ideal of freedom, so recently purchased by buckets of blood. The Black Codes imposed terrible burdens on the unfettered blacks, struggling against mistreatment and poverty to make their way as free people. Thousands of impoverished former slaves slipped into virtual **peonage** as **sharecropper** farmers, as did many landless whites.

The Black Codes made an ugly impression in the North. If the former slaves were being re-enslaved, people asked one another, had not the Boys in Blue spilled their blood in vain? Had the North really won the war?

peonage *A system in which debtors are held in servitude, to labor for their creditors.*

sharecropper *An agricultural system in which a tenant receives land, tools, and seed on credit and pledges in return a share of the crop to the creditor.*

Congressional Reconstruction

These questions grew more insistent when the congressional delegations from the newly reconstituted Southern states presented themselves in the Capitol in December 1865. To the shock and disgust of the Republicans, many former Confederate leaders were on hand to claim their seats.

The appearance of these ex-rebels was a natural but costly blunder. Voters of the South, seeking able representatives, had turned instinctively to their experienced statesmen. But most of the Southern leaders were tainted by active association with the "lost cause." Among them were four former Confederate generals, five colonels, and various members of the Richmond cabinet and Congress. Worst of all, there was the shrimpy but brainy Alexander Stephens, ex–vice president of the Confederacy, still under indictment for treason.

The presence of these "whitewashed rebels" infuriated the Republicans in Congress. The war had been fought to restore the Union, but not on these kinds of terms. Most Republicans balked at giving up the political advantage they had enjoyed while the South had been "out" from 1861 to 1865. They had passed much legislation that favored the North, such as the Morrill Act, the Pacific Railroad Act, and the Homestead Act. On the first day of the congressional session, December 4, 1865, they banged shut the door in the face of the newly elected Southern delegations.

Looking to the future, the Republicans were alarmed to realize that a restored South would be stronger than ever in national politics. Before the war a black slave had counted as three-fifths of a person in apportioning congressional representation. But now, owing to full counting of free blacks, the eleven rebel states were entitled to twelve more votes in Congress, and twelve more presidential electoral votes, than they had previously enjoyed. Again, angry voices in the North raised the cry, Who won the war?

Republicans had good reason to fear that ultimately they might be elbowed aside. Southerners might join hands with Democrats in the North and win control of Congress or maybe even the White House. If that happened, they could perpetuate the Black Codes, virtually re-enslaving the blacks. They could dismantle the economic program of the Republican party and possibly even repudiate the national debt. President Johnson thus deeply disturbed the congressional Republicans when he announced on December 6, 1865, that the recently rebellious states had satisfied his conditions and that in his view the Union was now restored.

Johnson Clashes with Congress

A clash between president and Congress was now inevitable. It exploded into the open in February 1866, when the president vetoed a bill (later repassed) extending the life of the controversial Freedmen's Bureau.

Aroused, the Republicans swiftly struck back. In March 1866 they passed the Civil Rights Bill, which conferred on blacks the privileges of American citizenship and struck at the Black Codes. President Johnson resolutely vetoed this forward-looking measure, but in April congressmen steamrollered it over his veto—something they repeatedly did henceforth. The hapless president, dubbed "Andy Veto," had his presidential wings clipped short, as Congress increasingly assumed the dominant role in running the government.

The Republicans now undertook to rivet the principles of the Civil Rights Bill into the Constitution as the Fourteenth Amendment. The proposed amendment, as approved by Congress and sent to the states in June 1866, was sweeping. It (1) conferred civil rights, including citizenship but excluding the franchise, on the freedmen; (2) reduced proportionately the representation of a state in Congress and in the Electoral College if it denied blacks the ballot; (3) disqualified from federal and state office former Confederates who as federal officeholders had once sworn to "support the Constitution of the United States"; and (4) guaranteed the federal debt, while repudiating all Confederate debts. (See the text of the Fourteenth Amendment in the Appendix.)

The radical faction was disappointed that the Fourteenth Amendment did not grant the right to vote, but all Republicans agreed that no state should be welcomed back into the Union fold without first ratifying the Fourteenth Amendment. Yet President Johnson advised the Southern states to reject it, and all of the "sinful eleven," except Tennessee, defiantly spurned the amendment.

Swinging 'Round the Circle with Johnson

As 1866 lengthened, the battle grew between Congress and the president. Now the issue was whether Reconstruction was to be carried on with or without the Fourteenth Amendment. The Republicans would settle for nothing less.

The crucial congressional elections of 1866—more crucial than some presidential elections—were fast approaching. Johnson was naturally eager to escape from the clutch of Congress by securing a majority favorable to his soft-on-the-South policy. Invited to dedicate a Chicago monument to Stephen A. Douglas, he undertook to speak at various cities en route in support of his views.

Johnson's famous "swing 'round the circle," beginning in the late summer of 1866, was a seriocomedy of errors. The president delivered a series of "give 'em hell" speeches, in which he accused the radicals in Congress of having planned large-scale antiblack riots and murder in the South. As he spoke, hecklers hurled insults at him. Reverting to his stump-speaking days in Tennessee, he shouted back angry retorts, amid cries of "You be damned!" and "Don't get mad, Andy!" The dignity of his high office sank to a new low.

As a vote-getter, Johnson was highly successful—for the opposition. His inept speechmaking heightened the cry to "Stand by Congress" against the "Tailor of the Potomac." When the ballots were counted, the Republicans had rolled up more than a two-thirds majority in both houses of Congress.

Republican Reconstruction

The Republicans now had a veto-proof Congress and virtually unlimited control of Reconstruction policy. But moderates and radicals still disagreed over the best course to pursue in the South.

The radicals were led in the Senate by the courtly and principled idealist Charles Sumner, and in the House by crusty and vindictive Pennsylvania Congressman Thaddeus Stevens. Both tirelessly labored not only for black freedom but for racial equality. Still opposed to rapid restoration of the Southern states, the radicals wanted to keep them out as long as possible and apply federal power to bring about a drastic social and economic transformation in the South.

But moderate Republicans, more attuned to time-honored Republican principles of states' rights and self-government, preferred policies that restrained the states from abridging citizens' rights, rather than policies that directly involved the federal government in individual lives. The actual policies adopted by Congress showed the influence of both these schools of thought, though the moderates, as the majority faction, had the upper hand. And one thing both groups had come to agree on by 1867 was the necessity to enfranchise black voters, even if it took federal troops to do it.

Against a backdrop of vicious and bloody race riots that had erupted in several Southern cities, Congress passed the Reconstruction Act on March 2, 1867. This drastic legislation divided the South into five military districts, each commanded by a Union general and policed by blue-clad soldiers, about twenty thousand all told.

Congress additionally laid down stringent requirements for the readmission of the seceded states. The wayward states were required to ratify the Fourteenth Amendment, giving the former slaves their rights as citizens, and to guarantee in their state constitutions full suffrage for their former adult male slaves. Yet the act, reflecting moderate sentiment, stopped short of giving the freedmen land or education at federal expense. The overriding purpose of the moderates was to create an electorate in Southern states that would vote those states back into the Union on acceptable terms and thus free the federal government from direct responsibility for the protection of black rights. As later events would demonstrate, this approach proved woefully inadequate to the cause of justice for the blacks.

The radical Republicans still worried that once the unrepentant states were readmitted, they would amend their constitutions to withdraw the ballot from the blacks. They therefore sought the ironclad safeguard of incorporating black suffrage in the federal Constitution. This goal was finally achieved by the Fifteenth Amendment, passed by Congress in 1869 and ratified by the required number of states in 1870 (see the Appendix).

Military Reconstruction of the South not only usurped certain functions of the president as commander in chief but set up a martial regime of dubious legality. The Supreme Court had already ruled, in the case *Ex parte Milligan* (1866), that military tribunals could not try civilians,

Online Study Center

Primary source
Union as It Was, The
college.hmco.com/pic/kennedybrief7e

The prominent suffragist and abolitionist Susan B. Anthony (1820–1906) was outraged over the proposed exclusion of women from the Fourteenth Amendment. In a conversation with her former male allies Wendell Phillips and Theodore Tilton, she reportedly held out her arm and declared,

"Look at this, all of you. And hear me swear that I will cut off this right arm of mine before I will ever work for or demand the ballot for the negro and not the woman."

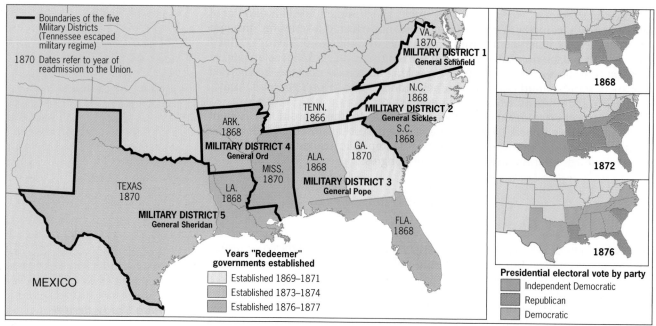

■ **Military Reconstruction, 1867 (five districts and commanding generals)** For many white Southerners, military Reconstruction amounted to turning the knife in the wound of defeat. An often-repeated story of later years had a Southerner remark, "I was sixteen years old before I discovered that damnyankee was two words."

Online Study Center

Interactive map
The Reconstruction
college/hmco.com/pic/kennedybrief7e

even during wartime, in areas where the civil courts were open. Peacetime military rule seemed starkly contrary to the spirit of the Constitution, but for the time being the Supreme Court avoided offending the Republican Congress.

Prodded into line by federal bayonets, the Southern states got on with the task of constitution making. By 1870 all of them had reorganized their governments and had been accorded full rights. The hated "bluebellies" remained until the new regimes—usually called "radical" regimes—appeared to be firmly entrenched. Yet when the federal troops finally left a state, its government swiftly passed into the hands of white "Redeemer" regimes, which were inevitably Democratic. Finally, in 1877, the last federal muskets were removed from state politics, and the "solid" Democratic South congealed.

The passage of the three Reconstruction-era Amendments—the Thirteenth, Fourteenth, and Fifteenth—delighted former abolitionists but deeply disappointed advocates of women's rights. Women had played a prominent part in the prewar abolitionist movement, and in the eyes of many women the struggle for black freedom and the crusade for women's rights were one and the same. Now, feminist leaders reeled with shock when the Fourteenth Amendment, which defined equal national citizenship, for the first time inserted the word *male* into the Constitution in referring to a citizen's right to vote. When the Fifteenth Amendment proposed to prohibit denial of the vote on the basis of "race, color, or previous condition of servitude," women's rights leaders Susan B. Anthony and Elizabeth Cady Stanton wanted the word *sex* added to the list. They lost this battle, too. Fifty years would pass before the Constitution granted women the right to vote.

The Realities of Radical Reconstruction in the South

scalawag *A white Southerner who supported Republican Reconstruction after the Civil War.*

carpetbagger *A Northerner who moved to the South after the Civil War; hence, any politician who relocates for political advantage.*

Blacks now had freedom, of a sort. By 1867 Republican hesitation over black voting had given way to a hard determination to enfranchise the former slaves wholesale and immediately, while thousands of white Southerners were being denied the right to vote. By glaring contrast, most of the Northern states, before ratification of the Fifteenth Amendment in 1870, withheld the ballot from their tiny black minorities. White Southerners naturally concluded that the Republicans were hypocritical in insisting that blacks in the South be allowed to vote.

Having gained their right to suffrage, Southern black men seized the initiative and began to organize politically. Their primary vehicle became the Union League, originally a pro-Union organization based in the North. Assisted by Northern blacks, freedmen turned the League into a network of political clubs that educated members in their civic duties and campaigned for Republican candidates. The League's mission soon expanded to include building black churches and schools, representing black grievances before local employers and governments, and recruiting militias to protect black communities from white retaliation.

Though African American women did not obtain the right to vote, they too assumed new political roles. Black women faithfully attended the parades and rallies common in black communities during the early years of Reconstruction and helped assemble mass meetings in the newly constructed black churches. They even showed up at the constitutional conventions held throughout the South in 1867, monitoring the proceedings and participating in informal votes outside the convention halls.

But black men elected as delegates to the state constitutional conventions held the greater political authority. They formed the backbone of the black political community. At the conventions, they sat down with whites to hammer out new state constitutions, which most importantly provided for universal male suffrage.

The sight of former slaves holding office deeply offended their onetime masters, who lashed out with fury at the freedmen's white allies, labeling them "**scalawags**" and "**carpetbaggers.**" The so-called scalawags were Southerners, often former Unionists and Whigs, whom former Confederates wildly accused of plundering the treasuries of the Southern radical governments. The carpetbaggers were supposedly sleazy Northerners who had packed all their worldly goods into a carpetbag suitcase at war's end and had come South to seek personal power and profit. In fact, most were former Union soldiers and Northern businessmen and professionals who wanted to play a role in modernizing the "New South."

How well did the radical regimes rule? White southerners regularly portrayed the "Black Reconstruction" governments as run by ignorant and corrupt former slaves. Black voters did make up a majority of the electorate in five states, but only in South Carolina did blacks predominate in the lower house of the legislature. Many of the newly elected black legislators were literate and able; more than a few came from the ranks of the prewar free blacks who had acquired considerable education. More than a dozen black congressmen and two black United States senators, Hiram Revels and Blanche K. Bruce, both of Mississippi, did creditable work in the national capital.

In some radical regimes, there was truth to the charges of graft and corruption. This was especially true in South Carolina and Louisiana, where conscienceless promoters and other pocket-padders used politically inexperienced blacks as cat's-paws. The worst "black-and-white" legislatures purchased as "legislative supplies" such "stationery" as hams, perfumes, suspenders, bonnets, corsets, champagne, and a coffin. Yet this sort of corruption was no more outrageous than the scams and felonies being perpetrated in the North at the same time, especially in Boss Tweed's New York.

The radical legislatures also passed much desirable legislation. For the first time in Southern history, steps were taken toward establishing adequate public schools. Tax systems were streamlined; public works were launched; and property rights were guaranteed to women. Many of these reforms were so welcome that they were retained by the all-white "Redeemer" governments that later returned to power.

The Ku Klux Klan

Deeply embittered, some Southern whites resorted to savage measures against "radical" rule. Many whites resented the success and ability of black legislators as much as they resented alleged "corruption." A number of secret organizations mushroomed forth, the most notorious of which was the "Invisible Empire of the South," or Ku Klux Klan, founded in Tennessee in 1866. Besheeted nightriders, their horses' hoofs muffled, would pound and hammer on blacks' cabin doors or

⊙ Map Skill-Builder:
Understanding Political Maps

On page 330, the map of military Reconstruction, along with the three sidebar maps on the vote in three presidential elections, provides a wealth of political information on the relationship between the rise and decline of radical Reconstruction in the South. To understand this political information requires examining all *four* maps to look for patterns and correlations.

1. In the election of 1868, which *three* former Confederate states had not yet been readmitted to the Union, and therefore cast no electoral votes for president?

2. In 1872—the peak of radical Reconstruction—*two* states that had already been "redeemed" by conservative whites (color-coded yellow on the main Military Reconstruction map) nevertheless *still* voted Republican (Grant) in the election of 1872—suggesting the continuing strength of the radicals. Which were they?

3. By the election of 1876, radical Reconstruction had declined, and all but four southern states had been "redeemed." Three of those were the only southern states to vote Republican (Hayes) that year, but even one state still under radical rule voted Democratic. Which state was it?

4. Only *one* southern state voted consistently Democratic throughout Reconstruction, even when it was under radical rule, suggesting the weakness of Reconstruction there. Which was it? Recalling Civil War military events, what might explain the especially deep hostility to Republicans in that state?

---

terror (terrorist) *Using violence or the threat of violence in order to create intense fear and attempt to promote some political policy or objectives.*

use other tactics to frighten them. Those stubborn souls who persisted in their "upstart" ways were flogged, mutilated, or even murdered. In one Louisiana parish in 1868, whites in two days killed or wounded two hundred victims; a pile of twenty-five bodies was found half-buried in the woods. Such atrocious **terror** tactics proved partially effective in keeping many blacks from the polls.

Congress, outraged by this night-riding lawlessness, passed the harsh Force Acts of 1870 and 1871. Federal troops were able to stamp out much of the "lash law," but by this time the Invisible Empire had already done its work of intimidation. The Klan remained a refuge for numerous scoundrels and cutthroats who hid under its sheets, often continuing to operate under the guise of "dancing societies," "missionary clubs," and "rifle clubs."

White resistance undermined attempts to empower the blacks politically. The white South for many decades openly flouted the Fourteenth and Fifteenth Amendments. Wholesale disfranchisement of the blacks, starting conspicuously about 1890, was achieved by intimidation, fraud, and trickery. Among various underhanded schemes were the literacy tests, unfairly administered by whites to the advantage of illiterate whites. In the eyes of white Southerners, the goal of white supremacy fully justified these dishonorable devices.

Impeachment and Acquittal for Johnson

Radicals meanwhile had been sharpening their hatchets for President Johnson. Not content with curbing his authority, they decided to remove him altogether by constitutional processes.*

As an initial step, Congress in 1867 passed the Tenure of Office Act—as usual over Johnson's veto. Contrary to precedent, the new law required the president to secure the consent of the Senate before he could remove his cabinet members, including the secretary of war, Edwin M. Stanton, a holdover from the Lincoln administration. Although outwardly loyal to Johnson, Stanton was secretly serving as a spy and informer for the radicals.

Johnson provided the radicals with a pretext to begin impeachment proceedings when he abruptly dismissed Stanton early in 1868. The House of Representatives immediately voted 126 to 47 to impeach Andrew Johnson for "high crimes and misdemeanors," as required by the Constitution, charging him with various violations of the Tenure of Office Act. Two additional articles related to Johnson's verbal assaults on the Congress, involving "disgrace, ridicule, hatred, contempt, and reproach."

With evident zeal the radical-led Senate now sat as a court to try Johnson on the dubious impeachment charges. The House conducted the prosecution. The trial aroused intense public interest and, because only one thousand tickets for seats were printed, proved to be the biggest show of 1868. Johnson kept his dignity and maintained a discreet silence. His battery of attorneys argued that the president had fired Stanton merely to put a test case before the Supreme Court. The House prosecutors, including oily-tongued Benjamin F. Butler and embittered Thaddeus Stevens, had a harder time building a compelling case for impeachment.

On May 16, 1868, the day for voting in the Senate, the tension was electric, and heavy breathing could be heard in the galleries. By a margin of only one vote, the radicals failed to muster the two-thirds majority for Johnson's removal. Seven independent-minded Republican senators, courageously putting country above party, voted "not guilty."

Diehard radicals were infuriated. "The Country is going to the Devil!" cried the crippled Stevens as he was carried from the hall. But the nation, though violently aroused, accepted the verdict with a good temper that did credit to its political maturity.

The nation thus narrowly avoided a bad precedent that would have gravely weakened one of the three branches of the federal government. Johnson was

---

*For impeachment, see Art. I, Sec. II, para.5; Art. I, Sec. III, paras. 6, 7; Art. II, Sec. IV, in the Appendix.

clearly guilty of bad speeches, bad judgment, and bad temper, but not of "high crimes and misdemeanors." From the standpoint of the radicals, his greatest crime had been to stand inflexibly in their path.

The Purchase of Alaska

Johnson's administration, though largely reduced to a figurehead, achieved its most enduring success in the field of foreign relations. The Russians by 1867 were in a mood to sell the vast and chilly expanse of land now known as Alaska. The region had been ruthlessly "furred out" and was a growing economic liability to them. The Russians were therefore eager to unload their "frozen asset" on the Americans. They preferred the United States to any other purchaser primarily because they wanted to strengthen further the Republic as a barrier against their ancient enemy, Britain.

In 1867 Secretary of State William Seward, an ardent expansionist, signed a treaty with Russia that transferred Alaska to the United States for the bargain price of $7.2 million. But Seward's enthusiasm for these frigid wastes was not shared by his ignorant or uninformed countrymen, who jeered at "Seward's Folly," "Seward's Icebox," and "Walrussia."

Then why did Congress and the American public sanction the purchase? For one thing Russia, alone among the great powers, had been conspicuously friendly to the North during the recent Civil War. Americans did not feel that they could offend their good friend the tsar by hurling his walrus-covered icebergs back into his face. Besides, the territory was rumored to be still teeming with furs, fish, and gold, and it might yet "pan out" profitably—as it later did with natural resources that included oil and gas.

■ **Freedmen Voting, Richmond, Virginia, 1871** The exercise of democratic rights by former slaves constituted a political and social revolution in the South, and was bitterly resented by whites.

The Heritage of Reconstruction

Many white Southerners regarded Reconstruction as a more grievous wound than the war itself. It left a festering scar that would take generations to heal. They resented the upending of their social and racial system, the political empowerment of blacks, and the insult of federal intervention in their local affairs. Yet given the explosiveness of the issues that had caused the war, and the bitterness of the fighting, the wonder is that Reconstruction was not far harsher than it was. Northern policymakers groped for the right policies, influenced as much by Southern responses to defeat and emancipation as by any specific plans of their own.

The Republicans acted from a mixture of idealism and political expediency. They wanted both to protect the freed slaves and to promote the fortunes of the Republican party. In the end their efforts backfired badly. Reconstruction conferred only fleeting benefits on the blacks, and it virtually extinguished the Republican party in the South for nearly one hundred years.

■ **Impeachment Drama** The impeachment proceedings against President Andrew Johnson, among the most severe constitutional crises in the Republic's history, were high political theater, and tickets were in sharp demand.

The remarkable ex-slave Frederick Douglass (1817?–1895) wrote in 1882,

"Though slavery was abolished, the wrongs of my people were not ended. Though they were not slaves, they were not yet quite free. No man can be truly free whose liberty is dependent upon the thought, feeling, and action of others, and who has himself no means in his own hands for guarding, protecting, defending, and maintaining that liberty. Yet the Negro after his emancipation was precisely in this state of destitution. . . . He was free from the individual master, but the slave of society. He had neither money, property, nor friends. He was free from the old plantation, but he had nothing but the dusty road under his feet. He was free from the old quarter that once gave him shelter, but a slave to the rains of summer and the frosts of winter. He was, in a word, literally turned loose, naked, hungry, and destitute, to the open sky."

Moderate Republicans never fully appreciated the extensive effort necessary to make the freed slaves completely independent citizens, nor the lengths to which Southern whites would go to preserve their system of racial dominance. Had Thaddeus Stevens's radical program of drastic economic reforms and heftier protection of political rights been enacted, things might well have been different. But deep-seated racism, ingrained American resistance to tampering with property rights, and rigid loyalty to the principle of local self-government, combined with spreading indifference in the North to the plight of blacks, formed too formidable an obstacle. Despite good intentions by Republicans, the Old South was in many ways more resurrected than reconstructed.

★ Chapter Summary ★

With the Civil War over, the nation faced the difficult problems of rebuilding the South, assisting the freed slaves, reintegrating the Southern states into the Union, and deciding who would direct the Reconstruction process.

The South was economically devastated and socially revolutionized by emancipation. As slaveowners reluctantly confronted the end of slave labor, blacks took their first steps in freedom. Black churches and freedmen's schools helped the former slaves begin to shape their own destiny.

The new President Andrew Johnson was politically inept and personally contentious. His attempt to implement a moderate plan of Reconstruction, along the lines originally suggested by Lincoln, fell victim to Southern whites' severe treatment of blacks and his own political blunders.

Republicans imposed harsh military Reconstruction on the South after their gains in the 1866 congressional elections. The Southern states reentered the Union with new radical governments, which rested partly on the newly enfranchised blacks, but also had support from some sectors of Southern society These governments were sometimes corrupt, but they also implemented important reforms, especially in education. For a time, acting from a mixture of idealism and political expediency, Republicans tried seriously to build a new Republican party in the South to guarantee black rights. But the divisions between moderate and radical Republicans meant that Reconstruction's aims were often limited and confused, despite successful passage of the important Fourteenth and Fifteenth Amendments guaranteeing black civil and voting rights.

Embittered whites hated the radical governments and mobilized reactionary terrorist organizations like the Ku Klux Klan to restore white supremacy. The radical Republican House of Representatives impeached Johnson, but the Senate failed narrowly to convict him. In the end, the inadequate Reconstruction policy, which never really addressed the deep economic and social legacy of slavery and the Civil War, failed disastrously and created as much or more bitterness than the war itself.

VARYING VIEWPOINTS

How Radical Was Reconstruction?

Few topics have triggered as much intellectual warfare as the "dark and bloody ground" of Reconstruction. The period provoked questions—sectional, racial, and constitutional—about which people felt deeply and remain deeply divided even today. Scholarly argument goes back conspicuously to a Columbia University historian, William A. Dunning, who wrote about Reconstruction as a kind of national disgrace, foisted on a prostrate region by vindictive and self-seeking radical Republican politicians.

In the 1920s, widespread suspicion that the Civil War itself had been a tragic and unnecessary blunder shifted attention to Northern politicians. Scholars like Howard Beale argued that the radical Republicans had masked a ruthless desire to exploit Southern resources and expand Republican power in the South behind a false "front" of concern for the freed slaves.

Although ignored by his contemporaries, the scholar and founder of the National Association for the Advancement of Colored People, W. E. B. Du Bois, wrote a sympathetic history of Reconstruction in 1935 that became the basis of historians' interpretations ever since. Following World War II, Kenneth Stampp and others, influenced by the modern civil rights movement, built on Du Bois's argument and claimed that Reconstruction had been a noble though ultimately failed attempt to extend American principles of equity and justice. By the early 1970s, this view had become orthodoxy, and it generally holds sway today. Yet some scholars, such as Michael Benedict and Leon Litwack, disillusioned with the inability to achieve full racial justice in the 1960s and 1970s, claimed to discover that Reconstruction was never really very radical, and argued that the Freedmen's Bureau and other agencies had merely allowed white planters to maintain local political and economic control.

More recently, Eric Foner has powerfully reasserted the argument that Reconstruction was a truly radical and noble attempt to establish an interracial democracy. Drawing on the work of Du Bois, Foner has emphasized that Reconstruction allowed blacks to form political organizations and churches and to establish some measure of economic independence. Many of the benefits of Reconstruction were erased by white Southerners during the Gilded Age, but in the twentieth century, constitutional principles and organizations developed during Reconstruction provided the foundation for the modern civil rights movement—which some have called the Second Reconstruction.

Steven Hahn's *A Nation Under Our Feet: Black Political Struggles in the Rural South from Slavery to the Great Migration* (2003) is the latest contribution to the literature on Reconstruction. Hahn emphasizes the assertiveness and ingenuity of African Americans in creating new political opportunities for themselves after emancipation.

PART FOUR

Forging an Industrial Society

1865–1899

A nation of farmers fought the Civil War in the 1860s. By the time the Spanish-American War broke out in 1898, America was an industrial nation. For generations Americans had plunged into the wilderness and plowed their fields. Now they settled in cities and toiled in factories. Between the Civil War and the century's end, economic and technological change came so swiftly and massively that it seemed to many Americans that a whole new civilization had emerged.

In some ways it had. The sheer scale of the new industrial civilization was dazzling. Transcontinental railroads knit the country together from sea to sea. New industries like oil and steel grew to staggering size—and made mega-millionaires out of entrepreneurs like oilman John D. Rockefeller and steelmaker Andrew Carnegie.

Drawn by the allure of industrial employment, Americans moved to the city. In 1860 only about 20 percent of the population were city dwellers. By 1900 that proportion had doubled, as rural Americans and European immigrants alike flocked to mill town and metropolis in search of steady jobs.

These sweeping changes challenged the spirit of individualism that Americans had celebrated since the seventeenth century. Even on the western frontier, that historic bastion of rugged loners, the hand of government was increasingly felt, as large armies were dispatched to subdue the Plains Indians and federal authority was invoked to regulate the use of natural resources. The rise of powerful monopolies called into question the government's traditional hands-off policy toward business, and a growing band of reformers increasingly clamored for government regulation of private enterprise. The mushrooming cities, with their needs for transport systems, schools, hospitals, sanitation, and fire and police protection, required bigger governments and budgets than an earlier generation could have imagined. As never before, Americans struggled to adapt old ideals of private autonomy to the new realities of industrial civilization.

With economic change came social and political turmoil. Labor violence brought bloodshed to places such as Chicago and Homestead, Pennsylvania. Small farmers, squeezed by debt and foreign competition, rallied behind the People's, or "Populist," party, a radical movement of the 1880s and 1890s that attacked the power of Wall Street, big business, and the banks. Anti-immigrant sentiment swelled. Bitter disputes over tariffs and monetary policy deeply divided the country, setting debtors against lenders, farmers against manufacturers, the West and South against the Northeast. And in this unfamiliar era of big money and expanding government, corruption flourished, from town hall to Congress, fueling loud cries for political reform.

The bloodiest conflict of all pitted Plains Indians against the relentless push of westward expansion. As railroads drove their iron arrows through the heart of the West, the Indians lost their land and life-sustaining buffalo herds. By the 1890s, after three decades of fierce fighting with the U.S. Army, the Indians who had once roamed across the vast rolling prairies were struggling to preserve their shattered cultures within the confinement of reservations.

The South remained the one region largely untouched by the Industrial Revolution sweeping the rest of America. For the most part, the South's rural way of life and its peculiar system of race relations were largely unperturbed by the changes happening elsewhere. On African Americans, the vast majority of whom continued to live in the Old South, the post-emancipation era inflicted new forms of racial injustice. State legislatures systematically deprived black Americans of their political rights, including the right to vote. Segregation of schools, housing, and all kinds of public facilities made a mockery of African Americans' Reconstruction-era hopes for equality before the law.

The new wealth and power of industrial America nurtured a growing sense of national self-confidence. Literature flowered, and a golden age of philanthropy dawned. The reform spirit spread. So did a restless appetite for overseas expansion. In a brief war against Spain in 1898, the United States, born in a revolutionary war of independence and long the champion of colonial peoples yearning to breathe free, seized control of the Philippines and itself became an imperial power. Uncle Sam's venture into empire touched off a bitter national debate about America's role in the world and ushered in a long period of argument over the responsibilities, at home and abroad, of a modern industrial state.

What if . . . ?

■ **What if industrial workers and small farmers in the post-Reconstruction era had joined in a political movement strong enough to challenge the "Captains of Industry" for control of the American economy?**

How would the course of American economic, social, and political development, and the character of America's foreign policy, have been different?

23

Political Paralysis in the Gilded Age

1869–1896

GRANT . . . HAD NO RIGHT TO EXIST. HE SHOULD HAVE BEEN
EXTINCT FOR AGES. . . . THAT, TWO THOUSAND YEARS AFTER
ALEXANDER THE GREAT AND JULIUS CAESAR, A MAN LIKE
GRANT SHOULD BE CALLED—AND SHOULD ACTUALLY AND
TRULY BE—THE HIGHEST PRODUCT OF THE MOST ADVANCED
EVOLUTION, MADE EVOLUTION LUDICROUS. . . . THE PROGRESS
OF EVOLUTION, FROM PRESIDENT WASHINGTON TO PRESIDENT
GRANT, WAS ALONE EVIDENCE ENOUGH TO UPSET DARWIN. . . .
GRANT . . . SHOULD HAVE LIVED IN A CAVE AND WORN SKINS.

HENRY ADAMS, *THE EDUCATION OF HENRY ADAMS*, 1907

The population of the post–Civil War Republic continued to vault upward by vigorous leaps, despite the awful bloodletting in both Union and Confederate ranks. Census takers reported over 39 million people in 1870, a gain of 26.6 percent over the preceding decade, as the immigrant tide surged again. The United States was now the third-largest nation in the Western world, ranking behind Russia and France.

But the civic health of the United States did not keep pace with its physical growth. The Civil War and its aftermath spawned waste, extravagance, speculation, and graft. Disillusionment ran deep among idealistic Americans in the postwar era. They had spilled their blood for the Union, emancipation, and Abraham Lincoln, who had promised "a new birth of freedom." Instead, they got a bitter dose of corruption and political stalemate—beginning with Ulysses S. Grant, a great soldier but an utterly inept politician.

Focus Questions

1. Why was the Gilded Age, by and large, a period of political patronage, corruption, and stalemate between the two major parties? Given these negative factors, why did political participation achieve high levels never seen before or since?
2. How did the disputed Hayes-Tilden election of 1877 lead to the Compromise of 1877 and the end of Reconstruction?
3. What did the end of Reconstruction mean for blacks, and how did the South's racial system perpetuate an economic and social backwardness that trapped both whites and blacks?
4. What caused the rise of industrial and agricultural conflict in the 1880s and 1890s, and why was Grover Cleveland unable to address growing farmer and labor discontent?
5. How did the depression of the 1890s stir growing social protest and class conflict, and fuel the rise of the radical Populist party?

Chronology

1868	Grant defeats Seymour for the presidency.		**1884**	Cleveland defeats Blaine for presidency.
1869	Fisk and Gould corner the gold market.		**1888**	Harrison defeats Cleveland for presidency.
1871	Tweed scandal in New York.		**1890**	"Billion Dollar" Congress. McKinley Tariff Act. Sherman Silver Purchase Act (repealed 1893).
1872	Crédit Mobilier scandal exposed. Liberal Republicans break with Grant. Grant defeats Greeley for presidency.		**1892**	Homestead steel strike. Coeur d'Alene (Idaho) silver miners' strike. People's party candidate James B. Weaver wins twenty-two electoral votes. Cleveland defeats Harrison and Weaver for presidency.
1873	Panic of 1873.			
1875	Whiskey Ring scandal. Civil Rights Act of 1875. Resumption Act.		**1893**	Depression of 1893 begins.
1876	Hayes-Tilden election standoff and crisis.		**1894**	Wilson-Gorman Tariff (contains income-tax provision; declared unconstitutional 1895). Republicans regain House of Representatives.
1877	Compromise of 1877. Reconstruction ends. Railroad strikes paralyze nation.		**1895**	J.P. Morgan's banking syndicate loans $65 million in gold to federal government.
1880	Garfield defeats Hancock for presidency.		**1896**	*Plessy* v. *Ferguson* legitimizes "separate but equal" doctrine.
1881	Garfield assassinated; Arthur assumes presidency.			
1882	Chinese Exclusion Act.			
1883	*Civil Rights Cases.* Pendleton Act sets up Civil Service Commission.			

The "Bloody Shirt" Elects Grant

Wrangling between Congress and Andrew Johnson had soured the people on professional politicians, and the notion still prevailed that a good general would make a good president. Stubbly-bearded General Grant was by far the most popular northern hero to emerge from the war. Grateful citizens of Philadelphia, Washington, and New York showered him with gifts of houses and cash, which the general, silently puffing on his cigar, unapologetically accepted.

Grant was a hapless greenhorn in the political arena. His one presidential vote had been cast for the Democratic ticket in 1856. A better judge of horseflesh than of humans, his cultural background was breathtakingly narrow. He once reportedly remarked that Venice, Italy, would be a fine city if only it were drained.

The Republicans, freed from the Union party **coalition** of war days, enthusiastically nominated Grant for the presidency in 1868. The party's platform sounded a clarion call for continued Reconstruction of the South under the glinting steel of federal bayonets. Yet Grant, always a man of few words, coined a popular campaign slogan when he declared, "Let us have peace."

Expectant Democrats, meeting in their own nominating convention, denounced military Reconstruction but could agree on little else. Wealthy eastern delegates demanded a platform promising that federal war bonds be redeemed in gold, while the poorer midwesterners backed the "Ohio Idea" calling for redemption in greenbacks. Debt-burdened agrarian Democrats thus hoped to keep more money in circulation and to keep interest rates lower. This dispute introduced a

⭐ **Makers of America: The Chinese**

⭐ **Varying Viewpoints: The Populists: Radicals or Reactionaries?**

coalition *A temporary alliance of political factions or parties for some specific purpose.*

bitter contest over monetary policy that continued to convulse the Republic until the century's end.

Midwestern delegates got the platform but not the candidate. The nominee, former New York governor Horatio Seymour, scuttled the Democrats' faint hope for success by repudiating the Ohio Idea. Republicans whipped up enthusiasm for Grant by energetically "waving the bloody shirt"—that is, reviving gory memories of the Civil War—which became for the first time a prominent feature of a presidential campaign.* "Vote as You Shot" was a powerful Republican slogan aimed at Union army veterans.

Grant won, with 214 electoral votes to 80 for Seymour. But despite his great popularity, the former general scored a majority of only 300,000 in the popular vote (3,013,421 to 2,706,829). Most white voters apparently supported Seymour, and the ballots of three still-unreconstructed southern states (Mississippi, Texas, and Virginia) were not counted at all. An estimated 500,000 former slaves gave Grant his margin of victory. To remain in power, the Republican party somehow had to continue to control the South—and to keep the ballot in the hands of the grateful freedmen. Republicans could not take future victories "for Granted."

The Era of Good Stealings

A few skunks can pollute a large area. Although the great majority of businesspeople and government officials were decent and honest, the whole postwar atmosphere was fetid. The Man in the Moon, it was said, had to hold his nose when passing over America. Freewheeling railroad promoters sometimes left gullible bond buyers with only "two streaks of rust and a right of way." Unscrupulous stock-market manipulators were a cinder in the public eye. Too many judges and legislators put their power up for hire. Cynics defined an honest politician as one who, when bought, would stay bought.

Notorious in the financial world were two millionaire partners, "Jubilee Jim" Fisk and Jay Gould. The corpulent and unscrupulous Fisk provided the "brass," while the undersized and cunning Gould provided the brains. The crafty pair concocted a plot in 1869 to **corner** the gold market. Their slippery game would work only if the federal Treasury refrained from selling gold. The conspirators worked on President Grant directly, and also through his brother-in-law, who received $25,000 for his complicity. On "Black Friday" (September 24, 1869), Fisk and Gould madly bid the price of gold skyward, while scores of honest businesspeople were driven to the wall. The bubble finally broke when the Treasury, contrary to Grant's supposed assurances, released gold for sale. A congressional probe concluded that Grant had done nothing crooked, though he had acted stupidly and indiscreetly.

The infamous Tweed Ring in New York City vividly displayed the ethics (or lack of ethics) typical of the age. Burly "Boss" Tweed—240 pounds of rascality—employed bribery, graft, and fraudulent elections to milk the metropolis of as much as $200 million. Honest citizens were cowed into silence. Protesters found their tax assessments raised.

Tweed's luck finally ran out. The *New York Times* secured damning evidence in 1871 and courageously published it, though offered $5 million not to do so. Gifted cartoonist Thomas Nast pilloried Tweed mercilessly, after spurning a heavy bribe to desist. New York attorney Samuel J. Tilden headed the prosecution, gaining fame that later paved the path to his presidential nomination. Unbailed and unwept, Tweed died behind bars.

More serious than Boss Tweed's peccadilloes were the misdeeds of the federal government. President Grant's cabinet was a rodent's nest of grafters and incompetents. Favor seekers haunted the White House, plying Grant himself with cigars, wine, and horses. Several dozen of his in-laws attached themselves to the public payroll.

corner *To gain exclusive control of a commodity in order to fix its price.*

---

*The expression is said to have derived from a speech by Representative Benjamin F. Butler of Massachusetts, who allegedly waved before the House the bloodstained nightshirt of a Klan-flogged carpetbagger.

The easygoing Grant was first tarred by the Crédit Mobilier scandal, which erupted in 1872. Union Pacific Railway insiders had formed the Crédit Mobilier construction company and then cleverly hired themselves at inflated prices to build the railroad line, earning dividends as high as 348 percent. Fearing that Congress might blow the whistle, the company furtively distributed shares of its valuable stock to key congressmen. A newspaper exposé and congressional investigation of the scandal led to the formal **censure** of two congressmen and the revelation that the vice president of the United States had also accepted payments from Crédit Mobilier.

The breath of scandal in Washington also reeked of alcohol. In 1874–1875 a sprawling Whiskey Ring robbed the Treasury of millions in excise tax revenues. When President Grant's own private secretary turned up among the culprits, the president volunteered a written statement to a jury that helped exonerate the thief. Further rottenness in the Grant administration came to light in 1876, forcing Secretary of War William Belknap to resign after pocketing bribes from suppliers to the Indian reservations. Grant, ever loyal to his crooked cronies, accepted Belknap's resignation "with great regret."

The Liberal Republican Revolt of 1872

By 1872 a powerful wave of disgust with Grantism was beginning to build up throughout the nation, even before some of the worst scandals had been exposed. Reform-minded citizens banded together in the Liberal Republican party. Voicing the slogan "Turn the Rascals Out," they urged purification of the Washington administration as well as an end to military Reconstruction.

The Liberal Republicans muffed their chance when their Cincinnati nominating convention astounded the country by nominating the brilliant but erratic Horace Greeley for the presidency. Although Greeley was a fearless editor of the *New York Tribune,* he was dogmatic, emotional, petulant, and notoriously unsound in his political judgments.

More astonishing still was the action of the office-hungry Democrats, who foolishly proceeded to endorse Greeley's candidacy. In swallowing Greeley the Democrats "ate crow" in large gulps, for the eccentric editor had long blasted them as traitors, slave drivers, saloon keepers, horse thieves, and idiots. Yet Greeley pleased the Democrats, North and South, when he pleaded for clasping hands across "the bloody chasm." The Republicans dutifully renominated Grant. The voters were thus presented with a choice between two candidates who had made their careers in fields other than politics and who were both eminently unqualified, by temperament and lifelong training, for high political office.

In the mud-spattered campaign that followed, regular Republicans denounced Greeley as an atheist, a free-lover, and a vegetarian, while Democrats derided Grant as a drunken swindler. But the regular Republicans, chanting "Grant us another term," pulled the president through. The count in the electoral column was 286 to 66, in the popular column 3,596,745 to 2,843,446.

Liberal Republican agitation frightened the regular Republicans into cleaning their own house before they were thrown out of it. The Republican Congress in 1872 passed a general **amnesty** act, removing political disabilities from all but some five hundred former Confederate leaders. Congress also moved to reduce

■ **Can the Law Reach Him?** 1872 Cartoonist Thomas Nast attacked "Boss" Tweed in a series of cartoons like this one that appeared in *Harper's Weekly* in 1872. Here Nast depicts the corrupt Tweed as a powerful giant, towering over a puny law force.

censure *An official statement of condemnation passed by a legislative body against one of its members or some other official of government. While severe, a censure itself stops short of penalties or **expulsion** from office.*

amnesty *A general pardon for offenses or crimes against a government.*

high Civil War tariffs and to fumigate the Grant administration with mild civil-service reform. Like many American third parties, the Liberal Republicans left some enduring footprints, even in defeat.

Depression and Demands for Inflation

Grant's woes deepened in the paralyzing economic panic that broke in 1873. Bursting with startling rapidity, the crash was one of those periodic plummets that roller-coastered the economy in this age of unbridled capitalist expansion. Boom times became gloom times as more than fifteen thousand businesses went bankrupt. In New York City, an army of unemployed riotously battled the police.

Black Americans were hard hit. The Freedman's Savings and Trust Company had made **unsecured loans** to several companies that went under. Black depositers, who had entrusted over $7 million to the bank, lost their savings, and black economic development and black confidence in savings institutions went down with it.

Hard times inflicted the worst punishment on debtors, who intensified their clamor for inflationary policies. Proponents of inflation breathed new life into the issue of greenbacks. During the war $450 million of the "folding money" had been issued, but it had depreciated under a cloud of popular mistrust and dubious legality.* By 1868 the Treasury had already withdrawn $100 million of the "battle-born currency" from circulation, and "hard-money" people everywhere looked forward to its complete disappearance. But now afflicted agrarian and debtor groups—"cheap-money" supporters—pressed for a reissuance of the greenbacks. With a crude but essentially accurate grasp of monetary theory, they reasoned that more money meant cheaper money and, hence, rising prices and easier-to-pay debts. Creditors, of course, reasoning from the same premises, advocated precisely the opposite policy.

The "hard-money" advocates took a notable step in 1874 when they persuaded Grant to veto a bill to print more paper money. They scored another victory in the Resumption Act of 1875, which pledged the government to the further withdrawal of greenbacks from circulation and to the redemption of all paper currency in gold at face value, beginning in 1879.

Down but not out, debtors now looked for relief to another precious metal, silver. The "sacred white metal," they claimed, had received a raw deal. In the early 1870s, the Treasury stubbornly and unrealistically maintained that an ounce of silver was worth only one-sixteenth as much as an ounce of gold. Silver miners thus stopped selling their shiny product to the federal mints, and Congress dropped the coinage of silver dollars in 1873. Fate then played a sly joke when new silver discoveries later in the 1870s shot production up and forced silver prices down. Westerners from silver-mining states now joined with debtors in assailing the "Crime of '73," demanding a return to the "Dollar of Our Daddies." Like the demand for more greenbacks, the demand for the coinage of more silver was nothing more nor less than another scheme to promote inflation.

Hard-money Republicans resisted this scheme and counted on Grant to hold the line against it. He did not disappoint them. The Treasury began to accumulate gold stocks against the appointed day for resumption of metallic-money payments. Coupled with the reduction of greenbacks, this policy was called "**contraction.**" It had a noticeable deflationary effect—the amount of money per capita in circulation actually decreased between 1870 and 1880, from $19.42 to $19.37. Contraction probably worsened the impact of the depression. But the new policy did restore the government's credit rating, and it brought the

---

unsecured loans *Money loaned without identification of collateral (existing assets) to be forfeited in case the borrower defaults on the loan.*

contraction *In finance, reducing the available supply of money, thus tending to raise interest rates and lower prices.*

---

* The Supreme Court in 1870 declared the Civil War Legal Tender Act unconstitutional. With the concurrence of the Senate, Grant thereupon added to the bench two justices who could be counted on to help reverse that decision, which happened in 1871. This is how the Court grew to its current size of nine justices.

embattled greenbacks up to their full face value. When Redemption Day came in 1879, few greenback holders bothered to exchange the lighter and more convenient bills for gold.

Republican hard-money policy had a political backlash. It helped elect a Democratic House of Representatives in 1874, and in 1878 it spawned the Greenback Labor party, which polled over a million votes and elected fourteen members of Congress. The contest over monetary policy was far from over.

Pallid Politics in the Gilded Age

The political seesaw was delicately balanced throughout most of the Gilded Age (a sarcastic name given to the three-decade-long post–Civil War era by Mark Twain in 1873). Even a slight nudge could tip the teeter-totter to the advantage of the opposition party. Every presidential election was a squeaker, and the majority party in the House of Representatives switched six times in the eleven sessions between 1869 and 1891. Wobbling in such shaky equilibrium, politicians tiptoed timidly, producing a political record that was often trivial and petty.

Few significant economic issues separated the major parties. Democrats and Republicans saw very nearly eye-to-eye on questions like the tariff and civil-service reform, and majorities in both parties substantially agreed even on the much-debated currency question. Yet despite their rough agreement on these national matters, the two parties were ferociously competitive with each other. They were tightly and efficiently organized, and they commanded fierce loyalty from their members. Voter turnouts reached heights unmatched before or since. Nearly 80 percent of eligible voters cast their ballots in presidential elections in the three decades after the Civil War. On election days droves of the party faithful tramped behind marching bands to the polling places, and "ticket splitting," or failing to vote the straight party line, was as rare as a silver dollar.

How can this apparent paradox of political **consensus** and partisan fervor be explained? The answer lies in the sharp ethnic and cultural differences in the membership of the two parties—in distinctions of style and tone, and especially of religious sentiment. Republican voters tended to adhere to those creeds that traced their lineage to Puritanism. They stressed strict codes of personal morality and believed that government should play a role in regulating both the economic and the moral affairs of society. Democrats, among whom immigrant Lutherans and Roman Catholics figured heavily, were more likely to adhere to faiths that took a less stern view of human weakness. Their religions professed toleration of differences in an imperfect world, and they spurned government efforts to impose a single moral standard on the entire society. These differences in temperament and religious values often produced raucous political contests at the local level, where issues like prohibition and education loomed large.

Democrats had a solid electoral base in the South and in the northern industrial cities, teeming with immigrants and controlled by well-oiled political machines. Republican strength lay largely in the Midwest and the rural and small-town Northeast. Grateful freedmen in the South continued to vote Republican in significant numbers. Another important bloc of Republican ballots came from the members of the Grand Army of the Republic (GAR)—a politically potent organization of several hundred thousand Union veterans of the Civil War.

The lifeblood of both parties was patronage—disbursing jobs by the bucketful in return for votes, **kickbacks,** and party service. Boisterous infighting over patronage beset the Republican party in the 1870s and 1880s. A "Stalwart" faction, led by the handsome and imperious Senator Roscoe ("Lord Roscoe") Conkling of New York, unblushingly embraced the time-honored system of swapping jobs for votes. Opposed to the Conklingites were the so-called Half-Breeds, who flirted coyly with civil-service reform, but whose real quarrel with the Stalwarts was over who should grasp the ladle that dished out the spoils. The champion of the Half-Breeds was James G. Blaine, a radiantly personable congressman from Maine with a fine physical presence, a thrilling speaking voice, and an elastic conscience. But

Online Study Center

Primary source
Political Symbols
college.hmco.com/pic/kennedybrief7e

consensus *Common or near-unanimous opinion.*

kickback *The return of a portion of the money received in a sale or contract, often secretly or illegally, in exchange for favors.*

despite all the color of their personalities, Conkling and Blaine succeeded only in stalemating each other and deadlocking their party.

The Hayes-Tilden Standoff, 1876

Hangers-on around Grant, like fleas urging their ailing dog to live, begged the "Old Man" to try for a third term in 1876. The general, blind to his own ineptitudes, showed a disquieting willingness. But the House, by a lopsided bipartisan vote of 233 to 18, spiked the third-term boom. It passed a resolution that sternly reminded the country—and Grant—of the antidictator implications of the two-term tradition.

With Grant out of the running and with the Conklingites and Blaineites neutralizing each other, the Republicans turned to a compromise candidate, Rutherford B. Hayes, who was obscure enough to be dubbed "the Great Unknown." His foremost qualification was having served as three-term governor of the potent "swing" state of Ohio, which was so crucial to the cliffhanging electoral contests of the day that it regularly produced presidential candidates.

Pitted against the humdrum Hayes was the Democratic nominee, Samuel J. Tilden, who had risen to fame as the man who bagged Boss Tweed in New York. Campaigning against Republican scandal, Tilden racked up 184 electoral votes of the needed 185, with 20 votes in four states doubtful because of irregular returns. Oregon eventually fell completely to Hayes, but surely Tilden could pick up at least one of the other three, especially in view of the fact that he had polled 247,448 more popular votes than Hayes, 4,284,020 to 4,036,572.

Both parties scurried to send "visiting statesmen" to the still-contested southern states of Louisiana, South Carolina, and Florida. All three disputed states submitted two sets of returns, one Democratic and one Republican. As the weeks drifted by, the paralysis tightened, generating a dramatic constitutional crisis. The Constitution merely specifies that the electoral returns from the states shall be sent to Congress, and in the presence of the House and Senate they shall be opened by the president of the Senate (see the Twelfth Amendment). But who should count them? On this point the Constitution was silent. If counted by the president of the Senate (a Republican), the Republican returns would be selected. If counted by the Speaker of the House (a Democrat), the Democratic returns would be chosen. How could the impasse be resolved?

The Compromise of 1877 and the End of Reconstruction

Clash or compromise was the stark choice. The danger loomed that there would be no president on inauguration day, March 4, 1877. "Tilden or Blood!" cried Democratic hotheads, and some of their "Minute Men" began to drill with arms. But behind the scenes, frantically laboring statesmen gradually hammered out an agreement in the Henry Clay tradition—the Compromise of 1877.

The election deadlock itself was to be broken by the Electoral Count Act, which passed Congress early in 1877. It set up an electoral commission consisting of fifteen men selected from the Senate, the House, and the Supreme Court.

In February 1877, about a month before Inauguration Day, the Senate and House met together in an electric atmosphere to settle the dispute. The roll of the states was tolled off alphabetically. When Florida was reached, the disputed documents were referred to the electoral commission, which sat in a nearby chamber. After prolonged discussion the members agreed, by the partisan vote of eight Republicans to seven Democrats, to accept the Republican returns. Outraged Democrats in Congress, smelling defeat, undertook to launch a filibuster "until hell froze over."

Renewed deadlock was avoided by the rest of the complex Compromise of 1877, already partially concluded behind closed doors. The Democrats reluctantly agreed that Hayes might take office in return for his withdrawing intimidating federal troops from the two states in which they remained,

Online Study Center

Primary source
Disputed Election of 1876, The
college.hmco.com/pic/kennedybrief7e

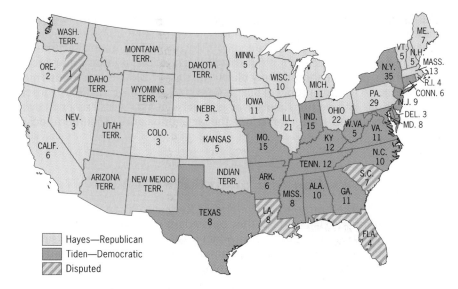

Louisiana and South Carolina. Among various concessions, the Republicans assured the Democrats a place at the presidential patronage trough and support for a bill subsidizing the Texas and Pacific Railroad's construction of a southern transcontinental line. Not all of these promises were kept in later years, including the Texas and Pacific subsidy. But the deal held together long enough to break the dangerous electoral standoff.

The compromise bought peace at a price. Violence was averted by sacrificing the black freedmen in the South. With the Hayes-Tilden deal, the Republican party quietly abandoned its commitment to black equality. That commitment had been weakening, in any case. The Civil Rights Act of 1875 was in a sense the last feeble gasp of the congressional radical Republicans. The act supposedly guaranteed equal accommodations in public places and prohibited racial discrimination in jury selection, but the law was born toothless and stayed that way for nearly a century. The Supreme Court pronounced much of the act unconstitutional in the *Civil Rights Cases* (1883), declaring that the Fourteenth Amendment prohibited only *government* violations of civil rights, not the denial of civil rights by *individuals.* Hayes clinched the bargain by withdrawing the last federal troops that were propping up carpetbag governments. The bayonet-backed Republican regimes collapsed as the blue-clad soldiers departed.

The Birth of Jim Crow in the South

Reconstruction was officially ended. Relying shamelessly on fraud and intimidation, white Democrats ("Redeemers") resumed political power in the South and ruthlessly suppressed the now-friendless blacks. For generations to come, blacks (as well as poor whites) were forced into sharecropping and tenant farming under conditions scarcely better than slavery. Through the "crop-**lien**" system, storekeepers extended credit to small farmers for food and supplies and in return took a lien on their customers' harvests. Shrewd merchants manipulated the system so that farmers remained perpetually in debt to them.

With white southerners back in the political saddle, daily discrimination against blacks grew increasingly oppressive. What had started as the informal separation of blacks and whites in the immediate postwar years developed by the 1890s into systematic state-level codes of segregation known as Jim Crow laws. Southern states also enacted literacy requirements, voter-registration laws, and poll taxes to ensure full-scale disfranchisement of the South's black population. The Supreme Court validated the South's segregationist social order in the case of *Plessy* v. *Ferguson* (1896). It ruled that "separate but equal" facilities were constitutional under the "equal protection" clause of the Fourteenth Amendment.

lien *A legal claim by a lender or another party on a borrower's property as a guarantee against repayment, and prohibiting any sale of the property.*

But in reality the quality of African American life was grotesquely unequal to that of whites. Segregated in inferior schools and separated from whites in virtually all public facilities, blacks were assaulted daily by reminders of their second-class citizenship. To ensure the stability of this political and economic "new order," southern whites dealt harshly with any black who dared to violate the South's racial code of conduct. A record number of blacks were lynched during the 1890s, most often for the "crime" of asserting themselves as equals. It would take a second Reconstruction, nearly a century later, to redress the racist imbalance of southern society.

Class Conflicts and Ethnic Clashes

The year 1877 marked more than the end of Reconstruction. As the curtains officially closed on regional warfare, they opened on scenes of class warfare. The explosive atmosphere was largely a by-product of the long years of depression and **deflation** following the panic of 1873. Railroad workers faced particularly hard times. When the presidents of the nation's four largest railroads collectively decided in 1877 to cut employees' wages by 10 percent, the workers struck back. President Hayes's decision to call in federal troops to quell the unrest brought the striking laborers an outpouring of working-class support. Work stoppages spread like wildfire in cities from Baltimore to St. Louis. When the battling between workers and soldiers ended after several weeks, over one hundred people were dead.

The failure of the great railroad strike exposed the weakness of the labor movement. Racial and ethnic fissures among workers fractured labor unity and were particularly acute between the Irish and Chinese in California (see "Makers of America: The Chinese," pp. 348–349). By 1880 the Golden State counted seventy-five thousand Asian newcomers, about 9 percent of its entire population.

Mostly single males from K'uang-t'ung (Guangdong) province in southern China, these newcomers had originally come to labor in the gold fields and on the transcontinental railroads across the West. When those jobs ended, the Chinese who remained worked at the most menial jobs, often as cooks, laundrymen, or domestic servants. Without women or families, these Chinese males faced extraordinary hardships and lived lonely lives.

In San Francisco, Irish-born demagogue Denis Kearney incited his followers, many of them recently arrived European immigrants, to violent abuse of the hapless Chinese. Taking to the streets, gangs of Kearneyites terrorized the Asians by shearing off precious pigtails. Some victims were murdered outright.

Congress finally slammed the door on Chinese immigrant laborers when it passed the Chinese Exclusion Act in 1882, prohibiting all further immigration from China. The door stayed shut until 1943. Some exclusionists even tried to strip native-born Chinese-Americans of their citizenship, but the Supreme Court ruled in *U.S.* v. *Wong Kim Ark* in 1898 that the Fourteenth Amendment guaranteed citizenship to all persons born in the United States. This doctrine of "birthright citizenship" provided important protections to Chinese-Americans as well as to other immigrant communities.

Garfield and Arthur

As the presidential campaign of 1880 approached, "Rutherfraud" Hayes was a man without a party, repudi-

---

deflation (ary) *An increase in the value of money in relation to available goods, causing prices to fall.* **Inflation,** *a decrease in the value of money in relation to goods, causes prices to rise.*

Online Study Center

Primary source
What Shall We Do with Our Boys
college.hmco.com/pic/kennedybrief7e

Online Study Center

Primary source
Chinese Exclusion Act
college.hmco.com/pic/kennedybrief7e

■ The First Blow at the Chinese Question, 1877
Caucasian workers, seething with economic anxiety and ethnic prejudice, savagely mistreated the Chinese in California in the 1870s.

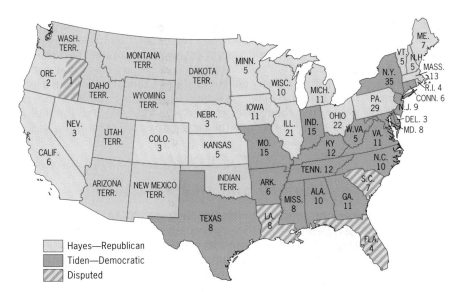

Hayes-Tilden Disputed Election of 1876 (with electoral vote by state) Nineteen of the twenty disputed votes composed the total electoral count of Louisiana, South Carolina, and Florida. The twentieth was one of Oregon's three votes, cast by an elector who turned out to be ineligible because he was a federal officeholder (a postmaster), contrary to the Constitution (see Art. II, Sec. I, para. 2).

Louisiana and South Carolina. Among various concessions, the Republicans assured the Democrats a place at the presidential patronage trough and support for a bill subsidizing the Texas and Pacific Railroad's construction of a southern transcontinental line. Not all of these promises were kept in later years, including the Texas and Pacific subsidy. But the deal held together long enough to break the dangerous electoral standoff.

The compromise bought peace at a price. Violence was averted by sacrificing the black freedmen in the South. With the Hayes-Tilden deal, the Republican party quietly abandoned its commitment to black equality. That commitment had been weakening, in any case. The Civil Rights Act of 1875 was in a sense the last feeble gasp of the congressional radical Republicans. The act supposedly guaranteed equal accommodations in public places and prohibited racial discrimination in jury selection, but the law was born toothless and stayed that way for nearly a century. The Supreme Court pronounced much of the act unconstitutional in the *Civil Rights Cases* (1883), declaring that the Fourteenth Amendment prohibited only *government* violations of civil rights, not the denial of civil rights by *individuals*. Hayes clinched the bargain by withdrawing the last federal troops that were propping up carpetbag governments. The bayonet-backed Republican regimes collapsed as the blue-clad soldiers departed.

The Birth of Jim Crow in the South

Reconstruction was officially ended. Relying shamelessly on fraud and intimidation, white Democrats ("Redeemers") resumed political power in the South and ruthlessly suppressed the now-friendless blacks. For generations to come, blacks (as well as poor whites) were forced into sharecropping and tenant farming under conditions scarcely better than slavery. Through the "crop-**lien**" system, storekeepers extended credit to small farmers for food and supplies and in return took a lien on their customers' harvests. Shrewd merchants manipulated the system so that farmers remained perpetually in debt to them.

With white southerners back in the political saddle, daily discrimination against blacks grew increasingly oppressive. What had started as the informal separation of blacks and whites in the immediate postwar years developed by the 1890s into systematic state-level codes of segregation known as Jim Crow laws. Southern states also enacted literacy requirements, voter-registration laws, and poll taxes to ensure full-scale disfranchisement of the South's black population. The Supreme Court validated the South's segregationist social order in the case of *Plessy* v. *Ferguson* (1896). It ruled that "separate but equal" facilities were constitutional under the "equal protection" clause of the Fourteenth Amendment.

lien *A legal claim by a lender or another party on a borrower's property as a guarantee against repayment, and prohibiting any sale of the property.*

But in reality the quality of African American life was grotesquely unequal to that of whites. Segregated in inferior schools and separated from whites in virtually all public facilities, blacks were assaulted daily by reminders of their second-class citizenship. To ensure the stability of this political and economic "new order," southern whites dealt harshly with any black who dared to violate the South's racial code of conduct. A record number of blacks were lynched during the 1890s, most often for the "crime" of asserting themselves as equals. It would take a second Reconstruction, nearly a century later, to redress the racist imbalance of southern society.

Class Conflicts and Ethnic Clashes

The year 1877 marked more than the end of Reconstruction. As the curtains officially closed on regional warfare, they opened on scenes of class warfare. The explosive atmosphere was largely a by-product of the long years of depression and **deflation** following the panic of 1873. Railroad workers faced particularly hard times. When the presidents of the nation's four largest railroads collectively decided in 1877 to cut employees' wages by 10 percent, the workers struck back. President Hayes's decision to call in federal troops to quell the unrest brought the striking laborers an outpouring of working-class support. Work stoppages spread like wildfire in cities from Baltimore to St. Louis. When the battling between workers and soldiers ended after several weeks, over one hundred people were dead.

The failure of the great railroad strike exposed the weakness of the labor movement. Racial and ethnic fissures among workers fractured labor unity and were particularly acute between the Irish and Chinese in California (see "Makers of America: The Chinese," pp. 348–349). By 1880 the Golden State counted seventy-five thousand Asian newcomers, about 9 percent of its entire population.

Mostly single males from K'uang-t'ung (Guangdong) province in southern China, these newcomers had originally come to labor in the gold fields and on the transcontinental railroads across the West. When those jobs ended, the Chinese who remained worked at the most menial jobs, often as cooks, laundrymen, or domestic servants. Without women or families, these Chinese males faced extraordinary hardships and lived lonely lives.

In San Francisco, Irish-born demagogue Denis Kearney incited his followers, many of them recently arrived European immigrants, to violent abuse of the hapless Chinese. Taking to the streets, gangs of Kearneyites terrorized the Asians by shearing off precious pigtails. Some victims were murdered outright.

Congress finally slammed the door on Chinese immigrant laborers when it passed the Chinese Exclusion Act in 1882, prohibiting all further immigration from China. The door stayed shut until 1943. Some exclusionists even tried to strip native-born Chinese-Americans of their citizenship, but the Supreme Court ruled in *U.S.* v. *Wong Kim Ark* in 1898 that the Fourteenth Amendment guaranteed citizenship to all persons born in the United States. This doctrine of "birthright citizenship" provided important protections to Chinese-Americans as well as to other immigrant communities.

deflation (ary) *An increase in the value of money in relation to available goods, causing prices to fall.* **Inflation,** *a decrease in the value of money in relation to goods, causes prices to rise.*

Online Study Center

Primary source
What Shall We Do with Our Boys
college.hmco.com/pic/kennedybrief7e

Online Study Center

Primary source
Chinese Exclusion Act
college.hmco.com/pic/kennedybrief7e

■ **The First Blow at the Chinese Question, 1877**
Caucasian workers, seething with economic anxiety and ethnic prejudice, savagely mistreated the Chinese in California in the 1870s.

Garfield and Arthur

As the presidential campaign of 1880 approached, "Rutherfraud" Hayes was a man without a party, repudiated by the Republican Old Guard. Seeking a new standard-bearer, the Republicans finally settled on a "dark-horse" candidate, Congressman James A. Garfield of Ohio. His vice-presidential running mate was a notorious Stalwart henchman, Chester A. Arthur of New York.

Energetically waving the bloody shirt, Garfield barely squeaked out a victory over the Democratic candidate, Civil War hero Winfield Scott Hancock. Garfield polled only 39,213 more votes than Hancock—4,453,295 to 4,414,082—but his margin in the electoral column was a comfortable 214 to 155.

The new president was an energetic and able man, but he was immediately ensnared in political conflict between his secretary of state, James G. Blaine, and Blaine's Stalwart nemesis, Senator Roscoe Conkling. Then, as the Republican factions dueled, tragedy struck. A disappointed and mentally deranged office seeker, Charles J. Guiteau, shot President Garfield in the back in a Washington railroad station. Garfield died eleven weeks later, on September 19, 1881, and Chester Arthur assumed the presidency.

Garfield's death did have one positive outcome: it shocked politicians into reforming the shameful spoils system. The unlikely instrument of reform was Chester Arthur. Arthur's record of cronyism and fondness for fine wines and elegant clothing (including eighty pairs of trousers) suggested that he was little more than a foppish dandy. But as the new president, Arthur surprised his critics by prosecuting several fraud cases and giving his former Stalwart pals the cold shoulder.

Disgust with Garfield's murder also gave the Republican party itself a previously undetected taste for reform. The medicine finally applied to the longsuffering federal government was the Pendleton Act of 1883—the so-called Magna Carta of civil-service reform. It made compulsory campaign contributions from federal employees illegal, and it established the Civil Service Commission to make appointments to federal jobs on the basis of competitive examinations rather than party pull.

Although at first covering only about 10 percent of federal jobs, **civil service** did rein in the most blatant political abuses. Yet like many well-intentioned reforms, it bred unintended problems of its own. With the "plum" federal posts now beyond their reach, politicians were forced to look elsewhere for money, the "mother's milk of politics." Increasingly, they turned to the bulging coffers of the big corporations. A new breed of boss emerged—less skilled at mobilizing small armies of immigrants and other voters on election day, but more adept at milking dollars from manufacturers and lobbyists.

Online Study Center

Primary source
Plunkitt Scorns Reform
college.hmco.com/pic/kennedybrief7e

civil service *Referring to regular employment by government according to a standardized system of job descriptions, merit qualifications, pay, and promotion, as distinct from* **political appointees** *who receive positions based on affiliation and party loyalty.*

The Blaine-Cleveland Mudslingers of 1884

President Arthur's surprising display of integrity offended too many powerful Republicans, and his ungrateful party refused to nominate him in 1884. Instead they turned to James G. Blaine, whose persistence in pursuit of the presidential nomination finally paid off. The dashing Maine politician, blessed with almost every asset except a reputation for honesty, was enthusiastically nominated by the regulars at the Republican convention in Chicago, though reformers gagged at his candidacy.

Blaine's enemies publicized the Republican nominee's fishy-smelling "Mulligan letters," written by Blaine to a Boston businessman. These damning documents linked Blaine to a corrupt deal involving federal favors to a southern railroad, and one of them ended with the furtive warning "Burn this letter." Some reformers, unable to swallow Blaine, bolted to the Democrats. They were sneeringly dubbed Mugwumps, a word of Indian derivation meaning "sanctimonious" or "holier than thou."

Victory-starved Democrats turned enthusiastically to a noted reformer, Grover Cleveland. A burly bachelor with a soup-straining mustache and a taste for chewing tobacco, Cleveland was a solid but not brilliant lawyer

New York political "boss" Roscoe Conkling (1829–1888) denounced the civil-service reformers in the New York World *(1877):*

"[The reformers'] vocation and ministry is to lament the sins of other people. Their stock in trade is rancid, canting self-righteousness. They are wolves in sheep's clothing. Their real object is office and plunder. When Dr. Johnson defined patriotism as the last refuge of a scoundrel, he was unconscious of the then undeveloped capabilities and uses of the word 'Reform.'"

The Chinese

In the late nineteenth century, the burgeoning industries and booming frontier towns of the United States' Pacific Coast hungered for laborers. In faraway Asia the Chinese answered the call. Contributing their muscle to the building of the West, they dug in the gold mines and helped to lay the transcontinental railroads that stitched together the American nation.

The first major wave of Chinese came in response to the discovery of gold in California in 1848. The fortune-hungry immigrants who sailed into San Francisco named the city the "golden mountain." A treaty negotiated with China in 1868 by the American diplomat Anson Burlingame guaranteed important civil rights to Chinese immigrants.

The California boom coincided with years of tumult and suffering in China. As the once-great Chinese Empire disintegrated, the European imperial powers forced their way into the unstable country. Faced with economic hardship and political turmoil, more than 2 million Chinese left their homeland between 1840 and 1900, for destinations as diverse as Southeast Asia, Peru, Hawaii, and Cuba. More than 300,000 entered the United States. Although their numbers included a few merchants and artisans, most were desperately poor and unskilled country folk.

The Chinese America of the late-nineteenth-century West was overwhelmingly a bachelor society. Women of good repute rarely made the passage. Of the very few Chinese women who did venture to California at this time, most became prostitutes. Many of them had been deceived by the false promise of honest jobs.

Although a stream of workers returned to China, many Chinese stayed. "Chinatowns" sprang up wherever

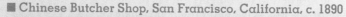
■ Chinese Butcher Shop, San Francisco, California, c. 1890

economic opportunities presented themselves. Chinese in these settlements spoke their own language, enjoyed the fellowship of their own compatriots, and sought safety from prejudice and violence. Many immigrant clubs and associations were American adaptations of Chinese traditions of loyalty to clan. The poorest and most alienated immigrants also established *tongs*—literally, "meeting halls"—secret societies that acquired a sinister reputation among non-Chinese.

Mounting anti-Chinese agitation forced the repudiation of the Burlingame Treaty in 1880, and in 1882 the Chinese Exclusion Act barred nearly all Chinese from the United States for six decades. Many of the bachelors died or returned home. Slowly, however, those men and the few women who remained raised families and reared a new generation of Chinese Americans. This second generation still suffered from discrimination, eking out their living in jobs despised by Caucasian laborers or taking daunting risks in small entrepreneurial ventures. Yet many hard-working Chinese did manage to open their own restaurants, laundries, and other small businesses. Such enterprises formed a solid economic foundation for their small community and remain a source of livelihood for many Chinese Americans even today.

of forty-seven. He had rocketed from the Buffalo mayor's office to the governorship of New York and the presidential nomination in three short years. Known as "Grover the Good," he enjoyed a well-deserved reputation for probity in office.

But Cleveland's admirers soon got a shock. Resolute Republicans, digging for dirt in the past of bachelor Cleveland, unearthed the report that he had been involved in an amorous affair with a Buffalo widow. Cleveland had provided financial support for her illegitimate son, now eight years old. Demoralized Democratic elders hurried to Cleveland and urged him to lie like a gentleman, but their ruggedly honest candidate insisted, "Tell the truth."

■ *"I Want My Pa!"* Malicious anti-Cleveland cartoon.

The campaign of 1884 sank to perhaps the lowest level in American experience, as the two parties grunted and shoved for the hog trough of office. Few fundamental differences separated them. Even the bloody shirt had faded to pale pink.* Personalities, not principles, claimed the headlines. Crowds of Democrats surged through city streets, chanting—to the rhythm of left, left, left, right, left—"Burn, burn, burn this letter!" Republicans taunted in return, "Ma, ma, where's my pa?" Defiant Democrats shouted back, "Gone to the White House, ha, ha, ha!"

The contest hinged on the state of New York, where Blaine blundered badly in the closing days of the campaign. A witless Republican clergyman damned the Democrats in a speech as the party of "Rum, Romanism, and Rebellion"—insulting with one swift stroke the culture, the faith, and the patriotism of New York's numerous Irish-Americans. Blaine was present at the time but lacked the presence of mind to repudiate the statement immediately. The pungent phrase, shortened to "RRR," stung and stuck. Blaine's silence seemed to give assent, and the wavering Irishmen who then deserted his camp helped to account for Cleveland's paper-thin plurality of about a thousand votes in New York State, enough to give him the presidency. Cleveland swept the solid South and squeaked into office with 219 to 182 electoral votes and 4,879,507 to 4,850,293 popular votes.

"Old Grover" Takes Over

Bull-necked Cleveland in 1885 was the first Democrat to take the oath of presidential office since Buchanan, twenty-eight years earlier. Huge question marks hung over his portly frame (5 feet 11 inches, 250 pounds). Could the "party of disunion" be trusted to govern the Union? Would desperate Democrats, ravenously hungry after twenty-four years of exile, trample the frail sprouts of civil-service reform in a stampede to the patronage trough? Could Cleveland restore a measure of respect and power to the maligned and enfeebled presidency?

Cleveland was a man of principles, most of them safely orthodox by the standards of the day. A staunch apostle of the hands-off creed of **laissez-faire**, the new president summed up his political philosophy in 1887 when he vetoed a bill to provide seeds for drought-ravaged Texas farmers. "Though the people support the government," he declared, "the government should not support the people." As tactless as a mirror and as direct as a bulldozer, Cleveland was outspoken, unbending, and profanely hot-tempered.

At the outset Cleveland narrowed the North-South chasm by naming to the cabinet two former Confederates. As for the civil service, Cleveland was whipsawed between the demands of the Democratic faithful for jobs and the demands of the Mugwumps, who had helped elect him, for reform. Believing in the merit system, Cleveland at first favored the cause of the reformers, but he eventually caved in to the carpings of Democratic bosses and fired almost two-thirds of the 120,000 federal employees, including 40,000 incumbent (Republican) postmasters, to make room for "deserving Democrats."

Military pensions gave Cleveland some of his most painful political headaches. The politically powerful Grand Army of the Republic (GAR) routinely lobbied hundreds of often questionable private pension bills through a compliant Congress. As a non-veteran, Cleveland was in an awkward position to fight the pension grabbers, but he conscientiously read each bill and ended up vetoing several hundred of them.

Cleveland also risked his political neck by prodding the hornet's nest of the tariff issue. Jacked up to new high levels during the Civil War, the tariff duties were producing enormous revenues while comfortably sheltering American industry.

laissez-faire *The doctrine of noninterference, especially by the government, in matters of economics or business (literally, "leave alone").*

---

* Neither candidate had served in the Civil War. Cleveland had hired a substitute to go in his stead while he supported his widowed mother and two sisters. Blaine was the only candidate nominated by the Republicans from Grant through McKinley (1868–1900) who had not been a Civil War officer.

By 1881 the Treasury was running an annual surplus amounting to an embarrassing $145 million. Congress could reduce the surplus either by squandering it on pensions or other "**pork-barrel**" bills or by lowering the tariff—something big industrialists vehemently opposed.

With his characteristic bluntness, Cleveland tossed an appeal for lower tariffs like a bombshell into the lap of Congress in late 1887. The response was electric. Democrats were deeply distressed at the obstinacy of their chief. Republicans rejoiced at his apparent recklessness. The old warrior Blaine gloated, "There's one more president for us in [tariff] protection." For the first time in years, a real issue divided the two parties as the 1888 presidential election loomed.

Dismayed Democrats, seeing no alternative, dejectedly nominated Cleveland at their St. Louis convention, while eager Republicans turned to Benjamin Harrison of Indiana, the grandson of former president William Henry ("Tippecanoe") Harrison. The tariff was the prime issue, and the two parties flooded the country with some 10 million pamphlets on the subject. Republicans raised an unprecedented $3 million war chest, largely by "frying the fat" out of nervous industrialists. The money was widely used to line up corrupt "voting cattle," known as "repeaters" or "floaters," especially in crucial swing states like Indiana.

On election day, Harrison nosed out Cleveland, 233 to 168 electoral votes. A change of about 7,000 ballots in New York would have reversed the outcome. Cleveland actually polled more popular votes, 5,537,857 to 5,447,129, but he nevertheless became the first sitting president to be voted out of his chair since Martin Van Buren in 1840.

> *On the night before the inauguration of Harrison, a crowd of jubilant Republicans tauntingly serenaded the darkened White House with a popular campaign ditty directed at Grover Cleveland:*
>
> Down in the cornfield
> Hear that mournful sound;
> All the Democrats are weeping—
> Grover's in the cold, cold ground!
>
> *But Grover was to rise again and serve as president for a second term of four more years.*

pork-barrel *In American politics, government appropriations for political purposes, especially projects designed to please a legislator's local constituency.*

Online Study Center
Primary source
Keep the Ball Rolling
college.hmco.com/pic/kennedybrief7e

Republicans Return Under Harrison

After a four-year famine, the Republicans under Harrison licked their lips hungrily for federal offices to lavish upon the party faithful. But in the House of Representatives they had only three votes more than the necessary quorum of 163 members, and the Democrats were preparing to obstruct all House business by refusing to answer roll calls, demanding roll calls to determine the presence of a quorum, and other similar delaying tactics.

Into this tense cockpit stepped the new Republican Speaker of the House, Thomas B. Reed of Maine. A tall, hulking figure, Reed was a master debater who spoke with a harsh nasal drawl and wielded a verbal harpoon of sarcasm. To one congressman who quoted Henry Clay's saying that he would "rather be right than president," Reed caustically retorted that he "would never be either." Opponents cringed at the crack of his quip.

"Czar" Reed soon bent the intimidated House to his imperious will. Employing clever parliamentary tactics to the full, Reed utterly dominated the "Billion-Dollar" Congress—the first in history to appropriate that sum. Congress showered pensions on Civil War veterans and increased government purchases of silver. To keep the revenues flowing in—and to protect Republican industrialists from foreign competition—the Billion-Dollar Congress also passed the McKinley Tariff Act of 1890, boosting rates to their highest peacetime level ever (an average of 48.4 percent on dutiable goods).

Sponsored in the House of Representatives by rising Republican star William McKinley of Ohio, the new tariff act brought fresh woes to farmers. Debt-burdened farmers had no choice but to buy high-priced manufactured goods from protected American industrialists, but they were compelled to sell their own agricultural products into highly competitive, unprotected world markets. Mounting discontent against Bill McKinley and his McKinley Bill caused many rural voters to rise in wrath. In the congressional elections of 1890, Republicans lost their precarious majority and were reduced to just 88 seats, compared with 235 Democrats. Ominously for conservatives, the new Congress also included nine members of the Farmers' Alliance, a militant organization of southern and western farmers.

The Drumbeat of Discontent

Politics was no longer "as usual" in 1892, when the newly formed People's party, or "Populists," burst upon the scene. Rooted in the Farmers' Alliances in the great agricultural belts of the West and South, the Populists met in Omaha and adopted a scorching platform that denounced the "prolific womb of governmental injustice." They demanded inflation through free and unlimited coinage of silver at the ratio of sixteen ounces of silver to one ounce of gold. They further called for a graduated income tax; government ownership of the railroads, telephone, and telegraph; the direct election of U.S. senators; a one-term limit on the presidency; the adoption of the initiative and referendum to allow citizens to shape legislation more directly; a shorter workday; and immigration restrictions. As their presidential candidate the Populists uproariously nominated the eloquent old Greenbacker, General James B. Weaver.

An epidemic of nationwide strikes in the summer of 1892 raised the prospect that the Populists could weld together a coalition of aggrieved workers and indebted farmers in a revolutionary joint assault on the capitalist order. At Andrew Carnegie's Homestead steel plant near Pittsburgh, company officials called in three hundred armed Pinkerton detectives in July to crush a strike by steelworkers angry over pay cuts. Defiant strikers, armed with rifles and dynamite, forced their assailants to surrender after a vicious battle that left ten people dead and some sixty wounded. Troops were eventually summoned, and both the strike and the union were broken. That same month, federal troops bloodily smashed a strike among silver miners in Idaho's Coeur d'Alene district.

The Populists made a remarkable showing in the 1892 presidential election. Singing "Good-bye, Party Bosses," they rolled up 1,029,846 popular votes and 22 electoral votes for General Weaver. They thus became one of the few third parties in U.S. history to break into the electoral column. But they fell far short of an electoral majority. Industrial laborers, especially in the urban East, did not rally to the Populist banner in appreciable numbers. Populist electoral votes came from only six midwestern and western states, four of which (Kansas, Colorado, Idaho, and Nevada) fell completely into the Populist basket.

The South, although a hotbed of agrarian agitation, proved especially unwilling to throw in its lot with the new party. Race was the reason. The more than one million southern black farmers, organized in the Colored Farmers' National Alliance, shared a host of complaints with poor white farmers, and for a time their common economic goals promised to overcome their racial differences. Recognizing the crucial edge that black votes could give them in the South, Populist leaders like Georgia's Tom Watson reached out to the black community. Watson was a wiry redhead who could "talk like the thrust of a Bowie knife." He declared, "There is no reason why the black man should not understand that the law that hurts me, as a farmer, hurts him, as a farmer." Many blacks were disillusioned enough with the Republican party to respond. Alarmed, the conservative white "Bourbon" elite in the South played cynically upon historic racial antagonisms to counter the Populists' appeal for interracial solidarity and woo back poor whites.

Southern blacks were heavy losers. The Populist-inspired reminder of potential black political strength led to the near-total extinction of what little African American suffrage remained in the South. White southerners more aggressively than ever used literacy tests and poll taxes to deny blacks the ballot. The notorious "grandfather clause" exempted from those requirements anyone whose forebear had voted in 1860—when, of course,

A popular protest song of the 1890s among western farmers was titled "The Hayseed." One stanza ran,

I once was a tool of oppression,
And as green as a sucker could be,
And monopolies banded together
To beat a poor hayseed like me.

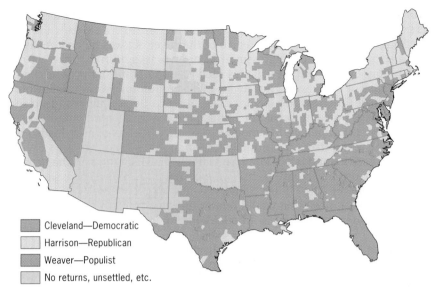

■ **Presidential Election of 1892 (showing vote by county)** Notice the concentration of Populist strength in the semiarid farming regions of the western half of the country. People living in territories (unsettled areas—see key) could not vote.

Cleveland—Democratic
Harrison—Republican
Weaver—Populist
No returns, unsettled, etc.

black slaves had not voted at all. More than half a century would pass before southern blacks could again vote in considerable numbers. Accompanying this disfranchisement were more severe Jim Crow laws designed to enforce racial segregation in public places, including hotels and restaurants, and backed up by atrocious lynchings and other forms of intimidation.

The conservative crusade to eliminate the black vote also had dire consequences for the Populist party itself. Even Tom Watson abandoned his interracial appeals and, in time, became a vociferous racist himself. After 1896 the Populist party lapsed increasingly into vile racism and staunchly advocated black disfranchisement. Such were the bitterly ironic fruits of the Populist campaign in the South.

Grover, Grim Times, and Gold

With the Populists divided and the Republicans discredited, Grover Cleveland took office once again in 1893, the only president ever reelected after defeat. He was the same old bull-necked and bull-headed Cleveland, with a little more weight, polish, conservatism, and self-assertiveness.

But though it was the same old Cleveland, it was not the same old country. Debtors were up in arms, workers were restless, and the advance shadows of panic were falling. Hardly had Cleveland seated himself back in the presidential chair when the devastating depression of 1893 burst about his burly frame. Lasting for about four years, it was the most punishing economic downturn of the nineteenth century. Contributing causes were the splurge of overbuilding and speculation, labor disorders, and the ongoing agricultural depression.

Distress ran deep and far. About eight thousand American businesses collapsed in six months. Dozens of railroad lines went into receivership. Soup kitchens fed the unemployed, while gangs of hoboes ("tramps") wandered aimlessly about the country. Local charities did their feeble best, but the federal government, bound by the let-nature-take-its-course philosophy of the times, saw no legitimate way to relieve the suffering masses.

Cleveland, who had earlier been bothered by a surplus, now faced a deepening deficit and a financial crisis. Owners of the paper currency issued under the Sherman Silver Purchase Act of 1890 were presenting the notes for redemption in gold. By law the notes then had to be reissued, and the new holders would then repeat the process, draining away gold in an "endless chain" operation.

Alarmingly, the gold reserve in the Treasury dropped below the $100 million regarded as the safe minimum for supporting about $350 million in outstanding

Online Study Center

Primary source
Sacrilegious Candidate, The
college.hmco.com/pic/kennedybrief7e

paper currency. Cleveland saw no alternative but to halt the bleeding away of gold by asking Congress to repeal the Sherman Silver Purchase Act of 1890.

The Congressional debate over repeal of the silver act was heated. A silver-tongued young Democratic congressman from Nebraska, thirty-three-year-old William Jennings Bryan, held the galleries spellbound for three hours as he championed the cause of free silver. The friends of silver announced that "hell would freeze over" before Congress passed the repeal measure. But an angered Cleveland used his patronage power to break the filibuster in the Senate and ram the measure through. He thus alienated Democratic silverites like Bryan and divided his own party at the very outset of his administration.

Repeal of the Sherman Silver Purchase Act only partially stopped the hemorrhaging of gold from the Treasury. In February 1894 the gold reserve sank to a dismaying $41 million. The United States was now in grave danger of going off the gold standard—a move that would render the nation's currency volatile and unreliable and also mortally cripple America's international trade.

Early in 1895 Cleveland turned in desperation to J. P. Morgan, "the bankers' banker" and the head of a Wall Street syndicate. After tense negotiations at the White House, Morgan and his fellow bankers agreed to lend the government $65 million in gold. They were obviously in business for profit, so they charged a commission amounting to about $7 million. The loan, at least temporarily, helped restore confidence in the nation's finances.

But the gold deal stirred up a storm. In the eyes of the silverites and other debtors, the Wall Street ogre represented all that was wicked and grasping in American politics. President Cleveland's secretive dealings with the mighty "Jupiter" Morgan were savagely condemned as a "sellout" of the national government. But Cleveland was certain that he had done no wrong. Sarcastically denying that he was "Morgan's errand boy," Cleveland asserted, "Without shame and without repentance I confess my share of the guilt."

Cleveland suffered further embarrassment with the passage of the Wilson-Gorman Tariff in 1894. The Democrats had pledged to lower tariffs, but by the time the measure made it through Congress, it had been so loaded with special-interest protection that it made scarcely a dent in the high McKinley Tariff rates. An outraged Cleveland grudgingly allowed the bill, which also contained a 2 percent tax on incomes over $4,000, to become law without his signature. When the Supreme Court struck down the income-tax provision in 1895,* the Populists and other disaffected groups found further proof that the courts were only the tools of the plutocrats.

Democratic political fortunes naturally suffered in the face of these setbacks. The tariff dynamite that had blasted the Republicans out of the House in 1890 now dislodged the Democrats, with a strong helping hand from the depression. The revitalized Republicans, singing "Times Are Mighty Hard," won the congressional elections of 1894 in a landslide—244 seats to 105 for the Democrats. Republicans looked forward to the 1896 presidential elections with unconcealed glee.

Despite his gruff integrity and occasional courage, Grover Cleveland failed utterly to cope with the serious economic crisis that befell the country in 1893. He was tied down in office by the same threads that held all the presidents of the day to Lilliputian levels. Grant, Hayes, Garfield, Arthur, Harrison, and Cleveland are often referred to as the "forgettable presidents." Bewhiskered and bland in person, they left mostly blanks—or blots—on the nation's political record, as issues like the tariff, the money question, and the rights of labor continued to fester. What little political vitality existed in Gilded Age America was to be found in local settings or in Congress, which overshadowed the White House for most of this period. But before the century ended, down-and-out debtors and disgruntled workers would make one last titanic effort to wring reform out of the political system—in the momentous election of 1896.

---

*It violated the "direct tax" clause. See Art. I, Sec. IX, para. 4 in the Appendix. The Sixteenth Amendment to the Constitution, adopted in 1913, permitted an income tax.

✪ Chapter Summary ✪

After the soaring ideals and tremendous sacrifices of the Civil War, the post–Civil War era was generally one of political disillusionment and even cynicism. Politicians from the White House to the courthouse were deeply enmeshed in corruption and scandal, while the actual economic, ethnic, and racial problems afflicting industrializing America festered beneath the surface without being seriously addressed.

The popular war hero Grant was a poor politician and his administration was rife with corruption. Despite occasional futile reform efforts by both high-minded "mugwumps" and third-party agrarians, politics in the Gilded Age was monopolized by the two patronage-fattened parties, which competed vigorously for spoils while essentially agreeing on most national policies. Cultural differences, different ethnic and religious constituencies, and deeply felt local issues fueled intense party competition and unprecedented voter participation. Periodic complaints by political reformers and "soft-money" farmers' advocates failed to make much of a dent on politics or the laissez-faire business economics of the time.

The deadlocked and bitterly contested 1876 election led to the crass Compromise of 1877, which put an end to Reconstruction at the price of abandoning southern blacks. An oppressive system of tenant farming and racial supremacy and segregation was thereafter fastened on the South, enforced by sometimes lethal violence. Racial prejudice against Chinese immigrants was also linked with labor unrest in the 1870s and 1880s.

Garfield's assassination by a disappointed office seeker spurred the beginnings of civil-service reform, but made politics more dependent on big business. Cleveland, the first Democratic president since the Civil War, proposed a lower tariff, creating the first real issue in national politics for some time. But the weakness of conventional politics was exposed by a major economic depression that began in 1893. This crisis, the worst of the nineteenth century, deepened the growing outcry from suffering farmers and workers against a government and economic system that seemed biased toward big business and the wealthy.

VARYING VIEWPOINTS

The Populists: Radicals or Reactionaries?

Taking their cue from contemporary satirical commentaries like Mark Twain and Charles Dudley Warner's *The Gilded Age* (1873), the first historians who wrote about the post–Civil War era judged it harshly. They condemned its politicians as petty and corrupt, lamented the emergence of a new plutocratic class, and railed against the arrogance of corporate power. Such a view is conspicuous in Charles and Mary Beard's *The Rise of American Civilization* (4 vols., 1927–1942) and in Vernon Louis Parrington's classic *Main Currents in American Thought* (3 vols. 1927–1930), in which the entire post–Civil War period is contemptuously dismissed as "the great barbecue."

The Beards and Parrington were leaders of the anti-business and pro-reform progressive school of historical writing that flourished in the early years of the twentieth century. Progressive historians identified Populism as virtually the only organized opposition to the social, economic, and political order that took shape in the last decades of the nineteenth century. The Populists thus became heroes to historians like John D. Hicks, whose work *The Populist Revolt* (1931) is the classic portrayal of the Populists as embattled farmers hurling defiance at Wall Street and the robber barons in defense of their simple, honest way of life. Bowed but unbroken by the defeat of their great champion, William Jennings Bryan, in the election of 1896, the Populists, Hicks claimed, left a reformist legacy that flourished again in the progressive era and the New Deal.

Hicks's point of view was the dominant one until the 1950s, when it was sharply criticized by Richard Hofstadter in *The Age of Reform* (1955). The city-born-and-bred Hofstadter argued that the Populists were best understood not as picturesque protesters, but as "harassed little country businessmen" bristling with provincial prejudices not just against Wall Street, but also irrationally against urbanism, immigrants, the East, and modernity itself. Hofstadter thus exposed a "dark side" of Populism that contained elements of backwoods anti-intellectualism, paranoia, and even anti-Semitism.

In the 1960s several scholars, inspired by the work of C. Vann Woodward, as well as by sympathy with the protest movements of that turbulent decade, began to rehabilitate the Populists as authentic reformers with genuine grievances. Especially notable in this vein was Lawrence Goodwyn's *Democratic Promise: The Populist Moment in America* (1976), which portrayed Populism as the last gasp of popular political revolt against urban industrialism and finance capitalism, a democratic "moment" in American history that expired with the Populists' absorption into the Democratic party.

Two subsequent works, Edward L. Ayers's *Promise of the New South* (1992) and Robert C. McMath's *American Populism* (1993), synthesized many of the older perspectives and presented a balanced view of the Populists as radical in many ways but also limited by their nostalgia for a lost agrarian past.

24

Industry Comes of Age

1865–1900

THE WEALTHY CLASS IS BECOMING MORE WEALTHY, BUT THE
POORER CLASS IS BECOMING MORE DEPENDENT. THE GULF
BETWEEN THE EMPLOYED AND THE EMPLOYER IS GROWING
WIDER; SOCIAL CONTRASTS ARE BECOMING SHARPER; AS
LIVERIED CARRIAGES APPEAR, SO DO BAREFOOTED CHILDREN.

HENRY GEORGE, 1879

Chapter Outline

⭐ The Railroad Boom

⭐ Speculators and Financiers

⭐ Early Efforts at Government Regulation

⭐ Lords of Industry

⭐ Industry in the South

⭐ Workers and Unions

⭐ Makers of America: The Knights of Labor

⭐ Varying Viewpoints: Industrialization: Boon or Blight?

As the nineteenth century drew toward a close, observers were asking, "Why are the best men not in politics?" One answer was that they were being lured away from public life by the lusty attractions of the booming private economy. As America's Industrial Revolution slipped into high gear, talented men ached for profits, not the presidency. They dreamed of controlling corporations, not Congress. What the nation lost in civic leadership, it gained in an astounding surge of economic growth. Although in many ways still a political dwarf, the United States was about to stand up before the world as an industrial colossus—and the lives of millions of working Americans would be transformed in the process.

Focus Questions

1. How did the transcontinental railroad network promote the post–Civil War transformation of American industry?
2. How did the American economy come to be dominated by monopolistic corporations in industries like steel and oil, and what was the public and governmental response to these huge combinations?
3. Why was the South generally excluded from industrial development, and what were the economic and social consequences for that region?
4. How did industrialization alter American society, particularly the role of the working class and of women?
5. Why did late nineteenth century American labor unions generally fail to mobilize American workers?

The Iron Colt Becomes an Iron Horse

The government-business entanglements that increasingly shaped politics after the Civil War also undergirded the industrial development of the nation. The unparalleled outburst of railroad construction was a crucial case. When Lincoln was shot in 1865, there were only 35,000 miles of steam railways in the United States, mostly east of the Mississippi. By 1900 the figure had spurted up to 192,556 miles, or more than that for all Europe combined, and much of the new trackage ran west of the Mississippi.

Transcontinental railroad building was so costly and risky as to require governmental subsidies. Congress began to advance liberal loans to two favored cross-continent companies in 1862 and added enormous donations of acreage paralleling the tracks. All told, Washington rewarded the railroads with 155,504,994 acres, and the western states contributed 49 million more—a total area larger than Texas.

Deadlock in the 1850s over the location of the proposed transcontinental railroad was broken when the South seceded, leaving the field to the North. In 1862, the year after the guns first spoke at Fort Sumter, Congress made provision for starting the long-awaited line. One weighty argument for action was the urgency of bolstering the Union, already disrupted, by binding the Pacific Coast more securely to the rest of the Republic.

The Union Pacific Railroad—note the word *Union*—was thus commissioned by Congress to thrust westward from Omaha, Nebraska. The laying of rails began in earnest after the Civil War ended in 1865, and with juicy loans and land grants available, the "groundhog" promoters made all possible haste.

Sweaty construction gangs, containing many Irish "Paddies" (Patricks), worked at a frantic pace. On one record-breaking day, a sledge-and-shovel army of some five thousand men laid ten miles of track. A favorite song was

> *Then drill, my Paddies, drill;*
> *Drill, my heroes, drill;*
> *Drill all day,*
> *No sugar in your tay [tea]*
> *Workin' on the U.P. Railway.*

When hostile Indians attacked, the laborers would drop their picks and seize their rifles. At rail's end, workers tried to find relaxation and conviviality in tented towns known as "hells on wheels," often teeming with as many as ten thousand men and a sprinkling of painted prostitutes and performers.

Rail laying at the California end was undertaken by the Central Pacific Railroad. This line pushed boldly eastward from boomtown Sacramento, over and through the towering, snow-clogged Sierra Nevada. Four farseeing men—the so-called Big Four—were the chief financial backers of the enterprise.

Online Study Center

Interactive map
Transcontinental Railroads and
Federal Loan Grants, 1850–1900
college.hmco.com/pic/kennedybrief7e

Online Study Center

Primary source
Union Pacific Railway Poster
college.hmco.com/pic/kennedybrief7e

■ Snow Sheds on the Central Pacific Railroad in the Sierra Nevada Mountains, by Joseph H. Becker, c. 1869 Formidable obstacles of climate and terrain confronted the builders of the Central Pacific Railroad in the mountainous heights of California. Note the Chinese laborers in the foreground.

Chronology

1862	Congress authorizes a transcontinental railroad.
1866	National Labor Union organized.
1869	Transcontinental railroad joined near Ogden, Utah. Knights of Labor organized.
1870	Standard Oil Company organized.
1876	Bell invents telephone.
1879	Edison invents electric light.

1886	Haymarket Square bombing. *Wabash* case. American Federation of Labor formed.
1887	Interstate Commerce Act.
1890	Sherman Anti-Trust Act.
1901	United States Steel Corporation formed.

The quartet included the heavyset, enterprising ex-governor Leland Stanford of California, who had useful political connections, and the burly, energetic Collis P. Huntington, an adept lobbyist.

The Central Pacific, which was granted the same princely subsidies as the Union Pacific, had the same incentive to haste. Some ten thousand Chinese laborers sweated from dawn to dusk under their basket hats. Hundreds lost their lives in premature explosions and other mishaps. The towering Sierra Nevada presented a formidable barrier; and the nerves of the Big Four were strained when their workers could chip only a few inches a day through solid rock, while the Union Pacific was sledgehammering westward across the plains.

A "wedding of the rails" was finally consummated near Ogden, Utah, in 1869, as the two locomotives gently kissed cowcatchers. The colorful ceremony included the breaking of champagne bottles and the driving of a last ceremonial (golden) spike, with ex-governor Stanford clumsily wielding a silver sledgehammer.* In all, the Union Pacific built 1,086 miles, the Central Pacific 689 miles.

Completion of the transcontinental line welded the West Coast more firmly to the Union and facilitated a flourishing trade with Asia. It penetrated the arid barrier of the deserts, paving the way for the phenomenal growth of the Great West. Americans compared this electrifying achievement with the Declaration of Independence and the emancipation of the slaves; jubilant Philadelphians again rang the cracked bell of Independence Hall.

Binding the Country with Railroad Ties

With the westward trail now blazed, four other transcontinental lines were completed before the century's end. None of them secured monetary loans from the federal government, as had the Union Pacific and the Central Pacific. But all of them except the Great Northern received generous grants of land.

The Northern Pacific Railroad, stretching from Lake Superior to Puget Sound, reached its terminus in 1883. The Atchison, Topeka, and Santa Fe—stretching through the southwestern deserts to California—was completed in 1884. The Southern Pacific ribboned from New Orleans to Los Angeles and was consolidated in the same year.

The last of the five nineteenth-century transcontinental railroads, the Great Northern, ran north of the Northern Pacific from Duluth to Seattle. Its creator was James J. Hill, a far-visioned Canadian-American who perceived that the prosperity of his railroad depended on the prosperity of the area that it served. Hill's sound principles of organization enabled his railroad to ride through later financial storms with flying colors.

---

* The spike was promptly removed and is now exhibited at the Stanford University Museum.

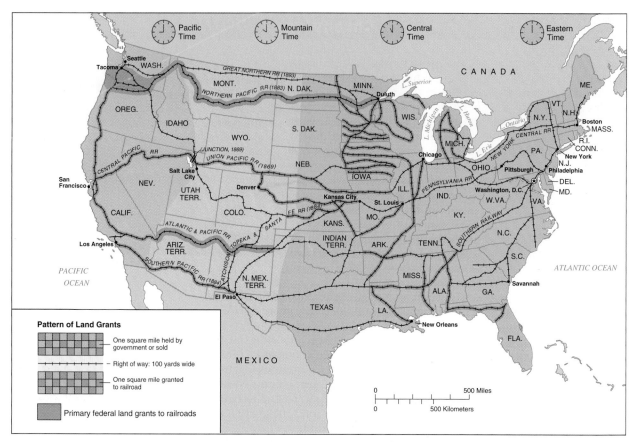

■ **Federal Land Grants to Railroads** The heavy red lines indicate areas within which the railroads might be given specific parcels of land. As shown in the inset, land was reserved in belts of various widths on either side of a railroad's right of way. Until the railroad selected the individual mile-square sections it chose to possess, *all* such sections within the belt were withdrawn from eligibility for settlement. The "time zones" were introduced in 1883 (see p. 361), and their boundaries have since been adjusted.

Yet the romance of the rails was not without its sordid side. Pioneer builders were often guilty of gross overoptimism, laying down rails that went "from nowhere to nothing" in order to get the lavish federal land bounties. When prosperity failed to smile, railroad companies went into bankruptcy, carrying down with them the savings of trusting investors. Many of the large railroads in the post–Civil War decades passed through seemingly endless bankruptcies, mergers, or reorganizations.

Revolution by Railways

The metallic fingers of the railroads intimately touched countless phases of American life. For the first time, a sprawling nation became physically bound with ribs of iron and steel. By stitching North America together from sea to sea, the transcontinental lines created an enormous market for American raw materials and manufactured goods—a huge empire of commerce that beckoned to foreign and domestic investors alike.

More than any other single factor the railroad network spurred the amazing industrialization of the post–Civil War years. The puffing locomotives opened up

In 1892 James Baird Weaver (1833–1912), nominee of the Populists, wrote regarding the railroad magnates,

"In their delirium of greed the managers of our transportation systems disregard both private right and the public welfare. Today they will combine and bankrupt their weak rivals, and by the expenditure of a trifling sum possess themselves of properties which cost the outlay of millions. Tomorrow they will capitalize their booty for five times the cost, issue their bonds, and proceed to levy tariffs upon the people to pay dividends upon the fraud."

fresh markets for manufactured goods and sped raw materials to the factory. The forging of the rails themselves provided the largest single source of orders for the adolescent steel industry.

The screeching iron horse likewise stimulated mining and agriculture, especially in the West. It took farmers out to their land, carried the fruits of their toil to market, and brought them their manufactured necessities. Clusters of farm settlements paralleled the railroads, just as earlier they had followed the rivers.

Railways were a boon for cities and played a leading role in the great cityward movement of the last decades of the century. The iron monsters could carry food to enormous concentrations of people and at the same time ensure them a livelihood by providing both raw materials and markets.

Railroad companies also stimulated the mighty stream of immigration. Seeking settlers to whom their land grants might be sold at a profit, they advertised seductively in Europe and sometimes offered to transplant the newcomers free to their farms.

The land also felt the impact of the railroad—especially the broad, ecologically fragile midsection of the continent. Settlers following the railroads plowed up the tallgrass prairies of Iowa, Illinois, Kansas, and Nebraska and planted well-drained, rectangular cornfields. On the shortgrass prairies of the high plains in the Dakotas and Montana, range-fed cattle rapidly displaced the buffalo, which were hunted to near-extinction. The white pine forests of Michigan, Wisconsin, and Minnesota disappeared into lumber that was rushed by rail to prairie farmers who used it to build houses and fences.

Time itself was bent to the railroads' needs. Until the 1880s every town in the United States had its own "local" time, dictated by the sun's position. When it was noon in Chicago, it was 11:50 a.m. in St. Louis and 12:18 p.m. in Detroit. For railroad operators worried about keeping schedules and avoiding wrecks, this patchwork of local times was a nightmare. Thus on November 18, 1883, the major rail lines decreed that the continent would henceforth be divided into four "time zones." Most communities quickly adopted railroad "standard" time.

Finally, the railroad, more than any other single factor, was the maker of millionaires. A raw new aristocracy, consisting of "lords of the rail" like eastern railroad magnate Cornelius Vanderbilt and "palace car" inventor George Pullman, replaced the old southern "lords of the lash." The multi-webbed lines became the playthings of Wall Street; and colossal wealth was amassed by stock speculators and corporate railroad manipulators.

Wrongdoing in Railroading

Corruption lurks nearby when fabulous fortunes can materialize overnight. The fleecings administered by the railroad construction companies, such as the Crédit Mobilier, were but the first of the bunco games that the railroad promoters learned to play. Methods soon became more refined, as fast-fingered financiers executed multimillion-dollar maneuvers beneath the noses of a bedazzled public. Jay Gould was the most adept of these ringmasters of rapacity. For nearly thirty years he boomed and busted the stocks of the Erie, the Kansas Pacific, the Union Pacific, and the Texas and Pacific in an incredible circus of speculative skullduggery.

One of the favorite devices of the moguls of manipulation was "stock watering." The term originally referred to the practice of making cattle thirsty by feeding them salt, and then having them bloat themselves with water before they were weighed in for sale. Using a variation of this technique, railroad stock promoters grossly inflated their claims about a given line's assets and profitability and sold stocks and bonds far in excess of the railroad's actual value. "Promoters' profits" were often the tail that wagged the iron horse itself. Railroad managers were forced to charge extortionate rates and wage ruthless competitive battles in order to pay off the exaggerated financial obligations with which they were saddled.

The public interest was frequently trampled underfoot as the railroad titans waged their brutal wars. Crusty old Cornelius Vanderbilt, when told that the law stood in his way, reportedly exclaimed: "Law! What do I care about the law? Hain't

Map Skill-Builder:
Understanding Economic Maps
The map on page 360, Federal Land Grants to Railroads, shows the relationship between federal land grants and the economic development of the American rail network in the decades after the Civil War.

1. Which two transcontinental railroads received the largest federal land grants?
2. Which major transcontinental railroad received no federal land grants over most of its route?
3. In which two midwestern states were railroads granted numerous federal land grants for "short-haul" rail lines?
4. In which region of the country were the railroads constructed entirely without federal land grants?

■ **The Modern Colossus of Railroads, 1879**
William H. Vanderbilt, flanked by Cyrus Field
(left) and Jay Gould (right), towers over the scene.
With the Interstate Commerce Act in 1887, the
government began to weaken the magnates' grip
over the nation's transportation system.

---

pool *In business, an agreement to divide
a given market in order to avoid
competition.*

rebates *A return of a portion of the
amount paid for goods or services.*

plutocracy *Government by the wealthy.*

free enterprise *An economic system that
permits unrestricted entrepreneurial
business activity; capitalism.*

Online Study Center

**Primary source
Farmers' Movement in the West,
The**
college.hmco.com/pic/kennedybrief7e

I got the power?" His son, William H. Vanderbilt, when asked in
1883 about the discontinuance of a fast mail train, reportedly
snorted, "The public be damned!"

While abusing the public, the railroaders blandly bought and
sold people in public life. They bribed judges and legislatures,
elected their own agents to high office, and showered free passes
on journalists and politicians.

Railroad kings were, for a time, virtual industrial monarchs.
As manipulators of a huge natural monopoly, they exercised
more direct control over the lives of more people than did the
president of the United States—and their terms were not limited
to four years. They increasingly shunned the crude bloodletting
of cutthroat competition and began to cooperate with one another to rule the railroad dominion. Sorely pressed to show at
least some returns on their bloated investments, they entered
into defensive alliances to protect precious profits.

The earliest form of combination was the "**pool**"—an agreement to divide the business in a given area and share the profits.
Other rail barons granted secret **rebates** or kickbacks to powerful
shippers in return for steady and assured traffic. Often they
slashed their rates on competing lines, but they more than made
up the difference on noncompeting ones, where they might
actually charge more for a short haul than for a long one.

Government Bridles the Iron Horse

It was neither healthy nor politically acceptable that so many
people should be at the mercy of so few. Impoverished farmers,
especially in the Midwest, began to wonder if the nation had not
escaped from the slavery power only to fall into the hands of the
money power, as represented by the railroad **plutocracy.**

But the American people, though quick to respond to political
injustice, were slow to combat economic injustice. Dedicated to
free enterprise and to the principle that competition is the soul of
trade, they remembered that Jefferson's ideals were hostile to governmental interference with business. Above all, there shimmered
the "American dream": the hope that in a catch-as-catch-can
economic system, anyone might become a millionaire.

The depression of the 1870s finally goaded the farmers into
protesting against being "railroaded" into bankruptcy. Under pressure from organized agrarian groups like the Grange (see p. 410), many midwestern legislatures
tried to regulate the railroad monopoly. The scattered state efforts screeched to a
halt in 1886. The Supreme Court, in the *Wabash* case, decreed that individual
states had no power to regulate *inter*state commerce. If the mechanical monster
were to be corralled, the federal government would have to do the job.

Congress ignored President Cleveland's grumbling indifference to the problem and passed the Interstate Commerce Act in 1887. It prohibited rebates and
pools and required the railroads to publish their rates openly. It also forbade unfair
discrimination against shippers and outlawed charging more for a short haul
than for a long one over the same line. Most important, it set up the Interstate
Commerce Commission (ICC) to administer and enforce the new legislation.

Despite acclaim, the Interstate Commerce Act emphatically did not represent a
popular victory over corporate wealth. One of the leading corporation lawyers of the
day, Richard Olney, shrewdly noted that the new commission "can be made of great
use to the railroads. It satisfies the popular clamor for a government supervision
of railroads, at the same time that such supervision is almost entirely nominal. . . .
The part of wisdom is not to destroy the Commission, but to utilize it."

What the new legislation did do was provide an orderly forum where competing business interests could resolve their conflicts in peaceable ways. The
country could now avoid ruinous rate wars among the railroads, and deflect angry

"confiscatory" attacks on the lines by pitchfork-prodded state legislatures. The Interstate Commerce Act tended to stabilize, not revolutionize, the existing business system.

Yet the act still ranks as a red-letter law. It was the first large-scale attempt by Washington to regulate business in the interest of society at large. It foreshadowed the doom of freewheeling, buccaneering business practices and served full notice that there was a public interest in private enterprise that the government was bound to protect.

Miracles of Mechanization

Postwar industrial expansion, partly a result of the railroad network, rapidly began to assume mammoth proportions. When Lincoln was elected in 1860, the Republic ranked only fourth among the manufacturing nations of the world. By 1894 it had bounded into first place. Why the sudden upsurge?

Liquid capital, previously scarce, was now becoming abundant. The word *millionaire* had not been coined until the 1840s, and in 1861 only a handful of individuals composed this class. But the Civil War, partly through profiteering, created immense fortunes, and these accumulations could now be combined with the customary borrowings from foreign capitalists.

The amazing natural resources of the nation, including coal, oil, and iron, were now about to be fully exploited. Massive immigration helped make unskilled labor cheap and plentiful. Steel, the keystone industry, built its strength largely on the sweat of low-priced immigrant labor from southern and eastern Europe, working in two twelve-hour shifts, seven days a week.

American ingenuity at the same time played a vital role in the second American industrial revolution. American inventiveness flowered luxuriantly in the postwar years: between 1860 and 1890 some 440,000 patents were issued. Business operations were facilitated by such new machines as the cash register, the stock ticker, and the typewriter ("literary piano"), which attracted women to industry. Urbanization was speeded by the refrigerator car, the electric dynamo, and the electric railway, which displaced animal-drawn cars.

The ingenious telephone was introduced in 1876 by Alexander Graham Bell, a teacher of the deaf who remarked that if he could make the mute talk, he could make iron speak. His invention had a great social impact on the nation, especially when it attracted many women from the home to become the "number, please" operators in the gigantic communications network.

The most versatile inventor of all was Thomas Alva Edison (1847–1931), who as a boy had been considered so dull-witted that he was taken out of school. Edison was a gifted tinkerer and a tireless worker, not a pure scientist. "Genius," he said, "is one percent inspiration and ninety-nine percent perspiration." Wondrous devices poured out of his "invention factory" in New Jersey—the phonograph, the mimeograph, the dictaphone, and the moving picture. He is probably best known for his perfection in 1879 of the electric light bulb, which he unveiled after experimenting with some six thousand different filaments. The electric light turned night into day and transformed ancient human habits as well. People had previously slept an average of nine hours a night; now they slept just a bit more than seven hours.

The Trust Titan Emerges

Despite pious protests to the contrary, competition was the bugbear of most business leaders of the day. Tycoons such as Andrew Carnegie, the steel king; John D. Rockefeller, the oil baron; and J. Pierpont Morgan, the bankers' banker, exercised their genius in devising ways to circumvent competition. Carnegie pioneered the "vertical integration" of production by directly controlling every phase of his steel-making operation from mining to marketing. His miners dug the ore from Minnesota's Mesabi range; Carnegie ships floated it across the Great Lakes;

Carnegie railroads delivered it to blast furnaces at Pittsburgh. When the molten metal finally poured from the glowing crucibles into the waiting ingot molds, no other hands but those in Carnegie's employ had touched the product.

Rockefeller pursued the less economically justifiable technique of "horizontal integration," which simply meant allying with competitors to monopolize a given market. He perfected a device for controlling bothersome rivals—the **"trust."** Stockholders in various smaller oil companies assigned their stock to the board of directors of Rockefeller's Standard Oil Company, formed in 1870. It then consolidated and concerted the operations of the previously competing enterprises. "Let us prey" was said to be Rockefeller's unwritten motto. Ruthlessly wielding vast power, Standard Oil soon cornered virtually the entire world petroleum market. Weaker competitors, left out of the trust agreement, were forced to the wall. Rockefeller's stunning success inspired many imitators, and the word *trust* came to be generally used to describe any large-scale business combination.

The imperial Morgan devised still other schemes for eliminating "wasteful" competition. The depression of the 1890s drove into his welcoming arms many bleeding businesspeople, wounded by cutthroat competition. His prescribed remedy was to consolidate rival enterprises and to ensure future harmony by placing officers of his own banking **syndicate** on their various boards of directors. These came to be known as "interlocking directorates."

The Supremacy of Steel

"Steel is king!" might well have been the exultant war cry of the new industrialized generation. The mighty metal ultimately held together the new civilization, from skyscrapers to coal scuttles, while providing it with food, shelter, and transportation. Steel making, notably rails for railroads, typified the dominance of heavy industry, which concentrated on making "capital goods," as distinct from the production of "consumer goods" such as clothes and shoes.

Now taken for granted, steel was a scarce commodity in the wood-and-brick America of Abraham Lincoln. Yet within an amazing twenty years after 1870, the United States outdistanced all foreign competitors and was pouring out more than one-third of the world's supply of steel. By 1900 the Americans were producing as much as Britain and Germany combined.

What wrought the transformation? Chiefly the invention in the 1850s of a method of making cheap steel. William Kelly, a Kentucky manufacturer of iron kettles, had earlier discovered that cold air blown on red-hot iron caused the metal to become white-hot by igniting the carbon and thus eliminating impurities. But Kelly was unable to win acceptance for the product. Only after Bessemer, a British inventor, joined forces with Kelly did the Bessemer-Kelly process make possible the new steel civilization.

Kingpin among steelmasters was Andrew Carnegie, an undersized, charming Scotsman. As a towheaded lad of thirteen, he was brought to America by his impoverished parents in 1848 and got a job as a bobbin boy at $1.20 a week. Mounting the ladder of success so fast that he was said to have scorched the rungs, he forged ahead by working hard, doing extra chores, cheerfully assuming responsibility, and smoothly cultivating influential people.

After accumulating some capital, Carnegie entered the steel business in the Pittsburgh area. By 1900 he was producing one-fourth of the nation's Bessemer steel, and his partners were dividing the profits of $40 million a year, with the "Napoleon of the Smokestacks" himself receiving a cool $25 million. These were the pre–income-tax days, when millionaires made real money and profits represented take-home pay.

Into the picture now stepped the financial giant of the age, J. Pierpont Morgan. "Jupiter" Morgan had made a legendary reputation for himself and his Wall Street banking house by financing the reorganization of railroads, insurance companies, and banks. An impressive figure of a man, with massive shoulders, shaggy brows, piercing eyes, and a bulbous, acne-cursed red nose, he had established an enviable reputation for integrity. He did not believe that "money

---

trust *A combination of corporations, usually in the same industry, in which stockholders trade their stock to a central board in exchange for trust certificates. (By extension, the term came to be applied to any large, semi-monopolistic business.)*

syndicate *An association of financiers organized to carry out projects requiring very large amounts of capital.*

power" was dangerous, except when in dangerous hands—and he did not regard his own hands as dangerous.

The force of circumstances brought Morgan and Carnegie into collision. By 1900 the canny little Scotsman, weary of turning steel into gold, was eager to sell his holdings. Morgan had meanwhile plunged heavily into the manufacture of steel pipe tubing. Carnegie, cleverly threatening to invade the same business, was ready to ruin his rival if he did not receive his price. The steelmaster's agents haggled with the imperious Morgan for eight agonizing hours, and the financier finally agreed to buy out Carnegie for over $400 million. Fearing that he would die "disgraced" with so much wealth, Carnegie dedicated the remaining years of his life to giving it away for public libraries, pensions for professors, and other such philanthropic purposes—in all disposing of about $350 million.

Morgan moved rapidly to expand his new industrial empire. He took the Carnegie holdings, added others, "watered" the stock liberally, and in 1901 launched the enlarged United States Steel Corporation. Capitalized at $1.4 billion, it was America's first billion-dollar corporation—a larger sum than the total estimated wealth of the nation in 1800. The Industrial Revolution had come into its own.

Rockefeller Grows an American Beauty Rose

Online Study Center

Primary source
Rockefeller and the American
Beauty Rose
college.hmco.com/pic/kennedybrief7e

Another new industry was born almost overnight when in 1859 the first oil well— "Drake's Folly" in Pennsylvania—poured out its liquid "black gold." Kerosene, derived from petroleum, was the first major product of the infant oil industry. Replacing whale oil as the fuel for America's lamps, kerosene became the country's fourth most valuable export by the 1870s.

But what technology gives, technology takes away. By 1885 Thomas Edison's new electric light bulbs had rendered kerosene largely obsolete. Oil might thus have remained a modest, even a shrinking, industry but for yet another turn of the technological tide—the invention of the automobile. By 1900 the gasoline-burning internal combustion engine had clearly bested its rivals, steam and electricity, and the oil business got a new, long-lasting, and hugely profitable lease on life.

John D. Rockefeller—lanky, shrewd, ambitious, abstemious (he neither drank, smoked, nor swore)—came to dominate the oil industry. Born to a family of precarious income, he became a successful businessman at age nineteen. One upward stride led to another, and in 1870 he organized the Standard Oil Company of Ohio, nucleus of the great trust formed in 1882.

In the jungle world of big business, a kind of primitive savagery prevailed. Rockefeller—"Reckafellow," as Carnegie had once called him—showed little mercy to his competitors. His son later explained that the giant American Beauty rose could be produced "only by sacrificing the early buds that grew up around it." His father pinched off the small buds with complete ruthlessness. By 1877 Rockefeller controlled 95 percent of all the oil refineries in the country. Employing spies and extorting secret rebates from the railroads, he even forced the lines to pay him rebates on the freight bills of his competitors!

Rockefeller thought he was simply obeying a law of nature. "The time was ripe" for aggressive consolidation, he later reflected. "The day of combination is here to stay. Individualism has gone, never to return." On the other side of the ledger, Rockefeller's oil monopoly did turn out a superior product at a relatively cheap price achieved through its large-scale methods of production and distribution. This, in truth, was the tale of the other trusts as well. The efficient use of expensive machinery called for bigness, and consolidation proved more profitable than ruinous price wars.

Other trusts blossomed along with the American Beauty of oil. These included the sugar trust, the tobacco trust, the leather trust, and the harvester trust, which amalgamated some two hundred competitors. The meat industry arose on the backs of bawling western herds, and meat kings like Gustavus F. Swift and Philip Armour took their places among the new royalty. Wealth was coming to dominate the commonwealth.

These untrustworthy trusts, and the "pirates" who captained them, were disturbingly new. They eclipsed an older American aristocracy of modestly

patrician *Characterized by noble or high social standing.*

successful merchants and professionals. An arrogant class of "new rich" was now elbowing aside the **patrician** families in the mad scramble for power and prestige. Not surprisingly, the ranks of the antitrust crusaders were frequently spearheaded by the "best men"—genteel old-family do-gooders who were not radicals but conservative defenders of their own vanishing influence.

The Gospel of Wealth

Monarchs of yore invoked the divine right of kings, and America's industrial plutocrats took a somewhat similar stance. Some candidly credited heavenly help and justified their social position with what came to be known as the "Gospel of Wealth." "Godliness is in league with riches," preached the Episcopal bishop of Massachusetts, and hard-fisted John D. Rockefeller piously acknowledged that "the good Lord gave me my money."

But most defenders of wide-open capitalism relied more heavily on the survival-of-the-fittest theories of English philosopher Herbert Spencer and Yale Professor William Graham Sumner. Later mislabeled "Social Darwinists," Spencer and Sumner owed less to British evolutionary naturalist Charles Darwin than to laissez-faire economists David Ricardo and Thomas Malthus. In fact, Spencer, not Darwin, coined the phrase "survival of the fittest." Whereas Darwin stressed adaptation, these social thinkers emphasized the rigidity of natural law, while occasionally borrowing evolutionary jargon to engage contemporary audiences. "The millionaires are a product of natural selection," Sumner declared. "What do social classes owe each other?" he asked in 1883, then answered his own question: nothing.

Self-justification by the wealthy inevitably involved contempt for the poor. Many of the rich, especially the newly rich, had pulled themselves up by their own bootstraps; hence they concluded that those who stayed poor must be lazy and lacking in enterprise. The Reverend Russell Conwell of Philadelphia became rich by delivering his lecture "Acres of Diamonds" thousands of times. In it he charged, "There is not a poor person in the United States who was not made poor by his own shortcomings." Such attitudes were a formidable roadblock to social reform.

Plutocracy, like the earlier slavocracy, took its stand firmly on the Constitution. The clause that gave Congress sole jurisdiction over interstate commerce was a godsend to the monopolists; their high-priced lawyers used it time and again to thwart controls by the state legislatures. Giant trusts likewise sought refuge behind the Fourteenth Amendment, which had been originally designed to protect the rights of the ex-slaves as persons. The courts ingeniously interpreted a corporation to be a legal "person" and decreed that, as such, it could not be deprived of its property by a state without "due process of law" (see Art. XIV, para. 1 in the Appendix).

> *Industrial millionaires were condemned in the Populist platform of 1892:*
>
> "The fruits of the toil of millions are boldly stolen to build up colossal fortunes for a few . . . and the possessors of these, in turn despise the Republic and endanger liberty. From the same prolific womb of governmental injustice we breed the two great classes—tramps and millionaires."

Government Tackles the Trust Evil

At long last the masses of the people began to mobilize against monopoly. They first tried to control the trusts through state legislation, as they had earlier attempted to curb the railroads. Failing here, as before, they were forced to appeal to Congress. After prolonged pulling and hauling, the Sherman Anti-Trust Act of 1890 was finally signed into law.

The Sherman Act flatly forbade combinations in restraint of trade, without making any distinction between "good" trusts and "bad" trusts. Bigness, not badness, was the sin. The law proved ineffective, largely because it had only baby teeth or no teeth at all, and because it contained legal loopholes through which clever corporation lawyers

■ **Washington as Seen by the Trusts, 1900** "What a funny little government," John D. Rockefeller observes in this satirical cartoon. His own wealth and power are presumed to dwarf the resources of the federal government.

could wriggle. But it was unexpectedly effective in one respect. Contrary to its original intent, it was used to curb labor unions or labor combinations that were deemed to be restraining trade.

Early prosecutions of the trusts by the Justice Department under the Sherman Act of 1890, as it turned out, were neither vigorous nor successful. Not until 1914 were the paper jaws of the Sherman Act fitted with reasonably sharp teeth. Until then, there was some question as to whether the government would control the trusts or the trusts the government.

But the iron grip of monopolistic corporations was being threatened. A revolutionary new principle had been written into the law books by the Sherman Anti-Trust Act of 1890, as well as by the Interstate Commerce Act of 1887. Private greed must henceforth be subordinated to public need.

The South in the Age of Industry

The industrial tidal wave that washed over the North after the Civil War caused only feeble ripples in the backwater of the South. The plantation system had degenerated into a pattern of absentee landownership. White and black share-croppers now tilled the soil for a share of the crop, or they became tenants, in bondage to landlords who controlled needed credit and supplies.

Southern agriculture received a welcome boost in the 1880s, when machine-made cigarettes replaced the roll-your-own variety and tobacco consumption shot up. James Buchanan Duke took full advantage of the new technology to mass-produce the dainty "coffin nails." In 1890, in what was becoming a familiar pattern, he absorbed his main competitors into the American Tobacco Company. The cigarette czar later showed such generosity to Trinity College, near his birthplace in Durham, North Carolina, that the trustees gratefully changed its name to Duke University.

Industrialists tried to coax the agricultural South out of the fields and into the factories, but with only modest success. The region remained overwhelmingly rural. Prominent among the boosters of a "new South" was silver-tongued Henry W. Grady, editor of the *Atlanta Constitution.* He tirelessly exhorted the ex-Confederates to become "Georgia Yankees" and outplay the North at the commercial and industrial game.

Yet formidable obstacles lay in the path of southern industrialization. One was the paper barrier of regional rate-setting systems imposed by the northern-dominated railroad interests. Railroads gave preferential rates to manufactured

Henry W. Grady (1851–1889), editor of the Atlanta Constitution, *urged the new South to industrialize. In a Boston speech in 1889, he described the burial in Georgia of a Confederate veteran:*

"The South didn't furnish a thing on earth for that funeral but the corpse and the hole in the ground. . . . They buried him in a New York coat and a Boston pair of shoes and a pair of breeches from Chicago and a shirt from Cincinnati, leaving him nothing to carry into the next world with him to remind him of the country in which he lived, and for which he fought for four years, but the chill of blood in his veins and the marrow in his bones."

———

Third World *Term developed during the Cold War for nations that were not part of either the Western (First World) or Communist (Second World) blocs; most were Asian, African, or Latin American countries formerly under colonial rule and still economically poor and dependent.*

goods moving southward from the North, but in the opposite direction they discriminated in favor of southern raw materials. The net effect was to keep the South in a kind of "**Third World**" servitude to the Northeast—as a supplier of raw materials to the manufacturing metropolis, unable to develop a substantial industrial base of its own.

A bitter example of this economic discrimination against the South was the "Pittsburgh plus" pricing system in the steel industry. Rich deposits of coal and iron ore near Birmingham, Alabama, worked by low-wage southern labor, should have given steel manufacturers there a competitive edge, especially in southern markets. But the steel lords of Pittsburgh brought pressure to bear on the compliant railroads. As a result, Birmingham steel, no matter where it was delivered, was charged a fictional fee, as if it had been shipped from Pittsburgh. This stunting of the South's natural economic advantages throttled the growth of the Birmingham steel industry.

In manufacturing cotton textiles, the South fared considerably better. Southerners had long resented shipping their fiber to New England, and now their cry was, "Bring the mills to the cotton." Beginning about 1880, northern capital began to erect cotton mills in the South, largely in response to tax benefits and the prospect of cheap and nonunionized labor.

The textile mills proved a mixed blessing to the economically blighted South. Cheap labor was the South's major attraction for potential investors, and keeping labor cheap became almost a religion among southern industrialists. The mills took root in the chronically depressed Piedmont region of southern Appalachia. Blacks were excluded from the mills, so rural southern whites, often derided as "hillbillies" or "lint-heads," worked from dawn to dusk amid the whirring spindles. Paid at half the rate of their northern counterparts, most were perpetually in debt to the company store. But despite their depressed working conditions and poor pay, many southerners saw employment in the mills as a salvation. With many mills anxious to tap the cheap labor of women and children, mill work often offered destitute farm-fugitive families their only chance to remain together.

The Impact of the New Industrial Revolution on America

Economic miracles wrought during the decades after the Civil War enormously increased the wealth of the Republic. The standard of living rose sharply, and well-fed American workers enjoyed more physical comforts than their counterparts in any other industrial nation. Urban centers mushroomed as the insatiable factories demanded more American labor, and as immigrants swarmed like honeybees to the new jobs (see "Makers of America: The Poles," pp. 492–493).

Early Jeffersonian ideals were withering before the smudgy blasts from the smokestacks. As agriculture declined in relation to manufacturing, America could no longer aspire to be a nation of small freehold farms. Jefferson's concepts of free enterprise, with neither help nor hindrance by Washington, were being thrown out the factory window.

Older ways of life also wilted in the heat of the factory furnaces. The very concept of time was revolutionized. Rural American migrants and peasant European immigrants, used to living by the languid clock of nature, now had to regiment their lives by the factory whistle. The seemingly arbitrary discipline of industrial labor did not come easily and sometimes had to be forcibly taught by corporate managers.

Probably no single group was more profoundly affected by the new industrial age than women. Propelled into industry by recent inventions, chiefly the typewriter and the telephone switchboard, millions of stenographers and "hello girls" discovered new economic and social opportunities. The "Gibson Girl," a magazine image of an independent and athletic "new woman" created in the 1890s by the artist Charles Dana Gibson, became the romantic ideal of the age. For middle-class women, careers often meant delayed marriages and smaller families. Most women workers, however, toiled neither for independence nor for glamour but out of economic necessity. They faced the same long hours and dangerous working conditions as did their mates and brothers, and they earned less because wages for "women's jobs" were usually set below men's.

The clattering machine age likewise accentuated class division. "Industrial buccaneers" flaunted bloated fortunes, and their rags-to-riches spouses displayed glittering diamonds. Such extravagances evoked bitter criticism. Some of it was envious, but much of it rose from the small and increasingly vocal group of **socialists** and other **radicals,** many of whom were recent European immigrants. The existence of an oligarchy of money was amply demonstrated by the fact that in 1900 about one-tenth of the people owned nine-tenths of the nation's wealth.

Finally, strong pressures for foreign trade developed as the tireless industrial machine threatened to saturate the domestic market. American products radiated out all over the world—notably the five-gallon kerosene can of the Standard Oil Company. The flag follows trade, and empire tends to follow the flag—a harsh lesson that America was soon to learn.

In Unions There Is Strength

The sweat of the laborer lubricated the vast new industrial machine. Yet wage workers did not share proportionately with their employers the benefits of the age of big business.

The worker, suggestive of the Roman galley slave, was becoming a lever-puller in a giant mechanism. Individual originality and creativity were being stifled, and less value than ever before was being placed on manual skills. Before the Civil War, the worker might have toiled in a small plant whose owner hailed the employee in the morning by first name and inquired after the family's health. But now the factory hand was employed by a corporation—depersonalized, bodiless, soulless, and often conscienceless. Employers could take advantage of the vast new railroad network and bring in unemployed workers from the four corners of the country and beyond to beat down high wage levels. During the 1880s and 1890s, several hundred thousand unskilled immigrant workers poured into the country from Europe, creating a labor market more favorable to the boss than the worker.

Individual workers were powerless to battle single-handedly against giant industry. The corporation could dispense with the individual worker much more easily than the worker could dispense with the corporation. Employers could retain high-priced lawyers, buy up the local press, import strikebreakers ("scabs"), and employ thugs to beat up labor organizers. In 1886 Jay Gould reputedly boasted, "I can hire one-half of the working class to kill the other half."

Corporations had still other weapons in their arsenals. They could call upon conservative federal judges to issue injunctions against strikers, and if defiance continued, could then request state or federal authorities to send in troops. Employers could lock the doors of their plants—a procedure called the "**lockout**"—and starve rebellious workers into submission. They could compel them to sign "ironclad oaths" or "**yellow dog contracts**," both solemn agreements not to join a labor union. They could put the names of labor agitators on a "black list" and circulate it among fellow employers. A corporation might even own the "company town," where high-priced grocery stores and "easy" credit often sank workers into perpetual debt—a status that strongly resembled serfdom.

The middle-class public, annoyed by recurrent strikes, grew deaf to the outcry of the worker. Carnegie and Rockefeller had battled their way to the top, and the view was common that the laborer could do likewise. Somehow the strike seemed like a foreign importation—socialistic and hence unpatriotic. Big business might combine into trusts to raise prices, but the worker must not combine into unions to raise wages. Unemployment seemed to be an act of God, who somehow would take care of the laborer.

Online Study Center

**Primary source
Gibson Girl**
college.hmco.com/pic/kennedybrief7e

socialists (socialism) *Political belief in promoting social and economic equality through the ownership and control of the major means of production by the whole community rather than by individuals or corporations.*

radicals *Those who believe in fundamental change in the political, economic, or social system.*

lockout *The refusal by an employer to allow employees to work unless they agree to his or her terms.*

yellow dog contract *A labor contract in which an employee must agree not to join a union as a condition of holding the job.*

EXAMINING THE EVIDENCE

The Photography of Lewis W. Hine The pell-mell onrush of industrialization after the Civil War spawned countless human abuses, few more objectionable than the employment of children, often in hazardous jobs. For decades, reformers tried to arouse public outrage against child labor, and they made significant headway at last with the help of photography—especially the photographs of Lewis W. Hine (1874–1940). A native of Wisconsin, Hine in 1908 became the staff photographer for the National Child Labor Committee, an organization committed to ending child labor. This 1909 photo of young "doffers," whose job it was to remove fully wound bobbins from textile spinning machines, is typical of Hine's work. He shows the boys climbing dangerously on the whirling mechanism, and his own caption for the photo names the mill—"Bibb Mill No. 1, Macon, Georgia"—but not the boys, as if to underline the impersonal, dehumanizing nature of their work and the specific responsibilities of their employer. His other subjects included child workers on Colorado beet farms, in Pennsylvania coal mines and Gulf Coast fish canneries, and in the glass, tobacco, and garment trades. Hine's images contributed heavily to the eventual success of the campaign to end child labor in the New Deal era. He is also celebrated as one of the fathers of documentary photography.

Online Study Center

Primary source
Child Worker Dies Headline
college.hmco.com/pic/kennedybrief7e

Online Study Center

Primary source
Child Glass Factory Worker
college.hmco.com/pic/kennedybrief7e

1. Why might Hine's graphic images have succeeded in stirring public opinion more powerfully than factual and statistical demonstrations of the evil of child labor?

2. Given Hine's own reform objectives, can his photographs—or any so-called documentary images—be taken at face value as literal, accurate information about the past?

3. Which details in Lewis Hine's photo especially emphasize the exploitation and dangers experienced by child laborers?

Labor Limps Along

Labor unions, which had been few and disorganized in 1861, were given a strong boost by the Civil War. By 1872, there were several hundred thousand organized workers and thirty-two national unions, representing such crafts as the bricklayers, typesetters, and shoemakers.

The National Labor Union, organized in 1866, represented a giant boot stride by the workers. The union lasted six years and attracted the impressive total of some 600,000 members, including the skilled, unskilled, and farmers, though it excluded the Chinese and made only nominal efforts to include women and blacks. Black workers organized their own Colored National Labor Union, but persistent white racism prevented the two national unions from working together. The National Labor Union agitated for the arbitration of industrial disputes and the eight-hour workday, and won the latter for government workers. But the devastating depression of the 1870s dealt it a knockout blow. Wage reductions in 1877 touched off such disruptive strikes on the railroads that nothing short of federal troops could restore order.

A new organization—the Knights of Labor—seized the torch dropped by the defunct National Labor Union (see "Makers of America: The Knights of Labor," p. 372). Officially known as the Noble and Holy Order of the Knights of Labor, it began inauspiciously in 1869 as a secret society, with a private ritual, passwords, and a secret grip. Secrecy, which continued until 1881, would forestall possible reprisals by employers.

The Knights of Labor, like the National Labor Union, sought to include all workers in "one big union." Their slogan was "An injury to one is the concern of all." A welcome mat was rolled out for the skilled and unskilled, for men and women, for whites and underprivileged blacks, some ninety thousand of whom joined. The Knights barred only liquor dealers, professional gamblers, lawyers, bankers, and stockbrokers.

Setting up broad goals, the embattled Knights campaigned for economic and social reform, including producers' **cooperatives** and codes for safety and health. The ordinary workday was then ten hours or more, and the Knights waged a determined campaign for the eight-hour stint.

Under the eloquent but often erratic leadership of Terence V. Powderly, an Irish American of nimble wit and fluent tongue, the Knights won a number of strikes for the eight-hour day. When the Knights staged a successful strike against Jay Gould's Wabash Railroad in 1885, membership mushroomed to about three-quarters of a million workers.

Unhorsing the Knights of Labor

Despite their outward success, the Knights were riding for a fall. They became involved in a number of May Day strikes in 1886, about half of which failed. A focal point was Chicago, home to about eighty thousand Knights. The city was also honeycombed with a few hundred **anarchists,** many of them foreign-born, who were advocating a violent overthrow of the American government.

Tensions rapidly built up to the bloody Haymarket Square episode. Labor disorders had broken out, and on May 4, 1886, the Chicago police advanced on a meeting called to protest alleged brutalities by the authorities. Suddenly a dynamite bomb was thrown that killed or injured several dozen people including police.

Hysteria swept the Windy City. Eight anarchists were rounded up. Although nobody proved that they had anything to do directly with the bomb, a judge and jury held that since they had preached incendiary doctrines, they could be charged with conspiracy. Five were sentenced to death: one of these men committed suicide, and four were executed. The other three anarchists were given stiff prison terms. They were eventually pardoned in 1892 by Illinois governor John P. Altgeld, a German-born Democrat of strong liberal tendencies.

Online Study Center

Primary source
American Federation of Labor Badge
college.hmco.com/pic/kennedybrief7e

---

cooperatives *An organization for producing, marketing, or purchasing goods in which the members share the benefits.*

anarchists (anarchism) *Political belief that all organized, coercive government is wrong in principle, and that society should be organized solely on the basis of free cooperation. (Some anarchists practiced violence against the state, while others were nonviolent pacifists.)*

The Knights of Labor

It was 1875. The young worker was guided into a room, where his blindfold was removed. Surrounding him were a dozen men, their faces covered by hoods. One of the masked figures solemnly asked three questions: "Do you believe in God?" "Do you gain your bread by the sweat of your brow?" "Are you willing to take a solemn vow, binding you to secrecy, obedience, and mutual assistance?" Yes, came the reply. The men doffed their hoods and joined hands in a circle. Their leader, the Master Workman, declared, "On behalf of the toiling millions of earth, I welcome you to this Sanctuary, dedicated to the service of God, by serving humanity." Then the entire group burst into song:

> Storm the fort, ye Knights of Labor,
> Battle for your cause;
> Equal rights for every neighbor,
> Down with tyrant laws!

The carefully staged pageantry then drew to a close. The worker was now a full-fledged member of the Knights of Labor.

He had just joined a loose-knit organization of some 100,000 working people, soon to swell to nearly one million following several successful strikes in the 1880s. The first women Knights joined in 1881, and there were female organizers, too. Fiery Mary Harris ("Mother") Jones got her start agitating for the Knights in the Illinois coalfields. The first all-black local was founded among coal miners in Ottumwa, Iowa. The Knights preached tolerance and the solidarity of all working men and women, and they meant it, though they supported restrictions on immigration, including the Chinese Exclusion Act of 1882.

Terence V. Powderly, born to Irish immigrant parents in Carbondale, Pennsylvania, in 1849, became the Grand Master Workman of the Knights. He had dropped out of school at age thirteen to take a job guarding railroad track switches and rose to mayor of Scranton, Pennsylvania. A complex, colorful, and sometimes cynical man, he denounced the "multimillionaires [for] laying the foundation for their colossal fortunes on the bodies and souls of living men." In the eyes of Powderly and the Knights, only the economic and political independence of American workers could preserve republican traditions and institutions from corruption by monopolists and other "parasites."

Powderly denounced "wage-slavery" and dedicated the Knights to achieving the "cooperative commonwealth." Shunning socialism, Powderly urged laborers to save enough from their wages to purchase mines, factories, railroads, and stores. Because labor would own and operate these enterprises, workers would be owner-producers, and the conflict between labor and capital would evaporate.

Powderly's vision of the cooperative commonwealth reflected the persistent dream of many nineteenth-century American workers that they would all one day become producers. As expectant capitalists, they lacked "class consciousness"—that is, a sense of themselves as a permanent working class that must organize to coax what benefits it could out of the capitalist system. Samuel Gompers, by contrast, followed that conservative strategy, and his American Federation of Labor, not Powderly's utopian dream, eventually carried the day. The swift decline of the Knights in the 1890s underscored the obsolescence of their unrealistic view that a bygone age of independent producers could be restored. Yet the Knights' commitment to unifying all workers in one union—regardless of race, gender, ethnicity, or skill level—produced a blueprint for the eventual success of similarly committed unions like the Congress of Industrial Organizations in the 1930s.

The Haymarket Square bomb helped blow the props from under the Knights of Labor. They were associated in the public mind, though mistakenly, with the anarchists. The eight-hour movement suffered correspondingly, and subsequent strikes by the Knights met with scant success. By the 1890s the Knights had melted away to 100,000 members, and these gradually fused with other protest groups of that decade.

The AF of L to the Fore

The elitist American Federation of Labor, born in 1886, was largely the brainchild of squat, square-jawed Samuel Gompers. This colorful Jewish cigar maker, born in a London tenement and removed from school at age ten, was brought to America when thirteen. Taking his turn at reading informative literature to fellow cigar makers in New York, he was pressed into overtime service because of his strong voice. Rising spectacularly in the labor ranks, he was elected president of the American Federation of Labor every year except one from 1886 to 1924.

Gompers adopted a down-to-earth approach, soft-pedaling attempts to engineer sweeping social reform. A bitter foe of socialism, he shunned politics for economic strategies and goals. Gompers had no quarrel with capitalism, but he demanded a fairer share for labor. All he wanted, he said, was "more." Promoting what he called "pure and simple" unionism, he sought better wages, hours, and working conditions.

The AF of L thus established itself on solid but narrow foundations. Although attempting to speak for all workers, it fell far short of being representative of them. Composed of skilled craftsmen, like the carpenters and bricklayers, it was willing to let unskilled laborers, including women and especially blacks, fend for themselves. The AF of L weathered the panic of 1893 reasonably well, and by 1900 it could boast a membership of 500,000.

Labor disorders continued, peppering the years from 1881 to 1900 with an alarming total of over 23,000 strikes. These disturbances involved 6,610,000 workers, with a total loss to both employers and employees of $450 million. The strikers lost about half their strikes and won or compromised the remainder. Perhaps the gravest weakness of organized labor was that it still embraced only a small minority of all working people—about 3 percent in 1900.

But attitudes toward labor had begun to change perceptibly by 1900. The public was beginning to concede the right of workers to organize, to bargain collectively,

■ **The Strike, by Robert Koehler, 1886** Scenes like this were becoming more typical of American life in the late nineteenth century as industrialism advanced spectacularly and sometimes ruthlessly. Here Koehler (1850–1917) shows an entire community of men, women, and children—many of them apparently immigrant newcomers—challenging the power of the "boss." The scene is tense but orderly, though violence seems to be imminent as one striker reaches for a rock.

and to strike. As a sign of the times, Labor Day was made a legal holiday by act of Congress in 1894. A few enlightened industrialists had come to perceive the wisdom of avoiding costly economic warfare by bargaining with the unions and signing agreements. But the vast majority of employers continued to fight organized labor, which achieved its grudging gains only after recurrent strikes and frequent reverses. Several trouble-fraught decades were to pass before labor was to gain a position of relative equality with capital. If the age of big business had dawned, the age of big labor was still some distance over the horizon.

✪ Chapter Summary ✪

Aided by government land grant subsidies and loans, the first transcontinental rail line was completed in 1869, soon followed by others. This rail network opened vast new markets and prompted industrial growth. The power and corruption of the railroads led to public demands for regulation. State regulation was declared unconstitutional, but the federal government took a small step with the Interstate Commerce Act (1887).

New technology and types of business organization, sometimes employing harsh competitive practices, led to the growth of huge corporate trusts. Andrew Carnegie and John D. Rockefeller led the way in the steel and oil industries. Initially, the oil industry supplied kerosene for lamps; it eventually expanded by providing gasoline to fuel automobiles. Cheap steel transformed industries from construction to rail building, and the powerful railroads dominated the economy and reshaped American society. Many sectors of the economy came to be dominated by monopolistic trusts that used "interlocking directorates" and other pressure tactics to control competitors. Business-oriented ideologies like the religious "gospel of wealth" and H. Spencer's "laissez-faire" cele-

brated the wealthy as "fittest" to survive, and denigrated poverty as a sign of moral and natural failure.

While industrialization did raise the general economy and standard of living, its benefits were very unevenly distributed. The South remained in underdeveloped "Third World" dependence, despite "New South" proclamations, while the industrial working class struggled at the bottom of the growing class divisions of American society. Increasingly transformed from independent producers and farmers to dependent wage earners, America's workers became vulnerable to illness, industrial accidents, and unemployment.

Workers' attempts at labor organization were generally ineffective, hindered by corporate and governmental opposition and their own backward-looking ideologies. The National Labor Union enjoyed a brief success before its collapse, and the Knights of Labor also disappeared after the Haymarket bombing. Gompers's AF of L successfully organized skilled craft laborers but ignored most industrial workers, women, and blacks. Middle class public attitudes toward organized labor slowly became more positive after 1900.

VARYING VIEWPOINTS

Industrialization: Boon or Blight?

The capitalists who forged an industrial America in the late nineteenth century were once called captains of industry—a respectful title that bespoke the awe due their wondrous material accomplishments. But these economic innovators have never been universally admired. During the Great Depression of the 1930s, when the entire industrial order they had created seemed to have collapsed utterly, it was fashionable to speak of them as robber barons—a term implying scorn for their high-handed methods. This sneer often issued from the lips and pens of leftist critics like Matthew Josephson, who sympathized with the working classes allegedly brutalized by the factory system.

Criticism has also come from writers nostalgic for the preindustrial past. These critics believe that industrialization stripped away the traditions, values, and pride of native farmers and immigrant craftspeople. Conceding that economic development elevated the material standard of living for working Americans, this interpretation contends that the Industrial Revolution diminished their spiritual "quality of life." Accordingly, historians like Herbert Gutman and David Montgomery portray labor's struggle for control of the workplace as the central drama of industrial expansion.

Nevertheless, even these historians concede that class-based protest has never been as powerful a force in the United States as in certain European countries. Many historians believe that this is so because greater social mobility in America dampened class tensions.

In the 1960s, historians led by Stephan Thernstrom began to test this long-standing belief. Looking at such factors as occupation, wealth, and geographic mobility, they tried to gauge the nature and extent of social mobility in the United States. Most of these historians concluded that although relatively few Americans made rags-to-riches leaps, large numbers experienced small improvements in their economic and social status. Few sons of laborers became corporate tycoons, but many more became line bosses and white-collar clerks.

In recent years such studies have been criticized by historians who point out the difficulties involved in defining "social status." For instance, some white-collar clerical workers received lower wages than manual laborers did. But were they higher or lower on the social scale? Furthermore, James Henretta has pointed out that different groups defined success differently: whereas Jewish immigrants often struggled to give their sons professional educations, the Irish put more emphasis on acquiring land, and Italians on building small family-run businesses.

Meanwhile, leftist historians such as Michael Katz have argued that the degree of social mobility in America has been overrated. These historians argue that industrial capitalism created two classes: a working class that sold its labor, and a business class that controlled resources and bought labor. Although most Americans took small steps upward, they generally remained within the class in which they began. Thus, these historians argue, the inequality of a capitalistic class system persisted in America's seemingly fluid society.

25

America Moves to the City

1865–1900

WHAT SHALL WE DO WITH OUR GREAT CITIES? WHAT WILL OUR GREAT CITIES DO WITH US . . . ? [T]HE QUESTION . . . DOES NOT CONCERN THE CITY ALONE. THE WHOLE COUNTRY IS AFFECTED . . . BY THE CONDITION OF ITS GREAT CITIES.

LYMAN ABBOT, 1891

Born in the country, America moved to the city in the decades following the Civil War. By the year 1900 the United States' upsurging population nearly doubled from the 40 million people enumerated in the census of 1870. Yet in the very same period the population of American cities *tripled.* This cityward drift affected not only the United States but most of the Western world. European peasants, pushed off the land in part by competition from cheap American foodstuffs, were pulled into cities—in both Europe and America—by the new lure of industrial jobs. A revolution in American agriculture thus fed the industrial and urban revolutions in Europe, as well as in the United States.

Focus Questions

1. What features characterized the new industrial city, and what was its impact on American Society?
2. Why did the massive "New Immigration" stir opposition from many native-born Americans, and how did political machines, social reformers, and churches adapt to the new urban and immigrant era?
3. What were the major changes in American religious life in the late nineteenth century, and how did the churches respond to the challenges of Darwinism, biblical criticism, and the dramatic growth of Catholicism, Judaism, and other "immigrant" faiths?
4. What were the major changes in American educational and cultural life in the late nineteenth century, and how did the turns toward "realism" and "pragmatism" reflect the new conditions of an urban and scientific civilization?
5. Why were there such fierce debates over morality in the late nineteenth century, especially issues concerning sex, women, and the family?

Chronology

1859	Charles Darwin publishes *On the Origin of Species*.
1862	Morrill Act provides public land for higher education.
1869	Wyoming Territory grants women the right to vote.
1871	*Woodhull and Claflin's Weekly* published.
1873	Comstock Law passed.
1874	Women's Christian Temperance Union (WCTU) organized. Chautauqua education movement launched.
1876	Johns Hopkins University graduate school established.
1879	Henry George publishes *Progress and Poverty*. Dumbbell tenement introduced. Mary Baker Eddy establishes Christian Science. Salvation Army begins work in America.
1881	Booker T. Washington becomes head of Tuskegee Institute.
1882	First immigration-restriction laws passed.
1883	Brooklyn Bridge completed.
1884	Mark Twain publishes *The Adventures of Huckleberry Finn*.
1885	Louis Sullivan builds the first skyscraper, in Chicago.
1886	Statue of Liberty erected in New York harbor.
1887	American Protective Association (APA) formed. Hatch Act supplements Morrill Act.
1888	Edward Bellamy publishes *Looking Backward*.
1889	Jane Addams founds Hull House in Chicago.
1890	National American Woman Suffrage Association formed.
1891	Basketball invented.
1893	Lillian Wald opens Henry Street Settlement in New York.
1897	Library of Congress opens.
1898	Charlotte Perkins Gilman publishes *Women and Economics*.
1899	Kate Chopin publishes *The Awakening*.
1900	Theodore Dreiser publishes *Sister Carrie*.
1907	Henry Adams privately publishes *The Education of Henry Adams*.
1910	National Association for the Advancement of Colored People (NAACP) founded.

The Urban Frontier

The growth of American metropolises was spectacular. In 1860 no city in the United States could boast a million inhabitants; by 1890 New York, Chicago, and Philadelphia had spurted past the million mark. By 1900 New York, with some 3.5 million people, was the second largest city in the world, outranked only by London.

Cities grew both up and out. The cloud-brushing skyscrapers allowed more people and workplaces to be packed onto a parcel of land. Appearing first as a ten-story building in Chicago in 1885, the skyscraper was made usable by the perfecting of the electric elevator. An opinionated Chicago architect, Louis Sullivan (1856–1924), contributed formidably to the further development of the skyscraper with his famous principle that "form follows function."

Cities also spread out, turning many Americans into commuters who traveled daily by mass-transit electric trolleys between urban job and suburban home. The compact and communal "walking city" gave way to the immense and impersonal **megalopolis,** carved into distinctly different districts for business, industry, and residential neighborhoods—which in turn were segregated by race, ethnicity, and social class.

Online Study Center

Interactive map
Urbanization, 1880 and 1929
college/hmco.com/pic/kennedybrief7e

megalopolis *An extensive, heavily populated area, containing several dense urban centers.*

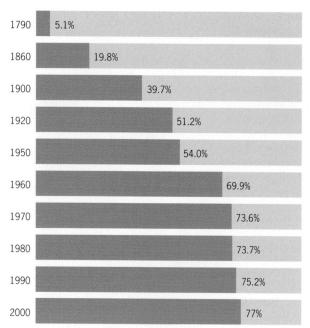

1790	5.1%
1860	19.8%
1900	39.7%
1920	51.2%
1950	54.0%
1960	69.9%
1970	73.6%
1980	73.7%
1990	75.2%
2000	77%

■ **The Shift to the City** Percentage of total population living in cities of twenty-five hundred or more. Notice the slowing pace of the cityward trend since the 1970s.

Online Study Center

Primary source
Department Store,
The: Another View
college.hmco.com/pic/kennedybrief7e

Rural America could not compete with the siren song of the city. Industrial jobs, above all, drew country folks off the farms and into factory centers. But the urban lifestyle also held powerful attractions. The predawn milking of cows had little appeal when compared with the late-night glitter of city lights. Electricity, indoor plumbing, and telephones all made life in the big city more alluring. Engineering marvels like the skyscraper and New York's awesome Brooklyn Bridge, a harplike suspension span dedicated in 1883, further added to the seductive glamour of the gleaming cities.

Cavernous department stores such as Macy's in New York and Marshall Field's in Chicago attracted urban middle-class shoppers and provided urban working-class jobs, many of them for women. The bustling emporiums also heralded a dawning era of consumerism and accentuated widening class divisions. When Carrie Meeber, novelist Theodore Dreiser's fictional heroine in *Sister Carrie* (1900), escapes from rural boredom to Chicago, it is the spectacle of the city's dazzling department stores that awakens her fateful yearning for a richer, more elegant way of life.

The move to the city also introduced Americans to new ways of living. Household products sold in bulk at the local store, without wrapping, gave way to city goods that came in throwaway bottles, boxes, bags, and cans. Apartment houses had no adjoining barnyards where residents might toss garbage to the hogs. Waste disposal, in short, was an issue new to the urban age. And the mountains of waste that urbanites generated further testified to a cultural shift away from the virtues of thrift to the convenience of consumerism.

The jagged skyline of America's perpendicular civilization could not fully conceal the canker sores of feverish growth. Criminals flourished like lice in the teeming asphalt jungles. Impure water, uncollected garbage, unwashed bodies, and droppings from draft animals enveloped many cities in a satanic stench.

The cities were monuments of contradiction. They represented "humanity compressed," remarked one observer, "the best and the worst combined, in a strangely composite community." They harbored merchant princes and miserable paupers, stately banks and sooty factories, green-grassed suburbs and

■ **Mulberry Street on New York City's Lower East Side,** c. 1900 Population densities in early-twentieth-century American cities were among the highest in the world. Mulberry Street, shown in this photo, was at the heart of New York's "Little Italy" neighborhood.

stinking **tenements.** The glaring contrasts that assaulted the eye in New York reminded one visitor of "a lady in ball costume, with diamonds in her ears, and her toes out at the boots."

Worst of all were the human pigsties known as slums. They seemed to grow ever more crowded, more filthy, and more rat infested, especially after the perfection in 1879 of the "dumbbell" tenement. So named because of the outline of its floor plan, the dumbbell was usually seven or eight stories high, with shallow, sunless, and ill-smelling air shafts providing minimal ventilation. Several families were sardined onto each floor of the barrackslike structures, and they shared a malodorous toilet in the hall. Small wonder that slum dwellers strove mightily to escape their wretched surroundings—as many of them did. The slums remained foul places, inhabited by successive waves of newcomers. To a remarkable degree hard-working people moved up and out of them. The wealthiest left the cities altogether and headed for the semirural suburbs. These leafy "bedroom communities" eventually ringed the brick-and-concrete cities with a greenbelt of **affluence.**

tenement *A multi-dwelling building, often poor or overcrowded.*

affluence *An abundance of wealth.*

The New Immigration

The powerful pull of the American urban magnet was felt even in faraway Europe. A brightly colored stream of immigrants continued to pour in from the old "mother continent." In each of the three decades from the 1850s through the 1870s, more than 2 million migrants had stepped onto America's shores. By the 1880s the stream had swelled to a rushing torrent, as more than 5 million cascaded into the country.

Until the 1880s, most immigrants had come from the British Isles and western Europe, chiefly Germany and Scandinavia. They were usually Protestant, except for the Catholic Irish and many Catholic Germans. They boasted a comparatively high rate of literacy and fitted relatively easily into American society.

But in the 1880s the character of the immigrant stream changed drastically. The so-called New Immigrants—Italians, Croats, Slovaks, Greeks, Poles—came from southern and eastern Europe. Many of them worshiped in Roman Catholic or Eastern Orthodox churches or in Jewish synagogues. Largely illiterate and impoverished, most new immigrants hived together in the "Little Italys" and "Little Polands" of the jam-packed cities. These new peoples totaled only 19 percent of newcomers in the 1880s; but by the first decade of the twentieth century, they constituted an astonishing 66 percent of the total inflow. (See "Makers of America: The Italians," p. 380.)

Why were these bright-shawled and quaint-jacketed strangers hammering on the gates? In part they left their native countries because Europe seemed to have no room for them. Rapid population growth, American food imports, and European industrialization shook the peasantry loose from its ancient habitats and customary occupations, creating a vast, footloose army of the unemployed. Europeans by the millions drained out of the countryside and into European cities. Most stayed there, but some kept moving and left Europe altogether. About 60 million Europeans abandoned the Old Continent in the nineteenth and early twentieth centuries. More than half of them moved to the United States. But that striking fact should not obscure the important truth that masses of people were already in motion in Europe before they felt the tug of the American magnet. Immigration to America was, in many ways, a by-product of the urbanization of Europe.

"America fever" proved highly contagious in Europe. The United States was often painted as a land of fabulous opportunity in the "America letters" sent by friends and relatives already transplanted.

The land of the free was also blessed with freedom from military conscription and institutionalized religious persecution. Beginning in the 1880s, savage persecution of minorities in Europe, especially of Jews in Russia, drove tens of thousands of battered refugees to American shores. Virtually unique among the New Immigrants, Jews had experienced city life in Europe, and many of them brought

Online Study Center

Interactive map
Percent of Foreign-Born Whites and Native Whites of Foreign or Mixed Parentage in Total Populations, by Counties, 1910
college/hmco.com/pic/kennedybrief7e

Online Study Center

Primary source
Because You're a Jew
college.hmco.com/pic/kennedybrief7e

Mary Antin (1881–1949), who came to America from Russian Poland in 1894 when thirteen years of age, later wrote in The Promised Land *(1912),*

"So at last I was going to America! Really, really going, at last! The boundaries burst. The arch of heaven soared. A million suns shone out for every star. The winds rushed in from outer space, roaring in my ears, 'America! America!'"

The Italians

Who were the "New Immigrants"? Who were these southern and eastern European birds of passage that flocked to the United States between 1880 and 1920? Prominent and typical among them were Italians, some 4 million of whom sailed to the United States during the four decades of the New Immigration.

They came from the southern provinces of their native land, the heel and toe of the Italian boot. These areas had lagged behind the prosperous, industrial region of northern Italy. Unification of the nation of Italy had raised hopes of similar progress in the downtrodden south, but it was slow in coming. Southern peasants tilled their fields without fertilizer or machinery, using hand plows and rickety hoes that had been passed down for generations.

From such demeaned conditions, southern Italians set out for the New World. Almost all of them were young men who intended to spend only a few months in America, stuff their pockets with dollars, and return home. Almost half of Italian immigrants did indeed repatriate—as did comparable numbers of the other New Immigrants, with the conspicuous exception of the Jews, who had fled their native lands to escape religious persecution. Almost all Italian immigrants sailed through New York harbor, sighting the Statue of Liberty as they debarked from crowded ships. Many soon moved on to other large cities, but so many remained that, in the early years of the twentieth century, more Italians resided in New York than in Florence, Venice, and Genoa combined.

Although most Italian immigrants huddled in the cities, they did not abandon their rural upbringings entirely. Much to their neighbors' consternation, they often kept chickens and raised vegetables in small garden plots nestled between decaying tenement houses.

Those who bade a permanent farewell to Italy clustered in tightly knit communities that boasted opera clubs, Italian-language newspapers, and courts for playing bocci—a version of lawn bowling imported from the Old Country. Pizza emerged from the hot wood-burning ovens of these Little Italys, its aroma and flavor wafting into the hearts and stomachs of all Americans.

Italians typically earned their daily bread as industrial laborers—most famously as longshoremen and construction workers. They owed their prominence in the building trades to the "padrone system." The *padrone*, or labor boss, met immigrants upon arrival and secured jobs for them in New York, Chicago, or wherever there was an immediate demand for industrial labor.

Lacking education, the Italians, as a group, remained in blue-collar jobs longer than some of their fellow New Immigrants. Many Italians, valuing vocation over schooling, sent their children off to work as early in their young lives as possible. Before World War I, less than 1 percent of Italian children were enrolled in high school. Over the next fifty years, Italian-Americans and their offspring gradually prospered, moving out of the cities into the more affluent suburbs. Many served heroically in World War II and availed themselves of the GI Bill to finance the college educations and professional training their immigrant forebears had lacked.

their urban skills of tailoring and shopkeeping to American cities. Destitute and devout, eastern European Jews were frequently given a frosty reception not only by old-stock Americans but also by those German Jews who had arrived decades earlier and prospered in the United States, some of them as garment manufacturers who now condescendingly employed their coreligionists as cheap labor.

The new immigrants struggled heroically to preserve their traditional cultures. Catholics expanded their **parochial** school system and Jews established Hebrew schools. Foreign-language newspapers abounded. Yiddish theaters, kosher food stores, Polish parishes, Greek restaurants, and Italian social clubs all attested to the desire to keep old ways alive. Yet time took its toll on these efforts to preserve Old World customs. The children of the immigrants grew up speaking fluent English, sometimes mocking the broken grammar of their parents. They often rejected the Old Country manners of their mothers and fathers in their desire to plunge headlong into the mainstream of American life.

parochial *Concerning a religious parish or small district. (By extension, the term is used, often negatively, to refer to narrow or local perspectives as distinct from broad or cosmopolitan outlooks.)*

sweatshop *A factory where employees are forced to work long hours under difficult conditions for meager wages.*

Reactions to the New Immigration

America's government system, nurtured in wide-open spaces, was ill-suited to the cement forests of the great cities. Beyond minimal checking to weed out criminals and the insane, the federal government did virtually nothing to ease the assimilation of immigrants into American society. State governments, usually dominated by rural representatives, did even less. City governments, overwhelmed by the sheer scale of rampant urban growth, proved woefully inadequate to the task. By default, the business of ministering to the immigrants' needs fell to the unofficial "governments" of the urban political machines, led by "bosses" like New York's notorious Boss Tweed.

Taking care of the immigrants was big business, indeed. Trading jobs and services for votes, a powerful boss might claim the loyalty of thousands of followers. In return for their support at the polls, the boss provided jobs on the city's payroll, found housing for new arrivals, tided over the needy with gifts of food and clothing, patched up minor scrapes with the law, and helped get schools, parks, and hospitals built in immigrant neighborhoods. Reformers gagged at this cynical exploitation of the immigrant vote, but the political boss gave valuable assistance that was forthcoming from no other source.

The nation's social conscience gradually awakened to the plight of the cities and their immigrant masses. Prominent in this awakening were some Protestant clergymen like Walter Rauschenbusch of New York City and Washington Gladden of Columbus, Ohio, who both sought to apply the lessons of Christianity to the slums and factories. Preaching the "social gospel," they insisted that churches tackle the burning social issues of the day.

One middle-class woman who was deeply dedicated to uplifting the urban masses was Jane Addams (1860–1935). Born into a prosperous Illinois family, Addams was one of the first generation of college-educated women and sought suitable outlets for her large talents. Inspired by a visit to England, in 1889 she established Hull House in Chicago as the most prominent American settlement house. Located in a poor immigrant neighborhood of Greeks, Italians, Russians, and Germans, Hull House offered instruction in English, counseling to help newcomers cope with American big-city life, child-care services for working mothers, and cultural activities for neighborhood residents.

Following Jane Addams's lead, women founded settlement houses in other cities as well—notably Lillian Wald's Henry Street Settlement in New York, which opened its doors in 1893. The settlement houses became centers of women's activism and of social reform on behalf of women, children, blacks, and consumers. The women of Hull House, for example, successfully lobbied in 1893 for an Illinois anti-**sweatshop** law that protected women workers and prohibited child labor. They were led by Florence Kelley, a guerrilla warrior in the urban jungle who battled for decades on behalf of the underprivileged at both Hull House and the Henry Street Settlement.

The pioneering work of Addams, Wald, and Kelley vividly demonstrated the truth that the city was the frontier of opportunity for women, just as the wilderness had been for men. The urban frontier opened new possibilities for women. More than a million women joined the work force in the single decade of the 1890s. Strict social codes prescribed which women might work and what jobs they might hold. Because employment for wives and mothers was considered taboo, the vast majority of working women were single. Their jobs depended on their race, ethnicity, and class. Black women had few opportunities beyond domestic service. White collar jobs as social workers, secretaries, department store clerks, and telephone operators were largely reserved for native-born women. Immigrant women tended to cluster in particular industries. Although hours were often long, pay low, and advancement limited, a job still bought working women some economic and social independence.

Narrowing the Welcome Mat

Antiforeignism, or "nativism," earlier touched off by the Irish and German arrivals in the 1840s and 1850s, bared its ugly face in the 1880s with fresh ferocity. The New Immigrants had come for much the same reasons as the Old—to escape the poverty and squalor of Europe and to seek new opportunities in America. But "nativists" viewed the eastern and southern Europeans as culturally and religiously exotic hordes and often gave them a rude reception. The newest newcomers aroused widespread alarm. Their high birthrate, common among people with a low standard of living, raised worries that the original Anglo-Saxon stock would soon be outbred and outvoted. Still more horrifying was the prospect that it would be "mongrelized" by a mixture of "inferior" southern European blood and that the fairer Anglo-Saxon types would disappear. One New England writer cried out in anguish,

> O Liberty, white Goddess! is it well
> To leave the gates unguarded?

"Native" Americans voiced additional fears. They blamed the immigrants for the degradation of urban government. Trade unionists assailed the alien arrivals for their willingness to work for "starvation" wages that seemed to them like princely sums and for importing in their intellectual baggage such dangerous doctrines as socialism, communism, and anarchism. Many business leaders who had welcomed the flood of cheap manual labor began to fear that they had embraced a Frankenstein's monster.

Antiforeign organizations, reminiscent of the "Know-Nothings" of antebellum days, were now revived in a different guise. Notorious among them was the American Protective Association (APA), which was created in 1887 and soon claimed a million members. In pursuing its nativist goals, the APA urged voting against Roman Catholic candidates for office and sponsored the publication of lustful fantasies about runaway nuns.

Organized labor was quick to throw its growing weight behind the move to choke off the rising tide of foreigners. Frequently used as strike-breakers, the wage-depressing immigrants were hard to unionize because of the language barrier. Labor leaders argued, not illogically, that if American industry was entitled to protection from foreign goods, the American worker was entitled to protection from foreign laborers.

Congress finally nailed up partial bars against the inpouring immigrants. The first restrictive law, in 1882, banged the gate shut in the faces of

LOOKING BACKWARD.

■ **Looking Backward** Older immigrants, trying to keep their own humble arrival in America "in the shadows," sought to close the bridge that had carried them and their ancestors across the Atlantic.

Examining the Evidence

Manuscript Census Data, 1900 Article I of the Constitution requires that a census of the American people be taken every ten years, in order to provide a reliable basis for congressional apportionment. Early censuses gathered little more than basic population numbers, but over the years the census takers have collected information on other matters as well, including occupational categories, educational levels, and citizenship status, yielding copious raw data for historical analysis. The census of 1890 was the first to use punch cards and electric tabulating machines, which greatly expanded the range of data that could be assembled and correlated— though the basic information was still hand-recorded by individual canvassers who went door-to-door to question household members and fill out the census forms. Those handwritten forms, as much as the aggregate numbers printed in the final census tally, can furnish invaluable insights to the historian. Despite its apparent bureaucratic formality, the form shown here richly details the lives of the residents of a tenement house on New York's Lower East Side in 1900. See in particular the entries for the Goldberg family.

1. In what ways does this document reflect the great demographic changes that swept late-nineteenth-century America?

2. What light does it shed on the character of immigrant "ghettos"?

3. What is the most common occupation of those listed? What is second? What might you conclude about the economic status of these residents of Manhattan?

TWELFTH CENSUS OF THE UNITED STATES.

SCHEDULE No. 1.—POPULATION.

[Handwritten census form showing residents of a New York tenement house, 1900. State: New York; County: New York; Boro: Manhattan; Enumerated on the 1st day of June, 1900, by Harman Wechsler, Enumerator. The form lists numerous individuals including the Ginsberg, Siegel, Reigar, Lurie, Levin, and Goldberg families, with columns for Location, Name, Relation, Personal Description, Nativity, Citizenship, Occupation, Education, and Ownership of Home.]

paupers, criminals, and convicts, all of whom had to be returned at the expense of the greedy or careless shipper. Congress further responded to pained outcries from organized labor when in 1885 it prohibited the importation of foreign workers under contract—usually for substandard wages.

In later years other federal laws lengthened the list of undesirables to include the insane, polygamists, prostitutes, alcoholics, anarchists, and people carrying contagious diseases. A proposed literacy test, long a favorite of nativists because it favored the Old Immigrants over the New, met vigorous opposition. It was not

pauper *A poor person, often one who lives on tax-supported charity.*

enacted until 1917, after three presidents had vetoed it on the grounds that literacy was more a measure of opportunity than of intelligence.

The year 1882, in addition to the first federal restrictions on immigration, brought forth a law to bar completely one ethnic group—the Chinese (see p. 346). Hitherto America had embraced the oppressed and underprivileged of all races and creeds. Now the gates were padlocked against defective undesirables—plus the Chinese.

Four years later, in 1886, the Statue of Liberty arose in New York harbor, a gift from the people of France. On its base were inscribed the words of Emma Lazarus:

> *Give me your tired, your poor,*
> *Your huddled masses yearning to breathe free,*
> *The wretched refuse of your teeming shore.*

To many nativists, those noble words described only too accurately the "scum" washed up by the New Immigrant tides. Yet the uprooted immigrants, unlike "natives" lucky enough to have had parents who caught an earlier ship, became American citizens the hard way. These new immigrants stepped off the boat ready to put their shoulders to the nation's industrial wheels. The Republic owes much to these latecomers—for their brawn, their brains, their courage, and the yeasty diversity they brought to American society.

Churches Confront the Urban Challenge

The swelling size and changing character of the urban population posed sharp challenges to American churches, which, like other national institutions, had grown up in the country. Protestant churches in particular suffered heavily from the shift to the city, where many of their traditional doctrines and pastoral approaches seemed irrelevant.

As they lost their bearings in the new urban world, some churches were tending to become merely sacred diversions or amusements. Reflecting the wealth of their prosperous parishioners, many of the old-line churches were distressingly slow to raise their voices against social and economic vices. John D. Rockefeller was a pillar of the Baptist Church; J. Pierpont Morgan, of the Episcopal Church. Cynics remarked that the Episcopal church had become "the Republican party at prayer." The mounting emphasis was on materialism; too many devotees worshiped at the altar of avarice. Money was the accepted measure of achievement, and the new gospel of wealth proclaimed that God caused the righteous to prosper.

Into this spreading moral vacuum stepped a new generation of liberal Protestants, whose ideas came to dominate American Protestantism between 1875 and 1925, despite frequent and bitter controversies. Entrenched in the leadership and seminaries of the mainstream denominations, liberal Protestants adapted religious ideas to modern culture and called for modest reforms. They rejected biblical literalism, questioned the idea of original sin, and supported the social gospel. Friendly to urban revivalists like Dwight Moody, a former shoe salesman who captivated audiences with his message of forgiveness, optimistic liberal Protestants sought to mediate between labor and capital, sciences and faith, religious and secular values. Their focus on fellowship and personal growth helped many Protestant Americans reconcile their religious faith with modern, cosmopolitan ways of thinking.

Simultaneously, the Roman Catholic and Jewish faiths were gaining enormous strength from the New Immigration. By 1900 Roman Catholics had become the largest single denomination, numbering nearly 9 million communicants. Cardinal James Gibbons (1834–1921) of Baltimore, an urban Catholic leader devoted to American unity, was immensely popular with Roman Catholics and Protestants alike. Acquainted with every president from Andrew Johnson to Warren Harding, he employed his liberal sympathies to assist the American labor movement.

By 1890 the variety-loving Americans could choose from 150 religious denominations, 2 of them newcomers. One was the band-playing Salvation Army, whose soldiers without swords invaded America from England in 1879 and established a beachhead on the street corners. Appealing frankly to the down-and-outers, the boldly named Salvation Army did much practical good, especially with free soup.

The other important new faith was the Church of Christ, Scientist (Christian Science), founded by Mary Baker Eddy in 1879 after she had suffered much ill health. Preaching that the true practice of Christianity heals sickness, she set forth her views in a book entitled *Science and Health with Key to the Scriptures* (1875), which sold an amazing 400,000 copies before her death. A fertile field for converts was found in America's hurried, nerve-wracked, and urbanized civilization. By the time Eddy died in 1910, she had founded an influential church that embraced several hundred thousand devoted worshipers.

The old-time religion received many blows from modern trends, including a boom sale of books on comparative religion and on historical criticism as applied to the Bible. Most unsettling of all was *On the Origin of Species* (1859), in which the English naturalist Charles Darwin set forth the sensational theory that higher forms of life had slowly evolved from lower forms, through a process of random biological mutation and adaptation.

Darwin's idea of "natural selection" broke new ground. Nature, in his view, blindly selected organisms for survival or death based on random, inheritable variations that they happened to possess. Some traits conferred advantages in the struggle for life, and hence better odds of passing them on to offspring. By providing a material explanation for the evolutionary process, Darwin's theory explicitly rejected the "dogma of special creation," which ascribed the design of each fixed species to divine agency.

Darwin's radical ideas evoked the wrath of scientists and laymen alike. Many zoologists, like Harvard's Louis Agassiz, held fast to the old doctrine of "special creation." By 1875, however, the majority of scientists in America and elsewhere had embraced the theory of organic evolution, though not all endorsed natural selection as its agent.

Clergymen and theologians responded to Darwin's theory in several ways. At first most believers joined scientists in rejecting his ideas outright. After 1875, by which time most natural scientists had embraced evolution, the religious community split into two camps. A conservative minority condemned what they thought was the "bestial hypothesis" of Darwinism. Their rejection of scientific consensus spawned a muscular view of biblical authority that eventually gave rise to **fundamentalism** in the twentieth century.

Most religious thinkers parted company with conservatives and sought ways to reconcile Darwinism with Christianity. These "accommodationists" eventually heralded the revolutionary theory as a newer and grander revelation of the Almighty. As one commentator observed,

> *Some call it Evolution,*
> *Others call it God.*

While the liberal efforts at compromise did succeed in keeping many Americans in the pews, these compromises also tended to relegate religious teaching to matters of personal faith, private conduct, and family life. As science began to explain more of the external world, commentators on nature and society increasingly refrained from adding religious perspectives to the discussion.

> *As a student at Harvard Medical School, William James (1842–1910) was influenced by Darwinian science. He reviewed Darwin's theory in his first published article in 1865:*
>
> "A doctrine like that of Transmutation of Species . . . cannot but be treated with some respect; and when we find that such naturalists, . . . many of whom but a few days ago were publicly opposing it, are now coming round, one by one, to espouse it, we may well doubt whether it may not be destined eventually to prevail."

fundamentalism *The conservative Protestant movement and ideology that rejects religious modernism and adheres to a strict and literal interpretation of Christian doctrine and Scriptures.*

The Lust for Learning

Public education continued its upward climb. The ideal of tax-supported elementary schools was still gathering strength. Beginning about 1870, more and more states were making at least a grade-school education compulsory, and this gain, incidentally, helped check the frightening abuses of child labor.

Spectacular indeed was the spread of the high schools, especially by the 1880s and 1890s. By 1900 some six thousand high schools were educating teenage boys and girls. In addition, the states provided free textbooks in increasing numbers during the last two decades of the century.

Other trends were noteworthy. Teacher-training schools, then called "normal schools," experienced a striking expansion after the Civil War. In 1860 only twelve normal schools were operating; in 1910, over three hundred. Kindergartens, earlier borrowed from Germany, began to gain strong support. The New Immigration in the 1880s and 1890s brought vast new strength to the private Catholic parochial schools, which were fast becoming a major pillar of the nation's educational structure.

Public schools, though showering benefits on children, excluded millions of adults. This deficiency was partially remedied by the Chautauqua movement, launched in 1874 on the shores of Lake Chautauqua in New York. The organizers achieved gratifying success through nationwide public lectures, often held in tents and featuring such well-known speakers as the witty Mark Twain. In addition, Chautauqua offered extensive home study courses, for which 100,000 people enrolled in 1892 alone.

Crowded cities, despite their cancers, generally provided better educational facilities than the old one-room, one-teacher red schoolhouse. The success of the public schools is confirmed by the falling of the illiteracy rate from 20 percent in 1870 to 10.7 percent in 1900. Americans were developing a profound faith, often misplaced, in formal education as the sovereign remedy for their ills.

Booker T. Washington and Education for Black People

Online Study Center

Primary source
Booker T. Washington and Others
college.hmco.com/pic/kennedybrief7e

War-torn and impoverished, the South lagged far behind other regions in public education, and African Americans suffered most severely. A staggering 44 percent of nonwhites were illiterate in 1900. Some help came from northern philanthropists, but the foremost champion of black education was an ex-slave, Booker T. Washington, who had slept under a board sidewalk to save pennies for his schooling. Called in 1881 to head the black normal and industrial school at Tuskegee, Alabama, he began with forty students in a tumbledown shanty. Undaunted, he taught black students useful trades so that they could gain self-respect and economic security. But Washington stopped short of advocating *social* equality with whites, acquiescing in segregation in return for the right to develop economic and educational resources of the black community.

Washington's commitment to training young blacks in agriculture and the trades guided the curriculum at Tuskegee Institute and made it an ideal place for slave-born George Washington Carver to teach and research. After Carver joined the faculty in 1896, he became an internationally famous agricultural chemist who

■ Booker T. Washington in His Office at Tuskegee Institute, c. 1902 In a famous speech in Atlanta, Washington accepted social separateness for blacks: "In all things that are purely social, we can be as separate as the fingers, yet one as the hand in all things essential to mutual progress."

■ **W. E. B. Du Bois** At the end of a long lifetime of struggle for racial justice in the United States, Du Bois renounced his American citizenship in 1961, at the age of 93, and took up residence in the newly independent African state of Ghana.

helped the economy of the South by discovering hundreds of new uses for the lowly peanut (shampoo, axle grease), sweet potato (vinegar), and soybean (paints).

Other black leaders, notably Dr. W. E. B. Du Bois, assailed Booker T. Washington as an "Uncle Tom" who was condemning their race to manual labor and perpetual inferiority. Born in Massachusetts, Du Bois was a mixture of African, French, Dutch, and Indian blood ("Thank God, no Anglo-Saxon," he would add). After a determined struggle, he earned a Ph.D. at Harvard, the first of his race to achieve that goal. He demanded complete equality for blacks, social as well as economic, and helped to found the National Association for the Advancement of Colored People (NAACP) in 1910. Rejecting Washington's gradualism and separatism, he demanded that the "talented tenth" of the black community be given full and immediate access to the mainstream of American life. An exceptionally skilled historian, sociologist, and poet, he died as a self-exile in Africa in 1963, at the age of ninety-five.

The Hallowed Halls of Ivy

Colleges and universities also shot up like lusty young saplings in the decades after the Civil War. The educational battle for women, only partially won before the war, turned into a rout of the masculine diehards. Women's colleges such as Vassar were gaining ground, and universities open

---

W. E. B. Du Bois (1868–1963) wrote in his 1903 classic, The Souls of Black Folk,

"It is a peculiar sensation, this double consciousness, this sense of always looking at one's self through the eyes of others, of measuring one's self through the eyes of others. . . . One ever feels his two-ness—an American, a Negro; two souls, two thoughts, two unreconciled strivings; two warring ideals in one dark body, whose dogged strength alone keeps it from being torn asunder."

to both genders were blossoming, notably in the Midwest. By 1900 every third college graduate was a woman. By the turn of the century the black institutes and academies planted during Reconstruction had blossomed into a crop of southern black colleges. Howard University in Washington, D.C., Hampton Institute in Virginia, Atlanta University, and numerous others nurtured higher education for blacks until the civil rights movement of the 1960s made attendance at white institutions possible.

The truly phenomenal growth of higher education owed much to the Morrill Act of 1862. This enlightened law provided a generous grant of public lands to the states for support of public higher education. The Hatch Act of 1887 extended the Morrill Act by providing federal funds for the establishment of agricultural experiment stations. Together these two pieces of legislation spawned over a hundred "land-grant colleges" that evolved into state universities, including such institutions as the University of California (1868), Ohio State University (1870), and Texas A&M (1876).

Private philanthropy richly supplemented federal grants to higher education. Many of the new industrial millionaires, developing tender social consciences, donated immense fortunes to educational enterprises. In the twenty years from 1878 to 1898 these money barons gave away about $150 million. Among the noteworthy new private universities were Cornell (1865) and Leland Stanford Junior (1891), the latter founded in memory of the deceased fifteen-year-old only child of a builder of the Central Pacific Railroad. The University of Chicago, opened in 1892, speedily forged into a front-rank position, owing largely to the lubricant of John D. Rockefeller's oil millions.

Towering among the new professionalized institutions of higher learning was Johns Hopkins University, opened in 1876, which developed the nation's first high-grade graduate school. Several generations of American scholars, repelled by snobbish English cousins and attracted by painstaking Continental methods, had attended German universities. Reputable scholars no longer had to go abroad for a gilt-edged graduate degree; Dr. Woodrow Wilson, among others, received his Ph.D. from Johns Hopkins.

Homegrown influences shaped the modern American university as much as Continental models. Antebellum colleges had stressed the "unity of truth," or the idea that knowledge and morality existed in a single system united by theology and moral philosophy. After the Darwinian challenge made religion and science seem less compatible, university reformers struggled to preserve the unity of moral and intellectual purpose. When that effort failed, university educators abandoned moral instruction and divorced "facts" from "values."

Other pressures also helped doom the traditional curriculum. Industrialization and science brought insistent demands for "practical" courses, and specialization, not synthesis, became the primary goal of a university education. The turn toward electives and pre-professional training received a powerful boost in the 1870s when Dr. Charles W. Eliot became president of Harvard College. As a sign of the secularizing times, Eliot changed Harvard's motto from *Christo et Ecclesiae* (for Christ and Church) to *Veritas* (Truth).

One of America's most brilliant intellectuals, the slight and sickly William James (1842–1910), served for thirty-five years on the Harvard faculty. Through his numerous writings he made a deep mark on many fields. His *Principles of Psychology* (1890) helped to establish the modern discipline of psychology. In *The Will to Believe* (1897) and *Varieties of Religious Experience* (1902), he explored the philosophy and psychology of religion. In his most famous work, *Pragmatism* (1907), he colorfully described America's greatest contribution to the history of philosophy. The concept of pragmatism held that truth was to be tested, above all, by its practical consequences.

The Appeal of the Press

Books continued to be a major source of edification and enjoyment for both juveniles and adults. Public libraries—the poor person's university—made encouraging progress in the late nineteenth century, especially in Boston and

Online Study Center

Primary source
Morrill Act
college.hmco.com/pic/kennedybrief7e

Educational Levels, 1870–2000

Year	Number Graduating from High School	Number Graduating from College	Median School Years Completed* (Years)	
1870	16,000	9,371		
1880	24,000	12,896		
1890	44,000	15,539		
1900	95,000	27,410		
1910	156,000	37,199	8.1†	
1920	311,000	48,622	8.2†	
1930	667,000	122,484	8.4†	
1940	1,221,000	186,500	8.6	
1950	1,199,700	432,058	9.3	
1960	1,858,000	392,440	10.5	
1970	2,889,000	792,656	12.2	
1980	3,043,000	929,417	12.5	
1990	2,503,000	1,048,631	12.7	74.2
2001	2,545,000	1, 823,036	N.A.	N.A.

* People twenty-five years and over.
† 1910–1930 based on retrogressions of 1940 data; 1940 was the first year measured (Folger and Nam, *Education of the American Population,* a 1960 Census Monograph).

Sources: Digest of Education Statistics, 1992, a publication of the National Center for Education Statistics, and *Statistical Abstract of the United States,* relevant years.

New York. The magnificent Library of Congress building, which opened its doors in 1897, provided thirteen acres of floor space in the largest and costliest edifice of its kind in the world. A new era was inaugurated by the generous gifts of Andrew Carnegie, who contributed $60 million for the construction of public libraries all over the country. By 1900 there were about nine thousand free public libraries in America.

Roaring newspaper presses, spurred by the invention of the Linotype in 1885, more than kept pace with the demands of a word-hungry public. But the heavy investment in machinery and plant was accompanied by a growing fear of offending advertisers and subscribers. Bare-knuckle editorials were, to an increasing degree, being supplanted by feature articles and noncontroversial **syndicated** material. The day of slashing journalistic giants like Horace Greeley was passing.

Sensationalism, at the same time, was capturing the public taste. The semiliterate immigrants, combined with straphanging urban commuters, created a profitable market for news that was simply and punchily written. Stories of sex, scandal, and other human-interest stories burst into the headlines, as a vulgarization of the press accompanied the growth of circulation. Critics complained in vain about these "presstitutes."

Two new journalistic **tycoons** emerged. Joseph Pulitzer, Hungarian-born and near-blind, was a leader in the techniques of sensationalism in St. Louis and in his *New York World.* His use of the colored comic supplements, featuring the "Yellow Kid," gave the name *yellow journalism* to his lurid sheets. A close and ruthless competitor was youthful William Randolph Hearst, who had been expelled from Harvard College for a crude prank. Able to draw on his California father's mining millions, he built up a powerful chain of newspapers, beginning with the *San Francisco Examiner* in 1887. Unfortunately, Pulitzer and Hearst both prostituted the press in their struggle for increased circulation; they "stooped, snooped, and scooped to conquer." Their flair for scandal and sensation was happily somewhat offset by the strengthening of the news-gathering Associated Press, which had been founded in the 1840s.

syndicated *In journalism, material that is sold by an organization for publication in several newspapers.*

tycoon *A wealthy businessperson, especially one who openly displays power and position.*

Apostles of Reform

Magazines partly satisfied the public appetite for good reading, notably old standbys like *Harper's,* the *Atlantic Monthly,* and *Scribner's Monthly.* Possibly the most influential journal was the liberal and highly intellectual *Nation,* whose modest circulation of 10,000 consisted largely of professors, preachers, and publicists. Launched in 1865 by the Irish-born critic Edwin L. Godkin, the *Nation* crusaded for civil-service reform, honesty in government, and a moderate tariff. Godkin believed that by reaching the nation's leaders his ideas might through them reach millions.

Another journalist-author, Henry George, was an original thinker who left an enduring mark. Poor in formal schooling, he was rich in idealism and in the milk of human kindness. After seeing poverty at its worst in India and land-grabbing at its greediest in California, he penned his classic treatise *Progress and Poverty* (1879), which undertook to solve "the great enigma of our times"—"the association of progress with poverty." According to George, property owners unjustifiably profited from the pressure of growing population on a fixed supply of land. A single 100 percent tax on those windfall profits would eliminate unfair inequalities and stimulate economic growth.

George's controversial single-tax ideas so horrified the propertied classes that his manuscript was rejected by numerous publishers. Finally published in 1879, the book ultimately sold some 3 million copies. George also lectured widely in America, where he influenced thinking about the maldistribution of wealth, and in Britain, where he left an indelible mark on Fabian socialism.

Edward Bellamy, a quiet Massachusetts Yankee, was another journalist-reformer of remarkable power. In 1888 he published a socialistic novel, *Looking Backward,* in which the hero, falling into a hypnotic sleep, awakens in the year 2000. He "looks backward" and finds that the social and economic injustices of 1887 have melted away under an idyllic government, which has nationalized big business to serve the public interest. To a nation already alarmed by the trust evil, the book had a magnetic appeal and sold over a million copies. Scores of Bellamy Clubs sprang up to discuss this mild utopian socialism, and they heavily influenced American reform movements near the end of the century.

Postwar Writing

As literacy increased, so did book reading. Post–Civil War Americans devoured millions of "dime novels," usually depicting the wild West. Paint-bedaubed Indians and quick-triggered gunmen like "Deadwood Dick" shot off vast quantities of gunpowder, and virtue invariably triumphed. These lurid "paperbacks" were frowned on by parents, but goggle-eyed youths read them in haylofts or in schools behind the broad covers of geography books. The king of dime novelists was Harlan F. Halsey, who made a fortune by dashing off about 650 novels, often one in a day.

General Lewis Wallace—lawyer, soldier, and author—was a colorful figure. Having fought with distinction in the Civil War, he sought to combat the prevailing wave of Darwinian skepticism with his novel *Ben Hur: A Tale of the Christ* (1880). A phenomenal success, the book sold an estimated 2 million copies in many languages, including Arabic and Chinese, and later appeared on stage and screen. It was the *Uncle Tom's Cabin* of the anti-Darwinists, who found in it support for the Holy Scriptures.

An even more popular writer was Horatio ("Holy Horatio") Alger, a Puritan-reared New Englander, who in 1866 forsook the pulpit for the pen. He wrote more than a hundred volumes of juvenile fiction that sold over 100 million copies. His stock formula was that virtue, honesty, and industry are rewarded with wealth and success (especially if one is lucky enough to save the life of the boss's daughter and marry her).

In poetry Walt Whitman was one of the few luminaries of yesteryear who remained active. The assassination of Lincoln inspired him to write two of the most moving poems in American literature, "O Captain! My Captain!" and "When Lilacs Last in the Dooryard Bloom'd."

The curious figure of Emily Dickinson, one of America's most gifted lyric poets, did not emerge until 1886, when she died and her poems were discovered. A Massachusetts recluse, she wrote over a thousand short lyrics on odd scraps of paper. Only two were published during her lifetime, and those without her consent. As she wrote,

> *How dreary to be somebody!*
> *How public, like a frog*
> *To tell your name the livelong day*
> *To an admiring bog!*

Literary Landmarks

In novel writing, the romantic sentimentality of a youthful era was giving way to a rugged realism that reflected more faithfully the materialism of an industrial society. American authors now turned increasingly to the coarse human comedy and tragedy of the world around them to find their subjects.

Two Missouri-born authors with deep connections to the South brought altogether new voices to the late-nineteenth-century literary scene. The daring **feminist** author Kate Chopin (1851–1904) wrote candidly about adultery, suicide, and women's ambitions in *The Awakening* (1899). Largely ignored in her own day, Chopin was rediscovered by later readers who cited her work as suggestive of the feminist yearnings that stirred beneath the surface of "respectability" in the Gilded Age.

feminist (feminism) *One who promotes complete political, social, and economic equality of opportunity for women.*

Mustachioed Mark Twain (1835–1910) leapt to fame with his comic short story "The Celebrated Jumping Frog of Calaveras County" (1867) and *The Innocents Abroad* (1869). He teamed up with Charles Dudley Warner in 1873 to write *The Gilded Age,* an acid satire on post–Civil War politicians and speculators that gave a name to an era. With his scanty formal schooling in frontier Missouri, Twain typified a new breed of American authors in revolt against the elegant refinements of the old New England school of writing. Christened Samuel Langhorne Clemens, he had served for a time as a Mississippi riverboat pilot and later took his pen name, Mark Twain, from the boatman's cry that meant two fathoms. After a brief stint in the armed forces, Twain journeyed to California, a trip he described, with a mixture of truth and tall tales, in *Roughing It* (1872).

Many other books flowed from Twain's busy pen. *The Adventures of Tom Sawyer* (1876) preceded *The Adventures of Huckleberry Finn* (1884), an American masterpiece that defied Twain's own definition of a classic as "a book which people praise and don't read." His later years were soured by bankruptcy growing out of unwise investments, and he was forced to take to the lecture platform and amuse what he called "the damned human race." Twain made his most enduring contribution in recapturing frontier realism and humor in the authentic American dialect.

William Dean Howells (1837–1920), a printer's son from Ohio, could boast of little schoolhouse education, but his busy pen carried him high into the literary circles of the East. In 1871 he became the editor of the prestigious Boston-based *Atlantic Monthly.* Howells wrote about ordinary people and about contemporary and sometimes controversial social themes. *A Modern Instance* (1882) deals with the once-taboo subject of divorce. *The Rise of Silas Lapham* (1885) describes the trials of a newly rich paint manufacturer caught up in the caste system of Brahmin Boston. *A Hazard of New Fortunes* (1890) portrays reformers, strikers, and socialists in Gilded Age New York.

Stephen Crane (1871–1900), the fourteenth son of a Methodist minister, also wrote about the seamy underside of life in urban, industrial America. His *Maggie: A Girl of the Streets* (1893), a brutal tale about a poor prostitute driven to suicide, was too grim to find a publisher. Crane had to have it printed privately. He rose quickly to prominence with *The Red Badge of Courage* (1895), the stirring story of a bloodied young Civil War recruit under fire. Crane himself had never seen a battle and wrote entirely from the printed Civil War records. He died of tuberculosis in 1900, when only twenty-nine.

Not all authors came from humble stock. The gifted Henry Adams (1838–1918)—grandson and great-grandson of American presidents—turned unrivaled family connections into a prolific career as a historian, novelist, and critic. His nine-volume *History of the United States During the Administrations of Jefferson and Madison* (1889–1891) made his mark as an historian. In *Mont-Saint Michel and Chartres* (1905) Adams penned a paean to the bygone beauty and unity of the High Middle Ages. His well-known autobiography, *The Education of Henry Adams* (1907) similarly reflects his anxieties about modernity and the chaotic forces of twentieth-century life.

Henry James (1843–1916), brother of Harvard philosopher William James, was a New Yorker who took as his dominant literary theme the confrontation of innocent Americans with subtle Europeans, James penned a remarkable number of brilliant novels, including *Daisy Miller* (1879), *The Portrait of a Lady* (1881), and *The Wings of the Dove* (1902). *The Bostonians* (1886) was one of the first novels about the rising feminist movement. James frequently made women his central characters, exploring their inner reactions to complex situations with a deftness that marked him as a master of "psychological realism." Long resident in England, he became a British subject shortly before his death.

Candid portrayals of contemporary life and social problems were the literary order of the day by the turn of the century. Jack London (1876–1916) turned from his popular nature books such as *The Call of the Wild* (1903) to depicting a possible fascistic revolution in *The Iron Heel* (1907). Frank Norris (1870–1902), like London a Californian, wrote *The Octopus* (1901), an earthy saga of the stranglehold of the railroad and corrupt politicians on California wheat ranchers.

Two black writers, Paul Laurence Dunbar (1872–1906) and Charles W. Chesnutt (1858–1932), brought another kind of realism to late nineteenth century literature. In Dunbar's acclaimed book of poetry, *Lyrics of Lowly Life* (1896), he used black dialect and folklore to capture the spontaneity and richness of southern black culture. Chesnutt did the same through his short stories, collected in *Conjure Women* (1899).

Conspicuous among the new "social novelists" rising in the literary firmament was Theodore Dreiser (1871–1945), a homely, gangling writer from Indiana. He burst on the literary scene in 1900 with *Sister Carrie,* a graphically realistic narrative of a poor working girl in Chicago and New York. She becomes one man's mistress, then elopes with another, and finally strikes out on her own to make a career on the stage. The fictional Carrie's disregard for prevailing moral standards so offended Dreiser's publisher that the book was soon withdrawn from circulation, though it later re-emerged as an acclaimed American classic.

The New Morality

Online Study Center

Primary source
Beauty and the Beast
college.hmco.com/pic/kennedybrief7e

Victoria Woodhull, who was real flesh and blood, also shook the pillars of conventional morality when she publicly proclaimed her belief in free love in 1871. Woodhull was a beautiful and eloquent divorcée, sometime stockbroker, and tireless feminist propagandist. Together with her sister Tennessee Claflin she published a far-out periodical, *Woodhull and Claflin's Weekly.* The sisters again shocked "respectable" society in 1872 when their journal struck a blow for the new morality by charging that Henry Ward Beecher, the most famous preacher of his day, had for years been carrying on an adulterous affair.

Pure-minded Americans sternly resisted these affronts to their moral principles. Their foremost champion was a portly crusader, Anthony Comstock, who made lifelong war on the "immoral." Armed after 1873 with a federal statute—the notorious Comstock Law—this self-appointed defender of sexual purity boasted that he had confiscated no fewer than 202,679 "obscene pictures and photos"; 4,185 "boxes of pills, powders, etc., used by abortionists"; and 26 "obscene pictures, framed on walls of saloons."

The antics of the Woodhull sisters and Anthony Comstock exposed to daylight the battle going on in late-nineteenth-century America over sexual attitudes and the place of women. Women's growing economic freedom encouraged sexual freedom, and the "new morality" began to be reflected in soaring divorce rates, the spreading practice of birth control, and increasingly frank discussion of sexual topics. By 1913, said one popular magazine, the chimes had struck "sex o'clock in America."

Families and Women in the City

The new urban environment was hard on families. Paradoxically, the crowded cities were emotionally isolating places. Urban families had to go it alone, separated from clan, kin, and village. Many families cracked under the strain of providing the virtually exclusive arena for intimate companionship and emotional satisfaction. The late-nineteenth-century urban era launched the "divorce revolution" that transformed the United States' social landscape in the twentieth century.

Urban life also dictated changes in work habits and even in family size. Not only fathers but mothers and even children as young as ten years old often worked, and usually in widely scattered locations. In the city more children meant more mouths to feed, more crowding in sardine-tin tenements, and more human baggage to carry in the uphill struggle for social mobility. Not surprisingly, birthrates were still dropping, and family size continued to shrink as the nineteenth century lengthened. Marriages were being delayed, and more couples learned the techniques of birth control.

Women were growing more independent in the urban environment, and in 1898 they heard the voice of a major feminist prophet, Charlotte Perkins Gilman. In that year the freethinking and original-minded Gilman published *Women and Economics.* In this classic of feminist literature, Gilman called on women to abandon their dependent status and contribute to the larger life of the community through productive involvement in the economy. Rejecting all claims that biology gave women a fundamentally different character from men, she argued that "our highly specialized motherhood is not so advantageous as believed." She advocated centralized nurseries and cooperative kitchens to facilitate women's participation in the work force—anticipating by more than half a century the day-care centers and convenience-food services of a later day.

Fiery feminists also continued to insist on the ballot. They had been demanding the vote since before the Civil War, but many high-minded female reformers had temporarily shelved the cause of women to battle for the rights of blacks. In 1890 militant suffragists formed the National American Woman Suffrage Association. Its founders included aging pioneers like Elizabeth Cady Stanton, who had helped organize the first women's rights convention in 1848, and her long-time comrade Susan B. Anthony, the radical Quaker who had courted jail by trying to cast a ballot in the 1872 presidential election.

By 1900 a new generation of women had taken command of the suffrage battle. Their most effective leader was Carrie Chapman Catt, a pragmatic and businesslike reformer of relentless dedication. Significantly, under Catt the suffragists de-emphasized the argument that women deserved the vote as a matter of right, because they were in all respects the equals of men. Instead Catt stressed the desirability of giving women the vote if they were to continue to discharge their traditional duties as homemakers and mothers in the increasingly public world of the city.

By thus linking the ballot to a traditional definition of women's role, suffragists registered encouraging gains as the new century opened, despite continuing showers of rotten eggs and the jeers of male critics. Women were increasingly permitted to vote in local elections. Wyoming Territory—later called "the Equality State"—granted the

In 1906 progressive reformer Jane Addams (1860–1935) argued that granting women the vote would improve the social and political condition of American cities:

"City housekeeping has failed partly because women, the traditional housekeepers, have not been consulted as to its multiform activities. The men have been carelessly indifferent to much of the civic housekeeping, as they have been indifferent to the details of the household. . . . City government demands the help of minds accustomed to detail and a variety of work, to a sense of obligation to the health and welfare of young children, and to a responsibility for the cleanliness."

first unrestricted suffrage to women in 1869. This important breach in the dike once made, many states followed Wyoming's example. Paralleling these triumphs, most of the states by 1890 had passed laws to permit wives to own or control their property after marriage.

The reborn suffrage movement and other women's organizations excluded black women from their ranks. Fearful that an integrated campaign would handicap its efforts to get the vote, the National American Woman Suffrage Association limited membership to whites. Black women, however, created their own associations. Journalist and teacher Ida B. Wells inspired black women to mount a nationwide antilynching crusade. She also helped launch the black women's club movement, which culminated in the establishment of the National Association of Colored Women in 1896.

Women also took a lead in the growing crusade against alcohol and the saloon. In 1874 the Women's Christian Temperance Union (WCTU) was organized with the white ribbon as its symbol of purity. The saintly Frances E. Willard—also a champion of planned parenthood—was its leading spirit. Less saintly was the mentally deranged "Kansas Cyclone," Carrie A. Nation, who smashed saloon bottles and bars with her hatchet. Female prohibitionists, singing "The Lips That Touch Liquor Must Never Touch Mine," began sweeping new states into the "dry column"—setting the stage for the great, but temporary, triumph of 1919 when the national prohibition amendment (Eighteenth) was attached to the Constitution.

Artistic Triumphs

John Adams had anticipated that his generation's preoccupation with nation-building would allow art to flourish in the future, but the results long proved unspectacular. Portrait painting continued to appeal, as it had since the colonial era, but many of America's finest painters made their livings abroad. James Whistler (1834–1903) did much of his work, including the celebrated portrait of his mother, in England. This eccentric and quarrelsome Massachusetts Yankee had earlier been dropped from West Point after failing chemistry. "Had silicon been a gas," he later jested, "I would have been a major general." Another American painter resident in England, John Singer Sargent (1856–1925), painted highly prized portraits of the British nobility. Mary Cassatt, an American exile in Paris, painted sensitive portrayals of women and children that earned her a place in the pantheon of the French impressionist painters.

Other brush wielders, no less talented, brightened the artistic horizon. Self-taught George Inness (1825–1894) became America's leading landscapist. Thomas Eakins (1844–1916) attained a high degree of realism in his paintings, a quality not appreciated by portrait sitters who wanted their moles overlooked. Boston-born Winslow Homer (1836–1910), who as a youth had secretly drawn sketches in school, was perhaps the greatest painter of the group. Earthily American and largely resistant to foreign influences, he revealed rugged realism and boldness of conception. His canvases of the sea and of fisherfolk were masterly, and probably no American artist has excelled him in portraying the awesome power of the ocean.

Probably the most gifted sculptor yet produced by America was Augustus Saint-Gaudens (1848–1907). Born in Ireland of an Irish mother and a French father, he became an adopted American. Among his most moving works is the Robert Gould Shaw memorial, erected in Boston in 1897. It depicts Colonel Shaw, a young white "Boston Brahmin" officer, leading his black troops into battle in the Civil War.

Music, too, was gaining popularity. America of the 1880s and 1890s was assembling high-quality symphony orchestras, notably in Boston and Chicago. The famed Metropolitan Opera House of New York was erected in 1883. In its fabled "Diamond Horseshoe" the newly rich, often under the pretense of enjoying the imported singers, would flaunt their jewels, gowns, and furs. While symphonies and operas were devoted to bringing European music to elite American audiences, new strains of homegrown American music were sprouting in the South. Black folk traditions like spirituals and "ragged music" were evolving into the blues, ragtime, and jazz that would transform American popular music in the twentieth century.

A marvelous discovery was the reproduction of music by mechanical means. The phonograph, though a squeakily imperfect instrument when invented by the deaf Edison, had by 1900 reached over 150,000 homes. Americans were rapidly being dosed with "canned music," as the "sitting room" piano increasingly gathered dust.

In addition to skyscraper builder Louis Sullivan, a famous American architect of the age was Henry H. Richardson. Born in Louisiana, Richardson settled in Boston and from there spread his immense influence throughout the eastern half of the United States. He popularized a distinctive, ornamental style that came to be known as "Richardsonian." His masterpiece and most famous work was the Marshall Field Building (1885) in Chicago.

■ **Buffalo Bill's Wild West Show, c. 1907** By the late 1800s, the "wild" West was already passing into the realm of myth—and popular entertainment. Famed frontiersman William F. ("Buffalo Bill") Cody made his fortune showing off his tame cowboys and Indians to urban audiences. Buffalo Bill Historical Center, Cody, Wyoming; Gift of The Coe Foundation, 1.69.74

The Business of Amusement

Fun and frolic were not neglected by the workaday American. The legitimate stage still flourished, as appreciative audiences responded to the lure of the footlights. Vaudeville, with its coarse jokes and graceful acrobats, continued to be immensely popular during the 1880s and 1890s, as were minstrel shows in the South, now performed by black singers and dancers rather than by whites wearing blackface.

The circus—high-tented and multiringed—finally emerged full-blown. Phineas T. Barnum, the master showman who had early discovered that "the public likes to be humbugged," joined hands with James A. Bailey in 1881 to stage the "Greatest Show on Earth."

Colorful "Wild West" shows, first performed in 1883, were even more distinctively American. Headed by the knightly, goateed, and free-drinking William F. ("Buffalo Bill") Cody, the troupe included war-whooping Indians, live buffalo, and deadeye sharpshooters like the girlish Annie Oakley. Rifle in hand, at thirty paces she could perforate a tossed-up card half a dozen times before it fluttered to the ground.

Baseball, already widely played before the Civil War, was clearly emerging as the national pastime, if not a national mania. A league of professional players was formed in the 1870s, and in 1888 an all-star baseball team toured the world, using the pyramids as a backstop while in Egypt. Basketball was invented in 1891 by James Naismith, a YMCA instructor in Springfield, Massachusetts. Designed as an active indoor sport that could be played during the winter months, it spread rapidly and enjoyed enormous popularity in the next century.

The trend toward spectator sports was exemplified by football, a rugged game that used the dangerous flying wedge formation. The Yale-Princeton game of 1893 drew fifty thousand cheering fans, while foreigners jeered that the nation was getting "sports on the brain."

Even pugilism, with its long background of bare-knuckle brutality, gained a new gloved respectability in 1892. Agile "Gentleman Jim" Corbett wrested the world championship from the aging and alcoholic John L. Sullivan, the "Boston Strong Boy."

Online Study Center

Primary source
Shoeless Joe Jackson
college.hmco.com/pic/kennedybrief7e

Online Study Center

Primary source
Women Playing Basketball
college.hmco.com/pic/kennedybrief7e

Two crazes swept the country in the closing decades of the century. Croquet became enormously popular, though condemned by moralists of the "naughty nineties" because it exposed feminine ankles and promoted flirtation. Cycling flourished when the low-framed "safety" bicycle replaced the high-seated model. By 1893 a million bicycles were in use, and thousands of young women especially turned to this new "spinning wheel" that offered freedom, not tedium.

The land of the skyscraper was plainly becoming more standardized, owing largely to the new industrialization. Despite their distinct ethnic and racial neighborhoods, Americans increasingly shared a common culture—playing, reading, shopping, and talking alike. As the century drew to a close, the explosion of cities paradoxically made Americans more diverse and more similar at the same time.

✪ Chapter Summary ✪

The United States moved from the country to the city in the post-Civil War decades. Mushrooming urban development was attractive and exciting for many who migrated from farms and small towns, but also created severe social problems, including overcrowding and slums.

After the 1880s the cities were also flooded with the "New Immigrants" from southern and eastern Europe. With their culturally different customs and non-Protestant religions, the newcomers often met with nativist hostility and discrimination. Congress began to throw up barriers to immigration, including a complete ban on the Chinese.

Religion had to adjust to social, cultural, and intellectual changes. The immigrant faiths of Roman Catholicism and Judaism gained considerable strength, while conflicts over evolution and biblical interpretation divided American Protestantism into fundamentalist and modernist wings.

American education expanded rapidly, especially at the secondary and collegiate levels, where major new research universities were founded, often by wealthy industrialists. Women's opportunities for education advanced in both separate institutions and coeducation. Black leaders Washington and Du Bois divided over the question of manual education versus development of an elite "talented tenth."

Significant conflicts over moral values, especially relating to sexuality and the role of women, began to appear. The new urban environment provided expanded opportunities for women but also created difficulties for the family. Families grew more isolated from society, the divorce rate rose, and average family size shrank.

American literature and art reflected a new social realism, often addressing the social and moral problems of the new urban, industrial age. American culture became more sophisticated and respected. Leisure-time amusements and sports became enormously popular but also more standardized, in keeping with the new industrial nation.

26

The Great West and the Agricultural Revolution

—◦⊶◦—

1865–1896

UP TO OUR OWN DAY AMERICAN HISTORY HAS BEEN IN A LARGE
DEGREE THE HISTORY OF THE COLONIZATION OF THE GREAT
WEST. THE EXISTENCE OF AN AREA OF FREE LAND, ITS
CONTINUOUS RECESSION, AND THE ADVANCE OF AMERICAN
SETTLEMENT WESTWARD, EXPLAIN AMERICAN DEVELOPMENT.

FREDERICK JACKSON TURNER, 1893

When the Civil War crashed to a close, the frontier line was still wavering westward. A long fringe of settlement, bulging outward here and there, ran roughly north through central Texas and on to the Canadian border. Between this jagged line and the settled areas on the Pacific slope, there were virtually no white people. The few exceptions were the islands of Mormons in Utah, occasional trading posts and gold camps, and several scattered Mexican settlements throughout the Southwest.

Sprawling in expanse, the Great West was a rough square that measured about a thousand miles on each side. Embracing mountains, plateaus, deserts, and plains, it was the habitat of the Indian, the buffalo, the wild horse, and the coyote. Twenty-five years later—that is, by 1890—the entire domain had been carved into states and the four territories of Utah, Arizona, New Mexico, and "Indian Territory," or Oklahoma. Pioneers flung themselves greedily on this enormous prize, as if to ravish it. Probably never before in human experience had so huge an area been transformed so rapidly.

Focus Questions

1. What features characterized the major military and cultural conflicts between the expanding United States and the Indians of the Great West in the decades after the Civil War? What were the causes and consequences of the Indians' defeat?
2. What were the principal stages of frontier settlement in the West, and how did each affect the region's development?
3. What was the significance of the closing of the frontier in 1890 for American history? Why did the West remain such a distinctive American region even after the frontier era ended?
4. How did the agricultural revolution on the Great Plains transform the economics of farming, and what were the consequences of those transformations for farmers?
5. What were the fundamental causes of western and southern farmers' protests, and how did their grievances eventually find powerful political expression in the Populist Party?

Online Study Center

Interactive map
The American West, 1860–1890
college.hmco.com/pic/kennedybrief7e

> *One disheartened Indian complained to the white Sioux Commission created by Congress,*
>
> "Tell your people that since the Great Father promised that we should never be removed we have been moved five times. . . . I think you had better put the Indians on wheels and you can run them about wherever you wish."

nomadic (nomad) *A way of life characterized by frequent movement from place to place for economic sustenance.*

immunity *Freedom or exemption from some imposition.*

Online Study Center

Interactive map
Western Indian Reservations, 1890
college.hmco.com/pic/kennedybrief7e

The Clash of Cultures in the West

Native Americans numbered about 360,000 in 1860, many of them scattered across the vast grasslands of the trans-Missouri West. But to their misfortune, the Indians stood in the path of the advancing white pioneers. An inevitable clash loomed between an acquisitive, industrializing civilization and the Indians' highly evolved lifeways, adapted over centuries to the demanding environment of the sparsely watered western plains.

Migration and conflict—and sometimes dramatic cultural change—were no strangers to the arid West, even before the whites began to arrive. The Comanches had driven the Apaches off the central plains into the upper Rio Grande valley in the eighteenth century. Harried by the Mandans and Chippewas, the Cheyenne had abandoned their villages along the upper reaches of the Mississippi and Missouri Rivers in the century before the Civil War. The Sioux, displaced from the Great Lakes woodlands in the late eighteenth century, emerged onto the plains to prey upon the Crows, Kiowas, and Pawnees. Mounted on Spanish-introduced horses, peoples like the Cheyenne and the Sioux transformed themselves into wide-ranging **nomadic** traders and deadly efficient buffalo hunters.

When white soldiers and settlers edged onto the plains just before the Civil War, they accelerated a fateful cycle that exacerbated already fierce enmities among the Indians and ultimately undermined the foundations of Native American culture. White intruders unwittingly spread cholera, typhoid, and smallpox among the native peoples of the plains, with devastating results. Equally harmful, whites put further pressure on the shrinking bison population by hunting and by grazing their own livestock on the prairie grasses. As the once-mammoth buffalo herds dwindled, warfare intensified among the Plains tribes for ever-scarcer hunting grounds.

The federal government tried to sign treaties with various "chiefs" at Fort Laramie in 1851. But the white treaty makers misunderstood both Indian government and Indian society. Whites could not grasp the fact that Native Americans, living in scattered bands, usually recognized no authority beyond their immediate family or perhaps a village elder. And the nomadic culture of the Plains Indians was utterly alien to the concept of living out one's life in the confinement of a defined territory.

In the 1860s the federal government tried to herd the Plains Indians into confines like the "Great Sioux Reservation" in the Dakotas and the Indian Territory of present-day Oklahoma, where dozens of southern Plains tribes were forced to move. Promises from Washington that they would be left alone and provided with food, clothing, and other supplies were often violated by corrupt federal agents who regularly cheated the Indians.

For more than a decade after the Civil War, fierce warfare between Indians and the U.S. Army raged in various parts of the West. Army troops, many of them recent immigrants, met formidable adversaries in the Plains Indians, whose superb horsemanship gave them baffling mobility. Fully one-fifth of all U.S. Army personnel on the frontier were African American—dubbed "Buffalo Soldiers" by the Indians, supposedly because of the resemblance of their hair to the bison's furry coat.

Receding Native Population

The Indian wars in the West were often savage clashes. Aggressive whites sometimes shot peaceful Indians on sight. At Sand Creek, Colorado, in 1864, Colonel J. M. Chivington's militia massacred in cold blood some four hundred Indians who apparently thought they had been promised **immunity**. Women were shot pray-

Chronology

1858	Pike's Peak gold rush.
1859	Nevada Comstock lode discovered.
1862	Homestead Act.
1864	Sand Creek massacre. Nevada admitted to Union.
1867	National Grange organized.
1876	Battle of the Little Bighorn. Colorado admitted to Union.
1877	Nez Percé Indian War.
1881	Helen Hunt Jackson publishes *A Century of Dishonor.*
1884	Federal government outlaws Indian Sun Dance.
1885–1890	Local chapters of Farmers' Alliances formed.
1887	Dawes Severalty Act.
1889	Oklahoma opened to settlement.
1889–1890	North Dakota, South Dakota, Montana, Washington, Idaho, and Wyoming admitted to the Union.
1890	Census Bureau declares frontier line ended. Emergence of People's party (Populists). Battle of Wounded Knee.
1892	Populist party candidate James B. Weaver polls more than 1 million votes in presidential election.
1893	Frederick Jackson Turner publishes "The Significance of the Frontier in American History."
1894	"Coxey's Army" marches on Washington. Pullman strike.
1896	McKinley defeats Bryan for presidency. Utah admitted to Union.
1897	Dingley Tariff Act.
1900	Gold Standard Act.
1907	Oklahoma admitted to Union.
1924	Indians granted U.S. citizenship.
1934	Indian Reorganization Act.

ing for mercy, children had their brains dashed out, and braves were tortured, scalped, and unspeakably mutilated.

Cruelty begot cruelty. In 1866 a Sioux war party ambushed Captain William Fetterman's command of eighty-one soldiers and civilians in Wyoming's Bighorn Mountains, killing every man and mutilating the corpses. As the cycle of ferocious warfare intensified, the federal government in 1868 abandoned its attempt to construct the Bozeman Trail through Montana. The sprawling "Great Sioux **Reservation**" was guaranteed to the Sioux tribes.

But in 1874 a new round of warfare with the Plains Indians began when Colonel George Armstrong Custer, a famed Civil War officer, led a "scientific" expedition into the Black Hills of South Dakota and announced that he had discovered gold. Hordes of greedy gold-seekers swarmed into the Sioux lands. The aggrieved Sioux took to the warpath, inspirited by the influential and wily Sitting Bull.

Colonel Custer's Seventh Cavalry set out to suppress the Indians and force them onto the reservation. Attacking what turned out to be a superior force of some 2,500 well-armed warriors camped along the Little Bighorn River in present-day Montana, the "White Chief with Yellow Hair" and his 264 officers and men were completely wiped out in 1876 when two supporting columns failed to come to their rescue.* But in a series of battles across the northern plains in the ensuing months, the U.S. Army relentlessly hunted down the Indians who had destroyed Custer's troops.

Online Study Center

Primary source
Sand Creek Massacre
college.hmco.com/pic/kennedybrief7e

---

reservation *Public lands designated for use by Indians.*

---

* When whites annihilated Indians, the engagement (in white history books) was usually a "battle"; when Indians slaughtered whites, it was a "massacre." "Strategy," when practiced by Indians, was "treachery."

■ **Indian Wars, 1860–1890** Surrending in 1877, Chief Joseph of the Nez Percés declared: "Our chiefs are killed. . . . The old men are all dead. . . . The little children are freezing to death. . . . I want to have time to look for my children. . . . Hear me, my chiefs. My heart is sick and sad. From where the sun now stands I will fight no more forever."

ward(s) *Someone considered incompetent to manage his or her own affairs and therefore placed under the legal guardianship of another person or group.*

The Nez Percé Indians of northeastern Oregon were goaded into a daring fight in 1877, when U.S. authorities tried to herd them onto a reservation. Chief Joseph finally surrendered his band after a tortuous, seventeen-hundred-mile, three-month trek across the Continental Divide toward Canada. There Chief Joseph hoped to rendezvous with Sitting Bull, who had taken refuge north of the border after the Battle of Little Bighorn. Betrayed into believing that they would be returned to their ancestral lands in Idaho, the Nez Percés instead were sent to a dusty reservation in Kansas, where 40 percent of them perished from disease. The survivors eventually returned to Idaho.

Fierce Apache tribes of Arizona and New Mexico were the most difficult to subdue. Led by Geronimo, whose eyes blazed hatred of the whites, they were pursued into Mexico by federal troops. Scattered remnants of the warriors were finally persuaded to surrender after the Apache women had been exiled to Florida.

This relentless fire-and-sword policy of the whites at last shattered the spirit of the Indians. The vanquished Native Americans were finally ghettoized on reservations, where they were compelled to eke out an existence as **wards** of the government.

The "taming" of the Indians was engineered by a number of factors. Of cardinal importance was the railroad, which shot an iron arrow through the heart of the West. The Indians were also ravaged by the white people's diseases and liquor, to which they showed little resistance.

Above all, the virtual extermination of the buffalo doomed the Plains Indians' nomadic way of life. When the white Americans ventured onto the Great Plains after the Civil War, some 15 million buffalo, or American bison, still blackened the prairies. In 1868 a Kansas Pacific locomotive had to wait eight hours for a herd to amble across the tracks. These huge, shaggy, lumbering beasts were the staff of life for the Native Americans (see "Makers of America: The Plains Indians," p. 402). Their flesh provided food; their dried dung provided fuel ("buffalo chips"); their hides provided clothing, lariats, and harnesses.

With the building of the railroad, the massacre of the herds began in deadly earnest. The creatures were slain for their hides, for a few choice cuts of meat, or for sheer amusement. The telescope-eyed crack shot William "Buffalo Bill" Cody killed over 4,000 buffalo in eighteen months while employed by the Kansas Pacific. "Sportsmen" on lurching railroad trains would lean out the windows and blaze away at the animals to satisfy their lust for slaughter or excitement. Such wholesale butchery left fewer than a thousand buffalo alive by 1885, and the once-numerous beasts were in danger of complete extinction. The whole story is a shocking example of the greed and waste that accompanied the conquest of a continent.

The End of the Trail

By the 1880s the national conscience began to stir uneasily over the plight of the Indians. Helen Hunt Jackson, a Massachusetts writer of children's literature, pricked the moral sense of Americans in 1881 when she published *A Century of Dishonor.* The book chronicled the sorry record of governmental ruthlessness and chicanery in dealing with the Indians. Her later novel *Ramona* (1884), a story of injustice to the California Indians, sold some 600,000 copies and further inspired sympathy for the Indians.

Debate seesawed. Humanitarians wanted to treat the Indians kindly and persuade them thereby to "walk the white man's road." Yet hard-liners insisted on the current policy of forced containment and brutal punishment. Neither side showed much respect for Native American culture. Christian reformers, who often administered educational facilities on the reservations, sometimes withheld food to force the Indians to give up their tribal religion and assimilate to white society. In 1884 these zealous white souls joined with military men in successfully persuading the federal government to outlaw the sacred Sun Dance. When the "Ghost Dance" cult later spread to the Dakota Sioux, the army bloodily stamped it out in 1890 at the so-called Battle of Wounded Knee. In the fighting thus provoked, an estimated two hundred Indian men, women, and children were killed, as well as twenty-nine soldiers.

The misbegotten offspring of the movement to reform Indian policy was the Dawes Severalty Act of 1887. Reflecting the forced-civilization views of the reformers, the act dissolved many tribes as legal entities, wiped out tribal ownership of land, and set up individual Indian family heads with 160 free acres. If the Indians behaved themselves like "good white settlers," they would get full title to their holdings, as well as citizenship, in twenty-five years. The **probationary** period was later extended, but full citizenship was granted to all Indians in 1924.

The federal efforts at forced assimilation included boarding schools for Indian children, beginning in 1879 with the Carlisle Indian School in Pennsylvania. "Kill the Indian and save the man" was the motto for these schools, where Native American children, separated from their tribes, were taught English and inculcated with white values and customs. The government also sent "field matrons" to the reservations to teach Native American women the art of sewing and to preach the virtues of chastity and hygiene.

The Dawes Act struck directly at tribal organization and tried to make rugged individualists out of the Indians. This legislation ignored the inherent reliance of traditional Indian culture on tribally held land. The forced-assimilation doctrine of the Dawes Act remained the

Online Study Center

**Primary source
Carlisle Indian Industrial School
Football Team**
college.hmco.com/pic/kennedybrief7e

---

probationary *Concerning a period of testing or trial, after which a decision is made based on performance.*

The Indian spokesman Plenty Coups said in 1909,

"I see no longer the curling smoke rising from our lodge poles. I hear no longer the songs of the women as they prepare the meal. The antelope have gone; the buffalo wallows are empty. Only the wail of the coyote is heard. The white man's medicine is stronger than ours. . . . We are like birds with a broken wing."

The Plains Indians

The last of the native peoples of North America to bow before the military might of the whites, the Indians of the northern Great Plains long defended their lands and their ways of life against the American cavalry. After the end of the Indian wars, toward the close of the nineteenth century, the Plains tribes struggled on, jealously guarding their communities against white encroachment and preserving much of their ancestral culture to this day.

Before Europeans first appeared in North America in the sixteenth century, the vast plain from northern Texas to Saskatchewan was home to some thirty different tribes. There was no typical Plains Indian; each tribe spoke a distinct language, practiced its own religion, and formed its own government.

Indians had first trod the arid plains to pursue sprawling herds of antelope, elk, and especially buffalo, but they were not exclusively hunters. The women were expert farmers, coaxing lush gardens of pumpkins, squash, corn, and beans from the dry but fertile soil. Still, the shaggy pelt and heavy flesh of the buffalo constituted the staff of life on the plains. Hunted by men, the great bison were butchered by women, who used every part of the beast. They fashioned horns into spoons, turned sinews into strong bowstrings, and wove buffalo hair into ropes. Meat not immediately eaten was pounded into pemmican—thin strips of smoked or sun-dried buffalo flesh.

The nomadic Plains Indians dispersed in small bands during the winter, gathering together in the summer for larger-scale religious ceremonies, socializing, and communal buffalo hunts. Then in the sixteenth century, the mounted Spanish *conquistadores* ventured into the New World, and their steeds quickly spread over the plains. The horse revolutionized Indian societies, turning the Plains tribes into efficient hunting machines that promised to banish hunger from the prairies. But the plains pony also ignited a furious competition for grazing land and for ever more horses, so that wars became increasingly bitter and frequent.

The European invasion soon eclipsed the short-lived era of the horse. After many battles the Plains Indians found themselves crammed together on tiny reservations, clinging with tired but determined fingers to their traditions. Although much of Plains Indian culture persists to this day, the Indians' free-ranging way of life passed into memory. As Black Elk, an Oglala Sioux, put it, "Once we were happy in our own country and we were seldom hungry, for then the two-leggeds and the four-leggeds lived together like relatives, and there was plenty for them and for us. But then the Wasichus [white people] came, and they made little islands for us . . . and always these islands are becoming smaller, for around them surges the gnawing flood of Wasichus."

■ A Comanche Village, by George Catlin, 1834

cornerstone of the government's official Indian policy until the Indian Reorganization Act ("the Indian New Deal") of 1934 partially reversed the individualistic approach and belatedly tried to restore the tribal basis of Indian life (see p. 528).

Under these new federal policies, defective though they were, the Indian population started to mount slowly. The total number had been reduced by 1887 to about 243,000—the result of bullets, bottles, and bacteria—but the census of 2000 counted more than 1.5 million Native Americans, urban and rural.

Mining: From Dishpan to Ore-Breaker

The conquest of the Indians and the coming of the railroad were life-giving boons to the mining frontier. The golden gravel of California continued to yield "pay dirt," and in 1858 an electrifying discovery of gold convulsed Colorado. Avid "fifty-niners" rushed west with "Pike's Peak or Bust" inscribed on the canvas of their covered wagons. But there were more miners than minerals, and many gold-grubbers creaked wearily back with the added inscription, "Busted, by Gosh." But some bearded fortune seekers stayed on in Colorado to strip away silver deposits or extract nonmetallic wealth from the earth in the form of golden grain.

"Fifty-niners" also poured feverishly into Nevada in 1859, after the fabulous Comstock lode had been uncovered. A fantastic amount of gold and silver, worth more than $340 million, was mined by the "Kings of the Comstock" from 1860 to 1890. The scantily populated state of Nevada was prematurely railroaded into the Union in 1864, partly to provide three electoral votes for President Lincoln.

Smaller "lucky strikes" drew frantic gold and silver seekers into Montana, Idaho, and other western states. Boomtowns, known as "Helldorados," sprouted like magic. Every third cabin was a saloon, where sweat-stained miners drank adulterated liquor ("rotgut") in the company of accommodating women. Lynch law and vigilante justice, as in early California, preserved a crude semblance of order. And when the "diggings" petered out, the gold seekers decamped, leaving behind picturesque "ghost towns," such as Virginia City, Nevada. Begun with a boom, these towns ended with a whimper.

Once the loose surface gold was gobbled up, ore-breaking machinery was imported to smash the gold-bearing quartz. This operation was so expensive that it could ordinarily be undertaken only by corporations pooling the wealth of stockholders. Gradually the age of big business came to the mining industry. Dusty, bewhiskered miners, dishpans in hand, were replaced by impersonal corporations with their costly machinery and trained engineers.

Yet the mining frontier had played a vital role in subduing the continent. Magnetlike, it attracted population and wealth while advertising the wonders of the Wild West. Women as well as men found opportunity, running boardinghouses or working as prostitutes. They earned a kind of equality on the rough frontier that earned them the vote in Wyoming (1869), Utah (1870), Colorado (1893), and Idaho (1896) long before their sisters in the East could cast a ballot. The amassing of precious metals helped finance the Civil War, facilitated the building of railroads, and injected the silver issue into American politics. Finally, the mining frontier added to American **folklore** and literature, as the writings of Mark Twain so colorfully attest.

Beef Bonanzas and the Long Drive

When the Civil War ended, the grassy plains of Texas supported several million tough, longhorn cattle. These scrawny beasts were killed primarily for their hides. There was no way to get their meat profitably to market.

Online Study Center

Interactive map
Natural Resources and the Development of the West
college.hmco.com/pic/kennedybrief7e

folklore *The common traditions and stories of a people.*

■ Dance-Hall Girl, Virginia City, Nevada, c. 1890 Women as well as men sought their fortunes in the frontier West—especially in wide-open mining towns like Virginia City.

The problem of marketing was neatly solved when the transcontinental railroads thrust their iron fingers into the West. Cattle could now be shipped bodily to the stockyards, and "beef barons" like the Swifts and Armours turned the highly industrialized meatpacking business into a main pillar of the economy. Drawing on the gigantic stockyards at Kansas City and Chicago, the packers could ship their fresh products to the East Coast in the newly perfected refrigerator cars.

A spectacular feeder of the new slaughterhouses was the "Long Drive." Texas cowboys—black, white, and Mexican—drove herds numbering from one thousand to ten thousand head slowly over the unfenced and unpeopled plains until they reached a railroad terminal. The bawling beasts grazed en route on the free government grass. Favorite terminal points were fly-specked "cow towns" like Dodge City and Abilene (Kansas), Ogallala (Nebraska), and Cheyenne (Wyoming). From 1866 to 1888, bellowing herds totaling over 4 million steers were driven northward from the beef bowl of Texas.

What the Lord giveth, the Lord also can take away. The railroad made the Long Drive; and the railroad unmade the Long Drive, primarily because the locomotives ran both ways. The same rails that bore the cattle from the open range to the kitchen range brought out the homesteader and the sheepherder. Both of these intruders, sometimes amid flying bullets, built barbed-wire fences that were too numerous to be cut down by the cowboys. Furthermore, the terrible winter of 1886–1887, with blinding blizzards reaching 68° below zero, left thousands of dazed cattle starving and freezing. The only escape for the stockman was to make cattle-raising a big business and avoid the perils of overproduction. Breeders learned to fence their ranches, lay in winter feed, import blooded bulls, and produce fewer and meatier animals. They also learned to organize. The Wyoming Stock-Growers' Association, especially in the 1880s, virtually controlled the territory and its legislature.

This was the heyday of the cowboy. The equipment of the lone cowhand—from "shooting irons" and ten-gallon hat to chaps and high-heeled boots—served a useful, not an ornamental, function. A "genuwine" gun-toting cowpuncher, riding where men were men and smelled like horses, could justifiably boast of his toughness.

These bowlegged Knights of the Saddle, with colorful trappings and cattle-lulling songs, became part of American folklore. Many of them, perhaps five thousand, were blacks, who especially enjoyed the newfound freedom of the open range.

■ **Nebraska Homesteaders in Front of Their Sod House, 1887** These two brothers and their families had escaped to Canada from the slave South during the Civil War. Returning to the United States in the 1880s, they took advantage of the Homestead Act to stake out farms in Custer County, Nebraska.

The Farmers' Frontier

Miners and cattlemen created the romantic legend of the West, but it was the sober sodbuster who wrote the final chapter of frontier history. A fresh day dawned for western farmers with the Homestead Act of 1862. The new law allowed a settler to acquire as much as 160 acres of land (a quarter-section) by living on it for five years, improving it, and paying a nominal fee of about $30.

The Homestead Act marked a drastic departure from previous policy. Before the act, public land had been sold primarily for revenue; now it was to be given away to encourage a rapid filling of empty spaces and to provide a stimulus to the family farm—"the backbone of democracy." During the forty years after its passage, about half a million families took advantage of the Homestead Act to carve out new homes in the vast open stretches. Yet five times that many families *purchased* their land from the railroads, land companies, or the states.

The Homestead Act often turned out to be a cruel hoax. The standard 160 acres, quite adequate in the well-watered Mississippi basin, frequently proved pitifully inadequate on the rain-scarce Great Plains. Thousands of homesteaders, perhaps two out of three, were forced to give up the one-sided struggle against drought.

Naked fraud was spawned by the Homestead Act and similar laws. Perhaps ten times more of the public domain wound up in the clutches of land-grabbing promoters than in the hands of bona fide farmers. Unscrupulous corporations would use "dummy" homesteaders—often their employees or immigrants bribed with cash or beer—to grab the best properties, containing timber, minerals, and oil. Settlers would later swear that they had "improved" the property by erecting a "twelve-by-fourteen" dwelling, which turned out to measure twelve by fourteen *inches.*

The railways also played a major role in developing the agricultural West, largely through the profitable marketing of crops. Some railroad companies induced Americans and European immigrants to buy the cheap land earlier granted to the railroads by the government. The Northern Pacific Railroad at one time had nearly a thousand paid agents in Europe distributing roseate leaflets in various languages.

Agriculture expanded once the myth of the Great American Desert was shattered. Pioneer explorers had assumed that the soil must be sterile, simply because it was not heavily watered and did not support immense forests. But once the prairie sod was broken with heavy iron plows pulled by four yokes of oxen, the earth proved astonishingly fruitful.

Lured by higher wheat prices resulting from crop failures elsewhere in the world, settlers in the 1870s rashly pushed still farther west, onto the poor, marginal lands beyond the 100th **meridian**. Geologist John Wesley Powell, explorer of the Colorado River's Grand Canyon, warned in 1874 that beyond the 100th meridian so little rain fell that agriculture was impossible without massive **irrigation**. Ignoring Powell's advice, farmers heedlessly chewed up the crusty earth in western Kansas, eastern Colorado, and Montana. They quickly went broke as a six-year drought in the 1880s further desiccated the already dusty region. In the wake of the drought, some pioneers tried the new "dry farming" technique of frequent shallow cultivation. But over time "dry farming" pulverized the surface soil and contributed to the "Dust Bowl" several decades later (see p. 528).

Other adaptations to the western environment were more successful. Tough strains of wheat, resistant to cold and drought, were imported from Russia and blossomed into billowing yellow carpets. Barbed wire, perfected by Joseph F. Glidden in 1874, solved the problem of how to build fences on the treeless prairies. Eventually, federally

meridian *In geography, any of the imaginary lines of longitude running north and south on the globe.*

irrigation *Watering land artificially, through canals, pipes, or other means.*

In making the arduous journey across the western prairies, many women settlers discovered new confidence in their abilities. Early on in her trek, Mary Richardson Walker (1811–1897) confided in her diary that

"my circumstances are rather trying. So much danger attends me on every hand. A long journey before me, going I know not whither, without mother or sister to attend me, can I expect to survive it all?"

Only a month later, she recorded that

"in the afternoon we rode thirty-five miles without stopping. Pretty well tired out, all of us. Stood it pretty well myself."

contiguous *Joined together by common borders.*

safety valve *Anything, such as the American frontier, that allegedly serves as a necessary outlet for built-up pressure, energy, and so on.*

Online Study Center

Interactive map
The Oklahoma Land Rush,
1889–1906
college.hmco.com/pic/kennedybrief7e

Online Study Center

Primary source
Settlement of the Frontier, The
college.hmco.com/pic/kennedybrief7e

financed irrigation projects on a colossal scale caused the Great American Desert to bloom. In the long run, hydraulic engineers had more to do with shaping the modern West than all the trappers, miners, cavalrymen, and cowboys ever did.

The Great West experienced a fantastic growth in population from the 1870s to the 1890s. A parade of new western states proudly joined the Union. Boomtown Colorado, offspring of the Pikes Peak gold rush, was greeted in 1876 as the "Centennial State." In 1889–1890 a Republican Congress, eagerly seeking more Republican electoral and congressional votes, admitted in a wholesale lot six new states: North Dakota, South Dakota, Montana, Washington, Idaho, and Wyoming. The Mormon church formally banned polygamy in 1890, but not until 1896 was Utah deemed worthy of admission. Only Oklahoma, New Mexico, and Arizona remained to be lifted into statehood from **contiguous** territory on the mainland of North America.

In a last gaudy fling, the federal government made available to settlers vast stretches of fertile plains formerly occupied by the Indians in Oklahoma ("the Beautiful Land"). Scores of overeager and well-armed "sooners," illegally jumping the gun, had entered Oklahoma Territory before the opening date. They had to be evicted repeatedly by federal troops, who on occasion would shoot the intruders' horses. On April 22, 1889, all was in readiness for the legal opening, and some 50,000 "boomers" were poised expectantly on the boundary line. At high noon the bugle shrilled, and a horde of "eighty-niners" poured in on lathered horses or careening vehicles. That night a lonely spot on the prairie had mushroomed into the tent city of Guthrie, with over 10,000 people. By the end of the year Oklahoma boasted 60,000 inhabitants, and Congress made it a territory. In 1907 it became the "Sooner State."

The Fading Frontier

In 1890—a watershed date—the superintendent of the census announced that for the first time in America's experience a frontier line was no longer discernible. All the unsettled areas were now broken into by isolated bodies of settlement. The "closing" of the frontier inspired one of the most influential essays ever written about American history—Frederick Jackson Turner's "The Significance of the Frontier in American History," in 1893.

As the nineteenth century neared its sunset, the westward-tramping American people were disturbed to find that their fabled free land was going or had gone. The secretary of war had prophesied in 1827 that five hundred years would be needed to fill the West. But as the nation finally recognized that its land was not inexhaustible, seeds were planted to preserve the vanishing resource. The government set aside lands for national parks—first Yellowstone in 1872, followed by Yosemite and Sequoia in 1890.

The frontier was more than a place: it was also a state of mind and a symbol of opportunity. Its passing ended a romantic phase of the nation's internal development and created new economic and psychological problems. Traditionally footloose, Americans have been notorious for their mobility. The nation's farmers, unlike the peasants of Europe, seldom remained rooted to their soil.

Much has been said about the frontier as a "**safety valve**." The theory is that when hard times came, the unemployed who cluttered the city pavements merely moved west, took up farming, and prospered. In truth, relatively few eastern city dwellers migrated to the frontier during depressions. Most of them did not know how to farm; few of them could raise enough money to transport themselves west and then pay for livestock and expensive machinery.

But the safety-valve theory does have some validity. Free acreage did lure to the West a host of immigrant farmers who otherwise might have remained in the eastern cities to clog the job markets and crowd the slums. And the very *possibility* of westward migration may have induced urban employers to maintain wage rates high enough to discourage workers from leaving.

But the real safety valve by the late nineteenth century was in western cities like Denver, San Francisco, and Seattle, where failed farmers, busted miners, and displaced easterners found the best places to seek their fortunes. Indeed, after

EXAMINING THE EVIDENCE

Robert Louis Stevenson's Transcontinental Journey, 1879   The celebrated Scottish writer Robert Louis Stevenson, author of such enduring classics as *Treasure Island, Kidnapped,* and *The Strange Case of Dr. Jekyll and Mr. Hyde,* journeyed from Scotland to California in 1879 to rendezvous with his American fiancée, Frances Osbourne. Between New York and San Francisco, Stevenson traveled on the transcontinental railroad line completed just ten years earlier, and he dutifully recorded his impressions of America, the West in particular, as he made his way toward California. Stevenson's account of his trip provides an unusually gifted writer's vivid portrait of the trans-Mississippi West at the close of the era of the Indian wars. Like all travelogues, Stevenson's colorful tale may reveal as much about the traveler as it does about the things he saw. Yet historians frequently make use of such documents to reconstruct the original appearance and texture of places that were once the exotic destinations of adventurous travelers, before they were transformed by the onrush of modernity.

1. In the passages reproduced here, inspired by the view as Stevenson's train passed through Nebraska and Wyoming, what features of the landscape does the author find most remarkable?

2. What does Stevenson's extended comparison of traveling across the plains to being "at sea" convey about cultured European views of the American West in the late nineteenth century? Why do the buffalo and the few cabins he sees not disrupt his perception of the West's "emptiness"?

3. What is Stevenson's view of the Indians, as well of those who built the railroad (including Chinese laborers)?

THE PLAINS OF NEBRASKA

. . . We were at sea—there is no other adequate expression—on the plains of Nebraska. . . . It was a world almost without a feature; an empty sky, an empty earth; front and back, the line of railway stretched from horizon to horizon, like a cue across a billiard-board; on either hand, the green plain ran till it touched the skirts of heaven. . . . [G]razing beasts were seen upon the prairie at all degrees of distance and diminution; and now and again we might perceive a few dots beside the railroad which grew more and more distinct as we drew nearer till they turned into wooden cabins, and then dwindled and dwindled in our wake until they melted into their surroundings, and we were once more alone upon the billiard-board. The train toiled over this infinity like a snail; and being the one thing moving, it was wonderful what huge proportions it began to assume in our regard. . . .

[That] evening we left Laramie [Wyoming]. . . . And yet when day came, it was to shine upon the same broken and unsightly quarter of the world. Mile upon mile, and not a tree, a bird, or a river. Only down the long, sterile cañons, the train shot hooting and awoke the resting echo. That train was the one piece of life in all the deadly land; it was the one actor, the one spectacle fit to be observed in this paralysis of man and nature. And when I think how the railroad has been pushed through this unwatered wilderness and haunt of savage tribes, and now will bear an emigrant for some £12 from the Atlantic to the Golden Gates; how at each stage of the construction, roaring, impromptu cities, full of gold and lust and death, sprang up and then died away again, and are now but wayside stations in the desert; how in these uncouth places pig-tailed Chinese pirates worked side by side with border ruffians and broken men from Europe, talking together in a mixed dialect, mostly oaths, gambling, drinking, quarrelling and murdering like wolves; how the plumed hereditary lord of all America heard, in this last fastness, the scream of the 'bad medicine waggon' charioting his foes; and then when I go on to remember that all this epical turmoil was conducted by gentlemen in frock coats, and with a view to nothing more extraordinary than a fortune and a subsequent visit to Paris, it seems to me, I own, as if this railway were the one typical achievement of the age in which we live, as if it brought together into one plot all the ends of the world and all the degrees of social rank, and offered to some great writer the busiest, the most extended, and the most varied subject for an enduring literary work. . . .

Source: *Across the Plains,* by Robert Louis Stevenson (New York: Charles Scribner's Sons, 1897).

---

about 1880 the area from the Rocky Mountains to the Pacific Coast was the most urbanized region in America, measured by the percentage of people living in cities.

U.S. history cannot be properly understood unless it is viewed in light of the westward-moving experience. As Frederick Jackson Turner wrote, "American history has been in a large degree the history of the colonization of the Great West." The story of settling and taming the trans-Mississippi West in the late nineteenth century was but the last chapter in the saga of the colonizing of various American "wests" since Columbus's day.

And yet the trans-Mississippi West formed a distinct chapter in that saga and retains even to this day much of its uniqueness. There the Native American peoples made their last struggle against colonization, and there most Native Americans live

Online Study Center

Interactive map
Settlement of the Trans-Mississippi West, 1860–1890

college.hmco.com/pic/kennedybrief7e

today. There "Anglo" culture collided most directly with Hispanic culture, and the Southwest remains the most Hispanicized region in America. There America faced across the Pacific to Asia, and there most Asian Americans dwell today. There the scale and severity of the environment posed their largest challenges to human ambitions, and there the environment continues to mold social and political life, and the American imagination, as in no other part of the nation.

The westward-moving pioneers and the country they confronted have assumed mythic proportions in the American mind. For better or worse, those pioneers planted the seeds of civilization in the immense western wilderness. The life we live, they dreamed of; the life they lived, we can only dream.

The Farm Becomes a Factory

The situation of American farmers, once jacks-and-jills-of-all-trades, was rapidly changing. They had raised their own food, fashioned their own clothing, and bartered for other necessities with neighbors. Now high prices persuaded farmers to concentrate on growing single "cash" crops, such as wheat or corn, and use their profits to buy foodstuffs at the general store and manufactured goods in town or by mail order. The Chicago firm of Aaron Montgomery Ward sent out its first catalogue—a single sheet—in 1872.

Large-scale farmers were now both specialists and businesspeople. As cogs in the vast industrial machine, they were intimately tied to banking, railroading, and manufacturing. They had to buy expensive machinery to plant and to harvest their crops. The speed of harvesting wheat was immensely increased in the 1870s by the twine binder and then in the 1880s by the "combine"—the combined reaper-thresher, which was drawn by twenty to forty horses and both reaped and bagged the grain.

This amazing mechanization of agriculture in the postwar years was almost as striking as the mechanization of industry. Those who remained on the farms achieved miracles of production, making America the world's breadbasket and butcher shop. The farm was attaining the status of a factory—an outdoor grain factory. The enormous bonanza wheat farms of the Minnesota–North Dakota area foreshadowed the gigantic agribusinesses of the next century. By 1890 at least a half-dozen of them were larger than fifteen thousand acres.

Agriculture was a big business from the outset in California's phenomenally productive (and phenomenally irrigated) Central Valley. California farms, carved out of giant Spanish-Mexican land grants and the railroads' huge holdings, were from the outset more than three times larger than the national average. With the advent of the railroad refrigerator car in the 1880s, California fruits and vegetable crops, raised on sprawling tracts by ill-paid migrant Mexican and Chinese farmhands, sold at a handsome profit in the rich urban markets of the East.

Deflation Dooms the Debtor

Once the farmers became chained to a one-crop economy—wheat or corn—they were in the same leaky boat with the southern cotton growers. The grain farmers were no longer the masters of their own destinies. They were engaged in one of the most fiercely competitive of businesses, for the price of their product was determined in a world market by the world output. If the wheat fields of Argentina, Russia, and other foreign countries flourished, the price of the farmers' grain would fall and American sodbusters would face ruin, as they did in the 1880s and 1890s.

Low prices and a deflated currency were the chief worries of the frustrated farmer in all regions. If a family had borrowed $1,000 in 1855, when wheat was worth about a dollar a bushel, they expected to pay back the equivalent of one thousand bushels, plus interest, when the mortgage fell due. But if they let their debt run to 1890, when wheat had fallen to about fifty cents a bushel, they would have to pay back the price two thousand bushels for the $1,000 they had borrowed,

Online Study Center

**Interactive map
Mining and Cattle Frontiers,
1860–1890**
college.hmco.com/pic/kennedybrief7e

plus interest. This unexpected burden struck them as unjust, though their steely-eyed creditors often branded the complaining farmers as slippery and dishonest rascals.

The deflationary pinch on the debtor flowed partly from the static money supply. There were simply not enough dollars to go around, and as a result prices were forced down. In 1870 the currency in circulation for each person was $19.42; in 1890 it was only up to $22.67. Yet during these twenty years, business and industrial activity, increasing manyfold, had intensified the scramble for available currency.

The forgotten farmers were caught on a treadmill. Despite unremitting toil, they operated year after year at a loss. In a vicious circle, their farm machinery increased their output of grain, lowered the price, and drove them even deeper into debt. Mortgages engulfed homesteads at an alarming rate; by 1890 Nebraska alone reported more than 100,000 farms blanketed with mortgages. The repeated crash of the sheriff-auctioneer's hammer kept announcing to the world that another sturdy American farmer had become landless in a landed nation.

Ruinous rates of interest, running from 8 to 40 percent, were charged on mortgages, largely by agents of eastern loan companies. The windburned sons and daughters of the sod, who felt that they deserved praise for developing the country, cried out in despair against the **loan sharks** and the Wall Street octopus.

Farm tenancy rather than farm ownership was spreading like stinkweed. The trend was especially marked in the sharecropping South, where cotton prices also sank dismayingly. By 1880 one-fourth of all American farms were operated by tenants. The United States was ready to feed the world, but under the new industrial feudalism the farmers were about to sink into a status suggesting Old World **serfdom**.

loan shark *A person who lends money at an exorbitant or illegal rate of interest.*

serfdom *The feudal condition of being permanently bound to land owned by someone else.*

Unhappy Farmers

Even Mother Nature ceased smiling as her powerful forces conspired against agriculture. Mile-wide clouds of grasshoppers, leaving "nothing but the mortgage," periodically ravaged prairie farms. The terrible cotton-boll weevil was also wreaking havoc in the South by the early 1890s.

The good earth was going sour. Floods washed the topsoil off millions of once-lush southern acres. A long succession of droughts seared the trans-Mississippi West, beginning in the summer of 1887. Whole towns were abandoned. "Going home to the wife's folks" and "in God we trusted, in Kansas we busted" were typical laments of many impoverished farmers as they fled their weather-beaten shacks and sunbaked sod houses.

To add to their miseries, the soil-tillers were gouged by their government—local, state, and national. Their land was overassessed, and they paid painful local taxes, whereas wealthy easterners could conceal their stocks and bonds in safe-deposit boxes. High protective tariffs in these years poured profits into the pockets of manufacturers. Farmers, on the other hand, had no choice but to sell their low-priced products in a fiercely competitive, unprotected world market, while buying high-priced manufactured goods in a protected home market.

The farmers were also "farmed" by the corporations. Trusts raised prices on farmers' machinery and supplies to extortionate levels, while operators pushed storage rates to the ceiling at grain warehouses and elevators. The railroad octopus often pushed freight rates so high that the farmers sometimes lost less if they burned their corn for fuel than if they shipped it.

Farmers still made up nearly one-half of the population in 1890, but they were hopelessly disorganized. The manufacturers and the railroad barons knew how to combine to promote their own interests, and so, increasingly, did industrial workers. But the farmers were by nature independent and individualistic—dead set against consolidation or regimentation. They never did organize successfully to restrict production until forced to do so by the federal government nearly half a century later, in Franklin Roosevelt's New Deal days. What they did manage to organize was a monumental political uprising.

The Farmers Take Their Stand

Agrarian unrest had flared forth earlier, in the Greenback movement shortly after the Civil War. Prices sagged in 1868, and a host of farmers unsuccessfully sought relief from low prices and high indebtedness by demanding an inflation of the currency with paper money.

The National Grange of the Patrons of Husbandry—better known as the Grange—was organized in 1867. Its leading spirit was Oliver H. Kelley, a shrewd and energetic Minnesota farmer then working as a clerk in Washington. Kelley's first objective was to enhance the lives of isolated farmers through social, educational, and fraternal activities. The Grange spread like an old-time prairie fire and by 1875 claimed some 800,000 members, chiefly in the Midwest and South.

The Grangers gradually raised their goals from individual self-improvement to improvement of the farmers' collective plight. In a determined effort to escape the clutches of the trusts, they established cooperatively owned stores, grain elevators, and warehouses, and even made a failed attempt to manufacture harvesting machinery.

Embattled Grangers also went into politics, enjoying their most gratifying success in the grain-growing regions of the upper Mississippi Valley. There, through state legislation, they strove to regulate railway rates and the storage fees charged by railroads and grain elevator operators. Many of the state courts, notably in Illinois, were disposed to recognize the principle of public control of private business for the general welfare. A number of the so-called Granger Laws, however, were bitterly fought through the high courts by the well-paid lawyers of the "interests." Following judicial reverses, most severely at the hands of the Supreme Court in the *Wabash* decision of 1886 (see p. 362), the Grangers' influence faded.

Farmers' grievances likewise found a vent in the Greenback Labor party, which combined the inflationary appeal of the earlier Greenbackers with a program for improving the lot of labor. In 1878, the high-water mark of the movement, the Greenback-Laborites polled over a million votes and elected fourteen members of Congress. In the presidential election of 1880 the Greenbackers ran General James B. Weaver, an old Granger who spoke to perhaps a half-million citizens, but he polled only 3 percent of the popular vote.

Prelude to Populism

A striking manifestation of rural discontent came through the Farmers' Alliance, founded in Texas in the late 1870s (see p. 352). Farmers came together in the Alliance to socialize, but more importantly they hoped to break the strangling grip of the railroads and manufacturers through cooperative buying and selling. Local chapters spread throughout the South and the Great Plains during the 1880s, until by 1890 members numbered more than a million hard-bitten souls.

Unfortunately, the Alliance weakened itself by ignoring the plight of landless tenant farmers, sharecroppers, and farmworkers. Even more debilitating was the Alliance's exclusion of blacks, who counted for nearly half the agricultural population of the South. In the 1880s a separate Colored Farmers' National Alliance emerged to attract black farmers, and by 1890 membership numbered more than 250,000. The long history of racial division in the South, however, made it difficult for white and black farmers to work together in the same organization.

Out of the Farmers' Alliances a new political party emerged in the early 1890s—the People's Party. Better known as the Populists, these frustrated farmers attacked Wall Street and the "money trust." They called for nationalizing the railroads, telephones, and telegraph; instituting a graduated income tax; and building government-owned warehouses where they could store their grain until market prices rose. They also wanted the free and unlimited coinage of silver—yet another of the debtors' demands for inflation that echoed continuously throughout the Gilded Age.

Numerous fiery **prophets** leapt forward to trumpet the Populist cause. William Hope Harvey produced an enormously popular pamphlet called *Coin's*

---

prophet(s) *A person believed to speak with divine power or special gifts, sometimes including predicting the future (hence any specially talented or eloquent advocate of a cause).*

Financial School (1894). Illustrated by clever woodcuts, the booklet showed how "Coin" Harvey overwhelmed the bankers and professors of economics with his brilliant arguments on behalf of free silver. Another notorious spellbinder was red-haired Ignatius Donnelly of Minnesota, three times elected to Congress. The queen of the Populist "calamity howlers" was Mary Elizabeth ("Mary Yellin'") Lease, a tall, athletic woman known as the "Kansas Pythoness." She reportedly demanded that Kansans should raise "less corn and more hell." The *New York Evening Post* snarled, "We don't want any more states until we can civilize Kansas." To many easterners, complaint, not corn, was rural America's staple crop.

Yet the Populists, despite their oddities, were not to be laughed away. They were leading a deadly earnest and impassioned campaign to relieve the farmers' many miseries. Smiles faded from Republican and Democratic faces alike as countless thousands of Populists began to sing "Good-bye, My Party, Good-bye."

In 1892 the Populists had jolted the traditional parties by winning several congressional seats and polling more than 1 million votes for their presidential candidate, James B. Weaver. Racial divisions continued to hobble the Populists in the South, but in the West their ranks were swelling. Could the People's Party now reach beyond its regional bases in agrarian America, join hands with urban workers, and mount a successful attack on the northeastern **citadels** of power?

citadel(s) *A fortress occupying a commanding height.*

Coxey's Army and the Pullman Strike

The panic of 1893 and the severe ensuing depression strengthened the Populists' argument that farmers and laborers alike were being victimized by an oppressive economic and political system. Ragged armies of the unemployed began marching to protest their plight. In the growing hordes of displaced industrial toilers, the Populists saw potential political allies.

The most famous marcher was "General" Jacob S. Coxey, a wealthy Ohio quarry owner who set out for Washington in 1894 with a small band of supporters. His platform included a demand that the government relieve unemployment by an inflationary five-hundred-million-dollar federal public works program. Coxey himself rode in a carriage with his wife and infant son, appropriately named Legal Tender Coxey, while his tiny "army" tramped along behind, singing:

> *We're coming, Grover Cleveland,*
> *500,000 strong.*
> *We're marching on to Washington*
> *to right the nation's wrong.*

The "Commonweal Army" of Coxeyites finally straggled into the nation's capital, but the "invasion" took on the aspects of a comic opera when "General" Coxey and his "lieutenants" were arrested for walking on the grass.

Elsewhere, violent flare-ups accompanied labor protests, notably in Chicago. Most dramatic was the crippling Pullman strike of 1894. Eugene V. Debs, a charismatic labor leader, had helped organize the American Railway Union of about 150,000 members. The Pullman Palace Car Company, which maintained a model town near Chicago for its employees, was hit hard by the depression and cut wages by about one-third, while holding the line on rent for company houses. The workers finally struck—in some places overturning Pullman cars—and paralyzed railway traffic from Chicago to the Pacific Coast.

The turmoil in Chicago was serious but not completely out of hand. At least this was the judgment of Governor John Peter Altgeld of Illinois, a friend of the downtrodden, who had pardoned the Haymarket Square anarchists the year before (see p. 370). But U.S. attorney general Richard Olney, an archconservative and an ex-railroad attorney, urged the dispatch of federal troops on the legal grounds that the strikers were interfering with the U.S. mail. President Cleveland supported Olney with

After the Pullman strike collapsed, Eugene Debs (1855–1926) said,

"No strike has ever been lost."
In 1897 he declared,

"The issue is Socialism versus Capitalism. I am for Socialism because I am for humanity."

the ringing declaration, "If it takes the entire army and navy to deliver a postal card in Chicago, that card will be delivered."

To the delight of conservatives, federal troops, bayonets fixed, crushed the Pullman strike. Debs was sentenced to six months' imprisonment for contempt of court because he had defied a federal court injunction to cease striking. Ironically, the lean labor agitator spent much of his enforced leisure reading radical literature, which led to his later leadership of the socialist movement in America.

Embittered cries of "government by injunction" now burst from organized labor. This was the first time that such a legal weapon had been used conspicuously by Washington to break a strike, and it was all the more distasteful because defiant workers who were held in contempt could be imprisoned without jury trial. Signs multiplied that employers were striving to smash labor unions by court action. Nonlabor elements of the country, including the Populists and other debtors, were likewise incensed. They saw in the brutal Pullman episode further proof of an unholy alliance between business and the courts.

Golden McKinley and Silver Bryan

The smoldering grievances of the long-suffering farmers and depression-plagued laborers gave ominous significance to the election of 1896. Conservatives of all stripes feared an impending upheaval, while down-and-out husbandmen and discontented workers cast about desperately for political salvation. Increasingly, monetary policy—whether to maintain the gold standard or inflate the currency by monetizing silver—loomed as the issue on which the election would turn.

The leading candidate for the Republican presidential nomination in 1896 was former Congressman William McKinley of Ohio, sponsor of the ill-starred tariff bill of 1890 (see p. 351). He had established a record as a Civil War officer; he hailed from the electorally potent state of Ohio; and he could point to long years of honorable service in Congress.

As a presidential candidate, McKinley was largely the creature of a fellow Ohioan, Marcus Alonzo Hanna, who had made his fortune in the iron business and now coveted the role of president-maker. As a wholehearted Hamiltonian, Hanna believed that a prime function of government was to aid business. He also believed that in some measure prosperity "trickled down" to the laborer, whose dinner pail was full when business flourished. Critics assailed this idea as equivalent to feeding the horses in order to feed the sparrows.

The hardheaded Hanna, although something of a novice in politics, organized his preconvention campaign for McKinley with consummate skill and a liberal outpouring of his own money. The convention steamroller, well lubricated with Hanna's dollars, nominated McKinley on the first ballot at St. Louis in June 1896. The Republican platform condemned Democratic incapacity in hard times and declared for the gold standard.

Dissension riddled the Democratic camp. Cleveland no longer led his party. The depression had driven the last nail into his political coffin. Dubbed "the Stuffed Prophet," he was undeniably the most unpopular man in the country. Labor-debtor groups remembered too vividly his intervention in the Pullman strike, the backstairs Morgan bond deal, and especially his stubborn hard-money policies. Ultraconservative in finance, Cleveland now looked more like a Republican than a Democrat on the money issue.

Rudderless, the Democratic convention met in Chicago in July 1896, with the silverites lusting for victory. Shouting insults at the absent Cleveland, the delegates refused to endorse their own administration. They had the enthusiasm and the numbers; all they lacked was a leader.

A new Moses suddenly appeared in the person of William Jennings Bryan of Nebraska. Then only thirty-six years of age and known as "the Boy Orator of the Platte,"* he stepped confidently onto the platform before fifteen thousand people.

---

* One contemporary sneered that Bryan, like the Platte River, was "six inches deep and six miles wide at the mouth."

His masterful presence was set off by a peninsular jaw, and raven-black hair. He radiated honesty, sincerity, and energy.

The convention-hall setting was made to order for a magnificent oratorical effort. A hush fell over the delegates as Bryan stood before them. With an organlike voice that rolled into the outer corners of the huge hall, he delivered a fervent plea for silver. Rising to supreme heights of eloquence, he thundered, "We will answer their demands for a gold standard by saying to them: 'You shall not press down upon the brow of labor this crown of thorns, you shall not crucify mankind upon a cross of gold.'"

The Cross of Gold speech was a sensation. Swept off its feet in a tumultuous scene, the Democratic convention nominated Bryan the next day on the fifth ballot. The platform demanded inflation through the unlimited coinage of silver at the ratio of 16 ounces of silver to 1 of gold, though the market ratio was about 32 to 1. This meant that the silver in a dollar would be worth about fifty cents.

Democratic "Gold Bugs," unable to swallow Bryan, bolted their party over the silver issue. A conservative senator from New York, when asked if he was a Democrat still, reportedly replied, "Yes, I am a Democrat still—very still." The Democratic minority, including Cleveland, charged that the Populist-silverites had stolen both the name and the clothes of their party. Many of them, including Cleveland, not too secretly hoped for a McKinley victory.

The Populists now faced a dilemma because the Democratic majority had appropriated their main plank—"16 to 1," that "heaven-born ratio." The bulk of the Populists, fearing a hard-money McKinley victory, endorsed "fusion" with the Democrats and Bryan for president, sacrificing their identity in the mix. Singing "The Jolly Silver Dollar of the Dads," they became in effect the "Demo-Pop" or "Popocratic" party, though a handful of the original Populists refused to support Bryan and went down with their colors nailed to the mast.

■ **The Sacrilegious Candidate** A hostile cartoonist makes sport of Bryan's flamboyant Cross of Gold speech in 1896.

Class Conflict: Plowholders Versus Bondholders

Mark Hanna smugly assumed that he could make the tariff the focus of the campaign. But Bryan, a dynamo of energy, forced the free-trade issue into a back seat when he took to the stump in behalf of free silver. Sweeping through 27 states and traveling 18,000 miles, he made nearly 600 speeches—36 in one day—and even invaded the East, "the enemy's country." Vachel Lindsay caught the spirit of his oratorical orgy:

> *Prairie avenger, mountain lion,*
> *Bryan, Bryan, Bryan, Bryan,*
> *Gigantic troubadour, speaking like a siege gun,*
> *Smashing Plymouth rock with his boulders from the West.* *

Free silver became almost as much a religious as a financial issue. Hordes of fanatical free-silverites, singing "No Crown of Thorns, No Cross of Gold," hailed Bryan as the messiah to lead them out of the wilderness of debt.

Bryan created panic among eastern conservatives with his threat of converting their holdings overnight into fifty-cent dollars. "In God we trust, with Bryan we bust," the Republicans sneered, while one clergyman cried, "That platform was made in Hell." Widespread fear of Bryan and the "silver lunacy" enabled "Dollar Mark" Hanna, now chairman of the Republican National Committee, to shine as a money-raiser. He "shook down" the trusts and plutocrats and piled up an enormous "slush fund" for a "campaign of education"—or of propaganda, depending on one's point of view. Republicans appealed to the "belly vote" with their prize

---

* Reprinted with the permission of Scribner, an imprint of Simon & Schuster Adult Publishing Group, from *The Collected Poems*, Revised Edition by Vachel Lindsay. (New York: Macmillan, 1925). All rights reserved.

■ **Campaign Gimcracks, 1896** These mechanical cards predicted Republican prosperity with McKinley and economic ruin with Bryan.

slogan, "McKinley and the full dinner pail." The McKinleyites amassed the most formidable political campaign chest thus far in American history—about $16 million, as contrasted with about $1 million for the poorer Democrats (roughly "16 to 1"). With some justification, the Bryanites accused Hanna of "buying" the election and of floating McKinley into the White House on a tidal wave of mud and money.

Bryan's cyclonic campaign began to lose steam as the weeks passed. Fear was probably Hanna's strongest ally, as it was Bryan's worst enemy. Some Republican businesspeople threatened wage reductions or told their workers not to come to work on Wednesday morning if Bryan won. Such were some of the "dirty tricks" of the "Stop Bryan, Save America" crusade.

Hanna's campaign methods paid off. On election day McKinley triumphed decisively. The vote was 271 to 176 in the Electoral College, and 7,102,246 to 6,492,559 in the popular vote. Driven by fear and excitement, an unprecedented outpouring of voters flocked to the polls. McKinley ran strongly in the populous East, where he carried every county of New England, and in the upper Mississippi Valley. Bryan's states, concentrated in the debt-burdened South and the trans-Mississippi West, involved more acreage than McKinley's but less population.

The free-silver election of 1896 was perhaps the most significant political turning point since Lincoln's victories in 1860 and 1864. Despite Bryan's strength in the South and West, the results vividly demonstrated his lack of appeal to the unmortgaged farmer and especially to the eastern urban laborer. Many wage earners in the East, threatened as they were by free silver, voted for their jobs and full dinner pails. Living precariously on a fixed wage, the factory workers had no reason to favor inflation, which was the heart of the Bryanites' program.

The Bryan-McKinley battle heralded the advent of a new era in American politics. The outcome represented a resounding victory for big business, the big

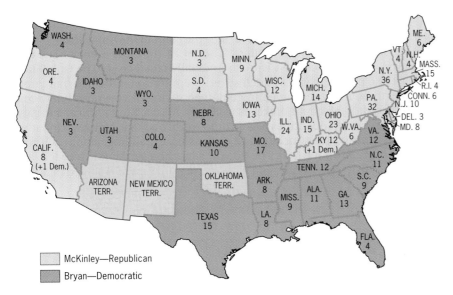

■ **Presidential Election of 1896 (with electoral vote by state)** This election tolled the death knell of the Gilded Age political system, with its razor-close elections, strong party loyalties, and high voter turnouts. For years after 1896, Republicans predominated, and citizens showed declining interest in either joining parties or voting.

cities, middle-class values, and financial conservatism. Bryan's defeat marked the last serious effort to win the White House with mostly agrarian votes. The future of presidential politics lay not on the farms, with their dwindling populations, but in the mushrooming cities, with their growing hordes of freshly arriving immigrants.

The smashing Republican victory of 1896 also heralded a Republican grip on the White House for sixteen consecutive years—indeed, for all but eight of the next thirty-six years. McKinley's election thus imparted a new character to the American political system. The long reign of Republican political dominance that it ushered in was accompanied by diminishing voter participation in elections, the weakening of party organizations, and the fading away of issues like the money question and civil-service reform, which came to be replaced by concern for industrial regulation and the welfare of labor. Scholars have dubbed this new political era the period of the "fourth party system."*

Online Study Center

Primary source
Tom Watson Indicts
Corporate Plunder
college.hmco.com/pic/kennedybrief7e

Republican Stand-pattism Enthroned

An eminently "safe" McKinley took the inaugural oath in 1897. Though a man of considerable ability, he was an ear-to-the-ground politician who seldom got far out of line with majority opinion. His cautious, conservative nature caused him to shy away from the flaming banner of reform. Business was given a free rein, and the trusts, which had trusted him in 1896, were allowed to develop more mighty muscles without serious restraints.

Almost as soon as McKinley took office, the tariff issue, which had played second fiddle to silver in the "Battle of '96," quickly forced itself to the fore. In due course the Dingley Tariff Bill was jammed through the House in 1897 under the pounding gavel of the rethroned "Czar" Reed. The proposed new rates were high, but not high enough to satisfy the paunchy lobbyists, who once again descended upon the Senate. Over 850 amendments were tacked onto the overburdened bill. The resulting piece of patchwork finally established the average rates at 46.5 percent, substantially

---

* The so-called first party system, marked by doubts about the very legitimacy of parties, embraced the Federalist-Republican clashes of the 1790s and early 1800s. The second party system took shape with the emergence of mass-based politics in the Jacksonian era, pitting Democrats against Whigs. The third party system was characterized by the precarious equilibrium between Republicans and Democrats, as well as the high electoral participation, that lasted from the end of the Civil War to McKinley's election. The fourth party system is described above. The fifth party system emerged in Franklin Roosevelt's New Deal, which initiated a long period of Democratic ascendancy. Each "system," except the fifth, lasted about forty years. Debate continues as to whether the nation has entered or is about to enter the era of the sixth party system.

higher than the Democratic Wilson-Gorman Act of 1894 and in some categories even higher than the McKinley Act of 1890. (See the chart in the Appendix.)

With the return of prosperity under McKinley in 1897, the money issue that overshadowed politics since the Civil War gradually faded away. The Gold Standard Act of 1900, passed over last-ditch silverite opposition, provided that paper currency was to be freely redeemed in gold. Electrifying discoveries of new gold deposits in Canada's fabled Klondike, as well as in Alaska, South Africa, and Australia, brought huge new quantities of gold onto world markets. Moderate inflation thus took care of the currency needs of an explosively expanding nation, as its circulatory system greatly improved. The tide of "silver heresy" rapidly receded, and the "Popocratic" fish were left gasping high and dry on a golden-sanded beach.

✪ Chapter Summary ✪

At the close of the Civil War, the Great Plains and Mountain West were still controlled by Indians who hunted buffalo on horseback and fiercely resisted white encroachment on their land and way of life. But the whites' railroads, mining, and livestock activities gradually broke up the Indians' territory, while diseases and the destruction of the buffalo reduced their numbers and ended their way of life. The federal government eventually forced the Indians onto largely barren reservations where their very existence was threatened.

Attempting to coerce Indians into adopting white ways, the government passed the Dawes Act, which eliminated tribal ownership of land, while often insensitive "humanitarians" created a network of Indian boarding schools that further assaulted traditional culture.

The mining and cattle frontiers created colorful chapters in western history. Farmers carried out the final phase of settlement, lured by free homesteads, railroads, and irrigation. The census declared the end of the frontier in 1890, concluding a formative phase of American history. The frontier was less of a "safety valve" than many believed, but may have had some impact on keeping American wage rates relatively high. The newest western frontier was actually in cities like Denver, San Francisco, and Seattle, which helped make the West the most urbanized region of the United States by the 1890s.

Beginning in the 1870s, farmers began pushing into the treeless prairies beyond the 100th meridian, using techniques of dry farming that gradually contributed to soil erosion. Irrigation projects, later financed by the federal government, allowed specialized farming in some areas of the arid West, including California. The "closing" of the frontier in 1890 signified the end of traditional westward expansion, but the Great West remained a unique social and environmental region.

As the farmers opened vast new lands, agriculture was becoming a mechanized business dependent on specialized production and international markets. Once declining prices and other woes doomed the farmers to permanent debt and dependency, they began to protest their lot, first through the Grange and then through the Farmers' Alliances, the prelude to the People's (Populist) Party. The Populists made spectacular gains in the West and the South, but racial divisions undermined southern Populism.

The major depression of the 1890s accelerated farmer and labor strikes and unrest, leading to a growing class conflict. In 1896 pro-silverite William Jennings Bryan captured the Democratic Party's nomination, and led a fervent campaign against the "goldbug" Republicans and their candidate William McKinley. McKinley's success in winning urban workers away from Bryan proved a turning point in American politics, signaling the triumph of the city, the middle class, and a new party system. The return of prosperity ended the preoccupation with monetary issues and made Republicans the dominant party for two generations.

VARYING VIEWPOINTS

Was the West Really "Won"?

For more than half a century, the Turner thesis dominated historical writing about the West. In his famous essay of 1893, "The Significance of the Frontier in American History," historian Frederick Jackson Turner argued that not only the West but the national character had been uniquely shaped by the westward movement. The struggle to overcome the hazards of the western wilderness had transformed *Europeans* into tough, inventive, and self-reliant *Americans.*

Written just three years after the superintendent of the census declared the frontier closed, Turner's thesis is surely among the most provocative statements ever made about formative influences on the nation's development and character. But as the frontier era recedes ever further into the past, scholars are less persuaded that Turner's thesis adequately explains the character of American society and its differences from Europe.

Modern historians such as David J. Weber challenge Turner's assumptions by suggesting that the line of the frontier did not define the quavering edge of "civilization," but instead marked the boundary between diverse and equally legitimate cultures. The frontier should therefore be understood not as the place where "civilization" triumphed over "savagery," but as the principal site of interaction between those cultures.

Several so-called New Western historians take this argument still further. Scholars such as Patricia Nelson Limerick, Richard White, and Donald Worster suggest that the cultural and ecological damage inflicted by advancing "civilization" must be reckoned with in any final accounting of what these pioneers accomplished. These same scholars insist that the West did not lose its regional identity after 1890. The West, they argue, is still a unique part of the national mosaic, a region whose history, culture, and identity remain every bit as distinctive as those of New England or the Old South.

But where Turner saw the frontier as the principal shaper of the region's character, the New Western historians emphasize the effects of ethnic and racial confrontation, topography, climate, and the roles of government and big business as the factors that have made the modern West. The pioneer "conquests" of Native Americans and Hispanics were less than complete, they contend, and the West therefore remains, uniquely among American regions, an unsettled arena of commingling and competition among these groups. Moreover, in these accounts the West's distinctively challenging climate and geography yielded to human habitation not through the efforts of heroic individual pioneers, but only through massive corporate—and especially federal government—investments in projects like the transcontinental railroads and irrigation systems. Such developments still give western life its special character today.

27

Empire and Expansion

1890–1909

WE ASSERT THAT NO NATION CAN LONG ENDURE HALF
REPUBLIC AND HALF EMPIRE, AND WE WARN THE AMERICAN
PEOPLE THAT IMPERIALISM ABROAD WILL LEAD QUICKLY AND
INEVITABLY TO DESPOTISM AT HOME.

DEMOCRATIC NATIONAL PLATFORM, 1900

Chapter Outline

In the years immediately following the Civil War, Americans remained astonishingly indifferent to the outside world. Enmeshed in struggles over Reconstruction and absorbed in efforts to heal the wounds of civil war, build an industrial economy, make their cities habitable, and settle the sprawling West, most citizens took little interest in international affairs. But the sunset decades of the nineteenth century witnessed a momentous shift in U.S. foreign policy. America's new diplomacy reflected the far-reaching changes that were reshaping agriculture, industry, and the social structure. American statesmen also responded to the intensifying scramble of other nations for international advantage in the dawning "age of empire." By the beginning of the twentieth century, America had acquired its own empire, an astonishing departure from its venerable anticolonial traditions. The world now had to reckon with a new great power, potentially powerful but with diplomatic ambitions and principles that remained to be defined.

Focus Questions

1. Why did the United States abandon its historic isolationism and turn outward to develop imperial great power ambitions at the end of the nineteenth century?
2. What were the causes of the Spanish-American War, and how did it lead to the acquisition of an American empire in the Philippines and Puerto Rico?
3. Why was there such a vigorous national debate over imperialism, and how did the Filipino rebellion against U.S. rule contribute to doubts about America's overseas role?
4. How did the United States become increasingly involved in China and the rest of East Asia, and what were the Open Door policy toward China and Theodore Roosevelt's diplomacy with Japan intended to achieve?
5. How did Theodore Roosevelt vigorously assert American power in Panama and elsewhere in Latin America, and why did the "Roosevelt Corollary" to the Monroe Doctrine stir controversy?

Chronology

1820	New England missionaries arrive in Hawaii.
1889	Samoa crisis with Germany.
1890	Mahan publishes *The Influence of Sea Power upon History.*
1891	New Orleans crisis with Italy.
1892	Valparaiso crisis with Chile.
1893	White planter revolt in Hawaii. Cleveland refuses Hawaii annexation.
1895	Cubans revolt against Spain.
1895–1896	Venezuelan boundary crisis with Britain.
1898	*Maine* explosion in Havana harbor. Spanish-American War. Teller Amendment. Dewey's victory at Manila Bay. Hawaii annexed.
1899	Senate ratifies treaty acquiring Philippines. Aguinaldo launches rebellion against United States in the Philippines. First American Open Door note.
1900	Hawaii receives full territorial status. Foraker Act for Puerto Rico. Boxer Rebellion and U.S. military expedition to China. Second Open Door note. McKinley defeats Bryan for the presidency.

1901	Supreme Court *Insular Cases.* Platt Amendment. McKinley assassinated; Roosevelt becomes president. Hay-Pauncefote Treaty with Britain gives United States exclusive right to build Panama Canal.
1902	U.S. troops leave Cuba. Colombian senate rejects U.S. proposal for canal across Panama.
1903	Panamanian revolution against Colombia. Hay-Bunau-Varilla Treaty gives United States control of Canal Zone in newly independent Panama.
1904	Roosevelt Corollary to the Monroe Doctrine.
1904–1914	Construction of the Panama Canal.
1905	United States takes over Dominican Republic customs service. Roosevelt mediates Russo-Japanese peace treaty.
1906	San Francisco Japanese education crisis. Roosevelt arranges Algeciras conference.
1906–1909	U.S. Marines occupy Cuba.
1907	Great White Fleet makes world voyage.
1907–1908	"Gentlemen's Agreement" with Japan.
1908	Root-Takahira agreement.
1917	Puerto Ricans granted U.S. citizenship.

Imperialist Stirrings

Many developments fed the nation's ambition for overseas expansion. Both farmers and factory owners began to look beyond American shores as agricultural and industrial production boomed. Many Americans believed that the United States had to expand or explode. Their country was bursting with a new sense of power generated by the robust growth in population, wealth, and productive capacity—and it was trembling from the hammer blows of labor violence and agrarian unrest. Overseas markets might provide a safety valve to relieve those pressures.

Other forces whetted the popular appetite for overseas involvement. The lurid "yellow press" of Joseph Pulitzer and William Randolph Hearst described foreign exploits as manly adventures, the kind of dashing derring-do that was the stuff of young boys' dreams. Pious missionaries, inspired by books like the Reverend

- ⭐ **The Roosevelt Corollary to the Monroe Doctrine, 1904**
- ⭐ **Roosevelt and East Asia**
- ⭐ **Makers of America: The Puerto Ricans**
- ⭐ **Makers of America: The Filipinos**
- ⭐ **Varying Viewpoints: Why Did America Become a World Power?**

Online Study Center

Interactive map
**The Expansion of Agriculture,
1860–1900**
college.hmco.com/pic/kennedybrief7e

Online Study Center

Interactive map
Imperialism in Asia
college.hmco.com/pic/kennedybrief7e

Online Study Center

Primary source
**Mahan Defines Security in Terms
of Sea Power**
college.hmco.com/pic/kennedybrief7e

indemnity *A payment assessed to compensate for an injury or illegal action.*

arbitration *An arrangement in which a neutral third party conclusively determines the outcome of a dispute between two parties. (In **mediation** the third party only proposes solutions that the disputing parties may or may not accept.)*

Online Study Center

Primary source
Keep Off!
college.hmco.com/pic/kennedybrief7e

The undiplomatic note to Britain by Secretary of State Richard Olney (1835–1917) read,

"To-day the United States is practically sovereign on this continent, and its fiat is law upon the subjects to which it confines its interposition. . . . Its infinite resources combined with its isolated position render it master of the situation and practically invulnerable as against any or all other powers."

Josiah Strong's *Our Country: Its Possible Future and Its Present Crisis,* looked overseas for new souls to harvest. Strong trumpeted the superiority of Anglo-Saxon civilization and summoned Americans to spread their religion and their values to "backward" peoples. At the same time, aggressive Americans like Theodore Roosevelt and Congressman (later Senator) Henry Cabot Lodge were interpreting Darwinism to mean that the earth belonged to the strong and the fit—that is, to Uncle Sam. This view was strengthened as latecomers to the colonial scramble began to scoop up leavings from the banquet table of earlier diners in Africa, China, and elsewhere. If America was to survive in the competition of modern nation-states, perhaps it, too, would have to become an imperial power.

The development of a new steel navy also focused attention overseas. Captain Alfred Thayer Mahan's book of 1890, *The Influence of Sea Power upon History, 1660–1783,* argued that control of the sea was the key to world dominance. Mahan helped stimulate the naval race among the great powers that gained momentum around the turn of the century. Red-blooded Americans joined in the demands for a mightier navy and for an American-built isthmian canal between the Atlantic and the Pacific.

America's new international interest manifested itself in a number of diplomatic crises or near-wars in the late 1880s and early 1890s. The American and German navies nearly came to blows in 1889 over the faraway Samoan Islands in the South Pacific, which were formally divided between the two nations in 1899. (German Samoa eventually became an independent republic; American Samoa remains an American possession.) The lynching of eleven Italians in New Orleans in 1891 brought America and Italy to the brink of war, until the United States agreed to pay compensation. In the ugliest affair, American demands on Chile after the deaths of two American sailors in the port of Valparaiso in 1892 made hostilities between the two countries seem inevitable. The threat of attack by Chile's modern navy spread alarm on the Pacific Coast, until American power finally forced the Chileans to pay an **indemnity**. The willingness of Americans to risk war over such distant and minor disputes demonstrated the aggressive new national mood.

America's new belligerence combined with old-time anti-British feeling to create a serious crisis between the United States and Britain in 1895–1896. The jungle boundary between British Guiana and Venezuela had long been in dispute, but the discovery of gold in the contested area brought the conflict between Britain and Venezuela to a head. President Cleveland and his pugnacious secretary of state, Richard Olney, stepped into the affair with a combative note to Britain invoking the Monroe Doctrine and declaring that the United States was now calling the tune in the Western Hemisphere. Unimpressed British officials shrugged off Olney's salvo as just another twist of the lion's tail and replied that the affair was none of Uncle Sam's business. President Cleveland—"mad clear through," as he put it—sent a bristling special message to Congress that called for a U.S. commission to determine where the line ought to go and threatened war if the British would not accept the boundary it set.

The entire country, irrespective of political party, was swept off its feet in an outburst of hysteria. War seemed inevitable. Fortunately, sober second thoughts prevailed on both sides of the Atlantic. A rising challenge from Kaiser Wilhelm's Germany and a looming war with the Dutch-descended Boers in South Africa left Britain in no mood for war with America. London backed off and consented to **arbitration**.

The chastened British, their eyes fully opened to the European peril, now cultivated Yankee friendship and inaugurated an era of "patting the Eagle's head," which replaced a century or so of America's "twisting the lion's tail." Sometimes called the Great Rapprochement—or reconciliation—between the United States and Britain, the new Anglo-American cordiality became a cornerstone of both nations' foreign policies as the twentieth century opened.

Spurning the Hawaiian Pear

Enchanted Hawaii had early attracted the attention of Americans. In the morning years of the nineteenth century, the breeze-brushed islands were a way station and provisioning point for Yankee shippers, sailors, and whalers. In 1820 the first New England missionaries arrived, preaching the twin blessings of Protestant Christianity and protective calico. As American sugar production flourished on the Hawaiian Islands, the U.S. government assumed a greater interest. The State Department, beginning in the 1840s, sternly warned other powers to keep their hands off the islands. America's grip was further tightened in 1887 by a treaty with the native government guaranteeing priceless naval-base rights at spacious Pearl Harbor.

But trouble was brewing in the insular paradise. Old World pathogens had scythed the indigenous Hawaiian population to one-sixth of its size at the time of first European contact, leading the American sugar lords to import large numbers of Asian laborers. By century's end Chinese and Japanese immigrants outnumbered both whites and native Hawaiians, prompting fears that Tokyo might intervene on behalf of its often-abused nationals. Then sugar markets went sour in 1890 when the McKinley Tariff Act raised barriers against the Hawaiian product. White American planters' mounting efforts to secure annexation by the United States were blocked by Queen Liliuokalani, who insisted that native Hawaiians should control the islands. Though only a tiny minority, the white planters staged a successful coup early in 1893. They were openly assisted by American troops, who landed under the unauthorized orders of the expansionist American minister to Honolulu. "The Hawaiian pear is now fully ripe," he wrote exultantly to his superiors in Washington, "and this is the golden hour for the United States to pluck it."

A treaty of annexation was rushed to Washington, but before it could be railroaded through the Senate, Republican president Harrison's term expired and Democratic president Cleveland came in. Suspecting that his powerful nation had gravely wronged the deposed Queen Liliuokalani and her people, "Old Grover" abruptly withdrew the treaty. A subsequent investigation determined that a majority of Hawaiian natives opposed annexation. Although Queen Liliuokalani could not be reinstated, the sugarcoated move for annexation had to be temporarily abandoned. The Hawaiian pear continued to ripen until 1898.

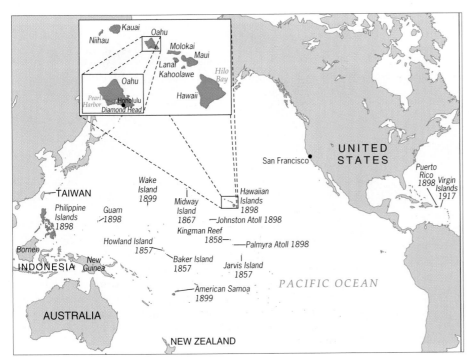

■ **The Pacific** The enlargements show the Hawaiian Islands and the Samoas, both areas of American imperialistic activity in the late nineteenth century.

War with Spain over Cuba

Cuba's masses, frightfully misgoverned, again rose against their Spanish oppressors in 1895. The roots of their revolt were partly economic. Sugar production—the backbone of the island's prosperity—was crippled when the American tariff of 1894 restored high duties on the toothsome product.

The desperate *insurrectos* sought to drive out their Spanish overlords by adopting a scorched-earth policy, torching canefields and sugar mills and dynamiting passenger trains. American sympathies went out to the Cuban underdogs. Sentiment aside, American business had about $50 million of investment in Cuba and conducted annual trade of about $100 million.

Fuel was added to the Cuban conflagration in 1896 with the coming to power of the Spanish General ("Butcher") Weyler. He undertook to crush the rebellion by herding many civilians into barbed-wire **reconcentration** camps, where they could not give assistance to the armed *insurrectos*. Lacking proper sanitation, these enclosures turned into deadly pestholes; the victims died miserably.

Atrocities in Cuba were red meat for the sensational new "yellow journalism." William R. Hearst and Joseph Pulitzer, then engaged in a titanic duel for circulation, attempted to outdo each other with screeching headlines and hair-raising "scoops." Where **atrocity** stories did not exist, they were invented. Hearst sent the gifted artist Frederic Remington to Cuba to draw sketches, allegedly with the pointed admonition, "You furnish the pictures and I'll furnish the war." Among other outrages, Remington depicted Spanish customs officials brutally disrobing and searching an American woman. Most readers of Hearst's *Journal,* their indignation soaring, had no way of knowing that such tasks were performed by female attendants.

Then early in 1898 Washington sent the battleship *Maine* to Cuba, ostensibly for a "friendly visit," but actually to protect and evacuate Americans if a dangerous flare-up should occur. Tragedy struck on February 15, 1898, when the *Maine* mysteriously blew up in Havana harbor, with a loss of 260 sailors.

Two investigations of the iron coffin ensued, one by U.S. naval officers and the other by Spanish officials. The Spaniards concluded that the explosion had been internal and presumably accidental; the Americans argued that the blast had been caused by a submarine mine. Not until 1976 did U.S. Navy Admiral H. G. Rickover confirm the original Spanish finding with overwhelming evidence that the initial

---

reconcentration *The policy of forcibly removing a population to confined areas in order to deny support to enemy forces.*

atrocity *An act of deliberate and extreme cruelty, often intended to terrorize or destroy its target.*

Online Study Center

Primary source
Yellow Kid
college.hmco.com/pic/kennedybrief7e

Online Study Center

Primary source
***Maine* Explosion**
college.hmco.com/pic/kennedybrief7e

■ **The Explosion of the *Maine*, February 15, 1898** Encouraged and amplified by the "yellow press," the outcry over the tragedy of the *Maine* helped drive the country into an impulsive war against Spain.

explosion had resulted from spontaneous combustion in one of the coal bunkers adjacent to a powder magazine.

But Americans in 1898, now mad for war, blindly embraced the less likely explanation. Lashed to fury by the yellow press, they leapt to the inaccurate conclusion that the Spanish government had been guilty of intolerable treachery. The battle cry of the hour became,

> *Remember the Maine!*
> *To hell with Spain!*

Nothing would do but to hurl the "dirty" Spanish flag from the hemisphere.

The national war fever burned ever higher, even though American diplomats had already gained Madrid's agreement to Washington's two basic demands: an end to reconcentration and an armistice with the Cuban rebels. The cautious McKinley found himself in a jam. He did not want hostilities, but neither did he want continuing Spanish control or a fully independent Cuba. More impetuous souls denounced the president as "Wobbly Willy" McKinley. Fight-hungry Theodore Roosevelt reportedly snarled that the "white-livered" occupant of the White House did not have "the backbone of a chocolate eclair." McKinley, recognizing the inevitable, eventually yielded and gave the people what they wanted.

But public pressure did not fully explain McKinley's course. He did not trust Spanish promises, and worried that Democrats would win the upcoming presidential election of 1900 if he remained indecisive. On April 11, 1898, McKinley sent his war message to Congress, urging armed intervention to free the oppressed Cubans. The legislators responded uproariously with what was essentially a declaration of war. In a burst of self-righteousness, they likewise adopted the hand-tying Teller Amendment. This **proviso** proclaimed to the world that when the United States had overthrown Spanish misrule, it would give the Cubans their freedom—a declaration that caused imperialistic Europeans to smile skeptically.

proviso *An article or clause in a statute, treaty, or contract establishing a particular stipulation or condition affecting the whole document.*

Dewey's May Day Victory at Manila

The American people plunged into the war lightheartedly, like schoolchildren off to a picnic. Bands blared incessantly "There'll Be a Hot Time in the Old Town Tonight" and "Hail, Hail, the Gang's All Here," thus leading some foreigners to believe that those were the national anthems.

The war got off to a giddy start for American forces. Even before the declaration of war, on February 25, 1898, while Navy Secretary John D. Long was away from the office, his hot-blooded assistant secretary Theodore Roosevelt took matters into his own hands. Roosevelt cabled Commodore George Dewey, commanding the American Asian squadron, to descend upon Spain's Philippines in the event of war.

Dewey carried out his orders magnificently on May 1, 1898. Sailing boldly with his six warships at night into the fortified harbor of Manila, he trained his guns the next morning on the Spanish fleet. The entire collection of antiquated and overmatched vessels was quickly destroyed.

Taciturn George Dewey became a national hero overnight. An amateur poet blossomed forth with this:

> *Oh, dewy was the morning*
> *Upon the first of May,*
> *And Dewey was the Admiral*
> *Down in Manila Bay.*
> *And dewy were the Spaniards' eyes,*
> *Them orbs of black and blue;*
> *And dew we feel discouraged?*
> *I dew not think we dew!*

Yet Dewey was in a perilous position. He had destroyed the enemy fleet, but he could not storm the forts of Manila with his sailors. His nerves frayed, he was forced to wait in the sweltering bay while troop reinforcements were slowly assembled in America. The appearance of German warships in Manila harbor added to the tension.

Long-awaited American troops, finally arriving in force, captured Manila on August 13, 1898, in collaboration with Filipino insurgents commanded by their well-educated, part-Chinese leader, Emilio Aguinaldo. Dewey, to his later regret, had brought this shrewd and magnetic revolutionary from exile in Asia so that he might weaken Spanish resistance.

These thrilling events in the Philippines had meanwhile focused attention on Hawaii. An impression spread that America needed the archipelago as a coaling and provisioning way station in order to send supplies and reinforcements to Dewey. A joint resolution of annexation was rushed through Congress and approved by McKinley on July 7, 1898. Hawaii received full territorial status in 1900.

The Confused Invasion of Cuba

Shortly after the outbreak of war, the Spanish government ordered a fleet of warships to Cuba. But the decrepit Spanish "armada" was soon forced into bottle-shaped Santiago harbor, where it was blockaded by the much more powerful American fleet. Sound strategy seemed to dictate that an American army be sent in from the rear to drive out the Spanish ships. Leading the ill-equipped American invading force was the grossly overweight General William R. Shafter, a would-be warrior so blubbery that he had to be carried about on a door.

The "Rough Riders," a part of the invading army, now charged onto the stage of history. This colorful regiment of volunteers, short on discipline but long on dash, consisted largely of western cowboys and other hardy characters, with a sprinkling of ex–polo players and ex-convicts. Commanded by Colonel Leonard Wood, the group was organized principally by the glory-hungry Theodore Roosevelt, who had resigned from the Navy Department to serve as lieutenant colonel.

About the middle of June a bewildered American army of seventeen thousand men finally embarked from Tampa, Florida, amid scenes of indescribable confusion. Shafter's landing near Santiago, Cuba, met little opposition. Brisk fighting broke out on July 1 at El Caney and Kettle Hill, up which Colonel Roosevelt and his horseless Rough Riders charged, with strong support from two crack black regiments. They suffered heavy casualties, but the colorful colonel, having the time of his life, shot a Spaniard with his revolver and rejoiced to see his victim double up like a jackrabbit. He later wrote a book on his exploits, which, humorist Finley Peter Dunne's fictional "Mr. Dooley" remarked, ought to have been entitled *Alone in Cubia* [*sic*].

■ **Colonel Theodore Roosevelt with Some of the "Rough Riders"** Roosevelt later described his first encounter with the Spanish enemy: "Soon we came to the brink of a deep valley. There was a good deal of cracking of rifles way off in front of us, but as they used smokeless powder we had no idea as to exactly where they were, or who they were shooting at. Then it dawned on us that we were the target. The bullets began to come overhead, making a sound like the ripping of a silk dress, with sometimes a kind of pop. . . . We advanced, firing at them, and drove them off."

The American army, fast closing in on Santiago, spelled doom for the Spanish fleet. On July 3 the Spanish fleet steamed out of the harbor and into the teeth of the waiting American warships. "Don't cheer, men," Captain Philip of the *Texas* admonished his seamen. "The poor devils are dying." Shortly thereafter Santiago surrendered.

Hasty preparations were then made for a descent on Puerto Rico before the war should end. There the American army met even less resistance. By this time Spain was ready for an armistice, which was signed on August 12, 1898.

If the Spaniards had held out a few months longer in Cuba, the American army might have melted away. Malaria, typhoid fever, dysentery, and yellow fever incapacitated numerous soldiers and sailors. Others suffered from malodorous canned meat known as "embalmed beef." All told, nearly four hundred men lost their lives to bullets; over five thousand succumbed to bacteria and other causes.

America's Course (Curse?) of Empire

Late in 1898 Spanish and American negotiators met in Paris. War-racked Cuba, as expected, was freed from its Spanish overlords. The Americans had little difficulty in securing the remote Pacific island of Guam, which they had captured early in the conflict from astonished Spaniards who had not known that a war was on. Spain also ceded Puerto Rico to the United States. Ironically, the last remnant of Spain's vast New World empire thus became the first territory ever annexed to the United States without the express promise of eventual statehood. In the decades to come, American investment in the island and Puerto Rican immigration to the United States would make this acquisition one of the weightier consequences of this somewhat carefree war (see "Makers of America: The Puerto Ricans," pp. 426–427).

Knottiest of all was the problem of the Philippines, a veritable apple of discord. These lush islands not only embraced an area larger than the British Isles but also contained a completely alien population of some 7 million souls. McKinley was confronted with a devil's dilemma. He did not feel that America could honorably give the islands back to Spanish misrule, especially after it had fought a war to free Cuba. And America would be turning its back on its responsibilities, he believed, if it simply pulled up anchor and sailed away.

McKinley viewed all the choices open to him as trouble-fraught. The Filipinos, if left to govern themselves, might fall into anarchy. One of the major powers, possibly aggressive Germany, might then seize them and suck the United States into a major war. Seemingly the least of the evils was to acquire all the Philippines and then perhaps give the Filipinos their freedom later.

President McKinley, ever sensitive to public opinion, kept a carefully attuned ear to the ground. The rumble that he heard seemed to call for the entire group of islands. Zealous Protestant missionaries were eager to win Filipino converts from Catholicism. (The Philippines had been substantially Christianized by Spanish Catholics before the founding of Jamestown in 1607.) Wall Street had generally opposed the war; but awakened by the booming of Dewey's guns, it was clamoring for profits in the Philippines.

A tormented McKinley later claimed that he went down on his knees seeking divine guidance and heard an inner voice telling him to take all the Philippines and Christianize and civilize them. Accordingly, he decided for outright annexation of the islands. Because Manila had been captured *after* the armistice was signed, the Americans agreed to pay Spain $20 million for the Philippine Islands—the last great Spanish haul from the New World.

President William McKinley (1843–1901) later described his decision to annex the Philippines:

"When next I realized that the Philippines had dropped into our laps, I confess I did not know what to do with them. . . . I went down on my knees and prayed Almighty God for light and guidance. . . . And one night late it came to me this way. . . . That there was nothing left for us to do but to take them all, and to educate the Filipinos, and uplift and civilize and Christianize them and by God's grace do the very best we could by them, as our fellow men, for whom Christ also died. And then I went to bed and went to sleep, and slept soundly."

The Puerto Ricans

At dawn on July 26, 1898, the U.S. warship *Gloucester* steamed into Puerto Rico's Guanica harbor, fired at the Spanish blockhouse, and landed some thirty-three hundred troops. Within days, the Americans had taken possession of the Caribbean island a thousand miles southeast of Florida. In so doing they set in motion changes on the island that ultimately brought a new wave of immigrants to U.S. shores.

Puerto Rico had been a Spanish possession since Christopher Columbus claimed it for Castile in 1493. The Spaniards enslaved many of the island's forty thousand Taino Indians and set them to work on farms and in mines. Many Tainos died of exhaustion and disease, and in 1511 the Indians rebelled. The Spaniards crushed the uprising, killed thousands of Indians, and began importing African slaves—thus establishing the basis for Puerto Rico's multiracial society.

The first Puerto Rican immigrants to the United States arrived as political exiles in the nineteenth century. From their haven in America, they agitated for the island's independence from Spain. The Puerto Rican political émigrés in the United States returned home after the Americans conquered the island in 1898.

But they were soon replaced by poor islanders looking for work. When Congress granted Puerto Ricans U.S. citizenship in 1917, thereby eliminating immigration hurdles, many islanders hurried north to find jobs. Over the ensuing decades, Puerto Ricans went to work in Arizona cotton fields, New Jersey soup factories, and Utah mines. The majority, however, clustered in New York City and found work in the city's cigar factories, shipyards, and garment industry. Migration slowed somewhat after the 1920s as the Great Depression shrank the job market on the mainland and as World War II made travel hazardous.

When World War II ended in 1945, the sudden advent of cheap air travel sparked an emigration explosion. As late as the 1930s, the tab for a boat trip to the mainland exceeded the average Puerto Rican's yearly earnings. But with an airplane surplus after World War II, the six-hour flight from Puerto Rico to New York cost under fifty dollars. The Puerto Rican population on the mainland quadrupled between 1940 and 1950 and tripled again by

■ The First Puerto Ricans The Spanish *conquistadores* treated the native Taino Indian peoples in Puerto Rico with extreme cruelty, and the Indians were virtually extinct by the mid–1500s.

1960. In 1970, 1.5 million Puerto Ricans lived in the United States, one-third of the island's total population.

U.S. citizenship and affordable air travel made it easy for Puerto Ricans to return home. Thus to a far greater degree than most immigrant groups, Puerto Ricans kept one foot in the United States and the other on their native island. By some estimates, 2 million people a year journeyed to and from the island during the postwar period. Puerto Rico's gubernatorial candidates sometimes campaigned in New York for the thousands of voters who were expected to return to the island in time for the election.

Puerto Ricans have fared better economically in the United States than on the island, where, in 1970, 60 percent of all inhabitants lived below the poverty line. In recent years Puerto Ricans have attained more schooling, and many have attended college. Invigorated by the civil rights movement of the 1960s, Puerto Ricans also became more politically active, electing growing numbers of congressmen and state and city officials.

The signing of the pact of Paris touched off one of the most impassioned foreign-policy debates in American history. Except for glacial Alaska, coral-reefed Hawaii, and a handful of Pacific atolls, the Republic had hitherto absorbed only contiguous territory on the continent. All previous acquisitions had been thinly peopled and eligible for ultimate statehood. But in the Philippines the nation had on its hands a distant tropical area, thickly populated by Asians of a different culture, tongue, and government institutions.

Opponents of annexation argued that such a step would dishonor and ultimately destroy American's venerable commitments to self-determination and anticolonialism. "Goddamn the United States for its vile conduct in the Philippine Isles!" burst out the usually mild-mannered Professor William James. The Harvard philosopher could not believe that the United States could "puke up its ancient soul in five minutes without a wink of squeamishness." The Anti-Imperialist League sprang into being to fight the McKinley administration's expansionist moves. The organization counted among its members some of the most prominent people in the United States, including the presidents of Stanford and Harvard Universities and the novelist Mark Twain. The anti-imperialist blanket even stretched over such strange bedfellows as the labor leader Samuel Gompers and the steel titan Andrew Carnegie.

Anti-imperialists raised many objections. The Filipinos thirsted for freedom; to annex them would violate the "consent of the governed" philosophy of the Declaration of Independence and the Constitution. Despotism abroad might well beget despotism at home. Imperialism was costly and unlikely ever to turn a profit. Finally, annexation would propel the United States into the political and military cauldron of East Asia.

Yet the expansionists or imperialists could sing a seductive song. They appealed to patriotism, invoked America's "civilizing mission," and played up possible trade profits. Manila, in fact, might become another Hong Kong. Rudyard Kipling, the British poet laureate of imperialism, urged America down the slippery path with a quotable poem:

Take up the White Man's burden—
Ye dare not stoop to less—
Nor call too loud on Freedom
To cloak your weariness.

In short, the wealthy Americans must help to uplift (and exploit) the underprivileged, underfed, and underclad of the world.

Over heated protests, the Senate approved the treaty with Spain with just one vote to spare on February 6, 1898. America was now officially an empire.

Online Study Center

Primary source
American Anti-Imperialist
League Program
college.hmco.com/pic/kennedybrief7e

Perplexities in Puerto Rico and Cuba

From the outset, the status of Puerto Rico was anomalous—neither a state nor a territory, and with little prospect of eventual independence. The Foraker Act of 1900 accorded the Puerto Ricans a limited degree of popular government, and in

■ **The Imperial Menu** A pleased Uncle Sam gets ready to place his order with headwaiter William McKinley. Swallowing some of these possessions eventually produced political indigestion. (Sandwich Islands was an earlier European name for Hawaii.)

1917 Congress granted Puerto Ricans U.S. citizenship but withheld full self-rule. Although the American regime worked wondrous improvements in education, sanitation, and transportation, many of the inhabitants still aspired to independence. Great numbers of Puerto Ricans ultimately moved to New York City, where they added to the complexity of the melting pot.

The annexation of Puerto Rico (and the Philippines) posed a thorny legal problem: Did the Constitution follow the flag? Did American laws, including tariff laws and the Bill of Rights, apply with full force to the newly acquired possessions? "Who are we?" a group of Puerto Rican petitioners asked Congress in 1900. "Are we citizens or are we subjects?" Beginning in 1901 with the *Insular Cases,* a badly divided Supreme Court decreed, in effect, that the flag did outrun the Constitution, and that the outdistanced document did not necessarily extend with full force to the new windfall. Puerto Ricans (and Filipinos) might be subject to American rule, but they did not enjoy all American rights.

Cuba, scorched and chaotic, presented another headache. An American military government under General Leonard Wood of Rough Rider fame wrought miracles in government, finance, education, agriculture, and public health. Wood and Colonel William C. Gorgas also launched a frontal attack on yellow fever. Spectacular experiments performed by Dr. Walter Reed and others on American soldiers, who volunteered as human guinea pigs, proved that the stegomyia mosquito was the lethal carrier. Cleaning up breeding places for mosquitoes wiped out yellow fever in Havana.

The United States, honoring its self-denying Teller Amendment of 1898, withdrew from Cuba in 1902. Old World imperialists could scarcely believe their eyes. But the Washington government feared that if Cuba were left on its own a grasping power like Germany might secure dangerous lodgment near America's soft underbelly. The Cubans were therefore forced to write into their own constitution of 1901 the so-called Platt Amendment.

The Cubans loathed the amendment, which served McKinley's ultimate purpose of bringing Cuba under American control. ("Plattism" survives as a colloquial term of derision even in modern-day Cuba.) The Platt amendment placed restrictions on Cubans' political and financial autonomy, and permitted the United States to intervene with troops to restore order when it saw fit. The Cubans also promised to sell or lease coaling or naval stations to their powerful "benefactor." The United States finally abrogated the amendment in 1934, although Uncle Sam still occupies one remaining base, Guantanamo, under an agreement that can be revoked only by the consent of both parties (see p. 540).

New Horizons in Two Hemispheres

In essence, the Spanish-American War was a kind of colossal coming-out party. Dewey's thundering guns merely advertised the fact that the nation was already a world power. The war itself was short (113 days), spectacular, low in casualties, and theatrically successful—despite the bungling. Secretary of State John Hay called it a "splendid little war." American prestige rose sharply, and the European great powers grudgingly accorded the Republic more respect.

An exhilarating new martial spirit thrilled America, buoyed along by the newly popular military marching-band music of John Philip Sousa. Most Americans did not start the war with consciously imperialistic motives, but after falling through the cellar door of imperialism in a drunken fit of idealism, they wound up with imperialistic and colonial fruits in their grasp. Captain Mahan's big-navyism seemed vindicated, and popular support grew for more and better battleships. A masterly organizer, Secretary of War Elihu Root established a general staff and founded the War College in Washington.

One of the happiest results of the conflict was the further closing of the "bloody chasm" between North and South. Thousands of patriotic southerners had flocked to the Stars and Stripes, and gray-bearded General Joseph ("Fighting Joe") Wheeler—a Confederate cavalry hero—was given a command in Cuba. He allegedly cried, in the heat of battle, "To hell with the Yankees! Dammit, I mean the Spaniards."

Even so, the newly imperial nation was not yet prepared to pay the full bill for its new status. By taking on the Philippine Islands, the United States became a full-fledged East Asian power. But the distant islands eventually became a "heel of Achilles"—a kind of indefensible **hostage** given to Japan, as events proved in World War II. Here and elsewhere, the Americans had shortsightedly assumed burdensome commitments that they proved unwilling to defend with appropriate naval and military outlays.

hostage *A person or thing forcibly held in order to obtain certain goals or agreements.*

"Little Brown Brothers" in the Philippines

The liberty-loving Filipinos assumed that they, like the Cubans, would be granted their freedom after the Spanish-American War. They were tragically deceived. Washington excluded them from the peace negotiations with Spain and made clear its intention to stay in the Philippines indefinitely. Bitterness toward the American troops erupted into open insurrection on February 4, 1899, under Emilio Aguinaldo. Having plunged into war with Spain to free Cuba, the United States was now forced to deploy some 126,000 troops ten thousand miles away to rivet shackles onto a people who asked for nothing but freedom—in the American tradition.

The poorly equipped Filipino rebels soon melted into the jungle to wage vicious guerrilla warfare. Both sides perpetrated sordid atrocities. Uncle Sam's soldiers adopted the "water cure"—forcing water down victims' throats until they yielded information or died. American-built reconcentration camps rivaled those of "Butcher" Weyler in Cuba. Having begun the Spanish war with noble ideals, America now dirtied its hands. One New York newspaper published a reply to Rudyard Kipling's famous poem:

> We've taken up the white man's burden
> Of ebony and brown;
> Now will you kindly tell us, Rudyard,
> How we may put it down?

The Americans broke the back of the Filipino insurgency in 1901 when they captured Aguinaldo. But sporadic fighting dragged on for many dreary months, eventually claiming the lives of 4,234 Americans and as many as 600,000 Filipinos.

Future president William H. Taft, an able and amiable Ohioan who weighed some 350 pounds, became civil governor of the Philippines in 1901. Forming a strong attachment to the Filipinos, he called them his "little brown brothers."

The Filipinos

At the beginning of the twentieth century, the United States, its imperial muscles just flexed in the war with Spain, found itself in possession of the Philippines. Uncertain of how to manage this empire, which seethed resentfully against its new masters, the United States promised to build democracy in the Philippines and to ready the islanders for home rule. Almost immediately after annexation, the American governor of the archipelago sent a corps of Filipino students to the United States, hoping to forge future leaders steeped in American ways who would someday govern an independent Philippines.

Most Filipino immigrants to the United States in these years, however, came not to study but to toil. With Chinese immigration banned, Hawaii and the Pacific Coast states turned to the Philippines for cheap agricultural labor. Beginning in 1906, the Hawaiian Sugar Planters Association aggressively recruited Filipino workers. Enlistments grew slowly at first, but by the 1920s thousands of young Filipino men had reached the Hawaiian Islands and been assigned to sugar plantations or pineapple fields.

Those Filipinos venturing as far as the American mainland found work less arduous but also less certain than did their countrymen on Hawaiian plantations. Many mainlanders worked seasonally—in winter as domestic servants, busboys, or bellhops; in summer journeying to the fields to harvest lettuce, strawberries, sugar beets, and potatoes. Eventually Filipinos, along with Mexican immigrants, came to make up the largest share of California's agricultural work force.

A mobile society, Filipino Americans also were overwhelmingly male; there was only one Filipino woman for every fourteen Filipino men in California in 1930. Thus the issue of intermarriage became acutely sensitive. California and many other states prohibited the marriage of Asians and Caucasians in demeaning laws that remained on the books until 1948. Undeterred by such overt discrimination and the vigilante violence sometimes directed at them, especially in Washington and California, Filipinos challenged restrictive state laws and the hooligans who found in them an excuse for mayhem. But Filipinos, who did not become eligible for American citizenship until 1946, long lacked political leverage.

After World War II, Filipino immigration accelerated. Between 1950 and 1970, the number of Filipinos in the United States nearly doubled, with women and men stepping aboard the new transpacific airliners in roughly equal numbers. Many of these recent arrivals were solidly middle class and sought in America a better life for their children. Today, the war-torn and perpetually depressed archipelago sends more immigrants to American shores than does any other Asian nation.

But McKinley's "benevolent assimilation" of the Philippines proceeded with painful slowness. Millions of American dollars did lead to better roads, improved public sanitation, and an unusually good school system. But all this vast expenditure was ill received. The Filipinos hated compulsory Americanization and pined for liberty. They finally got their freedom on the Fourth of July, 1946. In the meantime, thousands of Filipinos emigrated to the United States (see "Makers of America: The Filipinos," p. 430).

Hinging the Open Door in China

Ominous events had meanwhile been brewing in enfeebled China. After its defeat by Japan in 1894–1895, the imperialistic European powers, notably Russia and Germany, moved in. Like sharks attacking a wounded whale, they began to tear away valuable leaseholds and economic **spheres of influence** from the Manchu government.

sphere of influence *In international affairs, the territory where a powerful state exercises the dominant control over weaker states or territories.*

A growing group of Americans viewed the vivisection of China with alarm. Churches were worried about their missionary strongholds. Merchants feared that Europeans would monopolize Chinese markets. An alarmed American public demanded that Washington do something. Secretary of State John Hay, a witty poet-novelist-diplomat, finally decided upon a dramatic move.

In the summer of 1899, Hay dispatched to all the great powers a communication soon known as the Open Door note. He urged them to announce that in their leaseholds or spheres of influence they would respect certain Chinese rights and the ideal of fair competition. Tellingly, Hay had not bothered to consult the Chinese themselves.

The phrase *Open Door* quickly caught the American public's fancy. But Hay's proposal caused much squirming in the leading world capitals, though all the great powers except Russia eventually agreed to it.

Open Door or not, patriotic Chinese did not care to be used as a doormat by the Europeans. In 1900 a superpatriotic group, known as the "Boxers" for their training in martial arts, broke loose with the cry, "Kill Foreign Devils." They murdered more than two hundred foreigners and thousands of Chinese Christians and besieged the foreign diplomatic community in the capital, Beijing (Peking).

A multinational rescue force of some eighteen thousand soldiers, including several thousand Americans, arrived in the nick of time to quell the rebellion and prop the Open Door open. The victorious allied invaders acted angrily and

■ **American Missionary Grace Roberts Teaching in China, 1903** A long history of American missionary involvement in China nurtured a sentimental affection for that country among Americans that persisted well into the twentieth century.

The contest over American imperialism took place on the Senate floor as well as around the globe. In 1900 Senator Albert J. Beveridge (1862–1927), Republican from Indiana, returned from an investigative trip to the Philippines to defend its annexation.

"The Philippines are ours forever. . . . And just beyond the Philippines are China's illimitable markets. We will not retreat from either. We will not abandon our opportunity in the Orient. We will not renounce our part in the mission of our race: trustee, under God, of the civilization of the world."

Two years later Senator George F. Hoar (1826–1904), Republican from Massachusetts, broke with his party to denounce American annexation of the Philippines and other territories:

"You cannot maintain despotism in Asia and a republic in America. If you try to deprive even a savage or a barbarian of his just rights you can never do it without becoming a savage or a barbarian yourself."

partition *In politics, the act of dividing a weaker territory or government among several more powerful states.*

vindictively. They assessed prostrate China an excessive indemnity of $333 million, of which America's share was to be $24.5 million. When Washington discovered that this sum was much more than enough to pay damages and expenses, it remitted about $18 million to be used for the education of a selected group of Chinese students in the United States—a not-so-subtle initiative to further the westernization of Asia.

Secretary Hay let fly another paper broadside in 1900, announcing that henceforth the Open Door would embrace the territorial integrity of China. Those principles helped spare China from possible **partition** in these troubled years and were formally incorporated into the Nine-Power Treaty of 1922, only to be callously violated by Japan's takeover of Manchuria a decade later (see p. 518).

Imperialism or Bryanism in 1900?

President McKinley's renomination by the Republicans in 1900 was a foregone conclusion. He had won a war, acquired rich though burdensome real estate, and brought the promised prosperity of the full dinner pail. An irresistible vice-presidential boom had developed for "Teddy" Roosevelt (TR), the cowboy-hero of the Cuban campaign. Capitalizing on his war-born popularity, he had been elected governor of New York, where the local political bosses had found him headstrong and difficult to manage. They therefore devised a scheme to kick the colorful colonel upstairs into the vice presidency.

This plot to railroad Roosevelt worked beautifully. Gesticulating wildly, he sported a cowboy hat that made him stand out like a white crow. To cries of "We Want Teddy!" he was handily nominated. A wary Mark Hanna reportedly moaned that there would now be only one heartbeat between "that damned cowboy" and the presidency of the United States.

William Jennings Bryan was the odds-on choice of the Democrats, meeting at Kansas City. Their platform proclaimed that the paramount issue was Republican overseas imperialism.

McKinley, the soul of dignity, once again campaigned safely from his front porch. Bryan again took to the stump in a cyclonic campaign. Lincoln, he charged, had abolished slavery for 3.5 million Africans; McKinley had reestablished it for 7 million Filipinos. Roosevelt out-Bryaned Bryan, touring the country with revolver-shooting cowboys. Flashing his monumental teeth and pounding his fist into his palm, Roosevelt denounced all the dastards who would haul down Old Glory.

McKinley handily triumphed by a much wider margin than in 1896: 7,218,491 to 6,356,734 popular votes, and 292 to 155 electoral votes. But victory for the Republicans was not a mandate for imperialism. If there was any mandate at all it was for the two Ps: prosperity and protectionism. Meanwhile, the New York bosses gleefully looked forward to watching the nettlesome Roosevelt "take the veil" as vice president.

TR: Brandisher of the Big Stick

Kindly William McKinley had scarcely served another six months when, in September 1901, he was murdered by a deranged anarchist in Buffalo, New York. Roosevelt rode a buckboard out of his campsite in the Adirondack Mountains to take the oath of office, becoming, at age forty-two, the youngest president thus far in American history.

Born into a wealthy and distinguished New York family, Roosevelt, a red-blooded **blue blood**, had fiercely built up his spindly, asthmatic body by a stern and self-imposed routine of exercise. He graduated from Harvard with Phi Beta Kappa honors and published, at the age of twenty-four, the first of some thirty volumes of muscular prose. He worked as a ranch owner and cowboy in the Dakotas before pursuing his political career full time. Barrel-chested, bespectacled, with mulelike molars, squinty eyes, droopy mustache, and piercing voice, he was ever the delight of cartoonists.

The Rough Rider's high-voltage energy was electrifying. Believing that it was better to wear out than to rust out, he would shake the hands of some six thousand people at one stretch or ride long miles on horseback. Incurably boyish and **bellicose**, Roosevelt ceaselessly preached the virile virtues and denounced pacifistic "flubdubs" and "mollycoddles." An ardent champion of military and naval **preparedness**, he adopted as his pet proverb, "Speak softly and carry a big stick, [and] you will go far."

His outsized ego caused it to be said of him that he wanted to be the bride at every wedding and the corpse at every funeral. He loved people and mingled with those of all ranks—from Catholic cardinals to professional prizefighters, one of whom blinded a Rooseveltian eye in a White House bout. "TR" commanded an idolatrous personal following. After visiting him, a journalist wrote, "You go home and wring the personality out of your clothes."

Above all, TR believed that the president should lead, boldly. He had no real respect for the delicate checks and balances among the three branches of government. The president, he felt, may take any action in the general interest that is not specifically forbidden by the laws or the Constitution.

blue blood *A person of supposedly "pure blood," presumed to be descended from nobility or aristocracy.*

bellicose *Disposed to fight or go to war.*

preparedness *The accumulation of sufficient armed forces and matériel to go to war.*

Online Study Center

Primary source
Bully Pulpit, The
college.hmco.com/pic/kennedybrief7e

Building the Panama Canal

Roosevelt soon applied his bullish energy to foreign affairs. The Spanish-American War had reinvigorated interest in the long-talked-about canal across the Central American isthmus. An isthmian canal would plainly augment the strength of the navy by increasing its mobility. Such a waterway would also make easier the defense of such recent acquisitions as Puerto Rico, Hawaii, and the Philippines.

Initial obstacles in the path of the canal builders were legal rather than geographical. By the terms of the ancient Clayton-Bulwer Treaty, concluded with Britain in 1850, the United States could not secure exclusive control over an isthmian route. But by 1901 America's British cousins were willing to yield ground. Confronted with an unfriendly Europe and bogged down in the South African Boer War, they consented to the Hay-Pauncefote Treaty in 1901. It not only gave the United States a free hand to build the canal but conceded the right to fortify it as well.

But where exactly should the canal be dug? Many American experts favored a route across Nicaragua, but agents of an old French canal company were eager to salvage something from their costly failure in S-shaped Panama. Represented by a young, energetic, and unscrupulous engineer, Philippe Bunau-Varilla, the New Panama Canal Company suddenly dropped the price of its holdings from $109 million to the fire sale price of $40 million.

Congress in June 1902 finally decided on the Panama route. The scene now shifted to Colombia, of which Panama was a restive part. The Colombian senate rejected an American offer of $10 million and annual payment of $250,000 for a six-mile-wide zone across Panama. Roosevelt railed against "those dagos" who were frustrating his ambitions. Meanwhile, impatient Panamanians were ripe for a revolt. Scheming Bunau-Varilla was no less disturbed by the prospect of losing the company's $40 million. Working hand in glove with the Panama revolutionists, he helped incite a rebellion on November 3, 1903. U.S. naval forces prevented Colombian troops from cross the isthmus to quell the uprising.

Roosevelt moved rapidly to make steamy Panama a virtual outpost of the United States. Just three days after the insurrection, he hastily extended the right hand of recognition. Fifteen days later, Bunau-Varilla, who was now the Panamanian minister despite his French citizenship, signed the Hay–Bunau-Varilla Treaty

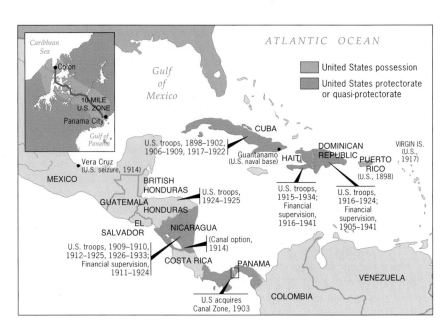

■ **Big Stick in the Caribbean** In 1901 Roosevelt declared: "If a man continually blusters . . . a big stick will not save him from trouble; and neither will speaking softly avail, if back of the softness there does not lie strength, power. . . . If the boaster is not prepared to back up his words his position becomes absolutely contemptible."

Online Study Center

Interactive map
The Panama Canal
college.hmco.com/pic/kennedybrief7e

in Washington. The price of the canal strip was left the same, but the zone was widened from six to ten miles. The French company gladly pocketed its $40 million from the U.S. Treasury.

Roosevelt, it seems clear, did not actively plot to tear Panama from the side of Colombia. But the conspirators knew of his angrily expressed views, and they counted on his using the big stick to hold Colombia at bay. The Rough Rider became so indiscreetly involved in the Panama affair as to create the impression that he had been a secret party to the intrigue, and the so-called rape of Panama marked an ugly downward lurch in U.S. relations with Latin America.

Canal construction began in 1904, in the face of daunting difficulties ranging from labor troubles to landslides and lethal tropical diseases. Colonel William C. Gorgas, the quiet and determined exterminator of yellow fever in Havana, ultimately made the Canal Zone "as safe as a health resort." At a cost of some $400 million, an autocratic West Point engineer, Colonel George Washington Goethals, ultimately brought the project to completion in 1914, just as World War I was breaking out.

TR's Perversion of Monroe's Doctrine

Latin American debt defaults prompted further Rooseveltian involvement in affairs south of the border. Nations such as Venezuela and the Dominican Republic were chronically in arrears in their payments to European creditors.

Roosevelt feared that if the Germans or British got their foot in the door as bill collectors, they might remain in Latin America, in flagrant violation of the Monroe Doctrine. He therefore declared a brazen policy of "preventive intervention," better known as the Roosevelt Corollary to the Monroe Doctrine. He announced that in the event of future financial malfeasance by the Latin American nations, the United States itself would intervene, take over the customshouses, pay off the debts, and keep the troublesome Europeans on the other side of the Atlantic. In short, no outsiders could push around the Latin American nations except Uncle Sam, Policeman of the Caribbean. This new brandishing of the big stick in the Caribbean became effective in 1905 when the United States took over management of the Dominican Republic's tariff collections. It was vigorously wielded again in 1906 when revolutionary disorders in Cuba led to the sending of U.S. marines, who policed the country until they were temporarily withdrawn in 1909.

Online Study Center

Interactive map
U.S. Hegemony in the Caribbean and Latin America
college.hmco.com/pic/kennedybrief7e

■ **Theodore Roosevelt and His Big Stick in the Caribbean, 1904** Roosevelt's policies seemed to be turning the Caribbean into a Yankee pond.

TR's rewriting of the Monroe Doctrine probably did more than any other single step to promote the "Bad Neighbor" policy begun in these years. As time wore on, the new **corollary** was used to justify wholesale interventions and repeated landings of the marines, all of which helped turn the Caribbean into a "Yankee pond." To Latin Americans it seemed as though the revised Monroe Doctrine, far from providing a shield, was a cloak behind which the United States sought to strangle them.

corollary *A secondary inference or deduction from a main proposition that is assumed to be established or proven.*

Online Study Center

**Primary source
Roosevelt Corollary to the Monroe Doctrine**
college.hmco.com/pic/kennedybrief7e

★

Roosevelt on the World Stage

Booted and spurred, Roosevelt charged into international affairs far beyond Latin America. The outbreak of war between Russia and Japan in 1904 gave him a chance to perform as a global statesman. The Russians' threatened seizure of China's Manchuria would be a pistol pointed at Japan's strategic heart. The Japanese responded in 1904 with a devastating surprise pounce on the Russian fleet. They proceeded to administer a humiliating series of beatings to the inept Russians. But as the war dragged on, Japan began to run short of men and yen. Tokyo officials therefore approached Roosevelt in the deepest secrecy and asked him to help sponsor peace negotiations.

Roosevelt was happy to oblige, as he wanted to avoid a complete Russian collapse so that the tsar's empire could remain a counterweight to Japan's growing power. At Portsmouth, New Hampshire, in 1905, TR guided the warring parties to a settlement that satisfied neither side. Japan was forced to drop its demands for a cash indemnity and Russian evacuation of Sakhalin Island, though it did gain effective control over Korea, which it formally annexed in 1910.

For achieving this agreement, as well as for helping arrange an international conference at Algeciras, Spain, in 1906 to mediate North African disputes, TR received the Nobel Peace Prize in 1906. But the price of his diplomatic glory was high for U.S. foreign relations. Two historic friendships withered on the windswept plains of Manchuria. America's relations with Russia, once friendly, soured as the Russians implausibly accused Roosevelt of robbing them of military victory.

Japan, once America's protégé, felt robbed of its due compensation. Both newly powerful, Japan and America now became rivals in Asia, as fear and jealousy between them grew.

Japanese Laborers in California

America's Pacific Coast soon felt the effects of the Russo-Japanese War. The conflict's dislocations and tax burdens sent a new wave of Japanese immigrants into the spacious valleys of California. Although Japanese residents never amounted to more than 3 percent of the state's population, white Californians ranted about a new "yellow peril" and feared being drowned in an Asian sea.

A showdown on the influx came in 1906 when San Francisco's school board, coping with the aftermath of a frightful earthquake and fire, ordered the segregation of Chinese, Japanese, and Korean students in a special school to free more space for whites. Instantly the incident boiled into an international crisis. The people of Japan, highly sensitive on questions of race, regarded this discrimination as an insult to them and their beloved children. On both sides of the Pacific, irresponsible war talk sizzled in the yellow press—the real "yellow peril." Roosevelt, the often-bellicose Rough Rider, was in this case unhappy that California might start up a war. He therefore invited the entire San Francisco Board of Education to the White House.

TR finally broke the deadlock, but not until he had brandished his big stick and bared his big teeth. The Californians were induced to repeal the offensive school order and to accept what came to be known as the "Gentlemen's Agreement." By this secret understanding, worked out during 1907–1908, Tokyo agreed to stop the flow of laborers to the American mainland by withholding passports.

Worried that his intercession might be interpreted in Tokyo as prompted by fear, Roosevelt hit upon a dramatic scheme to impress the Japanese with the heft of his big stick. He daringly decided to send the entire U.S. battleship fleet on a highly visible voyage around the world.

Online Study Center

Interactive map
U.S. Territorial Expansion in the Late 19ᵗʰ Century
college.hmco.com/pic/kennedybrief7e

■ Japanese Workers Building a Road in California, c. 1910

Late in 1907, sixteen smoke-belching battleships started from Virginia waters. Their commander pointedly declared that he was ready for "a feast, a frolic, or a fight." The Great White Fleet received tumultuous welcomes in Latin America, Hawaii, New Zealand, and Australia. The high point of the trip was an overwhelming reception in Japan, as tens of thousands of kimonoed schoolchildren turned out to wave tiny American flags and sing "The Star Spangled Banner."

In the warm diplomatic atmosphere created by the visit of the fleet, the U.S. signed the ~~the~~ Root-Takahira agreement with Japan in 1908. It pledged both powers to respect each other's territorial possessions in the Pacific and to uphold the Open Door in China. For the moment, at least, the two rising rival powers had found a means to maintain the peace.

⭐ Chapter Summary ⭐

The previously isolated United States dramatically turned attention overseas in the 1890s, leading to a sudden burst of imperialism. Among the stimuli for the new imperialism were the desire for new economic markets, the sensationalistic "yellow press," Protestant missionary fervor, "Social Darwinist" ideology, great-power rivalry, and naval competition.

American intervention in the Venezuelan boundary dispute of 1895–1896 demonstrated an aggressive new assertion of the Monroe Doctrine and led to an American-British rapprochement after a severe war scare. Longtime American involvement in Hawaii climaxed in 1893 with a revolution against native rule by white American planters. The new government sought annexation by the United States, but President Cleveland blocked the effort.

The "splendid little" Spanish-American War began in 1898 over American outrage about Spanish oppression of Cuba. American support for the Cuban rebellion was whipped up into intense popular fervor by the "yellow press." After the mysterious *Maine* explosion in February 1898, this public passion pushed a reluctant President McKinley into war, even though Spain was ready to concede on the major issues.

An astounding first development of the war was Admiral Dewey's naval victory in May 1898 in the rich Spanish islands of the Philippines in the Pacific. American troops, assisted by Filipino rebels, captured the Philippine city of Manila in another dramatic victory. Despite military confusion and many deaths from disease, American forces also easily and quickly overwhelmed the Spanish in Cuba and Puerto Rico.

McKinley's decision to take the Philippines precipitated a long and bitter national debate in Congress and the country over the wisdom and justice of American imperialism. The narrow proimperialist victory in the Senate made the Philippines and Puerto Rico American colonial possessions. Despite continuing doubts about the wisdom of imperialism, the United States had asserted itself as a new international power, including in East Asia.

America's decision to take the Philippines aroused violent resistance from the Filipinos, who had expected independence. The brutal war to defeat the Filipino rebels was longer and costlier than the Spanish-American conflict.

Economic interests, missionary efforts, and European imperialistic intrusion led to growing American involvement in China and East Asia. Hay's Open Door policy helped prevent the European great powers from dismembering and colonizing China. The United States joined the international expedition to suppress the Boxer Rebellion.

McKinley readily defeated Bryan's anti-imperialist campaign in 1900 to win reelection. Assuming the presidency after McKinley's death, Theodore Roosevelt brought a new energy and assertiveness to American foreign policy. When his plans to build a canal in Panama were frustrated by the Colombian Senate, he supported a Panamanian revolt that enabled the strategically important canal to be built. He also revised the Monroe Doctrine by adding a "Roosevelt Corollary" that declared an American right to intervene in Latin America, stirring considerable resentment south of the U.S. border.

Roosevelt successfully negotiated an end to the Russo-Japanese War but angered both parties in the process. The United States and Japan were now competitors in the Pacific. Japanese immigration and Pacific Coast fears of a "yellow peril" added to tensions, but Roosevelt's diplomacy enabled the two countries to maintain a fragile peace.

VARYING VIEWPOINTS

Why Did America Become a World Power?

American imperialism has long been an embarrassing topic for students of American history, who remember the Republic's own revolutionary origins and anticolonial tradition. Perhaps for that reason, many historians have tried to explain the dramatic overseas expansionism of the 1890s as some kind of aberration—a sudden, singular, and short-lived departure from time-honored American principles and practices. Various explanations have been offered to account for this spasmodic lapse. Scholars such as Julius Pratt pointed to the irresponsible behavior of the yellow press. Richard Hofstadter ascribed America's imperial fling to the "psychic crisis of the 1890s," a crisis brought on, he argued, by the strains of the decade's economic depression and the Populist upheaval. Howard K. Beale emphasized the contagious scramble for imperial possessions by the European powers, as well as Japan, in these years.

In Beale's argument, the United States—and Theodore Roosevelt in particular—succumbed to a kind of international peer pressure: if other countries were expanding their international roles and even establishing colonies around the globe, could the United States safely refrain from doing the same?

Perhaps the most controversial interpretation of American imperialism has come from a so-called New Left school of writers, inspired by William Appleman Williams (and before him by V. I. Lenin's 1916 book *Imperialism: The Highest Stage of Capitalism*). Historians such as Williams and Walter LaFeber argue that the explanation for political and military expansion abroad is to be found in economic expansion at home. Increasing industrial output, so the argument goes, required ever more raw materials and, especially, overseas markets. That "revisionist" interpretation, in turn, has been sharply criticized by scholars who point out that foreign trade accounted for only a tiny share of American output and that the diplomacy of this period was far too complex to be reduced to "economic need."

Most recently, historians have highlighted the importance of race and gender in the march toward empire. Roosevelt and other imperialists perceived their world in gendered terms. Many feared American society had lost touch with manly virtues and grown soft and "feminine" since the closing of the frontier. Imperialists also saw the nations of the world in a strict racial hierarchy, with "primitive" blacks and Indians at the bottom and "civilized" Anglo-Saxons at the top. In this world-view the conquest of "inferior" peoples seemed a natural tonic to restore the nation's masculine virility. Scholars who emphasize these explanations of imperialism are less likely to see the expansionism of the 1890s as an aberration in American history. Instead, they argue, these overseas adventures were part of a long tradition of race-fueled militarism, from the nation's earliest Indian wars to Cold War engagements in Korea and Vietnam.

PART FIVE

Struggling for Justice at Home and Abroad

1899–1945

The new century brought astonishing changes to the United States. Victory in the Spanish-American War made it clear that the United States was a world power. Industrialization ushered in giant corporations, sprawling factories, sweatshop labor, and the ubiquitous automobile. A huge wave of immigration was altering the face of the nation, especially the cities, where a majority of Americans lived by 1920. With bigger cities came bigger fears—of crime, vice, poverty, and disease.

Changes of such magnitude raised vexing questions. What role should the United States play in the world? How could the enormous power of industry be controlled? How would the millions of new immigrants make their way in America? What should the country do about poverty, disease, and the continuing plague of racial inequality? All these issues turned on a fundamental point: should government remain narrowly limited in its powers, or did the times require a more potent government that would actively shape society and secure American interests abroad?

The progressive movement represented the first attempt to answer those questions. Reform-minded men and women from all walks of life and from both major parties shared in the progressive crusade for greater government activism. Buoyed by this outlook, Presidents Theodore Roosevelt, William Howard Taft, and

Woodrow Wilson enlarged the capacity of government to fight graft, "bust" business trusts, regulate corporations, and promote fair labor practices, child welfare, conservation, and consumer protection. Progressive reformers, convinced that women would bring greater morality to politics, bolstered the decades-long struggle for female suffrage. Women finally secured the vote in 1920 with the ratification of the Nineteenth Amendment.

The progressive-era presidents also challenged America's tradition of isolationism in foreign policy. They felt the country had a moral obligation to spread democracy and an economic opportunity to reap profits in foreign markets. Roosevelt and Taft launched diplomatic initiatives in the Caribbean, Central America, and East Asia. Wilson aspired to "make the world safe for democracy" by rallying support for American intervention in the First World War.

The progressive spirit waned, however, as the United States retreated during the 1920s into what President Harding called "normalcy." Isolationist sentiment revived with a vengeance. Blessed with a booming economy, Americans turned their gaze inward to baseball heroes, radio, jazz, movies, and the first mass-produced American automobile, the Model T Ford. Presidents Harding, Coolidge, and Hoover backed off from the economic regulatory zeal of their predecessors.

"Normalcy" also had a brutal side. Thousands of suspected radicals were jailed or deported in the red scare of 1919 and 1920. Anti-immigrant passions flared until immigration quotas in 1924 squeezed the flow of newcomers to a trickle. Race riots scorched several northern cities in the summer of 1919, a sign of how embittered race relations had become in the wake of the "great migration" of southern blacks to wartime jobs in northern industry. A reborn Ku Klux Klan staged a comeback, not just in the South but in the North and West as well.

"Normalcy" itself soon proved short-lived, a casualty of the stock market crash of 1929 and the Great Depression that followed. As Americans watched banks fail, businesses collapse, and millions of people lose their jobs, they asked with renewed urgency what role the government should play in rescuing the nation. President Franklin D. Roosevelt's answer was the "New Deal"—an ambitious array of relief programs, public works, and economic regulations that failed to cure the depression but furnished an impressive legacy of social reforms.

Most Americans came to accept an expanded federal governmental role at home under FDR's leadership in the 1930s, but they still clung stubbornly to isolationism. The United States did little in the 1930s to check the rising military aggression of Japan and Germany. By the early 1940s, events forced Americans to reconsider. Once Hitler's Germany had seized control of most of Europe, Roosevelt, who had long opposed the isolationists, found ways to aid a beleaguered Britain. When Japan attacked the American naval base at Pearl Harbor in December 1941, isolationists at last fell silent. Roosevelt led a stunned but determined nation into the Second World War, and victory in 1945 positioned the United States to assume a commanding position in the postwar world order

The Great Depression and the Second World War brought to a head a half-century of debate over the role of government and the place of the United States in the world. In the name of a struggle for justice, FDR established a new era of government activism at home and internationalism abroad. The New Deal's legacy set the terms of debate in American political life for the rest of the century.

What If . . . ?

■ **What if the Great Depression had never occurred, or had been swiftly overcome, in America and abroad? Would there then have been a New Deal—or a Second World War?**

28

Progressivism and the Republican Roosevelt

⟨∽⟩

1901–1912

WHEN I SAY I BELIEVE IN A SQUARE DEAL I DO NOT MEAN . . .
TO GIVE EVERY MAN THE BEST HAND. IF THE CARDS DO NOT
COME TO ANY MAN, OR IF THEY DO COME, AND HE HAS NOT GOT
THE POWER TO PLAY THEM, THAT IS HIS AFFAIR. ALL I MEAN IS
THAT THERE SHALL BE NO CROOKEDNESS IN THE DEALING.

THEODORE ROOSEVELT, 1905

Nearly 76 million Americans greeted the new century in 1900. Almost one in seven of them was foreign-born. In the fourteen years of peace that remained before the Great War of 1914 engulfed the globe, 13 million more migrants would carry their bundles down the gangplanks to the land of promise.

Hardly had the twentieth century dawned on the ethnically and racially mixed American people than they were convulsed by a reform movement, the likes of which the nation had not seen since the 1840s. The new crusaders, who called themselves "**progressives**," waged war on many evils, notably monopoly, corruption, inefficiency, and social injustice. The progressive army was large, diverse, and widely deployed, but it had a single battle cry: "Strengthen the State." The "real heart of the movement," explained one progressive reformer, was to "use the government as an agency of human welfare."

Focus Questions

1. What were the origins and character of the progressive movement?
2. What were the primary achievements of progressivism at the local, state, and national levels, and what role did female reformers play in its success?
3. How did President Theodore Roosevelt apply progressive principles to the American economy, and to distinctively progressive causes like consumer protection and conservation?
4. How did Roosevelt's chosen successor William Howard Taft deeply alienate the progressive movement, and why did TR lead a progressive revolt that openly split the Republican party?

Progressive Roots

The groundswell of the new reformist wave went far back—to the Greenback Labor party of the 1870s and the Populists of the 1890s, to the mounting unrest throughout the land as grasping industrialists concentrated more and more power in fewer and fewer hands. An outworn philosophy of hands-off individualism seemed increasingly out of place in the modern machine age. Progressive theorists were insisting

Chronology

1901	Commission system established in Galveston, Texas.		**1907**	"Roosevelt panic."
	Progressive Robert La Follette elected governor of Wisconsin.		**1908**	*Muller* v. *Oregon*.
				Taft defeats Bryan for presidency.
1902	Lincoln Steffens and Ida Tarbell publish muckraking exposés.		**1909**	Payne-Aldrich Tariff.
	Anthracite coal strike.		**1910**	Ballinger-Pinchot affair.
	Newlands Act.		**1911**	Triangle Shirtwaist Company fire.
1903	Department of Commerce and Labor established.			Standard Oil antitrust case.
	Elkins Act.			U.S. Steel Corporation antitrust suit.
1904	*Northern Securities* case.		**1912**	Taft wins Republican nomination over Roosevelt.
	Roosevelt defeats Alton B. Parker for presidency.		**1913**	Seventeenth Amendment passed (direct election of U.S. senators).
1905	*Lochner* v. *New York*.			
1906	Hepburn Act.			
	Upton Sinclair publishes *The Jungle*.			
	Meat Inspection Act.			
	Pure Food and Drug Act.			

that society could no longer afford the luxury of a limitless "let-alone" (laissez-faire) policy. The people, through government, must substitute mastery for drift.

Well before 1900, perceptive politicians and writers had begun to pinpoint targets for the progressive attack. Bryan, Altgeld, and the Populists loudly branded the "bloated trusts" with the stigma of corruption and wrongdoing. In 1894 Henry Demarest Lloyd charged headlong into the Standard Oil Company with his book entitled *Wealth Against Commonwealth*. Eccentric economist Thorstein Veblen assailed the new rich with his prickly pen in *The Theory of the Leisure Class* (1899), a savage attack on "predatory wealth" and "**conspicuous consumption**."

Other pen-wielding knights likewise entered the fray. The keen-eyed Danish immigrant Jacob A. Riis, a reporter for the *New York Sun*, shocked middle-class Americans in 1890 with *How the Other Half Lives*. His account was a damning indictment of the dirt, disease, vice, and misery of those rat-gnawed human rookeries known as the New York slums. Novelist Theodore Dreiser used his blunt prose to batter promoters and profiteers in *The Financier* (1912) and *The Titan* (1914).

Socialists, many of whom were European immigrants inspired by the strong movements for state socialism in the Old World, began to register appreciable strength at the ballot box. High-minded messengers of the social gospel used Christian teachings to demand better housing and living conditions for the poor. Feminists in multiplying numbers added social justice to suffrage on their list of needed reforms. With urban pioneers like Jane Addams blazing the way, women entered the fight to improve the lots of families living and working in the festering cities.

progressive(s) *In politics, one who believes in continuing social advancement, scientific and technological improvement, and morally based reform.*

conspicuous consumption *The theory, developed by economist Thorstein Veblen, that much spending by the affluent occurs primarily to display wealth and status to others rather than from enjoyment of the goods or services themselves.*

Primary source
Reform Record
college.hmco.com/pic/kennedybrief7e

Primary source
Almost Thru the Dark Valley
college.hmco.com/pic/kennedybrief7e

Primary source
Give Mother the Vote
college.hmco.com/pic/kennedybrief7e

Raking Muck with the Muckrakers

Beginning about 1902 the exposing of evil became a flourishing industry among American publishers. A group of aggressive popular magazines surged to the front, notably *McClure's, Cosmopolitan, Collier's,* and *Everybody's*. Waging fierce circulation wars, they dug deep for the dirt that the public loved to hate. Enterprising editors financed extensive research and encouraged pugnacious writing by their bright young reporters, whom President Roosevelt branded as "muckrakers" in 1906.

■ **Child Workers** Two young girls tend a thread-winding machine. The boy is already a veteran coal miner.

Online Study Center

Primary source
McClure's Magazine
college.hmco.com/pic/kennedybrief7e

Online Study Center

Primary source
Muckrakers
college.hmco.com/pic/kennedybrief7e

Online Study Center

Primary source
Roosevelt Insists on Regulatory Legislation
college.hmco.com/pic/kennedybrief7e

Online Study Center

Primary source
Child Labor in Tenements
college.hmco.com/pic/kennedybrief7e

Online Study Center

Primary source
Patent Medicine Fraud, The
college.hmco.com/pic/kennedybrief7e

Despite presidential scolding, these muckrakers boomed circulation, and some of their most scandalous exposures were published as best-selling books. In 1902 a brilliant New York reporter, Lincoln Steffens, launched a series of articles in *McClure's* entitled "The Shame of the Cities." He fearlessly unmasked the corrupt alliance between big business and municipal government. Steffens was followed in the same magazine by Ida M. Tarbell, a pioneering woman journalist who published a devastating factual exposé of the Standard Oil Company. (Her father had been ruined by the oil interests.)

Plucky muckrakers fearlessly tilted their pen-lances at varied targets. They assailed the malpractices of life insurance companies and tariff lobbies. They roasted the beef trust, the "money trust," the railroad barons, and the corrupt amassing of American fortunes. David G. Phillips shocked an already startled nation by his series in *Cosmopolitan* entitled "The Treason of the Senate" (1906). He boldly charged that seventy-five of the ninety senators did not represent the people at all but the railroads and trusts.

Some of the most effective fire of the muckrakers was directed at social evils. The ugly list included the immoral "white slave" traffic in women, the rickety slums, and the appalling number of industrial accidents. The sorry subjugation of America's 9 million blacks—of whom 90 percent still lived in the South and one-third were illiterate—was spotlighted in Ray Stannard Baker's *Following the Color Line* (1908). The abuses of child labor were brought luridly to light by John Spargo's *The Bitter Cry of the Children* (1906).

Vendors of potent patent medicines (often heavily spiked with alcohol) likewise came in for bitter criticism. These conscienceless vultures sold incredible quantities of adulterated or habit-forming drugs. Muckraking attacks in *Collier's* were substantiated by Dr. Harvey W. Wiley, chief chemist of the Department of Agriculture, who even performed experiments on himself.

Full of sound and fury, the muckrakers signified much about the nature of the progressive reform movement. They were long on lamentation and short on sweeping remedies. To right social wrongs they counted on publicity and an aroused public conscience, not drastic political change. They sought not to overthrow capitalism but to cleanse it. The cure for the ills of American democracy, they earnestly believed, was more democracy.

Political Progressivism

Progressive reformers were mainly middle-class men and women who felt themselves squeezed from above and below. They sensed pressure from the new giant corporations, the restless immigrant hordes, and the aggressive labor unions. The progressives simultaneously sought two goals: to use state power to curb the trusts, and to stem the socialist threat by generally improving the common person's conditions of life and labor. Progressives emerged in both major parties, in all regions, and at all levels of government. The truth is that progressivism was less a minority movement and more a majority mood.

One of the first objectives of progressives was to regain the power that had slipped from the hands of the people into those of the "interests." These ardent reformers pushed for **direct primary** elections so as to undercut power-hungry party bosses. They favored the "**initiative**" so that voters could directly propose legislation themselves, thus bypassing the boss-bought state legislatures. Progressives also agitated for the "**referendum**," which would give the people the right to reject laws pushed through by free-spending agents of big business. The "**recall**" would enable the voters to remove faithless elected officials who had been bribed by bosses or lobbyists. The secret Australian ballot was likewise introduced in the states to counteract boss rule.

Direct election of U.S. senators became a favorite goal of progressives, especially after muckrakers had exposed the scandalous intimacy between greedy corporations and Congress. Direct election was finally achieved by the Seventeenth Amendment to the Constitution, approved in 1913 (see the Appendix). But the expected improvement in caliber was slow in coming.

Woman suffrage, the goal of feminists for many decades, likewise received powerful new support from the progressives early in the 1900s. The political reformers believed that women's votes would elevate the political tone, and the foes of the saloon felt that they could count on the support of enfranchised females. Many of the states, especially the more liberal ones in the West, gradually extended the vote to women. But by 1910 nationwide female suffrage was still a decade away.

direct primary *In politics, the nomination of a party's candidates for office through a special election of that party's voters.*

initiative *In politics, the procedure whereby voters can, through petition, present proposed legislation directly to the electorate.*

referendum *The submission of a law, proposed or already in effect, to a direct vote of the electorate.*

recall *In politics, a procedure for removing an official from office through popular election or other means.*

city manager *An administrator appointed by the city council or other elected body to manage affairs, supposedly in a nonpartisan or professional way.*

red-light district *A section of a city where prostitution is officially or unofficially tolerated.*

franchise *In government, a special privilege or license granted to a company or group to perform a specific function, sometimes for a specified period of time.*

Online Study Center

Interactive map
Woman Suffrage before 1920
college.hmco.com/pic/kennedybrief7e

Progressivism in the Cities and States

Progressives scored some of their most impressive gains in the cities. Frustrated by the inefficiency and corruption of machine-oiled city government, many localities followed the pioneering example of Galveston, Texas. In 1901 it had appointed expert-staffed commissions to manage urban affairs. Other communities adopted the **city manager** system, also designed to take politics out of municipal administration. Some of these "reforms" obviously valued efficiency more highly than democracy, as control of civic affairs was further removed from the people's hands.

Urban reformers likewise attacked "slumlords," juvenile delinquency, and wide-open prostitution (vice-at-a-price), which flourished in **red-light districts** unchallenged by bribed police. Public-spirited city dwellers also moved to halt the corrupt sale of **franchises** for streetcars and other public utilities.

Progressivism naturally bubbled up to the state level, notably in Wisconsin, which became a yeasty laboratory of reform. Pompadoured Governor Robert M. ("Fighting Bob") La Follette was an undersized but overbearing crusader who emerged as the most militant of the progressive Republican leaders. Elected governor in 1901, he waged a desperate fight to win control of Wisconsin from crooked lumber and railroad interests

The suffrage campaign of the early twentieth century benefited from a new generation of women who considered themselves "feminists." At a mass meeting in New York in 1914, Marie Jenny Howe (1870–1934), a minister by training as well as a prominent early feminist, proclaimed,

"We intend simply to be ourselves, not just our little female selves, but our whole big human selves."

■ **Jane Addams and Fellow Pacifists, 1915** Addams co-founded the Women's Peace party in 1915. Its pacifist platform was said to represent the views of the "mother half of humanity." Although the party initially attracted twenty-five thousand members, America's entry into the war two years later eroded popular support, as pacifist internationalism became suspect as anti-American.

and return it to the people. He also perfected a scheme for regulating public utilities while laboring in close association with experts on the faculty of the University of Wisconsin at Madison.

Other states marched steadily toward the progressive camp, as they undertook to regulate railroads and trusts, chiefly through public utilities commissions. Oregon was not far behind Wisconsin, and California made giant boot strides under the stocky Hiram W. Johnson. Elected Republican governor in 1910, this dynamic prosecutor of grafters helped break the dominant grip of the Southern Pacific Railroad on California politics and then, like La Follette, set up a political machine of his own.

Progressive Women

Women proved themselves an indispensable part of the progressive army. A crucial focus for women's activism was the settlement house movement (see p. 381). At a time when women could neither vote nor hold political office, settlement houses offered a side door to public life. They exposed middle-class women to the numerous problems plaguing American cities and gave them the skill and confidence to tackle those evils. The women's club movement also turned from literary self-improvement to engagement with social issues and current events. "Dante has been dead for several centuries," observed the president of the General Federation of Women's Clubs in 1904. "I think it is time that we dropped the study of his *Inferno* and turned our attention to our own."

Nineteenth-century notions of "separate spheres" dictated that a woman's place was in the home, so most female progressives defended their new activities as an extension—not a rejection—of the traditional roles of wife and mother. Thus they were often drawn to moral and "maternal" issues like keeping children out of sweatshops or ensuring that only safe food products found their way to the family table. Female activists agitated through organizations like the Women's Trade

Online Study Center

**Primary source
Election Day!**
college.hmco.com/pic/kennedybrief7e

Union League and the National Consumers League, as well as through two new federal agencies, the Children's Bureau (1912) and the Women's Bureau (1920), both in the Department of Labor.

Campaigns for factory reform and temperance particularly attracted women foot soldiers. Unsafe and unsanitary sweatshops—factories where workers toiled long hours for low wages—were a public scandal in many cities. Florence Kelley, a former resident of Jane Addams's Hull House, became the state of Illinois's first chief factory inspector and one of the leading advocates for improved factory conditions. In 1899 Kelley took control of the newly founded National Consumers League, which mobilized female consumers to pressure for laws safeguarding women and children in the workplace. In the landmark case *Muller* v. *Oregon* (1908), crusading attorney Louis D. Brandeis persuaded the Supreme Court to accept the constitutionality of laws protecting women workers by presenting evidence of the harmful effects of factory labor on women's bodies. Although this argument calling for special protection for women seemed discriminatory by later standards, progressives at the time hailed Brandeis's achievement as a triumph. The American welfare state that emerged from female activism focused more on protecting women and children than on granting benefits to everyone, as was the case in much of western Europe, with its stronger labor overtones.

Crusaders for these humane measures did not always have smooth sailing. One dismaying setback came in 1905, when the Supreme Court in *Lochner* v. *New York* invalidated a New York law establishing a ten-hour day for bakers. Yet the reformist progressive wave finally washed up into the judiciary, and in 1917 the Court upheld a ten-hour law for factory workers.

Laws regulating factories were worthless if not enforced, a truth horribly demonstrated by a lethal fire in 1911 at the Triangle Shirtwaist Company in New York City. Locked doors and other flagrant violations of the fire code turned the factory into a death trap, incinerating one hundred forty-six workers, most of them young immigrant women. Lashed by the public outcry, the legislature of New York and later other legislatures passed much stronger laws regulating the hours and conditions of sweatshop toil. By 1917 thirty states had put **workers' compensation** laws on their books, providing insurance to workers injured in industrial accidents. Gradually, the concept of the employer's responsibility to society was replacing the old dog-eat-dog philosophy of unregulated free enterprise.

Corner saloons naturally attracted the ire and fire of progressives, especially because they were often intimately connected with prostitution and voter corruption. By 1900 cities like New York and San Francisco had one saloon for about every two hundred people. Antiliquor campaigners received powerful support from several militant organizations, notably the Woman's Christian Temperance Union (WCTU). Founder Frances E. Willard, who would fall on her knees in prayer on saloon floors, mobilized nearly 1 million women to "make the world homelike" and built the WCTU into the largest organization of women in the world. She found a vigorous ally in the Anti-Saloon League, which was aggressive, well organized, and well financed.

Caught up in the crusade, some states and counties passed "dry" laws to control, restrict, or abolish alcohol. The big cities were generally "wet," for they had a large immigrant vote accustomed in the Old Country to the free flow of wine and beer. When World War I erupted in 1914, nearly one-half of the population lived in "dry" territory. Demon Rum was groggy and about to be floored—temporarily—by the Eighteenth Amendment in 1919.

TR's Square Deal for Labor

Theodore Roosevelt, although something of an imperialistic busybody abroad, was touched by the progressive wave at home. Like other reformers, he feared that the "public interest" was being submerged in the drifting seas of indifference. Everybody's interest was nobody's interest. Roosevelt decided to make it his. His sportsman's instincts spurred him into demanding a "square deal" for capital, labor, and the public at large. Broadly speaking, his program embraced three C's: control of the corporations, consumer protection, and conservation of natural resources.

Online Study Center

Primary source
Factory System's Influence, The
college.hmco.com/pic/kennedybrief7e

Online Study Center

Primary source
Triangle Shirtwaist Fire Victims
college.hmco.com/pic/kennedybrief7e

workers' (workmen's) compensation
Insurance, provided either by government or employers or both, providing benefits to employees suffering work-related injury or disability.

The Square Deal for labor received its acid test in 1902, when a crippling strike broke out in the anthracite coal mines of Pennsylvania. Some 140,000 besooted workers, many of them illiterate immigrants, had long been frightfully exploited and accident-plagued. They demanded, among other improvements, a 20 percent increase in pay and a reduction of the working day from ten to nine hours.

Unsympathetic mine owners, confident that a chilled public would react against the miners, refused to arbitrate or even negotiate. One of their spokesmen, multimillionaire George F. Baer, wrote that workers would be cared for "not by the labor agitators, but by the Christian men to whom God in his infinite wisdom has given the control of the property interests of this country."

As coal supplies dwindled, factories and schools were forced to shut down, and even hospitals felt the icy grip of winter. Profoundly annoyed by "extraordinary stupidity and bad temper" of the "wooden-headed" mine owners, Roosevelt threatened to seize the mines and operate them with federal troops. Faced with this first-time-ever threat to use federal bayonets against capital, rather than labor, the owners grudgingly consented to arbitration. A compromise decision ultimately gave the miners a 10 percent pay boost and a working day of nine hours. But their union was not officially recognized as a bargaining agent.

Keenly aware of the mounting antagonisms between capital and labor, Roosevelt urged Congress to create a new Department of Commerce and Labor. This goal was achieved in 1903. (Ten years later the agency was split into two.) An important arm of the new cabinet agency was the Bureau of Corporations, which was authorized to probe businesses engaged in interstate commerce. The bureau was highly useful in helping to break the stranglehold of monopoly and in clearing the road for the era of "trustbusting."

TR Corrals the Corporations

The sprawling railroad octopus sorely needed restraint. The Interstate Commerce Commission, created in 1887 as a feeble sop to the public, had proved woefully inadequate. Railroad barons could simply appeal the commission's decisions on rates to the federal courts—a process that might take ten years.

Spurred by the former-cowboy president, Congress passed effective railroad legislation, beginning with the Elkins Act of 1903. This curb was aimed primarily at the rebate evil. Heavy fines could now be imposed both on the railroads that gave rebates and on the shippers that accepted them.

Still more effective was the Hepburn Act of 1906. Free passes, with their hint of bribery, were severely restricted. The once-infantile Interstate Commerce Commission was expanded, and its reach was extended to include express companies, sleeping-car companies, and pipelines. For the first time, the commission was given real molars when it was authorized to nullify existing shipping rates and stipulate maximum rates.

Railroads also provided Roosevelt with an opportunity to brandish his antitrust bludgeon. *Trusts* had come to be a fighting word in the progressive era. TR was determined to respond to the public outcry against the trusts by curbing but not eliminating them. He believed that there were "good" trusts with public consciences and "bad" trusts greedy for power, and that the goal was not to throw out the baby with the bathwater.

Roosevelt, as a trustbuster, first burst into the headlines in 1902 with an attack on the Northern Securities Company, a railroad holding company organized by financial titan J. P. Morgan and empire builder James J. Hill. These Napoleonic moguls of money sought to achieve a virtual monopoly of the railroads in the Northwest. Roosevelt was therefore challenging the most regal potentates of the industrial aristocracy.

The railway promoters appealed to the Supreme Court, which in 1904 upheld Roosevelt's antitrust suit and ordered the Northern Securities Company to be dissolved. The *Northern Securities* decision jolted Wall Street and angered big business but greatly enhanced Roosevelt's reputation as a trust smasher. Roosevelt's big stick crashed down on other giant monopolies, as he initiated over forty legal proceedings against the beef, sugar, fertilizer, harvester, and other monopolies.

EXAMINING THE EVIDENCE

***Muller v. Oregon,* 1908** Court records provide notably fruitful sources for historians. They not only tell often-colorful stories about the lives of ordinary men and women caught up in the legal system; they also by their very nature testify to the norms and values that lawyers employ to make their cases and that judges invoke to explain their decisions. The case of *Muller* v. *Oregon* (see p. 447) is especially instructive on both counts. The official Supreme Court records tell how on September 4, 1905, Joe Haselbock, a supervisor in Curt Muller's Grand Laundry in Portland, Oregon, asked an employee, Mrs. E. Gotcher, to remain after hours to do an extra load of laundry. That request violated Oregon's law prohibiting women from working more than ten hours per day. Mrs. Gotcher later complained to the authorities, and Muller was fined $10.

Muller refused to pay and took his case all the way to the U.S. Supreme Court. In its landmark decision (below), the Court upheld the constitutionality of the Oregon statute, and Muller at last had to cough up his fine.

1. On what grounds did the Court justify its ruling?

2. What does Justice David J. Brewer's argument on behalf of the Court's decision suggest about the cultural identity and social role of women in early-twentieth-century American society?

3. Was Brewer's ruling really a "progressive" one? Why might progressives in the early twentieth century have regarded *Muller* as a great step forward, while Americans of the early twenty-first century might not?

(208 U.S. 412) CURT MULLER, Plff. in Err., v. STATE OF OREGON.

. . . That woman's physical structure and the performance of material functions place her at a disadvantage in the struggle for subsistence is obvious. This is especially true when the burdens of motherhood are upon her. . . . and as healthy mothers are essential to vigorous offspring, the physical well-being of woman becomes an object of public interest and care in order to preserve the strength and vigor of the race.

Still again, history discloses the fact that woman has always been dependent upon man. He established his control at the outset by superior physical strength, and this control in various forms, with diminishing intensity, has continued to the present. . . . It is still true that in the struggle for subsistence she is not an equal competitor with her brother. . . . Differentiated by these matters from the other sex, she is properly placed in a class by herself, and legislation designed for her protection may be sustained, even when like legislation is not necessary for men, and could not be sustained. It is

impossible to close one's eyes to the fact that she still looks to her brother and depends upon him. . . . The two sexes differ in structure of body, in the functions to be performed by each, in the amount of physical strength, in the capacity for long continued labor, particularly when done standing, the influence of vigorous health upon the future well-being of the race, the self-reliance which enables one to assert full rights, and in the capacity to maintain the struggle for subsistence. This difference justifies a difference in legislation, and upholds that which is designed to compensate for some of the burdens which rest upon her.

We have not referred in this discussion to the denial of the elective franchise in the state of Oregon, for while that may disclose a lack of political equality in all things with her brother, that is not of itself decisive. The reason runs deeper, and rests in the inherent difference between the two sexes, and in the different functions in life which they perform. . . .

Much mythology has inflated Roosevelt's reputation as a trustbuster. The Rough Rider understood the political popularity of monopoly-smashing, but he did not consider it sound economic policy. Combination and integration, he felt, were the hallmarks of the age, and to try to stem the tide of economic progress by political means he considered the rankest folly. Bigness was not necessarily badness, so why punish success? Roosevelt's real purpose in assaulting the Goliaths of industry was to prove conclusively that the government, not private business, ruled the country. He believed in regulating, not fragmenting, the big business combines. The threat of dissolution, he felt, might make the sultans of the smokestacks more amenable to federal regulation—and it did.

In truth, Roosevelt never swung his trust-crushing stick with maximum force. His successor, William Howard Taft, actually "busted" more trusts than TR did. In one celebrated instance in 1907, Roosevelt even gave his personal blessing to

Online Study Center

Primary source
Taft Cartoon
college.hmco.com/pic/kennedybrief7e

Online Study Center

Primary source
Nauseating Job, But It Must Be Done, A
college.hmco.com/pic/kennedybrief7e

Online Study Center

Primary source
Attack on the Meatpackers
college.hmco.com/pic/kennedybrief7e

J. P. Morgan's plan to have United States Steel Corporation absorb the Tennessee Coal and Iron Company, without fear of antitrust reprisals. When Taft then launched a suit against United States Steel in 1911, the political reaction from TR was explosive (see p. 455).

Caring for the Consumer

Roosevelt backed a noteworthy measure in 1906 that benefited both corporations and consumers. Big meatpackers were being shut out of certain European markets because some American meat had been found to be tainted. Foreign governments were threatening to ban all American meat imports.

At the same time, American consumers hungered for safer products. Their appetite for reform was whetted by Upton Sinclair's sensational novel *The Jungle*, published in 1906. Sinclair intended his revolting tract to focus attention on the plight of the workers in the big meat canning factories, but instead he appalled the public with his description of disgustingly unsanitary food products. (As he put it, he aimed for the nation's heart but hit its stomach.) The book described in noxious detail the filth, disease, and putrefaction in Chicago's damp, ill-ventilated slaughterhouses. A cynical jingle of the time ran,

> *Mary had a little lamb,*
> *And when she saw it sicken,*
> *She shipped it off to Packingtown,*
> *And now it's labeled chicken.*

Backed by a nauseated public, Roosevelt induced Congress to pass the Meat Inspection Act of 1906. It decreed that the preparation of meat shipped over state lines would be subject to federal inspection from corral to can. The largest packers accepted the act as an opportunity to drive their smaller, fly-by-night competitors out of business. At the same time, they could receive the government's seal of approval on their exports. As a companion to the Meat Inspection Act, the Pure Food and Drug Act of 1906 was designed to prevent the adulteration and mislabeling of foods and pharmaceuticals.

Earth Control

Wasteful Americans, assuming that their natural resources were inexhaustible, had looted and polluted their incomparable domain with unparalleled speed and greed. Western ranchers and timber men were especially eager to accelerate the destructive process, for they panted to build up the country, and the environmental consequences be hanged. But even before the end of the nineteenth century, far-visioned leaders saw that such a squandering of the nation's birthright would have to be halted or America would sink from resource richness to despoiled dearth.

A first serious step toward conservation was the Forest Reserve Act of 1891, authorizing the president to set aside public forest land as national forests and other reserves. Under this statute some 46 million acres of magnificent trees were rescued from the lumberman's saw in the 1890s and preserved for posterity.

A new day in the history of conservation dawned with the advent of Roosevelt (see "Makers of America: The Environmentalists," p. 452). Huntsman, naturalist, rancher, lover of the great outdoors, he was appalled by the pillaging of timber and mineral resources. Other dedicated conservationists, notably Gifford Pinchot, head of the federal Division of Forestry, had broken important ground before him. But Roosevelt seized the banner of

In his annual message to Congress in 1907, Roosevelt declared prophetically,

"We are prone to speak of the resources of this country as inexhaustible; this is not so. The mineral wealth of the country, the coal, iron, oil, gas, and the like, does not reproduce itself, and therefore is certain to be exhausted ultimately; and wastefulness in dealing with it to-day means that our descendants will feel the exhaustion a generation or two before they otherwise would."

leadership and charged into the fray with all the weight of his prestige, his energy, his firsthand knowledge, and his slashing invective.

Congress responded to the whip of the Rough Rider by passing the Newlands Act of 1902. This landmark legislation authorized Washington to use funds from the sale of public lands in the sun-baked western states for irrigation projects. Settlers repaid the cost of **reclamation** from their now-productive soil, and the money was put into a revolving fund to finance more such enterprises.

Roosevelt pined to preserve the nation's shrinking forests. By 1900 only about a quarter of the once-vast virgin timberlands remained standing. Lumbermen had already logged off most of the first-growth timber from Maine to Michigan, and the sharp thud of their axes was beginning to split the silence in the great fir forests of the Pacific slope. Roosevelt proceeded to set aside in federal reserves some 125 million acres, or almost three times the acreage thus saved from the saw by his three predecessors. He similarly earmarked millions of acres of coal deposits, as well as water resources useful for irrigation and power.

Conservation may have been Roosevelt's most enduring tangible achievement. He was buoyed in this effort by an upwelling national mood of concern about the disappearance of the frontier. An increasingly citified people worried that too much civilization might not be good for the national soul. City dwellers snapped up Jack London's *Call of the Wild* (1903) and other books about nature, and urban youngsters made the outdoor-oriented Boy Scouts of America the country's largest youth organization. The Sierra Club, founded in 1892, dedicated themselves to preserving the wildness of the western landscape.

The preservationists lost a major battle in 1913 when the federal government allowed the city of San Francisco to build a dam for its municipal water supply in the spectacular, high-walled Hetch Hetchy Valley in Yosemite National Park. The Hetch Hetchy controversy laid bare a deep division among conservationists that persists to this day. To the preservationists of the Sierra Club, including famed naturalist John Muir, Hetch Hetchy was a "temple" of nature that should be held inviolable by the civilizing hand of humanity. But other conservationists, including President Roosevelt and his chief forester, Gifford Pinchot, wanted to use the nation's natural endowment intelligently rather than lock it away as wilderness. They sought to combine recreation, sustained-yield logging, watershed protection, and summer stock grazing on the same expanse of federal land.

At first many westerners resisted the federal management of natural resources, but they soon learned how to take advantage of new agencies like the Forest Service and especially the Bureau of Reclamation. The largest ranches and timber companies in particular figured out how to work hand in glove with federal conservation programs devoted to the rational, large-scale, and long-term use of natural resources. The one-man-and-a-mule logger or the one-man-and-a-dog sheepherder had little clout in the new resources **bureaucracy** . Single-person enterprises were shouldered aside, in the interest of efficiency, by the combined bulk of big business and big government.

The Rough Rider's Second Term

Roosevelt was handily elected president in his own right in 1904 and entered his new term buoyed by his enormous personal popularity. Yet the conservative Republican bosses grew increasingly restive as Roosevelt in his second term called ever more loudly for regulating the corporations, taxing incomes, and protecting workers. Roosevelt, meanwhile, had partly defanged himself after his election in 1904 by announcing that under no circumstances would he be a candidate for a third term.

Roosevelt suffered a sharp setback in 1907, when a short but punishing panic descended on Wall Street. The financial flurry

reclamation *The process of bringing or restoring wasteland to productive use.*

bureaucracy (bureaucrat) *The management of government or business through organized departments and subdivisions manned by a system of officials (bureaucrats) following defined rules and processes. (The term is often, though not necessarily, disparaging.)*

Online Study Center

Primary source
John Muir on the Dominion of Nature
college.hmco.com/pic/kennedybrief7e

■ **High Point for Conservation** Conservationist Roosevelt and famed naturalist-conservationist John Muir visit Glacier Point, on the rim of Yosemite Valley, California. In the distance is Yosemite Falls; a few feet behind Roosevelt is a sheer drop of 3,254 feet (992 meters).

The Environmentalists

Humans have long been awed by nature, but they have also yearned to be its masters. The earliest European colonists saw North America as a "howling wilderness" and toiled mightily with ax and plow to tame it. By the mid-nineteenth century, Americans commanded powerful new technologies that promised unbridled dominion over the natural world. Only then did voices begin to be heard in defense of the wounded earth—the first faint stirrings of what would come to be called "environmentalism."

In a pattern that would often be repeated, nature's earliest defenders tended to be well-off townsfolk and city dwellers like Henry David Thoreau and Ralph Waldo Emerson. The Americans most likely to appreciate the value of pristine wilderness, it seemed, were those who had ceased to struggle against it. For the loggers, miners, and farmers who continued to sweat their living out of nature's grudging embrace, concern for environmental niceties often seemed like the sanctimonious piety of a privileged elite.

By the dawn of the twentieth century, many genteel, urban Americans had come to romanticize their pioneer forebears. Preservationists like John Muir waxed lyrical about the mystic allure of unspoiled nature. Seizing the popular mood, Theodore Roosevelt deliberately constructed an image of himself as a manly outdoorsman, and as president he greatly expanded the system of national forests. Roosevelt also pioneered the progressive conservation movement, which believed that nature must be neither uncritically reverenced nor wastefully exploited. Thus the same TR who admired the wonders of Yosemite Valley in the company of John Muir also promoted the "rational use" philosophy that justified the systematic harvesting of millions of trees and the drowning of vast river valleys behind massive dams. This attitude toward nature triumphed in the New Deal era of the 1930s, when the federal government initiated colossal projects that undertook nothing less than reengineering the face of the continent—including the Tennessee Valley Authority, the Soil Conservation Service, and the Shelterbelt tree-planting on the Great Plains.

The rise of ecological science in the post–World War II era fundamentally changed the debate about the relation of nature to civilization. Ecologists charged that the apparent "rationality" of the earlier conservationists dangerously neglected the stunningly complex interrelationships that linked together seemingly unrelated organisms—and to the perils of tampering even slightly with the delicate biological fabrics that nature had taken millennia to weave. Rachel Carson helped to popularize this new outlook in her sensational 1962 exposé, *Silent Spring,* about the far-reaching effects of pesticides on birds, plants, and animals—including humans.

The advent of ecological studies coincided with a revival of preservationist sentiment, especially in the suburbs, where Americans increasingly dwelled. Membership in environmental organizations such as the Sierra Club and the Audubon Society soared, as a generation infatuated with nature demanded a clean and green world. The first celebration of Earth Day on April 22, 1970, marked the maturation of modern-day environmentalism, which wedded scientific analysis with respect for nature's majesty. That same year saw the creation of the federal Environmental Protection Agency (EPA), soon to be followed by the Endangered Species Act and other legislation designed to regulate the relationship between humans and nature.

At the outset of the twenty-first century, developments like global warming served dramatic notice that planet earth was an ecological system that did not recognize national boundaries. Yet while Americans took pride in the efforts they had made to clean up their own turf, who were they, having long since consumed their timberlands and tamed their free-flowing waters, to tell the Brazilians that they should not cut down their Amazon forest or the Chinese that they should not dam their rivers? For the peoples of the developing world, struggling to match America's standard of living, environmentalists often seemed like spoiled spoilers, preaching the same privileged pieties that had infuriated generations of working Americans.

■ Sunrise, Yosemite Valley, by Albert Bierstadt, c. 1870 A German-born artist, Bierstadt romanticized the already awesome beauty of the American West.

featured frightened "runs" on banks, suicides, and criminal indictments against speculators. The financial world hastened to blame Roosevelt for the storm. It cried that this "quack" had unsettled industry with his boat-rocking tactics and branded the current distress the "Roosevelt panic." The hot-tempered president angrily lashed back at his critics when he accused "certain malefactors of great wealth" of having deliberately engineered the crisis to force the government to relax its assaults on trusts.

Still warmly popular in 1908, Roosevelt could easily have won a second presidential nomination and almost certainly the election. But he felt bound by his impulsive postelection promise after his victory in 1904. The departing president thus naturally sought a successor who would carry out "my policies." The man of his choice was amiable and ample-girthed, William Howard Taft, secretary of war and a mild progressive.

As heir apparent, Taft had often been called upon in Roosevelt's absence to "sit on the lid"—all 350 pounds of him. At the Republican convention of 1908 in Chicago, Roosevelt used his control of the party machinery—the "steamroller"—to push through Taft's nomination on the first ballot. Three weeks later, in mile-high Denver, in the heart of silver country, the Democrats nominated twice-beaten William Jennings Bryan.

The dull campaign of 1908 featured the rotund Taft and the now-balding "Boy Orator" both trying to claim the progressive Roosevelt mantle. The solid Judge Taft read cut-and-dried speeches, while Bryan griped that Roosevelt had stolen his policies from the Bryanite camp. A majority of voters chose stability with Roosevelt-endorsed Taft, who polled 321 electoral votes to 162 for Bryan. The victor's popular count was 7,675,320 to 6,412,294. The election's only surprise came from the Socialists, who amassed 420,793 votes for Eugene V. Debs, the hero of the Pullman strike of 1894 (see pp. 411–412).

Roosevelt, ever in the limelight, left soon after the election for a lion hunt in Africa. His numerous enemies clinked glasses while toasting "Health to the lions," and a few irreverently prayed that some big cat would "do its duty." But TR survived, still bursting with energy at the age of fifty-one in 1909.

Roosevelt was branded by his adversaries as a wild-eyed radical, but his reputation as an eater of errant industrialists now seems inflated. He fought many a sham battle, and the number of laws that he inspired was certainly not in proportion to the amount of noise he emitted. He was often under attack from the reigning business lords, but the more enlightened of them knew that they had a friend in the White House. Roosevelt should be remembered first and foremost as the

cowboy who started to tame the bucking bronco of adolescent capitalism, thus ensuring it a long adult life.

TR's enthusiasm and perpetual youthfulness, like an overgrown Boy Scout's, appealed to the young of all ages. "You must always remember," a British diplomat cautioned his colleagues, "that the president is about six." He served as a political lightning rod to protect capitalists against popular indignation—and against socialism, which Roosevelt regarded as "ominous." He strenuously sought the middle road between unbridled individualism and paternalistic **collectivism**. His conservation crusade, which tried to mediate between the romantic wilderness-preservationists and the rapacious resource-predators, was probably his most typical and his most lasting achievement.

Several other contributions of Roosevelt lasted beyond his presidency. First, he greatly enlarged the power and prestige of the presidential office—and masterfully developed the technique of using the big stick of publicity as a political bludgeon. Second, he helped shape the progressive movement and beyond it the liberal reform campaigns later in the century. His Square Deal, in a sense, was the grandfather of the New Deal later launched by his fifth cousin, Franklin D. Roosevelt. Finally, to a greater degree than any of his predecessors, TR opened the eyes of Americans to the fact that they shared the world with other nations. As a great power, they had fallen heir to great responsibilities—and had been seized by great ambitions—from which there was no escaping.

■ **Baby, Kiss Papa Good-bye** Theodore Roosevelt leaves his baby, "My Policies," in the hands of his chosen successor, William Howard Taft. Friction between Taft and Roosevelt would soon erupt, however, prompting Roosevelt to return to politics and challenge Taft for the presidency.

---

collectivism *A political or social system in which individuals are subordinated to mass organization and direction.*

> *Roosevelt, who preached the doctrine of the "strenuous life," practiced it until almost the end. In 1913 he sent a political message on a still-preserved phonograph recording to the Boys' Progressive League:*
>
> *"Don't flinch, don't foul, and hit the line hard."*

Taft: A Round Peg in a Square Hole

William Howard Taft, with his ruddy complexion and upturned mustache, at first inspired widespread confidence. "Everybody loves a fat man," the saying goes, and the jovial Taft, with "mirthquakes" of laughter bubbling up from his abundant abdomen, was personally popular. He had graduated second in his class at Yale and established an admirable reputation as a lawyer and judge, though he was widely regarded as hostile to labor unions. He had served as a trusted administrator and troubleshooter under Roosevelt—in the Philippines, at home, and in Cuba.

But "good old Will" suffered from lethal political handicaps. Roosevelt had led the conflicting elements of the Republican party by the sheer force of his personality. Taft, in contrast, had none of the arts of a dashing political leader and none of Roosevelt's zest for the fray. Recoiling from the clamor of controversy, he generally adopted an attitude of passivity toward Congress. He was a poor judge of public opinion, and his candor made him a chronic victim of "foot-in-mouth" disease.

"Peaceful Bill" was no doubt a mild progressive, but at heart he was more wedded to the status quo than to change. Significantly, his cabinet did not contain a single representative of the party's "insurgent" wing, which was on fire for reform of current abuses, especially the tariff.

The Dollar Goes Abroad as a Diplomat

Though ordinarily lethargic, Taft bestirred himself to use the lever of American investments to boost American political interests abroad. Washington warmly encouraged Wall Street bankers to sluice their surplus dollars into foreign areas of strategic concern to the United States. New York bankers would thus strengthen American defenses and foreign policies while bringing further prosperity to their homeland—and to themselves. The almighty dollar thereby supplanted the big stick.

China's Manchuria was the object of Taft's most spectacular effort to practice "dollar diplomacy." Newly ambitious Japan and imperialistic Russia, recent foes, controlled the railroads of this strategic province. President Taft saw in the Manchurian railway monopoly a possible slamming of the Open Door in the faces of U.S. merchants. But Secretary of State Philander Knox's attempt in 1909 to persuade U.S. investors to buy the Manchurian railroads and then turn them over to China ran into blunt Japanese and Russian opposition. Taft was showered with ridicule.

Another dangerous new trouble spot was the revolution-riddled Caribbean—now virtually a Yankee lake. Hoping to head off trouble, Washington urged Wall Street bankers to pump dollars into the financial vacuums in Honduras and Haiti. Again necessity was the mother of armed Caribbean intervention. Sporadic disorders in palm-fronded Cuba, Honduras, and the Dominican Republic brought American forces to these countries to restore order and protect American investments. A revolutionary upheaval in Nicaragua, partly fomented by American interests, resulted in the landing of twenty-five hundred marines in 1912. The marines remained in Nicaragua for thirteen years (see the map on p. 463).

Taft the Trustbuster

Taft managed to gain some fame as a smasher of monopolies. The ironic truth is that the colorless Taft brought 90 suits against the trusts during his four years in office, compared with some 44 for Roosevelt in $7\frac{1}{2}$ years.

By fateful happenstance the most sensational judicial actions during the Taft regime came in 1911. In that year the Supreme Court ordered dissolution of the mighty Standard Oil Company, which was judged to be a combination in restraint of trade in violation of the Sherman Anti-Trust Act of 1890. At the same time the Court handed down its famous "rule of reason." This doctrine held that only those combinations that "unreasonably" restrained trade were illegal. This fine-point proviso ripped a huge hole in the government's antitrust net.

Even more explosively, in 1911 Taft decided to press an antitrust suit against the U.S. Steel Corporation. This initiative infuriated Roosevelt, who had personally been involved in one of the mergers that prompted the suit. Once Roosevelt's protégé, President Taft was increasingly taking on the role of his antagonist. The stage was being set for a bruising confrontation.

Taft Splits the Republican Party

Lowering the barriers of the formidable protective tariff—the "Mother of Trusts"—was high on the agenda of the progressive members of the Republican party, and they at first thought they had a friend and ally in Taft. When the president called Congress into special session in March 1909, the House passed a moderately reductive bill. But senatorial reactionaries, led by Senator Nelson Aldrich of Rhode Island, tacked on hundreds of upward tariff revisions. Only such items as hides, sea moss, and canary seed were left on the duty-free list.

After much hand-wringing, Taft signed the Payne-Aldrich Bill, thus betraying his campaign promises and outraging the progressive wing of his party, heavily drawn from the Midwest. Taft rubbed salt in the wound by proclaiming it "the best bill that the Republican party ever passed."

Taft revealed a further knack for shooting himself in the foot in his handling of conservation. The portly president was a dedicated conservationist, and his contributions actually equaled or surpassed those of Roosevelt. He established the

Bureau of Mines to control mineral resources, rescued millions of acres of western coal lands from exploitation, and protected water-power sites from private development. But those praiseworthy accomplishments were largely erased in the public mind by the noisy Ballinger-Pinchot quarrel that erupted in 1910.

When Secretary of the Interior Richard Ballinger opened public lands in Wyoming, Montana, and Alaska to corporate development, he was sharply criticized by Gifford Pinchot, chief of the Agriculture Department's Division of Forestry and a stalwart Rooseveltian. When Taft dismissed Pinchot on the narrow grounds of **insubordination**, a storm of protest arose from conservationists and from Roosevelt's friends, who were legion. The whole unsavory episode further widened the growing rift between the president and the former president, onetime bosom political partners.

The reformist wing of the Republican party was now up in arms, as Taft was increasingly drawn into the embrace of the stand-pat Old Guard. By the spring of 1910, the Grand Old Party was split wide open, owing largely to the clumsiness of Taft. A suspicious Roosevelt returned triumphantly to New York in June 1910 and shortly thereafter stirred up a tempest. In a flaming speech at Osawatamie, Kansas, he proclaimed a doctrine—popularly known as the "New Nationalism"—that urged the national government to increase its power to remedy economic and social abuses.

Weakened by these internal divisions, the Republicans lost badly in the congressional elections of 1910. The Democrats emerged from their landslide victory with 228 seats to only 161 for the once-dominant Republicans. In a further symptom of the reforming temper of the times, a Socialist representative, Austrian-born Victor L. Berger, was elected from Milwaukee. (Berger was eventually denied his seat in 1919, during a wave of anti-red hysteria.) The Republicans, by virtue of holdovers, retained the Senate, 51 to 41, but the insurgents in their midst were numerous enough to make that hold precarious.

The Taft-Roosevelt Rupture

The sputtering uprising in Republican ranks had now blossomed into a full-fledged revolt. Early in 1911 the National Progressive Republican League was formed, with the fiery, white-maned Senator Robert La Follette of Wisconsin its leading candidate for the Republican presidential nomination. The assumption was that Roosevelt, an anti–third-termer, would not permit himself to be "drafted."

But the restless Rough Rider began to change his views about third terms as he saw Taft, hand in glove with the hated Old Guard, discard "my policies." In February 1912 Roosevelt formally wrote to seven state governors that he was willing to accept the Republican nomination. His reasoning was that the third-term tradition applied to three *consecutive elective* terms. Exuberantly he cried, "My hat is in the ring!" and "The fight is on and I am stripped to the buff!"

Roosevelt forthwith seized the Progressive banner, while La Follette, who had served as a convenient pathbreaker, was protestingly elbowed aside. Girded for battle, the Rough Rider came clattering into the presidential primaries then being held in many states. He shouted through half-clenched teeth that the president had fallen under the thumb of the reactionary bosses and that although Taft "means well, he means well feebly." The once-genial Taft, now in a fighting mood, branded Roosevelt supporters "emotionalists and neurotics."

A Taft-Roosevelt explosion was near in June 1912, when the Republican convention met in Chicago. The Rooseveltites, who were about 100 delegates short of winning the nomination, challenged the right of some 250 Taft delegates to be seated. Most of these contests were arbitrarily settled in favor of Taft, whose supporters held the throttle of the convention steamroller. The Roosevelt adherents, crying "fraud" and "naked theft," in the end refused to vote, and Taft triumphed.

Roosevelt, the supposedly good sportsman, refused to quit the game. Having tasted for the first time the bitter cup of defeat, he was now on fire to lead a third-party crusade.

insubordination *Deliberate disobedience of proper authority.*

★ Chapter Summary ★

The progressive movement of the early twentieth century became the greatest American reform crusade since abolitionism. Inaugurated by Populists, socialists, social gospelers, female reformers, and muckraking journalists, progressivism became a widely popular effort to strengthen government's power to correct the many social and economic problems associated with industrialization and urbanization.

Progressivism began at the city and state level, where it initially focused "good government" political reforms to corral corrupt bosses. It also turned to correcting a host of social and economic evils that seemed to require national action by the federal government. Women played an especially critical role in galvanizing progressive social concern. Seeing involvement in such issues as reforming child labor, poor tenement housing, and consumer causes as a natural extension of their traditional roles as wives and mothers, female activists brought significant changes in both law and public attitudes in these areas.

At the national level, Roosevelt's Square Deal vigorously deployed the federal government to promote the public interest and mediate conflicts between labor interests on one hand and the corporate trusts on the other. Rooseveltian progressivism also inspired attention to consumer and environmental concerns. Conservation became an important public crusade under Roosevelt, although sharp disagreements divided wilderness "preservationists" from moderate conservationists like Roosevelt who favored the "multiple use" of nature.

Roosevelt personally selected his longtime subordinate Taft as his political successor, expecting him to carry out "my policies." But Taft proved to be a poor politician who fell under the thumb of the conservative Republican Old Guard and rapidly lost public support. The progressives' hostility to Taft split the Republican party, and when Roosevelt failed to win the nomination he launched a fiery third-party crusade in the 1912 election.

Online Study Center

Primary source
Tenement Question, The—Inside and Out
college.hmco.com/pic/kennedybrief7e

Online Study Center

Primary source
Yard of Tenement
college.hmco.com/pic/kennedybrief7e

29

Wilsonian Progressivism at Home and Abroad

1912–1916

AMERICAN ENTERPRISE IS NOT FREE; THE MAN WITH ONLY A
LITTLE CAPITAL IS FINDING IT HARDER AND HARDER TO GET INTO
THE FIELD, MORE AND MORE IMPOSSIBLE TO COMPETE WITH THE
BIG FELLOW. WHY? BECAUSE THE LAWS OF THIS COUNTRY DO
NOT PREVENT THE STRONG FROM CRUSHING THE WEAK.

WOODROW WILSON, THE NEW FREEDOM, 1913

Office-hungry Democrats—the "outs" since 1897—were jubilant over the disruptive Republican brawl at Chicago. If they could come up with an outstanding reformist leader, they had an excellent chance to win the White House. Such a leader appeared in Dr. Woodrow Wilson, once a mild conservative but now a militant progressive. Beginning professional life as a brilliant academic scholar of government, Wilson had risen in 1902 to the presidency of Princeton University, where he achieved some sweeping educational reforms.

Wilson entered politics in 1910 when New Jersey bosses, needing a respectable "front" candidate for the governorship, offered him the nomination. They expected to lead the academic novice by the nose, but to their surprise, Wilson waged a passionate reform campaign in which he assailed the "predatory" trusts and promised to return state government to the people. Riding the crest of the progressive wave, the "Schoolmaster in Politics" was swept into office.

Once in the governor's chair, Wilson drove through the legislature a sheaf of forward-looking measures that made reactionary New Jersey one of the more liberal states. Filled with righteous indignation, Wilson revealed irresistible reforming zeal, burning eloquence, superb powers of leadership, and a refreshing habit of appealing over the heads of the scheming bosses to the sovereign people. Now a figure of national eminence, Wilson was being widely mentioned for the presidency.

Focus Questions

1. What made the election of 1912, more than most American elections, a debate on fundamental political philosophies rather than a disagreement about particular issues or policies?
2. How did Wilsonian progressivism successfully assault the "triple wall of privilege"?
3. What were the fundamental features of Wilson's highly moralistic foreign policy, and how did he apply those principles in Latin America?
4. What was America's response to the outbreak of World War I, and why did Wilson's initial attempts at neutrality and mediation turn into an increasingly critical stance toward Germany?
5. What were the basic issues in the election of 1916, and why did Hughes's attempt to straddle isolationist and anti-German sentiment fail?

Chronology

1912	Wilson defeats Taft and Roosevelt for presidency.
1913	Underwood Tariff Act.
	Sixteenth Amendment (income tax).
	Federal Reserve Act.
	Huerta takes power in Mexico.
	Seventeenth Amendment (direct election of senators).
1914	Clayton Anti-Trust Act.
	Federal Trade Commission established.
	U.S. occupation of Vera Cruz, Mexico.
	World War I begins in Europe.
1915	La Follette Seamen's Act.
1915	*Lusitania* torpedoed and sunk by German U-boat.
	U.S. Marines sent to Haiti.
1916	*Sussex* ultimatum and pledge.
	Workingmen's Compensation Act.
	Federal Farm Loan Act.
	Adamson Act.
	Jones Act.
	Pancho Villa raids New Mexico.
	Brandeis appointed to Supreme Court.
	U.S. Marines sent to Dominican Republic.
	Wilson defeats Hughes for presidency.
1917	United States buys Virgin Islands from Denmark.

The "Bull Moose" Campaign of 1912

When the Democrats met at Baltimore in 1912, Wilson was nominated on the forty-sixth ballot, aided by William Jennings Bryan's switch to his side. The Democrats gave Wilson a strong progressive platform to run on; dubbed the "New Freedom" program, it included calls for antitrust legislation, banking reform, and tariff reductions.

Surging events had meanwhile been thrusting Roosevelt to the fore as a candidate for the presidency on a third-party Progressive Republican ticket. The fighting ex-cowboy, angered by his recent rebuff, was eager to lead the charge. A pro-Roosevelt Progressive convention, with about two thousand delegates from forty states, assembled in Chicago in August 1912. Dramatically symbolizing the rising political status of women, as well as Progressive support for the cause of social justice, settlement-house pioneer Jane Addams placed Roosevelt's name in nomination for the presidency. The audience wildly cheered Roosevelt as he fervently cried, "We stand at Armageddon, and we battle for the Lord!" A religious revival atmosphere suffused the convention, as the hoarse delegates sang, "Onward Christian Soldiers" and the "Battle Hymn of the Republic."

Fired-up Progressives entered the campaign with righteousness and enthusiasm. Roosevelt boasted that he felt "as strong as a bull moose," so the bull moose took its place with the donkey and the elephant in the American political zoo. As one poet whimsically put it,

> *I want to be a Bull Moose,*
> *And with the Bull Moose stand*
> *With antlers on my forehead*
> *And a Big Stick in my hand.*

Roosevelt and Taft were bound to slit each other's political throats; by dividing the Republican vote they virtually guaranteed a Democratic victory. The two antagonists tore into each other as only former friends can. "Death alone can take me out now!" cried the once-jovial Taft, as he branded Roosevelt a "dangerous egotist" and a "demagogue." Roosevelt, fighting mad, assailed Taft as a "fathead" with "the brain of a guinea pig."

Beyond the clashing personalities, the overshadowing question of the 1912 campaign was which of two varieties of progressivism would prevail—Roosevelt's New Nationalism or Wilson's New Freedom. Both men favored a

■ GOP Divided by Bull Moose Equals Democratic Victory, 1912

more active government role in economic and social affairs, but they disagreed sharply over specific strategies. Roosevelt preached the theories spun out by the progressive thinker Herbert Croly in his book *The Promise of American Life* (1910). Croly and TR both favored continued consolidation of trusts and labor unions, paralleled by the growth of powerful regulatory agencies in Washington. Roosevelt and his "bull moosers" also campaigned for woman suffrage and a broad program of social welfare, including minimum-wage laws and social insurance. Clearly, the bull moose Progressives looked forward to the kind of activist welfare state that Franklin Roosevelt's New Deal would one day make a reality.

Wilson's New Freedom, by contrast, favored small enterprise, **entrepreneurship**, and the free functioning of unregulated and unmonopolized markets. The Democrats shunned social welfare proposals and pinned their economic faith on competition—on the "man on the make," as Wilson put it. The keynote of Wilson's campaign was not regulation but fragmentation of the big industrial combines, chiefly by means of vigorous enforcement of the antitrust laws. The election of 1912 thus offered the voters a choice not merely of policies but of political and economic philosophies—a rarity in United States history.

The heat of the campaign cooled a bit when, in Milwaukee, Roosevelt was shot in the chest by a fanatic. The Rough Rider suspended active campaigning for more than two weeks after delivering, with bull moose gameness and a bloody shirt, his scheduled speech.

entrepreneurship *The process whereby an individual initiates a business at some risk in order to expand it and thereby earn a profit.*

Online Study Center

Primary source
President Wilson Is with Us
college.hmco.com/pic/kennedybrief7e

★

Woodrow Wilson: A Minority President

Former professor Wilson won handily, with 435 electoral votes and 6,296,547 popular votes. The "third-party" candidate, Roosevelt, finished second, with 88 electoral votes and 4,118,571 popular votes. Taft won only 8 electoral votes and 3,486,720 popular votes (see the map on p. 468).

The election figures are fascinating. Wilson, with only 41 percent of the popular vote, was clearly a minority president, though his party won a majority in Congress. His popular total was actually smaller than Bryan had amassed in any of his three defeats, despite the increase in population. Taft and Roosevelt together polled over 1.25 million more votes than the Democrats. Progressivism rather than Wilson was the runaway winner. Although the Democratic total obviously included many conservatives in the solid South, the combined progressive vote for Wilson and Roosevelt exceeded the tally of the more conservative Taft. To the progressive tally must be added some support for the Socialist candidate, persistent Eugene V. Debs, who rolled up 900,672 votes, or more than twice as many as he had netted four years earlier. Starry-eyed Socialists dreamed of being in the White House within eight years.

The Presidential Vote, 1912

Candidate Percentage	Party	Electoral Vote	Popular Vote	Approximate
Woodrow Wilson	Democratic	435	6,296,547	41%
Theodore Roosevelt	Progressive	88	4,118,571	27
William H. Taft	Republican	8	3,486,720	23
Eugene V. Debs	Socialist	—	900,672	6
E. W. Chafin	Prohibition	—	206,275	1
A. E. Reimer	Socialist-Labor	—	28,750	0.2

Roosevelt's lone-wolf course was tragic both for himself and for his former Republican associates. The Progressive party, which was primarily a one-man show, had no future because it had elected few candidates to state and local offices; the Socialists, in contrast, elected more than a thousand. Without patronage plums to hand out to faithful party workers, death by slow starvation was inevitable. Yet the Progressives made a tremendous showing for a hastily organized third party and helped spur the enactment of many of their pet reforms by the Wilsonian Democrats.

As for the Republicans, they were thrust into unaccustomed minority status in Congress for the next six years and were frozen out of the White House for eight years. Taft himself had a fruitful old age. He taught law for eight pleasant years at Yale University and in 1921 became chief justice of the Supreme Court—a job for which he was far more happily suited than the presidency.

Wilson: The Idealist in Politics

(Thomas) Woodrow Wilson, the second Democratic president since 1861, looked like the ascetic intellectual he was, with clean-cut features, pinched-on eyeglasses, and trim figure. Born in Virginia shortly before the Civil War and reared in Georgia and the Carolinas, the professor-politician was the first man born and raised in one of the seceded southern states to reach the White House since Zachary Taylor, sixty-four years earlier. Wilson's admiration for the Confederacy's attempt to win independence partly inspired his ideal of self-determination for people of other countries. Steeped in the traditions of Jeffersonian democracy, he shared Jefferson's faith in the masses—if they were properly informed.

Son of a Presbyterian minister, Wilson was reared in an atmosphere of fervent **piety**. He later used the presidential pulpit to preach his inspirational political sermons. A moving orator, Wilson could rise on the wings of spiritual power to soaring eloquence. Skillfully using a persuasive voice, he relied not on arm waving but on sincerity and moral appeal. As a lifelong student of finely chiseled words, he turned out to be a "phraseocrat" who coined many noble epigrams. Someone has remarked that he was born halfway between the Bible and the dictionary and never strayed far from either.

Splendid though Wilson's intellectual equipment was, he suffered from serious defects of personality. Though jovial and witty in private, he could be cold and standoffish in public. Incapable of unbending and acting the showman, like "Teddy" Roosevelt, he lacked the common touch. He loved humanity in the mass rather than the individual in person. His academic background caused him to feel most at home with scholars, although he had to work with politicians. An austere and somewhat arrogant intellectual, he looked down his nose through pince-nez glasses upon lesser minds, including journalists. He was especially intolerant of stupid senators, whose "bungalow" minds made him "sick."

Wilson's burning idealism—especially his desire to reform ever-present wickedness—drove him forward faster than lesser spirits were willing to go. His sense of moral righteousness was such that he often found compromise difficult: black was black, wrong was wrong, and one should never compromise with wrong. Wilson's Scottish Presbyterian ancestors had passed on to him an inflexible stubbornness. When convinced that he was right, Wilson would break before he would bend, unlike the pragmatic Roosevelt.

piety *Devotion to religious duty and practices.*

Wilson Attacks the "Triple Wall of Privilege"

Few presidents have arrived at the White House with a clearer program than Wilson's or one destined to be so completely achieved. The new president called for an all-out assault on what he called the "triple wall of privilege": the tariff, the banks, and the trusts.

He tackled the tariff first. In a precedent-shattering move, he appeared in person before a joint session of Congress in 1913 and presented his appeal with

graduated income tax *A tax on income in which the taxation rates grow progressively higher for those with higher income.*

levy *A forcible tax or other imposition.*

inelasticity *The inability to expand or contract rapidly.*

commercial paper *Any business document having monetary or exchangeable value.*

promissory note *A written pledge to pay a certain person a specified sum of money at a certain time.*

stunning eloquence and effectiveness. Moved by Wilson's aggressive leadership, the House swiftly passed the Underwood Tariff Bill, which provided for a substantial reduction of rates. It was also a landmark in tax legislation. Under authority granted by the recently ratified Sixteenth Amendment, Congress enacted a **graduated income tax**, beginning with a modest **levy** on incomes over $3,000 (then considerably higher than the average family's income). By 1917 revenue from the income tax shot ahead of receipts from the tariff, a gap that has since vastly widened.

A second bastion of the "triple wall of privilege" was the antiquated and inadequate banking and currency system, long since outgrown by the Republic's lusty economic expansion. The most serious shortcoming of the country's financial structure, still creaking along under the Civil War National Banking Act, was the **inelasticity** of the currency. Banking reserves were heavily concentrated in New York and a handful of other large cities, and could not be mobilized in times of financial stress into areas that were badly pinched.

A House committee chaired by Congressman Arsene Pujo had already stirred public concern about the concentration of financial power by tracing the tentacles of the "money monster" into the hidden vaults of American banking and business. President Wilson's confidant, progressive-minded Massachusetts attorney Louis D. Brandeis, further fanned the flames of reform with his incendiary though scholarly book *Other People's Money and How the Bankers Use It.*

In June 1913, in a second dramatic personal appearance before Congress, the president issued a ringing call for a decentralized bank in government hands, as opposed to mossback Republican Senator Nelson Aldrich's demands for a gigantic private bank—in effect, a third Bank of the United States. Again appealing to the sovereign people, Wilson scored another triumph. In 1913 he signed the Federal Reserve Act, the most important piece of economic legislation between the Civil War and the New Deal.

The new Federal Reserve Board, appointed by the president, oversaw a nationwide system of twelve regional reserve banks. These regional banks were owned by member financial institutions, but the final authority of the Federal Reserve Board guaranteed public control. The board was also empowered to issue paper money—"Federal Reserve notes"—backed by **commercial paper**, such as the **promissory notes** of businesspeople. Thus the amount of money in circulation could be swiftly increased as needed for the legitimate requirements of business.

The Federal Reserve Act was a red-letter achievement. It carried the nation with flying banners through the financial crises of the First World War of 1914–1918. Without it, the Republic's progress toward the modern economic age would have been seriously retarded.

Without pausing for breath, Wilson pushed toward the last remaining rampart in the "triple wall of privilege"—the trusts. His third personal appearance before Congress in 1914 led to passage of the Federal Trade Commission Act of 1914. The new law empowered a presidentially appointed commission to turn a searchlight on industries engaged in interstate commerce, such as the meatpackers.

■ **Woodrow Wilson (1856–1924) at Princeton Commencement with Andrew Carnegie, 1906** Before his election to the presidency of the United States in 1912, Wilson (left) served as president of Princeton University (1902–1910) and governor of New Jersey (1910–1912). In all three offices he undertook substantial reforms. Fighting desperately later for the League of Nations, at the cost of his health, Wilson said, "I would rather fail in a cause that I know some day will triumph than to win in a cause that I know some day will fail."

The commissioners were expected to crush monopoly at the source by rooting out unfair trade practices, including unlawful competition, false advertising, mislabeling, adulteration, and bribery.

The knot of monopoly was further cut by the Clayton Anti-Trust Act of 1914. It lengthened the Sherman Act's list of objectionable business practices to include price discrimination and interlocking directorates (whereby the same individuals served as directors of supposedly competing firms). The Clayton Act also conferred long-overdue benefits on workers by exempting labor organizations from antitrust prosecutions under the Sherman Act and explicitly legalizing strikes and peaceful picketing. Union leader Samuel Gompers hailed the act as the **Magna Carta** of labor because it legally lifted human labor out of the category of "a commodity or article of commerce." But the rejoicing was premature, as conservative judges in later years continued to clip the wings of the union movement.

Magna Carta *The "Great Charter" of England, which feudal nobles forced King John to sign in 1215. As the first written guarantee of certain rights, such as trial by a jury of peers, against arbitrary royal power, it served as a model for later claims of Anglo-American liberties.*

Wilsonian Progressivism at High Tide

Energetically scaling the "triple wall of privilege," Woodrow Wilson had treated the nation to a dazzling demonstration of vigorous presidential leadership. He proved nearly irresistible in his first eighteen months in office. For once, a political creed was matched by deed, as the progressive reformers racked up victory after victory.

Standing at the peak of his powers at the head of the progressive forces, Wilson pressed ahead with further reforms. The Federal Farm Loan Act of 1916 made credit available to farmers at low rates of interest—as long demanded by the Populists. The La Follette Seamen's Act of 1915 required decent treatment and a living wage for often-abused sailors on American merchant ships.

Wilson further helped workers with the Workingmen's Compensation Act of 1916, granting assistance to federal civil-service employees during periods of disability. In the same year the president approved an act restricting child labor on products flowing into interstate commerce, though the stand-pat Supreme Court soon invalidated the law. The Adamson Act of 1916 established an eight-hour workday for all employees on trains in interstate commerce, with extra pay for overtime.

Wilson earned the enmity of businesspeople and bigots but endeared himself to progressives when in 1916 he nominated for the Supreme Court the prominent reformer Louis D. Brandeis—the first Jew to be called to the high

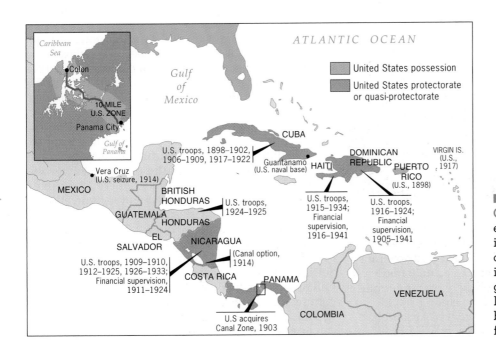

■ **The United States in the Caribbean 1898–1941** This map explains why many Latin Americans accused the United States of turning the Caribbean Sea into a Yankee lake. It also suggests that Uncle Sam was much less "isolationist" in his own backyard than he was in faraway Europe or Asia.

bench. Yet even Wilson's progressivism had its limits, and it clearly stopped short of better treatment for blacks. The southern-bred Wilson actually presided over accelerated segregation in the federal bureaucracy. When a delegation of black leaders personally protested to him, the schoolmasterish president virtually froze them out of his office.

Despite these limitations, Wilson knew that to be reelected in 1916, he needed to identify himself clearly as the candidate of progressivism. Wilson's election in 1912 had been something of a fluke, owing largely to the Taft-Roosevelt split in the Republican ranks. To remain in the White House, the president would have to woo the bull moose voters into the Democratic fold.

New Directions in Foreign Policy

In one important area, Wilson chose not to answer the trumpet call of the bull moosers. In contrast to Roosevelt and even Taft, Wilson recoiled from an aggressive foreign policy. Hating imperialism, he was repelled by TR's big stickism. Suspicious of Wall Street, he detested the so-called dollar diplomacy of Taft.

In office only a week, Wilson declared war on dollar diplomacy. He proclaimed that the government would no longer support American investors in Latin America and China. Shivering from this Wilsonian bucket of cold water, American bankers pulled out of the Taft-engineered six-nation loan to China the next day. Wilson's anti-imperialism also produced the Jones Act of 1916, which granted territorial status to the Philippines and promised independence as soon as a "stable government" could be established.

Events in the Caribbean soon forced Wilson to eat some of his anti-imperialist words. In response to disorders in Haiti in 1914–1915, the president reluctantly dispatched marines to protect American lives and property. In 1916 he stole a page from the Roosevelt Corollary to the Monroe Doctrine as the U.S. took over supervision of Haiti's finances and police. In the same year, Wilson sent the leathernecked marines to quell riots in the Dominican Republic, and that debt-cursed land came under the shadow of the American eagle's wings for the next eight years. In 1917 Wilson purchased from Denmark the Virgin Islands in the West Indies. Increasingly the Caribbean Sea, with its vital approaches to the now-completed Panama Canal, was taking on the earmarks of a Yankee preserve.

Moralistic Diplomacy in Mexico

Rifle bullets whining across the southern border served as a constant reminder that all was not quiet in Mexico. For decades Mexico had been sorely exploited by foreign investors in oil, railroads, and mines. By 1913 American capitalists had sunk about a billion dollars into the underdeveloped but generously endowed country.

But if Mexico was rich, the Mexicans were poor. Fed up with their miserable lot, they at last revolted. Their revolution took an ugly turn in 1913, when a conscienceless clique murdered the popular new revolutionary president and installed General Victoriano Huerta, an Indian, in the president's chair. All this chaos accelerated a massive migration of Mexicans to the United States. More than a million Spanish-speaking newcomers tramped across the southern border in the first three decades of the twentieth century. Settling mostly in Texas, New Mexico, Arizona, and California, they helped to create a unique borderland culture that blended Mexican and American folkways.

The revolutionary bloodshed also menaced American lives and property in Mexico. Cries for intervention

A Republican congressman voiced complaints against Wilson's Mexican policy in 1916:

"It is characterized by weakness, uncertainty, vacillation, and uncontrollable desire to intermeddle in Mexican affairs. He has not had the courage to go into Mexico nor the courage to stay out. . . . I would either go into Mexico and pacify the country or I would keep my hands entirely out of Mexico. If we are too proud to fight, we should be too proud to quarrel. I would not choose between murderers."

burst from the lips of American jingoes like publisher William Randolph Hearst, himself the owner of a Mexican ranch larger than Rhode Island.

But though he refused to intervene, Wilson also refused to recognize officially the murderous government of "that brute" Huerta. "I am going to teach the South American republics to elect good men," the former professor declared. He put his munitions where his mouth was in 1914, when he allowed American arms to flow to Huerta's principal rivals, white-bearded Venustiano Carranza and the firebrand Francisco ("Pancho") Villa.

The Mexican volcano erupted at the Atlantic seaport of Tampico in April 1914, when a small party of American sailors was arrested. The Mexicans promptly released the captives and apologized, but they refused the affronted American admiral's demand for a twenty-one gun salute. Wilson then ordered the navy to seize the Mexican port of Vera Cruz. Huerta as well as Carranza hotly protested against this high-handed Yankee maneuver.

Just as a full-dress shooting conflict seemed inevitable, Wilson was rescued by an offer of mediation from the ABC powers—Argentina, Brazil, and Chile. Huerta collapsed in July 1914 under pressure from within and without. He was succeeded by his archrival, Venustiano Carranza, still fiercely resentful of Wilson's military meddling. The whole sorry episode did not augur well for the future of United States–Mexican relations.

"Pancho" Villa, a combination of bandit and Robin Hood, had meanwhile emerged as the chief rival of President Carranza, whom Wilson now reluctantly supported. Challenging Carranza'a authority while also punishing the gringos, Villa's men ruthlessly killed sixteen American mining engineers in northern Mexico. A month later Villa and his followers, hoping to provoke a war between Wilson and Carranza, blazed across the border into Columbus, New Mexico, and murdered another nineteen Americans.

General John J. ("Black Jack"*) Pershing, a ramrod-erect veteran of the Cuban and Philippine campaigns, was ordered to break up the bandit band. His hastily organized force of several thousand mounted troops penetrated deep into rugged Mexico with surprising speed. They clashed with Carranza's forces and mauled the Villistas but missed capturing Villa himself. As the threat of war with Germany loomed larger, the invading army was withdrawn in January 1917.

A Precarious Neutrality

Europe's powder magazine, long smoldering, blew up in the summer of 1914, when the flaming pistol of a Serb patriot killed the heir to the throne of Austria-Hungary in Sarajevo. An outraged Vienna government, backed by Germany, forthwith presented a stern ultimatum to Serbia.

An explosive chain reaction followed. Russian mobilization in support of Serbia threatened Germany in the east, even as the tsar's ally, France, confronted Germany in the west. In alarm, the Germans struck suddenly at France through unoffending Belgium. Great Britain in turn was sucked into the conflagration on the side of France.

Almost overnight most of Europe was locked in a fight to the death. On one side were arrayed the Central Powers: Germany and Austria-Hungary, and later Turkey and Bulgaria. On the other side were the Allies, principally France, Britain, and Russia, and later Japan and Italy. Americans thanked God for the ocean moats and self-righteously congratulated themselves on having had ancestors wise enough to have abandoned the hell pits of Europe. Americans felt strong, snug, smug, and secure—but not for long.

President Wilson issued the routine neutrality proclamation and called on Americans to be neutral in thought as well as deed. But such scrupulous even-handedness proved difficult. Both sides wooed the United States, the great neutral in the West. The British enjoyed the boon of close cultural, linguistic, and economic ties with America and had the added advantage of controlling most of the

Online Study Center

Primary source
Mobile Address
college.hmco.com/pic/kennedybrief7e

Online Study Center

Interactive map
Europe Goes to War,
Summer 1914
college.hmco.com/pic/kennedybrief7e

---

* So called from his earlier service as an officer with the crack black Tenth Cavalry.

censor *An official who examines publications, mail, literature, and so forth in order to remove or prohibit the distribution of material deemed dangerous or offensive.*

torpedo *To launch from a submarine or airplane a self-propelled underwater explosive designed to detonate on impact.*

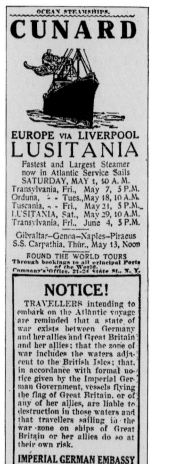

■ Advertisement from the *New York Herald*, May 1, 1915 Six days later the *Lusitania* was sunk. Notice the German warning.

The Fatherland, *the chief German-American propaganda newspaper in the United States, cried,*

"We [Americans] prattle about humanity while we manufacture poisoned shrapnel and picric acid for profit. Ten thousand German widows, ten thousand orphans, ten thousand graves bear the legend 'Made in America.'"

transatlantic cables. Their **censors** sheared away war stories harmful to the Allies and drenched the United States with tales of German bestiality.

Most Americans were anti-German from the outset, although some German Americans expressed noisy sympathy for the fatherland. With his villainous upturned mustache, Kaiser Wilhelm II seemed the embodiment of arrogant autocracy, an impression strengthened by Germany's ruthless strike at neutral Belgium. The discovery in 1915 of German plans for industrial sabotage in the United States further inflamed opinion against the kaiser and Germany. Yet the great majority of Americans earnestly hoped to stay out of the horrible war.

America Earns Blood Money

When Europe burst into flames in 1914, the United States was bogged down in a worrisome business recession. But British and French war orders soon pulled American industry out of the morass of hard times and onto a peak of war-born prosperity. Part of this boom was financed by American bankers, notably the Wall Street firm of J. P. Morgan and Company, which eventually advanced to the Allies the enormous sum of $2.3 billion during the period of American neutrality. The Central Powers protested bitterly against the immense trade between America and the Allies, but this traffic did not in fact violate international neutrality laws. Germany was technically free to trade with the United States, but the tight British naval blockade prevented it from doing so.

Hard-pressed Germany did not tamely consent to being starved out. In retaliation for the British blockade, in February 1915 Berlin announced a submarine war area around the British Isles. The submarine was a weapon so new that existing international law could not be made to fit it. The old rule that a warship must stop and board merchant ships could hardly apply to submarines, which could easily be rammed or sunk if they surfaced.

The cigar-shaped marauders posed a dire threat to the United States—as long as Wilson insisted on maintaining America's neutral rights. Berlin officials declared that they would try not to sink *neutral* shipping, but they warned that mistakes would probably occur. Wilson now determined on a policy of calculated risk. He would continue to claim profitable neutral trading rights while hoping that no high-seas incident would force his hand to grasp the sword of war. He emphatically warned Germany that it would be held to "strict accountability" for any attacks on American vessels or citizens.

The German submarines (known as U-boats, from the German *Unterseeboot,* or "underseas boat") meanwhile began their deadly work. In the first months of 1915, they sank about ninety ships in the war zone. Then the submarine issue became acute when the British passenger liner *Lusitania* was **torpedoed** and sank off the coast of Ireland on May 7, 1915, with the loss of 1,198 lives, including 128 Americans.

The *Lusitania* was carrying forty-two hundred cases of small-arms ammunition, a fact the Germans used to justify the sinking. But Americans were swept by a wave of shock and anger at this act of "mass murder" and "piracy." The eastern United States, closer to the war, seethed with talk of fighting, but the rest of the country showed a strong distaste for hostilities. The peace-loving Wilson had no stomach for leading a disunited nation into war, and relied instead on a series of increasingly strong notes to bring the German warlords sharply to book. "There is such a thing," he said, "as a man being too proud to fight."

Yet Wilson, sticking to his verbal guns, made some diplomatic progress. After another British liner, the *Arabic,* was sunk in August 1915, with the loss of two American lives, Berlin reluctantly agreed not to sink unarmed and unresisting passenger ships *without warning.*

This pledge appeared to be violated in March 1916, when the Germans torpedoed a French passenger steamer, the *Sussex.* The infuriated Wilson informed the

Germans that unless they renounced the inhuman practice of sinking merchant ships without warning he would break diplomatic relations—an almost certain prelude to war.

Germany reluctantly knuckled under to President Wilson's *Sussex* ultimatum, agreeing not to sink passenger ships and merchant vessels without giving warning. But the Germans attached a long string to their *Sussex* pledge: the United States would have to persuade the Allies to modify what Berlin regarded as their illegal blockade. This, obviously, was something that Washington could not do. Wilson promptly accepted the German pledge, without accepting the "string." He thus won a temporary but precarious diplomatic victory—precarious because Germany could pull the string whenever it chose, and the president might suddenly find himself tugged over the cliff of war.

Wilson Wins Reelection in 1916

Against this ominous backdrop, the presidential campaign of 1916 gathered speed. Both the bull moose Progressives and the Republicans met in Chicago. The Progressives uproariously renominated Theodore Roosevelt, but the Rough Rider, who loathed Wilson and all his works, had no stomach for splitting the Republicans again and ensuring the reelection of his hated rival. In refusing to run, he sounded the death knell of the Progressive party.

Roosevelt's Republican admirers also clamored for "Teddy," but the Old Guard detested the renegade who had ruptured the party in 1912. Instead, they **drafted** Supreme Court Justice Charles Evans Hughes, the cold, intellectual former governor of New York. The Republican platform condemned the Democratic tariff, assaults on the trusts, and Wilson's wishy-washiness in dealing with Mexico and Germany.

The thick-whiskered Hughes ("an animated feather duster") left the bench for the campaign stump, where he was not at home. In anti-German areas of the country, he assailed Wilson for not standing up to the kaiser, whereas in isolationist areas he took a softer line. This fence-straddling operation led to the jeer, "Charles Evasive Hughes."

Hughes was further plagued by Roosevelt, who was delivering a series of skin-'em-alive speeches against "that damned Presbyterian hypocrite Wilson." Frothing for war, TR privately sneered at Hughes as a "whiskered Wilson." The only difference between the two, he said, was "a shave."

Wilson, nominated by acclamation at the Democratic convention in St. Louis, ignored Hughes on the theory that one should not try to murder a man who is committing suicide. His campaign was built on the slogan "He Kept Us Out of War." Democratic orators warned that by electing Charles Evans Hughes, the nation would be electing a fight—with a certain frustrated Rough Rider leading the charge. A Democratic advertisement appealing to American workers read,

> *You are Working;*
> *—Not Fighting!*
> *Alive and Happy;*
> *—Not Cannon Fodder!*
> *Wilson and Peace with Honor?*
> *or*
> *Hughes with Roosevelt and War?*

On election day, Hughes swept the East and looked like a surefire winner. Wilson went to bed that night prepared to accept defeat, while New York newspapers displayed huge portraits of "The President-Elect—Charles Evans Hughes." But the rest of the country turned the tide. Midwesterners and westerners, attracted by Wilson's progressive reforms and antiwar policies, flocked to the polls for the president. The final result, in doubt

draft *In politics, to choose an individual to run for office without that person's prior solicitation or approval of the nomination. (A military draft, or conscription, legally compels individuals into the armed services.)*

During the 1916 campaign, J. A. O'Leary, the head of a pro-German and pro-Irish organization, sent a scorching telegram to Wilson condemning him for having been pro-British in approving war loans and ammunition traffic. Wilson shot back an answer:

"Your telegram received. I would feel deeply mortified to have you or anybody like you vote for me. Since you have access to many disloyal Americans and I have not, I will ask you to convey this message to them."

President Wilson's devastating and somewhat insulting response probably won him more votes than it lost.

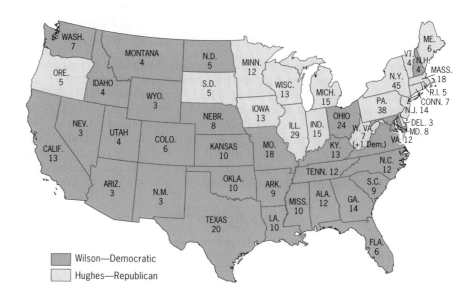

■ **Presidential Election of 1916 (with electoral vote by state)** Wilson was so worried about being a lame duck president in a time of great international tensions that he drew up a plan whereby Hughes, if victorious, would be appointed secretary of state, Wilson and the vice president would resign, and Hughes would thus succeed immediately to the presidency.

for several days, hinged on California, which Wilson carried by some 3,800 votes out of about a million cast.

Wilson barely squeaked through, with a final vote of 277 to 254 in the Electoral College and 9,127,695 to 8,533,507 in the popular column. The pro-labor Wilson received strong support from the working class and from renegade bull moosers, whom Republicans failed to lure back into their camp. Wilson had not specifically promised to keep the country out of war, but probably enough voters relied on such implicit assurances to ensure his victory. Their hopeful expectations were soon rudely shattered.

★ Chapter Summary ★

Advocating the "New Freedom," Democrat Woodrow Wilson defeated the Progressive Party candidate Roosevelt and the Republican Taft in the three-way election of 1912. The contest represented an unusual philosophical choice between alternative forms of progressivism. The eloquent, idealistic, but often ideologically self-righteous President Wilson successfully carried out a sweeping program of economic reform of the tariff, money and banking, and the trusts—what Wilson called the "triple wall of privilege." He also achieved substantial social reforms that benefited women and the working classes, but his lack of sympathy for blacks actually furthered segregation.

Wilson's attempt to implement similar progressive moral goals in foreign policy was less successful, as he stumbled into military involvements in the Caribbean and revolutionary Mexico. The outbreak of World War I in Europe brought growing risks of American involvement, especially because of the threat to neutral shipping from German submarine warfare. Led by President Wilson, most Americans earnestly sought to stay clear of the war, though all but a minority sympathized with the Allies more than the Germans.

Wilson temporarily avoided war by extracting the precarious *Sussex* pledge from Germany. His progressive campaign of 1916, appealing to workers and former bull moose supporters, narrowly won him reelection over Charles Evans Hughes and the Republicans, plagued by TR's disaffection and Hughes's deficiencies as a campaigner.

VARYING VIEWPOINTS

Who Were the Progressives?

Debate about progressivism has revolved mainly around a question that is simple to ask but devilishly difficult to answer: who were the progressives? It was once taken for granted that progressive reformers were simply the heirs of the Jeffersonian-Jacksonian-Populist reform crusades; they were the oppressed and downtrodden common folk who finally erupted in wrath and demanded their due.

But in his influential *Age of Reform* (1955), Richard Hofstadter astutely challenged that view. Progressive leaders, he argued, were not drawn from the ranks of society's poor and marginalized. Rather, they were middle-class people threatened from above by the emerging power of new corporate elites and from below by a restless working class. It was not economic deprivation, but "status anxiety," Hofstadter insisted, that prompted these people to become reformers. Their psychological motivation, Hofstadter concluded, rendered many of their reform efforts quirky and ineffectual.

By contrast, New Left historians, notably Gabriel Kolko, argue that progressivism was dominated by established business leaders who successfully directed "reform" to their own conservative ends. In this view, government regulation (as embodied in new agencies like the Federal Reserve Board and the Federal Tariff Commission, and in legislation like the Meat Inspection Act) simply accomplished what two generations of private efforts had failed to accomplish: dampening cutthroat competition, stabilizing markets, and making America safe for monopoly capitalism.

Still other scholars, notably Robert H. Wiebe and Samuel P. Hays, argue that the progressives were neither the psychologically or economically disadvantaged nor the old capitalist elite, but were, rather, members of a rapidly emerging, self-confident social class possessed of the new techniques of scientific management, technological expertise, and organizational know-how. This "organizational school" of historians does not see progressivism as a struggle of the "people" against the "interests," as a confused and nostalgic campaign by status-threatened reformers, or as a conservative coup d'état. The progressive movement, in this view, was by and large an effort to rationalize and modernize many social institutions by introducing the wise and impartial hand of government regulation.

This view has much to recommend it. Yet despite its widespread acceptance among historians, it is an explanation that cannot adequately account for the titanic political struggles of the progressive era over the very reforms that the "organizational school" regards as simple adjustments to modernity. The organizational approach also brushes over the deep philosophical differences that divided progressives themselves—such as the ideological chasm that separated Roosevelt's New Nationalism from Wilson's New Freedom.

Recently, scholars such as Robyn Muncy, Linda Gordon, and Theda Skocpol have stressed the role of women in advocating progressive reforms. Building the American welfare state in the early twentieth century, they argue, was fundamentally a gendered activity inspired by a "female dominion" of social workers and "social feminists." Moreover, in contrast to many European countries where labor movements sought a welfare state to benefit the working class, American female reformers promoted welfare programs specifically to protect women and children.

30

The War to End War

---❦---

1917–1918

THE WORLD MUST BE MADE SAFE FOR DEMOCRACY. ITS PEACE
MUST BE PLANTED UPON THE TESTED FOUNDATIONS OF
POLITICAL LIBERTY. WE HAVE NO SELFISH ENDS TO SERVE. WE
DESIRE NO CONQUEST, NO DOMINION. WE SEEK NO
INDEMNITIES FOR OURSELVES, NO MATERIAL COMPENSATION
FOR THE SACRIFICES WE SHALL FREELY MAKE.

WOODROW WILSON, WAR MESSAGE, APRIL 2, 1917

Destiny dealt cruelly with Woodrow Wilson. The lover of peace, as fate would have it, was forced to lead a hesitant and peace-loving nation into war. As the last days of 1916 slipped through the hourglass, the president made one final, futile attempt to mediate between the embattled belligerents. On January 22, 1917, he delivered one of his most moving addresses, restating America's conviction that only a negotiated "peace without victory" would prove durable.

Germany's warlords responded with a blow of the mailed fist. On January 31, 1917, they announced to an astonished world that they intended to wage *unrestricted* submarine warfare, sinking *all* ships, including America's, in the war zone.

Why this rash act? War with America was the last thing Germany wanted. But after three ghastly years in the trenches, Germany's leaders decided that making distinctions between combatants and noncombatants was a luxury they could no longer afford. Thus they jerked on the string they had attached to their *Sussex* pledge in 1916, desperately hoping to bring Britain to its knees before the United States entered the war. Wilson, his bluff called, broke diplomatic relations with Germany but refused to move closer to war unless the Germans undertook "overt" acts against American lives.

Focus Questions

1. Why did America enter World War I?
2. Why did Woodrow Wilson proclaim America's entry into the war as an ideological crusade for democracy and freedom, and how did that crusade both inspire fervor and crush domestic dissent?
3. How did America mobilize for war, and what was the war's impact on labor, women, and African Americans?
4. What was America's economic, military, and diplomatic contribution to the Allied victory, and why was Wilson forced to compromise his idealistic plan for a peace based on the Fourteen Points?
5. Why was the battle over ratifying the Treaty of Versailles so fierce and bitter, and how did Wilson's refusal to compromise with Lodge and others doom the treaty?

Chronology

1915	Council of National Defense established.
1917	Germany resumes unrestricted submarine warfare. Zimmermann note. United States enters World War I. Espionage Act of 1917.
1918	Wilson proposes the Fourteen Points. Sedition Act of 1918. Battle of Château-Thierry. Second Battle of the Marne.

	Meuse-Argonne offensive. Armistice ends World War I.
1919	Paris Peace Conference and Treaty of Versailles. Wilson's pro-League tour and collapse. Eighteenth Amendment (prohibition of alcohol) passed.
1920	Final Senate defeat of Versailles Treaty. Nineteenth Amendment (woman suffrage) passed. Harding defeats Cox for presidency.

War by Act of Germany

To defend American interests short of war, the president asked Congress for authority to arm American merchant ships. When a band of midwestern senators launched a filibuster to block the measure, Wilson denounced them as a "little group of willful men" who were rendering a great nation "helpless and contemptible." But their obstructionism was a powerful reminder of the continuing strength of American **isolationism**.

Meanwhile, the sensational Zimmermann note was intercepted and published on March 1, 1917, infuriating Americans, especially westerners. German foreign secretary Arthur Zimmermann had secretly proposed a German-Mexican alliance, tempting anti-Yankee Mexico with veiled promises of recovering Texas, New Mexico, and Arizona.

On the heels of this provocation came the long-dreaded "overt" acts in the Atlantic, where German U-boats sank four unarmed American merchant vessels in the first two weeks of March. As one Philadelphia newspaper observed, "The difference between war and what we have now is that now we aren't fighting back." Simultaneously came the rousing news that a revolution in Russia had toppled the cruel regime of the tsars. America could now fight foursquare for democracy on the side of the Allies without the black sheep of Russian despotism in the Allied fold.

Subdued and solemn, Wilson at last stood before a hushed joint session of Congress on the evening of April 2, 1917, and asked for a declaration of war. He had lost his gamble that America could pursue the profits of neutral trade without being sucked into the ghastly maelstrom. A myth developed in later years that America was dragged unwittingly into war by munitions makers and Wall Street bankers, desperate to protect their profits and loans. Yet the weapons merchants and financiers were already thriving, unhampered by wartime government restrictions and heavy taxation. The simple truth is that British harassment of American commerce had been galling but endurable; Germany had resorted to the mass killing of civilians. President Wilson had drawn a clear, if risky, line against the depredations of the submarine. The German high command, in a last desperate throw of the dice, chose to cross it. In a figurative sense, America's war declaration of April 6, 1917, bore the unambiguous trademark "Made in Germany."

isolationism *In American diplomacy, the traditional belief that the United States should refrain from involvement in overseas politics, alliances, or wars, and confine its national security interest to its own borders (sometimes along with the Caribbean and Central America).* **Internationalism** *or* **Wilsonianism** *is the contrasting belief that America's national security requires continuing involvement in global affairs and diplomatic or military alliances overseas.*

Online Study Center

Primary source
Zimmermann Telegram
college.hmco.com/pic/kennedybrief7e

Wilsonian Idealism Enthroned

"It is a fearful thing to lead this great peaceful people into war," Wilson said in his war message. It was fearful indeed, not least of all because of the formidable challenge it posed to Wilson's leadership skills. Ironically, it fell to the scholarly Wilson, deeply respectful of American traditions, to shatter one of the most sacred of those traditions by entangling America in a distant European war.

How could the president arouse the American people to shoulder this unprecedented burden? Isolationism remained strong, and no fewer than six senators and fifty representatives (including the first congresswoman, Jeannette Rankin of Montana) had voted against the war resolution. Wilson could whip up no enthusiasm, especially in the landlocked Midwest, for fighting to make the world safe from the submarine.

To galvanize the country, Wilson would have to proclaim more glorified aims. Radiating the spiritual fervor of his Presbyterian ancestors, he declared the twin goals of "a war to end war" and a crusade "to make the world safe for democracy." Brandishing the sword of righteousness, Wilson virtually hypnotized the nation with his lofty ideals. He contrasted the selfish war aims of the other belligerents, Allied and enemy alike, with America's shining altruism. America, he preached, did not fight for the sake of riches or territorial conquest. The Republic sought only to shape an international order in which democracy could flourish without fear of power-crazed autocrats and militarists.

In Wilsonian idealism the personality of the president and the necessities of history were perfectly matched. The high-minded Wilson genuinely believed in the principles he so eloquently intoned—especially that the modern world could not afford the kind of hyper-destructive war that advanced industrial states were now capable of waging. In this, Wilson's vision was prophetic. In any case, probably no other appeal could have successfully converted the American people from their historic hostility to involvement in European squabbles. Americans, it seemed, could be either isolationists or crusaders, but nothing in between.

Wilson's appeal worked—perhaps too well. Holding aloft the torch of idealism, the president fired up the public mind to a fever pitch. "Force, force to the utmost, force without stint or limit," he cried, while the country responded less elegantly with, "Hang the kaiser!" Lost on the gale was Wilson's earlier plea for "peace without victory."

Wilson's Fourteen Potent Points

Wilson quickly came to be recognized as the moral leader of the Allied cause. He scaled a summit of inspiring oratory on January 8, 1918, when he delivered his famed Fourteen Points Address to an enthusiastic Congress. Wilson's vision inspired all the drooping Allies to make mightier efforts and demoralized the enemy governments by holding out alluring promises to their dissatisfied minorities.

The first five of the Fourteen Points were broad in scope. (1) A proposal to abolish secret treaties pleased liberals of all countries. (2) Freedom of the seas appealed to the Germans, as well as to Americans who distrusted British sea power. (3) A removal of economic barriers among nations had long been the goal of liberal internationalists everywhere. (4) Reduction of armament burdens was gratifying to taxpayers of all countries. (5) An adjustment of colonial claims in the interests of both native peoples and the colonizers was a potentially revolutionary appeal that helped delegitimize old empires and inspire "subject peoples."

Other points among the fourteen proved to be no less seductive. They held out the promise of independence ("self-determination") to oppressed minority groups, such as the Poles, millions of whom lay under the heel of Germany and Austria-Hungary. The capstone point, number fourteen, foreshadowed the League of Nations—an international organization that Wilson dreamed would provide a system of **collective security**. Wilson earnestly prayed that this new scheme would effectively guarantee the political independence and territorial integrity of all countries, whether large or small.

Yet Wilson's appealing points, though raising hopes the world over, were not everywhere applauded. Certain leaders of the Allied nations, with an eye to territorial booty, were less than enthusiastic. Some hard-nosed Republicans at home openly mocked the "fourteen commandments" of "God Almighty Wilson."

collective security *In international affairs, reliance on a group of nations or an international organization as protection against aggressors, rather than on national self-defense alone.*

Creel Manipulates Minds

Mobilizing people's minds for war, both in America and abroad, was an urgent task facing the Washington authorities. The Committee on Public Information, headed by journalist George Creel, was therefore created to sell America on the war and sell the world on Wilsonian war aims. Though outspoken and tactless, Creel was gifted with zeal and imagination. His organization, employing 150,000 workers at home and overseas, proved that words were indeed weapons. It sent out an army of 75,000 "four-minute men"—often longer-winded than that—who delivered countless speeches full of "patriotic pep."

Creel's propaganda took varied forms. Posters were splashed on billboards in the "Battle of the Fences," as artists "rallied to the colors." Millions of leaflets and pamphlets containing the most pungent Wilsonisms were showered like confetti upon the world. Propaganda booklets with red-white-and-blue covers were printed by the millions. Hang-the-kaiser movies, carrying such titles as *The Kaiser, the Beast of Berlin* and *To Hell with the Kaiser,* revealed the "Hun" at his bloodiest. Arm-waving conductors by the thousands led huge audiences in songs that poured scorn on the enemy and glorified the "boys" in uniform.

The entire nation, catching the frenzied spirit of a religious revival, burst into song. Most memorable of many anthems was George M. Cohan's spine-tingling "Over There":

> *Over there, over there*
> *Send the word, send the word over there,*
> *That the Yanks are coming, the Yanks are coming*
> *The drums rum-tumming everywhere.*

Creel typified American war **mobilization** , which relied more on aroused passion and voluntary compliance than on formal laws. But he oversold the ideals of Wilson and led the world to expect too much. When the president proved to be a mortal and not a god, the resulting disillusionment at home and abroad was disastrous.

■ **Anti-German Propaganda** The government relied extensively on emotional appeals and hate propaganda to rally support for the First World War, which most Americans regarded as a distant "European" affair.

Enforcing Loyalty and Stifling Dissent

German Americans numbered over 8 million, counting those with at least one parent foreign-born, out of a total population of 100 million. Most proved to be loyal to the United States. But as emotion mounted, hate hysteria against Germans and things Germanic swept the nation. Orchestras found it unsafe to present German-composed music, like that of Wagner and Beethoven. German books were removed from library shelves, and German classes were canceled in high schools and colleges. Sauerkraut became "liberty cabbage," hamburger "liberty steak." Even beer became suspect, as patriotic Americans fretted over the loyalty of breweries with names like Schlitz or Pabst. A few German Americans were tarred, feathered, and beaten; a German Socialist in Illinois was lynched by a drunken mob.

Both the Espionage Act of 1917 and the Sedition Act of 1918 reflected current fears about Germans and antiwar Americans. Especially visible among the nineteen hundred prosecutions undertaken under these laws were antiwar Socialists and members of the radical union Industrial Workers of the World (IWW). Kingpin Socialist Eugene V. Debs was convicted under the Espionage Act in 1918 and sentenced to ten years in a federal penitentiary. IWW leader William D. ("Big Bill") Haywood and ninety-nine associates were similarly convicted. Some leftist journals like *The Masses* were denied use of the mails.

Virtually any criticism of the government could be censored and punished. Some critics claimed the new laws were bending, if not breaking, the First Amendment. But in *Schenck* v. *United States* (1919), the Supreme Court affirmed

Online Study Center

Primary source
World's Greatest Adventure in Advertising
college.hmco.com/pic/kennedybrief7e

mobilization *The organization of a nation and its armed forces for war.*

Online Study Center

Primary source
Terror in the Wisconsin Hinterlands
college.hmco.com/pic/kennedybrief7e

Online Study Center

Primary source
Socialist Critique of World War I
college.hmco.com/pic/kennedybrief7e

pardon *The official release of a person from punishment for a crime.*

their legality, arguing that freedom of speech could be revoked when such speech posed a "clear and present danger" to the nation.

These prosecutions form an ugly chapter in the history of American civil liberty. With the dawn of peace, presidential **pardons** were rather freely granted, including President Harding's to Eugene Debs in 1921. Yet a few victims lingered behind bars into the 1930s.

Factories and Workers in Wartime

Victory was no foregone conclusion, especially since the Republic was caught flatfootedly unready for its leap into global war. Wilson had only belatedly backed some mild preparedness measures beginning in 1915, including a shipbuilding program and a civilian Council of National Defense. It would take a herculean effort to mobilize America's daunting but disorganized resources and throw them into the field quickly enough to bolster the Allied war effort.

Towering obstacles confronted economic mobilizers. Sheer ignorance was among the biggest roadblocks. No one knew how much steel or explosive powder the country was capable of producing. Traditional fears of big government hamstrung efforts to orchestrate the economy from Washington.

Late in the war, Wilson finally succeeded in imposing some order on this economic confusion. In March 1918 he appointed Wall Street's Bernard Baruch to head the War Industries Board, but that agency never had more than feeble formal powers. Even in a globe-girdling crisis, the American preference for laissez-faire and for a weak central government proved amazingly strong.

Spurred by the slogan "Labor Will Win the War," American workers sweated their way to victory. In 1918 the War Department threatened to draft any unemployed male, but for the most part the government tried to treat labor fairly. The National War Labor Board, chaired by former president Taft, pressed employers to pay higher wages and adopt the eight-hour workday.

Samuel Gompers and his American Federation of Labor (AF of L) loyally supported the war, though some smaller and more radical labor organizations, including the Industrial Workers of the World, known as the "Wobblies," became war resisters. The Wobblies, who were mostly poorly treated workers in the lumber and fruit industries, engineered some damaging industrial sabotage. Mainstream labor's loyalty was rewarded, as union membership doubled to over 3 million and real wages (adjusting for inflation) had risen 20 percent by war's end.

Yet labor harbored grievances. Recognition of the right to organize still eluded labor's grasp. Some six thousand strikes, several stained by blood, broke out in the war years. In 1919 the greatest strike in American history rocked the steel industry. More than a quarter of a million workers walked off the job in a bid to force their employers to recognize their right to organize and bargain collectively. The steel companies resisted mercilessly. They brought in thirty thousand African American strikebreakers to keep the mills running. After bitter confrontations that left more than a dozen workers dead, the steel strike collapsed, a grievous setback that crippled the union movement for more than a decade.

The black workers who entered the steel mills in 1919 were but a fraction of the tens of thousands of southern blacks drawn to the North by the magnet of war-industry employment. Their sudden appearance in previously all-white areas sometimes sparked interracial violence. An explosive riot in East St. Louis, Illinois, in July 1917 left nine whites and at least forty blacks dead. An equally gruesome riot ripped through Chicago in July 1919, fanned by tensions between white working-class neighborhoods and African Americans who had found jobs as strikebreakers in meatpacking plants. Fifteen whites and twenty-three blacks were killed during nearly two weeks of terror.

Suffering Until Suffrage

Women also heeded the call of patriotism and opportunity. Thousands of female workers flooded into factories and fields, taking up jobs vacated by men who left

■ **In the Trenches** U.S. Army nurses at the fighting front in France, 1918. The war also opened many opportunities for women's work on the home front, but the conflict ended too soon for many women to secure a permanent foothold in occupations traditionally dominated by men.

the assembly line for the front line. But the war split the women's movement deeply. Many progressive feminists were pacifists, inclined to oppose both the participation of America in the war and women in the war effort. This group found a voice in the National Woman's party, led by Quaker activist Alice Paul, which demonstrated against "Kaiser Wilson" with marches and hunger strikes.

But the larger part of the suffrage movement, represented by the National American Woman Suffrage Association, supported Wilson's war. Leaders echoed Wilson's justification for fighting by arguing that women must take part in the war effort to earn a role in shaping the peace. The fight for democracy abroad was women's best chance for winning true democracy at home.

War mobilization gave new momentum to the suffrage fight. Impressed by women's war work, President Wilson endorsed woman suffrage as "a vitally necessary war measure." In 1917 New York voted for suffrage at the state level; Michigan, Oklahoma, and South Dakota followed. Eventually the groundswell could no longer be contained. In 1920, eighty years after the first calls for suffrage at Seneca Falls, the Nineteenth Amendment was ratified, giving all American women the right to vote (see the Appendix).

Despite political victory, women's wartime economic gains proved fleeting. When peace arrived, most women workers soon gave up their war jobs. Meanwhile,

Online Study Center

Primary source
Ford Motor Company Plant
Women Assembling Magnets

college.hmco.com/pic/kennedybrief7e

In an open address to Congress in 1917, suffragist Carrie Chapman Catt (1859–1947) capitalized on the idealism of the day and invoked the founding principles of American democracy in arguing the case for women's right to vote:

"How can our nation escape the logic it has never failed to follow, when its last unenfranchised class calls for the vote? Behold our Uncle Sam floating the banner with one hand, 'Taxation without representation is tyranny,' and with the other seizing the billions of dollars paid in taxes by women to whom he refuses 'representation.' . . . Is there a single man who can justify such inequality of treatment, such outrageous discrimination? Not one."

ration *A fixed allowance of food or other scarce commodity.*

Congress reaffirmed its support for women in their traditional role as mothers when it passed the Sheppard-Towner Maternity Act of 1921, providing federally financed instruction in maternal and infant health care.

Forging a War Economy

Mobilization relied more on the heated emotions of patriotism than on the cool majesty of the laws. The largely voluntary and somewhat haphazard character of economic war organization testified unequivocally to ocean-insulated America's safe distance from the fighting—as well as to the still-modest scale of government powers in the progressive-era Republic.

As the larder of democracy, America had to feed itself and its allies. By a happy inspiration, the man chosen to head the Food Administration was the Quaker humanitarian Herbert C. Hoover, already a hero for leading a massive drive to feed the starving people of war-racked Belgium.

In common with other American war administrators, Hoover preferred to rely on voluntary compliance rather than on formal edicts. Instead of **rationing** food supplies, he waged a whirlwind propaganda campaign through posters, billboards, newspapers, pulpits, and movies. To save food for export, Hoover proclaimed wheatless Wednesdays and meatless Tuesdays—all on a voluntary basis. Even children, when eating apples, were urged to be "patriotic to the core."

The country soon broke out in a rash of backyard "victory gardens." Congress severely restricted the use of foodstuffs for manufacturing alcoholic beverages. The wartime drive against German-descended brewers aided in the passage of the Eighteenth Amendment in 1919, which prohibited not only beer but all alcoholic drinks.

Thanks to the fervent patriotic wartime spirit, Hoover's voluntary approach worked. Farm production increased by one-fourth, and food exports to the Allies tripled in volume. Hoover's methods were widely imitated in other war agencies. The Fuel Administration exhorted Americans to save fuel with "heatless Mondays" and "gasless Sundays." The Treasury Department sponsored huge parades and invoked slogans like "Halt the Hun" to promote four great Liberty Loan drives, followed by a Victory Loan campaign in 1919. Together these efforts netted the then-fantastic sum of about $21 billion, or two-thirds of the current cost of the war to the United States. The remainder was raised by increased taxes.

Despite the Wilson administration's preference for voluntary means of mobilizing the economy, the government on occasion reluctantly exercised its sovereign formal power, notably when it took over the nation's railroads following indescribable traffic snarls in late 1917. Washington also launched a gigantic shipbuilding program, though it was slow to get under way.

Making Plowboys into Doughboys

Most citizens, at the outset, did not dream of sending a mighty force to France. They expected America to ship war materials to the Allies and to supply them with loans. But in April and May of 1917, the Europeans confessed that they were scraping the bottom not only of their money chests but, more ominously, of their manpower barrels. A huge American army would have to be raised, trained, and transported, or the whole western front would collapse.

Conscription was the only answer to the need for raising an immense army with all possible speed. Wilson disliked a draft, but he eventually accepted and eloquently supported conscription as a disagreeable and temporary necessity. After six weeks of criticism and debate, Congress grudgingly passed conscription.

The draft act required the registration of all males between the ages of eighteen and forty-five. The draft machinery, on the whole, worked effectively. No draftee could purchase an exemption or hire a substitute, as in the days of the Civil War. Within a few frantic months the army grew to over 4 million men. For the first time, women were admitted to the armed forces: some 11,000 to the navy and 269 to the marines. African Americans also served in the armed forces, though in strictly segregated units and usually under white officers.

Recruits were supposed to receive six months of training in America and two more months overseas. But so great was the urgency that many "doughboys" were swept swiftly into battle scarcely knowing how to handle a rifle, much less a bayonet.

America Helps Hammer the Hun

Russia's collapse underscored the need for haste. As the communistic **Bolsheviks** withdrew their beaten country from the "capitalistic" war early in 1918, Germany moved its battle-tested forces from the eastern front facing Russia to the western front in France. The Germans hoped to deliver the knockout blow to the Allies in about six months, long before America could get into the struggle.

Berlin's calculations as to American tardiness were surprisingly accurate. No really effective American fighting force reached France until about a year after Congress declared war. Nevertheless, France gradually began to bustle with American doughboys. The first trainees to reach the front were used as replacements in the Allied armies. The newcomers soon made friends with the French girls—or tried to—and one of the most sung-about women in history was the fabled "Mademoiselle from Armentières." One of the printable stanzas ran

> *She was true to me, she was true to you,*
> *She was true to the whole damned army, too.*

American operations were not confined solely to France; small detachments fought in Belgium, Italy, and notably Russia. The United States, hoping to keep munitions out of German hands, contributed some 5,000 troops to an Allied

Ignoring grisly tales of the agonies of trench warfare, many young American men saw an opportunity for adventure and seized it. Author John Dos Passos (1896–1970) recollected how he felt going off to war in 1917:

"We had spent our boyhood in the afterglow of the peaceful nineteenth century. . . . What was war like? We wanted to see with our own eyes. We flocked into the volunteer services. I respected the conscientious objectors, and occasionally felt I should take that course myself, but hell, I wanted to see the show."

Bolsheviks *The radical majority faction of the Russian Socialist party that seized power in the October 1917 revolution; they later took the name Communist. (Bolshevik is the Russian word for "majority"; their rivals for power were **Mensheviks,** or minority.)*

■ **Over There** American troops ("doughboys") man a machine gun in a bomb-blasted forest.

salient *A portion of a battle line that extends forward into enemy territory.*

Online Study Center

Interactive map
American Troops at the Western Frontier, 1918
college.hmco.com/pic/kennedybrief7e

⭐ Map-reading Skill Builder:
Understanding Military Maps

1. In which country did almost all of the major battles of the Western front in 1918 take place? Through which two other countries did smaller portions of the front run between Switzerland and the sea?

2. What critical city was the apparent object of the German offensive in spring 1918 that was halted in part by the American troops at Belleau Wood and Chateau-Thierry?

3. Which two cities—one in France and one in Germany—were the American troops in the Meuse-Argonne offensive approaching when the armistice was declared in November 1918?

invasion of northern Russia. Wilson likewise sent nearly 10,000 troops to Siberia as part of an Allied expedition. The Bolsheviks long resented these "capitalistic" interventions as high-handed efforts to suffocate their infant communist revolution in its cradle.

The dreaded German drive on the western front exploded in the spring of 1918. Spearheaded by about half a million troops, the enemy rolled forward with terrifying momentum. So dire was the peril that the Allies for the first time united under a supreme commander, the quiet Frenchman Marshal Ferdinand Foch.

At last the ill-trained "Yanks" were coming—and not a moment too soon. Late in May 1918, the forward-rolling Germans, smashing to within forty miles of Paris, threatened to knock out France. Newly arrived American troops, numbering fewer than thirty thousand, were thrown into the breach at Château-Thierry, right in the teeth of the German advance. This was a historic moment—the first significant engagement of American troops in a European war. With their arrival, it was clear that a new American giant had arisen in the West to replace the dying Russian titan in the East.

American weight in the scales was now being felt. By July 1918 the awesome German drive had spent its force, and keyed-up American men participated in a Foch counteroffensive in the Second Battle of the Marne. This engagement marked the beginning of a German withdrawal that was never effectively reversed. In September 1918 nine American divisions (about 243,000 men) joined four French divisions to push the Germans from the St. Mihiel **salient**, a German dagger in France's flank.

The Americans meanwhile demanded and got a separate army. General John J. ("Black Jack") Pershing was finally assigned a front stretching from the Swiss border to the French lines. As part of the last mighty Allied assault, involving several million men, Pershing's army undertook the Meuse-Argonne offensive, from September 26 to November 11, 1918. This battle, the most gargantuan thus far in American history, lasted forty-seven days and engaged 1.2 million American troops. With especially heavy fighting in the rugged Argonne Forest, the killed and wounded mounted to 120,000, or 10 percent of the Americans involved.

Victory was in sight—and fortunately so. The slowly advancing American armies in France were eating up their supplies so rapidly that they were in grave danger of running short. But the battered Germans were staggering under the sledgehammer blows of the Allies and suffering from critical food shortages caused by the British blockade. Propaganda leaflets containing seductive Wilsonian promises rained upon their crumbling lines from balloons, shells, and rockets.

■ **Major U.S. Operations in France, 1918** One doughboy recorded in his diary his baptism of fire at St. Mihiel: "Hiked through dark woods. No lights allowed, guided by holding on the pack of the man ahead. Stumbled through underbrush for about half mile into an open field where we waited in soaking rain until about 10:00 P.M. We then started on our hike to the St. Mihiel front, arriving on the crest of a hill at 1:00 A.M. I saw a sight which I shall never forget. It was the zero hour and in one instant the entire front as far as the eye could reach in either direction was a sheet of flame, while the heavy artillery made the earth quake."

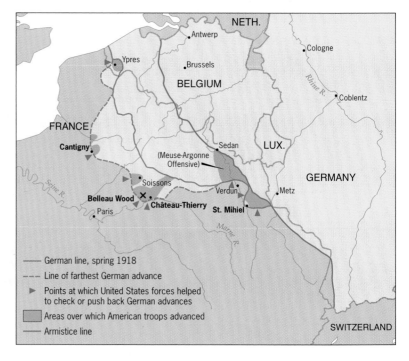

EXAMINING THE EVIDENCE

"Mademoiselle from Armentières" Some familiar songs, such as Julia Ward Howe's stirring Civil War–era melody "Battle Hymn of the Republic," were penned by known composers and have well-established scores and lyrics. But many ballads have no specific author. Songwriters may fit new verses to known tunes, but the songs essentially grow out of the soil of popular culture and take on a life of their own. "Yankee Doodle Dandy," for example, originated during the seventeenth-century English Civil War, was adapted by the American revolutionaries more than a century later, and was parodied by Southerners during the American Civil War:

> *Yankee Doodle had a mind*
> *To whip the Southern "traitors,"*
> *Because they didn't choose to live*
> *On codfish and potaters.*

"Stagger Lee," or "Stagolee," a blues ballad supposedly based on a murder in Memphis in the 1930s, has been played in countless renditions, with its homicidal subject variously portrayed as a ruthless badman or a civil rights hero.

This process of accretion and adaptation can furnish valuable clues to historians about changing sentiments and sensibilities, just as the ballads themselves give expression to feelings not always evident in the official record. Folklorist Alan Lomax spent a lifetime tracking down American ballads, documenting layers of life and experience not usually excavated by traditional scholars. In the case of the First World War's most notorious song, "Mademoiselle from Armentières" (or "Hinky Dinky, Parley-Voo?"), he compiled from various sources more than six hundred soldier-authored stanzas, some of which are reproduced here (others he delicately described as "not mailable").

> *Mademoiselle from Armentières,*
> *She hadn't been kissed in forty years.*
> *She might have been young for all we knew,*
> *When Napoleon flopped at Waterloo....*
> *You'll never get your croix de Guerre,*
> *If you never wash your underwear....*

> *The French, they are a funny race,*
> *They fight with their feet and save their face.*
> *The cootie [louse] is the national bug of France.*
> *The cootie's found all over France,*
> *No matter wear you hang your pants....*
> *Oh, the seventy-seventh went over the top,*
> *A sous lieutenant, a Jew, and a Wop....*
> *The officers get all the steak,*
> *And all we get is the belly-ache.*
> *The general got a Croix de Guerre,*
> *The son-of-a-gun was never there....*
> *There's many and many a married man,*
> *Wants to go back to France again.*
> *'Twas a hell of a war as we recall,*
> *But still 'twas better than none at all.*

1. What fresh—and irreverent—perspectives do these stanzas reveal about the soldier's-eye view of military life?

2. What view of France and the French people is implied in the lyrics? How do the ordinary American soldiers view their own experience of being in France?

3. What does the implied sexual content of the song and the "Mademoiselle" who supposedly inspired it reveal about this war as a "gendered" activity?

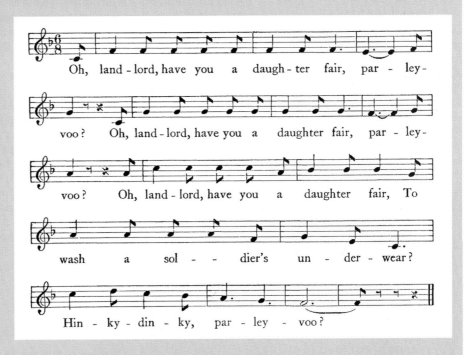

Oh, land-lord, have you a daugh-ter fair, par-ley-voo? Oh, land-lord, have you a daughter fair, par-ley-voo? Oh, land-lord, have you a daughter fair, To wash a sol-dier's un-der-wear? Hin-ky-din-ky, par-ley-voo?

Berlin was now ready to hoist the white flag. The Germans first sought a peace based on the Fourteen Points in October 1918. But Wilson made it clear that the kaiser must be thrown overboard before an armistice could be negotiated. The war-weary Germans then forced the disgraced kaiser to flee to Holland.

The exhausted Germans were through. They laid down their arms at eleven o'-clock on the eleventh day of the eleventh month of 1918, and an eerie, numbing silence fell over the western front. War-taut America burst into a delirium of around-the-clock rejoicing, as streets were jammed with laughing, whooping, milling, dancing masses. The war to end wars had ended.

The United States' main contribution to the ultimate victory had been food-stuffs, munitions, credits, oil, and manpower—but not battlefield victories. The Yanks fought only two major battles, at St. Mihiel and the Meuse-Argonne. It was the *prospect* of endless U.S. troop reserves, rather than America's actual military performance, that eventually demoralized the Germans.

Ironically enough, General Pershing in some ways depended more on the Allies than they depended on him. His army purchased more of its supplies in Europe than it shipped from the United States. The United States was no arsenal of democracy in this war; that role awaited it in the next global conflict, two decades later.

Wilson Steps Down from Olympus

Woodrow Wilson had helped to win the war. What role would he now play in shaping the peace? Expectations ran extravagantly high. As the fighting in Europe crashed to a close, the American president towered at the peak of his popularity and power. No other man had ever occupied so dizzy a pinnacle as moral leader of the world. Wilson also had behind him the prestige of victory and the economic resources of the mightiest nation on earth. But at this fateful moment, his sureness of touch deserted him, and he began to make a series of tragic fumbles.

Under the slogan "Politics is Adjourned" partisan political strife had been kept below the surface during the war crisis. Hoping to strengthen his hand at the Paris peace table, Wilson broke the truce by personally appealing for a Democratic victory in the congressional elections of November 1918. But the maneuver backfired when voters instead returned a narrow Republican majority to Congress. Having staked his reputation on the outcome, Wilson went to Paris as a diminished leader. Unlike all the **parliamentary** statesmen at the table, he did not command a legislative majority at home.

Wilson's decision to go in person to Paris to help make the peace infuriated Republicans, who saw it as flamboyant grandstanding. He further ruffled Republican feathers when he neglected to include a single Republican senator in his official peace delegation. The logical choice was the new chairman of the Senate Committee on Foreign Relations, slender and aristocratically be-whiskered Henry Cabot Lodge of Massachusetts, a Harvard Ph.D. But including Lodge would have been problematic for the president. The senator's mind, quipped one critic, was like the soil of his native New England: "naturally barren but highly cultivated." Wilson loathed him, and the feeling was hotly reciprocated. An accomplished author, Lodge had been known as "the scholar in politics" until Wilson came on the scene. The two men were at daggers drawn, personally and politically.

parliamentary *Concerning political systems in which the government is constituted from the controlling party's members in the legislative assembly.*

Grave concern was expressed by General Tasker H. Bliss (1853–1930), one of the five American peace commissioners (December 18, 1918):

"I am disquieted to see how hazy and vague our ideas are. We are going to be up against the wiliest politicians in Europe. There will be nothing hazy or vague about their ideas."

Hammering Out the Treaty

Woodrow Wilson, the great prophet arisen in the West, received tumultuous welcomes from the masses of France, Britain, and Italy late in 1918 and early in 1919. But the

 Wilson in Dover, England, 1919 Hailed by many Europeans in early 1919 as the savior of the Western world, Wilson was a fallen idol only a few months later, when his own countrymen repudiated the peace treaty he had helped to craft.

realistic statesmen of Italy and France were determined that Wilsonian idealism should not upset their fine-spun imperialistic plans.

The Paris Conference of great and small nations fell into the hands of an inner clique, known as the "Big Four." Wilson, representing the richest and freshest great power, more or less occupied the driver's seat. He was joined by Vittorio Orlando of Italy, David Lloyd George of Britain, and cynical, hard-bitten Georges Clemenceau of France, the seventy-eight-year-old "organizer of victory" known as "the Tiger."

Speed was urgent when the conference opened on January 18, 1919. Europe seemed to be slipping into anarchy; the red tide of communism was licking westward from Bolshevist Russia.

Wilson's ultimate goal was a world parliament to be known as the League of Nations, but he first bent his energies to preventing any cynical parceling out of the former colonies and **protectorates** of the vanquished powers. He forced through a compromise between naked imperialism and Wilsonian idealism, in which the victors received conquered territory only as **trustees** of the League of Nations. But in practice this half-loaf solution was little more than the old prewar colonialism, thinly disguised.

Wilson envisioned a League of Nations containing an assembly with seats for all nations and a council to be controlled by the great powers. He gained a signal victory over the skeptical Old World diplomats in February 1919, when they agreed to make the League Covenant, Wilson's brainchild, an integral part of the final peace treaty.

On a quick trip to America, Wilson discovered that certain Republican senators, led by Senator Lodge, were sharpening their knives. To them the League was either a useless "sewing circle" or an overpotent "superstate." Their hard core was composed of a dozen or so isolationists, led by Senators William Borah of Idaho and Hiram Johnson of California, who were known as the "irreconcilables" or "the battalion of death."

Thirty-nine Republican senators or senators-elect—enough to defeat the treaty—proclaimed that the Senate would not approve the League of Nations in its existing imperfect form. These difficulties delighted Wilson's Allied adversaries in Paris. They were now in a stronger bargaining position because Wilson would have to beg them for changes in the covenant that would safeguard the Monroe Doctrine and other U.S. interests dear to the senators.

As soon as Wilson was back in Paris, hardheaded Premier Clemenceau pressed French demands for the German-inhabited Rhineland and the Saar Valley, a rich coal area. Faced with fierce Wilsonian opposition to this violation of

protectorate *In international affairs, a weaker or smaller country held to be under the guidance or protection of a major power; the arrangement is a weaker form of imperialism or colonialism. (A* **colony** *is a territory owned outright by a more powerful nation.)*

trustee *A nation that holds the territory of a former colony as the conditional agent of an international body under defined terms.*

Online Study Center

Interactive map
Postwar Boundary Changes in Europe and the Middle East
college.hmco.com/pic/kennedybrief7e

self-determination, France settled for a compromise whereby the Saar basin would remain under the League of Nations for fifteen years, and then a popular vote would determine its fate. (The Saar population voted overwhelmingly to rejoin Germany in 1935.) In exchange for dropping its demands for the Rhineland, France got a security treaty in which both Britain and America pledged to come to its aid in the event of another German invasion. The French later felt betrayed when the pact was quickly pigeonholed by the U.S. Senate, which shied away from all entangling alliances.

Wilson's next battle was with Italy over Fiume, a valuable seaport inhabited by both Italians and Yugoslavs. When Italy demanded Fiume, Wilson insisted that the seaport go to Yugoslavia and appealed over the heads of Italy's leaders to the country's masses. The maneuver fell flat. The Italian delegates went home in a huff, and the Italian masses turned savagely against Wilson.

Another crucial struggle was with Japan over China's Shandong (Shantung) Peninsula and the German islands in the Pacific, which the Japanese had seized during the war. Japan was conceded the strategic Pacific islands under a League of Nations **mandate**,* but Wilson staunchly opposed Japanese control of Shandong as a violation of **self-determination** for its 30 million Chinese residents. But when the Japanese threatened to walk out, Wilson reluctantly accepted a compromise whereby Japan kept Germany's economic holdings in Shandong and pledged to return the peninsula to China at a later date. The Chinese were outraged by this imperialistic solution, while Clemenceau jeered that Wilson "talked like Jesus Christ and acted like Lloyd George."

Wilson's Battle for Ratification

A completed Treaty of Versailles was handed to the Germans in June 1919—almost literally on the point of a bayonet. A careful analysis of the treaty shows that only four of the original Wilsonian points were fully honored. Vengeance, not reconciliation, was the treaty's dominant tone. Loud and bitter cries of betrayal burst from German throats—charges that Adolf Hitler would soon reiterate during his meteoric rise to power in Germany.

Wilson, of course, was guilty of no conscious betrayal. He had been forced to compromise away some of his less cherished Fourteen Points in order to salvage the more precious League of Nations. He was much more like the mother who had to throw her sickly younger children to the pursuing wolves to save her sturdy firstborn. Greeted a few months earlier with frenzied acclaim in Europe, Wilson was now a fallen idol, condemned alike by disillusioned liberals and frustrated imperialists. He was keenly aware that some injustices had been forced into the treaty. But he was hoping that a potent League of Nations, led by America, would iron out the inequities.

Yet the loudly condemned treaty actually had much to commend it. Not least among its merits was its liberation of many oppressed peoples, such as the Poles, from the yoke of imperial dynasties. Wilson's critics to the contrary, the settlement was almost certainly a fairer one because he had gone to Paris.

Returning to America, Wilson sailed straight into a political typhoon. Isolationists raised a whirlwind of protest against Wilson's commitment to usher the United States into his newfangled League of Nations. Rabid Hun-haters, regarding the pact as not harsh enough, voiced their discontent. Principled liberals, like the editors of the *Nation* and the *New Republic,* thought it too harsh—and a gross betrayal to boot. German Americans, Italian Americans, Irish Americans, and others whom Wilson termed "hyphenated Americans" were aroused because the peace settlement was not sufficiently favorable to their native lands.

Despite mounting discontent, a strong majority of the people still seemed favorable to the treaty, with the "Wilson League" firmly riveted as Part I. At this time—early July 1919—Senator Lodge had no real hope of defeating the Treaty of

---

mandate *Under the League of Nations (1919–1939), a specific commission that authorized a trustee to administer a former colonial territory.*

self-determination *The Wilsonian doctrine that each people should have the right to freely choose its own political affiliation and national future, such as independence or incorporation into another nation.*

---

* In due time the Japanese illegally fortified these islands—the Marshalls, Marianas, and Carolines—and used them as bases against the United States in World War II.

Versailles. His strategy was merely to amend it in such a way as to "Americanize," "Republicanize," or "senatorialize" it.

Lodge effectively used delay to muddle and divide public opinion. He read the entire 264-page treaty aloud in the Senate Foreign Relations Committee and held protracted hearings in which people of various nationalities aired their grievances. With the treaty bogged down in the Senate, Wilson decided to take his case to the country in a spectacular speechmaking tour. The strenuous barnstorming campaign was undertaken in the face of protests by physicians and friends. Never robust, Wilson's frail body had begun to sag under the strain of partisan strife, a global war, and a stressful peace conference. But he declared that he was willing to die, like the soldiers he had sent into battle, for the sake of the new world order.

The presidential tour, begun in September 1919, got off to a rather lame start in the Midwest, where German American influence was strong. Trailing after him like bloodhounds came two "irreconcilable" senators, Borah and Johnson, who spoke in the same cities a few days later. Hat-tossing crowds answered their attacks on Wilson, crying, "Impeach him, impeach him!"

But the reception was different in the Rocky Mountain region and the Pacific Coast. These areas, which had elected Wilson in 1916, welcomed him with heartwarming outbursts. The high point—and the breaking point—of the return trip was at Pueblo, Colorado, on September 25, 1919. Wilson, with tears coursing down his cheeks, pleaded for the League of Nations as the only real hope of preventing future wars. That night he collapsed from physical and nervous exhaustion.

Wilson was whisked back in the "funeral train" to Washington, where several days later a stroke paralyzed one side of his body. During the next few weeks he lay in a darkened room in the White House, as much a victim of the war as the unknown soldier buried at Arlington. For seven months he did not meet his cabinet.

Defeat Through Deadlock

Senator Lodge, coldly calculating, was now at the helm. After failing to amend the treaty outright, he came up with fourteen formal **reservations** to protect American sovereignty and guard Congress's constitutional war-declaring power against the League. Wilson, hating Lodge, saw red at the mere suggestion of the Lodge reservations, which he insisted "emasculated" the entire pact.

reservation *A portion of a deed, contract, or treaty that places conditions or restrictions on the general obligations.*

Although too feeble to lead, Wilson was still strong enough to obstruct. When the day finally came for voting in the Senate, he sent word to all true Democrats to vote *against* the treaty with the odious Lodge reservations attached. Loyal Democrats in the Senate, on November 19, 1919, blindly did Wilson's bidding. Combining with the "irreconcilables," mostly Republicans, they rejected the treaty with the Lodge reservations appended, 55 to 39.

The nation was so shocked at this outcome that the Senate was forced to vote a second time in March 1920. There was only one possible path to success. Unless the Senate approved the pact with the Lodge reservations, the entire document would be rejected. But the sickly Wilson signed the treaty's death warrant by again sending word to all loyal Democrats to vote down the treaty with the obnoxious Lodge reservations. On March 19, 1920, the treaty netted a simple majority but failed to get the necessary two-thirds majority by a count of 49 yeas to 35 nays.

Who defeated the treaty? The Lodge-Wilson personal feud, traditionalism, isolationism, disillusionment, and partisanship all contributed to the confused picture. But Wilson himself must bear a substantial share of the responsibility. He asked for all or nothing—and got nothing.

The "Solemn Referendum" of 1920

Wilson's own pet solution for the deadlock was to settle the treaty issue by appealing to the people for a "solemn referendum" in the presidential election of 1920. This was sheer folly, for a true mandate on the League in the noisy arena of politics was clearly an impossibility.

Gathering in Chicago in June 1920, jubilant Republicans devised a masterfully ambiguous platform that could appeal to both pro-League and anti-League sentiment in the party. The nominee would run on a teeter-totter rather than a platform. As the leading presidential contestants jousted with one another, a group of Senate bosses, meeting rather casually in the historic "smoke-filled" Room 404 of the Blackstone Hotel, informally decided on affable, malleable Senator Warren G. Harding of Ohio as the candidate. To run with the "folksy," back-slapping former newspaper editor, the party nominated frugal, grim-faced Governor Calvin ("Silent Cal") Coolidge of Massachusetts.

Meeting in San Francisco, Democrats nominated earnest Governor James M. Cox of Ohio, who strongly supported the League. His running mate was Assistant Navy Secretary Franklin D. Roosevelt, a young, handsome, vibrant New Yorker.

Democratic attempts to make the campaign a referendum on the League were thwarted by Senator Harding, who issued muddled and contradictory statements on the issue from his front porch. Pro-League and anti-League Republicans both claimed that Harding's election would advance their cause, while the candidate suggested that if elected he would work for a vague Association of Nations—*a* league but not *the* League.

With newly enfranchised women swelling the vote totals, Harding was swept into power with a prodigious plurality of over 7 million votes—16,143,407 to 9,130,328 for Cox. The electoral count was 404 to 127. Eugene V. Debs, federal prisoner number 9653 at the Atlanta Penitentiary, rolled up the largest vote ever for the left-wing Socialist party—919,799.

Public desire for a change found vent in a resounding repudiation of "high and mighty" Wilsonianism. People were tired of professional high-browism, star-reaching idealism, bothersome do-goodism, moral overstrain, and constant self-sacrifice. Eager to lapse back into "normalcy," they were willing to accept a second-rate president—and they got a third-rate one.

Although the election could not be considered a true referendum, Republican isolationists successfully turned Harding's victory into a death sentence for the League. Politicians increasingly shunned the League as they would a leper. When the legendary Wilson died in 1924, admirers knelt in the snow outside his Washington home. His "great vision" of a league for peace had died long before.

Online Study Center

Primary source
Interrupting the Ceremony
college.hmco.com/pic/kennedybrief7e

The Betrayal of Great Expectations

America's spurning of the League was tragically shortsighted. The Republic had helped to win a costly war, but it foolishly kicked the fruits of victory under the table. Whether a strong international organization would have averted World War II in 1939 will always be a matter of dispute. But there can be no doubt that the orphaned League of Nations was undercut at the start by the refusal of the mightiest power on the globe to join it. The Allies themselves were largely to blame for the new world conflagration that flared up in 1939, but they found a convenient justification for their own shortcomings by pointing an accusing finger at Uncle Sam.

The ultimate collapse of the Treaty of Versailles must be laid, at least in some degree, at America's doorstep. This complicated pact, tied in with the four other peace treaties through the League Covenant, was a top-heavy structure designed to rest on a four-legged table. The fourth leg, the United States, was never put into place. This rickety structure teetered for over a decade and then crashed in ruins—a debacle that played into the hands of German **demagogue** Adolf Hitler.

The United States, as the tragic sequel proved, hurt its own cause when it buried its head in the sand. Granted that the conduct of its Allies had been disillusioning, it had its own ends to serve by carrying through the Wilsonian program. It would have been well advised if it had forthrightly assumed its war-born responsibilities and resolutely embraced the role of global leader proffered by the hand of destiny. In the interests of its own security, if for no other reason, the United States should have used its enormous strength to shape world-shaking events. Instead it permitted itself blithely to drift toward the abyss of a second and even more bloody international disaster.

demagogue *A politician who arouses fervor by appealing to the lowest emotions of a mass audience, such as fear, hatred, and greed.*

★ Chapter Summary ★

Germany's declaration of unlimited submarine warfare, as well as the Zimmermann note proposing a German alliance with Mexico, finally caused the United States to declare war. Wilson aroused the country to patriotic heights by declaring the war an idealistic crusade for democracy and a just peace, based on his ideologically liberal Fourteen Points.

Vigorous wartime propaganda stirred voluntary commitment to the war effort, but at the cost of suppressing dissent. American voluntary mobilization worked wonders in organizing industry, producing food, and financing the war. Labor, including women, made substantial wartime gains. Some progressive women opposed the war, but women's wartime efforts helped spur passage of the Nineteenth (Suffrage) Amendment. The beginnings of black migration to northern cities led to racial tensions and riots.

America's soldiers took nearly a year to arrive in Europe, and they fought in only two major battles at the end of the war. America's main contribution to the Allied victory was to provide new enthusiasm and morale, along with the threat of endless supplies of men and matériel to follow. Wilson's immense prestige created high expectations for an idealistic peace based on his Fourteen Points. But his own political blunders and the clever, stubborn opposition of European statesmen forced him to compromise his lofty aims and made the Versailles Treaty considerably harsher than he intended.

Republican opposition to Wilson and the League of Nations grew stronger, particularly in the U.S. Senate. As Lodge stalled the treaty, Wilson tried to rouse the country on behalf of his cherished League. A stroke ended his pro-League speaking tour, and his stubborn refusal to compromise with Lodge and the Republicans finally killed the treaty and the League. Wilson sought a "solemn referendum" on the League in the election of 1920, but the public delivered a harsh repudiation of Wilsonianism. Republican isolationists turned Harding's victory into a death sentence for the League.

Woodrow Wilson: Realist or Idealist?

As the first president to take the United States into a foreign war, Woodrow Wilson was obliged to make a systematic case to the American people to justify his unprecedented European intervention. His ideas have largely defined the character of American foreign policy ever since—for better or worse.

"Wilsonianism" comprised three closely related principles: (1) the era of American isolation from world affairs had irretrievably ended; (2) the United States must infuse its own founding political and economic ideas—including democracy, the rule of law, free trade, and national self-determination (or anticolonialism)—into the international order; and (3) American influence could eventually steer the world away from rivalry and warfare and toward a cooperative and peaceful international system, maintained by the League of Nations or, later, the United Nations.

Whether that Wilsonian vision constituted hard-nosed realism or starry-eyed idealism has excited scholarly debate for nearly a century. "Realists," such as George F. Kennan and Henry Kissinger, insist that Wilson was anything but a realist. They criticize the president as a naive, impractical dreamer who failed to understand that the international order was, and always will be, an anarchic, unruly arena, outside the rule of law, where only military force can effectively protect the nation's security. In a sharp critique in his 1950 study, *American Diplomacy,* Kennan condemned Wilson's vision as "moralism-legalism." In this view Wilson dangerously threatened to sacrifice American self-interests on the altar of his admirable but ultimately unworkable ideas.

Wilson's defenders, including conspicuously his principal biographer, Arthur S. Link, argue that Wilson's idealism was in fact a kind of higher realism, recognizing as it did that armed conflict on the scale of World War I could never again be tolerated and that some framework of peaceful international relations simply had to be found. The development of nuclear weapons in a later generation gave this argument more force. This "liberal" defense of Wilsonianism derives from the centuries-old liberal faith that, given sufficient intelligence and willpower, the world can be made a better place. Realists reject this notion of moral and political progress as hopelessly innocent, especially as applied to international affairs.

Some leftist scholars, such as William Appleman Williams, have argued that Wilson was in fact a realist of another kind: a subtle and wily imperialist whose stirring rhetoric cloaked a grasping ambition to make the United States the world's dominant economic power. Sometimes called "the imperialism of free trade," this strategy allegedly sought not to decolonialize the world and open up international commerce for the good of peoples elsewhere, but to create a system in which American economic might would irresistibly prevail. This criticism rests on the naive assumption that international relations are a "zero-sum game," in which one nation's gain must necessarily be another nation's loss. By contrast, Wilson's defenders claim that in a Wilsonian world, *all* parties would be better off; altruism and self-interest need not be mutually exclusive.

Still other scholars, especially John Milton Cooper, Jr., emphasize the absence of economic factors in shaping Wilson's diplomacy. Isolationism, so this argument goes, held such sway over American thinking precisely because the United States had such a puny financial stake abroad—no hard American economic interests were mortally threatened in 1917, nor for a long time thereafter. In these circumstances Wilson—and the Wilsonians who came after him, such as Franklin D. Roosevelt—had no choice but to appeal to abstract ideals and high principles. The "idealistic" Wilsonian strain in American diplomacy, in this view, may have been an unavoidable heritage of America's historically isolated situation. If so, it was Wilson's genius to make practical use of those ideas in his bid for popular support of his diplomacy.

31

American Life in the Roaring Twenties

1919–1929

AMERICA'S PRESENT NEED IS NOT HEROICS BUT HEALING; NOT NOSTRUMS BUT NORMALCY; NOT REVOLUTION BUT RESTORATION; . . . NOT SURGERY BUT SERENITY.

WARREN G. HARDING, 1920

Bloodied by the war and disillusioned by the peace, Americans turned inward in the 1920s. Shunning diplomatic commitments to foreign countries, they also denounced radical foreign ideas, condemned un-American lifestyles, and clanged shut the immigration gates against foreign peoples. They partly sealed off the domestic economy from the rest of the world and plunged headlong into a dizzying decade of homegrown prosperity.

The boom of the golden twenties showered genuine benefits on Americans, as incomes and living standards rose for many. But there seemed to be something incredible about it all, even as people sang,

My sister she works in the laundry,
My father sells bootlegger gin,
My mother she takes in the washing,
My God! how the money rolls in!

New technologies, new consumer products, and new forms of leisure and entertainment made the twenties roar. Yet just beneath the surface lurked widespread anxieties about the future and fears that America was losing sight of its traditional ways.

Focus Questions

1. Why was there such a strong movement toward social conservatism in the wake of World War I?
2. What were the major cultural conflicts that occurred over immigration, cultural pluralism, prohibition, and evolution? Why did these issues create such strong polarization among Americans?
3. What were the major features of the new "mass consumer economy," and what effects did it have on the way Americans lived?
4. How did the "new media" of radio, film, and recorded music transform American culture, including sexuality and the standardization of mass popular taste?
5. How were the new ideas of the times reflected in the American literary renaissance of the 1920s? How was the Harlem Renaissance of black writers similar to and different from artistic movements in the white literary world?

Seeing Red

Hysterical fears of red Russia continued to color American thinking for several years after the Bolshevik revolution of 1917, which spawned a tiny Communist party in America. Tensions were heightened by an epidemic of strikes that convulsed the Republic at war's end, many of them the result of high prices and frustrated union-organizing drives. Upstanding Americans jumped to the conclusion that labor troubles were fomented by bomb-and-whisker Bolsheviks. A general strike in Seattle in 1919, though modest in its demands and orderly in its methods, prompted a call from the mayor for federal troops to head off "the anarchy of Russia." Fire-and-brimstone evangelist Billy Sunday said he would like to "fill the jails so full of [Bolsheviks] that their feet would stick out the window."

The big "red scare" of 1919–1920 resulted in a nationwide crusade against left-wingers whose Americanism was suspect. Attorney General A. Mitchell Palmer earned the title of the "Fighting Quaker" for his excess zeal in rounding up suspects. When a bomb shattered both the nerves and the Washington home of Palmer in June 1919, the "Fighting Quaker" was dubbed the "Quaking Fighter." Late in December 1919, a shipload of 249 alleged alien radicals was deported on the *Buford* ("the Soviet Ark") to the "workers' paradise" of Russia. Hysteria was revived in September 1920 when a still-unexplained bomb blast on Wall Street killed thirty-eight people and wounded several hundred others.

Various states joined the pack in the outcry against radicals. In 1919–1920 a number of legislatures passed criminal **syndicalism** laws that outlawed the mere *advocacy* of violence to secure social change. Critics protested that mere words were not criminal deeds, that there was a great gulf between throwing fits and throwing bombs, and that "free screech" was for the nasty as well as the nice. Violence was done to traditional American concepts of free speech as IWW members and other radicals were vigorously prosecuted. The hysteria went so far that in 1920 five members of the New York legislature, all lawfully elected, were denied their seats simply because they were Socialists.

The red scare was a godsend to conservative businesspeople, who used it to break the backs of the fledgling unions. Labor's call for the "closed," or all-union, shop was denounced as "Sovietism in disguise." Employers, in turn, hailed their own antiunion campaign for the "open" shop as "the American plan."

Anti-redism and antiforeignism were reflected in a notorious case regarded by liberals as a "judicial lynching." Nicola Sacco, a shoe-factory worker, and Bartolomeo Vanzetti, a fish peddler, were convicted in 1921 of the murder of a Massachusetts paymaster and his guard. The jury and judge were prejudiced in some degree against the defendants because they were Italians, atheists, anarchists, and draft dodgers.

Liberals and radicals the world over rallied to the defense of the two aliens doomed to die. The case dragged on for six years until 1927, when the condemned men were electrocuted. Communists and other radicals were thus presented with two martyrs in the "class struggle," while many American liberals hung their heads.

syndicalism *A theory or movement that advocates bringing all economic and political power into the hands of labor unions by means of strikes.*

Hiram Wesley Evans (1881–1966), imperial wizard of the Ku Klux Klan, in 1926 poignantly described the cultural grievances that fueled the Klan and lay behind much of the Fundamentalist revolt against "Modernism":

"Nordic Americans for the last generation have found themselves increasingly uncomfortable and finally deeply distressed. . . . One by one all our traditional moral standards went by the boards, or were so disregarded that they ceased to be binding. The sacredness of our Sabbath, of our homes, of chastity, and finally even of our right to teach our own children in our own schools fundamental facts and truths were torn away from us. Those who maintained the old standards did so only in the face of constant ridicule. . . . We found our great cities and the control of much of our industry and commerce taken over by strangers. . . . We are a movement of the plain people, very weak in the matter of culture, intellectual support, and trained leadership. . . . This is undoubtedly a weakness. It lays us open to the charge of being 'hicks' and 'rubes' and 'drivers of second-hand Fords.'"

Hooded Hoodlums of the KKK

A new Ku Klux Klan, spawned by the postwar reaction, mushroomed fearsomely in the early 1920s. Despite the familiar sheets and hoods, it more closely resembled the

Chronology

1903	Wright brothers fly the first airplane. First story-sequence motion picture.
1919	Eighteenth Amendment (prohibition). Volstead Act. Seattle general strike. Anderson publishes *Winesburg, Ohio.*
1919-1920	"Red scare."
1920	Radio broadcasting begins. Fitzgerald publishes *This Side of Paradise.* Lewis publishes *Main Street.*
1921	Sacco-Vanzetti trial. Emergency Quota Act of 1921.
1922	Lewis publishes *Babbitt.* Eliot publishes "The Waste Land."
1923	Equal Rights Amendment (ERA) proposed.
1924	Immigration Act of 1924.
1925	Scopes trial. Florida real estate boom. Fitzgerald publishes *The Great Gatsby.* Dreiser publishes *An American Tragedy.*
1926	Hughes publishes *The Weary Blues.* Hemingway publishes *The Sun Also Rises.*
1927	Lindbergh flies the Atlantic solo. First talking motion pictures. Sacco and Vanzetti executed.
1929	Faulkner publishes *The Sound and the Fury.* Hemingway publishes *A Farewell to Arms.*

antiforeign nativist movements of the 1850s than the antiblack nightriders of the 1860s. It was antiforeign, anti-Catholic, antiblack, anti-Jewish, antipacifist, anti-communist, anti-internationalist, antievolutionist, anti-adultery, and anti–birth control. It was also pro-Anglo-Saxon, pro-native American, and pro-Protestant. In short, the besheeted Klan betokened an extremist, ultraconservative uprising against many of the forces of diversity and modernity that were transforming American culture.

As reconstituted, the Klan spread with astonishing rapidity, especially in the Midwest and the "**Bible Belt**" South. At its peak in the mid-1920s, it claimed about 5 million dues-paying members and wielded potent political influence. The "Knights" of the "Invisible Empire" included among their officials Imperial Wizards, Grand Goblins, and King Kleagles. The Klan's most impressive displays were "konclaves" and huge flag-waving parades. The chief warning was the blazing cross. The principal weapon was the bloodied lash, supplemented by tar and feathers.

This reign of hooded horror, so repulsive to the best American ideals, collapsed rather suddenly in the late 1920s. The Klan's bubble burst as decent people at last recoiled from its terrorism, while scandalous embezzling by Klan officials launched a congressional investigation that exposed the movement as a vicious racket. The KKK was an alarming manifestation of the intolerance and prejudice plaguing people anxious about the dizzying pace of social change in the 1920s.

Stemming the Foreign Flood

Isolationist America of the 1920s, ingrown and **provincial**, had little use for the immigrants who began to flood into the country again as peace settled soothingly on the war-torn world. Some 800,000 stepped ashore in 1920–1921, about two-thirds of them from southern and eastern Europe. The "one-hundred-percent Americans," shuddering at the sight of this resumed "New Immigration," once again cried that the famed poem at the base of the Statue of Liberty was all too literally true: they claimed that a sickly Europe was indeed vomiting on America "the wretched refuse of its teeming shore."

Online Study Center

Primary source
Ku Klux Klan on Parade
college.hmco.com/pic/kennedybrief7e

Bible Belt *The region of the American South, extending roughly from North Carolina west to Oklahoma and Texas, where Protestant Fundamentalism and belief in literal interpretation of the Bible were traditionally strongest.*

provincial *Narrow and limited; isolated from cosmopolitan influences.*

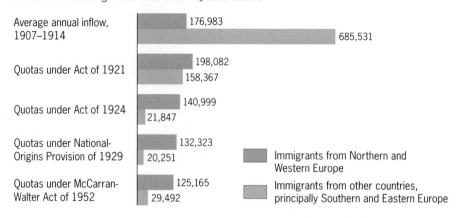

■ Annual Immigration and the Quota Laws

Average annual inflow, 1907–1914: 176,983 / 685,531

Quotas under Act of 1921: 198,082 / 158,367

Quotas under Act of 1924: 140,999 / 21,847

Quotas under National-Origins Provision of 1929: 132,323 / 20,251

Quotas under McCarran-Walter Act of 1952: 125,165 / 29,492

■ Immigrants from Northern and Western Europe
■ Immigrants from other countries, principally Southern and Eastern Europe

> *A recognized expert on American immigration, Henry P. Fairchild (1880–1956), wrote in 1926,*
>
> "The typical immigrant of the present does not really live in America at all, but, from the point of view of nationality, in Italy, Poland, Czecho-Slovakia, or some other foreign country."

Congress temporarily plugged the breach with the Emergency Quota Act of 1921. This stopgap legislation was soon replaced by the Immigration Act of 1924. Quotas for foreigners were drastically cut to 2 percent of persons of each nationality living in the United States in 1890, when comparatively few southern Europeans had arrived.* The purpose was clearly to freeze America's existing ethnic composition, which was largely northern European. A flagrantly discriminatory section of the Immigration Act of 1924 slammed the door absolutely against Japanese immigrants. Only Canadians and Latin Americans were exempt from the quota system.

The quota system effected a pivotal departure in American policy, as the country sacrificed something of its tradition of freedom and opportunity. The Immigration Act of 1924 marked the end of an era—a period of virtually unrestricted immigration that in the previous century had brought some 35 million newcomers to the United States, mostly from Europe. The immigrant tide now dwindled to a mere trickle, but it left on American shores by the 1920s a patchwork of ethnic communities separated from the larger society and from each other by language, religion, and customs. Many Italians, Jews, Poles, and others lived in isolated enclaves with their own houses of worship, newspapers, and theaters (see "Makers of America: The Poles," pp. 492–493). Efforts to organize labor unions repeatedly foundered on the rocks of ethnic rivalries, which were often played upon by cynical employers. Ethnic variety thus undermined class and political solidarity in America.

Immigration restriction did not appeal to reformers. Particularly opposed was the chorus of "cultural pluralists" who had long criticized the idea than an American "melting pot" would eliminate ethnic differences. Two intellectuals, the philosopher Horace Kallen and critic Randolph Bourne, championed alternative conceptions of the immigrant role in American society. Kallen defended German and Austrian immigrants' right to practice their ancestral customs even during the World War I anti-German hysteria. In Kallen's vision America's ethnic groups should be like the instruments in a symphony orchestra, each harmonizing with the other while retaining its own identity.

If Kallen stressed the preservation of identity, Bourne advocated greater cross-fertilization among immigrants. Cosmopolitan interchange, Bourne believed, was destined to make America "not a nationalist but a trans-nationality, a

---

*Five years later the Immigration Act of 1929, using 1920 as the quota base, virtually cut immigration in half by limiting the total to 152,574 a year. In 1965 Congress abolished the national-origins quota system.

 Klanswomen on Parade, 1928 Founded in the Reconstruction Era, the Ku Klux Klan enjoyed a remarkable resurgence in the 1920s. Here, women members, unmasked and unapologetic, march down Pennsylvania Avenue under the very shadow of the Capitol Dome.

weaving back and forth . . . of many threads of all sizes and colors." In this view the United States should serve as the vanguard of a more internationalized and multicultural age.

Other intellectuals, including progressives like John Dewey, Jane Addams, and Louis Brandeis, joined Kallen and Bourne in their defense of ethnic diversity. Vastly outnumbered in the debate over immigration in the 1920s, these early proponents of "cultural pluralism" planted the seeds for the blooming of "multiculturalism" in the last quarter of the twentieth century.

The Prohibition Experiment

One of the last peculiar spasms of the progressive reform movement was prohibition, loudly supported by crusading churches and by many women. The arid new order was authorized in 1919 by the Eighteenth Amendment (see the Appendix), as implemented by the Volstead Act passed by Congress later that year. Together these laws made the world safe for hypocrisy.

The legal abolition of alcohol was especially popular in the South and the West. Southern whites were eager to keep stimulants out of the hands of blacks, lest they burst out of "their place." In the West, prohibition represented an attack on all

Makers of America, The Poles

The Poles were among the largest immigrant groups to respond to industrializing America's call for badly needed labor after the Civil War. Between 1870 and World War I, some 2 million Polish-speaking peasants boarded steamships bound for the United States. By the 1920s, when antiforeign feeling led to restrictive legislation that choked the immigrant stream to a trickle, Polish immigrants and their American-born children began to develop new identities as Polish Americans.

The first Poles to arrive in the New World had landed in Jamestown in 1608 and helped to develop that colony's timber industry. Over the ensuing two and a half centuries, scattered religious dissenters and revolutionary nationalists also made their way from Poland to America. During the Revolution about one hundred Poles, including two officers recruited by Benjamin Franklin, served in the Continental Army.

But the Polish hopefuls who poured into the United States in the late nineteenth century came primarily to stave off starvation and to earn money to buy land. Known in their homeland as *za chlebem* ("for bread") emigrants, they belonged to the mass of central and eastern European

■ Polish Coal Miners, c. 1905 It was common practice in American mines to segregate mining crews by ethnicity and race.

peasants who had been forced off their farms by growing competition from large-scale, mechanized agriculture. An exceptionally high birthrate among the Catholic Poles compounded this economic pressure, creating an army of the land-poor and landless. With wages in the United States more than eight times higher than in Poland, the American magnet was irresistible.

Many Polish immigrants were also lured by glowing letters from friends and relatives already living in the United States. The first wave of Polish immigrants had established a thriving network of self-help and fraternal associations, organized around Polish Catholic parishes. Often Polish American entrepreneurs helped their European compatriots make travel arrangements or find jobs in the United States. One of the most successful of these, the energetic Chicago grocer Anton Schermann, is credited with "bringing over" a hundred thousand Poles and causing the Windy City to earn the nickname "the American Warsaw."

Most of the Poles arriving in the United States in the late nineteenth century headed for booming industrial cities such as Buffalo, Pittsburgh, Detroit, Milwaukee, and Chicago. In 1907 four-fifths of the men toiled as unskilled laborers in coal mines, meatpacking factories, textile and steel mills, oil refineries, and garment-making shops. Although married women usually stayed home and contributed to the family's earnings by taking in laundry and boarders, children and single girls often joined their fathers and brothers on the job.

When an independent Poland was created after World War I, few Poles chose to return to their Old World homeland. Instead, like other immigrant groups in the 1920s, they redoubled their efforts to integrate into American society. Polish institutions like churches and fraternal organizations, which had served to perpetuate a distinctive Polish culture in the New World, now facilitated the transformation of Poles into Polish Americans. When Poland was absorbed into the Communist bloc after World War II, Polish Americans clung still more tightly to their American identity, pushing for landmarks like Chicago's Pulaski Road to memorialize their culture in the New World.

the vices associated with the ubiquitous western saloon: public drunkenness, prostitution, and crime. But despite the overwhelming ratification of the "dry" amendment, strong opposition persisted in the larger eastern cities. For many "wet" foreign-born people, sociability was built around beer gardens and corner taverns.

Prohibitionists were naive in the extreme. They overlooked the tenacious American tradition of weak control by the central government, especially over private lives. They forgot that the federal authorities had never satisfactorily enforced a law that the majority of the people—or a strong minority—were hostile to. Lawmakers could not legislate away a thirst.

Prohibition simply did not prohibit. The old-time "men-only" corner saloons were replaced by thousands of "speakeasies," each with its tiny grilled window through which the thirsty spoke softly before the barred door was opened. Because of the difficulty of transporting and concealing bottles, hard liquor of high alcoholic content gained in popularity. Illegal rumrunners operating from the West Indies or Canada had their inning. "Home brew" and "bathtub gin" became popular, as law-evading adults engaged in "alky cooking" with toy stills.

Yet the "noble experiment" was not entirely a failure. Bank savings increased, and absenteeism in industry decreased, presumably because of the newly sober ways of formerly soused barflies. On the whole, probably less alcohol was consumed than in the days before prohibition, though strong drink continued to be available. As a legendary tippler remarked, prohibition was "a darn sight better than no liquor at all."

Prohibition also spawned shocking crimes. The lush profits of illegal alcohol led to bribery of the police. Violent wars broke out in the big cities between rival gangs—often rooted in immigrant neighborhoods—seeking to corner the rich market in booze. Rival triggermen used their sawed-off shotguns and chattering "typewriters" (machine guns) to "erase" bootlegging competitors who were trying to "muscle in" on their "racket." In the gang wars of the 1920s in Chicago, about five hundred mobsters were murdered.

Chicago was by far the most spectacular example of lawlessness. In 1925 "Scarface" Al Capone, a grasping and murderous booze distributor, began six years of gang warfare that netted him millions of blood-spattered dollars. He zoomed through the streets in an armor-plated car with bulletproof windows. Capone could not be convicted of the cold-blooded massacre, on St. Valentine's Day in 1929, of seven rival gang members, but he was finally sent to jail in 1932 for income tax fraud.

Online Study Center

Primary source
Genius of Advertising, The
college.hmco.com/pic/kennedybrief7e

racketeer *A person who obtains money illegally by fraud, bootlegging, gambling, or threats of violence.*

underworld *Those who live outside society's laws, by vice or crime; organized crime.*

Gangsters rapidly moved into other profitable and illicit activities: prostitution, gambling, and narcotics. Honest merchants were forced to pay "protection money" to prevent thugs from destroying their property. **Racketeers** even invaded the ranks of labor unions as organizers and promoters. Organized crime had come to be one of the nation's most gigantic businesses. By 1930 the annual "take" of the **underworld** was estimated to be from $12 billion to $18 billion—several times the income of the Washington government.

Monkey Business in Tennessee

Education in the 1920s continued to make giant boot-strides. More and more states were requiring young people to remain in school until age sixteen or eighteen, or until graduation from high school. The proportion of seventeen-year-olds who finished high school almost doubled in the 1920s, to more than one in four.

The most revolutionary contribution to educational theory during these yeasty years was made by mild-mannered Professor John Dewey, who served on the faculty of Columbia University from 1904 to 1930. By common consent one of America's few front-rank philosophers, he set forth the principles of "learning by doing" that formed the foundation of so-called progressive education, with its greater "permissiveness." Dewey believed that the workbench was as essential as the blackboard and that "education for life" should be a primary goal of the teacher.

Science also scored wondrous advances in these years. A massive public health program, launched by the Rockefeller Foundation in the South in 1909, had virtually wiped out the ancient affliction of hookworm by the 1920s. Better nutrition and health care helped to increase the life expectancy of a newborn infant from fifty years in 1901 to fifty-nine years in 1929.

■ **The Battle over Evolution** Opponents of Darwin's theories set up shop at the opening of the famed "Scopes Trial" in Dayton, Tennessee in 1925. The trial was an early battle in an American "culture war" that was still being waged nearly a century later.

Yet both science and progressive education in the 1920s were subjected to unfriendly fire from Fundamentalists. These devoted religionists charged that the teaching of Darwinian evolution was destroying faith in God and the Bible while contributing to the moral breakdown of youth in the jazz age. Numerous attempts were made to secure laws prohibiting the teaching of evolution, "the bestial hypothesis," in the public schools, and three southern states adopted such shackling measures. The trio of states included Tennessee, in the heart of the so-called Bible Belt South, where evangelical religion was especially robust.

The stage was set for the memorable "Monkey Trial" in the hamlet of Dayton, Tennessee, in 1925. A likable high school biology teacher, John T. Scopes, was indicted for teaching evolution. Batteries of newspaper reporters, armed with notebooks and cameras, descended upon the quiet town to witness the spectacle. Scopes was defended by nationally known attorneys, while former presidential candidate William Jennings Bryan, an ardent Presbyterian Fundamentalist, joined the prosecution. Taking the stand as an expert on the Bible, Bryan was made to appear foolish by the famed criminal lawyer, Clarence Darrow. Five days after the trial was over, Bryan died of a stroke, no doubt brought on by the wilting heat and witness-stand strain.

This historic clash between theology and biology proved inconclusive. Scopes, the forgotten man of the drama, was found guilty and fined $100. But the supreme court of Tennessee, while upholding the law, set aside the fine on a technicality. (The law itself was not formally repealed until 1967.) The Fundamentalists at best won only a hollow victory, for the absurdities of the trial cast ridicule on their cause. Yet even though increasing numbers of Christians were coming to reconcile the revelations of religion with the findings of modern science, Fundamentalism, with its emphasis on literal reading of the Bible, remained a vibrant force in American spiritual life. It was especially strong in the Baptist Church and in the rapidly growing Churches of Christ, organized in 1906.

> *The bombastic Fundamentalist evangelist W. A. (Billy) Sunday (1862–1935) declared in 1925,*
>
> "If a minister believes and teaches evolution, he is a stinking skunk, a hypocrite, and a liar."

Online Study Center

Primary source
Scopes Trial, The
college.hmco.com/pic/kennedybrief7e

The Mass-Consumption Economy

Prosperity—real, sustained, and widely shared—put much of the roar into the twenties. The economy kicked off its war harness in 1919, faltered a few steps in the recession of 1920–1921, and then sprinted forward for nearly seven years. Both the recent war and Treasury Secretary Andrew Mellon's tax policies favored the rapid expansion of capital investment. Ingenious machines, powered by cheap energy from newly tapped oil fields, dramatically increased the productivity of the laborer. Assembly-line production was so advanced at Henry Ford's famed Rouge River plant near Detroit that a finished automobile emerged every ten seconds.

Great new industries suddenly sprouted forth. Supplying electrical power for the humming new machines became a giant business in the 1920s. Above all the automobile, once the horseless chariot of the rich, now became the carriage of the common citizen. By 1930 Americans owned almost 30 million cars. The nation's deepening love affair with the automobile headlined a momentous shift in the character of the economy. American manufacturers seemed to have mastered the problems of production; their worries now focused on consumption. Could they find the mass markets for the goods they had contrived to spew forth in such profusion?

Responding to this need, a new arm of American commerce came into being: advertising. By persuasion and ploy, allure and sexual suggestion, advertisers sought to make Americans chronically discontented with their paltry possessions and want more, more, more. A founder of this new Madison Avenue "profession" was Bruce Barton, who published a best seller, *The Man Nobody Knows* (1925), portraying Jesus Christ as the greatest adman of all time. Christ was also an executive who "picked up twelve men from the bottom ranks of business and forged them into an organization that conquered the world."

Sports became big business in the consumer economy of the 1920s. Ballyhooed by the image makers, home-run heroes like George H. (Babe) Ruth were far better known than most statesmen. In 1921 a Jersey City crowd paid more than a million dollars to watch heavyweight champion Jack Dempsey knock out challenger George Carpentier—the first in a series of million-dollar gates in the golden 1920s.

Buying on **credit** was another innovative feature of the postwar economy. "Possess today and pay tomorrow" was the message directed at buyers. Once frugal descendants of Puritans went ever deeper into debt to own all kinds of newfangled marvels—refrigerators, vacuum cleaners, and especially cars and radios—*now*. Prosperity thus accumulated an overhanging cloud of debt, and the economy became increasingly vulnerable to disruptions of the credit structure.

Putting America on Rubber Tires

A new industrial revolution slipped into high gear in America in the 1920s. Machinery was the new messiah—and the automobile was its principal prophet. It heralded an amazing new industrial system based on assembly-line methods and mass-production techniques.

Europeans invented the gasoline engine, but Americans quickly adapted it. By the 1890s a few daring American inventors and promoters, including Henry Ford and Ransom E. Olds (Oldsmobile), were developing the infant automotive industry. By 1910 sixty-nine car companies rolled out a total annual production of 181,000 units. Soon an enormous industry sprang into being, as Detroit became the motorcar capital of America.

It was the lean and silent Ford, the best known of all the industrial wizards, who put America on rubber tires. This ill-educated, multimillionaire mechanic was socially and culturally narrow. "History is bunk," he once testified. But he dedicated himself with one-track devotion to the gospel of standardization, and erected an enormous personal empire on the cornerstone of his mechanical genius. After two early failures, he grasped and applied fully the techniques of standardization and assembly-line production—"Fordism." He is supposed to have remarked that the purchaser could have his Model T car in any color he desired just as long as it was black.

The flood of Fords was phenomenal. In 1914 the "Automobile Wizard" turned out his 500,000th Model T. By 1929, when the great bull market collapsed, Ford had produced nearly 20 million vehicles, and a total of 26 million were registered in the United States. This figure, averaging 1 for every 4.9 Americans, represented far more automobiles than existed in all the rest of the world.

The impact of the self-propelled carriage on various aspects of American life was tremendous. A gigantic new industry emerged, employing directly or indirectly about 6 million people by 1930. Thousands of new jobs, moreover, were created in supporting industries like rubber, glass, and fabrics, to say nothing of thousands of service stations and garages. America's standard of living, responding to this infectious vitality, rose to an enviable level.

Zooming motorcars were agents of social change. At first a luxury, they rapidly became a necessity. Essentially devices for needed transportation, they soon developed into a badge of freedom and equality—a necessary prop for self-respect. Women were further freed from their dependence on men. Buses made possible the consolidation of schools and to some extent of churches. Virtuous home life partially broke down as joyriders of all ages forsook the parlor for the highway. And what might young people get up to in the privacy of a closed-top Model T? An Indiana juvenile judge voiced parents' worst fears when he condemned the automobile as "a house of prostitution on wheels." Yet no sane American would plead for a return of the old horse and buggy, complete with fly-breeding manure. The automobile contributed notably to improved air and environmental quality, despite its later notoriety as a polluter. Life might be cut short on the highways, and smog might poison the air, but the automobile brought more convenience, pleasure, and excitement into more people's lives than almost any other single invention.

credit *In business, the arrangement of purchasing goods or services immediately but making the payment at a later date; a consumer loan.*

Online Study Center

Primary source
Ford Weekly Purchase Plan
college.hmco.com/pic/kennedybrief7e

Humans Develop Wings

Gasoline engines also provided the power that enabled humans to fulfill the age-old dream of sprouting wings. After near-successful experiments by others with heavier-than-air craft, the Wright brothers, Orville and Wilbur, performed "the miracle at Kitty Hawk," North Carolina. On a historic day—December 17, 1903—Orville Wright took aloft a feebly engined plane that stayed airborne for twelve seconds and 120 feet. Thus the air age was launched by two obscure bicycle repairmen.

Airplanes, once "flying coffins" for stuntmen, were first used with marked success for a serious purpose during the Great War of 1914–1918. Shortly thereafter private companies began to operate passenger lines with airmail contracts, which were in effect a subsidy from Washington. The first transcontinental airmail route was established from New York to San Francisco in 1920.

In 1927 modest and skillful Charles A. Lindbergh electrified the world with the first solo west-to-east conquest of the Atlantic. Seeking a prize of $25,000, the lanky flier courageously piloted his single-engine plane, the *Spirit of St. Louis,* from New York to Paris in a grueling thirty-three hours and thirty-nine minutes.

Lindbergh's exploit swept Americans off their feet. Fed up with the cynicism and debunking of the jazz age, they found in this wholesome and handsome youth a genuine hero. "Lucky Lindy" received an uproarious welcome in the canyons of lower Broadway, as eighteen hundred tons of ticker tape and other confetti showered upon him. Lindbergh's achievement did much to dramatize and popularize flying while giving a strong boost to the infant aviation industry.

The impact of the airplane was tremendous. The floundering railroads received another sharp setback through the loss of passengers and mail. A lethal new weapon was given to the gods of war with the coming of city-busting aerial bombs. The Atlantic Ocean was shriveling to about the size of the Aegean Sea in the days of Socrates, while isolation behind ocean moats was becoming a bygone dream.

The Radio and Film Revolutions

The speed of the airplane was far eclipsed by the speed of radio waves. Guglielmo Marconi, an Italian, invented wireless telegraphy in the 1890s, and his brainchild was used for long-range communication during World War I. Next came the voice-carrying radio, a triumph of many minds. A red-letter day was posted in November 1920, when the Pittsburgh station KDKA broadcast the news of the Harding landslide. Radio knitted the nation together. By the late 1920s, national commercial networks gained control of the new industry and drowned out much local programming. Various regions heard voices with standardized accents, and countless millions tuned in to perennial comedy favorites like "Amos 'n' Andy." Advertising "commercials" made radio another vehicle for American free enterprise, and brand-named programs like the "A&P Gypsies" and the "Eveready Hour" helped make radio-touted labels household words and purchases.

The flickering movie, the inventive fruit of Thomas Edison and others, first attracted attention in the naughty peep-show arcades in the 1890s. The first story-sequence movie, a breathless melodrama called *The Great Train Robbery,* was featured in the five-cent theaters, popularly called nickelodeons. Spectacular among the first full-length classics was D. W. Griffith's *The Birth of a Nation* (1915), which glorified the Ku Klux Klan of Reconstruction days and defamed both blacks and northern carpetbaggers.

A fascinating industry was thus launched. Hollywood, California, quickly became the movie capital of the world, for it enjoyed a maximum of sunshine and other advantages. Early movies featured nudity and heavy-lidded female vampires ("vamps"), and an outraged public forced the screen magnates to set up their own rigorous code of censorship. The motion picture really arrived during the World War of 1914–1918, when it was used as an engine of anti-German propaganda.

Online Study Center

Primary source
Great Train Robbery, The
college.hmco.com/pic/kennedybrief7e

A new era began in 1927 with the first "talkie"—*The Jazz Singer,* starring white performer Al Jolson in blackface. About the same time, color films began to be produced. Movies eclipsed all other new forms of amusement in the phenomenal growth of their popularity. Movie stars of the first pulchritude commanded much larger salaries than the president of the United States, in some cases as much as $100,000 for a single picture.

Critics bemoaned the vulgarization of popular taste wrought by the technologies of radio and movies. Much of the rich diversity of immigrant cultures was lost, as children, especially, turned away from Grandma's Yiddish storytelling to visit the downtown movie theater or tune in "Amos 'n' Andy." But the effects of the new mass media were not all negative. The standardization of tastes and language hastened immigrants' entry into the American mainstream— and set the stage for the emergence of a working-class political coalition that, for a time, would overcome the divisive ethnic differences of the past.

The Dynamic Decade

Far-reaching changes in lifestyles and values paralleled the dramatic upsurge of the economy. The census of 1920 revealed that for the first time most Americans no longer lived in the countryside but in urban areas. Women continued to find new opportunities for employment in the cities, though they tended to cluster in a few low-paying jobs (such as retail clerking and office typing) that quickly became classified as women's work. An organized birth control movement, led by fiery feminist Margaret Sanger, openly championed the use of contraceptives. Alice Paul's National Woman's party began in 1923 to campaign for an Equal Rights Amendment to the Constitution. To some defenders of traditional ways, it seemed that the world had suddenly gone mad.

Even the churches were affected. Fundamentalists lost ground to Modernists, who liked to think that God was a "good guy." To compete with automobiles and golf, some churches turned to providing entertainment of their own, including wholesome moving pictures for young people.

Even before the war, one observer thought the chimes had struck "sex o'clock in America," and the 1920s witnessed what many old-timers thought was a veritable erotic eruption. Advertisers exploited sexual allure to sell everything from soap to car tires. Once-modest maidens now proclaimed their new freedom as "flappers" in bobbed tresses and dresses. Young women appeared with hemlines

Online Study Center

**Primary source
Birth Control Clinic Circular**
college.hmco.com/pic/kennedybrief7e

■ **King Oliver's Creole Jazz Band, Early 1920s** Joseph "King" Oliver arrived in Chicago from New Orleans in 1918. His band became the first important black jazz ensemble and made Chicago's Royal Garden Café a magnet for jazz lovers. Left to right: Honoré Dutrey, trombone; Baby Dodds, drums; King Oliver, cornet; Lil Hardin, piano; Bill Johnson, banjo; and Johnny Dodds, clarinet. Kneeling in the foreground is the young Louis Armstrong, playing a trombone.

EXAMINING THE EVIDENCE

The Jazz Singer, 1927

The Jazz Singer was the first feature-length "talkie," a motion picture in which the characters actually speak, and its arrival spelled the end for "silent" films, where the audience read subtitles with live or recorded music as background. Although moviegoers flocked to *The Jazz Singer* to hear recorded sound, when they got there they found a movie concerned with themes of great interest to the urban, first or second-generation immigrant audiences who were Hollywood's major patrons. *The Jazz Singer* told the story of a poor, assimilating Jewish immigrant torn between following his father's wish that he train as an Orthodox cantor and his own ambition to make a success for himself as a jazz singer, performing in the popular blackface style. The movie's star, Al Jolson, was himself an immigrant Jew who had made his name as a blackface performer. White actors had gradually taken over the southern black minstrel show during the nineteenth century. By the early twentieth century, Jewish entertainers had entirely monopolized these roles. Jolson, like other Jewish blackface performers, used his ability to impersonate a black person to force his acceptance into mainstream white American society. This use of blackface seems ironic since black Americans in the 1920s were struggling with their own real-life battles against Jim Crow–era segregation, a blatant form of exclusion from American society.

1. Besides the novelty of being a "talkie," what may have made *The Jazz Singer* a box office hit in 1927?

2. How might different types of viewers in the audience have responded to the story?

3. Was the "blackface" tradition of performance by white actors an entirely racist one? Or is there a way in which it acknowledged the great importance of blacks within the wider American culture?

elevated, stockings rolled, breasts taped flat, cheeks rouged, and lips a crimson gash that held a dangling cigarette. Thus did the "flapper" symbolize a yearned-for and devil-may-care independence (some said wild abandon) in some American women.

Justification for this new sexual frankness could be found in the recently translated writings of Dr. Sigmund Freud. This Viennese physician appeared to

repression *In psychology, the forcing of instincts or ideas painful to the conscious mind into the unconscious, where they continue to exercise influence.*

charismatic *Concerning the personal magnetism or appeal of a leader for his or her followers; literally, "gift of grace."*

Online Study Center

**Primary source
Impossible Interview: Sigmund
Freud vs. Jean Harlow**
college.hmco.com/pic/kennedybrief7e

argue that sexual **repression** was responsible for a variety of nervous and emotional ills. Thus not pleasure alone but health demanded sexual gratification and liberation.

Many taboos flew out the window as sex-conscious Americans let themselves go. As unknowing Freudians, teenagers pioneered the sexual frontiers. Glued together in rhythmic embrace, they danced to jazz music squeaking from phonographs. The youthful "neckers" and "petters" also poached upon the forbidden territory of each others' bodies in darkened movie houses or in automobiles.

If the flapper was the goddess of the era, jazz was its sacred music. With its virtuoso wanderings and tricky syncopation, jazz moved up from New Orleans along with migrating blacks during World War I. Tunes like W. C. Handy's "St. Louis Blues" became instant classics, as the wailing saxophone became the trumpet of the new era. Blacks such as Handy, "Jelly Roll" Morton, and Joseph "King" Oliver gave birth to jazz, but the entertainment industry soon spawned all-white bands—notably Paul Whiteman's. Caucasian impresarios cornered the profits, though not the creative soul, of America's most native music.

A new racial pride also blossomed in the northern black communities that grew so rapidly during and after the war. Harlem in New York City, counting some 100,000 African American residents in the 1920s, was one of the largest black communities in the world. Harlem sustained a vibrant, creative culture that nourished poets like Langston Hughes, whose first volume of verse, *The Weary Blues,* appeared in 1926.

Harlem in the 1920s also spawned a **charismatic** leader, Marcus Garvey. The Jamaican-born Garvey founded the United Negro Improvement Association (UNIA) to promote the resettlement of American blacks in Africa. His Black Star Steamship Company and other enterprises failed financially, and Garvey himself was convicted of mail fraud in 1927 and deported by a nervous United States government. But the race pride that Garvey inspired among his 4 million UNIA followers helped these newcomers to northern cities gain self-confidence and self-reliance. And his example proved important to the later founding of the Nation of Islam (Black Muslim) movement.

Literary Liberation

Likewise in literature, an older era seemed to have ground to a halt with the recent war. By the dawn of the 1920s, most of the custodians of an aging genteel culture had died—Henry James in 1916, Henry Adams in 1918, and William Dean Howells ("the Dean of American literature") in 1920. A few novelists who had been popular in the previous decades continued to thrive, notably the well-to-do, cosmopolitan New Yorker Edith Wharton and the Virginia-born Willa Cather, esteemed for her stark but sympathetic portrayals of pioneering on the prairies.

But in the decade after the war, a new generation of writers burst on the scene. Many of them hailed from ethnic and regional backgrounds different from that of the Protestant New Englanders who traditionally had dominated American cultural life. The newcomers exhibited the energy of youth, the ambition of excluded outsiders, and, in many cases the smoldering resentment of ideals betrayed. They bestowed on American literature a new vitality, imaginativeness, and artistic quality.

A patron saint of many young authors was H. L. Mencken, the "Bad Boy of Baltimore." In the pages of his green-covered monthly *American Mercury,* Mencken assailed marriage, patriotism, democracy, prohibition, Rotarians, and the middle-class American "booboisie." The South he contemptuously dismissed as "the Sahara of the Bozart" (a bastardization of *beaux arts,* French for fine arts), and he scathingly attacked do-gooders as Puritans. Puritanism, he jibed, was "the haunting fear that someone, somewhere, might be happy."

The war had jolted many young writers out of their complacency about traditional values and literary standards. With their pens they probed for new codes of morals and understanding, as well as fresh forms of expression. F. Scott Fitzgerald, a handsome Minnesota-born Princetonian then only twenty-four years old, became an overnight celebrity when he published *This Side of Paradise* in 1920. The book became a kind of Bible for the young. It was eagerly devoured by aspiring flappers and their ardent wooers, many of whom affected an air of bewildered abandon toward life. Catching the spirit of the hour (often about 4 A.M.), Fitzgerald found "all gods dead, all wars fought, all faiths in man shaken." He followed this melancholy success with *The Great Gatsby* (1925), a brilliant commentary on the illusory American ideal of the self-made man. Theodore Dreiser's masterpiece of 1925, *An American Tragedy*, explored the pitfalls of social striving, as it dealt with the murder of a pregnant working girl by her socially ambitious young lover.

Ernest Hemingway, who had seen action on the Italian front in 1917, was among the writers most affected by the war. He responded to pernicious propaganda and the overblown appeal of patriotism by devising his own lean, word-sparing but word-perfect style. In *The Sun Also Rises* (1926) Hemingway told of disillusioned, spiritually numb American expatriates in Europe. In *A Farewell to Arms* (1929) he crafted one of the finest novels in any language about the war experience. A troubled soul, he finally blew out his brains with a shotgun blast in 1961.

Other writers turned to a caustic probing of American small-town life. Sherwood Anderson dissected various fictional personalities in *Winesburg, Ohio* (1919), finding them all in some way warped by their cramped psychological surroundings. Sinclair Lewis, a hotheaded, heavy-drinking writer from Sauk Centre, Minnesota, sprang into prominence in 1920 with *Main Street*, the story of one woman's unsuccessful war against provincialism. In *Babbitt* (1922) Lewis affectionately pilloried George F. Babbitt, a prosperous, vulgar, slavishly conformist real estate broker. The word "Babbittry" was quickly coined to describe his all-too-familiar lifestyle.

William Faulkner, a dark-eyed, pensive Mississippian turned his attention to a fictional chronicle of an imaginary, history-rich Deep South county he named "Yoknapatawpha." In powerful books like *The Sound and the Fury* (1929) and *As I Lay Dying* (1930), Faulkner peeled back layers of time and consciousness from the constricted souls of his ingrown southern characters. His extended meditations on southern themes culminated in what some readers consider his greatest work, *Absalom, Absalom* (1936).

Nowhere was innovation in the 1920s more obvious than in poetry. Ezra Pound, a brilliantly erratic Idahoan who deserted America for Europe, rejected what he called "an old bitch civilization, gone in the teeth," and proclaimed his doctrine: "Make It New." Pound strongly influenced Missouri-born and Harvard-educated T. S. Eliot. After taking up permanent residence in England, Eliot produced "The Waste Land" (1922), one of the most influential poems of the century. Robert Frost, a San Francisco-born poet, wrote hauntingly about his adopted New England.

On the stage, Eugene O'Neill, a New York dramatist and Princeton dropout of globe-trotting background, laid bare Freudian notions of sex in plays like *Strange Interlude* (1928). A prodigious playwright, he authored more than a dozen productions in the 1920s and won the Nobel Prize in 1936.

■ **F. Scott Fitzgerald and His Wife, Zelda** They are shown here in the happy, early days of their stormy marriage.

Langston Hughes (1902–1967) celebrated Harlem's role in energizing a generation of artists and writers in his poem "Aesthete in Harlem" (1930):

> "Strange,
> That in this nigger place
> I should meet Life face to face;
> When, for years, I had been seeking
> Life in places gentler speaking,
> Until I came to this vile street
> And found Life stepping on my feet!"

functionalism *The theory that a plan or design should be derived from its practical purpose.*

surtax *A special tax, usually involving a raised rate on an already existing tax.*

O'Neill arose from New York's Greenwich Village, which before and after the war was a seething cauldron of writers, painters, musicians, actors, and other would-be artists. After the war a black cultural renaissance also took root uptown in Harlem, led by such gifted writers as Claude McKay, Langston Hughes, and Zora Neale Hurston, and by jazz artists like Louis Armstrong and Eubie Blake. In an outpouring of creative expression called the Harlem Renaissance, they proudly exulted in their black culture and argued for a "New Negro" who was a full citizen and a social equal to whites.

Architecture also married itself to the new materialism and **functionalism**. Architects such as Frank Lloyd Wright were advancing the theory that buildings should grow from their sites and not slavishly imitate Greek and Roman importations. The machine age outdid itself in 1931 in New York City when it thrust upward the cloud-brushing Empire State Building, 102 stories high.

Wall Street's Big Bull Market

Signals abounded that the economic joyride might end in a crash; even in the best years of the 1920s several hundred banks failed annually. This something-for-nothing craze was well illustrated by real estate speculation, especially the fantastic Florida boom that culminated in 1925. Numerous underwater lots were sold to eager purchasers for preposterous sums. The whole wildcat scheme collapsed when the peninsula was devastated by a hurricane.

The stock exchange provided even greater sensations. Speculation ran wild. An orgy of boom-or-bust trading pushed the bull market to dizzying peaks, as Wall Street gamblers gored one another and fleeced greedy lambs. The stock market became a veritable gambling den.

As the 1920s lurched forward, everybody seemed to be buying stocks "on margin"—that is, with a small down payment. Barbers, stenographers, and elevator boys cashed in on hot tips picked up while on duty. One valet was reported to have parlayed his wages into a quarter of a million dollars. Rags-to-riches Americans eagerly worshiped at the altar of the ticker-tape machine. So powerful was the intoxicant of quick profits that few heeded the voices raised in certain quarters to warn that this kind of tinsel prosperity could not last forever.

Little was done by Washington to curb money-mad speculators. In the wartime days of Wilson, the national debt had rocketed from the 1914 figure of $1,188,235,400 to the 1921 peak of $23,976,250,608. Conservative principles of money management pointed to a diversion of surplus funds to reduce this financial burden. But to Secretary of the Treasury Andrew Mellon and his fellow millionaires, the burdensome taxes inherited from the war were especially distasteful. Their theory was that such high levies forced the rich to invest in tax-exempt securities rather than in factories that dispensed prosperous payrolls. The Mellonites also argued, with considerable persuasiveness, that high taxes not only discouraged business but also brought a smaller net return to the Treasury than moderate taxes.

Seeking to succor the "poor" rich people, Mellon helped engineer a series of tax reductions from 1921 to 1926. Congress followed his lead by repealing the excess-profits tax, abolishing the gift tax, and reducing excise taxes, the **surtax**, the income tax, and estate taxes. In 1921 a wealthy person with an income of $1 million had paid $663,000 in income taxes; in 1926 the same person paid about $200,000. Mellon's spare-the-rich policies thus shifted much of the tax burden from the wealthy to middle-income groups.

Mellon, lionized by conservatives as "the greatest Secretary of the Treasury since Hamilton," remains a controversial figure. True, he reduced the national debt by $10 billion—from about $26 billion to $16 billion. But foes of the emaciated multimillionaire charged that he should have bitten an even larger chunk out of the debt, especially while the country was pulsating with prosperity. He was also accused of indirectly encouraging the bull market. If he had absorbed more of the national income in taxes, there would have been less money left for frenzied speculation. His refusal to do so typified the single-mindedly probusiness regime that dominated the political scene throughout the postwar decade.

Online Study Center

**Primary source
Aspects of the Financial
Merry-Go-Round**
college.hmco.com/pic/kennedybrief7e

⭐ Chapter Summary ⭐

After the crusading idealism of World War I, America sharply turned inward, as many citizens became hostile to anything foreign or different. Radicals and immigrants were targeted in the red scare and the Sacco-Vanzetti case, while the resurgent Ku Klux Klan reflected many Protestant Americans' fears of change. New restrictions on immigration reflected prejudice against "non-Anglo-Saxon" groups. Sharp cultural and religious conflicts also occurred over the prohibition experiment and evolution.

A new mass-consumption economy fueled the spectacular prosperity of the 1920s. The automobile industry, led by Henry Ford, transformed the economy and altered American lifestyles. Charles Lindbergh's flight symbolized the persistence of individual heroism in an age of cynicism and mass standardization.

The pervasive media of radio and film dramatically altered popular culture and values. Jazz music, the Harlem Renaissance, and Marcus Garvey's movement all reflected African-Americans' new cultural energy. Birth control and Freudian psychology overturned traditional sexual standards, especially for women. Young literary rebels, many originally from the Midwest, scorned genteel New England and small-town culture and searched for new values, sometimes as expatriates in Europe. The stock-market boom symbolized the free-wheeling spirit of the decade.

32

The Politics of Boom and Bust

---❧---

1920–1932

WE IN AMERICA TODAY ARE NEARER TO THE FINAL TRIUMPH
OVER POVERTY THAN EVER BEFORE IN THE HISTORY OF ANY
LAND. WE HAVE NOT YET REACHED THE GOAL—BUT . . . WE
SHALL SOON, WITH THE HELP OF GOD, BE IN SIGHT OF THE DAY
WHEN POVERTY WILL BE BANISHED FROM THIS NATION.

HERBERT HOOVER, 1928

Three Republican presidents—Warren G. Harding, Calvin Coolidge, and Herbert Hoover—steered the nation on the roller-coaster ride of the 1920s, a thrilling ascent from the depths of post–World War I recession to breathtaking heights of prosperity, followed by a terrifying crash into the Great Depression. In a retreat from progressive reform, Republicans sought to serve the public good less by direct government action and more through cooperation with big business. Some corrupt officials served themselves as well, exploiting public resources for personal profit. Meanwhile, the United States retreated from its brief international fling during World War I and resumed with a vengeance its traditional foreign policy of military unpreparedness and political isolationism.

Focus Questions

1. How did the political conservatism and economic prosperity of the 1920s lead to policies advancing the interests of business and attempting to isolate America from the world?
2. What was consistent and what was different in the leadership and policies of the three Republican presidents of the 1920s—Harding, Coolidge, and Hoover?
3. How successfully did the United States address the international economic tangle of loans, war debts, and reparations? Why was there so much resentment of America's actions in Europe?
4. What were the immediate and more fundamental causes of the stock market crash and the Great Depression?
5. In what ways was Hoover's response to the Great Depression a reflection of the older ideology of individualism and *laissez-faire*, and in what ways did his actions reflect a newer view of government responsibility for the nation's collective economic well-being?

Chronology

1919	American Legion founded.
1920	Esch-Cummins Transportation Act.
1921	Veterans Bureau created.
1922	Five-Power Naval Treaty. Four-Power and Nine-Power Treaties on East Asia.
1923	*Adkins* v. *Children's Hospital.* Teapot Dome scandal. Harding dies; Coolidge assumes presidency.
1924	Adjusted Compensation Act for veterans. Dawes Plan for international finance. U.S. troops leave Dominican Republic. Coolidge wins three-way presidential election.
1926	U.S. troops occupy Nicaragua.
1928	Kellogg-Briand Pact. Hoover defeats Smith for presidency.
1929	Stock-market crash.
1930	Hawley-Smoot Tariff.
1931	Japanese invade Manchuria.
1932	Reconstruction Finance Corporation (RFC) established. Norris–La Guardia Anti-Injunction Act. "Bonus Army" dispersed from Washington, D.C.

The Republican "Old Guard" Returns

Warren G. Harding, inaugurated in 1921, *looked* presidential. With erect figure, broad shoulders, bushy eyebrows, and graying hair, he was one of the best-liked men of his generation. An easygoing, warm-handed backslapper, he exuded graciousness and love of people. Yet the charming, smiling exterior concealed a weak, inept interior. With a mediocre mind, Harding quickly found himself beyond his depth in the presidency. "God! What a job!" was his anguished cry on one occasion.

Harding, like Grant, was unable to detect moral halitosis in his evil associates, and he was soon surrounded by his poker-playing, shirt-sleeved cronies of the "Ohio gang." Harding hated to hurt his friends' feelings by saying no, and designing political leeches capitalized on this weakness. He "was not a bad man," said one Washington observer. "He was just a slob."

Admitting his own scant mental furnishings, Harding appointed to his cabinet some strong and capable Republicans: imperious and brilliant Charles Evans Hughes as secretary of state; lean and elderly Andrew W. Mellon as secretary of the treasury; and chubby-faced Herbert Hoover, famed wartime feeder of the Belgians, as secretary of commerce. But Harding also brought into his cabinet such corrupt characters as Secretary of the Interior Albert B. Fall, a scheming anti-conservationst, and Attorney General Harry M. Daugherty, a member of the "Ohio gang" and a big-time crook.

Well intentioned but weak-willed, Harding was a perfect "front" for enterprising industrialists. A McKinley-style old order settled back into place at war's end, crushing the reform seedlings that had sprouted in the progressive era. This new Old Guard hoped to improve on the old business doctrine of laissez-faire. Their plea was not simply for government to keep its hands off business but for government to help guide business along the path to profits. They subtly and effectively achieved their ends by putting the courts and the administrative bureaus into the safekeeping of fellow stand-patters for the duration of the decade.

The Supreme Court was a striking example of this trend. In his short presidency Harding appointed four justices who were or became deep-dyed reactionaries. In the first years of the 1920s, the Supreme Court axed progressive legislation. It killed a federal child-labor law, stripped away many of labor's hard-won gains, and rigidly restricted governmental intervention in the economy. In the

Justice Oliver Wendell Holmes (1841–1935), wryly dissenting in the Adkins *case, said,*

"It would need more than the Nineteenth Amendment to convince me that there are no differences between men and women, or that legislation cannot take those differences into account."

landmark case of *Adkins* v. *Children's Hospital* (1923), the Court reversed its own reasoning in *Muller* v. *Oregon* (see p. 447) and invalidated a minimum-wage law for women. Its strained ruling was that because females now had the vote (Nineteenth Amendment), they were the legal equals of men and could no longer be protected by special legislation. The contradictory premises of the *Muller* and *Adkins* cases framed a debate over gender differences that would continue for the rest of the century: Were women sufficiently different from men that they merited special legal and social treatment, or were they effectively equal in the eyes of the law and therefore undeserving of special protection and preferences?

Under Harding, corporations could once more relax and expand. Antitrust laws were often ignored, circumvented, or feebly enforced by friendly prosecutors in the attorney general's office. The Interstate Commerce Commission, to single out one agency, came to be dominated by members who were sympathetic to the managers of the railroads.

Big industrialists, striving to lessen competition, now had a free hand to set up trade associations. Cement manufacturers, for example, would use these agencies to agree upon standardization of product, publicity campaigns, and a united front in dealing with the railroads and labor. Although many of these associations ran counter to the spirit of existing antitrust legislation, their formation was encouraged by Secretary of Commerce Herbert Hoover. His sense of engineering efficiency led him to condemn the waste resulting from cutthroat competition and to encourage business self-regulation.

The Aftermath of War

Wartime government controls on the economy were swiftly dismantled. The War Industries Board disappeared with almost indecent haste. With its passing, progressive hopes for more government regulation of big business evaporated.

Washington likewise returned the railroads to private management in 1920. The Esch-Cummins Transportation Act of 1920 encouraged private consolidation of the railroads and obligated the federal Interstate Commerce Commission to guarantee their profitability.

Labor, suddenly deprived of its wartime crutch of friendly government support, limped along badly in the postwar decade. The Railway Labor Board, a successor body to the wartime labor boards, ordered a wage cut of 12 percent in 1922, provoking a two-month strike. It ended when Attorney General Daugherty, who fully shared Harding's big-business bias, clamped on the strikers one of the most sweeping injunctions in American history. Unions wilted in this hostile political environment, and membership dropped by nearly 30 percent between 1920 and 1930.

Needy veterans were among the few nonbusiness groups to reap lasting gains from the war. In 1921 Congress created the Veterans Bureau to operate hospitals and provide vocational rehabilitation for the disabled. The American Legion, founded in Paris in 1919 by Colonel Theodore Roosevelt, Jr., became known for its militant conservative patriotism and aggressive lobbying for veterans' benefits. It demanded "adjusted compensation" to make up for the wages veterans had "lost" while in uniform. Harding vetoed one such bill in 1922, but in 1924 Congress passed the Adjusted Compensation Act over President Calvin Coolidge's veto. It gave every former soldier a paid-up insurance policy due in twenty years—adding about $3.5 billion to the total cost of the war.

America Seeks Benefits Without Burdens

Isolation was enthroned in Washington. The Harding administration, with the Senate "irreconcilables" holding a hatchet over its head, continued to regard the League of Nations as a thing unclean.

But disarmament was one international issue on which Harding set isolationism aside and seized the initiative. He was prodded by businesspeople unwilling to dig deeper into their pockets for money to finance the ambitious naval building program started during the war. A deadly contest was shaping up with Britain and Japan, which watched with alarm as the oceans filled with American vessels. Public agitation in America, fed by worries about British and Japanese cooperation in the Pacific, brought about the headline-making Washington Disarmament Conference in 1921–1922. The double agenda included naval disarmament and the situation in East Asia.

At the outset, Secretary of State Charles Evans Hughes dramatically proposed a ten-year "holiday" on construction of battleships, and even the scrapping of some of the huge **dreadnoughts** already built or being built. He proposed that the scaled-down navies of America and Britain should enjoy parity in battleships and aircraft carriers, with Japan on the small end of a 5-5-3 ratio.

dreadnought *A heavily armored battleship with large batteries of twelve-inch guns.*

The conference's Five-Power Naval Treaty of 1922 embodied Hughes's ideas on ship ratios, but only after face-saving compensation for the insecure Japanese. The British and Americans both conceded that they would refrain from fortifying their East Asian possessions, including the Philippines. The Japanese were not subjected to such restraints in their possessions. In addition, a Four-Power Treaty bound Britain, Japan, France, and the United States to preserve the status quo in the Pacific—another concession to the Japanese. Finally, the Washington Conference gave chaotic China—"the sick man of East Asia"—a shot in the arm with the Nine-Power Treaty of 1922, whose signatories agreed to nail wide open the Open Door in China.

The Hardingites boasted of this globe-shaking achievement in disarmament, but their satisfaction was somewhat illusory. No restrictions had been placed on small warships, and the other powers churned ahead with the construction of cruisers, destroyers, and submarines, while penny-pinching Uncle Sam lagged dangerously behind. Ominously, the American people seemed content to rely for their security on words and wishful thinking rather than on weapons and hard-headed realism.

A similar sentimentalism welled up later in the decade, when millions of Americans signed petitions calling for the "outlawry of war." Calvin Coolidge's secretary of state, Frank B. Kellogg, and the French foreign minister, Aristide Briand, signed the Kellogg-Briand Pact forswearing war in 1928, and it was ultimately ratified by sixty-two nations. Lacking both muscles and teeth, this parchment peace was illusory in the extreme. Yet it accurately—and dangerously—reflected the American mind in the 1920s, which was all too ready to be lulled into a false sense of security. This mood took even deeper hold in the ostrich-like neutralism of the 1930s.

Online Study Center

Primary source
Kellogg-Briand Pact
college.hmco.com/pic/kennedybrief7e

Hiking the Tariff Higher

A comparable lack of realism afflicted foreign economic policy in the 1920s. Businesspeople, shortsightedly obsessed with the dazzling prospects in the prosperous home market, sought to keep that market to themselves by flinging up insurmountable tariff walls around the United States. Congress passed the Fordney-McCumber Tariff Law of 1922, which boosted schedules from the average of 27 percent under Wilson's Underwood Tariff of 1913 to an average of 38.5 percent.

The high-tariff course thus charted by the Republican regimes set off an ominous chain reaction. European producers felt the squeeze, for the American tariff walls prolonged the postwar chaos. An impoverished Europe needed to sell manufactured goods to the United States, particularly if it hoped to achieve economic recovery and to pay its huge war debt to Washington. America needed to give foreign nations a chance to make a profit from it so that they could buy U.S. manufactured articles and repay debts. International trade, Americans were slow to learn, is a two-way street.

Erecting tariff walls was a game that two could play. The American example spurred European nations, throughout the feverish 1920s, to pile up higher barriers themselves. The whole vicious circle further deepened the international economic distress, providing one more rung on the ladder by which Adolf Hitler scrambled to power.

⬥

The Stench of Scandal

The loose morality and get-rich-quickism of the Harding era manifested themselves spectacularly in a series of scandals. Early in 1923 the head of the Veterans Bureau, Colonel Charles R. Forbes, was caught with his hand in the till. An appointee of the gullible Harding, he and his **accomplices** looted the government to the tune of about $200 million, chiefly in connection with the building of veterans' hospitals. Forbes was convicted and sentenced to two years in a federal penitentiary.

Most shocking of all was the Teapot Dome scandal, an affair that involved priceless naval oil reserves at Teapot Dome (Wyoming) and Elk Hills (California). In 1921 the slippery secretary of the interior, Albert B. Fall, induced his careless colleague, the secretary of the navy, to transfer these valuable properties to the Interior Department. Harding indiscreetly signed the secret order. Fall then quietly leased the lands to oilmen Harry F. Sinclair and Edward L. Doheny, but not until they had paid him some $400,000 in bribes ("loans").

Teapot Dome, no tempest in a teapot, finally came to a whistling boil. Details of the crooked transaction leaked out in March 1923. Fall, Sinclair, and Doheny were indicted in 1924. Fall was found guilty of taking a bribe and sentenced to one year in jail. The two bribe givers were acquitted, though Sinclair served time in jail for "shadowing" jurors and for refusing to testify before a Senate committee.

Still more scandals erupted. Persistent reports about the underhanded doings of Attorney General Daugherty brought a Senate investigation in 1924 of the illegal sale of pardons and liquor permits. Forced to resign, the accused official was tried in 1927 but released after a jury twice failed to agree. During the trial, Daugherty hid behind the trousers of the now-dead Harding by implying that persistent probing might uncover crookedness in the White House.

Harding was mercifully spared the full revelation of these iniquities. Just as news of the scandals was beginning to break, he died in San Francisco on August 2, 1923, of pneumonia and thrombosis.

The brutal fact is that Harding simply was not a strong enough man for the presidency—as he himself privately admitted. Such was his weakness that he tolerated people and conditions that subjected the Republic to its worst disgrace since the days of President Grant.

accomplice *An associate or partner of a criminal who shares some degree of guilt.*

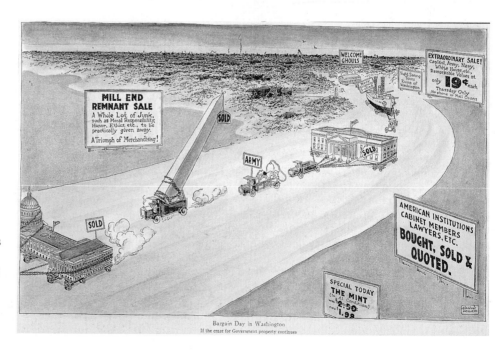

■ The Harding Scandals This 1924 cartoon satirizing the misdemeanors of the Harding administration shows the sale of the Capitol, the White House, and even the Washington Monument.

"Silent Cal" Coolidge

News of Harding's death was sped to Vice President Coolidge, then visiting at his father's New England farmhouse. By the light of two kerosene lamps the elder Coolidge, a justice of the peace, used the old family Bible to administer the presidential oath to his son.

This homespun setting was symbolic of Coolidge. Quite unlike Harding, the stern-faced Vermonter, with his thin nose and tightly set lips, embodied the New England virtues of honesty, morality, industry, and frugality. His dour visage prompted the acerbic observation that he had been "weaned on a pickle."

Coolidge seemed to be a crystallization of the commonplace. Painfully shy, he was blessed with only mediocre powers of leadership. He would occasionally display a dry wit in private; but his speeches, delivered in a nasal New England twang, were invariably boring. A staunch apostle of the status quo, he became the "high priest of the great god Business." He believed that "the man who builds a factory builds a temple" and that "the man who works there worships there." The hands-off temperament of "Cautious Cal" perfectly suited the times, and Coolidge's "luck" held during his five and a half prosperity-blessed years.

Ever a profile in caution, Coolidge slowly gave the Harding regime a badly needed moral fumigation. Teapot Dome had scalded the Republican party badly, but so transparently honest was the vinegary Vermonter that the scandalous oil did not rub off on him.

■ Calvin Coolidge, Gentleman Angler Coolidge "was a real conservative, a fundamentalist in religion, in the economic and social order, and in fishing," said his successor, Herbert Hoover, who had a fly fisherman's disdain for Coolidge's bait-fishing tactics—and for his predecessor's laissez-faire politics as well.

Frustrated Farmers

Sun-bronzed farmers were caught squarely in a boom-or-bust cycle in the postwar decade. While the fighting had raged, they had raked in money, hand over gnarled fist. But peace brought an end to high farm prices and to massive purchases by other nations, as foreign production reentered the stream of world commerce.

Machines also threatened to plow the farmer under an avalanche of his own overabundant crops. The gasoline-engine tractor was working a revolution on American farms. This steel mule was to cultivation and sowing what the McCormick reaper was to harvesting. Blue-denimed farmers could sit on their chugging mechanized chariots and harrow many acres in a single day. But such improved efficiency and expanded agricultural production helped to pile up more price-dampening surpluses. A withering depression swept through agricultural districts in the 1920s, when one farm in four was sold for debt or taxes.

Schemes abounded for bringing relief to the hard-pressed farmers. A bipartisan "farm bloc" from the agricultural states coalesced in Congress in 1921 and succeeded in driving through some helpful laws. Noteworthy was the Capper-Volstead Act, which exempted farmers' marketing cooperatives from antitrust prosecution. The farm bloc's favorite proposal was the McNary-Haugen Bill, pushed energetically from 1924 to 1928. It sought to keep agricultural prices high by authorizing the government to buy up surpluses and sell them abroad. Congress twice passed the bill, but frugal Coolidge twice vetoed it. Farm prices stayed low, and the farmers' political temperatures stayed high, reaching fever pitch in the election of 1924.

A Three-Way Race for the White House in 1924

Self-satisfied Republicans, chanting "Keep Cool and Keep Coolidge," nominated "Silent Cal" for the presidency at their convention in Cleveland in the simmering summer of 1924. Squabbling Democrats had more difficulty choosing a candidate when they met in New York's sweltering Madison Square Garden. Reflecting many of the cultural tensions of the decade, the party was hopelessly split between "wets" and "drys," urbanites and farmers, Fundamentalists and Modernists, northern liberals and southern stand-patters, immigrants and old-stock

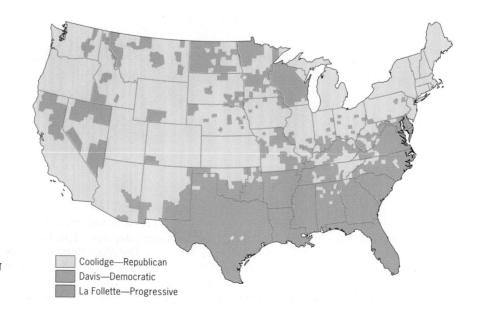

■ **Presidential Election of 1924 (showing popular vote by county)** Notice the concentration of La Follette's votes in the old Populist strongholds of the Midwest and the mountain states. His ticket did especially well in the grain-growing districts battered by the postwar slump in agricultural prices.

☐ Coolidge—Republican
◼ Davis—Democratic
◼ La Follette—Progressive

Americans. Deadlocked for an unprecedented 102 ballots, the convention at last turned wearily, sweatily, and unenthusiastically to John W. Davis. A wealthy Wall Street lawyer, the polished nominee was no less conservative than cautious Calvin Coolidge.

The field was now wide open for a liberal candidate, and white-pompadoured Senator Robert ("Fighting Bob") La Follette of Wisconsin sprang forward to lead a new Progressive grouping. He gained the support of both the American Federation of Labor and the Socialist party, but his major constituency was the price-pinched farmers. La Follette's new Progressive party, only a shadow of the robust progressive coalition of prewar days, called for government ownership of railroads and relief for farmers, lashed out at monopoly and antilabor injunctions, and urged a constitutional amendment to limit the Supreme Court's power to invalidate laws passed by Congress.

La Follette turned in a respectable showing, polling nearly 5 million votes. But "Cautious Cal" and the oil-smeared Republicans slipped easily back into office, overwhelming Davis, 15,718,211 votes to 8,385,283. The electoral count stood at 382 for Coolidge, 136 for Davis, and 13 for La Follette, all from his home state of Wisconsin.

Foreign-Policy Flounderings

Isolation continued to reign in the Coolidge era. Despite presidential proddings, the Senate proved unwilling to allow America to adhere to the World Court—the judicial arm of the still-suspect League of Nations. Coolidge only halfheartedly—and unsuccessfully—pursued further naval disarmament after the loudly trumpeted agreements worked out at the Washington Conference in 1922.

A glaring exception to the United States' inward-looking indifference to the outside world in the 1920s was the armed interventionism in the Caribbean and Central America. American troops were withdrawn (after an eight-year stay) from the Dominican Republic in 1924, but they remained in Haiti from 1914 to 1934. President Coolidge in 1925 briefly removed American bayonets from troubled Nicaragua, where they had glinted intermittently since 1909, but in 1926 he sent them back, five thousand strong, and they stayed until 1933. When U.S. oil companies clamored for intervention in Mexico in 1926 to protect their interests there, Coolidge kept cool and defused the crisis with some skillful diplomatic negotiating. But his mailed-fist tactics elsewhere bred sore resentments south of the Rio Grande, where angry critics loudly assailed "*yanqui* imperialism."

Overshadowing all other foreign-policy problems in the 1920s was the knotty issue of international debts, a complicated tangle of private loans, Allied war debts, and German **reparations**. The key knot in the debt tangle was the $10 billion that the U.S. Treasury had loaned to the Allies during and immediately after the war. Uncle Sam held their IOUs—and he wanted to be paid. The Allies, in turn, protested that they had held up a wall of flesh and bone against the common foe until America the Unready had finally entered the fray. America, they argued, should write off its loans as war costs, just as the Allies had been tragically forced to write off the lives of millions of young men. And the final straw, protested the Europeans, was that America's postwar tariff walls made it almost impossible for them to sell the goods to earn the dollars to pay their debts.

reparations *Compensation by a defeated nation for damage done to civilians and their property during a war.*

Unraveling the Debt Knot

America's tightfisted insistence on getting its money back helped to harden the hearts of the Allies against conquered Germany. The French and the British demanded that the Germans make enormous reparations payments, totaling some $32 billion, as compensation for war-inflicted damages. The Allies hoped to settle their debts to America with the money received from Germany. The French, seeking to extort lagging reparations payments, sent troops into Germany's industrialized Ruhr Valley in 1923. Berlin responded by permitting its currency to inflate

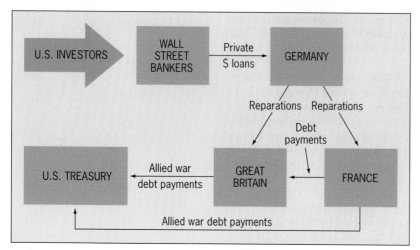

■ **Aspects of the Financial Merry-Go-Round, 1921–1933** Great Britain, with a debt of over $4 billion to the U.S. Treasury, had a huge stake in proposals for inter-Allied debt cancellation, but France's stake was even larger. Less prosperous than Britain in the 1920s, and more battered by the war, which had been fought on its soil, France owed nearly $3.5 billion to the United States and additional billions to Britain.

astronomically. At one point in October 1923, a loaf of bread cost 480 million marks, or about $120 million in preinflation money. German society teetered on the brink of mad anarchy, and the whole international house of financial cards threatened to flutter down in colossal chaos.

Sensible statesmen now urged that the war debts and reparations alike be drastically scaled down or canceled outright. But to Americans such proposals smacked of "welshing" on a debt. Scroogelike Calvin Coolidge turned aside suggestions of debt cancellation with a typically terse question: "They hired the money, didn't they?"

Reality finally dawned in the Dawes Plan of 1924. Negotiated largely by Charles Dawes, about to be Coolidge's running mate, it rescheduled German reparations payments and opened the way for further American private loans to Germany. The whole financial cycle now became still more complicated as U.S. bankers loaned money to Germany, Germany paid reparations to France and Britain, and the former Allies paid war debts to the United States. Clearly the source of this monetary merry-go-round was the flowing well of American credit. When that well dried up after the great crash in 1929, the tangled jungle of international finance quickly turned into a desert.

The United States never did get its money, but it harvested a bumper crop of ill will. Throughout Europe Uncle Sam was caricatured as Uncle Shylock, greedily whetting his knife for the last pound of Allied flesh. The bad taste left in American mouths by the whole sorry episode contributed powerfully to the storm-cellar neutrality legislation passed by Congress in the 1930s.

The Triumph of Herbert Hoover in 1928

Poker-faced Calvin Coolidge, the tight-lipped "Sphinx of the Potomac," bowed out of the 1928 presidential race when he announced, "I do not choose to run." His logical successor was super-Secretary (of Commerce) Herbert Hoover. He was nominated on a platform that clucked contentedly over both prosperity and prohibition.

Still-squabbling Democrats nominated Alfred E. Smith, the wisecracking, glad-handing governor of New York and one of the most colorful personalities in American politics. "Al(cohol)" Smith was soakingly "wet" on prohibition, abrasively urban, and Roman Catholic in an overwhelmingly Protestant—and unfortunately prejudiced—land. Many dry, rural, and Fundamentalist Democrats gagged on his candidacy, and they saddled the wet Smith with a dry running mate and a dry platform.

Radio figured prominently in this campaign for the first time, and it helped Hoover more than Smith. The New Yorker had more personal sparkle, but he could not project it through the radio. Iowa-born Hoover, with his double-breasted dignity, came out of the microphone better than he went in.

Chubby-faced, ruddy-complexioned Herbert Hoover, with his painfully high starched collar, was a living example of the American success story, and an intriguing mixture of two centuries. As a poor orphan boy who had worked his way through Stanford University, he had absorbed the nineteenth-century copybook maxims of industry, thrift, and self-reliance. As a fabulously successful mining engineer and businessman, he had honed to a high degree the efficiency doctrines of the progressive era.

A small-town boy from Iowa and Oregon, he had traveled and worked abroad extensively. His experiences there had further strengthened his faith in American individualism, free enterprise, and small government. With his unshaken dignity and Quaker restraint, Hoover was a far cry from the typical backslapping politician. Personally colorless in public, he had been accustomed during much of his life to giving orders to subordinates, and did not adapt readily to the necessary give-and-take of political accommodation.

As befitted America's newly mechanized civilization, Hoover was the ideal businessperson's candidate. A self-made millionaire, he recoiled from anything suggesting socialism, paternalism, or "planned economy." Yet as secretary of commerce, he had exhibited some progressive instincts. He endorsed labor unions and supported federal regulation of the new radio broadcasting industry. He even flirted for a time with the idea of government-owned radio, similar to the British Broadcasting Corporation (BBC).

Despite the best efforts of Hoover and Smith, below-the-belt tactics were employed to a disgusting degree by their lower-level campaigners. Religious bigotry raised its hideous head over Smith's Catholicism. An irresponsible whispering campaign claimed that "A vote for Al Smith is a vote for the Pope" and that the White House, under Smith, would become a branch of the Vatican.

Hoover triumphed in a landslide. He bagged 21,391,993 popular votes to 15,016,169 for his embittered opponent, while rolling up an electoral count of 444 to 87. A huge Republican majority was returned to the House of Representatives. Tens of thousands of dry southern Democrats—"Hoovercrats"—rebelled against Al Smith. Hoover carried all the Border States and five states of the former Confederacy, the first Republican candidate in fifty-two years, except for Harding's Tennessee victory, to carry a state that had seceded.

Online Study Center

Primary source
Herbert Hoover Embraces Individualism
college.hmco.com/pic/kennedybrief7e

Online Study Center

Primary source
Heavy Load for Al, A
college.hmco.com/pic/kennedybrief7e

President Hoover's First Moves

Prosperity in the late 1920s smiled broadly as the Hoover years began. Soaring stocks on the bull market continued to defy the laws of financial gravitation. But two immense groups of citizens were not getting their share of the riches flowing from the national cornucopia: the unorganized wage earners and especially the disorganized farmers.

Hoover's administration, in line with its philosophy of promoting self-help, responded to the outcry of the farmers with the Agricultural Marketing Act. Passed by Congress in June 1929, it was designed to help the farmers help themselves, largely through producers' cooperatives. It also set up a Federal Farm Board that provided generous loans to farm organizations seeking to buy, sell, and store agricultural surpluses.

Farmers also clutched at the tariff as a possible straw to keep their heads above the water of financial ruin. But the Hawley-Smoot Tariff of 1930, which started out in the House as a fairly reasonable measure designed to assist farmers, acquired more than a thousand amendments in the Senate and turned into the highest protective tariff in the nation's peacetime history. The average duty was raised from 38.5 percent to nearly 60 percent. To angered foreigners, the Hawley-Smoot Tariff seemed like a declaration of economic warfare. It widened the yawning trade gaps and plunged both America and other nations deeper into the terrible depression that had already begun. It increased international financial chaos and forced the United States further into the bog of economic isolationism, thus directly abetting Adolf Hitler's demagogic rise to power in Germany.

■ Index of Common Stock Prices (1926 = 100)

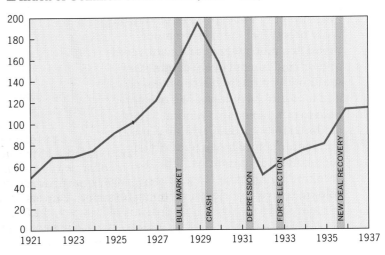

The Great Crash Ends the Golden Twenties

When Herbert Hoover confidently took the presidential oath on March 4, 1929, America's productive colossus—stimulated by the automobile, radio, movie, and other new industries—was roaring along at a breathtaking speed that suggested a permanent plateau of prosperity. Prices on the stock exchange continued to spiral upward and create a fool's paradise of paper profits. A few prophets of disaster sounded warnings, but they were drowned out by the mad chatter of the ticker-tape machine.

A catastrophic crash came on "Black Tuesday," October 29, 1929, when 16,410,030 shares of stock were sold in a save-who-may scramble. Wall Street became a wailing wall as gloom and doom replaced boom. Losses, even in blue-chip securities, were unbelievable. By the end of 1929—two months after the initial crash—stockholders had lost $40 billion in paper values, or more than the total cost of World War I to the United States.

The stock-market collapse heralded a business depression, at home and abroad, that was the most prolonged and prostrating in American or world experience. No other industrialized nation suffered so severe a setback. By the end of 1930, more than 4 million workers in the United States were jobless; two years later the figure had about tripled. Hungry and despairing workers pounded pavements in search of nonexistent jobs ("We're firing, not hiring"). Where employees were not discharged, wages and salaries were often slashed. A current jingle ran,

> *Mellon pulled the whistle,*
> *Hoover range the bell*
> *Wall Street gave the signal*
> *And the country went to hell.*

The misery and gloom were incalculable, as forests of dead chimneys stood stark against the sky. Over five thousand banks collapsed in the first three years of the depression, carrying down with them the life savings of tens of thousands of ordinary citizens. Countless thousands of honest, hard-working people lost their homes and farms to the forecloser's hammer. Breadlines formed, soup kitchens dispensed food, and apple sellers stood shivering on street corners trying to peddle their wares for five cents.

Families felt the stress, as jobless fathers nursed their guilt and shame at not being able to provide for their households. Breadless breadwinners often blamed themselves for their plight, despite abundant evidence that the economic system, not individual initiative, had broken down. Mothers meanwhile nursed fewer babies as hard times reached even into the nation's bedrooms, precipitating a decade-long dearth of births. As cash registers gathered cobwebs, the song "My God, How the Money Rolls In" was replaced by "Brother, Can You Spare a Dime?"

The Depression spectacle of want in the shadow of surplus moved an observer to write in Current History *(1932),*

"We still pray to be given each day our daily bread. Yet there is too much bread, too much wheat and corn, meat and oil and almost every commodity required by man for his subsistence and material happiness. We are not able to purchase the abundance that modern methods of agriculture, mining and manufacture make available in such bountiful quantities. Why is mankind being asked to go hungry and cold and poverty stricken in the midst of plenty?"

The Horn of Plenty Runs Dry

What caused the Great Depression? One basic explanation was overproduction by both farm and factory. Ironically, the depression of the 1930s was one of abundance, not want. It was the "great glut" or the "plague of plenty."

The nation's ability to produce goods had clearly outrun its capacity to consume or pay for them. Too much money was going into the hands of a few wealthy people, who invested it in factories and other agencies of production. Not enough was going into salaries and wages, where revitalizing purchasing power could be more quickly felt. Overexpansion of credit on so-called easy terms also caused many consumers to dive in beyond their depth.

■ "Hooverville" in Seattle, 1934 In the early years of the depression, desperate, homeless people constructed shacks out of scavenged materials. These shantytowns sprang up in cities across the country.

This already bleak picture was further darkened by economic anemia abroad. Britain and the Continent had never fully recovered from the upheaval of World War I. A drying up of international trade, moreover, had been hastened by the shortsighted Hawley-Smoot Tariff of 1930.

By 1930 the depression had become a national calamity. Through no fault of their own, a host of industrious citizens had lost everything. They wanted to work—but there was no work. The insidious effect of all this dazed despair on the spirit was incalculable and long lasting. Hitherto the people had grappled with storms, trees, stones, and other physical obstacles. But the depression was a baffling wraith they could not grasp. Initiative and self-respect were stifled, as panhandlers begged for food or "charity soup." In extreme cases "ragged individualists" slept under "Hoover blankets" (old newspapers), fought over the contents of garbage cans, or cooked their findings in old oil drums in tin-and-paper shanty-towns cynically named "Hoovervilles." The very foundations of America's social and political structure trembled.

Hoover's exalted reputation as a wonder-worker and efficiency engineer crashed about as dismally as the stock market. The perplexed president was impaled on the horns of a cruel dilemma. As a deservedly famed humanitarian, he was profoundly distressed by the widespread misery about him. Yet as a "rugged individualist," deeply rooted in an earlier era of free enterprise, he shrank from the heresy of government handouts. Convinced that industry, thrift, and self-reliance were the virtues that had made America great, he feared that a government doling out doles would weaken, or perhaps destroy, the national fiber.

As the depression nightmare steadily worsened, Hoover was finally forced to turn reluctantly from his doctrine of log-cabin individualism and accept the proposition that the welfare of the people was a direct concern of the national government. The president now worked out a compromise between the old hands-off philosophy and the "soul-destroying" handouts then being used in Britain. He would assist the hard-pressed railroads,

Herbert Hoover (1874–1964) spoke approvingly in a campaign speech in 1928 of "the American system of Rugged Individualism." In 1930 he referred to Cleveland's 1887 veto of a bill to appropriate seed grain for the drought-stricken farmers of Texas:

"I do not believe that the power and duty of the General Government ought to be extended to the relief of individual suffering. . . . The lesson should be constantly enforced that though the people support the Government the Government should not support the people."

■ Home Relief Station, by Louis Ribak, 1935–1936 Destitute and despairing, millions of hard-working Americans like these had to endure the degradation and humiliation of going on relief as the pall of depression descended over the land.

pump-priming *In economics, the spending or lending of a small amount of funds in order to stimulate a larger flow of economic activity.*

banks, and rural credit corporations, in the hope that if financial health were restored at the top of the economic pyramid, unemployment would be relieved at the bottom on a trickle-down basis.

Early in 1932 Congress, responding to Hoover's belated appeal, established the Reconstruction Finance Corporation (RFC). With an initial working capital of half a billion dollars, this agency became a government lending bank that provided indirect relief to insurance companies, banks, agricultural organizations, railroads, and even struggling state and local governments. But to preserve individualism and character, there would be no loans to individuals from this "billion-dollar soup kitchen."

"**Pump-priming**" loans by the RFC were of widespread benefit, but the organization was established many months too late for maximum usefulness. Projects that it supported were largely self-liquidating, and the government as a banker actually profited to the tune of many millions of dollars. Giant corporations so obviously benefited from this assistance that the RFC was dubbed—rather unfairly—"the millionaires' dole."

Hoover's administration also provided some indirect benefits for labor. After stormy debate, Congress passed the Norris–La Guardia Anti-Injunction Act in 1932, and Hoover signed it. The measure outlawed "yellow dog" (antiunion) contracts and forbade the federal courts to issue injunctions to restrain strikes, boycotts, and peaceful picketing.

The truth is that Herbert Hoover, despite criticism of his "heartlessness," did inaugurate a significant new policy. In previous panics the masses had been forced to "sweat it out." Slow though Hoover was to abandon this nineteenth-century bias, by the end of his term he had started down the road toward government assistance for needy citizens—a road that Franklin Roosevelt would travel much farther.

Many veterans of World War I were numbered among the hard-hit victims of the depression. A drive developed for the premature payment of the deferred bonus voted by Congress in 1924 and payable in 1945. Thousands of impoverished veterans, both of war and of unemployment, prepared to move on Washington, there to demand of Congress the immediate payment of their *entire* bonuses. The "Bonus Expeditionary Force," which mustered about twenty thousand men, converged on the capital in the summer of 1932. These supplicants promptly set up unsanitary public camps on vacant lots—a gigantic "Hooverville."

Online Study Center

Primary source
Hoover and the Bonus Marchers
college.hmco.com/pic/kennedybrief7e

EXAMINING THE EVIDENCE

Lampooning Hoover, 1932 The pages of *The American Pageant* are filled with political cartoons that provide pungent commentary on historical events. With one image rather than many words, a cartoonist can convey a point of view much the way an editorial writer does. This cartoon appeared in the *Washington Daily News* on July 25, 1932, three and a half months before Republican president Hoover lost the presidential election to his Democratic challenger, Franklin D. Roosevelt. The cartoonist foretells Hoover's defeat in November and departure from the White House the following March (not January, as at present), and expresses his support for the Home Loan Bank Bill. With this proposal, Hoover sought to come to the aid of home mortgage lenders in order to forestall them from foreclosing on homeowners. The cartoonist jokes that Hoover supported this bill because he identified with homeowners about to lose their homes, but he also cleverly insinuates that Hoover's banking reform was motivated by electoral opportunism. Surely Hoover sought to win public support in return for his new banking program as he battled for reelection, but the Home Loan Bank Bill also reflected Hoover's growing recognition that the federal government had to take direct action to remedy flaws that had precipitated the crisis of the Great Depression. As Hoover later recorded in his memoirs, "All this seems dull economics, but the poignant American drama revolving around the loss of the old homestead had a million repetitions straight from life, not because of the designing villain but because of a fault in our financial system."

1. How does the cartoonist use caricature to make his point?

2. What accounts for the political cartoon's special power?

3. Are there limitations to this genre? Find another cartoon in this book and subject it to similar analysis.

Following riots that cost two lives, Hoover ordered the army to evacuate the unwanted guests. The eviction was carried out by General Douglas MacArthur with bayonets and tear gas in the inglorious "Battle of Anacostia Flats." The veterans' shantytown was put to the torch, a few of the former soldiers were injured, and an eleven-month-old "bonus baby" allegedly died from exposure to tear gas.

This brutal episode brought down additional abuse on the once-popular Hoover, who by now was the most loudly booed man in the country. Cynics sneered that the "Great Engineer" had in a few months "ditched, drained, and damned the country." The existing panic was unfairly branded "the Hoover depression." In truth, Hoover had been oversold as a wizard, and the public grumbled when his magician's wand failed to produce rabbits. The time was ripening for the Democratic party—and Franklin D. Roosevelt—to cash in on Hoover's calamities.

Japanese Aggression

The Great Depression, which brewed enough distress at home, added immensely to difficulties abroad. Militaristic Japan stole the East Asian spotlight. In September 1931 Japanese imperialists, noting that the Western world was badly mired down in depression, plunged into Manchuria. Alleging provocation, they rapidly overran the coveted Chinese province and proceeded to bolt shut the Open Door in the conquered area.

Americans were stunned by this act of naked aggression. Many, though by no means a majority, urged strong measures, ranging from boycotts to blockades. Possibly a tight blockade by the League of Nations, backed by the United States, would have brought Japan sharply to book. But the League was handicapped in taking two-fisted action by the nonmembership of the United States. Washington flatly rebuffed initial attempts in 1931 to secure American cooperation in applying economic pressure on Japan.

Washington and Secretary of State Henry L. Stimson in the end decided to fire only paper bullets at the Japanese aggressors. The so-called Stimson Doctrine, proclaimed in 1932, declared that the United States would not recognize any territorial acquisitions achieved by force. Righteous indignation would substitute for solid initiatives. But there was no real sentiment for stronger measures among a depression-ridden people, who remained strongly isolationist during the 1930s.

⭐ Chapter Summary ⭐

The Republican governments of the 1920s carried out active, probusiness policies while undermining much of the progressive legacy by neglect or lack of enforcement. The Washington Naval Conference indicated America's strong desire in the 1920s to withdraw from international involvements. Sky-high tariffs protected America's booming industry but caused severe economic troubles elsewhere in the world and deepened the woes of farmers, who did not share in the nation's prosperity.

As the Harding scandals broke, Harding died and the puritanical Calvin Coolidge took office, thus avoiding political repercussions for the Republicans. Bitterly feuding Democrats—divided by region, religion, and culture—and La Follette Progressives fell easy victims to Republican-managed prosperity.

American demands for strict repayment of war debts created international economic difficulties and resentment of the United States. The Dawes plan provided temporary relief, but the Hawley-Smoot Tariff proved another devastating blow to international trade. Herbert Hoover, a renowned businessman and humanitarian, won a landslide victory over Catholic Al Smith.

The stock-market crash of 1929 brought a sudden end to prosperity and plunged America into a horrible depression. Herbert Hoover's reputation collapsed as he failed to relieve national suffering, although he did make unprecedented but limited efforts to revive the economy through federal assistance.

33

The Great Depression and the New Deal

— ✤ —

1933–1939

THE COUNTRY NEEDS AND . . . DEMANDS BOLD, PERSISTENT EXPERIMENTATION. IT IS COMMON SENSE TO TAKE A METHOD AND TRY IT. IF IT FAILS, ADMIT IT FRANKLY AND TRY ANOTHER. BUT ABOVE ALL, TRY SOMETHING.

FRANKLIN D. ROOSEVELT, CAMPAIGN SPEECH, 1932

Chapter Outline

⭐ Franklin D. Roosevelt as President

⭐ The Hundred Days Congress, 1933

⭐ The National Recovery Administration, 1933–1935

⭐ The Agricultural Adjustment Administration, 1933–1936

⭐ The Tennessee Valley Authority

⭐ The Social Security Act, 1935

⭐ Gains for Organized Labor

⭐ The Election of 1936 and the "Roosevelt Coalition"

⭐ The Supreme Court Fight, 1937

⭐ The New Deal Assessed

Voters were in an ugly mood as the presidential campaign of 1932 neared. Countless factory chimneys remained ominously cold, while more than 11 million unemployed workers and their families sank ever deeper into the pit of poverty.

Hoover, sick at heart, was renominated by the Republican convention in Chicago without great enthusiasm. The rising star in the Democratic firmament was Governor Franklin Delano Roosevelt of New York, a fifth cousin of Theodore Roosevelt. Like the Rough Rider, he had been born to a wealthy New York family, had graduated from Harvard, had been elected as a kid-gloved politician to the New York legislature, had served as governor of the Empire State, had been nominated for the vice presidency (though not elected), and had served capably as assistant secretary of the navy. Although both men were master politicians, adept with the colorful phrase, TR was pugnacious and confrontational, whereas FDR was suave and conciliatory—qualities that appealed strongly to a people traumatized by one of the greatest crises in American history.

Focus Questions

1. What qualities did Franklin Roosevelt bring to the presidency and to his "New Deal" efforts to alleviate the Depression and reform American society?
2. What were the primary New Deal efforts to achieve relief, recovery, and reform?
3. How did the early New Deal affect business, agriculture, and labor? Why did it meet such strong opposition from some quarters, including the Supreme Court?
4. How did Roosevelt politically mobilize the "New Deal coalition" of Southerners, Catholics, Jews, African Americans, and women to achieve his goals and and lay the foundations for the future success of the Democratic party?
5. What were the New Deal's greatest successes and failures, in both the short term and in the decades since?

Online Study Center

Primary source
Untitled Caricature of FDR and Hoover
college.hmco.com/pic/kennedybrief7e

---

dispossessed *The economically deprived.*

FDR: Politician in a Wheelchair

Infantile paralysis, while putting steel braces on Franklin Roosevelt's legs, put additional steel into his soul. Until 1921, when the dread disease struck, young Roosevelt—tall, athletic, and handsome—impressed observers as charming and witty yet at times as a superficial and arrogant "lightweight." But suffering humbled him to the level of common clay. In courageously fighting his way back from complete helplessness to a hobbling mobility, he schooled himself in patience, tolerance, compassion, and strength of will. He once remarked that after trying for two years to wiggle one big toe, all else seemed easy.

Another of Roosevelt's great personal and political assets was his wife, Eleanor. The niece of Theodore Roosevelt, she was Franklin Roosevelt's distant cousin as well as his spouse. Tall, ungainly, and toothy, she overcame the misery of an unhappy childhood and emerged as a champion of the **dispossessed**—and ultimately as the "conscience of the New Deal." She was to become the most active First Lady in history. Through her lobbying of her husband, her speeches, and her syndicated newspaper column, she powerfully influenced the policies of the national government. Always she battled for the impoverished and the oppressed. At one meeting in Birmingham, Alabama, she confounded local authorities and flouted the segregation statutes by deliberately straddling the aisle separating the black and white seating sections. Sadly, her personal relationship with her husband was often rocky due to his occasional infidelity. Condemned by conservatives and loved by liberals, she was one of the most controversial—and consequential—public figures of the twentieth century.

Franklin Roosevelt's political appeal was amazing. His commanding presence and his golden speaking voice, despite a sophisticated accent, combined to make him the premier American orator of his generation. He could turn on charm in private conversations as one would turn on a faucet. As a popular depression governor of New York, he had sponsored heavy state spending to relieve human suffering. Though favoring frugality, he believed that money, rather than humanity, was expendable. He revealed a deep concern for the plight of the "forgotten man"—a phrase he used in a 1932 speech—although he was assailed by the rich as a "traitor to his class."

Exuberant Democrats met in Chicago in June 1932 and speedily nominated Roosevelt, who flew daringly through stormy weather to Chicago where he smashed precedent to accept the nomination in person. He electrified the delegates and the public with these words: "I pledge you, I pledge myself to a new deal for the American people."

Roosevelt Routs Hoover in 1932

In the campaign that followed, Roosevelt consistently preached a New Deal for the "forgotten man," but he was annoyingly vague and somewhat contradictory. Many of his speeches were ghostwritten by the "Brains Trust" (popularly the "Brain Trust"), a small group of reform-minded intellectuals. They were predominantly youngish college professors who, as a kind of kitchen cabinet, later authored much of the New Deal legislation. Roosevelt rashly

■ **Eleanor Roosevelt (1884–1962)** America's most active First Lady, she commanded enormous popularity and influence during FDR's presidency. Here she emerges, miner's cap in hand, from an Ohio coal mine.

Chronology

1932	Roosevelt defeats Hoover for presidency.
1933	Bank holiday.
	Emergency Banking Relief Act.
	Hundred Days Congress enacts HOLC, AAA, NRA, PWA, and TVA.
	Federal Securities Act.
	Glass-Steagall Banking Reform Act.
	CWA established.
	Twentieth Amendment (changed calendar of congressional sessions and date of presidential inauguration).
	Twenty-first Amendment (prohibition repealed).
1934	Securities and Exchange Commission authorized.
	Indian Reorganization Act.
	FHA established.
	Frazier-Lemke Farm Bankruptcy Act.
1935	WPA established.
	Wagner Act.
	Resettlement Administration.
	Social Security Act.
	Public Utility Holding Company Act.
	Schechter "sick chicken" case.
	CIO organized.
1936	Soil Conservation and Domestic Allotment Act.
	Roosevelt defeats Landon for presidency.
1937	USHA established.
	Roosevelt announces "Court-packing" plan.
1938	Second AAA.
	Fair Labor Standards Act.
1939	Hatch Act.
	Reorganization Act.

promised a balanced budget and berated heavy Hooverian deficits. All of this was to make ironic reading in later months.

The high spirits of the Democrats found expression in the catchy air, "Happy Days Are Here Again." This theme song fit FDR's indestructible smile, his jauntily angled cigarette holder, his breezy optimism, and his promises to do something, even at the risk of bold experimentation. Meanwhile, grim-faced Herbert Hoover predicted on the campaign trail that if the Hawley-Smoot Tariff were repealed, the grass would grow "in the streets of a hundred cities." Such down-at-the-mouth gloom contrasted sharply with Roosevelt's tooth-flashing optimism and sparkling promises.

Hoover had been swept into office on the rising tide of prosperity; he was swept out by the receding tide of depression. The flood of votes totaled 22,809,638 for Roosevelt and 15,758,901 for Hoover; the electoral count stood at 472 to 59. In all, the loser carried only six rock-ribbed Republican states.

One striking feature of the election was a distinct shift of blacks from their traditional home in the Republican party of Lincoln to the Roosevelt camp. Beginning with the election of 1932, they became, notably in the great urban centers of the North, a vital element in the Democratic party.

Defeated and repudiated, Hoover continued to be president for four long months, until March 4, 1933. But he was helpless to embark on any long-range policies without the cooperation of Roosevelt. In two meetings with Roosevelt, Hoover tried to bind his successor to anti-inflationary policies that would have made impossible many of the later New Deal experiments. But Roosevelt refused to assume responsibility without authority and airily remarked to the press, "It's not my baby."

With Washington deadlocked, the vast and vaunted American economic machine clanked to a virtual halt. One worker in four tramped the streets, feet weary and hands idle. Banks were locking their doors all over the nation as people nervously stuffed paper money under their mattresses.

> *In his successful campaign for the governorship of New York in 1928, Franklin Roosevelt (1882–1945) had played down alleged Democratic "socialism":*
>
> "We often hear it said that government operation of anything under the sun is socialistic. If that is so, our postal service is socialistic, so is the parcel post which has largely taken the place of the old express companies; so are the public highways which took the place of the toll roads."

Online Study Center

Primary source
New Deal Overview
college.hmco.com/pic/kennedybrief7e

FDR and the Three Rs: Relief, Recovery, and Reform

Great crises often call forth gifted leaders, and the hand of destiny tapped Roosevelt on the shoulder. On a dreary inauguration day, March 4, 1933, his vibrant voice provided the American people with inspirational new hope. He denounced the "money changers" who had brought on the calamity, and he declared that the government must wage war on the Great Depression as it would wage war on an armed foe. His clarion note was, "Let me assert my firm belief that the only thing we have to fear is fear itself."

Roosevelt moved decisively. Now that he had full responsibility, he boldly declared a nationwide bank holiday, March 6–10, as a prelude to opening the banks on a sounder basis. He then summoned the overwhelmingly Democratic Congress into special session to cope with the national emergency. For the so-called Hundred Days (March 9–June 16, 1933), members hastily ground out an unprecedented basketful of remedial legislation.

Roosevelt's New Deal program aimed at three *R*'s—relief, recovery, and reform. Short-range goals were relief and immediate recovery, especially in the first two years. Long-range goals were permanent recovery and reform of current abuses, particularly those that had produced the boom-or-bust catastrophe. The three-*R* objectives often overlapped and got in one another's way. But amid all the topsy-turvy haste, the gigantic New Deal program lurched forward.

Firmly ensconced in the driver's seat, President Roosevelt cracked the whip. A green Congress so fully shared the panicky feeling of the country that it was ready to **rubber-stamp** bills drafted by White House advisers. More than that, Congress gave the president extraordinary **blank-check** powers: some laws it passed expressly delegated legislative authority to the chief executive.

rubber-stamp *To approve a plan or law quickly or routinely, without examination.*

blank-check *Referring to permission to use an unlimited amount of money or authority.*

■ **The Champ: FDR Chatting with Reporters** Roosevelt mastered the press as few presidents before or since have been able to do.

Roosevelt was delighted to exert executive leadership. He was inclined to do things by intuition—off the cuff. He was like the quarterback, as he put it, whose next play depends on the outcome of the previous play. So desperate was the mood of an action-starved public that any movement, even in the wrong direction, seemed better than no movement at all.

The frantic Hundred Days Congress passed many essentials of the New Deal's "three *R*'s," though important long-range measures were added in later sessions. These reforms owed much to the legacy of the pre–World War I progressive movement. Many of them were long overdue. The New Dealers, sooner or later, embraced such progressive ideas as unemployment insurance, old-age insurance, minimum-wage regulations, conservation and development of natural resources, and restrictions on child labor. Many of these forward-looking social welfare measures had already been adopted a generation or so earlier by the more advanced countries of western Europe.

Roosevelt Tackles Money and Banking

Banking chaos cried aloud for immediate action. Congress pulled itself together and in an incredible eight hours had the Emergency Banking Relief Act of 1933 ready for Roosevelt's busy pen. The new law invested the president with power to regulate banking transactions and **foreign exchange** and to reopen solvent banks.

Roosevelt, the master showman, next turned to the radio to deliver the first of thirty famous "fireside chats." As some 35 million people hung on his soothing words, he gave assurances that it was now safer to keep money in a reopened bank than "under the mattress." Confidence returned with a gush, and the banks unlocked their doors.

The Hundred Days Congress also buttressed public reliance on the banking system by enacting the memorable Glass-Steagall Banking Reform Act. This measure provided for the Federal Deposit Insurance Corporation, which insured individual deposits up to $5,000 (later raised).

Roosevelt moved swiftly elsewhere on the financial front, seeking to protect the melting gold reserve and to prevent panicky **hoarding**. He ordered all private holdings of gold to be surrendered to the Treasury in exchange for paper currency and then took the nation off the gold standard.

The goal of Roosevelt's "managed currency" was inflation, which he believed would relieve debtors' burdens and stimulate new production. Roosevelt's principal instrument for achieving inflation was gold buying. He instructed the Treasury Department to purchase gold, ratcheting its price up from $21 an ounce in 1933 to $35 an ounce in 1934, a price that held for nearly four decades. This policy did increase the amount of dollars in circulation, as holders of gold cashed it in at the newly elevated prices, although "sound-money" critics gagged on the "baloney dollar." The gold-buying scheme came to an end in February 1934, when FDR returned the nation to a limited gold standard for purposes of international trade only. Thereafter, the United States pledged itself to pay foreign bills, if requested, in gold at the rate of one ounce of gold for every $35 due. But domestic circulation of gold continued to be prohibited, and gold coins became collectors' items.

Creating Jobs for the Jobless

Overwhelming unemployment clamored for prompt remedial action. One out of every four workers was jobless when FDR took his inaugural oath—the highest level of unemployment in the nation's history. Roosevelt had no hesitancy about using federal money to assist the unemployed and at the same time to "prime the pump" of industrial recovery. (A farmer has to pour a little water into a dry pump—that is, "prime it"—to start the flow.)

foreign exchange *The transfer of credits or accounts between the citizens or financial institutions of different nations.*

hoarding *Secretly storing up quantities of goods or money.*

Online Study Center

Primary source
FDR's First Inaugural Address
college.hmco.com/pic/kennedybrief7e

Principal New Deal Acts During Hundred Days Congress, 1933 (items in parentheses indicate secondary purposes)

Recovery	Relief	Reform
FDR closes banks, March 6, 1933		
Emergency Banking Relief Act, March 9, 1933		
(Beer Act)	(Beer Act)	Beer and Wine Revenue Act, March 22, 1933
(CCC)	Unemployment Relief Act March 31, 1933, creates Civilian Conservation Corps (CCC)	
FDR orders gold surrender April 5, 1933		
FDR abandons gold standard April 19, 1933		
(FERA)	Federal Emergency Relief Act May 12, 1933, creates Federal Emergency Relief Administration (FERA)	
(AAA)	Agricultural Adjustment Act (AAA), May 12, 1933	
(TVA)	(TVA)	Tennessee Valley Authority Act (TVA) May 18, 1933
		Federal Securities Act May 27, 1933
Gold-payment clause repealed, June 5, 1933		
(HOLC)	Home Owners' Refinancing Act June 13, 1933, creates Home Owners' Loan Corporation (HOLC)	
National Industrial Recovery Act, June 16, 1933, creates National Recovery Administration (NRA), Public Works Administration (PWA)	(NRA, PWA)	(NRA)
(Glass-Steagall Act)	(Glass-Steagall Act)	Glass-Steagall Banking Reform Act, June 16 1933, creates Federal Deposit Insurance Corporation

For later New Deal measures, see p. 536.

The Hundred Days Congress responded to Roosevelt's spurs when it created the Civilian Conservation Corps (CCC). This agency provided employment in fresh-air government camps for about 3 million uniformed young men. Their useful work included reforestation, fire fighting, flood control, and swamp drainage. The recruits were required to help their parents by sending home most of their pay. Both human resources and natural resources were thus conserved.

The first major effort of the new Congress to grapple with the millions of adult unemployed was the Federal Emergency Relief Act. Its chief aim was immediate relief rather than long-range recovery. The resulting Federal Emergency Relief Administration (FERA) was handed over to zealous Harry L. Hopkins, a painfully thin, shabbily dressed, chain-smoking New York social worker who had earlier won Roosevelt's friendship and who became one of his most influential advisers. Hopkins's agency finally granted about $3 billion to the states for direct dole payments or preferably for wages on work projects.

Immediate relief was also given to two large and hard pressed special groups by the Hundred Days Congress. One section of the Agricultural Adjustment Act (AAA) made available many millions of dollars to help farmers meet their mortgages. Another law created the Home Owners' Loan Corporation (HOLC). Designed to refinance mortgages on nonfarm homes, it ultimately assisted about a million badly pinched households while simultaneously bailing out mortgage-holding banks.

Harassed by the continuing plague of unemployment, FDR himself established the Civil Works Administration (CWA) under Hopkins's direction late in 1933. Designed to provide temporary jobs during the cruel winter emergency, it employed tens of thousands of jobless people in leaf raking and other make-work tasks. The CWA served a useful purpose, although it was heavily criticized as "**boondoggling**."

Direct relief from Washington to needy families helped pull the nation through the ghastly winter of 1933–1934. But the disheartening persistence of unemployment and suffering demonstrated that emergency relief measures must be not only continued but supplemented.

boondoggle *To engage in trivial or useless work; any enterprise characterized by such work.*

fascist (fascism) *A political system or philosophy that advocates a mass-based party dictatorship, extreme nationalism, racism, and the glorification of war.*

A Day for Every Demagogue

One danger signal was the appearance of various demagogues, notably a magnetic "microphone messiah," Father Charles Coughlin, a Catholic priest in Michigan who began broadcasting in 1930 with the slogan "Social Justice." His anti–New Deal harangues to some 40 million radio fans finally became so anti-Semitic, fascistic, and demagogic that he was silenced in 1942 by his ecclesiastical superiors.

Also notorious among the new brood of agitators were those who capitalized on popular discontent to make pie-in-the-sky promises. Most conspicuous of these individuals was Senator Huey P. ("Kingfish") Long of Louisiana, who used his abundant rabble-rousing talents to publicize his "Share Our Wealth" program, which promised to make "Every Man a King." Every family was to receive $5,000, supposedly at the expense of the prosperous. H.L. Mencken called Long's chief lieutenant, former clergyman Gerald L.K. Smith, "the deadliest and damndest orator ever heard on this or any other earth, the champion boob-bumper of all time." Fear of Long's becoming a **fascist** dictator ended when he was shot by an assassin in the Louisiana state capitol in 1935.

Another Pied Piper was gaunt Dr. Francis E. Townsend of California, a retired physician whose savings had recently been wiped out. He attracted the trusting support of perhaps 5 million "senior citizens" with his fantastic plan, which nonetheless spoke to earthly need. Each oldster sixty years of age or over was to receive $200 a month, provided that the money was spent within the month. One estimate had the scheme costing one-half of the national income.

In 1935 Father Charles Coughlin (1891–1979) single-handedly defeated President Roosevelt's effort to win Senate ratification of a treaty providing for American membership in the World Court, a judicial body of limited authority established by the League of Nations. What FDR saw as a symbolic embrace of international responsibility Coughlin convinced his radio listeners was a conspiracy of international moneyed interests against American sovereignty:

"Our thanks are due to Almighty God in that America retains her sovereignty. Congratulations to the aroused people of the United States who, by more than 200,000 telegrams containing at least 1,000,000 names, demanded that the principles established by Washington and Jefferson shall keep us clear from foreign entanglements and European hatreds."

Partly to quiet the groundswell of unrest produced by such crackbrained proposals, Congress authorized the Works Progress Administration (WPA) in 1935. The objective was employment on useful projects. Launched under the supervision of the ailing but energetic Hopkins, this remarkable agency ultimately spent about $11 billion on thousands of public buildings, bridges, and hard-surfaced roads. It also controlled crickets in Wyoming and built a monkey pen in Oklahoma City. Predictably, missions like these caused critics to sneer that WPA meant "We Provide Alms." But the fact is that over a period of eight years nearly 9 million persons were given jobs, not handouts.

Agencies of the WPA also found part-time occupations for needy high school and college students and for such unemployed white-collar workers as actors, musicians, and writers. John Steinbeck, future Nobel Prize novelist, counted dogs in his California county. Cynical taxpayers condemned lessons in tap dancing, as well as the painting of scenes on post office walls. But much precious talent was nourished, self-respect was preserved, and more than a million pieces of art were created, many of them publicly displayed.

New Visibility for Women

Just over a decade after the ratification of the Nineteenth Amendment, American women began to carve a larger space for themselves in the nation's political and intellectual life. First Lady Eleanor Roosevelt may have been the most visible woman in the Roosevelt White House, but she was hardly the only female voice. Secretary of Labor Frances Perkins (1880–1965) became the first woman cabinet member. Mary McLeod Bethune (1875–1955), director of the Office of Minority Affairs in the National Youth Administration, served as the highest ranking African American in the Roosevelt administration.

Women also made important contributions in the social sciences, and especially relatively new and open field of anthropology. The landmark book by Ruth Benedict (1887–1948), *Patterns of Culture,* established the study of cultures as collective personalities. One of Benedict's students, Margaret Mead (1901–1978), drew from her own scholarly studies of adolescence among Pacific island peoples to advance bold new ideas about sexuality, gender roles, and intergenerational relationships.

Pearl S. Buck, raised in China by missionary parents, gained fame as a novelist by introducing American readers to Chinese peasant society. Her best-selling novel, *The Good Earth* (1931), earned her the Nobel Prize for literature in 1938.

A Helping Hand for Industry and Labor

A daring attempt to stimulate a nationwide comeback was initiated when the Hundred Days Congress authorized the National Recovery Administration (NRA). This ingenious scheme was by far the most complex and far-reaching effort by the New Dealers to combine immediate relief with long-range recovery and reform. Triple-barreled, it was designed to assist industry, labor, and the unemployed.

Individual industries—over two hundred in all—were to work out codes of "fair competition," under which hours of labor would be reduced so that employment could be spread over more people. A ceiling was placed on the maximum hours of labor; a floor was placed under wages to establish minimum levels.

Labor, under the NRA, was granted additional benefits. Workers were formally guaranteed the right to organize and bargain collectively through representatives *of their own choosing.* The hated "yellow dog," or antiunion, contract was expressly forbidden, and certain safeguarding restrictions were placed on the use of child labor.

Enthusiasm for industrial recovery through the NRA by patriotic mass meetings and huge parades, which included 200,000 marchers on New York City's Fifth Avenue. A handsome blue eagle was designed as the symbol of the NRA, and a newly formed professional football team was named the Philadelphia Eagles. Such was the enthusiasm for the NRA that for a brief period there was a marked upswing of business activity.

But the high-flying eagle gradually fluttered to earth. The "fair competition" codes required too much self-denial by labor, industry, and the public for such a scheme to work. Critics began to brand the NRA "Nuts Running America," symbolized by what Henry Ford called "that damn Roosevelt buzzard." Complete collapse was imminent when, in 1935, the Supreme Court shot down the dying eagle in the *Schechter* "sick chicken" decision. The learned justices unanimously held that Congress could not "delegate legislative powers" to the executive. They further declared that congressional control of interstate commerce could not properly apply to a local fowl business, like that of the Schechter brothers in Brooklyn. Roosevelt was incensed by this "horse and buggy" interpretation of the Constitution, but actually the Court helped him out of a bad jam.

The same act of Congress that hatched the NRA eagle also authorized the Public Works Administration (PWA), likewise intended both for industrial recovery and for unemployment relief. The agency was headed by acid-tongued Secretary of the Interior Harold L. Ickes, a free-swinging former bull mooser. Long-range recovery was the primary purpose of the new agency, and in time over $4 billion was spent on some thirty-four thousand projects, which included public buildings, highways, and parkways.

One spectacular PWA achievement was the Grand Coulee Dam on the Columbia River. In the depths of the depression, the towering dam seemed the height of folly. It made possible the irrigation of millions of acres of new farmland—at a time when the government was desperately trying to reduce farm surpluses. It created vast amounts of electrical power—in a region with little industry and virtually no market for additional power. But with the outbreak of World War II and then postwar prosperity, the dam would come to seem a stroke of genius, transforming the entire region with abundant water and power.

Special stimulants aided the recovery of one segment of business—the liquor industry. The Hundred Days Congress, in one of its earliest acts, legalized and taxed "light" wine and beer (3.2 percent alcohol), providing new employment and federal revenue. Prohibition was officially repealed by the Twenty-first Amendment late in 1933 (see Appendix)—and the saloon doors swung open.

Paying Farmers Not to Farm

Ever since the war-boom days of 1918, farmers had suffered from low prices and overproduction, especially in grain. During the depression, conditions became desperate as innumerable mortgages were foreclosed, corn was burned for fuel, and embattled farmers tried to prevent shipment of crops to glutted markets. In Iowa several volatile counties were placed under martial law.

A radical new approach to farm recovery was embraced when the Hundred Days Congress established the Agricultural Adjustment Administration (AAA). Through "artificial scarcity" this agency was to establish "**parity** prices" for basic commodities. "Parity" was the price set for a product that gave it the same real value, in purchasing power, that it had enjoyed during the period from 1909 to 1914. The AAA would eliminate price-depressing surpluses by paying growers to reduce their crop acreage.

Unhappily, the AAA got off to a wobbly start. It was begun after much of the cotton crop for 1933 had been planted, and balky mules, trained otherwise, were forced to plow under countless young plants. Several million squealing pigs were purchased and slaughtered. Much of their meat was distributed to persons on relief, but some of it was used for fertilizer. This "sinful" destruction of food, at a time when thousands of citizens were hungry, increased condemnation of the American economic system by many left-leaning voices. The much-criticized AAA was itself plowed under in 1936 by the Supreme Court, which declared its regulatory taxation provisions unconstitutional.

parity *Equivalence in monetary value under different conditions; specifically, in the United States, the price for farm products that would give them the same purchasing power as in the period 1909–1914.*

> *Novelist John Steinbeck (1902–1968) related in his novel* The Grapes of Wrath *(1939) that when the "Okies" and "Arkies" reached California, they found the big growers unwilling to pay more than twenty-five cents an hour for work in the fields. One owner mutters,*
>
> **"A Red is any son-of-a-bitch that wants thirty cents an hour when we're paying twenty-five!"**

The New Deal recovered from this blow by passing the Soil Conservation and Domestic Allotment Act (1936), which paid subsidies to farmers if they planted soil-conserving crops, like soybeans, or let their land lie fallow. The Second Agricultural Adjustment Act of 1938 permitted parity payments if farmers observed acreage restrictions on commodities such as cotton and wheat. Other provisions of the new AAA were designed to give farmers not only a fairer price but a more substantial share of the national income. Both goals were partially achieved.

Dust Bowls and Black Blizzards

Nature meanwhile had been providing some unplanned scarcity. Late in 1933 a prolonged drought struck the states of the trans-Mississippi Great Plains. Rainless weeks were followed by furious, whining winds, while the sun was darkened by millions of tons of powdery topsoil torn from homesteads that stretched from eastern Colorado to western Missouri—soon to be dubbed the "Dust Bowl." Despondent citizens sat on front porches with protective masks on their faces, watching their farms swirl by. Overawed victims of the Dust Bowl predicted the end of the world or the second coming of Christ.

Burned and blown out of the Dust Bowl, tens of thousands of refugees fled their ruined acres (see "Makers of America: The Dust Bowl Migrants," pp. 530–531). In five years about 350,000 Oklahomans and Arkansans—"Okies" and "Arkies"—trekked to southern California in "junkyards on wheels." The dismal story of these human tumbleweeds was realistically portrayed in John Steinbeck's best-selling novel *The Grapes of Wrath* (1939), which proved to be the *Uncle Tom's Cabin* of the Dust Bowl.

Zealous New Dealers, sympathetic toward these desperate soil-tillers, made various efforts to relieve their burdens. The Frazier-Lemke Farm Bankruptcy Act, passed in 1934, made possible a suspension of mortgage foreclosures for five years; a revised version was upheld by the Supreme Court. In 1935 the president set up the Resettlement Administration to help farmers move to better land. And more than 200 million young trees were successfully planted on the bare prairies as windbreaks by the young men of the Civilian Conservation Corps.

Native Americans also felt the far-reaching hand of New Deal reform. Commissioner of Indian Affairs John Collier ardently sought to reverse the forced-assimilation policies in place since the Dawes Act of 1887 (see pp. 401–402). The Indian Reorganization Act of 1934 (the "Indian New Deal") encouraged tribes to establish local self-government, helped stop the loss of Indian lands, and revived tribes' interest in their identity and culture. Nearly two hundred tribes established governments under its provisions, though seventy-seven others refused to organize.

Reforming Business and Creating Public Power

Reformist New Dealers were determined from the outset to curb the "money changers" who had played fast and loose with gullible investors before the Wall Street crash of 1929. The Hundred Days Congress passed the "Truth in Securities Act" (Federal Securities Act), which required promoters to transmit to the investor sworn information regarding the soundness of their stocks and bonds. In 1934 Congress took further steps to protect the public against fraud, deception, and inside manipulation. It authorized the Securities and Exchange Commission (SEC), which was designed as a watchdog administrative agency. Stock markets henceforth were to operate more as trading marts and less as gambling casinos.

New Dealers likewise directed their fire at public utility holding companies, those supercorporations. When Chicagoan Samuel Insull's multibillion-dollar financial empire crashed in 1932, citizens rebelled against such pyramided layers of big business. The Public Utility Holding Company Act of 1935 delivered a "death sentence" to this type of bloated growth.

Inevitably, the sprawling electric-power industry also attracted the fire of New Deal reformers. Within a few decades it had risen from nothingness to a behemoth

Online Study Center

Interactive map
The Dust Bowl
college.hmco.com/pic/kennedybrief7e

Online Study Center

Primary source
Oct. 29, Dies Irae
college.hmco.com/pic/kennedybrief7e

A landslide overwhelmed Landon as the demoralized Republicans carried only two states, Maine and Vermont. The popular vote was 27,752,869 to 16,674,665; the electoral count was 523 to 8—the most lopsided in 116 years. Democratic majorities were again returned to Congress. Jubilant Democrats could now claim more than two-thirds of the seats in the House and a like proportion in the Senate.

The battle of 1936, perhaps the most bitter since Bryan's defeat in 1896, partially bore out Republican charges of class warfare. Even more than in 1932, the needy economic groups were lined up against the so-called greedy economic groups. CIO units contributed generously to FDR's campaign chest. Many **left-wingers** turned to Roosevelt, as the customary third-party protest vote sharply declined. Blacks, several million of whom had also appreciated relief checks, had by now largely shaken off their traditional allegiance to the Republican party. To them, Lincoln was "finally dead."

FDR won primarily because he appealed to the "forgotten man," whom he never forgot. Roosevelt in fact had forged a powerful and enduring coalition of the South, blacks, urbanites, and the poor. He proved especially effective in marshaling the support of the multitudes of "New Immigrants"—mostly Catholics and Jews who had swarmed into the great cities since the turn of the century. These once-scorned newcomers, with their now-numerous sons and daughters, had at last come politically of age. In the 1920s, one out of every twenty-five federal judgeships went to a Catholic; Roosevelt appointed Catholics to one out of every four.

left (or left-wingers) *In politics, groups or parties that traditionally advocate progress, social change, greater economic and social equality, and the welfare of the common person. (The **right** or **right-wingers** are traditionally groups or parties that advocate adherence to tradition, established authorities, and acceptance of a greater degree of economic and social hierarchy.)*

Conflict over the Court

Bowing his head to the sleety blasts, Roosevelt took the presidential oath on January 20, 1937, instead of the traditional March 4. The Twentieth Amendment to the Constitution had been ratified in 1933. (See the Appendix.) It swept away the post-election lame duck session of Congress and shortened by six weeks the awkward period before inauguration.

Flushed with victory, Roosevelt interpreted his reelection as a mandate to continue New Deal reforms. But in his eyes the cloistered old men on the supreme bench, like fossilized stumbling blocks, stood stubbornly in the pathway of progress. In nine major cases involving the New Deal, the Roosevelt administration had been thwarted seven times. The Supreme Court was ultraconservative, and six of the nine oldsters in black were over seventy. As luck would have it, not a single member had been appointed by FDR in his first term.

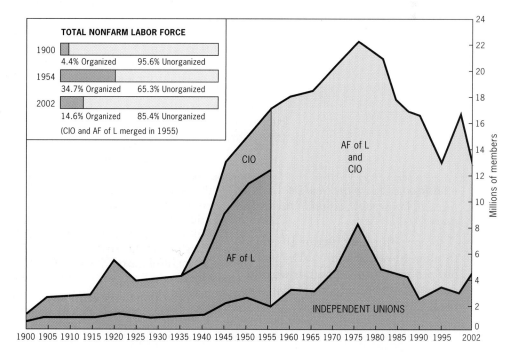

■ **The Rise and Decline of Organized Labor, 1900–2002** The percentage of the total labor force that was organized increased until 1954, and it has declined ever since, except for a brief rise in the 1990s among service and government workers. (*Source:* Bureau of Labor Statistics, *Statistical Abstract of the United States,* 2003.)

Online Study Center

Primary source
Of Course He Can't Want This
college.hmco.com/pic/kennedybrief7e

---

checks and balances *In American politics, the interlocking system of divided and counterweighted authority among the executive, legislative, and judicial branches of government.*

Roosevelt, his "Dutch up," viewed with mounting impatience what he regarded as the obstructive conservatism of the Court. To overcome such obstructionism, Roosevelt finally hit upon a Court scheme that he regarded as "the answer to a maiden's prayer." In fact, it proved to be one of the most costly political misjudgements of his career. Roosevelt's brainstorm, which caught Congress and the country by complete surprise, was a call for legislation that would permit him to add a new justice to the Supreme Court for every member over seventy who would not retire. The maximum membership could then be fifteen.

Congress and the nation were promptly convulsed over the scheme to "pack" the Supreme Court with a "dictator bill," which one critic called "too damned slick." Franklin "Double-crossing" Roosevelt was savagely condemned for attempting to break down the delicate **checks and balances** among the three branches of the government.

The Court had meanwhile seen the ax hanging over its head. Whatever his motives, Justice Owen J. Roberts, formerly regarded as a conservative, began to vote on the side of his liberal colleagues. "A switch in time saves nine" was the classic witticism inspired by this change. By a five-to-four decision, the Court, in March 1937, upheld the principle of a state minimum wage for women, thereby reversing its stand on a different case a year earlier. In succeeding decisions a Court more sympathetic to the New Deal upheld the National Labor Relations Act (Wagner Act) and the Social Security Act.

With these changes under way, Congress refused to endorse the Court-packing scheme, and Roosevelt suffered his first major legislative defeat at the hands of his own party. Yet in losing this battle, Roosevelt incidentally won his campaign. The Court, as he had hoped, became markedly more friendly to New Deal reforms. Furthermore, a succession of deaths and resignations enabled him to make nine appointments to the tribunal.

Yet in a sense FDR lost both the Court battle and the war. He so aroused conservatives of both parties in Congress that few New Deal reforms were passed after 1937, the year of the fight to "pack" the Supreme Court. With this catastrophic miscalculation, he squandered much of the political goodwill that had carried him to such a resounding victory in the 1936 election.

The Twilight of the New Deal

Roosevelt's first term, from 1933 to 1937, did not banish the depression from the land. Unemployment stubbornly persisted in 1936 at about 15 percent, down from the grim 25 percent of 1933 but still miserably high. Despite the inventiveness of New Deal programs and the billions of dollars in "pump priming," recovery had been dishearteningly modest, though the country seemed to be inching its way back to economic health.

Then, in 1937 the economy took another sharp downturn, a surprisingly severe depression-within-the-depression that the president's critics quickly dubbed the "Roosevelt recession." In fact, government policies had caused the nosedive, as new Social Security taxes began to bite into payrolls and as the administration cut back on spending out of continuing reverence for the orthodox economic doctrine of the balanced budget.

A basic objective of the New Deal was featured in Roosevelt's second inaugural address (1937):

"I see one-third of a nation ill-housed, ill-clad, ill-nourished. . . . The test of our progress is not whether we add more to the abundance of those who have much; it is whether we provide enough for those who have too little."

Only at this late date did Roosevelt at last frankly and deliberately embrace the recommendations of the British economist John Maynard Keynes. The New Deal had run deficits for several years, but all of them had been rather small and none was intended. Now, in April 1937, FDR announced a bold program to stimulate the economy by planned deficit spending. Although the deficits were still undersized for the Herculean task of conquering the depression, this abrupt policy reversal endorsing "Keynesianism" marked a turning point in the government's relation to the economy.

Roosevelt had meanwhile been pushing the remaining reform measures of the New Deal. But only a few of his proposals made it through an increasingly conservative

Congress. The Reorganization Act gave him limited administrative reforms, including the key new Executive Office in the White House. The Hatch Act of 1939 barred federal officials from political campaigning, soliciting, or using government funds for political purposes. But such clever ways of getting around it were found that the legislation proved disappointing.

By 1938 the New Deal had clearly lost most of its early momentum. Magician Roosevelt could find few dazzling new reform rabbits to pull out of his tall silk hat. In the congressional elections of 1938 the Republicans, for the first time, cut heavily into the New Deal majorities in Congress, though failing to gain control of either house. The international crisis that came to a boil in 1938–1939 shifted public attention away from domestic reform and no doubt helped save the political hide of the Roosevelt "spendocracy." The New Deal, for all practical purposes, had shot its bolt.

New Deal or Raw Deal?

Foes of the New Deal condemned its alleged radicalism, incompetence, confusion, and cross-purposes. New Dealers conceded some weaknesses but defended their record as a necessary and effective response to the depression.

To some conservatives, the New Deal was a radical attempt to make America over in a Bolshevik-Marxist image. They condemned "Rooseveltski" for bringing to Washington "crackpot" college professors, leftist "**pinkos**," and outright communists. The Hearst newspapers lambasted,

> The Red New Deal with a Soviet seal
> Endorsed by a Moscow hand,
> The strange result of an alien cult
> In a liberty-loving land.

Roosevelt was further accused by conservatives of tapping too many bright young leftists for his "Jew Deal," or even of being Jewish himself ("Rosenfeld").

More widespread was the charge that the New Deal brought bureaucracy, waste, and a welfare-state mentality that undermined the old American virtues of individualism, thrift, self-reliance, and limited government. The federal government, with its hundreds of thousands of employees, became incomparably the largest single business in the country, as the states faded farther into the background. Promises of budget balancing went out the window as the national debt skyrocketed from $19,487,000,000 in 1932 to $40,440,000,000 by 1939. Critics charged that the lavish benefactions of the "handout state" were turning once self-reliant Americans into relief-seeking loafers with wishbones larger than their backbones.

Business was bitter. Accusing the New Deal of fomenting class strife, countless businesspeople, especially Republicans, declared that they could pull themselves out of the depression if they could only get an interventionist big government off their back. Private enterprise, they charged, was being stifled by a "planned economy" and "creeping socialism." Roosevelt's aggressive leadership also came in for denunciation and charges that he was trying to create a "one-man supergovernment."

The most damning indictment of the New Deal was that it failed to cure the depression. Despite some $20 billion poured out in six years of **deficit spending** and lending, many economists came to believe that better results would have been achieved by much greater deficit spending. The New Deal had merely administered aspirin, sedatives, and Band-Aids, with the result that in 1939 millions of dispirited men and women were still unemployed. Not until World War II increased the national debt from $40 billion in 1939 to $258 billion in 1945 was the unemployment headache solved.

New Dealers staunchly defended their record. Admitting imperfection, they argued that the bureaucratic inefficiency and waste had been trivial in view of the immense sums spent and the obvious need for haste. The New Deal, they insisted, relieved a crisis by demonstrating that the Washington regime was to be used, not feared. The collapse of America's economic system was averted; a

pinko(s) *Disparaging term for someone who is not a "red," or Communist, but is presumed to be sympathetic to communism.*

deficit spending *The spending of public funds beyond the amount of income.*

**Later Major New Deal Measures, 1933–1939
(items in parentheses indicate secondary purposes)**

Recovery	Relief	Reform
(CWA)	FDR establishes Civil Works Administration (CWA), November 9, 1933	
Gold Reserve Act, January 30, 1934, authorizes FDR's devaluation, January 31, 1934		
		Securities and Exchange Commission (SEC) authorized by Congress, June 6, 1934
(Reciprocal Trade Agreements)	(Reciprocal Trade Agreements)	Reciprocal Trade Agreements Act, June 12, 1934
		Indian Reorganization Act June 18, 1934
(FHA)	National Housing Act, June 28, 1934, authorizes Federal Housing Administration (FHA)	(FHA)
(Frazier-Lemke Act)	Frazier-Lemke Farm Bankruptcy Act, June 28, 1934	
(Resettlement Administration)	FDR creates Resettlement Administration April 30, 1935	
(WPA)	FDR creates Works Progress Administration (WPA), May 6, 1935 under act of April 8, 1935	
(Wagner Act)	(Wagner Act)	(Wagner) National Labor Relations Act, July 5, 1935
		Social Security Act August 14, 1935
		Public Utility Holding Company Act August 26, 1935
(Soil Conservation Act)	Soil Conservation and Domestic Allotment Act, February 29, 1936	
(USHA)	(USHA)	United States Housing Authority (USHA) established by Congress September 1, 1937
(Second AAA)	Second Agricultural Adjustment Act, February 16, 1938	
(Fair Labor Standards)	(Fair Labor Standards)	Fair Labor Standards Act (Wages and Hours Bill) June 25, 1938
		Reorganization Act, April 3, 1939
		Hatch Act, August 2, 1939

fairer distribution of the national income was achieved; and the citizens were enabled to regain and retain their self-respect.

Though hated by business tycoons, FDR should have been their patron saint, so his admirers claimed. He deflected popular resentments against business and may have saved the American system of free enterprise. Roosevelt's quarrel was not with capitalism but with capitalists; he purged American capitalism of some of its worst abuses so that it might be saved from itself. He may even have headed off a more radical swing to the left by a mild dose of what was mistakenly reviled as "socialism." The head of the American Socialist party, when once asked if the New Deal had carried out the Socialist program, reportedly replied that it had indeed—on a stretcher.

Roosevelt, like Jefferson, provided reform without a bloody revolution—at a time in history when some foreign nations were suffering armed uprisings and when many Europeans were predicting either communism or fascism for America. He was upbraided by the left-wing radicals for not going far enough, by the right-wing radicals for going too far. Choosing the middle road, he has been called the greatest American conservative since Hamilton. He was in fact Hamiltonian in his espousal of big government, but Jeffersonian in his concern for the "forgotten man." Demonstrating anew the value of powerful presidential leadership, he exercised that power to relieve the erosion of the nation's greatest physical resource—its people. He helped preserve democracy in America at a time when democracies abroad were disappearing down the sinkhole of dictatorship. And in playing this role, he unwittingly girded the nation for its part in the titanic war that loomed on the horizon—a war in which democracy the world over would be at stake.

Millions

Unemployment, 1929–1942 The cold figures can only begin to suggest the widespread human misery caused by mass unemployment. One man wrote to a newspaper in 1932: "I am forty-eight; married twenty-one years; four children, three in school. For the last eight years I was employed as a Pullman conductor. Since September, 1930, they have given me seven months of part-time work. Today I am an object of charity. . . . My small, weak, and frail wife and two small children are suffering and I have come to that terrible place where I could easily resort to violence in my desperation."

⭐ Chapter Summary ⭐

Franklin Roosevelt, a confident aristocrat with a common touch, swept into office with an urgent mandate to cope with the depression emergency. His bank holiday and frantic Hundred Days legislation lifted America's spirits and created a host of new agencies to provide relief to the unemployed, economic recovery, and hoped-for permanent reform of a largely unregulated capitalist system.

Roosevelt's early programs put millions of the unemployed back on the job through federal action, but failed to achieve the economic recovery he sought. As popular demagogues like Huey Long and Father Charles Coughlin gained followings among the suffering population, Roosevelt developed sweeping programs to reform American industry, labor, and agriculture. The Supreme Court declared unconstitutional the most sweeping effort, the National Recovery Administration, and farmers continued to suffer from the Dust Bowl. But the TVA, Social Security, and the Wagner Act brought far-reaching social changes that especially benefited the economically disadvantaged.

Conservatives furiously denounced the New Deal, but Roosevelt formed a powerful coalition of urbanites, labor, "new immigrants," blacks, and the South that swept him to victory in 1936. FDR and especially his vigorously reformist wife Eleanor brought new visibility to women in his administration and the country.

Roosevelt's overreaching Court-packing plan failed, but the Supreme Court finally began approving New Deal legislation. The later New Deal encountered mounting conservative opposition and the stubborn persistence of unemployment. Although the New Deal was highly controversial, it steered a middle course between unregulated capitalism and socialism that prevented America from turning toward dictatorship or extreme right-wing or left-wing solutions.

VARYING VIEWPOINTS

How Radical Was the New Deal?

The Great Depression was both a great calamity and a great opportunity. How effectively Franklin Roosevelt responded to the calamity and what use he made of the opportunity are the two questions that have animated historical debate about the New Deal.

Some historians have denied that there was much of a connection between the depression and the New Deal. Arthur M. Schlesinger, Jr., for example, who believes in "cycles" of reform and reaction in American history, has written that "there would very likely have been some sort of New Deal in the 1930s even without the Depression." But most of the first generation of historians who wrote about the New Deal (in the 1940s, 1950s, and early 1960s) agreed with Carl Degler's judgment that the New Deal was "a revolutionary response to a revolutionary situation." In this view, though Roosevelt never found a means short of war to bring about economic recovery, he shrewdly utilized the stubborn economic crisis as a means to enact sweeping reforms.

Some leftist scholars writing in the 1960s, however, notably Barton J. Bernstein, charged that the New Deal did not reach far enough. This criticism echoed the socialist complaint in the 1930s that the depression represented the total collapse of American capitalism, and that the New Deal muffed the chance truly to remake American society. Roosevelt had the chance, these historians argue, to redistribute wealth, improve race relations, and bring the giant corporations to heel. Instead, say these critics, the New Deal simply represented a conservative holding action to shore up a sagging and corrupt capitalist order.

Those charges against the New Deal stimulated another generation of scholars in the 1970s, 1980s, and 1990s to look closely at the concrete institutional, attitudinal, and economic circumstances in which the New Deal unfolded. Historians such as James Patterson, Alan Brinkley, Kenneth Jackson, Harvard Sitkoff, and Lizabeth Cohen—sometimes loosely referred to as the "constraints school"—conclude that the New Deal offered just about as much reform as circumstances allowed and as the majority of Americans wanted. The findings of these historians are impressive: the system of checks and balances limited presidential power; the disproportionate influence of southern Democrats in Congress stalled attempts to move toward racial justice; the federal system, in fact, inhibited all efforts to initiate change from Washington. Most important, a majority of the American people at the time wanted to reform capitalism, not overthrow it.

The best proof of the soundness of that conclusion is probably the durability of the political alliance that Roosevelt assembled. The great "New Deal coalition" that dominated American politics for nearly four decades after Roosevelt's election in 1932 represented a broad consensus in American society about the legitimate limits of government efforts to shape the social and economic order. William Leuchtenburg has offered the most balanced historical assessment in his description of the New Deal as a "half-way revolution," neither radical nor conservative but accurately reflecting the American people's needs and desires in the 1930s—and for a long time thereafter.

34

Franklin D. Roosevelt and the Shadow of War

—◦§◦—

1933–1941

THE EPIDEMIC OF WORLD LAWLESSNESS IS SPREADING. WHEN AN EPIDEMIC OF PHYSICAL DISEASE STARTS TO SPREAD, THE COMMUNITY APPROVES AND JOINS IN A QUARANTINE OF THE PATIENTS IN ORDER TO PROTECT THE HEALTH OF THE COMMUNITY AGAINST THE SPREAD OF THE DISEASE. . . . THERE MUST BE POSITIVE ENDEAVORS TO PRESERVE PEACE.

FRANKLIN D. ROOSEVELT, CHICAGO QUARANTINE SPEECH, 1937

Americans in the 1930s tried to turn their backs on the world's problems. Their president at first seemed to share these views. The only battle Roosevelt fought was against the depression. America had its own burdens to shoulder, and the costs of foreign involvement, whether in blood or treasure, simply seemed too great.

But as the clouds of war gathered over Europe, Roosevelt eventually concluded that the United States could no longer remain aloof. Events gradually brought the American people around to his thinking: no nation was safe in an era of international anarchy, and the world could not remain half-enchained and half-free.

Focus Questions

1. What were the motives and effects of Franklin Roosevelt's early foreign policy?
2. How and why did isolationism come to dominate American public opinion and foreign policy in the 1930s?
3. How did the United States gradually awaken to the threat of totalitarian aggression in the late 1930s while still attempting to avoid foreign entanglements?
4. Why did FDR's increasingly bold moves to aid Britain in the fight against Hitler stir such a fierce national debate over the risk of being drawn into war and the best way to preserve America's security?
5. What issues and developments in Japanese-American relations led up to the surprise Japanese attack on Pearl Harbor?

Roosevelt's Early Foreign Policies

The sixty-six nation London Economic Conference in the summer of 1933 revealed how thoroughly Roosevelt's early foreign policy was subordinated to his strategy for domestic economic recovery. The delegates hoped to organize a coordinated international attack on the global depression by stabilizing national currencies. But Roosevelt, unwilling to subordinate his gold-juggling and other inflationary policies to an international agreement that might tie his hands, torpedoed the conference with a bombshell message that scolded the delegates for even trying to stabilize currencies. Whether the conference could have arrested the worldwide economic slide is debatable, but Roosevelt's every-man-for-himself attitude plunged the planet even deeper into economic crisis. The collapse of the London Conference also strengthened the global trend toward extreme nationalism—a trend that played directly into the hands of power-mad dictators who were determined to shatter the peace of the world.

Roosevelt matched isolationism from Europe with withdrawal from Asia. With the descent into hard times, American taxpayers were eager to throw overboard their expensive tropical liability in the Philippine Islands. Congress passed the Tydings-McGuffie Act in 1934, which provided for the independence of the Philippines in 1946. In truth, the American people were not so much giving freedom to the Philippines as they were freeing themselves *from* the Philippines by imposing economic terms so ungenerous as to threaten the islands with economic prostration. American isolationists rejoiced once again, and Japanese **militarists** calculated that they had little to fear from an inward-looking America.

Closer to home, Roosevelt inaugurated a refreshing new era in relations with Latin America. He proclaimed in his inaugural address, "I would dedicate this nation to the policy of the Good Neighbor." He made it clear from the outset that he was going to renounce armed intervention, particularly the vexatious corollary to the Monroe Doctrine devised by his cousin Theodore Roosevelt.

Accordingly, the United States withdrew the last marines from Haiti in 1934. That same year, after military strongman Fulgencia Batista had come to power, restive Cuba was released from the worst hobbles of the interventionist Platt Amendment, although the United States retained its naval base at Guantanamo (see p. 428). The U.S. similarly relaxed its grip on Panama in 1936. When the Mexican government seized Yankee oil properties in 1938, Roosevelt successfully resisted business pressure to intervene and eventually thrashed out a settlement in 1941. These earnest acts of friendliness paid rich dividends in goodwill among the peoples to the south, and Roosevelt was cheered with tremendous enthusiasm when he traveled to an Inter-American Conference at Buenos Aires, Argentina, in 1936. The Colossus of the North now seemed less a vulture and more an eagle.

Taken together, Roosevelt's noninvolvement in Europe and withdrawal from Asia, along with his brotherly embrace of his New World neighbors, suggested that the United States was giving up its ambition to be a world power and would content itself instead with being merely a regional power, its interests and activities confined exclusively to the Western Hemisphere.

Turning Toward Isolationism

Post-1918 chaos in Europe, followed by the Great Depression, spawned the ominous spread of **totalitarianism**. The individual was nothing; the state was everything. The Communist USSR led the way, with the crafty and ruthless Joseph Stalin finally emerging as dictator. Blustery Benito Mussolini, a swaggering fascist, seized the reins of power in Italy during 1922. And Adolf Hitler, a fanatic with a toothbrush mustache, plotted and harangued his way into control of Germany in 1933 with liberal use of the "big lie."

Hitler was the most dangerous of the dictators because he combined tremendous power with impulsiveness. A frustrated Austrian painter, with hypnotic talents as an orator and leader, he had led the Nazi party to power in Germany by making political capital of the Treaty of Versailles and Germany's depression-spawned unemployment. The desperate German people had fallen in behind the new Pied Piper, for they saw no other hope of escape from the plague of economic chaos and national disgrace. Hitler began clandestinely rearming in 1933, and in 1936 the Nazi Hitler and the Fascist Mussolini allied themselves in the Rome-Berlin Axis.

International gangsterism was likewise spreading in East Asia, where imperial Japan was on the make. Like Germany and Italy, Japan was a so-called have-not power. Like them, it resented the ungenerous Treaty of Versailles. Like them, it demanded additional space for its teeming millions, cooped up in their crowded

militarists *Someone who glorifies military values or institutions and extends them into the political and social spheres.*

totalitarianism *A political system of absolute control, in which all social, moral, and religious values and institutions are put in direct service of the state.*

Chronology

1933	FDR torpedoes London Economic Conference. FDR declares Good Neighbor policy toward Latin America.
1934	Tydings-McDuffie Act provides for Philippine independence on July 4, 1946.
1935	Mussolini invades Ethiopia. U.S. Neutrality Act of 1935.
1936	U.S. Neutrality Act of 1936.
1936-1939	Spanish Civil War.
1937	U.S. Neutrality Act of 1937. *Panay* incident. Japan invades China.
1938	Hitler seizes Austria. Munich Conference.
1939	Hitler seizes all of Czechoslovakia. Nazi-Soviet pact. World War II begins in Europe with Hitler's invasion of Poland. U.S. Neutrality Act of 1939.
1940	Hitler invades Denmark, Norway, Netherlands, and Belgium. Fall of France. United States invokes first peacetime draft. Battle of Britain. Bases-for-destroyers deal with Britain. FDR defeats Willkie for presidency.
1941	Lend-Lease Act. Hitler attacks Soviet Union. Atlantic Charter. Japan attacks Pearl Harbor.

island nation. Determined to find a place in the Asian sun, Tokyo terminated the Washington Naval Treaty in 1934 and in the following year accelerated its construction of giant battleships. In 1940 it joined arms with Germany and Italy in the Tripartite Pact.

Jut-jawed Mussolini, seeking both glory and empire in Africa, brutally attacked Ethiopia in 1935. The members of the League of Nations could have halted Mussolini's war machine with an oil embargo. But fearing global hostilities they failed to act, and the brave Ethiopians were speedily crushed.

Isolationism, long festering in America, received a strong boost from these alarms abroad. Though disapproving of the dictators, Americans still believed that their encircling seas conferred a kind of mystic immunity. They were continuing to suffer the disillusionment born of their participation in World War I, which they now regarded as a colossal blunder. They likewise nursed bitter memories of the ungrateful and defaulting debtors.

Mired down in the Great Depression, Americans had no real appreciation of the revolutionary forces being harnessed by the dictators. Americans were not so much afraid that totalitarian aggression would cause trouble as they were fearful that they might be drawn into it. Strong nationwide sentiment welled up for a constitutional amendment to forbid a declaration of war by Congress—except in case of invasion—unless there was a favorable popular referendum. As the gloomy 1930s lengthened, an avalanche of lurid articles and books condemning the munitions manufacturers as war-fomenting "merchants of death" poured forth from American presses. A Senate committee headed by Senator Gerald Nye of North Dakota sensationalized evidence regarding America's entry into World War I, thus shifting the blame away from the German submarines onto the American bankers and arms manufacturers. Because the munitions makers had obviously made money out of the war, many a naive citizen leaped to the illogical conclusion that these soulless scavengers had *caused* the war in order to make money. This kind of reasoning suggested that if the profits could only be removed from the arms traffic—"one hell of a business"—the country could steer clear of any future world conflict.

■ **Adolf Hitler Reviewing Troops, Berlin, 1939** Egging his people on with theatrical displays of pomp and ceremony, Hitler had created a vast military machine by 1939, when he started World War II with a brutal attack against Poland.

The thirst of Benito Mussolini (1883–1945) for national glory in Ethiopia is indicated by his remark in 1940:

"To make a people great it is necessary to send them to battle even if you have to kick them in the pants." (The Italians were notoriously unwarlike.)

In 1934 Mussolini proclaimed in a public speech,

"We have buried the putrid corpse of liberty."

Responding to overwhelming popular pressure, Congress made haste to legislate the nation out of war. Action was spurred by the danger that Mussolini's Ethiopian assault would plunge the world into a new bloodbath. The Neutrality Acts of 1935, 1936, and 1937, taken together, stipulated that *when the president proclaimed* the existence of a foreign war, certain restrictions would automatically go into effect: no American could legally sail on a belligerent ship, sell or transport munitions to a belligerent, or make loans to a belligerent.

This storm-cellar neutrality proved to be tragically shortsighted. Through its neutrality laws, America served notice that it would make no distinction between brutal aggressors and innocent victims. By striving to hold the scales even, it actually overbalanced them in favor of the dictators, who had armed themselves to the teeth. By declining to use its vast industrial strength to aid its democratic friends and defeat its totalitarian foes, America helped goad the aggressors along their blood-spattered path of conquest.

The Spanish Civil War of 1936–1939—a proving ground and dress rehearsal in miniature for World War II—was a painful object lesson in the folly of neutrality-by-legislation. Spanish rebels, who rose against the left-leaning republican government in Madrid, were headed by fascistic General Francisco Franco. Generously aided by his fellow conspirators Hitler and Mussolini, he undertook to overthrow the established Loyalist regime, which in turn was assisted on a smaller scale by the Soviet Union. This pipeline from communist Moscow chilled the natural sympathies of many Americans, especially Roman Catholics.

Washington continued official relations with the Loyalist government. In accordance with previous American practice, this regime should have been free to purchase desperately needed munitions from the United States. But Congress, with the encouragement of Roosevelt and with only one dissenting vote, amended the existing neutrality legislation so as to apply an arms embargo to both Loyalists and rebels.

Uncle Sam thus sat on the sidelines while Franco, abundantly supplied with arms and men by his fellow dictators, strangled the republican government of Spain. The democracies, including the United States, were so determined to stay out of war that they helped to condemn a fellow democracy to death. In so doing they further encouraged the dictators to take the dangerous road that led over the precipice to World War II.

Appeasing Japan and Germany

Sulfurous war clouds had meanwhile been gathering in tension-taut East Asia. In 1937 the Japanese militarists, at the Marco Polo Bridge near Beijing (Peking), touched off the explosion that led to an all-out invasion of China. In a sense this attack was the curtain raiser of World War II.

Roosevelt shrewdly declined to invoke the recently passed neutrality legislation by refusing to call the China incident an officially declared war. If he had put the existing restrictions into effect, he would have cut off the tiny trickle of munitions on which the Chinese were desperately dependent. The Japanese, of course, could continue to buy mountains of war supplies in the United States.

In Chicago—unofficial isolationist "capital" of America—President Roosevelt delivered his sensational "Quarantine Speech" in the autumn of 1937. Alarmed by the recent aggression of Italy and Japan, he called for "positive endeavors" to "**quarantine**" the aggressors—presumably by economic embargoes. The speech triggered a cyclone of protest from isolationists and other foes of involvement; they feared that a moral quarantine would lead to a shooting quarantine. Startled by this angry response, Roosevelt retreated and sought less direct means to curb the dictators.

quarantine *In politics, isolating a nation by refusing to have economic or diplomatic dealings with it.*

America's isolationist mood intensified in December 1937 when Japanese aviators bombed and sank an American gunboat, the *Panay,* in Chinese waters. Tokyo apologized and paid an indemnity, and Americans breathed a sigh of relief that they need not respond to the outrage.

Adolf Hitler meanwhile grew louder and bolder in Europe. In 1935 he had openly flouted the Treaty of Versailles by introducing compulsory military service in Germany. The next year he boldly marched into the demilitarized German Rhineland, likewise contrary to the detested treaty, while France and Britain looked on in an agony of indecision. Lashing his following to a frenzy, Hitler undertook to persecute and then exterminate the Jewish population in the areas under his control. In the end, he wiped out about 6 million innocent victims, mostly in gas chambers (see "Makers of America: Refugees from the Holocaust," p. 544). Calling upon his people to sacrifice butter for guns, he whipped the new German air force and mechanized ground **divisions** into the most devastating military machine the world had yet seen.

Suddenly, in March 1938, Hitler bloodlessly occupied German-speaking Austria, his birthplace. The democratic powers, wringing their hands in despair, prayed that this last grab would satisfy his passion for conquest. But like a drunken reveler calling for madder music and stronger wine, Hitler could not stop. Intoxicated by his recent gains, he began to make bullying demands for the German-inhabited Sudetenland of neighboring Czechoslovakia.

British and French leaders, eager to appease Hitler, frantically arranged a conference with Hitler and Mussolini at Munich, Germany, in September 1938. There they betrayed Czechoslovakia by consenting to the shearing away of the Sudetenland. Europeans and Americans alike hoped that these concessions would bring "peace in our time." Indeed, Hitler publicly promised that the Sudetenland "is the last territorial claim I have to make in Europe."

"Appeasement" of the dictators, symbolized by the ugly word *Munich,* turned out to be merely surrender on the installment plan. It was like giving a cannibal a finger in the hope of saving an arm. In March 1939, scarcely six months later, Hitler suddenly erased the rest of Czechoslovakia from the map, contrary to his solemn vows. The democratic world was again stunned.

divisions *The major unit of military organization, usually consisting of about 3,000 to 10,000 soldiers, into which most modern armies are organized.*

Hitler's Belligerency and U.S. Neutrality

Joseph Stalin, the sphinx of the Kremlin, was a key to the peace puzzle. When his efforts to secure a mutual defense treaty with Britain and France fell through in the summer of 1939, the Soviet Union astounded the world by signing, on August 23, 1939, a nonaggression treaty with the German dictator. The notorious Hitler-Stalin pact meant that, contrary to hopes of wishful thinkers in western Europe, the two menaces would not bleed each other to death, but rather join hands to share the spoils.

With the signing of the Nazi-Soviet pact, World War II was only hours away. Hitler now demanded from neighboring Poland a return of the areas wrested from Germany after World War I. Failing to secure satisfaction, he sent his mechanized divisions crashing into Poland at dawn on September 1, 1939. Honoring their commitments, Britain and France promptly declared war. But they were powerless to aid Poland, which was quickly divided between Hitler and his partner in crime, Stalin. Long-dreaded World War II was now fully launched, and the long truce of 1919–1939 had come to an end.

Americans were overwhelmingly anti-Nazi and anti-Hitler, but they were desperately determined to stay out of war; they were not going to be "suckers" again. Neutrality promptly became a heated issue in the United States. Britain and France urgently needed American airplanes and weapons, but the Neutrality Act of 1937 raised a sternly forbidding hand. Roosevelt summoned Congress into special session, and after six weeks of hectic debate it came up

President Roosevelt was roused at 3 A.M. on September 1, 1939, by a telephone call from Ambassador William Bullitt (1891–1967) in Paris:

"Mr. President, several German divisions are deep in Polish territory. . . . There are reports of bombers over the city of Warsaw."

"Well, Bill," FDR replied, "it has come at last. God help us all."

Refugees from the Holocaust

The ancient demon of anti-Semitism brutally bared its fangs when the Nazis came to power in 1933. Fortunately, many German Jews managed to escape from Hitler's racist juggernaut, including the world's premier nuclear physicist, Albert Einstein, the Nobel laureate whose plea to Franklin Roosevelt helped initiate the top-secret atomic bomb project; the philosopher Hannah Arendt; the painter Marc Chagall; and the composer Kurt Weill. Although America embraced some 150,000 Jews who fled the Nazi Third Reich in the 1930s, they represented only a tiny fraction of the 6 millions of Jews who eventually perished under the Nazi heel. Could America have done more to save them?

The answer to that question must begin with a sharp distinction between the prewar and war periods. Before the outbreak of the war in September 1939, the problem was how to accommodate refugees from the Third Reich. When the war began, Hitler closed off all emigration from Nazi-occupied Europe, and the problem then became how to rescue Jews trapped inside the Nazi death machine.

In the prewar period, the International Rescue Committee, founded by Eleanor Roosevelt in 1933, brought thousands of victims of persecution to sanctuary in the United States. President Roosevelt also speeded up the visa application process for Jewish immigrants, publicly condemned Nazi anti-Jewish policies, and in 1938 recalled the U.S. ambassador from Berlin to protest Nazi assaults on Jews. In the end the United States took in more Jews during the 1930s than any other country. But why did America not make room for still more refugees?

For one thing, the restrictive American immigration law of 1924 had set rigid national quotas and made no provision for asylum seekers. Opening America's gates to Germany's half-million Jews also risked unleashing a deluge of millions more Jews from countries like Poland and Romania, which were advertising their eagerness to be rid of their Jewish populations. And, of course, no one yet knew just how fiendish a destiny Hitler was preparing for Europe's Jews.

When reports of the Holocaust were verified in late 1942, the United States had yet to land a single soldier on the continent of Europe, so its options were few. Roosevelt did warn that the perpetrators of genocide would be brought to justice at war's end, and his War Refugee Board saved thousands of Jews from deportation to the death camp at Auschwitz. Yet, in what has become the most controversial symbol of America's alleged indifference to the plight of the Jews, American officials rejected requests in 1944 to bomb the rail lines leading to Auschwitz on the grounds that the diversion of airpower to such a mission might jeopardize the imminent invasion of Normandy, prolong the war, and thus put even more Jewish lives at risk.

Both before and during the war, anti-Semitism also colored American attitudes, dulling humanitarian sympathies and blocking more vigorous measures on behalf of Europe's Jews. Yet in the last analysis, the failure to extend more effective help may have owed as much to a failure of moral imagination as to a lack of either empathy or means. The Holocaust was a horror on such a scale that it literally surpassed understanding. When one death-camp escapee told his tale in 1943 to the Jewish Supreme Court justice Felix Frankfurter, Frankfurter said, "I am unable to believe you." When a friend objected that Frankfurter could not call such a man a liar, the justice replied, "I did not say that this young man is lying. I said that I am unable to believe him. There is a difference." The difference was the difference between knowledge and understanding. To this day it plagues all efforts to reckon with the enormity of the Holocaust's evil—and of all genocides since.

with the makeshift Neutrality Act of 1939. This law provided that henceforth the European democracies might buy American war materials, but only on a "cash-and-carry" basis. This meant that they would have to pay for munitions in cash and transport them in their own ships. America would thus avoid loans, war debts, and the torpedoing of American arms-carriers.

Despite its defects, this unneutral neutrality law clearly favored the democracies against the dictators. Because the British and French navies controlled the Atlantic, the European aggressors could not send their ships to buy America's munitions. The United States not only improved its moral position but simultaneously helped its economic position. Overseas demand for war goods brought a sharp upswing from the recession of 1937–1938 and ultimately solved the decade-long unemployment crisis (see the chart on p. 537).

The Fall of France and the Destroyer Deal (1940)

The months following the collapse of Poland, while France and Britain marked time, were known as the "phony war." An ominous silence fell on Europe as Hitler shifted his victorious divisions from Poland for a knockout blow at France. Inaction during this anxious period was relieved by the Soviets, who wantonly attacked neighboring Finland in an effort to secure strategic buffer territory.

An abrupt end to the "phony war" came in April 1940 when Hitler, again without warning, overran his weaker neighbors, Denmark and Norway. Hardly pausing for breath, the next month he attacked the Netherlands and Belgium, followed by a paralyzing blow at France. By late June, France was forced to surrender, but not until Mussolini had pounced on its rear for a jackal's share of the loot. In a pellmell but successful evacuation from the French port of Dunkirk, the British managed to salvage the bulk of their shattered army. The crisis providentially brought forth an inspired leader in Prime Minister Winston Churchill, the bulldog-jawed orator who nerved the British to fight off the fearful air bombings of their cities.

France's sudden collapse shocked Americans out of their daydreams. Stouthearted Britons, singing "There'll Always Be an England," were all that stood between Hitler and the death of constitutional government in Europe. If Britain went under, Hitler would have at his disposal the workshops, shipyards, and slave labor of western Europe. He might even have the powerful British fleet as well. This frightening possibility, which seemed to pose a dire threat to American security, steeled the American people to a tremendous effort.

Roosevelt moved with electrifying energy and dispatch. He called upon an already debt-burdened nation to build huge airfleets and a two-ocean navy, which could also check Japan. Congress, jarred out of its apathy toward preparedness, within a year appropriated the astounding sum of $37 billion, more than the total cost of fighting World War I. Congress also passed a conscription law on September 6, 1940, America's first peacetime draft.

As the Battle of Britain raged in the air over the British Isles, debate intensified in the United States over what foreign policy to embrace. Radio broadcasts from London beamed directly into American homes increased sympathy for Britain, but not yet sufficiently to push the United States into war. Roosevelt faced a historic decision: whether to hunker down in a "Fortress America" posture in the Western Hemisphere, or to bolster beleaguered Britain by all means short of war itself.

Both sides had their advocates. Supporters of aid to Britain formed propaganda groups, the most potent of which was the Committee to Defend America by Aiding the Allies. The isolationists, both numerous and sincere, were by no means silent. Determined to avoid bloodshed at all costs, they organized the America First Committee. Their basic philosophy was "the Yanks are not coming," and their most effective speechmaker was the famed

Online Study Center

Interactive map
The German Advance, 1939–1942
college.hmco.com/pic/kennedybrief7e

Adolf Hitler (1889–1945) promised to win his fellow Germans Lebensraum, *or "living space," and to win it by war if necessary. In his eyes, his nationalist and racist crusade justified every violent means at hand. As he told his commanders,*

"When you start a war, what matters is not who is right, but who wins. Close your hearts to pity. Act with brutality. Eighty million Germans must get what is their due. Their existence must be made secure. The stronger man is in the right."

aviator Colonel Charles A. Lindbergh, who, ironically, had narrowed the Atlantic in 1927.

Britain was in critical need of destroyers, for German submarines were again threatening to starve it out with attacks on shipping. Roosevelt moved boldly when, on September 2, 1940, he agreed to transfer to Great Britain fifty old destroyers left over from World War I. In return, the British promised to hand over to the United States eight valuable defensive base sites, stretching from Newfoundland to South America. These strategically located outposts were to remain under the Stars and Stripes for ninety-nine years.

Shifting warships from a neutral United States to a belligerent Britain was, beyond question, a flagrant violation of neutral obligations. But public-opinion polls demonstrated that a majority of Americans were determined to provide the battered British with "all aid short of war."

FDR Shatters the Two-Term Tradition (1940)

In the midst of this crisis came the distracting presidential election of 1940. The two leading Republican candidates were Senator Robert Taft of Ohio, son of the former president, and the energetic boy wonder, Thomas E. Dewey of New York. But in one of the miracles of American political history, the Philadelphia convention was swept off its feet by Wendell L. Willkie, a colorful German-descended son of Hoosier Indiana. This dynamic lawyer and public utilities corporation executive—tousle-headed, broad-faced, and large-framed—was a complete novice in politics. With the convention galleries wildly chanting "We Want Willkie," the delegates finally accepted this magnetic political upstart as the only candidate who could possibly beat Roosevelt. The outspoken Willkie was opposed not so much to the New Deal as to its extravagances and inefficiencies. Democratic critics branded him "the simple barefoot Wall Street lawyer."

Roosevelt delayed to the last minute the announcement of his decision to challenge the sacred two-term tradition. Despite what he described as his personal yearning for retirement, he avowed that in so grave a crisis he owed his experienced hand to the service of his country and humanity.

With the country already badly split between interventionists and isolationists, Willkie might have widened the breach dangerously by a violent attack on Roosevelt's aid-to-Britain policies. But the statesmanlike Republican candidate refrained from assailing the president's interventionism and accepted the essential premises of an internationalist foreign policy. Willkie campaigned hard against Rooseveltian "dictatorship" and the third term. Roosevelt, busy at his desk with mounting problems, stayed close to the White House and generally ignored Willkie. But in a speech in Boston he emphatically declared, "Your boys are not going to be sent into any foreign wars"—a pledge that later came back to plague him.

The time-honored argument that one should not change horses in the middle of a stream was strong, especially in an era of war-pumped prosperity. Roosevelt triumphed, although Willkie ran a strong race. The electoral count was 449 to 82. The popular vote was much closer—27,307,819 to 22,321,018. Democratic majorities in Congress remained about the same.

Congress Passes the Landmark Lend-Lease Law

By late 1940 embattled Britain was nearing the end of its financial tether. But Roosevelt, who had bitter memories of the wrangling over the Allied debts of World War I, was determined, as he put it, to eliminate "the silly, foolish, old dollar sign." He finally hit on the scheme of lending or leasing American arms to the reeling democracies. When the shooting was over, to use his comparison, the guns and tanks could be returned, just as one's next-door neighbor would return a garden hose when the threatening fire was put out. But isolationist Senator Robert Taft (who was reputed to have the finest mind in Washington until he made it up) retorted that lending arms was like lending chewing gum: "You don't want it back."

EXAMINING THE EVIDENCE

Public Opinion Polling in the 1930s   In 1936 the prominent news publication *Literary Digest* made a monumental gaffe when it relied on public-opinion polling data to forecast a victory for the Republican candidate, Alf Landon, over the incumbent, Franklin D. Roosevelt. As it happened, Roosevelt racked up a monstrous majority, winning the electoral votes of all but two states. The *Digest*'s error had been to compile its polling lists from records of automobile registration and telephone directories—unwittingly skewing its sample toward relatively well-off voters in an era when fewer than half of American families owned either a car or a telephone. The *Digest*'s embarrassing mistake ended an era of informal polling techniques, as new, scientifically sophisticated polling organizations founded by George Gallup and Elmo Roper forged to the fore. From this date forward, polling became a standard tool for marketers and advertisers—as well as for political strategists and historians. Yet controversy has long clouded the relationship between pollsters and politicians, who are often accused of abdicating their roles as leaders and slavishly deferring to public opinion, rather than trying to shape it. Franklin Roosevelt confronted this issue in the 1930s, as polls seemed to confirm the stubborn isolationism of the American people, even as the president grew increasingly convinced that the United States must play a more active international role.

1. What do the poll results suggest about Roosevelt's handling of this issue? About the reliability of polling data?

2. What are the legitimate political uses of public-opinion polls? How valuable are they to the historian?

3. How might the pollsters' wording of the questions have influenced the results, or made them difficult to interpret? Is it possible for polls to avoid terms like "everything possible" (Question #1) or "becomes necessary" (Question #6) that contain elements of subjective interpretation?

[1.] (U.S. Oct 3 '39) Do you think the United States should do everything possible to help England and France win the war, except go to war ourselves? (AIPO)

Yes 62%   No 38%

[2.] (U.S. Oct 3 '39) If it appears that Germany is defeating England and France, should the United States declare war on Germany and send our army and navy to Europe to fight? (AIPO)

	Yes	No
National total	29%	71%
BY GEOGRAPHICAL SECTION		
New England	33%	67%
Middle Atlantic	27	73
East central	25	75
West central	26	74
South	47	53
West	28	72
(Jan 30 '40) National		
Total	23%	77%

[3.] (U.S. May 29 '40) If the question of the United States going to war against Germany came up for a national vote to go to war (go into the war or stay out of the war)? (AIPO)

Yes 16%   No 84%

(June 11 '40)   Go in 19%   Stay out 81%

[4.] (U.S. Aug 5 '41) Should the United States go to war now against Japan? (AIPO)

	Yes	No	No opinion
	22%	78% = 100%	11%
(Oct 22 '41)	13	74	13

[5.] (U.S. Sept 17 '41) Should the United States go into the war now and send an army to Europe to fight? (AIPO)

Yes 9%   No 87%   No opinion 4%

[6.] (U.S. Nov 5 '41) If, in trying to defeat Germany, it becomes necessary to send a large American army to Europe, would you favor this step? (AIPO)

Yes 47%   No 46%   No opinion 7%

Source: From Hadley Cantril, ed. *Public Opinion, 1935–1946* (Princeton: Princeton University Press, 1951).

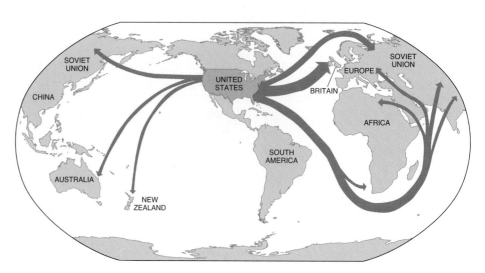

■ **Main Flow of Lend-Lease Aid** (width of arrows indicates relative amount) The proud but desperate British prime minister, Winston Churchill, declared in early 1941: "Give us the tools and we will finish the job." Lend-lease eventually provided the British and other Allies with $50 billion worth of "tools."

Online Study Center

Primary source
Main Flow of Lend-Lease Aid
college.hmco.com/pic/kennedybrief7e

convoy *(v.) To escort militarily, for purposes of protection. (The escorting ships or troops are called a* **convoy (n.).**)

The Lend-Lease Bill, patriotically numbered 1776, was entitled "An Act Further to Promote the Defense of the United States." The underlying concept was "Send guns, not sons" or "Billions, not bodies." America, so President Roosevelt promised, would be the "arsenal of democracy." It would send a limitless supply of arms to the victims of aggression, who in turn would finish the job and keep the war on their side of the Atlantic. Isolationists assailed the lend-lease scheme as "the blank-check bill." Isolationist Senator Burton Wheeler called it "the new triple-A [Agricultural Adjustment Act] bill"—a measure designed to "plow under every fourth American boy." Nevertheless, lend-lease was finally approved in March 1941 by sweeping majorities in both houses of Congress.

Lend-lease was one of the most momentous laws ever to pass Congress; it was a challenge hurled squarely into the teeth of the Axis dictators. America eventually sent about $50 billion worth of arms and equipment to those nations fighting aggressors. By its very nature, the Lend-Lease Bill marked the abandonment of any pretense of neutrality. It was no destroyer deal arranged privately by President Roosevelt. The bill was universally debated over drugstore counters and cracker barrels from California to Maine; and the sovereign citizen at last spoke through convincing majorities in Congress. Lend-lease had the somewhat incidental result of gearing U.S. factories for all-out war production. The enormously increased capacity thus achieved helped to save America's own skin when, at long last, the shooting war burst around its head.

Hitler himself evidently recognized lend-lease as an unofficial declaration of war. Until then, Germany had avoided attacking U.S. ships; memories of America's decisive intervention in 1917–1918 were still fresh in German minds. But after the passing of lend-lease there was less point in trying to curry favor with the United States. On May 21, 1941, the *Robin Moor*, an unarmed American merchant ship, was torpedoed and destroyed by a German submarine in the South Atlantic, outside a war zone. The sinkings had started, but on a limited scale.

> *Senator (later president) Harry S Truman (1884–1972) expressed a common reaction to Hitler's invasion of the Soviet Union in 1941:*
>
> "If we see that Germany is winning, we ought to help Russia, and if we see Russia is winning, we ought to help Germany, and that way let them kill as many as possible."

U.S. Destroyers and Hitler's U-Boats Clash

Lend-lease shipments of arms to Britain on British ships were bound to be sunk by German wolf-pack submarines. If the intent was to get the munitions to Britain, not to dump them into the ocean, the freighters would have to be escorted by U.S. warships. Britain simply did not have enough destroyers. Roosevelt made the fateful decision to **convoy** in July 1941, ordering the U.S. Navy to escort lend-lease shipments as far as Iceland. The British would then shepherd them the rest of the way.

Inevitable clashes with submarines ensued on the Iceland run, even though Hitler's orders were to strike American warships only in self-defense. In September 1941, the U.S. destroyer *Greer,* provocatively trailing a German U-boat, was attacked by the underseas craft, without damage to either side. Roosevelt then proclaimed a shoot-on-sight policy. On October 17 the escorting destroyer *Kearny,* while engaged in a battle with U-boats, lost eleven men when it was crippled but not sent to the bottom. Two weeks later the destroyer *Reuben James* was torpedoed and sunk off southwestern Iceland, with the loss of more than a hundred officers and enlisted men.

Neutrality was still inscribed on the statute books, but not on American hearts. The submarine attacks and Hitler's invasion of the Soviet Union in June 1941 led to closer collaboration between the United States and all of Nazi Germany's foes. With the surrender of the Soviet Union a dread possibility, the United States extended $1 billion of lend-lease aid to help halt the invaders—the first installment on an ultimate total of $11 billion.

Franklin Roosevelt and cherub-faced British Prime Minister Winston Churchill also met on a warship off the foggy coast of Newfoundland in August 1941, where they agreed to the eight-point Atlantic Charter. This covenant, suggestive of Wilson's Fourteen Points, outlined the aspirations of the democracies for a better world at war's end. Among its key features were self-determination for all peoples, disarmament, and eventually a "permanent system of general security" (a new League of Nations). The Atlantic Charter was cheered by liberals and subject peoples the world over, although roundly condemned by isolationists in the United States.

In November 1941 Congress pulled the teeth from the now-useless Neutrality Act of 1939. Merchant ships could henceforth be legally armed and could enter combat zones. Americans braced themselves for wholesale attacks by Hitler's submarines.

Surprise Assault at Pearl Harbor

The blowup came not in the Atlantic, but in the faraway Pacific. This explosion should have surprised no close observer, for Japan, since September 1940, had been a formal military ally of Nazi Germany—America's shooting foe in the North Atlantic.

Japan's position in East Asia had grown more perilous by the hour. It was still mired down in the costly and exhausting "China incident," from which it could extract neither honor nor victory. Its war machine was fatally dependent on immense shipments of steel, scrap iron, oil, and aviation gasoline from the United States. Such assistance to the Japanese aggressor was highly unpopular in America. But Roosevelt had resolutely held off an embargo, lest he goad the Tokyo **warlords** into a descent upon the oil-rich but defense-poor Dutch East Indies (present-day Indonesia).

Washington, late in 1940, finally imposed the first of its embargoes on Japan-bound supplies. This blow was followed in mid-1941 by a freezing of Japanese assets in the United States and a cessation of all shipments of gasoline and other sinews of war. As the oil gauge dropped, the squeeze on Japan grew steadily more nerve-racking. Japanese leaders were faced with two painful alternatives. They could either knuckle under to the Americans or break out of the embargo ring by a desperate attack on the oil supplies and other riches of Southeast Asia.

Final tense negotiations with Japan took place in Washington during November and early December of 1941. The State Department insisted that the Japanese clear out of China, but to sweeten the pill offered to renew trade relations on a limited basis. Japanese imperialists, after waging a bitter war against the Chinese for more than four years, were unwilling to lose face by withdrawing at the behest of the United States. Faced with capitulation or continued conquest, they chose the sword.

Officials in Washington, having "cracked" the top-secret code of the Japanese, knew that Tokyo's decision was for war. But the United States, as a democracy committed to public debate and action by Congress, could not shoot first.

Online Study Center

Interactive map
Japanese Advances, 1941–1942
college.hmco.com/pic/kennedybrief7e

---

warlord(s) *An armed leader or ruler who maintains power by continually waging war, often against other similar petty rulers or local military leaders lacking constitutional or legal legitimacy.*

■ The Battleship *West Virginia*, Wrecked at Pearl Harbor

hara-kiri *Traditional Japanese ritual suicide*

Roosevelt, misled by Japanese ship movements in the western Pacific, evidently expected the blow to fall on British Malaya or on the Philippines. No one in high authority in Washington seems to have believed that the Japanese were either strong enough or foolhardy enough to strike Hawaii.

But the paralyzing blow struck Pearl Harbor, while Tokyo was deliberately prolonging negotiations in Washington. Japanese bombers, winging in from distant aircraft carriers, attacked without warning on the "Black Sunday" morning of December 7, 1941. It was a date, as Roosevelt told Congress, "which will live in infamy." About three thousand casualties were inflicted on American personnel, many aircraft were destroyed; the battleship fleet was virtually wiped out when all eight of the craft were sunk or otherwise immobilized, and numerous small vessels were damaged or destroyed.

The next day an angered Congress, with only one dissenting vote, officially recognized that war had been "thrust" upon the United States. When Japan's allies, Germany and Italy, also declared war on December 11, 1941, the challenge was accepted by Congress the same day. The unofficial war was now official.

Japan's **hara-kiri** gamble in Hawaii paid off only in the short run. True, the Pacific fleet was largely destroyed or immobilized, but the sneak attack aroused and united America as almost nothing else could have done. To the very day of the blowup, a strong majority of Americans still wanted to keep out of war. But the bombs that pulverized Pearl Harbor blasted the isolationists into silence. The only thing left to do, growled isolationist Senator Wheeler, was "to lick hell out of them."

But Pearl Harbor was not the full answer to the question as to why the United States went to war. This treacherous attack was but the last explosion in a long chain reaction. Following the fall of France, Americans were confronted with a devil's dilemma. They desired above all to stay out of the conflict, yet they did not want Britain to be knocked out. They also wished to halt Japan, which menaced American security and international peace. To keep Britain from collapsing, the Roosevelt administration felt compelled to extend the unneutral aid that invited attacks from German submarines. To keep Japan from expanding, Washington undertook to cut off vital Japanese supplies with embargoes that invited possible retaliation. Rather than let democracy die and dictatorship rule supreme, most citizens were evidently determined to support a policy that might lead to war. It did.

✪ Chapter Summary ✪

Roosevelt's early foreign policies, such as wrecking the London economic conference and establishing the Good Neighbor policy in Latin America, were governed by his determination to make domestic recovery the national priority and to turn the United States away from commitments elsewhere in the world. America virtually withdrew from all European affairs, and promised independence to the Philippines in an attempt to avoid future involvement in East Asia.

Depression-spawned chaos and war in Europe and Asia strengthened the isolationist impulse, as Congress passed a series of Neutrality Acts designed to prevent America from being drawn into foreign wars. The United States adhered to this policy for a time, despite the spreading aggression of Italy, Germany, and Japan. But after the outbreak of World War II in Europe, Roosevelt cautiously began to provide some aid to the Allies.

After the fall of France in June 1940, Roosevelt provided greater assistance to desperate Britain in the destroyers-for-bases deal, and Congress passed the lend-lease program. Still-powerful isolationists protested these measures, but dark-horse Republican nominee Wendell Willkie refrained from attacking Roosevelt's foreign policy in the 1940 campaign.

By the summer of 1941, the United States was fighting an undeclared naval war with Nazi Germany in the North Atlantic. Roosevelt and Winston Churchill issued the Atlantic Charter upholding shared democratic principles and outlining plans for future peace and security. Meanwhile, American pressure against the Japanese invasion of China made Japanese militarists desperate. After negotiations with Japan failed, the surprise attack on Pearl Harbor plunged the United States into World War II.

35

America in World War II

—⟡—

1941–1945

NEVER BEFORE HAVE WE HAD SO LITTLE TIME IN WHICH TO DO
SO MUCH.

FRANKLIN D. ROOSEVELT, 1942

The United States was plunged into the inferno of World War II with the most stupefying and humiliating military defeat in its history. In the dismal months that ensued, the democratic world teetered on the edge of disaster.

Japan's fanatics forgot that whoever stabs a king must stab to kill. A wounded but still potent American giant pulled itself out of the mud of Pearl Harbor, grimly determined to avenge the bloody treachery. "Get Japan first" was the cry that rose from millions of infuriated Americans, especially on the Pacific Coast. These outraged souls regarded America's share in the global conflict as a private war of vengeance in the Pacific, with the European front a kind of holding operation.

But Washington, in the so-called ABC-1 agreement with the British, had earlier and wisely adopted the grand strategy of "getting Germany first." If America diverted its main strength to the Pacific, Hitler might crush both the Soviet Union and Britain and then emerge unconquerable in Fortress Europe. But if Germany was knocked out first, the combined Allied forces could be concentrated on Japan, and its daring game of conquest would be up. Meanwhile, just enough American strength would be sent to the Pacific to prevent Japan from digging in too deeply.

The get-Germany-first strategy was the solid foundation on which all American military strategy was built. But it encountered much unwarranted criticism from two-fisted Americans who thirsted for revenge against Japan. Aggrieved protests were also registered by shorthanded American commanders in the Pacific and by Chinese and Australian allies. But President Roosevelt, a competent strategist in his own right, wisely resisted these pressures.

Focus Questions

1. How did the government and the American people mobilize to wage a total war against both Germany and Japan?
2. What was the war's impact on American society, including regional migration, race relations, and women's roles?
3. What were the major American strategic decisions of the war? What challenges and obstacles did they meet, and why was the decision to postpone the "Second Front" in favor of invading North Africa and Italy so controversial?

Chronology

1941 The United States declares war on Japan.
Germany declares war on the United States.
Randolph plans black march on Washington.
Fair Employment Practices Commission (FEPC) established.

1942 Japanese-Americans sent to internment camps.
Japan conquers the Philippines.
Battle of the Coral Sea.
Battle of Midway.
United States invades North Africa.
Congress of Racial Equality (CORE) founded.

1943 Allies hold Casablanca conference.
Japanese driven from Guadalcanal.
Allies invade Italy.
Teheran conference.
"Zoot suit" riots in Los Angeles.
Race riot in Detroit.

1944 *Korematsu* v. *United States.*
D-Day invasion of France.
Battle of Marianas.
Roosevelt defeats Dewey for presidency.

1944-1945 Battle of the Bulge.

1945 Roosevelt dies; Truman assumes presidency.
Germany surrenders.
Battles of Iwo Jima and Okinawa.
Potsdam conference.
Atomic bombs dropped on Hiroshima and Nagasaki.
Japan surrenders.

---

4. How did the strategy of "island hopping" enable the United States to turn the Japanese tide in the Pacific and advance to within striking distance of the Japanese home islands?
5. How did the British-American and Soviet armies together conquer Nazi Germany and force its surrender, and why was the surrender of Japan so sudden and unprecedented?

⭐ **Makers of America: The Japanese**

⭐ **Examining the Evidence: Franklin Roosevelt at Teheran, 1943**

⭐ **Varying Viewpoints: World War II: Triumph or Tragedy?**

The Allies Trade Space for Time

Given time, the Allies seemed bound to triumph. But would they be given time? True, they had on their side the great mass of the world's population, but the wolf is never intimidated by the number of the sheep.

Time, in a sense, was the most needed munition. Expense was no limitation. The overpowering problem confronting America was to retool itself for all-out war production, while praying that the dictators would not meanwhile crush their adversaries who remained in the field—notably Britain and the Soviet Union. Haste was all the more imperative because the highly skilled German scientists might turn up with unbeatable secret weapons, including rocket bombs and perhaps even atomic arms.

America's task was far more complex and backbreaking than during World War I. It had to feed, clothe, and arm itself, as well as transport its forces to regions as far separated as Britain and Burma. More than that, it had to send a vast amount of food and munitions to its hard-pressed allies, who stretched all the way from the USSR to Australia. Could the American people, reputedly "gone soft," measure up to this herculean task? Was democracy "rotten" and "decadent," as the dictators sneeringly proclaimed?

The Shock of War

National unity was no worry, thanks to the electrifying blow by the Japanese at Pearl Harbor. American Communists had denounced the Anglo-French "imperialist"

Monica Sone (b. 1919), a college-age Japanese-American woman in Seattle, recorded the shock she and her brother felt when they learned of Executive Order No. 9066, which authorized the War Department to remove Japanese—aliens and citizens alike—from their homes:

"In anger, Henry and I read and reread the Executive Order. Henry crumbled the newspaper in his hand and threw it against the wall. 'Doesn't my citizenship mean a single blessed thing to anyone? Why doesn't somebody make up my mind for me? First they want me in the army. Now they're going to slap an alien 4-C on me because of my ancestry. . . .' Once more I felt like a despised, pathetic two-headed freak, a Japanese and an American, neither of which seemed to be doing me any good."

Online Study Center

Primary source
He CAN'T Forget Pearl Harbor—Can You?
college.hmco.com/pic/kennedybrief7e

Online Study Center

Primary source
Propaganda in Films
college.hmco.com/pic/kennedybrief7e

war before Hitler attacked Stalin in 1941, but they now clamored for an unmitigated assault on the Axis powers. A handful of strutting pro-Hitlerites in the United States melted away, while millions of Italian Americans and German Americans loyally supported the nation's war program. In contrast to World War I, when the patriotism of millions of immigrants was hotly questioned, World War II actually speeded the assimilation of many ethnic groups into American society. Immigration had been choked off for almost two decades before 1941, and America's ethnic communities were now composed of well-settled members, whose votes were crucial to Franklin Roosevelt's Democratic party. Consequently, there was virtually no governmental witch-hunting of minority groups, as had happened in World War I.

A painful exception was the plight of some 110,000 Japanese-Americans, concentrated on the Pacific Coast (see "Makers of America: The Japanese," pp. 556–557). The Washington top command, fearing that they might act as saboteurs for Japan in case of invasion, forcibly herded them together in concentration camps, though about two-thirds of them were American-born U.S. citizens. This brutal precaution was both unnecessary and unfair, as the loyalty and combat record of Japanese-Americans proved to be admirable. But a wave of post–Pearl Harbor hysteria, backed by the long historical swell of anti-Japanese prejudice on the West Coast, temporarily robbed many Americans of their good sense—and their sense of justice. The internment camps deprived these uprooted Americans of dignity and basic rights; the internees also lost hundreds of millions of dollars in property and foregone earnings. The wartime Supreme Court in 1944 upheld the constitutionality of the Japanese relocation in *Korematsu* v. *United States.* But more than four decades later in 1988, the U.S. government officially apologized for its actions and approved the payment of reparations of $20,000 to each camp survivor.

The war prompted other changes in the American mood. Many programs of the once-popular New Deal were wiped out by the conservative Congress elected in 1942, and even President Roosevelt declared in 1943 that "Dr. New Deal" was going into retirement, to be replaced by "Dr. Win-the-War." The era of New Deal reform was over.

World War II was no idealistic crusade, as World War I had been. The Washington government emphasized action rather than propaganda. According to opinion polls during the war, a majority or near-majority of citizens confessed to having "no clear idea what the war is about." All Americans knew was that they had a dirty job on their hands and that the only way out was forward. They went about their bloody task with astonishing efficiency.

Building the War Machine

The war crisis made the drooping American economy snap to attention. Massive military orders—over $100 billion in 1942 alone—almost instantly soaked up the idle industrial capacity of the still-lingering Great Depression. Orchestrated by the War Production Board, American factories poured forth an avalanche of weaponry: 40 billion bullets, 300,000 aircraft, 76,000 ships, 86,000 tanks, and 2.6 million machine guns.

Farmers, too, rolled up their sleeves and increased their output. The armed forces drained the farms of workers, but heavy new investment in agricultural machinery and improved fertilizers more than made up the difference. In 1944 and 1945, blue-jeaned farmers hauled in record-breaking billion-bushel wheat harvests.

These wonders of production also brought economic strains. Full employment and scarce consumer goods fueled a sharp inflationary surge in 1942. The

Office of Price Administration eventually brought ascending prices under control with extensive regulations. Rationing held down the consumption of critical goods, such as meat and butter, though some "black marketeers" and "meatleggers" cheated the system. The War Labor Board (WLB) imposed ceilings on wage increases.

Labor unions, whose memberships grew from about 10 million to more than 13 million workers during the war, fiercely resented the government-dictated wage ceilings. Despite the no-strike pledges of most major unions, a rash of labor walkouts plagued the war effort. Threats of lost production through strikes became so worrisome that Congress, in June 1943, passed the Smith-Connally Anti-Strike Act, which authorized the federal government to seize and operate tied-up industries. Under the act, Washington took over the coal mines and, for a brief period, the railroads. Yet work stoppages accounted for less than 1 percent of the total working hours of the United States' wartime laboring force.

Manpower and Womanpower

The armed services enlisted nearly 15 million men in World War II, and some 216,000 women, who were employed for noncombat duties. Best known of these "women in arms" were the WAACS (army), WAVES (navy), and SPARS (Coast Guard).

Despite exemptions for key categories of industrial and agricultural workers, the draft left the nation's farms and factories so short of personnel that new workers had to be found. An agreement with Mexico in 1942 brought thousands of Mexican agricultural workers, called **braceros**, across the border to harvest the fruit and grain crops of the West. The *bracero* program outlived the war by some twenty years, becoming a fixed feature of the agricultural economy in many western states.

Even more dramatic was the march of women onto the factory floor. More than 6 million women took up jobs outside the home; over half of them had never before worked for wages. Many of them were mothers, and the government was obliged to set up some three thousand day-care centers to care for "Rosie the Riveter's" children while Rosie drilled the fuselage of a heavy bomber or joined the links of a tank track. When the war ended, Rosie and many of her sisters wanted to keep on working and often did. The war thus foreshadowed an eventual revolution in the roles of women in American society.

Yet the war's immediate impact on women's lives has frequently been exaggerated. The great majority of women—especially those with husbands present in the home or with small children to care for—did not work for wages in the wartime economy but continued in their traditional roles. In both Britain and the Soviet Union, a far greater percentage of women, including mothers, were pressed into industrial employment as the gods of war laid a much heavier hand on those societies than they did on the United States.

At war's end, two-thirds of women war workers left the labor force. Many of them were forced out of their jobs by employers or unions, but half of them quit their jobs voluntarily because of family obligations. The immediate postwar period witnessed not a permanent widening of women's employment opportunities but a widespread rush into suburban domesticity and the mothering of the "baby boomers," who were born by the tens of millions in the decade and a half after 1945. America was destined to experience a revolution in women's status later in the postwar period, but that epochal change was only beginning to gather momentum in the war years.

The war also proved to be a demographic cauldron, churning and shifting the American population. Many of the 15 million men and women in uniform, having seen new sights and glimpsed new horizons, chose not to go home again at war's

  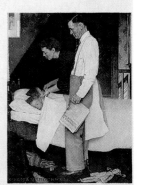

Freedom of Speech   *Freedom of Worship*

Freedom from Want   *Freedom from Fear*

■ **The Four Freedoms, by Norman Rockwell** In his January 6, 1941, speech to Congress requesting lend-lease aid to the Allies, President Roosevelt spoke eloquently of the "four freedoms" then threatened by Nazi and Japanese aggression. They are here given pictorial representation by Norman Rockwell, probably the most popular and best-loved American artist of the time.

bracero A Mexican farm laborer temporarily brought into the United States.

Online Study Center

Primary source
Women Welders at the Landers, Frary, and Clark Plant
college.hmco.com/pic/kennedybrief7e

The Japanese

In 1853 the American commodore Matthew Perry sailed four gunboats into Japan's Uraga Bay and demanded that the nation open itself to diplomatic and commercial exchange with the United States. Within two decades of Perry's arrival, Japan's new "Meiji" government had launched the nation on an ambitious program of industrialization and militarization designed to make it the economic and political equal of the Western powers.

As Japan rapidly modernized, its citizens increasingly took ship for America. A steep land tax drove more than 300,000 Japanese farmers off their land. In 1884 the Meiji government permitted Hawaiian planters to recruit contract laborers from among this displaced population. By the 1890s many Japanese were sailing beyond Hawaii to the ports of Long Beach, San Francisco, and Seattle.

Between 1885 and 1924, roughly 200,000 Japanese migrated to Hawaii, and around 180,000 more ventured to the U.S. mainland. They were a select group: because the Meiji government saw overseas Japanese as representatives of their homeland, it strictly regulated emigration. Thus Japanese immigrants to America arrived with more money and better education than their European counterparts.

Women as well as men migrated. The Japanese government, wanting to avoid the problems of an itinerant bachelor society that it observed among the Chinese in the United States, actively promoted women's migration. Although most Japanese immigrants were young men in their twenties and thirties, thousands of women also ventured to Hawaii and the mainland as contract laborers or "picture brides," so called because their courtships had consisted exclusively of exchanges of photographs with their prospective husbands.

In Hawaii most Japanese labored on the vast sugar cane plantations. On the mainland they initially found migratory work on the railroads or in fish, fruit, or vegetable canneries. A separate Japanese economy of restaurants, stores, and boardinghouses soon sprang up in cities to serve the immigrants' needs.

From such humble beginnings, many Japanese—particularly those on the Pacific Coast—quickly moved into farming. In the late nineteenth century, the spread of irrigation shifted California agriculture from grain to fruits and vegetables, and the invention of the refrigerated railcar opened hungry new markets in the East. The Japanese, with centuries of experience in intensive farming, arrived just in time to take advantage of these developments. By 1940 Japanese farmers produced most of the state's strawberries, beans, and tomatoes.

But the very success of the Japanese proved a lightning rod for trouble. On the West Coast, Japanese immigrants had long endured racist barbs and social

■ Japanese American Evacuees, 1942 After the U.S. Army's Western Defense Command ordered the forced evacuation of all Japanese and Japanese Americans living on the Pacific Coast, families had no choice but to pack up whatever they could carry and move to the "relocation centers" hastily erected farther inland.

Online Study Center

Primary source
Window Sign After Relocation
college.hmco.com/pic/kennedybrief7e

Online Study Center

Primary source
Japanese Americans Arrive at Assembly Center
college.hmco.com/pic/kennedybrief7e

segregation. Increasingly, white workers and farmers, jealous of Japanese success, pushed for immigration restrictions. Bowing to this pressure, President Theodore Roosevelt in 1908 negotiated the "Gentlemen's Agreement," under which the Japanese government voluntarily agreed to limit emigration. In 1913 the California legislature denied Japanese immigrants already living in the United States the right to own land.

Legally barred from becoming citizens, Japanese immigrants (the "Issei," from the Japanese word for *first*) became more determined than ever that their American-born children (the "Nissei," from the Japanese word for *second*) would reap the full benefits of their birthright. Japanese parents encouraged their children to learn English, to excel in school, and to get a college education. Many Nissei grew up in two worlds, a fact they often recognized by Americanizing their Japanese names. Although education and acculturation did not protect the Nissei from the hysteria of World War II, those assets did give them a springboard to success in the postwar era.

end. War industries sucked people into boomtowns like Los Angeles, Detroit, Seattle, and Baton Rouge. California's population grew by nearly 2 million. The South experienced especially dramatic changes. The states of the old Confederacy received a disproportionate share of defense contracts, including nearly $6 billion of federally financed industrial facilities. Here were the seeds of the postwar blossoming of the "Sunbelt."

Despite this economic stimulus in the South, some 1.6 million blacks left the land of their past enslavement to seek jobs in the war plants of the West and North. Forever after, race relations constituted a national, not a regional, issue. Explosive tensions developed over employment, housing, and segregated facilities. Black leader A. Philip Randolph, head of the Brotherhood of Sleeping Car Porters, threatened a massive "Negro March on Washington" in 1941 to demand equal opportunities for blacks in war jobs and in the armed forces. Roosevelt's response was to issue an executive order forbidding discrimination in defense industries and to establish the Fair Employment Practices Commission (FEPC) to monitor compliance with his edict.

Blacks were also drafted into the armed forces, though they were generally assigned to service branches rather than combat units. But in general the war helped to embolden blacks in their long struggle for equality. Membership in the National Association for the Advancement of Colored People (NAACP) shot up almost to the half-million mark, and a new militant organization, the Congress of Racial Equality (CORE), was founded in 1942.

The northward migration of African Americans accelerated after the war, thanks to the advent of the mechanical cotton picker—an invention whose impact rivaled that of Eli Whitney's cotton gin. Overnight, the Cotton South's historic need for cheap labor disappeared. Their muscle no longer required in Dixie, some 5 million black tenant farmers and sharecroppers headed north in the three decades after the war. Within a single generation, a near-majority of African Americans gave up their historic homeland and their rural way of life. By 1970 half of all blacks lived outside the South, and *urban* had become almost a synonym for *black*.

The war also prompted an exodus of Native Americans from the reservations. Thousands of Indian men and women found war work in the major cities, and thousands more answered Uncle Sam's call to arms. More than 90 percent of Indians resided on reservations in 1940; six decades later almost half lived in cities.

The sudden rubbing against one another of unfamiliar peoples produced some distressingly violent friction. In 1943 young "zoot-suit"–clad Mexicans and Mexican Americans in Los Angeles were viciously attacked by Anglo sailors who cruised the streets in taxicabs, searching for victims. At almost the same time, an even more brutal race riot that killed twenty-five blacks and nine whites erupted in Detroit.

Online Study Center

Interactive map
The Home Front
college.hmco.com/pic/kennedybrief7e

Online Study Center

Primary source
Zoot-Suiter
college.hmco.com/pic/kennedybrief7e

An African American soldier angrily complained about segregation in the armed forces during World War II:

"Why is it we Negro soldiers who are as much a part of Uncle Sam's great military machine as any cannot be treated with equality and the respect due us? The same respect which white soldiers expect and demand from us? . . . There is great need for drastic change in this man's Army! How can we be trained to protect America, which is called a *free* nation, when all around us rears the ugly head of segregation?"

Holding the Home Front

☀ Map Skill-Builder:
Understanding Demographic-Political Maps

With its combination of demographic and political information, this map conveys both a broad impression of the wartime migration (through the graphic arrows) and specific quantitative data that can be further analyzed if the reader chooses.

1. During World War II, what was the approximate *net* migration of civilian population from the East to the West? (Net migration is the number of westward migrants minus the number of those who moved east.)

2. Of the nine fastest-growing cities during the 1940s, how many were located in the West and South? (Consider Washington, D.C., as a southern city.) Which were the two fastest-growing cities in the North?

Despite these ugly episodes, Americans on the home front suffered little from the war, compared with the peoples of the other fighting nations. By war's end much of the planet was a smoking ruin. But in America the war invigorated the economy and lifted the country out of a decade-long depression. The gross national product vaulted from less than $100 billion in 1940 to more than $200 billion in 1945. Corporate profits approximately doubled during the war. Despite wage ceilings, overtime pay fattened pay envelopes. On December 7, 1944, the third anniversary of Pearl Harbor, Macy's department store rang up the biggest sales day in its history. Americans had never had it so good—and they wanted it a lot better.

The hand of government touched more American lives more intimately during the war than ever before. The war, perhaps even more than the New Deal, pointed the way to the post-1945 era of big-government interventionism. Millions of men and women worked for Uncle Sam in the armed forces or defense industries, and their personal needs were cared for by government-sponsored housing projects, day-care facilities, and health plans. The Office of Scientific Research and Development channeled hundreds of millions of dollars into university-based scientific research, establishing the partnership between the government and universities that underwrote America's technological and economic leadership in the postwar era.

The flood of war dollars—not the relatively modest rivulet of New Deal spending—at last swept the plague of unemployment from the land. War, not enlightened social policy, cured the depression. As the postwar economy continued to depend dangerously on military spending for its health, many observers looked back to the years 1941–1945 and saw the origins of a "warfare-welfare state."

The conflict was phenomenally expensive. The wartime bill amounted to more than $330 billion—ten times the direct cost of World War I and twice as much as *all* previous federal spending since 1776. Despite an expanded income tax and

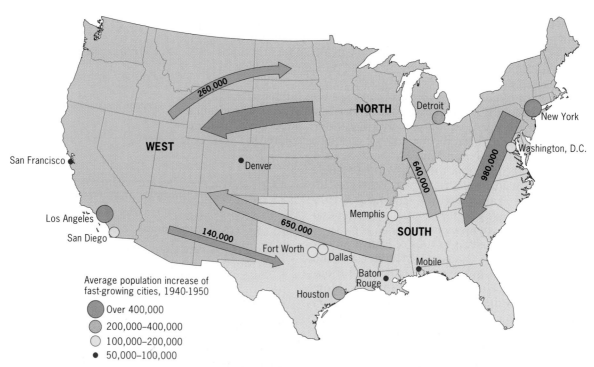

■ **Internal Migration in the United States During World War II** Few events in American history have moved the American people about so massively as World War II. The West and the South boomed, and several war-industry cities grew explosively. A majority of migrants from the South were blacks; 1.6 million African Americans left the region in the 1940s. (Source: United States Department of Labor, Bureau of Labor Statistics.)

higher tax rates, only about two-fifths of the war costs were paid from current revenues. The remainder was borrowed. The national debt skyrocketed from $49 billion in 1941 to $259 billion in 1945.

The Rising Sun in the Pacific

Early successes of the efficient Japanese militarists were breathtaking: they realized that they would have to win quickly or lose slowly. Simultaneously with the assault on Pearl Harbor, the Japanese launched widespread and uniformly successful attacks on various **bastions** in the Pacific and East Asia. These included the American outposts of Guam, Wake, and the Philippines, as well as Hong Kong and British Malaya, with its critically important supplies of rubber and tin.

Nor did the Japanese tide stop there. The soldiers of the emperor, plunging into the snake-infested jungles of Burma, cut the famed Burma road. This was the route over which the United States had been trucking a trickle of munitions to the armies of Chinese generalissimo Jiang Jieshi (Chiang Kai-shek), who was still resisting the Japanese invader in China. Thereafter, intrepid American aviators were forced to fly a handful of war supplies to Jiang "over the hump" of the towering Himalaya Mountains from the India-Burma theater. Meanwhile, the Japanese had lunged southward against the oil-rich Dutch East Indies, which speedily fell to the assailants.

In the Philippines General Douglas MacArthur, the eloquent and egotistical American commander, slowed the invading Japanese army's advance for five months. Twenty thousand American troops and a larger force of Filipinos withdrew to a strong defensive position at Bataan, near Manila, where they held off violent Japanese attacks until April 9, 1942. Before the inevitable American surrender, MacArthur was ordered to depart secretly for Australia, but he proclaimed as he departed, "I shall return." The battered remnants of his army were treated with vicious cruelty in the infamous eighty-mile Bataan death march to prisoner-of-war camps. The island fortress of Corregidor, in Manila harbor, held out until May 6, 1942, when it surrendered and left Japanese forces in complete control of the Philippine archipelago.

> **bastion** *A fortified stronghold, often including earthworks or stoneworks, that guards against enemy attack.*

Japan's High Tide at Midway

The aggressive warriors from Japan, making hay while the Rising Sun shone, pushed relentlessly southward. They invaded the turtle-shaped island of New Guinea, north of Australia, and landed on the Solomon Islands, from which they threatened Australia itself. Their onrush was finally checked by a crucial naval battle in the Coral Sea, in May 1942. An American carrier task force, with Australian support, inflicted heavy losses on the victory-flushed Japanese. For the first time in history, the fighting was all done by carrier-based aircraft.

Japan next undertook to seize Midway Island, more than a thousand miles northwest of Honolulu. From this strategic base, it could launch devastating assaults on Pearl Harbor and perhaps force the weakened American Pacific fleet into destructive combat. An epochal naval battle was fought near Midway on June 3–6, 1942. Admiral Chester W. Nimitz, a high-grade naval strategist, directed a smaller but skillfully maneuvered carrier force against the powerful invading fleet. The fighting was all done by aircraft, and the Japanese broke off action after losing four vitally important carriers.

Midway was a pivotal victory. Combined with the Battle of Coral Sea, the U.S. success at Midway halted Japan's juggernaut. But the thrust of the Japanese into the eastern Pacific did net them America's fog-girt islands of Kiska and Attu in the Aleutian archipelago, off Alaska. This easy conquest aroused fear of an invasion of the United States from the northwest. Much American strength was consequently diverted to the defense of Alaska.

Yet the Japanese imperialists, overextended in 1942, suffered from "victory disease." Their appetites were bigger than their stomachs. If they had only dug in and consolidated their gains, they would have been much more difficult to dislodge once the tide turned.

■ **United States Thrusts in the Pacific, 1942–1945** American strategists had to choose among four proposed plans for waging the war against Japan:

1. Defeating the Japanese in China by funneling supplies over the Himalayan "hump" from India
2. Carrying the war into Southeast Asia (a proposal much favored by the British, who could thus regain Singapore)
3. Heavy bombing of Japan from Chinese air bases
4. "Island-hopping" from the South Pacific to within striking distance of the Japanese home islands. The fourth strategy, favored by General Douglas MacArthur, was the one finally emphasized.

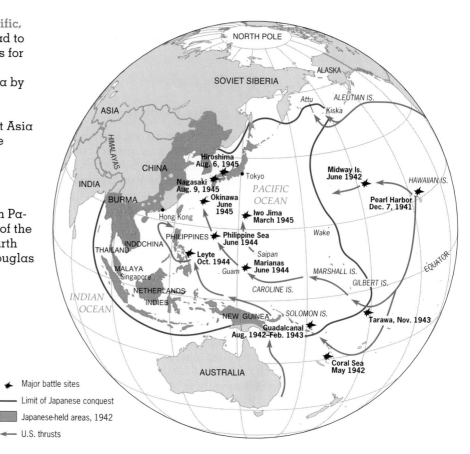

Online Study Center

Interactive map
World War II in the Pacific
college.hmco.com/pic/kennedybrief7e

★ Major battle sites
— Limit of Japanese conquest
▨ Japanese-held areas, 1942
← U.S. thrusts

American Leapfrogging Toward Tokyo

Following the heartening victory at Midway, the United States for the first time was able to seize the initiative in the Pacific. In August 1942 American ground forces gained a toehold on Guadalcanal Island, in the Solomons, in an effort to protect the lifeline from America to Australia through the Southwest Pacific. After several desperate sea battles for naval control of the area, the Japanese troops evacuated Guadalcanal in February 1943.

American and Australian forces, under General MacArthur, meanwhile had been hanging on courageously to the southeastern tip of New Guinea, the last buffer protecting Australia. Aided by American naval forces, MacArthur eventually fought his way westward through the tropical jungle hells and completed the conquest of New Guinea by August 1944.

The U.S. Navy, with marines and army divisions doing the meat-grinder fighting, had meanwhile been "leapfrogging" the Japanese-held islands in the Pacific. Old-fashioned strategy dictated that the American forces, as they drove toward Tokyo, should reduce the fortified Japanese outposts on their flank. The new American strategy of island-hopping called for bypassing some of the most heavily fortified Japanese posts, capturing nearby islands, setting up airfields on them, and then neutralizing the enemy bases through heavy bombing. Deprived of essential supplies from the homeland, Japan's outposts would slowly wither on the vine—as they did.

With Admiral Nimitz skillfully coordinating the efforts of naval, air, and ground units, the American attacks achieved brilliant success. In May and August 1943, Attu and Kiska in the Aleutians were easily retaken. In November 1943 "bloody Tarawa" and Makin in the Gilbert Islands fell after suicidal resistance, and key outposts in the Marshall Islands succumbed after savage fighting in January and February 1944. The conquest of Guam and other islands in the Marianas in July and August 1944 provided airfields for America's new B-29 superbombers to

Online Study Center

Interactive map
The Pacific War
college.hmco.com/pic/kennedybrief7e

carry out round-trip bombing raids on Japan's home islands. With these unsinkable aircraft carriers now available, virtual around-the-clock bombing of Japan began in November 1944.

The Allied Halting of Hitler

Early setbacks for America in the Pacific were paralleled in the Atlantic. Hitler had entered the war with a formidable fleet of ultramodern submarines, which ultimately operated in "wolf packs" with frightful effect. During ten months of 1942 more than 500 merchant ships were lost. Not until the spring of 1943 did the Allies clearly gain the upper hand against the **U-boat.**

The turning point of the land-air war against Hitler came late in 1942. The British, who had launched a thousand-plane raid on Cologne in May, were joined by the American air force in cascading bombs on German cities. The Germans under Marshal Erwin Rommel—the "Desert Fox"—had driven eastward across the hot sands of North Africa into Egypt, perilously close to the Suez Canal. A breakthrough would have spelled disaster for the Allies. But late in October 1942, British general Bernard Montgomery delivered a withering attack at El Alamein, west of Cairo. With the aid of several hundred hastily shipped American Sherman tanks, he speedily drove the enemy back to Tunisia, more than a thousand miles away.

On the Soviet front, the unexpected successes of the red army gave a new lift to the Allied cause. In September 1942 the Russians halted the German steamroller at rubble-strewn Stalingrad, graveyard of Hitler's hopes. In November 1942 the resilient Russians unleashed a crushing counteroffensive, which was never seriously reversed. A year later, Stalin had regained about two-thirds of the blood-soaked Soviet motherland wrested from him by the German invader.

A Second Front from North Africa to Rome

Soviet losses were already staggering in 1942; millions of soldiers and civilians lay dead, and Hitler's armies had laid waste a vast territory equivalent in the United States to the area from Chicago to the Atlantic seaboard. Small wonder that Kremlin leaders clamored for a second front to divert the German strength westward.

Many Americans, including FDR, were eager to begin an invasion of France in 1942 or 1943. They feared that the Soviets might make a separate peace with Germany, as they had in 1918, and leave the Western Allies to face Hitler's fury alone. But British military planners, remembering their appalling losses in France in 1914–1918, preferred to attack Hitler's Fortress Europe through the "soft underbelly" of the Mediterranean. Faced with British boot-dragging, the Americans reluctantly agreed to postpone a massive invasion of Europe.

An assault on French-held North Africa was a compromise second front. The highly secret attack, launched in November 1942, was headed by a gifted and easy-smiling American general, Dwight D. ("Ike") Eisenhower, a master of organization and conciliation. The joint Allied operation, ultimately involving some 400,000 men and about 850 ships, was highly successful. After savage fighting, the remnants of the German-Italian army were finally trapped in Tunisia and surrendered in May 1943.

At Casablanca, in newly occupied French Morocco, President Roosevelt met with Winston Churchill in January 1943 to plan new blows. The Big Two agreed to step up the Pacific war, invade Sicily, increase pressure on Italy, and insist on "unconditional surrender" by the enemy. Designed to hearten the ultrasuspicious Soviets, who professed to fear separate Allied peace negotiations, "unconditional surrender" proved to be one of the most controversial moves of the war. The main criticism was that it steeled the enemy to fight to a last-bunker resistance, while complicating the problems of postwar reconstruction.

Allied forces, victorious in Africa, now turned against the not-so-soft underbelly of Europe. Sicily fell in August 1943 after sporadic but sometimes bitter resistance. Shortly before the conquest of the island, Mussolini was **deposed**, and Italy surrendered unconditionally soon thereafter, in September, 1943.

U-boat *A German submarine (from the German* Unterseeboot *or underseas boat).*

depose *Forcibly remove from office or position.*

Online Study Center

Interactive map
World War II in Europe and North Africa
college.hmco.com/pic/kennedybrief7e

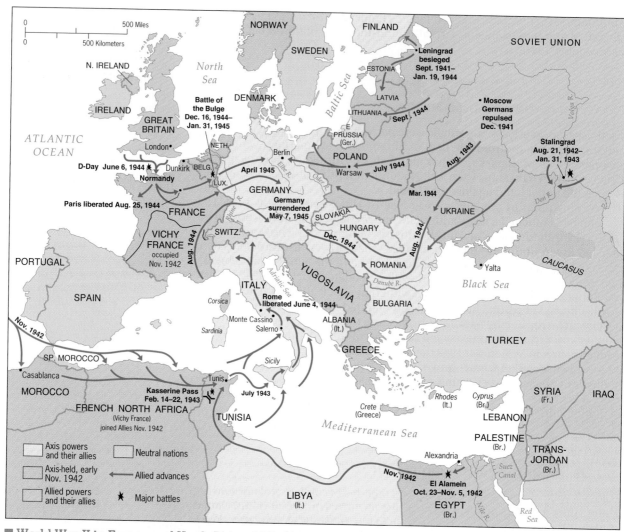

■ World War II in Europe and North Africa, 1939–1945

beachhead *The first position on a beach secured by an invading force and used to land further troops and supplies.*

But if Italy dropped out of the war, the Germans did not drop out of Italy. Hitler's well-trained troops stubbornly resisted the Allied invaders now pouring into the toe of the Italian boot. "Sunny Italy" proceeded to belie its name, for in the snow-covered and mud-caked mountains of its elongated peninsula occurred some of the filthiest, bloodiest, and most frustrating fighting of the war. After a touch-and-go assault on the Anzio **beachhead**, Rome was finally taken on June 4, 1944. But painful fighting continued in northern Italy, and not until May 2, 1945, did several hundred thousand Axis troops in Italy lay down their arms. While the Italian second front opened the Mediterranean and diverted some German divisions from the blazing Soviet and French battle lines, it also may have delayed the main Allied invasion of France by many months—allowing more time for the Soviet army to advance into Eastern Europe.

D-Day: June 6, 1944

The Soviets never ceased their clamor for an all-out second front. Plans for a major Allied invasion were finally settled at a conference of Stalin, Churchill, and Roosevelt in Teheran, Iran, held from November 28 to December 1, 1943. The Soviets agreed to launch attacks on Germany from the east simultaneously with the prospective Allied assault from the west.

Online Study Center

Interactive map
German and Italian Expansion,
1933–1942

college.hmco.com/pic/kennedybrief7e

Preparations for the cross-channel invasion of France were gigantic. Britain's fast-anchored isle virtually groaned with munitions, supplies, and troops, as nearly 3 million fighting men were readied. Because the United States was to provide most of the Allied warriors, the overall command was entrusted to an American, General Eisenhower.

French Normandy, less heavily defended than other parts of the European coast, was pinpointed for the invasion assault. On D-Day, June 6, 1944, the enormous operation, which involved some forty-six hundred vessels, unwound. Stiff resistance was encountered from the Germans, who had been misled by a feint into expecting the blow to fall farther north.

The Allied beachhead, at first clung to with fingertips, was gradually enlarged, consolidated, and reinforced. After desperate fighting, the invaders finally broke out of the German iron ring that enclosed the Normandy landing zone. Most spectacular were the lunges across France by American armored divisions, brilliantly commanded by blustery and profane General George S. ("Blood 'n' Guts") Patton. The retreat of the German defenders was hastened when an American-French force landed in August 1944 on the southern coast of France and swept northward. With the assistance of the French "**underground**," Paris was liberated in August 1944.

Allied forces rolled irresistibly toward Germany. The first important German city (Aachen) fell to the Americans in October 1944, and the days of Hitler's "thousand-year Reich" were numbered.

Online Study Center

Primary source
Parisian Girl Cheers U.S. Troops
college.hmco.com/pic/kennedybrief7e

Online Study Center

Interactive map
The Fall of the Third Reich
college.hmco.com/pic/kennedybrief7e

underground *A secret or illegal movement organized in a country to resist or overthrow the government.*

■ **Allies Landing in Normandy, June 6, 1944** Nine-foot ocean swells on invasion day made loading the assault landing craft, such as the one pictured here, treacherous business. Many men were injured or tossed into the sea as the bathtublike amphibious vessels bobbed wildly up and down alongside the troop transports. As the vulnerable boats churned toward the beach, some officers led their tense, grim-faced troops in prayer. One major, recalling the remarkable Battle of Agincourt in 1415, quoted from Shakespeare's *Henry V*: "He that outlives this day, and comes safe home / Will stand a tip-toe when this day is named."

FDR: The Fourth-Termite of 1944

The presidential campaign of 1944 came awkwardly as the awful conflict roared to its climax. Meeting in Chicago, victory-starved Republicans nominated short, mustachioed, and dapper Thomas Dewey, the popular governor of New York. A former prosecutor, Dewey was only forty-two years old, causing one veteran New Dealer to sneer that the candidate had cast his diaper into the ring. To offset Dewey's mild internationalism, the convention nominated for the vice presidency a strong isolationist, Senator John W. Bricker of Ohio.

FDR, aging under the strain but still the "indispensable man," was nominated by **acclamation** for a fourth term. The scramble for the vice-presidential plum turned into a free-for-all. Roosevelt's third-term vice president, former agriculture secretary Henry A. Wallace, was a committed liberal who desired renomination. Conservative Democrats concocted a "ditch Wallace" movement that developed tremendous momentum and finally won Roosevelt's blessing. The vice-presidential nomination then went to smiling and self-assured Senator Harry S Truman of Missouri, who had recently attained national visibility as the efficient chairman of a Senate committee investigating wasteful war expenditures.

A dynamic Dewey took the offensive in the campaign, proclaiming in his beautiful baritone voice that it was "time for a change" after "twelve long years" of New Dealism. In the closing weeks of the campaign, Roosevelt left his desk for the stump. He was eager to show himself, even in chilling rains, to spike well-founded rumors of failing health.

Democrats relied heavily on the new political action committee of the CIO, which provided union funds and campaign workers. Roosevelt, as customary, won a sweeping victory: 432 to 99 in the Electoral College, 25,606,585 to 22,014,745 in the popular totals. Elated, he quipped that "the first twelve years are the hardest."

The Last Days of Hitler

By mid-December 1944, the month after Roosevelt's fourth-term victory, Germany seemed to be wobbling on its last legs. The Soviet surge had penetrated eastern Germany. Allied aerial "blockbuster" bombs, making the "rubble bounce" with around-the-clock attacks, were falling like giant explosive hailstones on cities, factories, and transportation arteries. The German western front seemed about to buckle under the sledgehammer blows of the United States and its Allies.

Hitler then staked everything on one last throw of his reserves. Secretly concentrating a powerful force, he hurled it, on December 16, 1944, against the thinly held American lines in the heavily befogged and snow-shrouded Ardennes Forest. Caught off guard, the outmanned Americans were driven back, creating a deep "bulge" in the Allied line. The ten-day penetration was finally halted after the 101st Airborne Division had stood firm at the vital bastion of Bastogne. The commander, Brigadier General A. C. McAuliffe, defiantly answered the German demand for surrender with one word: "Nuts." Reinforcements were rushed up, and the last-gasp Hitlerian offensive was at length bloodily stemmed in the Battle of the Bulge.

In March 1945, forward-driving American troops reached Germany's Rhine River, where, by incredibly good luck, they found one strategic bridge undemolished. Pressing their advantage, General Eisenhower's troops reached the Elbe River in April 1945. There, a short distance south of Berlin, American and Soviet advance guards dramatically clasped hands.

The conquering Americans were horrified to find blood-bespattered **concentration camps**, where the German Nazis had engaged in scientific mass murder of "undesirables," including an estimated 6 million Jews. The Washington government had long been informed about Hitler's campaign of **genocide** against the Jews and had been reprehensibly slow to take steps against it—such as bombing rail lines that carried the victims to the camps. But until the war's end, the full dimensions of the "Holocaust" were not known. When the details were revealed, the whole world was aghast.

acclamation *A general and unanimous action of approval or nomination by a large public body, without a vote.*

concentration camp *A place of confinement for prisoners or others a government considers dangerous or undesirable.*

genocide *The systematic extermination or killing of an entire people.*

EXAMINING THE EVIDENCE

Franklin Roosevelt at Teheran, 1943 In late 1943 the "Big Three" wartime leaders—British prime minister Winston Churchill, American president Franklin Roosevelt, and Soviet leader Marshal Joseph Stalin—gathered together for the first time. They met amid growing Soviet frustration with the British and the Americans for their failure thus far to open a "second front" against Germany in Western Europe, while the Soviets continued to suffer horrendous losses in the savage fighting in Eastern Europe. American military planners were eager to open a second front as soon as possible, but the British, who would necessarily have to supply most of the troops until America was fully mobilized, balked. Tension among the three leaders over the second-front plan—code-named OVERLORD, the operation that resulted in the Anglo-American invasion of Normandy on "D-Day," June 6, 1944—is evident in this report of their discussions in the Iranian city of Teheran on November 28, 1943. The excerpts printed here are actually taken from two separate accounts: one composed by the American diplomat and Roosevelt's official translator Charles Bohlen, the other written by a military officer on behalf of the United States Joint Chiefs of Staff. Both versions were published in *Foreign Relations of the United States,* a compilation of American diplomatic records since 1861. The Soviets and the British also kept their own records of the Teheran meetings, giving historians remarkably rich sources with which to reconstruct the crucial negotiations and decisions that shaped wartime diplomacy.

1. Why might the history of diplomacy be so lavishly documented?

2. At this meeting, what were the principal objectives that each leader pursued? How did each man address his task?

3. In what ways was the future of the war—and the postwar world—here foreshadowed?

FIRST PLENARY MEETING, NOVEMBER 28, 1943, 4 P. M., CONFERENCE ROOM, SOVIET EMBASSY

Bohlen Minutes

SECRET

THE PRESIDENT said as the youngest of the three present he ventured to welcome his elders. He said he wished to welcome the new members to the family circle and tell them that meetings of this character were conducted as between friends with complete frankness on all sides with nothing that was said to be made public. . . .

Chief of Staff Minutes

MARSHAL STALIN asked who will be the commander in this Operation Overlord. (THE PRESIDENT and PRIME MINISTER interpolated this was not yet decided.) MARSHAL STALIN continued, "Then nothing will come out of these operations." . . .

THE PRESIDENT said we again come back to the problem of the timing for OVERLORD. It was believed that it would be good for OVERLORD to take place about 1 May, or certainly not later than 15 May or 20 May, if possible.

THE PRIME MINISTER said that he could not agree to that. . . .

. . . He said he (the Prime Minister) was going to do everything in the power of His Majesty's Government to begin OVERLORD at the earliest possible moment. However, he did not think that the many great possibilities in the Mediterranean should be ruthlessly cast aside as valueless merely on the question of a month's delay in OVERLORD.

MARSHAL STALIN said all the Mediterranean operations are diversions, . . .

THE PRESIDENT said he found that his staff places emphasis on OVERLORD. While on the other hand the Prime Minister and his staff also emphasize OVERLORD, nevertheless the United States does not feel that OVERLORD should be put off.

THE PRESIDENT questioned whether it would not be possible for the **ad hoc** committee to go ahead with their deliberations without any further directive and to produce an answer by tomorrow morning.

MARSHAL STALIN questioned, "What can such a committee do?" He said, "We Chiefs of State have more power and more authority than a committee. General Brooke cannot force our opinions and there are many questions which can be decided only by us." He said he would like to ask if the British are thinking seriously of OVERLORD only in order to satisfy the U.S.S.R.

THE PRIME MINISTER replied that if the conditions specified at Moscow regarding OVERLORD should exist, he firmly believed it would be England's duty to hurl every ounce of strength she had across the Channel at the Germans.

THE PRESIDENT observed that in an hour a very good dinner would be awaiting all and people would be very hungry. He suggested that the staffs should meet tomorrow morning and discuss the matter. . . .

The vengeful Soviets, clawing their way forward from the east, reached Berlin in April 1945. After desperate house-to-house fighting, followed by an orgy of pillage and rape, they captured the bomb-shattered city. Adolf Hitler, after a hasty marriage to his mistress, committed suicide in an underground bunker on April 30, 1945.

Tragedy had meanwhile struck the United States. President Roosevelt, while relaxing at Warm Springs, Georgia, suddenly died from a massive cerebral hemorrhage on April 12, 1945. Knots of confused, leaderless citizens gathered to discuss the future anxiously, as bewildered, unbriefed Vice President Truman took the helm.

On May 7, 1945, what was left of the German government surrendered unconditionally. May 8 was officially proclaimed V-E (Victory in Europe) Day and was greeted with frenzied rejoicing in the Allied countries.

Japan Dies Hard

Japan's rickety bamboo empire meanwhile was tottering to its fall. American submarines—"the silent service"—were sending the Japanese merchant marine to the bottom so fast they were running out of prey. All told, these underseas craft destroyed 1,042 ships, or about 50 percent of Japan's entire life-sustaining merchant fleet.

Giant bomber attacks were more spectacular. Launched from Saipan and other captured Mariana islands, they were reducing the enemy's fragile cities to cinders. The massive fire-bomb raid on Tokyo, March 9–10, 1945, was annihilating. It destroyed over 250,000 buildings, gutted a quarter of the city, and killed an estimated 83,000 people—a loss comparable to that later inflicted by the atomic bombs.

General MacArthur was also on the move. Completing the conquest of jungle-draped New Guinea, he headed northwest for the Philippines, en route to Japan, with six hundred ships and 250,000 men. In a scene well staged for the photographers, he splashed ashore at Leyte Island, on October 20, 1944, with the summons, "People of the Philippines, I have returned . . . Rally to me." The ravaged city of Manila on the main island of Luzon fell in March 1945, but the Philippines were not finally conquered until July, after bitter fighting against holed-in Japanese, who took a toll of over sixty thousand American casualties.

America's steel vise was tightening mercilessly around Japan. The tiny island of Iwo Jima was captured in March 1945, after a desperate assault that cost over four thousand American dead. The island of Okinawa, well defended by Japanese soldiers who fought with incredible courage from their caves, was finally taken in June 1945, at the cost of fifty thousand American casualties and far heavier Japanese losses. The U.S. Navy, which covered the invasion of Okinawa, sustained severe damage. Japanese suicide pilots ("kamikazes"), in an exhibition of mass hara-kiri for their emperor, smashed their bomb-laden planes onto the decks of the invading fleet, sinking over thirty ships and damaging scores more.

The Atomic Bombs

Strategists in Washington were meanwhile planning an all-out invasion of the main islands of Japan—an invasion that presumably would cost hundreds of thousands of American (and even more Japanese) casualties. Tokyo, recognizing imminent defeat, had secretly sent peace feelers to Moscow, which had not yet entered the East Asian war. But bomb-scorched Japan still showed no outward willingness to surrender *unconditionally* to the Allies.

The Potsdam conference, held near Berlin in July 1945, sounded the death knell of the Japanese. There President Truman, still new on his job, met in a seventeen-day parley with Joseph Stalin and the British leaders. The conferees issued a stern ultimatum to Japan: surrender or be destroyed. But no encouraging response was forthcoming.

America had a fantastic ace up its sleeve. Early in 1940, after Hitler's wanton assault on Poland, Roosevelt was persuaded by American and exiled scientists, notably German-born Albert Einstein, to push ahead with preparations for unlocking the secret of an atomic bomb. Congress, at Roosevelt's blank-check request, blindly made available nearly $2 billion.

What was called the Manhattan Project pushed feverishly forward, as American know-how and industrial power were combined with the most advanced scientific knowledge. Much technical skill was provided by refugee scientists who had fled the torture chambers of the dictators. Finally, in the desert near Alamogordo, New Mexico, on July 16, 1945, the experts detonated the first awesome and devastating atomic device.

With Japan still refusing to surrender, the Potsdam threat was fulfilled. On August 6, 1945, a lone American bomber dropped one atomic bomb on the city of Hiroshima, Japan. In a blinding flash of death, followed by a funnel-shaped cloud, about 180,000 people were left killed, wounded, or missing. Some 70,000 of them died instantaneously. Sixty thousand more soon perished from burns and radiation disease.

Two days later, on August 8, Stalin entered the war against Japan, exactly on the deadline date previously agreed upon with his allies. Soviet armies speedily overran the depleted Japanese defenses in Manchuria and Korea in a six-day "victory parade" that involved several thousand Russian casualties. Stalin was evidently determined to be in on the kill, lest he lose a voice in the final division of Japan's holdings.

On August 9, American aviators dropped a second atomic bomb on the city of Nagasaki. The explosion took a horrible toll of about eighty thousand people killed or missing (see "Varying Viewpoints," p. 569). The Japanese nation could endure no more. On August 10, 1945, Tokyo sued for peace on one condition: that Hirohito, the bespectacled Son of Heaven, be allowed to remain on his ancestral throne as nominal emperor. Despite their "unconditional surrender" policy, the Allies accepted this condition on August 14, 1945. The official surrender ceremonies took place on the battleship *Missouri* on September 2, 1945. At the same time, Americans at home celebrated V-J (Victory in Japan) Day, after the most horrible war in history had ended in mushrooming atomic clouds.

The Scientific director of the Manhattan Project, J. Robert Oppenheimer (1904–1967), recalled his reaction as he witnessed the detonation of the first atomic bomb at the Trinity test site in Alamogordo, New Mexico, in July 1945. He was not only awed by the extraordinary force of this new weapon. He also feared the power to do harm that it gave to humans:

"I remembered the line from the Hindu scripture, the *Bhagavad-Gita:* 'Now I am become Death, the destroyer of Worlds.'"

Online Study Center

Primary source
Announcing the Use of the A-Bomb at Hiroshima
college.hmco.com/pic/kennedybrief7e

Online Study Center

Primary source
Unconditional Surrender of Japan
college.hmco.com/pic/kennedybrief7e

The Allies Triumphant

World War II proved to be terribly costly. American forces suffered some 1 million casualties, about one-third of which were deaths. Compared with other wars, the proportion killed by wounds and disease was sharply reduced, owing in part to the use of blood plasma and "miracle" drugs, notably penicillin.

America was fortunate in emerging with its mainland virtually unscathed. Much of the rest of the world was utterly destroyed and destitute. America alone was untouched and healthy—oiled and muscled like a prize bull, standing astride the world's ruined landscape.

This complex conflict was the best-fought war in America's history. Though unprepared for it at the outset, the nation was better prepared than for the others, partly because it had begun to buckle on its armor about a year and a half before the war officially began. In the end the United States showed itself to be resourceful, tough, adaptable—able to accommodate itself to the tactics of an enemy who was relentless and ruthless.

American military leadership proved to be of the highest order. A new crop of war heroes emerged in brilliant generals like Eisenhower, MacArthur, and George Marshall (chief of staff) and in imaginative admirals like Nimitz. President Roosevelt and Prime Minister Churchill, as kindred spirits, collaborated closely in planning strategy. "It is fun to be in the same decade with you," FDR once cabled Churchill.

bazooka *A metal-tubed weapon from which armor-piercing rockets are electronically fired.*

Industrial leaders were no less skilled, for marvels of production were performed almost daily. Assembly lines proved as important as battle lines, and victory went again to the side with the most smokestacks. The enemy was almost literally smothered by bayonets, bullets, **bazookas**, and bombs. Hitler and his Axis coconspirators had chosen to make war with machines, and the ingenious Yankees could ask for nothing better. They demonstrated again, as they had in World War I, that the American way of war was simply more—more men, more weapons, more machines, more technology, and more money than any enemy could hope to match. From 1940 to 1945, the output of American factories was simply phenomenal.

Hermann Goering, a Nazi leader, had sneered, "The Americans can't build planes—only electric iceboxes and razor blades." Democracy had given its answer, as the dictators, despite long preparation, were overthrown and discredited. It is true that an unusual amount of direct control was exercised over the individual by the Washington authorities during the war emergency. But the American people preserved their precious liberties without serious impairment.

★ Chapter Summary ★

America was badly wounded but roused to national unity and determination by Pearl Harbor. Roosevelt and Churchill settled on a fundamental strategy of dealing with Hitler first, while doing just enough in the Pacific to block the Japanese advance.

With the ugly exception of the Japanese-American concentration camps, World War II proceeded in the United States without the fanaticism and violations of civil liberties that occurred in World War I. The economy was effectively mobilized, using new sources of labor such as women and Mexican *braceros.* Numerous African Americans and Indians also left their traditional rural homelands and migrated to war-industry jobs in the cities of the North and West. The war brought full employment and prosperity, as well as enduring social changes, as millions of Americans were uprooted and thrown together in the military and in new communities across the country. Unlike European and Asian nations, however, the United States experienced relatively little economic and social devastation from the war. The federal government became vastly more powerful, and touched Americans' lives in numerous new ways.

The tide of Japanese conquest was stemmed at the Battles of Midway and the Coral Sea, and American forces then began a slow strategy of "island hopping" toward Tokyo. Allied troops first invaded North Africa and Italy in 1942–1943, providing a small, compromise "second front" that attempted to appease the badly weakened Soviet Union as well as the anxious British. The real second front came in June 1944 with the D-Day invasion of France. The Allies moved rapidly across France, but faced a setback in the Battle of the Bulge in the Low Countries.

Meanwhile, American capture of the Marianas Islands enabled the use of ground bases for extensive bombing of the Japanese home islands. The seriously ill Roosevelt won a fourth term just as Allied troops entered Germany and finally met the Russians, bringing an end to Hitler's rule in May 1945. After a last round of brutal warfare on Okinawa and Iwo Jima, the dropping of two atomic bombs ended the war against Japan in August 1945.

VARYING VIEWPOINTS

The Atomic Bombs: Were They Justified?

No episode of the World War II era has provoked sharper controversy than the atomic bombings of Japan in August 1945. Lingering moral misgivings about the nuclear incineration of Hiroshima and Nagasaki have long threatened to tarnish America's crown of military victory. Some critics have accused the United States of racist motives because the bombs were dropped on a nonwhite people. Others believe the bombs—especially the second bomb dropped on Nagasaki—were unnecessary because the Japanese were already on the verge of collapse. Still other scholars, notably Gar Alperovitz, have charged that the atomic bombs were not the last shots of World War II but the first salvos in the emerging Cold War. Alperovitz argues that President Truman dropped the bomb because he wanted to intimidate and isolate the Soviet Union.

Each of these accusations has been vigorously rebutted. Richard Rhodes's history of the making of the atomic bomb emphasizes that the Anglo-American atomic project began as a race against the Germans. From the outset, British and American planners believed this ultimate weapon of destruction would deliver victory into the hands of whoever possessed it. They consequently assumed that it would be used at the earliest possible moment, and that German cities could well have been the target.

It is true that American intelligence sources knew in the early summer of 1945 that some Japanese statesmen were trying to enlist the neutral Russians' good offices to negotiate a surrender. But as R.J. C. Butow's fine-grained study of Japan's decision to surrender demonstrates, the Japanese clung to several unacceptable conditions, including no military occupation of the home islands and no international trials of war criminals. All this flew squarely in the face of America's demand for nothing less than an *unconditional* surrender. As for the Nagasaki bomb (dropped on August 9), Butow notes that it conclusively dispelled the Japanese government's original assessment that the Hiroshima attack on August 6 was a one-time-only stunt.

Could the use of the atomic bombs have been avoided? Martin J. Sherwin, Barton J. Bernstein, and McGeorge Bundy have shown that few policymakers of the time seriously asked that question. In fact, the "decision" to use the bomb was not made in 1945, but in 1942, when the United States committed itself to a crash program to build—and use—a nuclear weapon as swiftly as possible. Intimidating the Soviets might have been a "bonus" to using the bomb against Japan, but influencing Soviet behavior was never the *primary* reason for the fateful decision.

Doubt and remorse about the atomic conclusion of World War II have plagued the American conscience ever since. Less often remarked on are the deaths of four times more Japanese noncombatants than died at Hiroshima and Nagasaki in the fire-bombing of some five dozen Japanese cities in 1945. Those deaths suggest that the deeper moral questions should perhaps not be addressed to the particular technology of nuclear weaponry, but to the quite deliberate decision, made by several combatants—including the Germans, the British, the Americans, and the Japanese themselves—to designate civilian populatons as legitimate military targets.

Online Study Center

Primary source
Truman Announces the Atomic
Bomb Attack
college.hmco.com/pic/kennedybrief7e

PART SIX

Making Modern America

—⁂—

1945 to the Present

World War II broke the back of the Great Depression in the United States and also ended the century-and-a-half-old American tradition of isolationism in foreign affairs. Alone among the warring powers, the United States managed to emerge from the great conflict physically unscarred, economically healthy, and diplomatically strengthened. Yet if Americans faced a world full of promise at the war's end, it was also a world full of dangers, none more disconcerting than Soviet communism. These two themes of promise and menace mingled uneasily throughout the nearly five decades of the Cold War era, from the end of World War II in 1945 to the collapse of the Soviet Union in 1991.

Truman in 1948, John F. Kennedy in 1960, and Lyndon Johnson in 1964). The Democratic party, the party of the liberal New Deal at home and of an activist foreign policy abroad, comfortably remained the nation's majority party. Americans trusted their government and had faith in the American dream that their children's lives would be richer than their own lives had been. Anything and everything seemed possible.

The rising curve of expectations, propelled by economic growth, ascended through the 1950s. It peaked in the 1960s, an exceptionally stormy decade during which faith in government, in the wisdom of American foreign policy, and in the American dream itself began to sour. Lyndon Johnson's "Great Society" reforms, billed as the completion of the unfinished work of the New Deal, foundered on the rocks of fiscal limitations and stubborn racial resentments. Johnson, the most ambitious reformer in the White House since Franklin Roosevelt, eventually saw his presidency destroyed by the furies unleashed over the Vietnam War.

At home, unprecedented prosperity in the postwar quarter-century nourished a robust sense of national self-confidence and fed a revolution of rising expectations. Invigorated by the prospect of endlessly spreading affluence, Americans in the 1940s, '50s, and '60s had record numbers of babies, aspired to ever-higher standards of living, generously expanded the welfare state (especially for the elderly), widened opportunities for women, welcomed immigrants, and even found the will to grapple at long last with the nation's grossest legacy of injustice, its treatment of African Americans. With the exception of Dwight Eisenhower's presidency in the 1950s, Americans elected liberal Democratic presidents (Harry

When economic growth flattened in the 1970s, the horizon of hopes for the future seemed to sink as well. The nation entered a frustrating period of stalled expectations, increasingly rancorous racial tensions, disillusion with government, and political stalemate, although in one important area idealism survived. As "second-wave feminism" gathered steam, women burst through barriers that had long excluded them from male domains, from the factory floor to the U.S. Army to the Ivy League. Not content with private victories, they also called on the government for help—to ensure women equal opportunity as workers, fair treatment as consumers, and the right to choose an abortion.

With the exceptions of Jimmy Carter in the 1970s and Bill Clinton in the 1990s, Americans after 1968 elected conservative Republicans to the White House (Richard Nixon in 1968 and 1972, Ronald Reagan in 1980 and 1984, George Bush in 1988, and George W. Bush in 2000 and 2004), but, until the 1990s, they continued to elect mostly Democratic congresses. As the twenty-first century dawned, a newly invigorated conservative Republican party was bidding to achieve long-term majority status, while the Democratic party teetered on a tightrope between its liberal policies and the conservative demands of the day for tax cuts and welfare reform.

Abroad, competition with the Soviet Union and after 1949 with communist China as well, colored every aspect of America's foreign relations and shaped domestic American life too. Unreasoning fear of communists at home unleashed the destructive force of McCarthyism in the 1950s—a modern-day witch hunt in which careers were capsized and lives ruined by reckless accusations of communist sympathizing. The FBI encroached on sacred American liberties in its zeal to uncover communist "subversives."

The Cold War remained cold, in the sense that no shooting conflict broke out between the great-power rivals. But the United States did fight two shooting wars, in Korea in the 1950s and in Vietnam in the 1960s. Vietnam, the only foreign war in which the United States was defeated, cruelly convulsed American society, ending not only Lyndon Johnson's presidency but the thirty-five-year era of the Democratic party's political dominance as well. Vietnam also touched off the most vicious inflationary cycle in American history, and it embittered and disillusioned an entire generation.

Uncle Sam in the Cold War era also built a fearsome arsenal of nuclear weapons, great air and missile fleets to deliver them, a two-ocean navy, and, for a time, a large army raised by conscription. Whether the huge expenditures necessary to maintain that gigantic defense establishment stimulated or distorted the economy was long a controversial question. When the Cold War ended, Americans turned their attention in the 1990s to developing the potential of a new "global economy." But as the twenty-first century dawned, a terrorist assault on American soil required a new turn to issues of national defense and international security.

What if . . . ?

■ **What if the United States had not fought the Vietnam War?**

Would the era of liberal Democratic rule and faith in government have continued for decades more?

Would the modern American conservative movement have risen to power?

36

The Cold War Begins

1945–1952

AMERICA STANDS AT THIS MOMENT AT THE
SUMMIT OF THE WORLD.

WINSTON CHURCHILL, 1945

The American people, 140 million strong, cheered their nation's victories in Europe and Asia at the conclusion of World War II. But when the shouting faded away, many Americans began to worry about their futures. Four fiery years of global war had not entirely driven from their minds the painful memories of twelve desperate years of the Great Depression. Still more ominously, victory celebrations had barely ended before America's crumbling relations with its wartime ally, the Soviet Union, threatened a new and even more terrible international conflict.

Focus Questions

1. What were the causes and consequences of the post–World War II economic boom?
2. What were the principal short-term and long-term changes in American society caused by the postwar "baby boom"?
3. What were the sources of the emerging Cold War between the United States and the Soviet Union, and what key events in Germany and Eastern Europe brought the two sides to the brink of confrontation?
4. How did the United States attempt to "contain" the Soviet Union, and later Communist China, and what were the effects of this policy in Europe and East Asia (including Korea)?
5. How did the Cold War affect domestic American society, and what were the results of the widespread fear of both Soviet spying and domestic Communist subversion?

Postwar Economic Anxieties

The decade of the 1930s had left deep scars. Joblessness and insecurity had dampened the marriage rate. Babies went unborn as pinched budgets and sagging self-esteem wrought a sexual depression in American bedrooms. The war had banished the blight of depression, but grim-faced observers warned that peace would bring the return of hard times.

The faltering economy in the initial postwar years threatened to confirm the worst predictions of the doomsayers who foresaw another Great Depression. Real **gross national product** (GNP) slumped sickeningly in 1946 and 1947 from its wartime peak. With the removal of wartime price controls, prices giddily levitated by 33 percent in 1946–1947. An epidemic of strikes swept the country. During 1946 alone some 4.6 million laborers laid down their tools, fearful that soon they would barely be able to afford the autos and other goods they themselves were manufacturing.

Chronology

1944	Servicemen's Readjustment Act (GI Bill). Bretton Woods economic conference.	**1948**	United States officially recognizes Israel. Hiss case begins. Truman defeats Dewey for presidency.
1945	Spock publishes *The Common Sense Book of Baby and Child Care.* Yalta conference. United Nations established.	**1948- 1949**	Berlin crisis.
1945- 1946	Nuremberg war crimes trials in Germany.	**1949**	NATO established. Communists defeat Nationalists in China.
1946	Employment Act creates Council of Economic Advisers. Iran crisis. Kennan's "Long Telegram" lays out "Containment Doctrine."	**1950**	American economy begins postwar growth. McCarthy red hunt begins. McCarran Internal Security Act passed by Congress over Truman's veto.
1946- 1948	Tokyo war crimes trials.	**1950- 1953**	Korean War.
1947	Truman Doctrine. Marshall Plan. Taft-Hartley Act. National Security Act creates Department of Defense, National Security Council (NSC), and Central Intelligence Agency (CIA).	**1951**	Truman fires MacArthur. Rosenbergs convicted of treason.
		1952	United States explodes first hydrogen bomb.
		1957	Postwar peak of U.S. birthrate.
		1973	U.S. birthrate falls below replacement level.

The growing muscle of organized labor deeply annoyed many conservatives. They had their revenge against labor's New Deal gains in 1947, when a Republican-controlled Congress (the first in fourteen years) passed the Taft-Hartley Act over President Truman's vigorous veto. Labor leaders condemned the Taft-Hartley Act as a "slave-labor law." It outlawed the "closed" (all-union) shop, made unions liable for damages resulting from jurisdictional disputes, and required union leaders to take a noncommunist oath.

The Democratic administration meanwhile took steps of its own to forestall an economic downturn. It sold war factories and other government installations to private businesses at fire-sale prices. It secured passage in 1946 of the Employment Act, which created a three-member Council of Economic Advisers to advise the president on government policy to "promote maximum employment, production, and purchasing power."

Most dramatic was the passage of the Servicemen's Readjustment Act of 1944—better known as the GI Bill of Rights, or the GI Bill. Enacted partly out of fear that the employment markets would never be able to absorb 15 million returning veterans at war's end, the GI Bill made generous provisions for sending the former soldiers to school. In the postwar decade, some 8 million veterans advanced their educations at Uncle Sam's expense. The majority attended technical and vocational schools, but colleges and universities were crowded to the blackboards as more than 2 million ex-GIs stormed the halls of higher learning. The total eventually spent for education was some $14.5 billion in taxpayer dollars. The act also enabled the Veterans Administration (VA) to guarantee about $16 billion in loans for veterans to buy homes, farms, and small businesses. By raising educational levels and stimulating the construction industry, the GI Bill powerfully nurtured the robust and long-lived economic expansion that eventually took hold in the late 1940s and that profoundly shaped the entire history of the postwar era.

gross national product *The total value of a nation's annual output of goods and services.*

■ **The GI Bill** Financed by the federal government, thousands of World War II veterans crowded into college classrooms in the 1940s. Here a fresh crop of ex-soldier students lays in supplies for the new term.

The Long Economic Boom, 1950–1970

Gross national product began to climb haltingly in 1948. Then, beginning about 1950, the American economy surged onto a dazzling plateau of sustained growth that was to last virtually uninterrupted for two decades. America's economic performance became the envy of the world. National income nearly doubled in the 1950s and almost doubled again in the 1960s, shooting through the trillion-dollar mark in 1973. Americans, some 6 percent of the world's people, were enjoying about 40 percent of the planet's wealth. Nothing loomed larger in the history of the post–World War II era than this fantastic eruption of affluence. It did not enrich all Americans, and it did not touch all people evenly, but it transformed the lives of a majority of citizens and molded the agenda of politics and society for at least two generations. Prosperity underwrote social mobility, funded vast new welfare programs like Medicare, and gave Americans the confidence to exercise unprecedented international leadership in the Cold War era.

As the gusher of prosperity poured forth its riches, Americans drank deeply from the gilded goblet. Millions of depression-pinched souls sought to make up for the sufferings of the 1930s. They determined to "get theirs" while the getting was good. A people who had once considered a chicken in every pot the standard of comfort and security now hungered for two cars in every garage, swimming pools in their backyards, vacation homes, and gas-guzzling recreational vehicles. The size of the "middle class," defined as households earning between $3,000 and $10,000 a year, doubled from pre–Great Depression days and included 60 percent of the American people by the mid-1950s. By the end of that decade, the vast majority of American families owned their own cars and washing machines, and nearly 90 percent owned a television set. In another revolution of sweeping consequences, almost 60 percent of American families owned their own homes by 1960, compared with less than 40 percent in the 1920s.

Of all the beneficiaries of postwar prosperity, none reaped greater rewards than women. More than ever, urban offices and shops provided them with a bonanza of employment, as the service sector of the economy dramatically outgrew the old industrial and manufacturing sectors. Women accounted for a quarter of the American work force at the end of World War II and for nearly half the labor pool five decades later. Yet even as women continued their march into the workplace in the 1940s and 1950s, popular culture glorified the traditional feminine roles of homemaker and mother. The clash between the demands of suburban housewifery and the realities of employment eventually sparked a feminist revolt in the 1960s.

What propelled this unprecedented economic explosion? The Second World War itself provided a powerful stimulus. While other countries had been ravaged by years of fighting, the United States had used the war crisis to fire up its smokeless factories and rebuild its depression-plagued economy. Invigorated by battle, America had almost effortlessly come to dominate the ruined global landscape of the postwar period.

Ominously, much of the glittering prosperity of the 1950s and 1960s rested on the underpinnings of colossal military budgets, leading some critics to speak of a "permanent war economy." The economic upturn of 1950 was fueled by massive appropriations for the Korean War, and defense spending accounted for some 10 percent of the GNP throughout the ensuing decade. Pentagon dollars primed the pumps of high-technology industries such as aerospace, plastics, and electronics, and also financed much of the scientific research and development ("R and D") that spurred the economy.

Cheap energy also fed the economic boom. American and European companies controlled the flow of abundant petroleum from the Middle East, and they kept their prices low. Americans doubled their consumption of inexpensive and seemingly inexhaustible oil in the quarter-century after the war. Anticipating a limitless future of low-cost fuels, they flung out endless ribbons of highways, installed air conditioning in their homes, and engineered a sixfold increase in the country's electricity-generating capacity between 1945 and 1970.

With the forces of nature increasingly harnessed in their hands, workers chalked up spectacular gains in productivity—the amount of output per hour of work. In the two decades after the outbreak of the Korean War in 1950, productivity increased at an average rate of more than 3 percent per year. Gains in productivity were also enhanced by the rising educational level of the work force. By 1970 nearly 90 percent of the school-age population were enrolled in educational institutions—a dramatic contrast with the opening years of the century, when only half of this age group had attended school. Better educated and better equipped, American workers in 1970 could produce nearly twice as much in an hour's labor as they had done in 1950. Productivity was the key to prosperity. Rising productivity in the 1950s and 1960s virtually doubled the average American's standard of living in the postwar quarter-century.

The Smiling Sunbelt

The convulsive economic changes of the post-1945 period shook and shifted the American people, amplifying the population redistribution set in motion by World War II. As immigrants and westward-trekking pioneers, Americans had always been a people on the move, but they were astonishingly footloose in the postwar years. For some three decades after 1945, an average of 30 million persons changed residences every year. Families especially felt the strain, as distance divided parents from children, and brothers and sisters from one another. One sign of this sort of stress was the phenomenal popularity of advice books on child-rearing, especially Dr. Benjamin Spock's *The Common Sense Book of Baby and Child Care.* First published in 1945, it instructed millions of parents during the ensuing decades in the kind of homely wisdom that was once transmitted naturally from grandparent to parent, and from parent to child.

Especially striking was the growth of the "Sunbelt"—a fifteen-state area stretching in a smiling crescent from Virginia through Florida and Texas to Arizona and California. This region increased its population at a rate nearly double that of the old industrial zones of the Northeast (the "Frostbelt"). In the 1950s California alone accounted for one-fifth of the entire nation's population growth and by 1963 had outdistanced New York as the most populous state—a position still held in the early twenty-first century.

Online Study Center

Interactive map
Population Increase in the Sunbelt States, 1950–1994
college.hmco.com/pic/kennedybrief7e

■ **Sunbelt Prosperity** The old and new West are evident in this view of booming Dallas.

A Niagara of federal dollars accounted for much of the Sunbelt region's new prosperity, though, ironically, southern and western politicians led the cry against government spending. By the 1990s the South and West were annually receiving some $125 billion more in federal funds than the Northeast and Midwest. North-easterners and their allies from the hard-hit region of the Ohio Valley tried to rally political support with the sarcastic slogan "The North shall rise again."

These dramatic shifts of population and wealth further broke the historic grip of the North on the nation's political life. Every occupant of the White House since 1964 has hailed from the Sunbelt, and the region's congressional representation rose as its population grew. With their frontier ethic of unbridled individualism and their devotion to unregulated economic growth, the Sunbelters were redrawing the Republic's political map.

The Rush to the Suburbs

In all regions, America's modern migrants—if they were white—fled from the cities to the burgeoning new suburbs (see "Makers of America: The Suburbanites," p. 578). Government policies encouraged this momentous movement. Federal Housing Authority (FHA) and Veterans Administration (VA) home-loan guarantees made it more economically attractive to own a home in the suburbs than to rent an apartment in the city. Tax deductions for interest payments on home mortgages provided additional financial incentive. And government-built highways that sped commuters from suburban homes to city jobs further facilitated this mass migration. By 1960 one of every four Americans dwelt in suburbia, and the same leafy neighborhoods held more than half the nation's population as the twentieth century neared its end.

■ **America on the Move, 1953** Millions of Americans migrated to the suburbs and the Sunbelt in the years after World War II. Here a new housing development has just opened near Los Angeles.

The construction industry boomed in the 1950s and 1960s to satisfy this demand. Pioneered by innovators such as the Levitt brothers, whose first "Levittown" sprouted on New York's Long Island in the 1940s, builders developed efficient new techniques of mass-produced housing construction.

EXAMINING THE EVIDENCE

Advertising Prosperity, 1956   This Ford advertisement in a popular magazine encouraged readers to buy a second car. By the mid-1950s, once manufacturers had met the demand for cars, homes, appliances, and other consumer goods that a decade and a half of depression and world war had pent up, they worried about how to keep expanding their markets. "Planned obsolescence"—changing design frequently enough to necessitate replacement purchasing—was one strategy. Altering expectations about what consumers needed was another. This advertisement suggests that the up-to-date family, living in its modern-style suburban home, had no choice but to own two cars, one for the male breadwinner's business, the other for the wife's "ferrying the family."

1. What gender role prescriptions are reinforced in this advertisement?

2. What assumptions has Ford made about prospective buyers of its cars?

3. How much can mass advertising tell us about the actual values of Americans living at a particular time?

The only problem in posing this picture was getting the two Fords to stand still.

Seven good reasons for two FORDS

To free their family from one-car captivity the Bremers got two Fords: a Country Sedan and a Thunderbird—the car that inspired the styling and performance of all '56 Fords.

"We saw the need for a second car even before our first youngster arrived. If you're married you know why. The five children just made two Fords more necessary. I need a car for business. My wife needs one for ferrying the family.

"*Why are they Fords?* In the first place, you can't beat Ford's looks at *twice* the price. You get extra zip in a Ford V-8, too. That's why it's the world's best seller! It's a good investment, too. Nothing at the price keeps its value like a Ford. And, of course, you don't need children to appreciate the extra safety of Ford Lifeguard Design," *says Mr. Bremer.*

SEE YOUR LOCAL FORD DEALER

The Country Sedan, one of six Ford do-it-alls, has 4-doors, lots of room. And its 200-h.p. V-8 is the most powerful standard "8" in its field.

The Ford Thunderbird inspired the styling for all Fords. And you can have its 225-h.p. Special V-8 in most of them.

Join the 300,000 TWO FORD families!

Snooty critics wailed about the aesthetic monotony of the suburban "tract" developments, but eager homebuyers nevertheless moved into them by the millions.

"White flight" to the leafy green suburbs left the inner cities—especially in the Northeast and Midwest—black, brown, and broke. Migrating blacks from the South filled up the urban neighborhoods abandoned by the departing white middle class (See Makers of America: The Great African American Migration, p. 600). Taxpaying businesses fled with their affluent customers from downtown shops to suburban shopping malls.

Online Study Center

**Primary source
Levittown**
college.hmco.com/pic/kennedybrief7e

The Suburbanites

Few images evoke more vividly the prosperity of the postwar era than aerial photographs of sprawling suburbs. Neat rows of look-alike tract houses, each with driveway and lawn and here and there a backyard swimming pool, came to symbolize the capacity of the economy to deliver the "American dream" to millions of families.

Suburbanization was hardly new. Well-off city dwellers had beaten paths to leafy outlying neighborhoods since the nineteenth century. But after 1945 the steady flow became a stampede. The baby boom, new highways, government guarantees for mortgage lending, and favorable tax policies all made suburbia blossom.

Who were the Americans racing to the new postwar suburbs? War veterans led the way in the immediate postwar years, aided by low-interest Veterans Administration mortgages. People of all kinds followed, heading for neighborhoods that varied from the posh to the plain. Yet the overwhelming majority of suburbanites were white and middle-class. In 1967 sociologist Herbert Gans published *The Levittowners*, based on his own move to a Levitt-built community outside Philadelphia. He described suburban families in tract developments as predominantly third-or fourth-generation Americans with some college education and at least two children. Men tended to work in either white-collar jobs or upper-level blue-collar positions. Women usually worked in the home, so much so that suburbia came to symbolize domestic confinement for feminists of the 1960s and 1970s.

The house itself became more important than ever as postwar suburbanites built their leisure lives around television, home improvement projects, and barbecues on the patio. The center of family life shifted to the fenced-in backyard, and institutions that had thrived as social centers in the city—churches, women's clubs, fraternal organizations, taverns—had a tougher time attracting patrons in the privatized world of postwar surburbia.

Life in the suburbs was a boon to the automobile, as parents jumped behind the wheel to shuttle children, groceries, and golf clubs to and fro. Drive-thru restaurants and drive-in movies sprang up, and roadside shopping centers edged out downtowns as places to shop. Meanwhile, the new interstate highway system enabled breadwinners to live far from their jobs and still commute to work daily.

Wherever they worked, suburbanites turned their backs on the city and its problems. They fought to maintain their independent municipalities as secluded retreats, with their own taxes, schools, and zoning restrictions designed to keep out public housing and the poor. Even the naming of towns like Elmwood Park and Maple Grove Village reflected the pastoral ideal. With a majority of Americans living in suburbs by the 1980s, cities lost their political clout. Bereft of state and federal aid, cities festered with worsening social problems: poverty, drug addiction, and crime.

Middle-class African Americans began to move to the suburbs in substantial numbers by the 1980s, but even that migration failed to alter dramatically the racial divide of metropolitan America. Black suburbanites settled in black middle-class suburbs within white-majority counties. By the end of the twentieth century, suburbia as a whole was more racially diverse than at midcentury. But old patterns of urban "white flight" and residential segregation endured.

Government policies sometimes aggravated this spreading pattern of residential segregation. FHA administrators often refused home mortgage loans to blacks and "other unharmonious racial or nationality groups," thus limiting black mobility out of the inner cities. Even public housing programs frequently built housing for blacks in neighborhoods that were already predominantly black—thus solidifying racial separation.

The Postwar Baby Boom

Of all the upheavals in postwar America, none was more dramatic than the "baby boom"—the huge leap in the birthrate in the decade and a half after 1945. Confident young men and women tied the nuptial knot in record numbers at war's end, and they began immediately to fill the nation's empty cradles. They thus touched off a demographic explosion that added more than 50 million bawling babies to the nation's population by the end of the 1950s. The soaring birthrate finally crested in 1957 and was followed by a deepening birth dearth. By 1973 fertility rates had dropped below the point necessary to maintain existing population figures. If the downward trend persisted, only further immigration would lift the U.S. population above its 1996 level of some 264 million.

This boom-or-bust cycle of births begot a bulging wave along the American **population curve**. As the oversize postwar generation grew to maturity, it was destined—like the fabled pig passing through the python—to strain and distort many aspects of American life. Elementary-school enrollments, for example, swelled to nearly 34 million pupils in 1970. Then began a steady decline, as the onward-marching age group left in its wake closed schools and unemployed teachers.

The maturing babies of the postwar boom sent economic shock waves undulating through the decades. The baby boomers created lucrative markets for toys and baby food in the 1940s and 1950s and for clothes and recorded rock music in the 1960s. In the 1980s the hordes of baby boomers bumped and jostled one another in the job market, struggling to get a foothold on the crowded ladder of social mobility. In the 1990s the boom generation began raising its own "secondary boom" of children. The impact of the huge postwar generation will continue to ripple through American society well into the twenty-first century, when its members pass eventually into retirement, placing enormous strains on the Social Security system.

population curve *The varying size and age structure of a given nation or other group, measured over time.*

precinct *The smallest subdivision of a city, as it is organized for purposes of police administration, politics, voting, and so on.*

protégé *Someone under the patronage, protection, or tutelage of another person or group.*

Truman: The "Gutty" Man from Missouri

Presiding over the opening of the postwar period was the "accidental president"—Harry S Truman. "The moon, the stars, and all the planets" had fallen on him, he remarked when he was called upon to shoulder Roosevelt's awesome burdens of leadership. Trim and owlishly bespectacled, with graying hair and a friendly, toothy grin, Truman was called "the average man's average man." The first president in many years without a college education, he had farmed, served as an artillery officer in France during World War I, and failed as a haberdasher. He then tried his hand at **precinct**-level Missouri politics, through which he rose from a judgeship to the U.S. Senate. Though a **protégé** of a notorious political machine in Kansas City, he had managed to keep his own hands clean.

The problems of the postwar period were staggering, and the suddenly burdened new president at first approached his tasks with humility. But he gradually evolved from a shrinking pipsqueak into a scrappy little cuss, gaining confidence to the point of cockiness. A smallish man thrust suddenly into a giant job, Truman permitted designing old associates of the "Missouri gang" to gather around him and, like Grant, was stubbornly loyal to them when they were caught with cream on their whiskers. On occasion he would send critics hot-tempered and profane "s.o.b." letters. Most troubling, in trying to demonstrate to a skeptical public his decisiveness and power of command, he was inclined to go off half-cocked or stick mulishly to some wrongheaded notion.

But if Truman was sometimes small in the small things, he was often big in the big things. He had down-home authenticity, few pretensions, rock-solid probity, and a lot of that old-fashioned character trait called moxie. Not one to dodge responsibility, he placed a sign on his White House desk that read, "The buck stops here." Among his favorite sayings was, "If you can't stand the heat, get out of the kitchen."

Yalta: Bargain or Betrayal?

Vast and silent, the Soviet Union continued to be the great enigma. The conference in Teheran in 1943, where Roosevelt had first met Stalin man to man, had done something to clear the air, but much had remained unresolved—especially questions about the postwar fates of Germany, Eastern Europe, and Asia.

A final fateful conference of the Big Three had taken place in February 1945 at Yalta. At this former tsarist resort on the relatively warm shores of the Black Sea, Stalin, Churchill, and the fast-failing Roosevelt reached momentous agreements. Stalin agreed that Poland, with revised boundaries, should have a representative government based on free elections—a pledge he soon broke. Bulgaria and Romania were likewise to have free elections—a promise also flouted. The Big Three further announced plans for fashioning a new international peacekeeping organization—the United Nations.

■ **The Communist Menace** First appearing in the *New York Daily News* on January 6, 1946, this map reflected the rising anxiety in post–World War II America that the Soviet Union was an aggressively expansionist power, relentlessly gobbling up territory and imposing its will across both Europe and Asia.

The most controversial decision at Yalta concerned Moscow's entry into the war against Japan. Uncertain of the untested atomic bomb, and expecting frightful American casualties in the projected assault on Japan, Roosevelt was willing to offer inducements to the Soviets to enter the Asian war and pin down Japanese troops in Manchuria and Korea. Horse trader Stalin was in a position at Yalta to exact a high price. He agreed to attack Japan within three months after the collapse of Germany, but only if the Soviets were promised the southern half of Sakhalin Island, Japan's Kurile Islands, and control of key industrial centers in China's Manchuria. The Americans agreed, and Stalin later redeemed his pledge in full.

As it turned out, Moscow's muscle was not necessary to knock out Japan. Critics charged that Roosevelt had sold Jiang Jieshi (Chiang Kai-shek) down the river and contributed to his overthrow by the Chinese communists four years later. Roosevelt's defenders countered that Stalin's mighty red army could have secured much more of China if he had wished, and that the Yalta conference really set limits to his ambitions. Apologists for Roosevelt also noted that Soviet troops had already occupied much of Eastern Europe and a war to throw them out was unthinkable.

The fact is that the Big Three at Yalta were not drafting a comprehensive peace settlement; at most they were sketching general intentions and testing one another's reactions. In the case of Poland, Roosevelt admitted that the Yalta agreement was "so elastic that the Russians can stretch it all the way from Yalta to Washington without ever technically breaking it." More specific understandings among the wartime allies—especially the two emerging **superpowers**, the United States and the Soviet Union—awaited the arrival of peace.

Online Study Center

Primary source
Red Menace, The
college.hmco.com/pic/kennedybrief7e

superpower(s) *One of the two overwhelmingly dominant international powers after World War II—the United States and the Soviet Union.*

The United States and the Soviet Union

History provided little hope that the United States and the Soviet Union would reach cordial understandings about the shape of the postwar world. Mutual suspicions were ancient, abundant, and deep. Communism and capitalism were historically hostile social philosophies. The United States had refused officially to recognize the Bolshevik revolutionary government in Moscow until 1933. Soviet skepticism was also aroused by American delays in opening a second front against Germany, by the abrupt termination of vital lend-lease aid in 1945, and by the refusal of Moscow's plea for a $6 billion reconstruction loan—while approving a similar loan of $3.75 billion to Britain in 1946.

Different visions of the postwar world also separated the two superpowers. Stalin aimed above all to guarantee the security of the Soviet Union by establishing friendly governments along its western border, especially in Poland. By maintaining an extensive Soviet sphere of influence in eastern and central Europe, the USSR could protect itself and consolidate its revolutionary base as the world's leading communist country.

To many Americans, that "sphere of influence" looked like an ill-gained "empire." Doubting that Soviet goals were purely defensive, they remembered the earlier Bolshevik call for world revolution. Stalin's emphasis on "spheres" also clashed with Franklin Roosevelt's Wilsonian dream of an "open world," decolonized, demilitarized, and democratized, with a strong international organization to oversee the global peace.

Even the ways in which the United States and the Soviet Union resembled each other were troublesome. Both countries had been largely isolated from world affairs before World War II. Both nations also had a history of conducting a kind of "missionary" diplomacy—of trying to export to all the world the political doctrines precipitated out of their respective revolutionary origins.

Unaccustomed to their great-power roles, America and the USSR suddenly found themselves staring eyeball-to-eyeball over the prostrate body of battered Europe—a Europe that had been the traditional center of international affairs. The wartime "Grand Alliance" of the United States, the Soviet Union, and Britain had been a child of necessity. When the hated Hitler fell, suspicion and rivalry between communistic, despotic Russia and capitalistic, democratic America were all but

Online Study Center

Interactive map
The Global Cold War
college.hmco.com/pic/kennedybrief7e

inevitable. In a fateful progression of events, marked often by misperceptions as well as by genuine conflicts of interest, the two powers provoked each other into a tense standoff known as the Cold War. Enduring four and a half decades, the Cold War not only shaped Soviet-American relations; it overshadowed the entire postwar international order in every corner of the globe.

Shaping the Postwar World

Despite these obstacles, the United States did manage at war's end to erect some of the structures that would support Roosevelt's vision of an open world. Meeting at Bretton Woods, New Hampshire, in 1944, the Western Allies established the International Monetary Fund (IMF) to encourage world trade and the International Bank for Reconstruction and Development (World Bank) to promote economic growth in war-ravaged and **underdeveloped** areas. In contrast to its behavior after World War I, the United States took the lead in creating these important international bodies.

underdeveloped *Economically and industrially deficient.*

Meeting in San Francisco in April 1945, representatives from fifty nations fashioned the United Nations Charter. The U.N. was a successor to the old League of Nations, but it differed from its predecessor in significant ways. The League had adopted rules denying veto power to any party in a dispute. The U.N., by contrast, more realistically provided that no member of the Security Council, dominated by the Big Five powers (the United States, Britain, the USSR, France, and China), could have action taken against it without its consent. The League, in short, presumed great-power conflict; the U.N. presumed great-power cooperation. The U.N. also featured an Assembly, which could be controlled by smaller countries. In contrast to the U.S. rejection of the League in 1919, the Senate overwhelmingly approved the U.N. Charter on July 28, 1945, by a vote of 89 to 2.

The United Nations had some gratifying initial successes. It helped preserve peace in Iran, Kashmir, and other trouble spots. It played a large role in creating the new Jewish state of Israel. The U.N. Trusteeship Council guided former colonies to independence. Through such arms as UNESCO (United Nations Educational, Scientific, and Cultural Organization), FAO (Food and Agricultural Organization), and WHO (World Health Organization), the U.N. brought benefits to peoples the world over.

But it proved far less successful in controlling the fearsome new technology of the atom. The Soviets rejected an American proposal in 1946 for a U.N. agency to prevent the manufacture of nuclear weapons. The atomic clock ticked ominously on for the next forty-five years, shadowing all relations between the Soviet Union and the United States and threatening the very future of the human race.

Online Study Center

Interactive map
The Rise of the Third World: Newly Independent Nations Since 1943
college.hmco.com/pic/kennedybrief7e

The Problem of Germany

Hitler's ruined Reich posed especially thorny problems for all the wartime Allies. They agreed only that the cancer of Nazism had to be cut out of the German body politic, which involved punishing Nazi leaders for war crimes. The Allies tried twenty-two top culprits at Nuremberg, Germany, during 1945–1946 for crimes against the laws of war and humanity. Justice, Nuremberg-style, was harsh. Twelve of the accused Nazis swung from the gallows, and seven were sentenced to long jail terms.

Beyond punishing the top Nazis, the Allies could agree on little about postwar Germany. Some American Hitler-haters wanted to deindustrialize Germany, while the Soviets sought to extract enormous reparations from the Germans. Both these desires clashed headlong with the reality that an industrial, healthy German economy was indispensable to the recovery of Europe. The Americans

Former prime minister Winston Churchill (1874–1965), in a highly controversial speech at Fulton, Missouri (March 1946), warned of Soviet expansionism:

"From Stettin in the Baltic to Trieste in the Adriatic an iron curtain has descended across the Continent."

soon came to appreciate that fact, but the fearful Soviets resisted all efforts to revitalize Germany.

Along with Austria, Germany had been divided at war's end into four **military occupation** zones, each assigned to one of the Big Four powers (France, Britain, America, and the USSR). Before long, it was apparent that Germany would remain indefinitely divided. West Germany eventually became an independent country, wedded to the West. East Germany and the other Soviet-dominated Eastern European countries became nominally independent "satellite" states, bound to the Soviet Union. Eastern Europe virtually disappeared from Western sight behind the "iron curtain" of secrecy and isolation that Stalin clanged down across Europe from the Baltic to the Adriatic. The division of Europe would endure for more than four decades.

With Germany now split in two, there remained the problem of the rubble heap known as Berlin. Lying deep within the Soviet zone (see the map on p. 584), this beleaguered isle in a red sea had been broken, like Germany as a whole, into sectors occupied by troops of each of the four victorious powers. In 1948 the Soviets abruptly choked off all rail and highway access to Berlin, evidently reasoning that the Allies would be starved out.

Berlin became a hugely symbolic issue as well as a test of wills for both sides. The Americans organized a gigantic airlift in the midst of hair-trigger tension. For nearly a year American pilots ferried thousands of tons of supplies to the grateful Berliners, their former enemies. The Soviets, their bluff dramatically called, finally lifted their blockade in May 1949. In the same year the governments of the two Germanies, East and West, were formally established. The Cold War had icily congealed.

Crystallizing the Cold War

A crafty Stalin also probed the West's resolve at other sensitive points, including oil-rich Iran. In 1946 he broke an agreement to remove his troops from Iran's northernmost province, which the USSR had occupied, with British and American approval, during World War II. Truman sent off a stinging protest, and the Soviet dictator backed down.

Moscow's hard-line policies in Germany, Eastern Europe, and the Middle East wrought a psychological Pearl Harbor. Any remaining goodwill from the period of comradeship-in-arms evaporated in a cloud of dark distrust. "I'm tired of babying the Soviets," Truman remarked privately in 1946, as attitudes on both sides began to harden frostily.

Truman's piecemeal responses to various Soviet challenges took on intellectual coherence in 1947 with the formulation of the "**containment** doctrine." Crafted by a brilliant young diplomat and Soviet specialist, George F. Kennan, this concept held that Russia, whether tsarist or communist, was relentlessly expansionary. But the Kremlin was also cautious, Kennan argued, and the flow of Soviet power into "every nook and cranny available to it" could be stemmed by "firm and vigilant containment."

Truman embraced Kennan's advice when he formally and publicly adopted a "get-tough-with-Russia" policy in 1947. His first dramatic move was triggered by word that heavily burdened Britain could no longer bear the financial and military load of defending Greece against communist pressures. If Greece fell, Turkey would presumably collapse, and the strategic eastern Mediterranean would pass into the Soviet orbit.

In a surprise appearance before Congress on March 12, 1947, the president announced what came to be called the Truman Doctrine. He requested $400 million to bolster Greece and Turkey, which Congress quickly granted, More generally, he declared that "it must be the policy of the United States to support free peoples who are resisting attempted subjugation by armed minorities or outside pressures"—a sweeping and open-ended commitment of vast and worrisome proportions.

Critics then and later charged that the Truman Doctrine committed the United States to backing any tinhorn despot who claimed to be resisting "Communist aggression," needlessly polarized the world into pro-Soviet and pro-American

military occupation *The holding and control of a territory and its citizenry by the conquering forces of another nation.*

containment *In international affairs, the blocking of another nation's expansion through the application of military and political pressure short of war.*

Online Study Center

Primary source
Josef Stalin Eats Greek Crow
college.hmco.com/pic/kennedybrief7e

Online Study Center

Interactive map
Divided Europe
college.hmco.com/pic/kennedybrief7e

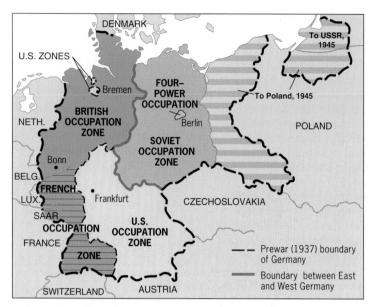

■ **Postwar Partition of Germany** Germany lost much of its territory in the east to Poland and the Soviet Union. The military occupation zones were the bases for the formation of two separate countries in 1949, when the British, French, and American zones became West Germany, and the Soviet zone became East Germany. (The two Germanies were reunited in 1990.) Berlin remained under joint four-power occupation from 1945 to 1990 and became a focus and symbol of Cold War tensions.

camps, and unwisely construed the Soviet threat as primarily military in nature. Apologists for Truman have explained that it was Truman's fear of a revived isolationism that led him to exaggerate the Soviet threat and to pitch his message in the charged language of a holy global war against godless communism—a description of the Cold War that straitjacketed future policymakers who would seek to tone down Soviet-American competition and animosity.

Truman found support for casting the Cold War as a battle between good and evil from theologians like the influential liberal Protestant clergyman Reinhold Niebuhr (1892–1971). In the 1940s and 1950s, Niebuhr raised a Christian voice against fascism, pacifism, and communism. Niebuhr divided the world into the "children of light" and the "children of darkness." He argued that Christian justice, including force if necessary, required a "realist" response to "children of darkness" like Hitler and Stalin.

A threat of a different sort loomed in Western Europe—especially France, Italy, and Germany. Still suffering from the hunger and economic chaos spawned by the war, these key nations were in grave danger of being taken over from the inside by Communist parties that could exploit these hardships. President Truman responded with a bold policy. On June 5, 1947, Secretary of State George C. Marshall invited the Europeans to work out a *joint* plan for their economic recovery. If they did so, then the United States would provide substantial financial assistance. The democratic nations of Europe enthusiastically accepted the life-giving Marshall Plan at a Paris conference in July 1947. Marshall offered the same aid to the Soviet Union and its allies, but nobody was surprised when the Soviets denounced the "Martial Plan" as one more capitalist trick.

Congress at first balked at the Marshall Plan's proposal for spending the mammoth sum of $12.5 billion over four years in sixteen countries. But a Soviet-sponsored communist coup in Czechoslovakia finally awakened the legislators to reality, and they voted the initial appropriations in April 1948. Truman's Marshall Plan was a spectacular success. American dollars pumped reviving blood into the economic veins of the anemic Western European nations. Within a few years, an "economic miracle" drenched Europe in prosperity. The Communist parties in Italy and France lost ground, and these two keystone countries were saved from the westward thrust of communism.

A resolute Truman made another fateful decision in 1948. Access to Middle Eastern oil was crucial to European recovery and, increasingly, to the U.S. economy. Yet the Arab oil countries adamantly opposed the creation of the Jewish state of Israel in the British mandate territory of Palestine. Defying Arab wrath and his own State and Defense Departments, Truman officially recognized the state of Israel on the day of its birth, May 14, 1948. Humanitarian sympathy for the Jewish survivors of the Holocaust ranked high among his reasons, as did his wishes to preempt Soviet influence in the Jewish state and to retain the support of American Jewish voters. Truman's policy of strong support for Israel would vastly complicate U.S. relations with the Arab world in the decades ahead.

America Begins to Rearm

The Cold War, the struggle to contain Soviet communism, was not war, yet it was not peace. The standoff with the Kremlin banished the dreams of tax-fatigued Americans that tanks could be beaten into automobiles.

The Soviet menace spurred the unification of the armed services as well as the creation of a huge new national security apparatus. Congress in 1947 passed the

National Security Act, creating the Department of Defense. The uniformed heads of each service were brought together as the Joint Chiefs of Staff. The National Security Act also established the National Security Council (NSC) to advise the president on security matters and the Central Intelligence Agency (CIA) to coordinate the government's foreign fact-gathering. In the same year, Congress resurrected the military draft, providing for the conscription of selected young men from nineteen to twenty-five years of age. The forbidding presence of the Selective Service System shaped millions of young people's educational, marital, and career plans in the following quarter-century. One shoe at a time, a war-weary America was reluctantly returning to a war footing.

The Soviet threat was also forcing the democracies of Western Europe into an unforeseen degree of unity under the leadership of the United States. On April 4, 1949, twelve nations signed the North Atlantic Treaty, which pledged the signatories to regard an attack on one as an attack on all, and to respond with "armed force" if necessary. Despite last-ditch howls from immovable isolationists, the U.S., Senate approved the treaty on July 21, 1949, by a vote of 82 to 13.

The NATO pact was epochal. The formation of the North Atlantic Treaty Organization (NATO) marked a dramatic departure from the traditional American avoidance of entangling alliances, especially in peacetime, and a significant step in the militarization of the Cold War. NATO became the cornerstone of all Cold War American policy toward Europe. With good reason, pundits summed up NATO's threefold purpose: "to keep the Russians out, the Germans down, and the Americans in."

Reconstruction and Revolution in Asia

Reconstruction in Japan was simpler than in Germany, primarily because it was largely a one-man show. The occupying American army, led by General Douglas MacArthur as a kind of Yankee *mikado*, implemented his program for the democratization of Japan with stunning success. The Japanese cooperated to an astonishing degree. They saw that good behavior and the adoption of democracy would speed the end of occupation—and it did. A MacArthur-dictated constitution, adopted in 1946, paved the way for a phenomenal economic recovery that within a few decades made Japan one of the world's mightiest industrial powers.

If Japan was a success story for American policymakers, the opposite was true in China, where a bitter civil war had raged for years between Nationalists and communists. Washington had halfheartedly supported the Nationalist government of Generalissimo Jiang Jieshi in his struggle with the communists under Mao Zedong (Mao Tse-tung). But ineptitude and corruption within the generalissimo's regime eroded his people's confidence and enabled the communist armies to sweep to victory late in 1949. Jiang was forced to flee with the remnants of his force to the island of Taiwan.

The collapse of Nationalist China was a depressing defeat for America and its allies in the Cold War. At one fell swoop nearly one-fourth of the world's population—some 500 million people—was swept into the communist camp. Seeking scapegoats, the Republicans charged that President Truman and his British-appearing secretary of state, Dean Acheson, had "lost China." Democrats heatedly replied that when a regime has forfeited the support of its people, no amount of outside help will save it. Truman, the argument ran, did not "lose" China because he never had China to lose.

More bad news came in September 1949, when President Truman shocked the nation by announcing that the Soviets had exploded an atomic bomb—approximately three years earlier than many experts had thought possible. To outpace the Soviets in nuclear weaponry, Truman ordered the development of the "H-bomb" (hydrogen bomb)—a city-smashing device many times more lethal than the atomic bomb. The United States exploded its first

In August 1949 Secretary of State Dean Acheson (1893–1971) explained publicly why America had "dumped" Jiang Jieshi:

"The unfortunate but inescapable fact is that the ominous result of the civil war in China was beyond the control of the government of the United States. Nothing that this country did or could have done within the reasonable limits of its capabilities could have changed that result; nothing that was left undone by this country has contributed to it. It was the product of internal Chinese forces, forces which this country tried to influence but could not."

Online Study Center

Primary source
USSR's First Atomic Bomb
college.hmco.com/pic/kennedybrief7e

hydrogen device on a South Pacific atoll in 1952. Not to be outdone, the Soviets exploded their first H-bomb in 1953, and the nuclear arms race entered a perilously competitive cycle. Nuclear "superiority" became a dangerous and elusive dream, as each side tried to outdo the other in the scramble to build more destructive weapons. If the Cold War should ever blaze into a hot war, there might be no world left for the communists to communize or the democracies to democratize—a chilling thought that constrained both camps. Peace through mutual terror brought a shaky stability to the superpower standoff.

★ Ferreting Out Alleged Communists

One of the most active Cold War fronts was at home, where a new anti-red chase was in full cry. Many nervous citizens feared that communists were undermining the government and treacherously misdirecting foreign policy. In 1947 Truman launched a massive "loyalty" program. A Loyalty Review Board investigated more than 3 million federal employees, some three thousand of whom either resigned or were dismissed, none under formal indictment.

Individual states likewise became intensely security-conscious. Loyalty oaths in increasing numbers were demanded of employees, especially teachers. The gnawing question for many earnest Americans was, Could the nation continue to enjoy traditional freedoms in a Cold War climate?

In 1949 eleven communists were convicted of advocating the overthrow of the American government under the Smith Act of 1940 and sent to prison. In 1948 Congressman Richard M. Nixon, a member of the House Un-American Activities Committee (HUAC) and an ambitious red-catcher, led the chase after Alger Hiss, a prominent ex–New Dealer and a distinguished member of the "eastern establishment." Accused of being a communist agent in the 1930s, Hiss dramatically confronted his chief accuser before the committee and denied everything. But Hiss was caught in embarrassing falsehoods, convicted of perjury in 1950, and sentenced to five years in prison.

Was America really riddled with Soviet spies? Soviet agents did infiltrate certain government agencies, and espionage may have helped the Soviets develop an atomic bomb somewhat sooner than they would have otherwise. But for many ordinary Americans, the hunt for communists was not just about fending off the military threat of the Soviet Union. Unsettling dangers lurked closer to home. While men like Nixon and Senator Joseph McCarthy led the search for communists in Washington, conservative politicians at the state and local levels discovered that all manner of real or perceived social changes—including declining religious sentiment, increased sexual freedom, and agitation for civil rights—could be tarred with a red brush. Anticommunist crusaders ransacked school libraries for "subversive" books and drove debtors, drinkers, and homosexuals, all alleged to be security risks, from their jobs.

Some Americans, including President Truman, realized that the red hunt was turning into a witch hunt. In 1950 Truman vetoed the McCarran Internal Security Bill, which authorized the president to arrest and detain suspicious persons during an "internal security emergency." But the congressional guardians of the Republic's liberties enacted the bill over Truman's veto.

The stunning success of Soviet scientists in developing an atomic bomb was attributed by many to the cleverness of communist spies in stealing American secrets. In 1951 two American citizens, Julius and Ethel Rosenberg, were convicted of "leaking" atomic data to Moscow. Their sensational trial and eventual electrocution in 1953 began to sour some sober citizens on the excesses of the red-hunters.

★ Democratic Divisions in 1948

Attacking high prices and "High-Tax Harry" Truman, the Republicans had won control of Congress in the congressional elections of 1946. Their prospects had seldom looked rosier as they gathered in Philadelphia to choose their 1948 presidential candidate. They noisily renominated New York governor Thomas E. Dewey, still as debonair as if he had stepped out of a bandbox.

Also gathering in Philadelphia, Democratic politicos looked without enthusiasm on their hand-me-down president and sang "I'm Just Mild About Harry." But their "dump Truman" movement collapsed when war hero Dwight D. Eisenhower refused to be drafted. The peppery president, unwanted but undaunted, was then chosen in the face of vehement opposition by southern delegates. They were alienated by his strong stand in favor of civil rights for blacks, who now mustered many votes in the big-city ghettoes of the North.

Truman's nomination split the party wide open. Embittered southern Democrats from thirteen states, like their "fire-eating" forebears of 1860, met in their own convention in Birmingham, Alabama, with Confederate flags brashly in evidence. Amid scenes of heated defiance, these "Dixiecrats" nominated Governor J. Strom Thurmond of South Carolina on a States' Rights party ticket.

To add to the confusion within Democratic ranks, former vice president Henry A. Wallace threw his hat into the ring. Having parted company with the administration over its get-tough-with-Russia policy, he was nominated at Philadelphia by the new Progressive party—a bizarre collection of disgruntled former New Dealers, starry-eyed pacifists, well-meaning liberals, and **communist-fronters**.

Wallace, a vigorous if misguided liberal, assailed Uncle Sam's "dollar imperialism" from the stump. This so-called Pied Piper of the **Politburo** took an apparently pro-Soviet line that earned him drenchings with rotten eggs in hostile cities. But to many Americans, Wallace raised the only hopeful voice in the deepening gloom of the Cold War.

With the Democrats deeply split three ways and the Republican congressional victory of 1946 just past, Dewey's victory seemed assured. Succumbing to overconfidence engendered by his massive lead in public-opinion polls, the cold, smug Dewey confined himself to dispensing soothing-syrup trivialities like "Our future lies before us."

The seemingly doomed Truman, with little money and few active supporters, had to rely on his "gut-fighter" instincts and folksy personality. Traveling the country by train to deliver some three hundred "give 'em hell" speeches, he lashed out at the Taft-Hartley "slave labor" law and the "do-nothing" Republican Congress while whipping up support for his program of civil rights, improved labor benefits, and health insurance. "Pour it on 'em, Harry!" cried increasingly large and enthusiastic crowds as the pugnacious president rained a barrage of verbal uppercuts on his opponent.

On election night the *Chicago Tribune* ran off an early edition with the headline "DEWEY DEFEATS TRUMAN." But in the morning it turned out that "President" Dewey had embarrassingly snatched defeat from the jaws of victory. Truman had swept to a stunning triumph, to the complete bewilderment of politicians, pollsters, prophets, and pundits. Even though Thurmond took away 39 electoral votes in the South, Truman won 303 electoral votes, primarily from the South, Midwest, and West. Dewey's 189 electoral votes came principally from the East. The popular vote was 24,179,345 for Truman, 21,991,291 for Dewey, 1,176,125 for Thurmond, and 1,157,326 for Wallace. To make the victory sweeter, the Democrats regained control of Congress as well.

Truman's victory rested on farmers, workers, and blacks, all of whom were Republican-wary. Republican overconfidence and Truman's lone-wolf, never-say-die campaign also won him the support of many Americans who admired his "guts." No one wanted him, someone remarked, except the people.

Smiling and self-assured Truman sounded a clarion note in his inaugural address, when he called for a "bold new program" ("Point Four") to lend U.S. money and technical aid to underdeveloped lands to help them help themselves. Truman wanted to spend millions to keep underprivileged peoples from becoming communists rather than to spend billions to shoot them after they had become

> *In his inaugural address, January 1949, President Harry S Truman (1884–1972) said,*
>
> "Communism is based on the belief that man is so weak and inadequate that he is unable to govern himself, and therefore requires the rule of strong masters. . . . Democracy is based on the conviction that man has the moral and intellectual capacity, as well as the inalienable right, to govern himself with reason and justice."

communist-fronter(s) *One who belongs to an ostensibly independent political, economic, or social organization that is secretly controlled by the Communist party.*

Politburo *The small ruling executive body that controlled the Central Committee of the Soviet Communist party, and hence dictated the political policies of the Soviet party, and other Communist parties (from "Political Bureau").*

Online Study Center

Primary source
Tipping the Scales (1948)
college.hmco.com/pic/kennedybrief7e

 That Ain't the Way I Heard It!
Truman wins.

communists. This farseeing program was officially launched in 1950, and it brought badly needed assistance to impoverished countries, notably in Latin America, Africa, the Middle East, and East Asia.

At home Truman outlined a sweeping "Fair Deal" program in his 1949 message to Congress. It called for improved housing, full employment, a higher minimum wage, better farm price supports, new TVAs, and an extension of Social Security. But most of the Fair Deal fell victim to congressional opposition from Republicans and southern Democrats. The only major successes came in raising the minimum wage, providing for public housing in the Housing Act of 1949, and extending old-age insurance to many more beneficiaries in the Social Security Act of 1950.

The Korean Volcano Erupts (1950)

Online Study Center

Primary source
Korea—The War That Could Have Set Off World War III
college.hmco.com/pic/kennedybrief7e

perimeter *The outer boundary of a defined territory.*

Korea, the Land of the Morning Calm, heralded a new and more ominous phase of the Cold War—a shooting phase—in June 1950. When Japan collapsed in 1945, Soviet troops had accepted the Japanese surrender north of the thirty-eighth parallel on the Korean peninsula, and American troops had done likewise south of that line. Both superpowers professed to want the reunification and independence of Korea, a Japanese colony since 1910. But, as in Germany, each helped to set up rival regimes above and below the parallel. When the Soviets and Americans withdrew in 1949, the entire peninsula was a bristling armed camp.

Secretary of State Acheson seemed to wash his hands of the dispute early in 1950, when he declared that Korea was outside the essential United States defense **perimeter** in the Pacific. But when North Korean army columns rumbled across the thirty-eighth parallel on June 25, 1950, shoving the South Koreans southward into a tiny defensive area around Pusan, President Truman sprang quickly into the breach. The invasion seemed to provide devastating proof of a fundamental premise in the "containment doctrine" that shaped Washington's foreign policy: that even a slight relaxation of America's guard was an invitation to communist aggression somewhere.

The Korean invasion also provided the occasion for a vast expansion of the American military. Truman's National Security Council had recommended in a document of 1950 (known as National Security Council Memorandum Number

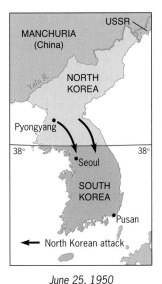
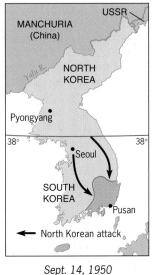
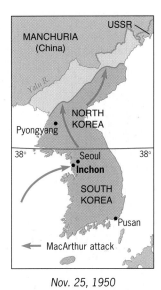
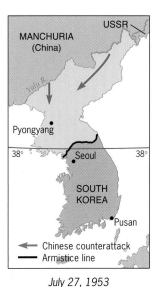

| June 25, 1950 | Sept. 14, 1950 | Nov. 25, 1950 | July 27, 1953 |

■ **The Shifting Front in Korea**

68, or NSC-68) that the United States should quadruple defense spending. Buried at the time, NSC-68 was resurrected by the Korean crisis. Truman now ordered a massive military buildup, well beyond what was necessary for the immediate purposes of the Korean War. Soon the United States had 3.5 million men under arms and was spending $50 billion per year on the defense budget—some 13 percent of the GNP.

NSC-68 was a key document of the Cold War period, not only because it marked a major step in the militarization of American foreign policy, but also because it vividly reflected the sense of almost limitless possibility that pervaded postwar American society. NSC-68 rested on the assumption that the enormous American economy could bear without strain the huge costs of a gigantic rearmament program.

Truman took full advantage of a temporary Soviet absence from the United Nations Security Council to obtain a unanimous condemnation of North Korea as an aggressor. The Council also called upon all U.N. members, including the United States, to "render every assistance" to restore peace. Two days later, without consulting Congress, Truman ordered American armed forces under General Douglas MacArthur to support South Korea. Officially, the United States was simply participating in a United Nations "police action," but in fact the United States made up the overwhelming bulk of the U.N. contingents.

The Military Seesaw in Korea

Rather than fight his way out of the southern Pusan perimeter, MacArthur launched a daring amphibious landing behind the enemy's lines at Inchon. This bold gamble, on September 15, 1950, succeeded brilliantly; within two weeks the North Koreans had scrambled back behind the "sanctuary" of the thirty-eighth parallel. Truman's avowed intention was to restore South Korea to its former borders, but there seemed little point in permitting the North Koreans to regroup north of the parallel and come again. The U.N. General Assembly tacitly authorized a crossing by MacArthur, whom President Truman ordered northward, provided that there was no intervention in force by the Chinese or Soviets.

The Americans thus raised the stakes in Korea, and in so doing they quickened the fears of another potential player in this dangerous game. The Chinese communists had publicly warned that they would not sit idly by and watch hostile troops approach the strategic Yalu River boundary between Korea and China. But MacArthur pooh-poohed all predictions of an effective intervention by the Chinese and reportedly boasted that he would "have the boys home by Christmas."

MacArthur erred badly. In November 1950 hordes of Chinese fell upon his rashly overextended lines and hurled the U.N. forces reeling back down the peninsula. The fighting then sank into a frostbitten stalemate on the icy terrain near the thirty-eighth parallel.

An imperious MacArthur, humiliated by this rout, pressed for drastic retaliation. He favored a blockade of the China coast and bombardment of Chinese bases in Manchuria. But Washington policymakers, with anxious eyes on Moscow, refused to enlarge the already costly conflict. The chairman of the Joint Chiefs of Staff declared that a wider clash in Asia would be "the wrong war, at the wrong place, at the wrong time, and with the wrong enemy." Europe, not Asia, was the administration's first concern; and the USSR, not China, loomed as the more sinister foe.

Two-fisted General MacArthur felt that he was being asked to fight with one hand tied behind his back. He sneered at the concept of a "limited war" and insisted that "there is no substitute for victory." When the general began to take issue publicly with presidential policies, Truman had no choice but to remove the insubordinate MacArthur from command (April 11, 1951). MacArthur, a legend in his own mind, returned to the United States to an uproarious welcome, whereas Truman was condemned as an "imbecile," a "Judas," and an appeaser of Communist Russia and Communist China.

In July 1951 truce discussions began in a rude field tent near the firing line but were almost immediately snagged on the issue of prisoner exchange. Talks dragged on unproductively for nearly two years while men continued to die.

✪ Chapter Summary ✪

In the immediate postwar years there were widespread fears of a return to depression. But fueled by cheap energy, increased worker productivity, and government programs like the GI Bill of Rights, the economy began a spectacular expansion that lasted from 1950 to 1970. This burst of affluence transformed American industry and society. More women joined the work force even as popular culture glorified the roles of mother and homemaker.

Footloose Americans migrated to the Sunbelt of the South and West, and to the growing suburbs, leaving the northeastern cities with poorer populations. Families grew rapidly, as the "baby boom" created a population bulge that would last for decades.

The Yalta agreement near the end of World War II left major issues undecided and created controversy over postwar relations with the Soviet Union. With feisty Truman in the White House, the two new superpowers soon found themselves at odds over Eastern Europe, Germany, and the Middle East.

The Truman Doctrine announced military aid and an ideological crusade against international communism. The Marshall Plan provided economic assistance to starving and communist-threatened Europe, which soon joined the United States in the NATO military alliance.

The Cold War and revelations of Soviet spying aroused deep fears of communist subversion at home, which spread into a general assault on the socially "deviant." Issues of the Cold War and civil rights fractured the Democratic party three ways in 1948, but a gutsy Truman campaign overcame the divisions to win a triumphant underdog victory over Dewey, Thurmond, and Wallace.

The Communist Chinese won a civil war against the Nationalists. North Korea invaded South Korea, and the Americans and Chinese joined in the fighting. The seesaw war settled into a bloody stalemate. MacArthur's insubordination and threats to expand the war to China led Truman to fire him.

VARYING VIEWPOINTS

Who Was to Blame for the Cold War?

Whose fault was the Cold War? (And, for that matter, who should get credit for ending it?) For two decades after World War II, American historians generally agreed that the aggressive Soviets were solely responsible. This "orthodox" or "official" appraisal squared with the traditional view of the United States as a virtuous, innocent land with an idealistic foreign policy. This point of view also justified America's Cold War containment policy, which cast the Soviet Union as an aggressor that must be confined by the ever-vigilant United States. America supposedly had only defensive intentions, with no expansionary ambitions of its own.

In the 1960s a vigorous revisionist interpretation flowered, powerfully influenced by disillusion over U.S. involvement in Vietnam. The revisionists stood the orthodox view on its head. The Soviets, they argued, had only defensive intentions at the end of World War II; it was the Americans who behaved provocatively by brandishing their new atomic weaponry. Some of these critics pointed an accusing finger at President Truman, alleging that he abandoned Roosevelt's conciliatory approach to the Soviets and adopted a bullying attitude, emboldened by the American atomic monopoly. More radical revisionists like Gabriel and Joyce Kolko even claimed to have found the roots of Truman's alleged belligerence in long-standing American policies of economic imperialism—policies that eventually resulted in the tragedy of Vietnam.

In the 1970s a "postrevisionist" interpretation emerged that is widely agreed upon today. Historians such as John Lewis Gaddis and Melvyn Leffler pooh-pooh the economic determinism of the revisionists, while frankly acknowledging that the United States did have vital security interests at stake in the post–World War II era. The postrevisionists analyze the ways in which inherited ideas (like isolationism) and the contentious nature of post–World War II domestic politics, as well as miscalculations by American leaders, led a nation in search of security into seeking not simply a sufficiency but a "preponderance" of power. The American *overreaction* to its security needs, these scholars suggest, exacerbated U.S.-Soviet relations and precipitated the four-decade-long nuclear arms race that formed the centerpiece of the Cold War.

In the case of Vietnam, the postrevisionist historians focus not on economic necessity but on a failure of political intelligence, induced by the stressful conditions of the Cold War, that made the dubious domino theory—the belief that failure in Vietnam would cause other nations to tumble like dominoes into the Soviet camp—seem plausible. Misunderstanding Vietnamese intentions, exaggerating Soviet ambitions, and fearing to appear "soft on communism" in the eyes of their domestic political rivals, American leaders plunged into Vietnam, sadly misguided by their own Cold War obsessions.

Most postrevisionists, however, still lay the lion's share of the blame for the Cold War on the Soviet Union. By the same token, they credit the Soviets with ending the Cold War—a view hotly disputed by Ronald Reagan's champions, who claim it was his anti-Soviet policies in the 1980s that brought the Russians to their knees (see pp. 653–654). The great unknown, of course, is the precise nature of Soviet thinking in the Cold War years. Were Soviet aims predominantly defensive, or did the Kremlin incessantly plot world conquest? Was there an opportunity for reconciliation with the West following Stalin's death in 1953? Should Mikhail Gorbachev or Ronald Reagan be remembered as the leader who ended the Cold War? With the opening of Soviet archives, scholars are eagerly pursuing answers to such questions.

37

The Eisenhower Era

1952–1960

EVERY WARSHIP LAUNCHED, EVERY ROCKET FIRED SIGNIFIED
. . . A THEFT FROM THOSE WHO HUNGER AND ARE NOT FED,
THOSE WHO ARE COLD AND ARE NOT CLOTHED.

DWIGHT D. EISENHOWER, APRIL 16, 1953

In President Dwight D. Eisenhower, the man and the hour met. Americans yearned for a period of calm, in which they could pursue without distraction their new visions of consumerist affluence. The nation sorely needed a respite from twenty years of depression and war. Yet the American people unexpectedly found themselves in the early 1950s dug into the frontlines of the Cold War abroad and dangerously divided at home over the explosive issues of communist subversion and civil rights. They longed for reassuring leadership. "Ike" seemed ready both to reassure and to lead.

Focus Questions

1. What changes occurred in the American consumer economy of the 1950s, and how did those changes fuel the rise of mass "popular culture"?
2. What caused the sudden rise and equally sudden fall of Senator Joseph McCarthy and "McCarthyism"?
3. What were the origins of the modern American civil rights movement, and what successes and challenges did it face in the generally conservative political and social environment of the 1950s?
4. What were the fundamental principles of Dwight Eisenhower's Cold War foreign policy toward the Soviet Union as well as Vietnam, Cuba, and the Middle East?
5. What were the central issues in the tight Kennedy-Nixon presidential campaign of 1960? In what ways did the candidates differ, and in what ways did they reflect the general American consensus of the times?

Changing Economic Patterns

The continuing post–World War II economic boom wrought wondrous changes in American society in the 1950s. Prosperity triggered a fabulous surge in home construction: one of every four homes standing in America in 1960 had been built in the 1950s, and 83 percent of those new homes were in the suburbs.

More than ever, science and technology drove economic growth. The invention of the transistor in 1948 sparked a revolution in electronics, and especially in

Chronology

1952	Eisenhower defeats Stevenson for presidency. Eillison publishes *Invisible Man*.	**1957**	Little Rock school desegregation crisis. Southern Christian Leadership Conference (SCLC) formed. Eisenhower Doctrine. Soviet Union launches *Sputnik* satellite.
1953	CIA-engineered coup installs shah of Iran.	**1958**	U.S. troops sent to Lebanon. NDEA authorizes loans and grants for science and language education.
1954	French defeated in Vietnam. Army-McCarthy hearings. *Brown* v. *Board of Education*. CIA-sponsored coup in Guatemala.	**1958– 1959**	Berlin crisis.
1955	Montgomery bus boycott by blacks begins; emergence of Martin Luther King, Jr. Warsaw Pact signed. AF of L merges with CIO. Geneva summit meeting.	**1959**	Castro leads Cuban revolution. Landrum-Griffin Act. Alaska and Hawaii attain statehood.
1956	Soviets crush Hungarian revolt. Suez crisis. Eisenhower defeats Stevenson for presidency.	**1960**	Sit-in movement for civil rights begins. U-2 incident sabotages Paris summit. OPEC formed. Kennedy defeats Nixon for presidency.

computers. The first electronic computers in the 1940s were massive machines, but transistors and, later, printed circuits on silicon wafers made possible dramatic miniaturization and phenomenal computational speed. Eventually personal computers contained more computing power than room-size earlier models.

Aerospace industries also grew fantastically in the 1950s, thanks both to Eisenhower's aggressive buildup of the Strategic Air Command and to a robustly expanding passenger airline business. Connections between military and civilian aircraft production were evident when Seattle-based Boeing Company brought out the first large passenger jet, the "707," in 1957. Its design owed much to the previous development of SAC's long-range strategic bomber.

The nature of the work force was also changing. A quiet revolution was marked in 1956 when "white-collar" workers for the first time outnumbered "blue-collar" workers, signaling the passage from an industrial to a postindustrial era. Keeping pace with that fundamental transformation, organized labor withered as a percentage of the labor force, after peaking at about 35 percent in 1954.

The surge in white-collar employment opened special opportunities for women. Postwar popular culture developed a "cult of domesticity" celebrating the conventional female roles of wife and mother. Popular television programs like "Ozzie and Harriet" and "Leave It to Beaver" depicted idyllic suburban homes with a working husband, two children, and a wife who did not work outside the home. But they did so without irony; much of middle-class America really did live that way.

But as the 1950s progressed another quiet revolution was gaining momentum that was destined to transform women's roles and even the character of the American family. Of some 40 million new jobs created in the three decades after 1950, more than 30 million were in clerical and service work. Women filled the huge majority of these new positions.

Exploding employment opportunities for women unleashed a groundswell of social and psychological change that mounted to tidal-wave proportions in the decades that followed. In the new urban age, women's dual role as *both* workers and homemakers raised urgent questions about family life and about traditional definitions of gender differences.

★ **Makers of America: The Great African-American Migration**

★ **Examining the Evidence: The Shopping Mall as New Town Square, 1960**

Feminist Betty Friedan gave focus and fuel to women's feelings in 1963 when she published *The Feminine Mystique*, a runaway best-seller and a classic of the modern women's movement. Friedan spoke in rousing accents to millions of able, educated women who were already working for wages but also struggling against the guilt and frustration of trying to live up to the feminine "ideal" as defined by the postwar "cult of domesticity."

Consumer Culture in the Fifties

The 1950s witnessed a huge expansion of the middle class and the blossoming of a consumer culture. Diner's Club introduced the plastic credit card in 1950, and four years later the first McDonald's hamburger stand opened in San Bernardino, California. In 1955 Disneyland opened its doors in Anaheim, California. These innovations—easy credit, high-volume "fast-food" production, and new forms of recreation—were harbingers of an emerging new lifestyle of affluence that was in full flower by the decade's end.

Crucial to the development of that lifestyle was the rapid rise of the new technology of television. Only 6 TV stations were broadcasting in 1946; a decade later 442 stations were operating. TV sets were rich people's novelties in the 1940s, but 7 million sets were sold in 1951. By 1960 virtually every American home had one, in a stunning display of the speed with which new technologies can pervade and transform modern societies. By the mid-1950s advertisers annually spent $10 billion to hawk their wares on television, while critics fumed that the wildly popular new mass medium was degrading the public's aesthetic, moral, political, and educational standards.

Even religion capitalized on the powerful new electronic pulpit. "Televangelists" like the Baptist Billy Graham, the **Pentecostal** and Holiness preacher Oral Roberts, and the Roman Catholic Fulton J. Sheen took to the airwaves to spread the Christian gospel. Television also catalyzed the commercialization of professional sports, as viewing audiences that once numbered in the stadium-capacity thousands could now be counted in the couch-potato millions.

Sports also reflected the shift in population toward the West and South. In 1958 baseball's New York Giants moved to San Francisco and the Brooklyn Dodgers abandoned Flatbush for Los Angeles. Those moves touched off a new westward and southward movement of sports franchises. Shifting population and spreading affluence led eventually to substantial expansion of the major baseball leagues and the principal football and basketball leagues as well.

Popular music was also dramatically transformed in the 1950s. The chief revolutionary was Elvis Presley, a white singer born in 1935 in Tupelo, Mississippi. Fusing black rhythm and blues with white bluegrass and country styles, Elvis created a new musical idiom known forever after as rock and roll. Rock was "crossover" music, carrying its heavy beat and driving rhythms across the cultural divide that separated black and white musical traditions. Listening and dancing to it quickly became a kind of religious rite for the millions of baby boomers coming of age in the 1950s.

Traditionalists were repelled by Presley, and they found much more to upset them in the affluent decade. Movie star Marilyn Monroe, with her ingenuous smile and mandolin-curved hips, helped to popularize—and commercialize—new standards of sensuous sexuality. So did *Playboy* magazine, first published in 1953. As the decade closed, Americans were well on their way to becoming free-spending consumers of mass-produced, standardized products advertised on the electronic medium of television and often sold for their alleged sexual allure.

Many critics lamented the implications of this new consumerist lifestyle. Harvard sociologist David Riesman criticized the postwar generation as a pack of conformists in *The Lonely Crowd* (1950), as did William H. Whyte, Jr., in *The Organization Man*. Harvard economist John Kenneth Galbraith highlighted the troublesome connection between private opulence and public squalor in a series of books beginning with *The Affluent Society* (1958). Americans had televisions in their homes but garbage in their streets. They ate rich food but breathed foul air.

Pentecostal *A family of Protestant Christian churches that emphasize a "second baptism" of the holy spirit, speaking in tongues, faith healing, and intense emotionalism in worship.*

Online Study Center

Primary source
Report on the Baby Boom
college.hmco.com/pic/kennedybrief7e

■ The King Rock star Elvis Presley revolutionized popular music in the 1950s.

But Galbraith's call for social spending to match private purchasing fell on mostly deaf ears in the giddily affluent 1950s.

The Advent of Eisenhower

Democratic prospects in the presidential election of 1952 were blighted by the military deadlock in Korea, Truman's clash with MacArthur, war-bred inflation, and whiffs of scandal from the White House. Dispirited Democrats nominated a reluctant Adlai E. Stevenson, the witty, eloquent, and idealistic governor of Illinois. Republicans enthusiastically chose war hero General Dwight D. Eisenhower. As Ike's running mate the convention selected California senator Richard M. Nixon, who had gained notoriety as a relentless red-hunter.

Eisenhower was already the most popular American of his time, as "I Like Ike" buttons everywhere testified. Striking a grandfatherly, nonpartisan pose, Eisenhower left the rough campaigning to Nixon, who relished bare-knuckle political combat. The vice-presidential candidate lambasted his opponents with charges that they had cultivated corruption, caved in on Korea, and coddled communists. He particularly blasted the cerebral Stevenson as "Adlai the appeaser," with a "Ph.D. from [Secretary of State] Dean Acheson's College of Cowardly Communist Containment."

Nixon himself faltered when reports surfaced of a secretly financed "slush fund" he had tapped while in the Senate. He responded with a mawkish, self-pitying speech on television, during which he referred shamelessly to the family cocker spaniel Checkers. The maudlin "Checkers speech" demonstrated the awesome political potentialities of television. Soon even Eisenhower was reluctantly appearing in the short televised "spots" that amounted, one critic observed, to "selling the President like toothpaste." Television allowed politicians to bypass the traditional political party organizations and speak directly to the voters. But its origins in entertaining and advertising meant that political messages would be increasingly tuned to the standards of show business and commercialism.

The outcome of the presidential election of 1952 was never really in doubt. Given an extra prod by Eisenhower's last-minute pledge to go personally to Korea to end the war, the voters overwhelmingly declared for Ike. He garnered 33,963,234 votes to Stevenson's 27,314,992. He cracked the solid South wide open, ringing up 442 electoral votes to 89 for his opponent. Ike not only ran far ahead of his ticket but pulled enough Republicans into office on his military coattails to ensure GOP control of the new Congress by a paper-thin margin.

True to his campaign pledge, president-elect Eisenhower undertook a flying three-day visit to Korea in December 1952. But it took seven more months of hard negotiations before an armistice was finally signed. The brutal and futile fighting had lasted three years. About fifty-four thousand Americans lay dead, joined by perhaps more than a million Chinese, North Koreans, and South Koreans. Tens of billions of American dollars had been poured down the Asian sinkhole. Yet this terrible toll in blood and treasure bought only a return to the conditions of 1950; Korea remained divided at the thirty-eighth parallel. Americans took what little comfort they could from the fact that communism had been "contained" and that the bloodletting had been "limited" to something less than full-scale global war. The shooting had ended, but the Cold War remained frigidly frozen.

As a military commander, Eisenhower had cultivated a leadership style that self-consciously projected an image of sincerity, fairness, and optimism. Ike thus seemed ideally suited to soothe the anxieties of troubled Americans, much as a distinguished and well-loved grandfather brings stability to his family. He played this role well as he presided over a decade of shaky peace and shining prosperity. Yet critics charged that he unwisely hoarded the "asset" of his immense popularity, rather than spend it for a good cause (especially civil rights), and that he cared much more for social harmony than for social justice.

The Rise and Fall of Joseph McCarthy

One of the first problems Eisenhower faced was the swelling popularity and swaggering power of an obstreperous anticommunist crusader, Wisconsin Republican Senator Joseph R. McCarthy. Elected to the Senate on the basis of a trumped-up war record, McCarthy had crashed into the limelight in February 1950 when he accused Secretary of State Dean Acheson of knowingly employing 205 Communist party members. Pressed to reveal the names, McCarthy later conceded that there were only 57 genuine communists and in the end failed to root out even one. McCarthy's Republican colleagues nevertheless realized the usefulness of this kind of attack on the Democratic administration. Ohio's Senator John Bricker reportedly said, "Joe, you're a dirty s.o.b., but there are times when you've got to have an s.o.b. around, and this is one of them."

McCarthy's rhetoric grew bolder and his accusations spread more wildly after the Republican victory in 1952. McCarthy saw the red hand of Moscow everywhere. Incredibly, he even denounced General George Marshall, former army chief of staff and ex–secretary of state, as "part of a conspiracy so immense and an infamy so black as to dwarf any previous venture in the history of man."

McCarthy flourished in the seething Cold War atmosphere of suspicion and fear. He was neither the first nor the most effective red-hunter, but he was surely the most ruthless, and he did the most damage to American traditions of fair play and free speech. The careers of countless officials, writers, and actors were ruined after "Low-Blow Joe" had "named" them, often unfairly, as communists or communist sympathizers. Politicians trembled in the face of such onslaughts, especially when opinion polls showed that a majority of the American people approved of McCarthy's crusade.

Eisenhower privately loathed McCarthy but publicly tried to stay out of his way. Trying to appease the brash demagogue from Wisconsin, Eisenhower allowed him, in effect, to control personnel policy at the State Department. One baleful result was severe damage to the morale and effectiveness of the professional foreign service. In particular, McCarthyite purges deprived the government of a number of Asian specialists who might have counseled a wiser course in Vietnam in the fateful decade that followed.

McCarthy finally bent the bow too far when he attacked the U.S. Army. The embattled military men fought back in thirty-five days of televised hearings in the spring of 1954. The political power of the new broadcast medium was again demon-

Online Study Center

Primary source
Red Menace, The
college.hmco.com/pic/kennedybrief7e

strated as up to 20 million Americans watched in fascination while a boorish, surly McCarthy cut his own throat by parading his essential meanness and irresponsibility. A few months later the Senate condemned him for "conduct unbecoming a member." Three years later McCarthy died unwept and unsung. But "**McCarthyism**" passed into the English language as a label for the dangerous forces of unfairness and fear that a democratic society can unleash only at its peril.

Desegregating the South

America counted some 15 million black citizens in 1950, two-thirds of whom still made their homes in the South. There they lived bound by the iron folkways of a segregated society. A rigid set of antiquated rules known as "Jim Crow" laws governed all aspects of their existence, from the schoolroom to the restroom. Blacks everywhere in the South not only attended segregated schools but were compelled to use separate public toilets, drinking fountains, restaurants, and waiting rooms. Trains and buses had "whites only" and "colored only" seating. Only about 20 percent of eligible southern blacks were registered to vote, and fewer than 5 percent in some Deep South states such as Mississippi and Alabama.

Where the law proved insufficient to enforce this regime, vigilante violence did the job. Six black war veterans, claiming the rights for which they had fought overseas, were murdered in the summer of 1946. In 1955 a fourteen-year-old black boy, Emmett Till, was lynched in Mississippi for allegedly leering at a white woman. It is small wonder that a black clergyman declared that "everywhere I go in the South the Negro is forced to choose between his hide and his soul."

Somewhat more racial progress was made in the North after the war. In a growing number of northern cities and states African Americans agitated for—and secured—equal access to public accommodations like restaurants, theaters, and beaches. Jack Roosevelt ("Jackie") Robinson cracked the racial barrier in big-league baseball when the Brooklyn Dodgers signed him in 1947. In his landmark 1944 book *An American Dilemma*, Swedish scholar Gunnar Myrdal had exposed the scandalous contradiction between the "American Creed" of "liberty, equality, and humanitarianism" and the nation's shameful treatment of black citizens. The national conscience was slowly awakening from its centuries-long slumber, but blacks still suffered.

> *In a moment of high drama during the Army-McCarthy hearings, attorney Joseph Welch (1890–1960) reproached McCarthy in front of a huge national television audience for threatening to slander a young lawyer on Welch's staff:*
>
> "Until this moment, Senator, I think I never really gauged your cruelty or your recklessness. Little did I dream you could be so cruel as to do an injury to that lad. . . . If it were in my power to forgive you for your reckless cruelty, I would do so. I like to think that I am a gentleman, but your forgiveness will have to come from someone other than me. . . . Have you no decency, sir, at long last? Have you left no sense of decency?"

McCarthyism *The practice of making sweeping, unfounded charges against innocent people with consequent loss of reputation, job, and so on.*

■ **Exposing "Reds"** Senator McCarthy makes a point at the army-McCarthy hearings in 1954 while army counsel Joseph Welch ponders a reply. McCarthy declared in a speech in 1951: "Let me assure you that regardless of how high-pitched becomes the squealing and screaming of those leftwing, bleeding-heart, phony liberals, this battle is going to go on."

A black woman described the day-in, day-out humiliations of life in a Jim Crow South:

"You could not go to a white restaurant; you sat in a special place at the movie house; and Lord knows, you sat in the back of the bus. It didn't make any difference if you were rich or poor, if you were black you were nothing. You might have a hundred dollars in your pocket, but if you went to the store you would wait at the side until all the clerks got through with all the white folks, no matter if they didn't have change for a dollar. Then the clerk would finally look at you and say, 'Oh, did you want something? I didn't see you there.'"

---

taboo *A social prohibition or rule that results from strict tradition or convention.*

■ **The Face of Segregation** These women in the segregated South of the 1950s were compelled to enter the movie theater through the "Colored Entrance." Once inside, they were restricted to a separate seating section, usually in the rear of the theater.

Increasingly, however, African Americans refused to suffer in silence. The war had generated a new militancy and restlessness among many members of the black community (see "Makers of America: The Great African-American Migration," p. 600). The National Association for the Advancement of Colored People (NAACP) had for years pushed doggedly to dismantle the legal underpinnings of segregation and now enjoyed some success. In 1950 NAACP chief legal counsel Thurgood Marshall (himself later a Supreme Court justice), in the case of *Sweatt* v. *Painter*, wrung from the High Court a ruling that separate professional schools for blacks failed to meet the test of equality.

On a chilly day in December 1955, Rosa Parks, a college-educated black seamstress, made history in Montgomery, Alabama. She boarded a bus, took a seat in the "whites only" section, and refused to give it up to a white person, as the law required. Her arrest for violating the city's Jim Crow statutes sparked a yearlong black boycott of the city buses and served notice throughout the South that blacks would no longer submit meekly to the absurdities and indignities of segregation.

The Montgomery bus boycott also catapulted to prominence a young pastor at Montgomery's Dexter Avenue Baptist Church, the Reverend Martin Luther King, Jr. Barely twenty-seven years old, King became a champion of the downtrodden and disfranchised. His oratorical skill, his passionate devotion to biblical and constitutional conceptions of justice, and his devotion to the nonviolent principles of India's Mohandas Gandhi thrust him to the forefront of the black revolution that soon pulsed across the South and the rest of the nation.

Seeds of the Civil Rights Revolution

In 1946 President Harry Truman commissioned a report on blacks entitled "To Secure These Rights." Following the report's recommendations, Truman in 1948 ended segregation in federal civil service and ordered "equality of treatment and opportunity" in the armed forces. Yet Congress stubbornly resisted passing civil rights legislation, and Truman's successor, Dwight Eisenhower, showed no real interest in the racial issue.

It was the Supreme Court that assumed civil rights leadership. Chief Justice Earl Warren, former governor of California, shocked traditionalists with his active judicial intervention in previously **taboo** social issues. Publicly snubbed and privately criticized by President Dwight Eisenhower, Warren courageously led the Court to address urgent issues that Congress and the president preferred to avoid.

The unanimous decision of the Warren Court in *Brown* v. *Board of Education of Topeka, Kansas* in May 1954 was epochal. In a forceful opinion, the learned justices ruled that segregation in the public schools was "inherently unequal" and thus unconstitutional. The uncompromising sweep of the decision startled conservatives like an exploding time bomb, for it reversed the Court's earlier declaration of 1896 in *Plessy* v. *Ferguson* (see p. 345) that "separate but equal" facilities were allowable under the Constitution. That doctrine was now dead. Desegregation, the justices insisted, must go ahead with "all deliberate speed."

The Border States generally made reasonable efforts to comply with this ruling, but in the Deep South diehards organized "massive resistance" against the Court's annulment of the princi-

■ **Martin Luther King, Jr., and His Wife, Coretta, Arrested** King and his wife were arrested for the first time in Montgomery, Alabama, in 1955 while organizing a bus boycott.

ple of "separate but equal." More than a hundred southern congressmen and senators pledged their unyielding resistance to desegregation, and several states diverted funds to hastily created "private" schools. Throughout the South, white citizens' councils, sometimes with fire and hemp, thwarted attempts to make integration a reality. Ten years after the Court's momentous ruling, fewer than 2 percent of the eligible blacks in the Deep South were sitting in classrooms with whites.

President Eisenhower remained reluctant to promote integration. He shied away from employing his vast popularity and the prestige of his office to educate white Americans about the need for racial justice. He complained that the Supreme Court's decision in *Brown* v. *Board of Education* had upset "the customs and convictions of at least two generations of Americans," and he steadfastly refused to issue a public statement endorsing the Court's conclusions. "I do not believe," he explained, "that prejudices, even palpably unjustifiable prejudices, will succumb to compulsion."

But in September 1957 Ike was forced to act. Arkansas Governor Orval Faubus mobilized the National Guard to prevent nine black students from enrolling in Little Rock's Central High School. Confronted with a direct challenge to federal authority, Eisenhower sent troops to escort the children to their classes. In the same year Congress passed the first civil rights bill since Reconstruction, setting up a Civil Rights commission to investigate violations of civil rights. Eisenhower characteristically reassured a southern senator that the legislation represented "the mildest civil rights bill possible."

Blacks meanwhile continued to take the civil rights movement into their own hands. Martin Luther King, Jr., formed the Southern Christian Leadership Conference (SCLC) in 1957. The churches were the largest and best-organized black institutions that had been allowed to flourish in a segregated society, and the SCLC aimed to mobilize their vast power on behalf of black rights.

More spontaneous was the "sit-in" movement launched on February 1, 1960, by four black college freshmen in Greensboro, North Carolina. Without a detailed plan or institutional support, they demanded service at a whites-only Woolworth's lunch counter. The following day, eighty-five students joined in; by the end of the week, a thousand. The sit-in movement rolled swiftly across the South, swelling into a wave of wade-ins, lie-ins, and pray-ins to compel equal treatment in restaurants, transportation, employment, housing, and voter registration. In April 1960 southern black students formed the Student Non-Violent Coordinating Committee (SNCC, pronounced "snick") to give more focus and force to these efforts. Young and impassioned, SNCC members would eventually lose patience with the more stately tactics of the SCLC and the even more deliberate legalisms of the NAACP.

Online Study Center

Primary source
Rosa Parks Sits in Front Again
college.hmco.com/pic/kennedybrief7e

Online Study Center

Primary source
Greensboro Sit-In
college.hmco.com/pic/kennedybrief7e

The Great African American Migration

Among the groups most affected by the great social upheavals of World War II were African Americans. Predominantly a rural, southern people before 1940, African Americans were propelled by the war into the cities of the North and West, and by 1970 a majority lived outside the states of the Old Confederacy. The results of that massive demographic shift were momentous, for African Americans and for all of American society.

So many black southerners took to the roads during World War II that local officials lost track of the numbers. Black workers on the move crowded into boardinghouses, camped out in cars, and clustered in the juke joints of roadside America en route to their new lives.

Southern cotton fields and tobacco plantations had yielded but slender sustenance to African American farmers, most of whom struggled to make ends meet as tenants and sharecroppers. The Great Depression dealt yet another blow, for when New Deal farm programs paid growers to leave their land fallow, many landlords simply pocketed the money and evicted their tenants—white as well as black. As the Depression deepened, dispossessed former sharecroppers toiled as seasonal farmworkers or languished without jobs.

The spanking new munitions plants and bustling shipyards of the South offered little solace to African Americans. In 1940 and 1941 the labor-hungry war machine soaked up unemployed white workers but commonly denied jobs to blacks. Fed up with such injustices, many African Americans headed for shipyards, factories, and foundries on the Pacific Coast or north of the Mason-Dixon line, where their willing hands found work awaiting them.

Angered by continuing racism, black leaders cajoled President Roosevelt into issuing Executive Order 8802 in June 1941 declaring that "there shall be no discrimination in the employment of workers in defense industries or government because of race, creed, color, or national origin." Roosevelt's action was a tenuous, hesitant step, yet it was the first time since Reconstruction that the federal government had committed itself to ensuring justice for African Americans.

By war's end the great wartime exodus had scattered hundreds of thousands of African Americans to new regions and ways of life. In western and northern cities, blacks now competed for housing and jobs, and they also voted—many of them for the first time in their lives.

As early as 1945, NAACP leader Walter White concluded that the war "immeasurably magnified the Negro's awareness of the disparity between the American profession and practice of democracy." The wartime migration thus set the stage for the success of the civil rights movement. With their new political base outside the Old South, and with new support from the Democratic party, African Americans eventually forced an end to the hated segregationist practices that kept them from enjoying their full rights as citizens.

■ Detroit Race Riot, 1943 A black passenger is dragged from a streetcar.

Eisenhower Republicanism at Home

The balding, sixty-two-year-old General Eisenhower had entered the White House in 1953 pledging his administration to a philosophy of "dynamic conservatism." Above all, he strove to balance the federal budget and guard the Republic from what he called "creeping socialism." True to his small-government philosophy, Eisenhower supported the transfer of control over offshore oil fields from the federal government to the states. Ike also tried to curb the TVA by encouraging a private power company to build a generating plant to compete with the massive public utility spawned by the New Deal. Eisenhower's secretary of health, education, and welfare condemned free distribution of Salk antipolio vaccine as "socialized medicine."

Eisenhower responded to the Mexican government's worry that illegal Mexican immigration to the United States would undercut the *bracero* program of legally imported farmworkers inaugurated during World War II (see p. 555). In a massive roundup of illegal aliens, as many as 1 million Mexicans were apprehended and returned to Mexico in 1954.

In yet another of the rude and arbitrary reversals that have long afflicted the government's relations with Native Americans, Eisenhower sought to cancel the tribal preservation policies of the "Indian New Deal," in place since 1934 (see p. 528). He proposed to "terminate" the tribes as legal entities and to return to the assimilationist goals of the Dawes Severalty Act of 1887 (see pp. 401–402). Most Indians resisted termination, and the policy was abandoned in 1961.

Eisenhower obviously could not unscramble all the eggs that had been fried by New Dealers and Fair Dealers for twenty long years. He pragmatically accepted and thereby legitimated many New Dealish programs. In some ways Eisenhower even did the New Deal one better. In a public works project that dwarfed anything the New Deal had ever dreamed of, Ike backed the Interstate Highway Act of 1956, a $27 billion plan to build forty-two thousand miles of sleek, fast, motorways. The construction of these modern, multilane roads created countless construction jobs, speeded the suburbanization of America, and exacerbated problems of air quality and energy consumption.

Ike's Foreign Policies

The 1952 Republican platform condemned the mere "containment" of communism as "negative, futile, and immoral." Incoming secretary of state John Foster Dulles promised not just to stem the red tide but to "roll back" its gains and "liberate captive peoples." At the same time, the new administration promised to balance the budget by cutting military spending.

How were these two contradictory goals to be reached? Dulles answered with a "policy of boldness" in early 1954. Eisenhower would relegate the army and navy to the back seat and build up an air fleet of superbombers (called the Strategic Air Command, or SAC) with city-flattening nuclear bombs. These fearsome weapons would inflict "massive retaliation" on the Soviets or the Chinese if they got out of hand, with a much cheaper price tag than conventional forces—"more bang for the buck." At the same time, Eisenhower sought a thaw in the Cold War through negotiations with the new Soviet leaders who came to power after dictator Joseph Stalin's death in 1953.

In the end, the touted "new look" proved illusory. The burly new Soviet premier, Nikita Khrushchev, rudely rejected Ike's call in 1955 for "open skies" over both the Soviet Union and the United States. In 1956 the Hungarians rose up against their Soviet masters and felt badly betrayed when the United States refused their desperate appeals for aid. The brutally crushed Hungarian uprising revealed the sober truth that America's mighty nuclear sledgehammer was too heavy a weapon to be used in such a relatively minor crisis.

Western Europe, thanks to the Marshall Plan and NATO, seemed reasonably secure by the early 1950s, but Southeast Asia was a different can of worms. In Vietnam and elsewhere, nationalist movements had fought for years to throw off the yoke of French colonialism. The legendary Vietnamese leader, goateed Ho Chi Minh, had

Online Study Center

Primary source
Rosa Maria Urbina and Jose Luis
Describe Life as Illegals
college.hmco.com/pic/kennedybrief7e

■ East Asia, 1955–1956

tried to appeal personally to Woodrow Wilson as early as 1919 to support self-determination for the people of Southeast Asia.

But Cold War events dampened the dreams of anticolonial Asian peoples. Their leaders—including Ho Chi Minh—became increasingly communist while the United States became increasingly anticommunist. By 1954 American taxpayers were financing nearly 80 percent of the costs of a bottomless French colonial war in Vietnam. The United States' share amounted to about $1 billion a year.

Despite this massive aid, French forces continued to crumble under Viet Minh guerrilla pressure. In March 1954 a key French garrison was trapped hopelessly in the fortress of Dienbienphu. The new "policy of boldness" was now put to the test. Secretary Dulles, Vice President Nixon, and the chairman of the Joint Chiefs of Staff favored intervention with American bombers to help bail out the beleaguered French. But Eisenhower, wary about another war in Asia soon after Korea, held back.

Dienbienphu fell to the nationalists, and a multination conference at Geneva roughly halved Vietnam at the seventeenth parallel (see map). The victorious Ho Chi Minh in the north consented to this arrangement on the assurance that Vietnam-wide elections would be held within two years. In the south a pro-Western government under Ngo Dinh Diem was soon entrenched in Saigon. The Vietnamese never held the promised elections, primarily because the communists seemed certain to win, and Vietnam remained a dangerously divided country. American aid continued as communist guerrillas heated up their campaign against Diem. The Americans had evidently backed a losing horse but could see no easy way to call off their bet.

Cold War Crises in Europe and the Middle East

The United States had initially backed the French in Vietnam in part to win French approval of a plan to rearm West Germany. Despite French fears, the Germans were finally welcomed into the NATO fold in 1955. In the same year, the Eastern European countries and the Soviets signed the Warsaw Pact, creating a red military counterweight to the newly bolstered NATO forces in the West.

Despite these hardening military lines, the Cold War seemed to be thawing a bit in 1955. In May the Soviets rather surprisingly agreed to end their occupation of Austria. A summit conference in Geneva, Switzerland, in July produced little progress on the burning issues, but it bred a conciliatory "spirit of Geneva" that caused a modest blush of optimism to pass over the face of the Western world.

Violent events late in 1956 ended the post-Geneva lull. When the liberty-loving Hungarians struck for their freedom, they were ruthlessly overpowered by Soviet tanks while the Western world looked on in horror.

Fears of Soviet penetration in the oil-rich Middle East also heightened Cold War tensions. The government of Iran, supposedly influenced by the Kremlin, began to resist the power of the gigantic Western companies that controlled Iranian petroleum. In response, the American Central Intelligence Agency (CIA) engineered a coup in 1953 that installed the youthful shah of Iran, Mohammad Reza Pahlavi, as a kind of dictator. Though successful in the short run in securing Iranian oil for the West, the American intervention left a bitter legacy of resentment among many Iranians. More than two decades later, they took their revenge on the shah and his American allies (see p. 644).

The Suez crisis proved far messier than the swift strike in Iran. President Nasser of Egypt, an ardent Arab nationalist, had tentatively obtained American and British aid to build an immense dam on the Nile. But when Nasser began to flirt openly with the communist camp, Secretary of State Dulles dramatically withdrew the dam offer. Nasser promptly regained face by nationalizing the Suez Canal, owned chiefly by British and French stockholders.

Nasser's action placed a razor's edge at the jugular vein of Western Europe's oil supply. America's jittery British and French allies, deliberately keeping Washington in the dark, joined with Israel in an attack on Egypt late in October 1956. The French and British had calculated that the oil-rich United States would supply them while their Middle Eastern supplies were disrupted. But a furious President Eisenhower resolved to let them "boil in their own oil" and refused to release emergency supplies. The oilless French and British resentfully withdrew their troops.

The Suez crisis marked the last time in history that the United States could brandish its "oil weapon." As recently as 1940, the United States had produced two-thirds of the world's oil, but by 1948 America had become a net oil importer. Its days as an "oil power" clearly were numbered as the economic and strategic importance of the Middle East oil region grew dramatically.

The U.S. president and Congress proclaimed the Eisenhower Doctrine in 1957, pledging U.S. military and economic aid to Middle Eastern nations threatened by communist aggression. The real threat to U.S. interests in the Middle East, however, was not communism but nationalism. The poor Arab countries increasingly resolved to reap for themselves the lion's share of the enormous oil wealth that Western companies pumped out of the scorching Middle Eastern deserts. In a portentous move, Saudi Arabia, Kuwait, Iraq, and Iran joined with Venezuela in 1960 to form the Organization of Petroleum Exporting Countries (OPEC). In the next two decades, OPEC's stranglehold on the Western economies would tighten.

Round Two for Ike

The election of 1956 was a replay of the 1952 contest, with President Eisenhower pitted once more against Adlai Stevenson. The Democrats were hard-pressed to find issues with which to attack the genial general in a time of prosperity and peace, and the voters made it clear that they still liked Ike. Eisenhower piled up an enormous majority of 35,590,472 popular votes to Stevenson's 26,022,752; in the Electoral College the vote was even more unbalanced at 457 to 73. But the general's coattails this time were not so stiff or broad. He failed to win for his party either house of Congress.

Eisenhower began his second term in fragile health, and critics charged that he had his hands on his golf clubs, fly rod, and shotgun more often than on the levers of power. But in his last years in office Ike rallied himself to do less golfing and more governing.

A key area in which the president bestirred himself was labor legislation. Congressional investigations produced scandalous revelations of gangsterism and brass-knuckle tactics in many American unions, especially the Teamsters Union. The AF of L-CIO had already expelled the Teamsters for choosing leaders like two-fisted James R. Hoffa. Hoffa was later convicted for **jury tampering**, served part of his sentence, and disappeared—evidently the victim of gangsters he had crossed.

Even labor's friends agreed that the house of labor needed a thorough cleaning. Eisenhower persuaded Congress in 1959 to pass the Landrum-Griffin Act. It was designed to bring labor leaders to book for financial shenanigans and to prevent bullying tactics. The law also prohibited "**secondary boycotts**" and certain kinds of picketing.

Soviet scientists astounded the world on October 4, 1957, by lofting into orbit around the globe a beep-beeping "baby moon" (*Sputnik I*), weighing 184 pounds. A month later they sent aloft an even larger satellite (*Sputnik II*), weighing 1,120 pounds and carrying a dog. This amazing scientific breakthrough rattled American self-confidence. It cast doubts on America's vaunted scientific superiority and raised sobering military questions. If the Soviets could fire heavy objects into outer space, they certainly could reach America with intercontinental ballistic missiles (ICBMs).

"Rocket fever" swept the nation. Eisenhower established the National Aeronautics and Space Administration (NASA) and directed billions of dollars to missile development. After humiliating and well-advertised failures—notably the Vanguard missile, which blew up on national television just a few feet above the ground in 1957—in February 1958 the United States managed to put into orbit a

jury tampering *The felony of bribing, threatening, or otherwise interfering with the autonomous deliberations and decisions of a jury.*

secondary boycotts *A boycott of goods, aimed not at the employer or company directly involved in a dispute but at those who do business with that company.*

grapefruit-sized satellite weighing 2.5 pounds. By the end of the decade, several satellites had been launched, and the United States had successfully tested its own ICBMs.

The *Sputnik* success led to a critical comparison of the American educational system, which was already under fire as too easygoing, with that of the Soviet Union. A strong move now developed in the United States to replace "frills" with solid subjects—to substitute square roots for square dancing. Congress rejected demands for federal scholarships, but late in 1958 the National Defense and Education Act (NDEA) authorized $887 million for college student loans and grants for the improvement of teaching the sciences and languages.

The Continuing Cold War

The fantastic race toward nuclear annihilation continued unabated. Humanity-minded scientists urged that nuclear tests be stopped before the atmosphere became so polluted as to produce generations of deformed mutants. The Soviets, after completing an intensive series of exceptionally "dirty" tests, proclaimed a suspension in March 1958 and urged the Western world to follow. Beginning in October 1958, Washington did halt both underground and atmospheric testing. But attempts to regularize such suspensions by proper inspection sank on the reef of mutual mistrust.

Thermonuclear suicide seemed nearer in July 1958, when both Egyptian and communist plottings threatened to engulf Western-oriented Lebanon. After its president had called for aid under the Eisenhower Doctrine, the United States boldly landed several thousand troops and helped restore order.

The burly Khrushchev, seeking new propaganda laurels, was eager to meet with Eisenhower and pave the way for a "summit conference" with Western leaders. Despite grave misgivings as to any tangible results, the president invited him to America in 1959. Khrushchev appeared before the U.N. General Assembly in New York and then went to Camp David, the presidential retreat in Maryland, to meet with Eisenhower. Khrushchev emerged saying that his ultimatum for the evacuation of Berlin would be extended indefinitely. The relieved world gave prayerful but premature thanks for the "spirit of Camp David."

The Camp David spirit quickly evaporated when the follow-up Paris "summit conference," scheduled for May 1960, turned out to be an incredible fiasco. Both Moscow and Washington had publicly taken a firm stand on the burning Berlin issue, and neither could risk a public back down. Then, on the eve of the conference, an American U-2 spy plane was shot down deep in the heart of Russia. After bungling bureaucratic denials in Washington, "honest Ike" took the unprecedented step of assuming personal responsibility. Khrushchev stormed into Paris filling the air with invective, and the conference collapsed before it could get off the ground. The concord of Camp David was replaced with the grapes of wrath.

thermonuclear *Concerning the heat released in nuclear fission; specifically, the use of that heat in hydrogen bombs.*

HERBLOCK
©1960 THE WASHINGTON POST CO.

■ **What's So Funny? 1960** Premier Khrushchev gloats over Ike's spying discomfiture.

Cuba's Castroism Spells Communism

Latin Americans bitterly resented Uncle Sam's lavishing of billions of dollars on Europe while doling out only millions to the poor relations to the south. They also chafed at Washington's habit of intervening in

Latin American affairs—as in a CIA-directed coup that ousted a leftist government in Guatemala in 1954. On the other hand Washington continued to support bloody dictators who claimed to be combating communists.

Most ominous of all was the communist beachhead in Cuba. Ironfisted Cuban dictator Fulgencio Batista, in power since the 1930s, had encouraged huge investments of American capital, and Washington in turn had given him some support. But early in 1959 black-bearded Fidel Castro engineered a revolution that ousted Batista. Castro then denounced the Yankee imperialists and began to expropriate valuable American properties in pursuing a land-distribution program. Washington, finally losing patience, released Cuba from "imperialistic slavery" by cutting off the heavy U.S. imports of Cuban sugar. Castro retaliated with further wholesale **confiscations** of Yankee property and in effect made his leftwing dictatorship an economic and military satellite of Moscow. An exodus of anti-Castro Cubans headed for the United States, especially Florida. Nearly 1 million arrived between 1960 and 2000. Washington broke diplomatic relations with Cuba early in 1961 and imposed a strict trade embargo that has been in place ever since.

Americans talked seriously of invoking the Monroe Doctrine before the Soviets set up a communist base only ninety miles from their shores. Khrushchev angrily proclaimed that the Monroe Doctrine was dead and indicated that he would shower missiles on the United States if it attacked his new friend Castro.

Online Study Center

Primary source
Duck Test
college.hmco.com/pic/kennedybrief7e

confiscation *The seizure of property by a public authority, often as a penalty.*

Kennedy Challenges Nixon for the Presidency

Republicans approached the 1960 presidential campaign with Vice President Richard Nixon as their heir apparent. The "old" Nixon had been a no-holds-barred campaigner, especially in assailing Democrats and left-wingers. The "new" Nixon was represented as a mature, seasoned statesman who had gained stature with his global travels. Nixon handily won the Republican nomination; his running mate was the patrician Henry Cabot Lodge, Jr., of Massachusetts (grandson of Woodrow Wilson's arch-foe).

By contrast, the Democratic race for the presidential nomination started as a free-for-all. John F. Kennedy—a tall, youthful, dark-haired millionaire senator from Massachusetts—won impressive victories in the primaries. He then scored a first-ballot triumph in Los Angeles over his closest rival, Senator Lyndon B. Johnson, the Senate majority leader from Texas. A disappointed South was not completely appeased when Johnson accepted second place on the ticket.

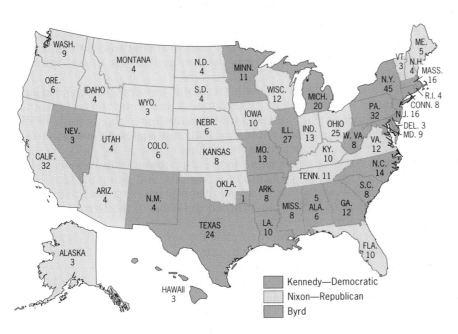

■ **Presidential Election of 1960 (with electoral vote by state)** Kennedy owed his hairbreadth triumph to his victories in twenty-six of the forty largest cities—and to Lyndon Johnson's strenuous campaigning in the South, where Kennedy's Catholic religion may have been a hotter issue than his stand on civil rights.

> *Candidate John F. Kennedy (1917–1963), in a speech to a Houston group of Protestant ministers (September 12, 1960), declared,*
>
> "I believe in an America where the separation of church and state is absolute—where no Catholic prelate would tell the President, should he be a Catholic, how to act, and no Protestant minister would tell his parishioners for whom to vote . . . and where no man is denied public office because his religion differs from the President who might appoint him or the people who might elect him."

Online Study Center

Primary source
Kennedy/Nixon Presidential Debate
college.hmco.com/pic/kennedybrief7e

Bigotry inevitably showed its snarling face. Senator Kennedy was a Roman Catholic, the first to be nominated since Al Smith's ill-starred campaign in 1928. Smear artists revived the ancient charges about the Pope's controlling the White House. Kennedy pointed to his fourteen years of service in Congress, denied that he would be swayed by Rome, and asked if some 40 million Catholic Americans were to be condemned to second-class citizenship from birth.

Kennedy's Catholicism aroused misgivings in the Protestant Bible Belt South, which was ordinarily Democratic. "I fear Catholicism more than I fear communism," declaimed one Baptist minister in North Carolina. But the religious issue largely canceled itself out. If many southern Democrats stayed away from the polls because of Kennedy's Catholicism, northern Democrats in unusually large numbers supported Kennedy because of the bitter attacks on their Catholic faith.

Kennedy charged that the Soviets, with their nuclear bombs and circling *Sputniks*, had gained on America in prestige and power. Nixon retorted that the nation's prestige had not slipped, although Kennedy was causing it to do so by his unpatriotic talk. A series of television debates between the contestants may have tipped the scales. Nobody "won" the debates, but Kennedy held his own with the more experienced Nixon. The debates once again demonstrated the importance of image over substance in a television age. Many viewers found Kennedy's glamour and vitality far more appealing than Nixon's tired and pallid appearance.

Kennedy squeezed through by the rather comfortable margin of 303 electoral votes to 219,* but with a breathtakingly close popular margin of only 118,574 votes out of over 68 million cast. He was the first Roman Catholic and the youngest person to date to be elected president. Like Franklin Roosevelt, Kennedy ran well in the large industrial centers, where he had strong support from workers, Catholics, and African Americans. (He had solicitously telephoned the pregnant Coretta King, whose husband, Martin Luther King, Jr., was then imprisoned in Georgia for participating in a sit-in.) Although losing a few seats, the Democrats swept both houses of Congress by wide margins.

An Old General Fades Away

President Eisenhower continued to enjoy extraordinary popularity to the final curtain. Despite Democratic gibes about "eight years of golfing and goofing," Eisenhower was universally admired and respected for his dignity, decency, sincerity, goodwill, and moderation.

Pessimists had predicted that Eisenhower would be a seriously crippled lame duck during his second term, owing to the barrier against reelection erected by the Twenty-second Amendment, ratified in 1951 (see the Appendix). In truth, he displayed more vigor, more political know-how, and more aggressive leadership during his last two years as president than ever before.

America was fabulously prosperous in the Eisenhower years, despite pockets of poverty and unemployment, recurrent recessions, and perennial farm problems. To the north the vast St. Lawrence waterway project, constructed jointly with Canada and completed in 1959, had turned the cities of the Great Lakes into bustling ocean seaports.

"Old Glory" could now proudly display fifty stars. Alaska and Hawaii both attained statehood in 1959. Alaska, though gigantic, was thinly populated and non-

---

*Six Democratic electors in Alabama, all eight unpledged Democratic electors in Mississippi, and one Republican elector in Oklahoma voted for Virginia Senator Harry F. Byrd.

EXAMINING THE EVIDENCE

The Shopping Mall as New Town Square, 1960 In this photograph Democratic presidential candidate John F. Kennedy is campaigning at the Bergen Mall in Paramus, New Jersey. Just one presidential contest earlier, a regional shopping center would have been a rare campaign stop. The Bergen Mall opened in 1957, a time when similar shopping centers were popping up in suburbanizing metropolitan areas all over the United States. Real estate developers watched Americans flee cities for suburbs, and they followed the money, locating shopping centers strategically at new highway intersections or along the busiest thoroughfares. As suburbanites increasingly found branches of their favorite department and chain stores closer to home during the 1950s and 1960s, they found it less and less necessary to go downtown. Shopping centers for their part went out of their way to sell themselves as modern-style downtowns worthy of being the public core of new suburban communities, even though legally they were privately owned space. They provided the full range of shops and services once found in city centers, including restaurants, post offices, Laundromats, banks, and even chapels. They offered entertainment, from movie theaters and skating rinks to free open-air concerts, carnivals, and exhibitions. They made auditoriums available for community meetings. And they attracted public events like Kennedy on the stump.

1. Look closely at this photograph. What kind of audience greeted candidate Kennedy at the Bergen Mall in 1960? How different might the crowd have looked in a more socially diverse urban center like Manhattan or in nearby Newark, the largest city in New Jersey at the time?

2. What did it mean for sites of consumption, such as privately owned shopping centers, to take on the roles and responsibilities previously associated with urban streets, squares, and parks?

3. How might current struggles of downtown merchants against "big-box" chain stores like Wal-Mart be compared to this history of continuing changes in American public and consumer spaces?

contiguous, but these objections were overcome in a Democratic Congress that expected Alaska to vote Democratic. Hawaii had ample population (largely of Asian descent), advanced democratic institutions, and more acreage than Rhode Island, Delaware, or Connecticut. As the first noncontiguous states to join the Union, Alaska and Hawaii helped turn America's face toward the Pacific and East Asia.

Though a crusading general, Eisenhower as president mounted no moral crusade for civil rights. This was perhaps his greatest failing. Yet he was no bigot, and he had done far more than grin away problems. As a Republican president, he had further woven the reforms of the Democratic New Deal and Fair Deal into the fabric of national life. As a former general, he had exercised wise restraint in his use of military power and had soberly guided foreign policy away from countless threats to peace. He had ended one war and avoided all others. As the decades lengthened, appreciation of him grew.

The Life of the Mind in Postwar America

America's affluence in the heady post–World War II decades was matched by a mother lode of literary gems. In fiction writing some of the prewar realists continued to ply their trade, notably Ernest Hemingway in *The Old Man and the Sea* (1952). A Nobel laureate in 1954, Hemingway was dead by his own duck gun in 1961. John Steinbeck, another prewar writer who persisted in graphic portrayals of American society, such as *East of Eden* (1952) and *Travels with Charley* (1962), received the Nobel Prize for literature in 1962, the seventh American to be so honored.

Curiously, World War II did not inspire the same kind of literary outpouring that World War I had. Searing realism, the trademark style of war writers in the 1920s, characterized the earliest novels that portrayed soldierly life in World War II, such as Norman Mailer's *The Naked and the Dead* (1948) and James Jones's *From Here to Eternity* (1951). But as time passed, realistic writing fell from favor. Authors tended increasingly to write about the war in fantastic and even psychedelic prose. Joseph Heller's *Catch-22* (1961) dealt with the improbable antics and anguish of American airmen in the wartime Mediterranean. A savage satire, it made readers hurt when they laughed. The supercharged imagination of Kurt Vonnegut, Jr., produced works of sometimes impenetrably inventive prose, including the dark comedy war tale *Slaughterhouse Five* (1969).

The dilemmas created by the new mobility and affluence of American life were explored by Pennsylvania-born John Updike in books like *Rabbit, Run* (1960) and *Couples* (1968), and by Massachusetts-bred John Cheever in *The Wapshot Chronicle* (1957) and *The Wapshot Scandal* (1964). These writers represented the rear guard of an older WASP (White Anglo-Saxon Protestant) elite that had long dominated American writing.

Younger poets were also coming to the fore during the postwar period. Pacific northwesterner Theodore Roethke wrote lyrically about the land until his premature death in a Seattle suburb in 1963. Robert Lowell, descended from a long line of patrician New Englanders, sought to apply the wisdom of the Puritan past to the perplexing present in allegorical poems like *For the Union Dead* (1964). Troubled Sylvia Plath crafted the moving verses of *Ariel* (published posthumously in 1966) and a disturbing novel, *The Bell Jar* (1963), but her career was cut short when she took her own life in 1963. Anne Sexton produced brooding autobiographical poems until her death by apparent suicide in 1974. Another brilliant poet of the period, John Berryman, ended it all in 1972 by leaping from a Minneapolis bridge onto the frozen bank of the Mississippi River. Writing poetry seemed to be a dangerous pursuit in modern America. The life of the poet, it was said, began in sadness and ended in madness.

Playwrights were also active. Tennessee Williams wrote a series of searing dramas about psychological misfits struggling to hold themselves together amid the disintegrating forces of modern life. Noteworthy were *A Streetcar Named Desire* (1947) and *Cat on a Hot Tin Roof* (1955). Arthur Miller brought to the stage searching probes of American values, notably *Death of a Salesman* (1949) and *The Crucible* (1953), which treated the Salem witch trials as a dark parable warning against the dangers of McCarthyism. Lorraine Hansberry offered an affecting portrait of African American life in *A Raisin in the Sun* (1959). In the 1960s Edward Albee exposed the rapacious underside of middle-class life in *Who's Afraid of Virginia Woolf?* (1962).

Books by black authors also made the best-seller lists, beginning with Richard Wright's chilling portrait of a black Chicago killer in *Native Son* (1940). Ralph Ellison depicted the black individual's quest for personal identity in *Invisible Man* (1952), a haunting novel narrated by a nameless black person who finds that none of his supposed supporters—white philanthropists, black nationalists, and Communist party members—can see him as a real man. James Baldwin won plaudits as a novelist and essayist, particularly for his sensitive reflections on the racial question in *The Fire Next Time* (1963). Black nationalist LeRoi Jones, who changed his name to Imamu Amiri Baraka, crafted powerful plays like *Dutchman* (1964).

After Nobel Prize recipient William Faulkner died in 1962, his fellow Mississippians Walker Percy and Eudora Welty grasped the torch of southern letters. Tennesseean Robert Penn Warren immortalized Louisiana politico Huey Long in *All the King's Men* (1946). Flannery O'Connor wrote perceptively of her native Georgia, and Virginian William Styron confronted the harsh history of his home state in a controversial fictional representation of an 1831 slave rebellion, *The Confessions of Nat Turner* (1967).

Especially bountiful was the harvest of books by Jewish novelists. Some critics quipped that a knowledge of Yiddish was becoming necessary to understanding much of the dialogue presented in modern American novels. J. D. Salinger painted an unforgettable portrait of a sensitive, upper-class, Anglo-Saxon adolescent in *Catcher in the Rye* (1951), but other Jewish writers found their favorite subject matter in the experience of lower- and middle-class Jewish immigrants. Bernard Malamud rendered a touching portrait of a family of New York Jewish storekeepers in *The Assistant* (1957). Philip Roth penned an uproarious account of a sexually obsessed middle-aged New Yorker in *Portnoy's Complaint* (1969). Chicagoan Saul Bellow contributed masterful sketches of Jewish urban and literary life in *The Adventures of Augie March* (1953) and *Herzog* (1962). Bellow became the eighth American Nobel laureate for literature in 1976.

✪ Chapter Summary ✪

Using the new medium of television to enhance his already great popularity, grandfatherly "Ike" was ideally suited to soothe an America badly shaken by the Cold War and Korea. Eisenhower was slow to go after Joseph McCarthy, but the demagogue's bubble finally burst when he attacked the U.S. Army. Eisenhower also reacted cautiously to the beginnings of the civil rights movement but sent troops to Little Rock to enforce court orders for desegregation. Eisenhower's domestic policies were moderately conservative; they left most of the New Deal in place.

Despite John Dulles's tough talk, Eisenhower's foreign policies were also generally cautious. He avoided military involvement in Vietnam, although aiding Diem, and pressured Britain, France, and Israel to resolve the Suez crisis.

He also refused to intervene in the Hungarian revolt and sought negotiations to thaw the frigid Cold War. Dealing with Nikita Khrushchev proved difficult, as *Sputnik*, the Berlin Crisis, the U-2 incident, and Fidel Castro's Cuban revolution all kept Cold War tensions high. In a tight election, Senator John Kennedy defeated Eisenhower's vice president, Richard Nixon, by calling for the country to "get moving again" by more vigorously countering the Soviets.

American society grew ever more prosperous in the Eisenhower era, as science, technology, and the Cold War fueled burgeoning new industries like electronics and aviation. Women joined the movement into the increasingly white-collar workforce, and chafed at widespread restrictions they faced.

A new consumer culture, centered around television, fostered a new ethic of leisure and enjoyment, including more open expressions of sexuality in popular entertainment. Intellectuals and artists criticized the focus on private affluence rather than the public good. Jewish, African American, and southern writers had a striking new impact on American thought and writing.

The Stormy Sixties

❦

1960–1968

LET THE WORD GO FORTH FROM THIS TIME AND PLACE,
TO FRIEND AND FOE ALIKE, THAT THE TORCH HAS
BEEN PASSED TO A NEW GENERATION OF AMERICANS.

JOHN F. KENNEDY, INAUGURAL, 1961

Chapter Outline

Complacent and comfortable as the 1950s closed, Americans elected in 1960 a young, vigorous president who pledged "to get the country moving again." Neither the nation nor the new president had any inkling, as the new decade opened, of just how action-packed it would be, both at home and abroad. The 1960s would bring a sexual revolution, a civil rights revolution, the emergence of a "youth culture," a devastating war in Vietnam, and the beginnings, at least, of a feminist revolution. By the end of the stormy sixties, many Americans would yearn nostalgically for the comparative calm of the fifties.

Focus Questions

1. Why did John F. Kennedy's "New Frontier" raise such high expectations, and to what extent were those expectations met?
2. How was Lyndon Johnson able to pass the flood of legislation intended to achieve his "Great Society"?
3. How was the idealistic and nonviolent spirit of the civil rights movement overcome in the mid-1960s by white racial "backlash," black power, and urban rioting?
4. How did Lyndon Johnson and his advisers lead the United States deeper into the Vietnam quagmire, and why did that war create such deep divisions in American politics and society?
5. What were the roots of the cultural rebellion of the 1960s, and what were its short-term and long-term consequences?

Kennedy's New Frontier

Hatless and topcoatless in the twenty-two-degree chill, John F. Kennedy delivered a stirring inaugural address on January 20, 1961. Tall, elegantly handsome, speaking crisply and with staccato finger jabs at the air, Kennedy personified the glamour and vitality of the new administration. The youngest president ever elected, he assembled one of the youngest cabinets, including his thirty-five-year-old brother, Robert, as attorney general. "Bobby," the president quipped, would find "some legal experience" useful when he began to practice law.

610

Chronology

1961 Berlin crisis and construction of the Berlin Wall.
Bay of Pigs.
Alliance for Progress.
Kennedy sends "military advisers" to South Vietnam.

1962 Pressure from Kennedy results in a rollback of steel prices.
Laos neutralized.
Cuban missile crisis.

1963 Anti-Diem coup in South Vietnam.
Civil rights march in Washington, D.C.
Kennedy assassinated; Johnson assumes presidency.

1964 Twenty-fourth Amendment (abolishing poll tax in federal elections) ratified.
"Freedom Summer" voter registration in the South.
Tonkin Gulf Resolution.
Johnson defeats Goldwater for presidency.

War on Poverty begins.
Civil Rights Act.

1965 Great Society legislation.
Voting Rights Act.
U.S. troops occupy Dominican Republic.

1965–1968 Race riots in U.S. cities.
Escalation of Vietnam War.

1967 Six-Day War between Israel and Egypt.

1968 Tet offensive in Vietnam.
Martin Luther King, Jr., and Robert Kennedy assassinated.
Nixon defeats Humphrey and Wallace for presidency.

1969 Astronauts land on moon.
Stonewall riot in New York City.

From the outset Kennedy inspired high expectations, especially among the young. His challenge of a "New Frontier" quickened patriotic pulses. He brought a warm heart to the Cold War when he proposed the Peace Corps, an army of idealistic and mostly youthful volunteers to bring American skills to underdeveloped countries. He summoned citizens to service with his clarion call to "ask not what your country can do for you but what you can do for your country." The president's personal grace and wit won him the deep affection of many of his fellow citizens.

Kennedy came into office with fragile Democratic majorities in Congress. Southern Democrats threatened to team up with Republicans and ax New Frontier proposals such as medical assistance for the aged and increased federal aid to education. Kennedy forced an expansion of the conservative-dominated House Rules Committee, but despite this victory his key medical and education bills remained stalled in Congress.

Another vexing problem was the economy. Kennedy had campaigned on the theme of revitalizing the economy after the recessions of the Eisenhower years. His administration helped negotiate a noninflationary wage agreement in the steel industry in early 1962. The assumption was that the companies, for their part, would keep the lid on prices. But almost immediately, steel management announced significant price increases, thereby seemingly demonstrating bad faith. The president erupted in wrath, remarking that his father had once said that "all businessmen were sons of bitches." He called the "big steel" men onto the Oval Office carpet and unleashed his Irish temper. Overawed, the steel operators backed down.

The steel episode provoked fiery attacks by big business on the New Frontier, but Kennedy soon appealed to believers in free enterprise when he announced his support of a general tax-cut bill. He chose to stimulate the economy by slashing taxes and putting more money directly into private hands. When he announced his policy

⭐ **Examining the Evidence: Conflicting Press Accounts of the March on Washington, 1963**

⭐ **Varying Viewpoints: The Sixties: Constructive or Destructive?**

Online Study Center

Primary source
CORE demonstration (unknown)
college.hmco.com/pic/kennedybrief7e

Richard Goodwin (b. 1931), a young Peace Corps staffer, eloquently summed up the buoyantly optimistic mood of the early 1960s:

"For a moment, it seemed as if the entire country, the whole spinning globe, rested, malleable and receptive, in our beneficent hands."

before a big-business group, one observer called it "the most Republican speech since McKinley."

Kennedy also promoted a multibillion-dollar project to land an American on the moon. When skeptics objected that the money could best be spent elsewhere, Kennedy "answered" them in a speech at Rice University in Texas: "But why, some say, the moon? . . . And they may well ask, why climb the highest mountain? Why, thirty-five years ago, fly the Atlantic? Why does Rice play Texas?" Twenty-four billion dollars later, in 1969, two American astronauts triumphantly planted human footprints on the moon's dusty surface.

Rumblings in Europe

A few months after settling into the White House, the new president met Soviet Premier Nikita Khrushchev at Vienna in June 1961. The tough-talking Soviet leader adopted a belligerent attitude, threatening to cut off Western access to Berlin. Though visibly shaken, the president refused to be bullied. The Soviets backed off from their most bellicose threats but suddenly began to construct the Berlin Wall in August 1961. A barbed-wire-and-concrete barrier, the "Wall of Shame" looked to the **free world** like a gigantic enclosure around a concentration camp. The Wall stood for almost three decades as an ugly scar symbolizing the post–World War II division of Europe into two hostile camps.

Kennedy meanwhile turned his attention to Western Europe, now miraculously prospering after the Marshall Plan and the growth of the Common Market, a free-trade area that evolved into the European Union. He finally secured passage of the Trade Expansion Act in 1962, authorizing tariff cuts of up to 50 percent to promote trade with the Common Market countries.

But not all of Kennedy's ambitious designs for Europe were realized. American policymakers were dedicated to an economically and militarily united "Atlantic Community," with the United States the dominant partner. But they found their way blocked by towering, stiff-backed Charles de Gaulle, president of France. De Gaulle vetoed British membership in the Common Market with a haughty "*non*," and sought to preserve French freedom of action by developing his own small atomic force. Despite the perils of **nuclear proliferation** or Soviet domination, de Gaulle demanded an independent Europe, free of Yankee influence.

Foreign Flare-ups and "Flexible Response"

Special problems for U.S. foreign policy emerged from the worldwide decolonization of European overseas possessions after World War II. Sparsely populated Laos, freed of its French colonial overlords in 1954, was teetering dangerously under pressure from an aggressive communist movement by the time Kennedy came into office. A red Laos, many observers feared, would be a river on which the influence of communist China would flood into all of Southeast Asia.

As the Laotian civil war raged, Kennedy's military advisers seriously considered sending in American troops. But the president sought a diplomatic escape hatch in the fourteen-power Geneva conference, which imposed a shaky peace in Laos in 1962.

These "brushfire wars" intensified the pressure for a shift away from Secretary Dulles's dubious doctrine of "massive retaliation." Kennedy felt hamstrung by the knowledge that in a crisis he had the Devil's choice between humiliation and nuclear incineration. With Defense Secretary Robert McNamara, he pushed the strategy of "flexible response"—that is, developing an array of military "options" that could be precisely matched to the gravity of the crisis at hand. To this end, Kennedy increased spending on conventional military forces and bolstered the Special Forces (Green Berets). They were an elite antiguerrilla outfit trained to survive on snake meat and to kill with scientific finesse.

free world *During the Cold War, the noncommunist democracies of the Western world, as opposed to the communist states.*

nuclear proliferation *The spreading of nuclear weapons to nations that have not previously had them.*

Stepping into the Vietnam Quagmire

The doctrine of "flexible response" seemed sane enough, but it contained lethal logic. It potentially lowered the level at which diplomacy would give way to shooting. It also provided a mechanism for a progressive, and possibl y endless, stepping-up of the use of force. Vietnam soon presented a grisly proof of these pitfalls.

The corrupt, right-wing Diem government in Saigon, despite a deluge of American dollars, had ruled shakily since the partition of Vietnam in 1954 (see p. 602). Anti-Diem agitators noisily threatened to topple the pro-American government from power. In a fateful decision late in 1961, Kennedy ordered a sharp increase in the number of "military advisers" (U.S. troops) in South Vietnam.

American forces allegedly entered Vietnam to foster political stability—to help protect Diem from the communists long enough to allow him to enact basic social reforms favored by the Americans. But the Kennedy administration eventually despaired of the reactionary Diem and encouraged a successful coup against him in November 1963. Ironically, the United States thus contributed to a long process of political disintegration that its original policy had meant to prevent. Kennedy still told the South Vietnamese that it was "their war," but he had made dangerously deep political commitments. By the time of his death, he had ordered more than fifteen thousand American men into the far-off Asian slaughter pen. A graceful pullout was becoming increasingly difficult.

■ "Backbone" The United States supports South Vietnam.

Cuban Confrontations

Although the United States regarded Latin America as its backyard, its southern neighbors feared and resented the powerful Colossus of the North. In 1961 Kennedy extended the hand of friendship with the Alliance for Progress (*Alianza para el Progreso*), hailed as a Marshall Plan for Latin America. But results were disappointing; there was little alliance and even less progress. American handouts had little positive impact on Latin America's immense social problems.

President Kennedy also struck below the border with the mailed fist. He had inherited from the Eisenhower administration a CIA-backed scheme to topple Fidel Castro from power by invading Cuba with anticommunist **exiles**. On April 17, 1961, some twelve hundred exiles landed at Cuba's Bay of Pigs. When the ill-starred invasion quickly bogged down, Kennedy stood fast in his decision to keep hands off, and the bullet-riddled band of anti-Castroites surrendered. President Kennedy assumed full responsibility for the failure, remarking that "victory has a hundred fathers, and defeat is an orphan."

The Bay of Pigs blunder, along with continuing American covert efforts to assassinate Castro and overthrow his government, naturally pushed the Cuban leader even further into the Soviet embrace. Wily Chairman Khrushchev lost little time taking full advantage of his Cuban comrade's position just ninety miles off Florida's coast. In October 1962 the aerial photographs of American spy planes revealed that the Soviets were secretly and speedily installing nuclear-tipped missiles in Cuba.

≋ Online Study Center

Interactive map
The U.S. in the Caribbean & Central America
college.hmco.com/pic/kennedybrief7e

▬▬▬

exiles *A person who has been banished or driven from her or his country by the authorities.*

Kennedy and Khrushchev now began a nerve-racking game of "nuclear chicken." The president, on October 22, 1962, ordered a naval "quarantine" of Cuba and demanded immediate removal of the threatening weaponry. He also served notice on Khrushchev that any attack on the United States from Cuba would be regarded as coming from the Soviet Union and would trigger nuclear retaliation against the Russian heartland. For an anxious week, Americans waited while Soviet ships approached the patrol line established by the U.S. Navy off Cuba. The world teetered breathlessly on the brink of global atomization.

In this tense eyeball-to-eyeball confrontation, Khrushchev finally flinched. On October 28 he agreed to a partially face-saving compromise, by which he would pull the missiles out of Cuba. The United States in return indicated that it would not invade the island and would quietly remove some of its own missiles from Turkey.

Fallout from the Cuban missile crisis was considerable. A disgraced Khrushchev was ultimately hounded out of the Kremlin and became an "unperson." Kennedy, apparently sobered by the appalling risks he had just run, pushed harder for a nuclear test-ban treaty with the Soviet Union. After prolonged negotiations in Moscow, a pact prohibiting trial nuclear explosions in the atmosphere was signed in late 1963.

Most significant was Kennedy's speech at American University, Washington, D.C., in June 1963. The president urged Americans to abandon a view of the Soviet Union as a Devil-ridden land filled with fanatics and instead to deal with the world "as it is, not as it might have been had the history of the last eighteen years been different." Kennedy thus tried to lay the foundations for a realistic policy of **peaceful coexistence** with the Soviet Union. Here were the modest origins of the policy that later came to be known as *détente* (French for "relaxation of tension").

The Struggle for Civil Rights

Kennedy had campaigned with a strong appeal to black voters, but he proceeded gingerly to redeem his promises. Although he had pledged to eliminate racial discrimination in housing "with a stroke of the pen," it took him nearly two years to find the right pen. Civil rights groups meanwhile sent thousands of pens to the White House in an "Ink for Jack" protest against the president's slowness.

Political concerns stayed the president's hand on civil rights. Elected by a wafer-thin margin and with shaky control over Congress, Kennedy needed the support of southern legislators to pass his economic and social legislation, especially his medical and educational bills.

But events soon scrambled these careful calculations. After the wave of **sit-ins** that surged across the South in 1960, groups of Freedom Riders fanned out to end segregation in facilities serving interstate bus passengers. A white mob torched a Freedom Ride bus near Anniston, Alabama, in May 1961, and Attorney General Robert Kennedy's personal representative was beaten unconscious in another anti–Freedom Ride riot in Montgomery. When southern officials proved unwilling or unable to stem the violence, Washington dispatched federal marshals to protect the Freedom Riders.

Reluctantly but fatefully, the Kennedy administration had now joined hands with the civil rights movement. For the most part, the relationship between Martin Luther King, Jr., and the Kennedys was a fruitful one. Encouraged by Robert Kennedy, SNCC and other civil rights groups inaugurated a Voter Education Project to register the South's historically disfranchised blacks.

Integrating southern universities threatened to provoke wholesale slaughter. Some desegregated painlessly, but the University of Mississippi ("Ole Miss") became a volcano. A twenty-nine-year-old air force veteran, James Meredith, encountered violent opposition when he

---

peaceful coexistence *The principle or policy that communists and noncommunists—specifically, the United States and the Soviet Union—ought to live together without trying to dominate or destroy each other.*

détente *In international affairs, a period of relaxation of tension and agreement in areas of mutual interest between rival powers—but something short of alliance or friendship.*

sit-in *A demonstration in which people occupy a facility for a sustained period to achieve political or economic goals.*

Primary source
Montgomery March
college.hmco.com/pic/kennedybrief7e

In his civil rights address of June 11, 1963, President John F. Kennedy (1917–1963) said,

"If an American, because his skin is dark, cannot eat lunch in a restaurant open to the public; if he cannot send his children to the best public school available; if he cannot vote for the public officials who represent him; if, in short, he cannot enjoy the full and free life which all of us want, then who among us would be content to have the color of his skin changed and stand in his place?"

■ **Freedom Ride, 1961** Rampaging whites near Anniston, Alabama, burned this bus carrying an interracial group of Freedom Riders on May 14, 1961.

attempted to register in October 1962. In the end President Kennedy was forced to send in four hundred federal marshals and three thousand troops to enroll Meredith in his first class—in colonial American history.

In the spring of 1963, Martin Luther King, Jr., launched a campaign against discrimination in Birmingham, Alabama, the most segregated big city in America. Although they constituted nearly half the city's population, blacks made up fewer than 15 percent of the city's voters. Knowing that cross burnings and bomb attacks on civil rights activists were common, King told his organizers that "some of the people sitting here will not come back alive from this campaign." Events soon confirmed this grim prediction. Watching developments on television screens, a horrified world saw peaceful civil rights marchers repeatedly repelled by police with attack dogs and electric cattle prods. Most fearsome were the high-pressure fire hoses that delivered water with enough force to knock bricks loose from buildings or strip bark from trees at a distance of one hundred feet. Water from the hoses bowled little children down the street like tumbleweed.

Jolted by these vicious confrontations, President Kennedy delivered a memorable televised speech to the nation on June 11, 1963. Pleading for new civil rights legislation, he called the situation a "moral crisis" and declared that the principle at stake "is as old as the Scriptures and as clear as the American Constituion. In August Martin Luther King, Jr., led 200,000 black and white demonstrators in a peaceful "March on Washington" in support of the proposed legislation. Still the violence continued. On the very night of Kennedy's stirring television address a white gunman shot down Medgar Evers, a black Mississippi civil rights worker. In September 1963 an explosion blasted a Baptist church in Birmingham, killing four black girls who had just finished their Sunday school lesson called "The Love That Forgives."

The Killing of Kennedy

Violence haunted America in the mid-1960s, and it stalked onto center stage on November 22, 1963. While riding in an open limousine in downtown Dallas, Texas, President Kennedy was shot in the brain by a concealed rifleman and died within seconds. As a stunned nation grieved, the tragedy grew still more unbelievable. The alleged assassin, a furtive figure named Lee Harvey Oswald, was himself shot to death in front of the television cameras by a self-appointed avenger, Jack Ruby.

Online Study Center

Interactive map
African Americans and the Southern Vote, 1960–1971
college.hmco.com/pic/kennedybrief7e

So bizarre were the events surrounding the two murders that even an elaborate official investigation conducted by Chief Justice Warren could not quiet all doubts and theories about what had really happened. Vice President Johnson, sworn in as president on an airplane in Dallas, managed a dignified and efficient transition and pledged continuity with his slain predecessor's policies.

For several days, the nation was steeped in sorrow. Not until then did many Americans realize how fully their young, vibrant president and his captivating wife had cast a spell over them. Chopped down in his prime after only slightly more than a thousand days in the White House, Kennedy was acclaimed more for the ideals he had enunciated and the spirit he had kindled than for his concrete achievements. He had laid one myth to rest forever—that a Catholic could not be trusted with the presidency of the United States.

In later years revelations about Kennedy's womanizing and allegations about his involvement with organized crime figures tarnished his reputation. But despite those accusations, his vigor, charisma, and idealism made him an inspirational figure for the generation of Americans who came of age in the 1960s—including Bill Clinton, who as a boy had briefly met President Kennedy and would himself be elected president in 1992.

The LBJ Brand on the Presidency

The torch passed to craggy-faced Lyndon Baines Johnson, a Texan who towered six feet three inches. The new president hailed from the populist hill country of Texas, and had supported New Deal measures as a young Congressman. But Johnson had trimmed his sails to the right in order to win statewide elections in Texas, and as Senate Majority Leader he developed into a master wheeler-dealer. He could move political mountains or checkmate opponents as the occasion demanded, using what came to be known as the "Johnson treatment"—a flashing display of backslapping, flesh-pressing, and arm-twisting that overbore friend and foe alike. His ego and vanity were legendary.

As president, Johnson quickly shed the conservative coloration of his Senate years to reveal the latent liberal underneath. Seeking to carry on his predecessor's legacy, Johnson rammed Kennedy's stalled tax-cut and civil rights bills through an initially resistant Congress, and added proposals of his own for a billion-dollar "War on Poverty."

Johnson dubbed his popular domestic program the "Great Society"—a sweeping set of New Dealish economic and welfare measures aimed at transforming the American way of life. Public support for LBJ's antipoverty war was aroused by Michael Harrington's *The Other America* (1962), which revealed that in affluent America 20 percent of the population—and over 40 percent of the black population—suffered in poverty.

Johnson's nomination by the Democrats in 1964 was a foregone conclusion, and he was chosen by acclamation at the party's convention in Atlantic City. The Republicans, convening in San Francisco, nominated box-jawed Senator Barry Goldwater of Arizona, a bronzed and bespectacled champion of rock-ribbed conservatism. The American stage was thus set for a historic clash of political principles.

Goldwater's forces had galloped out of the Southwest to ride roughshod over the moderate Republican "eastern **establishment**." Goldwater attacked the federal income tax, the Social Security system, the Tennessee Valley Authority, civil rights legislation, the nuclear test-ban treaty, and, most loudly, the Great Society. His fiercely dedicated followers proclaimed, "In Your Heart You Know He's Right," which prompted the Democratic response, "In Your Guts You Know He's Nuts." Goldwater warmed right-wing hearts when he announced that "extremism in the defense of liberty is no vice. And . . . moderation in the pursuit of justice is no virtue."

Johnson cultivated the contrasting image of a resolute statesman by seizing upon the Tonkin Gulf episode early in August 1964. Unbeknownst to the American public or Congress, U.S. Navy ships had been cooperating with South Vietnamese gunboats in provocative raids along the coast of North Vietnam. Two of these American destroyers were allegedly fired upon by the North Vietnamese on August 2 and 4, although exactly what happened remains unclear. Later investigations

establishment *The ruling inner circle of a nation and its principal institutions.*

EXAMINING THE EVIDENCE

Conflicting Press Accounts of the March on Washington, 1963 The day after the March on Washington of August 28, 1963 (see p. 615), newspapers all over the country carried reports of this historic assembly of more than 200,000 people to demand civil rights and equal job opportunities for African Americans. Although the basic outlines of the story were the same in most papers, ancillary articles, photographs, and editorials revealed deep-seated biases in coverage. Shown here are continuations from the front-page stories in the *New York Times,* a bastion of northeastern liberalism (below), and the *Atlanta Constitution,* a major southern newspaper (right). While the *Times* called the march "orderly" in its headline, the *Constitution*'s story in its right columns highlighted the potential for violence and the precautions taken by police. The article read: "There was such a force of uniformed officers on hand to cope with any possible trouble that one senator was prompted to comment: 'It almost looks like we had a military coup d'état during the night.'" In addition to stressing the march's potential for disruption, the *Constitution* ran an advertisement right below the March on Washington story for a National Ku Klux Klan Rally two days hence, featuring prominent speakers and a cross burning. This comparison of newspaper coverage of a controversial event serves as a reminder that press reporting must always be scrutinized for biases when it is used as historical evidence.

1. What other differences in coverage separated these two newspapers?

2. What factors contribute to press biases?

3. How are both President Kennedy and the marchers and their leaders portrayed in the two stories? Which portrays the marchers as taking more initiative, and why?

March a Big Boost for Bill, Kennedy Tells 10 Leaders

Dr. King Names Ex-Red Cross Official as Aide

A former official of the American Red Cross has been appointed special assistant to Dr. Martin Luther King Jr. head of the Southern Christian Leadership Conference.

SCLC announced the appointment of Harry G. Boyte 52, of Atlanta, who served 17 years with the Red Cross.

Boyte was born in Charlotte N.C. He joined the Red Cross in 1942 and subsequently became administrative assistant chief of personnel.

(PAID ADVERTISEMENT)

NATIONAL KU KLUX KLAN RALLY

Prominent Speakers
Cross Burning

STONE MOUNTAIN, GA.

AUGUST 31, 1963
7:30 P.M.

Largest Ever Held in the Country
Delegations from 46 States
Press Representatives from 5 Foreign Countries

PUBLIC INVITED
Klansmen and families urged to attend

FREE PARKING

200,000 Join Orderly March in Capital for Civil Rights; Kennedy Sees Negro Gain

LEADERS OF RALLY URGE ACTION 'NOW'

Ask Laws Against Inequity
—Picnic Air Prevails as
Crowds Clap and Sing

President Meets March Chiefs; Urges Bipartisan Aid on Rights

LEADERS MEET WITH KENNEDY: From left Whitney M. Young Jr., of National Urban League; the Rev. Dr. Martin Luther King Jr., Southern Christian Leadership Conference; John Lewis, partly hidden, Student Nonviolent Coordinating Committee; Rabbi Joachim Prinz, American Jewish Congress; the Rev. Dr. Eugene Carson Blake, United Presbyterian Church in U.S.A.; A. Philip Randolph, Negro American Labor Council; the President; Walter P. Reuther, the United Automobile Workers; Vice President Johnson, almost hidden, and Roy Wilkins, N.A.A.C.P. Mr. Kennedy and Mr. Johnson met with leaders of the civil rights march at the White House after the ceremonies at the Lincoln Memorial.

strongly suggested that the North Vietnamese fired in self-defense on August 2 and that the "attack" of August 4 never happened. Johnson later wisecracked, "For all I know, the Navy was shooting at whales out there."

Johnson nevertheless promptly called the attacks "unprovoked" and moved swiftly to make political hay out of this episode. He ordered a "limited" retaliatory air raid against the North Vietnamese bases, loudly proclaiming that he sought "no wider war"—thus implying that the truculent Goldwater did. Johnson also used the incident to spur congressional passage of the all-purpose Tonkin Gulf Resolution. With only two dissenting votes in both houses, the lawmakers virtually abdicated their war-declaring powers and handed the president a blank check to use further force in Southeast Asia.

The towering Texan rode to a spectacular victory in November 1964. The voters were herded into Johnson's column by fondness for the Kennedy legacy, faith in Great Society promises, and fear of Goldwater. A stampede of 43,129,566 Johnson votes trampled the Republican ticket, with its 27,178,188 supporters. The tally in the Electoral College was 486 to 52. Goldwater carried only his native Arizona and five other states—all of them, significantly, in the racially restless South. Johnson's record-breaking 61 percent of the popular vote swept lopsided Democratic majorities into both houses of Congress.

The Great Society Congress

Johnson's huge victory temporarily smashed the conservative congressional coalition of southern Democrats and northern Republicans. A wide-open legislative road stretched before the Great Society programs, as the president skillfully ringmastered his two-to-one Democratic majorities. Congress poured out a flood of legislation, comparable only to the output of the New Dealers in the Hundred Days Congress of 1933, as Johnson fully delivered on long-delayed Democratic promises of social reform.

Besides a greatly expanded War on Poverty, a tireless Johnson also prodded the Congress into creating two new cabinet offices: the Department of Transportation and the Department of Housing and Urban Development (HUD). He named noted economist Robert C. Weaver to be secretary of HUD and the nation's first black cabinet member. Other noteworthy laws established the National Endowment for the Arts and the National Endowment for the Humanities, designed to lift the level of American cultural life.

Even more impressive were the Big Four legislative achievements that crowned LBJ's Great Society: aid to education, medical care for the elderly and indigent, immigration reform, and a new voting rights bill.

Johnson's federal program for education neatly avoiding the thorny question of church and state by channeling educational aid to students, thus allowing funds to flow to hard-pressed parochial institutions. With a keen eye for the dramatic, LBJ signed the education bill in the humble one-room Texas schoolhouse he had attended as a boy.

Medicare for the elderly, accompanied by Medicaid for the poor, became a reality in 1965. Like the New Deal's Social Security program, Medicare and Medicaid created "entitlements." That is, they conferred rights on certain categories of Americans virtually in perpetuity. These programs materially improved the lives of millions of Americans—but also eventually undermined the federal government's financial health.

Immigration reform was the third of Johnson's Big Four feats. The Immigration and Nationality Act of 1965 abolished at last the "national-origins" quota that had been in place since 1921 (see p. 489), doubled to 290,000 the number of immigrants allowed to enter annually, and provided for the admission of close relatives of U.S. citizens without limits. The "family unification" provision swelled immigration, and to the surprise of the act's sponsors, the sources of immigration shifted heavily from Europe to Latin America and Asia.

Great Society programs came in for rancorous political attack in later years. Conservatives charged the billions spent for "social engineering" had simply been flushed down the waste pipe. Yet the poverty rate declined measurably in the ensuing decade. Medicare dramatically reduced poverty among America's elderly, and antipoverty programs like Project Head Start sharply improved the educational performance of underprivileged youth. Lyndon Johnson was not fully victorious in the war against poverty, but he did win several noteworthy battles.

Battling for Black Rights

With the last of his Big Four reforms, the Voting Rights Act of 1965, Johnson made heartening headway against one of the most persistent American evils, racial discrimination. The Civil Rights Act of 1964 had prohibited racial discrimination in public accommodations and employment and strengthened school desegregation. But the problem of voting rights remained. In Mississippi and throughout the South, only about 5 percent of eligible blacks were registered to vote. Ballot-denying devices like the poll tax, **literacy tests**, and bare-faced intimidation still barred black people from the political process.

Beginning in 1964, opening up the polling booths became the chief goal of the black movement in the South. The Twenty-fourth Amendment, ratified in January 1964, abolished the poll tax in federal elections. (See the Appendix.) Singing "We Shall Overcome," blacks joined hands with white civil rights workers—many of them student volunteers from the North—in a massive voter-registration drive in Mississippi during the "Freedom Summer" of 1964.

But events soon blighted bright hopes. In late June 1964, one black and two white civil rights workers disappeared in Mississippi. Their badly beaten bodies were later found buried beneath an earthen dam. In August an integrated "Mississippi Freedom Democratic Party" delegation was denied its seat at the national Democratic convention.

Early in 1965 Martin Luther King, Jr., resumed the voter-registration campaign in Selma, Alabama. State troopers with tear gas and whips assaulted King's peaceful demonstrators. A Boston Unitarian minister was killed, and a few days later a white Detroit woman was shotgunned to death by Klansmen on the highway near Selma.

As the nation recoiled in horror before these violent scenes, President Johnson, speaking in soft southern accents, delivered a compelling address on television. What happened in Selma, he insisted, concerned all Americans, "who must overcome the crippling legacy of bigotry and injustice." Then, in a stirring adaptation of the anthem of the civil rights movement, the president concluded: "And we shall overcome." Following words with deeds, Johnson speedily shepherded through Congress the landmark Voting Rights Act of 1965, signed into law on August 6. It outlawed literacy tests and sent federal voter registrars into several southern states.

The passage of the Voting Rights Act, exactly one hundred years after the conclusion of the Civil War, climaxed a century of awful abuse and robust resurgence for African Americans in the South. The act did not end discrimination and oppression overnight, but it placed an awesome lever for change in blacks' hands. Black southerners now had power and began to wield it without fear of reprisals. In the following decade, for the first time since emancipation, African Americans began to migrate *into* the South.

Black Power

The Voting Rights Act of 1965 marked the end of an era in the history of the civil rights movement—the era of nonviolent demonstrations, focused on the South, led by peaceful moderates like Martin Luther King, Jr., and aimed at integrating blacks into American society. As if to symbolize the turn of events, just five days after President Johnson signed the landmark voting law, a bloody riot erupted in Watts, a black **ghetto** in Los Angeles. The week-long violence left thirty-one blacks and three whites dead, more than a thousand people injured, and hundreds of buildings charred and gutted. The Watts explosion heralded a new phase of the black struggle—increasingly marked by militant confrontation, focusing on northern and western cities, led by radical and sometimes violent spokespersons, and often aiming not at interracial cooperation but at black separatism.

literacy test *A literacy examination that a person must pass before being allowed to vote.*

ghetto *The district of a city where members of a religious or racial minority are forced to live, either by legal restriction or by informal social pressure. (Originally, ghettoes were enclosed Jewish districts in Europe.)*

Online Study Center

Primary source
Selma, Alabama
college.hmco.com/pic/kennedybrief7e

Dr. Martin Luther King, Jr. (1929–1968) and Malcolm X (1925–1965) not only differed in the goals they held out to their fellow African Americans—King urging racial integration and Malcolm X black separatism—but also in the means they advocated to achieve them. In his famous "I Have a Dream" speech during the interracial March on Washington on August 28, 1963, King proclaimed to a quarter of a million people assembled at the Lincoln Memorial,

"In the process of gaining our rightful place we must not be guilty of wrongful deeds. Let us not seek to satisfy our thirst for freedom by drinking from the cup of bitterness and hatred. . . . We must not allow our creative protest to degenerate into physical violence. Again and again we must rise to the majestic heights of meeting physical force with soul force."

militant *In politics, someone who pursues political goals in a belligerent way, often using paramilitary means.*

black separatism *The doctrine that blacks in the United States ought to separate themselves from whites, either in separate institutions or in a separate political territory.*

The pious Christian moderation of Martin Luther King, Jr., came under heavy fire from this second generation of younger black leaders. Deepening division among black leaders was highlighted by the career of Malcolm X. Born Malcolm Little, he was at first inspired by the **militant** black nationalist Nation of Islam founded by Elijah Muhammad. A brilliant and charismatic preacher, Malcolm X trumpeted **black separatism** and inveighed against the "blue-eyed white devils." Eventually, Malcolm distanced himself from Elijah Muhammad's separatist preachings and moved toward mainstream Islam. In early 1965 he was cut down by Nation of Islam gunmen while speaking to a large crowd in New York City.

The Black Panther party meanwhile openly brandished weapons in the streets of Oakland, California. Then in 1966 Trinidad-born Stokely Carmichael, a leader of the Student Non-Violent Coordinating Committee (SNCC), began to preach the doctrine of "Black Power," which, he said, "will smash everything Western civilization has created." Some advocates of Black Power insisted that they simply intended the slogan to describe a broad-front effort to exercise the political and economic rights gained by the civil rights movement. But other African Americans, recollecting previous black nationalist movements like that of Marcus Garvey earlier in the century (see p. 500), breathed a vibrant separatist meaning into the concept of Black Power. They emphasized African American distinctiveness, shed their "white" names for new African identities, and demanded black studies programs in colleges and universities.

Ironically, just as the civil rights movement had achieved its greatest legal and political triumphs, city-shaking riots erupted in the black ghettoes of several American cities. A bloody outburst in Newark, New Jersey, in the summer of 1967, took twenty-five lives. Federal troops restored order in Detroit, Michigan, after forty-three people died in the streets. As in Los Angeles, black rioters torched their own neighborhoods, attacking police officers, and even firefighters, who had to battle both flames and mobs chanting, "Burn, baby, burn." These outbursts angered many white Americans, who threatened to retaliate with their own "backlash" against ghetto arsonists and killers. Inner-city anarchy baffled many northerners, who had considered racial problems a purely "southern" question. But black concerns had moved north—as had nearly half the nation's black people. In the North the Black Power movement now focused less on civil rights and more on economic demands. Black unemployment, for example, was nearly double that for whites. These oppressive problems seemed even less likely to be solved peaceably than the struggle for voting rights in the South.

Despair deepened when the magnetic and moderate voice of Martin Luther King, Jr., was forever silenced by a sniper's bullet in Memphis, Tennessee, on April 4, 1968. A martyr for justice, he had bled and died against the peculiarly American thorn of race. The killing of King cruelly robbed the American people of one of the most inspirational leaders in their history—at a time when they could least afford to lose him. This outrage triggered a nationwide orgy of ghetto-gutting and violence that cost over forty lives.

Rioters noisily made news, but thousands of other blacks quietly made history. Their voter registration had shot upward, and by the late 1960s several hundred blacks held elected office in the Old South. Cleveland, Ohio, and Gary, Indiana, elected black mayors. By 1972 nearly half of southern black children sat in integrated classrooms. Actually, more schools in the South were integrated than in the North. About a third of black families had risen economically into the ranks of the middle class—though an equal proportion remained below the "poverty line." King left a shining legacy of racial progress, but he was cut down when the job was far from completed.

Combating Communism in Two Hemispheres

Violence at home eclipsed Johnson's legislative triumphs, while foreign flare-ups threatened his political life. Discontented Dominicans rose in revolt against their military government in April 1965. Johnson speedily announced that the Dominican Republic was the target of a Castro-like coup by "Communist conspirators," and he dispatched some twenty-five thousand American troops to restore order. But the evidence of a communist takeover was fragmentary at best. Johnson was widely condemned, at home and in Latin America, for his temporary reversion to "gunboat diplomacy."

About the same time, Johnson was sinking deeper into the monsoon mud of Vietnam. Viet Cong guerrillas attacked an American air base at Pleiku, South Vietnam, in February 1965. The president immediately ordered retaliatory bombing raids against military installations in North Vietnam and for the first time ordered U.S. troops to land. By the middle of March 1965, the Americans had "Operation Rolling Thunder" in full swing—regular full-scale bombing attacks against North Vietnam. Before 1965 ended, some 184,000 American troops were slogging through the jungles and rice paddies of South Vietnam searching for guerrillas.

Johnson had now taken the first fateful steps down a slippery path. He and his advisers believed that a fine-tuned, step-by-step escalation in American force would drive the enemy to defeat with a minimum loss of life. But the enemy matched every increase in American firepower with more men and more wiliness in the art of guerrilla warfare.

The South Vietnamese themselves were meanwhile becoming spectators in their own war, as the fighting became increasingly Americanized. Corrupt and collapsible governments succeeded each other in Saigon with bewildering rapidity. Yet American officials continued to talk of defending a faithful democratic ally. Washington spokespeople also defended the action as a test of Uncle Sam's "commitment" and of the reliability of his numerous treaty pledges to resist communist encroachment. Persuaded by such panicky thinking, Johnson steadily raised the military stakes in Vietnam. By 1968 he had poured more than half a million troops into Southeast Asia, and the annual bill for the war was exceeding $30 billion. Yet the end was nowhere in sight.

Vietnam Vexations

America could not defeat the enemy in Vietnam but seemed to be defeating itself. World opinion grew increasingly hostile; the blasting of an underdeveloped country by a mighty superpower struck many critics as obscene.

Overcommitment in Southeast Asia also tied America's hands elsewhere. Bealeaguered Israel stunned the Soviet-backed Egyptians in a devastating Six-Day War in June 1967, occupying new territories in the Sinai Peninsula, the Golan Heights, the Gaza Strip, and the West Bank of the Jordan River. Although the Israelis eventually withdrew from the Sinai, they began moving Jewish settlers into the heavily Arab West Bank. The Six Day War markedly intensified the problems of the already volatile Middle East, compressing and focusing the Arab-Israeli conflict into an intractable standoff between Israelis and Palestinians, now led by Yasir Arafat (1929–2004). The Middle East became an ever more dangerously packed powder keg that the war-plagued United States proved powerless to defuse.

Domestic discontent festered as the Vietnamese entanglement dragged on. Antiwar demonstrations had begun on a small scale with campus "teach-ins" in 1965, and gradually these protests mounted to tidal-wave proportions. As the long arm of the military draft dragged more and more young men off to the Southeast Asian slaughterpen, resistance stiffened. Thousands of draft registrants fled to Canada; others publicly burned their draft cards. Hundreds of thousands of chanting marchers filled the streets of New York, San Francisco, and other cities. Many Americans felt pangs of conscience at the ghastly spectacle of their countrymen burning peasant huts and blistering civilians with ghastly napalm.

Online Study Center

Primary source
President Lyndon Johnson's Defense of the American . . .
college.hmco.com/pic/kennedybrief7e

Online Study Center

Interactive map
The Vietnam War, 1954–1975
college.hmco.com/pic/kennedybrief7e

Online Study Center

Primary source
Child from Vietnam War on TV Screen
college.hmco.com/pic/kennedybrief7e

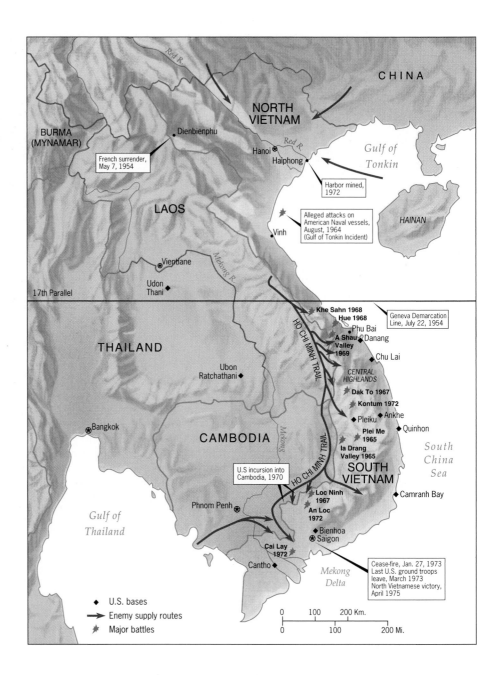

■ Vietnam and Southeast Asia, 1954–1975

doves *During the Vietnam War, someone who opposed the war and favored de-escalation or withdrawal by the United States.*

Opposition in Congress to the Vietnam involvement centered in the influential Senate Committee on Foreign Relations, headed by Senator J. William Fulbright of Arkansas. A constant thorn in the side of the president, he staged a series of widely viewed televised hearings in 1966 and 1967, during which prominent personages aired their views, largely antiwar. Gradually the public came to feel that it had been lied to about both the causes and the "winnability" of the war. A yawning "credibility gap" opened between the government and the people. New flocks of antiwar "**doves**" were hatching daily.

By early 1968 the brutal and futile struggle had become the longest and most unpopular foreign war in the nation's history. The government had failed utterly to explain to the people what was supposed to be at stake in Vietnam. Casualties, killed and wounded, already exceeded 100,000. More bombs had been dropped on Vietnam than on all enemy territory in World War II.

The war was ripping apart the fabric of American society and even threatening to shred the Constitution. In 1967 President Johnson ordered the CIA, in clear violation of its charter as a *foreign* intelligence agency, to spy on domestic antiwar activities. He also encouraged the FBI to turn its counterintelligence program against the peace movement, subverting leading "doves" with false accusations that they were communist sympathizers. These clandestine tactics made the FBI look like a totalitarian state police rather than a guardian of American democracy.

As the war dragged on, evidence mounted that America had been entrapped in an Asian civil war, fighting against highly motivated rebels who were striving to overthrow an oppressive regime. Yet Johnson clung to his basic strategy of ratcheting up the pressure bit by bit. He stubbornly assured doubting Americans that he could see "the light at the end of the tunnel." But to growing numbers of Americans, it seemed that Johnson was bent on "saving" Vietnam by destroying it.

★ Vietnam Topples Johnson

Hawkish illusions that the struggle was about to be won were shattered by a blistering communist offensive launched in late January 1968, during Tet, the Vietnamese New Year. At a time when the Viet Cong were supposedly licking their wounds, they suddenly and simultaneously mounted savage attacks on twenty-seven key South Vietnamese cities, including the capital, Saigon. Although eventually beaten off with heavy losses, they demonstrated anew that victory could not be gained by Johnson's strategy of gradual escalation. With an increasingly insistent voice, American public opinion demanded a speedy end to the war. But American military leaders responded to the Tet attacks with a request for 200,000 more troops. The size of the request staggered many policymakers.

Meanwhile, Senator Eugene J. McCarthy of Minnesota was sharply challenging the president from within his own party for the 1968 Democratic presidential nomination. McCarthy, a sometime poet and devout Catholic, gathered a small army of antiwar college students as campaign workers. Going "clean for Gene," with shaven faces and shortened locks, they helped him gain an impressive 42 percent of the Democratic vote in the New Hampshire presidential primary on March 12, 1968. Four days later, Senator Robert F. Kennedy of New York, the murdered president's younger brother and by now himself a "dove" on Vietnam, threw his hat into the ring. The charismatic Kennedy, heir to his fallen brother's mantle of leadership, stirred a passionate response among workers, African Americans, Hispanics, and young people.

These startling events abroad and at home were not lost on LBJ. In a bombshell address on March 31, 1968, he announced that he would freeze American troop levels and scale down the bombing. Johnson startled his vast audience by firmly declaring that he would not be a candidate for the presidency in 1968.

Johnson's "abdication" had the effect of preserving the military status quo. The United States could maintain the maximum *acceptable* level of military activity in Vietnam with one hand, while trying to negotiate a settlement with the other. North Vietnam shortly agreed to negotiations in Paris, but progress was glacially slow, as prolonged bickering developed over the very shape of the conference table.

★ The Presidential Sweepstakes of 1968

The summer of 1968 was one of the hottest political seasons in the nation's history. Johnson's heir apparent for the Democratic nomination was his loyal vice president, Hubert Humphrey. Senators McCarthy and Kennedy meanwhile dueled in several state primaries, with Kennedy's bandwagon gathering ever-increasing speed. But on June 5, 1968, on the night of an exciting victory in the California primary, Kennedy was shot to death by a young Arab immigrant.

■ **The Agony of War, 1965** A U.S. marine carries a South Vietnamese baby to safety. The child was wounded by American jets during the opening stages of a military operation at Cape Batangan, Vietnam.

Angry antiwar forces, deprived by an assassin's bullet of their leading candidate, streamed menacingly into Chicago for the Democratic convention in August 1968. Mayor Richard Daley responded by arranging for barbed-wire barricades around the convention hall, as well as thousands of police and National Guard reinforcements. Some militant demonstrators baited the officers in blue by calling them "pigs," shouting obscenities, and hurling bags of excrement at police lines. As people the world over watched on television, the exasperated "peace officers" broke into a "police riot," clubbing and manhandling innocent and guilty alike. Acrid tear gas fumes hung over the city even as Humphrey steamrolled to a first-ballot nomination. The Humphrey forces blocked the dovish McCarthyites' attempt to secure an antiwar platform plank and rammed through their own declaration that armed force would be relentlessly applied until the enemy showed more willingness to negotiate.

Scenting victory over the badly divided Democrats, the Republicans convened in plush Miami Beach, Florida, where former vice president Richard Nixon rose from his political grave to win the nomination. As a "**hawk**" on Vietnam and a right-leaning middle-of-the-roader on domestic policy, Nixon pleased the Goldwater conservatives and was acceptable to party moderates. He appealed to white southern voters and to the "law and order" element when he tapped as his running mate Maryland governor Spiro T. Agnew, noted for his tough stands against **dissidents** and black militants. The Republican platform called for victory in Vietnam and a strong anticrime policy.

Adding color and confusion to the campaign was the third-party candidacy of the segregationist former Alabama governor George C. Wallace. Wallace jabbed repeatedly at "pointy-headed bureaucrats" and taunted hecklers as "bums" who needed a bath. He also called for prodding blacks back into their place. He and his running mate, former air force general Curtis LeMay, also proposed smashing the North Vietnamese to smithereens by "bombing them back to the Stone Age."

Between the positions of the Republicans and the Democrats on Vietnam, there was little choice. Both candidates were committed to keeping on the war until the enemy would settle for an "honorable peace," which seemed to mean an "American victory." The millions of "doves" had no place to roost, and many refused to vote at all. Humphrey, scorched by the LBJ brand, went down to defeat as a loyal prisoner of his chief's policies.

Nixon, who had lost a cliffhanger to Kennedy in 1960, won one in 1968. He garnered 301 electoral votes with 43.4 percent of the popular tally (31,785,480), compared with 191 electoral votes and 42.7 percent of the popular votes (31,275,166) for Humphrey. Wallace won an impressive 9,906,473 popular votes and 46 electoral votes, all from five states of the Deep South, four of which the Republican Goldwater had carried in 1964. Nixon was a minority president who owed his election to divisions over the war and protests against crime and rioting. Wallace's large third-party vote resoundingly demonstrated the continuing power of "populist" politics, which appealed to voters' fears and resentments rather than to the better angels of their nature. His candidacy foreshadowed a coarsening of American political life that would take deep root in the ensuing decades.

■ **Robert F. Kennedy Campaigning for the Presidency, 1968** Wrapped in the Kennedy family mystique and exuding his own boyish charm, Kennedy excited partisan crowds to wildly adulatory outpourings.

Online Study Center

Primary source
Police Riot in the Streets of Chicago, A
college.hmco.com/pic/kennedybrief7e

──────

hawk *During the Vietnam War, someone who favored vigorous prosecution or escalation of the conflict.*

dissidents *Someone who dissents, especially from an established or normative institution or position.*

The Obituary of Lyndon Johnson

Talented but tragedy-struck Lyndon Johnson returned to his Texas ranch in January 1969 and died there four years later. His party was defeated, and his "me-too" Hubert Humphrey was repudiated. Yet Johnson's legislative leadership for a time had

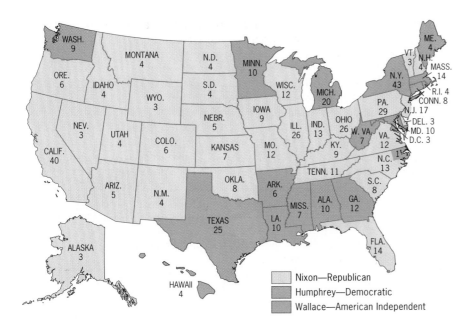

■ **Presidential Election of 1968 (with electoral vote by state)** George Wallace won in five states and denied a clear majority to either of the two major-party candidates in twenty-five other states. A shift of some fifty thousand votes might have thrown the election into the House of Representatives, giving Wallace the strategic bargaining position that he sought.

been remarkable. No president since Lincoln worked harder or did more for civil rights. None showed more compassion for the poor, blacks, and the ill educated.

But by 1966 Johnson was already sinking into the Vietnam quicksands. Great Society programs began to wither on the vine as soaring war costs sucked tax dollars into the military machine. Johnson promised guns and butter but could not deliver both. The War on Poverty met resistance as stubborn as the Viet Cong and eventually went down to defeat. Great want persisted alongside great wealth.

The Southeast Asian quagmire engulfed Johnson's noblest intentions. He was evidently persuaded by his brightest advisers, both civilian and military, that massive aerial bombing and limited troop commitments would make a "cheap" victory possible. His decision not to escalate the fighting further offended the "hawks," and his refusal to back off altogether antagonized the "doves." Like the Calvinists of colonial days, luckless Lyndon Johnson was damned if he did and damned if he did not.

The Cultural Upheaval of the 1960s

The struggles of the 1960s against racism, poverty, and the war in Vietnam had momentous cultural consequences. The decade came to be seen as a watershed dividing two distinct eras in terms of values, morals, and behavior.

Everywhere in 1960s America, a newly negative attitude toward all kinds of authority began to take hold. Disillusioned by the discovery that American society was not free of racism, sexism, imperialism, and oppression, many young people lost their traditional moral rudders. Neither families nor churches nor schools seemed to be able to define values and shape behavior with the certainty of shared purpose that many people believed had once existed.

The nation's mainstream Protestant denominations, which had dominated American religious life for centuries, lost their grip and many of their churchgoing parishioners. The liberal Protesant churches suffered the most. They increasingly ceded religious authority to conservative evangelicals while surrendering cultural authority to secular professionals and academic social scientists. A new cultural divide began to take shape, as educated Americans became increasingly secular and the less educated became more religious. Religious upheaval even churned the tradition-bound Roman Catholic Church, among the world's oldest and most conservative institutions. Clerics abandoned their Roman collars and the Latin Mass; folk songs replaced Gregorian chants; and meatless Fridays became ancient history. No matter what the topic, conventional wisdom and inherited ideas came under fire. "Trust no one over thirty" was a popular sneer of rebellious youth.

 The "Free Speech Movement," Berkeley, California, December 4, 1964 Student leader Mario Savio addresses a crowd at the University of California at Berkeley. The Free Speech Movement marked the first of the large-scale student mobilizations that would rock campuses across the country throughout the rest of the 1960s.

Online Study Center

Interactive map
Disturbances on College and
University Campuses, 1967–1969
college.hmco.com/pic/kennedybrief7e

Online Study Center

Primary source
Port Huron Statement Sets the
Social Agenda for SDS, The
college.hmco.com/pic/kennedybrief7e

Skepticism about authority had deep historical roots in American culture, and it had even bloomed in the supposedly complacent and conformist 1950s. "Beat" poets such as Allen Ginsberg and iconoclastic novelists like Jack Kerouac had voiced dark disillusion with the materialistic pursuits of "establishment" culture in the Eisenhower era. In movies like *Rebel Without a Cause* (1955), the attractive young actor James Dean expressed the restless frustration of many young people.

The disaffection of the young reached crisis proportions in the tumultuous 1960s. One of the first organized protests against established authority broke out at the University of California at Berkeley in 1964, in the aptly named Free Speech Movement. Students objected to an administrative ban on the use of campus space for political debate, and accused the Cold War "megaversity" of promoting corporate interests rather than humane values.

But in only a few years, the clean-cut Berkeley activists and their sober-minded sit-ins would seem downright quaint. Fired by outrage against the war in Vietnam, some sons and daughters of the middle class became radical political rebels. Others turned to mind-bending drugs, tuned in to "acid rock," and dropped out of "straight" society. Others "did their own thing" in communes or "alternative" institutions. Patriotism became a dirty word. Beflowered women in trousers and long-haired men with earrings heralded the rise of a self-conscious "counterculture" vehemently opposed to traditional American ways.

The 1960s also witnessed a "sexual revolution," though its novelty and scale are often exaggerated. Without doubt, the introduction of the birth-control pill in 1960 made unwanted pregnancies much easier to avoid and sexual appetites much easier to satisfy. Gay men and lesbians increasingly demanded sexual tolerance. A brutal attack on gay men by off-duty police officers at New York's Stonewall Inn in 1969 powerfully energized gay and lesbian militancy.

Launched in youthful idealism, many of the cultural "revolutions" of the 1960s sputtered out in violence and cynicism. Students for a Democratic Society (SDS), once at the forefront of the antipoverty and antiwar campaigns, had by decade's end spawned an underground terrorist group called the Weathermen. Peaceful civil rights demonstrations had given way to blockbusting urban riots. What started as apparently innocent experiments with drugs like marijuana and LSD had fried many youthful brains and spawned a loathsome underworld of drug lords and addicts.

Strait-laced guardians of respectability denounced the self-indulgent romanticism of the "flower children" as the beginning of the end of modern civilization. Sympathetic observers hailed the "greening" of America—the replacement of materialism and imperialism by a new consciousness of human values.

But the upheavals of the 1960s could be largely attributed to three *P*'s: the youthful population bulge, protest against racism and the Vietnam War, and the apparent permanence of prosperity. As the decade flowed into the 1970s, the flower children grew older and had children of their own, the civil rights movement fell silent, the war ended, and economic stagnation blighted the bloom of prosperity. Young people in the 1970s seemed more concerned with finding a job in the system than with tearing the system down. But if the counterculture had not managed fully to replace older values, it had weakened their grip, perhaps permanently.

✪ Chapter Summary ✪

Kennedy's vigorous New Frontier initiatives stirred a spirit of idealism, but many of his programs became bogged down in Congress. Cold War confrontations over Berlin and Russian missiles in Cuba created threats of nuclear war but were successfully defused. Countering Third World communism through flexible response led the administration into dangerous involvement in Vietnam and elsewhere.

Johnson succeeded Kennedy and overwhelmingly defeated the militantly conservative Goldwater in the 1964 election. The black movement for integration and voting rights won great victories with Johnson's support. Johnson also used his huge congressional majorities to push through a mass of liberal Great Society legislation. Martin Luther King's nonviolent civil rights movement was overshadowed by more militant voices, as Northern ghettos erupted in violence amid calls for black power and black nationalism. A growing white backlash reduced sympathies for further integration and civil rights gains.

Johnson escalated military involvement in the Dominican Republic and especially Vietnam. As the number of troops and casualties grew without producing military success, dovish protests against the war gained strength. Political opposition forced Johnson not to seek reelection, and the deep Democratic divisions over the war allowed Nixon to win the White House. The third party candidacy of George Wallace revealed the growth of an angry "populist" politics. The political upheavals of the 1960s also produced a youthful "counterculture" that revolted against authority and weakened all mainstream American institutions, including government and religion. The counterculture, which began in idealism, eventually faded amidst growing cynicism and economic anxiety in the 1970s.

VARYING VIEWPOINTS
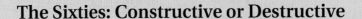

The Sixties: Constructive or Destructive

The 1960s were convulsed by controversy, and they have remained controversial ever since. Conflicts raged in that turbulent decade between social classes, races, sexes, and generations. More than three decades later, the conservative Republicans who gained power sought nothing less than a wholesale repudiation of the government activism that marked the sixties decade and a resounding reaffirmation of the "traditional values" that sixties culture supposedly trashed. Liberal Democrats, on the other hand, continued to press for affirmative action for women and minorities, protection for the environment, an expanded welfare state, and sexual tolerance—all legacies of the stormy sixties. Four issues dominate historical discussion of the 1960s: the civil rights struggle; the Great Society's "War on Poverty"; the Vietnam War and the antiwar movement; and the emergence of the counterculture.

Although most scholars praise the civil rights achievements of the 1960s, they disagree over the civil rights movement's turn away from nonviolence toward separatism and Black Power. The Freedom Riders and Martin Luther King, Jr., find much more approval in most history books than do Malcolm X or the Black Panther party. But some scholars, notably William L. Van Deburg in *New Day in Babylon: The Black Power Movement and American Culture, 1965–1975* (1992), argue that the "flank effect" of radical Black Power advocates like Stokely Carmichael actually enhanced the bargaining position of moderates like Dr. King.

Johnson's War on Poverty has liberal defenders in scholars like Allen Matusow (*The Unraveling of America*, 1984) and John Schwarz (*America's Hidden Success*, 1988). Schwarz demonstrates, for example, that Medicare and Social Security reforms virtually eliminated poverty among America's elderly. But conservative critics like Charles Murray (*Losing Ground*, 1984) and Lawrence Meade (*Beyond Entitlements*, 1986) see the Great Society, in a phrase popular in the 1960s, as part of the problem, not part of the solution. In their view, the War on Poverty did not simply fail to eradicate poverty among the so-called underclass; it actually deepened the dependency of the poor on the welfare state and even generated a multigenerational "cycle" of poverty.

For many young people of the 1960s, the antiwar movement protesting America's policy in Vietnam provided an initiation into politics and an introduction to "movement culture," with its sense of community and shared purpose. But scholars disagree over the movement's real effectiveness in checking the war. Writers like John Lewis Gaddis (*Strategies of Containment*, 1982) explain America's eventual withdrawal from Vietnam essentially without reference to the protesters in the streets. Others, like Todd Gitlin (*The Sixties: Years of Hope, Days of Rage*, 1987), insist that mass protest was the force that finally pressed the war to a conclusion.

Debate over the counterculture not only pits liberals against conservatives but also pits liberals against radicals. A liberal historian like William O'Neill (*Coming Apart*, 1971) might sympathize with what he considers some of the worthy values pushed by student activists, such as racial justice, nonviolence, and the antiwar movement, but he also claims that much of the sixties "youth culture" degenerated into hedonism, arrogance, and social polarization. In contrast, historians such as Michael Kazin and Maurice Isserman argue that cultural radicalism and political radicalism were two sides of the same coin. Many young people in the sixties made little distinction between the personal and the political. As Sara Evans demonstrates in *Personal Politics* (1980), "the personal *was* the political" for many women.

Critics may argue over the "good" versus the "bad" sixties, but there is no denying the degree to which that tumultuous time, for better or worse, shaped the world in which we now live.

39

The Stalemated Seventies

—◈—

1968–1980

IN ALL MY YEARS OF PUBLIC LIFE, I HAVE NEVER
OBSTRUCTED JUSTICE. PEOPLE HAVE GOT TO KNOW
WHETHER OR NOT THEIR PRESIDENT IS A CROOK. WELL,
I'M NOT A CROOK; I EARNED EVERYTHING I'VE GOT.

RICHARD NIXON, 1973

As the 1960s lurched to a close, the fantastic quarter-century economic boom of the post–World War II era also showed signs of petering out. By increasing their productivity, American workers had doubled their average standard of living in the twenty-five years since the end of World War II. Now, fatefully, productivity gains slowed to the vanishing point. The entire decade of the 1970s did not witness a productivity advance equivalent to even one year's progress in the preceding two decades. At the new rate, it would take five hundred more years to bring about another doubling of the average worker's standard of living. The median income of the average American family stagnated in the two decades after 1970 and failed to decline only because of the addition of working wives' wages to the family income. The rising baby-boom generation now faced the depressing prospect of a living standard that would be lower than that of their parents. As the postwar years of robust economic growth crested by the early 1970s, at home and abroad the "can do" American spirit gave way to an unaccustomed sense of limits.

Focus Questions

1. How did the economy's poor performance throughout the 1970s affect the political atmosphere and public policies of the decade?
2. What were Richard Nixon's primary foreign policy initiatives, and how did they affect the war in Vietnam and Cambodia as well as relations with the Soviet Union and China?
3. How did the Watergate scandal lead to Nixon's resignation, and why did it contribute to the deepening public disillusionment with government, already fueled by the Vietnam War?
4. How were the economy, energy, and Middle East foreign policy all linked in the 1970s, and why did both Republican and Democratic administrations have so little success in addressing these issues?
5. How did the Iranian crisis intensify public disaffection with the Carter administration?

Online Study Center

**Interactive map
Southeast Asia and the Vietnam War
college.hmco.com/pic/kennedybrief7e**

Sources of Stagnation

What caused the sudden slump in productivity? Some observers cited the increasing presence in the work force of women and teenagers, who typically had fewer skills than male adult workers and were less likely to take the full-time, long-term jobs by which skills might be developed. Other commentators blamed declining investment in new machinery, the heavy costs of compliance with government-imposed safety and health regulations, and the general shift of the economy from manufacturing to services, where productivity gains were allegedly more difficult to achieve.

The Vietnam War also precipitated painful economic distortions. The disastrous conflict in Southeast Asia drained tax dollars from needed improvements in education, deflected scientific skill and manufacturing capacity from the civilian sector, and touched off a sickening spiral of inflation. Sharply rising oil prices in the 1970s also fed inflation, but its deepest roots lay in government policies of the 1960s—especially Lyndon Johnson's insistence on simultaneously fighting the war in Vietnam and funding the Great Society programs at home, all without a tax increase to finance the added expenditures. The cost of living more than tripled in the dozen years following Richard Nixon's inauguration, in the longest and steepest inflationary cycle in American history.

Other weaknesses in the nation's economy were also laid bare by the abrupt reversal of America's financial fortunes in the 1970s. The competitive advantage of many American businesses had been so enormous after World War II that they had small incentive to modernize plants and seek more efficient methods of production. The defeated German and Japanese people had meanwhile scratched their way out of the ruins of war and built wholly new factories with the most up-to-date technology and management techniques. By the 1970s their efforts paid handsome rewards, as they came to dominate industries like steel, automobiles, and consumer electronics—fields in which the United States had once been unchallengeable.

The poor economic performance of the 1970s hung over the decade like a pall. It frustrated both policymakers and citizens who keenly remembered the growth and optimism of the quarter-century since World War II. Now a stalemated, unpopular war and a stagnant, unresponsive economy heralded the end of the self-confident postwar era. With it ended the liberal dream, vivid since New Deal days, that an affluent society could spend its way to social justice.

Nixon "Vietnamizes" the War

Inaugurated on January 20, 1969, Richard Nixon urged the American people, torn with dissension over Vietnam and race relations, to "stop shouting at one another." Yet the new president seemed an unlikely conciliator of the clashing forces that appeared to be ripping apart American society. Solitary and suspicious by nature, Nixon could be brittle and testy in the face of opposition. He also harbored bitter resentments against the "liberal establishment." Yet Nixon brought one hugely valuable asset with him to the White House—his broad knowledge and thoughtful expertise in foreign affairs.

The first burning need of American foreign policy was to quiet the public uproar over Vietnam. President Nixon's announced policy, called "Vietnamization," was to withdraw the 540,000 U.S. troops in South Vietnam over an extended period. The South Vietnamese—with American money, weapons, training, and advice—could then gradually take over the burden of fighting their own war. The so-called Nixon Doctrine furthermore proclaimed that in the future, Asians and others would have to fight their own wars without the support of large bodies of American ground troops.

Nixon sought not to end the war but to win it without the further spilling of American blood. But even this much involvement was distasteful to the American "doves," many of whom demanded a withdrawal that was prompt, complete, unconditional, and irreversible. Antiwar protesters staged a massive national

Chronology

1970 Nixon orders invasion of Cambodia.
Kent State and Jackson State incidents.
Environmental Protection Agency (EPA) created.
Clean Air Act.

1971 Pentagon Papers published.
Twenty-sixth Amendment (lowering voting age to eighteen) ratified.

1972 Nixon visits China and the Soviet Union.
ABM and SALT I treaties ratified.
Nixon defeats McGovern for presidency.
Equal Rights Amendment passes Congress.
Title IX of Education Amendments passed.

1973 Vietnam cease-fire and U.S. withdrawal.
Agnew resigns; Ford appointed vice president.
War Powers Act.
Arab-Israeli war and Arab oil embargo.
Endangered Species Act.
Frontiero v. *Richardson*.
Roe v. *Wade*.

1973-
1974 Watergate hearings and investigations.

1974 Nixon resigns; Ford assumes presidency.
First OPEC oil-price increase.

1975 Helsinki accords.
South Vietnam falls to communists.

1976 Carter defeats Ford for presidency.

1978 Egyptian-Israeli Camp David agreement.
United States v. *Wheeler*.

1979 Iranian revolution and oil crisis.
SALT II agreements signed (never ratified by Senate).
Soviet Union invades Afghanistan.

1979-
1981 Iranian hostage crisis.

Vietnam **moratorium** in October 1969, as nearly 100,000 people jammed Boston Common and some 50,000 filed by the White House carrying lighted candles.

Undaunted, Nixon launched a counteroffensive by appealing to the "silent majority" who presumably supported the war. Though ostensibly conciliatory, Nixon's approach was in fact deeply divisive. His intentions became clear when he unleashed tough-talking Vice President Agnew to attack the "nattering nabobs of negativism" who demanded quick withdrawal from Vietnam. Nixon himself in 1970 sneered at the student antiwar demonstrators as "bums."

By January 1970 the Vietnam conflict had become the longest in American history and, with some 40,000 killed and over 250,000 wounded, the third most costly foreign war in the nation's experience. Especially in the war's early stages, African Americans were disproportionately represented in the army and accounted for a disproportionately high share of combat casualties. Black and white soldiers alike floundered through booby-trapped swamps and steaming jungles, often unable to distinguish friend from foe among the Vietnamese peasants. Morale plummeted, as drug abuse, mutiny, and sabotage dulled the army's fighting edge.

Domestic disgust with the war was further deepened in 1970 by revelations that in 1968 American troops had massacred innocent women and children in the village of My Lai. Increasingly desperate for a quick end to the demoralizing conflict, Nixon widened the war in 1970 by ordering an attack on Vietnam's neighbor, Cambodia.

moratorium *A period in which economic or social activity is suspended, often to achieve certain defined goals.*

Online Study Center

Primary source
Eisenhower, Kennedy, Johnson, Nixon
college.hmco.com/pic/kennedybrief7e

Online Study Center

Primary source
Letters Home from Vietnam
college.hmco.com/pic/kennedybrief7e

"Cambodianizing" the Vietnam War

Suddenly, on April 29, 1970, without consulting Congress, Nixon ordered American troops to invade officially neutral Cambodia, which the North Vietnamese and Viet Cong had long used as a springboard for troops, weapons, and supplies. Angry students nationwide responded to the Cambodian invasion with rock throwing,

A Marine Corps officer expressed the disillusion that beset many American troops in Vietnam:

"For years we disposed of the enemy dead like so much garbage. We stuck cigarettes in the mouths of corpses, put *Playboy* magazines in their hands, cut off their ears to wear around our necks. We incinerated them with napalm, atomized them with B-52 strikes, shoved them out the doors of helicopters above the South China Sea. . . . All we did was count, count bodies. Count dead human beings. . . . That was our fundamental military strategy. Body count. And the count kept going up."

Kremlin *The extensive palace complex in Moscow that housed the Soviet (Russian) government; hence, a shorthand term for the Soviet or Russian government.*

antiballistic missile *A defensive missile designed to intercept and destroy an offensive missile in flight.*

■ **The War at Home** Antiwar students clash with police in Ann Arbor, Michigan, in 1970.

window smashing, and arson. At Kent State University in Ohio, jumpy members of the National Guard fired into a noisy crowd, killing four and wounding many more; at historically black Jackson State College in Mississippi, the highway patrol killed two students.

Nixon withdrew the American troops from Cambodia after only two months. But in America the Cambodian invasion deepened the bitterness between "hawks" and "doves," as right-wing groups physically assaulted leftists. Disillusionment with "whitey's war" increased ominously among African Americans in the armed forces. The Senate (though not the House) overwhelmingly repealed the Gulf of Tonkin blank check that Congress had given Johnson in 1964 and sought ways to restrain Nixon. The youth of America were only slightly mollified when the government reduced draft calls, introduced a draft lottery, and lowered the voting age to eighteen through approval of the Twenty-sixth Amendment in 1971 (see the Appendix).

New combustibles fueled the fires of antiwar discontent in June 1971, when a former Pentagon official leaked to the *New York Times* the "Pentagon Papers," a topsecret Pentagon study that documented the blunders and deceptions of the Kennedy and Johnson administrations, especially the provoking of the 1964 North Vietnamese attack in the Gulf of Tonkin.

Nixon's Détente with Beijing and Moscow

As the antiwar firestorm flared ever higher, Nixon concluded that the road out of Vietnam ran through Beijing and Moscow. He perceived that tensions between the Chinese and the Soviets afforded the United States an opportunity to play off one antagonist against the other and to enlist the aid of both in pressuring North Vietnam into peace. Nixon's thinking was reinforced by his bespectacled and German-accented national security adviser, Dr. Henry A. Kissinger, who in 1969 began negotiating secretly with North Vietnamese officials in Paris while preparing the president's path to Beijing and Moscow.

Nixon, heretofore an uncompromising anticommunist, startled the nation by making an historic journey to China in February 1972. He capped the visit with the Shanghai Communiqué, in which the two nations agreed to "normalize" their relationship. Nixon next traveled to Moscow in May 1972 to play his "China card" in a game of high-stakes diplomacy in the **Kremlin**. The Soviets, hungry for American foodstuffs and alarmed over the possibility of intensified rivalry with an American-backed China, were ready to deal.

Nixon's visits ushered in an era of *détente*, or relaxed tension, with the two communist powers and produced several significant agreements in 1972, including the sale of $750 million worth of wheat, corn, and other grain to the Soviet Union. More important, the United States and the USSR agreed to an **antiballistic missile** (ABM) treaty, which limited each nation to two clusters of defensive missiles, and to a series of arms-reduction agreements known as SALT (Strategic Arms Limitations Talks) aimed at freezing the numbers of long-range nuclear missiles for five years.

These accords constituted long-overdue first steps toward slowing the arms race. Yet even though the ABM treaty forbade elaborate defensive systems, the United States forged ahead with the development of "MIRVs" (multiple independently targeted reentry vehicles), designed to overcome any defense by "saturating" it with large numbers of warheads, several to a rocket. Predictably, the Soviets proceeded to "MIRV" their own missiles, and the arms race ratcheted up to a still more perilous plateau, with over sixteen thousand nuclear warheads deployed by both sides by the end of the 1980s.

Nixon's détente diplomacy did, to some extent, de-ice the Cold War. Yet Nixon remained staunchly anticommunist when the occasion seemed to demand it. He strongly opposed the election of the outspoken Marxist Salvador Allende as president of Chile in 1970. His administration and the Central Intelligence Agency worked covertly to undermine the legitimately elected leftist president. When the Chilean army overthrew and killed Allende in 1973, many observers smelled a Yankee rat. Even so, by checkmating and co-opting the two great communist powers, the president had cleverly set the stage for America's exit from Vietnam, although the concluding act in that wrenching tragedy still remained to be played.

Nixon on the Home Front

Nixon had lashed out during the campaign at the "permissiveness" and "judicial activism" of the Supreme Court presided over by Chief Justice Earl Warren. The Warren Court's controversial decisions on sexual freedom, civil rights, criminal law, the practice of religion, and the structure of political representation had reflected its deep concern for the individual, no matter how lowly.

In *Griswold* v. *Connecticut* (1965), the Court struck down a state law that prohibited the use of contraceptives, even among married couples. The Court proclaimed (critics said "invented") a "right of privacy" that soon provided the basis for decisions protecting women's abortion rights. Controversial decisions in the cases of *Escobedo* (1964) and *Miranda* (1966) gave accused criminals the right to remain silent. In two stunning decisions, *Engel* v. *Vitale* (1962) and *School District of Abingdon Township* v. *Schempp* (1963), the Court outraged religious conservatives when it invoked the First Amendment, which requires separation of church and state, to prohibit required prayers and Bible readings in public schools.

Because these divisive decisions affected stubborn social problems spawned by mid-century tensions, the Court came under relentless criticism, the bitterest since New Deal days. Fulfilling campaign promises, President Nixon undertook to change the Court's philosophical complexion. He sought appointees who would strictly interpret the Constitution, cease "meddling" in social and political questions, and not coddle radicals or criminals. The Senate in 1969 speedily confirmed his nomination of white-maned Warren E. Burger of Minnesota to succeed the retiring Earl Warren as chief justice. Before the end of 1971 the Court counted four conservative Nixon appointments out of nine members.

Yet Nixon was to learn the ironic lesson that many presidents have learned about their Supreme Court appointees: once seated on the high bench, the justices are fully free to think and decide according to their own beliefs, not according to the president's expectations. The Burger Court that Nixon shaped proved reluctant to dismantle the "liberal" rulings of the Warren Court; it even produced the most controversial judicial opinion of modern times, the momentous *Roe* v. *Wade* decision in 1973, which legalized abortion (see p. 641).

Surprisingly Nixon presided over significant expansion of the welfare programs that conservative Republicans routinely denounced. He approved increased funds for entitlements like Food Stamps, Medicaid, and Aid to Families with Dependent Children (AFDC), and he added a generous new program, Supplemental Security Income (SSI), to aid the indigent, blind, and disabled. Nixon also signed legislation in 1972 guaranteeing automatic Social Security cost-of-living increases to protect the elderly against the ravages of inflation. Ironically, this "indexing" actually helped to fuel the inflationary fires.

Amid much controversy, Nixon in 1969 implemented his so-called Philadelphia Plan requiring construction unions to establish "goals and timetables" for the hiring of black apprentices. Soon extended to all federal contracts, the Philadelphia Plan required employers to meet hiring quotas or to establish "set-asides" for minority contractors. Nixon's policy had far-reaching implications, because it went beyond earlier definitions of "affirmative action" designed to aid *individuals*, and instead conferred privileges on certain *groups*. While opening broad employment and educational opportunities for minorities and women, this approach opened a Pandora's box of protest from critics who assailed this "reverse discrimination" created by executive orders and unelected courts, not by democratically elected representatives.

Among other legacies of the Nixon years was the creation in 1970 of the Environmental Protection Agency (EPA) and a companion body, the Occupational Safety and Health Administration (OSHA). Their births climaxed two decades of mounting concern for the environment. Author Rachel Carson gave the environmental movement a huge boost in 1963 when she published *Silent Spring*, an enormously effective piece of latter-day muckraking that exposed the poisonous effects of pesticides. Legislatively armed by the Clean Air Act of 1970, the Endangered Species Act of 1973, and similar laws, the EPA and OSHA stood on the frontline of the battle for ecological sanity. They made notable progress in the ensuing decades in reducing automobile emissions and cleaning up befouled waterways and waste sites.

Elected as a minority president, with only 43 percent of the vote in 1968, Nixon devised a clever but cynical plan—called the "southern strategy"—to achieve a solid majority in 1972. Appointing conservative Supreme Court justices, soft-pedaling civil rights, and opposing school busing to achieve racial balance were all parts of the strategy.

The Nixon Landslide of 1972

But the southern strategy became superfluous as foreign policy dominated the presidential campaign of 1972. Vietnam continued to be the burning issue. Nearly four years had passed since Nixon had promised, as a presidential candidate, to end the war and "win" the peace. Yet in the spring of 1972 the fighting escalated anew to alarming levels when the North Vietnamese, heavily equipped with foreign tanks, burst through the demilitarized zone separating the two Vietnams. Nixon reacted promptly by launching massive bombing attacks on strategic centers in North Vietnam, including Hanoi, the capital. Gambling heavily on Moscow's and Beijing's forbearance, he also ordered the dropping of contact mines to blockade the principal harbors of North Vietnam.

The continuing Vietnam conflict spurred the rise of South Dakota senator George McGovern to the 1972 Democratic nomination. McGovern's promise to pull the remaining American troops out of Vietnam in ninety days earned him the backing of the large antiwar element in the party. But his appeal to racial minorities, feminists, leftists, and youth alienated the traditional working-class backbone of his party. Moreover, the discovery shortly after the convention, that McGovern's running mate, Missouri senator Thomas Eagleton, had undergone psychiatric care forced Eagleton's removal from the ticket and virtually doomed McGovern's candidacy.

Nixon's campaign emphasized that he had wound down the "Democratic war" in Vietnam from some 540,000 troops to about 30,000. His candidacy received an added boost just twelve days before the election when the high-flying Dr. Kissinger announced that "peace is at hand" in Vietnam and that an agreement would be settled in a few days.

Nixon won the election in a landslide. His lopsided victory encompassed every state except Massachusetts and the nonstate District of Columbia. He piled up 520 electoral votes to 17 and a popular majority of 47,169,911 votes to 29,170,383. McGovern had counted on a large vote from young people, but less than half the 18–21 group even bothered to vote.

The dove of peace, "at hand" in Vietnam just before the balloting, took flight after the election. After the fighting on both sides had again escalated, Nixon launched a furious two-week bombing of North Vietnam. This merciless pounding drove North Vietnamese negotiators to agree to cease-fire arrangements on January 23, 1973, nearly three months after peace was prematurely proclaimed.

Nixon hailed the face-saving cease-fire agreement as "peace with honor," but the boast rang hollow. The United States was to withdraw its remaining 27,000 or so troops and could reclaim some 560 American prisoners of war. The North Vietnamese were allowed to keep some 145,000 troops in South Vietnam, where they still occupied about 30 percent of the country. This shaky "peace" was in reality little more than a thinly disguised American retreat.

The Secret Bombing of Cambodia and the War Powers Act

The constitutionality of Nixon's continued aerial battering of Cambodia had meanwhile been coming under increasing fire. In July 1973 America was shocked to learn that the U.S. Air Force had already secretly conducted some thirty-five hundred bombing raids against North Vietnamese positions in Cambodia, beginning in March 1969 and continued for some fourteen months prior to the open American incursion in May 1970. The most disturbing feature of these sky **forays** was that, while they were going on, American officials, including the president, had sworn that Cambodian neutrality was being respected. Countless Americans began to wonder what kind of representative government they had if they were fighting a war they knew nothing about.

Defiance followed secretiveness. After the Vietnam cease-fire in January 1973, Nixon brazenly continued large-scale bombing of communist forces in order to help the rightist Cambodian government, and he repeatedly vetoed congressional efforts to stop him. The years of bombing inflicted grisly wounds on Cambodia, blasting its people and revolutionizing its politics. The long-suffering Cambodians soon groaned under the sadistic heel of Pol Pot, a murderous tyrant who dispatched as many as 2 million of his people to their graves.

Congressional opposition to the expansion of presidential war-making powers by Johnson and Nixon led to the War Powers Act in November 1973. Passed over Nixon's veto, it required the president to report to Congress within forty-eight hours after committing troops to a foreign conflict. Such a limited authorization would have to end within sixty days unless Congress extended it for thirty more days.

The War Powers Act was but one manifestation of what came to be called the "New Isolationism," a mood of caution and restraint in the conduct of the nation's foreign affairs after the bloody and futile misadventure in Vietnam. Meanwhile, the draft ended in January 1973, although it was retained on a standby basis. The armed forces were to be all volunteers.

> *The* Washington Post *(July 19, 1973) carried this news item:*
>
> "American B-52 bombers dropped about 104,000 tons of explosives on Communist sanctuaries in neutralist Cambodia during a series of raids in 1969 and 1970.... The secret bombing was acknowledged by the Pentagon the Monday after a former Air Force major ... described how he falsified reports on Cambodian air operations and destroyed records on the bombing missions actually flown."

foray *A single, defined movement or attack by a military unit.*

recession *A moderate and short-term economic downturn, less severe than a depression. (Economists define a recession as two consecutive quarters, i.e., six months, of declining gross domestic product.)*

The Arab Oil Embargo and the Energy Crisis

The long-rumbling Middle East erupted anew in October 1973, when the rearmed Syrians and Egyptians unleashed surprise attacks on Israel. Kissinger, who had become secretary of state in September, hastily flew to Moscow in an effort to restrain the Soviets, who were arming the attackers. Believing that the Kremlin was poised to fly combat troops to the Suez area, Nixon placed America's nuclear forces on alert and ordered a gigantic airlift of nearly $2 billion in war materials to the Israelis. This assistance helped save the day, as the Israelis aggressively turned the tide and threatened Cairo until American diplomacy brought about an uneasy cease-fire.

America's policy of backing Israel against its oil-rich neighbors exacted a heavy penalty. Late in October 1973, the Arab nations suddenly clamped an embargo on oil for the United States and other countries supporting Israel. Americans had to suffer through a long, cold winter of lowered thermostats and speedometers. Lines of automobiles at service stations lengthened as tempers shortened and a business **recession** deepened.

The "energy crisis" suddenly energized a number of long-deferred projects. Congress approved a costly Alaska pipeline and a national speed limit of fifty-five miles per hour to conserve fuel. Agitation mounted for heavier use of coal and nuclear power, despite the environmental threat they posed.

The five months of the Arab "blackmail" embargo in 1974 clearly signaled the end of an era—a period of cheap and abundant energy. American oil production peaked in 1970 and then began an irreversible decline. Blissfully unaware of their dependence on foreign suppliers, Americans, like revelers on a binge, had more than tripled their oil consumption since the end of World War II. The number of automobiles increased 350 percent between 1949 and 1972, and Detroit's engineers gave nary a thought to building more fuel-efficient engines.

By 1974 America was addicted to oil and extremely vulnerable to any interruption in supplies. That stark fact deeply colored the diplomatic and economic history of the next decades. The Middle East loomed ever larger on the map of America's strategic interests, until the United States in 1991 at last found itself pulled into a shooting war with Iraq to protect its oil supplies (see pp. 659–661).

The Middle Eastern sheiks quadrupled their price for crude oil after lifting the embargo in 1974. The huge new oil bills wildly disrupted the U.S. balance of international trade and added further fuel to the already raging fires of inflation. Various sectors of the economy, including Detroit's carmakers, began their slow, grudging adjustment to the rudely dawning age of energy dependency. But full reconciliation to that uncomfortable reality was a long time coming.

Watergate Woes

attorney general *The presidentially appointed head of the Department of Justice and chief legal officer of the federal government.*

Nixon's electoral triumph in 1972 was almost immediately sullied—and eventually undone—by the Watergate scandal. On June 17, 1972, five men were arrested inside the Watergate office complex in Washington after attempting to plant electronic "bugs" in the Democratic party's headquarters. They were working for the Republican Committee for the Re-election of the President—popularly known as CREEP. The Watergate break-in turned out to be just one in a series of Nixon administration "dirty tricks" that included forging documents to discredit Democrats, using the Internal Revenue Service to harass innocent citizens named on a White House "enemies list," burglarizing the office of the psychiatrist who had treated the leaker of the Pentagon Papers, and perverting the FBI and CIA to cover the tricksters' track.

Meanwhile, the moral stench hanging over the White House worsened when Vice President Spiro Agnew was forced to resign in October 1973 for taking bribes from Maryland contractors. Congress invoked the Twenty-fifth Amendment (see the Appendix) to replace Agnew with a twelve-term congressman from Michigan, Gerald ("Jerry") Ford.

Amid a mood of growing national outrage, a select Senate committee conducted widely televised hearings about the Watergate affair in 1973–1974. Nixon indignantly denied any prior knowledge of the break-in and any involvement in the legal proceedings against the burglars. But John Dean III, a former White House lawyer with a remarkable memory, accused top White House officials, including the president, of obstructing justice by trying to cover up the Watergate break-in and silence its perpetrators. Then another former White House aide revealed that a secret taping system had recorded most of Nixon's Oval Office conversations. Now Dean's sensational testimony could be checked against the White House tapes, and the Senate committee could better determine who was telling the truth. But Nixon stubbornly refused to produce the taped evidence. Moreover, on October 20, 1973, he ordered the "Saturday Night Massacre," firing the special prosecutor who demanded the evidence, as well as his **attorney general** and deputy attorney general, who had refused orders to dismiss the prosecutor.

Nixon finally acceded in the spring of 1974 to the House Judiciary Committee's demand for the Watergate

■ Nixon, the Law-and-Order-Man

tapes, though with many sections missing (including Nixon's frequent obsceni-ties, which were excised with the phrase "expletive deleted"). But on July 24, 1974, the president suffered a disastrous setback when the Supreme Court unanimously ruled that **"executive privilege"** gave him no right to withhold from the special prosecutor portions of tapes relevant to criminal activity. Skating on thin ice over hot water, Nixon reluctantly complied.

Nixon now made public three subpoenaed tapes of conversations with his chief aide on June 23, 1972. One of them revealed the president giving orders, six days after the Watergate break-in, to use the CIA to hold back an inquiry by the FBI. Nixon's own tape-recorded words convicted him of having been an active party to the attempted cover-up. The House Judiciary Committee proceeded to draw up articles of impeachment, based on obstruction of justice, abuse of the powers of the presidential office, and contempt of Congress.

The public's wrath proved to be overwhelming. Republican leaders in Congress concluded that the guilty and unpredictable Nixon was a loose cannon on the deck of the ship of state. They frankly informed the president that his im-peachment by the full House and removal by the Senate were foregone conclu-sions and that he would do best to resign.

Left with no better choice, Nixon choked back his tears and announced his resignation in a dramatic television appearance on August 8, 1974. Few presidents had flown so high, and none had sunk so low. In his Farewell Address, Nixon ad-mitted having made some "judgments" that "were wrong" but insisted that he had always acted "in what I believed at the time to be the best interests of the nation." Unconvinced, countless Americans would change the song "Hail to the Chief" to "Jail to the Chief."

The nation had survived a wrenching constitutional crisis, which proved that the impeachment machinery forged by the Founding Fathers could work when public opinion overwhelmingly demanded that it be implemented. The principles that no person is above the law and that presidents must be held to strict account-ability for their acts were strengthened. The United States of America, on the eve of its two-hundredth birthday as a republic, had eventually cleaned its own sullied house, giving an impressive demonstration of self-discipline and self-government to the rest of the world.

executive privilege *In American govern-ment, the claim that certain information known to the president or the executive branch of government should be unavail-able to Congress or the courts because of the principle of separation of powers.*

Primary source
Nixon Incriminates Himself
college.hmco.com/pic/kennedybrief7e

Primary source
House Judiciary Committee's
Conclusion on Impeachment
college.hmco.com/pic/kennedybrief7e

The First Unelected President

Gerald Rudolph Ford, the first man to be made president solely by a vote of Congress, entered the besmirched White House in August 1974 with serious handi-caps. He was widely—and unfairly—suspected of being little more than a dim-witted former college football player. President Johnson had sneered that "Jerry" was so lacking in brainpower that he could not walk and chew gum at the same time. Worse, Ford had been selected, not elected, vice president, following Spiro Agnew's resignation in disgrace. The sour odor of illegitimacy hung about this president without precedent.

Then, out of a clear sky, Ford granted a complete pardon to Nixon for any crimes he may have committed as president, discovered or undiscovered. Democrats were outraged, and lingering suspicions about the pardon cast a dark shadow over Ford's prospects of being elected president in his own right in 1976.

Ford at first sought to enhance the so-called détente with the Soviet Union that Nixon had crafted. In July 1975 President Ford joined leaders from thirty-four other nations in Helsinki, Finland, to sign several sets of historic accords. One group of agreements officially wrote an end to World War II by finally legitimizing the Soviet-dictated boundaries of Poland and other Eastern European countries. In return, the Soviets signed a "third basket" of agreements, guaranteeing more liberal exchanges of people and information between East and West and protect-ing certain basic human rights. The Helsinki accords kindled small dissident movements in Eastern Europe and even in the USSR itself, but the Soviets soon poured ice water on these sputtering flames of freedom.

Western Europeans cheered the Helsinki conference as a milestone of détente. But in the United States critics increasingly charged that détente was proving to be a one-way street. American grain and technology flowed to the USSR, and little of comparable importance flowed back. Moscow also continued its human rights violations, including restrictions on Jewish emigration. Despite these difficulties, Ford at first clung stubbornly to détente. But the American public's fury over Moscow's double-dealing steadily mounted. The thaw in the Cold War was threatening to prove chillingly brief.

Defeat in Vietnam

Early in 1975 the North Vietnamese gave full throttle to their long-expected drive southward. President Ford urged Congress to vote still more weapons for Vietnam. But his plea was in vain, and without the crutch of massive American aid, the South Vietnamese quickly and ingloriously collapsed.

The dam burst so rapidly that the remaining Americans had to be frantically evacuated by helicopter, the last of them on April 29, 1975. Also rescued were about 140,000 South Vietnamese, most of them so dangerously identified with the Americans that they feared a bloodbath by the victorious communists. Ford compassionately admitted these people to the United States, adding further seasoning to the melting pot. Eventually some 500,000 arrived (see "Makers of America: The Vietnamese," pp. 640–641).

America's longest, most frustrating war thus ended not with a bang but a whimper. In a technical sense the Americans had not lost the war; their client nation had. The United States had fought the North Vietnamese to a standstill and had then withdrawn its troops in 1973, leaving the South Vietnamese to fight their own war, with generous shipments of costly American weaponry. The estimated cost to America was $118 billion in current outlays, together with some 56,000 dead and 300,000 wounded. The people of the United States had in fact provided just about everything, except the will to win—and that could not be injected by outsiders.

Technicalities aside, America had lost more than a war. It had lost face in the eyes of foreigners, lost its own self-esteem, lost confidence in its military prowess—and lost much of the economic muscle that had made possible its global leadership since World War II. Americans reluctantly came to realize that their power as well as their pride had been deeply wounded in Vietnam and that recovery would be slow and painful.

Feminist Victories and Defeats

As the army limped home from Vietnam, most of the protest movements of the 1960s, including the antiwar movement, had long since splintered and stalled. One major exception to this pattern stood out: the American feminist movement.

■ **Passing the Buck** A satirical view of where responsibility for the Vietnam debacle should be laid.

EXAMINING THE EVIDENCE

The "Smoking Gun" Tape, June 23, 1972, 10:04–11:39 A.M. The technological capability to record Oval Office conversations combined with Richard Nixon's obsession with documenting his presidency to give the public—and the Senate committee investigating his role in the break-in of the Democratic National Committee headquarters in the Watergate Office Tower—rare access to personal conversations between the president and his closest advisers. This tape, which undeniably exposed Nixon's central role in constructing a "cover-up" of the Watergate break-in, was made on Nixon's first day back in Washington after the botched burglary of June 17, 1972. In this conversation with White House Chief of Staff H. R. Haldeman, Nixon devised a plan to block a widening FBI investigation by instructing the director of the CIA to deflect any further FBI snooping on the grounds that it would endanger sensitive CIA operations. Nixon refused to turn over this and other tapes to Senate investigators until so ordered by the Supreme Court on July 24, 1974. Within four days of its release on August 5, Nixon was forced to resign. After eighteen months of protesting his innocence of the crime and his ignorance of any effort to obstruct justice, Nixon was finally undone by the evidence in this incriminating "smoking gun" tape. While tapes documented two straight years of Nixon's Oval Office conversations, other presidents, such as Franklin Roosevelt, John F. Kennedy, and Lyndon Baines Johnson, recorded important meetings and crisis deliberations. Since Watergate, however, it is unlikely that any president has permitted extensive tape recording, depriving historians of a unique insight into the inner workings of the White House.

1. Should taped White House discussions be part of the public record of a presidency, and if so, who should have access to them?

2. What else might historians learn about a president and the administration from a tape like this one, besides the specific details of the Watergate cover-up?

3. Why did this conversation especially lead to near-unanimous calls for Nixon's impeachment or resignation from Republicans and Democrats alike?

Haldeman: . . . yesterday, they concluded it was not the White House, but are now convinced it is a CIA thing, so the CIA turn off would . . .

President: Well, not sure of their analysis, I'm not going to get that involved. I'm (unintelligible).

Haldeman: No, sir. We don't want you to.

President: You call them in.

President: Good. Good deal! Play it tough. That's the way they play it and that's the way we are going to play it.

Haldeman: O.K. We'll do it.

President: Yeah, when I saw that news summary item, I of course knew it was a bunch of crap, but I thought ah, well it's good to have them off on this wild hair [sic] thing because when they start bugging us, which they have, we'll know our little boys will not know how to handle it. I hope they will though. You never know. Maybe, you think about it. Good!

President: When you get in these people when you . . . get these people in, say: "Look, the problem is that this will open the whole, the whole Bay of Pigs thing, and the President just feels that" ah, without going into the details . . . don't, don't lie to them to the extent to say there is no involvement, but just say this is sort of a comedy of errors, bizarre, without getting into it, "the President believes that it is going to open the whole Bay of Pigs thing up again. And, ah because these people are plugging for, for keeps and that they should call the FBI in and say that we wish for the country, don't go any further into this case," period!

Although they had their differences, feminists showed vitality and momentum by winning legislative and judicial victories and provoking an intense rethinking of gender roles. (On the roots of this movement, see "Makers of America: The Feminists," p. 642).

Thousands of women marched in the Women's Stride for Equality on the fiftieth anniversary of woman suffrage in 1970. In 1972 Congress passed Title IX of the Education Amendments, prohibiting sex discrimination in any federally assisted educational program. This act created opportunities for girls' and women's athletics at schools and colleges, giving birth to a new "Title IX generation" that would reach maturity in the 1980s and 1990s and help professionalize women's sports as well. The Equal Rights Amendment (ERA) to the Constitution won congressional

Online Study Center

Primary source
Women's Liberation March
college.hmco.com/pic/kennedybrief7e

The Vietnamese

At first glance, the towns of Westminster and Fountain Valley, California, seem to resemble other California communities nearby. Tract homes line residential streets; shopping centers flank the busy thoroughfares. But these are no ordinary American suburbs. Instead, they make up "Little Saigons," vibrant outposts of Vietnamese culture in the contemporary United States.

Before South Vietnam fell in 1975, few Vietnamese ventured across the Pacific. Only in 1966 did U.S. immigration authorities even designate "Vietnamese" as a separate category of newcomers, and most early immigrants were the wives and children of U.S. servicemen. But as the communists closed in on Saigon, many Vietnamese, particularly those who had worked closely with American or South Vietnamese authorities, feared for their future. Gathering together as many of their extended-family members as they could assemble, thousands of Vietnamese fled for their lives. In a few hectic days in 1975, some 140,000 escaped before the approaching gunfire, a few dramatically clinging to the bottoms of departing helicopters. Another 60,000 less fortunate refugees escaped at the same time over land and sea to Hong Kong and Thailand, where they waited nervously for permission to move on.

To accommodate the refugees, the U.S. government set up camps across the nation. Arrivals were crowded into army barracks affording little room and less privacy. These were boot camps not for military service but for assimilation into American society. A rigorous program trained the Vietnamese in English, forbade children from speaking their native language in the classroom, and even immersed them in American slang. Many resented this attempt to mold them and strip them of their culture.

Their discontent boiled over when authorities prepared to release the refugees from camps and board them with families around the nation. The resettlement officials had decided to find a sponsor for each Vietnamese family—an American family that would provide food, shelter, and assistance for the refugees until they could fend for themselves. But the Vietnamese people cherish their traditional extended families—grandparents, uncles, aunts, and cousins living communally with parents and children.

■ **Preserving the Past** A Vietnamese American boy learns classical calligraphy from his grandfather.

As soon as refugees could, they relocated from the rural districts where they had been scattered to established Vietnamese enclaves around San Francisco, Los Angeles, and Dallas.

Soon a second throng of Vietnamese immigrants pushed into these Little Saigons. Fleeing from the ravages of poverty and from the oppressive communist government, these stragglers had crammed themselves and their few possessions into little boats, hoping to reach Hong Kong or get picked up by friendly ships. Eventually, many of these "boat people" reached the United States. Usually less educated than the first arrivals and receiving far less resettlement aid from the U.S. government, they were, however, more willing to start at the bottom. Today these two groups total more than half a million people. Differing in experience and expectations, the Vietnamese share a new home in a strange land. Their uprooting is an immense, unreckoned consequence of America's longest war.

approval in 1972. It declared, "Equality of rights under the law shall not be denied or abridged by the United States or by any State on account of sex." Twenty-eight states quickly ratified the amendment, first proposed by suffragists in 1923. Hopes rose that the ERA would soon be the law of the land.

Even the Supreme Court seemed to be on the movement's side. In *Reed* v. *Reed* and *Frontiero* v. *Richardson* (1973), the Court challenged sex discrimination in legislation and employment. And in the landmark case of *Roe* v. *Wade* (1973), the Court struck down laws prohibiting abortion, arguing that a woman's decision to terminate a pregnancy was protected by the constitutional right of privacy.

But the feminist movement soon faced a formidable backlash. In 1972 President Nixon vetoed a proposal to set up nationwide public day care, saying it would weaken the American family. The Catholic Church and the religious right organized a powerful grassroots movement to oppose the legalization of abortion. The most bitter defeat for feminists was a campaign, orchestrated by conservative spokeswoman Phyllis Schlafly, that killed the ERA. Its advocates, Schlafly charged, were just "bitter women seeking a constitutional cure for their personal problems." In 1979 Congress extended the deadline for ratification, but ERA opponents dug in their heels. The amendment died in 1982, three states short of success.

The Seventies in Black and White

Although the civil rights movement had fractured, race remained an explosive issue in the 1970s. The Supreme Court in *Milliken* v. *Bradley* blind-sided school integrationists when it ruled that desegregation plans could not require students to move across school-district lines. The decision effectively exempted suburban districts from shouldering any part of the burden of desegregating inner-city schools, thereby reinforcing "white flight" to the suburbs and forcing all the problems of desegregation into the least prosperous districts. Conflicts over desegregation often pitted the poorest, most disadvantaged elements of the white and black communities against one another.

Affirmative action programs also remained highly controversial. White workers who were denied advancement and white students who were refused college admission cried "reverse discrimination," charging that race or ethnic background was now outweighing ability in employment or admissions. In 1978 the Supreme Court, by a narrow five-to-four margin, upheld the claim of one white Californian, Allan Bakke, that he had been denied admission to medical school because of a program that favored minority applicants. In a tortured decision, the Court ordered the University of California at Davis medical school to admit Bakke, and declared that preference in admissions could not be based on ethnic or racial identity alone. Yet at the same time, the Court said that racial factors might be taken into account in a school's overall admissions policy for purposes of assembling a diverse student body. In an impassioned dissent, the Court's only black justice, Thurgood Marshall, warned that denial of racial preferences might sweep away years of civil rights progress. But many conservatives cheered the decision as affirming the principle that justice is colorblind.

Online Study Center

Interactive map
Continued Shift to the Sunbelt
college.hmco.com/pic/kennedybrief7e

The Feminists

A well-to-do housewife and mother of seven, Elizabeth Cady Stanton (1815–1902) was an unlikely revolutionary. Yet this founding mother of American feminism devoted seven decades of her life to the fight for women's rights.

Young Elizabeth Cady drew her inspiration from the fight against slavery. When she and her new husband, abolitionist Henry Stanton, attended the World Anti-Slavery Convention in London, she was insulted that women were forced to sit in a screened-off balcony above the convention floor. Stanton went on to organize the Seneca Falls Convention in 1848. There she presented her Declaration of Sentiments, which proclaimed that "all men *and women* are created equal" and demanded women's rights to own property, enter the professions, and vote.

Early feminists encountered a mountain of hostility to their cause. Stanton failed to have women included in the Fourteenth Amendment to the Constitution, which granted equal citizenship to African Americans, and she died nearly twenty years before her dream of woman suffrage was realized in the Nineteenth Amendment (1920). Yet by imagining women's emancipation as an expansion of America's founding principles of citizenship, Stanton charted a path that other feminists would follow a century later.

Historians use the terms "first wave" and "second wave" to distinguish the women's movement of the nineteenth century from that of the late twentieth century. The woman most often credited with launching the "second wave" is Betty Friedan (1921–2006). Friedan had seen her mother sacrifice her own career in journalism to raise a family, and wrote the best-seller *The Feminine Mystique* to expose the quiet desperation of millions of her housewives trapped in the "comfortable concentration camp" of the suburban home. In 1966 Friedan cofounded the National Organization for Women (NOW), the chief political arm of second-wave feminism.

Just as first-wave feminism grew out of abolitionism, the second wave drew ideas, leaders, and tactics from the civil rights movement of the 1960s. Civil rights workers and feminists alike focused on equal rights. NOW campaigned vigorously for an Equal Rights Amendment, which in 1982 fell just three states short of ratification.

Second-wave feminism also had an avowedly radical wing, supported by younger women eager to challenge almost every traditional male and female gender role and to take the feminist cause to the streets. Among these women was Robin Morgan, a civil rights activist in organizations like the Congress of Racial Equality (CORE) and SNCC (Student Non-Violent Coordinating Committee). Women in the movement who protested against gender discrimination met ridicule, as in SNCC leader Stokely Carmichael's retort that "the only position for women in SNCC is prone." Morgan went on to found WITCH (Women's International Terrorist Conspiracy from Hell), made famous by its protest at the 1968 Miss America pageant in Atlantic City, New Jersey. There demonstrators threw symbols of women's oppression—bras, girdles, dishcloths—into trash cans. (Contrary to news stories, they did not burn the bras.)

As the contrast between WITCH and NOW suggests, second-wave feminism was a remarkably diverse movement. Feminists in the late twentieth century disagreed over many issues—from pornography and marriage to how much to expect from government, capitalism, and men. Some feminists placed a priority on gender equality, whereas others defended a feminism of gender difference.

Still, beyond these differences feminists had much in common. Most advocated a woman's right to choose abortion and regarded the law as a key weapon against gender discrimination. By century's end radical and moderate feminists alike could take pride in a host of achievements that had changed the landscape of gender relations. Yet, like Elizabeth Cady Stanton, second-wave feminists also shared the burden of understanding that the goals of genuine equality would take more than a lifetime to achieve.

Inspired by the civil rights movement, Native Americans in the 1970s gained remarkable power through using the courts and well-planned acts of civil disobedience. But while blacks had fought against segregation, Indians used the tactics of the civil rights movement to assert their status as separate semisovereign peoples. Indian activists captured the nation's attention by seizing the island of Alcatraz in 1970 and the village of Wounded Knee, South Dakota, in 1972. In the case of *United States* v. *Wheeler* (1978), the Supreme Court declared that Indian tribes possessed a "unique and limited" sovereignty, subject to the will of Congress but not to individual states.

Online Study Center

Primary source
Sioux Indian Protester
college.hmco.com/pic/kennedybrief7e

The Bicentennial Campaign and the Carter Victory

America's two-hundredth birthday, in 1976, fell during a presidential election year—a fitting coincidence for a proud democracy. Gerald Ford energetically sought nomination for the presidency in his own right and won the Republican nod at the Kansas City convention.

The Democratic standard-bearer was fifty-one-year-old James Earl Carter, Jr., a dark-horse candidate who galloped out of obscurity during the long primary-election season. A former Georgia governor who insisted on humble "Jimmy" as his first name, this **born-again** Baptist touched many people with his down-home sincerity. Untainted by ties with a corrupt and cynical Washington, Carter ran against the memory of Nixon and Watergate as much as he ran against Ford. His most effective campaign pitch was his promise that "I'll never lie to you."

Carter squeezed out a narrow victory on election day, with 51 percent of the popular vote. The electoral count stood at 297 to 240. The winner swept every state except Virginia in his native South. Especially important were the votes of African-Americans, 97 percent of whom cast their ballots for Carter.

Carter enjoyed hefty Democratic majorities in both houses of Congress. Hopes ran high that the stalemate of the Nixon-Ford years between a Republican White House and a Democratic Capitol Hill would now be ended. At first Carter enjoyed notable political success, as Congress granted his requests to create a new cabinet-level Department of Energy and to cut taxes. But Carter's honeymoon did not last long. An inexperienced outsider, he had campaigned against the Washington "establishment" and never quite made the transition to being an insider himself. He repeatedly rubbed congressional fur the wrong way, and critics charged that he isolated himself in a shallow pool of fellow Georgians whose ignorance of the ways of Washington compounded the problems of their greenhorn chief.

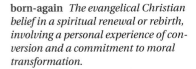

born-again *The evangelical Christian belief in a spiritual renewal or rebirth, involving a personal experience of conversion and a commitment to moral transformation.*

Online Study Center

Primary source
First Success of the Religious Right
college.hmco.com/pic/kennedybrief7e

Carter's Humanitarian Diplomacy

As a committed Christian, President Carter displayed from the outset an overriding concern for human rights as the guiding principle of his foreign policy. In the African nations of Rhodesia (later Zimbabwe) and South Africa, Carter and his eloquent United Nations ambassador, Andrew Young, championed the oppressed black majority.

The president's most spectacular foreign-policy achievement came in September 1978 when he invited President Anwar Sadat of Egypt and Prime Minister Menachem Begin of Israel to the woodsy presidential retreat at Camp David, Maryland, in an attempt to prevent another blowup in the misery-drenched Middle East. Skillfully serving as go-between, Carter persuaded the two visitors to sign an accord (September 17, 1978) under whose terms Israel agreed to withdraw from territory conquered in the 1967 war and Egypt promised to respect Israel's borders. Both parties pledged themselves to sign a formal peace treaty within three months.

Carter achieved further diplomatic success by resuming full diplomatic relations with China in 1979. He also concluded two treaties turning over complete ownership and control of the Panama Canal to the Panamanians by the year 2000.

Despite these dramatic accomplishments, trouble stalked Carter's foreign policy. Overshadowing all international issues was the ominous reheating of the Cold War with the Soviet Union. Détente fell into disrepute as thousands of Cuban troops, assisted by Soviet advisers, appeared in Angola, Ethiopia, and elsewhere in Africa to support revolutionary factions. Arms-control negotiations with Moscow stalled in the face of this Soviet military meddling.

Economic and Energy Woes

Adding to Carter's mushrooming troubles was the failing health of the economy. A stinging recession during Gerald Ford's presidency had temporarily slowed inflation, but virtually from the moment of Carter's inauguration, prices resumed their dizzying ascent, driving the inflation rate well above 13 percent by 1979. The soaring bill for imported oil plunged America's **balance of payments** deeply into the red (an unprecedented $40 billion in 1978).

The "oil shocks" of the 1970s taught Americans a painful but necessary lesson: they could never again seriously consider a policy of economic isolation, as they had tried to do between the two world wars. For most of American history, foreign trade had accounted for no more than 10 percent of gross national product (GNP). But huge foreign-oil bills drove that figure upward in the 1970s so that, by century's end, some 27 percent of GNP depended on foreign trade. Unable to dominate international trade and finance as they once had, Americans would have to master foreign languages and study foreign cultures if they wanted to prosper in the rapidly globalizing economy.

Yawning deficits in the federal budget, reaching nearly $60 billion in 1980, further aggravated the U.S. economy's inflationary ailments. The elderly and other Americans living on fixed incomes suffered from the shrinking dollar. People with money to lend pushed interest rates ever higher. The "prime rate" (the rate of interest that banks charged their very best customers) vaulted to an unheard-of 20 percent in early 1980. The high cost of borrowing money shoved small businesses to the wall and strangled the construction industry.

Carter diagnosed America's economic disease as stemming primarily from the nation's costly dependence on foreign oil. Unfortunately, his legislative proposals in April 1977 for energy conservation ignited a blaze of indifference among the American people, who had already forgotten the long gasoline lines of 1973.

Events in Iran jolted Americans out of their complacency about energy supplies in 1979. The imperious Mohammed Reza Pahlevi, installed as shah of Iran with help from America's CIA in 1953, had long ruled his oil-rich land with a will of steel. His repressive regime was finally overthrown in January 1979 in a violent revolution spearheaded by Muslim fundamentalists. The revolutionary upheavals soon crippled Iran's oil fields. As Iranian oil supplies stopped flowing, Americans once more found themselves waiting impatiently in long lines at gas stations or buying high-priced gasoline only on specified days.

As the oil crisis deepened, President Carter sensed the rising temperature of popular discontent. In July 1979 he retreated to the mountain hideaway of Camp David, where he remained largely out of public view for ten days. Like a royal potentate of old summoning the wise men of the realm for their counsel in a time of crisis, Carter called in over one hundred leaders from all walks of life to give him their views. Meanwhile, the nation anxiously awaited the results of these extraordinary deliberations.

balance of payments *The net ratio, expressed as a positive or negative sum, of a nation's exports in relation to its imports. (It may be calculated in relation to one particular foreign nation, or to all foreign states collectively.)*

President Jimmy Carter (b. 1924) delivered what became known as his "malaise" speech (although he never used the word) on television in 1979. In time cultural conservatives would take up his theme to support their call for a return to "traditional values":

"In a nation that was proud of hard work, strong families, close-knit communities, and our faith in God, too many of us now tend to worship self-indulgence and consumption. Human identity is no longer defined by what one does, but by what one owns. But we've discovered that owning things and consuming things does not satisfy our longing for meaning. We've learned that piling up material goods cannot fill the emptiness of lives which have no confidence or purpose. . . . The symptoms of this crisis of the American spirit are all around us."

When Carter finally came down from the mountaintop on July 15, 1979, he stunned and perplexed the nation by chiding his fellow citizens for falling into a "moral and spiritual crisis" and for being too concerned with "material goods." A few days later, the president fired four of his cabinet secretaries and circled the wagons of his Georgia advisers more tightly about the White House. Critics began to wonder aloud whether Carter, the professed man of the people, was losing touch with the popular mood of the country.

Foreign Affairs and the Iranian Imbroglio

Hopes for a less dangerous world rose slightly in June 1979, when President Carter met with Soviet leader Leonid Brezhnev in Vienna to sign the long-stalled SALT II agreements, limiting the levels of lethal strategic weapons in the Soviet and American arsenals. But conservative critics of the president's defense policies, still regarding the Soviet Union as the Wicked Witch of the East, unsheathed their long knives to carve up the SALT treaty when it came to the Senate for debate in the summer of 1979.

Political earthquakes in the petroleum-rich Persian Gulf region finally buried all hopes of ratifying the SALT II treaty. On November 4, 1979, a howling mob of rabidly anti-American Muslim militants stormed the United States embassy in Teheran, Iran, and took all of its occupants hostage. The captors demanded that American authorities ship the exiled shah from the United States back to Iran. Americans agonized over both the fate of the hostages and the stability of the entire Persian Gulf region, so dangerously close to the Soviet Union. The Soviet army then aroused the West's worst fears on December 27, 1979, when it blitzed into the mountainous nation of Afghanistan, next door to Iran, and appeared to be poised for a thrust at the oil jugular of the gulf.

President Carter reacted vigorously to these alarming events. He slapped an embargo on the export of grain and high-technology machinery to the USSR, called for a boycott of the upcoming Olympic Games in Moscow, and requested that young people (including women) be made to register for a possible military draft. Proclaiming that the United States would "use any means necessary, including force," to protect the Persian Gulf against Soviet incursions, Carter grimly conceded that he had misjudged the Soviets. The SALT treaty became a dead letter in the Senate. Meanwhile, the Soviet army met unexpectedly stiff resistance in Afghanistan and became bogged down in a nasty, decade-long guerrilla war that came to be called "Russia's Vietnam."

The Iranian hostage crisis was Carter's—and America's—bed of nails. The captured Americans languished in cruel captivity, while the nightly news broadcasts showed humiliating scenes of Iranian mobs burning the American flag and spitting on effigies of Uncle Sam.

Carter at first tried to apply economic sanctions and the pressure of world opinion against the Iranians. But the president's frustration grew as the political turmoil in Iran rumbled on endlessly. Carter at last ordered a daring rescue mission. A highly trained **commando** team penetrated deep into Iran's sandy interior, but when equipment failures prevented some members of the team from reaching their destination, the mission had to be scrapped. As the commandos withdrew in the dark desert night, two of their aircraft collided, killing eight of the would-be rescuers.

commando *Member of a small, elite military force trained to carry out difficult missions, often within territory controlled by the enemy.*

The disastrous failure of the rescue raid proved anguishing for Americans. The episode seemed to underscore the nation's helplessness and even incompetence in the face of a mortifying insult to the national honor. The stalemate with Iran dragged on throughout the rest of Carter's term, providing an embarrassing backdrop to the embattled president's struggle for reelection.

★ Chapter Summary ★

Nixon's "Vietnamization" policy reduced American ground participation in the war, but his Cambodia invasion sparked massive protest. Nixon's journeys to Communist Moscow and Beijing (Peking) established a new rapprochement with these powers. In domestic policy, Nixon and the Supreme Court promoted affirmative action and environmental protection.

Nixon's landslide 1972 election victory was negated as the widespread Watergate scandal erupted. A cease-fire provided cover for withdrawal of the last American troops from Vietnam, but Congressional protest over the secret bombing of Cambodia led to the War Powers Act. The Middle East War of 1973 and the Arab oil embargo created an energy and economic crisis that lasted through the decade and ended the long era of postwar prosperity. Americans gradually awoke to their costly and dangerous dependence on Middle Eastern oil, and began to take tentative steps toward conservation and alternative energy sources.

Nonelected Gerald Ford took over after Watergate forced Nixon to resign. The Communist Vietnamese finally overran the South Vietnamese government in 1975. The defeat in Vietnam added to a general sense of disillusionment with government and society and a new sense of the limits of American power. The major social movement to survive the sixties was feminism, which achieved widespread social breakthroughs though failing to pass the Equal Rights Amendment. Race remained an explosive issue, as divisive issues of busing and affirmative action eroded the good will created by the civil rights movement.

Campaigning against Watergate and a corrupt Washington, outsider Jimmy Carter won a slender victory over Ford in 1976, but proved unable to work with Congress or improve the economy once he took office. His Camp David agreement brought peace between Egypt and Israel, but the Iranian revolution led to a new energy crisis that compounded already severe inflation and recession. The Soviet invasion of Afghanistan and the holding of American hostages in Iran added to Carter's woes and a general American sense of frustration and helplessness.

40

The Resurgence of Conservatism

1980–1992

IT WILL BE MY INTENTION TO CURB THE SIZE AND INFLUENCE
OF THE FEDERAL ESTABLISHMENT AND TO DEMAND
RECOGNITION OF THE DISTINCTION BETWEEN THE POWERS
GRANTED TO THE FEDERAL GOVERNMENT AND THOSE RESERVED
TO THE STATES OR TO THE PEOPLE.

RONALD REAGAN, INAUGURAL ADDRESS, 1981

Chapter Outline

- ⭐ The "New Right" and Reagan's Election, 1980
- ⭐ Budget Battles and Tax Cuts
- ⭐ Reagan and the Soviets
- ⭐ The Iran-Contra Scandal
- ⭐ Reagan's Economic Legacy
- ⭐ Reagan and the "Social Issues"
- ⭐ The Election of George Bush, 1988
- ⭐ The End of the Cold War
- ⭐ The Persian Gulf War, 1991
- ⭐ Bush's Battles at Home
- ⭐ Varying Viewpoints: Where Did Modern Conservatism Come From?

"It's morning in America" was the slogan of Republican candidate Ronald Reagan in his 1980 presidential campaign. Certainly the 1980s were a new day for America's conservative right. Census figures confirmed that the average American was older than in the stormy sixties and much more likely to live in the South or West, the traditional bastions of the "Old Right," where many residents harbored suspicions of federal power. The conservative cause drew added strength from the emergence of a "New Right" movement, partly in response to the countercultural protests of the 1960s. Spearheading the New Right were evangelical Christian groups such as the Moral Majority, dedicated believers who enjoyed startling success as political fund-raisers and organizers.

Many New Right activists were far less agitated about economic questions than about cultural concerns—the so-called social issues. They denounced abortion, pornography, homosexuality, feminism, and especially affirmative action. They championed prayer in the schools and tougher penalties for criminals. Together, the Old and New Right added up to a powerful political combination, devoted to changing the very character of American society.

Focus Questions

1. What social and cultural developments led to the dramatic rise of Ronald Reagan and the "new right" in the early 1980s?
2. What were the essential elements of the "Reagan revolution" in economic and social policy, and what were Reaganism's short-term and long-term consequences?
3. How did the renewed Cold War of the early 1980s eventually lead to the Reagan-Gorbachev agreements of the late 1980s and the end of the Cold War? What caused the collapse of communism and the Soviet Union in 1989–1991?
4. How did the religious right transform American politics, and how did issues like abortion and affirmative action create disagreement in the Supreme Court and the country?
5. How did the United States become more involved in the Middle East, leading up to the military intervention of the Persian Gulf War?

> *In a speech to the National Association of Evangelicals on March 8, 1983, President Ronald Reagan (1911–2004) defined his stand on school prayer:*
>
> "The Declaration of Independence mentions the Supreme Being no less than four times. 'In God We Trust' is engraved on our coinage. The Supreme Court opens its proceedings with a religious invocation. And the Members of Congress open their sessions with a prayer. I just happen to believe the schoolchildren of the United States are entitled to the same privileges as Supreme Court Justices and Congressmen."

Online Study Center

Primary source
Re-elect Carter-Mondale
college.hmco.com/pic/kennedybrief7e

■ **President Ronald Reagan** The oldest man ever elected to the presidency, Reagan displayed youthful vigor both on the campaign trail and in office.

The Election of Ronald Reagan, 1980

Ronald Reagan was well suited to lead the gathering conservative crusade. Reared in a generation whose values were formed well before the upheavals of the 1960s, he naturally sided with the New Right on social issues. In economic and social matters alike, he denounced the activist government and failed "social engineering" of the 1960s. Just as his early political hero, Franklin Roosevelt, had championed the "forgotten man" against big business, Reagan championed the "common man" against big government. He aimed especially to win over from the Democratic column working-class and lower-middle-class white voters by implying that the Democratic party had become the exclusive tool of its minority constituents.

Though Reagan was no intellectual, he drew on the ideas of a small but influential group of thinkers known as "**neoconservatives.**" Their ranks included Norman Podhoretz, editor of *Commentary* magazine, and Irving Kristol, editor of *The Public Interest*. Reacting against what they saw as the excesses of 1960s liberalism, the neoconservatives championed free-market capitalism liberated from government restraints, and they took tough, harshly anti-Soviet positions in foreign policy. They also questioned liberal welfare programs and affirmative-action policies and called for reassertion of traditional values of individualism and the centrality of the family.

An actor-turned-politician, Reagan enjoyed enormous popularity with his crooked grin and aw-shucks manner. The son of an impoverished Irish-American father from a small Illinois town, Reagan got his start in the depressed 1930s as a radio sports announcer. He became a B-grade Hollywood star in the 1940s, and helped purge communists from the Screen Actors Guild as the organization's president in the 1950s. In 1954 he became a spokesman for General Electric and began preaching a conservative, antigovernment line. Reagan's growing skill at promoting the conservative cause inspired a group of wealthy California businessmen to help him launch his political career as governor of California from 1966 to 1974.

By 1980 the Republican party was ready to challenge the Democrats' hold on the White House. Bedeviled abroad and becalmed at home, Jimmy Carter's administration struck many Americans as bungling and befuddled. Carter's inability to control double-digit inflation was especially damaging. Disaffection with Carter's apparent ineptitude ran deep even in his own Democratic party, where an "ABC" (Anybody But Carter) movement gathered steam. The liberal wing of the party found their champion in Senator Edward Kennedy of Massachusetts, the last survivor of the assassin-plagued Kennedy brothers. He and Carter slugged it out in a series of bruising primary elections, while delighted Republicans decorously proceeded to name Reagan their presidential nominee. In the end Kennedy's candidacy fell victim to the country's conservative mood and to lingering suspicions about a 1969 automobile accident on Chappaquiddick Island, Massachusetts, in which a young woman assistant was drowned when Kennedy's car plunged off a bridge. A badly battered Carter, his party divided and in disarray, was left to do battle with Reagan.

Chronology

1980	Reagan defeats Carter for presidency.
1981	Iran releases American hostages. "Reaganomics" spending and tax cuts passed. Solidarity movement in Poland. O'Connor appointed to Supreme Court (first woman justice).
1981–1991	United States aids anti-leftist forces in Central America.
1982	Recession hits U.S. economy.
1983	Reagan announces SDI plan (Star Wars). U.S. marines killed in Lebanon. U.S. invasion of Grenada.
1984	Reagan defeats Mondale for presidency.
1985	Gorbachev comes to power in Soviet Union. First Reagan-Gorbachev summit meeting, in Geneva.
1986	Iran-contra scandal revealed. Second Reagan-Gorbachev summit meeting, in Reykjavik, Iceland.
1987	Stock-market plunges 508 points. Senate rejects Supreme Court nomination of Robert Bork.

	Third Reagan-Gorbachev summit meeting, in Washington, D.C.; INF Treaty signed.
1988	Fourth Reagan-Gorbachev summit meeting, in Moscow. Bush defeats Dukakis for presidency.
1989	Chinese government suppresses prodemocracy demonstrators. *Webster* v. *Reproductive Health Services.* Eastern Europe throws off communist regimes. Berlin Wall torn down.
1990	Iraq invades Kuwait. East and West Germany reunite. Americans with Disabilities Act (ADA).
1991	Persian Gulf War. Thomas appointed to Supreme Court. Gorbachev resigns as Soviet president. Soviet Union dissolves.
1992	Twenty-seventh Amendment (prohibiting congressional pay raises from taking effect until an election seats a new session of Congress) ratified. *Planned Parenthood* v. *Casey.*

The Republican candidate proved to be a formidable campaigner. Using his professional acting skills to great advantage, Reagan attacked the incumbent's fumbling performance in foreign policy and blasted the Democratic party's "big-government philosophy." Galloping inflation, sky-high interest rates, and a faltering economy also put the incumbent president on the defensive. Carter countered ineffectively with charges that Reagan was a trigger-happy cold warrior who might push the country into nuclear war.

Carter's spotty record in office was no defense against Reagan's popular appeal. On election day the Republican rang up a spectacular victory, bagging over 51 percent of the popular vote, while 41 percent went to Carter and 7 percent to independent candidate John Anderson. The electoral count stood at 489 for Reagan and 49 for Carter, making him the first elected president to be unseated by the voters since Herbert Hoover in 1932. Equally startling, the Republicans gained control of the Senate for the first time in twenty-five years. Leading Democratic liberals who had been targeted for defeat by well-heeled New Right groups went down like dead timber in the conservative windstorm that swept the country.

Carter showed dignity in defeat. An unusually intelligent, articulate, and well-meaning president, he had been hampered by his lack of managerial talent and badly buffeted by events beyond his control, such as the soaring price of oil, runaway inflation, and the galling insult of the continuing hostage crisis in Iran. Though unsuccessful in the White House, Carter earned much admiration in later years for his humanitarian and human rights activities. He received the Nobel Peace Prize in 2002.

neoconservatives (neoconservatism) *Political activists and thinkers, mostly former liberals, who turned to a defense of traditional social and moral values and a strongly anticommunist foreign policy in the 1970s and 1980s.*

The Reagan Revolution

Reagan's arrival in Washington was triumphal. The Iranians contributed to the festive mood by releasing the hostages on Reagan's Inauguration Day, January 20, 1981, after 444 days of captivity. The new president, a hale and hearty sixty-nine-year-old, was devoted to fiscal fitness and a leaner federal government. He sought nothing less than the dismantling of the welfare state and the reversal of the political evolution of the preceding half century. Years of New Deal–style tax-and-spend programs, Reagan jested, had created a federal government that reminded him of the definition of a baby as a creature who was all appetite at one end, with no sense of responsibility at the other.

By the early 1980s, this antigovernment message found a receptive audience. In the two decades since 1960, federal spending had risen from about 18 percent of gross national product to nearly 23 percent. After four decades of advancing New Deal and Great Society programs, a strong countercurrent took hold. Californians staged a "tax revolt" in 1978 (known by its official ballot title of "Proposition 13") that slashed property taxes and forced painful cuts in government services. The California "tax quake" jolted other state capitals and rocked even Washington, D.C. Ronald Reagan had ridden this political shock wave to presidential victory in 1980 and proceeded to rattle the "**welfare state**" to its very foundations

Reagan pursued his smaller-government policies with near-religious zeal and remarkable effectiveness. He proposed a new federal budget that necessitated cuts of some $35 billion, mostly in social programs like food stamps and federally funded job-training centers. Reagan worked naturally in harness with the Republican majority in the Senate, while in the Democratic House he enterprisingly wooed a group of mostly southern conservative Democrats (dubbed "boll weevils"), who abandoned their own party's leadership to follow the president.

Then on March 30, 1981, a deranged gunman shot the president as he was leaving a Washington hotel. A .22-caliber bullet penetrated beneath Reagan's left arm and collapsed his left lung. With admirable courage and grace, and with impressive physical resilience for a man his age, Reagan seemed to recover rapidly from his violent ordeal. Twelve days after the attack, he walked out of the hospital and returned to work. When he appeared a few days later on national television to address the Congress and the public on his budget, the outpouring of sympathy and support was enormous.

welfare state *The political system, typical of modern industrial societies, in which government assumes responsibility for the economic well-being of its citizens by providing social benefits.*

supply-side *In economics, the theory that investment incentives such as lowered federal spending and tax cuts will stimulate economic growth and increased employment.*

The Battle of the Budget

Swept along on a tide of presidential popularity, Congress swallowed Reagan's budget proposals. The new president's triumph amazed political observers, especially defeated Democrats. He had descended on Washington like an avenging angel of conservatism, kicking up a blinding whirlwind of political change. His impressive performance demonstrated the power of the presidency with a skill not seen since Lyndon Johnson's day.

Reagan hardly rested to savor the sweetness of his victory. The second part of his economic program called for deep tax cuts, amounting to 25 percent across-the-board reductions over a period of three years. Thanks largely to Reagan's skill as a television performer and the continued defection of the "boll weevils" from the Democratic camp, the president again had his way. In late 1981 Congress approved a set of far-reaching tax reforms that lowered individual tax rates, reduced federal estate taxes, and created new tax-free savings plans for small investors. Reagan's "**supply-side**" economic advisers assured him that the combination of budgetary discipline and tax reduction would stimulate new investment, boost productivity, foster dramatic economic growth, and eventually even reduce the deficit.

But at first supply-side economics seemed to be a beautiful theory mugged by a gang of brutal facts, as the economy slid into its deepest recession since the 1930s. Unemployment reached nearly 11 percent in 1982, businesses folded, and several bank failures jolted the nation's entire financial system. The automobile industry, once the brightest jewel in America's industrial crown, reported losses in the hundreds of millions of dollars.

Ignoring the yawping pack of Democratic critics, President Reagan and his economic advisers serenely waited for their supply-side economic policies ("Reaganomics") to produce the promised results. The supply-siders seemed to be vindicated when a healthy economic recovery finally got under way in 1983. Yet the economy of the 1980s was not uniformly sound. For the first time in the twentieth century, income gaps widened between the richest and the poorest Americans. The poor got poorer and the very rich grew fabulously richer, while middle-class incomes largely stagnated. Symbolic of the new income stratification was the emergence of "yuppies," or young urban professionals. Sporting Rolex watches and BMW sports cars, they made a near-religion out of conspicuous consumption. Though numbering only about 1.5 million people, yuppies showcased the values of materialism and the pursuit of wealth that came to symbolize the high-rolling 1980s.

Some economists located the sources of the economic upturn neither in the president's budget cuts and tax reforms nor in the go-get-'em avarice of the yuppies. Rather, they pointed to his massive expenditures for the military. Reagan cascaded nearly 2 trillion dollars onto the Pentagon in the 1980s, asserting the need to close the "window of vulnerability" in the armaments race with the Soviet Union. Ironically, this conservative president thereby plunged the government into a red-ink bath of deficit spending that made the New Deal look downright stingy. Federal budget deficits topped $100 billion in 1982, and the government's books were nearly $200 billion out of balance in every subsequent year of the 1980s. Massive government borrowing to cover these deficits kept interest rates high. The soaring dollar caused by high interest rates dealt crippling blows to American exporters, as the American international trade deficit reached a record $152 billion in 1987. The masters of international commerce and finance for a generation after World War II, Americans suddenly became the world's heaviest borrowers in the global economy of the 1980s.

Online Study Center

Primary source
Federal Budget, The
college.hmco.com/pic/kennedybrief7e

Reagan Renews the Cold War

Hard as nails toward the Soviet Union in his campaign speeches, Reagan saw no reason to soften up after he checked in at the White House. He claimed that the Soviets were "prepared to commit any crime, to lie, to cheat" in pursuit of their goals of world conquest. He denounced the Soviet empire as "the focus of evil in the modern world."

Reagan believed in negotiating with the Soviets—but only from a position of overwhelming strength. Accordingly, his strategy for dealing with Moscow was simple: by enormously expanding U.S. military capabilities, he could threaten the Soviet leaders with a fantastically expensive new round of the arms race. Desperate to avoid economic ruin, Kremlin leaders would come to the bargaining table and sing Reagan's tune.

This strategy resembled a riverboat gambler's ploy. It wagered the enormous sum of Reagan's defense budgets on the hope that the other side would not call Washington's bluff and initiate a new cycle of arms competition. Reagan played his trump card in this risky game in March 1983 when he announced his intention to pursue a high-technology missile defense system called the Strategic Defense Initiative (SDI), popularly known as "Star Wars." The plan called for orbiting battle stations in space that could fire laser beams or other forms of concentrated energy to vaporize intercontinental missiles on liftoff. Most scientists considered this an impossible goal, but the deeper logic of SDI lay in its fit with Reagan's overall Soviet strategy. By pitching the arms contest onto a stratospherically high plane of technology and astronomical expense, it would further force the Kremlin's hand.

Relations with the Soviets further nose-dived in late 1981 when the government of Poland, needled by a popular union movement called "Solidarity," clamped martial law on the troubled country. Seeing the heavy fist of the Kremlin inside this Polish iron glove, Reagan imposed economic sanctions on Poland and the USSR alike.

oligarchs *A small, elite class of authoritarian rulers.*

Dealing with the Soviet Union was additionally complicated by the inertia and ill health of the aging **oligarchs** in the Kremlin, three of whom died between late 1982 and early 1985. Relations grew even more tense when the Soviets, in September 1983, blasted from the skies over their country a Korean airliner, plummeting hundreds of civilians, including many Americans, to their deaths. By the end of 1983, all arms-control negotiations with the Soviets were broken off. The deepening chill in the Cold War was further felt in 1984, when USSR and Soviet-bloc athletes boycotted the Olympic Games in Los Angeles.

Troubles Abroad

The volatile Middle Eastern pot continued to boil ominously. Israel badly strained its bonds of friendship with the United States by continuing to allow new settlements to be established in the occupied territory of the Jordan River's West Bank. Israel further raised the stakes in the Middle East in June 1982 when it invaded neighboring Lebanon, seeking to suppress once and for all the guerrilla bases from which Palestinian fighters harassed beleaguered Israel. The Palestinians were bloodily subdued, but Lebanon, already pulverized by years of episodic civil war, was plunged into armed chaos.

President Reagan sent American troops to Lebanon in 1983 as part of an international peacekeeping force, but their presence did not bring peace. A suicidal bomber crashed an explosives-laden truck into U.S. Marine Corps barracks on October 23, 1983, killing more than two hundred marines. President Reagan soon thereafter withdrew the remaining American troops, while miraculously suffering no political damage from this horrifying and humiliating attack. His mystified Democratic opponents began to call him a "Teflon president," to whom nothing hurtful could stick.

Central America, in the United States' own backyard, also rumbled menacingly. A leftist revolution had deposed the long-time dictator of Nicaragua in 1979. President Carter had tried to ignore the hotly anti-American rhetoric of the revolutionaries, known as "Sandinistas," and to establish good diplomatic relations with them. But cold warrior Reagan took their words at face value and hurled back at them some hot language of his own.

Reagan accused the Sandinistas of turning their country into a forward base for Soviet and Cuban military penetration of all of Central America. Brandishing

Online Study Center

Interactive map
The Mideast Crisis, 1980–2002
college.hmco.com/pic/kennedybrief7e

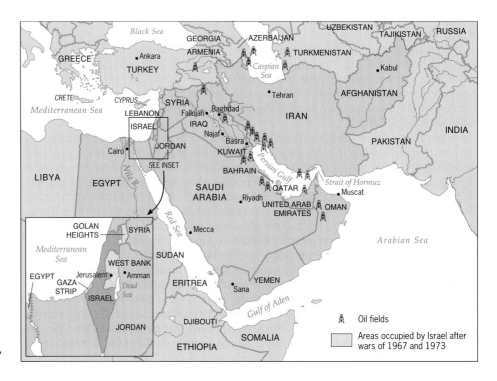

■ **The Middle East** A combination of political instability and precious petroleum resources has made the region from Egypt to Afghanistan an "arc of crisis."

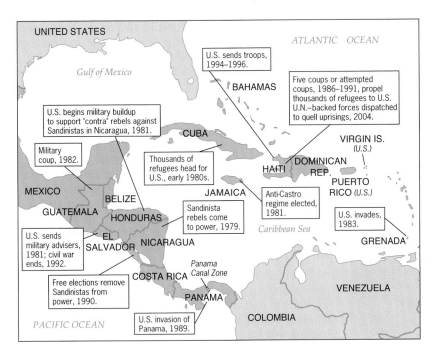

■ Central America and the Caribbean
This region of historic importance to the United States continued to be restless in the early twenty-first century.

photographs taken from high-flying spy planes, administration officials claimed that Nicaraguan leftists were shipping weapons to revolutionary forces in tiny El Salvador, torn by violence since a coup in 1979. Reagan sent military "advisers" to prop up the pro-American government of El Salvador. He also provided covert aid, including the CIA-engineered mining of harbors, to the "contra" rebels opposing the anti-American Sandinista government of Nicaragua.

Reagan flexed his military muscles elsewhere in the turbulent Caribbean. In a dramatic display of American might, in October 1983 he dispatched a heavy-firepower invasion force to the island of Grenada, where a military coup had killed the prime minister and brought Marxists to power. Swiftly overrunning the tiny island, American troops vividly demonstrated Reagan's determination to assert the dominance of the United States in the Caribbean, just as Theodore Roosevelt had done.

Round Two for Reagan

A confident Ronald Reagan, bolstered by a buoyant economy at home and by the popularity of his muscular posture abroad, handily won the Republican nomination in 1984 for a second White House term. His Democratic opponent was former Vice President Walter Mondale, who made history by naming as his own vice-presidential running mate Congresswoman Geraldine Ferraro of New York. She was the first woman ever to appear on a major party presidential ticket. But even this dramatic gesture could not salvage Mondale's candidacy. On election day Reagan walked away with 525 electoral votes to Mondale's 13, winning everywhere except in Mondale's home state of Minnesota and the District of Columbia. Reagan also overwhelmed Mondale in the popular vote—52,609,797 to 36,450,613.

Shrinking the federal government and reducing taxes had been the main objectives of Reagan's first term; foreign-policy issues dominated his second term. The president soon found himself contending for the world's attention with a charismatic new Soviet leader, Mikhail Gorbachev, installed as chairman of the Soviet Communist party in March 1985. Gorbachev was personable, energetic, imaginative, and committed to radical reforms in the Soviet Union. He announced two policies with remarkable, even revolutionary, implications. *Glasnost,* or "openness," aimed to ventilate the secretive, repressive stuffiness of Soviet society by introducing free speech and a measure of political liberty. *Perestroika,* or

■ **Contra Rebel Troops Head for Battle**   These rebels were long-seasoned and battle-scarred veterans of Nicaragua's civil war by the time this photograph was taken in 1987.

"restructuring," was intended to revive the moribund Soviet economy by adopting many of the free-market practices of the capitalist West.

Both *glasnost* and *perestroika* required that the Soviet Union shrink the size of its enormous military machine and redirect its energies to the civilian economy. That requirement, in turn, necessitated an end to the Cold War. Gorbachev accordingly made warm overtures to the West, including an announcement in April 1985 that the Soviet Union would cease to deploy intermediate-range nuclear forces (INF) targeted on Western Europe, pending an agreement on their complete elimination. He pushed this goal when he met with Ronald Reagan at their first of four summit meetings, in Geneva in November 1985. A second summit meeting in Reykjavik, Iceland, in October 1986 broke down in stalemate, but at a third summit in Washington, D.C., in December 1987, the two leaders at last signed the INF Treaty, banning all intermediate-range nuclear missiles from Europe.

Reagan and Gorbachev capped their new friendship in May 1988 at a final summit in Moscow. There President Reagan, who had entered office condemning the "evil empire" of Soviet communism, warmly praised Gorbachev. Reagan, the consummate cold warrior, had been flexible and savvy enough to seize a historic opportunity to join with the Soviet chief to bring the Cold War to a kind of conclusion. For this, history would give both leaders high marks.

The Iran-Contra Imbroglio

Two foreign-policy problems seemed insoluble to Reagan: the continuing captivity of a number of American hostages seized by Muslim extremist groups in bleeding, battered Lebanon; and the continuing grip on power of the left-wing Sandinista government in Nicaragua. The president repeatedly requested that Congress provide military aid to the contra rebels fighting against the Sandinista regime. Congress repeatedly refused, and the administration grew increasingly frustrated, even obsessed, in its search for a means to help the contras.

Unbeknownst to the American public, some Washington officials saw a possible linkage between the two thorny problems of the Middle Eastern hostages and the Central American Sandinistas. In 1985 American diplomats secretly arranged arms sales to embattled Iran in return for Iranian aid in obtaining the release of American hostages held by Middle Eastern terrorists. At least one hostage was eventually set free. Meanwhile, money from the payment for the arms was diverted to the contras. These actions brazenly violated a congressional ban on military aid to the Nicaraguan rebels—not to mention Reagan's repeated vow that he would never negotiate with terrorists.

News of these secret dealings broke in November 1986 and ignited a firestorm of controversy. President Reagan claimed he was innocent of wrongdoing and ignorant about the activities of his subordinates, but a congressional committee condemned the "secrecy, deception, and disdain for the law" displayed by administration officials and concluded that "if the president did not know what his national security advisers were doing, he should have."

The Iran-contra affair cast a dark shadow over Reagan's record in foreign policy, tending to obscure the president's achievement in establishing a new relationship with the

Online Study Center

Primary source
Oliver North Testimony
college.hmco.com/pic/kennedybrief7e

On March 4, 1987, President Ronald Reagan somewhat confusingly tried to explain his role (or lack of role) in the arms-for-hostages deal with Iran:

"A few months ago I told the American people I did not trade arms for hostages. My heart and my best intentions still tell me that is true, but the facts and the evidence tell me it is not."

Soviets. Although the several Iran-contra investigations presented damaging revelations of Reagan's weaknesses and laziness as a chief executive, he remained among the most popular and beloved presidents in modern American history.

Reagan's Economic Legacy

Ronald Reagan had taken office vowing to invigorate the American economy by rolling back government regulations, lowering taxes, and balancing the budget. He did ease many regulatory rules, and he pushed major tax-reform bills through Congress in 1981 and 1986. But a balanced budget remained grotesquely out of reach. The combination of tax reduction and huge increases in military spending opened a vast "revenue hole" of $200 billion in annual deficits. In his eight years in office, President Reagan added nearly $2 trillion to the national debt—more than all his predecessors combined.

The staggering deficits of the Reagan years assuredly constituted a great economic failure. And because foreign lenders, especially the Japanese, financed so much of the Reagan-era debt, the deficits virtually guaranteed that future generations of Americans would have to either work harder than their parents, lower their standard of living, or both to pay their foreign creditors.

But if the deficits represented an economic failure, they also constituted, strangely enough, a kind of political triumph. By making new social spending both practically and politically impossible, the deficits achieved one of Reagan's paramount goals: slowing the growth of government and blocking or even repealing the social programs launched in the era of Lyndon Johnson's Great Society. They achieved, in short, Reagan's highest political objective: the containment of the welfare state. Ronald Reagan thus ensured the long-term perpetuation of his values to a degree that few presidents have managed to achieve. For better or worse, the consequences of "Reaganomics" would be large and durable.

> *Hollywood director Oliver Stone's (b. 1946) film* Wall Street *both romanticized and vilified the business culture of the 1980s. The character of Gordon Gekko, inspired by real-life corporate raider Ivan Boesky, captured the spirit of the times:*
>
> "Ladies and gentlemen, greed is good. Greed works, greed is right. . . . Greed for life, money, love, knowledge, has marked the upward surge of mankind—and greed, mark my words, will save the malfunctioning corporation called the U.S.A."

The Religious Right

Religion pervaded American politics in the 1980s. Especially conspicuous was a coalition of conservative evangelical Christians known as the religious right. In 1979 the Reverend Jerry Falwell, an evangelical minister from Lynchburg, Virginia, founded a political organization called the Moral Majority. Falwell preached with great success against sexual permissiveness, abortion, feminism, and the spread of gay rights. In its first two years, the Moral Majority registered between 2 million and 3 million voters. Using radio, direct-mail marketing, and cable TV, "televangelists" reached huge audiences in the 1980s, collected millions of dollars, and became aggressive political advocates of conservative causes.

Members of the religious right were sometimes called "movement conservatives," a term that recalls the left-wing protest movements of the 1960s. In many ways the religious right of the 1980s was a reflection of, or an answer to, sixties radicalism. Feminists in the 1960s declared that "the personal was political." The religious right did the same. What had in the past been personal matters—gender roles, homosexuality, and prayer—became the organizing ground for a powerful political movement. Like advocates of multiculturalism and affirmative action, the religious right practiced a form of "identity politics." But rather than defining themselves as Latino voters or gay voters, they declared themselves Christian or pro-life voters. The New Right also mimicked the New Left in some of its tactics. If the left had consciousness-raising sessions, the right had prayer meetings. If protesters in the 1960s blocked entrances to draft offices, protesters in the 1980s blocked entrances to abortion clinics.

Online Study Center

Primary source
Teenagers Against Abortion
college.hmco.com/pic/kennedybrief7e

Several leaders of the religious right fell from grace by engaging in financial or sexual misconduct in the latter part of the decade. But such scandals would not shake the faith of America's conservative Christians or diminish the new political clout of activist, evangelical religionists.

Conservatism in the Courts

If the budget was Reagan's chief weapon in the war against the welfare state, the courts became his principal instrument in the "cultural wars" demanded by the religious right. By the time he left office, Reagan had appointed a near-majority of all sitting federal judges. Equally important, he had named three conservative-minded justices to the U.S. Supreme Court. They included Sandra Day O'Connor, a brilliant, public-spirited Arizona judge. When she was sworn in on September 25, 1981, she became the first woman to ascend to the high bench in the Court's nearly two-hundred-year history.

Reaganism repudiated two great icons of the liberal political culture: affirmative action and abortion. The Court showed its newly conservative colors in 1984, when it decreed, in a case involving Memphis fire fighters, that union rules about job seniority could outweigh affirmative-action concerns in guiding promotion policies in the city's fire department. In two cases in 1989 (*Ward's Cove Packing* v. *Antonia* and *Martin* v. *Wilks*), the Court made it more difficult to prove that an employer practiced racial discrimination in hiring and made it easier for white males to argue that they were the victims of reverse discrimination. Congress passed legislation in 1991 that partially limited the effects of these decisions.

The contentious issue of abortion also reached the Court in 1989. In the case of *Roe* v. *Wade* in 1973, the Supreme Court had prohibited states from making laws that interfered with a woman's right to an abortion during the early months of pregnancy. For nearly two decades, that decision had been the bedrock principle on which "pro-choice" advocates built their case for abortion rights. It had also provoked bitter criticism from Roman Catholics and various "right-to-life" groups, who wanted a virtually absolute ban on all abortions. In *Webster* v. *Reproductive Health Services*, the Court in July 1989 did not entirely overturn *Roe*, but it seriously compromised *Roe*'s protection of abortion rights. By approving a Missouri law that imposed certain restrictions on abortion, the Court signaled that it was inviting the states to legislate in an area in which *Roe* had previously forbidden them to legislate.

Right-to-life advocates were at first delighted by the *Webster* decision. But the Court's ruling also galvanized pro-choice organizations into a new militancy. Bruising, divisive battles loomed as state legislatures across the land confronted abortion. This painful cultural conflict over the unborn was also part of the Reagan era's bequest to the future.

Referendum on Reaganism in 1988

Republicans lost control of the Senate in the off-year elections of November 1986. Hopes rose among Democrats that the "Reagan revolution" might be showing signs of political vulnerability at last. The newly Democratic majority in the Senate flexed its political muscle in 1987 when it rejected Robert Bork, Reagan's ultraconservative nominee for a Supreme Court vacancy. Democrats also relished the prospect of making political hay out of both the Iran-contra scandal and the allegedly unethical behavior that tainted an unusually large number of Reagan's "official family."

Disquieting signs of economic trouble also seemed to open political opportunities for Democrats. The double mountain of deficits—the federal budget deficit and international trade deficit—continued to mount ominously. Falling real estate prices caused hundreds of savings and loan (S&L) institutions to fail, especially in the Southwest. A massive federal rescue operation for the S&Ls cost well over $500 billion. A wave of mergers, acquisitions, and **leveraged buyouts** washed over Wall Street, leaving many brokers and traders megarich and many companies saddled

leveraged buyouts *The purchase of one company by another using money borrowed on the expectation of selling a portion of assets after the acquisition.*

with megadebt. A cold spasm of fear struck the money markets on "Black Monday," October 19, 1987, when the leading stock-market index plunged 508 points—the largest one-day decline in history. This crash, said *Newsweek* magazine, heralded "the final collapse of the money culture . . ., the death knell of the 1980s." But as Mark Twain famously commented about his own obituary, this announcement proved premature.

Hoping to cash in on these ethical and economic anxieties, a pack of Democrats—dubbed the "Seven Dwarfs" by derisive Republicans—chased after their party's 1988 presidential nomination. The handsome and charismatic Democratic front runner, former Colorado senator Gary Hart, was forced to drop out of the race after charges of sexual misconduct. African American candidate Jesse Jackson, a rousing speechmaker who hoped to forge a "rainbow coalition" of minorities and the disadvantaged, campaigned energetically. But the Democratic nomination in the end went to the coolly cerebral governor of Massachusetts, Michael Dukakis. Republicans nominated Reagan's vice president, George Bush, who ran largely on the Reagan record of tax cuts, strong defense policies, toughness on crime, opposition to abortion, and a long-running if hardly robust economic expansion. Dukakis made little headway exploiting the ethical and economic sore spots and came across to television viewers as almost supernaturally devoid of emotion. On election day the voters gave him just 41,016,429 votes to 47,946,422 for Bush. The Electoral College count was 111 to 426.

Online Study Center

Primary source
ACT UP Activists at the DNC, Atlanta, GA
college.hmco.com/pic/kennedybrief7e

autocratic (autocracy) *Relating to authoritarian or repressive government or institutional practices.*

George Bush and the End of the Cold War

George Herbert Walker Bush was born with a silver spoon in his mouth. His father had served as a U.S. senator from Connecticut, and young George enjoyed a first-rate education at Yale. After service in World War II and success in the Texas oil business, he turned to public service. Bush served briefly as a congressman from Texas and then held various posts in several Republican administrations, including emissary to China, ambassador to the United Nations, director of the Central Intelligence Agency, and vice president. He capped this long political career when he was inaugurated as president of the United States in January 1989, promising to work for "a kinder, gentler America."

In the first months of the Bush administration, the communist world commanded the planet's fascinated attention. Everywhere in the communist bloc it seemed, astoundingly, that the season of democracy had arrived.

In China hundreds of thousands of prodemocracy demonstrators thronged Beijing's Tienanmen Square in the spring of 1989. But in June of that year, China's aging and **autocratic** rulers brutally crushed the prodemocracy movement. Tanks rolled over the crowds, and machine-gunners killed hundreds of protesters. World opinion roundly condemned the bloody suppression of the prodemocracy demonstrators. President Bush joined in the criticism. Yet despite angry demands in Congress for punitive restrictions on trade with China, the president insisted on maintaining normal relations with Beijing.

Stunning changes also shook Eastern Europe. Long oppressed by puppet regimes propped up by Soviet guns, the region was revolutionized in just a few startling months in 1989. The Solidarity movement in Poland led the way when it toppled Poland's communist government in August. With dizzying speed, communist regimes collapsed in Hungary, Czechoslovakia, East Germany, and even hyperrepressive Romania. In December 1989, jubilant Germans danced atop the hated Berlin Wall, symbol of the division of Germany and all of Europe into two armed and hostile camps. The Wall itself soon came down, heralding the imminent end of the forty-five-year-long Cold

■ **Tiananmen Square, Beijing, China, June 1989** Before they were brutally suppressed by Chinese authorities, student demonstrators paraded a homemade Statue of Liberty to signify their passion for democracy.

In his state of the union address on January 31, 1990, President George H. W. Bush (b. 1924) declared,

"The events of the year just ended, the revolution of '89, have been a chain reaction, changes so striking that it marks the beginning of a new era in the world's affairs."

Just six months later, speaking at Stanford University, Soviet president Mikhail Gorbachev (b. 1931) said,

"The Cold War is now behind us. Let us not wrangle over who won it. It is in the common interest of our two countries and nations not to fight this trend toward cooperation, but rather to promote it."

Online Study Center

Interactive map
End of the Cold War
college.hmco.com/pic/kennedybrief7e

Online Study Center

Primary source
Reagan in Front of Berlin Wall
college.hmco.com/pic/kennedybrief7e

Online Study Center

Primary source
McDonald's in Moscow
college.hmco.com/pic/kennedybrief7e

Online Study Center

Interactive map
The Fall of Communism
college.hmco.com/pic/kennedybrief7e

Online Study Center

Interactive map
The End of the Cold War Changes the Map of Europe
college.hmco.com/pic/kennedybrief7e

War. With the approval of the victorious Allied powers of World War II, the two Germanies, divided since 1945, were at last reunited in October 1990.

Most startling of all were the changes that rolled over the heartland of world communism, the Soviet Union itself. Mikhail Gorbachev's policies of *glasnost* and *perestroika* had set in motion a groundswell that surged out of his control. Old-guard hard-liners, in a last-gasp effort to preserve the tottering communist system, attempted to dislodge Gorbachev with a military coup in August 1991. With the support of Boris Yeltsin, president of the Russian Republic (one of several republics that composed the Union of Soviet Socialist Republics), Gorbachev foiled the plotters. But his days were numbered. In December 1991 Gorbachev resigned as president, and the Soviet Union dissolved into fifteen sovereign republics, with Russia the most powerful state and Yeltsin the dominant leader.

The demise of the Soviet Union wrote a definitive finish to the Cold War era. More than four decades of nail-biting tension between the two nuclear superpowers, the Soviet Union and the United States, evaporated when the USSR dismantled itself. With the Soviet Union swept into the dustbin of history and communism all but extinct, Bush spoke hopefully of a "new world order," where democracy would reign and diplomacy would supersede weaponry. Some observers even saw in these developments the "end of history," in the sense that democracy, victorious in its two-century-long struggle against foes on the left and right, had no ideological battles left to fight.

But the disintegration of the Soviet Union posed serious new questions. Who would honor arms-control agreements with the United States? Which of the successor states of the former Soviet Union would take command of the formidable Soviet nuclear arsenal?

Throughout the former Soviet empire, waves of nationalistic fervor and long-suppressed ethnic and racial hatred rolled across the vast land as communism's roots were wrenched out. A particularly nasty conflict erupted in 1991, when the Chechnyan minority tried to declare their independence from Russia, prompting President Yeltsin to send in Russian troops. Ethnic warfare flared in other former communist countries as well, notably in misery-drenched former Yugoslavia, racked by vicious "ethnic cleansing" against minorities. The cruel and paradoxical truth stood revealed that the calcified communist regimes of Eastern Europe, whatever their sins, had at least bottled up the ancient ethnic antagonisms that were the region's peculiar curse and that now erupted in all their historical fury.

Refugees from the strife-torn regions flooded into Western Europe. The sturdy German economy, the foundation of European prosperity, wobbled under the awesome burden of absorbing technologically backward, physically decrepit East Germany. The Western democracies, which for more than four decades had feared the military *strength* of the Eastern bloc, now saw their well-being threatened by the social and economic *weakness* of the former communist lands.

The end of the Cold War also proved a mixed blessing for the United States. The nearly half century of the Cold War had been the only lengthy period in American history when the United States had consistently pursued an internationalist foreign policy. With the Soviet threat canceled, would the United States revert to its traditional isolationism? The Soviet-American rivalry, with its demands for high levels of military preparedness, had also sustained huge sectors of the American economy such as aerospace. When the Pentagon in 1991 closed thirty-four military bases and canceled numerous weapons orders, unemployment soared in southern California and other areas that had once been deluged with Pentagon dollars. The problems of weaning the U.S. economy from its decades of dependence on defense spending tempered the euphoria of Americans as they welcomed the Cold War's long-awaited finale.

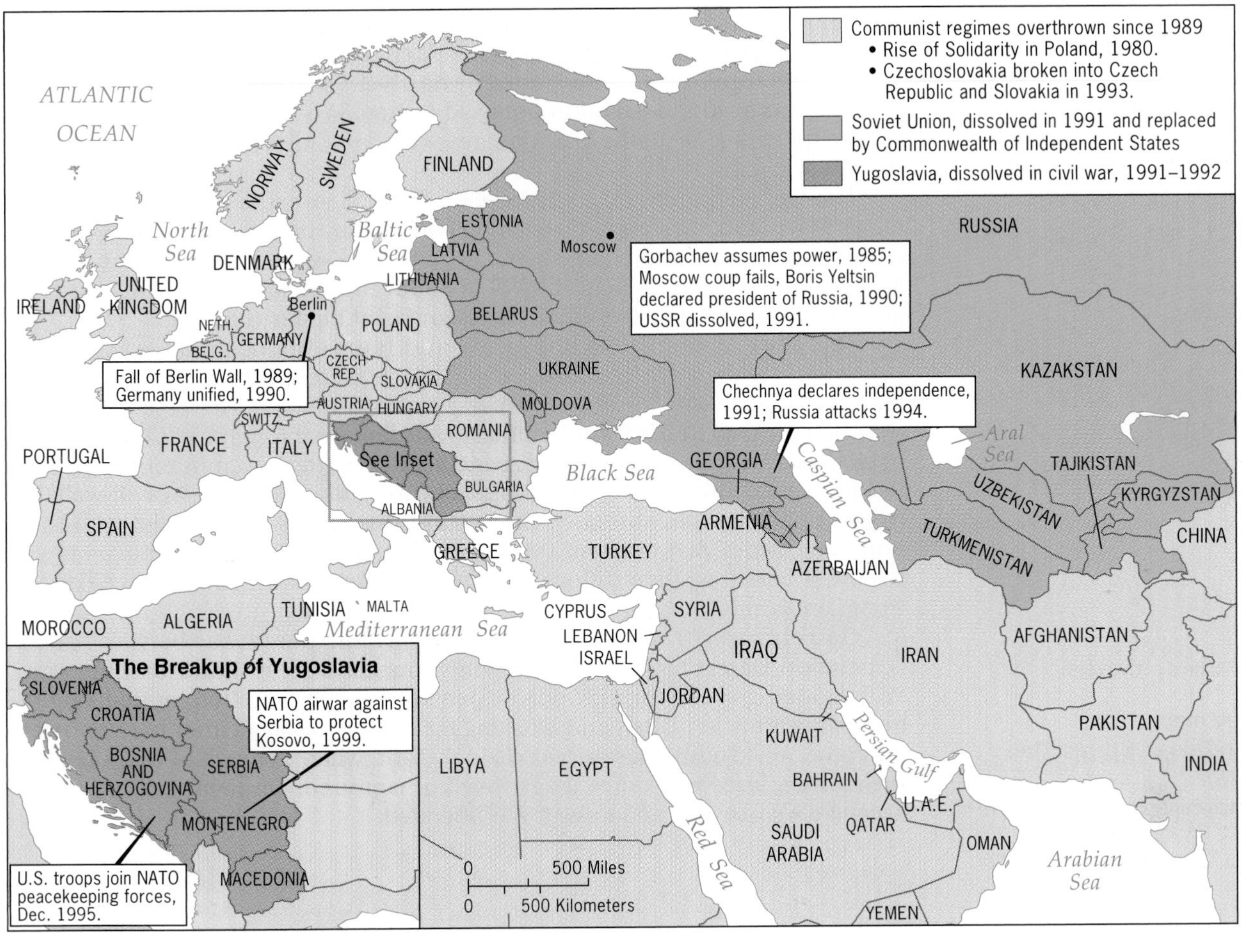
Communist regimes overthrown since 1989
• Rise of Solidarity in Poland, 1980.
• Czechoslovakia broken into Czech Republic and Slovakia in 1993.
Soviet Union, dissolved in 1991 and replaced by Commonwealth of Independent States
Yugoslavia, dissolved in civil war, 1991–1992
ATLANTIC OCEAN
North Sea
Baltic Sea
Black Sea
Caspian Sea
Aral Sea
Mediterranean Sea
Red Sea
Persian Gulf
Arabian Sea
Moscow
Berlin
Gorbachev assumes power, 1985; Moscow coup fails, Boris Yeltsin declared president of Russia, 1990; USSR dissolved, 1991.
Fall of Berlin Wall, 1989; Germany unified, 1990.
Chechnya declares independence, 1991; Russia attacks 1994.
See Inset
The Breakup of Yugoslavia
NATO airwar against Serbia to protect Kosovo, 1999.
U.S. troops join NATO peacekeeping forces, Dec. 1995.
SLOVENIA
CROATIA
BOSNIA AND HERZOGOVINA
SERBIA
MONTENEGRO
MACEDONIA
0 500 Miles
0 500 Kilometers

■ **The End of the Cold War Changes the Map of Europe**

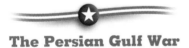

The Persian Gulf War

Sadly, the end of the Cold War did not mean the end of all wars. President Bush flexed the United States' still-intimidating military muscle in tiny Panama in December 1989, when he sent airborne troops to capture dictator Manuel Noriega.

Still more ominous events in the summer of 1990 severely tested Bush's dream of a democratic and peaceful new world order. On August 2 Saddam Hussein, the brutal and ambitious ruler of Iraq, sent his armies to overrun Kuwait, a tiny, oil-rich desert sheikdom on Iraq's southern frontier. Oil fueled Saddam's aggression. With his hand on the world's jugular vein, he would be able to dictate the terms of oil supplies to the industrial nations, and perhaps totally extinguish the Arabs' enemy, Israel.

The speed and audacity of the Iraqi invasion of Kuwait were stunning. But the world responded just as swiftly. The United Nations Security Council unanimously condemned the invasion on August 3 and demanded the immediate and unconditional withdrawal of Iraq's troops. In November the Security Council delivered an ultimatum: Saddam must leave Kuwait by January 15, 1991, or U.N. forces would "use all necessary means" to expel his troops. For perhaps the first time in the post–World War II era, the U.N. seemed to be fulfilling its founders' dreams that it could preserve international order by putting guns where its mouth was. In a **logistical** operation of astonishing complexity, meanwhile, the United States spearheaded a massive international military deployment on the sandy Arabian peninsula. As the January 15 deadline approached, some 539,000

logistical *Relating to the organization and movement of substantial quantities of people and material in connection with some defined objective.*

U.S. soldiers, sailors, and pilots—many of them women and all of them members of the new, post-Vietnam, all-volunteer American military—swarmed into the Persian Gulf region. They were joined by nearly 270,000 troops from twenty-eight other countries in the coalition opposed to Iraq. When all diplomatic efforts to resolve the crisis failed, the U.S. Congress voted on January 12, 1991, to approve the use of force.

The United States and its U.N. allies first unleashed a thirty-seven-day air attack that pummeled targets in occupied Kuwait and in Iraq itself. Iraq responded to this pounding by launching several dozen "Scud" short-range ballistic missiles against military and civilian targets in Saudi Arabia and Israel. These missile attacks claimed several lives but did no significant military damage.

The allied commander, the beefy and blunt American general Norman ("Stormin' Norman") Schwarzkopf, could take nothing for granted as he prepared for the ground phase of the war. Saddam, who had threatened to wage "the mother of all battles," had the capacity to inflict awful damage through the use of chemical or biological weapons. His tactics also included releasing a gigantic oil slick into the Persian Gulf to forestall amphibious assault, and igniting hundreds of oil-well fires whose smoky plumes shrouded the ground from aerial view. Faced with these horrifying tactics, Schwarzkopf's strategy was starkly simple: soften the Iraqis with relentless bombing, then suffocate them on the ground with a tidal-wave rush of troops and armor.

On February 23 the dreaded and long-awaited land war began. Dubbed "Operation Desert Storm," it lasted only four days—the "hundred-hour war." With lightning speed the U.N. forces penetrated deep into Iraq, outflanking the occupying army in Kuwait and blocking the enemy's ability either to retreat or to reinforce. Allied casualties were amazingly light, whereas much of Iraq's remaining fighting force was quickly destroyed or captured. On February 27 Saddam accepted a cease-fire, and Kuwait was liberated.

Online Study Center

**Interactive map
Operation Desert Storm: The
Ground War**
college.hmco.com/pic/kennedybrief7e

■ **The Highway of Death** The Allied coalition wreaked gruesome destruction on Iraqi forces fleeing back to Iraq after their defeat in Kuwait in 1991.

Most Americans cheered the war's rapid and enormously successful conclusion. But when the smoke cleared, Saddam Hussein had survived to menace the world another day. America's allies had agreed only to the liberation of Kuwait, not to regime change in Iraq. Bush was therefore obliged to call off the dogs of war before they could drive the Iraqi tyrant from power. The perpetually troubled Middle East knew scarcely less trouble after Desert Storm had ceased to thunder, and the United States, for better or worse, found itself more deeply ensnared in the region's web of mortal hatreds and intractable conflicts.

Bush on the Home Front

George Bush partly redeemed his promise to work for a "kinder, gentler America" when he signed the Americans with Disabilities Act (ADA) in 1990, a landmark law prohibiting discrimination against the 43 million U.S. citizens with physical or mental disabilities. The president also signed a major water projects bill in 1992 that put the interests of the environment ahead of agriculture, especially in California's heavily irrigated Central Valley.

The new president continued to aggravate the explosive "social issues" that had so divided Americans throughout the 1980s, especially the nettlesome questions of affirmative action and abortion. Bush challenged the legality of college scholarships targeted for racial minorities, and he only grudgingly accepted a watered-down civil rights bill in 1991 that made it easier for employees to prove discrimination in hiring and promotion.

Most provocatively, in 1991 Bush nominated for the Supreme Court the conservative African American jurist Clarence Thomas, a stern critic of affirmative-action policies. Thomas's nomination was loudly opposed by labor, civil rights, and women's organizations. Reflecting irreconcilable divisions over affirmative action and abortion, the Senate Judiciary Committee concluded its hearings with a divided 7-to-7 vote and forwarded the matter to the Senate without a recommendation.

Then, just days before the Senate was scheduled to vote in early October 1991, a press leak revealed that Anita Hill, a University of Oklahoma law professor, had accused Thomas of sexual harassment. The Senate Judiciary Committee was forced to reopen its hearings. For days, a prurient American public sat glued to their television sets as Hill graphically detailed her charges of sexual improprieties and Thomas angrily responded. In the end, by a 52-to-48 vote, the Senate narrowly confirmed Thomas as the second African American ever to sit on the supreme bench (Thurgood Marshall was the first). While many Americans hailed Hill as a heroine for focusing the nation's attention on issues of sexual harassment, Thomas maintained that Hill's widely publicized, unproved allegations amounted to "a high-tech lynching for uppity blacks who in any way deign to think for themselves, to do for themselves."

The furor over Clarence Thomas's confirmation suggested that the social issues that had helped produce three Republican presidential victories in the 1980s were losing some of their electoral appeal. Many women, enraged by the all-male judiciary committee's behavior in the Thomas hearings, grew increasingly critical of the president's uncompromising stand on abortion. A "gender gap" opened between the two political parties, as pro-choice women grew increasingly cool toward the strong anti-abortion stand of the Republicans.

Still more damaging to President Bush's political health, the economy sputtered and stalled almost at the outset of his administration. By 1992 the unemployment rate exceeded 7 percent, while the federal budget deficit continued to mushroom, topping $250 billion in each year of Bush's presidency. In a desperate attempt to stop the hemorrhage of **red ink**, Bush agreed in 1990 to a budget that included $133 billion in new taxes.

Bush's 1990 tax and budget package added up to a political catastrophe. In his 1988 presidential campaign, Bush had belligerently declared, "Read my lips—no new taxes." Now he had flagrantly broken that campaign promise.

Online Study Center

Interactive map
American Indian Reservations
college.hmco.com/pic/kennedybrief7e

red ink *A deficit in a financial account, with expenditures or debts larger than income or assets; from the early accounting practice of marking such deficits in red.*

⭐ **Chapter Summary** ⭐

Reagan led Republicans to sweeping victories in 1980 and 1984 over divided and demoralized Democrats. Riding a conservative national tide, Reagan pushed both his "supply-side" economic program of lower taxes and the "new-right" social policies, especially opposition to affirmative action, abortion, and drugs. These policies brought economic recovery and lower inflation, as well as record budget deficits that severely restricted "big government." The Supreme Court under Reagan and his successor, George Bush, became increasingly conservative, while the confirmation hearings of Justice Clarence Thomas highlighted issues of sexual harassment. Religious conservatives assumed growing influence on American politics, borrowing many tactics from the sixties New Left.

Reagan revived the Cold War confrontation with the Soviet Union, and engaged the United States in assertive military support for anti-leftist forces in Latin America and elsewhere. The ratcheting up of military spending, along with the attempted reforms led by Mikhail Gorbachev, contributed to the unraveling of Communism in Eastern Europe and the Soviet Union in 1989–1991. With America as the only remaining superpower, George Bush led an international coalition to victory in the Persian Gulf War, but the Middle East remained a dangerous tinderbox despite new efforts to resolve the Israel-Arab conflict. Bush supported the Americans with Disabilities Act, but also pushed conservative social issues and appointed the controversial Clarence Thomas to the Supreme Court. Economic recession and a growing "gender gap" raised Democrats' hopes as the election of 1992 approached.

VARYING VIEWPOINTS

Where Did Modern Conservatism Come From?

Ronald Reagan's elections surprised many historians. Reflecting a liberal political outlook that is common among academic scholars, they were long accustomed to understanding American history as an inexorable, almost evolutionary, unfolding of liberal principles, including the quests for economic equality, social justice, and active government. Progressive historians of the early twentieth century like Charles and Mary Beard portrayed conservatives as rich, privileged elites bent on preserving their wealth and power (see "Varying Viewpoints: The Populists: Radicals or Reactionaries? on p. 356).

Even the "New Left" revisionists of the 1960s, while critical of the celebratory tone of their progressive forebears, were convinced that the deep currents of American history flowed leftward. But whether they were liberal or revisionist, most scholars writing in the first three post–World War II decades dismissed conservatism as an obsolete political creed. Conservatives were seen as fringe wackos—paranoid McCarthyites or racist demagogues who, in the words of liberal critic Lionel Trilling, trafficked only in "irritable mental gestures which seem to resemble ideas." Such an outlook is conspicuous in books like Daniel Bell, ed., *The Radical Right* (1963), and Richard Hofstadter, *The Paranoid Style in American Politics* (1965).

Yet what flowed out of the turbulent decade of the 1960s was not a strengthened liberalism but a revived conservatism. Ronald Reagan's huge political success compelled a thorough reexamination of the tradition of American conservatism and the sources of its modern resurgence.

Historians such as Leo Ribuffo and Alan Brinkley have argued that characters once dismissed as irrational crackpots or colorful irrelevancies—including religious fundamentalists and depression-era figures like Huey Long and Father Charles Coughlin—articulated values deeply rooted and widely shared in American culture. These conservative spokespersons, whatever their peculiarities, offered a vision of free individuals, minimal government, and autonomous local communities that harkened back to the "civic republicanism" in the era of young nationhood.

But modern conservatism, however deep its roots, is also a product of the recent historical past. As scholars like Thomas Sugrue and Thomas Edsall have shown, the economic stagnation that set in after 1970 made many Americans insecure about their futures and receptive to new political doctrines. At the same time, as commentator Kevin Phillips has stressed, "social issues" with little or no apparent economic content, became increasingly prominent, as movements for sexual liberation, abortion on demand, women's rights, and race relations sharply challenged traditional beliefs. Finally, the failure of government policies in Vietnam, runaway inflation in the 1970s, as well as the disillusioning Watergate episode, cast doubt on the legitimacy and even the morality of "big government."

Many modern conservatives, including the pundit George Will, stress the deep historical roots of American conservatism. In their view, as Will once put it, it took sixteen years to count the ballots from the 1964 (Goldwater versus Johnson) election, and Goldwater won after all. But that argument is surely overstated. Goldwater ran against the legacy of the New Deal and was overwhelmingly defeated. Reagan ran against the consequences of the Great Society and won decisively. Many conservatives, in short, apparently acknowledge the legitimacy of the New Deal and the stake that many middle-class Americans feel they have in its programs of Social Security, home mortgage subsidies, farm price supports, and similar policies. But they reject the philosophy of the Great Society with its more focused attack on urban poverty and its vigorous support of affirmative action. Modern conservatism springs less from a repudiation of government per se and more from a disapproval of the particular priorities and strategies of the Great Society. The different historical fates of the New Deal and the Great Society suggest the key to the rise of modern conservatism.

America Confronts the Post–Cold War Era

⟨⟩

1992–2006

THERE IS NOTHING WRONG WITH AMERICAN THAT CANNOT BE
CURED WITH WHAT IS RIGHT IN AMERICA.

WILLIAM J. CLINTON, INAUGURAL, 1993

The collapse of the Soviet Union and the democratization of its client regimes in Eastern Europe ended the four-decade-old Cold War and left the United States the world's sole remaining superpower. Americans welcomed these changes but seemed unsure how to exercise their unprecedented economic and military might in this new international framework. The culture wars that had started in the 1960s fed ferociously partisan political squabbles that distracted the nation from its urgent task of clearly defining its role in the dawning age of globalization. In 2000, George W. Bush won a bitterly contested presidential election that left the nation more rancorously divided than ever, until a spectacular terrorist attack on September 11, 2001, called forth, at least temporarily, a resurgent sense of national unity. Bush responded to the 9/11 terrorist attacks by invading the terrorist haven of Afghanistan. He also invaded Iraq in 2003, despite serious controversy over his justifications for the invasion. Bush won reelection in 2004, but the on-going Iraq War, which claimed over 2,500 American lives by 2006, continued to bedevil the Bush presidency and breed unsettling questions about America's role in the world.

Focus Questions

1. How did Bill Clinton attempt to navigate between traditional liberal Democratic values and his claim to be a centrist "new Democrat"?
2. What were the causes and consequences of the economic boom of the 1990s?
3. What caused the growing partisanship and polarization between the conservative Republican movement and the Clinton administration, and how did these conflicts play out in Clinton's impeachment?
4. What was the impact of the September 11, 2001, attacks on American society and on U.S. national security policies in the Middle East and elsewhere?
5. What were the major successes and failures of George W. Bush's domestic and foreign policies, including the Iraq War?

Bill Clinton: The First Baby-Boomer President

Online Study Center

Primary source
Arsenio Hall and Bill Clinton
college.hmco.com/pic/kennedybrief7e

As the last decade of the twentieth century opened, the slumbering economy, the widening gender gap, and the rising anti-incumbent spirit spelled opportunity for Democrats, frozen out of the White House for all but four years since 1968. In a bruising round of primary elections, Governor William Jefferson Clinton of Arkansas weathered blistering accusations of womanizing and draft evasion to emerge as his party's standard-bearer, with another southern moderate, Tennessee Senator Albert Gore, as his vice-presidential running mate.

Clinton claimed to be a "new" Democrat, chastened by his party's long exile in the political wilderness. Clinton and other centrist Democrats attempted to point their party away from its traditional antibusiness, dovish, champion-of-the-underdog orientation and toward pro-growth, strong defense, and anti-crime policies. The youthful and phenomenally articulate Clinton campaigned vigorously on promises to stimulate the economy, reform the welfare system, and overhaul the nation's scandalously expensive and inefficient health-care apparatus.

Trying to wring one more win out of the social issues that had underwritten two Reagan and one Bush presidential victories, the Republican convention in Houston emphasized "family values" as it renominated George Bush and Vice President J. Danforth Quayle for a second term. Bush claimed credit for ending the Cold War and trumpeted his leadership in the Persian Gulf War. But with the average worker's earnings actually declining during Bush's presidency, fear for the economic problems of the future swayed more voters than pride in the foreign policies of the past. At Clinton's campaign headquarters, a simple sign reminded staffers of his principal campaign theme: "It's the economy, stupid."

Reflecting pervasive economic unease and the virulence of the throw-the-bums-out national mood, nearly 20 percent of voters cast their ballots for independent presidential candidate H. Ross Perot, a bantamweight, jug-eared Texas billionaire who harped incessantly on federal deficit problems and boasted of the fact that he had never held any public office. With a record turnout of voters on election day, the final tallies gave Clinton 43,728,275 popular votes and 370 in the Electoral College. Bush polled 38,167,416 popular and 168 electoral votes. Perot won no electoral votes but did gather 19,237,247 in the popular count—the strongest showing for an independent or third-party candidate since Theodore Roosevelt ran on the Bull Moose ticket in 1912. Democrats also racked up clear majorities in both houses of Congress. The new Congress included thirty-nine African Americans, and record numbers of Hispanics, Asian Americans, Indians, and women as well.

Women and minorities figured prominently in President Clinton's cabinet, as he fulfilled his pledge to shape a government that "looks like America." Janet Reno became the first female attorney general, and former University of Wisconsin president Donna Shalala was appointed secretary of health and human services. Clinton also seized the opportunity in 1993 to nominate Ruth Bader Ginsburg to the Supreme Court, where she joined Sandra Day O'Connor to give the Court a pair of women justices until O'Connor's retirement in 2005.

■ **Presidential Campaign Debate, 1992**
George Bush, Ross Perot, and Bill Clinton squared off at the University of Richmond (Virginia) on October 16, 1992. The telegenic Clinton handily dominated the television debates, especially in the "talk-show" format used on this occasion.

A False Start for Reform

Badly overestimating his electoral mandate for liberal reform, the young president made a series of costly blunders upon entering the White House. He stirred a hornet's nest of controversy by advocating an end to the ban on gays and lesbians in the armed forces. Confronted with fierce opposition, the president finally settled for a "don't ask, don't tell" policy that quietly accepted gay and lesbian soldiers and sailors without officially acknowledging their presence in the military.

Even more damaging to Clinton's political standing was the fiasco of his attempt to reform the nation's health-care system. In a dramatic but risky move, the president appointed his wife, Hillary Rodham Clinton, as director of a task force charged with redesigning the medical-service industry. Their stupefyingly complicated plan was dead on arrival when it was presented to Congress in October 1993. The First Lady was doused with a torrent of abuse, although she eventually rehabilitated herself and won election as U.S. senator from New York in 2000—the first First Lady ever to hold elective office.

Clinton had better luck with a deficit-reduction bill in 1993, which combined with an increasingly buoyant economy by 1996 to shrink the federal deficit to its lowest level in more than a decade. By 1998 Clinton's policies seemed to have caged the ravenous deficit monster, as Congress argued over the unfamiliar question of how to spend projected federal budget *surpluses.*

Clinton induced Congress to pass several new gun control laws, including a $30 billion anticrime bill that included a ban on many assault weapons. These measures aimed to hold the line against the epidemic of violence that rocked American society in the 1990s. A huge explosion destroyed a federal office building in Oklahoma City in 1995, taking 168 lives, presumably in retribution for a 1993 standoff in Waco, Texas, between federal agents and the fundamentalist Branch Davidians. That showdown ended in the destruction of the sect's compound and the deaths of many Branch Davidians, including women and children. These episodes brought to light a secretive underground of **paramilitary** private "militias," armed to the teeth and ultrasuspicious of all government.

Even many law-abiding citizens shared to some degree in the antigovernment attitudes that drove the militia members to murderous extremes. Thanks largely to the disillusioning agony of Vietnam and the naked cynicism of Richard Nixon in the Watergate scandal, the confidence in government that came naturally to the generation that licked the Great Depression and won the Second World War was in short supply by century's end. Reflecting the pervasive disenchantment with politics and politicians, several states passed term-limit laws for elected officials, although the Supreme Court ruled in 1995 that the restrictions did not apply to federal officeholders.

Before the decade was out, the logic of Clinton's emphasis on gun control was tragically confirmed. On an April morning in 1999, two students at Columbine High School in Littleton, Colorado, killed twelve fellow students and a teacher. Some observers blamed the violence in movies and video games for such school shootings, while others pointed to the failings of parents. But the culprit that attracted the most sustained political attention was guns—their abundance and accessibility. Clinton engaged in a pugnacious debate with the pro-gun National Rifle Association over the need to toughen gun laws. In May 2000 a "Million Mom March" in Washington demonstrated growing public support for new anti-gun measures, which, however, were slow in coming.

Online Study Center

**Primary source
U.S. Health Spending**
college.hmco.com/pic/kennedybrief7e

paramilitary *Unauthorized or voluntary groups that employ military organization, methods, and equipment outside the official military system of command and organization.*

The Politics of Distrust

Widespread antigovernment sentiment and Clinton's failed initiatives offered conservative Republicans a golden opportunity in 1994, and they seized it aggressively. Led by outspoken Georgia representative Newt Gingrich, Republicans offered voters a "Contract with America" that promised an all-out assault on budget deficits and radical reductions in welfare programs. Their campaign succeeded fabulously, as a right wing tornado roared across the land in the 1994 congressional elections. Republicans picked up eleven governorships, eight Senate seats, and fifty-three seats in the House, giving them control of both chambers of Congress for the first time in forty years.

But if President Clinton had overplayed his mandate for liberal reform in 1993, the congressional Republicans now proceeded to overplay their mandate for conservative retrenchment. The new Republican majority did achieve one long-standing conservative goal by restricting "unfunded mandates"—federal laws that imposed new obligations on state and local governments without providing new revenues. And in 1996 the new Congress achieved a major conservative victory

Chronology

1992	Clinton defeats Bush and Perot for presidency.
1993	NAFTA signed.
1994	Republicans win majorities in both houses of Congress.
1996	Welfare Reform Bill becomes law. Clinton defeats Dole for presidency.
1998	Clinton-Lewinsky scandal. House of Representatives impeaches Clinton.
1999	Senate acquits Clinton on impeachment charges. Kosovo crisis; NATO warfare with Serbia.
2000	"Million Mom March" against guns, in Washington, D.C. U.S. normalizes trade relations with China. George W. Bush wins presidency in Electoral College, although Albert Gore takes popular vote.
2001	Terrorists attack New York City and Washington, D.C., toppling World Trade Center towers and killing over 3,000 Americans and others. U.S. invades Afghanistan. Congress passes USA Patriot Act.
2002	Congress passes "No Child Left Behind" Act. Bush labels Iraq, Iran, and North Korea an "axis of evil." Congress authorizes use of force against Iraq. U.N. Security Council demands that Iraq comply with weapons inspections.
2003	U.S. invades Iraq. Supreme Court narrowly approves affirmative action.
2004	Gay marriage controversy erupts. Iraqi interim government is installed. George W. Bush defeats John Kerry for presidency.
2005	Bush appoints John Roberts as Supreme Court chief justice. Hurricane Katrina devastates New Orleans and Gulf Coast region. Iraqis approve new constitution.
2006	*Hamdan* v. *Rumsfeld* declares Congressionally unauthorized military tribunals unconstitutional.

when Clinton signed, over the howls of old-line liberal Democrats, a Welfare Reform Bill that severely slashed welfare grants and required able-bodied welfare recipients to find employment. President Clinton was at first stunned by the magnitude of the Republican congressional victory in 1994. But many Americans gradually came to feel that the Gingrich Republicans were bending the bow too far, especially when Speaker Gingrich advocated provocative ideas like sending the children of welfare families to orphanages. In a tense confrontation between the Democratic president and the Republican Congress, the federal government actually had to shut down for several days at the end of 1995, until a budget package was agreed upon. These outlandishly partisan antics bred a backlash that helped President Clinton rebound from his political near-death experience.

As the 1996 election approached, the Republicans chose Kansas Senator Robert Dole as their presidential candidate. A decorated World War II veteran, Dole ran a listless campaign. Clinton, buoyed by a healthy economy and his artful trimming to the conservative wind, breezed to an easy victory, with 47,401,898 popular votes to Dole's 39,198, 482. The Reform party's egomaniacal leader, Ross Perot, ran a sorry third, picking up less than half the votes he had garnered in 1992. Clinton won 379 electoral votes, Dole only 159. But Republicans retained control of Congress.

Clinton Again

As Clinton began his second term—the first Democratic president since Franklin Delano Roosevelt to be reelected—the heady promises of far-reaching reform with which he had entered the White House four years earlier were no longer heard. Still facing Republican majorities in both houses of Congress, he proposed only modest legislative goals, even though soaring tax revenues generated by the prosperous economy produced in 1998 a balanced federal budget for the first time in three decades.

Clinton cleverly managed to put Republicans on the defensive by claiming the political middle ground on contentious welfare and affirmative-action issues. He now warmly embraced the landmark Welfare Reform Bill of 1996 that he had initially been slow to endorse. Juggling the political hot potato of affirmative action, Clinton pledged to "mend it, not end it." When voters in California in 1996 approved Proposition 209, prohibiting affirmative-action preferences in government and higher education, the number of minority students in the state's public universities temporarily plummeted. A federal appeals court decision, *Hopwood* v. *Texas,* had similar effects in Texas, Mississippi, and Louisiana (the three states in the federal court's jurisdiction). Clinton criticized these broad assaults on affirmative action but stopped short of trying to reverse them, aware that public support for affirmative action, especially among white Americans, had diminished since the 1970s.

Clinton's major political advantage continued to be the roaring economy, which by 2000 had sustained the longest period of growth in American history, driven by new Internet ("dot.com") businesses and other high-tech and media companies. While unemployment crept down below 4 percent and businesses scrambled madly for workers, inflationary pressure remained remarkably low.

Prosperity did not make Clinton immune to controversy over trade policy. During his first term, he had displayed political courage by supporting the North American Free Trade Agreement (NAFTA), creating in 1993 a free-trade zone encompassing Mexico, Canada, and the United States. Clinton took another step in 1994 toward a global free-trade system when he vigorously promoted the creation of the World Trade Organization (WTO). But simmering discontent over the human and environmental costs of "globalization" spurred protests in the United States and elsewhere and hampered Clinton's push for further expansion of free trade.

Money spurred controversy of another sort in the late 1990s. Campaign finance reform, long smoldering as a potential issue, suddenly flared up after the 1996 presidential contest. Congressional investigators revealed that the Clinton campaign had milked many improper sources for funds, including contributors who paid to stay overnight in the White House and foreigners who were legally prohibited from giving to American campaigns. But Republicans and Democrats alike had reasons to avoid reform, having grown addicted to vast sums of money to finance television ads for their candidates. Only a few mavericks in both parties battled to eliminate the corrupting influence of big donors. Senator John McCain of Arizona made campaign finance reform a centerpiece of his surprisingly strong, though ultimately unsuccessful, bid for the Republican presidential nomination in the 2000 campaign.

Problems Abroad

The end of the Cold War dismantled the framework within which the United States had conducted foreign policy for nearly half a century. Clinton groped for a new formula to replace anticommunism as the basic premise of American diplomacy.

Absorbed by domestic issues, President Clinton at first seemed uncertain and even amateurish in his conduct of foreign policy. He followed his predecessor's lead in dispatching American peacekeeping troops to Somalia, but quietly withdrew them after Somali rebels killed more than a dozen Americans in late 1993. Burned in Somalia, Washington stood on the sidelines when catastrophic ethnic violence in the central African country of Rwanda killed half a million people. A similar reluctance afflicted American policy toward Haiti, where democratically elected president Jean-Bertrand Aristide had been deposed by a military coup in 1991. Clinton at last committed twenty thousand American troops to restore Aristide to the Haitian presidency in 1994.

Clinton also did an about-face on his China policy. Candidate Clinton had denounced George Bush in 1992 for not imposing economic sanctions on China as punishment for Beijing's wretched record of human rights abuses. But China's economic importance to the United States soon led President Clinton to soft-pedal his criticism of the Beijing regime. In 2000 he persuaded Congress to pass a controversial trade bill making the Asian giant a full-fledged trading partner of the United States.

Clinton's approach to the tormented Balkans in southeastern Europe showed a similar initial hesitation, followed eventually by firm leadership. In the former Yugoslavia, as vicious ethnic conflict raged through Bosnia, the Washington government dithered until finally deciding to commit American troops to a NATO peacekeeping contingent in late 1995. When Serbian president Slobodan Milosević in 1999 unleashed a new round of "ethnic cleansing" in the region, this time against ethnic Albanians in the province of Kosovo, U.S.-led NATO forces launched an air war against Serbia. The bombing campaign initially failed to stop ethnic terror, as refugees flooded into neighboring countries, but it eventually forced Milosević to accept a NATO peacekeeping force in Kosovo. With ethnic reconciliation still an elusive dream in the Balkans, Washington accepted the reality that American forces had an enduring role as peacekeepers in the region.

The Middle East remained a major focus of American diplomacy right up to the end of Clinton's tenure. At an historic White House meeting in 1993, Clinton persuaded Israeli prime minister Yitzhak Rabin and Palestinian Liberation Organization leader Yasir Arafat to agree in principle on self-rule for the Palestinians within Israel. But hopes flickered low two years later when Rabin fell to an assassin's bullet. Clinton and his second-term secretary of state, Madeleine Albright, spent the rest of the 1990s struggling in vain to broker the permanent settlement that continued to elude Israelis and Palestinians.

Seeking a legacy as a peacemaker, Clinton stepped up his personal efforts to resolve festering international conflicts in Northern Ireland, the Korean peninsula, and southern Asia. But the guiding principles of American foreign policy in the post-Cold War era remained ill-defined and elusive.

Scandal and Impeachment

Scandal had dogged Bill Clinton from the beginning of his presidency. Allegations of wrongdoing, reaching back to his pre-presidential days in Arkansas, included a failed real estate investment known as the Whitewater Land Corporation. The Clintons' role in that deal prompted the appointment of a federal special prosecutor to investigate—though an indictment for Whitewater wrongdoing never materialized.

All the previous scandals were overshadowed when it was revealed in January 1998 that Clinton had engaged in a sexual affair with a young White House intern, Monica Lewinsky, and then lied about it when he testified under oath in another woman's civil lawsuit accusing him of sexual harassment.

The accusation that Clinton had lied under oath presented a stunning windfall to the special prosecutor, Kenneth Starr. Clinton, now suddenly caught in a legal and political trap, issued repeated denials of involvement with "that woman," Ms. Lewinsky. But he was finally forced to make the humiliating admission that he had had an "inappropriate relationship" with her. In September 1998 Starr accordingly presented to the House of Representatives a stinging report, including lurid sexual details, charging Clinton with eleven possible grounds for impeachment, all related to the Lewinsky matter.

The House quickly cranked up the rusty machinery of impeachment. As an acrid partisan atmosphere enveloped the capital, House Republicans in December 1998 eventually passed two articles of impeachment against the president: perjury before a grand jury and obstruction of justice. Crying foul, the Democratic minority charged that, however deplorable Clinton's personal misconduct, sexual transgressions did not rise to the level of "high crimes and misdemeanors" prescribed as grounds for impeachment in the Constitution (see Art. II, Sec. IV in the Appendix). The House Republican managers (prosecutors) of impeachment replied that perjury and obstruction were grave public issues and that nothing less than "the rule of law" was at stake.

As cries of "honor the Constitution" and "sexual McCarthyism" filled the air, the nation debated whether the president's peccadilloes amounted to high crimes or low follies. Most Americans apparently leaned toward the latter conclusion. In the 1998 midterm elections, voters reduced the House Republicans' majority, causing fiery House Speaker Newt Gingrich to resign his post. Although Americans held a low opinion of Clinton's slipshod personal morals, most liked the president's political and economic policies and wanted him to stay in office.

In early 1999, for the first time in 130 years the nation witnessed an impeachment proceeding in the U.S. Senate. Dusting off ancient precedents from Andrew Johnson's trial, the one hundred senators solemnly heard arguments and evidence in the case, with Chief Justice William Rehnquist presiding. With the facts widely known and the two parties' political positions firmly locked in, the trial's outcome was a foregone conclusion. On the key obstruction of justice charge, five northeastern Republicans joined all forty-five Democratic senators in voting not guilty. The fifty Republican votes for conviction fell far short of the constitutionally required two-thirds majority. The vote on the perjury charge was forty-five guilty, fifty-five not guilty.

■ **The Legacy of Impeachment** *Time* magazine's cartoonist asked how future generations would judge the Clinton impeachment episode—and how it might be treated in history textbooks.

Clinton's Legacy

Beyond the obvious stain of impeachment, Clinton's legacy was a mixed one for his country and his party. He came to office in 1992 determined to make economic growth his first priority. Aided by a global expansion, he achieved notable successes. By decade's end, the country reached near-full employment, poverty rates inched down, and median income reached new highs.

Yet by governing successfully as a "New Democrat" and avowed centrist, Clinton did more to consolidate than reverse the Reagan-Bush revolution against New Deal liberalism that had for half a century provided the compass for the Democratic party and for the nation. As a brilliant communicator, Clinton kept alive a vision of social justice and racial harmony. But as an executive, he discouraged people from expecting government to remedy all the nation's ills. By setting such a low standard for his personal conduct, he replenished the sad reservoir of public cynicism about politics that Vietnam and Watergate had created a generation before. In the last days of his presidency, Clinton struck a deal with the special prosecutor to win immunity from further legal action over the Lewinsky scandal, and issued executive pardons that appeared to reward political backers and donors.

The Bush-Gore Presidential Battle

Clinton's loyal vice president, Al Gore, easily won the Democratic party's presidential nomination in 2000. A seasoned and savvy policy expert, Gore faced the tricky challenge of somehow associating himself with Clinton-era prosperity while detaching himself from Clinton-era scandal. Trying to distance himself from Clinton's foibles, he chose as his running mate Connecticut senator Joseph Lieberman, an outspoken critic of Clinton during the Lewinsky affair and the first Jew nominated to a national ticket by a major party. Meanwhile, consumer advocate Ralph Nader's candidacy on the Green party ticket threatened to siphon off environmentalist votes from the pro-environment Gore.

The Republicans nominated George W. Bush, well known as the elder son of former president George H.W. Bush and a popular two-term governor of Texas. Bush campaigned on a promise to "restore dignity to the White House"—a thinly veiled attack on Clinton's personal failings. Bush chose former defense secretary Richard Cheney as his vice presidential running mate, lending the ticket a much-needed aura of experience. Styling himself a "compassionate conservative," "George W." (or "dubbya") promised to end the strident partisan warfare that had paralyzed Washington in the Clinton years.

The campaign focused on how the federal government should spend the projected $2 trillion surplus over the coming decade. True to the Republican creed of smaller government, Bush championed huge tax cuts, along with private-sector initiatives like **vouchers** to improve education, and "faith-based" institutions to serve the poor. Gore countered with a more modest tax cut targeted at the middle and lower classes, and proposed using most of the surplus to reduce the national debt and better fund Social Security and Medicare.

The election turned out to be an epochal cliffhanger. Not since the Hayes-Tilden election of 1876 had the electoral mechanisms ground their gears so badly before yielding a definite conclusion. In the pivotal state of Florida, the vote was so close that state law compelled a recount. When that second tally confirmed Bush's paper-thin margin of victory, Democrats successfully petitioned the Florida Supreme Court for hand recounts in several contested counties where confusing ballots or faulty voting machines seemed to have denied Gore a legitimate majority. Crying foul, Republicans fought back by pushing the Republican-dominated legislature to name a set of pro-Bush electors, regardless of the vote retabulating under way, and also took their case to the U.S. Supreme Court.

There, with the eyes of an increasingly restive nation riveted on the proceedings, the nine justices broke into a bare-knuckle judicial brawl. Five tumultuous weeks after election day, the presidential campaign of 2000 finally ended when the

vouchers *Officially granted certificates for benefits of a particular kind, redeemable by a designated agency or service provider.*

■ **Making All the Votes Count** This African American father and daughter joined a rally in downtown Miami several weeks after the disputed 2000 election to demand a recount of dismissed presidential ballots. Many Florida blacks charged that election officials had turned them away from the polls or disproportionately disqualified their votes, resurrecting the kind of obstacles that had long kept blacks from voting in the South.

junta *A band of political intriguers, especially military figures, who seize power by force and rule without formal legal authority.*

high court's five most conservative members ruled in Bush's favor. They reasoned that the lack of uniform standards for evaluating disputed ballots meant that the hand counts amounted to an unconstitutional violation of the Fourteenth Amendment's "equal protection" clause. In a rare departure from high bench decorum, Justice John Stevens wrote scathingly for the minority that the Court's decision jeopardized "the nation's confidence in the judge as an impartial guardian of the rule of law."

The Supreme Court ruling gave Bush the victory but also cast a cloud of illegitimacy over his presidency. Bush's final official margin of victory in Florida was only 537 votes out of 6 million cast. With Florida's 25 electoral votes thus narrowly falling into Bush's column, he won the Electoral College by a slim margin of only five electoral votes—271 to 266 for Gore. Bush's popular vote, 50,456,002 fell short of Gore's 50,999,897, making Bush the first president since Benjamin Harrison to win the presidency while losing the popular count. The Senate was split fifty-fifty between Democrats and Republicans, with Vice President Cheney holding the tie-breaking vote.

The fiasco of the 2000 election severely tested American democracy, but in the end the Republic earned a passing grade. The nation's two-century-old electoral machinery might have shown its age, but it managed to wheeze and clank its way to a peaceful resolution of one of the most ferociously contested presidential races ever. Despite all the partisan maneuvering, no credible charges of serious chicanery or outright corruption wafted up out of the election's cauldron of controversy. And however unsettling the U.S. Supreme Court's intervention might have been, surely it was better to have the buck stop with the judges, not with a **junta.** The foresight of the Founders in crafting a system of elections and courts stood reaffirmed for the new century, though the imbroglio unquestionably demonstrated the need for modernized balloting procedures.

Bush Begins

As the son of the forty-first president, George W. Bush became the first presidential offspring since John Quincy Adams to reach the White House. Affecting the chummy manner of a self-made good ol' boy—though he held degrees from Yale and Harvard—Bush promised to bring to Washington the conciliatory skills he had honed as the Republican governor of Texas.

But as president, Bush soon proved to be more of a divider than a uniter, less a "compassionate conservative" than a crusading ideologue. Religious traditionalists cheered but liberals jeered when he withdrew American support from international health programs that sanctioned abortion. He pleased corporate chieftains but angered environmentalists by challenging scientific findings on global warming and repudiating the Kyoto Treaty limiting greenhouse gas emissions (negotiated by the Clinton administration but never ratified by the

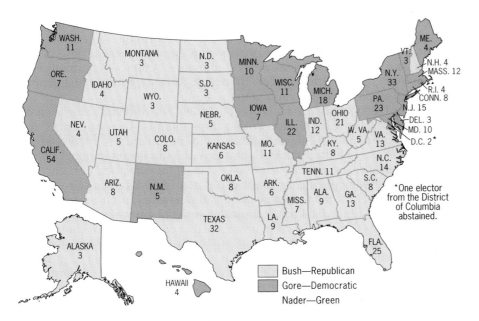

Bush—Republican
Gore—Democratic
Nader—Green

*One elector
from the District
of Columbia
abstained.

■ **Presidential Election of 2000
(with electoral vote by state)**
Although Democrat Albert Gore won the popular election for president by half a million votes, George W. Bush's contested 537-vote advantage in Florida gave him a slight lead in the Electoral College. The 2.7 million popular votes won by Green party candidate and consumer activist Ralph Nader almost surely deprived Gore of victory, casting Nader in the role of spoiler. Bush's failure to win the popular vote inspired critics to protest at his inauguration with placards reading "Hail to the Thief."

Senate). Bush pressed ahead with a whopping $1.3 trillion tax cut that, together with a softening economy, turned the federal budget surpluses of the late 1990s into yawning deficits that reached nearly $500 billion by 2006.

These polarizing policies both reflected and deepened the cultural chasm that increasingly divided "red-state"(conservative, Republican) from "blue-state"(liberal, Democratic) America. The new president's initiatives proved so divisive that a member of his own party, Vermont senator James Jeffords, left the Republican party in May 2001, thereby briefly returning control of the Senate to the Democrats—though Republicans regained control following the 2002 elections.

Online Study Center

**Interactive map
The Election of 2000**
college.hmco.com/pic/kennedybrief7e

Terrorism Comes to America

On September 11, 2001, the long era of America's impregnable national security violently ended. On a balmy late-summer morning, suicidal terrorists slammed two hijacked airliners, loaded with passengers and jet fuel, into the twin towers of New York City's World Trade Center. They flew a third plane into the military nerve-center of the Pentagon, near Washington, D.C., killing 189 people. Heroic passengers forced another hijacked aircraft to crash in rural Pennsylvania, killing all aboard but depriving the terrorists of a fourth weapon of mass destruction.

As the two giant New York skyscrapers thunderously collapsed, some three thousand innocent victims perished, including hundreds of New York's police and fire department rescue workers. A stunned nation blossomed with flags, as grieving and outraged Americans struggled to express their sorrow and solidarity in the face of catastrophic terrorism.

President Bush responded with a sober but stirring address to Congress nine days later. His solemn demeanor and the gravity of the situation helped to dissipate the cloud of illegitimacy that had shadowed his presidency since the disputed election of 2000.

While emphasizing his respect for the Islamic religion and Muslim peoples, Bush identified the principal enemy as Osama bin Laden, head of a shadowy terrorist network known as Al Qaeda. A wealthy extremist exiled from his native Saudi Arabia, bin Laden directed terrorist attacks

■ **The Toll of Terror** Grief overcame this exhausted fire fighter during the search for survivors in the wreckage of New York's World Trade Center.

Interactive map
Afghanistan
college.hmco.com/pic/kennedybrief7e

from landlocked Afghanistan, ruled by an Islamic fundamentalist party, the Taliban. Bin Laden harbored venomous resentment against the United States for its support of Israel and its military presence on the sacred soil of the Arabian peninsula, and he also fed on worldwide resentment of America's enormous economic, military, and cultural power. Ironically, America's most conspicuous strengths had made it a conspicuous target.

When the Taliban refused to hand over bin Laden, Bush ordered a massive military campaign against Afghanistan. Within three months, American forces and Afghani rebels overthrew the Taliban but failed to find bin Laden, and Americans continued to live in fear of future attacks. Confronted with this unconventional, diffuse menace, antiterrorism experts called for new tactics of "asymmetrical warfare," employing not just traditional military muscle, but innovative intelligence gathering, economic reprisals, infiltration of suspected organizations, and even assassinations.

The terrorists' blows diabolically coincided with the onset of a recession. The already-gathering economic downdraft worsened as edgy Americans shunned air travel and the tourist industry withered.

In the anxious atmosphere immediately after the September 11 attacks, Congress in 2001 rammed through the USA-Patriot Act (officially, "Uniting and Strengthening America by Providing Appropriate Tools Required to Intercept and Obstruct Terrorism"). The Act permitted extensive telephone and e-mail surveillance and authorized the detention and deportation of immigrants suspected of terrorism. The Justice Department meanwhile rounded up hundreds of immigrants and held them without habeas corpus (formal charges in an open court). As hundreds of Taliban fighters and other terrorism suspects captured in Afghanistan languished in legal limbo on the American military base at Guantanamo Bay, Cuba, public opinion polls showed Americans sharply divided on whether the terrorist threat fully warranted such drastic encroachments on America's venerable tradition of protecting civil liberties.

Catastrophic terrorism brought a long chapter in American history to a dramatic climax. All but unique among modern peoples, Americans for nearly two centuries had been spared from foreign attack on their homeland. That unusual degree of virtually cost-free national security had undergirded the values of openness and individual freedom that defined the distinctive character of American society. Now American security and American liberty alike were dangerously imperiled.

Bush Takes the Offensive Against Iraq

On only its second day in office, the Bush administration warned that it would not tolerate Iraq's continued defiance of United Nations weapons inspections, mandated after Iraq's defeat in the 1991 Persian Gulf War. Iraqi dictator Saddam Hussein had played hide-and-seek with the inspectors for years. After Saddam expelled all international inspectors in 1998, President Clinton declared that his removal ("regime change") was an official goal of U.S. policy, but no sustained military action against Iraq had followed.

In January 2002, just weeks after the September 11 attacks, President Bush claimed that Iraq, along with Iran and North Korea, constituted an "axis of evil" that gravely menaced American security. The Iraqi tyrant, defeated but not destroyed by Bush's father in 1991, became the principal object of the new president's wrath. Unlike the elder Bush, who had carefully assembled a broad international coalition to fight the Persian Gulf War, his son brashly determined to break with long-standing American traditions and wage a preemptive war against Iraq—and to go it alone if necessary.

In his 2002 state of the union address, President Bush declared:

"Iraq continues to flaunt its hostility toward America and to support terror. The Iraqi regime has plotted to develop anthrax, and nerve gas, and nuclear weapons for over a decade. . . . This is a regime that has agreed to international inspections, then kicked out the inspectors. This is a regime that has something to hide from the civilized world.

States like these, and their terrorist allies, constitute an axis of evil, arming to threaten the peace of the world. By seeking weapons of mass destruction, these regimes pose a grave and growing danger. They could provide these arms to terrorists, giving them the means to match their hatred. They could attack our allies or attempt to blackmail the United States. In any of these cases, the price of indifference would be catastrophic."

The younger Bush thus stood revealed as a daring risk-taker willing to embrace bold, dramatic policies, foreign as well as fiscal. Itching for a fight, and egged on by hawkish Vice President Cheney and other "neoconservative" advisers, Bush accused the Iraqi regime of developing weapons of mass destruction (WMD) and supporting terrorist organizations like Al Qaeda.

Most controversially, he also suggested that a liberated, democratic Iraq might provide a beacon of hope to the Islamic world and thereby begin to improve the political equation in the volatile Middle East. To skeptical observers, including America's European allies, his ambition to create a democracy in long-suffering Iraq seemed hopelessly utopian. Secretary of State Colin Powell warned about the consequences of invading and occupying an unstable, religiously and culturally divided nation of 25 million people. "You break it, you own it," he told the president. Congress passed a resolution in October 2002 authorizing the president to employ armed force to defend against Iraqi threats to America's national security. But with United Nations inspectors unable to find weapons of mass destruction in Iraq, the U.N. Security Council declined to authorize the use of force against Saddam Hussein.

In this tense and confusing atmosphere, Bush, with Britain his only major ally, launched the long-anticipated invasion of Iraq on March 19, 2003. Saddam Hussein's vaunted military machine collapsed almost immediately. In less than a month Baghdad had fallen. From the deck of a U.S. aircraft carrier off the California coast, speaking beneath a banner declaring "Mission Accomplished," Bush triumphantly announced on May 1, 2003, that "major combat operations in Iraq have ended."

Owning Iraq

Combat may have ended, but conflict did not. Contrary to rosy predictions that the Iraqi people would welcome the Americans as liberators and that democracy would sweetly blossom, Iraq became a seething cauldron of apparently endless violence. Iraqi factions jockeyed murderously for political position in the post-Saddam era. Iraqi insurgents, aided by militants from other Islamic nations, repeatedly attacked American troops, killing more than 2,500 by 2006. Revelations in April 2004 about American abuse of Iraqi prisoners in Baghdad's notorious Abu Ghraib prison further inflamed anti-American sentiment in Iraq and beyond. Once a model democracy, the United States was now reviled in many quarters as just another arrogant imperialist power. President Bush nevertheless pressed ahead with efforts to create stability in Iraq.

In the United States, controversy over the war and its rationale continued to swirl. No weapons of mass destruction were found in Iraq, and links between Saddam and Al Qaeda had proved impossible to substantiate. Little evidence had accumulated that Saddam's downfall would topple other autocratic regimes in the region or open the door to Middle East peace. As the casualty lists grew longer, antiwar critics wondered anew whether the war was necessary, and growing numbers of disillusioned Americans questioned what long-term burdens in the Middle East America had, perhaps unwittingly, assumed.

The Iraq War was only one of the issues that fostered sharp divisions among Americans in the first years of the twenty-first century. Disgruntled Democrats still fumed with resentment over the "stolen" 2000 election. Civil libertarians fulminated over the restrictions on citizen rights imposed by the USA Patriot Act and its zealous enforcer, Attorney General John Ashcroft. Antiwar skeptics felt duped and misled into the potential quagmire of Iraq. Revelations about flagrant corporate fraud at energy giant Enron and other prominent companies fed rampant popular disillusion with the business community. Pro-life and pro-choice champions still could not find common ground on the troubled issue of abortion. Controversies over the right of gays and lesbians to marry flared after the legalization of such marriages in Massachusetts in 2004. A number of states passed laws or constitutional amendments barring the practice, and President Bush also pushed for a federal constitutional amendment prohibiting gay marriage.

Affirmative action also continued to spark sharp debate between African Americans and other minorities, who viewed it as a necessary antidote to centuries

Supreme Court Justice Sandra Day O'Connor justified her decision in favor of affirmative action in the Grutter case as follows:

"By virtue of our Nation's struggle with racial inequality, [minority] students are both likely to have experiences of particular importance to the Law School's mission, and less likely to be admitted in meaningful numbers on criteria that ignore those experiences."

Justice Clarence Thomas dissented:

"Every time the government places citizens on racial registers and makes race relevant to the provision of burdens or benefits, it demeans us all . . . . When blacks take positions in the highest places of government, industry, or academia, it is an open question today whether their skin color played a part in their advancement . . . asking the question itself unfairly marks those blacks who would succeed without discrimination."

of oppression, and other Americans who saw it as unjustifiable violation of the Constitution's protection of equality before the law. The Supreme Court appeared to split the difference between these two positions in the twin cases of *Gratz* v. *Bollinger* and *Grutter* v. *Bollinger* in 2003. In the first case, the Court declared unconstitutional a numerical formula for admitting undergraduate students to the University of Michigan. In the second, it allowed to stand a more flexible, individually based minority admissions procedure for the Michigan law school, even while declaring, "We expect that 25 years from now, the use of racial preferences will no longer be necessary."

The Election of 2004

President Bush confidently sought reelection in 2004 by pursuing policies designed to bolster and expand his Republican base of support. He trumpeted his tax cuts as a way to throttle government expansion and urged making them permanent. He claimed success for his controversial No Child Left Behind Act of 2002, which mandated sanctions against schools that failed to meet federal performance standards. He resisted federally funded embryonic stem-cell research, which many researchers believed to hold the promise of cures for deadly diseases, as an immoral assault on human life. But most of all he cast himself as a war president and a stalwart, decisive commander-in-chief who was sternly facing down the terrorist threat.

To challenge Bush the Democrats turned to Massachusetts Senator John Kerry, a lanky and long-jawed patrician whose Vietnam war heroism was presumed to counter charges that he would lack vigor in the war against terror. But some veterans' groups nevertheless attacked him viciously (and irresponsibly), while Kerry's own statements that he had voted *for* a military spending bill before voting *against* it was distorted to portray him as a waffling flip-flopper.

On election day Bush nailed down the decisive election victory that had eluded him in 2000. His three-pronged strategy of emphasizing taxes, terror, and moral values paid off handsomely. He posted the first popular vote majority in more than a decade, 60,639,281 to Kerry's 57,355,978. The electoral count was 286 for Bush to 252 for Kerry.

In posting his victory, Bush spurred hopes that his party might be entering a period of political dominance. Bush was the first Republican to win a majority of the historically Democratic Catholic vote and he polled 43 percent of the Latino vote. He ran up heavy majorities among evangelical Christians and won a substantial majority of suburban voters, the most numerous and fastest growing part of the electorate.

Storms at Home and Abroad

Buoyed by his reelection, President Bush declared in his expansive inaugural address that "the survival of liberty in our land increasingly depends on the success of liberty in other lands" and proclaimed it the policy of the United States "to seek and support the growth of democratic movements and institutions in every nation and culture, with the ultimate goal of ending tyranny in our world." Seeing the Iraq War as a decisive test in the global war against terrorism, Bush urged Americans to display "patience" in taking on "obligations that are difficult to fulfill but that it would be dishonorable to abandon."

But within months of the inauguration polls showed that the lack of visible progress in the war and the continuing toll of American casualties were wearing public patience thin. Bush and his new secretary of state, Condoleezza Rice, accordingly pushed hard for Iraqis to create an effective government that could assume more responsibility for its own security. Under urgent American prodding, Iraqis managed to hold national elections and adopted a constitution. But fierce divisions among Iraq's religious and ethnic groups delayed the formation of a new government until May 2006.

American military strategy focused on handing over responsibility for battling insurgents to the Iraqi army. But factionalism plagued Iraq's military forces as well. Armed sectarian militias—sometimes operating under the cover of police uniforms—conducted vicious killings and reprisals against one another and against civilian targets, including the destruction of a major **Shi'ite** mosque in February 2006. Some American officials openly worried that civil conflict among Iraqis would cripple the war against the insurgents.

Shi'ite *One of the two major historic traditions within Islam, which adheres to a line of authority deriving from the prophet Muhammad's son-in-law Ali. The other tradition, the **Sunni**, derives authority primarily from Islamic law, judicial scholarship and interpretation, and the caliphate, i.e., Islamic rulers. It does not regard succession from Muhammad as important.*

On the domestic front, Bush successfully mobilized the Republican majorities in Congress to extend many of his tax cuts and pass an energy bill aimed at reducing what he called the country's "addiction" to imported oil. He also sought to confront the looming deficits in Social Security funding by proposing a limited "privatization" of the system, especially for younger workers. Despite Bush's urgent appeals and heavy expenditure of the political capital he had accumulated in the election, Republicans and Democrats alike quickly scampered away from his plan. Social Security once again proved to be a political untouchable.

In August 2005, a devastating storm, Hurricane Katrina, struck the U.S. Gulf Coast. Hurricane-spawned flooding broke through the levees protecting low-lying New Orleans, leaving 80 percent of the historic city under water. Nearly two thousand people perished in New Orleans and neighboring Mississippi and Alabama, while the rest of the population tried to flee, amidst scenes of incredible chaos. Tens of thousands of homeless evacuees soon strained resources in Texas and other states.

The slow response of government officials to the hurricane prompted much criticism, especially of the Federal Emergency Management Agency (FEMA) and the new Homeland Security department. After initially praising FEMA's efforts, President Bush fired the agency's director and promised extensive federal help in rebuilding New Orleans.

The Katrina disaster, deepening deficits, and flagrant scandals involving mostly Republican lawmakers and high-powered Washington **lobbyists** produced a sour public mood and slumping approval ratings for Bush. The simmering immigration issue burst to the fore in December 2005 when the House passed a bill containing a harsh crackdown on illegal immigrants and advocating fence-building along the 2000-mile Mexican border. Hundreds of thousands of immigrants and their allies took to the streets in protest. President Bush then proposed and the Senate passed a measure that provided a "path to citizenship" for illegals, while also tightening border security. But critics railed against anything that smacked of "amnesty," and the issue remained a hot political button as mid-term elections approached.

lobbyist *A person who works to persuade legislators to pass measures favorable to the special cause or interest that he or she represents.*

The death of Chief Justice William Rehnquist and the retirement of Sandra Day O'Connor in 2005 created the first Supreme Court vacancies since 1994. Bush named two conservative judges, John Roberts and Samuel Alito, as their replacements. With these appointments, and his renewed support for anti-gay marriage and anti-flag burning constitutional amendments, Bush sought to bolster his conservative base.

But it was the Iraq War and the fate of the larger "war against terrorism" that continued to define the Bush presidency. Critics of the war's impact on civil liberties grew noisier when it was learned in 2006 that government agencies had been tapping phones and tracking financial records of suspected terrorists without the necessary court approval. International criticism of the Guantanamo Bay prison camp grew so strong that even President Bush told European leaders that he wanted to close it, but could see no way to safely release such terrorism suspects.

The president's efforts to try some Guantanamo suspects before military tribunals and his claims of sweeping, inherent presidential powers to fight terrorism were checked by the Supreme Court in June 2006. In the case of *Hamdan* v. *Rumsfeld,* the Court ruled that a terrorism suspect captured in Afghanistan— Osama bin Laden's chauffeur—could not be tried by a presidentially ordered tribunal that had not been approved by Congress and that incorporated procedures contrary to international law. Debates over Iraq and terrorism, and their spillover effects on policies relating to American liberty and security, thus remained vigorous five years after the September 11 attacks.

The Iraq War became the dominant issue in the 2006 mid-term election campaign. President Bush vigorously defended his policy, but acknowledged the need to alter tactics and devise "benchmarks" to measure the Iraqi government's performance. With mounting U.S. casualties and few signs of progress, even some Republicans criticized the war's management by defense secretary Donald Rumsfeld, while Democrats hit hard at Bush and the increasingly unpopular war.

Scandals and anxiety over harsh Republican immigration policies added to the GOP undertow, giving the Democrats a clear victory. They claimed control of the House of Representatives for the first time since 1994, and gained enough seats to organize the Senate with the aid of two independent senators. In the wake of the election defeat, the discredited Rumsfeld resigned his post. The impact of his departure on Iraq policy was unclear. The loss of the Republican Congressional majorities that Bush had enjoyed for most of his presidency might lead either to greater stalemate or to a new spirit of compromise in his final two years in office.

⭐ Chapter Summary ⭐

The dynamic young "baby-boomer" Bill Clinton defeated President George H.W., Bush in 1992, and promoted an ambitious reform agenda within the context of his centrist "new Democrat" ideology. Clinton's efforts to reform health care and promote gun control met strong resistance, but his economic policies helped to spark a decade-long expansion. Presenting an aggressively conservative agenda, Republicans gained control of Congress in 1994 for the first time in fifty years. But over-reaching by the Newt Gingrich–led Republicans enabled Clinton to revive and win a second term by defeating Kansas Senator Robert Dole in 1996.

In his second term, Clinton downplayed reform and successfully claimed the political middle ground on issues like welfare reform, affirmative action, and gun control. The booming economy created budget surpluses, and enhanced Clinton's efforts to develop even more free trade agreements in line with the successful North American Free Trade Agreement (NAFTA). Clinton recovered from early foreign policy stumbles in African and Latin America with a successful intervention in the former Yugoslavia. But efforts at Middle East peace stalled. Clinton's affair with Monica Lewinsky led to his highly partisan impeachment in 1998 and acquittal in 1999.

Texas Governor George Walker Bush defeated Clinton's vice president, Albert Gore, in a cliffhanging election that was finally settled by the Supreme Court. Bush promoted an aggressive and divisive conservative agenda of deep tax cuts at home and unilateral assertion of American interests abroad.

The terrorist attacks of September 11, 2001, were a watershed in American history, ending centuries of nearly cost-free national security. Bush invaded the Al Qaeda stronghold of Afghanistan, ousting the Taliban regime, and Congress passed the USA Patriot Act over civil libertarian objects. A recession slowed economic growth and swelled federal budget deficits. With Congressional authorization but without U.N. authorization or a significant coalition, Bush invaded Iraq in March 2003. U.S. forces quickly crushed Saddam Hussein's army, but became entrapped in low-intensity warfare against determined Iraqi insurgents.

The United States became culturally and politically polarized in the early years of the twenty-first century. George W. Bush ran successfully as a wartime president leading the fight against terrorism, defeating Democrat John Kerry in the election of 2004. Bush began his second term committed to staying the course in Iraq, but growing public discontent with the war and the government's response to a hurricane caused his political support to erode.

42

The American People Face a New Century

◆

AS OUR CASE IS NEW, SO WE MUST THINK ANEW AND ACT
ANEW. WE MUST DISENTHRALL OURSELVES, AND THEN WE
SHALL SAVE OUR COUNTRY.

ABRAHAM LINCOLN, 1862

Well beyond its two-hundredth birthday as the twenty-first century began, the United States was both an old and a new nation. It boasted one of the longest uninterrupted traditions of democratic government of any country on earth. Indeed, it had pioneered the techniques of mass democracy and was, in that sense, the oldest modern polity. As one of the earliest countries to industrialize, America had also dwelled in the modern economic era longer than most nations.

But the Republic was in many ways still youthful as well. Innovation, entrepreneurship, and risk-taking—all characteristics of youth—were honored national values. The twenty-first century began much like the twentieth, with American society continuing to be rejuvenated by fresh waves of immigrants, full of energy and ambition. The U.S. economy, despite problems, pulsated as a driving engine of world economic growth. American inventions—especially computer and communications technologies—were transforming the face of global society. Consumers from Lisbon to Tokyo seemed to worship the icons of American culture—downing soft drinks and donning blue jeans, watching Hollywood films, listening to rock or country music, even adopting indigenous American sports such as baseball and basketball. In the realm of consumerism, American products appeared to have Coca-Colonized the globe—for better or worse.

The history of American society also seemed to have increased global significance as the third millennium of the Christian era opened. Americans were a pluralistic people who had struggled for centuries to provide opportunity and to achieve tolerance and justice for many different religious, ethnic, and racial groups. Their historical experience could offer valuable lessons to the rapidly internationalizing planetary society that was emerging at the dawn of the twenty-first century.

Much history remained to be made as the country entered its third century of nationhood. The great social experiment of American democracy was far from complete. The ethical challenges posed by science and technology, environmental stewardship of a fragile planet, and overcoming inequality and prejudice all posed formidable challenges for the future. And the terrorist attacks of September 11, 2001, violently heralded a new era of fear and anxiety.

But men and women make history only within the framework bequeathed to them by earlier generations. Whether they like it or not—indeed, whether they know it or not—they march forward along time's path bearing the burdens of the past. Understanding when they have come to a truly new turn in the road, when they can lay part of their burden down, and when they cannot, or should not—all this constitutes the kind of wisdom that only historical study can engender.

Focus Questions

1. How did economic and technological changes alter the American workplace and work force?
2. What ethical questions were raised by the revolutionary new knowledge in science and medicine?
3. What caused the growing economic inequality in the late twentieth and early twenty-first centuries, and what were the social and moral consequences of this trend for American society?
4. How has the feminist movement altered women's roles and transformed the character of American business, politics, education, and family life?
5. What major changes affected American family life in the half century since World War II, and what were the long-term economic and social consequences of the "aging of America"?
6. What lay behind the vast new wave of immigration from Latin America and Asia, and what challenges and opportunities did it pose for the future of American society?
7. How has American art, literature, and media reflected the dynamic character of American society in the late twentieth and early twenty-first centuries?

Economic Revolutions

When the twentieth century opened, United States Steel Corporation was the flagship business of America's industrial revolution. A generation later, General Motors' preeminence in automobile production signaled the historic shift to a mass consumer economy that began in the 1920s and flowered fully in the 1950s. Following World War II the rise of International Business Machines (IBM) symbolized the transformation to the fast-paced "information age." By century's end, the phenomenal growth of Microsoft Corporation and the Internet heralded an explosive communications revolution. Americans now rocketed down the "information superhighway" toward the uncharted terrain of an electronic global village.

The communications revolution was full of both promise and peril. In the blink of an eye, ordinary citizens could gain access to information once available only to privileged elites. Businesspeople instantaneously girdled the planet with transactions of prodigious scope and serpentine complexity. By the late 1990s a "dot-com" explosion of new commercial ventures quickly expanded the market (and the stock-market stakes) for entrepreneurs leading the way in making the Internet a twenty-first-century electronic mall, library, and entertainment center rolled into one.

But the very speed and efficiency of the new communications tools threatened to wipe out entire occupational categories. Postal letter-carriers, travel agents, booksellers, bank tellers, stockbrokers, and others whose business it was to mediate between product and client might find themselves roadkill on the information superhighway. White-collar jobs in financial services and high-tech engineering could now be "outsourced" to countries such as Ireland or India.

Increasingly, scientific research was the motor that propelled the economy, and new scientific knowledge raised new moral dilemmas and provoked new political arguments. Pioneering genetic discoveries, for instance, had yielded new strains of high-yield, pest-resistant crops, but also, unfortunately, had unleashed genetic mutations that might threaten the fragile balance of the wondrous **biosphere** in which humankind was delicately suspended. By the dawn of the new century, a revolution in biological engineering pointed the way to radical new medical therapies—and to mouth-watering profits for bioengineering firms.

biosphere *The earth's entire network of living plants and organisms, conceived as an interconnected whole.*

Research into human stem cells held out the promise of cures for afflictions like Parkinson's disease and Alzheimer's. But the Bush administration shared the concern of certain religious groups that harvesting stem cells involved the destruction of human life in embryonic form. Bush therefore limited government funding for stem cell research, as Americans continued to struggle with the ethical implications of their vast new technological powers.

Other unprecedented ethical questions clamored for resolution. What principles should govern the allocation of human organs for lifesaving transplants? How, if at all, should society regulate the increasingly lengthy and often painful process of dying?

Affluence and Inequality

Americans were still an affluent people at the beginning of the twenty-first century. Median household income declined somewhat in the early 1990s but rebounded by 2002 to about $42,400. Yet even those Americans with incomes below the government's official poverty level (defined in 2004 as $18,850 for a family of four) enjoyed a standard of living higher than that of two-thirds of the rest of humankind.

Americans were no longer the world's wealthiest people, as they had been in the quarter-century after World War II. Citizens of several other countries enjoyed higher average per capita incomes, and many nations boasted more equitable distributions of wealth. In an unsettling reversal of long-term trends in American society, during the last two decades of the twentieth century the rich got much richer while the poor got an ever-shrinking share of the pie. The richest 20 percent of Americans in the early 2000s raked in nearly half of the nation's income, whereas the poorest 20 percent received a mere 4 percent. The gap between rich and poor began to widen in the 1980s and widened further thereafter. Between 1968 and 2004 the share of the nation's income that flowed to the top 20 percent of its households swelled from 40 percent to just over 50 percent. Even more striking, in the same period the top 5 percent of income receivers saw their share of the national income grow from about 15 percent to a remarkable 22 percent.

Widening inequality could be measured in other ways as well. Chief executives in the 1970s typically earned forty-one times as much as the average worker in their corporations; by the early 2000s they earned 245 times as much. At the same time some 34 million people,

■ **Two Nations?** While decaying neighborhoods and the sad legions of the homeless blighted American urban life at the dawn of the twenty-first century, affluent Americans took refuge in gated communities like this one in the Brentwood section of Los Angeles.

12 percent of all Americans (8 percent of whites, 24 percent of African Americans, and 22 percent of Latinos), remained mired in poverty—a depressing indictment of the inequities afflicting an affluent and allegedly egalitarian republic.

What caused the widening income gap? Some critics pointed to the tax and fiscal policies of the Reagan and Bush (father and son) presidencies, which favored the wealthy. But deeper-running historical currents probably played a more powerful role, as suggested by similar trends toward inequality in other industrialized societies. Among the most conspicuous causes were intensifying global competition; the shrinkage in high-paying manufacturing jobs for semiskilled and unskilled workers; the greater economic rewards commanded by educated workers in high-tech industries; the decline of unions; the rising tide of relatively low-skill immigrants; and the increasing tendency of educated men and women to marry one another and both work, creating households with very high incomes. Educational opportunities also had a way of perpetuating inequality, starting with the underfunding of many schools in poor urban areas and the soaring cost of higher education. A 2004 study revealed that at the 146 most selective colleges, 74 percent of the students came from families with incomes in the top 25 percent, compared to 3 percent of the students from the bottom income quartile.

The Feminist Revolution

Online Study Center

**Primary source
Women in the Work Force**
college.hmco.com/pic/kennedybrief7e

All Americans were caught up in the great economic changes of the late twentieth century, but no group was more profoundly affected than women. When the twentieth century opened, women made up about 20 percent of all workers. Over the next five decades they increased their presence in the labor force at a fairly steady rate, except for a temporary spurt during World War II. Then, beginning in the 1950s, women's entry into the workplace accelerated dramatically. By the 1990s nearly half of all workers were women, and the majority of working-age women held jobs outside the home. Most astonishing was the upsurge in employment of mothers. In 1950, 90 percent of mothers with children under the age of six did not work for pay. But half a century later, a majority of women with children as young as one year old were wage earners. Women brought home the bacon and cooked it, too.

Beginning in the 1960s, many all-male strongholds—including Yale, Princeton, and West Point — opened their doors to women. By the 1980s, women became the majority on college campuses; by 2006 they made up 58 percent of the nation's college students. After graduation, women were piloting commercial airliners, orbiting outer space, governing states and cities, and writing Supreme Court decisions.

Yet despite those gains, many feminists remained frustrated. Women continued to receive lower wages, on average 77 cents on the dollar in 2002 compared with men doing the same full-time work—and they tended to concentrate in a few low-prestige, low-paying occupations (the "pink-collar ghetto"). Although they made up more than half the population, women in 2004 accounted for only 30 percent of lawyers and judges (up from 5 percent in 1970) and 25 percent of physicians (up from 10 percent in 1970). Overt sexual discrimination explained some of this occupational segregation, but most of it seemed attributable to the greater burdens of parenthood on women than on men. Women were far more likely than men to interrupt their careers to bear and raise children, and even to choose less demanding career paths to allow for fulfilling those traditional roles. Discrimination and a focus on children also helped account for the persistence of a "gender gap" in national elections. Women continued to vote in greater numbers than men for Democratic candidates, who were often perceived to be more willing to favor government support for health and child care, education, and job equality.

Online Study Center

**Primary source
U.S. Health Spending**
college.hmco.com/pic/kennedybrief7e

As the revolution in women's status rolled on in the 2000s, men's lives changed as well. Men assumed traditional female responsibilities such as cooking, laundry, and child care. Recognizing the new realities of the modern American household, Congress passed a Family Leave Bill in 1993, mandating job protection for working fathers as well as mothers who needed to take time off work for family-related reasons.

■ Women's World: Something Old, Something New

By the beginning of the twenty-first century, revolutionary changes in the economy and in social values had opened new career possibilities to women, while not fully relieving them of their traditional duties as mothers and homemakers. Dramatic changes in race relations and the redefinition of gender roles at the end of the twentieth century transformed even tradition-bound institutions like the U.S. Military Academy at West Point, New York, as this gathering of cadets suggests. Women's athletics came into their own in the wake of the feminist revolution. In 1999 the U.S. Women's World Cup Soccer Team brought home the trophy to a nation suddenly enthralled with women's soccer.

Changing Families and Aging Citizens

The **nuclear family,** once prized as the foundation of society and the nursery of the Republic, suffered heavy blows in postwar America. By the 1990s one out of every two marriages ended in divorce, although the divorce rate appeared to ebb a bit by the century's end. Seven times more children were affected by divorce than at the beginning of the twentieth century, and kids who commuted between separated parents were commonplace.

Traditional families were not only falling apart at an alarming rate but were also increasingly slow to form in the first place. The proportion of adults living alone tripled in the five decades after 1950, and by the 2000s about one-third of women age twenty-five to twenty-nine had never married. In the 1960s, 5 percent of all births were to unmarried women, but four decades later one out of four white babies, one out of three Hispanic babies, and two out of three African American babies were born to single mothers. Every fourth child in America was growing up in a household that lacked two parents. The collapse of the traditional family contributed heavily to the pauperization of many women and children, as single parents (usually mothers) struggled to keep their households economically afloat.

Child-rearing, the family's foremost function, was being increasingly assigned to "parent-substitutes" at day-care centers or schools—or to television, the modern age's "electronic babysitter." Estimates were that the average child by age sixteen had watched up to fifteen thousand hours of TV—more time than was spent in the classroom. Parental anxieties multiplied with the advent of the Internet,an electronic **cornucopia** where youngsters could surf through poetry and problem sets as well as pornography.

But if the *traditional* family was increasingly rare, the family itself remained a bedrock of American society in the early twenty-first century, as viable families

nuclear family *A parent or parents and their immediate offspring.*

cornucopia *An overflowing abundance of good things, as in the bountiful outpouring of fruits and flowers in Greek mythology's "horn of plenty."*

Online Study Center

Primary source
Changing Demographics
college.hmco.com/pic/kennedybrief7e

now assumed a variety of forms. Children in households led by a single parent, stepparent, or grandparent encountered a degree of acceptance that would have been unimaginable a generation earlier. Even the notion of gay marriage, which emerged as a major public controversy when the Massachusetts Supreme Court ruled it legal in 2003, signaled that the idea of marriage retained its luster.

Americans were living longer than ever before. A person born at the dawn of the twentieth century could expect to survive less than fifty years, whereas someone born in 2000 could expect a life span of seventy-seven years. Miraculous medical advances like the development of antibiotics after 1940 and Dr. Jonas Salk's discovery in 1953 of a polio vaccine lengthened and strengthened lives.

Longer lives spelled more older people. One American in eight was over sixty-five years of age in 2000, and projections were that one of every five people would be in the "sunset years" by 2050. This aging of the population raised a host of political, social, and economic questions. Elderly people formed a potent electoral bloc that aggressively lobbied for government favors and achieved real gains for senior citizens. As late as the 1960s nearly a quarter of Americans over the age of sixty-five lived in poverty; three decades later only about one in ten did.

These triumphs for senior citizens also brought fiscal strains, especially on the Social Security system, established in 1935 to provide income for retired workers. When Social Security began, most workers continued to toil after age sixty-five (if they were among the lucky few who lived that long). By century's end the majority of the elderly population relied primarily on Social Security checks for their living expenses. Contrary to popular mythology, Social Security payments were funded from the taxes of current workers, not from the retirees' own earlier payments. By the time the new century opened, the ratio of active workers to retirees had dropped so low that drastic adjustments were necessary.

At the beginning of the new century, as the huge wave of post–World War II baby boomers approached retirement age, it seemed that the "unfunded liability"—the difference between what the government promised to pay to the elderly and the taxes it expected to take in—might rise above $7 trillion, a sum that threatened to bankrupt the Republic unless sweeping reforms were adopted. Yet because of the electoral power of older Americans, Social Security and Medicare reform remained the "third rail" of American politics, which politicians dared not touch. President George W. Bush's proposal in 2005 to privatize a portion of Social Security by giving younger workers the option to invest some of their payroll taxes in individual retirement accounts failed in the face of strong opposition from most Republicans and Democrats alike. In the absence of bold reforms, a war between the generations loomed in the twenty-first century, as payments to the nonworking elderly threatened to soak up fully half the working population's income by about 2040.

The New Immigration

Online Study Center

**Primary source
Country of Origin and Year of
Entry into the U.S.**
college.hmco.com/pic/kennedybrief7e

Newcomers continued to flow into modern America. They washed ashore in waves that numbered nearly 1 million persons per year from the 1980s into the early twenty-first century—the largest inflow of immigrants in America's experience. In striking contrast to the historic pattern of immigration, Europe contributed far fewer people than did the countries of Asia and Latin America.

What prompted this new migration to America? The truth is that the newest immigrants came for many of the same reasons as the old. They typically left countries where populations were growing rapidly and where agricultural and industrial revolutions were shaking people loose from old habits of life—conditions almost identical to those in nineteenth-century Europe. And they came to America, as previous immigrants had done, in search of jobs and economic opportunity. Some came with skills and even professional degrees. But most came with meager skills and scant education, and started work in low-paying manual jobs.

The Southwest, from Texas to California, felt the immigrant impact especially sharply, as Mexican migrants—by far the largest contingent of modern immigrants—concentrated heavily in that region. By the turn of the century Latinos made up nearly one-third of the population in Texas, Arizona, and California and almost 40 percent in New Mexico—amounting to a demographic *reconquista* of the lands lost by Mexico in the war of 1846.

The size and geographic concentration of the Hispanic population in the Southwest had few precedents in the history of American immigration. Most previous groups had been so thinly scattered across the land that they had little choice but to learn English and make their way in the larger American society, however much they might have longed to preserve their native language and customs. But it seemed possible that Mexican Americans might succeed in creating a truly bicultural zone in the booming southwestern states.

Some old-stock Americans worried about the capacity of the modern United States to absorb these new immigrants. The Immigration Reform and Control Act of 1986 attempted to choke off illegal entry by penalizing employers of **undocumented** aliens and by granting **amnesty** to many of those already here. But the flow of immigrants, legal and illegal, continued to swell throughout the next two decades. In 2005, hostility to illegal immigration flared up across the country, leading the House of Representatives to pass a punitive anti-immigration bill that stirred massive protests by immigrants and their supporters. President George W. Bush's proposal for a more comprehensive reform, including a "path to citizenship" for the undocumented, also failed. But responding to the continuing public demand to stem illegal immigration, Congress in October 2006 passed a new law authorizing the construction of 700 miles of fencing along the 2000-mile border with Mexico.

Yet the fact was that foreign-born people accounted for about 12.4 percent of the American population in 2006—still a smaller proportion than the historical high point of nearly 15 percent recorded in the census of 1910. Somewhat inconsistently, critics charged both that immigrants robbed citizens of jobs and that they dumped themselves on the welfare rolls at the taxpayers' expense. But studies showed that immigrants took jobs scorned by Americans and that they paid more dollars in federal taxes (withholding and Social Security taxes, as well as sales taxes for things like gasoline, cigarettes, and alcoholic beverages) than they claimed in welfare payments. In some states, however, the cost of providing immigrants with social services like education and health care cost more than they contributed in taxes. Another worry was that unscrupulous employers might take cruel advantage of immigrant workers, who often had scant knowledge of their legal rights.

Online Study Center

Interactive map
Changing Latino Population
college.hmco.com/pic/kennedybrief7e

Online Study Center

Primary source
Interstate Pedestrians
college.hmco.com/pic/kennedybrief7e

---

undocumented *Lacking official certification of status as a legal immigrant or resident alien.*

amnesty *An official governmental act in which some general category of offenders is declared immune from punishment.*

Ethnic Pride

Thanks both to continued immigration and to their own high birthrate, Latinos were becoming an increasingly important minority (see "Makers of America: The Latinos," p. 688). The United States by 2003 was home to about 39 million Latinos. They included some 26 million Mexican Americans, 3 million Puerto Ricans, and 1 million Cubans, mostly in Florida.

Flexing their political muscles, Latinos elected mayors of Miami, Denver, and San Antonio. After years of struggle, the United Farmworkers Organizing Committee (UFWOC), headed by soft-spoken and charismatic César Chávez, succeeded in improving working conditions for the mostly Mexican American "stoop laborers" who followed the cycle of planting and harvesting across the American West. Latinos, newly confident and organized, became the nation's largest ethnic minority when their numbers surpassed African Americans in 2003. Indeed, by the first decade of the new century, most newborns in California were Latino, a powerful harbinger of the state's demographic future.

Asian Americans also made giant strides. By the 1980s they were America's fastest-growing minority. Once feared and hated as the "yellow peril" and consigned to the most menial jobs, citizens of Asian ancestry were now counted among the most prosperous Americans. Indians, the original Americans, numbered some 2.4 million in the 2000 census. Half of them had left their reservations to live in cities. Meanwhile, unemployment and alcoholism had blighted reservation life. Many tribes took advantage of their special legal status as independent nations by opening gambling casinos on reservation lands, but the cycle of discrimination and poverty proved hard to break.

Online Study Center

Primary source
Percent of the U.S. Population Who Were. . .
college.hmco.com/pic/kennedybrief7e

■ **The Oldest Americans** Members of the Cheyenne River Sioux Tribe celebrate the opening of the Smithsonian Institution's National Museum of the American Indian in Washington, D.C., 2004.

Cities and Suburbs

America's "alabaster cities" of song and story grew more sooty and less safe in the closing decades of the twentieth century. Crime was the great scourge of urban life. The rate of violent crimes committed in cities reached an all-time high in the drug-infested 1980s, then leveled off in the early 1990s. The number of violent crimes even began to decline substantially in many areas after 1995. Nevertheless, murders, robberies, and rapes remained shockingly common not only in cities but in suburbs and rural areas as well. America imprisoned a larger fraction of its citizens than almost any other country in the world, and some desperate citizens resorted to armed vigilante tactics to protect themselves.

The migration from cities to the suburbs was so swift and massive that by the mid-1990s a majority of Americans were suburban dwellers. The nation's rather brief "urban age" lasted little more than seven decades after 1920, and with its passing many observers saw a new fragmentation and isolation of American life. Some affluent suburban neighborhoods walled themselves off behind elaborate security systems in "gated communities." By the first decade of the twenty-first century, the suburban rings around big cities such as New York, Chicago, and Houston were becoming more racially and ethnically diverse, though individual schools and towns were often homogeneous.

Suburbs grew fastest in the West and Southwest. Newcomers came not only from nearby cities but from other regions of the United States as well. A momentous shift of the American population was under way, as inhabitants from the Northeast and the Midwest moved southward and westward to job opportunities and the sun. The Great Plains faced the sharpest decline, hollowing out the traditional American heartland.

Some major cities exhibited signs of renewal, including New York, Chicago, San Francisco, and even the classic "city without a center," Los Angeles. Well-to-do

Online Study Center

Interactive map
Living Patterns, 1990
college.hmco.com/pic/kennedybrief7e

residents reclaimed once-fashionable neighborhoods. But these latter-day homesteaders struggled to make their cities centers of residential integration. Cities stubbornly remained as divided by wealth and race as the suburban social landscape surrounding them.

Minority America

Racial and ethnic tensions exacerbated the problems of American cities. These stresses were especially evident in Los Angeles, which, like New York a century earlier, was a magnet for minorities, especially immigrants from Asia and Latin America. When in 1992 a mostly white jury exonerated white Los Angeles police officers who had been videotaped viciously beating a black suspect, the minority neighborhoods in South Central Los Angeles erupted in rage. Arson and looting laid waste entire city blocks, and scores of people were killed. Many black rioters vented their anger against white police by attacking Asian shopkeepers, who in turn formed armed patrols to protect their property.

> *In 1990 the African American intellectual Shelby Steele (b. 1946) declared in his provocative book,* The Content of Our Character,
>
> "What is needed now is a new spirit of pragmatism in racial matters where blacks are seen simply as American citizens who deserve complete fairness and in some cases developmental assistance, but in no case special entitlements based on color. We need deracinated social policies that attack poverty rather than black poverty and that instill those values that make for self-reliance."

The Los Angeles riots vividly testified to black skepticism about the American system of justice. Just three years later, again in Los Angeles, the televised spectacle of former football star O. J. Simpson's murder trial fed white disillusionment with the state of race relations. After months of testimony that seemed to point to Simpson's guilt, the jury acquitted him, presumably because certain Los Angeles police officers involved in the case had been shown to harbor racist sentiments. In a later **civil trial,** another jury unanimously found Simpson liable for the "wrongful deaths" of his former wife and another victim. The reaction to the Simpson verdicts revealed the yawning chasm that separated white and black America, as most whites continued to believe Simpson guilty, while a majority of African Americans told pollsters that the original not-guilty verdict was justified. Similarly, complaints by African Americans that they had been unlawfully kept from the polls during the 2000 presidential election in Florida reflected many blacks' conviction that they were still facing systematic racial disenfranchisement.

American cities have always held an astonishing variety of ethnic and racial groups, but in the early twenty-first century, minorities made up a majority of the population of many American cities, as whites fled to the suburbs. The most desperate black ghettos, housing a hapless "underclass" in the inner core of the old industrial cities, were especially problematic. Successful blacks who had benefited from the civil rights revolution of the 1950s and 1960s followed whites to the suburbs, leaving the poorest of the poor in the old ghettos. Without a middle class to sustain community institutions like schools and small businesses, the inner cities, plagued by unemployment and drug addiction, seemed bereft of leadership, cohesion, resources, and hope.

Some segments of the African American community did prosper in the wake of the civil rights gains of the 1950s and 1960s, and by the early 2000s over a third of all black families could be classified as firmly middle class. Blacks continued to make headway in political life as well. The number of black elected officials had risen above the nine thousand mark, including some three dozen members of Congress and the mayors of several large cities. Voting tallies demonstrated that successful black politicians were moving beyond isolated racial constituencies by appealing to a wide variety of voters. In 1989 Virginians, only 15 percent of whom were black, chose L. Douglas Wilder as the first African American state governor. In 2001 President Bush appointed Colin Powell secretary of state. In Bush's second administration Condoleezza Rice became the first African American woman to hold the post.

By the early twenty-first century blacks also dramatically advanced into higher education, though the educational gap between blacks and whites remained. The political assault against affirmative action in California and elsewhere in the 1990s only compounded obstacles to advanced training for many young African

civil trial *A trial before a judge or jury instigated by a private lawsuit in which one party seeks recovery of goods, financial compensation, or damages for loss or suffering from another private party or business. A* **criminal trial** *is instigated by an indictment for criminal law violations, and is brought by a state prosecutor on behalf of the government ("the people"); it may result in fines, imprisonment, or execution.*

The Latinos

Today Mexican food is handed through fast-food drive-up windows in all fifty states, Spanish-language broadcasts fill the airwaves, and the Latino community has its own telephone book, the *Spanish Yellow Pages.* Latinos send representatives to Congress and mayors to city hall, record hit songs, paint murals, and teach history. Latinos, among the fastest-growing segments of the U.S. population, include Puerto Ricans, frequent voyagers between their native island and northeastern cities; Cubans, many of them refugees from the communist dictatorship of Fidel Castro, concentrated in Miami and southern Florida; and Central Americans, fleeing the ravages of civil war in Nicaragua and El Salvador.

But the most populous group of Latinos derives from Mexico. The first significant numbers of Mexicans began heading for *El Norte* ("the North") around 1910, when the upheavals of the Mexican Revolution stirred and shuffled the Mexican population into more or less constant flux. Their northward passage was briefly interrupted during the Great Depression, when thousands of Mexican nationals were deported. But immigration resumed during World War II, and since then a steady flow of legal immigrants has passed through border checkpoints, joined by countless millions of their undocumented countrymen and countrywomen stealing across the frontier on moonless nights.

For the most part, these Mexicans came to work in the fields, following the ripening crops northward to Canada through the summer and autumn months. Others found work in the cities of the Southwest—El Paso, Los Angeles, Houston, and San Bernardino. Houses may have been shabby in the barrios, but these Mexican neighborhoods provided a sense of togetherness, a place to raise a family, and the chance to join a mutual aid society. Such societies, or *Mutualistas,* sponsored baseball leagues, helped the sick and disabled, and defended their members against discrimination.

Mexican immigrants lived so close to the border that their native country acted like a powerful magnet, drawing them back time and time again. Mexicans frequently returned to see relatives, and relatively few became U.S. citizens. In addition, the Mexican government sometimes intervened to discourage Mexicans from becoming citizens of their adopted country. In the 1910s and 1920s the Mexican consulate in Los Angeles launched a Mexicanization program among the immigrants, sponsoring parades to observe *Cinco de Mayo* ("Fifth of May"), celebrating Mexico's defeat of a French army in 1862. Since World War II, the American-born generation has carried on the fight for political representation, economic opportunity, and cultural preservation.

Fresh arrivals from Mexico and from other Latin American nations daily swell the Hispanic communities across America. As the United States moves through the twenty-first century, it is taking on a pronounced Spanish accent.

■ **Chicana Pride** A Mexican American girl celebrates her cultural heritage at the Texas Folklife Festival in San Antonio.

Americans. But defenders of affirmative action chalked up a major victory in 2003 when the Supreme Court, in a key case involving the University of Michigan, preserved affirmative action in university admissions as long as schools avoided using quotas or other mechanistic ways of diversifying their student bodies.

E Pluribus Plures

Controversial issues of color and culture also pervaded the realm of ideas at the turn of the twenty-first century. Echoing early-twentieth-century "cultural pluralists" like Horace Kallen and Randolph Bourne, many intellectuals after 1970 embraced the creed of "multiculturalism." The new mantra stressed the need to preserve and promote, rather than squash, a variety of distinct ethnic and racial cultures in the United States.

In the middle of the twentieth century, thinkers had tended to emphasize race-blind tolerance and universal qualities of the human species that transcended distinctions of nationality, color, or creed. In the 1970s and 1980s, however, ethnic pride became the catchword, and multiculturalism replaced the aging symbol of the "melting pot" with the colorful complexity of the "salad bowl."

The nation's classrooms became battlegrounds for the debate over America's commitment to pluralism. Multiculturalists attacked the traditional curriculum as "Eurocentric" and advocated greater focus on diverse ethnic traditions. In response, critics charged that too much stress on ethnic difference would come at the expense of national cohesion and an appreciation of common American values.

The Life of the Mind

Despite the mind-sapping chatter of the "boob tube," Americans in the late twentieth century read more, listened to more music, and were better educated than ever before. Colleges awarded some 2.5 million degrees in 2004. The expanding ranks of educated people lifted the economy to more advanced levels while creating consumers of "high culture." Americans annually made some 300 million visits to museums in the 1990s and patronized about a thousand opera companies and fifteen hundred symphony orchestras—as well as countless popular music groups.

What Americans read said much about the state of American society in the new century. Among the most striking developments in American letters was the rise of authors from once-marginal regions and ethnic groups coming into their own. Reflecting the general population shift westward, the West became the subject of a particularly rich literary outpouring. Larry McMurtry lovingly recollected the end of the cattle-drive era in *Lonesome Dove* (1985). Raymond Carver penned understated and powerful stories about working-class life in the Pacific Northwest, and Annie Dillard recreated the gritty frontier history of that same region. David Guterson wrote a moving tale of interracial anxiety and affection in the World War II–era Pacific Northwest in *Snow Falling on Cedars* (1994). Norman MacLean, a former English professor, left two unforgettable accounts of his boyhood in Montana: *A River Runs Through It* (1976) and *Young Men and Fire* (1992).

African American authors and artists also increasingly made their mark. Playwright August Wilson retold the history of black Americans in the twentieth century, with special emphasis on the psychic costs of the northward migration (*Fences*, 1985; *Joe Turner's Come and Gone*, 1988; *Jitney*, 1978). Alice Walker gave fictional voice to the experiences of black women in her hugely popular *The Color*

In her touching novel The Joy Luck Club, *Amy Tan explored the complex dilemmas of growing up as a Chinese American:*

"'A girl is like a young tree,' [my mother] said, 'You must stand tall and listen to your mother standing next to you. That is only way to grow strong and straight. But if you bend to listen to other people you will grow crooked and weak. . . .' Over the years I learned to choose from the best opinions. Chinese people had Chinese opinions. American people had American opinions. And in almost every case, the American version was much better. It was only later that I discovered there was a serious flaw with the American version. There were too many choices, so it was easy to get confused and pick the wrong thing."

Purple (1982). Toni Morrison wove a bewitching portrait of maternal affection in *Beloved* (1987) and in 1993 became the first African American woman to win the Nobel Prize for literature. Kiowa author N. Scott Momaday won a Pulitzer Prize for his portrayal of Indian life in *House Made of Dawn* (1968).

Asian American authors also flourished, among them playwright David Hwang, novelist Amy Tan, and essayist Maxine Hong Kingston, whose *Woman Warrior* (1976) and *China Men* (1980) imaginatively reconstructed the lives of the earliest Chinese immigrants. Jhumpa Lahiri's *Interpreter of Maladies* (1999) explored the sometimes painful relationship between immigrant Indian parents and their American-born children.

Latino writers made their mark as well. Sandra Cisneros drew on her own life as a Mexican American child to evoke Latino life in working-class Chicago in *The House on Mango Street* (1984). Women writers and women's themes forged to the fictional forefront as the feminist movement advanced. Jane Smiley modeled her searing narrative of a midwestern farm family, *A Thousand Acres* (1991), on Shakespeare's *King Lear* and followed up with a hilarious spoof on university life in *Moo* (1995). E. Annie Proulx won widespread acclaim with her comic yet tender portrayal of a struggling family in *The Shipping News* (1993). The rising interest in feminist and African American themes revived the popularity of the 1930s writer Zora Neale Hurston, especially her naturalist novel *Their Eyes Were Watching God,* first published in 1937.

New York became the art capital of the world after World War II, as well-heeled Americans supported a large number of painters and sculptors. The open and tradition-free American environment seemed especially congenial to the experimental mood of much modern art. Jackson Pollock pioneered abstract expressionism in the 1940s and 1950s, flinging paint on huge flats stretched on his studio floor. Realistic representation went out the window as artists like Pollock and Willem de Kooning strove to create "action paintings" that made the viewer a creative participant in defining the painting's meaning. Pop artists in the 1960s, notably Andy Warhol, canonized on canvas everyday items of consumer culture, such as soup cans. Claes Oldenburg tried to stun viewers into a new visual awareness with unfamiliar versions of familiar objects, such as giant plastic sculptures of pillow-soft telephones.

On the stage, playwright David Mamet analyzed the barbarity of American capitalism in plays like *Glengarry Glen Ross* and *American Buffalo,* in which he crafted a kind of poetry from the sludge of American slang. The AIDS epidemic inspired Tony Kushner's sensationally inventive *Angels in America,* a broad-ranging commentary, alternately hilarious and touching, about the condition of American life at century's end. Film, the most characteristic American art form, continued to flourish, especially as a wave of younger filmmakers like George Lucas, Steven

■ (left) Author Toni Morrison;
(right) Author Jhumpa Lahiri

Spielberg, Spike Lee, and the Coen brothers, as well as the innovative documentary artist, Ken Burns, made their influence felt.

Architecture also benefited from the building boom of the postwar era. Old master Frank Lloyd Wright produced strikingly original designs, as in the round-walled Guggenheim Museum in New York. Eero Saarinen, the son of a Finnish immigrant, contributed a number of imaginative structures, including two Yale University residential colleges that evoked the atmosphere of an Italian hill town. Chinese-born I. M. Pei designed numerous graceful buildings on several college campuses, as well as the John F. Kennedy Library in Boston. Philip Johnson artfully rendered huge edifices intimate in structures like New York City's Seagram Building and the New York State Theater at Lincoln Center in Manhattan. "Postmodernists" such as Robert Venturi and Michael Graves, inspired by the decorative details of earlier historical styles, rejected the spare functionalism that had dominated modern architecture for much of the century. The flight from stark modernism took fanciful forms in Frank Gehry's use of luminous, undulating sheets of metallic skin in his widely hailed Guggenheim Museum in Bilbao, Spain, and Walt Disney Concert Hall in Los Angeles.

The American Prospect

The American spirit pulsed with vitality in the twenty-first century, but grave problems continued to plague the Republic. Women still fell short of first-class economic citizenship, and American society groped for ways to adapt the traditional family to the new realities of women's work outside the home. A generation after the civil rights triumphs of the 1960s, full equality remained an elusive dream for countless Americans of color. Powerful foreign competitors challenged America's premier economic status. As job opportunities shrank in some of the nation's regions and expanded in others, as jobs shifted to cheaper labor markets abroad, and as giant corporations like Enron collapsed through corporate scandal, many Americans began to fear their economy as a treacherous landscape even as it offered some of them astounding prosperity. The alarmingly unequal redistribution of wealth and income threatened to turn America into a society of haves and have-nots, mocking the ideals of democracy and breeding seething resentments along the economic frontier that divided rich from poor.

Environmental worries clouded the country's future. Coal-fired electrical generating plants helped form acid rain and probably contributed to the greenhouse effect, an ominous warming in the planet's temperature. The planet was being drained of oil, and disastrous accidents like the grounding and subsequent oil spill of the giant tanker *Exxon Valdez* in 1989 in Alaska's pristine Prince William Sound demonstrated the ecological risks of oil exploration and transportation at sea. By the early twenty-first century, bolstered by the sharply escalating price of oil, the once-lonely cries for alternative fuel sources had escalated into mainstream public fascination with solar power and windmills, electric "hybrid" cars, and the pursuit of an affordable hydrogen fuel cell. Energy conservation remained another crucial but elusive strategy—much heralded at the politician's rostrum, but too rarely embodied in public policy, as witnessed in the Bush administration's rejection of the Kyoto "global warming treaty" in 2001.

As the human family grows at an alarming rate on a shrinking globe, new challenges still face America and its historic values. The task of cleansing Spaceship Earth of its abundant pollutants—including nuclear weapons—was one urgent mission confronting the American people in the new century. Another was seeking ways to resolve the ethnic and cultural conflicts that erupted with renewed virulence around the globe in the wake of the Cold War's end. At the same time, new opportunities beckon in outer space and on inner-city streets, at the artist's easel and in the concert hall, at the inventor's bench and in the scientist's laboratory, and in the unending quest for social justice, individual fulfillment, and international peace.

The terrorist attack on America on September 11, 2001, posed yet another challenge to the United States. Shielded for over two centuries against assaults on its soil, it would now have to preserve its security in a world made smaller by global communication and transportation, without altering its fundamental democratic values and way of life.

In facing those challenges, the world's oldest republic had an extraordinary tradition of resilience and resourcefulness to draw on. Born as a revolutionary force in a world of conservatism, the United States stood in the twenty-first century as a conservative force in a world of revolution. It had held aloft the banner of liberal democracy in a world wracked by revolutions of the right and left, including fascism, Nazism, and communism. Yet through it all, much that was truly revolutionary also remained a part of America's liberal democratic heritage, as its people pioneered in revolutions against colonialism, racism, sexism, ignorance, and poverty.

The dream of "making the world safe for democracy," articulated nearly a century earlier by Woodrow Wilson at the end of the First World War, gained a new poignancy after September 11, when Americans expressed a yearning for greater equality, opportunity, and democracy in the Middle East—all in the hope of diminishing the root causes of international terrorism. The capacity to nurture progress, however, depended on the ability of Americans to improve their own country, and to do so in the midst of threats to their own security. As Wilson wrote in 1892, long before he became president, "Democratic institutions are never done; they are like living tissue, always a-making. It is a strenuous thing, this living the life of a free people."

✪ Chapter Summary ✪

In the early years of the twenty-first century, the American culture and economy underwent further dynamic changes. Having passed from an age of heavy industry to one of information and mass culture, it now entered an era characterized by globalization and instant communication via the Internet and other media. Science and technology increasingly created the new forms of wealth, opening vast new human possibilities but also presenting serious ethical and environmental challenges. The benefits of the new wealth did not reach everyone, however, as the gaps between those with education and those without contributed to an increasingly severe inequality in Americans' wealth and income.

The decades-long movement into the work force of women, including mothers of young children, opened ever-wider doors of opportunity, and contributed to changes in men's roles as well as in family life. Women's continuing focus on issues of families and children made the issues of workplace discrimination and child care important features of the continuing struggle for equality. With fewer families being formed, the population began to age and the elderly became a potent lobbying force.

That the American population continued to grow was due primarily to a vast new wave of immigration, especially from Asia and Latin America. Though more racially and culturally diverse than earlier immigrants, the new arrivals were exactly like earlier groups in seeking economic opportunity and liberties unavailable in their homelands. Latinos, Asians, and Indians all asserted their own identity and pride. Mexican Americans were the largest of the diverse Latino groups, and their rapidly growing presence increasingly made the American Southwest a "bi-cultural zone." Some old-stock Americans feared that the new immigrants, particularly Latinos, were not assimilating as previous groups had.

The issues of "multiculturalism" came to the fore, and Americans debated whether too much emphasis on ethnic distinctiveness would undermine a sense of common culture and national identity.

The problems of poverty, increasingly concentrated in inner cities ringed by affluent suburbs, remained stubborn and frustrating to millions of Americans, including many minorities. The majority of Americans now lived in suburbs, mostly white and affluent, but with some minorities appearing in "inner-ring" communities. The African American community made great strides in education, politics, and other areas, but there was a growing gap between an upwardly mobile middle class and those left behind. America's cities were plagued by problems of drugs and crime, but in the 1990s and 2000s crime dropped and many cities began to show signs of renewal.

American culture remained incredibly dynamic and inventive, both in "high culture" and "pop culture." The new voices of westerners, women, African Americans, Asians, and others were increasingly influential and popular, contributing to the variety and energy of U.S. society. Beginning with the postwar "abstract expressionist" movement in New York City, American visual arts and architecture also led worldwide revolutions in taste and transformed the nature of urban life.

American democracy remains a dynamic force in a new global and technological age. Issues of economic inequality, environmental degradation, and ethnic conflict demand urgent attention and engagement by American citizens. Most critical of all, the nation must find a way to remain vigilant against terrorism without sacrificing the unique values and opportunities of democracy. Protecting the freedoms upon which the United States was built in an age rocked by instability locally and globally has become America's greatest challenge.

APPENDIX

SUGGESTED READINGS

CHAPTER 1

PRIMARY SOURCE DOCUMENTS

Various English editions of Hernán Cortés's correspondence from Mexico are available, including *Five Letters, 1519–1526* (1929), trans. by J. Bayard Morris.* An important source from a *conquistador*'s perspective is Bernal Diaz del Castillo, *Historia Verdadera de la Conquista de la Nueva España*, selections of which have been recently translated into English in *The Discovery and Conquest of Mexico, 1517–1521*, edited by Genaro Garcia (1996). Bartolomé de Las Casas, *Thirty Very Judicial Propositions** (1552), and Juan Ginés de Sepúlveda, *The Second Democrates** (1547), reflect the Spanish *conquistadores*' efforts to understand the native peoples of the New World. See also Las Casas's *The Destruction of the Indies* (1542). *The Broken Spears: The Aztec Account of the Conquest of Mexico,** edited by Miguel León-Portilla (1962), is an anthology of texts compiled from indigenous sources. Olaudah Equiano, *Equiano's Travels** (1789), is a fascinating account by an African in the New World in the eighteenth century.

SECONDARY SOURCES

Brian M. Fagan reviews the evidence concerning the earliest humans to arrive in the Americas in *The Great Journey: The Peopling of Ancient America* (1987). Archaeologist Tom Dillehay revises estimates of settlement of the New World in *The Settlement of the Americas: A New Prehistory* (2000), which presents exciting new archaeological evidence. Alice Beck Keyhoe gives an engaging account of American Indian nations during the fifteen thousand years before Columbus in *America Before the European Invasions* (2002). For more on the pre-Columbian history of the Americas, see Norman Hammond, *Ancient Maya Civilization* (1982); Brian M. Fagan, *Kingdoms of Gold, Kingdoms of Jade: The Americas Before Columbus* (1991); and Stuart J. Fiedel, *Prehistory of the Americas* (1992). For a terrific study in cross-cultural perceptions between Columbus and Indians, see Tzvetan Todorov, *The Conquest of America* (1984). Immanuel Wallerstein, *The Modern World System: Capitalist Agriculture and the Origins of the European World in the Sixteenth Century* (1974), provides a theoretical overview of European colonization's international economic background. Early African history is sketched in J. D. Fage, *A History of West Africa* (1969), and John Thornton discusses Africa's role in the world economy in *Africa and Africans in the Making of the Atlantic World, 1400–1800* (1992). A fascinating brief synthesis of early European contact with the Americas is J. H. Elliott, *The Old World and the New, 1492–1650* (1970). For a comparative study, see Anthony Pagen, *Lords of All Worlds: Ideologies of Empire in Spain, Britain, and France* (1995). Alfred W. Crosby, Jr., discusses *The Columbian Exchange: Biological and Cultural Consequences of 1492* (1972). See the same author's *Ecological Imperialism: The Biological Expansion of Europe, 900–1900* (1986). A marvelously illustrated volume portraying the impact of America on the European imagination is Hugh Honour, *The New Golden Land* (1975). See also Kirkpatrick Sale, *The Conquest of*

Paradise: Christopher Columbus and the Columbian Legacy (1990), and Herman J. Viola and Carolyn Margolis, *Seeds of Change: Five Hundred Years Since Columbus* (1991). D. W. Meinig presents a geographical overview of immigration in *The Shaping of America: A Geographical Perspective on 500 Years of History: Atlantic America, 1492–1800* (1986). Patricia Seed compares different forms of European conquest in *Ceremonies of Possession* (1995). For an engaging and comprehensive study of New World Iberian colonies from the preconquest period to the early nineteenth century, see Mark A. Burkholder and Lyman L. Johnson, *Colonial Latin America* (2000). Various aspects of the Spanish and Portuguese conquests of America are described in Charles Gibson, *Spain in America* (1966), and L. McAlister, *Spain and Portugal in the New World, 1492–1700* (1984). William H. Prescott, *History of the Conquest of Mexico* (1843) and *History of the Conquest of Peru* (1847) are two fascinating narrative histories of the nineteenth century. Nathan Wachtel presents the Indians' view of the Spanish conquest in *The Vision of the Vanquished* (1977). The spread of Spanish America northward is traced in Edward H. Spicer, *Cycles of Conquest: The Impact of Spain, Mexico, and the United States on the Indians of the Southwest, 1533–1960* (1962); Andrew L. Knaut, *The Pueblo Revolt of 1680: Conquest and Resistance in Seventeenth-Century New Mexico* (1997); Ramon A. Gutierrez, *When Jesus Came, the Corn Mothers Went Away* (1991); and David J. Weber's masterful synthesis, *The Spanish Frontier in North America* (1992).

CHAPTER 2

PRIMARY SOURCE DOCUMENTS

Richard Hakluyt, *Divers Voyages Touching the Discovery of America and the Islands Adjacent*, edited by J. W. Jones (1850), supplied the rationale for the establishment of English colonies in North America. John Smith, "Generall Historie of Virginia," in *Travels and Works of Captain John Smith,** edited by Edward Arber (1910), is an account by the amazing, vain man who steered Jamestown through its precarious first few years.

SECONDARY SOURCES

England's involvement in overseas settlement in the sixteenth century is described in David B. Quinn, *England and the Discovery of America, 1481–1620* (1974). In *The Elizabethans and the Irish* (1966), Quinn details the role of Ireland in the origins of Elizabethan colonization. The international economic background to colonization is sketched in Ralph Davis, *The Rise of the Atlantic Economies* (1973), and in Kenneth R. Andrews, *Trade, Plunder, and Settlement: Maritime Enterprise and the Genesis of the British Empire, 1480–1630* (1984). The immediate English backdrop is colorfully presented in Peter Laslett, *The World We Have Lost* (1965), and in Carl Bridenbaugh, *Vexed and Troubled Englishmen, 1590–1642* (1968). James Lang, *Conquest and Commerce: Spain and England in the Americas* (1975), is a comparative chronicle of colonial rivalries; Jack P. Greene, *Pursuits of Happiness: The Social Development of Early Modern British Colonies and the Formation of American Culture* (1988), compares the process of English colonization in different regions of North America and the Caribbean. Contact between Indian and European cultures is handled in Colin G. Calloway, *New Worlds for All: Indians, Europeans, and the Remaking of America* (1997), and James

---

*An asterisk indicates that the document, or an excerpt from it, can be found in David M. Kennedy and Thomas A. Bailey, eds., *The American Spirit: United States History as Seen by Contemporaries*, 11th ed. (Boston: Houghton Mifflin, 2006)

Axtell, *The Invasion Within: The Contest of Cultures in Colonial America* (1985). James Merrell, *The Indians' New World* (1989), which describes the wrenching experiences of the Catawba Indians, is the best ethnohistorical account of a single tribe for the early period. See also Daniel K. Richter, *The Ordeal of the Longhouse: The Peoples of the Iroquois League in the Era of European Colonization* (1992), and Richard White, *The Middle Ground: Indians, Empires, and Republics in the Great Lakes Region, 1650–1815* (1991). The Chesapeake region has continued to receive attention, especially in Paul G. E. Clemens, *The Atlantic Economy and Colonial Maryland's Eastern Shore* (1980); Lois Green Carr et al., eds., *Colonial Chesapeake Society* (1988); Lois Green Carr et al., *Robert Cole's World: Agriculture and Society in Early Maryland* (1991); Philip D. Morgan, *Slave Counterpoint: Black Culture in the Eighteenth-Century Chesapeake and Lowcountry* (1998); and James Horn, *Adapting to a New World: English Society in the Seventeenth-Century Chesapeake* (1994). Richard Dunn, *Sugar and Slaves: The Rise of the Planter Class in the English West Indies, 1624–1713* (1972), describes South Carolina society's West Indian roots. The most comprehensive account of the various colonial economies is contained in John J. McCusker and Russell R. Menard, *The Economy of British North America, 1607–1789* (1985). The role of slavery in early colonial society is examined perceptively in Edmund S. Morgan, *American Slavery, American Freedom* (1975). For a unique and important study of the role gender played in shaping racial ideologies in colonial Virginia, see Kathleen Brown, *Good Wives, Nasty Wenches, and Anxious Patriarchs* (1996). See also Peter Wood's account of South Carolina, *Black Majority* (1974), and Ira Berlin's overview, *Many Thousands Gone: The First Two Centuries of Slavery in North America* (1998). Gary Nash analyzes relations among Indians, European colonists, and blacks in *Red, White, and Black: The Peoples of Early America* (1974), as do Daniel H. Usner, Jr., in *Indians, Settlers, and Slaves in a Frontier Exchange Economy: The Lower Mississippi Valley Before 1783* (1992), and Timothy Silver in *A New Face on the Countryside: Indians, Colonists, and Slaves in South Atlantic Forests, 1500–1800* (1990). Daniel K. Richter examines European colonists through the eyes of Native Americans in *Facing East from Indian Country: A Native History of Early America* (2003).

CHAPTER 3

PRIMARY SOURCE DOCUMENTS

John Winthrop, "A Model of Christian Charity" (1630), in *The American Primer*, edited Daniel Boorstin, outlines the goals of the Puritan errand into the wilderness. Winthrop's "Speech on Liberty"* (1645), in his *History of New England* (1853), established the colony's fundamental political principles. William Bradford, *Of Plymouth Plantation,* * edited by Samuel E. Morison (1952), is a rich contemporary account.

SECONDARY SOURCES

New England has received more scholarly attention than any other colonial region. Harry Stout, *The New England Soul: Preaching and Culture in Colonial New England* (1986), is a comprehensive account. A brilliant and complex intellectual history is Perry Miller, *The New England Mind* (2 vols., 1939, 1953), a work that has long been a landmark for other scholars. Sacvan Bercovitch traces the heritage of the New England temperament in *The Puritan Origins of the American Self* (1975). Also see David Jaffe, *People of the Wachusett: Greater New England in History and Memory* (1999). Other interpretations of Puritanism include Charles Hambrick-Stowe, *The Practice of Piety* (1982), and Andrew Delbanco, *The Puritan Ordeal* (1989). David Hall, *Worlds of Wonder, Days of Judgment: Popular Religious Belief in Early New England* (1989), describes the relation between high Puritan doctrine and lay belief and practice. Jon Butler, *Awash in a Sea of*

Faith: Christianizing the American People (1990), is comprehensive. John T. Ellis pays special attention to religious issues in *Catholics in Colonial America* (1965), as does Edmund S. Morgan in *Roger Williams: The Church and State* (1967). On other religious minorities, see Carla Gardina Pestana, *Quakers and Baptists in Colonial Massachusetts* (1991). For analyses of Puritan-Indian relations, see Francis Jennings, *The Invasion of America* (1975), and Neal Salisbury, *Manitou and Providence* (1982). For a fascinating account of some settlers' assimilation into Indian society, see John Demos, *The Unredeemed Captive: A Family Story from Early America* (1994). David S. Lovejoy discusses the impact of England's Glorious Revolution on the colonies in *The Glorious Revolution in America* (1975). Areas outside New England are dealt with in Gary Nash, *Quakers and Politics: Pennsylvania, 1681–1726* (1971); Patricia Bonomi, *A Factious People: Politics and Society in Colonial New York* (1971); Richard and Mary Dunn, eds., *The World of William Penn* (1986); Oliver A. Rink, *Holland on the Hudson: An Economic and Social History of Dutch New York* (1986); and Joyce D. Goodfriend, *Before the Melting Pot: Society and Culture in Colonial New York City, 1664–1730* (1992). The essays in Michael Zuckerman, ed., *Friends and Neighbors: Group Life in America's First Plural Society* (1982), argue that the middle colonies provide the best early model for America as a whole. Timothy H. Breen, *Puritans and Adventurers* (1980), draws contrasts between Virginia and New England.

CHAPTER 4

PRIMARY SOURCE DOCUMENTS

The first slave laws of Virginia are collected in Warren M. Billings, ed., *The Old Dominion in the Seventeenth Century** (1975), as are first-hand accounts of Bacon's Rebellion. See also George L. Burr, ed., *Narratives of the Witchcraft Cases, 1648–1706** (1914).

SECONDARY SOURCES

On life and labor in the Chesapeake, consult Thad W. Tate and David L. Ammerman, eds., *The Chesapeake in the Seventeenth Century* (1979). Further probing economic conflicts and their role in the introduction of slavery is Timothy H. Breen and Stephen Innes, *Myne Owne Ground: Race and Freedom on Virginia's Eastern Shore, 1640–1676* (1980). Gloria Main chronicles *The Tobacco Colony: Life in Early Maryland, 1650–1719* (1982). Darrett B. Rutman and Anita H. Rutman examine Virginia in *A Place in Time: Middlesex County, Virginia 1650–1750* (1984). Daniel Blake Smith looks *Inside the Great House: Planter Family Life in Eighteenth-Century Chesapeake Society* (1980). Kenneth A. Lockridge analyzes the life of one of Virginia's most celebrated residents in *The Diary and Life of William Byrd II of Virginia, 1674–1744* (1987). Winthrop Jordan's fascinating *White over Black: American Attitudes Toward the Negro, 1550–1812* (1968) discusses the evolution of racial thought. Rhys Isaac's masterful *The Transformation of Virginia 1740–1790* (1999) explores the tumultuous role of religious and political conflicts in shaping colonial Virginia. Life in New England's towns and homes is scrutinized in John Demos, *A Little Commonwealth: Family Life in Plymouth Colony* (1970); Philip Greven, *Four Generations: Population, Land, and Family in Colonial Andover, Massachusetts* (1970); Kenneth Lockridge, *New England Town: Dedham* (1970); Christine Heyrman, *Commerce and Culture: The Maritime Communities of Colonial Massachusetts, 1690–1750* (1984); and Daniel Vickers, *Farmers and Fishermen: Two Centuries of Work in Essex County, Massachusetts, 1630–1850* (1994). For a less idealized portrait of early New England, see John F. Martin, *Profits in the Wilderness: Entrepreneurship and the Founding of New England Towns in the Seventeenth Century* (1991); Margret Ellen Newell, *From Dependency to Independence: Economic Revolution in Colonial New England* (1998); and Stephen Innes, *Creating the Com-*

monwealth: The Economic Culture of Puritan New England (1995). For more on the role of gender in seventeenth-century society, see Laurel T. Ulrich, *Good Wives: Image and Reality in the Lives of Women in Northern New England, 1650–1750* (1982); Marylynn Salmon, *Women and the Law of Property in Early America* (1986); Mary Beth Norton, *Founding Mothers and Fathers* (1996); Cornelia Hughes Dayton, *Women Before the Bar: Gender, Law, and Society in Connecticut, 1639–1789* (1995); Lisa Wilson, *Ye Heart of a Man: The Domestic Life of Men in Colonial New England* (1999); and Philip Greven, *The Protestant Temperament* (1977), which analyzes child-rearing practices. Edmund S. Morgan describes the crisis that beset the original Puritans when their children displayed a lesser degree of religiosity in *Visible Saints* (1963). David Grayson Allen emphasizes the persistence of English customs in *In English Ways: The Movement of Societies and the Transferral of English Local Law and Custom to Massachusetts Bay in the Seventeenth Century* (1981). See also David Cressy, *Coming Over: Migration and Communication Between England and New England in the Seventeenth Century* (1987), and David Hackett Fischer, *Albion's Seed: Four British Folkways in America* (1989). Witchcraft is the subject of Paul Boyer and Stephen Nissenbaum's *Salem Possessed* (1974), John Demos's *Entertaining Satan* (1982), and Carol F. Karlsen's *The Devil in the Shape of a Woman: Witchcraft in Colonial New England* (1987). Mary Beth Norton's recent reinterpretation of the Salem witchcraft trials, *In the Devil's Snare: The Salem Witchcraft Crisis of 1692* (2002), emphasizes New England's experience of frontier conflict in King William's War. See also Richard Godbeer, *The Devil's Dominion: Magic and Religion in Early New England* (1992), and Peter Charles Hoffer, *The Devil's Disciples: Makers of the Salem Witchcraft Trials* (1996). A sweeping survey that emphasizes the diversity of cultures already present in seventeenth-century America is E. Brooks Holifield, *Era of Persuasion: American Thought and Culture, 1521–1680* (1989). The relationship of Indians and New England whites to their environment is the subject of William Cronon's intriguing *Changes in the Land* (1983). David Konig, *Law and Society in Puritan Massachusetts: Essex County, 1629–1692* (1979), considers the role of law in mitigating social tensions.

CHAPTER 5

PRIMARY SOURCE DOCUMENTS

Noting the ethnic diversity of colonial American society, Michel-Guillaume Jean de Crèvecoeur, *Letters from an American Farmer** (1904), and Benjamin Franklin, "Observations on the Increase of Mankind,"* in Jared Sparks, ed., *The Works of Benjamin Franklin* (1840), respectively celebrate and express unease at that diversity. Franklin's entertaining *Autobiography** (1868) is an indispensable guide to the values and preoccupations of his time. It includes an account of George Whitefield's visit to Philadelphia during the Great Awakening.

SECONDARY SOURCES

Social history is painted with broad strokes in James Henretta, *The Evolution of American Society, 1700–1815* (1973), and Jack Greene, *Pursuits of Happiness* (1988). Population trends are detailed in Robert V. Wells, *The Population of the British Colonies in America before 1776* (1975). Philip D. Curtin studies black slaves and white indentured servants in *The African Slave Trade: A Census* (1969). For pioneering work in historical demography, see Russell Menard's *Migrants, Servants and Slaves: Unfree Labor in Colonial British America* (2001), and Sharon V. Salinger, *"To Serve Well and Faithfully": Labor and Indentured Servants in Pennsylvania, 1682–1800* (1987). Bernard Bailyn captures the human face of migration and settlement on the eve of the Revolution in his masterful *Voyagers to the West*

(1986). Several works detail the experiences of the very diverse groups who came to America during this period. The lives of convicts relocated to the United States are explored in A. Roger Ekirch, *Bound for America: The Transportation of British Convicts to the Colonies, 1718–1775* (1987); British immigrants in Bernard Bailyn, *The Peopling of British North America* (1986); Scottish immigrants in Alan L. Karras, *Sojourners in the Sun: Scottish Migrants in Jamaica and the Chesapeake, 1740–1800* (1992); German immigrants in Marianne S. Wokek, *Trade in Strangers: The Beginnings of Mass Migration to North America* (1999); and colonial immigration in general in Ida Altman and James Horn, eds., *"To Make America": European Emigration in the Early Modern Period* (1991). Large-scale economic patterns are traced in John J. McCusker and Russell R. Menard, *The Economy of British America, 1607–1789* (1991), and Alice H. Jones, *The Wealth of a Nation to Be: The American Colonies on the Eve of the Revolution* (1980). The complex interactions between whites and blacks are documented in Mechal Sobel, *The World They Made Together: Black and White Values in Eighteenth-Century Virginia* (1987), and William D. Piersen, *Black Yankees: The Development of an Afro-American Subculture in Eighteenth-Century New England* (1988). The toiling classes are probed in Gerald W. Mullin, *Flight and Rebellion: Slave Resistance in Eighteenth-Century Virginia* (1972); Gary B. Nash, *The Urban Crucible: Social Change, Political Consciousness and the Origins of the American Revolution* (1979); Allen Kulikoff, *Tobacco and Slaves: The Development of Southern Cultures in the Chesapeake, 1680–1800* (1986); Robert Orwell, *Masters, Slaves, and Subjects: The Culture of Power in the South Carolina Low Country* (1998); and Marcus Rediker, *Between the Devil and the Deep Blue Sea: Merchant Seamen, Pirates, and the Anglo-American Maritime World, 1700–1750* (1987). Nash links social conflict to the Great Awakening, as does Richard L. Bushman, *From Puritan to Yankee: Character and Social Order in Connecticut, 1690–1765* (1967). Patricia Bonomi also emphasizes religious conflict as a promoter of Revolutionary ideology in *Under the Cope of Heaven: Religion, Society, and Politics in Colonial America* (1986), as do the essayists in Ronald Hoffman and Peter J. Albert, eds., *Religion in a Revolutionary Age* (1994). Alan Heimert first explored the significance of the Great Awakening in *Religion and the American Mind* (1966); his interpretation has been revised by Jon Butler in *Awash in a Sea of Faith* (1992). Jon Butler has also written a cultural history of the development of American identity in the late eighteenth century in *Becoming America: The Revolution Before 1776* (2000). Other important works on religion include David S. Lovejoy, *Religious Enthusiasm in the New World: Heresy to Revolution* (1985), and Susan Juster, *Disorderly Women: Sexual Politics and Evangelicalism in Revolutionary New England* (1994). Cultural history is imaginatively presented in Howard M. Jones, *O Strange New World: American Culture in the Formative Years* (1964). Henry May's *The Enlightenment in America* is comprehensive (1976). The sometimes heroic dedication to education is portrayed by Lawrence Cremin, *American Education: The Colonial Experience, 1607–1783* (1970), and the general social implications of the early educational system are studied in James Axtell, *The School upon a Hill* (1974). Colonial politics are interpreted in a most suggestive way in Bernard Bailyn, *The Origins of American Politics* (1965). More fine-grained local studies are John Gilman Kolp, *Gentlemen and Freeholders: Electoral Politics in Colonial Virginia* (1998); Richard L. Bushman, *King and People in Provincial Massachusetts* (1985); Robert Zemsky, *Merchants, Farmers and River Gods: An Essay on Eighteenth-Century American Politics* (1971); Jackson Turner Main, *Society and Economy in Colonial Connecticut* (1985); Patricia Bonomi, *A Factious People: Politics and Society in Colonial New York* (1971); James T. Lemon, *The Best Poor Man's Country* (1972), which deals with Pennsylvania; and Daniel Blake Smith, *Inside the Great House: Planter Family Life in Eighteenth-Century Chesapeake Society* (1980). Timothy Breen examines the ways in which the increasing indebtedness of the Virginia planters changed their behavior in *Tobacco Culture: The Mentality of the Great Tidewater Planters on the Eve of Revolution* (1985).

CHAPTER 6

PRIMARY SOURCE DOCUMENTS

"The Albany Plan of the Union" was the first great statement of colonial unity; "The Proclamation of 1763" forbade settlement west of the Appalachians. Both are collected in Henry Steele Commager, *Documents of American History*. Adolph B. Benson, ed., *The America of 1750; Petar Kalm's Travels in North America* (1937),* records the observations of a visiting Swedish naturalist with a keen eye for the behavior of humans.

SECONDARY SOURCES

A cutting-edge study of the major themes in Atlantic history is presented in David Armitage, ed., *The British Atlantic World, 1500–1800* (2002). For an analysis of Britain's concept of empire, also see Armitage's *Ideological Origins of the British Empire* (2000) and David Hancock, *Citizens of the World: London Merchants and the Integration of the British Atlantic Community* (1995). Further efforts to analyze the colonial empire are James Henretta, *"Salutary Neglect": Colonial Administration under the Duke of Newcastle* (1972); Michael Kammen's especially interesting *Empire and Interest* (1970); and John Brewer, *The Sinews of Power: War, Money and the English State, 1688–1783* (1989). The empire as seen through British eyes is captured in Paul David Nelson, *William Tryon and the Course of Empire: A Life in British Imperial Service* (1990). The French colonial effort is described in George M. Wrong, *The Rise and Fall of New France* (2 vols., 1928). William John Eccles presents a vivid study of French exploration and settlement in North America and the West Indies in *The French in North America, 1500–1783* (1998). Calvin Martin, *Keepers of the Game* (1978), offers a provocative interpretation of the fur trade and its impact on Indian societies. Other works on the role of Indians in larger imperial struggles include Armstrong Starkey, *European and Native American Warfare, 1615–1815* (1998); Francis Jennings, *Empire of Fortune: Crowns, Colonies and Tribes in the Seven Years War in America* (1988); Gregory Evans Dowd, *A Spirited Resistance: The North American Indian Struggle for Unity, 1745–1815* (1992); and Richard White, *The Middle Ground: Indians, Empires, and Republics in the Great Lakes Region, 1650–1815* (1991). The wars for empire in the eighteenth century are vividly narrated by Fred Anderson in *Crucible of War: The Seven Years' War and the Fate of Empire in British North America, 1754–1766* (2001). Anderson's *A People's Army: Massachusetts Soldiers and Society in the Seven Years' War* (1984) discusses the experience of colonial soldiers in forging resistance to Britain. Alan Rogers, *Empire and Liberty: American Resistance to the British Authority, 1755–1763* (1974), investigates American participation in the Seven Years' War, as does Douglas E. Leach, *Roots of Conflict: British Armed Forces and Colonial Americans, 1677–1763* (1986). Classic accounts are Francis Parkman's several volumes, condensed in *The Battle for North America*, edited by John Tebbel (1948), and *The Parkman Reader*, edited by Samuel E. Morison (1955).

CHAPTER 7

PRIMARY SOURCE DOCUMENTS

Adam Smith, *An Inquiry into the Nature and Causes of the Wealth of Nations** (1776), is a penetrating analysis of British mercantilism. An intriguing Loyalist account of the Revolution, since reprinted, is Peter Oliver, *Origin and Progress of the American Rebellion* (1781). Patrick Henry, "Speech Before the Virginia House of Burgesses Against the Stamp Act"* (1765), was an influential statement of colonial opposition to British policy, as was John Dickinson's response to the Townshend Acts, *Letters from a Farmer in Pennsylvania* (1768). Revolutionary writings may also be found in Bernard Bailyn, ed., *Pamphlets of the American Revolution, 1750–1776* (1965). For con-

temporary accounts of the beginning of hostilities, see Peter Force, ed., *American Archives*, 4th series, vol. 2* (1839). For visual sources from the period, consult the edition compiled by Donald H. Cresswell, *The American Revolution in Drawings and Prints* (1975).

SECONDARY SOURCES

The Revolution is interpreted as a divinely ordained event in George Bancroft's *History of the United States of America* (1852). Edmund S. Morgan, *The Birth of the Republic, 1763–1789* (1959), is a brief account of the Revolutionary era. It stresses the happy coincidence of the revolutionaries' principles and their interests, as do Daniel Boorstin, *The Genius of American Politics* (1953), and Robert E. Brown, *Middle-Class Democracy and the Revolution in Massachusetts, 1691–1780* (1955). Lawrence Gipson, *The Coming of the Revolution, 1763–1775* (1954), summarizes his fifteen-volume masterwork. A more recent effort at a general synthesis is Robert Middlekauff, *The Glorious Cause: The American Revolution, 1763–1789* (1982). Robert R. Palmer, *The Age of the Democratic Revolution: A Political History of Europe and America, 1760–1800* (2 vols., 1959, 1964), places American events in the larger context of Western history. Two enlightening collections of essays are Jack P. Greene, ed., *The Reinterpretation of the American Revolution, 1763–1789* (1968), and Alfred F. Young, ed., *The American Revolution* (1976), which generally represents a "New Left" revisionist view, a perspective also found in Edward A. Countryman, *The American Revolution* (1987). A recent work that reinforces revisionist themes is Gary Nash, *The Unknown American Revolution: The Unruly Birth of Democracy and the Struggle to Create America* (2005). For an examination of ordinary people's experience in the Revolution, see Ray Raphael, *A People's History of the American Revolution* (2001). An interesting effort to blend British and American perspectives is Ian R. Christie and Benjamin W. Labaree, *Empire or Independence, 1760–1776* (1976). The sources of American dissatisfaction with the British imperial system can be traced in Carl Ubbelohde, *The American Colonies in the British Empire, 1607–1763* (1968), and Thomas C. Barrow, *Trade and Empire: The British Customs Service in Colonial America* (1967). Oliver M. Dickerson, *The Navigation Acts and the American Revolution* (1951), concludes that the navigation system did not put undue burdens on the colonies. Bernhard Knollenberg examines the effects of the British tightening of the imperial system in the 1760s in *Origin of the American Revolution, 1759–1766* (1960), as does Michael Kammen in *Empire and Interest* (1970). John Shy imaginatively explores an important aspect of the imperial system's effect on America in *Toward Lexington: The Role of the British Army in the Coming of the American Revolution* (1965). A perceptive short account of the American reaction to British initiatives is Edmund S. Morgan and Helen M. Morgan, *The Stamp Act Crisis* (1953). Benjamin W. Labaree discusses another instance of American reaction in *The Boston Tea Party* (1964). Pauline Maier focuses on the crucial role of the "mob" in *From Resistance to Revolution: Colonial Radicals and the Development of American Opposition to Britain, 1765–1776* (1972). The British side is told in Peter D. G. Thomas, *British Politics and the Stamp Act Crisis* (1975), *The Townshend Duties Crisis* (1987), and *Tea Party to Independence* (1991). Bernard Bailyn's seminal *Ideological Origins of the American Revolution* (1967) stresses the importance of ideas in pushing the Revolution forward, as well as the colonists' fears of a conspiracy against their liberties. John Philip Reid emphasizes legal ideas in *Constitutional History of the American Revolution: The Authority of Rights* (1987), as does Jerrilyn Greene Marston in *King and Congress: The Transfer of Political Legitimacy, 1774–1776* (1987). Useful local studies of American resistance are Richard D. Brown, *Revolutionary Politics in Massachusetts* (1970); Woody Holton, *Forced Founders: Indians, Debtors, Slaves, and the Making of the American Revolution in Virginia* (1999). Richard Ryerson, *The Revolution Is Now Begun: The Radical Committees of Philadelphia, 1765–1776* (1978); Joseph S. Tiedmann, *Reluctant Revolutionaries: New York City and the Road to Independence, 1763–1776* (1997); and David Hackett Fischer, *Paul*

Revere's Ride (1994). On the meaning of the Revolution for African Americans, see Sylvia R. Frey, *Water from the Rock: Black Resistance in a Revolutionary Age* (1991). Ordinary artisans' involvement in Revolutionary events is the subject of Alfred F. Young's *The Shoemaker and the Tea Party* (1999). Helpful biographies of key Revolutionary figures include Richard Beeman, *Patrick Henry* (1974); Merrill D. Peterson, *Thomas Jefferson and the New Nation* (1970); Dumas Malone, *Jefferson and His Time* (5 vols., 1948–1974); C. Bradley Thompson, *John Adams and the Spirit of Liberty* (1998); and Pauline Maier, *The Old Revolutionaries: Political Lives in the Age of Samuel Adams* (1980). Imaginative cultural history is found in Robert A. Gross, *The Minutemen and Their World* (1976). Edward A. Countryman emphasizes class conflict in *A People in Revolution: The American Revolution and Political Society in New York, 1760–1790* (1981). A psychological approach to the problem of the Revolutionary generation's assault on established authority is taken in Jay Fliegelman, *Prodigals and Pilgrims: The American Revolution Against Patriarchal Authority, 1750–1800* (1982).

CHAPTER 8

PRIMARY SOURCE DOCUMENTS

Thomas Paine's fiery *Common Sense** (1776) is the manifesto of the Revolution. "The Declaration of Independence"* (1776) is one of the foundations of American political theory. For eyewitness accounts of the war, see John C. Dann, *The Revolution Remembered* (1980). See also the "Treaty of Peace with Great Britain" (1783), in Henry Steele Commager, *Documents of American History*.

SECONDARY SOURCES

The war is sketched in Don Higginbotham's excellent military history, *The War of American Independence: Military Attitudes, Policies, and Practice, 1763–1789* (1971). On the implications of the Revolutionary conflict, see John Shy, *A People Numerous and Armed: Reflections on the Military Struggle for American Independence* (1976); E. Wayne Carp, *To Starve the Army at Pleasure: Continental Army Administration and American Political Culture, 1775–1783* (1984); Charles Royster, *A Revolutionary People at War: The Continental Army and the American Character* (1980); Mark V. Kwasny, *Washington's Partisan War, 1775–1783* (1996); and Ronald Hoffman et al., eds., *An Uncivil War: The Southern Backcountry During the American Revolution* (1985). The conflict is considered in its European setting in Piers Mackesy, *The War for America, 1775–1783* (1964). Carl Becker's classic *The Declaration of Independence* (1922) is masterful; on the same subject, see also Garry Wills, *Inventing America: Jefferson's Declaration of Independence* (1980), and Pauline Maier, *American Scripture: The Making of the Declaration of Independence* (1997). The role of the Loyalists is treated in Robert M. Calhoon, *The Loyalists in Revolutionary America* (1973); Mary Beth Norton, *The British-Americans: The Loyalist Exiles in England* (1972); John E. Ferling, *The Loyalist Mind: Joseph Galloway and the American Revolution* (1977); Robert M. Calhoon, *Loyalists and Community in North America* (1994); Janice Potter-MacKinnon, *While the Women Only Wept: Loyalist Refugee Women* (1993); and Bernard Bailyn's unusually sensitive biography of the governor of colonial Massachusetts, *The Ordeal of Thomas Hutchinson* (1974). General treatments of an often-neglected subject are Benjamin Quarles, *The Negro in the American Revolution* (1961); Ronald Hoffman and Ira Berlin, eds., *Slavery and Freedom in the Age of the American Revolution* (1983); and Sylvia R. Frey, *Water from the Rock: Black Resistance in a Revolutionary Age* (1991). See also Duncan J. MacLeod, *Slavery, Race and the American Revolution* (1974), and David B. Davis, *The Problem of Slavery in the Age of Revolution, 1770–1823* (1975), an able, gracefully written book. International implications are developed in James H. Hutson, *John Adams and the Diplomacy of the American Revolution* (1980), and Jonathan R. Dull, *A Diplomatic History of the American Revolution*

(1985). Attention to the social history of the Revolution has been largely inspired by John F. Jameson's seminal *The American Revolution Considered as a Social Movement* (1926). Jackson T. Main, *The Social Structure of Revolutionary America* (1969), takes the exploration further along the same lines, with conclusions somewhat at variance with Jameson's. Local studies of this issue include Alan Taylor, *Liberty Men and Great Proprietors: The Revolutionary Settlement on the Maine Frontier, 1760–1820* (1990); Steven Rosswurm, *Arms, Country, and Class: The Philadelphia Militia and the "Lower Sort" During the American Revolution* (1987); and Billy G. Smith, *The "Lower Sort": Philadelphia's Laboring People, 1750–1800* (1990). For information on the role of Indians in the Revolution, see Barbara Graymont, *The Iroquois in the American Revolution* (1972); Isabel T. Kelsay, *Joseph Brant, 1743–1807: Man of Two Worlds* (1984); and Colin G. Calloway, *The American Revolution in Indian Country* (1995). Thomas Doerflinger describes economic change during the Revolution in *A Vigorous Spirit of Enterprise: Merchants and Economic Development in Revolutionary Philadelphia* (1986). Interesting biographies are Samuel E. Morison's swashbuckling *John Paul Jones* (1959); Eric Foner, *Tom Paine and Revolutionary America* (1976); and James T. Flexner, *George Washington in the American Revolution, 1775–1783* (1968). British troubles are laid bare in William B. Willcox, *Portrait of a General: Sir Henry Clinton in the War of Independence* (1964). Women are the subject of Linda K. Kerber, *Women of the Republic: Intellect and Ideology in Revolutionary America* (1980); Mary Beth Norton, *Liberty's Daughters: The Revolutionary Experience of American Women* (1980); and Joy Day Buel and Richard Buel, Jr., *The Way of Duty: A Woman and Her Family in Revolutionary America* (1984). Michael Kammen brilliantly evokes the ways that the Revolution has been enshrined in the national memory in *A Season of Youth: The American Revolution and the Historical Imagination* (1978).

CHAPTER 9

PRIMARY SOURCE DOCUMENTS

A comparison of the text of the Articles of Confederation (1781), in Henry Steele Commager, *Documents of American History,* with the Constitution* makes an intriguing study. See also Madison, Hamilton, and Jay's explanations of the Constitution in *The Federalist* papers, especially *Federalist* No. 10.* Additional primary sources may be found in Bernard Bailyn, ed., *The Debate on the Constitution: Federalist and Antifederalist Speeches, Articles, and Letters During the Struggle over Ratification* (1993). For visual sources from the period, consult *The American Revolution in Drawings and Prints* (1975), a volume compiled by Donald H. Cresswell.

SECONDARY SOURCES

John Fiske, in *The Critical Period of American History* (1888), portrayed America under the Articles of Confederation as a crisis-ridden country. His view is sharply qualified by Merrill Jensen in *The New Nation* (1950). Jack N. Rakove's *The Beginnings of National Politics* (1979) offers a history of the Continental Congress that substantially revises Jensen's work. Especially informative is Gordon S. Wood's massive and brilliant study of the entire period, *The Creation of the American Republic, 1776–1787* (1969), and his equally compelling work, *The Radicalism of the American Revolution* (1991), which documents the relative egalitarianism that swept revolutionary society during and after the war. For a similar argument that relies on the material culture of the era, see Richard Bushman, *The Refinement of America: Persons, Houses, Cities* (1992). See also Richard B. Morris, *The Forging of the Union, 1781–1787* (1987). For the intellectual foundations of the political economy, see Cathy Matson and Peter Onuf, *A Union of Interests: Political and Economic Thought in Revolutionary America* (1990). An influential transatlantic perspective on the roots of American republicanism is J. G. A. Pocock, *The Machi-*

avellian Moment: Florentine Political Thought and the Atlantic Republican Tradition (1975). Edmund S. Morgan also looks at both Britain and America in *Inventing the People: The Rise of Popular Sovereignty in England and America* (1988). On the state constitutions, see Jackson T. Main, *The Sovereign States, 1775–1783* (1973), and Willi P. Adams, *The First American Constitutions* (1980). Peter S. Onuf carefully examines the Northwest Ordinance in *Statehood and Union: A History of the Northwest Ordinance* (1987). On the Constitutional Convention, see Richard Bernstein's superb synthesis of current scholarship, *Are We to Be a Nation? The Making of the Constitution* (1987). Bernstein's work was one of a host of useful studies inspired by the bicentennial of the drafting of the Constitution. Others include Ruth Bloch, *Visionary Republic: Millennial Themes in American Thought, 1756–1800* (1986); Richard Beeman et al., eds., *Beyond Confederation: Origins of the Constitution and American National Identity* (1987); Leonard Levy, *Original Intent and the Framers' Constitution* (1988); and Jack N. Rakove, *Original Meanings: Politics and Ideas in the Making of the Constitution* (1996). For a more general interpretation of the Constitution's role in American society, see Michael G. Kammen, *A Machine That Would Go of Itself* (1986). Thornton Anderson, *Creating the Constitution* (1993), and Robert A. Rutland, *The Ordeal of the Constitution* (1966), describe the ratification struggle. Charles A. Beard caused a stir with the class-based analysis he offered in *An Economic Interpretation of the Constitution of the United States* (1913). It is seriously weakened by two blistering attacks: Robert E. Brown, *Charles Beard and the Constitution* (1956), and Forrest McDonald, *We the People: The Economic Origins of the Constitution* (1958). See also McDonald's *E Pluribus Unum: The Formation of the American Republic, 1776–1790* (1965). Jackson T. Main, *The Anti-Federalists* (1961), partially rehabilitates Beard. Gary Nash's *Race and Revolution* (1990) offers a perceptive study of controversies over race and slavery in the making of the Constitution, as do the contributors to John P. Kaminski, ed., *A Necessary Evil? Slavery and the Debate over the Constitution* (1995). David Szatmary is perceptive on *Shays' Rebellion* (1980), as are the contributors to Robert Gross, ed., *In Debt to Shays* (1993). On similar episodes of agrarian radicalism, see Alan Taylor, *Liberty Men and Great Proprietors: The Revolutionary Settlement on the Maine Frontier, 1760–1820* (1990). Charles R. Kesler has edited a collection of essays on *The Federalist* papers entitled *Saving the Revolution: The Federalist Papers and the American Founding* (1987). Also see Morton White, *Philosophy, The Federalist, and the Constitution* (1987). A concise summary of the original federalist-antifederalist debate is Herbert J. Storing, *What the Anti-Federalists Were For* (1981). Relevant biographical studies of merit are Richard Brookhiser, *Alexander Hamilton, American* (1999), and Jack Rakove, *James Madison and the Creation of the American Republic* (2002). For an engaging study of the political negotiations and infighting among several members of the founding generations, see Joseph Ellis, *Founding Brothers: the Revolutionary Generation* (2001).

CHAPTER 10

PRIMARY SOURCE DOCUMENTS

"The Report on Manufactures" (in Daniel Boorstin, ed., *American Primer*), the last of Alexander Hamilton's messages to Congress, presented the case for the development of American industry. Thomas Jefferson expounded his views in *Notes on the State of Virginia* (1784). For further study of the Hamiltonian-Jeffersonian debate, see Harold C. Syrett, ed. *The Papers of Alexander Hamilton* (27 vols., 1961–1987), and Julian Boyd et al., eds., *The Papers of Thomas Jefferson* (30 vols., 1950–2003). Important salvos in the battle between national power and state sovereignty, and between Federalists and Jeffersonians, were the Virginia* and Kentucky resolutions (1798) and the reply of Rhode Island* (1799). Washington's Farewell Address* (1796) established the foundation for American attitudes about party politics and foreign policy. See also Benjamin Franklin Bache's stinging editorial on Washington's retirement, *Philadelphia Aurora** (1797).

SECONDARY SOURCES

Perceptive introductions are provided in James Roger Sharp's succinct *American Politics in the Early Republic: The New Nation in Crisis* (1993) and Stanley Elkins and Eric McKitrick's comprehensive work, *The Age of Federalism: The Early American Republic, 1788–1800* (1993). On administration, see Ronald Hoffman, *Launching the "Extended Republic": The Federalist Era* (1996). On the economy, see Paul Gilje, *Wages of Independence: Capitalism in the Early American Republic* (1997). Innovative work on political culture in the early national period can be found in James Sharp, *American Politics in the Early Republic* (1993), and Joanne Freeman, *Affairs of Honor* (2001). On the Bill of Rights, see Bernard Schwartz, *The Great Rights of Mankind: A History of the American Bill of Rights* (1991), and Patrick L. Conley and John P. Kaminski, eds., *The Bill of Rights and the States: The Colonial and Revolutionary Origins of American Liberties* (1992). On the use of party politics, see Richard Hofstadter's thoughtful *The Idea of a Party System* (1969); Richard Buel, Jr., *Securing the Revolution: Ideology in American Politics, 1789–1815* (1972); John Zvesper, *Political Philosophy and Rhetoric: A Study of the Origins of American Party Politics* (1977); John F. Hoadley, *Origins of American Political Parties, 1789–1803* (1986); and Lance Banning, ed., *After the Constitution: Party Conflict in the New Republic* (1989). Other interpretations of that subject, stressing the ideology of republicanism, are Drew McCoy, *The Elusive Republic: Political Economy in Jeffersonian America* (1980), and Lance Banning, *The Jeffersonian Persuasion* (1978). Charles G. Steffens examines the political beliefs of workers in *The Mechanics of Baltimore: Workers and Politics in the Age of Revolution, 1763–1812* (1984), as do Michael Merrill and Sean Wilentz in their introduction to the edited volume *The Key of Liberty: The Life and Democratic Writings of William Manning, "A Laborer," 1747–1814* (1992). For a trenchant analysis of Jeffersonianism, see Joyce Appleby, *Capitalism and a New Social Order: The Republican Vision* (1984), whose analysis emphasizes the role of liberalism in American political thought, a point previously made by Louis Hartz in *The Liberal Tradition in America* (1955). Also illuminating is Gerald Stourzh, *Alexander Hamilton and the Idea of Republican Government* (1970). Thomas P. Slaughter focuses on *The Whiskey Rebellion: Frontier Epilogue to the American Revolution* (1986). A comprehensive biography is James T. Flexner, *George Washington and the New Nation, 1783–1793* (1969). An engaging account is Joseph Ellis, *His Excellency: George Washington* (2004). Consult also Forrest McDonald, *The Presidency of George Washington* (1974), and Garry Wills, *Cincinnatus: George Washington and the Enlightenment* (1984). Of special interest is Richard H. Kohn, *Eagle and Sword: The Federalists and the Creation of the Military Establishment in America, 1783–1802* (1975). On aspects of foreign policy, see Alexander De Conde, *Entangling Alliance* (1958); Gilbert Lycan, *Alexander Hamilton and American Foreign Policy* (1970); Jerald Combs, *The Jay Treaty* (1970); Lawrence S. Kaplan, *Colonies into Nation: American Diplomacy, 1763–1801* (1972); and Daniel G. Lang, *Foreign Policy in the Early Republic: The Law of Nations and the Balance of Power* (1985). For the view from across the Atlantic, see Charles R. Ritcheson, *Aftermath of Revolution: British Policy Toward the United States, 1783–1795* (1969). On Adams, consult Page Smith, *John Adams* (2 vols., 1962), and Stephen G. Kurtz, *The Presidency of John Adams* (1957). James M. Smith, *Freedom's Fetters* (1956), treats the Alien and Sedition Acts, as does Leonard Levy in *Legacy of Suppression* (1960).

CHAPTER 11

PRIMARY SOURCE DOCUMENTS

Thomas Jefferson's "First Inaugural Address" (1801), in Henry Steele Commager, *Documents of American History*, echoed the themes of Washington's Farewell Address and set the tone for his presidency. Reuben G. Thwaites, ed., *Original Journals of the Lewis and Clark Ex-*

*pedition** (1904), chronicles the explorers' adventures. For the political flavor of the age, see the debate over the Embargo Act* (1807); for constitutional history, read the decision of John Marshall in *Marbury* v. *Madison** (1803). See James Madison, "War Message"* (1812), in James D. Richardson, ed., *Messages and Papers of the Presidents*, vol. 1 (1896), and the protest of thirty-four Federalist congressmen, *Annals of Congress*,* 12th Cong., 1st sess., 2219–2221 (1812). John Marshall's decision in *McCulloch* v. *Maryland*,* 4 Wheaton 316 (1819), is a leading statement of the era's surging nationalism.

SECONDARY SOURCES

A monument of American historical writing is Henry Adams, *History of the United States During the Administrations of Jefferson and Madison* (9 vols., 1889–1891), available in a one-volume abridgement edited by Ernest Samuels. Especially fascinating are Adams's prologue and epilogue on the United States in 1800 and 1817. A brief introduction is given in Marshall Smelser, *The Democratic Republic, 1801–1815* (1968). For a succinct study of Marshall's life and legal thought, see Jean Edward Smith, *John Marshall: Definer of a Nation* (1996). A helpful analysis of challenges faced by the judiciary is Richard E. Ellis, *The Jeffersonian Crisis: Courts and Politics in the New Republic* (1971). For a broad understanding of legal developments in this period, see Lawrence Friedman, *A History of American Law* (1973); Morton J. Horwitz, *The Transformation of American Law, 1780–1860* (1977); and Alfred H. Kelly, Winfred A. Harbison, and Herman Belz, *The American Constitution: Its Origins and Development* (6th ed., 1983). On the Supreme Court, see R. Kent Newmyer, *The Supreme Court Under Marshall and Taney* (1986), and G. Edward White, *The Marshall Court and Cultural Change, 1815–1835* (1988). Politics are treated in a broad, imaginative context in James S. Young, *The Washington Community, 1800–1829* (1966). For the important role women played in early America's political society, see Catherine Allgor, *Parlor Politics* (2000). See also Robert M. Johnstone, Jr., *Jefferson and the Presidency* (1979), and the Joyce Appleby, Lance Banning, and Drew McCoy volumes cited in Chapter 10. Other works include Joseph Ellis, *American Sphinx: The Character of Thomas Jefferson* (1997), and Robert B. Tucker and David Hendrickson, *Empire of Liberty: The Statecraft of Thomas Jefferson* (1990). Noble E. Cunningham, Jr., *In Pursuit of Reason: The Life of Thomas Jefferson* (1987), is a short biography. The standard scholarly biography is Merrill D. Peterson, *Thomas Jefferson and the New Nation* (1970). Peterson has also scrutinized *The Jefferson Image in the American Mind* (1960). Forrest McDonald is highly critical of his subject in *The Presidency of Thomas Jefferson* (1976). Leonard Levy debunks Jefferson's liberalism in *Jefferson and Civil Liberties* (1963); Anthony Wallace examines Jefferson's racial ideas and his policies toward Native Americans in *Jefferson and the Indians* (1999); and Garry Wills does the same for black slaves in *Negro President: Thomas Jefferson and the Slave Power* (2003). See also Reginald Horsman, *Expansion and American Indian Policy, 1783–1812* (1967), and Gregory Evans Dowd, *A Spirited Resistance: The North American Indian Struggle for Unity, 1745–1815* (1992). Donald Jackson, *Thomas Jefferson and the Stony Mountain: Exploring the West from Monticello* (1981), captures Jefferson's fascination with the West. See also Stephen E. Ambrose's spirited biography of Meriwether Lewis, *Undaunted Courage* (1996). An engaging and recent study of the origins and diplomacy of the Louisiana Purchase is Jon Kukla's *A Wilderness so Immense* (2003). The embargo is treated in Burton Spivak, *Jefferson's English Crisis: Commerce, Embargo and the Republican Revolution* (1979). See also Doron S. Ben-Atar, *The Origins of Jeffersonian Commercial Policy and Diplomacy* (1993). Daniel Boorstin vividly evokes the intellectual climate of the age in *The Lost World of Thomas Jefferson* (1948). Irving Brant looks at *James Madison, Secretary of State* (1953), and F. E. Ewing examines Jefferson's powerful Treasury secretary in *America's Forgotten Statesman: Albert Gallatin* (1959). An important work that sets the War of 1812 in a broad context of early American history is J. C. A. Stagg, *Mr. Madison's War: Politics, Diplomacy and Warfare in the Early Ameri-*

can Republic (1983). Also see Steven Watts, *The Republic Reborn: War and the Making of Liberal America, 1790–1820* (1987), and Donald R. Hickey, *The War of 1812: A Forgotten Conflict* (1989). On the causes of the war, Julius W. Pratt, *Expansionists of 1812* (1925), stresses western pressures; Bradford Perkins, *Prologue to War: England and the United States, 1805–1812* (1961), and Reginald Horsman, *The Causes of the War of 1812* (1962), discuss free seas; and Roger H. Brown, *The Republic in Peril, 1812* (1964), emphasizes the need for saving the republican form of government.

CHAPTER 12

PRIMARY SOURCE DOCUMENTS

Timothy Dwight offers a participant's view of the opposition to the War of 1812 in *The History of the Hartford Convention** (1833). Charles F. Adams, ed., *Memoirs of John Quincy Adams** (1875), offers a behind-the-scenes portrait of the creation of the Monroe Doctrine. See also the text of Monroe's public statement in James D. Richardson, ed., *Messages and Papers of the Presidents,** vol. 2 (1896). "The Missouri Compromise" (1819–1820), in Henry Steele Commager, *Documents of American History*, reveals the dangerous sectional animosities underlying such national pride.

SECONDARY SOURCES

On the War of 1812, see the books by J. C. A. Stagg, Steven Watts, and Donald R. Hickey cited in Chapter 11. Lester D. Langley, *The Americans in the Age of Revolution, 1750–1850* (1996), takes a comparative approach to the history of the Western Hemisphere. On Indian affairs and westward expansion, see Dorothy Jones, *License for Empire: Colonialism by Treaty in Early America* (1982), and the works of R. David Edmunds, *The Shawnee Prophet* (1983) and *Tecumseh and the Quest for Indian Leadership* (1984). The relevant volumes of Henry Adams's nine-volume *History of the United States* (1889–1891) still contain magnificent reading, both on the war and on the peace. Federalist reaction to Republican foreign policy is vividly etched in David H. Fisher, *The Revolution of American Conservatism* (1965), and James M. Banner, *To the Hartford Convention: The Federalists and the Origins of Party Politics in Massachusetts* (1970). Consult also James H. Broussard, *The Southern Federalists, 1800–1816* (1979). Irving Brant argues that James Madison was a strong president in *James Madison: Commander in Chief, 1812–1836* (1961). More recent treatments of Madison include Robert A. Rutland, *James Madison: The Founding Father* (1987); Drew R. McCoy, *The Last of the Fathers: James Madison and the Republican Legacy* (1989); and Jack N. Rakove, *James Madison and the Creation of the American Republic* (1990). Other useful biographical studies are Robert Remini, *Henry Clay: Statesman for the Union* (1991), and David Heidler, *Old Hickory's War: Andrew Jackson and the Quest for Empire* (2003). An excellent introduction to nationalism is George Dangerfield, *The Awakening of American Nationalism, 1815–1828* (1965). See also Robert H. Wiebe's ambitious *Opening of American Society: From the Adoption of the Constitution to the Eve of Disunion* (1984). Arand Otto Mayr and Robert C. Post, eds., detail *Yankee Enterprise: The Rise of the American System of Manufactures* (1981). Glover Moore, *The Missouri Controversy, 1819–1821* (1953), and Charles S. Sydnor, *The Development of Southern Sectionalism, 1819–1848* (1948), place the Missouri Compromise in a broader context. On the Monroe Doctrine, the classic text is Dexter Perkins, *A History of the Monroe Doctrine* (1955). James E. Lewis, *The American Union and the Problem of Neighborhood* (1998), places the Monroe Doctrine in a new interpretive context. Ernest R. May ties the doctrine to domestic politics, especially the impending election of 1824, in *The Making of the Monroe Doctrine* (1975). See also Harry Ammon, *James Monroe: The Quest for National Identity* (1971), as well as James Lewis, *John Quincy Adams: Policymaker for the Union* (2001).

CHAPTER 13

PRIMARY SOURCE DOCUMENTS

Davy Crockett, *Exploits and Adventures in Texas** (1836), is a lively description of the democratic political order of Jacksonian America. James Fenimore Cooper's *The American Democrat** (1838) offers an incisive commentary on the era's politics, while C. W. Janson, *The Stranger in America, 1793–1806** (1807), exposes the seamier aspects of American egalitarianism. A still-powerful classic treatise on the Jacksonian period is Alexis de Tocqueville, *Democracy in America* (1835, 1840). On the Bank War, see Andrew Jackson, "Veto Message"* (July 10, 1832), in James D. Richardson, ed., *Messages and Papers of the Presidents*, vol. 2 (1896); *The Nullification Era: A Documentary Record*, edited by William W. Freehling; and Daniel Webster's "Speech on Jackson's Veto of the U.S. Bank Bill" (1832), in Richard Hofstadter, ed., *Great Issues in American History*. On the "Tariff of Abominations" and its implications, see the "Webster-Hayne Debate"* (1830). *The Diary of Philip Hone, 1828–1851* (1927) presents the everyday reflections of a Whig mayor of New York.

SECONDARY SOURCES

Overviews of Jacksonian politics include Arthur M. Schlesinger, Jr., *The Age of Jackson* (1945); Harry L. Watson, *Liberty and Power: The Politics of Jacksonian America* (1990); and Charles Sellers, *The Market Revolution: Jacksonian America, 1815–1846* (1991). A sweeping narrative of early American politics that puts Jacksonian democracy at its center is Sean Wilentz, *The Rise of American Democracy: Jefferson to Lincoln* (2005). For a more temporally focused approach that still uses a broad lens, see Louis P. Masur, *1831: Year of Eclipse.* Edward Pessen, *Jacksonian America: Society, Personality, and Politics* (rev. ed., 1978), is a good general introduction that sharply disputes Tocqueville's findings. See also Frederick Jackson Turner, *The Frontier in American History* (1920), which casts Jackson as an exemplar of the democratic spirit of the frontier. Marvin Meyers, *The Jacksonian Persuasion* (1957), and John William Ward, *Andrew Jackson: Symbol for an Age* (1955), examine the broader cultural significance of "Old Hickory" and his supporters. Lee Benson, *The Concept of Jacksonian Democracy: New York as a Test Case* (1961), attacks Schlesinger's emphasis on eastern labor's support for Jackson. For a general overview of political participation, see Glenn C. Altschuler and Stuart M. Blumin, *Rude Republic: Americans and Their Politics in the Nineteenth Century* (2001). On the evolution of mass-based political parties, see Lawrence Kohl, *The Politics of Individualism: Parties and the American Character in the Jacksonian Era* (1989); Richard P. McCormick, *The Second American Party System* (1966); and two books by Ronald P. Formisano, *The Birth of Mass Political Parties: Michigan, 1827–1861* (1971) and *The Transformation of Political Culture: Massachusetts Parties, 1790s–1840s* (1983). See also Amy Bridges, *A City in the Republic: Antebellum New York and the Origins of Machine Politics* (1984), and Richard L. McCormick's general survey of party politics from Jackson into the twentieth century, *The Party Period and Public Policy: American Politics from the Age of Jackson to the Progressive Era* (1986). Four works that consider Jacksonian politics in the South are William J. Cooper, *The South and the Politics of Slavery, 1828–1856* (1978); J. Mills Thornton III, *Politics and Power in a Slave Society: Alabama, 1800–1860* (1978); William W. Freehling, *The Road to Disunion: Secessionists at Bay, 1776–1854* (1990); and Harry L. Watson, *Jacksonian Politics and Community Conflict: The Emergence of the Second American Party System in Cumberland County, North Carolina* (1981), which discusses the opponents of Jackson. Robert V. Remini has a three-volume biography of Jackson; *Andrew Jackson and the Course of American Freedom* (1981) and *Andrew Jackson and the Course of American Democracy* (1984) cover the presidential years. Remini also has a fine biography of Clay, *Henry Clay: Statesman for*

the Union (1991). A masterful analysis of the period's most celebrated statesmen is Merrill D. Peterson, *The Great Triumvirate: Webster, Clay, and Calhoun* (1987). On Van Buren, see John Niven, *Martin Van Buren: The Romantic Age of American Politics* (1983). Incisive analysis can be found in Richard Hofstadter's essay on Jackson in *The American Political Tradition and the Men Who Made It* (1948). See also Daniel Feller, *The Jacksonian Promise 1815–1840* (1995). On nullification, see Richard E. Ellis, *The Union at Risk: Jacksonian Democracy, States' Rights and the Nullification Crisis* (1987). An impressive study of the nullification crisis with a regionally specific focus is William W. Freehling's *Prelude to Civil War: The Nullification Controversy in South Carolina, 1816–1836* (1966). On Calhoun, see Gerald M. Capers, *John C. Calhoun, Opportunist* (1960), and John Niven, *John C. Calhoun and the Price of Union* (1988). Jacksonians are charged with ignorance and hypocrisy in Bray Hammond, *Banks and Politics in America from the Revolution to the Civil War* (1957). John McFaul looks at the broader picture in *The Politics of Jacksonian Finance* (1972), and Robert V. Remini focuses on political questions in *Andrew Jackson and the Bank War* (1967). For an insightful and imaginative personal biography of Jackson, see Andrew Burstein, *The Passions of Andrew Jackson* (2003). Jackson's Indian policies are scrutinized in Ronald N. Satz, *American Indian Policy in the Jacksonian Era* (1975). See also Michael D. Green, *The Politics of Indian Removal* (1982), and Anthony Wallace, *The Long, Bitter Trail: Andrew Jackson and the Indians* (1993). For studies of the so-called Five Civilized Tribes, see Charles Hudson, *The Southeastern Indians* (1976), and William G. McLaughlin, *Cherokee Renascence in the New Republic* (1986). Daniel W. Howe provides a stimulating analysis of Jackson's opponents in *The Political Culture of the American Whigs* (1980). For an illuminating and comprehensive study of the Whig party, see Michael F. Holt, *The Rise and Fall of the American Whig Party* (1999). Attempts to connect politics with the economic changes of the era include Charles Sellers's provocative synthesis, *The Market Revolution: Jacksonian America, 1815–1846* (1991), and Melvyn Stokes and Stephen Conway, eds., *The Market Revolution in America* (1996).

CHAPTER 14

PRIMARY SOURCE DOCUMENTS

Seth Luther, *An Address to the Working-Men of New England** (1833), is the eloquent appeal of an uneducated working-class labor reformer. On the transportation revolution, see John H. B. Latrobe, *The First Steamboat Voyage on the Western Waters** (1871), and Mark Twain's classic *Life on the Mississippi** (1883). Lemuel Shaw's decision of 1842 in *Commonwealth* v. *Hunt*, 4 Metc. III (in Henry Steele Commager, *Documents of American History*) is regarded as the "Magna Carta of American labor organization." Ralph Waldo Emerson's address "The Young American," printed in *The Dial* (April 1844), expresses his enthusiasm for a new era of technological advancement. Thomas Dublin has edited *Farm to Factory: Women's Letters, 1830–1860* (rev. ed., 1993), and Charles Dickens's *American Notes* (1842) offers a European perspective on American urbanization and growth.

SECONDARY SOURCES

On immigration, see Maldwyn Jones, *American Immigration* (1960); John Bodnar, *The Transplanted: A History of Immigrants in Urban America* (1985); Hasia Diner, *Erin's Daughters in America* (1983); and Kerby A. Miller, *Emigrants and Exiles: Ireland and the Irish Exodus to North America* (1985). Bruce Levine, *The Spirit of 1848: German Immigrants, Labor Conflict, and the Coming of the Civil War* (1992), discusses German refugees and their new place in America. Solid introductions are George R. Taylor, *The Transportation Revolution, 1815–1860* (1951); Clarence H. Danhoff, *Change in Agriculture: The Northern United States, 1820–1870* (1969); and Douglas C. North, *Economic Growth in the United States, 1790–1860* (1961). See also North's *Growth and Welfare in the American Past* (rev. ed., 1974). The events of the period are placed in a larger context of economic history in Stuart Bruchey, *The Roots of American Economic Growth, 1607–1861* (1965), and Albert W. Niemi, *U.S. Economic History: A Survey of the Major Issues* (1975). On government and private sponsorship of new technologies and infrastructure, see John Lauritz Larson, *Internal Improvement: National Public Works and the Promise of Popular Government in the Early United States* (2001). Thomas C. Cochran, *Frontiers of Change: Early Industrialism in America* (1981), treats industrialization as culturally inspired change. Two fascinating case studies of the coming of industrialism are Alan Dawley, *Class and Community: The Industrial Revolution in Lynn* (1977), and Anthony F. C. Wallace, *Rockdale: The Growth of an American Village in the Early Industrial Revolution* (1978). The laboring classes are chronicled in Bruce Laurie, *Artisans into Workers: Labor in Nineteenth-Century America* (1989). Consult also Herbert Gutman's pathbreaking *Work, Culture, and Society in Industrializing America* (1976); Sean Wilentz's insightful *Chants Democratic: New York City and the Rise of the American Working Class, 1788–1850* (1984); David A. Zonderman's *Aspirations and Anxieties: New England Workers and the Mechanized Factory System, 1815–1850* (1992); and David R. Roediger's *The Wages of Whiteness: Race and the Making of the American Working Class* (1991). The experiences of women workers are the focus of Thomas Dublin, *Women at Work: The Transformation of Work and Community in Lowell, Massachusetts, 1826–1860* (1979), and Christine Stansell, *City of Women: Sex and Class in New York, 1780–1860* (1986). Mary Blewett puts the gender identities of both men and women at the center of *Men, Women, and Work: Class, Gender, and Protest in the New England Shoe Industry, 1780–1910* (1988). On the introduction of technology, see David H. Hounshell, *From the American System to Mass Production, 1800–1932: The Development of Manufacturing Technology in the United States* (1984), and David F. Hawke, *Nuts and Bolts of the Past: A History of American Technology, 1776–1860* (1988). Ideological aspects of this process are described in John F. Kasson, *Civilizing the Machine: Technology and Republican Values in America, 1776–1900* (1976), and David Nye, *Consuming Power: A Social History of American Energies* (1998). For a fascinating study of how industrialization shaped daily routine and time, see Michael O'Malley, *Keeping Watch: A History of American Time* (1996). The canal era is comprehensively described in Carter Goodrich, *Government Promotion of American Canals and Railroads, 1800–1890* (1960), and Ronald E. Shaw, *Canals for a Nation: The Canal Era in the United States, 1790–1860* (1990). On the Erie Canal, see Carol Sheriff, *The Artificial River* (1996). On railroads, consult Robert Fogel, *Railroads and American Economic Growth* (1964), which presents the startling thesis that the iron horse in fact did little to promote growth. For a different view, see Albert Fishlow, *American Railroads and the Transformation of the Ante-Bellum Economy* (1965), and James A. Ward, *Railroads and the Character of America, 1820–1887* (1986). The organization and management of railroad corporations is treated in Alfred D. Chandler, Jr., *The Visible Hand: The Managerial Revolution in American Business* (1977). The legal foundation of the market revolution is discussed in Morton Horwitz, *The Transformation of American Law, 1780–1860* (1977). Steven Hahn and Jonathan Prude, eds., *The Countryside in the Age of Capitalist Transformation: Essays in the Social History of Rural America* (1985), is a provocative look at the impact of the transportation and industrial revolutions on the countryside. See also Christopher Clark, *The Roots of Rural Capitalism: Western Massachusetts, 1780–1860* (1990), and Alan Kulikoff, *The Agrarian Origins of American Capitalism* (1992). On urbanization, see Allan R. Pred, *Urban Growth and the Circulation of Information: The United States System of Cities, 1790–1840* (1973), and Elizabeth Blackmar, *Manhattan for Rent, 1785–1850* (1989).

CHAPTER 15

PRIMARY SOURCE DOCUMENTS

Alexis de Tocqueville, *Democracy in America** (1835, 1840), has stood for over a century and a half as the classic analysis of the American character. Joseph Smith, *The Pearl of Great Price** (1929), contains an account of the Mormon leader's religious visions, which capture the religious restiveness of the age. William H. McGuffey, *Fifth Eclectic Reader* (1879), was a popular school text. On the women's movement, see the "Seneca Falls Manifesto"* (1848), which laid the foundations of the feminist movement. Catharine Beecher and Harriet Beecher Stowe, *The American Woman's Home** (1869), discusses the role of women. Stowe's classic novel, *Uncle Tom's Cabin* (1852), offers an emotional appeal against slavery and a fascinating portrait of slavery, religion, and family life in antebellum America.

SECONDARY SOURCES

A magisterial synthesis is Daniel Boorstin, *The Americans: The National Experience* (1965). Satisfying detail is found in two Russell B. Nye books: *The Cultural Life of the New Nation, 1776–1830* (1960) and *Society and Culture in America, 1830–1860* (1974). Alexis de Tocqueville's classic account of life in the young Republic is brilliantly analyzed by James R. Schlieffer in *The Making of Tocqueville's "Democracy in America"* (1980). On the rise of the middle class, see Karen Halttunen, *Confidence Men and Painted Women* (1982); Richard L. Bushman, *The Refinement of America: Persons, Houses, Cities* (1992); and Stuart M. Blumin, *The Emergence of the Middle Class* (1989). Sydney E. Ahlstrom, *Religious History of the American People* (1972), is sweeping. On revivalism, see Nathan O. Hatch, *The Democratization of American Christianity* (1989), and Paul Johnson, *A Shopkeeper's Millennium: Society and Revivals in Rochester, New York, 1815–1837* (1978), which links revivals to economic change. Bushman describes the origins of Mormonism in *Joseph Smith and the Beginnings of Mormonism* (1984), and provides insights into Smith's extraordinary life in *Rough Stone Rolling: Joseph Smith* (2005). Leonard J. Arrington analyzes Joseph Smith's successor in *Brigham Young: American Moses* (1984). On the Shakers, see Stephen J. Stein, *The Shaker Experience in America* (1992). On reform broadly, see Ronald Walters, *American Reformers, 1815–1860* (1978), and Robert Abzug, *Cosmos Crumbling: American Reform and the Religious Imagination* (1994). For particular movements, consult David Rothman, *The Discovery of the Asylum* (1971); Gerald Grob, *Mental Institutions in America: Social Policy to 1875* (1973); and David Gallagher, *Voice for the Mad: The Life of Dorothea Dix* (1995). On the development of hospitals, see Charles Rosenberg, *The Care of Strangers: The Rise of America's Hospital System* (1987). On juvenile delinquency, see Joseph Hawes, *Children in Urban Society* (1971). On prohibition, see Ian Tyrrell, *Sobering Up: From Temperance to Prohibition in Antebellum America* (1979), and William Rorabaugh, *The Alcoholic Republic* (1979). On education, see Lawrence A. Cremin, *American Education: The National Experience, 1789–1860* (1980), and Carl F. Kaestle and Maris A. Vinovskis, *Education and Social Change in Nineteenth-Century Massachusetts* (1980). An alternative interpretation of the rise of public education can be found in Michael Katz, *The Irony of Early School Reform* (1968), and Samuel Bowles and Herbert Gintis, *Schooling in Capitalist America* (1976). Vinovskis offers a critique of these authors in *The Origins of Public High Schools: A Reexamination of the Beverly High School Controversy* (1985). A recent study of one Utopian community is Spencer Klaw, *Without Sin: The Life and Death of the Oneida Community* (1993). Women's history for this period is explored in a number of studies, including Carroll Smith-Rosenberg, *Religion and the Rise of the American City* (1971); Nancy Cott, *The Bonds of Womanhood: "Woman's Sphere" in New England: 1780–1835* (1977); Ellen Carol DuBois, *Feminism and Suffrage* (1978); Ruth Bordin, *Women and Temperance* (1981); Estelle B.

Freedman, *Their Sisters' Keepers: Women's Prison Reform in America, 1830–1930* (1981); Barbara Epstein, *The Politics of Domesticity* (1981); Nancy Hewitt, *Women's Activism and Social Change: Rochester, New York, 1822–1872* (1984); Lori D. Ginzberg, *Women and the Work of Benevolence* (1990); and Ann Douglas, T*he Feminization of American Culture* (1977). Family history is covered in Steven Mintz and Susan Kellogg, *Domestic Revolutions: A Social History of American Family Life* (1988); Jeanne Boydston, *Home and Work: Housework, Wages, and the Ideology of Labor in the Early Republic* (1990); Joseph F. Kett, *Rites of Passage: Adolescence in America* (1976); Lewis Perry, *Childhood, Marriage, and Reform: Henry Clarke Wright, 1797–1870* (1980); Carl N. Degler, *At Odds: Women and the Family in America from the Revolution to the Present* (1980); and Mary P. Ryan, *Cradle of the Middle Class: The Family in Oneida County, New York* (1981). See also Kathryn Kish Sklar, *Catharine Beecher: A Study in Domesticity* (1973). Suzanne Lebsock, *The Free Women of Petersburg* (1984), discusses these issues in a southern context. For the relationship of nature to the emerging American culture, see Henry Nash Smith, *Virgin Land: The American West as Symbol and Myth* (1950); Leo Marx, *The Machine in the Garden: Technology and the Pastoral Ideal in America* (1964); and Barbara Novak, *Nature and Culture: American Landscape and Painting, 1825–1875* (1980). Studies with a cultural focus include Joseph Ellis, *After the Revolution: Profiles of Early American Culture* (1979), and Anne Rose, *Voices of the Marketplace: American Thought and Culture, 1830–1860* (1995). See also Lawrence Buell, *New England Literary Culture: From Revolution Through Renaissance* (1986), and Kenneth Cmiel, *Democratic Eloquence: The Fight over Popular Speech in Nineteenth-Century America* (1990). Edward L. Widmer, *Young America: The Flowering of Democracy in New York City* (1999), explores the literary-political nexus at the heart of Gotham culture in the 1840s. On three critically important transcendentalist figures, see Charles Capper, *Margaret Fuller: An American Romantic Life* (1992), and Robert D. Richardson's excellent volumes, *Emerson: The Mind on Fire* (1995) and *Thoreau: A Life of the Mind* (1986). Perry Miller, *The Raven and the Whale: The War of Words and Wits in the Era of Poe and Melville* (1956), remains a classic account of the New York literati in the age of the "American Renaissance."

CHAPTER 16

PRIMARY SOURCE DOCUMENTS

Two influential abolitionist documents are Theodore Dwight Weld, *American Slavery As It Is** (1839), and the inaugural editorial of William Lloyd Garrison in *The Liberator** (1831). Roy P. Basler, ed., *The Collected Works of Abraham Lincoln* (1933), contains the Great Emancipator's assessment of abolitionism in 1854. For southern perspectives, see James Henry Hammond's famous "Cotton Is King" speech, *Congressional Globe*, 36th Cong., 1st sess., 961 (March 3, 1858).* Frederick Law Olmsted, *The Cotton Kingdom* (1861), chronicles the future landscape architect's observations while traveling through the South in the 1850s. Famous firsthand accounts of slavery include Frederick Douglass, *Narrative of the Life of Frederick Douglass* (1845), and Harriet Jacobs, *Incidents in the Life of a Slave Girl* (1861). John W. Blassingame, ed., *Slave Testimony* (1977), also offers a rich collection of slave narratives.

SECONDARY SOURCES

A good introduction to southern history is Clement Eaton, *A History of the Old South: The Emergence of a Reluctant Nation* (1975). For a discussion of the intellectual's place in a southern agrarian society, see Drew Gilpin Faust, *A Sacred Circle: The Dilemma of the Intellectual in the Old South, 1840–1860* (1977). Always incisive is C. Vann Woodward, *The Burden of Southern History* (1960). On white politics and society, see Bruce Collins, *White Society in the Antebellum South* (1985); Bertram Wyatt-Brown, *Honor and Violence in the Old South*

(1986); and Drew Gilpin Faust's perceptive biography, *James Henry Hammond and the Old South: A Design for Mastery* (1982). Nonslaveholding whites are documented in Frank L. Owsley, *Plain Folk of the Old South* (1949), and Stephanie McCurry, *Masters of Small Worlds: Yeoman Households, Gender Relations, and the Political Culture of the Antebellum South Carolina Low Country* (1995). Important interpretations of the "peculiar institution" include Eugene Genovese, *Roll, Jordan, Roll: The World the Slaves Made* (1974); Barbara Jeanne Fields, *Slavery and Freedom on the Middle Ground: Maryland During the Nineteenth Century* (1985); Gavin Wright, *The Political Economy of the Cotton South* (1978); and Eugene Genovese and Elizabeth Fox-Genovese, *Fruits of Merchant Capital* (1983). Genovese and Fox-Genovese present a dense account of the slaveholders' culture and religion in *The Mind of the Master Class: History and Faith in the Southern Slaveholders' Worldview* (2005). James Oakes has questioned many of Eugene Genovese's interpretations in *The Ruling Race: A History of American Slaveholders* (1982) and *Slavery and Freedom: An Interpretation of the Old South* (1990). Catherine Clinton examines *The Plantation Mistress* (1982); Elizabeth Fox-Genovese discusses southern women more generally in *Within the Plantation Household: Black and White Women of the Old South* (1988). See also Deborah Gray White, *Ar'n't I a Woman? Female Slaves in the Plantation South* (1985); Melton Alonza McLaurin, *Celia, a Slave* (1991); and Brenda E. Stevenson, *Life in Black and White: Family and Community in the Slave South* (1996). There is a rich and varied literature on slavery and African Americans; a good place to start is John Hope Franklin, *From Slavery to Freedom* (8th ed., 2000), and Peter J. Parish, *Slavery: History and Historians* (1989). The modern debate on slavery began with Ulrich B. Phillips's apologia *American Negro Slavery* (1918); a darker view of the same subject is found in Kenneth M. Stampp, *The Peculiar Institution* (1956). Consult also Stanley Elkins's controversial essay, *Slavery* (2nd ed., 1968), which also has interesting observations on the abolitionists. Considerable furor surrounded the publication of Robert Fogel and Stanley Engerman's *Time on the Cross: The Economics of American Slavery* (2 vols., 1974). For contrasting views and rebuttals, see John W. Blassingame, *The Slave Community* (rev. ed., 1979); Herbert Gutman, *The Black Family in Slavery and Freedom, 1750–1925* (1976); Paul David, *Reckoning with Slavery* (1976); Lawrence Levine, *Black Culture and Black Consciousness: Afro-American Folk Thought from Slavery to Freedom* (1977); Albert J. Raboteau, *Slave Religion: The "Invisible Institution" in the Antebellum South* (1978); and Sterling Stuckey, *Slave Culture: Nationalist Theory and the Foundations of Black America* (1987). Vincent Harding, *There Is a River: The Black Struggle for Freedom in America* (1981), discusses slave resistance and revolt, a subject handled rather differently in Peter Kolchin's fascinating comparative study, *Unfree Labor: American Slavery and Russian Serfdom* (1987). John Hope Franklin, *Runaway Slaves: Rebels on the Plantation* (1999), analyzes the motivations and consequences of slaves who escaped from their owners' farms and plantations. Manisha Sinha, *The Counterrevolution of Slavery: Politics and Ideology in Antebellum South Carolina* (2000), is an important new study that links political radicalism with the practice of slavery. Another political history of the South is Lacy K. Ford, Jr., *The Origins of Southern Radicalism: The South Carolina Upcountry, 1800–1860* (1988), which tells the story of this Unionist stronghold. A study that compares the development of race relations in South Africa and the United States is George M. Frederickson, *White Supremacy: A Comparative Study in American and South African History* (1981). Ira Berlin examines how the institution of slavery developed in discrete chronological stages in *Many Thousands Gone: The First Two Centuries of Slavery in North America* (1998) and tells the story of free blacks in *Slaves Without Masters* (1975), which should be supplemented by Michael P. Johnson and James L. Roark, *Black Masters: A Free Family of Color in the Old South* (1984). See also Harry Reed, *Platform for Change: The Foundation of the Northern Free Black Community, 1775–1865* (1994), for the situation of blacks outside the South. For an important study of interracial families in the antebellum South, see Joshua Rothman, *Notorious in* the *Neighborhood: Sex and Families Across the Color Line in Virginia, 1787–1861* (2003). On the experience of the antebellum slave trade, see Walter Johnson, *Soul by Soul: Life Inside the Antebellum Slave Market* (2001). Valuable community studies include Charles Joyner, *Down by the Riverside: A South Carolina Slave Community* (1984); Suzanne Lebsock, *The Free Women of Petersburg: Status and Culture in a Southern Town, 1784–1860* (1984); and Orville Vernon Burton, *In My Father's House Are Many Mansions: Family and Community in Edgefield, South Carolina* (1985). David B. Davis provides indispensable background to the history of abolitionism in *The Problem of Slavery in Western Culture* (1966) and *The Problem of Slavery in the Age of Revolution* (1975), as does Thomas Bender, ed., in *The Antislavery Debate* (1992). The best brief history of the abolitionists is James B. Stewart, *Holy Warriors* (1976). Ronald E. Walters emphasizes the constraints that American culture placed on abolitionists in *The Antislavery Appeal: American Abolitionism After 1830* (1976). Aileen Kraditor is favorably disposed toward William Lloyd Garrison in *Means and Ends in American Abolitionism: Garrison and His Critics* (1967). See also Julie Roy Jeffrey, *The Great Silent Army of Abolitionism: Ordinary Women in the Antislavery Movement* (1998). For provocative appraisals, see Lewis Perry and Michael Fellman, eds., *Antislavery Reconsidered: New Perspectives on the Abolitionists* (1979). Benjamin Quarles examines *Black Abolitionists* (1969), as do Jane H. Pease and William H. Pease in *They Who Would Be Free: Blacks Search for Freedom, 1830–1861* (1974), and Shirley J. Yee in *Black Women Abolitionists: A Study in Activism, 1828–1860* (1992). Sojourner Truth is the subject of Nell Irvin Painter, *Sojourner Truth: A Life, a Symbol* (1996). The most prominent black abolitionist is portrayed in Waldo E. Martin, Jr., *The Mind of Frederick Douglass* (1984), and William S. McFeely, *Frederick Douglass* (1990).

CHAPTER 17

PRIMARY SOURCE DOCUMENTS

Trader Josiah Gregg describes the Santa Fe trade in his 1845 book, *Commerce of the Prairies,* edited by Max L. Moorehead (1954), and historian Francis Parkman's classic *The California and Oregon Trail* (1849) draws a fascinating picture of the Pacific Coast. Colorful reminiscences of the pioneers are collected in Dale Morgan, ed., *Overland in 1846: Diaries and Letters of the California-Oregon Trail** (1963), and Sandra Myres, *Ho for California! Women's Overland Diaries from the Huntington Library* (1980). Stella M. Drumm, ed., *Down the Santa Fe Trail and into Mexico, 1846–1847,* is a fascinating firsthand account of New Mexico during the Mexican War written by the daughter of a prominent trader (1975). The outbreak and conduct of the war also come alive in Allan Nevins, ed., *Polk: The Diary of a President, 1845–1849* (1929).

SECONDARY SOURCES

Frederick Merk, *Manifest Destiny and Mission in American History* (1963), is a good introduction. For more recent explanations of American motivations during the imperialistic decade of the 1840s, see Thomas R. Hietala, *Manifest Design: Anxious Aggrandizement in Late Jacksonian America* (1985); Robert E. May, *Manifest Destiny's Underworld: Filibustering in Antebellum America* (2002); and Sam W. Haynes and Christopher Morris, eds., *Manifest Destiny and Empire: American Antebellum Expansionism* (1997). For explorations of the role racial thought played in Manifest Destiny, see Reginald Horsman, *Race and Manifest Destiny: The Origins of American Racial Anglo-Saxonism* (1981); the early chapters of Richard D. White, *"It's Your Misfortune and None of My Own": A History of the American West* (1992); and Michael A. Morrison, *Slavery and the American West: The Eclipse of Manifest Destiny* (1997). Norman A. Graebner, *Empire on the Pacific* (1955), discusses Polk's drive to acquire Cali-

fornia, and Theodore J. Karamanski, *Fur Trade and Exploration: Opening the Far Northwest, 1821–1852* (1983), gives a vivid depiction of the Pacific region (1983). The definitive account of the American Southwest before U.S. invasion is David Weber's *The Mexican Frontier, 1821–1846* (1982), which traces the gradual drift of the region away from Mexican control. David M. Pletcher's *The Diplomacy of the Annexation of Texas, Oregon, and the Mexican War* (1973) is a thorough, balanced account of annexation and the coming of the war. On the conflict with Mexico, see Richard Bruce Winders, *Crisis in the Southwest: The United States, Mexico, and the Struggle over Texas* (2002); James McCaffrey, *Army of Manifest Destiny: The American Soldier in the Mexican War* (1992); and Paul Foos, *A Short, Offhand Killing Affair: Soldiers and Social Conflict During the U.S.-Mexican War* (2002). The perspectives of Mexicans are analyzed in Josefina Zoraida Vázquez, *The United States and Mexico* (1985); Gene M. Brack, *Mexico Views Manifest Destiny, 1821–1846* (1976); and Iris Engstrand et al., *Culture y Cultura: Consequences of the U.S.-Mexican War, 1846–1848* (1998). John H. Schroeder analyzes an important aspect of the conflict in *Mr. Polk's War: American Opposition and Dissent, 1846–1848* (1973). Richard Francaviglia et al., eds., *Dueling Eagles: Reinterpreting the U.S.-Mexican War 1846–1848* (2000), compiles the most recent scholarly perspectives. The second volume of Charles Sellers's excellent three-volume biography of James K. Polk focuses on the years 1843 to 1846 (1966); Paul H. Bergeron scrutinizes Polk's administration in *The Presidency of James K. Polk* (1987); and William Dusinberre explores the influence of Polk's life as a slaveowner on his public policies in *Slavemaster President: The Double Career of James K. Polk* (2003). Robert W. Johannsen uses the war to investigate American culture in *To the Halls of the Montezumas: The Mexican War in the American Imagination* (1985). John Mack Faragher provides an in-depth look at the westward migration of one community in *Sugar Creek: Life on the Illinois Prairie* (1986). Linda S. Hudson, *Mistress of Manifest Destiny: A Biography of Jane McManus Storm Cazneau, 1807–1878* (2001), chronicles the life of a woman who propagandized for westward expansion. Gregg Cantrell, *Stephen F. Austin, Empresario of Texas* (1999), is a biography of the key figure in Anglo-American colonization in Texas. For an insightful look at the cultural exchange brought about by the gold rush, see Susan Lee Johnson, *Roaring Camp: The Social World of the California Gold Rush* (2001). Three works that explore the experiences of women in the West are Julie Roy Jeffrey, *Frontier Women* (1979); Glenda Riley, *The Female Frontier* (1988); and Susan Armitage and Elizabeth Jameson, eds., *The Women's West* (1987).

CHAPTER 18

PRIMARY SOURCE DOCUMENTS

The *Congressional Globe* for 1850 contains the dramatic orations of a dying generation of American statesmen on the Compromise of 1850. See the speeches by Webster,* Calhoun,* and Clay in Richard Hofstadter, ed., *Great Issues in American History.* The debate on the Kansas-Nebraska Bill can be found in the 1854 volume of the same source, which includes addresses by Stephen A. Douglas* and his opponent, Salmon P. Chase.*

SECONDARY SOURCES

Earlier interpretations of the sectional crisis include Charles A. and Mary R. Beard, *The Rise of American Civilization* (1927); Avery Craven, *The Repressible Conflict, 1830–1861* (1939); and Allan Nevins, *The Ordeal of the Union* (1947). A compelling account of the events of the 1850s is David M. Potter's masterful *The Impending Crisis, 1848–1861* (1976). A concise summary of the events leading to the war is also available in the opening chapters of James M. McPherson, *Battle Cry of Freedom: The Civil War Era* (1988). Comprehensive treatments may be found in David H. Donald, Jean H. Baker, and Michael

F. Holt, *The Civil War and Reconstruction* (rev. ed., 2001); William J. Cooper, *The South and the Politics of Slavery* (1978); Kenneth Stampp, ed., *The Imperiled Union: Essays on the Background of the Civil War* (1980); Richard H. Sewell, *A House Divided: Sectionalism and Civil War, 1848–1860* (1988); and William Freehling, *Road to Disunion: Secessionists at Bay, 1776–1854* (1990). The standard work is Holman Hamilton, *Prologue to Conflict: The Crisis and Compromise of 1850* (1964). See also Mark J. Stegmaier, *Texas, New Mexico, and the Compromise of 1850: Boundary Dispute and Sectional Crisis* (1996). On the southern view of events, see Kenneth S. Greenberg, *Masters and Statesmen: The Political Culture of American Slavery* (1985), and Eugene Genovese, *The World the Slaveholders Made* (1969). The emergence of the Republican party after 1854 can be studied in Eric Foner's brilliant discussion of ideology, *Free Soil, Free Labor, Free Men* (1970), and William Gienapp, *The Origins of the Republican Party, 1852–1856* (1987). Also see Michael Holt, *Forging a Majority: The Formation of the Republican Party in Pittsburgh* (1969); Paul Kleppner, *The Third Electoral System, 1853–1892: Parties, Voters, and Political Cultures* (1979); Bruce Levine, *Half Slave and Half Free: The Roots of the Civil War* (1992); and Frederick J. Blue, *The Free Soilers: Third Party Politics, 1848–1854* (1973). On the Know-Nothing party, see Tyler Anbinder, *Nativism and Slavery: The Northern Know-Nothings and the Politics of the 1850s* (1992). Holt has developed his views in *The Political Crisis of the 1850s* (1978), an unusually provocative book. Party politics are treated in two books by Joel H. Silbey, *The Shrine of Party: Congressional Voting Behavior, 1841–1852* (1967) and his unorthodox *Partisan Imperative: The Dynamics of American Politics Before the Civil War* (1985). Richard H. Sewell, *Ballots for Freedom: Antislavery Politics in the United States, 1837–1860* (1976), is a standard work. A biographical approach is taken in Merrill Peterson, *The Great Triumvirate: Webster, Clay, and Calhoun* (1987). Robert Trennert examines the impact of westward migration and the gold rush on U.S. Indian policy in *Alternative to Extinction: Federal Indian Policy and the Beginnings of the Reservation System, 1846–1851* (1975).

CHAPTER 19

PRIMARY SOURCE DOCUMENTS

Harriet Beecher Stowe, *Uncle Tom's Cabin** (1852), and Hinton R. Helper, *The Impending Crisis of the South** (1857), are vivid and important. The Lincoln-Douglas debates* (1858) frame the issues of the 1850s and remain classics of American oratory. William W. Freehling and Craig M. Simpson, eds., *Secession Debated: Georgia's Showdown in 1860* (1992), features a dramatic debate between Unionist Alexander Stephens and secessionist Robert Toombs.

SECONDARY SOURCES

For comprehensive treatments of events leading up to the Civil War, refer to Chapter 18 for the titles by David M. Potter, James M. McPherson, William J. Cooper, Kenneth Stampp, Richard H. Sewell, Allan Nevins, and David H. Donald, Jean H. Baker, and Michael F. Holt. Gabor S. Boritt, ed., *Why the Civil War Came* (1996), is an informative compilation of articles on the causes of the war. Leonard L. Richards, *The Slave Power: The Free North and Southern Domination, 1780–1860* (2000), and Ward M. McAfee, ed., *The Slaveholding Republic* (2001), give interpretations on the coming of the war. David H. Donald, *Charles Sumner and the Coming of the Civil War* (1960), is an outstanding biography. A more recent biography is Frederick J. Blue, *Charles Sumner and the Conscience of the North* (1994). On the literary attack on slavery, see Thomas F. Gossett, *Uncle Tom's Cabin and American Culture* (1985). Nicole Etcheson, *Bleeding Kansas: Contested Liberty in the Civil War Era* (2004), tells the story of the first frontier war over slavery expansion. On the Buchanan administration, see Kenneth M. Stampp, *America in 1857: A Nation on the Brink* (1990), and Michael J. Birkner, ed., *James Buchanan and the Political*

Crisis of the 1850s (1996). On the Lincoln-Douglas debates, see Harry V. Jaffa, *Crisis of the House Divided* (1959). Don E. Fehrenbacher brilliantly and thoroughly dissects *The Dred Scott Case* (1978). The final moments before fighting began are scrutinized in David M. Potter, *Lincoln and His Party in the Secession Crisis* (1942). The Southern side of the question appears in Steven A. Channing, *Crisis of Fear: Secession of South Carolina* (1970), and William L. Barney, *The Secessionist Impulse: Alabama and Mississippi* (1974). On Southern Unionists' role in beginning the war, see Daniel W. Crofts, *Reluctant Confederates: Upper South Unionists in the Secession Crisis* (1989). Jean H. Baker, *Affairs of Party: The Political Culture of Northern Democrats in the Mid-Nineteenth Century* (1983), and Robert W. Johannsen, *Stephen A. Douglas* (1973), present matters from the Democratic perspective. See also J. Mills Thornton III, *Power and Politics in a Slave Society: Alabama 1820–1860* (1978), and Marc W. Kruman, *Parties and Politics in North Carolina, 1836–1865* (1983). Stephen B. Oates paints a vivid portrait of John Brown in *To Purge This Land with Blood* (1970), as Joan Hedrick does of Harriet Beecher Stowe in *Harriet Beecher Stowe: A Life* (1994). For a broader view, see Paul Finkelman, *And His Soul Goes Marching On: Responses to John Brown and the Harpers Ferry Raid* (1995).

CHAPTER 20

PRIMARY SOURCE DOCUMENTS

The Constitution of the Confederacy (1861) makes an interesting contrast to the U.S. Constitution. Two diaries that describe life behind Confederate lines are those of John B. Jones, published as Earl S. Miers, ed., *A Rebel War Clerk's Diary** (1958), and C. Vann Woodward, ed., *Mary Chesnut's Civil War* (1981). A comprehensive collection of primary sources about every aspect of the war can be found in William Gienapp, ed., *The Civil War and Reconstruction: A Documentary Collection* (2001). It contains Lincoln's Gettysburg Address* (1863), which poetically proclaims the president's highest war aims.

SECONDARY SOURCES

Two extensive biographies of Abraham Lincoln are Stephen B. Oates, *With Malice Toward None: The Life of Abraham Lincoln* (1977), and William Gienapp, *Abraham Lincoln and Civil War America* (2002). See also Garry Wills, *Lincoln at Gettysburg: The Words That Remade America* (1992), David H. Donald, *Lincoln* (1995), and Allen Guelzo, *Abraham Lincoln: Redeemer President*. On Mary Todd Lincoln, see Jean H. Baker, *Mary Todd Lincoln: A Biography* (1987). In *Jefferson Davis, American* (2000), William J. Cooper provides a counterpoint to the rich literature on the life of Lincoln. Home-front politics are treated in James A. Rawley, *The Politics of Union* (1974), and Joel Silbey, *A Respectable Minority: The Democratic Party in the Civil War Era* (1977). See also Eric Foner, *Politics and Ideology in the Age of the Civil War* (1980). Mark Neely has written several books on Civil War politics, including *Southern Rights: Political Prisoners and the Myth of Confederate Constitutionalism* (1999) and *The Union Divided: Party Conflict in the Civil War North* (2002). George C. Rable's *The Confederate Republic* (1994) is a comprehensive study of politics in the Confederacy. Lincoln's problems are analyzed in LaWanda Cox, *Lincoln and Black Freedom* (1981). See also Hans L. Trefousse, *The Radical Republicans: Lincoln's Vanguard for Racial Justice* (1969). Eugene C. Murdoch analyzes the military draft in the North in *One Million Men* (1971). Iver Bernstein treats *The New York City Draft Riots* (1990). Gerald F. Linderman examines the motivations of soldiers in *Embattled Courage: The Experience of Combat in the Civil War* (1987). Mary E. Massey presents the interesting story of women in the Civil War in *Bonnet Brigades* (1966). That topic also figures in Elizabeth D. Leonard, *Yankee Women: Gender Battles in the Civil War* (1994). See also the essays in Catherine Clinton and Nina Silber, eds., *Divided Houses: Gender and the Civil War* (1992), and Drew Gilpin Faust, *Mothers of Invention: Women of the Slaveholding South in the Amer-*

ican Civil War (1996). William Freehling, *The South vs. The South: How Anti-Confederate Southerners Shaped the Course of the Civil War* (2001), argues that Southern social divisions contributed to the Union victory. For more on the Confederacy, see Emory M. Thomas, *The Confederate Nation, 1861–1865* (1979), and Drew Gilpin Faust, *The Creation of Confederate Nationalism* (1988). Economic matters are handled in Ralph L. Andreano, ed., *The Economic Impact of the American Civil War* (1962); David T. Gilchrist and W. David Lewis, eds., *Economic Change in the Civil War Era* (1965); and Heather Cox Richardson, *The Greatest Nation of the Earth: Republican Economic Policies During the Civil War* (1997). Two useful anthologies are David H. Donald, ed., *Why the North Won the Civil War* (1960), and Robert P. Swierenga, ed., *Beyond the Civil War Synthesis: Political Essays on the Civil War Era* (1975). Richard E. Beringer et al. present a different viewpoint in *Why the South Lost the Civil War* (1986). The war's literary legacy is keenly analyzed in Edmund Wilson's classic *Patriotic Gore* (1962) and in Daniel Aaron's *The Unwritten War: American Writers and the Civil War* (1973). On the religious impact of the war, see Randall M. Miller et al., *Religion and the American Civil War* (1998). David W. Blight, *Race and Reunion: The Civil War in American Memory* (2001), is a study of how Americans have remembered their bloodiest conflict.

CHAPTER 21

PRIMARY SOURCE DOCUMENTS

Abraham Lincoln's 1862 reply to Horace Greeley's "Prayer of Twenty Millions"* (*Collected Works of Abraham Lincoln*, edited by Roy P. Basler, 1953) is an early statement of the president's war aims. See also, in the same collection, the Emancipation Proclamation (1863). Reminiscences of the military struggle include Eliza Andrews, *The War-Time Journal of a Georgia Girl* * (1908) and *Memoirs of General William T. Sherman* * (1887). Also of interest is Stephen Crane's classic war novel, *The Red Badge of Courage* (1895).

SECONDARY SOURCES

A compelling single-volume account of the war is James M. McPherson, *Battle Cry of Freedom: The Civil War Era* (1988). Geoffrey C. Ward's *The Civil War* (1990) is beautifully illustrated, and James G. Randall, *Lincoln the President* (4 vols., 1945–1955), provides a wealth of rich detail. Other capable one-volume studies include Peter J. Parish, *The American Civil War* (1975), and Phillip S. Paludan, *"A People's Contest": The Union and the Civil War, 1861–1865* (1988). See also the multivolume study by Shelby Foote, *The Civil War* (3 vols., 1958–1974), and Allan Nevins's monumental *Ordeal of the Union* (8 vols., 1947–1971). Bruce Catton has a series of a dozen or so readable books on aspects of the Civil War, including *A Stillness at Appomattox* (1953) and *This Hallowed Ground* (1956). Herman Hattaway and Archer Jones discuss *How the North Won* (1983). For fascinating essays on the legacy of the Civil War, see Alice Fahs and Joan Waugh, eds., *The Memory of the Civil War in American Culture* (2004). On the home front, see Reid Mitchell, *The Vacant Chair: The Northern Soldier Leaves Home* (1993); William Blair, *Virginia's Private War: Feeding Body and Soul in the Confederacy, 1861–1865* (1998); and David Williams, *Rich Man's War: Class, Caste, and Confederate Defeat in the Lower Chattahoochee Valley* (1998). On the "modern" character of the war, see Charles B. Royster, *The Destructive War: William Tecumseh Sherman, Stonewall Jackson, and the Americans* (1991). David P. Crook, *The North, the South, and the Powers* (1974), discusses the relationship of the combatants to England. James M. McPherson, *Abraham Lincoln and the Second American Revolution* (1991), posits a fateful clash between competing ways of life in North and South. Bell I. Wiley's descriptions of common soldiers, *The Life of Johnny Reb* (1943) and *The Life of Billy Yank* (1952), are classics. See also Benjamin Quarles, *The Negro in the Civil War* (1953), and James M. McPherson's collection of documents, *The Negro's Civil War* (1965).

More recent accounts of the black experience include Ira Berlin et al., *Freedom: A Documentary History of Emancipation, 1861–1867*, Series 2: *The Black Military Experience* (1982), and Joseph Glatthaar, *Forged in Battle: The Civil War Alliance of Black Soldiers and White Officers* (1990). Emancipation is treated in Louis Gerteis, *From Contraband to Freedmen; Federal Policy Toward Southern Blacks, 1861–1865* (1973); Herman Belz, *Emancipation and Equal Rights: Politics and Constitutionalism During the Civil War Reconstruction* (1978); Willie Lee Rose, *Rehearsal for Reconstruction: The Port Royal Experiment* (1964); LaWanda Cox, *Lincoln and Black Freedom* (1981); and Leon Litwack's powerful *Been in the Storm So Long* (1979). On the abolitionists' role in securing emancipation, see James M. McPherson, *The Struggle for Equality* (1964), and David W. Blight, *Frederick Douglass' Civil War: Keeping Faith in Jubilee* (1989). The Southern response is discussed in Robert Durden, *The Gray and the Black: The Confederate Debate on Emancipation* (1973). The two leading Civil War generals are masterfully treated in Douglas S. Freeman, *R. E. Lee* (4 vols., 1934–1935), and William S. McFeely, *Grant* (1981). On the legal end to slavery in America, consult Michael Vorenberg, *Final Freedom: The Civil War, the Abolition of Slavery, and the Thirteenth Amendment* (2001).

CHAPTER 22

PRIMARY SOURCE DOCUMENTS

Booker T. Washington's classic autobiography, *Up from Slavery* * (1901), records one freedman's experiences. Contemporary comments on Reconstruction include the laments of editor Edwin L. Godkin, *The Nation* * (December 7, 1871), and Frederick Douglass, *Life and Times of Frederick Douglass* * (1882), as well as the debates in the *Congressional Globe* * (1867–1868) between radicals such as Thaddeus Stevens and moderates such as Lyman Trumbull.

SECONDARY SOURCES

Eric Foner, *Reconstruction: America's Unfinished Revolution, 1863–1877* (1988), is a superb synthesis of current scholarship. Overall accounts may be found in David H. Donald, Jean H. Baker, and Michael F. Holt, *The Civil War and Reconstruction* (rev. ed., 2001), and James M. McPherson, *Ordeal by Fire: The Civil War and Reconstruction* (1981), perhaps the best brief introduction. Lincoln's early efforts at Reconstruction are handled in Peyton McCrary, *Abraham Lincoln and Reconstruction* (1978), and Herman Belz, *Emancipation and Equal Rights* (1978). Willie Lee Rose engagingly describes *Rehearsal for Reconstruction: The Port Royal Experiment* (1964). Dan Carter, *When the War Was Over: The Failure of Self-Reconstruction in the South, 1865–1867* (1985), and Eric L. McKitrick, *Andrew Johnson and Reconstruction: Principle and Prejudice, 1865–1866* (1963), chart the first years of the period. Sympathetic to the radical Republicans are James M. McPherson, *The Struggle for Equality* (1964), and Hans L. Trefousse, *The Radical Republicans* (1969). See also David Montgomery, *Beyond Equality: Labor and the Radical Republicans, 1862–1872* (1967). Siding with the radicals in the impeachment fight are Michael L. Benedict, *The Impeachment and Trial of Andrew Johnson* (1973), and Hans L. Trefousse, *Impeachment of a President* (1975). Steven Hahn exhaustively examines the post–Civil War genesis of African American political traditions in *A Nation Under Our Feet* (2003). Conditions in the South are analyzed in W. E. B. Du Bois's controversial classic *Black Reconstruction* (1935) and Leon F. Litwack's brilliantly evocative *Been in the Storm So Long* (1979), a revealing study of the initial responses, by both blacks and whites, to emancipation. An excellent account of the southern economy after the war is Gavin Wright, *Old South, New South: Revolutions in the Southern Economy Since the Civil War* (1986). It can be usefully supplemented by Roger Ransom and Richard L. Sutch, *One Kind of Freedom: The Economic Consequences of Emancipation* (1977). Julie Saville, *The Work of Reconstruction* (1994), highlights the efforts of newly freed slaves to shape the economic arrangements of the postwar

South. See also James Roark, *Masters Without Slaves: Southern Planters in the Civil War and Reconstruction* (1977), and Lawrence Powell, *New Masters: Northern Planters During the Civil War and Reconstruction* (1980). Barbara Fields looks at the border state of Maryland in *Slavery and Freedom on the Middle Ground* (1985). William McFeely offers an excellent biography of *Frederick Douglass* (1991). Dewey W. Grantham, *Life and Death of the Solid South* (1988); Edward L. Ayers, *The Promise of the New South: Life After Reconstruction* (1992); Dwight Billings, *Planters and the Making of a "New South": Class, Politics and Development in North Carolina, 1865–1900* (1979); and Jonathan M. Wiener, *Social Origins of the New South: Alabama, 1860–1885* (1978), elucidate the political economy of the postbellum South. Joel Williamson offers a psychological portrait of race relations in *The Crucible of Race: Black-White Relations in the American South Since Emancipation* (1984). Consult also Thomas Holt, *Black over White: Negro Political Leadership in South Carolina During Reconstruction* (1977), and Martha Hodes, *White Women, Black Men: Illicit Sex in the Nineteenth-Century South* (1997). C. Vann Woodward, *The Strange Career of Jim Crow* (rev. ed., 1974), is a classic study of the origins of segregation. His views have drawn criticism in Harold O. Rabinowitz, *Race Relations in the Urban South, 1865–1890* (rev. ed., 1996). See also Rabinowitz's *Southern Black Leaders of the Reconstruction Era* (1982). The Freedmen's Bureau has been the subject of several studies, including Claude Oubré, *Forty Acres and a Mule: The Freedmen's Bureau and Black Land Ownership* (1978), and Donald Nieman, *To Set the Law in Motion: The Freedmen's Bureau and the Legal Rights of Blacks, 1865–1868* (1979). Nell Irvin Painter follows African Americans who chose to leave the South altogether in *Exodusters: Black Migration to Kansas After Reconstruction* (1976). Special studies of value are William P. Vaughn, *Schools for All* (1974); William C. Gillette, *The Right to Vote: Politics and the Passage of the 15th Amendment* (1965); Stanley I. Kutler, *Judicial Power and Reconstruction Politics* (1968); and Harold M. Hyman, *A More Perfect Union: The Impact of the Civil War and Reconstruction on the Constitution* (1973). Richard N. Current rehabilitates the maligned carpetbaggers in *Those Terrible Carpetbaggers* (1988). Provocative scholarship is presented in Kenneth M. Stampp and Leon Litwack, eds., *Reconstruction: An Anthology of Revisionist Writings* (1969), and Robert P. Swierenga, ed., *Beyond the Civil War Synthesis* (1975). J. Morgan Kousser and James M. McPherson, eds., *Region, Race, and Reconstruction: Essays in Honor of C. Vann Woodward* (1982), contains some intriguing essays. Eric Foner looks at emancipation in a comparative perspective in *Nothing but Freedom* (1983). A comprehensive study of the climax of this troubled period is William Gillette, *Retreat from Reconstruction, 1869–1879* (1979). Also see Michael Perman, *The Road to Redemption: Southern Politics, 1869–1879* (1984). David W. Blight's highly acclaimed *Race and Reunion: The Civil War in American Memory* (2001) details the postbellum battle to determine the way Americans remembered the war

CHAPTER 23

PRIMARY SOURCE DOCUMENTS

Henry Adams penned some perceptive and sour observations on the era in his autobiographical *Education of Henry Adams* (1907) and in his novel *Democracy* (1880). See also the classic satire by Mark Twain and Charles Dudley Warner, *The Gilded Age* (1873).

SECONDARY SOURCES

The scandal-rocked Grant era is treated with brevity in David H. Donald, Jean H. Baker, and Michael F. Holt, *The Civil War and Reconstruction* (rev. ed., 2001), and at greater length in William Gillette, *Retreat from Reconstruction* (1979), and James M. McPherson, *Ordeal by Fire* (1981). On Hayes, see Ari Hoogenboom, *Rutherford B. Hayes: Warrior and President* (1995). On the controversial Tilden-Hayes

contest, see Roy Morris, Jr., *Fraud of the Century: Rutherford B. Hayes, Samuel Tilden, and the Stolen Election of 1876* (2003). A general look at corruption as a political issue is Mark W. Summers, *The Era of Good Stealings* (1993). Consult also William S. McFeely, *Grant* (1981). Indicative of the recent trend toward more sympathetic evaluations of Ulysses Grant is Jean Edward Smith's readable biography, *Grant* (2001). Southern politics is detailed in C. Vann Woodward's classic *Origins of the New South, 1877–1913* (1951); Terry L. Seip, *The South Returns to Congress* (1983); and Michael Perman, *The Road to Redemption* (1984). Barry A. Crouch, *The Freedmen's Bureau and Black Texans* (1992), describes the hopes and frustrations of freedom for blacks in post–Civil War Texas. Brenda E. Stevenson traces slavery's lingering impact on post–Civil War black life and race relations in *Life in Black and White: Family and Community in the Slave South* (1996). The origins of racial segregation are analyzed in C. Vann Woodward, *The Strange Career of Jim Crow* (rev. ed., 1974). Michael Perman, *Struggle for Mastery: Disfranchisement in the South, 1888–1908* (2001), carefully considers the abrogation of black voting rights in this period. Dale Baum, *The Civil War Party System: The Case of Massachusetts, 1848–1876* (1984), and James C. Mohr, *The Radical Republicans and Reform in New York During Reconstruction* (1973), discuss the North. Heather Cox Richardson, *The Death of Reconstruction: Race, Labor, and Politics in the Post–Civil War North, 1865–1901* (2001), highlights economic and class interests in the waning of northern support for Reconstruction. Mark W. Summers analyzes *Railroads, Reconstruction, and the Gospel of Prosperity* (1984). Gary Brechin examines the West's largest city in *Imperial San Francisco: Urban Power, Earthly Ruin* (1999). On the party system, see Paul Kleppner, *The Third Electoral System, 1853–1892* (1979); Morton Keller, *Affairs of State: Public Life in Nineteenth-Century America* (1977); Peter McCaffery, *When Bosses Ruled Philadelphia: The Emergence of the Republican Machine, 1867–1933* (1993); Samuel McSeveney, *The Politics of Depression: Political Behavior in the Northeast, 1893–1896* (1972); and Richard Jensen, *The Winning of the Mid-West* (1971). Jon Teaford defends the record of municipal governments in *The Unheralded Triumph: City Government in America, 1870–1900* (1984). Money questions are treated in Irwin Unger, *The Greenback Era* (1964); Walter T. K. Nugent, *Money and American Society, 1865–1880* (1968); and Allen Weinstein's account of the *"Crime of '73," Prelude to Populism* (1970). C. Vann Woodward sharply analyzes the Compromise of 1877 in *Reunion and Reaction* (rev. ed., 1956). California receives special attention in Alexander Saxton, *The Indispensable Enemy: Labor and the Anti-Chinese Movement in California* (1975). Labor issues are cogently and compellingly discussed in Paul Krause, *The Battle for Homestead, 1880–1892: Politics, Culture, and Steel* (1992). Charles Hoffman examines *The Depression of the Nineties* (1970), an issue given much attention in David P. Thelen, *The New Citizenship: Origins of Progressivism in Wisconsin, 1885–1900* (1972). Three intriguing cultural histories of the period are Alan Trachtenberg, *The Incorporation of America: Culture and Society in the Gilded Age* (1982); Richard Slotkin, *The Fatal Environment: The Myth of the Frontier in American History, 1800–1890* (1985); and Lawrence Levine, *Highbrow/Lowbrow: The Emergence of Cultural Hierarchy in America* (1988).

CHAPTER 24

PRIMARY SOURCE DOCUMENTS

Andrew Carnegie, "Wealth,"* *North American Review* (June 1889), gives the philosophy of the Gilded Age's greatest entrepreneur. Henry Grady's Boston speech (1889), in Joel C. Harris, *Life of Henry W. Grady** (1890), dramatizes the plight of the South. Samuel Gompers penned his "Letter on Labor in Industrial Society," an open letter to Judge Peter Grossup, in 1894 (in Richard Hofstadter, *Great Issues in American History*). William Dean Howell's novel *The Rise of Silas Lapham* (1885) treats the moral impact of the new business culture on one New England businessman and his family.

SECONDARY SOURCES

A useful survey is Samuel P. Hays's penetrating study *The Response to Industrialism, 1885–1914* (1957). Stuart Bruchey puts the period in context in *The Growth of the Modern Economy* (1975). Business is the subject of Alfred D. Chandler, Jr., *The Visible Hand: The Managerial Revolution in American Business* (1978); Saul Engelbourg, *Power and Morality: American Business Ethics, 1840–1914* (1980); and Naomi R. Lamoreaux, *The Great Merger Movement in American Business, 1895–1904* (1985). Olivier Zunz surveys the development of corporate culture in *Making America Corporate, 1870–1920* (1990), while Scott M. Cutlip examines *The Unseen Power: Public Relations, a History* (1994). Thomas K. McCraw assesses government regulation in *Prophets of Regulation: Charles Francis Adams, Louis D. Brandeis, James M. Landis, Alfred E. Kahn* (1984). In *Control Through Communication: The Rise of System in American Management* (1989), Joanne Yates argues that big business was more efficient than Brandeis believed. Alternatively, Charles Perrow, *Organizing America: Wealth, Power, and the Origins of Corporate Capitalism* (2002), argues that the appeal of big corporations was more about power than efficiency. The thought and attitudes characteristic of the new industrial age are examined in Richard Hofstadter, *Social Darwinism in American Thought* (rev. ed., 1955); Daniel T. Rodgers, *The Work Ethic in Industrial America, 1850–1920* (1978); and Alan Trachtenberg, *The Incorporation of America: Culture and Society in the Gilded Age* (1982). Sven Beckert provides an insightful look into the creation and character of New York's powerful economic elite in *The Monied Metropolis: New York City and the Consolidation of the American Bourgeoisie, 1850–1896* (2001). On the railroads, see George R. Taylor and Irene D. Neu, *The American Railroad Network, 1861–1890* (1956), and Robert Fogel's provocative *Railroads and American Economic Growth* (1964). An important new study is David H. Bain, *Empire Express: Building the First Transcontinental Railroad* (1999). C. Vann Woodward has provided a masterful analysis in *Origins of the New South, 1877–1913* (1951), which can be profitably supplemented by Jonathan M. Wiener, *Social Origins of the New South* (1978); Don H. Doyle, *New Men, New Cities, New South: Atlanta, Nashville, Charleston, Mobile, 1860–1910* (1980); and Edward L. Ayers, *The Promise of the New South: Life After Reconstruction* (1992). Also see Gaines M. Foster, *Ghosts of the Confederacy: Defeat, the Lost Cause and the Emergence of the New South, 1865–1913* (1987). For more on race relations in the post-Reconstruction South, see Joel Williamson, *The Crucible of Race* (1984); Howard O. Rabinowitz, *Race Relations in the Urban South, 1865–1890* (new ed., 1996); and Neil R. McMillen, *Dark Journey: Black Mississippians in the Age of Jim Crow* (1989). Labor is the subject of Gerald Grob, *Workers and Utopia* (1961), and David Montgomery's innovative *The Fall of the House of Labor: The Workplace, the State, and American Labor Activism, 1865–1925* (1987). Paul Krause details *The Battle for Homestead, 1880–1892* (1992). Especially stimulating are two volumes by Herbert Gutman, *Work, Culture, and Society in Industrializing America* (1976) and *Power and Culture: Essays on the American Working Class* (1987). On women workers, see David Katzman, *Seven Days a Week: Women and Domestic Service in Industrializing America* (1978); Philip Foner, *Women and the American Labor Movement* (1979); and Alice Kessler-Harris, *Out to Work: A History of Wage-Earning Women in the United States* (1982). For a discussion of labor and race, see Gerald David Jaynes, *Branches Without Roots: Genesis of the Black Working Class in the American South, 1862–1882* (1986), and Tera W. Hunter, *To 'Joy My Freedom: Southern Black Women's Lives and Labors After the Civil War* (1997).

CHAPTER 25

PRIMARY SOURCE DOCUMENTS

Jacob Riis, *How the Other Half Lives** (1890), is a vivid account of life in America's slums. In *A Hazard of New Fortunes* (1890), William Dean Howells penned one of the first "urban novels" in American literature. Frances Willard, *Glimpses of Fifty Years** (1880), is the memoir of a leading prohibitionist. Victoria Woodhull, *The Scarecrows of Sexual Slavery** (1874), provocatively illustrates some changing ideas about women's roles. Henry James's novel *The Bostonians* (1886) vividly portrays feminists and suffragists.

SECONDARY SOURCES

The Rise of the City, 1878–1898 (1933) is a classic study by Arthur M. Schlesinger. More recent are Gunther Barth, *City People: The Rise of Modern City Culture in Nineteenth-Century America* (1980); Howard Chudacoff, *The Evolution of American Urban Society* (1975); the opening chapters of Kenneth T. Jackson, *Crabgrass Frontier: The Suburbanization of America* (1985); and Eric H. Monkkonen, *America Becomes Urban: The Development of Cities and Towns, 1780–1980* (1988). Specific cities are discussed in Sam Bass Warner, Jr.'s *The Private City: Philadelphia in Three Periods of Its Growth* (1968) and in his study of Boston, *Streetcar Suburbs* (1962). See also Karen Sawislak's graceful and insightful *Smoldering City: Chicagoans and the Great Fire, 1871–1874* (1995), and Philip J. Ethington, *The Public City: The Political Construction of Urban Life in San Francisco, 1850–1900* (1994). On architecture, see Robert Twombly, *Louis Sullivan: His Life and Work* (1986). On new urban spaces and their use by city dwellers, see Roy Rosenzweig and Elizabeth Blackmar, *The Park and the People: A History of Central Park* (1992); Kathy Peiss, *Cheap Amusements: Working Women and Leisure in Turn-of-the-Century New York* (1986); and David Nasaw, *Going Out: The Rise and Fall of Public Amusements* (1993). Martin Melosi, *The Sanitary City: Urban Infrastructure in America from Colonial Times to the Present* (2000), and Joel Tarr, *The Search for the Ultimate Sink: Urban Pollution in Historical Perspective* (1996), argue that waste disposal has been a key force shaping urban politics in American history. Oscar Handlin pioneered the study of immigrant communities in American cities with his *Boston's Immigrants* (rev. ed., 1959). More recent studies of the same topic include John Bodnar, *The Transplanted: A History of Immigrants in Urban America* (1985); Jon Gjerde, *From Peasants to Farmers: The Migration from Norway to the Upper Middle West* (1985); Kerby A. Miller, *Emigrants and Exile: Ireland and the Irish Exodus to North America* (1985); Donna Gabaccia, *From the Other Side: Women, Gender, and Immigrant Life in the U.S., 1820–1990* (1994); Thomas Kessner, *The Golden Door: Italian and Jewish Mobility in New York City, 1880–1915* (1977); Stephan Thernstrom, *The Other Bostonians* (1973); Virginia Yans-McLaughlin, *Family and Community: Italian Immigrants in Buffalo, 1880–1930* (1975); Dino Cinel, *From Italy to San Francisco: The Immigrant Experience* (1982); Humbert Nelli, *Italians of Chicago, 1880–1920* (1970); Ronald Takaki, *Strangers from a Different Shore: A History of Asian Americans* (1989); and Irving Howe's monumental and moving account of Jewish immigration, *World of Our Fathers* (1976). Maldwyn Jones, *American Immigration* (1960), is a well-written introduction, as is Thomas J. Archdeacon, *Becoming American* (1983). Oscar Handlin, *The Uprooted* (1951), is an imaginative account of the immigrant experience. John Higham examines the "nativist" reaction in *Strangers in the Land* (1955). On medicine, consult Morris J. Vogel, *The Invention of the Modern Hospital: Boston, 1870–1930* (1980); Paul Starr, *The Social Transformation of American Medicine* (1982); and John Duffy, *The Sanitarians: A History of American Public Health* (1990). On education, see Lawrence Cremin, *The Transformation of the School* (1961), and Laurence Veysey, *The Emergence of the American University* (1965). Black thought for this period is illuminated by three studies: August Meier, *Negro Thought in America, 1880–1915* (1963); Louis R. Harlan, *Booker T. Washington: The Making of a Black Leader, 1865–1901* (1972); and David Levering Lewis's two-volume biography *W. E. B. Du Bois* (1993, 2000). For blacks in northern cities before World War I, see Allan H. Spear, *Black Chicago: The Making of a Negro Ghetto, 1890–1920* (1967), and James Borchert, *Alley Life in Washington: Family, Community, Religion, and Folklife in the City* (1980).

On religion, see Susan Curtis, *A Consuming Faith: The Social Gospel and Modern American Culture* (1991). On women and the family, consult Carl Degler, *At Odds: Women and the Family from the Revolution to the Present* (1980); Steven Mintz, *A Prison of Expectations: The Family in Victorian Culture* (1983); Mari Jo Buhle, *Women and American Socialism, 1870–1920* (1981); Margaret W. Rossiter, *Women Scientists in America* (1982); Elisabeth Griffith, *In Her Own Right: The Life of Elizabeth Cady Stanton* (1984); Rosalind Rosenberg, *Beyond Separate Spheres* (1982) and *Divided Lives* (1992); Allen F. Davis, *American Heroine: The Life and Legend of Jane Addams* (1973); Elaine May, *Great Expectations: Marriage and Divorce in Post-Victorian America* (1980); Carroll Smith-Rosenberg, *Disorderly Conduct: Visions of Gender in Victorian America* (1985); and Estelle B. Freedman, *Their Sisters' Keepers: Women's Prison Reform in America, 1830–1930* (1981). John L. Thomas considers *Alternative America: Henry George, Edward Bellamy, Henry Demarest Lloyd, and the Adversary Tradition* (1983). Louis Menand tackles the cutting edge of American thought in this period in *The Metaphysical Club: A Story of Ideas in America* (2001). James Turner probes one aspect of the conflict between science and religion in *Without God, Without Creed: The Origins of Unbelief in America* (1985). Three fascinating studies document the rise of a "new" middle-class mentality: Burton J. Bledstein, *The Culture of Professionalism* (1976); Thomas Haskell, *The Emergence of Professional Social Science* (1977); and Stuart M. Blumin, *The Emergence of the Middle Class: Social Experience in the American City, 1760–1900* (1989). See also Alexandra Oleson and John Voss, eds., *The Organization of Knowledge in Modern America, 1860–1920* (1979).

CHAPTER 26

PRIMARY SOURCE DOCUMENTS

Black Elk Speaks, edited by John G. Neihardt (1932), is an eloquent Indian statement about the Sioux experience. Indian perspectives on the westward movement can be found in Jerome A. Greene, ed., *Lakota and Cheyenne: Indian Views of the Great Sioux Wars, 1876–1877** (1994). Theodore Roosevelt, *Hunting Trips of a Ranchman** (1885), offers the future president's views on the Indian question. Mary Lease's famous call to arms is recorded in William E. Connelley, ed., *History of Kansas, State and People** (1928). William H. Coin Harvey, *Coin's Financial School** (1894), expounded the silverite position. William Jennings Bryan's Cross of Gold speech* won him the Democratic presidential nomination in 1896 and a hallowed place in the annals of American oratory.

SECONDARY SOURCES

Vivacious chapters appear in Ray A. Billington, *Westward Expansion* (5th ed., 1982). Walter Prescott Webb, *The Great Plains* (1931), is a classic. Robert V. Hine, *The American West* (2nd ed., 1984), is a useful survey. Patricia Nelson Limerick traces regional themes across time in *Legacy of Conquest: The Unbroken Past of the American West* (1987). Richard White's fresh account, *"It's Your Misfortune and None of My Own": A New History of the American West* (1991), emphasizes the role of the federal government, corporations, and the market economy in the region's development and pays special attention to the twentieth century, as do Donald Worster, *Rivers of Empire: Water, Aridity, and the Growth of the American West* (1986), and Donald J. Pisani, *To Reclaim a Divided West: Water, Law, and Policy, 1848–1902* (1992). Women in the West are discussed in Glenda Riley, *The Female Frontier: A Comparative View of Women on the Prairie and Plains* (1988), and Beverly Beeton, *Women Vote in the West: The Woman Suffrage Movement, 1869–1896* (1986). Native Americans are discussed in Robert Utley, *The Indian Frontier of the American West, 1846–1890* (1984), and Dee Brown, *Bury My Heart at Wounded Knee: An Indian History of the American West* (1970). Consult also Francis

P. Prucha, *The Great Father: The United States Government and the American Indians* (1984); Frederick E. Hoxie, *A Final Promise: The Campaign to Assimilate the Indians* (1984); Joe S. Sando, *Pueblo Nations: Eight Centuries of Pueblo Indian History* (1992); Thomas Berger's novel *Little Big Man* (1964); and Albert Hurtado, *Indian Survival on the California Frontier* (1988). The military history of the "Indian wars" is covered in S. L. A. Marshall, *Crimsoned Prairie* (1972). Two intriguing studies of cross-cultural perception are Robert F. Berkhofer, Jr., *The White Man's Indian* (1978), and Richard Drinnon, *Facing West: The Metaphysics of Indian Hating and Empire Building* (1980). A sweeping look at Chicano history is Juan Gómez-Quiñones, *Roots of Chicago Politics, 1600–1940* (1994). David Alan Johnson explores *Founding the Far West: California, Oregon, and Nevada, 1840–1890* (1992). William Cronon explores the relationship between Chicago and the development of the "Great West" in *Nature's Metropolis* (1991), a book nicely complemented by John C. Hudson, *Making the Corn Belt* (1994). Sarah Jane Deutsch, *No Separate Refuge: Culture, Class, and Gender on an Anglo-Hispanic Frontier in the American Southwest, 1880–1940* (1987), and Neil Foley, *The White Scourge: Mexicans, Blacks, and Poor Whites in Texas Cotton Culture* (1997), explore the social histories of the Southwest borderlands. Donald J. Pisani looks at western agriculture in *From the Family Farm to Agribusiness: The Irrigation Crusade in California and the West, 1850–1931* (1984). For beef, see Philip Durham and Everett L. Jones, *The Negro Cowboys* (1965); Robert Dykstra, *The Cattle Town* (1968); and Gene M. Gressley, *Bankers and Cattlemen* (1966). A powerful work on the farmers' protest is Lawrence Goodwyn, *Democratic Promise* (1976), abridged as *The Populist Moment* (1978). See also John D. Hicks's classic *The Populist Revolt* (1931); Steven Hahn, *The Roots of Southern Populism* (1983); William A. Link, *The Paradox of Southern Progressivism, 1880–1930* (1992); and Robert C. McMath, *American Populism: A Social History, 1877–98* (1993). Richard Hofstadter's stimulating *The Age of Reform* (1955) sparked a long-running debate among historians about the nature of Populism. A more recent study is Michael Kazin, *The Populist Persuasion: An American History* (1995). Paolo Coletta's biography of William Jennings Bryan (3 vols., 1964–1969) is rich in detail. The election of 1896 is examined in Robert F. Durden, *The Climax of Populism: The Election of 1896* (1965), and Stanley Jones, *The Presidential Election of 1896* (1964). Also informative are Paul W. Glad, *McKinley, Bryan and the People* (1964), and H. Wayne Morgan, *William McKinley and His America* (1963). Kevin Starr probes the cultural history of California in both *Americans and the California Dream, 1850–1915* (1973) and *Inventing the Dream: California Through the Progressive Era* (1985). Henry Nash Smith, *Virgin Land: The American West as Symbol and Myth* (1950), is a landmark study of particular interest to students of literature.

CHAPTER 27

PRIMARY SOURCE DOCUMENTS

Examples of "yellow journalism" include Joseph Pulitzer's *New York World* and William R. Hearst's *New York Journal*. Particularly interesting is the editorial in the *World* of February 13, 1897,* and the article by Charles Duval in the *Journal* of October 10, 1897.* "McKinley's War Message,"* in James D. Richardson, ed., *Messages and Papers of the Presidents*, vol. 10 (1899), outlines the American rationale for intervention. The anti-imperialist answer can be found in Charles E. Norton's article in *Public Opinion** (June 23, 1898). Theodore Roosevelt's corollary* to the Monroe Doctrine, in *A Compilation of the Messages and Papers of the Presidents*, vol. 16, found its first expression in 1904. *The Annual Report* of the secretary of commerce and labor for 1908* contains the "Gentlemen's Agreement" with Japan. For the intrigue surrounding the independence of Panama and the building of the canal, see *Foreign Relations of the United States** (1903) and

Theodore Roosevelt to Albert Shaw, October 10, 1903,* in *The Letters of Theodore Roosevelt*, vol. 3, edited by Elting E. Morison (1951).

SECONDARY SOURCES

Main outlines are sketched in Thomas G. Paterson, *American Foreign Policy: A Brief History* (2nd ed., 1983). Two general (and quite contrasting) interpretations of modern American foreign policy are George F. Kennan, *American Diplomacy* (1951), and William Appleman Williams, *The Tragedy of American Diplomacy* (1959). For a thorough and concise survey of U.S. foreign affairs in this period, see Walter LaFeber, *The Cambridge History of American Foreign Relations, Volume 2: The American Search for Opportunity, 1865–1913* (1993). Consult also Ernest R. May, *American Imperialism: A Speculative Essay* (1968), and Walter LaFeber, *The New Empire* (1963) and *Inevitable Revolutions* (1983). E. S. Rosenberg's *Spreading the American Dream* (1982) examines U.S. economic and cultural expansion from 1890 to 1945. The racial and imperial ideologies shaping American policy are incisively considered in Matthew Frye Jacobson, *Barbarian Virtues: The United States Encounters Foreign Peoples at Home and Abroad, 1876–1917* (2000). Thoughtful perceptions can be found in Robert Seager II, *Alfred Thayer Mahan* (1977), and James L. Abrahamson, *America Arms for a New Century* (1981). On the Spanish-American War, see Frank Freidel, *The Splendid Little War* (1958), and David F. Trask, *The War with Spain in 1898* (1981). Fascinating reading is Hyman G. Rickover, *How the Battleship Maine Was Destroyed* (1976). Helpful studies of the opponents of expansion are Robert L. Beisner, *Twelve Against Empire: The Anti-Imperialists, 1898–1900* (1968); E. Berkeley Tompkins, *Anti-Imperialism in the United States: The Great Debates, 1890–1920* (1970); and Kendrick A. Clements, *William Jennings Bryan: Missionary Isolationist* (1983). Thomas McCormick sees a design for "informal" imperialism in *The China Market* (1967). David F. Healey examines *The United States in Cuba, 1898–1902* (1963), and Leon Wolff paints a grim picture of American involvement in the Philippines in *Little Brown Brother* (1961). For more on the Philippine imbroglio, see Peter W. Stanley, *A Nation in the Making: The Philippines and the United States, 1899–1921* (1975); H. W. Brands, *Bound to Empire: The United States and the Philippines* (1992); Richard E. Welch, Jr., *Response to Imperialism: The United States and the Philippine-American War, 1899–1902* (1979); Stuart C. Miller, *"Benevolent Assimilation": The American Conquest of the Philippines, 1899–1903* (1982); and Stanley Karnow, *In Our Image: America's Empire in the Philippines* (1989). Howard K. Beale describes *Theodore Roosevelt and the Rise of America to World Power* (1956). Analytical and sympathetic is John M. Blum, *The Republican Roosevelt* (new ed., 1977). An outstanding single-volume biography of TR is William H. Harbaugh, *Power and Responsibility* (rev. ed., 1975). Lewis L. Gould focuses on *The Presidency of Theodore Roosevelt* (1991), while especially good on the youthful Roosevelt is David McCullough, *Mornings on Horseback* (1981). On relations with Japan, see Charles E. Neu, *The Troubled Encounter: The United States and Japan* (1975). Also valuable are two books by Akira Iriye, *Across the Pacific* (1967) and *Pacific Estrangement: Japanese and American Expansion, 1897–1911* (1972). Michael H. Hunt thoroughly details the Open Door in *The Making of a Special Relationship: The United States and China to 1914* (1983), a book that may be profitably paired with James Reed, *The Missionary Mind and American East Asian Policy, 1911–1915* (1983). Also see William R. Hutchison, *Errand to the World: American Protestant Thought and Foreign Missions* (1987). On the treatment of the Japanese in the United States, see Ronald Takaki, *Strangers from a Different Shore* (1989). The canal issue is analyzed in Walter LaFeber, *The Panama Canal* (1978), and Richard H. Collin, *Theodore Roosevelt's Caribbean: The Panama Canal, the Monroe Doctrine, and the Latin American Context* (1990). On race relations and foreign policy, see Alexander DeConde, *Ethnicity, Race, and American Foreign Policy* (1992). On gender and imperialism, see Gail Bederman, *Manliness and Civi-*

lization (1995), and Kristen Hoganson, *Fighting for American Manhood* (1998).

CHAPTER 28

PRIMARY SOURCE DOCUMENTS

Lincoln Steffens, *The Shame of the Cities** (1904), is an exemplary muckraking document, as is Upton Sinclair's notorious novel *The Jungle* (1906). For a less than gracious assessment of the muckrakers, see Theodore Roosevelt, "The Man with the Muckrake,"* *Putnam's Monthly* and *The Critic* (October 1906). A revealing account of municipal politics is George Washington Plunkitt, *Plunkitt of Tammany Hall** (1905). See also the decision of the Supreme Court on state bakery regulations in *Lochner* v. *New York*, 198 U.S. 45 (1905). Oliver Wendell Holmes, Jr.'s thundering dissent in the *Lochner* case is reprinted in Richard Hofstadter, *Great Issues in American History*.

SECONDARY SOURCES

A brief introduction is John W. Chambers, *The Tyranny of Change: America in the Progressive Era, 1900–1917* (1980). Perceptive interpretations are Samuel P. Hays, *The Response to Industrialism, 1885–1914* (1957); Robert H. Wiebe, *The Search for Order* (1967); and Richard Hofstadter, *The Age of Reform* (1955). Valuable analyses of progressivism at the state level include Richard McCormick's exceptionally good *From Realignment to Reform: Political Change in New York State, 1893–1910* (1981); David Thelen's study of Wisconsin, *The New Citizenship* (1972); and Dewey W. Grantham, *Southern Progressivism* (1983). Robert D. Johnson zeros in on one western city's experience in *The Radical Middle Class: Populist Democracy and the Question of Capitalism in Progressive Era Portland, Oregon* (2003). Especially provocative are James Weinstein, *The Corporate Ideal in the Liberal State* (1968), and Gabriel Kolko, *The Triumph of Conservatism* (1963). Consult also Alfred D. Chandler, Jr., *The Visible Hand* (1977), and Morton Keller, *Regulating a New Economy: Public Policy and Economic Change in America, 1900–1933* (1990). On pure food and drugs, see James Harvey Young, *Pure Food: Securing the Federal Food and Drugs Act of 1906* (1989). Other social issues of importance are treated in James H. Timberlake, *Prohibition and the Progressive Movement* (1963); David J. Rothman, *Conscience and Convenience: The Asylum and Its Alternatives in Progressive America* (1980); Allen F. Davis, *Spearheads for Reform: The Social Settlements and the Progressive Movement, 1890–1914* (1967); Mina Carson, *Settlement Folk: Social Thought and the American Settlement Movement, 1885–1930* (1990); James T. Patterson, *America's Struggle Against Poverty, 1900–1980* (new ed., 2000); David B. Tyack, *The One Best System: A History of American Urban Education* (1974); and Lynn Gordon, *Gender and Higher Education in the Progressive Era* (1990). On religion, see Martin E. Marty, *Modern American Religion: The Irony of It All, 1893–1919* (1986). T. J. Jackson Lears takes a different perspective in *No Place of Grace: Antimodernism and the Transformation of American Culture* (1981). Municipal reform is the subject of Martin J. Schiesl, *The Politics of Efficiency* (1977), and two useful anthologies, Bruce Stave, ed., *Urban Bosses, Machines and Progressive Reformers* (1972), and Blaine A. Brownell and Warren E. Stickle, eds., *Bosses and Reformers* (1973). For a classic study of progressive conservation, see Samuel P. Hays, *Conservation and the Gospel of Efficiency* (1959). Karl Jacoby provides a bracingly fresh take in *Crimes Against Nature: Squatters, Poachers, Thieves, and the Hidden History of American Conservation* (2001). Socialism is discussed in Nick Salvatore, *Eugene V. Debs: Citizen and Socialist* (1982); James Weinstein, *The Decline of Socialism in America, 1912–1925* (1967); and Mari Jo Buhle, *Women and American Socialism, 1897–1920* (1981). On women and progressivism, see Robyn Muncy, *Creating a Female Dominion in American Reform* (1991); Theda Skocpol, *Protecting Soldiers and Mothers*

(1992); Ellen Fitzpatrick, *Endless Crusade: Women Social Scientists and Progressive Reform* (1990); and Rosalind Rosenberg, *Beyond Separate Spheres* (1982). Eric Rauchway examines *The Refuge of Affections: Family and American Reform Politics, 1900–1920* (2001). Jacqueline Jones focuses on black women in *Labor of Love, Labor of Sorrow: Black Women, Work, and the Family from Slavery to the Present* (1985). See also Glenda Gilmore's splendid *Gender and Jim Crow* (1996). The Taft era is summarized in Paolo Coletta, *The Presidency of William Howard Taft* (1973). See also Norman Wilensky, *Conservatives in the Progressive Era* (1965), and James Holt, *Congressional Insurgents and the Party System, 1909–1916* (1968). Otis Graham traces the progressive legacy in *Encore for Reform: The Old Progressives and the New Deal* (1967). Daniel T. Rodgers puts American progressivism in an international perspective in his masterful *Atlantic Crossings: Social Politics in a Progressive Age* (1998).

CHAPTER 29

PRIMARY SOURCE DOCUMENTS

Theodore Roosevelt's "Acceptance Speech"* at the Progressive convention of 1912 and Woodrow Wilson's collection of campaign speeches, *The New Freedom** (1913), give the substance and flavor of the critical 1912 campaign. Louis D. Brandeis, *Other People's Money and How the Bankers Use It** (1914), expresses the philosophy of a key Wilson adviser. On the *Lusitania* incident, see *Foreign Relations of the United States* (1915, Supplement).

SECONDARY SOURCES

See the titles by John W. Chambers, Samuel P. Hays, Richard Hofstadter, Robert H. Wiebe, and Daniel T. Rodgers cited in Chapter 28. Kendrick Clements, *The Presidency of Woodrow Wilson* (1992), in an elegant synthesis of the president and his age. John M. Cooper, Jr., *The Warrior and the Priest* (1983), deftly contrasts Wilson and Theodore Roosevelt. Biographies of Wilson include August Heckscher's voluminous *Woodrow Wilson: A Biography* (1991), Arthur Link's five-volume *Wilson* (1947–1965), and John M. Blum's *Woodrow Wilson and the Politics of Morality* (1956). Particularly interesting is Alexander and Juliette George's psychological study, *Woodrow Wilson and Colonel House* (1956). For a sharply contrasting view, see Edwin A. Weinstein, *Woodrow Wilson: A Medical and Psychological Biography* (1981). The road to World War I finds comprehensive treatment in Ernest May, *The World War and American Isolation, 1914–1917* (1959). Consult also Ross Gregory, *The Origins of American Intervention in the First World War* (1971), and Patrick Devlin, *Too Proud to Fight: Woodrow Wilson's Neutrality* (1975). Frank A. Ninkovich boldly reinterprets Wilson's diplomatic doctrines and their legacies in *The Wilsonian Century* (1999). Mira Wilkins traces *The History of Foreign Investment in the United States to 1914* (1989). Superb biographies of prominent intellectuals include David Levy, *Herbert Croly of the New Republic: The Life and Thought of an American Progressive* (1985); Edward A. Stettner, *Shaping Modern Liberalism: Herbert Croly and Progressive Thought* (1993); and Philippa Strum, *Brandeis: Justice for the People* (1984). Special studies of value include Thomas A. Bailey and Paul B. Ryan, *The* Lusitania *Disaster* (1975); Jeffrey J. Safford, *Wilsonian Maritime Diplomacy* (1978); Ronald Radosh, *American Labor and Foreign Policy* (1969); and Burton I. Kaufman, *Efficiency and Expansion* (1974). For the European background, see Laurence Lafore, *The Long Fuse* (1965), and Fritz Fisher, *Germany's Aims in the First World War* (1967). Social and intellectual currents are described in Henry F. May, *The End of American Innocence: A Study of the First Years of Our Own Time, 1912–1917* (1959). Michael C. Adams, *The Great Adventure: Male Desire and the Coming of World War I* (1990), is a provocative work that tries to link Victorian gender ideology to the martial enthusiasms of the early twentieth century.

CHAPTER 30

PRIMARY SOURCE DOCUMENTS

John J. Pershing, *My Experiences in the World War** (1931), recounts American fighting tactics. Woodrow Wilson's "Fourteen Points Address" to Congress on January 8, 1918* (*Congressional Record,* 65th Cong., 2nd sess., 691), defined the nation's war aims. William E. Borah, "Speech on the League of Nations" (1919), in Richard Hofstadter, *Great Issues in American History,* reveals the isolationist position. Ernest Hemingway's *A Farewell to Arms* (1929) is an outstanding war novel.

SECONDARY SOURCES

The home front is emphasized in David M. Kennedy, *Over Here: The First World War and American Society* (rev. ed., 2005). Economic mobilization is covered in Robert Cuff, *The War Industries Board* (1973), and Daniel R. Beaver, *Newton D. Baker and the American Financing of World War I* (1970). On labor, see David Brody, *Labor in Crisis: The Steel Strike of 1919* (1965); Julie Greene, *Pure and Simple Politics: The American Federation of Labor and Political Activism, 1881 to 1917* (1998); and Michael Kazin, *Barons of Labor: The San Francisco Building Trades and Union Power in the Progressive Era* (1987). Politics is treated in Seward Livermore, *Politics Is Adjourned: Woodrow Wilson and the War Congress, 1916–1918* (1966). American propaganda efforts are colorfully portrayed in James R. Mock and Cedric Larson, *Words That Won the War* (1939), and Stephen L. Vaughn, *Holding Fast the Inner Lines: Democracy, Nationalism, and the Committee on Public Information* (1980). The abuse of civil liberties is analyzed in Harry N. Scheiber, *The Wilson Administration and Civil Liberties, 1917–1921* (1960), and Paul L. Murphy, *World War I and the Origin of Civil Liberties in the United States* (1979). Military matters are handled in Edward M. Coffman, *The War to End All Wars: The American Military Experience in World War I* (1968); Arthur E. Barbeau and Florette Henri, *Unknown Soldiers: Black American Troops in World War One* (1974); and John Whiteclay Chambers II, *To Raise an Army: The Draft Comes to Modern America* (1987). The war experiences of women are captured in Maurine W. Greenwald, *Women, War, and Work* (1980). Gerd Hardach, *The First World War, 1914–1918* (1977), is a broad economic history. On Wilson's foreign economic policies, see Jeffrey J. Safford, *Wilsonian Maritime Diplomacy* (1978), and Burton I. Kaufman, *Efficiency and Expansion: Foreign Trade Organization in the Wilson Administration* (1974). The postwar international economic position of the United States is discussed in Carl Parrini, *Heir to Empire* (1969); Michael Hogan, *Informal Entente* (1977); and Joan Hoff Wilson, *American Business and Foreign Policy, 1920–1933* (1973). Paul P. Abrahams examines *The Foreign Expansion of American Finance and Its Relationship to the Foreign Economic Policies of the United States, 1907–1921* (1976). Works of cultural history include Stanley Cooperman, *World War I and the American Novel* (1966); Stuart Rochester, *American Liberal Disillusionment in the Wake of World War I* (1977); and Paul Fussell, *The Great War and Modern Memory* (1975). On the peace, see Arthur S. Link, *Woodrow Wilson: Revolution, War, and Peace* (1979), and two studies by Thomas A. Bailey, *Woodrow Wilson and the Lost Peace* (1944) and *Woodrow Wilson and the Great Betrayal* (1945). Lloyd E. Ambrosius updates the realist critique of Wilson in *Woodrow Wilson and Wilsonian Statecraft* (1991). Consult also N. Gordon Levin, Jr., *Woodrow Wilson and World Politics* (1968); Arno J. Mayer, *Politics and Diplomacy of Peacemaking* (1967); Thomas J. Knock, *To End All Wars: Woodrow Wilson and the Quest for a New World Order* (1992); Robert H. Ferrell, *Woodrow Wilson and World War I, 1917–1921* (1985); Lloyd C. Gardner, *Safe for Democracy: The Anglo-American Response to Revolution, 1913–1923* (1984); and John M. Cooper, *Breaking the Heart of the World* (2001). Lodge is somewhat rehabilitated in John A. Garraty, *Henry Cabot Lodge* (1953), and especially in William C. Widenor, *Henry Cabot Lodge and the Search for an American Foreign Policy* (1980). The end of this troubled period is sketched in Burl Noggle, *Into the Twenties: The United States from Armistice to Normalcy* (1974). Alan Dawley reforges the link between domestic and foreign affairs in this period in *Changing the World: American Progressives in War and Revolution* (2003).

CHAPTER 31

PRIMARY SOURCE DOCUMENTS

For provocative statements on assimilation and immigration, see Horace Kallen, *Culture and Democracy in the United States* (1924) and Philip Davis, ed., *Immigration and Americanization* (1920). For caustic fictional versions of the decade's social conditions, see the novels of Sinclair Lewis: *Main Street* (1920), *Babbitt* (1922), and *Arrowsmith* (1925).

SECONDARY SOURCES

The best introduction to the 1920s is William Leuchtenburg, *The Perils of Prosperity, 1914–1932* (1958). Also strong are Michael E. Parrish, *Anxious Decades: America in Prosperity and Depression, 1920–1941* (1992), and David J. Goldberg, *Discontented America: The United States in the 1920s* (1999). Frederick Lewis Allen, *Only Yesterday* (1931), is an evocative recollection of the texture of life in the decade. Equally informative are Robert S. Lynd and Helen M. Lynd's classic sociological studies, *Middletown* (1929) and *Middletown in Transition* (1937). Robert K. Murray, *Red Scare* (1955), is authoritative. On the same subject, see Stanley Coben, *A. Mitchell Palmer* (1963). Immigration restriction is dealt with in John Higham, *Strangers in the Land* (1955). The standard work on the revived Klan is David M. Chalmers, *Hooded Americanism* (rev. ed., 1981). Also valuable is Nancy MacLean, *Behind the Mask of Chivalry: The Making of the Second KKK* (1993), and Kathleen Blee, *Women of the Klan: Racism and Gender in the 1920s* (1991). The changing experiences of women are discussed in Winnifred Wandersee, *Women's Work and Family Values, 1920–1940* (1981); Lois Scharf and Joan M. Jensen, eds., *Decades of Discontent: The Women's Movement, 1920–1940* (1983); Nancy F. Cott, *The Grounding of Modern Feminism* (1987); and Phyllis Palmer, *Domesticity and Dirt: Housewives and Domestic Servants in the United States, 1920–1945* (1990). Prohibition is handled in Norman H. Clark's highly readable *Deliver Us from Evil* (1976). On a related subject, see Humbert S. Nelli, *The Business of Crime* (1976). Revealing on the Scopes trial are Lawrence W. Levine's sensitive study of William Jennings Bryan, *Defender of the Faith* (1965), and Edward J. Larsen, *Summer for the Gods: The Scopes Trial and America's Continuing Debate over Science and Religion* (1997). On the economy, see Alfred D. Chandler, Jr., *Strategy and Structure: Chapters in the History of Industrial Enterprise* (1962); Irving Bernstein, *The Lean Years: A History of the American Worker, 1920–1933* (1960); and Daniel Nelson, *Frederick Winslow Taylor and the Rise of Scientific Management* (1980). On the culture of the 1920s, see Stanley Coben, *Rebellion Against Victorianism: The Impetus for Cultural Change in 1920s America* (1991), and Lynn Dumenil, *The Modern Temper: American Culture and Society in the 1920s* (1995). On advertising, consult Stuart Ewen, *Captains of Consciousness* (1976), and Roland Marchand, *Advertising the American Dream: Making Way for Modernity* (1985). Susan Douglas, *Inventing American Broadcasting* (1987), and Susan Smulyan, *Selling Radio* (1994), describe the birth of the mass media. Movies are featured in Lary May, *Screening Out the Past: The Birth of Mass Culture and the Motion Picture Industry* (1980), and Robert Sklar, *Movie-Made America* (1975). The "youth culture" is the subject of Paula Fass, *The Damned and the Beautiful: American Youth in the 1920s* (1977). Changing sexual attitudes are analyzed in David M. Kennedy, *Birth Control in America: The Career of Margaret Sanger* (1970), and Linda Gordon, *Woman's Body, Woman's Right: A Social History of Birth Control in America* (1976). See also Ellen Chesler,

Woman of Valor: Margaret Sanger and the Birth Control Movement in America (1992). Gilbert Osofsky describes the background of the Harlem Renaissance in *Harlem: The Making of a Ghetto, 1890–1930* (1966). See also David Lewis, *When Harlem Was in Vogue* (1981). William M. Tuttle, *Race Riot: Chicago in the Red Summer of 1919* (1970), describes the violent side of race relations in the 1920s. The "great migration" of blacks to the North is described in James R. Grossman's *Land of Hope: Chicago, Black Southerners, and the Great Migration* (1989). Judith Stein, *The World of Marcus Garvey* (1986), discusses the most popular black leader of the period. Richard W. Fox and T. J. Jackson Lears have edited a fascinating collection of essays on American culture, *The Culture of Consumption: Critical Essays in American History, 1880–1980* (1983). Also see William Leach, *Land of Desire: Merchants, Power, and the Rise of a New American Culture* (1993), and Warren I. Susman, *Culture as History: The Transformation of American Society in the Twentieth Century* (1984). David M. Kennedy, *Over Here: The First World War and American Society* (rev. ed., 2005), pays special attention to the literature that emerged from the war experience.

CHAPTER 32

PRIMARY SOURCE DOCUMENTS

Herbert Hoover, *American Individualism* (1922), contains the philosophy of the man and his times. See also Hoover's "Rugged Individualism" speech (1928), in Richard Hofstadter, *Great Issues in American History*. As the Great Depression descended, Hoover fought to maintain his principles in a noteworthy speech at New York's Madison Square Garden* (*New York Times*, November 1, 1932). On foreign affairs, see the "Stimson Doctrine" (1931), in Henry Steele Commager, *Documents of American History*.

SECONDARY SOURCES

A lively introduction to the postwar decade is Burl Noggle, *Into the Twenties: The United States from Armistice to Normalcy* (1974). On Harding, see Robert K. Murray's balanced *Harding Era* (1969); consult also his *Politics of Normalcy: Government Theory and Practice in the Harding-Coolidge Era* (1973). John D. Hicks presents the standard liberal interpretation of the decade in *Republican Ascendancy* (1960). Burl Noggle looks at the chief scandal of the period in *Teapot Dome* (1962). David M. Kennedy, *Over Here: The First World War and American Society* (rev. ed., 2005), discusses postwar race relations and demobilization, as well as the international economic aftermath of the war, a subject treated at greater length in Joan Hoff Wilson, *American Business and Foreign Policy, 1920–1933* (1971). Robert Cohen explores *When the Old Left Was Young: Student Radicals and America's First Mass Student Movement, 1929–1941* (1993). On labor, see Robert H. Zieger, *American Worker, American Unions, 1920–1985* (1986), for a concise summary. On the Washington disarmament conference, see Thomas H. Buckley, *The United States and the Washington Conference, 1921–1922* (1970). The Democratic party is analyzed in Douglas Craig, *After Wilson: The Struggle for the Democratic Party, 1920–1934* (1992), and David Burner, *The Politics of Provincialism* (1967). The complicated international financial tangle of the 1920s is deftly discussed in Herbert Feis, *The Diplomacy of the Dollar* (1950), and in the early chapters of Charles Kindleberger, *The World in Depression* (1973). The cultural element of this economic story is treated in Emily S. Rosenberg, *Financial Missionaries to the World: The Politics and Culture of Dollar Diplomacy, 1900–1930* (1999). The drama of the 1928 election is captured in Allan J. Lichtman, *Prejudice and the Old Politics: The Presidential Election of 1928* (1979), and Oscar Handlin, *Al Smith and His America* (1958). The election is placed in a larger context in Samuel Lubell's classic *The Future of American Politics* (1952) and Paul Kleppner's *Who Voted? The Dynamics of Electoral Turnout, 1870–1980* (1982). George H. Nash's multivolume biography, *The Life of Herbert Hoover* (1988), is detailed, while the best brief biography of Hoover is Joan Hoff Wilson, *Herbert Hoover, Forgotten Progressive* (1975). Brilliantly unsympathetic toward Hoover is Arthur M. Schlesinger, Jr., *The Crisis of the Old Order, 1919–1933* (1957). On the depression itself, consult John K. Galbraith's breezy *The Great Crash, 1929* (1955); Maury Klein's *Rainbow's End* (2001); Peter Temin's trenchant *Did Monetary Factors Cause the Great Depression?* (1976); Robert McElvaine's *The Great Depression* (1984); and Lester V. Chandler's comprehensive *America's Greatest Depression* (1970).

CHAPTER 33

Primary Source Documents

James Agee and Walker Evans, *Let Us Now Praise Famous Men* (1940), brilliantly evokes the misery of the depression in words and photographs. Franklin D. Roosevelt's dramatic "First Inaugural Address" (1933), in Henry Steele Commager, *Documents of American History*, captured the imagination of the distressed nation. Less successful was Roosevelt's "Radio Address on Supreme Court Reform" (1937), in Richard Hofstadter, *Great Issues in American History*. See also Dorothy Thompson's attack on the Court plan in the *Washington Star*, February 10, 1937.* Clifford Odets's play *Waiting for Lefty* (1935) and John Steinbeck's novel *The Grapes of Wrath* (1939) exemplify the literature stimulated by the Great Depression. Robert S. McElvaine has collected a compelling set of letters in *Down and Out in the Great Depression* (1983).

Secondary Sources

A masterly summation is William E. Leuchtenburg, *Franklin D. Roosevelt and the New Deal, 1932–1940* (1963). See also Leuchtenburg's *Supreme Court Reborn: The Constitutional Revolution in the Age of Roosevelt* (1995). Briefer and more critical of the limitations of reform is Paul Conkin, *The New Deal* (rev. ed., 1975). A detailed biography is Frank Freidel, *Franklin D. Roosevelt* (4 vols., 1952–1973). Brilliantly pro-FDR are the three volumes of Arthur M. Schlesinger, Jr., *Age of Roosevelt: The Crisis of the Old Order* (1957), *The Coming of the New Deal* (1959), and *The Politics of Upheaval* (1960). For a newer account, see George T. McJimsey's *The Presidency of Franklin Delano Roosevelt* (2000). John M. Blum, *From the Morgenthau Diaries* (3 vols., 1959–1967), gives the perspective of an important New Deal insider, as does T. H. Watkins, *Righteous Pilgrim: The Life and Times of Harold L. Ickes, 1874–1952* (1990). The views of other contemporaries may be found in Frances Perkins, *The Roosevelt I Knew* (1946); Rexford G. Tugwell, *In Search of Roosevelt* (1972); and Raymond Moley, *After Seven Years* (1939). The long-lost memoir of Roosevelt's attorney general and close friend, Robert Jackson, has recently been discovered and published as *That Man: An Insider's Portrait of Franklin D. Roosevelt* (2003). A concise biography is Frank Freidel, *Franklin D. Roosevelt: Rendezvous with Destiny* (1990). The social impact of the depression is vividly etched in Studs Terkel, *Hard Times* (1970); Ann Banks, *First Person America* (1980); and James N. Gregory, *American Exodus: The Dust Bowl Migration and Okie Culture in California* (1989). For a comprehensive portrait of New Deal America, see David M. Kennedy's *Freedom from Fear: The American People in Depression and War* (1999). Two volumes by Lois Scharf are of interest: *To Work and to Wed: Female Employment, Feminism, and the Great Depression* (1980) and *Eleanor Roosevelt: First Lady of American Liberalism* (1987). Also see Susan Ware, *Beyond Suffrage: Women in the New Deal* (1981), and Blanche Wiesen Cook, *Eleanor Roosevelt: A Life* (1992). Alan Brinkley brilliantly chronicles *Voices of Protest: Huey Long, Father Coughlin, and the Great Depression* (1982). See also his treatment of the later New Deal in *The End of Reform* (1995). For a sharply critical portrayal, see William Ivy Hair, *The Kingfish and His Realm: The Life and Times of Huey P. Long* (1991). Greg Mitchell describes *The Campaign of the Century: Upton Sinclair's Race for Governor of California and the Birth of Media Politics* (1992). Labor is dealt with in Irving Bernstein, *Turbulent Years* (1970), and Lizabeth Cohen, *Making a New Deal: Industrial Workers in Chicago, 1919–1939* (1990). Ellis Hawley, *The New Deal and the Problem of Monopoly* (1966), is a superb analysis of the conflicting currents of economic policy in the Roosevelt administration. W. Andrew Achenbaum examines one of the era's most important pieces of legislation in *Social Security: Visions and Revisions* (1986). On the TVA, see Erwin C. Hargrave, *Prisoners of Myth, The Leadership of the Tennessee Valley Authority, 1933–1990* (1994). A comprehensive assessment by several noted scholars is Harvard Sitkoff, ed., *Fifty Years Later: The New Deal Evaluated* (1985). James Patterson, *The New Deal and the States* (1969), examines the local impact of the Roosevelt measures, as does Charles H. Trout, *Boston, the Great Depression, and the New Deal* (1977). Indians receive special attention in Graham D. Taylor, *The New Deal and American Indian Tribalism* (1980), and Kenneth R. Philip, *John Collier's Crusade for Indian Reform* (1977). On blacks, see Nancy J. Weiss, *Farewell to the Party of Lincoln: Black Politics in the Age of FDR* (1983), and Karen Ferguson, *Black Politics in New Deal Atlanta* (2002). Richard Lowitt analyzes *The New Deal and the West* (1984). On the impact of the Great Depression and the New Deal in the South, see Gavin Wright, *Old South, New South: Revolutions in the Southern Economy Since the Civil War* (1986); Bruce Schulman, *From Cotton Belt to Sunbelt* (1990); and James Cobb and Michael Namaroto, eds., *The New Deal and the South* (1984). Especially good on intellectual history is Richard H. Pells, *Radical Visions and American Dreams: Culture and Social Thought in the Depression Years* (1973). A trenchant appraisal of the New Deal legacy is Steven Fraser and Gary Gerstle, eds., *The Rise and Fall of the New Deal Order* (1989).

CHAPTER 34

Primary Source Documents

For background on the date that will live in infamy, see *Pearl Harbor Attack: Hearings Before the Joint Committee on the Investigation of the Pearl Harbor Attack*, 79th Cong., 1st sess.* (1946). Franklin D. Roosevelt's "Quarantine the Aggressors Speech" (1937), in Richard Hofstadter, *Great Issues in American History*, revealed what would become the goal of the president's foreign policy in succeeding years. See also Roosevelt's "Press Conference on Lend-Lease" (1940), in *The Public Papers and Addresses of Franklin D. Roosevelt, 1940 Volume* (1941). For opposition to lend-lease, see the speech of January 12, 1941, by Montana senator Burton K. Wheeler, *Congressional Record*, 77th Cong., 1st sess., Appendix, 178–179.* Charles A. Lindbergh elaborated the isolationist position in the *New York Times* (April 24, 1941).* Warren F. Kimball, ed., *Churchill and Roosevelt: The Complete Correspondence* (1984), is enlightening on many topics.

Secondary Sources

Indispensable and comprehensive is Robert Dallek, *Franklin D. Roosevelt and American Foreign Policy, 1932–1945* (rev. ed., 1995). Also strong is Kenneth S. Davis, *FDR: Into the Storm, 1937–1940* (1993). More specialized is Lloyd Gardner, *Economic Aspects of New Deal Diplomacy* (1964). B. J. C. McKercher details the *Transition of Power: Britain's Loss of Global Pre-eminence to the United States, 1930–1945* (1999). Isolationism is ably handled in Manfred Jonas, *Isolationism in America, 1935–1941* (1966), and Thomas Guinsburg, *The Pursuit of Isolationism in the United States Senate from Versailles to Pearl Harbor* (1982). Sympathetic to the isolationists is Wayne S. Cole, *Roosevelt and the Isolationists, 1932–1945* (1983). An updated treatment can be found in Justus D. Doenecke's exhaustively researched *Storm on the Horizon: The Challenge to American Intervention, 1939–1941* (2000). On Good Neighborism, consult Irwin F. Gellman, *Good Neighbor Diplomacy* (1979). The Spanish Civil War is dealt with in Allen Guttmann, *The Wound in the Heart: America and the Spanish Civil War* (1962), and Douglas Little, *Malevolent Neutrality: The*

United States, Great Britain, and the Origins of the Spanish Civil War (1985). On the Far East, see Dorothy Borg, *The United States and the Far Eastern Crisis of 1933–1938* (1964); P. W. Schroeder, *The Axis Alliance and Japanese-American Relations, 1941* (1958); Akira Iriye, *The Globalizing of America, 1913–1945* (1993); and Akira Iriye and Warren Cohen, eds., *American, Chinese, and Japanese Perspectives on Wartime Asia, 1931–49* (1990). Warren F. Kimball analyzes *The Most Unsordid Act: Lend Lease, 1939–1941* (1969). David L. Porter examines *The Seventy-Sixth Congress and World War II, 1939–1940* (1979). The Japanese attack on Pearl Harbor is considered in Gordon W. Prange, *At Dawn We Slept* (1981), and Michael Slackman, *Target: Pearl Harbor* (1990). A provocative analysis of the reasons (or lack thereof) for U.S. entry into the conflict is Bruce Russett, *No Clear and Present Danger* (1972). See also Donald Cameron Watt, *How War Came: The Immediate Origins of the Second World War, 1938–1939* (1989), and David Reynolds, *From Munich to Pearl Harbor* (2001).

CHAPTER 35

PRIMARY SOURCE DOCUMENTS

Vivid portraits of the fighting are found in Ernie Pyle, *Here Is Your War* (1943) and *Brave Men* (1944). On the atomic bomb, consult the reactions of the *Nippon Times** (August 10, 1945), *The Christian Century** (August 29, 1945), and President Truman's justification of the bombing in *Memoirs of Harry S. Truman** (1955).

SECONDARY SOURCES

See John M. Blum, *V Was for Victory: Politics and American Culture During World War II* (1976), and John W. Jeffries, *Wartime America: The World War II Home Front* (1996), for discussions of the home front. Consult also Doris Kearns Goodwin, *No Ordinary Time* (1994); William L. O'Neill, *A Democracy at War: America's Fight at Home and Abroad in World War II* (1993); Richard Polenberg, *War and Society: The United States, 1941–1945* (1972); and Harold G. Vatter, *The U.S. Economy in World War II* (1985). Ronald T. Takaki provides a multicultural perspective on the war in *Double Victory* (2000). Studs Terkel has compiled an interesting oral history of the war experience in *The Good War* (1984). On women, see William H. Chafe, *The American Woman: Her Changing Social, Economic, and Political Roles, 1920–1970* (1972); Susan M. Hartmann, *The Home Front and Beyond* (1982); and D'Ann Campbell, *Women at War with America: Private Lives in a Patriotic Era* (1984). On the internment of Japanese Americans, consult Roger Daniels, *Prisoners Without Trial* (1993) and *Concentration Camps U.S.A.* (1971); Peter Irons, *Justice at War: The Story of the Japanese-American Internment Cases* (1983); and the oral histories provided in John Tateishi, ed., *And Justice for All* (1984). On blacks, see Neil A. Wynn, *The Afro-Americans and the Second World War* (1976), and Nicholas Lemann, *The Promised Land: The Great Black Migration and How It Changed America* (1991). Nelson Lichtenstein examines *Labor's War at Home: The CIO in World War II* (1983), and Gerald Nash describes *The American West Transformed: The Impact of the Second World War* (1985). The military history of the war is capably summarized in H. P. Willmott, *The Great Crusade: A New Complete History of the Second World War* (1990), and in Gerhard Weinberg's massively detailed *A World at Arms* (1994). See also Russell F. Weigley, *Eisenhower's Lieutenants: The Campaigns of France and Germany, 1944–1945* (1981); Eric Larrabee, *Commander in Chief: Franklin Delano Roosevelt, His Lieutenants, and Their War* (1987); and David Eisenhower, *Eisenhower at War, 1943–45* (1986). Ed Cray profiles *General of the Army: George C. Marshall, Soldier and Statesman* (1990). A good introduction to wartime diplomacy is Gaddis Smith, *American Diplomacy During the Second World War* (1965). More detailed are Herbert Feis's three volumes: *Churchill, Roosevelt, Stalin* (2nd ed., 1967), *Between War and Peace: The Potsdam Conference* (1960), and *The Atomic Bomb and the End of World War II* (1966). Also valuable are Robert Dallek's work, cited in Chapter 34; John L.

Gaddis, *The United States and the Origins of the Cold War, 1941–1947* (1972); and two "revisionist" studies that are highly critical of American policy: Gabriel Kolko, *The Politics of War: The World and United States Foreign Policy, 1943–1945* (1968), and Lloyd Gardner, *Architects of Illusion: Men and Ideas in American Foreign Policy, 1941–1949* (1970). The war in Asia is covered in Ronald H. Spector's gracefully written *Eagle Against the Sun: The American War with Japan* (1985). John W. Dower explores the racial ideas that underlay the war against Japan in *War Without Mercy: Race and Power in the Pacific War* (1986) and the war's aftermath in his award-winning *Embracing Defeat: Japan in the Wake of World War II* (1999). Paul Fussell contrasts actual combat and wartime rhetoric in *Wartime: Understanding and Behavior in the Second World War* (1989). On the atomic bomb, the most comprehensive account is Richard Rhodes, *The Making of the Atomic Bomb* (1986). Also see Richard G. Hewlett and Oscar E. Anderson, Jr., *The New World* (1962); Martin J. Sherwin, *A World Destroyed: The Atomic Bomb and the Grand Alliance* (1975); and Gar Alperovitz's critiques of American nuclear strategy, *Atomic Diplomacy* (rev. ed., 1985) and *The Decision to Use the Atomic Bomb* (1995). Paul Boyer, *By the Bomb's Early Light* (1985), analyzes the bomb's impact on the American mind.

CHAPTER 36

PRIMARY SOURCE DOCUMENTS

George F. Kennan's "long telegram,"* in *Foreign Relations of the United States, 1946*, vol. 6 (1969), outlined the containment doctrine that would form the foundation of U.S. foreign policy in the Cold War era. Harry S Truman first applied the containment doctrine when he enunciated the Truman Doctrine,* *Congressional Record*, 80th Cong., 1st sess., 1981 (1947). On the changing postwar family, consult Dr. Benjamin Spock, *The Common Sense Book of Baby and Child Care** (1957).

SECONDARY SOURCES

Lucid overviews of the postwar years can be found in James Patterson, *Grand Expectations* (1996); William H. Chafe, *The Unfinished Journey: America Since World War II* (1986); John Patrick Diggins, *The Proud Decades: America in War and Peace, 1941–1960* (1988); and William O'Neill, *American High: The Years of Confidence, 1945–1960* (1986). Lizabeth Cohen, *A Consumers' Republic: The Politics of Mass Consumption in Postwar America* (2003), offers a trenchant examination of American society in this period and beyond. Harold G. Vatter gives a valuable account of *The United States Economy in the 1950s* (1963). Edward Denison, *The Sources of Economic Growth in the United States* (1962), argues that improved education was the key to economic growth. The southern economic boom is charted in two books by James C. Cobb: *The Selling of the South* (1982) and *Industrialization and Southern Society* (1984). The rise of the Sunbelt is dramatically portrayed in Kirkpatrick Sale, *Power Shift* (1975), and Kevin Phillips, *The Emerging Republican Majority* (1970). Suburbia is the subject of Herbert J. Gans, *The Levittowners* (1967); Zane Miller, *Suburb* (1981); Carol O'Connor, *A Sort of Utopia: Scarsdale, 1891–1981* (1983); and Kenneth T. Jackson's sweeping synthesis, *Crabgrass Frontier* (1985). On the baby boom and its implications, consult Landon Y. Jones, *Great Expectations: America and the Baby Boom Generation* (1980), and Michael X. Delli Carpini, *Stability and Change in American Politics: The Coming of Age of the Generation of the 1960s* (1986). Mark Silk chronicles the role of organized religion in America since the 1940s in *Spiritual Politics: Religion and America Since World War II* (1988). On the origins of the Cold War, see the titles cited in Chapter 35 by John L. Gaddis, Lloyd Gardner, Gar Alperovitz, Martin J. Sherwin, Herbert Feis, and Gabriel Kolko. Consult also Gaddis's *Strategies of Containment* (1982) and Joyce and Gabriel Kolko's *The Limits of Power: The World and United States Foreign Policy, 1945–1954* (1972), which roundly condemns Washington's actions.

For an ambitious revisionist synthesis, see Thomas J. McCormick, *America's Half-Century: U.S. Foreign Policy in the Cold War* (rev. ed., 1995). Useful surveys of the diplomatic history of the period, all of them in varying degrees critical of American policy, are Stephen Ambrose, *Rise to Globalism: American Foreign Policy Since 1938* (rev. ed., 1997); Walter LaFeber, *America, Russia, and the Cold War, 1945–1984* (9th ed., 2002); and Daniel Yergin, *Shattered Peace* (1977). Among the most comprehensive postrevisionist studies is Melvyn P. Leffler, *A Preponderance of Power: National Security, the Truman Administration, and the Cold War* (1992). On the first years of nuclear diplomacy, see Gregg Herken, *The Winning Weapon: The Atomic Bomb in the Cold War, 1945–1950* (1980). Broader accounts that include discussion of domestic events are David McCullough, *Truman* (1992), and Alonzo L. Hamby, *Beyond the New Deal: Harry S. Truman and American Liberalism* (1973). The implications of the election of 1948 are examined in Samuel Lubell's perceptive *The Future of American Politics* (1952). Various aspects of foreign policy are analyzed in Timothy P. Ireland, *Creating the Entangling Alliance: The Origins of the North Atlantic Treaty Organization* (1981); Gordon Chang, *Friends and Enemies: The United States, China, and the Soviet Union* (1990); Michael Schaller, *The American Occupation of Japan: The Origins of the Cold War in Asia* (1985); and Robert M. Blum, *Drawing the Line: The Origins of the American Containment Policy in East Asia* (1982). Korea is discussed in Callum A. MacDonald, *Korea: The War Before Vietnam* (1986); Bruce Cumings, ed., *Child of Conflict: The Korean-American Relationship, 1943–1953* (1983); and Bruce Cumings and Jon Halliday, *Korea: The Unknown War* (1988). On the "red scare" at home, see Richard Fried, *Nightmare in Red* (1990); Ellen Schrecker, *Many Are the Crimes* (1998); and David M. Oshinsky, *A Conspiracy So Immense: The World of Joe McCarthy* (1983). Daniel Bell, ed., *The Radical Right* (1963), places McCarthyism in a larger context. See also David W. Reinhard, *The Republican Right Since 1945* (1983). For more on J. Edgar Hoover, see Thomas Gid Powers, *Secrecy and Power: The Life of J. Edgar Hoover* (1987). Examinations of the impact of the Cold War on American culture include Nora Sayre, *Running Time: The Films of the Cold War* (1982); Ellen Schrecker, *No Ivory Tower: McCarthyism and the Universities* (1986); and Richard H. Pells, *The Liberal Mind in a Conservative Age* (1985). Valuable personal reflections by policymakers include Truman's own *Year of Decisions* (1955) and *Years of Trial and Hope* (1956); George F. Kennan, *Memoirs, 1925–1950* (1967); Dean Acheson, *Present at the Creation* (1969); and Charles Bohlen, *Witness to History* (1973).

CHAPTER 37

PRIMARY SOURCE DOCUMENTS

Earl Warren's decision in *Brown* v. *Board of Education of Topeka*, 347 U.S. 492–495* (1954), altered the course of race relations in the United States. It also sparked the opposition of one hundred southern congressmen, *Congressional Record*, 84th Cong., 2nd sess., 4515–4516* (1956). Eisenhower's Farewell Address* (1961) warned of the dangers of the "military-industrial complex." John Kenneth Galbraith criticized the consumer culture in *The Affluent Society** (1958). Joe McCarthy's vitriol can be found in his *McCarthyism: The Fight for America** (1952).

SECONDARY SOURCES

The era is surveyed readably in several works, including those titles by James Patterson, William H. Chafe, John Patrick Diggins, and William O'Neill cited in Chapter 36. Eisenhower is the subject of Stephen Ambrose's two-volume biography, *Eisenhower: Soldier, General of the Army, President-Elect, 1890–1952* (1983) and *Eisenhower: The President* (1984). See also Jeff Broadwater, *Eisenhower and the Anti-Communist Crusade* (1992), and Chester Pach and Elmo Richardson, *The Presidency of Dwight D. Eisenhower* (1991). Fred I.

Greenstein portrays Eisenhower as the master of *The Hidden Hand Presidency* (1982). Robert A. Divine, *Eisenhower and the Cold War* (1981), praises his diplomatic restraint. Various aspects of foreign policy are covered in Douglas Brinkley, *Dean Acheson: The Cold War Years, 1953–71* (1992); Richard Immerman, *The CIA in Guatemala: The Foreign Policy of Intervention* (1982); Walter Isaacson and Evan Thomas, *The Wise Men: Six Friends and the World They Made: Acheson, Bohlen, Harriman, Kennan, Lovett, McCloy* (1986); Richard E. Welch, Jr., *Response to Revolution: The United States and the Cuban Revolution, 1959–1961* (1985); Robert Schulzinger, *The Wise Men of Foreign Affairs: The History of the Council on Foreign Relations* (1984); and Herman Kahn's chilling *On Thermonuclear War* (1960). See also Gordon Chang's book cited in Chapter 36. The relation of Cold War politics to matters of race is skillfully developed in Mary L. Dudziak, *Cold War Civil Rights* (2000), and Thomas Borstelmann, *The Cold War and the Color Line* (2001). For background and consequences of the Supreme Court's 1954 desegregation decision, see Richard Kluger, *Simple Justice: The History of Brown v. Board of Education* (1976); Raymond Wolters, *The Burden of Brown: Thirty Years of School Desegregation* (1984); and Robert A. Margo, *Race and Schooling in the South, 1880–1950* (1990). Especially rich are Taylor Branch, *America in the King Years* (3 vols.; 1988, 1999, 2006), and David J. Garrow, *Bearing the Cross: Martin Luther King, Jr., and the Southern Christian Leadership Conference* (1986). The South before the civil rights movement is ably described in John Egerton, *Speak Now Against the Day: The Generation Before the Civil Rights Movement in the South* (1994), and Leon F. Litwack, *Trouble in Mind: Black Southerners in the Age of Jim Crow* (1998). For one man's experience of integration, see Jules Tygiel, *Baseball's Great Experiment: Jackie Robinson and His Legacy* (1983). Three excellent studies of race in northern cities are Thomas Sugrue, *Origins of the Urban Crisis* (1996); Arnold Hirsch, *Making the Second Ghetto: Race and Housing in Chicago, 1940–1960* (1983); and John T. McGreevy, *Parish Boundaries: The Catholic Encounter with Race in the Twentieth Century Urban North* (1996). Relevant memoirs and biographies include William O. Douglas, *The Court Years, 1939–1975* (1980); G. Edward White, *Earl Warren* (1982); John Bartlow Martin, *Adlai Stevenson* (2 vols., 1976–1977); and Townsend Hoopes, *The Devil and John Foster Dulles* (1973). On the election of 1960, see Theodore H. White's colorful *Making of the President, 1960* (1961). For more on cultural developments during the 1950s, see Lary May, ed., *Recasting America: Culture and Politics in the Age of the Cold War* (1989); Elaine May, *Homeward Bound: American Families in the Cold War Era* (1988); Stephanie Coontz, *The Way We Never Were* (1992); Tino Balio, ed., *Hollywood in the Age of Television* (1990); David Halberstam, *The Fifties* (1993); Stephen J. Whitfield, *The Culture of the Cold War* (1991); Tom Engelhardt, *The End of Victory Culture* (1995); and Eugenia Kaledin, *Mothers and More: American Women in the 1950s* (1984). On postwar literature, see Tony Tanner, *City of Words* (1971), and Alfred Kazin, *Bright Book of Life* (1973). On the arts, consult Edward Lucie-Smith, *Late Modern: The Visual Arts Since 1945* (1969). On television, see David Marc, *Demographic Vistas: Television in American Culture* (1984), and Lynn Spigel, *Make Room for TV: Television and the Family Ideal in Postwar America* (1992).

CHAPTER 38

PRIMARY SOURCE DOCUMENTS

Norman Mailer paints vivid portraits of the 1968 conventions in *Miami and the Siege of Chicago* (1968) and of the antiwar March on Washington in *Armies of the Night* (1968). Martin Luther King, Jr.'s Letter from Birmingham Jail* (1963) eloquently defends the civil rights movement. The progress of the war in Vietnam is chronicled in *The Pentagon Papers** (1971). Students for a Democratic Society (1962) and Young Americans for Freedom (1960) both issued manifestos* that suggest the political temper of the era. Stewart Alsop penned a notable editorial in *Newsweek** (1970) that reflects the "establishment's" disgust with the cultural upheavals of the decade. The two-volume documentary collection *Reporting Civil Rights* (2003), edited by Clayborne Carson et al., is an invaluable resource.

SECONDARY SOURCES

The tumultuous decade of the 1960s is treated in William L. O'Neill, *Coming Apart: An Informal History of America in the 1960s* (1971); Howard Brink, *Age of Contradiction* (1998); and John Morton Blum, *Years of Discord* (1991), as well as in the surveys cited in Chapter 37. On Kennedy, see Irving Bernstein, *Promises Kept: John F. Kennedy's New Frontier* (1991); Thomas Reeves, *A Question of Character: A Life of John F. Kennedy* (1991); Theodore C. Sorensen, *Kennedy* (1965); and Arthur M. Schlesinger, Jr., *A Thousand Days* (1965). More critical is Henry Fairlie, *The Kennedy Promise* (1973). Other useful biographies include Arthur M. Schlesinger, Jr., *Robert F. Kennedy and His Times* (1978), and Nigel Hamilton, *JFK: Reckless Youth* (1992). Seymour Harris is informative on *Economics of the Kennedy Years* (1964). Michael Beschloss details *The Crisis Years: Kennedy and Khrushchev, 1960–1963* (1991). The Cuban missile crisis is chronicled in Robert F. Kennedy, *Thirteen Days* (1969), and Graham Allison, *Essence of Decision* (1971). On the space program, consult Walter McDougall, *Heavens and the Earth: A Political History of the Space Age* (1985), and William E. Burrows, *This New Ocean: The Story of the First Space Age* (1998). Kennedy's assassination is scrutinized, not entirely satisfactorily, in *The Official Warren Commission Report* (1964). See also Gerald Posner, *Case Closed* (1993). On Johnson, a splendid short biography is Bruce J. Schulman, *Lyndon B. Johnson and American Liberalism* (1994). Johnson's own memoir, *The Vantage Point* (1971), is marred by excessive self-justification. Equally unbalanced antidotes are found in Robert Caro, *The Years of Lyndon Johnson* (3 vols; 1982, 1990, 2002). More revealing is *Taking Charge: The Johnson White House Tapes, 1963–1964,* edited by Michael Beschloss (1997). Highly favorable to Johnson is Randall B. Woods, *LBJ: Architect of American Ambition* (2006). For a complex portrait, see Robert Dallek, *Lyndon Johnson and His Times* (2 vols.; 1991, 1998). The conditions that called forth the Great Society programs are movingly described in Michael Harrington, *The Other America: Poverty in the United States* (1962). James T. Patterson summarizes *America's Struggle Against Poverty, 1900–1981* (new ed., 2000). Two superb chronicles of the civil rights movement focusing on Martin Luther King, Jr., are the books by Taylor Branch and David J. Garrow cited in Chapter 37. The racial upheavals of the decade are discussed in John Dittmer, *Local People: The Struggle for Civil Rights in Mississippi* (1994); Harvard Sitkoff, *The Struggle for Black Equality, 1954–1992* (1993); Clayborne Carson, *In Struggle: SNCC and the Black Awakening of the 1960s* (1981); and William H. Chafe, *Civilities and Civil Rights: Greensboro, North Carolina, and the Black Struggle for Freedom* (1980). See also Alex Haley, ed., *The Autobiography of Malcolm X* (1966), and Eldridge Cleaver, *Soul on Ice* (1968). On the New Left, consult two volumes by Todd Gitlin, *The Sixties: Years of Hope, Days of Rage* (1987) and *The Whole World Is Watching: Mass Media in the Making and Unmaking of the New Left* (1980); James Miller, *"Democracy Is in the Streets": From Port Huron to the Sea of Chicago* (1987); Sara Evans, *Personal Politics* (1979); Jerry Anderson *The Movement of the Sixties* (1995); and Doug Rossinow, *The Politics of Authenticity* (1998). On conservatism, see Dan Carter, *The Politics of Rage: George Wallace, the Origins of the New Conservatism, and the Transformation of American Politics* (1995); Jonathan Schoenwald, *A Time for Choosing: The Rise of Modern American Conservatism* (2001); and Lisa McGirr, *Suburban Warriors: The Origins of the New American Right* (2001). On Vietnam, consult Ronald Spector, *The United States Army in Vietnam* (1984); W. H. Brands, *Since Vietnam* (1996); and Stanley Karnow's encyclopedic *Vietnam: A History* (1983). Concise accounts are George Herring, *America's Longest War* (1986), and Marilyn B. Young, *The Vietnam Wars, 1945–1990* (1991). George Q. Flynn looks at *The Draft, 1940–1973* (1993). See also Christian Appy, *Working-Class War* (1993). Neil Sheehan, *A Bright Shining Lie: John Paul Vann and America in Vietnam* (1988), is a gripping account of one unorthodox commander. Jeffrey P. Kimball, ed., *To Reason Why: The Debate About the Causes of U.S. Involvement in the Vietnam War* (1990), contains readings from academic and public-policy figures. Robert S. McNamara, *In Retrospect: The Tragedy and Lessons of Vietnam* (1995), is the sorrowful apology of one of the war's principal architects for the "mistake" of Vietnam. Two works by John Lewis Gaddis shrewdly analyze the Cold War context of the Vietnam conflict: *The Long Peace* (1987) and *The United States and the End of the Cold War* (1992). See also his *Strategies of Containment* (1982). Presidential elections are described in Theodore H. White's *Making of the President, 1964* (1965) and *Making of the President, 1968* (1969). The emergence of a "youth culture" in the 1960s is illuminated in three studies by Kenneth Keniston: *The Uncommitted* (1965), *Young Radicals* (1968), and *Youth and Dissent* (1971). Popular books indicating the mood of the 1960s include Theodore Roszak, *The Making of a Counter-Culture* (1969), and Charles Reich, *The Greening of America* (1970). In *American Genesis: A Century of Invention and Technological Enthusiasm* (1989), Thomas Hughes argues that the sixties marked the end of a century-long national love affair with technology. Also intriguing on the 1960s is Morris Dickstein, *The Gates of Eden: American Culture in the Sixties* (1977). A lucid survey of the intellectual history of the postwar era is Richard Pells, *The Liberal Mind in a Conservative Age* (1984). Changes in attitudes toward sex are scrutinized in Daniel Yankelovich, *The New Morality* (1974); Morton Hunt, *Sexual Behavior in the 1970s* (1974); and Paul Robinson, *The Modernization of Sex* (1976). A useful overview of the decade is Maurice Isserman and Michael Kazin, *America Divided: The Civil War of the 1960s* (2000).

CHAPTER 39

PRIMARY SOURCE DOCUMENTS

Richard Nixon's vision of the international order is delineated in his *RN: The Memoirs of Richard Nixon** (1978). The articles of impeachment reported against Nixon can be found in *House of Representatives Report No. 93-1305,* 93rd Cong., 2nd sess., 1–2* (1974). Opposing opinions on the Panama Canal treaty were voiced by Cyrus Vance and Ronald Reagan, *Hearings Before the Committee on Foreign Relations,* United States Senate, 95th Cong., 1st sess., 10–15, 96–103 (1977). An influential text of the feminist movement was Robin Morgan's anthology *Sisterhood Is Powerful* (1970).

SECONDARY SOURCES

Melvin Small offers a brief, balanced study of *The Presidency of Richard Nixon* (1999). The most comprehensive account of Nixon's early career is Stephen E. Ambrose, *Nixon: The Education of a Politician, 1913–1962* (1987). See also his *Nixon: The Triumph of a Politician, 1962–1972* (1989). Nixon's intriguing personality is examined in Gary Wills, *Nixon Agonistes: The Crisis of the Self-Made Man* (1970). Theodore White continues his chronicle of presidential electioneering in *The Making of the President, 1972* (1973). Consult also Hunter S. Thompson's savagely masterful *Fear and Loathing on the Campaign Trail, 1972* (1973) and Timothy Crouse's insightful study of the political press, *The Boys on the Bus* (1973). A wide-ranging discussion of the home front is in Kim McQuaid, *The Anxious Years: America in the Vietnam-Watergate Era* (1989). Valuable background on U.S. foreign policy in the Nixon years can be found in David P. Calleo and Benjamin Rowland, *America and the World Political Economy* (1973). On multinational corporations, see Richard J. Barnet and Ronald E. Muller, *Global Reach* (1974). Retrospectives on Vietnam include George C. Herring, *America's Longest War* (1986); William Buckingham, *Operation Ranch Hand: The Air Force and Herbicides in Southeast Asia, 1961–1971* (1982); and William Shawcross's chilling account of U.S. involvement in Cambodia, *Sideshow* (2nd ed., 1981). Shawcross is vigorously rebutted in Henry Kissinger's rich memoirs,

White House Years (1979), *Years of Upheaval* (1982), and *Years of Renewal* (1999). A good biography of Nixon's secretary of state is Robert D. Schulzinger, *Henry Kissinger: Doctor of Diplomacy* (1989). On U.S. involvement in the Middle East, see Douglas Little, *American Orientalism: The United States and the Middle East Since 1945* (2002), and William B. Quandt, *Peace Process: American Diplomacy and the Arab-Israeli Conflict Since 1967* (rev. ed., 2001). Arthur M. Schlesinger, Jr., traces the growth of *The Imperial Presidency* (1973). The Watergate crisis is vividly described in two books by Carl Bernstein and Robert Woodward, *All the President's Men* (1974) and *The Final Days* (1976), and in Stanley I. Kutler, *The Wars of Watergate* (1990). Jonathan Schell, *The Time of Illusion* (1976), assesses the impact of the crisis on the nation's spirit and institutions. Many of the fallen president's former men have written of their involvement in the Watergate affair, including Jeb Stuart Magruder, John Dean, John Erlichman, and H. R. Haldeman. Robert Woodward and Scott Armstrong provide a behind-the-scenes look at key decisions of the Burger Court in *The Brethren: Inside the Supreme Court* (1979). John Robert Greene describes the Nixon and Ford administrations in *The Limits of Power* (1992). "Jerry" Ford, the first appointed president, is analyzed by his former press secretary in J. F. ter Horst, *Gerald Ford and the Future of the Presidency* (1974). For a sharply critical view, see Clark Mollenhoff, *The Man Who Pardoned Nixon* (1976). Consult also Richard Reeves, *A Ford, Not a Lincoln* (1975), and Ford's own *A Time to Heal: The Autobiography of Gerald Ford* (1979). On the extremes of the women's movement in the 1970s, see Alice Echols, *Daring to Be Bad: Radical Feminism in America, 1967–1975* (1989), and Susan Hartman, *The Other Feminists: Activists in the Liberal Establishment* (1998). Jimmy Carter wrote his autobiography, *Why Not the Best?* (1975), as did his wife, Rosalynn Carter, *First Lady from Plains* (1984). They should be supplemented by Burton Kaufman, *The Presidency of James Earl Carter* (1993), and John Dambrell, *The Carter Presidency* (1993). Sharply critical are Clark R. Mollenhoff, *The President Who Failed: Carter Out of Control* (1980), and Joseph A. Califano, Jr. (whom Carter fired from the cabinet), *Governing America: An Insider's Report from the White House and the Cabinet* (1981). Other useful memoirs are Carter's own *Keeping Faith* (1982) and National Security Adviser Zbigniew Brzezinski's *Power and Principle* (1983). Gaddis Smith, *Morality, Reason and Power* (1986), surveys Carter's foreign policy. The debate on Panama spawned two noteworthy books: Walter LaFeber's pro-withdrawal *Panama Canal: The Crisis in Historical Perspective* (1978) and Paul B. Ryan's anti-withdrawal *Panama Canal Controversy* (1977). On other aspects of Central American policy, see Richard Fagen, *The Nicaraguan Revolution* (1981), and Walter LaFeber's *Inevitable Revolutions: The United States in Central America* (2nd ed., 1993). The catastrophe in Iran is described in James Bill, *The Eagle and the Lion: The Tragedy of Americans' Iranian Relations* (1987); Michael Ledeen and William Lewis, *Debacle: The American Failure in Iran* (1981); and Barry M. Rubin, *Paved with Good Intentions: The American Experience and Iran* (1980).

CHAPTER 40

PRIMARY SOURCE DOCUMENTS

The debate over "Reaganomics" can be followed in Reagan's nationally televised address of July 27, 1981, *Weekly Compilation of Presidential Documents,** vol. 17, no. 31, and in the critical response of the *New York Times** (August 2, 1981). See also the comments of Budget Director David Stockman in William Greider, *The Education of David Stockman and Other Americans* (1982). On arms control, see the pastoral letter of the National Council of Catholic Bishops and the reply of Albert Wohlstetter in Charles Kegley and Eugene Wittkopf, eds., *The Nuclear Reader* (1985). On Central American policy, see Reagan's remarkable speech of March 16, 1986.* The inside workings of the Iran-contra scandal can be studied in *The Tower Commission Report* (1987).

SECONDARY SOURCES

Garry Wills, *Reagan's America: Innocents at Home* (1987), and Haynes Johnson, *Sleepwalking Through History: America in the Reagan Years* (1997), survey the Reagan era. Reagan is portrayed in Laurence Barrett, *Gambling with History* (1984); Fred Greenstein, *The Reagan Presidency* (1983); Michael Schaller, *Reckoning with Reagan* (1992); and Lou Cannon, *President Reagan: The Role of a Lifetime* (1992). Reagan's economic policies are discussed in Paul C. Roberts, *The Supply-Side Revolution* (1984), and John W. Sloan, *The Reagan Effect: Economics and Presidential Leadership* (1999), and are sharply criticized in David A. Stockman, *The Triumph of Politics: Why the Reagan Revolution Failed* (1986). Other views on the economy can be found in Lester Thurow, *The Zero-Sum Society* (1981), and Samuel Bowles et al., *Beyond the Wasteland* (1984). The debate over nuclear policy is covered in R. James Woolsey, *Nuclear Arms* (1984); Strobe Talbott, *The Russians and Reagan* (1984); and Charles Kegley and Eugene Wittkopf, eds., *The Nuclear Reader* (1985). The neoconservative movement is best elucidated by the writings of its leaders; see Norman Podhoretz, *Breaking Ranks* (1979), and Irving Kristol, *Reflections of a Neoconservative* (1983). For a critical view, consult Peter Steinfels, *The Neoconservatives* (1979). Issues of special concern to the neoconservatives are treated by Charles Murray, *Losing Ground* (1984), an indictment of federal government social programs. Its conclusions are sharply contested by John E. Schwartz, *America's Hidden Success* (rev. ed., 1988). This debate is put into historical perspective in James T. Patterson, *America's Struggle Against Poverty, 1900–1980* (new ed., 2000). Two studies of affirmative action are Allan P. Sindler, *Bakke, DeFinis and Minority Admissions* (1978), and J. Harvie Wilkinson, *From Brown to Bakke* (1979). The presidential election of 1980 is chronicled by Jules Witcover and Jack Germond in *Blue Smoke and Mirrors* (1981) and put into historical perspective in Theodore H. White, *America in Search of Itself* (1982). For more on conservatism in the last decades of the twentieth century, see William C. Berman, *America's Right Turn: From Nixon to Bush* (1994), and the titles by Schoenwald and McGirr in Chapter 38. Kevin P. Phillips is also insightful about the implications of the conservative revival in *Post-Conservative America* (1982). Eugene Genovese explores *The Southern Tradition: The Achievement and Limitations of an American Conservatism* (1994). Useful books on the role of religion in modern politics include William Martin, *With God on Our Side: The Rise of the Religious Right in America* (1996); Garry Wills, *Under God: Religion and American Politics* (1990); Robert Wuthrow, *The New Christian Right* (1983); and Richard John Neuhaus, *The Naked Public Square: Religion and Democracy in America* (1984). On the Supreme Court, see Richard L. Pacelle, Jr., *The Transformation of the Supreme Court's Agenda: From the New Deal to the Reagan Administration* (1991). Critical of Reagan are William Leuchtenburg, *In the Shadow of FDR: From Harry Truman to Ronald Reagan* (1983); Paul D. Erickson, *Reagan Speaks: The Making of an American Myth* (1985); Ronnie Duggar, *On Reagan* (1983); June Mayer and Doyle McManus, *Landslide: The Unmaking of the President, 1984–88* (1988); and Richard Reeves, *The Reagan Detour* (1985). More balanced are two books by John L. Palmer, *The Reagan Record* (coedited with Isabel V. Sawhill, 1984) and *Perspectives on the Reagan Years* (1986). Among the interesting memoirs by Reagan administration officials, in addition to David Stockman's book, are Martin Anderson's strongly pro-Reagan *Revolution* (1989); Secretary of State Alexander Haig's *Caveat* (1984); press secretary Larry Speakes's *Speaking Out* (1988); Michael Deaver's anecdotal *Behind the Scenes* (1987); Donald R. Regan's tattletale *For the Record* (1988); and speechwriter Peggy Noonan's somewhat bemused *What I Saw at the Revolution: A Political Life in the Reagan Era* (1990). Important topics in foreign policy are covered in John Ehrman, *The Rise of Neoconservatism: Intellectuals and Foreign Affairs, 1945–1994* (1995); Walter LaFeber, *Inevitable Revolutions* (2nd ed.,1993), which discusses Central America; Robert Pastor's more probing study, *Condemned to Repetition: The United States and Nicaragua* (1987); and Bob Woodward, *Veil: The Secret Wars of the*

CIA (1987). Theodore Draper details the Iran-contra affair in *A Very Thin Line* (1991). In *The Devil We Knew: Americans and the Cold War* (1993), H. W. Brands attempts to calculate how much it cost the United States to win the Cold War. The legacy of the Reagan era is the subject of Kevin P. Phillips's devastating *The Politics of Rich and Poor: Wealth and the American Electorate in the Reagan Aftermath* (1990) and Barbara Ehrenreich's *The Worst Years of Our Lives: Irreverent Notes from a Decade of Greed* (1990). John Lewis Gaddis offers a balanced appraisal of the historical character of the entire Cold War in *We Now Know: Rethinking Cold War History* (1997). The Clarence Thomas/Anita Hill hearings of 1991 are discussed in Toni Morrison, ed., *Race-ing Justice, En-gendering Power* (1992).

CHAPTER 41

PRIMARY SOURCE DOCUMENTS

President Bill Clinton's impeachment and trial can be followed in *The Impeachment and Trial of President Clinton: The Official Transcripts from the House Judiciary Committee Hearings to the Senate Trial*, ed. Merrill McLaughlin (1999).

SECONDARY SOURCES

Bob Woodward, *The Agenda* (1994), *The Choice* (1996) provide inside glimpses of politics in the Clinton years. Mixed reviews greeted Bill Clinton's autobiography, *My Life* (2004). For insightful analysis by a historian, see James MacGregor Burns and Georgia J. Sorenson, *Dead Center: Clinton-Gore Leadership and the Perils of Moderation* (1999). For a compelling study by a journalist, see Joe Klein, *The Natural* (2002). On the precedent-shattering First Lady, see David Brock, *The Seduction of Hillary Rodham* (1996). She has provided her own, relatively guarded memoirs in *Living History* (2003). James B. Stewart, *Blood Sport* (1996), is especially good on Clinton's complex relationship with the media. On Clinton's impeachment, see Richard Posner, *An Affair of State: The Investigation, Impeachment, and Trial of President Clinton* (1999). Clinton adviser Sidney Blumenthal provides passionate recollections of his years in the White House in *The Clinton Wars* (2003). Haynes Johnson offers a characteristically insightful overview of the 1990s in *The Best of Times: America in the Clinton Years* (2001). On the contested election between George W. Bush and Al Gore, see *The Unfinished Election of 2000*, edited by Jack Rakove.

CHAPTER 42

PRIMARY SOURCE DOCUMENTS

The classic book that launched the modern women's movement is Betty Friedan's *The Feminine Mystique* (1963). For the views of a Christian conservative on the abortion issue, see Ralph Reed, "We Stand at a Crossroads," *Newsweek** (May 13, 1996). *Statistical Abstract of the United States* is an annual government publication with a wealth of information on a variety of topics, including immigration, Social Security funding, and the social and economic condition of minorities.

SECONDARY SOURCES

A useful overview of recent history is Paul Boyer, *Promises to Keep: The United States Since World War II* (2005). On the American economy since the 1990s, see Joseph E. Stiglitz, *The Roaring Nineties: A New History of the World's Most Prosperous Decade* (2003); Alan S. Blinder and Janet L. Yellen, *The Fabulous Decade: Macroeconomic Lessons from the 1990s* (2001); and Paul Krugman, *The Great Unraveling: Losing Our Way in the New Century* (2003). Growing income in-

equality is discussed in Barbara Ehrenreich, *Fear of Falling: The Inner Life of the Middle Class* (1989) and *Nickle and Dimed: On (Not) Getting By in America* (2001), as well as in Kevin P. Phillips, *The Politics of Rich and Poor: Wealth and the American Electorate in the Reagan Aftermath* (1990) and *Wealth and Democracy: A Political History of the American Rich* (2002). The evolving social participation of women, and the dilemmas thereby created, are clearly spelled out in Rosalind Rosenberg, *Divided Lives* (1992), and William H. Chafe, *The Paradox of Change: American Women in the 20th Century* (1991). See also Betty Friedan, *The Second Stage* (1981); Sylvia Ann Hewlett, *A Lesser Life: The Myth of Women's Liberation in America* (1986); Susanne M. Bianchi, *American Women in Transition* (1987); Marion Faux, *Roe vs. Wade* (1988); Jean E. Friedman et al., eds., *Our American Sisters* (1987); Andrew Hacker, *Mismatch: The Growing Gulf Between Women and Men* (2003); and Susan Faludi's provocative best seller, *Backlash: The Undeclared War Against American Women* (1991). Faludi has also provided a view from the other side of America's gendered strife in *Stiffed: The Betrayal of the American Man* (1999). George Masnick and Mary Jo Bane, *The Nation's Families: 1960–1990* (1980), is rich in statistical information. For a brilliant discussion of the same subject from an economic perspective, see Victor R. Fuchs, *How We Live* (1983) and *Women's Quest for Economic Equality* (1988). On the looming problems in the Social Security system, see Peter G. Peterson, *Will America Grow Up Before It Grows Old?* (1996). For an analysis of the leading senior citizens' lobby, the American Association of Retired Persons, consult Charles R. Morris, *The AARP: America's Most Powerful Lobby and the Clash of Generations* (1996). George J. Borjas turns an economist's critical eye on recent immigration in *Friends or Strangers* (1990). To view recent debates about immigration in sweeping historical context, see Bill Ong Hing, *Defining America Through Immigration Policy* (2004). America's newest immigrants are the subjects of David M. Reimers, *Still the Golden Door: The Third World Comes to America* (1986). On Mexican Americans, see Carlos Munoz, Jr., *Youth, Identity, Power: The Chicano Movement* (1989); George J. Sanchez, *Becoming Mexican American* (1989); and Richard Rodriguez's poignant memoir, *Hunger of Memory* (1982). Asian Americans are discussed in Bill Ong Hing, *Making and Remaking Asian America Through Immigration Policy* (1993), and Ronald Takaki, *Strangers from a Different Shore* (1989). On blacks, see Andrew Hacker, *Two Nations: Black and White, Separate, Hostile, Unequal* (1992); Gerald David Jaynes and Robin M. Williams, Jr., *A Common Destiny: Blacks and American Society* (1989); and David J. Dent, *In Search of Black America: Discovering the African-American Dream* (2000). Regarding Native Americans, consult Alvin M. Josephy, *Now That the Buffalo Have Gone: A Study of Today's American Indians* (1982). The problems of the cities are examined in Jon C. Teaford, *The Rough Road to Renaissance: Urban Revitalization in America, 1940–1985* (1990), and Larry Bennett, *Fragments of Cities: The New American Downtowns and Neighborhoods* (1990). Suburbs are the subject of Dolores Hayden, *Building Suburbs: Green Fields and Urban Growth, 1820–2000* (2003). On crime, consult Elliott Currie, *Confronting Crime: An American Challenge* (1986). For penetrating analyses of the problems of the inner cities, consult three studies by William J. Wilson, *The Truly Disadvantaged: The Inner City, the Underclass, and Public Policy* (1987); *Poverty, Inequality, and the Future of Social Policy* (1995); and *When Work Disappears* (1996). The job limitations of inner-city residents who do work are the focus of Katherine Newman's *No Shame in My Game: The Working Poor in the Inner City* (1999) and *A Different Shade of Gray: Midlife and Beyond in the Inner City* (2003). Welfare reform is the subject of Mary Jo Bane, *Welfare Realities* (1994), as well as the essays collected in Barbara Ehrenreich, *Lost Ground: Welfare Reform, Poverty, and Beyond* (2002). Nicholas Lemann, *The Promised Land* (1991), provides a vivid account of the welfare system and the failed promises of Lyndon Johnson's "War on Poverty." The political implications of the debates over race and welfare policies are spelled out in Thomas Byrne Edsall and Mary D. Edsall, *Chain Reaction: The Impact of Race, Rights, and Taxes on American Politics* (1991). On the persistence of racial segregation in America, see Douglas S. Massey and Nancy A. Denton, *American Apartheid: Segregation and the Making of the Underclass* (1993), Alex Kotlowitz, *The Other Side of the River* (1999), and Gary Orfield, *Brown at 50: King's Dream or Plessy's Nightmare* (2004). The broader cultural controversies of the era are examined in Arthur M. Schlesinger, Jr., *The Disuniting of America* (1992); Robert Hughes, *Culture of Complaint: The Fraying of America* (1993); and Henry Louis Gates, Jr., *Loose Canons: Notes on the Culture Wars* (1993). David A. Hollinger offers a fresh analysis of how opinions toward interracial and interethnic marriage have evolved in America in "Amalgamation and Hypodescent: The Question of Ethnoracial Mixture in the History of the United States," *American Historical Review*, vol. 108, no. 5 (December 2003). A sensitive and intriguing study of the values of modern Americans is Robert N. Bellah, *Habits of the Heart: Individualism and Commitment in American Life* (1985). See also Allan Bloom's conservative critique of modern higher education, *The Closing of the American Mind* (1987), and the rejoinder by Lawrence Levine, *The Opening of the American Mind* (1996). On recent trends in religious practice, see Alan Wolfe, *The Transformation of American Religion: How We Actually Live Our Faith* (2003).

Declaration of Independence

In Congress, July 4, 1776

The Unanimous Declaration of the Thirteen United States of America

[Bracketed material in color has been inserted by the authors. For adoption background see pp. 99–100.]

When, in the course of human events, it becomes necessary for one people to dissolve the political bonds which have connected them with another, and to assume, among the powers of the earth, the separate and equal station to which the laws of nature and of nature's God entitle them, a decent respect to the opinions of mankind requires that they should declare the causes which impel them to the separation.

We hold these truths to be self-evident: That all men are created equal; that they are endowed by their Creator with certain unalienable rights; that among these are life, liberty, and the pursuit of happiness; that, to secure these rights, governments are instituted among men, deriving their just powers from the consent of the governed; that whenever any form of government becomes destructive of these ends, it is the right of the people to alter or to abolish it, and to institute new government, laying its foundation on such principles, and organizing its powers in such form, as to them shall seem most likely to effect their safety and happiness. Prudence, indeed, will dictate that governments long established should not be changed for light and transient causes; and accordingly all experience hath shown that mankind are more disposed to suffer, while evils are sufferable, than to right themselves by abolishing the forms to which they are accustomed. But when a long train of abuses and usurpations, pursuing invariably the same object, evinces a design to reduce them under absolute despotism, it is their right, it is their duty, to throw off such government, and to provide new guards for their future security. Such has been the patient sufferance of these colonies; and such is now the necessity which constrains them to alter their former systems of government. The history of the present King of Great Britain is a history of repeated injuries and usurpations, all having in direct object the establishment of an absolute tyranny over these states. To prove this, let facts be submitted to a candid world.

He has refused his assent to laws, the most wholesome and necessary for the public good. [See royal veto, p. 85.]

He has forbidden his governors to pass laws of immediate and pressing importance, unless suspended in their operation till his assent should be obtained; and, when so suspended, he has utterly neglected to attend to them.

He has refused to pass other laws for the accommodation of large districts of people [by establishing new countries], unless those people would relinquish the right of representation in the legislature, a right inestimable to them, and formidable to tyrants only.

He has called together legislative bodies at places unusual, uncomfortable, and distant from the depository of their public records, for the sole purpose of fatiguing them into compliance with his measures. [e.g., removal of Massachusetts Assembly to Salem, 1774.]

He has dissolved representative houses repeatedly, for opposing, with manly firmness, his invasions on the rights of the people. [e.g., Virginia Assembly, 1765.]

He has refused for a long time, after such dissolutions, to cause others to be elected; whereby the legislative powers, incapable of annihilation, have returned to the people at large for their exercise; the state remaining, in the mean time, exposed to all the dangers of invasions from without and convulsions within.

He has endeavored to prevent the population [populating] of these states; for that purpose obstructing the laws for naturalization of foreigners; refusing to pass others to encourage their migration hither, and raising the conditions of new appropriations of lands. [e.g., Proclamation of 1763, p. 82.]

He has obstructed the administration of justice, by refusing his assent to laws for establishing judiciary powers.

He has made judges dependent on his will alone, for the tenure of their offices, and the amount and payment of their salaries. [See Townshend Acts, p. 88.]

He has erected a multitude of new offices, and sent hither swarms of officers to harass our people and eat out their substance. [See enforcement of Navigation Laws, p. 90.]

He has kept among us, in times of peace, standing armies, without the consent of our legislatures. [See pp. 86, 91.]

He has affected to render the military independent of, and superior to, the civil power.

He has combined with others to subject us to a jurisdiction foreign to our constitution, and unacknowledged by our laws, giving his assent to their acts of pretended legislation:

> For quartering large bodies of armed troops among us [See Boston Massacre, p. 88];
>
> For protecting them, by a mock trial, from punishment for any murders which they should commit on the inhabitants of these states [See 1774 Acts, p. 91];
>
> For cutting off our trade with all parts of the world [See Boston Port Act, p. 91];
>
> For imposing taxes on us without our consent [See Stamp Act, pp. 86–87];
>
> For depriving us, in many cases, of the benefits of trial by jury;
>
> For transporting us beyond seas, to be tried for pretended offenses;
>
> For abolishing the free system of English laws in a neighboring province [Quebec], establishing therein an arbitrary government, and enlarging its boundaries, so as to render it at once an example and fit instrument for introducing the same absolute rule into these colonies [Quebec Act, p. 91];
>
> For taking away our charters, abolishing our most valuable laws, and altering fundamentally the forms of our governments [e.g., in Massachusetts, p. 91];
>
> For suspending our own legislatures, and declaring themselves invested with power to legislate for us in all cases whatsoever [See Stamp Act repeal, pp. 87–88.]

He has abdicated government here, by declaring us out of his protection and waging war against us. [Proclamation, p. 98.]

He has plundered our seas, ravaged our coasts, burned our towns, and destroyed the lives of our people. [e.g., the burning of Falmouth (Portland), p. 99.]

He is at this time transporting large armies of foreign mercenaries [Hessians, p. 98] to complete the works of death, desolation, and tyranny already begun with circumstances of cruelty and perfidy scarcely paralleled in the most barbarous ages, and totally unworthy the head of a civilized nation.

He has constrained our fellow-citizens, taken captive on the high seas [by impressment], to bear arms against their country, to become the executioners of their friends and brethren, or to fall themselves by their hands.

He has excited domestic insurrection among us [i.e., among slaves], and has endeavored to bring on the inhabitants of our frontiers the merciless Indian savages, whose known rule of warfare is an undistinguished destruction of all ages, sexes, and conditions.

In every stage of these oppressions we have petitioned for redress in the most humble terms; our repeated petitions have been answered only by repeated injury. [e.g., pp. 96–97.] A prince, whose character is thus marked by every act which may define a tyrant, is unfit to be the ruler of a free people.

Nor have we been wanting in our attentions to our British brethren. We have warned them, from time to time, of attempts by their legislature to extend an unwarrantable jurisdiction over us. We have reminded them of the circumstances of our emigration and settlement here. We have appealed to their native justice and magnanimity; and we have conjured them, by the ties of our common kindred, to disavow these usurpations, which would inevitably interrupt our connections and correspondence. They, too, have been deaf to the voice of justice and of consanguinity [blood relationship]. We must, therefore, acquiesce in the necessity which denounces [announces] our separation, and hold them, as we hold the rest of mankind, enemies in war, in peace friends.

We, therefore, the representatives of the United States of America, in General Congress assembled, appealing to the Supreme Judge of the world for the rectitude of our intentions, do, in the name and by the authority of the good people of these colonies, solemnly publish and declare, That these United Colonies are, and of right ought to be, FREE AND INDEPENDENT STATES; that they are absolved from all allegiance to the British crown, and that all political connection between them and the state of Great Britain is, and ought to be, totally dissolved; and that, as free and independent states, they have full power to levy war, conclude peace, contract alliances, establish commerce, and do all other acts and things which independent states may of right do. And for the support of this declaration, with a firm reliance on the protection of Divine Providence, we mutually pledge to each other our lives, our fortunes, and our sacred honor.

[Signed by]   JOHN HANCOCK [President]
                                              [and fifty-five others]

Constitution of the United States of America

[Boldface headings and bracketed explanatory matter and marginal comments (both in color) have been inserted for the reader's convenience. Passages that are no longer operative are printed in italic type.]

PREAMBLE

We the people of the United States, in order to form a more perfect union, establish justice, insure domestic tranquility, provide for the common defense, promote the general welfare, and secure the blessings of liberty to ourselves and our posterity, do ordain and establish this CONSTITUTION for the United States of America.

Article I. Legislative Department

SECTION I. Congress

Legislative power vested in a two-house Congress. All legislative powers herein granted shall be vested in a Congress of the United States, which shall consist of a Senate and a House of Representatives.

SECTION II. House of Representatives

1. The people elect representatives biennially. The House of Representatives shall be composed of members chosen every second year by the people of the several States, and the electors [voters] in each State shall have the qualifications requisite for electors of the most numerous branch of the State Legislature.

2. Who may be representatives. No person shall be a Representative who shall not have attained the age of twenty-five years, and been seven years a citizen of the United States, and who shall not, when elected, be an inhabitant of that State in which he shall be chosen.

See 1787 compromise, p. 124.

See 1787 compromise, p. 125.

3. Representation in the House based on population; census. Representatives and direct taxes[1] shall be apportioned among the several States which may be included within this Union, according to their respective numbers, *which shall be determined by adding to the whole number of free persons, including those bound to service for a term of years* [apprentices and indentured servants], *and excluding Indians not taxed, three-fifths of all other persons* [slaves].[2] The actual enumeration [census] shall be made within three years after the first meeting of the Congress of the United States, and within every subsequent term of ten years, in such manner as they shall by law direct. The number of Representatives shall not exceed one for every thirty thousand, but each State shall have at least one Representative; *and until such enumeration shall be made, the State of New Hampshire shall be entitled to choose three, Massachusetts eight, Rhode Island and Providence Plantations one, Connecticut five, New York six, New Jersey four, Pennsylvania eight, Delaware one, Maryland six, Virginia ten, North Carolina five, South Carolina five, and Georgia three.*

---

[1]Modified in 1913 by the Sixteenth Amendment re income taxes (see p. 462).

[2]The word *slave* appears nowhere in the original, unamended Constitution. The three-fifths rule ceased to be in force when the Thirteenth Amendment was adopted in 1865 (see p. 51 and amendments below).

4. Vacancies in the House are filled by election. When vacancies happen in the representation from any State, the Executive authority [governor] therefore shall issue writs of election [call a special election] to fill such vacancies.

See Johnson trial, p. 332; Nixon trial preliminaries, pp. 636–637; and discussion of Clinton's impeachment, pp. 669–670.

5. The House selects its Speaker; has sole power to vote impeachment charges (i.e., indictments). The House of Representatives shall choose their Speaker and other officers; and shall have the sole power of impeachment.

SECTION III.

Senate

1. Senators represent the states. The Senate of the United States shall be composed of two Senators from each State, *chosen by the legislature thereof,*[1] for six Years; and each Senator shall have one vote.

2. One-third of senators chosen every two years; vacancies. *Immediately after they shall be assembled in consequence of the first election, they shall be divided as equally as may be into three classes. The seats of the Senators of the first class shall be vacated at the expiration of the second year, of the second class at the expiration of the fourth year, and of the third class at the expiration of the sixth year,* so that one-third may be chosen every second year; *and if vacancies happen by resignation or otherwise, during the recess of the legislature of any State, the Executive* [governor] *thereof may make temporary appointments until the next meeting of the legislature, which shall then fill such vacancies.*[2]

3. Who may be senators. No person shall be a Senator who shall not have attained to the age of thirty years, and been nine years a citizen of the United States, and who shall not, when elected, be an inhabitant of that State for which he shall be chosen.

4. The vice president presides over the Senate. The Vice President of the United States shall be President of the Senate, but shall have no vote, unless they be equally divided [tied].

5. The Senate chooses its other officers. The Senate shall choose their other officers, and also a President *pro tempore,* in the absence of the Vice President, or when he shall exercise the office of the President of the United States.

See Johnson trial, p. 332; and discussion of Clinton's impeachment, pp. 669–670.

6. The Senate has sole power to try impeachments. The Senate shall have the sole power to try all impeachments. When sitting for that purpose, they shall be on oath or affirmation. When the President of the United States is tried, the Chief Justice shall preside[3]: and no person shall be convicted without the concurrence of two-thirds of the members present.

7. Penalties for impeachment conviction. Judgment in cases of impeachment shall not extend further than to removal from office, and disqualification to hold and enjoy any office of honor, trust or profit under the United States: but the party convicted shall nevertheless be liable and subject to indictment, trial, judgment and punishment, according to law.

SECTION IV.

Election and Meetings of Congress

1. Regulation of elections. The times, places and manner of holding elections for Senators and Representatives shall be prescribed in each State by the legislature thereof; but the Congress may at any time by law make or alter such regulations, except as to the places of choosing Senators.

2. Congress must meet once a year. The Congress shall assemble at least once in every year, and such meeting *shall be on the first Monday in December, unless they shall by law appoint a different day.*[4]

---

[1]Repealed in favor of popular election in 1913 by the Seventeenth Amendment.
[2]Changed in 1913 by the Seventeenth Amendment.
[3]The vice president, as next in line, would be an interested party.
[4]Changed in 1933 to January 3 by the Twentieth Amendment (see p. 533 and below).

SECTION V.   **Organization and Rules of the Houses**

1. Each house may reject members; quorums. Each house shall be the judge of the elections, returns and qualifications of its own members, and a majority of each shall constitute a quorum to do business; but a smaller number may adjourn from day to day, and may be authorized to compel the attendance of absent members, in such manner, and under such penalties, as each house may provide.

See "Bully" Brooks case, pp. 279–280.

2. Each house makes its own rules. Each house may determine the rules of its proceedings, punish its members for disorderly behavior, and with the concurrence of two-thirds, expel a member.

3. Each house must keep and publish a record of its proceedings. Each house shall keep a journal of its proceedings, and from time to time publish the same, excepting such parts as may in their judgment require secrecy; and the yeas and nays of the members of either house on any question shall, at the desire of one-fifth of those present, be entered on the journal.

4. Both houses must agree on adjournment. Neither house, during the session of Congress, shall, without the consent of the other, adjourn for more than three days, nor to any other place than that in which the two houses shall be sitting.

SECTION VI.   **Privileges of and Prohibitions upon Congressmen**

1. Congressional salaries; immunities. The Senators and Representatives shall receive a compensation for their services, to be ascertained by law and paid out of the treasury of the United States. They shall in all cases except treason, felony and breach of the peace, be privileged from arrest during their attendance at the session of their respective houses, and in going to and returning from the same; and for any speech or debate in either house, they shall not be questioned in any other place [i.e., they shall be immune from libel suits].

2. A congressman may not hold any other federal civil office. No Senator or Representative shall, during the time for which he was elected, be appointed to any civil office under the authority of the United States, which shall have been created, or the emoluments whereof shall have been increased, during such time; and no person holding any office under the United States shall be a member of either house during his continuance in office.

SECTION VII.   **Method of Making Laws**

See 1787 compromise, p. 124.

1. Money bills must originate in the House. All bills for raising revenue shall originate in the House of Representatives; but the Senate may propose or concur with amendments as on other bills.

Nixon, more than any predecessors, "impounded" billions of dollars voted by Congress for specific purposes, because he disapproved of them. The courts generally failed to sustain him, and his impeachment foes regarded wholesale impoundment as a violation of his oath to "faithfully execute" the laws.

2. The president's veto power; Congress may override. Every bill which shall have passed the House of Representatives and the Senate, shall, before it become a law, be presented to the President of the United States; if he approve he shall sign it, but if not he shall return it with his objections to that house in which it shall have originated, who shall enter the objections at large on their journal, and proceed to reconsider it. If after such reconsideration two-thirds of that house shall agree to pass the bill, it shall be sent, together with the objections, to the other house, by which it shall likewise be reconsidered, and, if approved by two-thirds of that house, it shall become a law. But in all such cases the votes of both houses shall be determined by yeas and nays, and the names of the persons voting for and against the bill shall be entered on the journal of each house respectively. If any bill shall not be returned by the President within ten days (Sundays excepted) after it shall have been presented to him, the same shall be a law, in like manner as if he had signed it, unless the Congress by their adjournment prevent its return, in which case it shall not be a law [this is the so-called pocket veto].

3. All measures requiring the agreement of both houses go to president for approval. Every order, resolution, or vote to which the concurrence of the Senate and House of Representatives may be necessary (except on a question of adjournment) shall be presented to the President of the United States; and before the same shall take effect, shall be approved by him, or being disapproved by him, shall be repassed by two-thirds of the Senate and House of Representatives, according to the rules and limitations prescribed in the case of a bill.

SECTION VIII.   Powers Granted to Congress

Congress has certain enumerated powers:

1. It may lay and collect taxes. The Congress shall have power to lay and collect taxes, duties, imposts, and excises, to pay the debts and provide for the common defense and general welfare of the United States; but all duties, imposts and excises shall be uniform throughout the United States;

2. It may borrow money. To borrow money on the credit of the United States;

3. It may regulate foreign and interstate trade. To regulate commerce with foreign nations, and among the several States, and with the Indian tribes;

For 1798 naturalization see p. 142.
4. It may pass naturalization and bankruptcy laws. To establish an uniform rule of naturalization, and uniform laws on the subject of bankruptcies throughout the United States;

5. It may coin money. To coin money, regulate the value thereof, and of foreign coin, and fix the standard of weights and measures;

6. It may punish counterfeiters. To provide for the punishment of counterfeiting the securities and current coin of the United States;

7. It may establish a postal service. To establish post offices and post roads;

8. It may issue patents and copyrights. To promote the progress of science and useful arts by securing for limited times to authors and inventors the exclusive right to their respective writings and discoveries;

9. It may establish inferior courts. To constitute tribunals inferior to the Supreme Court;

See Judiciary Act of 1789, p. 133.
10. It may punish crimes committed on the high seas. To define and punish piracies and felonies committed on the high seas [i.e., outside the three-mile limit] and offenses against the law of nations [international law];

11. It may declare war; authorize privateers. To declare war,[1] grant letters of marque and reprisal,[2] and make rules concerning captures on land and water;

12. It may maintain an army. To raise and support armies, but no appropriation of money to that use shall be for a longer term than two years;[3]

13. It may maintain a navy. To provide and maintain a navy;

14. It may regulate the army and navy. To make rules for the government and regulation of the land and naval forces;

15. It may call out the state militia. To provide for calling forth the militia to execute the laws of the Union, suppress insurrections, and repel invasions;

See Whiskey Rebellion, p. 136.
16. It shares with the states control of militia. To provide for organizing, arming, and disciplining the militia, and for governing such part of them as may be employed in the service of the United States, reserving to the States respectively the appointment of the officers, and the authority of training the militia according to the discipline prescribed by Congress;

---

[1]Note that presidents, though they can provoke war (see the case of Polk, p. 256) or wage it after it is declared, cannot declare it.

[2]Papers issued to private citizens in wartime authorizing them to capture enemy ships.

[3]A reflection of fear of standing armies earlier expressed in the Declaration of Independence.

17. It makes laws for the District of Columbia and other federal areas. To exercise exclusive legislation in all cases whatsoever, over such district (not exceeding ten miles square) as may, by cession of particular States, and the acceptance of Congress, become the seat of government of the United States,[1] and to exercise like authority over all places purchased by the consent of the legislature of the State, in which the same shall be, for the erection of forts, magazines, arsenals, dock-yards, and other needful buildings;—and

Congress has certain implied powers:

This is the famous "elastic clause"; See p. 136.

18. It may make laws necessary for carrying out the enumerated powers. To make all laws which shall be necessary and proper for carrying into execution the foregoing powers, and all other powers vested by this Constitution in the government of the United States, or in any departure or officer thereof.

SECTION IX.   **Powers Denied to the Federal Government**

See 1787 slave compromise, p. 125.

1. Congressional control of slave trade postponed until 1808. *The migration or importation of such persons as any of the States now existing shall think proper to admit shall not be prohibited by the Congress prior to the year 1808; but a tax or duty may be imposed on such importation, not exceeding $10 for each person.*

See Lincoln's unlawful suspension, p. 299.

2. The writ of habeas corpus[2] may be suspended only in cases of rebellion or invasion. The privilege of the writ of habeas corpus shall not be suspended, unless when in cases of rebellion or invasion the public safety may require it.

3. Attainders[3] and ex post facto laws[4] forbidden. No bill of attainder or ex post facto law shall be passed.

4. Direct taxes must be apportioned according to population. No capitation [head or poll tax] or other direct, tax shall be laid, unless in proportion to the census or enumeration herein before directed to be taken.[5]

5. Export taxes forbidden. No tax or duty shall be laid on articles exported from any State.

6. Congress must not discriminate among states in regulating commerce. No preference shall be given by any regulation of commerce or revenue to the ports of one State over those of another; nor shall vessels bound to, or from, one State, be obliged to enter, clear, or pay duties in another.

See Lincoln's unlawful infraction, p. 299.

7. Public money may not be spent without congressional appropriation; accounting. No money shall be drawn from the treasury, but in consequence of appropriations made by law; and a regular statement and account of the receipts and expenditures of all public money shall be published from time to time.

8. Titles of nobility prohibited; foreign gifts. No title of nobility shall be granted by the United States; and no person holding office of profit or trust under them, shall, without the consent of Congress, accept of any present, emolument, office, or title, of any kind whatever, from any king, prince, or foreign state.

---

[1] The District of Columbia, ten miles square, was established in 1791 with a cession from Virginia (see pp. 134–135).

[2] A writ of habeas corpus is a document that enables a person under arrest to obtain an immediate examination in court to ascertain whether he or she is being legally held.

[3] A bill of attainder is a special legislative act condemning and punishing an individual without a judicial trial.

[4] An ex post facto law is one that fixes punishments for acts committed before the law was passed.

[5] Modified in 1913 by the Sixteenth Amendment (see p. 462 and amendments below).

SECTION X. **Powers Denied to the States**

Absolute prohibitions on the states:

On contracts see Fletcher *v.*
Peck, p. 172.

1. The states are forbidden to do certain things. No State shall enter into any treaty, alliance, or confederation; grant letters of marque and reprisal [i.e., authorize privateers]; coin money; emit bills of credit [issue paper money]; make anything but gold and silver coin a [legal] tender in payment of debts; pass any bill of attainder,[1] ex post facto,[1] or law impairing the obligation of contracts, or grant any title of nobility.

Conditional prohibitions on the states:

Cf. Confederation chaos,
pp. 120–121.

2. The states may not levy duties without the consent of Congress. No State shall, without the consent of Congress, lay any imposts or duties on imports or exports, except what may be absolutely necessary for executing its inspection laws: and the net produce of all duties and imposts, laid by any State on imports or exports, shall be for the use of the treasury of the United States; and all such laws shall be subject to the revision and control of the Congress.

3. Certain other federal powers are forbidden the states except with the consent of Congress. No State shall, without the consent of Congress, lay any duty of tonnage [i.e., duty on ship tonnage], keep [nonmilitia] troops or ships of war in time of peace, enter into any agreement or compact with another State, or with a foreign power, or engage in war, unless actually invaded, or in such imminent danger as will not admit of delay.

Article II. *Executive Department*

SECTION I. **President and Vice President**

1. The president is the chief executive; term of office. The executive power shall be vested in a President of the United States of America. He shall hold his office during the term of four years,[2] and, together with the Vice President, chosen for the same term, be elected as follows:

See 1787 compromise,
p. 125.

See 1876 Oregon case, p. 345.

2. The president is chosen by electors. Each State shall appoint, in such manner as the legislature thereof may direct, a number of electors, equal to the whole number of Senators and Representatives to which the State may be entitled in the Congress; but no Senator or Representative, or person holding an office of trust or profit under the United States, shall be appointed an elector.

A majority of the electoral votes needed to elect a president. *The electors shall meet in their respective States, and vote by ballot for two persons, of whom one at least shall not be an inhabitant of the same State with themselves. And they shall make a list of all the persons voted for, and of the number of votes for each; which list they shall sign and certify, and transmit sealed to the seat of government of the United States, directed to the President of the Senate. The President of the Senate shall, in the presence of the Senate and House of Representatives, open all the certificates, and the votes shall be counted. The person having the greatest number of votes shall be the President, if such number be a majority of the whole number of electors appointed; and if there be more than one who have such majority, and have an equal number of votes, then the House of Representatives shall immediately choose by ballot one of them for President; and if no person have a majority, then from the five highest on the list the said house shall in like manner choose the President. But in choosing the President the votes shall be taken by States, the representation from each State*

See Burr-Jefferson disputed
election of 1800, p. 148.

---

[1]For definitions see footnotes 3 and 4 on preceding page.
[2]No reference to reelection; for anti–third term Twenty-second Amendment, see below.

See Jefferson as vice president in 1796, p. 140.

having one vote; a quorum for this purpose shall consist of a member or members from two-thirds of the States, and a majority of all the States shall be necessary to a choice. In every case, after the choice of the President, the person having the greatest number of votes of the electors shall be the Vice President. But if there should remain two or more who have equal votes, the Senate shall choose from them by ballot the Vice President.[1]

3. Congress decides time of meeting of Electoral College. The Congress may determine the time of choosing the electors and the day on which they shall give their votes; which day shall be the same throughout the United States.

To provide for foreign-born people, like Alexander Hamilton, born in the British West Indies.

4. Who may be president. No person except a natural-born citizen, *or a citizen of the United States at the time of the adoption of this Constitution,* shall be eligible to the office of President; neither shall any person be eligible to that office who shall not have attained to the age of thirty-five years, and been fourteen years a resident within the United States [i.e., a legal resident].

Modified by Twentieth and Twenty-fifth Amendments below.

5. Replacements for president. In case of the removal of the President from office or of his death, resignation, or inability to discharge the powers and duties of said office, the same shall devolve on the Vice President, and the Congress may by law provide for the case of removal, death, resignation, or inability, both of the President and Vice President, declaring what officer shall then act as President, and such officer shall act accordingly, until the disability be removed, or a President shall be elected.

6. The president's salary. The President shall, at stated times, receive for his services a compensation, which shall neither be increased or diminished during the period for which he shall have been elected, and he shall not receive within that period any other emolument from the United States, or any of them.

7. The president's oath of office. Before he enter on the execution of his office, he shall take the following oath or affirmation:—"I do solemnly swear (or affirm) that I will faithfully execute the office of the President of the United States, and will to the best of my ability preserve, protect and defend the Constitution of the United States."

SECTION II.   Powers of the President

See cabinet evolution, p. 134.

1. The president has important military and civil powers. The President shall be commander in chief of the army and navy of the United States, and of the militia of the several States, when called into the actual service of the United States; he may require the opinion, in writing, of the principal officer in each of the executive departments, upon any subject relating to the duties of their respective offices, and he shall have power to grant reprieves and pardons for offenses against the United States, except in cases of impeachment.[2]

For president's removal power, see p. 332.

2. The president may negotiate treaties and nominate federal officials. He shall have power, by and with the advice and consent of the Senate, to make treaties, provided two-thirds of the Senators present concur; and he shall nominate, and by and with the advice and consent of the Senate, shall appoint ambassadors, other public ministers and consuls, judges of the Supreme Court, and all other officers of the United States, whose appointments are not herein otherwise provided for, and which shall be established by law: but the Congress may by law vest the appointment of such inferior officers, as they think proper, in the President alone, in the courts of law, or in the heads of departments.

3. The president may fill vacancies during Senate recess. The President shall have power to fill up all vacancies that may happen during the recess of the Senate, by granting commissions which shall expire at the end of their next session.

---

[1] Repealed in 1804 by the Twelfth Amendment (for text see below).

[2] To prevent the president's pardoning himself or his close associates, as was feared in the case of Richard Nixon. See p. 637.

For president's personal appearances, see pp. 461–462.

SECTION III. **Other Powers and Duties of the President**

Messages; extra sessions; receiving ambassadors; execution of the laws. He shall from time to time give to the Congress information of the state of the Union, and recommend to their consideration such measures as he shall judge necessary and expedient; he may, on extraordinary occasions, convene both houses, or either of them, and in case of disagreement between them, with respect to the time of adjournment, he may adjourn them to such time as he shall think proper; he shall receive ambassadors and other public ministers; he shall take care that the laws be faithfully executed, and shall commission all the officers of the United States.

SECTION IV.

See discussion of Presidents Johnson, p. 332; Nixon, pp. 636–637; and Clinton, pp. 669–670.

Impeachment

Civil officers may be removed by impeachment. The President, Vice President and all civil officers[1] of the United States shall be removed from office on impeachment for, and on conviction of, treason, bribery, and other high crimes and misdemeanors.

Judicial Department

Article III.

The Federal Courts

SECTION I.

See Judiciary Act of 1789, p. 133.

The judicial power belongs to the federal courts. The judicial power of the United States shall be vested in one Supreme Court, and in such inferior courts as the Congress may from time to time ordain and establish. The judges, both of the Supreme and inferior courts, shall hold their offices during good behavior, and shall, at stated times, receive for their services a compensation which shall not be diminished[2] during their continuance in office.

Jurisdiction of Federal Courts

SECTION II.

1. Kinds of cases that may be heard. The judicial power shall extend to all cases, in law and equity, arising under this Constitution, the laws of the United States, and treaties made, or which shall be made, under their authority;—to all cases affecting ambassadors, other public ministers and consuls;—to all cases of admiralty and maritime jurisdiction;—to controversies to which the United States shall be a party;—to controversies between two or more States;—*between a State and citizens of another State*[3];—between citizens of different States;—between citizens of the same State claiming lands under grants of different States, and between a State, or the citizens thereof, and foreign states, citizens or subjects.

2. Jurisdiction of the Supreme Court. In all cases affecting ambassadors, other public ministers and consuls, and those in which a State shall be a party, the Supreme Court shall have original jurisdiction.[4] In all the other cases before mentioned, the Supreme Court shall have appellate jurisdiction,[5] both as to law and fact, with such exceptions, and under such regulations, as the Congress shall make.

3. Trial for federal crime is by jury. The trial of all crimes, except in cases of impeachment, shall be by jury; and such trial shall be held in the State where the said crimes shall have been committed; but when not committed within any State, the trial shall be at such place or places as the Congress may by law have directed.

---

[1] i.e., all federal executive and judicial officers, but not members of Congress or military personnel.

[2] In 1978, in a case involving federal judges, the Supreme Court ruled that diminution of salaries by inflation was irrelevant.

[3] The Eleventh Amendment (see below) restricts this to suits by a state against citizens of another state.

[4] i.e., such cases must originate in the Supreme Court.

[5] i.e., it hears other cases only when they are appealed to it from a lower federal court or a state court.

SECTION III.   **Treason**

See Burr trial, p. 154.

1. Treason defined. Treason against the United States shall consist only in levying war against them, or in adhering to their enemies, giving them aid and comfort. No person shall be convicted of treason unless on the testimony of two witnesses to the same overt act, or on confession in open court.

2. Congress fixes punishment for treason. The Congress shall have power to declare the punishment of treason, but no attainder of treason shall work corruption of blood, or forfeiture except during the life of the person attained.[1]

Article IV.   *Relations of the States to One Another*

SECTION I.   **Credit to Acts, Records, and Court Proceedings**

Each state must respect the public acts of the others. Full faith and credit shall be given in each State to the public acts, records, and judicial proceedings of every other State.[2] And the Congress may by general laws prescribe the manner in which such acts, records, and proceedings shall be proved [attested], and the effect thereof.

SECTION II.   **Duties of States to States**

1. Citizenship in one state is valid in all. The citizens of each State shall be entitled to all privileges and immunities of citizens in the several States.

This stipulation is sometimes openly flouted. In 1978 Governor Jerry Brown of California, acting on humanitarian grounds, refused to surrender to South Dakota an American Indian, Dennis Banks, who was charged with murder in an armed uprising.

Basis of fugitive-slave laws; see p. 268.

2. Fugitives from justice must be surrendered by the state to which they have fled. A person charged in any State with treason, felony, or other crime, who shall flee from justice, and be found in another State, shall on demand of the executive authority [governor] of the State from which he fled, be delivered up, to be removed to the State having jurisdiction of the crime.

3. Slaves and apprentices must be returned. *No person held to service or labor in one State, under the laws thereof, escaping into another, shall, in consequence of any law or regulation therein, be discharged from such service or labor, but shall be delivered up on claim of the party to whom such service or labor may be due.*[3]

SECTION III.   **New States and Territories**

e.g., Maine (1820); see p. 169.

1. Congress may admit new states. New States may be admitted by the Congress into this Union; but no new State shall be formed or erected within the jurisdiction of any other State; nor any State be formed by the junction of two or more States, or parts of States, without the consent of the legislatures of the States concerned as well as of the Congress.[4]

2. Congress regulates federal territory and property. The Congress shall have power to dispose of and make all needful rules and regulations respecting the territory or other property belonging to the United States; and nothing in this Constitution shall be so construed as to prejudice any claims of the United States, or of any particular State.

SECTION IV.   **Protection to the States**

See Cleveland and the Pullman strike, pp. 410–411.

United States guarantees to states representative government and protection against invasion and rebellion. The United States shall guarantee to every State in this Union a

---

[1] i.e., punishment only for the offender; none for his or her heirs.

[2] e.g., a marriage in one is valid in all.

[3] Invalidated in 1865 by the Thirteenth Amendment (for text see below).

[4] Loyal West Virginia was formed by Lincoln in 1862 from seceded Virginia. This act was of dubious constitutionality and was justified in part by the wartime powers of the president. See p. 293.

republican form of government, and shall protect each of them against invasion; and on application of the legislature, or of the executive [governor] (when the legislature cannot be convened), against domestic violence.

Article V. *The Process of Amendment*

The Constitution may be amended in four ways. The Congress, whenever two-thirds of both houses shall deem it necessary, shall propose amendments to this Constitution, or, on the application of the legislature of two-thirds of the several States, shall call a convention for proposing amendments, which, in either case, shall be valid to all intents and purposes, as part of this Constitution, when ratified by the legislatures of three-fourths of the several States, or by conventions in three-fourths thereof, as the one or the other mode of ratification may be proposed by the Congress; provided *that no amendments which may be made prior to the year one thousand eight hundred and eight shall in any manner affect the first and fourth clauses in the ninth section of the first article;*[1] and that no State, without its consent, shall be deprived of its equal suffrage in the Senate.

Article VI. *General Provisions*

This pledge honored by Hamilton, pp. 134–135.

1. The debts of the Confederation are taken over. All debts contracted and engagements entered into, before the adoption of this Constitution, shall be as valid against the United States under this Constitution, as under the Confederation.

2. The Constitution, federal laws, and treaties are the supreme law of the land. This Constitution, and the laws of the United States which shall be made in pursuance thereof; and all treaties made, or which shall be made, under the authority of the United States, shall be the supreme law of the land; and the judges in every State shall be bound thereby, anything in the Constitution or laws of any State to the contrary notwithstanding.

3. Federal and state officers bound by oath to support the Constitution. The Senators and Representatives before mentioned, and the members of the several State legislatures, and all executive and judicial officers, both of the United States and of the several States, shall be bound by oath or affirmation to support this Constitution; but no religious test shall ever be required as a qualification to any office or public trust under the United States.

Article VII. *Ratification of the Constitution*

See 1787 irregularity, pp. 126–129.

The Constitution effective when ratified by conventions in nine states. The ratification of the conventions of nine States shall be sufficient for the establishment of this Constitution between the States so ratifying the same.

Done in Convention by the unanimous consent of the States present, the seventeenth day of September in the year of our Lord one thousand seven hundred and eighty-seven and of the Independence of the United States of America the twelfth. In witness whereof we have hereunto subscribed our names.

[Signed by]

G° WASHINGTON
Presidt and Deputy from Virginia
[and thirty-eight others]

---

[1]This clause, regarding slave trade and direct taxes, became inoperative in 1808.

AMENDMENTS TO THE CONSTITUTION

Amendment I. *Religious and Political Freedom*

For background of Bill of Rights, see pp. 132–133.

Congress must not interfere with freedom of religion, speech or press, assembly, and petition. Congress shall make no law respecting an establishment of religion,[1] or prohibiting the free exercise thereof; or abridging the freedom of speech, or of the press; or the right of the people peaceably to assemble, and to petition the government for a redress of grievances.

Amendment II. *Right to Bear Arms*

The people may bear arms. A well-regulated militia being necessary to the security of a free State, the right of the people to keep and bear arms [i.e., for military purposes] shall not be infringed.[2]

Amendment III. *Quartering of Troops*

See Declaration of Independence and British quartering above.

Soldiers may not be arbitrarily quartered on the people. No soldier shall, in time of peace, be quartered in any house without the consent of the owner, nor in time of war, but in a manner to be prescribed by law.

Amendment IV. *Searches and Seizures*

A reflection of colonial grievances against the crown.

Unreasonable searches are forbidden. The right of the people to be secure in their persons, houses, papers, and effects, against unreasonable searches and seizures, shall not be violated, and no [search] warrants shall issue but upon probable cause, supported by oath or affirmation, and particularly describing the place to be searched, and the persons or things to be seized.

Amendment V. *Right to Life, Liberty, and Property*

When witnesses refuse to answer questions in court, they routinely "take the Fifth Amendment."

The individual is guaranteed certain rights when on trial and the right to life, liberty, and property. No person shall be held to answer for a capital, or otherwise infamous crime, unless on a presentment [formal charge] or indictment of a grand jury, except in cases arising in the naval forces, or in the militia, when in actual service in time of war or public danger; nor shall any person be subject for the same offense to be twice put in jeopardy of life or limb; nor shall be compelled in any criminal case to be a witness against himself, nor be deprived of life, liberty, or property, without due process of law; nor shall private property be taken for public use [i.e., by eminent domain] without just compensation.

Amendment VI. *Protection in Criminal Trials*

See Declaration of Independence above.

An accused person has important rights. In all criminal prosecutions, the accused shall enjoy the right to a speedy and public trial, by an impartial jury of the State and district

---

[1] In 1787 "an establishment of religion" referred to an "established church," or one supported by all taxpayers, whether members or not. But the courts have often acted under this article to keep religion, including prayers, out of the public schools.

[2] The courts, with "militia" in mind, have consistently held that the "right" to bear arms is a limited one.

wherein the crime shall have been committed, which district shall have been previously ascertained by law, and to be informed of the nature and cause of the accusation; to be confronted with the witnesses against him; to have compulsory process [subpoena] for obtaining witnesses in his favor, and to have the assistance of counsel for his defense.

Amendment VII.   *Suits at Common Law*

The rules of common law are recognized. In suits at common law, where the value in controversy shall exceed twenty dollars, the right of trial by jury shall be preserved, and no fact tried by a jury shall be otherwise re-examined in any court of the United States, than according to the rules of the common law.

Amendment VIII.   *Bail and Punishments*

Excessive fines and unusual punishments are forbidden. Excessive bail shall not be required, nor excessive fines imposed, nor cruel and unusual punishment inflicted.

Amendment IX.   *Concerning Rights Not Enumerated*

The Ninth and Tenth Amendments were bulwarks of southern states' rights before the Civil War.

The people retain rights not here enumerated. The enumeration in the Constitution, of certain rights, shall not be construed to deny or disparage others retained by the people.

Amendment X.   *Powers Reserved to the States and to the People*

A concession to states' rights, p. 133.

Powers not delegated to the federal government are reserved to the states and the people. The powers not delegated to the United States by the Constitution, nor prohibited by it to the States, are reserved to the States respectively, or to the people.

Amendment XI.   *Suits Against a State*

The federal courts have no authority in suits by citizens against a state. The judicial power of the United States shall not be construed to extend to any suit in law or equity, commenced or prosecuted against one of the United States by citizens of another State, or by citizens or subjects of any foreign state. [Adopted 1798.]

Amendment XII.   *Election of President and Vice President*

Forestalls repetition of 1800 electoral dispute, p. 148.

See 1876 disputed election. p. 334.

See 1824 election, pp. 177–178.

1. Changes in manner of electing president and vice president; procedure when no presidential candidate receives electoral majority. The electors shall meet in their respective States, and vote by ballot for President and Vice President, one of whom, at least, shall not be an inhabitant of the same state with themselves; they shall name in their ballots the person voted for as President, and in distinct ballots the person voted for as Vice President, and they shall make distinct lists of all persons voted for as President, and of all persons voted for as Vice President, and of the number of votes for each, which lists they shall sign and certify, and transmit sealed to the seat of government of the United States, directed to the President of the Senate;—the President of the Senate shall, in the presence of the Senate and House of Representatives, open all the certificates and the votes shall be counted;—the person having the greatest number of votes for President shall be the President, if such number be a majority of the whole number of electors appointed; and if no person have such majority, then from the persons having the highest numbers not exceeding three on the list of those voted for as President, the House of Representatives shall choose immediately, by ballot, the President. But in choosing the President, the votes shall be taken by States, the representation from each State having one vote; a quorum for this purpose shall consist of a member or members from two-thirds of the States, and a majority of all the States shall be necessary to a choice. And if the House of Representatives shall not choose a President whenever the right of choice shall devolve upon them, before *the fourth day of March*[1] next following, then the Vice President shall act as President, as in the case of the death or other constitutional disability of the President.

2. Procedure when no vice presidential candidate receives electoral majority. The person having the greatest number of votes as Vice President, shall be the Vice President, if such number be a majority of the whole number of electors appointed; and if no person have a majority, then from the two highest numbers on the list the Senate shall choose the Vice President; a quorum for the purpose shall consist of two-thirds of the whole number of Senators, and a majority of the whole number shall be necessary to a choice. But no person constitutionally ineligible to the office of President shall be eligible to that of Vice President of the United States. [Adopted 1804.]

Amendment XIII.   *Slavery Prohibited*

For background see pp. 309–310.

Slavery forbidden. 1. Neither slavery[2] nor involuntary servitude, except as a punishment for crime whereof the party shall have been duly convicted, shall exist within the United States, or any place subject to their jurisdiction.

2. Congress shall have power to enforce this article by appropriate legislation. [Adopted 1865.]

Amendment XIV.   *Civil Rights for Ex-slaves,[3] etc.*

For background see pp. 326–327.

For corporations as "persons," see p. 366.

Abolishes three-fifths rule for slaves, Art. I., Sec. II, para. 3.

1. Ex-slaves made citizens; U.S. citizenship primary. All persons born or naturalized in the United States, and subject to the jurisdiction thereof, are citizens of the United States and of the State wherein they reside. No State shall make or enforce any law which shall abridge the privileges or immunities of citizens of the United States; nor shall any State deprive any person of life, liberty, or property, without due process of law; nor deny to any person within its jurisdiction the equal protection of the laws.

2. When a state denies citizens the vote, its representation shall be reduced. Representatives shall be apportioned among the several States according to their respective numbers, counting the whole number of persons in each State, excluding Indians not taxed. But when the right to vote at any election for the choice of Electors for President and Vice President of the United States, Representatives in Congress, the executive and judicial officers of a State, or the members of the legislature thereof, is denied to any of the male inhabitants of such State, being twenty-one years of age and citizens of the United States, or in any way abridged, except for participation in rebellion, or other crime, the basis of representation therein shall be reduced in the proportion which the number of such make citizens shall bear to the whole number of male citizens twenty-one years of age in such State.[4]

Leading ex-Confederates denied office. See p. 326.

3. Certain persons who have been in rebellion are ineligible for federal and state office. No person shall be a Senator or Representative in Congress, or Elector of President and Vice President, or hold any office, civil or military, under the United States, or under any State, who, having previously taken an oath, as a member of Congress, or as an officer

---

[1]Changed to January 20 by the Twentieth Amendment (for text see below).

[2]The only explicit mention of slavery in the Constitution.

[3]Occasionally an offender is prosecuted under the Thirteenth Amendment for keeping an employee or other person under conditions approximating slavery.

[4]The provisions concerning "male" inhabitants were modified by the Nineteenth Amendment, which enfranchised women. The legal voting age was changed from twenty-one to eighteen by the Twenty-sixth Amendment.

of the United States, or as a member of any State legislature, or as an executive or judicial officer of any State, to support the Constitution of the United States, shall have engaged in insurrection or rebellion against the same, or given aid or comfort to the enemies thereof. But Congress may, by a vote of two-thirds of each house, remove such disability.

The ex-Confederates were thus forced to repudiate their debts and pay pensions to their own veterans, plus taxes for the pensions of Union veterans, their conquerors.

4. Debts incurred in aid of rebellion are void. The validity of the public debt of the United States, authorized by law, including debts incurred for payment of pensions and bounties for services in suppressing insurrection or rebellion, shall not be questioned. But neither the United States nor any State shall assume or pay any debt or obligation incurred in aid of insurrection or rebellion against the United States, or any claim for the loss or emancipation of any slave; but all such debts, obligations, and claims shall be held illegal and void.

5. Enforcement. The Congress shall have power to enforce, by appropriate legislation, the provisions of this article. [Adopted 1868.]

Amendment XV. *Suffrage for Blacks*

For background see pp. 328–329.

Black males are made voters. 1. The right of the citizens of the United States to vote shall not be denied or abridged by the United States or by any State on account of race, color, or previous condition of servitude.

2. The Congress shall have power to enforce this article by appropriate legislation. [Adopted 1870.]

Amendment XVI. *Income Taxes*

For background see p. 462.

Congress has power to lay and collect income taxes. The Congress shall have power to lay and collect taxes on incomes, from whatever source derived, without apportionment among the several States, and without regard to any census or enumeration. [Adopted 1913.]

Amendment XVII. *Direct Election of Senators*

Senators shall be elected by popular vote. 1. The Senate of the United States shall be composed of two Senators from each State, elected by the people thereof, for six years; and each Senator shall have one vote. The electors in each State shall have the qualifications requisite for electors of [voters for] the most numerous branch of the State legislatures.

2. When vacancies happen in the representation of any State in the Senate, the executive authority of such State shall issue writs of election to fill such vacancies: Provided, that the Legislature of any State may empower the executive thereof to make temporary appointments until the people fill the vacancies by election as the Legislature may direct.

3. This amendment shall not be so construed as to affect the election or term of any Senator chosen before it becomes valid as part of the Constitution. [Adopted 1913.]

Amendment XVIII. *National Prohibition*

For background see pp. 491–492.

The sale or manufacture of intoxicating liquors is forbidden. 1. *After one year from the ratification of this article the manufacture, sale, or transportation of intoxicating liquors within, the importation thereof into, or the exportation thereof from the United States and all territory subject to the jurisdiction thereof, for beverage purposes, is hereby prohibited.*

2. *The Congress and the several States shall have concurrent power to enforce this article by appropriate legislation.*

3. *This article shall be inoperative unless it shall have been ratified as an amendment to the Constitution by the legislatures of the several States, as provided by the Constitution,* *within seven years from the date of the submission thereof to the States by the Congress.* [Adopted 1919; repealed 1933 by Twenty-first Amendment.]

Amendment XIX.   *Woman Suffrage*

For background see p. 475.

Women guaranteed the right to vote.   1. The right of citizens of the United States to vote shall not be denied or abridged by the United States or by any State on account of sex.

2. Congress shall have power to enforce this article by appropriate legislation. [Adopted 1920.]

Amendment XX.   *Presidential and Congressional Terms*

Shortens lame duck periods by modifying Art. I, Sec. IV, para. 2.

1.   Presidential, vice presidential, and congressional terms of office begin in January. The terms of the President and Vice President shall end at noon on the 20th day of January, and the terms of Senators and Representatives at noon on the 3d day of January, of the years in which such terms would have ended if this article had not been ratified; and the terms of their successors shall then begin.

2.   New meeting date for Congress. The Congress shall assemble at least once in every year, and such meeting shall begin at noon on the 3d day of January, unless they shall by law appoint a different day.

3.   Emergency presidential and vice presidential succession. If, at the time fixed for the beginning of the term of the President, the President-elect shall have died, the Vice President–elect shall become President. If a President shall not have been chosen before the time fixed for the beginning of his term, or if the President-elect shall have failed to qualify, then the Vice President–elect shall act as President until a President shall have qualified; and the Congress may by law provide for the case wherein neither a President-elect nor a Vice President–elect shall have qualified, declaring who shall then act as President, or the manner in which one who is to act shall be selected, and such persons shall act accordingly until a President or Vice President shall have qualified.

4. The Congress may by law provide for the case of the death of any of the persons from whom the House of Representatives may choose a President whenever the right of choice shall have devolved upon them, and for the case of the death of any of the persons from whom the Senate may choose a Vice President whenever the right of choice shall have devolved upon them.

5. Sections 1 and 2 shall take effect on the 15th day of October following the ratification of this article.

6. This article shall be inoperative unless it shall have been ratified as an amendment to the Constitution by the Legislatures of three-fourths of the several States within seven years from the date of its submission. [Adopted 1993.]

Amendment XXI.   *Prohibition Repealed*

For background see p. 527.

1.   Eighteenth Amendment repealed. The eighteenth article of amendment to the Constitution of the United States is hereby repealed.

2.   Local laws honored. The transportation or importation into any State, Territory, or Possession of the United States for delivery or use therein of intoxicating liquors, in violation of the laws thereof, is hereby prohibited.

3. This article shall be inoperative unless it shall have been ratified as an amendment to the Constitution by conventions in the several States, as provided in the Constitution, within seven years from the date of the submission thereof to the States by the Congress. [Adopted 1933.]

Amendment XXII.   Anti–Third Term Amendment

Sometimes referred to as the anti–Franklin Roosevelt amendment.

1. Presidential term is limited. No person shall be elected to the office of President more than twice, and no person who has held the office of President, or acted as President, for more than two years of a term to which some other person was elected President shall be elected to the office of President more than once. But this article shall not apply to any person holding the office of President when this article was proposed by the Congress [i.e., Truman], and shall not prevent any person who may be holding the office of President, during the term within which this article becomes operative [i.e., Truman] from holding the office of President or acting as President during the remainder of such term.

2. This article shall be inoperative unless it shall have been ratified as an amendment to the Constitution by the legislatures of three-fourths of the several States within seven years from the date of its submission to the States by the Congress. [Adopted 1951.]

Amendment XXIII.   District of Columbia Vote

Designed to give the District of Columbia three electoral votes and to quiet the century-old cry of "No taxation without representation." Yet the District of Columbia still has only one nonvoting member of Congress.

1. Presidential electors for the District of Columbia. The District, constituting the seat of government of the United States, shall appoint in such manner as the Congress shall direct:

A number of electors of President and Vice President equal to the whole number of Senators and Representatives in Congress to which the District would be entitled if it were a State, but in no event more than the least populous State; they shall be in addition to those appointed by the States, but they shall be considered for the purposes of the election of President and Vice President, to be electors appointed by a State; and they shall meet in the District and perform such duties as provided by the twelfth article of amendment.

2. Enforcement. The Congress shall have the power to enforce this article by appropriate legislation. [Adopted 1961.]

Amendment XXIV.   Poll Tax

Designed to end discrimination against poor people, including southern blacks who were often denied the vote through inability to pay poll taxes. See p. 619.

1. Payment of poll tax or other taxes not to be prerequisite for voting in federal elections. The right of citizens of the United States to vote in any primary or other election for President or Vice President, for electors for President or Vice President, or for Senator or Representative in Congress, shall not be denied or abridged by the United States or any State by reason of failure to pay any poll tax or other tax.

2. Enforcement. The Congress shall have the power to enforce this article by appropriate legislation. [Adopted 1964.]

Amendment XXV.   Presidential Succession and Disability

Gerald Ford was the first "appointed president." See pp. 636–637.

1. Vice president to become president. In case of the removal of the President from office or of his death or resignation, the Vice President shall become President.[1]

2. Successor to vice president provided. Whenever there is a vacancy in the office of the Vice President, the President shall nominate a Vice President who shall take office upon confirmation by a majority vote of both Houses of Congress.

---

[1]The original Constitution (Art. II, Sec. I, para. 5) was vague on this point, stipulating that "the powers and duties" of the president, but not necessarily the title, should "devolve" on the vice president. President Tyler, the first "accidental president," assumed not only the powers and duties but the title as well.

3. Vice president to serve for disabled president. Whenever the President transmits to the President pro tempore of the Senate and the Speaker of the House of Representatives his written declaration that he is unable to discharge the powers and duties of his office, and until he transmits to them a written declaration to the contrary, such powers and duties shall be discharged by the Vice President as Acting President.

4. Procedure for disqualifying or requalifying president. Whenever the Vice President and a majority of either the principal officers of the executive departments or of such other body as Congress may by law provide, transmit to the President pro tempore of the Senate and the Speaker of the House of Representatives their written declaration that the President is unable to discharge the powers and duties of his office, the Vice President shall immediately assume the powers and duties of the office as Acting President.

Thereafter, when the President transmits to the President pro tempore of the Senate and the Speaker of the House of Representatives his written declaration that no inability exists, he shall resume the powers and duties of his office unless the Vice President and a majority of either the principal officers of the executive department[s] or of such other body as Congress may by law provide, transmit within four days to the President pro tempore of the Senate and the Speaker of the House of Representatives their written declaration that the President is unable to discharge the powers and duties of his office. Thereupon Congress shall decide the issue, assembling within forty-eight hours for that purpose if not in session. If the Congress, within twenty-one days after receipt of the latter written declaration, or, if Congress is not in session, within twenty-one days after Congress is required to assemble, determines by two-thirds vote of both Houses that the President is unable to discharge the powers and duties of his office, the Vice President shall continue to discharge the same as Acting President; otherwise, the President shall resume the powers and duties of his office. [Adopted 1967.]

Amendment XXVI.   *Lowering Voting Age*

A response to the current revolt of youth. See p. 632.

1. Ballot for eighteen-year-olds. The right of citizens of the United States, who are eighteen years of age or older, to vote shall not be denied or abridged by the United States or any state on account of age.

2. Enforcement. The Congress shall have the power to enforce this article by appropriate legislation. [Adopted 1971.]

Amendment XXVII.   *Restricting Congressional Pay Raises*

Reflects anti-incumbent sentiment of early 1990s. First proposed by James Madison in 1789; took 203 years to be ratified.

Congress not allowed to increase its current pay. No law varying the compensation for the services of the Senators and Representatives shall take effect, until an election of Representatives shall have intervened. [Adopted 1992.]

PHOTOGRAPH CREDITS

Chapter 1
p. 7, Library and Archives Canada / Maps, Plans and Charts Collection / NMC 93764; **p. 8,** Ansel Adams © by the Trustees of the Ansel Adams Publishing Rights Trust / Corbis; **p. 10,** Painting by Lloyd K. Townsend, Photo by Art Grossman; **p. 14,** © Bettmann / Corbis; **p. 16** Library of Congress; **p. 17,** © Bettmann / Corbis.

Chapter 2
p. 20, National Portrait Gallery, London; **p.23,** National Portrait Gallery / Smithsonian Institution, Washington, D.C. / Art Resource, New York; **p.28,** Phil Degginger / Bruce Coleman USA Photo Library.

Chapter 3
p. 33, Judith Cantz / Stock, Boston; **p. 37,** Mike Mazzaschi / Stock, Boston; **p. 39,** © British Library Board, All Rights Reserved, shelf-mark 121.35; **p. 41,** from the collection of Gilcrease Museum, Tulsa, Oklahoma; **p. 43,** Copyright of Christie's Images, Ltd., 2000.

Chapter 4
p. 49, The Colonial Williamsburg Foundation, Williamsburg, Virginia; **p. 51,** The Library of Congress; **p. 52,** Courtesy of the Historical Society of Pennsylvania Collection, Atwater Kent Museum of Philadelphia; **p. 53,** Abby Aldrich Rockefeller Folk Art Collection, Colonial Williamsburg Foundation, Williamsburg, Virginia; **p. 55,** Worcester Art Museum, Worcester, Massachusetts, Gift of Mr. and Mrs. Albert W. Rice.

Chapter 5
p. 62, The Granger Collection; **p. 67,** Private Collection / Bridgeman Art Library, Ltd.; **p. 68,** The Granger Collection.

Chapter 6
p. 76, Image © Board of Trustees, National Gallery of Art, Washington, Paul Mellon Collection; **p. 78,** The Granger Collection; **p. 80,** © Richard T. Nowitz / Corbis.

Chapter 7
p. 86, Gift of Joseph W., William B., and Edward H.R. Revere, Courtesy of the Museum of Fine Arts, Boston; **p. 89 (left)** Library of Congress; **p. 89 (right),** Courtesy of the American Antiquarian Society; **p. 90,** The Granger Collection.

Chapter 8
p. 98, The Henry Francis du Pont Winterthur Museum; **p. 99,** The Granger Collection; **p. 104,** Courtesy of the Massachusetts Historical Society; **p.105,** The Metropolitan Museum of Art, Gift of John S. Kennedy, 1897, Photograph © 1992 The Metropolitan Museum of Art, New York; **p. 109,** Courtesy of the Historical Society of Pennsylvania Collection, Atwater Kent Museum of Philadelphia.

Chapter 9
p. 116, Courtesy of the Massachusetts Historical Society; **p.117,** National Gallery of Art, Washington, Andrew W. Mellon Fund; **p.123,** Courtesy of the Historical Society of Pennsylvania Collection; **p. 125,** Fraunces Tavern ® Museum, New York City.

Chapter 10
p. 136, Credit Suisse Collection of Americana, New York City; **p. 137,** Henry Francis du Pont Winterthur Museum; **p.141,** Prints Collection, The New York Public Library, Astor, Lenox, and Tilden Foundations; **p.144,** Virginia Chamber of Commerce, photo by D'adamo.

Chapter 11
p. 149, Courtesy, American Antiquarian Society; **p. 150,** © Bettmann / Corbis; **p. 154,** Collection of The New-York Historical Society, neg. 51322; **p. 157,** AP-Wide World Photos.

Chapter 12
p. 162, © Bettmann / Corbis; **p. 166,** The Metropolitan Museum of Art, Joseph Pulitzer Bequest, 1942; **p. 167,** Maryland Historical Society; **p. 172,** Collection of the Supreme Court of the United States.

Chapter 13
p. 178, Nelson-Atkins Museum of Art, Kansas City, Missouri (Purchase: Nelson Trust); **p. 181,** Image © Board of Trustees, National Gallery of Art, Washington, D.C., Andrew W. Mellon Fund; **p. 185,** The Granger Collection; **p. 189,** Collection of The New-York Historical Society, neg. 44812; **p. 191,** Texas State Library and Archives Commission; **p. 193,** Franklin Delano Library, Hyde Park, New York.

Chapter 14
p. 198, The Granger Collection; **p. 202,** Collection of The New-York Historical Society, neg. 41082; **p. 204,** The Granger Collection; **p. 206,** Cincinnati Museum Center - Cincinnati Historical Society Library; **p. 210,** The Granger Collection; **p. 211,** National Museum of American History, Division of Work and Industry, Smithsonian Institution, Washington, D.C.; **p. 213,** Museum of Fine Arts, Boston, Gift of Maxim Karolik for the M. and M. Karolik Collection of American Watercolors and Drawings, 1800-1895; 53.245.

Chapter 15
p. 218, The Library of Congress; **p. 222,** Smithsonian Institution, Division of Cultural History, Washington, D.C.; **p. 224,** © Houghton Library, Harvard University; **p. 227,** © Bettmann / Corbis; **p. 231,** Berg Collection, The New York Public Library, Astor, Lenox and Tilden Foundations.

Chapter 16
p. 241, Musee de l'Homme, Paris / Art Resource, New York; **p. 243,** Missouri Historical Society, St. Louis; **p. 244,** National Portrait Gallery, Smithsonian Institution, Washington, D.C. / Art Resource, New York; **p. 245,** Historic New Orleans Collection, accession no. 1970.13.1.

Chapter 17
p. 254, Smithsonian American Art Museum, Washington, D.C. / Art Resource, New York; **p. 259,** Private Collection, photo Courtesy Masco Corporation; **p. 260,** Courtesy of The Bancroft Library, University of California, Berkeley.

Chapter 18
p. 266, The Granger Collection; **p. 268,** Brooklyn Museum of Art, 40.59a, Gift of Gwendolyn O. L. Conkling; **p. 273,** National Portrait Gallery, Smithsonian Institution, Washington, D.C. / Art Resource, New York.

Chapter 19
p.276, The Metropolitan Museum of Art, Gift of I.N. Phelps Stokes, Edward S. Hawes, and Marion Augusta Hawes, 1937 (37.14.00); **p. 278,** Print Collection, Miriam and Ira D. Wallach Division of Art, Prints and Photographs, The New York Public Library, Astor, Lenox and Tilden Foundations; **p. 283,** The Metropolitan Museum of Art. Gift of M. and M. Carl Stoeckel, 1897.

Chapter 20
p. 295, National Archives; **p. 302, (left)** Chicago History Museum, negative ICHi-15123; **p. 302, (right)** Decorative and Industrial Arts Department, Chicago History Museum, negative G1969.1737.

Chapter 21
p. 306, Library of Congress; **p. 309,** The Library of Congress; **p. 310,** three panels, *A Bit of War History: Contraband, Recruit, and Veteran,* The Metropolitan Museum of Art, Gift of Charles Stewart Smith, 1884; **p. 311,** John Hays Papers, Manuscript Division, the Library of Congress; **p. 316, (left)** The Granger Collection; **p.316, (right)** National Archives; **p. 318,** © Bettmann / Corbis.

INDEX

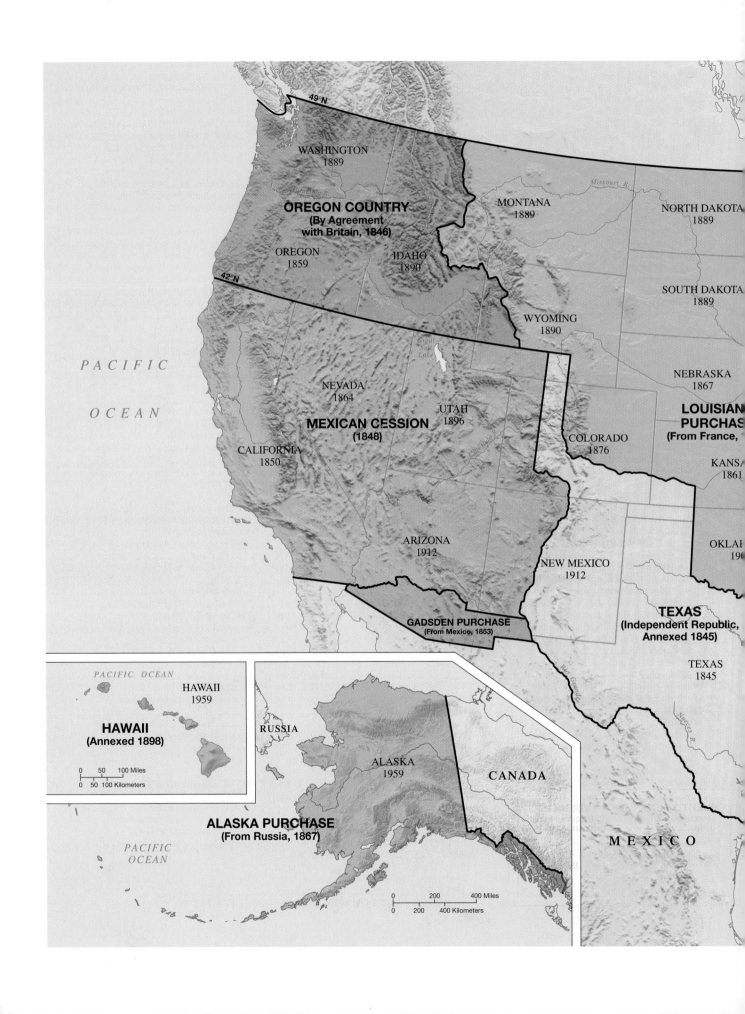

WASHINGTON
1889

OREGON COUNTRY
(By Agreement
with Britain, 1846)

OREGON
1859

IDAHO
1890

MONTANA
1889

NORTH DAKOTA
1889

SOUTH DAKOTA
1889

WYOMING
1890

49°N

42°N

Missouri R.

PACIFIC

OCEAN

NEVADA
1864

UTAH
1896

*Great
Salt
Lake*

NEBRASKA
1867

LOUISIAN
PURCHAS
(From France,

MEXICAN CESSION
(1848)

CALIFORNIA
1850

Colorado R.

COLORADO
1876

KANSA
1861

ARIZONA
1912

NEW MEXICO
1912

OKLAI
19(

GADSDEN PURCHASE
(From Mexico, 1853)

TEXAS
(Independent Republic,
Annexed 1845)

TEXAS
1845

Rio Grande

Nueces R.

PACIFIC OCEAN

HAWAII
1959

HAWAII
(Annexed 1898)

| 0 | 50 | 100 Miles |
| 0 | 50 | 100 Kilometers |

RUSSIA

ALASKA
1959

CANADA

ALASKA PURCHASE
(From Russia, 1867)

PACIFIC
OCEAN

MEXICO

| 0 | 200 | 400 Miles |
| 0 | 200 | 400 Kilometers |

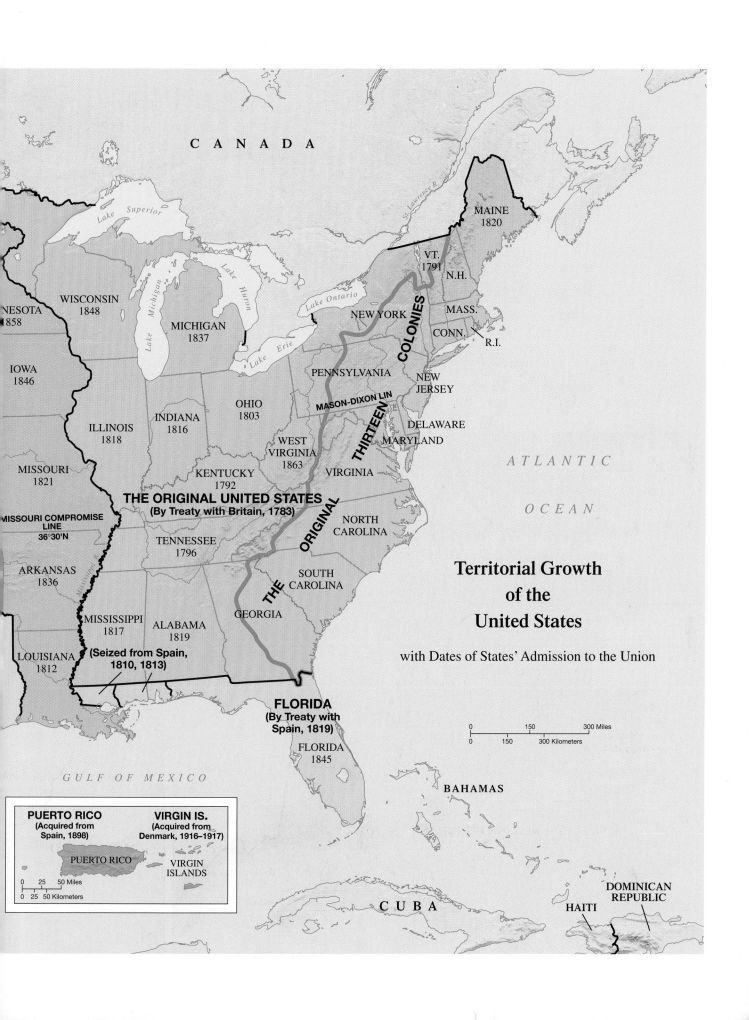

CANADA

Lake Superior

MAINE
1820

VT.
1791

N.H.

Lake Michigan

Lake Huron

WISCONSIN
1848

NESOTA
858

Lake Ontario

MICHIGAN
1837

NEW YORK

MASS.

CONN.

Lake Erie

R.I.

IOWA
1846

ILLINOIS
1818

INDIANA
1816

OHIO
1803

PENNSYLVANIA

NEW
JERSEY

MASON-DIXON LIN

DELAWARE

WEST
VIRGINIA
1863

MARYLAND

MISSOURI
1821

KENTUCKY
1792

VIRGINIA

THE ORIGINAL UNITED STATES
(By Treaty with Britain, 1783)

MISSOURI COMPROMISE
LINE
36°30′N

TENNESSEE

NORTH
CAROLINA

St. Lawrence R.

THIRTEEN COLONIES

THE ORIGINAL

ARKANSAS
1836

SOUTH
CAROLINA

ATLANTIC

OCEAN

Territorial Growth
of the
United States

with Dates of States' Admission to the Union

MISSISSIPPI
1817

ALABAMA
1819

GEORGIA

LOUISIANA
1812

(Seized from Spain,
1810, 1813)

| 0 | 150 | 300 Miles |
| 0 | 150 | 300 Kilometers |

FLORIDA
(By Treaty with
Spain, 1819)

FLORIDA
1845

GULF OF MEXICO

BAHAMAS

PUERTO RICO
(Acquired from
Spain, 1898)

VIRGIN IS.
(Acquired from
Denmark, 1916–1917)

PUERTO RICO

VIRGIN
ISLANDS

| 0 | 25 | 50 Miles |
| 0 | 25 | 50 Kilometers |

CUBA

HAITI

DOMINICAN
REPUBLIC

RUSSIA

WAY FINLAND
SWEDEN ESTONIA
LATVIA
LITHUANIA
BELARUS
MANY POLAND
CZ.
AUS. SLK. UKRAINE
SLN. HUNG. MOLDOVA
B. H. SE. ROMANIA
ITALY BULGARIA
MO.
ALBANIA MAC.
GREECE
MALTA
TUNISIA

KAZAKHSTAN

MONGOLIA

N. KOREA

GEORGIA
TURKEY ARMENIA
CYPRUS
UZBEKISTAN
TURKMENISTAN
KYRGYZSTAN
TAJIKISTAN
S. KOREA JAPAN

PACIFIC OCEAN

SYRIA AZERBAIJAN
LEBANON IRAQ
ISRAEL IRAN
JORDAN
AFGHANISTAN
PEOPLE'S REPUBLIC OF CHINA

LIBYA EGYPT
KUWAIT BAHRAIN
QATAR
SAUDI
ARABIA
UNITED
ARAB EMIRATES OMAN

PAKISTAN
BHUTAN
NEPAL
BANGLADESH
INDIA
MYANMAR
(BURMA)
LAOS

TAIWAN

Wake I.

GER CHAD
SUDAN
ERITREA
DJIBOUTI
YEMEN

THAILAND VIETNAM
CAMBODIA
(KAMPUCHEA)
PHILIPPINES

Mariana
Islands

Guam

MARSHALL
ISLANDS

RIA
CENTRAL
AFRICAN REP.
ETHIOPIA

SRI LANKA
BRUNEI
DARUSSALAM

PALAU

Caroline Islands

CAMEROON
SOMALIA
MALDIVES

MALAYSIA

KIRIBATI

GABON
UGANDA KENYA
RWANDA
DEM. REP.
OF CONGO
BURUNDI TANZANIA
SEYCHELLES

SINGAPORE

INDIAN OCEAN

NAURU

GO

ANGOLA
ZAMBIA
MALAWI

COMOROS

MADAGASCAR

INDONESIA

EAST TIMOR

PAPUA
NEW
GUINEA

SOLOMON IS.

TUVALU

NAMIBIA ZIMBABWE
MAURITIUS

VANUATU

FIJI

BOTSWANA

New Caledonia

MOZAMBIQUE
SWAZILAND
SOUTH
AFRICA
LESOTHO

AUSTRALIA

ABBREVIATIONS	
AUS.	AUSTRIA
BEL.	BELGIUM
B. H.	BOSNIA AND HERZEGOVINA
CR.	CROATIA
CZ.	CZECH REPUBLIC
DEN.	DENMARK
HUNG.	HUNGARY
LUX.	LUXEMBOURG
MAC.	FORMER YUGOSLAV REPUBLIC OF MACEDONIA
MO.	MONTENEGRO
NETH.	NETHERLANDS
SE.	SERBIA
SLK.	SLOVAKIA
SLN.	SLOVENIA
SWITZ.	SWITZERLAND

NEW
ZEALAND

20°E   40°E   60°E   80°E   100°E   120°E   140°E   160°E